ANNUAL

BIBLIOGRAPHY

OF

ENGLISH LANGUAGE

AND LITERATURE

FOR 1986

VOLUME 61

EDITOR
ELIZABETH ERSKINE

AMERICAN EDITORS
MARY JEAN DeMARR
D. GENE ENGLAND
Indiana State University, Terre Haute

Modern Humanities Research Association

1990

The *Annual Bibliography*
of English Language and Literature
may be ordered from the Hon. Treasurer MHRA
King's College, Strand, London WC2R 2LS, England

ISBN 0 947623 30 2
ISSN 0066-3786

Printed in Great Britain by
W. S. MANEY & SON LIMITED
HUDSON ROAD   LEEDS LS9 7DL

PREFACE

The Preface to the 1986 Bibliography must begin with an apology for its late publication, caused by the difficulties of computer-sorting a volume so complex as the categorized, sub-categorized, sub-sectioned, back- and forward-referenced *Annual Bibliography*. We do very much regret this long delay, and sincerely apologize to our users and contributors for it.

The academic world's prevailing economic climate does not encourage staffs of teaching departments or libraries to take on extra-departmental jobs, and we are grateful that in spite of it these new contributors have enlisted: Matthew Brennan, Michael D. Crane, James Kelly, D. J. Hall, Sheila Rainey, Hélène Redding, and Jean-Pierre van Noppen. The following are retiring with this volume: Margaret J. Arnold (1982–85), Edra Bogle (1968–85), Nancy Benson Carroll (1981–85), Pia Christensen (1985), C. Herbert Gilliland (1984–85), Stephen P. Heady (1982–85), F. M. Jorysz (1974–86), Elisabeth Leedham-Green (1985–86), Warren Loveless (1980–85), Lionel Madden (1968–86), Timothy S. Martin (1985), Gundel S. Mende-Kroczek (1984–86), Anda Olsen (1983–85), David Parker (1975–85), M. J. Pearce (1968–1985), Steve Roud (1982–86), Clive Scott (1974–85), Georges-Denis Zimmermann (1979–86). We thank them all for their support, but are under a particular obligation to the six longest-serving contributors (Mr Jorysz, Mr Madden, Ms Bogle, Mr Pearce, Dr Parker, and Dr Scott) for the work they have done for ABELL in a total of 91 volumes.

This year, Dr Reah, our Language Adviser since 1982, retires from this exacting and often tiresome task. He very generously agreed to continue in office for an extra year in order to see his sections of this first fully computerized volume through the press, and we are extremely grateful to him for this, and for all his advice.

An American critic recently took us to task for shortcomings in our subject indexing, implying that nowadays scholars search only in the sections labelled with the names or subjects of their particular concern, and ignore the general 'genre' categories at the beginning of the Language or Literature sections as a whole, and those preceding the Author sections in each century. This (if in fact it happens) is unwise. We have to balance bulk against comprehensiveness and cannot give a cross-reference to every author mentioned in a general article: *Maiden Aunts in the Nineteenth-Century Novel* would almost certainly be indexed *only* in the Nineteenth-Century Fiction section, and not under Jane Austen, Charles Dickens, Susan Ferrier *et al.*

Another warning: after its first appearance in ABELL, a book is categorized in subsequent years (e.g., for its reviews or trans-Atlantic publication) only in the earliest of the categories in which its first report was recorded. Thus a book originally categorized under Book

Illustration, Folk Drama, and Sir Osbert Sitwell will re-appear in Book Illustration only, and will there be back-referenced to the publication details in the original Book Illustration entry. This apparently harsh practice rules out value judgements as to the books most 'important' category — on which editor and researcher might well differ — and prevents an unmanageable multiplication of *See* entries.

We record, with many thanks, our usual indebtedness to the Staff of Cambridge University Library for all their kindness and help, and in particular to the Librarian for allotting us office accommodation, despite increasing demands on its now severely limited space, in a building which is for bibliographers an ideal environment.

E.E.

Details of unpublished British and Republic of Ireland theses are taken, by kind permission, from ASLIB's *Index to Theses, with Abstracts, Accepted for Higher Degrees by the Universities of Great Britain and Ireland and the Council for National Academic Awards*, edited by Geoffrey M. Paterson.

Contributors — *continued*

For Pakistan:	ALAMGIR HASHMI
Poland:	IRENA DOBRZYCKA, University of Warsaw
	JACEK FISIAK, Adam Mickiewicz University, Poznań
Romania:	ANGELA POPESCU-BRĂDICENI ⎱ Central State Library,
	IOANA CREȚEANU ⎰ Bucharest
Republic of South Africa:	FRANCES STOY, South African Library, Cape Town
	DOROTHY DRIVER, University of Cape Town
Spain:	PABLO DOMÍNGUEZ, University of La Laguna, Tenerife
Sweden:	GÖRAN EKROTH ⎱ Royal Library, Stockholm
	KERSTIN ASSARSSON-RIZZI ⎰
Switzerland:	GEORGES-DENIS ZIMMERMANN, Université de Neuchâtel
Syria:	SULEIMAN M. AHMAD, Tishreen University, Latakia
UK and Republic of Ireland:	J. H. ALEXANDER, University of Aberdeen
	JOHN R. ALLRED, Leeds Polytechnic
	CECILY CLARK
	J. G. W. ERSKINE, Stranmillis College, Belfast
	ISOBEL FOX, Library, Trinity College, Dublin
	PHILIP GROVER, University of Sheffield
	D. J. HALL, Cambridge University Library
	KEVIN HARRIS, Dickens House Museum, London
	MICHAEL C. HEAD, Robert Gordon's Institute of Technology, Aberdeen
	JOYCE M. HILL, University of Leeds
	ROBERT INGLESFIELD, University of London
	LESLEY JOHNSON, University of Leeds
	ELISABETH S. LEEDHAM-GREEN, Cambridge University Library
	LIONEL MADDEN, College of Librarianship Wales, Aberystwyth
	PETER MEREDITH, University of Leeds
	JAMES OGDEN, University College of Wales, Aberystwyth
	SHEILA RAINEY
	DEREK ROPER, University of Sheffield
	STEVE ROUD
	PRISCILLA SCHLICKE, Robert Gordon's Institute of Technology, Aberdeen
	STUART SILLARS
	P. S. SMITH, University of Sheffield
	JOHN TURNER, College of Librarianship Wales, Aberystwyth
	E. D. UNDERWOOD, University College of Wales, Aberystwyth
	ERIC VICKERS
	COLIN WILCOCKSON, Pembroke College, Cambridge
	ELIZABETH WILLIAMS, University of Leeds
USA:	B. J. ALEXANDER, Tarleton State University, Stephenville, TX
	MATTHEW BRENNAN, Indiana State University, Terre Haute, IN
	DAVID R. CHENEY, University of Toledo, Toledo, OH
	MICHAEL D. CRANE, United States Air Force Academy, Colorado Springs, CO
	EUGENE R. CUNNAR, New Mexico State University, Las Cruces, NM
	ALICE CUSHMAN, Tarleton State University, Stephenville, TX

Contributors — *continued*

LeAnne Daniels, Indiana University, Bloomington, IN
Thomas Derrick, Indiana State University, Terre Haute, IN
G. Ronald Dobler, Morehead State University, Morehead, KY
Raymond F. Dolle, Indiana State University, Terre Haute, IN
Alvin I. Dust, University of Waterloo, Waterloo, Ont.
Gordon Eriksen, Western Michigan University, Kalamazoo, MI
Marc Glasser, Morehead State University, Morehead, KY
Styron Harris, East Tennessee State University, Johnson City, TN
James A. Houck, Youngstown State University, Youngstown, OH
Harriet Hudson, Indiana State University, Terre Haute, IN
Fred Isaac, Berkeley, CA
Walter D. Lehrman, University of Akron, Akron, OH
James Kelly, Silver Springs, MD
Justyn Moulds, Marlboro, VT
Charles J. Nolan, Jr, United States Naval Academy,
    Annapolis, MD
Robert Perrin, Indiana State University, Terre Haute, IN
Betty Jo Hicks Peters, Morehead, KY
John S. Phillipson, University of Akron, Akron, OH
William L. Sipple, Robert Morris College, Coraopolis, PA
Charna Todd-Howson, Indiana State University, Terre Haute, IN
Peter A. Walker, Columbia University, New York
William White, Franklin, MI
Paula M. Woods, Baylor University, Waco, TX

For USSR: Peter Hellyer, Slavonic & East European Branch, British Library,
    London

CONTENTS

SOURCES AND ABBREVIATIONS 1986

While the editors make every effort to maintain regular coverage of the periodicals listed below, no undertaking is given that every journal listed has been fully reported. Issues which have not been available to contributors during the report year are covered as soon as possible thereafter. Articles may also be reported from periodicals not included in this list, for example when a magazine publishes a special literary number. In such cases the place of publication is given in each entry for that periodical. The editors will be glad to hear of errors and omissions, and of new journals requiring coverage.

In many cases journals are referred to in this volume by their main titles alone (e.g. Ariel, Bibliotheck), without this title being shown separately below as an abbreviation.

USSR serials. Titles of serials published in the USSR are sometimes cited differently in different sources. In particular 'gosudarstvennyĭ', etc., 'state', is sometimes included, sometimes not. This should be allowed for by users of the *Bibliography*.

AAA	Arbeiten aus Anglistik und Amerikanistik (Univ. of Graz)
AAAPSS	Annals of the American Academy of Political and Social Science (Philadelphia, PA)
AAnth	American Anthropologist (Washington, DC)
AArt	American Artist (New York)
AAS	Anglo-American Studies (Salamanca)
ABC	American Book Collector (Ossining, New York)
Abhath al-Yarmouk (Irbid, Jordan)	
ABN	Arnold Bennett Newsletter (Glencoe, IL)
ABPR	American Book Publishing Record (New York)
ABS	American Behavioral Scientist (Beverly Hills, CA)
ABV (Sofia)	
Academia Scientiarum Fennica, dissertationes humanarum litterarum (Helsinki)	
ACLSN	American Council of Learned Societies Newsletter (New York)
Acta Academiae Aboensis, Ser. A: Humaniora (Åbo, Finland)	
Acta Jutlandica (Aarhus Univ., Denmark)	
Acta Universitatis Tamperensis (Tampere, Finland)	
ActLitH	Acta Litteraria Academiae Scientiarum Hungaricae (Budapest)
AD	Armchair Detective (New York)
al-Ādāb al-Ajnabīyah (Syria)	
Adena (Louisville, KY)	
AEB	Analytical and Enumerative Bibliography (Northern Illinois Univ., DeKalb)
Agenda (London)	
Agora: a journal in the humanities and social sciences (State Univ. of New York, Potsdam)	
AH	American Heritage: the magazine of history (New York)
AHR	American Historical Review (Washington, DC)
AHum	American Humor: an interdisciplinary newsletter (Virginia Commonwealth Univ., Richmond)
AI	American Imago: a psychoanalytic journal for culture, science and the arts (Wayne State Univ., Detroit, MI)
AIQ	American Indian Quarterly (Univ. of California, Berkeley)
AJES	Aligarh Journal of English Studies (Aligarh Muslim Univ., India)
AJH	American Jewish History (Waltham, MA)
AJP	American Journal of Philology (Baltimore, MD)

AJPS   American Journal of Political Science (Austin, TX)
AJS   American Journal of Sociology (Chicago)
Aktual'nye problemy leksikologii i slovoobrazovaniiā (Novosibirsk Univ., USSR)
AL   American Literature: a journal of literary history, criticism and
                    bibliography (Durham, NC)
ʿĀlam al-Fikr (Kuwait)
AlaR   Alabama Review: a journal of Alabama history
                    (University, AL)
ALH   Acta Linguistica Hafniensia: international journal of general
                    linguistics (Copenhagen)
ALitA   American Literature Abstracts (San Jose State College, CA)
ALLC Bulletin   Association for Literary and Linguistic Computing Bulletin
                    (Cambridge)
ALLC Journal   Association for Literary and Linguistic Computing Journal
                    (Cambridge)
Allegorica (Univ. of Texas at Arlington)
Allt om böcker (Lund)
ALM   Archives des Lettres Modernes: études de critique et d'histoire
                    littéraire (Paris)
ALR   American Literary Realism, 1870–1910 (Univ. of Texas at
                    Arlington)
ALS   Australian Literary Studies (Univ. of Queensland, St Lucia)
AM   American Mercury (Torrance, CA)
America: national Catholic weekly review (New York)
AmerS   American Studies International (George Washington Univ.,
                    Washington, DC)
AmeSt   American Studies (Seoul National Univ., Korea)
Amfiteatru (Bucharest)
AmLib   American Libraries (Chicago)
AmQ   American Quarterly (Univ. of Pennsylvania, Philadelphia)
AmS   American Studies (Univ. of Kansas, Lawrence)
AmSS   American Studies in Scandinavia (Oslo)
Amst   Amerikastudien/American Studies (Munich)
Analecta cartusiana (Univ. of Salzburg)
Andvari (Reykjavik)
ANF   Arkiv för nordisk filologi/Archives for Scandinavian Philology
                    (Lund)
Ang   Anglia: Zeitschrift für englische Philologie (Tübingen)
Anglistik & Englischunterricht (Heidelberg)
Annales Universitatis Turkuensis, Ser.B. (Turku, Finland)
AnnMed   Annuale Mediaevale (Duquesne Univ., Pittsburgh, PA)
ANQ   American Notes and Queries (Lexington, KY)
AnthL   Anthropological Linguistics (Indiana Univ., Bloomington)
AnthQ   Anthropological Quarterly (Washington, DC)
Antic (Auckland)
Antwerp Papers in Linguistics
Anuario de filología (Univ. del Zulia, Maracaibo, Venezuela)
AnUBLLS   Analele Universităţii Bucureşti. Limbi şi literaturi străine.
                    (Bucharest)
AnUCFil   Analele Universităţii Craiova. Seria Ştiinţe filologice (Craiova,
                    Romania)
AnUGSU   Analele Universităţii din Galaţi. Fascicula I. Ştiinţe sociale şi
                    umaniste (Galaţi, Romania)
AnUILingv   Analele ştiinţifice ale Universităţii 'Al.I.Cuza' din Iaşi. (Serie
                    nouă.) Secţiunea III. e. Lingvistică (Jassy, Romania)
AnUILit   Analele ştiinţifice ale Universităţii 'Al.I.Cuza' din Iaşi. (Serie
                    nouă.) Secţiunea III. f. Literatură (Jassy, Romania)
AnUTFil   Analele Universităţii din Timişoara. Seria Ştiinţe
                    filologice (Timişoara, Romania)
AP   Acta Philologica (Warsaw)

APAIS — Australian Public Affairs Information Service (Canberra)
APC — Abstracts of Popular Culture (Univ. of Maryland, College Park)
Apollo: the international magazine of art and antiques (London)
APP — American Poetry and Poetics (Madison, SD)
APQ — American Philosophical Quarterly (Bowling Green State Univ., OH)
APR — American Poetry Review (Philadelphia, PA)
APSR — American Political Science Review (Washington, DC)
AQ — Arizona Quarterly (Univ. of Arizona, Tucson)
AR — Antioch Review (Yellow Springs, OH)
Arab Journal for the Humanities/al-Majallah al-ʿArabīyah li-l-ʿUlūn al Insānīyah (Kuwait)
Arab Journal of Language Studies (Sudan)
Arbor: revista general de investigacion y cultura (Madrid)
arcadia: Zeitschrift für vergleichende Literaturwissenschaft (Berlin)
Archiv — Archiv für das Studium der neueren Sprachen und Literaturen (Berlin)
Archiv für Geschichte des Buchwesens (Frankfurt)
Archiv für Kulturgeschichte (Cologne)
Archives et bibliothèques de Belgique (Brussels)
ArchivR — Archiv für Reformationsgeschichte/Archive for Reformation History (Gütersloh, W. Germany)
ArchL — Archivum Linguisticum: a review of comparative philology and general linguistics (Univ. of Leeds)
Arena: a Marxist journal of criticism and discussion (North Carlton, Vic.)
ArH — Archivo Hispalense: revista histórica, literaria y artística (Seville)
Ariadne: University of Crete School of Philosophy Yearbook (Rethymnon)
Ariel: a review of international English literature (Univ. of Calgary, Alta.)
ArizW — Arizona and the West: a journal of history (Univ. of Arizona, Tucson)
ArkHQ — Arkansas Historical Quarterly (Univ. of Arkansas, Fayetteville)
Arnoldian (U.S. Naval Academy, Annapolis, MD)
Artes: tidskrift för litteratur, konst och musik (Stockholm)
ArtJ — Art Journal (New York)
ASch — American Scholar (Washington, DC)
ASci — American Scientist (New Haven, CT)
ASE — Anglo-Saxon England (Emmanuel College, Cambridge)
ASocR — American Sociological Review (Washington, DC)
Aspirantski sbornik na Velikotărnovskija Universitet 'Kiril i Metodij' (Sofia)
Assays: critical approaches to medieval and Renaissance texts (Carnegie–Mellon Univ., Pittsburgh, PA)
Ateneu (Bacău, Romania)
Atlantis (Univ. of Oviedo, Spain)
AtlMon — Atlantic Monthly (Boston, MA)
ATQ — American Transcendental Quarterly: journal of New England writers (Univ. of Rhode Island, Kingston)
AUMLA — Journal of the Australasian Universities Language and Literature Association: a journal of literary criticism, philology and linguistics (Univ. of Tasmania, Hobart)
AUR — Aberdeen University Review
AusQ — Australian Quarterly (Sydney)
Australasian Journal of Philosophy (La Trobe Univ., Bundoora, Vic.)
Australian Academic and Research Libraries (Ultimo, N.S.W.)
Australian Author (Milsons Point, N.S.W.)
Australian Historical Bibliography (Univ. of New South Wales, Kensington)
Australian Journal of Education (Hawthorn, Vic.)
Australian Journal of Linguistics (Univ. of Queensland, St Lucia)
Australian Journal of Screen Theory (Univ. of New South Wales, Kensington)
Australian Library Journal (Ultimo, N.S.W.)

Australian National Bibliography (Canberra)
Australian Review of Applied Linguistics (Brisbane)
AWest   The American West (Palo Alto, CA)
AWR   Anglo-Welsh Review (Tenby, Dyfed)
BALF   Black American Literature Forum (Indiana State Univ.,
                        Terre Haute)
Bălgarski ezik (Sofia)
Bălgarski ezik i literatura (Sofia)
Bălgarski žurnalist (Sofia)
Balkan Studies (Thessaloniki)
Balkansko ezikoznanie/Linguistique Balkanique (Sofia)
Ball State Monographs: Publications in English (Muncie, IN)
BALLF   Bulletin de l'Académie de Langue et de Littérature Française
                        (Brussels)
BANQ   Biblionews and Australian Notes and Queries: journal for book
                        collectors (Cremorne, N.S.W.)
BAR   British Archaeological Reports (Oxford)
BaratR   Barat Review: a journal of literature and the arts (Barat
                        College, Lake Forest, IL)
BB   Bulletin of Bibliography (Westport, CT)
BBB   Black Books Bulletin (Chicago)
BC   Book Collector (London)
BDC   Barnhart Dictionary Companion (Cold Spring, NY)
Belgian Journal of Linguistics (Brussels)
Bethlehem University Journal (Jordan)
BF   Book Forum (New York)
BHM   Bulletin of the History of Medicine (Baltimore, MD)
BHS   Bulletin of Hispanic Studies (Liverpool)
Bibliographical Society of Australia and New Zealand Bulletin (Univ. of Adelaide)
Bibliographie de Belgique: Belgische Bibliografie (Brussels)
Bibliotekar (Sofia)
Bibliotheck: a Scottish journal of bibliography and allied topics (Edinburgh Univ.
    Library)
BIHS   Bulletin of the Institute for Humanistic Science (Inha Univ.,
                        Incheon, Korea)
Bildung und Erziehung (Düsseldorf)
BIS   Browning Institute Studies: an annual of Victorian literary and
                        cultural history (Univ. of Maryland, College Park, MD)
BJA   British Journal of Aesthetics (Oxford)
BJECS   British Journal for Eighteenth Century Studies (Oxford)
BJRL   Bulletin of the John Rylands University Library of Manchester
BkIA   Books at Iowa (Univ. of Iowa, Iowa City)
BkW   Book World (Washington Post, Washington, DC)
Blake: an illustrated quarterly (Univ. of New Mexico, Albuquerque)
BlakeS   Blake Studies (Memphis State Univ., TN)
BLJ   British Library Journal (London)
BLM: Bonniers litterära magasin (Stockholm)
BLR   Bodleian Library Record (Oxford)
BLSMPAB   Bulletin de la Classe des Lettres et Sciences Morales et
                        Politiques de l'Académie de Belgique (Brussels)
BN   Beiträge zur Namenforschung (Heidelberg)
Bókaormurinn (Reykjavik)
Boundary 2: a journal of postmodern literature and culture (State Univ. of New York,
    Binghamton)
BPJ   Beloit Poetry Journal (Ellsworth, ME)
BR   Bilingual Review/Revista bilingue (State Univ. of New York,
                        Binghamton)
BRH   Bulletin of Research in the Humanities (New York)
British National Bibliography (London)
Brno Studies in English (Univ. J. E. Purkyne, Brno, Czechoslovakia)

Broadsheet (Auckland)
Brussels Preprints in Linguistics

BSch	Black Scholar: journal of black studies and research (San Francisco, CA)
BSEAA	XVIIe–XVIIIe: Bulletin de la Société d'Études anglo-américains des XVIIᵉ et XVIIIᵉ siècles (Paris)
BSJ	Baker Street Journal: an irregular quarterly of Sherlockiana (New York)
BSN	Browning Society Notes (Platt, nr Sevenoaks, Kent)
BST	Brontë Society Transactions (Haworth)
BSUF	Ball State University Forum (Muncie, IN)

Bulletin (Sydney)
Bulletin des Anglicistes Médiévistes (Paris)
Bulletin de la Société linguistique de Paris

BuR	Bucknell Review: a scholarly journal of letters, arts and science (Cranbury, NJ)

Burlington Magazine (London)

BurnsC	Burns Chronicle and Club Directory (Kilmarnock)
BW	Book World (Chicago Tribune)
CAE	Collection of articles and essays (Hankuk Univ. of Foreign Studies, Korea)

Cahiers de l'APLIUT (Paris)
Cahiers de linguistique théorique et appliquée (Bucharest). *See* RRL
Cahiers de la Nouvelle (Angers, France). *See* JSSE
Cahiers Internationaux de Symbolisme (Univ. de l'État, Mons)
Calamus (Walt Whitman Quarterly International) (Tokyo)
Caliban (Univ. of Toulouse–Le Mirail, Toulouse)
Cambridge Review: a journal of University life and thought (Cambridge)

CamQ	Cambridge Quarterly
CanD	Canadian Drama/Art dramatique canadien (Univ. of Waterloo, Ont.)
CanL	Canadian Literature/Littérature canadienne: a quarterly of criticism and review (Univ. of British Columbia, Vancouver)
CanP	Canadian Poetry (Univ. of Western Ontario, London)
CanRCL	Canadian Review of Comparative Literature/Revue canadienne de littérature comparée (Univ. of Alberta, Edmonton)
CanTR	Canadian Theatre Review (Toronto)
CaQ	California Quarterly: a journal of fiction and poetry (Univ. of California, Davis)
CarnM	Carnegie Magazine (Pittsburgh, PA)

Carrell: journal of the Friends of the University of Miami Library (Coral Gables, FL)

CathHR	Catholic Historical Review (Washington, DC)

Cauce (Seville)

CB	Classical Bulletin (Asbury College, Wilmore, KY)
CC	Crosscurrents (West Nyack, NY)
CCC	College Composition and Communication (Urbana, IL)
CCTE	Proceedings of Conference of College Teachers of English at Texas (Commerce, TX)
CE	College English (Urbana, IL)
CEACrit	CEA Critic: an official journal of the College English Association (Bucknell Univ., Lewisburg, PA). *Formerly* CEAF
CEAF	CEA Forum. *See* CEACrit
CEBAL	Copenhagen School of Economics and Business Administration, Language Dept
CEl	Cahiers élisabethains: études sur la Pré-Renaissance et la Renaissance anglaises (Université Paul Valéry, Montpellier)

Cencrastus: Scottish and international literature, arts and affairs (Edinburgh)
Centrum: working papers of the Minnesota Center for Advanced Studies in Language, Style and Literary Theory (Univ. of Minnesota, Minneapolis)

CH	California History (San Francisco)

Chaucer Newsletter (New Chaucer Society, Univ. of Oklahoma, Norman)
ChauR   Chaucer Review (University Park, PA)
ChCen   Christian Century: an ecumenical weekly (Chicago)
Chelsea (New York)
ChiR   Chicago Review (Univ. of Chicago)
CHist   Church History (Wallingford, PA)
ChrisL   Christianity and Literature (Baylor Univ., Waco, TX)
ChronC   Chronicles of Culture (Rockford, IL)
Chronica (Scripps College, Claremont, CA)
ChronOkla   Chronicles of Oklahoma (Oklahoma City)
CHSB   Cincinnati Historical Society Bulletin. *See* Queen City Heritage
CHum   Computers and the Humanities (Osprey, FL)
CI   Critical Inquiry (Chicago)
CIF   Cuadernos de investigación filológica (Colegio Univ. de la
                          Rioja, Logroño, Spain)
CimR   Cimarron Review (Oklahoma State Univ., Stillwater)
Cithara: essays in Judaeo-Christian tradition (St Bonaventure Univ., NY)
CJ   Classical Journal (Florida State Univ., Tallahassee)
CJa   Cizí jazyky ve škole (Prague)
CJIS   Canadian Journal of Irish Studies (Univ. of British Columbia,
                          Vancouver)
CJL   Canadian Journal of Linguistics/Revue canadienne de
                          linguistique (Carleton Univ., Ottawa)
CL   Comparative Literature (Univ. of Oregon, Eugene)
CLAJ   College Language Association Journal (Morehouse College,
                          Atlanta, GA)
CLB   Charles Lamb Bulletin (Sevenoaks, Kent)
CLC   Columbia Library Columns (Columbia Univ., New York)
CLEd   Children's Literature in Education (New York)
CLIO: journal of literature, history, and the philosophy of history (Indiana Univ.–
   Purdue Univ., Fort Wayne, IN)
CLit   College Literature (West Chester Univ., PA)
CLQ   Colby Library Quarterly (Colby College, Waterville, ME)
CLS   Comparative Literature Studies (Univ. of Illinois, Urbana–
                          Champaign)
Clues: a journal of detection (Bowling Green State Univ., OH)
CM   Classica et Mediaevalia (Roskilde, Denmark)
CMF   Časopis pro moderní filologii (Prague). *See* PP
CML   Classical and Modern Literature: a quarterly (Terre Haute, IN)
ColJR   Columbia Journalism Review (Columbia Univ., New York)
Colloquium: the Australian and New Zealand theological review (Auckland)
ColoM   Colorado Magazine (Denver)
ColoQ   Colorado Quarterly (Univ. of Colorado, Boulder)
Comitatus: a journal of medieval and Renaissance studies (Univ. of California, Los
   Angeles)
CommEd   Communication Education (Annandale, VA)
Commentary: journal of significant thought and opinion on contemporary issues
   (New York)
ComMon   Communication Monographs (Annandale, VA)
Communication & Cognition (Ghent)
Communiqué (Univ. of the North, Pietersburg, South Africa)
CompCrit   Comparative Criticism: a yearbook (Cambridge)
CompDr   Comparative Drama (Western Michigan Univ., Kalamazoo)
ComQ   Communication Quarterly (Villanova Univ., PA)
Concerning Poetry (Western Washington State College, Bellingham)
ConLit   Contemporary Literature (Univ. of Wisconsin–Madison)
ConnHSB   Connecticut Historical Society Bulletin (Hartford)
Connoisseur (London)
Conradiana: a journal of Joseph Conrad studies (Texas Tech Univ., Lubbock)
Contemporanul (Bucharest)

Contrast: South African literary journal (Cape Town)
ConvLit   Convorbiri literare (Bucharest)
Coranto: journal of the Friends of the Libraries, University of Southern
    California (Los Angeles)
CP   Classical Philology (Chicago)
CR   Centennial Review (Michigan State Univ., East Lansing)
CREL   Cahiers roumains d'études littéraires (Bucharest)
Cresset: a review of literature, the arts and public affairs (Valparaiso Univ., IN)
Crit   Critique: studies in modern fiction (Washington, DC)
Critical Arts: a journal for media studies (Univ. of Natal, Durban, South Africa)
Critical Arts Monograph (Univ. of Natal, Durban, South Africa)
Critical Review (Australian National Univ., Canberra)
Criticism: a quarterly for literature and the arts (Detroit, MI)
Critique: revue générale des publications françaises et étrangères (Paris)
CritQ   Critical Quarterly (Manchester)
CRL   College and Research Libraries (Chicago)
Cronica (Jassy, Romania)
Crosscurrent (Hamilton, NZ). *Merger* of Pacific Quarterly *and* Rimu
Crux: a guide to teaching English language and literature (Pretoria)
CSR   Christian Scholar's Review: a Christian quarterly of the arts
                              and sciences (Union, ME)
Current Affairs Bulletin (Univ. of Sydney)
CVE   Cahiers victoriens et édouardiens (Univ. Paul Valéry,
                              Montpellier)
CW   Classical World (Duquesne Univ., Pittsburgh, PA)
Cweal   Commonweal (New York)
CWH   Civil War History: a journal of the middle period
                              (Kent State Univ., OH)
DA   Dissertation Abstracts International (Ann Arbor, MI)
Daedalus: journal of the American Academy of Arts and Sciences (Cambridge, MA)
DalR   Dalhousie Review: a Canadian quarterly of literature and
                              opinion (Dalhousie Univ., Halifax, N.S.)
Damascus University Journal
Dansk bogfortegnelse (Copenhagen)
Danske studier (Birkerød, Denmark)
Degrés (Brussels)
DelH   Delaware History (Wilmington)
Delta: revue du Centre d'Études et de Recherche sur les Écrivains du Sud aux
    États-Unis (Univ. Paul Valéry, Montpellier)
Descant: Texas Christian University literary journal (Fort Worth)
Deutsche Bibliographie (Frankfurt)
Deutsches Archiv für Erforschung des Mittelalters (Munich)
DHLR   D. H. Lawrence Review (Univ. of Delaware, Newark)
Diacritics: a journal of contemporary criticism (Baltimore, MD)
Dialog (Warsaw)
Diavazo (Athens)
Dic   Dictionaries: journal of the Dictionary Society of North America
                              (Univ. of Michigan, Ann Arbor)
Dick   Dickensian (London)
Dirasāt (Amman)
Direction   Direction Line: newsletter for bibliographers and textual critics
                              (Univ. of Texas at Austin)
Dix-huitième siècle (Paris)
DLAJ   DeKalb Literary Arts Journal (DeKalb Community Coll.,
                              Clarkston, GA)
Dodona: University of Ioannina School of Philosophy yearbook (Ioannina, Greece)
DQ   Denver Quarterly (Univ. of Denver, CO)
DQR: Dutch Quarterly Review of Anglo-American Letters (Amsterdam)
DreiS   Dreiser Studies (Indiana State Univ., Terre Haute)
DS   Dickinson Studies (Brentwood, MD)

DSA	Dickens Studies Annual: essays on Victorian fiction (Southern Illinois Univ., Carbondale)
DSN	Dickens Studies Newsletter (Univ. of Louisville, KY)
DUJ	Durham University Journal
DVLG	Deutsche Vierteljahrsschrift für Literaturwissenschaft und Geistesgeschichte (Stuttgart)
DWB	Dietsche Warande en Belfort: tijdschrift voor letterkunde, kunst en geestesleven (Antwerp)
EA	Études anglaises (Paris)
EAL	Early American Literature (Chapel Hill, NC)
EAS	Essays and Studies (London)
EC	Essays in Criticism: a quarterly journal of literary criticism (Oxford)
ECanW	Essays on Canadian Writing (Toronto)
ECent	Eighteenth Century: theory and interpretation (Texas Tech Univ., Lubbock). *Formerly* Studies in Burke and his Time
ECI	Eighteenth-Century Ireland (Trinity College Dublin)
ECL	Eighteenth-Century Life (College of William and Mary, Williamsburg, VA)
ECS	Eighteenth-Century Studies (St Olaf College, Northfield, MN)
Edda: nordisk tidsskrift for litteraturforskning (Oslo)	
EDH	Essays by Divers Hands (London)
Edinburgh Review (Edinburgh Univ.)	
EducF	Educational Forum (Ohio State Univ., Columbia)
EHR	English Historical Review (Harlow, Essex)
Éire–Ireland: journal of Irish studies (St Paul, MN)	
EJ	English Journal (Urbana, IL)
EL	Études de lettres (Univ. of Lausanne)
ELH (Baltimore, MD)	
ELit	Essays in Literature (Western Illinois Univ., Macomb)
ELN	English Language Notes (Univ. of Colorado, Boulder)
ELR	English Literary Renaissance (Univ. of Massachusetts, Amherst)
ELT	English Literature in Transition (1800–1920) (Arizona State Univ., Tempe)
Enc	Encounter (London)
Eng	English (Oxford)
EngA	English in Africa (Rhodes Univ., Grahamstown, South Africa)
English Academy Review (English Academy of Southern Africa, Johannesburg)	
English in Aotearoa (NZ Assn for the teaching of English, Wellington)	
English in Australia (Norwood, S. Australia)	
English Usage	English Usage in Southern Africa (Univ. of South Africa, Pretoria)
EngS	English Studies: a journal of English language and literature (Lisse, The Netherlands)
EngSt	English Studies (Seoul National Univ., Korea)
EON	Eugene O'Neill Newsletter (Suffolk Univ., Boston, MA)
Ephemera (Nancy, France)	
Epoch: a magazine of contemporary literature (Cornell Univ., Ithaca, NY)	
ERec	English Record (Buffalo, NY)
ERGS	ETC.: a review of general semantics (San Francisco)
ESA	English Studies in Africa: a journal of the humanities (Johannesburg)
ESCan	English Studies in Canada (Univ. of Alberta, Edmonton)
Esprit (Paris)	
ESQ: a journal of the American renaissance (Washington State Univ., Pullman)	
Esquire (New York)	
ESRS	Emporia State Research Studies (Emporia State Univ., KS)
ET	English Teaching (Seoul)
Ethics: an international journal of social, political and legal philosophy (Chicago)	

Études germaniques (Paris)
Études irlandaises (Université de Lille III, Villeneuve d'Ascq, France)
Études sur le XVIIIe siècle (Université Libre de Bruxelles)
Euphorion: Zeitschrift für Literaturgeschichte (Heidelberg)
Europe: revue littéraire mensuel (Paris)
EWeltyN   Eudora Welty Newsletter (Univ. of Toledo, OH)
EWN   Evelyn Waugh Newsletter (State Univ. of New York, Garden
         City)
Exp   Explicator (Washington, DC)
Explorations (Government College, Lahore)
ExRC   Explorations in Renaissance Culture (Univ. of Southern
         Mississippi, Hattiesburg)
Extrapolation: journal of the scholarly study of science fiction and fantasy
    (Kent, OH)
Ezik i literatura (Sofia)
Factotum (ESTC, British Library)
FAJ   Feminist Art Journal (Brooklyn, NY)
Familia (Oradea, Romania)
Fenix (Biblioteca Nacional, Lima)
FF   Folklore Forum (Bloomington, IN)
FHA   Fitzgerald/Hemingway Annual (Univ. of South Carolina,
         Columbia)
FHQ   Florida Historical Quarterly (Univ. of South Florida, Tampa)
Field: contemporary poetry and poetics (Oberlin College, OH)
Filologija (Sofia)
Fine Print (San Francisco)
FK   Filológiai Közlöny/Philological Review (Budapest)
FL   Folia linguistica: acta Societatis Linguisticae Europaeae
         (Vienna)
FLH   Folia Linguistica Historica (The Hague)
FM   Filosofska misăl (Sofia)
FMJ   Folk Music Journal (Sheffield)
FMod   Filología moderna (Univ. Complutense, Madrid)
FOB   Flannery O'Connor Bulletin (Georgia College, Milledgeville)
Focus   Focus on Robert Graves (Univ. of Colorado, Boulder)
Folk Life: a journal of ethnological studies (Cardiff)
Folklore (Univ. College, London)
Form (Dhaka)
Fort Hare Papers (Fort Hare Univ., Alice, South Africa)
Forum (Romania)
ForumH   Forum (Houston) (Univ. of Houston, TX)
ForumL   Forum der Letteren: Tijdschrift voor Taal- en Letterkunde
         (Leiden)
FQ   Four Quarters (La Salle College, Philadelphia, PA)
Frankfurter Hefte (Bonn)
French–American Review (Texas Christian Univ., Fort Worth)
FRP   Film Research in Progress (Univ. of North Carolina, Chapel
         Hill)
FS   Faulkner Studies: an annual of research, criticism, and reviews
         (Univ. of Miami, Coral Gables, FL)
Fund og forskning i det Kongelige Biblioteks Samlinger (Copenhagen)
FurmS   Furman Studies (Furman Univ., Greenville, SC)
GaHQ   Georgia Historical Quarterly (Savannah, GA)
Gambit: international theatre review (London)
GaR   Georgia Review (Univ. of Georgia, Athens)
Genre (Univ. of Oklahoma, Norman)
Germanica Olomucensia, Acta Universitatis Palackianae, Facultas Philosophica,
    Philologia (Palacký Univ., Olomouc, Czechoslovakia)
GGA   Göttingische gelehrte Anzeigen (Göttingen)
GHJ   George Herbert Journal (Sacred Heart Univ., Bridgeport, CT)

De Gids (Amsterdam)
GL   General Linguistics (University Park, PA)
GLOT: Tijdschrift voor taalwetenschap (Dordrecht)
GLR   Great Lakes Review: a journal of Midwest culture
                            (Central Michigan Univ., Mt Pleasant)
Glyph: textual studies (Minneapolis, MN)
Godišnik na VITIZ 'Krăstju Sarafov' (Sofia)
Gothic (Baton Rouge, LA)
GPJ   Great Plains Journal (Lawton, OK)
GPQ   Great Plains Quarterly (Lincoln, NB)
GR   Germanic Review (Washington, DC)
Gradiva: a journal of contemporary theory and practice (State Univ. of New York,
    Stony Brook)
Greyfriar: Siena studies in literature (Siena College, Loudonville, NY)
GRM   Germanisch-romanische Monatsschrift (Heidelberg)
Growing Point (Northampton)
GSB   General Semantics Bulletin (Institute of General Semantics,
                            Lakeville, CT)
GSUFNF   Godišnik na Sofijskija universitet. Fakultet po klasičeski i novi
                            filologii (Sofia)
GSUFSF   Godišnik na Sofijskija universitet. Fakultet po slavjanski filologii
                            (Sofia)
HAHR   Hispanic American Historical Review (Durham, NC)
Harper's (New York)
HC   Hollins Critic (Hollins College, Roanoke, VA)
Hecate: a women's interdisciplinary journal (Univ. of Queensland, St Lucia)
Helikon: vilagirodalmi figyelo (Budapest)
Helios (Texas Tech Univ., Lubbock)
Hellenika (Salonica)
Hemisphere: an Asian-Australian magazine (Canberra)
HemR   Hemingway Review (Ohio Northern Univ., Ada)
HGP   Heritage of the Great Plains (Emporia State Univ., KS)
Hist   History (London)
HistJ   Historical Journal (Cambridge)
Historian: a journal of history (Allentown, PA)
Historical News (Christchurch, N.Z.)
Historical Studies (Univ. of Melbourne)
Historiographica Linguistica (Amsterdam)
HJ   Higginson Journal (Brentwood, MD)
HJR   Henry James Review (Louisiana State Univ., Baton Rouge)
HLB   Harvard Library Bulletin (Harvard Univ., Cambridge, MA)
HLQ   Huntington Library Quarterly: a journal for the history and
                            interpretation of English and American civilization (San
                            Marino, CA)
HMPEC   Historical Magazine of the Protestant Episcopal Church
                            (Austin, TX)
Honest Ulsterman (Belfast)
HopQ   Hopkins Quarterly (Mohawk College, Hamilton, Ont.)
Horisont: organ för Svenska Osterbottens litteraturforening (Krylbo,
    Sweden)
Horizon (New York)
HR   Hudson Review (New York)
HSCL   Harvard Studies in Comparative Literature
                            (Harvard Univ., Cambridge, MA)
HSE   Hungarian Studies in English (Debrecen, Hungary)
HSJ   Housman Society Journal (Bromsgrove, Worcestershire)
HT   History Today (London)
HTR   Harvard Theological Review (Harvard Divinity School,
                            Cambridge, MA)
Humanist (Amherst, NY)

HUSL   Hebrew University Studies in Literature and the Arts
        (Jerusalem)
HZ   Historische Zeitschrift (Munich)
IAN   Izvestiîa Akademii nauk S.S.S.R. Seriîa literatury i îazyka
        (Moscow)
IARB   Inter-American Review of Bibliography/Revista interamericana
        de bibliografia (Washington, DC)
ICAME News: newsletter of the International Computer Archive of Modern English
        (Norwegian Computing Centre for the Humanities, Bergen)
ICarbS: journal of the Friends of the Morris Library at Southern Illinois University
        (Carbondale, IL)
IE   Indiana English (Indiana State Univ., Terre Haute)
IF   Indogermanische Forschungen: Zeitschrift für Indogermanistik
        und allgemeine sprachwissenschaft (Berlin)
IHB   Indiana History Bulletin (Indianapolis)
IIBE   Izvestija na Instituta za bǎlgarski ezik (Sofia)
IJAL   International Journal of American Linguistics (Chicago)
IJAS   Indian Journal of American Studies (Hyderabad)
IJPP   Interpretation: a journal of political philosophy (City Univ. of
        New York, Flushing)
IKS   Inmun Kwahak (The Journal of the Humanities)
        (Sungkyunkwan Univ., Korea)
IKY   Inmun Kwahak (The Journal of the Humanities) (Yonsei
        Univ., Korea)
Illusions: a New Zealand magazine of film, television and theatre criticism
        (Wellington)
IMH   Indiana Magazine of History (Indiana Univ., Bloomington)
Independent (London)
Indiana University Publications, Humanities Series (Bloomington)
IndS   Independent Shavian (New York)
Infini (Paris)
InL   Inostrannaîa literatura (Moscow)
Innsbrucker Beiträge zur Sprachwissenschaft (Innsbruck)
Inostrannye îazyki v shkole (Moscow)
Interlanguage (Rhodes Univ., Grahamstown)
International Folklore Review (London)
Interpretations: a journal of ideas, analysis, and criticism (Memphis State
        Univ., TN)
International Medieval Bibliography (Univ. of Leeds)
IowaR   Iowa Review (Univ. of Iowa, Iowa City)
IPQ   International Philosophical Quarterly (Fordham Univ.,
        Bronx, NY)
IR   Intercollegiate Review: a journal of scholarship and opinion
        (Bryn Mawr, PA)
IRAL   International Review of Applied Linguistics in Language
        Teaching (Heidelberg)
Irish Booklore (Belfast)
Irish Folk Music Studies (Dublin)
Isis (Philadelphia, PA)
ISJR   Iowa State Journal of Research (Iowa State Univ., Ames)
Islands: a New Zealand quarterly of arts and letters (Auckland)
Issledovaniîa po romano-germanskomu îazykozaniîû (Volgogradskiĭ pedagogicheskiĭ
        institut, Volgograd)
IT   Index to Theses accepted for higher degrees by the Universities
        of Great Britain and Ireland (and the Council for National
        Academic Awards) (ASLIB) (London)
ItalA   Italian Americana (State Univ. of New York, Buffalo)
Italian Studies (Univ. of Hull)
Italica (Univ. of Wisconsin, Madison)
ITL   ITL Review of Applied Linguistics (Leuven)

IUR   Irish University Review: a journal of Irish Studies (University
                           College, Dublin)
Izraz (Sarajevo, Yugoslavia)
Izvestija na Instituta za izkustvoznanie (Sofia)
Izvestija na Instituta za literatura (Sofia)
JA   Journal of Aesthetics and Art Criticism (Temple Univ.,
                           Philadelphia, PA)
JAC   Journal of American Culture (Bowling Green State Univ., OH)
JAE   Journal of Aesthetic Education (Univ. of Illinois at
                           Urbana-Champaign)
JAF   Journal of American Folklore (Washington, DC)
Jagger Journal (J.W. Jagger Library, Univ. of Cape Town)
JAH   Journal of American History (Bloomington, IN)
JAML   Journal of Arts Management and Law (Washington, DC)
JAR   Journal of Anthropological Research (Univ. of New Mexico,
                           Albuquerque)
JASAT   Journal of the American Studies Association of Texas
                           (Wayland College, Plainview)
JAStud   Journal of American Studies (Cambridge)
JazA   Jazykovědné aktuality (Prague)
JBCD   Journal of the Book Club of Detroit
JBecS   Journal of Beckett Studies (Ohio State Univ., Lima)
JBS   Journal of British Studies (Chicago)
JC   Journal of Communication (Philadelphia, PA)
JCanStud   Journal of Canadian Studies/Revue d'études canadiennes
                           (Trent Univ., Peterborough, Ont.)
JCF   Journal of Canadian Fiction (Montreal)
JCL   Journal of Commonwealth Literature (Oxford)
JCSJ   John Clare Society Journal (Peterborough)
JCT   Joseph Conrad Today (State Univ. College of New York,
                           Oswego)
JDJ   John Donne Journal: studies in the age of Donne (North
                           Carolina State Univ., Raleigh)
JEGP   Journal of English and Germanic Philology (Univ. of Illinois
                           at Urbana-Champaign)
JEL   Journal of English Linguistics (Univ. of Wisconsin,
                           Whitewater)
JELL   Journal of the English Language and Literature (Seoul)
JELLC   Journal of the English Language and Literature, Chungchong
                           (Daejeon, Korea)
JEPNS   Journal of the English Place-Name Society (Univ. of
                           Nottingham)
JES   Journal of Ethnic Studies (Western Washington Univ.,
                           Bellingham, WA)
JEurS   Journal of European Studies (Univ. of Exeter)
Jewish Affairs (Johannesburg)
JFR   Journal of Folklore Research (Bloomington, IN)
JGE   Journal of General Education (University Park, PA)
JH   Journal of the Humanities (Seoul National Univ., Korea)
JHI   Journal of the History of Ideas (Temple Univ., Phila-
                           delphia, PA)
JHK   Journal of Humanities (Kyungpook National Univ., Taegu,
                           Korea)
JHM   Journal of the History of Medicine and Allied Sciences (New
                           Haven, CT)
JHP   Journal of the History of Philosophy (Emory Univ.,
                           Atlanta, GA)
JHY   Journal of the Humanities (Yeungnam Univ., Gyongsan,
                           Korea)
JIES   Journal of Indo-European Studies (Butte, MT)

JISHS	Journal of the Illinois State Historical Society (Springfield)
JIWE	Journal of Indian Writing in English (Gulbarga, India)
JJQ	James Joyce Quarterly (Univ. of Tulsa, OK)
JLN	Jack London Newsletter (Southern Illinois Univ., Carbondale)
JMH	Journal of Modern History (Chicago)
JMissH	Journal of Mississippi History (Jackson)
JML	Journal of Modern Literature (Temple Univ., Phila-delphia, PA)
JMMLA	Journal of the Midwest Modern Language Association (Univ. of Iowa, Iowa City)
JMRS·	Journal of Medieval and Renaissance Studies (Durham, NC)
JNL	Johnsonian News Letter (Columbia Univ., New York)
JNPH	Journal of Newspaper and Periodical History (London)
JNT	Journal of Narrative Technique (Eastern Michigan Univ., Ypsilanti)
JNZL	Journal of New Zealand Literature (Wellington)

Journal of the English Literary Club (Peshawar, Pakistan)
Journal of Librarianship (London)
Journal of Literary Studies/Tydskrif vir Literatuurwetenskap (SAVAL, Pretoria)
Journal of Pacific History (Australian National Univ., Canberra)
Journal of Pragmatics: an interdisciplinary bi-monthly of language studies (Amsterdam)
Journal of Semantics (Dordrecht)
Journal of Social Sciences and Humanities (Karachi)

JP	Journal of Philosophy (Columbia Univ., New York)
JPC	Journal of Popular Culture (Bowling Green State Univ., OH)
JPH	Journal of Presbyterian History (Philadelphia, PA)
JPhon	Journal of Phonetics (Colchester)
JPHS	Journal of the Printing Historical Society (London)
JPol	Journal of Politics (Univ. of Florida, Gainesville)
JPR	Journal of Psycholinguistic Research (New York)
JPRS	Journal of Pre-Raphaelite Studies (Peterborough, NH)
JQ	Journalism Quarterly (Univ. of South Carolina, Columbia)
JR	Journal of Religion (Chicago)
JRead	Journal of Reading (Newark, DE)
JRMMRA	Journal of the Rocky Mountain Medieval and Renaissance Association (Northern Arizona Univ., Flagstaff)
JRUL	Journal of the Rutgers University Libraries (New Brunswick, NJ)
JSAA	Journal of Southern African Affairs (Univ. of Maryland, College Park)
JSH	Journal of Southern History (Rice Univ., Houston, TX)
JSHR	Journal of Speech and Hearing Research (Rockville, MD)
JSSE	Journal of the Short Story in English (Angers, France). *Formerly* Cahiers de la Nouvelle

Judaism: a quarterly journal of Jewish life and thought (New York)

JUJH	Jeju University Journal: humanities (Jeju, Korea)

Junior Bookshelf (Huddersfield)

JWCI	Journal of the Warburg and Courtauld Institutes (Univ. of London)
JWest	Journal of the West (Manhattan, KS)
JWMS	Journal of the William Morris Society (Kew, Surrey)

Kalki: studies in James Branch Cabell (Oradell, NJ)
Karamu (Eastern Illinois Univ., Charleston)

KF	Keystone Folklore (Univ. of Pennsylvania, Philadelphia)
KFR	Kentucky Folklore Record: a regional journal of folklore and life (Western Kentucky Univ., Bowling Green)
KH	Kansas History: a journal of the Central Plains (Topeka, KS)

Kirke og kultur (Oslo)

KJ	Kipling Journal (London)

Klagenfurter Beiträge zur Sprachwissenschaft (Klagenfurt, Austria)
KN   Kwartalnik Neofilologiczny (Warsaw)
Knizhnaiâ letopis' (Moscow)
Književna smotra (Zagreb)
Kp   Kunapipi (Univ. of Aarhus)
KQ   Kansas Quarterly (Kansas State Univ., Manhattan)
KR   Kenyon Review (Kenyon College, Gambier, OH)
Krăgozor (Sofia)
Kritik: tidsskrift for litteratur, forskning, undervisning (Copenhagen)
KSJ   Keats–Shelley Journal: Keats, Shelley, Byron, Hunt, and their
                             circles (Univ. of Pennsylvania, Philadelphia)
KSMB   Keats–Shelley Memorial Bulletin. See KSR
KSR   Keats–Shelley Review. Formerly Keats–Shelley Memorial
                             Bulletin (Univ. of York)
LaH   Louisiana History (Univ. of Southwestern Louisiana,
                             Lafayette)
Landfall: a New Zealand literary magazine (Christchurch)
Lang   Language (Washington, DC)
Langage et l'Homme (Brussels)
Langages: sémiotiques textuelles (Paris)
LangMono   Language Monographs (Arlington, VA)
LangS   Language and Style: an international journal (City Univ. of
                             New York, Flushing)
LankaG   Lanka Guardian (Colombo)
Lantern: journal for art, knowledge and culture (Pretoria)
LAR   Library Association Record (London)
La Trobe Library Journal (Bundoora, Vic.)
Laurels: a magazine devoted to French-American friendship (New York)
LC   Library Chronicle (Univ. of Pennsylvania, Philadelphia)
LCUT   Library Chronicle (Univ. of Texas at Austin)
LDeus   Letras de Deusto (Univ. of Deusto, Bilbao, Spain)
Leabharlann/Irish Library (Armagh)
Leeds Medieval Studies (Univ. of Leeds)
Leeds Studies in English (Univ. of Leeds)
Leeds Texts and Monographs (Univ. of Leeds)
Legacy: a journal of nineteenth-century American women writers (Univ. of
   Massachusetts, Amherst)
Letopis' zhurnal'nykh stateĭ (Moscow)
LeuB   Leuvense Bijdragen: tijdschrift voor Germaanse filologie
                             (Katholieke Univ. van Leuven)
Lexi (Athens)
LF   Literaturen front (Sofia)
LGJ   Lost Generation Journal (Salem, MO)
LH   Lincoln Herald: magazine of Lincoln and the Civil War
                             (Harrogate, TN)
LI   Linguistic Inquiry (Cambridge, MA)
Library (Oxford)
Library History (London)
Library Review: a quarterly devoted to information transfer, conservation and
   exploitation (Glasgow)
Libros (Madrid)
Linen Hall Review (Linen Hall Library, Belfast)
LingR   Linguistic Reporter (Arlington, VA)
Lingua: international review of general linguistics (Amsterdam)
Linguistic Review (Dordrecht)
Linguistica (Prague)
Linguistics and Philosophy: an international journal (Dordrecht)
Linguistics in the Netherlands (Dordrecht)
Linq: literature in North Queensland (James Cook Univ., Townsville, Qld.)
Listener (London)

Literární měsíčník (Prague)
Literator: bulletin van die letterkundige dept., Universiteit van Potchefstroom/
    Literator: bulletin of the literature dept., University of Potchefstroom (South
    Africa)
Literaturna misăl (Sofia)
LitEW   Literature East and West (Austin, TX)
LitFQ   Literature/Film Quarterly (Salisbury State College, MD)
LitR   Literary Review: international journal of contemporary writing
                        (Fairleigh Dickinson Univ., Madison, NJ)
Littératures (Univ. of Toulouse)
Livres de l'année (Paris)
Livres du mois (Paris)
Livres-Hebdo (Paris)
LJ   Library Journal (New York)
LL   Language Learning: a journal of applied linguistics
                        (Univ. of Michigan, Ann Arbor)
LM   Lesbók Morgunblaðsins (Reykjavik)
LMR   Literary Magazine Review (Kansas State Univ., Manhattan)
Long-Islander (Huntington, NY)
Long Room (Friends of Trinity Coll. Library, Dublin)
Lore and Language (Univ. of Sheffield)
LQ   Library Quarterly: a journal of investigation and discussion in
                        the field of library science (Chicago)
LRB   London Review of Books
LRN   Literary Research Newsletter (Manhattan College, Bronx, NY)
LU   ·   Lion and the Unicorn: a critical journal of children's literature
                        (Brooklyn College, NY)
Luceafărul (Bucharest)
LWU   Literatur in Wissenschaft und Unterricht (Univ. of Kiel)
MA   Moyen Âge: revue historique (Brussels)
Maal og minne (Oslo)
MÆ   Medium Ævum (Magdalen College, Oxford)
MalaR   Malahat Review (Victoria, BC)
Mankind (Univ. of Sydney)
Manuscripta: a journal devoted to manuscript studies (Saint Louis Univ., MO)
Manuscriptum: revista trimestriala editata de muzeul literaturii Romanae
    (Bucharest)
al-Ma'rifah (Syria)
MarkR   Markham Review (Wagner College, Staten Island, NY)
MassR   Massachusetts Review: a quarterly of literature, arts and public
                        affairs (Univ. of Massachusetts, Amherst)
MBL   Modern British Literature (Butler, PA)
MCMT   Main Currents in Modern Thought (New Rochelle, NY)
Meanjin: a magazine of literature, art and discussion (Univ. of Melbourne)
MEB   Missouri English Bulletin (Lincoln Univ., Jefferson City, MO)
MedArch   Medieval Archaeology (London)
MedHum   Medievalia et Humanistica: studies in medieval and
                        Renaissance culture (North Texas State Univ., Denton)
MedStud   Mediaeval Studies (Toronto)
MELUS: the journal of the Society for the Study of the Multi-Ethnic Literature of the
    United States (State Univ. of New York, Albany)
Mémoires   Mémoires de la Société Néophilologique de Helsinki
Menckeniana (Baltimore, MD)
Mentalities (Hamilton, N.Z.)
Meridian (La Trobe Univ., Bundoora, Vic.)
MESN   Medieval English Studies Newsletter (Tokyo)
METh   Medieval English Theatre (Univ. of Lancaster)
MF   Mystery Fancier (Memphis, TN)
MFR   Mississippi Folklore Register (East Central Junior College,
                        Decatur, MS)

MFS   Modern Fiction Studies (Purdue Univ., West Lafayette, IN)
MHM   Maryland Historical Magazine (Baltimore)
MHR   Missouri Historical Review (Columbia, MO)
MichA   Michigan Academician (Ann Arbor)
MichH   Michigan History (Lansing)
MichQR   Michigan Quarterly Review (Univ. of Michigan, Ann Arbor)
MidA   Mid-America: a historical review (Loyola Univ., Chicago)
Midamerica: the yearbook of the Society for the Study of Midwestern Literature
    (Michigan State Univ., East Lansing)
Mid-America Folklore (Batesville, AR)
Midland History (Chichester, Sussex)
MidQ   Midwest Quarterly: a journal of contemporary thought
                                (Pittsburg State Univ., KS)
Midwestern Miscellany (Michigan State Univ., East Lansing)
Miesięcznik Literacki (Warsaw)
MillNL   Mill News Letter (Univ. of Toronto)
MinnH   Minnesota History (St Paul)
MinnR   Minnesota Review: a journal of committed writing (State Univ.
                          of New York, Stony Brook)
Misc   Miscelánea (Univ. of Zaragoza)
MissQ   Mississippi Quarterly: the journal of Southern culture
                          (Mississippi State Univ.)
MJLF   Midwestern Journal of Language and Folklore (Indiana
                          State Univ., Terre Haute)
MLJ   Modern Language Journal (Madison, WI)
MLN (Baltimore, MD)
MLQ   Modern Language Quarterly (Univ. of Washington,
                                Seattle)
MLR   Modern Language Review (London)
MLS   Modern Language Studies (Brown Univ., Providence, RI)
MMN   Marianne Moore Newsletter (Philadelphia, PA)
MN   Mystery Nook (Wheaton, MD)
ModAge   Modern Age (Bryn Mawr, PA)
ModDr   Modern Drama (Univ. of Toronto)
Monist: an international quarterly of general philosophical inquiry
    (La Salle, IL)
Montana: the magazine of Western history (Helena, MT)
Moreana: time trieth truth (Angers, France)
Morgunblaðið (Reykjavik)
Mosaic: journal for the interdisciplinary study of literature (Univ. of Manitoba,
    Winnipeg)
Most (Mostar, Yugoslavia)
MP   Modern Philology (Chicago)
MPS   Modern Poetry Studies (Buffalo, NY)
MQ   Milton Quarterly (Ohio Univ., Athens)
MS   Moderna språk (Linkoping, Sweden)
MSE   Massachusetts Studies in English (Univ. of Massachusetts,
                          Amherst)
MsM   Ms.: the new magazine for women (New York)
MSS   Manuscripts (Burbank, CA)
MSSN   Medieval Sermon Studies Newsletter (Univ. of Warwick)
MStud   Milton Studies (Univ. of Pittsburgh, PA)
MTJ   Mark Twain Journal (College of Charleston, SC)
MULRN   McMaster University Library Research News (Hamilton,
                          Ont.)
Münchener Studien zur Sprachwissenschaft (Munich)
MundusA   Mundus Artium: a journal of international literature and the
                          arts (Univ. of Texas at Dallas, Richardson)
MusQ   Musical Quarterly (New York)
al-Muṣtanṣirīyah Literary Review (Baghdad)

MV   Minority Voices: an interdisciplinary journal of literature and the arts (University Park, PA)

Mythlore: a journal of J. R. R. Tolkien, C. S. Lewis, Charles Williams, general fantasy and mythic studies (Los Angeles, CA)

Nabokovian (Univ. of Kansas, Lawrence). *Formerly* Vladimir Nabokov Research Newsletter.

Nachrichten der Akademie der Wissenschaften in Göttingen

Nagyvilág (Budapest)

NAmerR   North American Review (Univ. of Northern Iowa, Cedar Falls)

Names (New York)

Nat   Nation (New York)

Natalia (Pietermaritzburg, South Africa)

National Times: Australia's national weekly newspaper of business and affairs (Sydney)

NatR   National Review: a journal of fact and opinion (New York)

Natural Language and Linguistic Theory (Dordrecht)

Nauchnye trudy Kubanskogo universiteta (Krasnodar, USSR)

Nauchnye trudy Kuĭbyshevskogo universiteta (Kuĭbyshev, USSR)

Naučni trudove. Filologija Plovidvski Universitet 'Paisij Hilendarski' (Plovdiv, Bulgaria)

NC   New Comparison (Univ. of Warwick)

NCarF   North Carolina Folklore Journal (Appalachian State Univ., Boone)

NCathW   New Catholic World (Mahwah, NJ)

NCF   Nineteenth-Century Fiction (Berkeley, CA)

NCHR   North Carolina Historical Review (Raleigh)

NCL   Notes on Contemporary Literature (West Georgia College, Carrollton)

NCrit   New Criterion (New York)

NDEJ   Notre Dame English Journal (Univ. of Notre Dame, IN)

NDFN   Nauchnye doklady vyssheĭ shkoly. Filologicheskie nauki (Moscow)

NDH   North Dakota History: journal of the Northern Plains (Bismarck, ND)

NDQ   North Dakota Quarterly (Univ. of N. Dakota, Grand Forks)

Nea Poreia (Thessalonika)

NebH   Nebraska History (Lincoln, NE)

Neohelicon: acta comparationis litterarum universarum (Akademiai Kiadó, Budapest)

Neophilologus (Groningen)

NEQ   New England Quarterly: an historical review of New England life and letters (Boston, MA)

NER   New England Review (Hanover, NH)

Neue Sammlung: Vierteljahres-Zeitschrift für Erziehung und Gesellschaft (Stuttgart)

NewL   New Leader: a bi-weekly of news and opinion (New York)

New Letters: a magazine of fine writing (Univ. of Missouri, Kansas City)

New Literature Review (Univ. of New England, Armidale, N.S.W.)

New Outlook (Auckland)

NewSt   New Statesman: an independent political and literary review (London)

New Zealand Journal of French Studies (Palmerston North)

New Zealand Monthly Review (Christchurch)

New Zealand National Bibliography (Wellington)

New Zealand Slavonic Journal (Victoria Univ., Wellington)

New Zealand Speech–Language Therapists' Journal (Christchurch)

New Zealand Women's Studies Journal (Auckland)

NGM   National Geographic (Washington, DC)

NHJ   Nathaniel Hawthorne Journal (Englewood, CO)

NHN   Nathaniel Hawthorne Society Newsletter. *See* NHR

NHR   Nathaniel Hawthorne Review (Bowdoin College,
              Brunswick, ME). *Formerly* Nathaniel Hawthorne Society
              Newsletter
Nieman Reports (Harvard Univ., Cambridge, MA)
NIF   Newsletter on Intellectual Freedom (Chicago)
Nimrod (Univ. of Tulsa, OK)
NJH   New Jersey History (Newark, NJ)
NJL   Nordic Journal of Linguistics (Oslo)
NK   Narodna kultura (Sofia)
NLB   Newberry Library Bulletin (Chicago)
NLH   New Literary History: a journal of theory and interpretation
              (Baltimore, MD)
NM   Neuphilologische Mitteilungen (Helsinki)
NMAL   Notes on Modern American Literature (St John's Univ.,
              Jamaica, NY)
NMS   Nottingham Medieval Studies (Univ. of Nottingham)
NMW   Notes on Mississippi Writers (Univ. of Southern Mississippi,
              Hattiesburg)
NoB   Namn och bygd: tidskrift för nordisk ortsnamnforskning/
              Journal for Nordic place-name research (Uppsala)
Nomina: journal of name studies relating to Great Britain and Ireland (Univ. of Hull)
NOR   New Orleans Review (Loyola Univ., New Orleans, LA)
Nordlyd: Tromsö University Working Papers on Language and Linguistics (Tromsö,
    Norway)
Norsk bokfortegnelse (Oslo)
Novel: a forum on fiction (Brown Univ., Providence, RI)
NovM   Novyĭ Mir (Moscow)
NOWELE   North-Western European Language Evolution: NOWELE
              (Odense Univ., Denmark)
NQ   Notes and Queries (Oxford)
NR   New Republic: a journal of opinion (Washington, DC)
NRam   New Rambler: the journal of the Johnson Society of London
              (Farningham, Kent)
NRF   Nouvelle revue française (Paris)
NSch   New Scholasticism (Catholic Univ. of America, Washington,
              DC)
NSG   Newsletter of Study Group on Eighteenth-Century Russia
              (Univ. of East Anglia, Norwich)
NwMSUS   Northwest Missouri State University Studies: bulletin of
              Northwest Missouri State University (Maryville)
NwOQ   Northwest Ohio Quarterly (Bowling Green State Univ., OH)
NWT   Nieuw Wereld Tijdschrift (Liezele-Purs, Belgium)
NY   New Yorker
NYF   New York Folklore (State Univ. of New York, Buffalo)
NYH   New York History (Cooperstown, NY)
NYHSQ   New York Historical Society Quarterly (New York)
NYRB   New York Review of Books
NYTB   New York Times Book Review
NYTM   New York Times Magazine
NZJH   New Zealand Journal of History (Univ. of Auckland)
NZLib   New Zealand Libraries (Wellington)
NZList   New Zealand Listener (Wellington)
NZZ   Neue Zürcher Zeitung (Zürich)
Ob   Obsidian: black literature in review (Detroit, MI)
Odyssey: a journal of the humanities (Oakland Univ., Rochester, MI)
OE   Ons Erfdeel: algemeen nederlands tweemaandelijks kultureel
              tijdschrift (Rekkem, Belgium)
OEN   Old English Newsletter (State Univ. of New York, Binghamton)
OhioanaQ   Ohioana Quarterly (Columbus, OH)
OhioH   Ohio History (Columbus)

OhioR — Ohio Review (Ohio Univ., Athens)
OL — Orbis litterarum: international review of literary studies (Copenhagen)
OldN — Old Northwest (Miami Univ., Oxford, OH)
OLSON: journal of the Charles Olson Archives (Univ. of Connecticut, Storrs)
OnS — On-Stage Studies (Univ. of Colorado, Boulder)
Opera News (New York)
OpL — Open Letter (Toronto)
Oral English (Le Moyne Coll., Syracuse, NY)
Oral History (Univ. of Essex)
Orana: journal for school and children's librarians (Ultimo, N.S.W.)
Orbis: bulletin international de documentation linguistique (Univ. Catholique de Louvain)
Ord och bild: nordisk kulturtidskrift (Stockholm)
OreHQ — Oregon Historical Quarterly (Portland)
Orizont (Timişoara, Romania)
Ortnamnssällskapets i Uppsala årsskrift (Uppsala)
Overland (Mt Eliza, Vic.)
PAAS — Proceedings of the American Antiquarian Society (Worcester, MA)
PacH — Pacific Historian (Univ. of the Pacific, Stockton, CA)
PacHR — Pacific Historical Review (Berkeley, CA)
Pacific Philosophical Quarterly (Univ. of Southern California, Los Angeles)
PacNQ — Pacific Northwest Quarterly (Univ. of Washington, Seattle)
PacQ — Pacific Quarterly. See Crosscurrent
PADS — Publications of the American Dialect Society (Univ. of Kansas, Lawrence)
Paideuma (Univ. of Maine, Orono)
Paintbrush: a journal of poetry, translations and letters (Georgia Southwestern College, Americus)
El país: panorama semanal (Madrid)
Palimpsest (Iowa City)
Pamiętnik Teatralny (Warsaw)
Panorama (Sofia)
PAPS — Proceedings of the American Philosophical Society (University Park, PA)
Parergon: bulletin of the Australian and New Zealand Association for Medieval and Renaissance Studies (Univ. of Sydney)
ParisR — Paris Review (Flushing, NY)
Parousia (Univ. of Athens)
Past and Present: a journal of historical studies (Corpus Christi College, Oxford)
Paunch (Buffalo, NY)
PBSA — Papers of the Bibliographical Society of America (Williamsburg, MA)
PBSC — Papers of the Bibliographical Society of Canada (Toronto)
PCL — Perspectives on Contemporary Literature (Univ. of Louisville, KY)
PCP — Pacific Coast Philology (San Diego State Univ., CA)
Pegasus (Soungjeon Univ., Korea)
PEW — Philosophy East and West: a quarterly journal of Asian and comparative thought (Univ. of Hawaii, Honolulu)
PH — Przegląd Humanistyczny (Warsaw)
PhilL — Philosophy and Literature (Baltimore, MD)
Philosophy (Cambridge)
PhilP — Philological Papers (West Virginia Univ., Morgantown)
PhilR — Philosophy and Rhetoric (University Park, PA)
PhilS — Philosophical Studies: an international journal for philosophy in the analytic tradition (Dordrecht)
PhilT — Philosophy Today (Celina, OH)
Phylon: Atlanta University review of race and culture (Atlanta, GA)

PJAS   Pakistan Journal of American Studies (Islamabad)
PL   Papers in Linguistics: international journal of human
                communication (Edmonton, Alta.)
Pl   Ploughshares: a journal of new writing (Cambridge, MA)
Plamăk (Sofia)
Planet (Aberystwyth)
Playboy (Chicago)
Plays and Players (Croydon, Surrey)
PLL   Papers on Language and Literature (Southern Illinois
                Univ., Edwardsville)
PMHB   Pennsylvania Magazine of History and Biography
                (Philadelphia)
PMHS   Proceedings of the Massachusetts Historical Society (Boston)
PMLA: Publications of the Modern Language Association of America
      (New York)
PMMLA   Papers of the Midwest MLA (New York)
PN Review (Manchester)
PoeS   Poe Studies (Pullman, WA)
PoetA   Poetica: Zeitschrift für Sprach- und Literaturwissenschaft
                (Bochum)
PoetC   Poet and Critic (Iowa State Univ., Ames)
Poetics: international review for the theory of literature (Amsterdam)
Poétique: revue de théorie et d'analyse littéraires (Paris)
Poetry (Chicago)
Poetry Wales: Cylchgrawn Cenedlaethol o Farddoniaeth Newydd (Bridgend)
PoetT   Poetica: an international journal of linguistic-literary studies
                (Tokyo)
Polycom (Carlton, Vic.)
PP   Philologica Pragensia: journal of modern philology (Prague).
                Includes, as supplement, CMF
PPQ   Pacific Philosophical Quarterly (Univ. of Southern California,
                Los Angeles)
PPR   Philosophy and Phenomenological Research (Buffalo, NY)
PQ   Philological Quarterly (Univ. of Iowa, Iowa City)
PR   Partisan Review (Boston Univ., MA)
Prague Studies in English
Praxis: a journal of cultural criticism (Univ. of California, Los Angeles)
Private Library (Pinner, Middlesex)
Problemi na izkistvoto (Bucharest)
Prose Studies (London)
Prospects: an annual journal of American cultural studies (Columbia Univ., New
      York)
PrS   Prairie Schooner (Univ. of Nebraska, Lincoln)
PRv   Philosophical Review (Cornell Univ., Ithaca, NY)
Przewodnik bibliograficzny (Warsaw)
PSiCL   Papers and Studies in Contrastive Linguistics (Poznań)
PSQ   Political Science Quarterly (New York)
PT   Poetics Today (Jerusalem)
PTFS   Publications of the Texas Folklore Society (Nacogdoches, TX)
PubH   Publishing History (Cambridge)
Publications of the Department of English and German, Tampere Univ. (Finland)
Publications of the Department of English, University of Turku (Finland)
PULC   Princeton University Library Chronicle (Princeton, NJ)
Puls (Sofia)
Push from the Bush (Clayton, Vic.)
QH   Quaker History (Haverford, PA)
QJLC   Quarterly Journal of the U.S. Library of Congress
                (Washington, DC)
QJS   Quarterly Journal of Speech (Annandale, VA)
QNL   Quarterly Newsletter (Book Club of California,
                San Francisco)

QQ Queen's Quarterly: a Canadian review (Queen's Univ., Kingston, Ont.)

Quadrant (Sydney)

Quaerendo: a quarterly journal from the Low Countries devoted to manuscripts and printed books (Leiden)

Quarry: new South African writing (Johannesburg)

Quarterly Bulletin of the South African Library (Cape Town)

Queen City Heritage: the journal of the Cincinnati Historical Society (Cincinnati, OH). *Formerly* Cincinnati Historical Society Bulletin

Quest: a feminist quarterly (Washington, DC)

RALS Resources for American Literary Study (Longwood College, Farmville, VA)

Ramuri (Craiova, Romania)

RANAM Recherches anglaises et américaines: a quarterly review (Univ. des Sciences Humaines, Strasbourg)

Rapports d'activités de l'Institut de Phonétique (Brussels)

Raritan: a quarterly review (Rutgers Univ., New Brunswick, NJ)

Ravi (Lahore)

RBPH Revue belge de philologie et d'histoire (Brussels)

RCEI Revista canaria de estudios ingleses (Univ. of La Laguna, Tenerife)

Reading Time (Curtin, A.C.T.)

REAL Re: Artes Liberales (Stephen F. Austin State Univ., Nacogdoches, TX)

RECTR Restoration and Eighteenth-Century Theatre Research (Loyola Univ. of Chicago)

REEDNewsletter Records of Early English Drama Newsletter (Univ. of Toronto)

Ren Renascence: essays on values in literature (Milwaukee, WI)

RenD Renaissance Drama (Univ. of New Orleans, LA)

Rendezvous: Idaho State University journal of arts and letters (Pocatello, ID)

RenP Renaissance Papers (Duke Univ., Durham, NC)

RenR Renaissance and Reformation/Renaissance et réforme (Univ. of Toronto)

Representations (Berkeley, CA)

Republika (Zagreb)

RES Review of English Studies: a quarterly journal of English literature and the English language (Oxford)

Restoration: studies in English literary culture, 1660–1700 (Univ. of Tennessee, Knoxville)

Review (Charlottesville, VA)

Revista interamericana de bibliografía. *See* IARB

RevL Revue de Louisiane/Louisiana Review (Lafayette)

Revue des lettres modernes: histoire des idées des littératures (Paris)

Revue du cinéma/Image et son: revue culturelle de cinéma (Paris)

Revue internationale de philosophie (Wetteren, Belgium)

Revue romane (Copenhagen)

RFil Revista de filología (Univ. of La Laguna, Tenerife)

RG Revue générale (Brussels)

RHT Revue d'histoire du théâtre (Paris)

RiceUS Rice University Studies (Houston, TX)

Rimu. *See* Crosscurrent

RITL Revista de istorie şi teorie literară (Bucharest)

RL Religion and Literature (Univ. of Notre Dame, IN)

RLC Revue de littérature comparée (Paris)

RMM Revue de métaphysique et de morale (Paris)

RMP Rheinisches Museum für Philologie (Frankfurt)

RMRLL Rocky Mountain Review of Language and Literature (Boise State Univ., ID)

RMS Renaissance and Modern Studies (Univ. of Nottingham)

RN Revue nouvelle (Brussels)

RNL   Review of National Literatures (Whitestone, NY)
RodR   Rodna reč (Sofia)
Romanskoe i germanskoe îâzykoznanie (Minskiĭ pedagogicheskiĭ institut, Minsk,
   USSR)
RomLit   România literară (Bucharest)
RomN   Romance Notes (Univ. of North Carolina, Chapel Hill)
RORD   Research Opportunities in Renaissance Drama (Univ. of
                    Kansas, Lawrence)
RPA   Revue de Phonétique appliquée (Paris)
RPF   Revue philosophique de la France et de l'étranger (Paris)
RPh   Romance Philology (Berkeley, CA)
RPP   Romanticism Past and Present (Northeastern Univ.,
                    Boston, MA)
RQ   Renaissance Quarterly (New York)
RR   Romanic Review (Columbia Univ., New York)
RRCNU   Research Review of Chungbuk National University (Chongju,
                    Korea)
RRL   Revue roumaine de linguistique (Bucharest). *Includes, as
                    supplement,* Cahiers de linguistique théorique et appliquée
RSWSU   Research Studies of Washington State University (Pullman)
RUC   Revista de la Universidad Complutense de Madrid
RULB   Revue de l'Université Libre de Bruxelles
RusL   Russkaîâ literatura (Leningrad)
RussR   Russian Review: an American quarterly devoted to Russia
                    past and present (Cambridge, MA)
SAC   Studies in the Age of Chaucer: the yearbook of the New Chaucer
                    Society (Univ. of Tennessee, Norman)
SAF   Studies in American Fiction (Northeastern Univ., Boston, MA)
SAH   Studies in American Humor (Southwest Texas State Univ.,
                    San Marcos)
SAL   Southwestern American Literature (Denton, TX)
Samlaren: tidskrift för svensk litteraturvetenskaplig forskning (Uppsala)
Samtiden (Oslo)
SAP   Studia Anglica Posnaniensia (Poznań)
SAQ   South Atlantic Quarterly (Durham, NC)
SaS   Slovo a slovesnost/Word and writing (Prague)
SAtlR   South Atlantic Review (Univ. of North Carolina, Chapel Hill)
SatR   Saturday Review: a review of literature and the creative arts
                    (Washington, DC)
Săvremennik (Sofia)
SB   Studies in Bibliography: papers of the Bibliographical Society of
                    the University of Virginia (Univ. of Virginia, Charlottesville)
SBrown   Studies in Browning and his Circle: a journal of criticism,
                    history and bibliography (Baylor Univ., Waco, TX)
ScanR   Scandinavian Review (New York)
SchM   Schweizer Monatshefte (Zurich)
SchP   Scholarly Publishing (Toronto)
Science Fiction: a review of speculative literature (Univ. of Western Australia,
   Nedlands)
SCL   Studii şi cercetări lingvistice (Bucharest)
SCN   Seventeenth-Century News (Pennsylvania State Univ.,
                    University Park)
Scottish Language: an annual review (Univ. of Aberdeen)
ScottN   Scott Newsletter (Univ. of Aberdeen)
SCR   South Central Review (Texas A & M Univ., College Station)
Scriblerian and Kit-Cats: a newsjournal devoted to Pope, Swift, and their circle, the
   Kit-Cats and Dryden (Temple Univ., Philadelphia, PA)
Scriptorium: international review of manuscript studies (Brussels)
SDR   South Dakota Review (Univ. of South Dakota, Vermillion)
SE   Southern Exposure (Durham, NC)

Secolul 20: revista de literatura universala (Bucharest)
SEEJ   Slavic and East European Journal (Univ. of Arizona, Tucson)
SEL   Studies in English Literature/Eibungaku Kenkyu (Tokyo)
SELit   Studies in English Literature 1500–1900 (Rice Univ., Houston, TX)
Septemvri (Sofia)
Seventeenth Century (Univ. of Durham)
SewR   Sewanee Review (Univ. of the South, Sewanee, TN)
SEz   Săpostavitelno ezikoznanie (Sofia)
SFN   Shakespeare on Film Newsletter (Univ. of Vermont, Burlington)
SFQ   Southern Folklore Quarterly (Univ. of Florida, Gainesville)
SFS   Science-Fiction Studies (McGill Univ., Montreal)
SGM   Scottish Geographical Magazine (Edinburgh)
Shaw: the annual of Bernard Shaw studies (University Park, PA)
Shen   Shenandoah (Washington and Lee Univ., Lexington, VA)
SHQ   Southwestern Historical Quarterly (Austin, TX)
ShS   Shakespeare Survey: an annual survey of Shakespearean study and production (Oxford)
SHum   Studies in the Humanities (Indiana Univ. of Pennsylvania, Indiana)
SIcon   Studies in Iconography (Arizona State Univ., Tempe)
Sigma (Univ. Paul Valéry, Montpellier)
Signs: journal of women in culture and society (Chicago)
Sinsear (Dublin)
Sistemnoe opisanie leksiki germanskikh îâzykov (Leningrad State Univ.)
Sites: a journal for radical perspectives (Palmerston North, NZ)
SixCT   Sixteenth Century Journal: an interdisciplinary journal for Renaissance and Reformation students and scholars (Northeast Missouri State Univ., Kirksville)
SJO   Jahrbuch der deutschen Shakespeare-Gesellschaft Ost (Weimar)
SJP   Southern Journal of Philosophy (Memphis State Univ., TN)
SJS   San Jose State Journal (San Jose State Univ., CA)
SJW   Jahrbuch der deutschen Shakespeare-Gesellschaft West (Univ. of Würzburg)
Skírnir (Reykjavik)
SL   Studies in Language (Amsterdam)
SlavR   Slavic Review: American quarterly of Soviet and East European studies (Stanford Univ., CA)
SLI   Studies in the Literary Imagination (Georgia State Univ., Atlanta)
SLJ   Scottish Literary Journal (Univ. of Aberdeen)
SLN   Sinclair Lewis Newsletter (St Cloud State College, MN)
Slovoobrazovanie i ego mesto v kurse obucheniîâ inostrannomu îâzyku (Leningrad State Univ.)
SLRC   Studii de literatură română și comparată Universitatea din Timişoara (Romania)
Smithsonian (Washington, DC)
Smjana (Sofia)
SN   Studia Neophilologica: a journal of Germanic and Romance philology (Stockholm)
SNL   Shakespeare Newsletter (Evanston, IL)
SNTM   Sbornik nauchnykh trudov Moskovskogo pedagogicheskogo instituta inostrannykh îâzykov (Moscow)
SNTT   Sbornik nauchnykh trudov Tashkentskogo universtiteta (Tashkent)
Societas Scientiarum Fennica: commentationes humanarum litterarum (Helsinki)
SoCR   South Carolina Review (Clemson Univ., SC)
SocSJ   Social Science Journal (Colorado State Univ., Fort Collins)

SoHR   Southern Humanities Review (Auburn Univ., AL)
SoLJ   Southern Literary Journal (Univ. of North Carolina, Chapel Hill)
SoQ   Southern Quarterly: a journal of the arts in the South (Univ. of Southern Mississippi, Hattiesburg)
SoR   Southern Review: a literary and critical quarterly magazine (Louisiana State Univ., Baton Rouge)
SoRA   Southern Review: literary and interdisciplinary essays (Univ. of Adelaide)
SoS   Southern Studies: an interdisciplinary journal of the South (Northwestern State Univ. of Louisiana, Natchitoches)
Soundings: an interdisciplinary journal (Vanderbilt Univ., Nashville, TN)
South African Journal of Linguistics (Lynn East)
South-Central Names Institute Publications (East Texas State Univ., Commerce)
Southerly: a review of Australian literature (Univ. of Sydney)
SP   Studies in Philology (Univ. of North Carolina, Chapel Hill)
Span (Christchurch, NZ)
Spec   Speculum: a journal of medieval studies (Cambridge, MA)
Spect   Spectator (London)
SpenN   Spenser Newsletter (State Univ. of New York, Albany)
Spenser Studies: a Renaissance poetry annual (Princeton Univ., NJ)
Spin (Palmerston North, NZ)
Spirit: a magazine of poetry (Seton Hall Univ., South Orange, NJ)
Splash (Auckland)
SPR   Southern Poetry Review (Univ. of North Carolina, Charlotte)
Die Sprache: Zeitschrift für Sprachwissenschaft (Wiesbaden)
Spr   Sprachkunst: Beiträge zur Literaturwissenschaft (Vienna)
SQ   Shakespeare Quarterly (Washington, DC)
SR   Studies in Romanticism (Boston Univ., MA)
Sravnitelno literaturoznanie (Sofia)
SRev   Southwest Review (Southern Methodist Univ., Dallas, TX)
SRO   Shakespearean Research and Opportunities: the report of the MLA Conference (City Univ. of New York)
SS   Scandinavian Studies (Urbana, IL)
SSF   Studies in Short Fiction (Newberry College, SC)
SShA: èkonomika, politika, ideologiiâ (Moscow)
SSJ   Southern Speech Communication Journal (Appalachian State Univ., Boone, NC)
SSL   Studies in Scottish Literature (Univ. of South Carolina, Columbia)
SSMLN   Society for the Study of Midwestern Literature Newsletter (Michigan State Univ., East Lansing)
SSQ   Social Science Quarterly (Austin, TX)
SStud   Shakespeare Studies (Univ. of New Mexico, Albuquerque)
SStudT   Shakespeare Studies (Tokyo)
Staffrider (Braamfontein, South Africa)
Standpunte (Auckland Park, South Africa)
Steaua (Cluj-Napoca, Romania)
SteiQ   Steinbeck Quarterly (Ball State Univ., Muncie, IN)
Streven (Antwerp)
StUCNPhil   Studia Universitatis Babes-Bolyai, Cluj–Napoca. Series Philologia (Cluj–Napoca, Romania)
StudAJL   Studies in American Jewish Literature (University Park, PA)
StudCanL   Studies in Canadian Literature (Univ. of New Brunswick, Fredericton)
StudECC   Studies in Eighteenth-Century Culture (Arizona State Univ., Tempe)
Studier fra sprog- og oldtidsforskning (Copenhagen)
Studier i modern språkvetenskap (Univ. of Stockholm)
Studies: an Irish quarterly review (Dublin)

Studies in Burke and his Time. *See* ECent
Studies in Language (Faculty of Arts, Univ. of Joensun, Finland)
StudL   Studia Linguistica: revue de linguistique générale et comparée
         (Malmo, Sweden)
StudME   Studies in Medieval English Language and Literature (Japan
         Society for Medieval English Studies, Tokyo)
StudN   Studies in the Novel (North Texas State Univ., Denton)
Style (Northern Illinois Univ., DeKalb)
Svensk bokförteckning/Swedish National Bibliography (Stockholm)
Svensk litteraturtidskrift (Stockholm)
Svenska tidskriftsartiklar (Lund)
SvL   Světová literatura (Prague)
SW   South and West: an international literary quarterly
         (Fort Smith, AR)
Swift Studies (Munster: Ehrenpreis Centre for Swift Studies)
SwS   Southwestern Studies (Univ. of Texas at El Paso)
Sydney Morning Herald (Broadway, N.S.W.)
Sydsvenska ortnamnssällskapets årsskrift: annual journal of the South Swedish Place-
    Name Society (Lund)
Symposium: a quarterly journal in modern foreign literatures (Washington, DC)
Synthesis: bulletin du Comité National de Littérature Comparée de la République
    Socialiste de Roumanie (Bucharest)
SZ   Stimmen der Zeit: Monatsschrift für das Geistesleben der
         Gegenwart (Freiburg im Breisgau)
T   Teatǎr (Sofia)
TamkR   Tamkang Review: a journal mainly devoted to comparative
         studies between Chinese and foreign literatures
         (Taipei, Taiwan)
TAPS   Transactions of the American Philosophical Society
         (Philadelphia, PA)
TBR   Texas Books in Review (Univ. of North Texas, Denton)
TCBS   Transactions of the Cambridge Bibliographical Society
         (Cambridge)
TCL   Twentieth-Century Literature: a scholarly and critical
         journal (Hofstra Univ., Hempstead, NY)
TDR   Drama Review: international journal documenting historical
         and contemporary trends in the performing arts (Cambridge,
         MA)
Te   Teatr (Moscow)
Te Reo: journal of the Linguistic Society of New Zealand (Univ. of Auckland)
Text & Context: a journal of interdisciplinary studies (North Staffs Poly.,
    Stoke-on-Trent)
TfL   Tidskrift för litteraturvetenskap (Umeå, Sweden)
TFSB   Tennessee Folklore Society Bulletin (Middle Tennessee
         State Univ., Murfreesboro)
TheatreS   Theatre Survey (State Univ. of New York, Albany)
Themes in Drama (Cambridge)
Theologie und Philosophie (Freiburg im Breisgau)
Theologische Zeitschrift (Basel Univ.)
Theoria: a journal of studies in the arts, humanities and social sciences
    (Univ. of Natal, Pietermaritzburg, South Africa)
THES   Times Higher Education Supplement (London)
This Australia (Collingwood, Vic.)
ThN   Thackeray Newsletter (Mississippi State Univ., Starkville)
Thomist: a speculative quarterly review of theology and philosophy (Washington,
    DC)
Thoreau Society Booklet (State Univ. College, Geneseo, NY)
Thoth (Syracuse Univ., NY)
Thought: a review of culture and ideas (Fordham Univ., Bronx, NY)
THQ   Tennessee Historical Quarterly (Nashville)

xlii   SOURCES AND ABBREVIATIONS

Threshold (Belfast)
Tijdschrift voor de Studie van de Verlichting en van het Vrije Denken (Centrum voor
  de Studie van de Verlichting en van het Vrije Denken, Vrije Universiteit, Brussels)
Time (New York)
Tíminn (Reykjavik)
TJ   Theatre Journal (Baltimore, MD)
TJQ   Thoreau Quarterly: a journal of literary and philosophical
                    studies (Univ. of Minnesota, Minneapolis)
TLR   Turnbull Library Record (Wellington, NZ)
TLS: Times Literary Supplement (London)
TM   Temps modernes (Paris)
TMM   Tímarit Máls og menningar (Reykjavik)
TN   Theatre Notebook: journal of the history and technique of
                    British theatre (London)
Tocher (Univ. of Edinburgh)
Topic: a journal of the liberal arts (Washington and Jefferson College,
  Washington, PA)
TPB   Tennessee Philological Bulletin: proceedings of the annual
                    meeting of the Tennessee Philological Association (Memphis,
                    TN)
TQ   Texas Quarterly (Univ. of Texas at Austin)
Traditio: studies in ancient and medieval history, thought, and religion
  (Bronx, NY)
Trans   Translation (Columbia Univ., New York)
Transilvania (Sibiu, Romania)
TRB   Tennyson Research Bulletin (Lincoln)
TRI   Theatre Research International (Oxford)
Tribuna (Cluj-Napoca, Romania)
TriQuarterly (Northwestern Univ., Evanston, IL)
Trudove na Velikotărnovskija universitet 'Kiril i Metodij' (Tărnovo, Bulgaria)
Trudy Samarkandskogo universiteta (Samarkand)
TS   Theatre Studies: the journal of the Ohio State University
                    Theatre Research Institute (Columbus, OH)
TSAR   Toronto South Asian Review
TSB   Thoreau Society Bulletin: devoted to the life and writings of
                    Henry David Thoreau (State Univ. College, Geneseo, NY)
TSE   Tulane Studies in English (Tulane Univ., New Orleans, LA)
TSL   Tennessee Studies in Literature (Univ. of Tennessee,
                    Knoxville)
TSLL   Texas Studies in Literature and Language: a journal of the
                    humanities (Univ. of Texas at Austin)
TSWL   Tulsa Studies in Women's Literature (Univ. of Tulsa, OK)
TTJE   Texas Tech Journal of Education (Texas Tech Univ., Lubbock)
Twainian (Perry, MO)
Twórczość (Warsaw)
TWR   Thomas Wolfe Review (Univ. of Akron, OH)
Tygodnik Powszechny (Cracow, Poland)
UASPY   University of Athens School of Philosophy Yearbook
Uchenye zapiski Tartuskogo universiteta. Trudi po romano-germanskoĭ filologii
  (Tartu, USSR)
UCTSE   University of Cape Town Studies in English (Univ. of Cape
                    Town)
UDR   University of Dayton Review (Dayton, OH)
UES   Unisa English Studies: journal of the Department of English
                    (Univ. of South Africa, Pretoria)
UHQ   Utah Historical Quarterly (Salt Lake City)
UHSL   University of Hartford Studies in Literature: a journal of
                    interdisciplinary criticism (West Hartford, CT)
UJH   University Journal: Humanities (Busan National Univ., Korea)
Ulster Folklife (Cultra, Co. Down)

UMPWS   University of Michigan Papers in Women's Studies (Ann Arbor)
UMSE   University of Mississippi Studies in English (University)
Unicorn: a miscellaneous journal (Brooklyn, NY)
Univ   Universitas: Zeitschrift für Wissenschaft, Kunst und Literatur (Stuttgart)
University of Colorado Studies, Series in Bibliography (Boulder)
University of Colorado Studies, Series in Language and Literature (Boulder)
University of Tulsa Monograph Series (Tulsa, OK)
Untold (Christchurch, NZ)
UPQ   University: a Princeton quarterly (Princeton, NJ)
Upstream (Cape Town)
UPub   University Publishing: an international quarterly review of books published by university presses (Berkeley, CA)
URLB   University of Rochester Library Bulletin (Rochester, NY)
USFLQ   University of South Florida Language Quarterly (Univ. of South Florida, Tampa)
USLL   Utah Studies in Literature and Linguistics (Univ. of Utah, Salt Lake City)
USP   Under the Sign of Pisces: Anaïs Nin and her circle (Ohio State Univ., Columbus)
UTQ   University of Toronto Quarterly: a Canadian journal of the humanities (Toronto)
UTSPY   University of Thessaloniki School of Philosophy Yearbook
UWR   University of Windsor Review (Univ. of Windsor, Ont.)
Vatra (Tîrgu-Mureş, Romania)
VC   Virginia Cavalcade (Richmond, VA)
Vestnik Khar'kovskogo universiteta. Inostrannye îazyki (Khar'kov, USSR)
VH   Vermont History (Montpelier, VT)
VÎA   Voprosy îazykoznaniîa (Moscow)
Viator: medieval and Renaissance studies (Univ. of California, Los Angeles)
Views on Language and Language Teaching (Athens)
VIJ   Victorians Institute Journal (East Carolina Univ., Greenville, NC)
Vinduet: Gyldendals tidsskrift för litteratur (Oslo)
VisCom   Visionary Company: a magazine of the Twenties (Mercy Coll., Dobbs Ferry, NY)
VKU   Vestnik Kievskogo universiteta. Romano-germanskaîa filologiîa (Kiev)
VLit   Voprosy literatury (Moscow)
VLU   Vestnik Leningradskogo universiteta. Istoriîa, îazyk, literatura (Leningrad)
VMHB   Virginia Magazine of History and Biography (Richmond, VA)
VMKANTL   Verslagen en mededelingen van de Koninklijke Academie voor Nederlandse Taal- en Letterkunde (Antwerp)
VMU   Vestnik Moskovskogo universiteta. Ser. 9: filologiîa (Moscow)
VN   Victorian Newsletter (Western Kentucky Univ., Bowling Green)
VNRN   Vladimir Nabokov Research Newsletter. See Nabokovian
VP   Victorian Poetry (West Virginia Univ., Morgantown)
VPR   Victorian Periodicals Review (Southern Illinois Univ., Edwardsville)
VQR   Virginia Quarterly Review: a national journal of literature and discussion (Univ. of Virginia, Charlottesville)
VR   Viaţa românească (Bucharest)
VS   Victorian Studies: a journal of the humanities, arts and sciences (Indiana Univ., Bloomington)
VWM   Virginia Woolf Miscellany (Rohnert Park, CA)
VWQ   Virginia Woolf Quarterly (Cherry Hill, NJ)
WAL   Western American Literature (Utah State Univ., Logan)

WBEP　　　　　　Wiener Beiträge zur englischen Philologie (Vienna)
WCR　　　　　　West Coast Review: a quarterly magazine of the arts
　　　　　　　　　　(Simon Fraser Univ., Burnaby, BC)
WCWR　　　　　William Carlos Williams Review (Swarthmore College, PA)
WD　　　　　　　Writer's Digest (Cincinnati, OH)
WE　　　　　　　Winesburg Eagle: the official publication of the Sherwood
　　　　　　　　　　Anderson Society (Univ. of Richmond, VA)
Westerly: a quarterly review (Univ. of Western Australia, Nedlands)
WF　　　　　　　Western Folklore (Glendale, CA)
Whimsy: proceedings of the Whim Conference (Tempe, AZ)
WHR　　　　　　Western Humanities Review (Univ. of Utah, Salt Lake City)
WIRS　　　　　　Western Illinois Regional Studies (Western Illinois Univ.,
　　　　　　　　　　Macomb)
WJSC　　　　　　Western Journal of Speech Communication (California State
　　　　　　　　　　Univ., Los Angeles)
WLB　　　　　　Wilson Library Bulletin (Bronx, NY)
WLT　　　　　　World Literature Today: a literary quarterly of the University
　　　　　　　　　　of Oklahoma (Norman)
WLWE　　　　　World Literature Written in English (Univ. of Guelph, Ont.)
WMH　　　　　　Wisconsin Magazine of History (Madison, WI)
WMQ　　　　　　William and Mary Quarterly: a magazine of early American
　　　　　　　　　　history and culture(Williamsburg, VA)
Women and Literature: a journal of women writers and the literary treatment of
　　women up to 1900 (Rutgers Univ., New Brunswick, NJ)
Women's Studies: an interdisciplinary journal (City Univ. of New York, Flushing)
WordsC　　　　　Wordsworth Circle (Temple Univ., Philadelphia, PA)
Working Papers (Speech and Language Research Centre, Macquarie University,
　　North Ryde, N.S.W.)
WPQ　　　　　　Western Political Quarterly (Salt Lake City, UT)
Writer (Boston, MA)
WSJ　　　　　　　Wallace Stevens Journal (Clarkson College, Potsdam, NY)
WT　　　　　　　Water Table (Seattle, WA)
WVH　　　　　　West Virginia History (Charleston, WV)
WWQR　　　　　Walt Whitman Quarterly Review (Univ. of Iowa, Iowa City)
Yankee (Dublin, NH)
YCC　　　　　　　Yearbook of Comparative Criticism (University Park, PA)
YCGL　　　　　　Yearbook of Comparative and General Literature (Indiana
　　　　　　　　　　Univ., Bloomington)
Yearbook of the Children's Literature Association, New Zealand (Auckland)
YER　　　　　　　Yeats Eliot Review: a journal of criticism and scholarship
　　　　　　　　　　(Univ. of Alberta, Edmonton)
YES　　　　　　　Yearbook of English Studies (Univ. of Warwick)
YFS　　　　　　　Yale French Studies (New Haven, CT)
YLG　　　　　　　Yale University Library Gazette (New Haven, CT)
YR　　　　　　　Yale Review (New Haven, CT)
YREAL　　　　　REAL: Yearbook of Research in English and American
　　　　　　　　　　Literature (Berlin)
YSE　　　　　　　Yale Studies in English (New Haven, CT)
YYY　　　　　　　Youngeo Youngmunhak (English Language and
　　　　　　　　　　Literature)(Yeungnam Univ., Korea)
ZAA　　　　　　　Zeitschrift für Anglistik und Amerikanistik (Leipzig)
Zagadnienia Rodzajów Literackich (Łódź)
ZDL　　　　　　　Zeitschrift für Dialektologie und Linguistik (Stuttgart)
Život (Sarajevo, Yugoslavia)
ZP　　　　　　　Zeitschrift für Phonetik, Sprachwissenschaft und
　　　　　　　　　　Kommunikationsforschung (Berlin, E. Germany)
ZRG　　　　　　　Zeitschrift für Religions- und Geistesgeschichte (Cologne)
ZVS　　　　　　　Zeitschrift für vergleichende Sprachforschung/Journal of
　　　　　　　　　　Comparative Linguistic Research into Indo-European
　　　　　　　　　　Philology (Göttingen)
Życie Literackie (Cracow)

ANNUAL BIBLIOGRAPHY OF ENGLISH LANGUAGE AND LITERATURE
1986

FESTSCHRIFTEN AND OTHER COLLECTIONS

Actes du congrès de Poitiers

1. SOCIÉTÉ DES ANGLICISTES DE L'ENSEIGNEMENT SUPÉRIEUR. Actes du congrès de Poitiers. Paris: Didier, 1984. pp. 701.

ARNAUD, RENÉ. Quelques observations quantitatives 'en temps réel' sur un changement: l'accroisement d'emploi de la forme progressive dans la 1re moitié du XIXe siècle. 67–75

BAR-DAVID, YORAM. Joyce et Kafka. 173–94

BOUCHER, PAUL. Time–space markers in oral discourse in English. 235–46

BREWER, DEREK. The place of medieval literature in English studies. 679–94

BROSSE, MONIQUE. Vrais ou faux gémeaux: Frederick Marryat et Édouard Corbière. 205–13

CAMÉE, JEAN-FRANÇOIS. La critique des conventions théâtrales dans *The Critic* de Sheridan. 317–26

CARLET, YVES. La religion transcendantale et la nouvelle Amérique. 23–36

CARRÉ, JACQUES. Architecture et société britanniques au XVIIIe siècle: pour une problématique. 7–19

CODACCIONI, MARIE-JOSÉ. L'autre vie de Bertha Rochester. 107–14

COHEN-SAFIR, C. Le doute chez K. Vonnegut, Jr. 567–77

CUSIN, MICHEL. D'un usage possible du schéma de Jakobson pour questionner les textes de fiction. 115–20

DEAN, JOHN. The city in science fiction since mid-century. 557–66

DEBAX, JEAN-PAUL. Ironie et cruauté dans *Measure for Measure*. 471–88

DE GUILLEBON, BRIGITTE. Problématique du personnage chez Dickens. 121–4

DELECHELLE, GÉRARD. La valeur causale de *as* et *with*. 249–58

DELMAS, CLAUDE. Remarques à propos de *the*. 259–70

DOMMERGUES, ANDRÉ. Patrick White et le thème aborigène. 663–74

ESCARBELT, BERNARD. 'Un peuple de *paysans*': difficultés de terminologie dans l'étude de l'Irlande au début du XIXe siècle. 155–65

GALLET, LILIANE. La traduction assistée par ordinateur (TAO): réalisations, perspectives, conséquences: 'How will it affect my job?' 621–35

GARBAGNATI, LUCILE. Une traduction anesthésiante pour un texte subversif: Mark Twain: *The Adventures of Huckleberry Finn* (1884) traduit par W. L. Hughes, 1886. 215–22

GOIZET, ANNETTE. *Helen O'Loy* de Lester Del Rey: Helen est-elle femme ou robot? 579–86

GUIERRE, LIONEL. Où en est l'accentuation du mot en anglais? 273–83

GURY, JACQUES. Shakespeare, du Globe au petit écran, en passant par Drury Lane: *Romeo and Juliet*, 1595 – 1748 – 1978. 327–31

JOLICŒUR, CLAUDE. Mythologie chrétienne et structure narrative dans *The Way of All Flesh* de Samuel Butler. 91–101

MARTINET, MARIE-MADELEINE. 'The sister arts' et le sens du temps. 417–32

MATHIS, GILLES. Rhétorique(s) et stylistique(s). 505–30

NORDON, PIERRE. Le fou sur la scène anglaise contemporaine. 333–39

PARRINDER, PATRICK. ''Tis new to thee': the strange and the familiar in the language of science fiction. 587–97

PIRONON, JEAN. Le thème de *La foire* de Ben Jonson à Defoe: changements de mentalité et typologie jungienne. 433–44

QUERE, HENRI. Retour aux lieux familiers de la fiction: personnage, narration, description. 125–35

RAMEL, JACQUES. Méta-diégèse et extra-diégèse dans le théâtre élisabéthain. 341–56

RAYNAUD, JEAN. Science-fiction: genre, ou vision? Introduction à une problématique. 599–609

SAHEL, PIERRE. Le spectateur de la fin du *Conte d'hiver*. 357–68

SESSA, JACQUELINE. *Les Antipodes* de Richard Brome, comédie anglaise et comédie européenne. 223–30

STRAUCH, GÉRARD. Monologue intérieur et style indirect libre. 531–53

SUHAMY, HENRI. À propos d'une phrase de Muriel Bradbrook: rhétorique et cruauté dans *Titus Andronicus*. 489–98

Age d'or et apocalypse

2. ELLRODT, ROBERT; BRUGIÈRE, BERNARD (eds). Age d'or et apocalypse. Paris: Publications de la Sorbonne. pp. 364. (Langue et langages, 13.)

AQUIEN, PASCAL. W. H. Auden: nostalgie de l'Eden et apocalypse du moi. 251–9

BLEIKASTEN, ANDRÉ.   Temps, mythe et histoire chez Faulkner. 173–93

BRUGIÈRE, BERNARD.   Qu'appelle-t-on aujourd'hui littérature apocalyptique? 113–28

CARLET, YVES.   Thoreau et le temps retrouvé: *A Week on the Concord and Merrimack Rivers.* 149–71

CARRIVE, LUCIEN.   Le royaume de Dieu, l'apocalypse et le millenium dans le protestantisme anglais classique. 31–46

DAYRAS, SOLANGE.   Apocalypse 1945: du thomisme à l'atomisme. 261–71

DUTRUCH, SUZANNE.   Les lendemains: variations sur l'enfer: à propos de quelques romans de science-fiction. 293–301

ELLRODT, ROBERT.   Milton et la vision édénique. 47–62

HIMY, ARMAND.   Blake et l'apocalyptique dans *Jérusalem.* 131–47

LAFOURCADE, BERNARD.   Wyndham Lewis ou l'apocalypse immobile. 195–212

LOJKINE, MONIQUE.   T. S. Eliot: entre l'aspiration à l'éternel présent de l'Eden retrouvé et apocalypse now. 213–29

MARTINET, MARIE-MADELEINE.   Iconologie élisabéthaine du temps mythique: l'homme au bord du jardin et la tour de feu. 25–30

NAUGRETTE, J.-P.   L'Afrique à la courbe du temps: l'Apocalypse selon V. S. Naipaul. 303–17

PETILLON, PIERRE.   *Day of Doom*: la rhétorique de la fin des temps dans la Nouvelle Angleterre du XVIIe siècle. 63–75

PORÉE, MARC.   Le roman des derniers jours: Anthony Burgess, *The End of the World News.* 273–92

PRUVOT, MONIQUE.   Apocalypse et temps mythique chez les peintres américains de l'école de New York. 335–55

RABATÉ, JEAN-MICHEL.   L'énonciation apocalyptique des *Cantos Pisans.* 231–49

SOUPEL, SERGE.   Visions édéniques et visions apocalyptiques chez James Hervey (1714–1758.) 77–87

TEYSSANDIER, HUBERT.   L'Apocalypse et le nouvel Eden dans *Riders in the Chariot* de Patrick White. 319–33

VENET, GISÈLE.   Temps mythiques et temps tragique: du Moyen Age au Baroque. 11–24

The American Short Story, 1900–1945: a Critical History

3. STEVICK, PHILIP (ed.).   The American short story, 1900–1945: a critical history. Boston, MA: G. K. Hall, 1985. pp. 168. (Twayne's critical history of the short story.) Rev. by Samuel Irving Bellman in SSF (23) 124–5.

GULLASON, THOMAS A.   The 'lesser' renaissance: the American short story in the 1920s. 71–101

KIMBEL, ELLEN.   The American short story: 1900–1920. 33–69

ROHRBERGER, MARY.   The question of regionalism: limitation and transcendence. 147–82

WATSON, JAMES G.   The American short story: 1930–1945. 103–46

Anglisticko-Amerikanistická Konference

4. HLADKÝ, JOSEF (ed.).   Anglisticko-Amerikanistická Konference. (Conference on English and American studies.) Brno: Purkyně UP. pp. 69.

ARBEIT, MARCEL.   Morální aspekty románů Flannery O'Connorové a Walkera Percyho. (The novels of Flannery O'Connor and Walker Percy: moral aspects.) 18

BÖHMEROVÁ, ADELA.   Neutralizácia negácie v angličtine a v slovenčine. (The neutralization of negation in English and in Slovak.) 19–20

CHAMONIKOLASOVÁ, JANA.   Volné elementy v hovorové angličtině. (Free elements in colloquial English.) 28–9

DUŠKOVÁ, LIBUŠE.   Ke klasifikaci vedlejších vět uvozených jednoduchými a složenými relativy. (Classification of subordinate clauses introduced by simple and complex relatives.) 20–1

FIRBAS, JAN.   Ilustrace k pojetí jazyka jako sytému systémů. (Illustrations of the conception of language as a system of systems.) 21–2

GOLKOVÁ, EVA.   O funkci anglického prvního větného členu ve funkční větné perspektivě. (The function of the English first clause element in functional sentence perspective.) 22–3

GRMELA, JOSEF.   Několik poznámek k interpretaci Maggie, dítě ulice Stephena Cranea. (Notes on the interpretation of Stephen Crane's *Maggie*.) 23–4

HAJIČOVÁ, IVANA.   Slovosledné pozice časových a místních určení. (The word-order of temporal and local adverbials.) 24–5

HILSKÝ, MARTIN.   Angus Wilson a nové tendence současné britské prózy. (Angus Wilson and the new trends in contemporary British prose.) 25–6

HLADKÝ, JOSEF.   Dělení slov a zvuková rovina. (Word-division and the phonic level of language.) 26–7

HORNÁT, JAROSLAV.   Pinterův návrat domů. (Pinter's *The Home-coming.*) 27–8

JAŘAB, JOSEF.   Modernismus a současná americká poezie. (Modernism and contemporary American poetry.) 30–1

JINDRA, MIROSLAV.   Hledání kořenů. (The search for roots.) 31–2

MAREK, JIŘÍ.   Současná literatura ve Skotsku. (Contemporary Scottish literature.) 38–9

MARKOVÁ, MILENA.   K poměru verbálních a nominálních rysů mezi češtinou a angličtinou z hlediska překladu. (The relation of verbal and nominal features in Czech and English.) 39–40

MASNEROVÁ, EVA. K problému vymezení prózy amerického Jihu: její historičnost a další charakteristické rysy. (The delimitation of fiction in the American South: its history and characteristics.) 40–1

NENADÁL, RADOSLAV. Násilí jako konstruktivní fabulační prvek u Johna Irvinga. (Violence as a constructional element in John Irving.) 42–3

NOSEK, JIŘÍ. Funkce a obsah v jazyce. (Function and content in language.) 43–4

PANTŮČKOVÁ, LIDMILA. Několik poznámek ke vztahu Jana Nerudy k americké literatuře. (Notes on the relation of Jan Neruda to American literature.) 44–5

PROCHÁZKA, MARTIN. K problému tvůrčí metody v poezii a estetice anglického romantismu. (Problems of creative methods in poetry and the aesthetics of English Romanticism.). 55–6

ŘEŘICHA, VÁCLAV. Metodologické problémy analýzy anglických substantivních kompozit. (Problems of analysis of English nounal compounds.) 57–8

RUŽIČKOVÁ, EVA. Verbonominálne konštrukcie a pomocné sloveso 'have'. (Verbo-nominal structures and the auxiliary 'have'.) 56–7

STAŠKOVÁ, JAROSLAVA. K problematike vymedzenia významu anglických temporálnych predložiek. (Problems in defining meanings of English temporal prepositions.) 60–1

STŘÍBRNÝ, ZDENĚK. Několik poznámek o dekonstruktivismu. (Notes on deconstructivism.) 61–2

TÁRNYIKOVÁ, JARMILA. Komunikativní přístup v syntaxi. (The communicative approach to syntax.) 64

TICHÝ, ALEŠ. Vypravěč a styl u Jamese Joyce a Virginie Woolfové. (Narrator and style in James Joyce and Virgina Woolf.) 64–5

TURBOVÁ, MILENA. Anglické překladové protějšky českého 'již/už'. (English equivalents of the Czech adverbs 'již/už'.) 65

VÁŇOVÁ, TAMARA. Ženské postavy v díle Margarety Atwoodové. (Margaret Atwood's female characters.) 65–6

VILIKOVSKÝ, JÁN. John Dryden, jeho teória a prax vnitroliterárného prekladu. (John Dryden, his theory and practice of internal translation.) 68

Les aspects littéraires du biculturalisme aux États-Unis

5. SANTRAUD, JEANNE-MARIE (ed.). Les aspects littéraires du biculturalisme aux États-Unis. Paris: Presses de l'Université de Paris–Sorbonne. pp. 174.

ATLAN, MADY. Manhattan: le nouveau Yiddishland d'Isaac Bashevis Singer. 143–56

BARDOT, JEAN. L'influence française dans la vie et l'œuvre de Kate Chopin. 31–46

CASTEX, PEGGY. Is there a reader in the house? The dilemma of Cajun literature. 47–76

FARHI, EMMANUELLE. Le yiddish, reflet de la conscience morale. 129–42

GERBAUD, COLETTE. Terre et culture: un pionnier. Saint Jean de Crèvecœur et divers aspects du phénomène culturel. 11–30

HUBNER, P. Henry James et *La Scène américaine* (1907): le drame transatlantique des cultures. 79–96

LAVABRE, SIMONE. Vladimir Nabokov: richesse et problèmes du biculturalisme. 99–106

MILLER, JAMES E., JR. Kosinski and the lessons of hate and revenge. 107–16

SANTRAUD, JEANNE-MARIE; SAPORTA, MARC. Introduction à une étude du biculturalisme. 3–10

SAPORTA, MARC. L'émigré de nulle part. 119–28

WEST, THOMAS. Culture, cultures and bi-culturalism. 159–69

The British Working-Class Novel in the Twentieth Century

6. HAWTHORN, JEREMY (ed.). The British working-class novel in the twentieth century. London; Baltimore, MD; Caulfield East, Vic.: Arnold, 1984. pp. xii, 162. (Stratford-upon-Avon studies, second ser.) Rev. by Felicity Horne in UES (24:2) 53–4.

BURTON, DEIRDRE. A feminist reading of Lewis Grassic Gibbon's *A Scots Quair*. 34–46

CRAIG, DAVID. The roots of Sillitoe's fiction. 94–109

DAVIES, TONY. Unfinished business: realism and working-class fiction. 124–36

HOLDERNESS, GRAHAM. Miners and the novel: from bourgeois to proletarian fiction. 18–32

MARTIN, GRAHAM. 'History' and 'myth' in D. H. Lawrence's Chatterley novels. 62–74

MILES, PETER. The painter's bible and the British workman: Robert Tressell's literary activism. xii, 1–17

PICKERING, MICHAEL; ROBINS, KEVIN. The making of a working-class writer: an interview with Sid Chaplin. 138–50

PICKERING, MICHAEL; ROBINS, KEVIN. 'A revolutionary materialist with a leg free': the autobiographical novels of Jack Common. 76–92

SHERRY, RUTH. The Irish working class in fiction. 110–23

WEBSTER, ROGER. *Love on the Dole* and the aesthetic of contradiction. 48–61

Canadian Writers and their Works: Fiction Series: Vol. 6

7. LECKER, ROBERT; DAVID, JACK; QUIGLEY, ELLEN (eds). Canadian writers and their works: fiction series: vol. 6. Downsview, Ont.: ECW Press, 1985. pp. 283. Rev. by W. J. Keith in CanL (110) 117–20; by Leslie Monkman in QQ (93:4) 874–9.

GREENSTEIN, MICHAEL.   Adele Wiseman. 239–72
McSWEENEY, KERRY.   Mordecai Richler. 129–79
MILLS, JOHN.   Robertson Davies. 19–78
MITCHELL, BEVERLEY.   Ethel Wilson. 181–238
STUEWE, PAUL.   Hugh Garner. 79–127

Canadian Writers and their Works: Fiction Series: Vol. 7

8. LECKER, ROBERT; DAVID, JACK; QUIGLEY, ELLEN (eds).   Canadian writers and their works: fiction series: vol. 7. Downsview, Ont.: ECW Press, 1985. pp. 326. Rev. by Leslie Monkman in QQ (93:4) 874–9; by W. J. Keith in CanL (110) 117–20.

CAMERON, BARRY.   Clark Blaise. 21–89
DAHLIE, HALLVARD.   Alice Munro. 215–56
GAREBIAN, KEITH.   Hugh Hood. 93–151
ROLLINS, DOUGLAS.   John Metcalf. 155–211
SCOBIE, STEPHEN.   Sheila Watson. 259–312

Canadian Writers and their Works: Poetry Series: Vol. 5

9. LECKER, ROBERT; DAVID, JACK; QUIGLEY, ELLEN (eds).   Canadian writers and their works: poetry series: vol. 5. Toronto: ECW Press, 1985. pp. 350. Rev. by J. M. Zezulka in CanP (19) 102–4; by Leslie Monkman in QQ (93:4) 874–9.

AICHINGER, PETER.   Earle Birney. 27–71
FRANCIS, WYNNE.   Irving Layton. 143–234
GOLDIE, TERRY.   Louis Dudek. 75–139
STEVENS, PETER.   Miriam Waddington. 279–329
WHITEMAN, BRUCE.   Raymond Souster. 237–76

Canadian Writers and their Works: Poetry Series: Vol. 9

10. LECKER, ROBERT; DAVID, JACK; QUIGLEY, ELLEN (eds).   Canadian writers and their works: poetry series: vol. 9. Toronto: ECW Press, 1985. pp. 288. Rev. by J. M. Zezulka in CanP (19) 102–4; by Leslie Monkman in QQ (93:4) 874–9.

BARTLEY, JAN.   Gwendolyn MacEwen. 231–71
BLODGETT, E. D.   D. G. Jones. 85–130
MALLINSON, JEAN.   Margaret Atwood. 17–81sscher
MIDDLEBRO', T. G.   Dennis Lcc. 189–228
. WOODCOCK, GEORGE.   Patrick Lane. 133–85

Classical Models in Literature/Les modèles classiques dans les littératures/Klassische Modelle in der Literatur

11. KONSTANTINOVIĆ, ZORAN; ANDERSON, WARREN; DIETZE, WALTER (eds).   Classical models in literature/Les modèles classiques dans les littératures/Klassische Modelle in der Literatur. Proceedings of the IXth Congress of the International Comparative Literature Association. Innsbruck: Inst. für Sprachwissenscraft der Universität Innsbruck, 1981. pp. 305. Rev. by Franco Meregalli in CanRCL (12:3) 1985, 481–7.

ANDERSON, WARREN.   'Influentia' and 'influence': the currents of Maeander. 35–42

AVERINCEV, SERGEJ S.   Das dauerhafte Erbe der Griechen: die rhetorische Grundeinstellung als Synthese des Traditionalismus und der Reflexion. 267–71

FOLEY, JOHN MILES.   Narrativity in *Beowulf*, the Odyssey, and the Serbo-Croatian 'return song'. 295–301

KRETZOI, CHARLOTTE.   Changes in the meaning and function of plain style. 249–53

LOY, J. ROBERT.   Attitudes toward authority in European literature to the eighteenth century. 65–9

MARINO, ADRIAN.   Interpréter et/est moderniser les classiques. 77–82

MORTIER, ROLAND.   Cent ans de littérature comparée: l'acquis, les perspectives. 11–17

PAXTON, NANCY L.   Daughters of Lucrece: Shakespeare's response to Ovid in *Titus Andronicus*. 217–24

RIEHLE, WOLFGANG.   The fragment in English Romantic poetry. 133–8

ROSENMEYER, THOMAS G.   Aristotelian ethos and character in modern drama. 119–25

ŠARČEVIĆ, SUSAN.   The classical hero and modern evolution. 127–32

TATLOW, ANTONY.   Classical and radical organicism: towards a rhetoric of social gesture. 83–8

VAN DELFT, LOUIS.   La notion de 'caractère' á l'âge classique. 59–63

WELLEK, RENÉ.   Literature, fiction and literariness. 19–25

Communiquer et traduire/Communicating and Translating

12. DEBUSSCHER, G.; VAN NOPPEN, J.-P. (eds).   Communiquer et traduire/Communicating and translating: essays in honour of Jean Dierickx. Brussels: Éditions de l'Université de Bruxelles, 1985. pp. 339. (Faculté de Philosophie et Lettres, 96.)

BAETENS BEARDSMORE, HUGO.   Medium and message orientated communication compared with the BICS/CALP theory in bilingual education. 191–9

BAGHDIKIAN, SONIA.   'He did not seeke' or 'He seeketh not': are you a queen or a country woman? 241–8

DEBUSSCHER, GILBERT.   *Educating Rita*, or an Open University *Pygmalion*. 303–17

DELBAERE-GARANT, JEANNE.   Prospero to-day: magus, monster or patriarch? 293–302

DELSEMME, PAUL.   Oscar Wilde et la Beligique fin de siècle. 277–91

DOMINICY, MARC.   Sur les emplois 'temporels' de *only*. 211–17

GOFFIN, ROGER.   La science de la traduction 1955–1985: une tentative de bilan provisoire. 27–36

GOOSSENS, LOUIS.   What's in an advertising name? 95–102

HEIDELBERGER-LEONARD, IRÈNE.   Translation as the prime art of communication? A note on George Steiner's *After Babel*. 19–25

JOLY, ANDRÉ.   Pour une analyse systématique des modalités non verbales de la communication. 131–41

MAUFORT, MARC.   Communication as translation of the self: Jamesian inner monologue in O'Neill's *Strange Interlude* (1927). 319–28

NOËL, J.; JANSSEN, J.; MERGEAI, J.-P.   Disambiguating definition language in two automatic dictionaries of English: outline of a computer-aided procedure. 143–9

SIMON, IRÈNE.   The theatre motif in William Golding's *Rites of Passage*. 261–7

THOVERON, GABRIEL.   Quality/popular: intraduisibles en français? 79–84

VANDENBERGEN, ANNE-MARIE.   Conjunction and continuity in newspaper reports. 85–94

VAN NOPPEN, JEAN-PIERRE.   In and beyond the glossary, or on making maps out of puzzles. 165–74

VAN ROEY, JACQUES.   Deceptive terminology for deceptive cognates. 159–64

VORLAT, EMMA.   'Your marriage is going through a rocky patch': on idioms in the Lonely Hearts column. 103–8

WHITBURN, M.   La chaînon manquant. 55–63

WILMET, MARC.   *A kiwi abounds in this area: note sur l'article 'indéfini générique'. 219–26

Contrasts: Comparative Essays on Italian-Canadian Writing

13.   PIVATO, JOSEPH (ed.).   Contrasts: comparative essays on Italian-Canadian writing. Montreal: Guernica, 1985. pp. 255.

AMPRIMOZ, ALEXANDRE L.; VISELLI, SANTE A.   Death between two cultures: Italian-Canadian poetry. 101–20

BILLINGS, ROBERT.   Contemporary influences on the poetry of Mary di Michele. 121–52

MINNI, C. D.   The short story as an ethnic genre. 61–76

PACI, F. G.   Tasks of the Canadian novelist writing on immigrant themes. 35–60

PIVATO, JOSEPH.   Ethnic writing and comparative Canadian literature. 17–34

SCIFF-ZAMARO, ROBERTA.   *Black Madonna*: a search for the Great Mother. 77–99

Le corps et l'âme en Grande-Bretagne au XVIIIe siècle. Colloques 1983–85 du Centre d'Études Anglaises du XVIIIe siècle

14.   BOUCÉ, PAUL-GABRIEL; HALIMI, SUZY (eds).   Le corps et l'âme en Grande-Bretagne au XVIIIe siècle. Colloques 1983–85 du Centre d'Études Anglaises du XVIIIe siècle. Paris: Publications de la Sorbonne. pp. 180.

BRUNETEAU, CLAUDE.   La maladie anglaise. 11–24

BULCKAEN-MESSINA, DENISE.   Jeu des acteurs et reflets de l'âme dans la *Rosciade* (1761) de Charles Churchill. 99–110

DENIZOT, PAUL.   Yorick et la quête du bonheur, ou les équivoques ludiques du corps et de l'âme. 157–66

DESFOND, HÉLÈNE.   Tyburn chez Mandeville et Fielding, ou le corps exemplaire du pendu. 61–70

DIXSAUT, JEAN.   'Uncommon gradations': l'amour, le corps et l'âme dans *Pamela*. 131–8

DU SORBIER, FRANÇOISE.   A la recherche de la femme perdue: Moll Flanders et Roxana. 121–30

DUHET, PAULE-MARIE.   Bonheur et douleur dans *Elements of Morality for the Use of Children* (1790–1791) de Mary Wollstonecraft. 167–76

DUTRUCH, SUZANNE.   Henry et John Fielding magistrates: âme de la ville et corps de la police. 71–86

HEROU, JOSETTE.   Jeux de l'âme et du corps sur la scène comique en Angleterre au XVIIIe siècle. 87–98

JOUVE, MICHEL.   Corps difformes et âmes perverses: quelques réflexions sur la pratique de la caricature. 111–20

LACROIX, JEAN-MICHEL.   La publicité des produits pharmaceutiques dans la presse anglaise du XVIIIe siècle. 37–50

LAMOINE, GEORGES.   L'âme et le corps en prison au XVIIIe siècle. 51–60

MITCHELL, BRIGITTE.   Le corps et l'âme du Révérend John Penrose. 25–36

WAGNER, PETER.   The assertion of body and instinct: John Cleland's *Memoirs of a Woman of Pleasure*. 139–56

Dialog der Texte: Literatur und Landeskunde. Beiträge zu Problemen einer integrativen Landes- und Kulturkunde des englischsprachigen Auslands

15.   KUNA, FRANZ; TSCHACHLER, HEINZ (eds).   Dialog der Texte: Literatur und Landeskunde. Beiträge zu Problemen einer integrativen Landes- und Kulturkunde des englischsprachigen Auslands. Tübingen: Narr. pp. 544.

GRÜNZWEIG, WALTER. Überlegungen zum Verhältnis von Literaturstudium und Landeskunde am Beispiel der Romane Charles Sealsfields. 315–34

HELLER, ARNO. Literarische Landes- und Kulturkunde als kommunikativer Prozeß: ein amerikanistisches Beispiel. 209–29

HÖBLING, WALTER. Fiktionale Texte in der Landes- und Kulturkunde: Pragmatische Überlegungen am Beispiel amerikanischer Romane zum Vietnamkonflikt. 231–53

KUNA, FRANZ. Dialog der Texte: Landeskunde als kultureller Prozess. 425–41

PEPER, JÜRGEN. Die Metapher als Kulturfigur: ein literarästhetischer Beitrag zur Landes- und Kulturkunde. 259–92

English in Speech and Writing: a Symposium
16. TOTTIE, GUNNEL; BÄCKLUND, INGEGERD (eds). English in speech and writing: a symposium. Uppsala: Acta Universitatis Upsaliensis; Stockholm: Almqvist & Wiksell. pp. 204. (Studia anglistica Upsaliensia, 60.)

AIJMER, KARIN. Why is 'actually' so popular in spoken English? 119–29

ALTENBERG, BENGT. Contrastive linking in spoken and written English. 13–40

BÄCKLUND, INGEGERD. 'Beat until stiff': conjunction-headed abbreviated clauses in spoken and written English. 41–55

ERMAN, BRITT. Some pragmatic expressions in English conversation. ('You know', 'you see', 'I mean'.) 131–47

HERMERÉN, LARS. Modalities in spoken and written English: an inventory of forms. 57–91

RENOUF, ANTOINETTE. The elicitation of spoken English. 177–97

STENSTRÖM, ANNA-BRITA. What does 'really' really do? Strategies in speech and writing. 149–63

TOTTIE, GUNNEL. The importance of being adverbial: adverbials of focusing and contingency in spoken and written English. 93–118

VIITANEN, OUTI. On the position of 'only' in English conversation. 165–75

English Language and Literature: Methods of Teaching and Research
17. BAŁUK-ULEWICZOWA, TERESA; KOROSADOWICZ, MARIA (eds). Proceedings of the third April Conference of University Teachers of English, Cracow 1984 (April 11–15). English language and literature: methods of teaching and research. Cracow: Uniwersytet Jagielloński. pp. 247. (Zeszyty Naukowe Uniwersytetu Jagiellońskiego. Prace historycznoliterackie, 64.)

BOLTON, FRANCES. George Eliot and Italian Renaissance painting. 159–67

DILLER, HANS-JURGEN.   The image of the Middle Ages in nineteenth-century scholarship and fiction. 147–58

GIBIŃSKA, MARTA.   'Travellers ne'er did lie, though fools at home condemn 'em': some remarks on the dramatic presentation of romance material in *The Tempest*. 115–26

GRUNZWEIG, WALTER.   Reminiscences of the Arkansas legislature, back fifty years ago: Mark Twain's use of Austrian politics in *Stirring Times in Austria*. 181–93

JĘDRZEJKIEWICZ, MARIA.   Escape from freedom: 'enchanters' in Iris Murdoch's fiction. 217–25

MILLER, MICHAEL T.   Virginia words: historical and geographical perspectives. 11–21

PIEŃKOWSKI, PIOTR.   The idea of the mental garden in William Wordsworth's poetry. 127–45

ROPER, DEREK.   'Practical criticism': fifty years of an English teaching method. 227–43

SIEDLECKI, PETER A.   Herman Melville and his untrustworthy metaphor. 170–9

SOKOLOVA, BOIKA.   Renaissance aesthetics and Marlowe's *Faustus*. 127–35

TABAKOWSKA, ELŻBIETA.   On the pragmatics of *the*. 23–32

WALCZUK, ANNA.   Gilbert Keith Chesterton's europeanism. 207–15

ZACHARASIEWICZ, WALDEMAR.   Jack Hodgins as a short story writer and the tradition of regional fiction in Canada. 195–206

Essays in Honour of Kristian Smidt

18.   BILTON, PETER, *et al.* (eds).   Essays in honour of Kristian Smidt. Oslo: Univ. of Oslo, Inst. of English studies. pp. 373.

BARNARD, ROBERT.   Charlotte Brontë's unfinished novels. 122–33

BEATTY, AUDREY.   List of Kristian Smidt's publications. 351–73

BEATTY, C. J. P.   Victor Hugo, Swinburne, and an Irish poet. 134–44

BERGE, MARIT.   Jimmy Porter – Osborne's Hedda Gabler? 201–12

BJØRHOVDE, GERD.   Transformation and subversion as narrative strategies in two fantasy novels of the 1920s: Sylvia Townsend Warner's *Lolly Willowes* and Virginia Woolf's *Orlando*. 213–24

BRADBROOK, MURIEL.   Social nuances in Shakespeare's early comedies. 1–8

BRØGGER, FREDERIK CHR.   Modernism and antimodernism: Eliot's *The Waste Land* as an 'American' poem. 225–38

CLAYBOROUGH, ARTHUR.   Arnold Kettle and *Wuthering Heights*: the anatomy of an argument. 146–56

DEROLEZ, R.   Focus on *Beowulf*: variation or meaning. 9–16

DIETRICHSON, JAN W.   Herman Melville in literary history. 157–73

ELLMANN, RICHARD.   Ulysses am Main. 239–49

ERIKSEN, ROY TOMMY.   A mannerist topos in Spenser and Shakespeare. 17–28

FRYKMAN, ERIK.   *Punch* cartoons and the Victorian lower classes. 174–80

GERRITSEN, JOHAN.   De Witt, van Buchell, the Swan and the Globe: some notes. 29–46

HARTVEIT, LARS.   Ideological stock-taking in J. G. Farrell's historical fiction. 251–62

HAUG, INGRID.   Art *vs* decay in Tina Howe's *Painting Churches*. 263–74

KENNEDY, ANDREW.   A young person's Eliot: a personal recollection, based on 1948–51. 275–83

MARGESON, JOHN.   Chapman's experiments with tragic form. 47–58

MELCHIORI, GIORGIO.   Reconstructing the ur-*Henry IV*. 59–77

NUTTALL, A. D.   Ovid immoralised: the method of wit in Marvell's *The Garden*. 79–89

OLSEN, STEIN HAUGOM.   A glimpse into the darkness? The epistemological and ontological theme in William Golding's *Darkness Visible*. 284–95

ØVERLAND, ORM.   Norwegian-American theater and drama 1865–1885. 189–200

POLLARD, ARTHUR.   Paternalism and liberty: Tory Southey and Whig Macaulay. 181–8

REINERT, OTTO.   The unmended gear: the 'problem' in *Troilus and Cressida*. 90–103

ROLL-HANSEN, DIDERIK.   Shaw's *Saint Joan* on the stage: a comparison of some early and some recent London productions. 296–304

SCHRICKX, WILLEM.   *The Revenger's Tragedy* and its contemporary Dutch adaptation by Theodore Rodenburg. 104–9

STAMM, RUDOLF.   The second orchard scene in Shakespeare's *Romeo and Juliet*. 110–21

TINDALE, JOAN.   Some observations on the situation of contemporary British women dramatists. 305–11

Evolution of the Novel/
L'évolution du roman/Die Entwicklung des Romans
19. KONSTANTINOVIĆ, ZORAN; KUSHNER, EVA; KÖPECZI, BÉLA (eds). Evolution of the novel/L'évolution du roman/Die Entwicklung des Romans. Proceedings of the IXth International Comparative Literature Association, Innsbruck 1979. Innsbruck: Instituts für Sprachwissenschaft der Universität Innsbruck, 1982. pp. 504. Rev. by Franco Meregalli in CanRCL (13:2) 293–6.

AARSETH, ASBJØRN.   Myth and metanarration in the modern novel:

remarks on Faulkner's *Absalom, Absalom!* and Simon's *La Route des Flandres.* 341-5

ARESU, BERNARD.   Gilbert Durand and the mythical structure of time in three novels by Faulkner, Simon and Kateb. 437-41

BAL, MIEKE; VAN ZOEST, AART.   Structure narrative et signification: le cas de *Wuthering Heights.* 317-27

BALL, ROLAND C.   The new forms of the novel in the period of Romanticism. 155-60

BEKER, MIROSLAV.   The attack on character in modern fiction. 255-9

BRADY-PAPADOPOULOU, VALENTINI.   The Christ figure as archetype in Kazantzakis' *Christ Recrucified* and Patrick White's *Riders in the Chariot.* 409-13

BRENNAN, JOSEPH G.   The imperceptive narrator. 233-9

DETWEILER, ROBERT.   Mass communication technology and postmodern fiction. 489-95

DOBRZYCKA, IRENA.   Literature for the masses and the rise of the English social novel. 459-63

GILLESPIE, GERALD.   The incorporation of history as content and form: anticipations of the Romantic and modern novel. 29-34

HALÁSZ, A. M.   The genealogical novel: a 20th century genre. 41-5

HORTON, ANDREW S.   Deconstructing the Oedipus myth in Malcolm Lowry's *Under the Volcano.* 391-5

KLEIN, H. M.   Fiction of the First World War and the problems of criticism. 109-14

KORENEVA, MARIJA M.   The novel of the First and Second World War in western Europe and the USA. 63-6

LEFERINK, HEIN; VAN DER WOUDE, MARIUS.   Comment faire, en 1979, l'histoire du roman? Quelques problèmes méthodologiques. 91-5

MUSGRAVE, MARIAN.   Black myth versus white myth in the novels of Ishmael Reed. 381-4

NWEZEH, E. C.   Satire in post-Independence West African fiction. 193-9

OGUNSANWO, OLATUBOSUN.   George Meredith and F. Scott Fitzgerald: literary affinities, narrative indirectness and realism. 245-8

OKAFOR, CLÉMENT A.   Igbo narrative tradition and the novels of Chinua Achebe: transition from oral to written literature. 483-7

PIKE, BURTON.   The myth of the city in the novel. 421-4

RHEIN, PHILLIP H.   The search for sin. 369-73

ROUSE, H. B.   Genesis, mimesis and Clio: history and the novel – the novel as history. 15-18

SCHAEFER, JACQUELINE T.   Two medieval myths in the work of Charles Morgan. 415-20

SCHIPPER, MINEKE.   Réalisme et roman africain. 193–205

SPIESS, REINHARD F.   Rezeptionstheorie und historischer Roman. Zum Beispiel: Charles Sealsfields historisches Nordamerika. 97–102

SUVIN, DARKO.   'Formal' and 'sociological' analysis in the aesthetics of the science-fiction novel. 453–8

SZANTO, GEORGE.   Fictions, societies and laws of equal and unequal development: notes for a sociology of literary comparison. 283–90

SZEGEDY-MASZÁK, MIHÁLY.   Four aspects of the narrative text. 129–33

SZILÁRD, LÉNA.   Der Mythos im Roman und der Wechsel der literarisch-stilistischen Formationen: von Joyce und A. Belyj zum späten Th. Mann und zu M. Bulgakov. 347–52

VERZEA, ILEANA.   The reception of the English historical novel in Romania. 103–7

VIDAN, IVO.   Time sequence in spatial fiction. 271–5

WARD, PATRICIA A.   Medievalism in the Romantic novel. 35–9

WEBER, ROBERT W.   Pour un mythopoétique du roman de l'inconscient. 353–6

WEIMANN, ROBERT.   Fictionality and the rise of realism: Rabelais and Nashe. 139–43

WONG, TAK-WAI.   The theme of initiation in Chinese and Anglo-American fiction. 375–80

Feminist Theorists:
Three Centuries of Women's Intellectual Traditions

20.   SPENDER, DALE (ed.).   Feminist theorists: three centuries of women's intellectual traditions. (Pub. in USA as *Feminist Theorists: Three Centuries of Key Women Thinkers.*) London: Women's Press, 1983; New York: Pantheon, 1983. pp. 402. Rev. by Marilyn J. Boxer in Signs (10) 1985, 806, 808–10.

BLACK, NAOMI.   Virginia Woolf: the life of natural happiness (1882–1941). 296–313

BRODY, MIRIAM.   Mary Wollstonecraft: sexuality and women's rights (1759–1797). 40–59

GOREAU, ANGELINE.   Aphra Behn: a scandal to modesty (*ca.*1640–1689). 8–27

KINNAIRD, JOAN K.   Mary Astell: inspired by ideas (1668–1731). 28–39

LANE, ANN J.   Charlotte Perkins Gilman: the personal is political (1860–1935). 203–17

MELLOWN, MURIEL.   Vera Brittain: feminist in a new age (1896–1970). 314–34

STANLEY, LIZ.   Olive Schreiner: new women, free women, all women (1855–1920). 229–43

URBANSKI, MARIE MITCHELL OLSEN. Margaret Fuller: feminist writer and revolutionary (1810–1850). 75–89

WEINER, GABY. Harriet Martineau: a reassessment (1802–1876). 60–74

Für eine offene Literaturwissenschaft: Erkundungen und Erprobungen am Beispiel US-amerikanischer Texte/Opening up Literary Criticism: Essays on American Prose and Poetry

21. TRUCHLAR, LEO (ed.). Für eine offene Literaturwissenschaft: Erkundungen und Erprobungen am Beispiel US-amerikanischer Texte/ Opening up literary criticism: essays on American prose and poetry. Salzburg: Neugebauer. pp. 139.

BACHINGER, KATRINA. The Tao of *Housekeeping*: reconnoitering the utopian ecological frontier in Marilynne Robinson's 'feminist' novel. 14–33

STEINER, DOROTHEA. Feminist criticism, poetic theory and American poetry historiography. 88–113

TRUCHLAR, LEO. Robert Coover, *Spanking the Maid*. Eine Leseerfahrung. 114–32

WALLINGER-NOWAK, HANNA. The wild zone in Paule Marshall's fiction. 69–87

Gaining Ground: European Critics on Canadian Literature

22. KROETSCH, ROBERT; NISCHIK, REINGARD M. (eds). Gaining ground: European critics on Canadian literature. Edmonton, Alta.: NeWest Press, 1985. pp. 303. (Western Canadian literary documents series, 6). Rev. by Tracy Ware in DalR (65:4) 1985/86, 575.

BADER, RUDOLF. Frederick Philip Grove and naturalism reconsidered. 222–33

CAPONE, GIOVANNA. *A Bird in the House*: Margaret Laurence on order and the artist. 161–70

FABRE, MICHEL. 'Orphans' progress', reader's progress: voice and understatement in Mavis Gallant's stories. 150–60

GOETSCH, PAUL. Margaret Atwood's *Life Before Man* as a novel of manners. 137–49

EL-HASSAN, KARLA. Reflections on the special unity of Stephen Leacock's *Sunshine Sketches of a Little Town*. 171–85

HOWELLS, CORAL ANN. Worlds alongside: contradictory discourses in the fiction of Alice Munro and Margaret Atwood. 121–36

KLOOS, WOLFGANG. Narrative modes and forms of literary perception in Rudy Wiebe's *The Scorched-Wood People*. 205–21

NISCHIK, REINGARD M. European publications on Canadian literature. 279–96

NISCHIK, REINGARD M. Narrative techniques in Aritha van Herk's novels. 107–20

PACHE, WALTER.   'The fiction makes us real': aspects of post-modernism in Canada. 64–78

SCHÄFER, JÜRGEN.   A farewell to Europe: Rudy Wiebe's *The Temptations of Big Bear* and Robert Kroetsch's *Gone Indian*. 79–90

SPRIET, PIERRE.   Structure and meaning in Rudy Wiebe's *My Lovely Enemy*. 53–63

STANZEL, FRANZ K.   Texts recycled: 'found' poems found in Canada. 91–106

VAUTHIER, SIMONE.   The dubious battle of story-telling: narrative strategies in Timothy Findley's *The Wars*. 11–39

ZACHARASIEWICZ, WALDEMAR.   The invention of a region: the art of fiction in Jack Hodgins' stories. 186–91

Identity of the Literary Text
23.   VALDÉS, MARIO J.; MILLER, OWEN (eds).   Identity of the literary text. Toronto; London: Toronto UP, 1985. pp. xxi, 330. Rev. by Joseph Adamson in ESCan (12:2) 246–50.

HAMLIN, CYRUS.   The faults of vision: identity and poetry (a dialogue of voices, with an essay on *Kubla Khan*). 119–45

MILLER, J. HILLIS.   Topography and tropography in Thomas Hardy's *In Front of the Landscape*. 73–91

PARKER, PATRICIA.   The (self-) identity of the literary text: property, propriety, proper place, and proper name in *Wuthering Heights*. 92–116

Jubinlejní Ročenka Kruhu Moderních Filologů
24.   KRUHU MODERNÍCH FILOLOGŮ.   Jubinlejní Ročenka Kruhu Moderních Filologů. (Jubilee anniversary report of the Czechoslovak Circle of Modern Philology.) Prague: Circle of Modern Philology. pp. 77.

JAŘAB, JOSEF.   The gradual advent of Emily Dickinson. 46–51

KLÉGR, ALEŠ.   Ke vztahu koordinace a asociace. (On coordination and association.) 18–22

KRÁMSKÝ, JIŘÍ.   The place of morphology in the system of language. 9–12

NOSEK, JIŘÍ.   Funkce a tvar v jazyce. (Function and form in language.) 5–8

PANTŮČKOVÁ, LIDMILA.   Několik poznámek k Nerudově vztahu k Shakespearovi. (Jan Neruda's relationship to Shakespeare.) 54–7

PŘIDAL, ANTONÍN.   K proměnám detektivky u G. K. Chestertona a K. Čapka. (Variations on the detective story in G. K. Chesterton's and Karel Čapek's work.) 51–4

Learning and Literature in Anglo-Saxon England
25.   LAPIDGE, MICHAEL; GNEUSS, HELMUT (eds).   Learning and literature in Anglo-Saxon England: studies presented to Peter Clemoes on the occasion of his sixty-fifth birthday. Cambridge: CUP, 1985. pp. xiv, 459.

BATELY, JANET. Linguistic evidence as a guide to the authorship of Old English verse: a reappraisal, with special reference to *Beowulf*. 409–31

BLAIR, PETER HUNTER. Whitby as a centre of learning in the seventh century. 3–32

CROSS, J. E. On the library of the Old English martyrologist. 227–49

GATCH, M. McC. The Office in late Anglo-Saxon monasticism. 341–62

GNEUSS, HELMUT. Liturgical books in Anglo-Saxon England and their Old English terminology. 91–141

GODDEN, M. R. Anglo-Saxon on the mind. 271–98

GREENFIELD, STANLEY B. Beowulf and the judgement of the righteous. 393–407

KEYNES, SIMON. King Athelstan's books. 143–201

KORHAMMER, MICHAEL. The orientation system in the Old English *Orosius*: shifted or not? 251–69

LAPIDGE, MICHAEL. Surviving booklists from Anglo-Saxon England. 33–89

RANKIN, SUSAN. The liturgical background of the Old English Advent lyrics: a reappraisal. 317–40

SCRAGG, D. G. The homilies of the Blickling manuscript. 299–316

SIMS-WILLIAMS, PATRICK. Thoughts on Ephrem the Syrian in Anglo-Saxon England. 205–26

STANLEY, E. G. *The Judgement of the Damned* (from Cambridge, Corpus Christi College 201 and other manuscripts), and the definition of Old English verse. 363–91

Linguistics across Historical and Geographical Boundaries

26. KASTOVSKY, DIETER; SZWEDEK, ALEKSANDER (eds); PŁOCIŃSKA, BARBARA (asst ed.). Linguistics across historical and geographical boundaries in honour of Jacek Fisiak on the occasion of his fiftieth birthday: vol. 1, Linguistic theory and historical linguistics; vol. 2, Descriptive, contrastive and applied linguistics. Berlin; New York; Amsterdam: Mouton de Gruyter. pp. xxiv, 1543. (Trends in linguistics, studies and monographs, 32.)

ANDERSON, JOHN. The English prosody /h/. 799–809

ANTTILA, RAIMO. An etymology for the aquatic '*acker/aiker*' in English, and other grains of truth? 177–82

AUSTERLITZ, ROBERT. Contrasting fact with fiction: the common denominator in internal reconstruction, with a bibliography. 183–92

BALD, WOLF-DIETRICH. Context in contrastive linguistics: *one* and *ein*. 1117–32

BAMMESBERGER, ALFRED. On Old English *gefrægnod* in *Beowulf* 1333a. 193–7

ROMAINE, SUZANNE. The effects of language standardization on deletion rules: some comparative Germanic evidence from *t/d*-deletion. 605–20

RUBACH, JERZY. Degemination in Old English and the formal apparatus of generative phonology. 621–35

RUSIECKI, JAN. The semantics of antonymic pairs of adjectives: elicitation test evidence from English and Polish. 1427–41

STEIN, DIETER. Old English Northumbrian verb inflection revisited. 637–50

STEIN, GABRIELE. Definitions and first person pronoun involvement in Thomas Elyot's *Dictionary*. 1465–74

STOCKWELL, ROBERT P. Grammar as speaker's knowledge versus grammar as linguists' characterization of norms. 125–33

STRAUSS, JÜRGEN. Concepts, fields, and 'non-basic' lexical items. 135–44

SUSSEX, ROLAND. Paraphrase strategies and the teaching of translation. 1475–83

SUZUKI, SEIICHI. Syllable theory and Old English verse: a preliminary observation. 651–7

SZWEDEK, ALEKSANDER. Sentence stress and category membership. 1051–61

TERASAWA, YOSHIO. Hebrew loan words in English. 659–69

THORNE, JAMES P. *Because*. 1063–6

THRANE, TORBEN. On delimiting the senses of near-synonyms in historical semantics: a case-study of adjectives of 'moral sufficiency' in the Old English *Andreas*. 671–92

VACHEK, JOSEF. An emotionally conditioned split of some personal names. 693–700

VAN DER AUWERA, JOHAN. The possibilities of *may* and *can*. 1067–76

VAN OIRSOUW, ROBERT R. Syntactic ambiguity: a systematic accident. 145–55

VIERECK, WOLFGANG. Dialectal speech areas in England: Orton's lexical evidence. 725–40

WAKELIN, MARTYN F. The *Exmoor Courtship* and *Exmoor Scolding*: an evaluation of two eighteenth-century dialect texts. 741–51

WATTS, RICHARD J. Generated or degenerate? Two forms of linguistic competence. 157–73

WEŁNA, JERZY. The Old English digraph <cg> again. 753–62

ZABROCKI, TADEUSZ. A processing explanation for a syntactic difference between English and Polish. 1485–99

Literary Theory / Renaissance Texts

27. PARKER, PATRICIA; QUINT, DAVID (eds). Literary theory /

Renaissance texts. Baltimore, MD; London: Johns Hopkins UP. pp. vi, 399.

ATTRIDGE, DEREK.   Puttenham's perplexity: nature, art, and the supplement in Renaissance poetic theory. 257–79

GIRARD, RENÉ.   Hamlet's dull revenge. 280–302

GREENBLATT, STEPHEN.   Psychoanalysis and Renaissance culture. 210–24

HALPERN, RICHARD.   John Skelton and the poetics of primitive accumulation. 225–56

KAHN, VICTORIA.   Humanism and the resistance to theory. 373–96

MONTROSE, LOUIS ADRIAN.   The Elizabethan subject and the Spenserian text. 303–40

NYQUIST, MARY.   Textual overlapping and Dalilah's harlot-lap. 341–72

PARKER, PATRICIA.   Deferral, dilation, différance: Shakespeare, Cervantes, Jonson. 182–209

Literature and Lore of the Sea

28.   CARLSON, PATRICIA ANN (ed.).   Literature and lore of the sea. Amsterdam: Rodopi. pp. 288. (Costerus, 52.)

BAGNALL, NORMA.   The selchie in legend and literature. 225–31

BERTHOLD, DENNIS.   Cape Horn passages: literary conventions and nautical realities. 40–50

BERTHOLD, DENNIS.   Deeper surroundings: the presence of *Walden* in Slocum's *Sailing Alone Around the World.* 161–75

DE GRAZIA, EMILIO.   A coming indistinctly into view: a familiar review of *Moby-Dick.* 133–42

DE GRAZIA, EMILIO.   The great plain: Rolvaag's New World sea. 244–55

DE GRAZIA, EMILIO.   Poe's other beautiful woman. 176–84

FOULKE, ROBERT.   The elegiac structure of Conrad's *The Mirror of the Sea.* 154–60

FOULKE, ROBERT.   Life in the dying world of sail, 1870–1910. 72–115

FOULKE, ROBERT.   The literature of voyaging. 1–13

GOODMAN, AILENE S.   The extraordinary being: death and the mermaid in baroque literature. 256–74

GUZLOWSKI, JOHN Z.   No more sea changes: four American novelists' responses to the sea. 232–43

HUGHES, JAMES M.   Inner and outer seas in Dickinson, Dana, Cooper and Roberts. 202–11

HUGHES, JAMES M.   Popular imagery of the sea: lore is a four-letter word. 215–24

MADISON, ROBERT D.   Cooper's *The Wind-And-Wing* and the concept of the Byronic pirate. 119–32

MEAD, JOAN TYLER.   'Spare me a few minutes I have Something to Say': poetry in manuscripts of sailing ships. 23–31

O'BRIEN, ELLEN J.   That 'insular Tahiti': Melville's truth-seeker and the sea. 193–201

QUINLAN, KIERAN.   Sea and sea-shore in *Song of Myself*: Whitman's liquid theme. 185–92

SPRINGER, HASKELL.   Call them all Ishmael? Fact and form in some nineteenth-century sea narratives. 14–22

WIXON, RICHARD L.   Herman Melville: critic of America and harbinger of ecological crisis. 143–53

Literature, Politics and Theory

29.   BARKER, FRANCIS, *et al.* (eds).   Literature, politics and theory: papers from the Essex Conference 1976–84. London; New York: Methuen. pp. xix, 259.

BALIBAR, RENÉE.   National language, education, literature. 126–47

BELSEY, CATHERINE.   The Romantic construction of the unconscious. 57–76

JAMESON, FREDRIC.   Religion and ideology: a political reading of *Paradise Lost*. 35–56

MUSSELWHITE, DAVID.   The trial of Warren Hastings. 77–103

PECHEY, GRAHAM.   Bakhtin, Marxism and post-structuralism. 104–25

WILLIAMS, RAYMOND.   Forms of English fiction in 1848. 1–16

Maître et serviteur dans le monde anglo-américain des XVIIe et XVIIIe siècles

30.   SOCIÉTÉ D'ÉTUDES ANGLO-AMÉRICAINES DES XVIIe ET XVIIIe SIÈCLES.

Maître et serviteur dans le monde anglo-américain des XVIIe et XVIIIe siècles. Actes du Colloque 1985. Paris: Didier. pp. 212. (Publications de l'Université de Rouen.)

ARNAUD, PIERRE.   Au service de Lucifer: le diable, la magie et le pacte dans *Le Moine* de M. G. Lewis. 133–51

BIRNBAUM, G.   Servants in England and America in the 17th century: the beginnings of slavery. 45–64

BLONDEL, MADELEINE.   Deux ecclésiastiques anglais et leurs domestiques au 18e siècle. 181–96

BONNEAU, DANIELLE.   Maîtres et serviteurs dans les comédies de Ben Jonson. 65–85

GIRARD, GAÏD.   Maîtres et serviteurs dans *Caleb Williams*: passage du témoin et figures du double. 197–209

HALIMI, SUZY.   Defoe au service de Guillaume III. 123–32

HEROU, JOSETTE.   Maîtres et valets dans la comédie anglaise du 18e siècle: ambiguïtés et inversions. 97–110

LANOIX, LOUIS.   Pope, poëte des lumières. 153–64

LANOIX, LOUIS.   Samuel Pepys: le serviteur et le maître. 165–79

POYET, ALBERT.   Poésie et théâtralité dans *All for Love* de John Dryden. 111–22

RIGAUD, NADIA.   L'évolution des relations entre maîtres et serviteurs dans le théâtre d'Etherege. 87–95

ROUX, LOUIS.   Les artistes et leurs protecteurs en Angleterre au 17e siècle. 5–30

VERDEIL, MARIE-HÉLÈNE.   La dynastie Winthrop: 'Covenant' et relations sociales en Nouvelle-Angleterre au 17e siècle. 31–43

Mapped but Not Known:
the Australian Landscape of the Imagination

31.   EADEN, P. R.; MORES, F. H. (eds).   Mapped but not known: the Australian landscape of the imagination. Essays and poems presented to Brian Elliott, 11 April 1985. Adelaide: Wakefield Press. pp. viii, 269.

BARNES, JOHN.   'Through clear Australian eyes': landscape and identity in Australian writing. 86–104

MITCHELL, ADRIAN.   No new thing: the concept of novelty and early Australian writing. 52–63

ROSS, BRUCE CLUNIES.   Landscape and the Australian imagination. 224–43

WILDING, MICHAEL.   'Weird melancholy': inner and outer landscapes in Marcus Clarke's stories. 128–45

Medieval English Religious and Ethical Literature

32.   KRATZMANN, GREGORY; SIMPSON, JAMES (eds).   Medieval English religious and ethical literature: essays in honour of G. H. Russell. Cambridge: Brewer. pp. vi, 250.

CURTIS, PENELOPE.   Some discarnational impulses in the *Canterbury Tales*. 128–45

DONALDSON, E. TALBOT.   Long Will's apology: a translation. 30–4

DOYLE, A. I.   Remarks on surviving manuscripts of *Piers Plowman*. 35–48

ELLIOTT, RALPH W. V.   Chaucer's clerical voices. 146–55

FINLAY, ALISON.   The warrior Christ and the unarmed hero. 19–29

GRAY, DOUGLAS.   Books of comfort. 209–21

KANE, GEORGE.   Some fourteenth-century 'political' poems. 82–91

KELLY, H. A.   The non-tragedy of Arthur. 92–114

KNIGHT, STEPHEN.   Chaucer's religious Canterbury Tales. 156–66

KRATZMANN, GREGORY.   *The Dialoges of Creatures Moralysed*: a sixteenth-century medieval book of ethics. 222–32

LYNCH, ANDREW.   'Taking keep' of the *Book of the Duchess*. 167–78

PRICE, JOCELYN.   'Inner' and 'outer': conceptualizing the body in *Ancrene Wisse* and Aelred's *De institutis inclusarum*. 192–208

SIMPSON, JAMES.   The role of *scientia* in *Piers Plowman*. 49–65

TRAPP, J. B.   An English late-medieval cleric and Italian thought: the case of John Colet, Dean of St Paul's (1467–1519). 233–50

TRIGG, STEPHANIE.   Israel Gollancz's *Wynnere and Wastoure*: political satire or editorial politics? 115–27

WALDRON, R. A.   Langland's originality: the Christ-knight and the Harrowing of Hell. 66–81

WALL, JOHN.   Penance as poetry in the late fourteenth century. 179–91

Medieval Literature: Criticism, Ideology and History

33.   AERS, DAVID (ed.).   Medieval literature: criticism, ideology and history. Brighton: Harvester Press. pp. 228.

AERS, DAVID.   Reflections on the 'allegory of the theologians', ideology and *Piers Plowman*. 58–73

BECKWITH, SARAH.   A very material mysticism: the medieval mysticism of Margery Kempe. 34–57

COOK, JON.   Carnival and *The Canterbury Tales*: 'only equals may laugh' (Herzen). 169–91

FERSTER, JUDITH.   Interpretation and imitation in Chaucer's Franklin's Tale. 148–68

GASH, ANTHONY.   Carnival against Lent: the ambivalence of medieval drama. 74–98

KNIGHT, STEPHEN.   The social function of the Middle English romances. 99–122

MOI, TORIL.   Desire in language: Andreas Capellanus and the controversy of courtly love. 11–33

PEARSALL, DEREK.   Chaucer's poetry and its modern commentators: the necessity of history. 123–47

SHARRATT, BERNARD.   John Skelton: finding a voice – notes after Bakhtin. 192–222

Mémoire et création dans le monde anglo-américain aux XVIIe et XVIIIe siècles

34.   SOCIÉTÉ D'ÉTUDES ANGLO-AMÉRICAINES DES XVIIe ET XVIIIe SIÈCLES.   Mémoire et création dans le monde anglo-américain aux XVIIe et XVIIIe siècles: Actes du Colloque tenu à Paris les 21 et 22 octobre 1983. Strasburg: Université de Strasbourg II, 1983. PP. 171.

BARIDON, MICHEL.   '"Copy for ever" is my rule': Blake lecteur de Reynolds dans le débat sur memoire et création. 75–87

CAMÉE, JEAN-FRANÇOIS.   Mémoire et création: de *Grace Abounding* au *Pilgrim's Progress*. 99–109

CHEVIGNARD, BERNARD.   Mémoire et création dans les *Letters from an American Farmer* de St John de Crèvecœur. 125–35

DHUICQ, BERNARD.   *Oroonoko*: expérience et création. 41–8

DUVAL, GILLES.   'History-histories': mémoire et création dans la littérature de colportage anglaise du 18e siècle. 111–23

LACASSAGNE, CLAUDE-LAURENCE.   *Grace Abounding* . . .: la narration et la grâce. 89–97

LESSAY, FRANCK.   L'état de nature selon Hobbes: point de départ ou point de dépassement de l'histoire. 3–14

MARTINET, MARIE-MADELEINE.   Les espaces de la mémoire créatrice en Angleterre aux XVIIe et XVIIIe siècles. 59–74

MATHIS, GILLES.   Mémoire et création dans *Le Paradis perdu*. 147–67

MORÈRE, PIERRE.   Mémoire et création dans les Préfaces des *Lyrical Ballads*: l'héritage du dix-huitième siècle. 23–39

PAVLOPOULOS, FRANÇOISE.   Mémoire, *Mémoires* et création chez Lord Hervey. 49–58

TRICAUD, FRANÇOIS.   Remarques sur le poids du passé et le pouvoir d'innover selon Hobbes et selon Hume. 15–21

VENET, GISÈLE.   Mémoire et création dans la poétique baroque. 137–46

Migrations

35.   CENTRE D'HISTOIRE DES IDÉÉS DANS LES ILES BRITTANIQUES. Migrations: communications faites au colloque des 12 et 14 octobre 1985: mélanges offerts à Olivier Lutaud. Paris: Centre d'histoire des idées dans les Iles Britanniques, Univ. de Paris IV-Sorbonne. pp. 168.

LAMOINE, GEORGES.   Le *True Born Englishman*: à la recherche de ses ancêtres. 46–54

LESSAY, FRANCK.   Joseph Conrad et les chemins de l'empire. 122–39

LUCAZEAU, MICHEL.   Y a-t-il une source patristique de *La Tempête?* Compte rendu d'enquête. 30–45

MORVAN, ALAIN.   Discours sur un exil intérieur: *The Jacobite's Journal* de Fielding. 55–68

Modes of Interpretation in Old English Literature

36.   BROWN, PHYLLIS RUGG; CRAMPTON, GEORGIA RONAN; ROBINSON, FRED C. (eds).   Modes of interpretation in Old English literature: essays in honour of Stanley B. Greenfield. Toronto; London; Buffalo, NY: Toronto UP. pp. xxi, 298.

ANDERSON, EARL R.   *The Battle of Maldon*: a reappraisal of possible sources, date, and theme. 247–72

BLOOMFIELD, MORTON W.   *Deor* revisited. 273–82

BROWN, GEORGE HARDIN.   Old English verse as a medium for Christian theology. 15–28

CALDER, DANIEL G. Figurative language and its contexts in *Andreas*: a study in medieval expressionism. 115–36

CLEMOES, PETER. 'Symbolic' language in Old English poetry. 3–14

CROSS, JAMES E. Identification: towards criticism. 229–46

FRANK, ROBERTA. 'Mere' and 'sund': two sea-changes in *Beowulf.* 153–72

FRESE, DOLORES WARWICK. Poetic prowess in *Brunanburh* and *Maldon*: winning, losing and literary outcome. 83–99

GNEUSS, HELMUT. King Alfred and the history of Anglo-Saxon libraries. 29–49

IRVING, EDWARD B., JR. Crucifixion witnessed, or dramatic interaction in *The Dream of the Rood*. 102–13

MELLINKOFF, RUTH. Serpent imagery in the illustrated Old English Hexateuch. 51–64

NELSON, MARIE. *The Battle of Maldon* and *Juliana*: the language of confrontation. 137–50

POPE, JOHN C. *Beowulf* 505, 'gehedde', and the pretensions of Unferth. 173–87

RENOIR, ALAIN. Old English formulas and themes as tools for contextual interpretation. 65–79

RISSANEN, MATTI. 'Sum' in Old English poetry. 197–225

STANLEY, E. G. Notes on the text of the Old English *Genesis*. 189–96

Mythe et histoire

37. JONES-DAVIES, M. T. (ed.). Mythe et histoire. Société Française Shakespeare, actes du congrès, 1983. Paris: Touzot, 1984. pp. 201.

BROCKBANK, J. P. Myth and history in Shakespeare's Rome. 95–111

CHAUCHAIX, J. Histoire et mythe dans la *Sophonisbe* de J. Marston. 127–45

DAVIES, OLIVER FORD. The Roman plays: an actor's view. 157–67

GOY-BLANQUET, DOMINIQUE. Des histoires tristes. 31–49

HABICHT, WERNER. Hamlet's prophetic soul: an obscured myth? 113–26

MARTINET, MARIE-MADELEINE. Les mythes historiques chez Shakespeare: rumeur ou silence? 21–9

PEYRE, YVES. Mythes de renaissance. 67–93

SAHEL, PIERRE. *Henri VI*: le mythe contre l'histoire. 51–66

SUHAMY, HENRI. Shakespeare historien: propagateur de mythes, ou recenseur sceptique? 9–19

New Directions in Linguistics and Semiotics

38. COPELAND, JAMES E. (ed.). New directions in linguistics and semiotics. Houston, TX: Rice UP, 1984. pp. xi, 269. (Rice Univ. studies, ns 2.) Rev. by Keith Arnold in CJL (31:2) 157–9.

FILLMORE, CHARLES J.   Lexical semantics and text semantics. 123–47

HAAS, MARY R.   Lessons from American Indian linguistics. 68–72

HALLIDAY, M. A. K.   Linguistics in the university: the question of social accountability. 51–67

HOCKETT, CHARLES F.   The uniqueness fallacy. 35–46

LAMB, SYDNEY M.   On the aims of linguistics. 1–11

LEHISTE, ILSE.   The many linguistic functions of duration. 96–122

LEHMANN, WINFRED P.   Mellow glory: see language steadily and see it whole. 17–34

LONGACRE, ROBERT E.   Reshaping linguistics: context and content. 79–95

PREZIOSI, DONALD.   Subjects + objects: the current state of visual semiotics. 179–205

SEBEOK, THOMAS A.   Symptom. 211–30

SHAUMYAN, SEBASTIAN.   Semiotic laws in linguistics and natural science. 231–57

STANKIEWICZ, EDWARD.   Linguistics, poetics, and the literary genres. 155–78

The Nineteenth-Century British Novel

39. HAWTHORN, JEREMY (ed.).   The nineteenth-century British novel. London; Baltimore, MD; Caulfield East, Vic.; Arnold. pp. viii, 192. Stratford-upon-Avon studies, second ser.)

BURNS, MARJORIE.   'This shattered prison': versions of Eden in *Wuthering Heights*. 30–45

EASSON, ANGUS.   Statesman, dwarf and weaver: Wordsworth and nineteenth-century narrative. 16–29

ERMARTH, ELIZABETH DEEDS.   'Th'observed of all observers': George Eliot's narrator and Shakespeare's audience. 126–40

FLINT, KATE.   The woman reader and the opiate of fiction: 1855–1870. 46–61

LOTHE, JAKOB.   Hardy's authorial narrative method in *Tess of the d'Urbervilles*. 156–70

MILLER, D. A.   'Cage aux folles': sensation and gender in Wilkie Collins's *The Woman in White*. 94–124

OLSEN, STEIN HAUGOM.   Appreciating *Pride and Prejudice*. viii, 1–14

RIGNALL, J. M.   Thackeray's *Henry Esmond* and the struggle against the power of time. 80–93

SELL, ROGER D.   Dickens and the new historicism: the polyvocal audience and discourse of *Dombey and Son*. 62–79

SKILTON, DAVID.   The Trollope reader. 142–155

Opening Texts: Psychoanalysis and the Culture of the Child

40. SMITH, JOSEPH H.; KERRIGAN, WILLIAM (eds).   Opening texts:

psychoanalysis and the culture of the child. Baltimore, MD; London: Johns Hopkins UP, 1985. pp. xix, 144. (Psychiatry and the humanities, 8.)

MacLeod, Anne Scott. An end to innocence: the transformation of childhood in twentieth-century children's literature. 100–17

Marcus, Steven. Some representations of childhood in Wordsworth's poetry. 1–16

Pickering, Samuel, Jr. Allegory and the first school stories. 42–68

Tatar, Maria. From nags to witches: stepmothers in the Grimms' fairy tales. 28–41

Tucker, Nicholas. Lullabies and child care: a historical perspective. 17–27

Zipes, Jack. Don't bet on the prince: feminist fairy tales and the feminist critique in America. 69–99

Papers from the 4th International Conference on English Historical Linguistics. Amsterdam, 10–13 April 1985

41. Eaton, Roger, et al. (eds). Papers from the 4th international conference on English historical linguistics. Amsterdam, 10–13 April 1985. Amsterdam; Philadelphia, PA: Benjamins, 1985. pp. xvii, 341.

Aitchison, Jean; Agnihotri, Rama Kant. 'I deny that I'm incapable of not working all night': divergence of negative structures in British and Indian English. 3–14

Austin, Frances O. Relative *which* in late 18th century usage: the Clift family correspondence. 15–29

Beal, Joan C. Lengthening of *a'* in Tyneside English. 31–44

Denison, David. The origins of periphrastic *do*: Ellegård and Visser reconsidered. 45–60

Ihalainen, Ossi. Synchronic variation and linguistic change: evidence from British English dialects. 61–72

Keyser, Samuel Jay; O'Neil, Wayne. The simplification of the Old English strong nominal paradigms. 85–107

Koopman, Willem F. Verb and particle combinations in Old and Middle English. 109–21

Lagerquist, Linnea M. The impersonal verb in context: Old English. 123–36

Lass, Roger; Wright, Susan. The South African chain shift: order out of chaos? 137–61

Minkova, Donka. Of rhyme and reason: some foot-governed quantity changes in English. 163–78

Nagucka, Ruta. Remarks on complementation in Old English. 195–204

Nevalainen, Terttu. Lexical variation of EModE exclusive adverbs: style switching or a change in progress? 179–94

PLANK, FRANS.   The interpretation and development of form alternations conditioned across word boundaries: the case of *wife's*, *wives*, and *wives'*. 205–33

POUSSA, PATRICIA.   A note on the voicing of initial fricatives in Middle English. 235–52

RISSANEN, MATTI.   Expression of exclusiveness in Old English and the development of the adverb *only*. 253–67

SAMUELS, M. L.   The great Scandinavian belt. 269–81

STEIN, DIETER.   Discourse markers in Early Modern English. 283–302

STOCKWELL, ROBERT P.   Assessment of alternative explanations of the Middle English phenomenon of high vowel lowering when lengthened in the open syllable. 303–18

TOON, THOMAS E.   Preliminaries to the linguistic analysis of the Old English glosses and glossaries. 319–29

TRAVIS, LISA DEMENA.   The role of INFL in word order change. 331–41

VAN KEMENADE, ANS.   Old English infinitival complements and West-Germanic V-raising. 73–84

Papers from the 6th International Conference on Historical Linguistics

42. FISIAK, JACEK (ed.).   Papers from the 6th International conference on historical linguistics. Amsterdam; Benjamins: Poznań; Adam Mickiewicz UP, 1985. pp. xxiii, 622. (Current issues in linguistic theory, 34.) (Amsterdam studies in the theory and history of linguistic science, 4.)

FRASER, THOMAS.   Did Old English have a middle voice? 129–38

GBUREK, HUBERT.   The vowel /a:/ in English. 139–48

GOOSSENS, LOUIS.   Framing the linguistic action in Old and present-day English: OE *cwepan, secgan, sp(r)ecan* and present-day English *speak, talk, say* and *tell* compared. 149–70

HICKEY, RAYMOND.   Velar segments in Old English and Old Irish. 267–79

NAGUCKA, RUTA.   For a diachrony-in-synchrony analysis. 395–407

ROMAINE, SUZANNE.   Variability in word formation patterns and productivity in the history of English. 451–65

SCHNEIDER, EDGAR W.   Regional variation in 19th century black English in the American South. 467–87

TRAUGOTT, ELIZABETH CLOSS.   Confrontation and association. 515–26

VIERECK, WOLFGANG.   On the origin and developments of American English. 561–9

Papers from the Third Scandinavian Symposium on Syntactic Variation, Stockholm, May 11–12, 1985

43. JACOBSON, SVEN (ed.). Papers from the third Scandinavian symposium on syntactic variation, Stockholm, May 11–12, 1985. Stockholm: Almqvist & Wiksell. pp. 180. (Stockholm studies in English, 65.)

AIJMER, KARIN. Polysemy, lexical variation and principles of semantic change: a study of the variation between *can* and *may* in Early Modern British English. 143–70

BREIVIK, LEIF EGIL. Variation in existential sentences in a synchronic-diachronic perspective. 171–80

JACOBSON, SVEN. Synonymy and hyponymy in syntactic variation. 7–17

JOHANNESSON, NILS-LENNART. Variable subject deletion in Late Middle English topic constructions. 119–29

JOHANSSON, STIG. Some observations on the order of adverbial particles and objects in the LOB Corpus. 51–62

KYTÖ, MERJA. *May* and *might* indicating 'epistemic possibility' in Early American English. 131–42

MONELL, SIV. The molecule strategy: a study of the description of character in *The Rainbow* by D. H. Lawrence. 75–87

NEVALAINEN, TERTTU; RISSANEN, MATTI. Do you support the *do*-support? Emphatic and non-emphatic *do* in affirmative statements in present-day spoken English. 35–50

NEVANLINNA, SAARA. Variation in the syntactic structure of simile in OE prose. 89–98

POUSSA, PATRICIA. Historical implications of the distribution of the zero-pronoun relative clause in Modern English dialects: looking backwards towards OE from Map S5 of *The Linguistic Atlas of England*. 99–117

ROMAINE, SUZANNE. Syntactic variation and the acquisition of strategies of relativization in the language of Edinburgh school children. 19–33

RUIN, INGER. About *today* and *tomorrow* in the past. 63–73

Play-Texts in Old Spelling

44. SHAND, G. B.; SHADY, RAYMOND C. (eds). Play-texts in old spelling: papers from the Glendon conference. New York: AMS Press, 1984. pp. ix, 161. (AMS studies in the Renaissance, 6.) Rev. by L. A. Beaurline in RQ (38:4) 1985, 573–6; by Thomas L. Berger in RenR (10:4) 382–4; by Jay L. Halio in JEGP (85:2) 258–60.

BEVINGTON, DAVID. Editorial indications of stage business in old-spelling editions. 105–12

EDWARDS, PHILIP. The function of commentary. 97–104

GAINES, BARRY. Textual apparatus – rationale and audience. 65–71

GAIR, REAVLEY.   In search of 'the mustie fopperies of antiquity'.
123–30

JANZEN, HENRY D.   Preparing a diplomatic edition: Heywood's *The Escapes of Jupiter*. 73–9

MCLEOD, RANDALL.   Spellbound. 81–96 (Renaissance typesetting problems.)

MORTON, RICHARD.   How many revengers in *The Revengers Tragedy*? Archaic spellings and the modern annotator. 113–22

SCHOENBAUM, S.   Old-spelling editions: the state of the art. 9–26

STALLWORTHY, JON.   Old-spelling editions: the state of the business in 1978. 141–51

TURNER, ROBERT KEAN.   Accidental evils. 27–33

WERSTINE, PAUL.   The editorial usefulness of printing house and compositor studies. 35–64

ZITNER, S. P.   Excessive annotation, or piling Pelion on Parnassus. 131–9

The Progress of Romance: the Politics of Popular Fiction

45. RADFORD, JEAN (ed.).   The progress of romance: the politics of popular fiction. London: Routledge & Kegan Paul. pp. x, 238. (History workshop.)

BRIDGWOOD, CHRISTINE.   Family romances: the contemporary popular family saga. 167–93

CLARK, ANNA.   The politics of seduction in English popular culture, 1748–1848. 47–70

JONES, ANN ROSALIND.   Mills & Boon meets femininism. 195–218

LIGHT, ALISON.   Writing fictions: femininity and the 1950s. 139–65

PRICE, DERRICK.   *How Green was My Valley*: a romance of Wales. 73–94

RADFORD, JEAN.   An inverted romance: *The Well of Loneliness* and sexual ideology. 97–111

TAYLOR, HELEN.   *Gone with the Wind*: the mammy of them all. 113–36

Realism in European Literature

46. BOYLE, NICHOLAS; SWALES, MARTIN (eds).   Realism in European literature: essays in honour of J. P. Stern. Cambridge; New York; Sydney: CUP. pp. ix, 224.

BAMBROUGH, RENFORD.   Ounces of example: Henry James, philosopher. 169–82

BARTON, ANNE.   'Enter mariners, wet': realism in Shakespeare's last plays. 28–49

HEATH, STEPHEN.   Realism, modernism, and 'language-consciousness'. 103–22

HELLER, ERICH.   Notes on language, its deconstruction and on translating. 1–11

HOUGH, GRAHAM.   Language and reality in *Bleak House*. 50–67

Reconstructing American Literary History

47. BERCOVITCH, SACVAN (ed.).   Reconstructing American literary history. Cambridge, MA; London: Harvard UP. pp. xii, 351. (Harvard studies in English, 13.) Rev. by Thomas Kent in Criticism (28:4) 470–4; by Alan Wald in NYTB, 28 Sept., 35; by Philip F. Gura in AL (58:4) 620–1.

DICKSTEIN, MORRIS.   Popular fiction and critical values: the novel as a challenge to literary history. 29–66

FERGUSON, ROBERT A.   'We hold these truths': strategies of control in the literature of the Founders. 1–28

FISHER, PHILIP.   Appearing and disappearing in public: social space in late-nineteenth-century literature and culture. 155–88

GILBERT, SANDRA M.   The American sexual poetics of Walt Whitman and Emily Dickinson. 123–54

LENTRICCHIA, FRANK.   On the ideologies of poetic modernism, 1980–1913: the example of William James. 220–49

MICHAELS, WALTER BENN.   Corporate fiction: Norris, Royce, and Arthur Machen. 189–219

PACKER, BARBARA.   Origin and authority: Emerson and the Higher Criticism. 67–92

SOLLORS, WERNER.   A critique of pure pluralism. 250–79

STEINER, WENDY.   Collage or miracle: historicism in a deconstructed world. 323–51

STEPTO, ROBERT B.   Distrust of the reader in Afro-American narratives. 300–22

SUNDQUIST, ERIC J.   *Benito Cereno* and New World slavery. 93–122

VON HALLBERG, ROBERT.   American poet–critics since 1945. 280–99

The Romantic Theatre

48. CAVE, RICHARD ALLEN (ed.).   The Romantic theatre: a symposium. Gerrards Cross: Smythe; Totowa, NJ: Barnes & Noble. pp. 130.

CAVE, RICHARD ALLEN.   Romantic drama in performance. 79–104

CURRAN, STUART.   Shelleyan drama. 61–77

GEE, CHRISTINA; KNIGHT, JUDITH.   Bibliography. (Byron, Coleridge, Keats, Shelley, Wordsworth.) 113–26

MELCHIORI, GIORGIO.   The dramas of Byron. 47–60

WEBB, TIMOTHY.   The Romantic poet and the stage: a short, sad, history. 9–46

Rome in the Renaissance: the City and the Myth

49. RAMSEY, P. A. (ed.).   Rome in the Renaissance: the city and the myth. Papers of the thirteenth Annual Conference of the Center for Medieval and Early Renaissance Studies. Binghamton, NY: Center for

Medieval and Early Renaissance Texts and Studies, 1982. pp. xvii, 431. (Medieval and Renaissance texts and studies, 18.) Rev. by Carolyn Valone in Manuscripta (29:3) 1985, 198–9.

KRANZ, DAVID L.   Shakespeare's new idea of Rome. 371–80

LAWRY, J. S.   *Catiline* and 'the sight of Rome in us'. 395–407

PATTERSON, ANNABEL.   'Roman-cast similitude': Ben Jonson and the English use of Roman history. 381–94

REVARD, STELLA P.   Milton and Classical Rome: the political context of *Paradise Regained*. 411–19

SIMMONS, J. L.   Shakespeare and the antique Romans. 77–92

Shakespeare and his Contemporaries: Essays in Comparison

50. HONIGMANN, E. A. J. (ed.).   Shakespeare and his contemporaries: essays in comparison. Manchester; Dover, NH: Manchester UP. pp. xii, 143. (Revels plays companion library.)

BECKERMAN, BERNARD.   Scene patterns in *Doctor Faustus* and *Richard III*. 31–41

DAVIES, H. NEVILLE.   *Pericles* and the Sherley brothers. 94–113

EDWARDS, PHILIP.   'Seeing is believing': action and narration in *The Old Wives Tale* and *The Winter's Tale*. 79–93

FOAKES, R. A.   The descent of Iago: satire, Ben Jonson, and Shakespeare's *Othello*. 16–30

HUNTER, GEORGE K.   Bourgeois comedy: Shakespeare and Dekker. 1–15

LEGGATT, ALEXANDER.   A double reign: *Richard II* and *Perkin Warbeck*. 129–39

MEHL, DIETER.   Corruption, retribution and justice in *Measure for Measure* and *The Revenger's Tragedy*. 114–28

PECHTER, EDWARD.   *Julius Caesar* and *Sejanus*: Roman politics, inner selves and the powers of the theatre. 60–78

TETZELI VON ROSADOR, K.   'Supernatural soliciting': temptation and imagination in *Doctor Faustus* and *Macbeth*. 42–59

Shakespeare and Southern Writers: a Study in Influence

51. KOLIN, PHILIP C. (ed.).   Shakespeare and Southern writers: a study in influence. Jackson: Mississippi UP, 1985. pp. x, 177. Rev. by Perry Lentz in WHR (40:3) 275–8.

CONLEY, TIMOTHY KEVIN.   Resounding fury: Faulkner's Shakespeare, Shakespeare's Faulkner. 83–124

DAVIS, J. MADISON.   Walker Percy's *Lancelot*: the Shakespearean threads. 159–72

HARDER, KELSIE B.   Southern formalism at Shakespeare: Ransom on the Sonnets. 125–36

MURPHY, CHRISTINA.   The artistic design of societal commitment: Shakespeare and the poetry of Henry Timrod. 29–47

RICHARDSON, THOMAS J.   Is Shakespeare dead? Mark Twain's irreverent question. 63–82

WATSON, CHARLES S.   Simms's use of Shakespearean characters. 13–28

WINCHELL, MARK ROYDEN.   Renaissance men: Shakespeare's influence on Robert Penn Warren. 137–58

YOUNG, THOMAS DANIEL.   Lanier and Shakespeare. 49–61

Silent but for the Word: Tudor Women as Patrons, Translators, and Writers of Religious Works

52. HANNAY, MARGARET PATTERSON (ed.).   Silent but for the word: Tudor women as patrons, translators, and writers of religious works. Kent, OH: Kent State UP, 1985. pp. 304. Rev. by Richard P. Batteiger in SCN (44:4) 72–3; by Brenda M. Hosington in Cithara (25:2) 76–8; by Katharina M. Wilson in Moreana (23:89) 56–61; by Eleanor Rosenberg in RQ (39:4) 769–73.

BEILIN, ELAINE V.   Anne Askew's self-portrait in the *Examinations*. 77-91

BORNSTEIN, DIANE.   The style of the Countess of Pembroke's translation of Philippe de Mornay's *Discours de la vie et de la mort*. 126–34

FISCHER, SANDRA K.   Elizabeth Cary and tyranny, domestic and religious. 225–37

FISKEN, BETH WYNNE.   Mary Sidney's *Psalmes*: education and wisdom. 166–83

HANNAY, MARGARET P.   'Doo what men may sing': Mary Sidney and the tradition of admonitory dedication. 149–65

KING, JOHN N.   Patronage and piety: the influence of Catherine Parr. 43–60

LAMB, MARY ELLEN.   The Cooke sisters: attitudes towards learned women in the Renaissance. 107–25

LEVIN, CAROLE.   Lady Jane Grey: protestant queen and martyr. 92–106

LEWALSKI, BARBARA K.   Of God and good women: the poems of Aemilia Lanyer. 203–24

PRESCOTT, ANNE LAKE.   The Pearl of the Valois and Elizabeth I: Marguerite de Navarre's *Miroir* and Tudor England. 61–76

QUITSLUND, JON A.   Spenser and the patroness of the *Fowre Hymnes*: 'Ornaments of all true love and beautie'. 184–202

VERBRUGGE, RITA.   Margaret More Roper's personal expression in the *Devout Treatise upon the Pater Noster*. 30–42

WALLER, GARY F.   Struggling into discourse: the emergence of Renaissance women's writing. 238–56

WAYNE, VALERIE.   Some sad sentence: Vives' *Instruction of a Christian Woman*. 15–29

Studies in the History of Western Linguistics

53. BYNON, THEODORA; PALMER, F. R. (eds). Studies in the history of Western linguistics: in honour of R. H. Robins. Cambridge: CUP. pp. x, 285.

AARSLEFF, HANS. Joseph de Maistre and Victorian thought on the origin of language and civilization. 96–108

BREKLE, HERBERT E. What is the history of linguistics and to what end is it studied? A didactic approach. 1–10

BYNON, THEODORA. August Schleicher: Indo-Europeanist and general linguist. 129–49

COVINGTON, MICHAEL A. Grammatical theory in the Middle Ages. 23–42

DAVIES, ANNA MORPURGO. Karl Brugmann and late nineteenth-century linguistics. 150–71

HOENIGSWALD, HENRY M. Nineteenth-century linguistics on itself. 172–88

LAW, VIVIEN. Originality in the medieval normative tradition. 43–55

LEPSCHY, GIULIO. European linguistics in the twentieth century. 189–201

MATTHEWS, P. H. Distributional syntax. 245–77

PERCIVAL, W. KEITH. Renaissance linguistics: the old and the new. 56–68

SALMON, VIVIAN. Effort and achievement in seventeenth-century British linguistics. 69–95

BIBLIOGRAPHY

GENERAL

54. FAHY, CONOR. The 'fingerprint' as a bibliographical aid. Factotum (9) 1980, 16–17.

55. HAGSTROM, JACK W. C. Collective poem by 103 American poets. BB (42) 1985, 222.

56. HILLYARD, BRIAN. The fingerprint in practice. Factotum (9) 1980, 18–21.

57. MAY, JAMES E. On the inclusiveness of descriptive bibliographies: limitations of bibliographical catalogues like the ESTC. AEB (8:4) 1984, 227–38.

58. SWANICK, ERIC L. New Brunswick literature and the pursuit of bibliography. StudCanL (11:2) 182–9.

59. WILLIAMS, WILLIAM PROCTOR; ABBOTT, CRAIG S. An introduction to bibliographical and textual studies. New York: Modern Language Association, 1985. pp. vi, 106. Rev. by Hugh Amory in PBSA (80:2) 243–53.

BINDING

60. BALL, DOUGLAS. Victorian publishers' bindings. London: Library Assn, 1985. pp. 214.

61. HICKIN, NORMAN. Bookworms: the insect pests of books. London: Sheppard Press. pp. 176. Rev. by Eric Korn in TLS, 20 June, 690.

62. JOHNSON, MARY-PARKE. An inventory of the Joseph T. Altemus bookbindery, Philadelphia, 1854. PBSA (80:2) 179–91.

63. WILLIAMS, FRANKLIN B., JR (ed.). The Gardyners passetaunce: (c.1512). With notes on the two unique editions in Westminster Abbey Library, descriptions of the bindings in which they were preserved and the other items found in these bindings, by HOWARD M. NIXON. London: Roxburghe Club, 1985. pp. xv, 75.

BOOK ILLUSTRATION

For work on the illustrations, etc., of William Blake, see under 'Eighteenth Century Authors: William Blake'.

64. ANDERSON, DOUGLAS. Reading the pictures in *Huckleberry Finn*. AQ (42:2) 100–20.

65. BATE, JONATHAN. Shakespearean allusion in English caricature in the age of Gillray. JWCI (49) 196–210.

66. BOGARDUS, RALPH F. Pictures and texts: Henry James, A. L. Coburn, and new ways of seeing in literary culture. (Bibl. 1985, 81.) Rev. by Charles Higgins in AL (58:3) 449–51.

67. BROWNE, RONALD. 'Curious cuts'. Factotum (10) 1980, 21–2.

68. CECH, JOHN. Remembering Caldecott: *The Three Jovial Huntsmen* and the art of the picture book. LU (7/8) 1983/84, 110–19.

69. DAVIS, PAUL.   Imaging *Oliver Twist*: Hogarth, illustration, and the part of darkness. Dick (82:3) 158–76.

70. DOWLING, LINDA.   Letterpress and picture in the literary periodicals of the 1890s. YES (16) 117–31.

71. ENGEN, RODNEY K.   Dictionary of Victorian wood engravers. Cambridge: Chadwyck-Healey, 1985. pp. xxi, 297.

72. —— The myth of Kate Greenaway. ABC (7:7) 3–11.

73. FILSTRUP, JANE MERRILL.   An interview with Edward St John Gorey at the Gotham Book Mart. LU (2:1) 1978, 17–37.

74. GARLICK, KENNETH.   Illustrations to *A Midsummer Night's Dream* before 1920. ShS (37) 1984, 41–53.

75. GOLDEN, CATHERINE JEAN.   The Victorian illustrated book: authors who composed with graphic images and words. Unpub. doct. diss., Univ. of Michigan. [Abstr. in DA (47) 1333A.]

76. GOULDEN, R. J.   William Darres, Claude du Bosc and the European market. Factotum (14) 1982, 17–20.

77. GRENVILLE, HUGO.   Book illustration: Edmund Dulac. LRev, Apr. 1985, 8–10.

78. ISON, MARY M.   Things nobody even heard of: Jessie Willcox Smith draws the water-babies. QJLC (39:2) 1982, 90–101.

79. KEITT, DIANE.   Charles Dickens and Robert Seymour: the battle of wills. Dick (82:1) 3–11.

80. MASLEN, ELIZABETH.   Scenes unseen in *Hamlet*. NC (2) 14–30.

81. RASMUSSEN, BONNIE.   Literary criticism: explication of the picture book. Orana (Wagga Wagga, N.S.W.) (21:3) 1985, 137–41.

82. TARRANT, DOROTHY; TARRANT, JOHN.   It was the Jazz Age and John Held Jr drew it and lived it. Smithsonian (17:6) 94–8, 100–5.

83. UCHIDA, ICHIGORO.   Edgar Allan Poe to seikimatu no illustration. (Edgar Allan Poe and *fin de siècle* illustrations.) Tokyo: Iwasaki Bijyutu. pp. 114.

84. VAN LEEUWEN, HENDRIK.   The liaison of visual and written Nonsense. DQR (16:3) 186–219.

85. WELCH, DENNIS M.   Imitation in Blake's *Night Thoughts* illustrations. CLQ (22:3) 165–84.

86. WOOD, J. L.   Pictures of printing presses: a genealogy. Factotum (10) 1980, 19–21.

BOOK PRODUCTION, PRINTING, AND TYPOGRAPHY

87. BAKER, DONALD C.   William Thynne's printing of the Squire's Tale: manuscript and printer's copy. SB (39) 125–32.

88. BARKER, NICOLAS; COLLINS, JOHN.   A sequel to *An Enquiry into the Nature of Certain Nineteenth Century Pamphlets* by JOHN CARTER and GRAHAM POLLARD. (Bibl. 1985, 99.) Rev. by William E. Fredeman in Review (7) 1985, 259–96.

89. —— —— (eds). An enquiry into the nature of certain nineteenth century pamphlets. By JOHN CARTER and GRAHAM POLLARD. (Bibl. 1985, 100.) Rev. by William E. Fredeman in Review (7) 1985, 259–96.

90. BECK, BRUCE (introd.). RHM: Robert Hunter Middleton, the man and his letters: eight essays on his life and career. Chicago: Caxton Club, 1985. pp. ix, 100. Rev. by John Dreyfus in TLS, 7 Mar., 259.

91. BILLINGSLEY, DALE B. The editorial design of the 1557 *English Works*. Moreana (23:89) 39–48. (Sir Thomas More's *Works*.)

92. BLAIR, SANDRA J. Australia's first printery. Heritage Australia (Canberra) (4:3) 1985, 2–4.

93. BOND, W. H. Thomas Hollis and Baron's Milton: a strange device. BC (35:3) 381.

94. CAVE, RODERICK. A common press in New Zealand. Bibliographical Society of Australia and New Zealand Bulletin (8:3) 1984, 172–3.

95. COPPENS, CHRIS. De International Paper Conservation Conference, Oxford 14–18 April 1986: enkele aantekeningen. (A few notes.) Archives et Bibliothèques de Belgique (Brussels)(57:3/4) 497–505.

96. CRUMP, M. J. Chatterton's Rowley poems: an unnoticed cancel. Factotum (4) 1978, 21.

97. DARBY, TRUDI. Rowley's hand in collaboration. Library (8:1) 68–9.

98. DeCANDIDO, GRACEANNE A. The book thought through: contemporary handmade books at the Metropolitan Museum of Art. ABC (7:2) 27–9.

99. EDDY, DONALD D. John Brown, *Essays on the Characteristics*. Factotum (5) 1979, 15.

100. ERICKSON, LEE. The poets' corner: the impact of technological changes in printing on English poetry, 1800–1850. ELH (52:4) 1985, 893–911.

101. FINNERAN, RICHARD J. Editing Yeats's poems. (Bibl. 1985, 108.) Rev. by Elizabeth Mackenzie in NQ (33:4) 566; by George Bornstein in MLS (16:2) 82–7.

102. FREDEMAN, WILLIAM E. The story of a lie: a sequel to *A Sequel*. Review (7) 1985, 259–96 (review-article).

103. HAMMOND, ANTONY. *The White Devil* in Nicholas Okes's Shop. SB (39) 135–76.

104. HANNA, RALPH, III. Booklets in medieval manuscripts: further considerations. SB (39) 100–11.

105. HARRIS, JOHN. Page cancels. Factotum (15) 1982, 10.

106. HENDEL, RICHARD. A book designer's odyssey. SchP (17:4) 349–54.

107. JANSSEN, FRANS A. Some notes on setting by formes. Quaerendo (16:3) 191–7.

108. JOHNSTON, W. T. A note on printing in Cupar. Bibliotheck (13:3) 82–91.

109. JONES, BERNARD. William Barnes' *Guide to Dorchester*. BC (35:3) 326–36.

110. KERNER, DAVID.   The alleged errors of dialogue indentation in *Islands in the Stream*. AEB (8:4) 1984, 239–41.

111. LEE, KYUNG-SHIK.   F *Troilus* eui inswae byeonchick e daehan seogihakjeok gochal. (Bibliographical explanation of printing irregularities in F *Troilus*.) JELL (32:4) 693–718.

112. LOVE, HAROLD.   Manuscript versus print in the transmission of English literature 1600–1700. Bibliographical Society of Australia and New Zealand Bulletin (9:3) 1985, 95–107.

113. McKITTERICK, DAVID.   Four hundred years of university printing and publishing in Cambridge 1584–1984: catalogue of the exhibition in the University Library Cambridge. (Bibl. 1985, 117.) Rev. by B. J. McMullin in Bibliographical Society of Australia and New Zealand Bulletin (9:2) 1985, 74–6.

114. McLEOD, RANDALL.   Spellbound. *In* (pp. 81–96) **44**. (Renaissance typesetting problems.)

115. McMULLIN, B. J.   A case for 'columniation'. Factotum (21) 1985, 19–20.

116. —— Page cancels. Factotum (14) 1982, 11–12.

117. —— Unsigned publications of the late eighteenth century. Factotum (18) 1984, 19–24.

118. MEYER, HORST.   Bibliographie der Buch- und Bibliotheksgeschichte (BBB): Band 3, 1983; Band 4, 1984. Bad Iburg: Bibliographischer Verlag Dr Horst Meyer, 1985; 1986. pp. 522; 556.

119. MILLS, TREVOR.   Signatures in *The Patriot*, 1792–3. Factotum (16) 1983, 10–11.

120. MOSLEY, JAMES.   British type-specimens before 1831: a hand-list. Oxford: Oxford Bibliographical Society, 1984. pp. 70. (Oxford Bibliographical Society occasional publications, 14.) Rev. by David McKitterick in Library (8:4) 377–9.

121. MULHOLLAND, PAUL.   Thomas Middleton's *The Two Gates of Salvation* (1609): an instance of running-title rotation. Library (8:1) 18–31.

122. NUTTALL, D.   English printers, 1600–1700, and their supra-text roman and italic types. Unpub. doct. diss., Univ. of Reading. [Abstr. in IT (36) 883.]

123. PARR, PHILIP J.   The Laurentius legend of the origin of printing. Levin, NZ: Aspect Press. pp. 8.

124. PERFECT, CHRISTOPHER; ROOKLEDGE, GORDON.   Rookledge's international typefinder: the essential handbook of typeface recognition and selection. New York: Beil, 1983. pp. 268.

125. RASMUSSEN, ERIC.   The relevance of cast-off copy in determining the nature of omissions: Q2 *Hamlet*. SB (39) 133–5.

126. RHEIN, DONNA E.   The handprinted books of Leonard and Virginia Woolf at the Hogarth Press, 1917–1932. Ann Arbor, MI: UMI Research Press; Epping: Bowker, 1985. pp. xvi, 166. (Studies in modern literature, 52.) Rev. by Brian MacInerny in ABC (7:10) 44.

127. RIDDELL, JAMES A.   Variant title-pages of the 1616 Jonson folio. Library (8:2) 152–6.

128. SMITH, BART. White on black. Factotum (16) 1983, 24–5. (Printing in white on black paper.)

129. TURNER, ROBERT KEAN. Accidental evils. *In* (pp. 27–33) **44.**

130. WALKER, KIM. Press variants and proof correction in Shirley's *The Dukes Mistris* (1638). Long Room (31) 19–33.

131. WERSTINE, PAUL. The editorial usefulness of printing house and compositor studies. *In* (pp. 35–64) **44.**

132. WETZEL, CLAUS-DIETER. Die Worttrennung am Zeilenende in altenglischen Handschriften. (Bibl. 1985, 123.) Rev. by Klaus Dietz in Archiv (222:2) 1985, 381–4.

133. WOOD, J. L. Pictures of printing presses: a genealogy. *See* **86.**

134. WRIGHT, GLENN P. The Raverat proofs of *Mrs Dalloway*. SB (39) 241–61.

135. YAMADA, AKIHIRO. The printing of King James I's *The True Lawe of Free Monarchies* with special reference to the 1603 editions. PoetT (23) 74–80.

MANUSCRIPTS

136. ACKER, PAUL. Harvard MS Eng 1032: exemplary verse concerning Charlemagne and Theobald. NM (87:3) 354–64.

137. ALEXANDER, J. J. G. (gen. ed.). A survey of manuscripts illuminated in the British Isles: vol. 5, Gothic manuscripts 1285–1385, by LUCY FREEMAN SANDLER, 1, Text and illustrations; 2 Catalogue. London: Miller. 2 vols. pp. 70, (plates) 128; 231.

138. BACKHOUSE, JANET. Books of hours. London: British Library, 1985. pp. 80.

139. BARON, HELEN. *Sons and Lovers*: the surviving manuscripts from three drafts dated by paper analysis. SB (38) 1985, 289–328.

140. BOFFEY, J. The manuscript context of English courtly love lyrics, *c.* 1450–1530. Unpub. doct. diss., Univ. of York, 1983.

141. BOFFEY, JULIA. Manuscripts of English courtly love lyrics in the later Middle Ages. Cambridge: Brewer, 1985. pp. x, 232. (Manuscript studies, 1.)

142. BOYLE, LEONARD E. Medieval Latin paleography: a bibliographical introduction. Buffalo, NY; London; Toronto: Toronto UP, 1984. pp. xvi, 399. (Toronto medieval bibliographies, 8.) Rev. by Broxton Ross in Spec (61:3) 623–4.

143. BROWN, MICHELLE P. Paris, Bibliothèque Nationale, lat. 10861 and the scriptorium of Christ Church, Canterbury. ASE (15) 119–37.

144. CARLEY, JAMES P. John Leland and the contents of English pre-dissolution libraries: Glastonbury Abbey. Scriptorium (40) 107–20.

145. CLANTON, STACY M. The 'number' of Sir Walter Ralegh's *Booke of the Ocean to Scinthia*. SP (82:2) 1985, 200–11.

146. COHEN-MUSHLIN, ALIZA. The making of a manuscript: the Worms Bible of 1148. (Bibl. 1985, 132.) Rev. by Kristine Edmondson Haney in Spec (61:2) 396–8.

147. COPPENS, CHRIS.   De International Paper Conservation Conference, Oxford 14–18 April 1986: enkele aantekeningen. (A few notes.) *See* **95.**

148. DOYLE, A. I.   Remarks on surviving manuscripts of *Piers Plowman. In* (pp. 35–48) **32.**

149. DUMVILLE, DAVID N.   The West Saxon genealogical regnal list: manuscripts and texts. Ang (104:1/2) 1–32.

150. DUNN, R. D.   Fragment of an unpublished essay on printing by William Camden. BLJ (12:2) 145–9.

151. FITZGERALD, WILMA.   *Ocelli nominum*: names and shelf marks of famous/familiar manuscripts (II). MedStud (48) 397–421.

152. GATCH, MILTON McC.   John Bagford, bookseller and antiquary. BLJ (12:2) 150–71.

153. HALL, J. R.   On the bibliographic unity of Bodleian MS Junius 11. ANQ (24:7/8) 104–7.

154. HANNA, RALPH, III.   Booklets in medieval manuscripts: further considerations. *See* **104.**

155. HIEATT, CONSTANCE B.; JONES, ROBIN F.   Two Anglo-Norman culinary collections edited from British Library manuscripts, Additional 32084 and Royal 12.C.xii. Spec (61:4) 859–82.

156. HORNER, PATRICK J. (comp.).   The index of Middle English prose: handlist 3, A handlist of manuscripts containing Middle English prose in the Digby Collection, Bodleian Library Oxford. Cambridge: Brewer. pp. xxiii, 86.

157. KELLIHER, HILTON; BROWN, SALLY.   English literary manuscripts. London: British Library. pp. 80.

158. KELLIHER, W. H. (introd.).   The manuscript of William Wordsworth's *Poems, in Two Volumes* (1807). London: British Library, 1984. pp. 71, 117 leaves. (Facsim. of BL MS 47864.) Rev. by A. R. Jones in Library (8:2) 184–6.

159. KIERNAN, KEVIN S.   Madden, Thorkelin, and MS Vitellius/Vespasian A xv. Library (8:2) 127–32.

160. LAPIDGE, MICHAEL.   Litanies of the saints in Anglo-Saxon manuscripts: a preliminary list. Scriptorium (40) 264–77.

161. LAWTON, L. S.   Text and image in late medieval English vernacular literary manuscripts. Unpub. doct. diss., Univ. of York, 1983.

162. LEINBAUGH, THEODORE H.   A damaged passage in Ælfric's *De creatore et creatura*: methods of recovery. Ang (104:1/2) 104–14.

163. LOVE, HAROLD.   Manuscript versus print in the transmission of English literature 1600–1700. *See* **112.**

164. McHANEY, THOMAS (ed.).   William Faulkner manuscripts: 14, *The Wild Palms*: vol. 1, Holograph manuscript and miscellaneous rejected holograph pages. New York; London: Garland. pp. xii, 238.

165. MEALE, C. M.   The social and literary contexts of a late medieval manuscript: a study of BL MS Harley 2252 and its owner John Colyns. Unpub. doct. diss., Univ. of York, 1984.

166. MELLINKOFF, RUTH.   Serpent imagery in the illustrated Old English Hexateuch. *In* (pp. 51–64) **36.**

167. MOSSER, DANIEL W.   The two scribes of the Cardigan manuscript and the 'evidence' of scribal supervision and shop production. SB (39) 112–25.

168. MOSSER, DANIEL WAYNE.   The Cardigan Chaucer manuscript and the process of fifteenth-century book production. Unpub. doct. diss., Univ. of Texas at Austin, 1985. [Abstr. in DA (46) 3041A.]

169. OHLGREN, THOMAS H.   London, British Library MS Harley 603, fol. 12. OEN (19:2) 42–3.

170. RAMSEY, R. VANCE.   Paleography and scribes of shared training. SAC (8) 107–44.

171. REIMAN, DONALD H. (ed.).   Percy Bysshe Shelley: vol. 2, *The Mask of Anarchy*. New York; London: Garland, 1985. pp. xxiii, 157. (Manuscripts of the younger Romantics.)

172. —— Percy Bysshe Shelley: vol. 3, *Hellas: a Lyrical Drama*: a facsimile of the press-copy transcript, and fair-copy transcripts of *Written on Hearing the News of the Death of Napoleon* and *Letters to Maria Gisborne*, as well as a fragment of the press-copy transcript of *Lines Written Among the Euganean Hills*: all in the Henry E. Huntington Library. New York; London: Garland, 1985. pp. 123. (Manuscripts of the younger Romantics.)

173. RONBERG, GERT.   The two manuscripts of *The Wars of Alexander*: a linguistic comparison. Neophilologus (69:4) 1985, 604–10.

174. ROSS, THOMAS W.; BROOKS, EDWARD (eds).   English glosses from British Library Additional Manuscript 37075. Norman, OK: Pilgrim, 1984. pp. xv, 160. Rev. by Lister M. Matheson in SAC (8) 237–9.

175. SCHACH, PAUL.   Instant saga style: the evidence of the manuscripts. JEGP (85:3) 404–20.

176. SCHIPPER, WILLIAM.   Orthography and dialect in Cambridge University Library MS Ii.1.33. StudME (1) 53–65.

177. SCRAGG, D. G.   The homilies of the Blickling manuscript. *In* (pp. 299–316) **25.**

178. SEYMOUR, M. C.   The manuscripts of John Capgrave's English works. Scriptorium (40) 248–55.

179. SHAILOR, BARBARA A.   Catalogue of medieval and Renaissance manuscripts in the Beinecke Rare Book and Manuscript Library, Yale University: vol. 1, MSS 1–250. Binghamton, NY: Center for Medieval and Early Renaissance Studies, 1984. pp. xxii, 420, (plates) 32. (Medieval and Renaissance texts & studies.) Rev. in BB (43:2) 122; by A. I. Doyle in AEB (8:4) 1984, 249–54; by Paul Saenger in CRL (47:5) 518–20.

180. SIEGEL, SANDRA F. (ed.).   *Purgatory*: manuscript materials including the author's [Yeats's] final text. Ithaca, NY; London: Cornell UP. pp. xi, 222.

181. SMALLWOOD, T. M.   Another example of the double-copying of a passage of Middle English. NM (87:4) 550–4.

182. SMITH, MARGARET M.; BOUMELHA, PENNY.   Index of English literary manuscripts: vol. 3, 1700–1800: part 1, Addison–Fielding. London: Mansell. pp. 350.

183. STANLEY, E. G.   *The Judgement of the Damned* (from Cambridge, Corpus Christi College 201 and other manuscripts), and the definition of Old English verse. *In* (pp. 363–91) **25.**

184. SULLIVAN, ERNEST W., II.   A fragment of a possible Byron poem in manuscript. PBSA (80:1) 55–73.

185. SZARMACH, PAUL E.   British Library, Cotton Vespasian D.vi. fol. 62v. OEN (20:1) 32–3.

186. THOMPSON, J. J.   Robert Thornton and his book producing activities: aspects of the transmission of certain late medieval texts in the light of their present context in Thornton's manuscripts. Unpub. doct. diss., Univ. of York, 1984.

187. TOON, THOMAS E.   Preliminaries to the linguistic analysis of the Old English glosses and glossaries. *In* (pp. 319–29) **41.**

188. WATSON, ANDREW G.   Catalogue of dated and datable manuscripts *c.*435–1600 in Oxford libraries. (Bibl. 1985, 255.) Rev. by A. I. Doyle in Library (8:4) 373–5.

189. ——John Twyne of Canterbury (d. 1581) as a collector of medieval manuscripts: a preliminary investigation. Library (8:2) 133–51.

COLLECTING AND THE LIBRARY

190. ADELMAN, SEYMOUR.   He didn't like us, but we like him: a book collector's A. E. Housman. NYTB, 14 Sept., 3.

191. ANON.   Milton bookplate. Factotum (2) 1978, 18.

192. ——Nabokov papers: U. S. Library of Congress. VNRN (4) 1980, 20–34.

193. ARELLANES, AUDREY SPENCER (ed.).   Bookplates in the news, 1970–1985: a collection of sixty issues of the Newsletter of the American Society of Bookplate Collectors and Designers. Detroit, MI: Gale Research. pp. 640. Rev. by Wesley McCann in Leabharlann (3:4) 122–3.

194. BATTIN, PATRICIA.   The library: centre of the restructured university. SchP (17:3) 255–67.

195. BELL, ALAN.   The foundation of the Elizabethan Club library. BC (35:3) 337–44.

196. BENSON, C. J.   Anatomizing early printed books in Trinity College, Dublin. ECI (1) 195–9.

197. BERCH, VICTOR A.   Notes on some unrecorded circulating libraries of eighteenth century London. Factotum (6) 1979, 15–19.

198. BLACK, JEREMY.   Diplomats as book procurers in the age of Walpole. Factotum (14) 1982, 14–16.

199. BRODSKY, LOUIS DANIEL.   Twenty-five years as a Faulkner collector. ABC (7:4) 3–11.

200. —— HAMBLIN, ROBERT W. Faulkner: a comprehensive guide to the Brodsky collection: vol. 4, *Battle Cry*: a screenplay by William Faulkner. Jackson: Mississippi UP, 1985. pp. xlix, 409.

201. —— —— Faulkner: a comprehensive guide to the Brodsky collection: vol. 3, *The De Gaulle Story* by William Faulkner. Jackson: Mississippi UP, 1984. pp. xxxix, 400. Rev. by Dawn Truard in SCR (3:1) 102–4.

202. BURGESS, MOIRA (comp.). Scottish Fiction Reserve: directory of authors included in the scheme. Edinburgh: National Library of Scotland. pp. 86.

203. BUSH, SARGENT, JR; RASMUSSEN, CARL J. The library of Emmanuel College, Cambridge, 1584–1637. Cambridge: CUP. pp. x, 223.

204. CARLEY, JAMES P. John Leland and the contents of English pre-Dissolution libraries: the Cambridge Friars. TCBS (9:1) 90–100.

205. —— John Leland and the contents of English pre-dissolution libraries: Glastonbury Abbey. *See* **144.**

206. CARL-MITCHELL, CHARLOTTE. Medieval and Renaissance manuscripts at the HRHRC. LCUT (35) 89–105.

207. —— GOULD, KAREN. A list of HRHRC medieval and Renaissance manuscripts. LCUT (35) 107–13.

208. CARPENTER, KENNETH E. The first 350 years of the Harvard University Library: description of an exhibition. HLB (34:1) iii–xii, 1–216.

209. CARTWRIGHT, GRAHAM. Pope's books: a postscript to Mack. NQ (33:1) 56–8.

210. CLINGHAM, G. J. Bolingbroke's copy of Pope's *Works 1717–1735* in Tonbridge School library. NQ (33:4), 500–2.

211. CROSS, J. E. On the library of the Old English martyrologist. *In* (pp. 227–49) **25.**

212. DICKINSON, DONALD C. Dictionary of American book collectors. Westport, CT: Greenwood Press. pp. 383. Rev. by Madeleine B. Stern in ABC (7:9) 39–41.

213. DIRDA, MICHAEL. Mold, mildew, and modern first editions. BkW, 13 July, 1, 14, 15.

214. ELIAS, A. C., JR. Lord Orrery's copy of *Memoirs of the Life and Writings of Swift* (1751). ECI (1) 111–25.

215. ELIOT, SIMON. Public libraries and popular authors, 1883–1912. Library (8:4) 322–50.

216. FABIAN, BERNHARD. Eighteenth-century English and American booksellers catalogues in Göttingen. Factotum (5) 1979, 23–6.

217. —— Libraries and humanistic scholarship. Journal of Librarianship (18) 79–92.

218. FOX, PETER (ed.). Treasures of the library: Trinity College Dublin. Dublin: Royal Irish Academy. pp. 258. Rev. by Wesley McCann in Linen Hall Review (3:3) 28–9; by David McKitterick in Leabharlann (3:4) 119–20.

219. FRASER, IAN H. C. The heir of Parham: Robert Curzon,

14th Baron Zouche. Harleston: Paradigm. pp. xviii, 230. Rev. by A. O. J. Cockshut in TLS, 1 Aug., 849.

220. GALLUP, DONALD.   The Ezra Pound archive at Yale. YLG (60:3/4) 161–77.

221. GARSIDE, PETER.   Thomas Lockett's catalogue of novels. . . (1790). Factotum Occasional Paper 3, 1983, 8–13.

222. GATCH, MILTON McC.   John Bagford, bookseller and antiquary. *See* **152.**

223. GILCHER, EDWIN.   A note on Arizona State University's George Moore collection. ELT (29:4) 386–7.

224. GNEUSS, HELMUT.   King Alfred and the history of Anglo-Saxon libraries. *In* (pp. 29–49) **36.**

225. GOULDEN, R. J.   Auction catalogue printing, 1715–1730. Factotum (10) 1980, 23–7.

226. —— *Ebrietatis encomium.* Factotum (6) 1979, 9.

227. GREANEY, VINCENT.   Libraries and reading for leisure. Leabharlann (3:3) 77–83.

228. GREGORY, P.   The popular fiction of the eighteenth-century commercial circulating libraries. Unpub. doct. diss., Univ. of Edinburgh, 1985. [Abstr. in IT (35) 1084.]

229. HAMBRICK, MARGARET.   A Chartist's library. London: Mansell. pp. 266.

230. HAMILTON, DAVID MIKE.   The tools of my trade: the annotated books in Jack London's library. Seattle; London: Washington UP. pp. xiv, 326.

231. HEWITT, DAVID.   The Magnum Opus and the Pforzheimer manuscripts. ScottN (8) 18–20.

232. HIND, CHARLES.   A coffin collector. Factotum (22) 11. (Sir Thomas Parkyns.)

233. HOBBS, A. S.; WHALLEY, J. I. (eds).   Beatrix Potter: the V & A Collection. London: Victoria & Albert Museum; Warne. pp. 240. Rev. by M. C. in Junior Bookshelf (50:4) 137.

234. HOLLAND, MERIDEL.   John Ruskin's lectionary. DUJ (78:2) 301–10.

235. HOOK, DAVID.   Mr Boswell's books and the Inquisition. Library (8:3) 265–8.

236. HOWELL, JOHN BRUCE.   A history of the Dublin Library Society, 1791–1881. Halifax, N.S.: Dalhousie Univ., School of Library Service, 1985. pp. 34.

237. HUGHES, MURIEL J.   The library of Margaret of York, Duchess of Burgundy. Private Library (7:2) 1985, 53–78.

238. HUMPHREYS, K. W.   The book and the library in society. Library History (7:4) 105–18.

239. HURST, CLIVE.   The Dunston collection. BLR (12:3) 176–204.

240. JANNETTA, M. J.   Footnotes on circulating libraries. Factotum (5) 1979, 16–17.

241. JESTIN, CATHERINE T.   Notes by 'A curious gentleman'. YLG (61:1/2) 61–5. (On the Lewis Walpole Library at Yale.)

242. JOHN RYLANDS UNIVERSITY LIBRARY OF MANCHESTER. Children's books of yesterday: a survey of 200 years of children's reading: an exhibition in the Deansgate Building, Winter 1985. Manchester: John Rylands Univ. Library, 1985. pp. 24.

243. JOHNSON, BARRY C. Lost in the Alps: a portrait of Robert Proctor, the 'great bibliographer' and of his career in the British Museum. (Bibl. 1985, 199.) Rev. by David McKitterick in TLS, 28 Feb., 229; by K. A. Manley in Library History (7:4) 1985, 123–5.

244. KASER, DAVID. Books and libraries in camp and battle: the Civil War experience. Westport, CT; London: Greenwood Press, 1984. pp. xiii, 141. (Contributions in librarianship and information science, 48.)

245. KER, N. R. Books, collectors and libraries: studies in the medieval heritage. Ed. by ANDREW G. WATSON. London; Roncevert, WV: Hambledon Press, 1985. pp. xiv, 528. (History ser. 36; Literature ser. 2.) Rev. by P. S. Morrish in Library History (7:3) 1985, 90–1; by David McKitterick in TLS, 4 Apr., 371.

246. KEYNES, SIMON. King Athelstan's books. *In* (pp. 143–201) **25.**

247. KJELLIN, GUNNAR. Lars von Engeström's collection. Factotum (6) 1979, 10–11. (Eighteenth-century Swedish collector of English books.)

248. KNOWLES, OWEN; MISKIN, G. W. S. Unpublished Conrad letters: the *HQS Wellington* collection. NQ (32) 1985, 370–6.

249. LAPIDGE, MICHAEL. Surviving booklists from Anglo-Saxon England. *In* (pp. 33–89) **25.**

250. LAURENCE, DAN H. A portrait of the author as a bibliography. BC (35:2) 165–77.

251. LEARMOUTH, TREVOR; MACWILLIAM, STUART (comps). Historic English dictionaries 1592–1899: a union catalogue of holdings in Exeter libraries. Exeter: University of Exeter, Dictionary Research Centre. pp. 100. (Exeter union catalogues of dictionaries publications, 1.)

252. McCANN, WESLEY. Swift at Tollymore Park. Linen Hall Review (3:4) 13–15.

253. McCARTHY, MURIEL. All graduates and gentlemen: Marsh's Library. (Bibl. 1980, 605.) Rev. by Antony Hammond in CJIS (12:1) 98–100.

254. McLEOD, MARGARET S. The cathedral libraries catalogue: books printed before 1701 in the libraries of the Anglican cathedrals of England and Wales: vol. 1. London: British Library; Bibliographical Soc., 1984. pp. xxii, 442. Rev. by Paul Morgan in BC (35:4) 527–30.

255. MARDER, LOUIS. Pforzheimer Shakespeareana sold to University of Texas–Austin. SNL (36:1) 12.

256. MATTESON, ROBERT S. An Irish archbishop and his library. Linen Hall Review (3:3) 15–17. (Archbishop William King, 1650–1729.)

257. MATTHEWS, JACK. Booking in the heartland. Baltimore, MD; London: Johns Hopkins UP. pp. ix, 161.

258. MAXTED, IAN.   All quiet on the western front? A report on ESTC activity in Devon. Factotum (19) 1984, 23–7.

259. MISENHEIMER, JAMES B., JR; O'NEILL, ROBERT K.   The Cordell collection of dictionaries and Johnson's lexicographic presence; the love of books in two centuries. NRam (24) 1983, 33–46.

260. MITCHELL, JEROME.   Scott holdings in the Library at Schloss Corvey. ScottN (8) 14–17.

261. MOLLAND, A. GEORGE.   Duncan Liddell (1561–1613): an early benefactor of Marischal College Library. AUR (51) 485–99.

262. MORGAN, JANET (comp.).   Victorian literature at St Deiniol's Library: a bibliography of poetry, plays and fiction. 1837–1901. Hawarden: The Library, 1985. pp. 55.

263. MORGAN, PENELOPE E.   Cathedral librarianship. Journal of Librarianship (18) 153–64.

264. NAIDITCH, P. G.   Corrections. HSJ (12) 143. (*Refers to* bibl. 1985, 11315.)

265. NICKSON, M. A. E.   Sloane's codes: the solution to a mystery. Factotum (7) 1979, 13–18.

266. OATES, J. C. T.   Cambridge University Library; a history: from the beginnings to the Copyright Act of Queen Anne. Cambridge: CUP. pp. xviii, 510. Rev. by Anthony Hobson in TLS, 7 Nov., 1244.

267. OFFICE OF THE CALIFORNIA SECRETARY OF STATE.   Archival and manuscript repositories in California. Sacramento: Soc. of California Archivists, 1984. pp. 180. Rev. by David S. Zeidberg in PacHR (55:3) 466–7.

268. PARKER, STEPHEN JAN.   Some Nabokov holdings in the Library of Congress. VNRN (3) 1979, 16–23.

269. PEARSON, DAVID.   The books of Peter Shaw in Trinity College, Cambridge. TCBS (9:1) 76–89.

270. —— The library of John Bowes of Durham. BC (35:4) 475–93.

271. —— An unrecorded book from the library of John Donne. BC (35:2) 246.

272. PEATTIE, ROGER W.   Whitman, Charles Aldrich and W. M. Rossetti in 1885: background to the Whitman subscription. AL (58:3) 413–21.

273. PINNEY, THOMAS.   Kipling in the libraries. ELT (29:1) 83–90.

274. POMEROY, ELIZABETH.   The Huntington: library, art gallery, botanical gardens. Florence: Scala; London: Wilson, 1983. pp. 144.

275. PRINGLE, LAUREN HELEN.   An annotated and indexed calendar and abstract of the Ohio State University collection of Simone de Beauvoir's letters to Nelson Algren. Unpub. doct. diss., Ohio State Univ., 1985. [Abstr. in DA (46) 3716A.]

276. QUARRIE, PAUL.   The library of Eton College. Factotum (5) 1979, 19–23.

277. ROBERTS, WARREN.   D. H. Lawrence at Texas: a memoir. LCUT (34) 23–37.

278. ROBINSON, PHILIP.   Recollections of moving a library: or, how the Phillipps collection was brought to London. BC (35:4) 431–42.

279. SHAILOR, BARBARA A.	Catalogue of medieval and Renaissance manuscripts in the Beinecke Rare Book and Manuscript Library, Yale University: vol. 1, MSS 1–250. *See* **179.**

280. SIMS, GEORGE.	The rare book game. Philadelphia, PA: Holmes, 1985. pp. 161. Rev. by Ralph B. Sipper in ABC (7:5) 47–9.

281. SOLHEIM, HELENE ELIZABETH.	Walter N. H. Harding and the Harding drama collection at the Bodleian Library, Oxford. Unpub. doct. diss., Univ. of Washington, 1985. [Abstr. in DA (46) 3044A.]

282. STAM, DAVID H.	The doors and windows of the library: Leigh Hunt and special collections. BC (35:1) 67–75.

283. STEWART, CHARLOTTE A.	The life of a Johnson collection. ABC (7:6) 9–17.

284. TITE, C. G. C. (ed.).	Thomas Smith: catalogue of the manuscripts in the Cottonian Library, 1696. (Bibl. 1985, 252.) Rev. by Leona Rostenberg in ABC (7:4) 42–4; by E. G. Stanley in NQ (33:3) 402.

285. VERVLIET, HENDRICK D. L. (ed.).	Annual bibliography of the printed book and libraries: vol. 14. Dordrecht: Nijhoff, 1985. pp. x, 401.

286. VOIGTS, LINDA EHRSAM.	A handlist of Middle English in Harvard manuscripts. HLB (33:1) 1985, 5–96.

287. WALDO, MICHAEL J.	A comparative analysis of nineteenth-century academic and literary society library collections in the Midwest. Unpub. doct. diss., Indiana Univ., 1985. [Abstr. in DA (46) 2845A.]

288. WATSON, ANDREW G.	Catalogue of dated and datable manuscripts c.435–1600 in Oxford libraries. *See* **188.**

289. ——John Twyne of Canterbury (d. 1581) as a collector of medieval manuscripts: a preliminary investigation. *See* **189.**

290. WILLIAMS, FRANKLIN B., JR (ed.).	The Gardyners passetaunce: (c. 1512). With notes on the two unique editions in Westminster Abbey Library, descriptions of the bindings in which they were preserved and the other items found in these bindings, by HOWARD M. NIXON. *See* **63.**

291. WILLIAMS, MOELWYN I. (ed.).	A directory of rare book and special collections in the United Kingdom and the Republic of Ireland. (Bibl. 1985, 258.) Rev. by David J. Shaw in Library (8:4) 390–2; by Joel H. Wiener in VPR (19:3) 111–12; by Alan Bell in TLS, 7 Mar., 259.

292. WOLFF, ROBERT LEE (comp.).	Nineteenth-century fiction: a bibliographical catalogue based on the collection formed by Robert Lee Wolff: vol. 5, Anonymous, pseudonymous, multiple-author fiction, annuals and periodicals, index. New York; London: Garland. pp. viii, 229. (Garland reference library of the humanities, 334.)

293. WOOD, J. L.	Sir Hans Sloane's books. Factotum (2) 1978, 15–18.

294. YEATS-EDWARDS, PAUL.	The Warden and Fellows' library at Winchester College. Factotum (6) 1979, 22–6.

TEXTUAL STUDIES

For textual studies of Shakespeare, see under 'William Shakespeare: Editions and Textual Criticism'.

295. ACKER, PAUL.	Harvard MS Eng 1032: exemplary verse concerning Charlemagne and Theobald. *See* **136.**

296. ALEXANDER, J. J. G. (gen. ed.).   A survey of manuscripts illuminated in the British Isles: vol. 5, Gothic manuscripts 1285–1385, by LUCY FREEMAN SANDLER, 1, Text and illustrations; 2 Catalogue. *See* **137.**

297. AMORY, HUGH.   The evidence of things not seen: concealed proofs of Fielding's Juvenal. PBSA (80:1) 15–53.

298. —— New, old, Anglo-American, textual criticism. PBSA (80:2) 243–53 (review-article).

299. BARON, HELEN.   *Sons and Lovers*: the surviving manuscripts from three drafts dated by paper analysis. *See* **139.**

300. BRATTIN, JOEL J.   Reading between the lines: interpreting Dickens's later manuscripts. Unpub. doct. diss., Stanford Univ. [Abstr. in DA (47) 534A.]

301. BUNING, MARIUS.   Ulysses's textual homecoming. DQR (16:2) 145–52 (review-article).

302. CLAREY, JOELLYN.   D. H. Lawrence's *Moby-Dick*: a textual note. MP (84:2) 191–5.

303. CREEL, JAMES MELTON.   The phonetic play: *Pygmalion* from manuscript to first printing. Unpub. doct. diss., Univ. of Texas at Austin, 1985. [Abstr. in DA (46) 3348A.]

304. DAALDER, JOOST.   Recovering the text of Wyatt's *Disdain Me Not without Desert*. SN (58:1) 59–66.

305. DUMVILLE, DAVID N.   The West Saxon genealogical regnal list: manuscripts and texts. *See* **149.**

306. EDWARDS, PHILIP.   The function of commentary. *In* (pp. 97–104) **44.**

307. GAINES, BARRY.   Textual apparatus – rationale and audience. *In* (pp. 65–71) **44.**

308. GAIR, REAVLEY.   In search of 'the mustie fopperies of antiquity'. *In* (pp. 123–30) **44.**

309. GELLERT, JAMES.   The sources of Davenant's *The Law Against Lovers*. Library (8:4) 351–7.

310. HALL, J. R.   The Conybeare *Cædmon*: a turning point in the history of Old English scholarship. HLB (33:4) 1985, 378–403.

311. HAMMOND, ANTONY.   *The White Devil* in Nicholas Okes's Shop. *See* **103.**

312. HIGDON, DAVID LEON.   'Word for word': the collected editions of Conrad's *Under Western Eyes*. Conradiana (18:2) 129–36.

313. HULT, DAVID F.   Lancelot's two steps: a problem in textual criticism. Spec (61:4) 836–58.

314. KELLIHER, W. H. (introd.).   The manuscript of William Wordsworth's *Poems, in Two Volumes* (1807). *See* **158.**

315. KERNER, DAVID.   The alleged errors of dialogue indentation in *Islands in the Stream*. *See* **110.**

316. KIERNAN, KEVIN S.   Madden, Thorkelin, and MS Vitellius/ Vespasian A xv. *See* **159.**

317. LEINBAUGH, THEODORE H.   A damaged passage in Ælfric's *De creatore et creatura*: methods of recovery. *See* **162.**

318.	LICH, GLEN E.	'Anything but a misprint': comments on an Oscar Wilde typescript. SCR (3:2) 46–54.

319.	LOVE, HAROLD.	Manuscript versus print in the transmission of English literature 1600–1700. *See* **112.**

320.	—— The text of Rochester's *Upon Nothing*. Melbourne: Monash Univ., 1985. pp. 46. (Occasional papers, 1.)

321.	McLEOD, RANDALL.	Spellbound. *In* (pp. 81–96) **44.** (Renaissance typesetting problems.)

322.	MORSE, RUTH.	Editing A. D. Hope: notes and documents. ALS (12:4) 499–509.

323.	MORTON, RICHARD.	How many revengers in *The Revengers Tragedy?* Archaic spellings and the modern annotator. *In* (pp. 113–22) **44.**

324.	MULHOLLAND, PAUL.	Thomas Middleton's *The Two Gates of Salvation* (1609): an instance of running-title rotation. *See* **121.**

325.	PEARSALL, DEREK (ed.).	Manuscripts and readers in fifteenth-century England: the literary implications of manuscript study. (Bibl. 1985, 276.) Rev. by N. F. Palmer in MLR (81:1) 160–2.

326.	RAMSEY, R. VANCE.	Paleography and scribes of shared training. *See* **170.**

327.	REIMAN, DONALD H. (ed.).	Percy Bysshe Shelley: vol. 2, *The Mask of Anarchy. See* **172.**

328.	—— Percy Bysshe Shelley: vol. 3, *Hellas: a Lyrical Drama*: a facsimile of the press-copy transcript, and fair-copy transcripts of *Written on Hearing the News of the Death of Napoleon* and *Letters to Maria Gisborne*, as well as a fragment of the press-copy transcript of *Lines Written Among the Euganean Hills*: all in the Henry E. Huntington Library. *See* **171.**

329.	ROBBINS, J. ALBERT.	A new manuscript of Poe's *For Annie*. SB (39) 261–5.

330.	RUDE, DONALD W.	Joseph Conrad's typescripts at Falls Library. Library (8:4) 360–2.

331.	SCHACH, PAUL.	Instant saga style: the evidence of the manuscripts. *See* **175.**

332.	SCHIPPER, WILLIAM.	Orthography and dialect in Cambridge University Library MS Ii.1.33. *See* **176.**

333.	SCHOENBAUM, S.	Old-spelling editions: the state of the art. *In* (pp. 9–26) **44.**

334.	SCHWARTZ, RICHARD ALAN.	A textual history of Wallace Stevens' *Three Travellers Watch a Sunrise*. SB (39) 269–76.

335.	SEED, DAVID.	*Ulysses*: the evolution of a definitive text. AEB (8:3) 1984, 173–83.

336.	SHEWAN, R.	Oscar Wilde's *Salome*: a critical variorum edition from three extant manuscripts, proofsheets and two early printed texts transcribed in parallel. Unpub. doct. diss., Univ. of Reading, 1982.

337.	SMALLWOOD, T. M.	Another example of the double-copying of a passage of Middle English. *See* **181.**

338.	STALLWORTHY, JON.	Old-spelling editions: the state of the business in 1978. *In* (pp. 141–51) **44.**

339. TANSELLE, G. THOMAS.   Historicism and critical editing. SB (39) 1–46.

340. TURNER, ROBERT KEAN.   Accidental evils. *In* (pp. 27–33) **44.**

341. UFFELMAN, LARRY; SCOTT, PATRICK.   Kingsley's serial novels: II, *The Water-Babies.* VPR (19:4) 122–31.

342. VANDER MOTTEN, J. P.   Another annotated copy of Sir William Killigrew's *Four New Playes* (1666). Library (8:1) 53–8.

343. WALKER, KIM.   Press variants and proof correction in Shirley's *The Dukes Mistris* (1638). *See* **130.**

344. WERSTINE, PAUL.   The editorial usefulness of printing house and compositor studies. *In* (pp. 35–64) **44.**

345. WILLIAMS, WILLIAM PROCTOR; ABBOTT, CRAIG S.   An introduction to bibliographical and textual studies. *See* **59.**

346. WRIGHT, GLENN P.   The Raverat proofs of *Mrs Dalloway. See* **134.**

347. YAMADA, AKIHIRO.   The printing of King James I's *The True Lawe of Free Monarchies* with special reference to the 1603 editions. *See* **135.**

348. ZITNER, S. P.   Excessive annotation, or piling Pelion on Parnassus. *In* (pp. 131–9) **44.**

HISTORY OF PUBLISHING AND BOOKSELLING

349. ACKLAND, MICHAEL.   Charles Harpur and his editors. Bibliographical Society of Australia and New Zealand Bulletin (9:1) 1985, 1–13.

350. ADAMS, J. R. R.   The Quota Press: a preliminary checklist. Linen Hall Review (3:1) 16–17.

351. ALSTON, R. C.   The Clays of Daventry: a footnote to booktrade history. Factotum (21) 1985, 10–11.

352. —— A provincial printer at work, 1793–1800. Factotum (10) 1980, 6–7. (Jasper Sprange of Tunbridge Wells.)

353. ALTICK, RICHARD D.   Nineteenth-century best-sellers: a third list. SB (39) 235–41.

354. ANON.   50 years on. Junior Bookshelf (50:2) 55–6. (H. J. B. Woodfield and *Junior Bookshelf.*)

355. BILLMAN, CAROL.   The secret of the Stratemeyer syndicate: Nancy Drew, the Hardy Boys, and the million dollar fiction factory. New York: Ungar. pp. 187. Rev. by Anita Susan Grossman in NYTB, 28 Sept., 12.

356. BLACK, M. H.   Cambridge University Press: 1584–1984. (Bibl. 1984, 455.) Rev. by B. J. McMullin in Bibliographical Society of Australia and New Zealand Bulletin (9:2) 1985, 61–73; by Stephen Lehmann in LQ (56:1) 75–7.

357. BLAIR, SANDRA J.   Australia's first printery. *See* **92.**

358. BOHN, MELVIN MICHAEL.   The Cummington Press and Abattoir Editions: a descriptive bibliography of the presswork of Harry Duncan, 1939–1985. Unpub. doct. diss., Univ. of Nebraska–Lincoln. [Abstr. in DA (47) 1310A.]

359. CAPRARO, ROCCO L. European booksellers and the London book trade. Factotum (15) 1982, 18–20.

360. CARR, R. P. (introd.). The Mandrake Press 1929–30: catalogue of an exhibition, Cambridge University Library, September–November 1985. Cambridge: Cambridge Univ. Library, 1985. pp. 53.

361. CAVE, RODERICK. The private press. (Bibl. 1971, 530.) New York; London: Bowker, 1983. pp. 389. (Second ed.: first ed. 1971.) Rev. by Paul J. Koda in BB (43:2) 114.

362. COLBY, ROBERT A. 'What fools authors be!': the Author's Syndicate, 1890–1920. LCUT (35) 61–87.

363. COLE, RICHARD CARGILL. Irish booksellers and English writers 1740–1800. London: Mansell. pp. xv, 266.

364. COLLIN, DOROTHY W. The composition and publication of Elizabeth Gaskell's *Cranford*. BJRL (69:1) 59–95.

365. CONNELL, CHARLES. They gave us Shakespeare: John Heminge and Henry Condell. Boston, MA; Henley; London: Routledge & Kegan Paul, 1982. (Cf. bibl. 1985, 299.) Rev. by Ann Jennalie Cook in MLR (81:3) 714–15.

366. DEGUCHI, YASUO. Igirisu bungei syuppan shi. (A history of literary publications in England.) Tokyo: Kenkyusha. pp. 232.

367. DOUGLAS, JANE. Citizen Lee and the Tree of Liberty. Factotum (7) 1979, 8–11.

368. DOYLE, JAMES. The Confederation poets and American publishers. CanP (17) 1985, 59–67.

369. DUNN, R. D. Fragment of an unpublished essay on printing by William Camden. *See* **150.**

370. DUVAL, GILLES. 'History-histories': mémoire et création dans la littérature de colportage anglaise du 18e siècle. *In* (pp. 111–23) **34.**

371. ENGLISH, J. S. The Mozleys of Gainsborough. Factotum Occasional Paper 3, 1983, 21–3.

372. ERICKSON, LEE. The poets' corner: the impact of technological changes in printing on English poetry, 1800–1850. *See* **100.**

373. FABIAN, BERNHARD. 'London' books? Factotum (4) 1978, 18–20.

374. FEATHER, JOHN. British publishing in the eighteenth century: a preliminary subject analysis. Library (8:1) 32–46.

375. —— The provincial book trade in eighteenth-century England. (Bibl. 1985, 304.) Rev. by Ian Maxted in BC (35:2) 249–51; by Robin Myers in JNPH (2:3) 42–4; by Pat Rogers in TLS, 17 Jan., 71.

376. FERDINAND, C. The illustrated pirate. Factotum (5) 1979, 18–19. (Gay's *Fables*.)

377. GARSIDE, PETER. Thomas Lockett's catalogue of novels. . . (1790). *See* **221.**

378. GASKELL, PHILIP. A bibliography of the Foulis Press. (Bibl. 1965, 161.) Winchester: St Paul's Bibliographies. pp. 484. (St Paul's bibliographies, 14.) (Second ed.: first ed. 1964.)

379. GATCH, MILTON McC. John Bagford, bookseller and antiquary. *See* **152.**

380. GOULDEN, R. J. John Baskett. Factotum (7) 1979, 19–24.

381. —— No fleas on Curll. Factotum (2) 1978, 7–8. (Mist.)

382. —— William Darres, Claude du Bosc and the European market. *See* **76.**

383. GROENING, LAURA.   Critic and publisher: another chapter in E. K. Brown's correspondence. CanL (110) 46–58.

384. HALL, MAX.   Harvard University Press: a history. Cambridge, MA: Harvard UP. pp. 257. Rev. by Michael Black in SchP (18:1) 72–5.

385. HARRIS, FRANCES.   Jacob Tonson and the *Advice to the Electors of Great Britain*. Factotum (16) 1983, 13–15.

386. —— Paper-round: the distribution of Whig propaganda in 1710. Factotum (9) 1980, 12–13.

387. —— Political verse by Francis Hoffman. Factotum (4) 1978, 13–15.

388. HERNLUND, PATRICIA.   A new work by Thomas Sheridan. Factotum (6) 1979, 6–8.

389. HIND, CHARLES.   News of the trade. Factotum (18) 1984, 10–13.

390. IKIN, BRIDGET.   Peter Pindar and the pirates. Factotum (9) 1980, 27–31.

391. —— A Sterne warning: false imprints and piracies in the 1780's. Factotum (4) 1978, 16–17.

392. ING, JANET.   A London shop of the 1850s: the Chiswick Press. PBSA (80:2) 153–78.

393. ING, JANET THOMPSON.   Charles Whittingham the Younger and the Chiswick Press, 1852–59. Unpub. doct. diss., Univ. of California, Berkeley, 1985. [Abstr. in DA (47) 696A–7A.]

394. JOHANSON, GRAEME.   'Cultural cringe' or colonial fringe? Melbourne Historical Journal (17) 1985, 78–85.

395. JOHNSON, GERALD D.   John Trundle and the book-trade 1603–1626. SB (39) 177–99.

396. JOSEPH, MICHAEL; RYLEY, ALISON; ROBOTHAM, JOHN S.   'All the leading sensations of the day': purple publishing in Victorian America. ABC (7:8) 3–10.

397. JOSEPH, RICHARD.   Michael Joseph: master of words. Southampton: Ashford. pp. xviii, 238.

398. KNOTT, DAVID.   Competition and co–operation in the Kent almanac trade: the Fisher–Simmons partnership. Factotum Occasional Paper 3, 1983, 14–20.

399. KRAUS, JOE W.   A history of Way & Williams, with a bibliography of their publications, 1895–1898. Philadelphia, PA: MacManus, 1984. pp. xii, 111. Rev. by Robert A. Tibbetts in BB (43:2) 117–18.

400. —— Messrs Copeland & Day, 69 Cornhill, Boston, 1893–1899. (Bibl. 1985, 316.) Rev. by Robert A. Tibbetts in BB (43:2) 117–18.

401. LAURENCE, DAN H.   A portrait of the author as a bibliography. *See* **250.**

402. LEE, HERMIONE (introd.).   The Hogarth letters. London: Chatto & Windus, 1985. pp. xxviii, 349. Rev. by L. H. Hugo in UES (24:2) 47–8.

403. McKenzie, D. F. Dealers in books outside the Stationers' Company, circa 1685. Factotum (8) 1980, 12–13.

404. McMinn, Joseph. Swift and George Faulkner, 'Prince of Dublin Printers'. Linen Hall Review (3:2) [misnumbered 3:3] 15–17.

405. McMullin, B. J. Four hundred years of university printing in Cambridge. Bibliographical Society of Australia and New Zealand Bulletin (9:2) 1985, 61–76 (review-article).

406. Mansbridge, Ronald. The Bentham folio Bible. Factotum (19) 1984, 14–16.

407. Maxted, Ian. . . . A most barbarous, dreadful, and shocking murder . . . . Factotum Occasional Paper 3, 1983, 2–6. (Exeter printing.)

408. Menikoff, Barry. Robert Louis Stevenson and *The Beach of Falesá*: a study in Victorian publishing with the original text. (Bibl. 1985, 324.) Rev. by Nicholas Rankin in LRev, Mar. 1985, 27–8; by David H. Jackson in Review (8) 79–92.

409. Miller, Leo. Milton's *Defensio* ordered wholesale for the States of Holland. NQ (33:1) 33.

410. Mitchell, Jim. Bible publishing in eighteenth-century Britain. Factotum (20) 1985, 11–19.

411. Myers, Robin. A rare Stationers' Company broadside summons. Factotum (18) 1984, 14–15.

412. —— Harris, Michael (eds). Bibliophily. Cambridge: Chadwyck-Healey. pp. 200. (Publishing history occasional ser., 2.)

413. —— —— Economics of the British book trade, 1605–1939. Cambridge: Chadwyck-Healey, 1985. pp. 248.

414. —— —— Maps and prints: aspects of the English book trade. Oxford: Oxford Polytechnic Press, 1984. pp. xiii, 124.

415. Myerson, Joel. New light on George Ripley and the *Harbinger's* New York years. HLB (33:3) 1985, 313–36.

416. Nichol, D. W. Pope, Warburton and the Kemptons: problems of literary legacy (with a book-trade correspondence). Unpub. doct. diss., Univ. of Edinburgh, 1984.

417. Nichol, Donald W. Piracy of Pope's Homer. NQ (33:1) 54–6.

418. Pancost, David W. How Washington Irving published *The Sketch Book* in England. SAF (14:1) 77–83.

419. Parker, George L. The beginnings of the book trade in Canada. (Bibl. 1985, 329.) Rev. by Paul Hjartarson in CanL (111) 164–6.

420. Parsons, Nicholas. The book of literary lists: a collection of annotated lists of fact, statistics and anecdote concerning books. London: Sidgwick & Jackson, 1985. pp. xii, 234.

421. Perkin, M. R. A note on the beginnings of letterpress printing in Chester. Factotum (5) 1979, 6–7.

422. —— A note on the survival of books with Liverpool imprints. Factotum Occasional Paper 3, 1983, 7.

423. Peterson, William S. A bibliography of the Kelmscott Press. (Bibl. 1985, 330.) Rev. by Joseph R. Dunlap in ABC (7:2) 40–5.

424. PICKFORD, CHRISTOPHER. Bedford stationers and booksellers. Factotum (15) 1982, 21–7. (Eighteenth century.)

425. RAVEN, J. R. English popular literature and the image of business, 1760–1790. Unpub. doct. diss., Univ. of Cambridge, 1985. [Abstr. in IT (35) 47.]

426. REITT, BARBARA BLACK. Modernization and the emerging book editor, 1865–1895: William Dean Howells as bench mark in a world of change. Unpub. doct. diss., Emory Univ., 1985. [Abstr. in DA (47) 181A.]

427. RHEIN, DONNA E. The handprinted books of Leonard and Virginia Woolf at the Hogarth Press, 1917–1932. *See* **126.**

428. RIVERS, ISABEL (ed.). Books and their readers in eighteenth-century England. (Bibl. 1985, 332.) Rev. by Philip Wheatley in NQ (33:1) 116–18.

429. SAVORY, JEROLD; MARKS, PATRICIA. The smiling Muse: Victoriana in the comic press. Philadelphia, PA: Art Alliance Press; London: Assoc. UPs, 1985. pp. 256. Rev. by Maurice Milne in JNPH (2:3) 38–9.

430. SHAHEEN, MOHAMMAD. Meredith to Evans and Thomson. ELN (24:1) 79–84.

431. SPIECKERMAN, MARIE-LUISE. The English reprints of Richter at Altenburg: some notes and a list. Factotum (7) 1979, 25–30.

432. STERN, MADELEINE B. Antiquarian bookselling in the United States: a history from the origins to the 1940s. Westport, CT: Greenwood Press, 1985. pp. 246. Rev. by Terence A. Tanner in CRL (47:2) 184–6; by Keith Arbour in ABC (7:6) 42–5.

433. STERNBERG, PAUL R. The publication of Thomas Morton's *New English Canaan* reconsidered. PBSA (80:3) 369–74.

434. STOCKDALE, ERIC. John Almon and the state-prisoner. Factotum (9) 1980, 22–4.

435. SUTHERLAND, JOHN. *Cornhill*'s sales and payments: the first decade. VPR (19:3) 106–8.

436. —— Henry Colburn, publisher. PubH (19) 59–84.

437. THOMSON, GEORGE MALCOLM. Martin Secker & Warburg: the first fifty years: a memoir. London: Secker & Warburg. pp. 86.

438. TIERNEY, JAMES E. More on George Faulkner and the London book trade. Factotum (19) 1984, 8–11.

439. TRAUB, EILEEN. The early years of the Hogarth Press. ABC (7:10) 32–6.

440. TREMAINE, MARIE. Early printing in Canada. PBSC (23) 1984, 32–9. (Repr. of essay pub. 1934 by Golden Dog Press, Toronto.)

441. VIPOND, MARY. Best sellers in English Canada: 1919–1928. JCF (35/36) 73–105.

442. WARNER, MICHAEL DAVID. The letters of the Republic: literature and print in republican America. Unpub. doct. diss., Johns Hopkins Univ. [Abstr. in DA (47) 532A.]

443. WEGNER, JURGEN. *Poetry Australia*: 21 years: 100 issues. BANQ (10:4) 1985, 112–14.

444. WEST, JAMES L. W., III. Authorship in America during the Progressive period. Review (8) 149–56 (review-article).

445. WHITEMAN, BRUCE; STEWART, CHARLOTTE; FUNNELL, CATHERINE. A bibliography of Macmillan of Canada imprints, 1906–1980. (Bibl. 1985, 396.) Rev. by E. J. Devereux in CanP (18) 145–7.

446. WILLIAMS, RAYMOND. Forms of English fiction in 1848. *In* (pp. 1–16) **29.**

447. WILSON, CHARLES. First with the news: the history of W. H. Smith, 1792–1972. London: Cape. pp. 510. Rev. by John Sutherland in TLS, 21 Feb., 186; by Asa Briggs in Listener (115) 2 Jan., 23.

448. WOOD, J. L. Who were the bondsmen. Factotum (22) 13–14. (Publishing by subscription.)

449. ZBORAY, RONALD J. The transportation revolution and antebellum book distribution reconsidered. AmQ (38:1) 53–71.

CONTEMPORARY PUBLISHING AND BOOKSELLING

450. ALLEN, WALTER C., *et al.* (eds). The quality of trade book publishing in the 1980s. Library Trends (Urbana, IL) (33:2) 1984, 95–223.

451. ANON. University presses select 'best' Westerns. AWest (24:3) 88, 90.

452. ATTWOOLL, DAVID. Developing a list of reference books. SchP (17:4) 317–26.

453. BAILEY, HERBERT S., JR. On the future of scholarly communication. SchP (17:3) 251–4.

454. BATTIN, PATRICIA. The library: centre of the restructured university. *See* **194.**

455. BLUMENTHAL, JOSEPH. Robert Frost and his printers. Austin, TX: Taylor, 1985. pp. xii, 126. Rev. by Ward Ritchie in ABC (7:6) 37–9.

456. BRINKMEYER, BOB. In print, out of print: book publishing in the '80's. SE (9:2) 1981, 86–7.

457. CARTER, E. GRAYDON. Leading the gliterary life. Esquire (106:6) 160–2, 165–6. (Gary Fisketjon, editorial director of the Atlantic Monthly Press.)

458. CHEAPE, CHARLES W. Family firm to modern multinational: Norton Company, a New England enterprise. Cambridge, MA: Harvard UP, 1985. pp. xii, 424. (Harvard studies in business history, 36.) Rev. by Arthur M. Johnson in NEQ (59:1) 126–9.

459. DENNISON, SALLY. [Alternative] literary publishing: five modern historics. Iowa City: Iowa UP, 1984. pp. 240. Rev. by Sam S. Baskett in CR (30:3) 422–3.

460. DOWNES, DAVID. Clouding the mirror. AWR (83) 81–5. (On censorship.)

461. EDELSTEIN, J. M. Claude Fredericks and the Banyan Press: a bibliographical checklist. ABC (7:3) 37–44.

462. Fox, Mary Frank (ed.).   Scholarly writing and publishing: issues, problems, and solutions. Boulder, CO: Westview Press, 1985. pp. x, 170. Rev. by Carol Orr in SchP (17:4) 375–8.

463. Geiger, Stephen R.   Electronics in publishing and the consequences. SchP (18:1) 29–31.

464. Geiser, Elizabeth A.; Dolin, Arnold; Topkis, Gladys S. (eds).   The business of book publishing: papers of practitioners. Boulder, CO: Westview Press, 1985. pp. 446. Rev. by Edward F. Rivinus in SchP (17:4) 372–3.

465. Greenbaum, Arlynn.   A newsletter for authors. SchP (17:4) 364–6.

466. Hano, Arnold.   J'étais un veinard, ou les souvenirs d'un directeur de paperbacks. Europe (62:664/65) 1984, 94–7.

467. Havighurst, Walter.   The book business then and now. OhioanaQ (29:2/3) 44–9, 96–100.

468. Hewitt, David.   The new Edinburgh Edition of the Waverley Novels. ScottN (8) 17–18.

469. Hogan, Judy.   Caroline Wren Press: flying against the wind. SE (9:2) 1981, 92–6.

470. Jerome, Judson.   Poet's market: 1986. Cincinnati, OH: Writer's Digest, 1985. pp. 371.

471. Katzen, May.   Electronic publishing in the humanities. SchP (18:1) 5–16.

472. Luey, Beth.   Sharp practice, penny wisdom, and future shock. SchP (17:4) 343–7.

473. Mattson, Francis O.   A rambling visit to San Francisco's book country. ABC (7:4) 25–9.

474. Meyers, Jeffrey.   On editing collections of original essays. SchP (17:2) 99–108.

475. Perry, Ralph Barton.   'Should there be a University Press?' SchP (17:2) 109–17.

476. Petro, Pamela.   A tour of private presses and the book arts in Britain: part 1, The fine presses; part 2, The experimental presses. ABC (7:8) 11–17; (7:9) 13–18.

477. —— Newman, Richard.   'Remarks called for and otherwise': the career of Charles F. Heartman, bookseller. ABC (7:10) 9–15.

478. Ravenscroft, Alison.   Write on women: women and publishing. Scarlet Woman (Melbourne) (21) 5–7.

479. Reid, Tony.   By the book. NZList, 20 Dec., 20–2.

480. Sanders, Charles Richard.   A brief history of the 'Duke–Edinburgh Edition of the Carlyle Letters'. SSL (17) 1982, 1–12.

481. Schriner, Delores Korb.   Editors at work: a study of the revision processes of professional editors. Unpub. doct. diss., Wayne State Univ., 1985. [Abstr. in DA (47) 163A.]

482. Seed, David.   *Ulysses*: the evolution of a definitive text. *See* **335.**

483. Stallworthy, Jon.   Old-spelling editions: the state of the business in 1978. *In* (pp. 141–51) **44.**

484. SUTHERLAND, JOHN.   The comeback of the hardback. TLS, 5 Dec., 1371–2.

485. TIMMERMAN, JOHN H.   Train of robes, plume of feathers: rhetoric in the religious publishing house. Cresset (49:9) 11–14.

486. WHITESIDE, THOMAS.   Conglomerates: swallowing up the industry. SE (9:2) 1981, 88–90.

487. WHITTINGTON, HARRY.   Temps de crise. Les débuts du marché des éditions originales en livres de poches. Trans. by J.-P. SCHWEIGHAEUSER. Europe (62:664/65) 1984, 91–4.

488. WILLIAMS, BRIDGET.   Publishing and the Literary Fund. Islands (3:1) 61–5.

489. WRIGHT, PAUL M.   The Library of America: an American Pléiade. AR (44:4) 467–80.

SCHOLARLY METHOD

See also relevant bibliographical sections above and 'Language, Literature, and the Computer' below.

490. ASH, RUSSELL. Indexes: having fun with. Bookseller (London) (4196) 2082.

491. BEVINGTON, DAVID. Editorial indications of stage business in old-spelling editions. *In* (pp. 105–12) **44.**

492. BOSTIAN, LLOYD R. Working with writers. SchP (17:2) 119–26.

493. BRERETON, JOHN C. (ed.). Traditions of inquiry. New York; Oxford: OUP, 1985. pp. xiv, 191.

494. BUDD, JOHN MASON. Characteristics of research materials used by American literature scholars: a citation study. Unpub. doct. diss., Univ. of North Carolina at Chapel Hill, 1985. [Abstr. in DA (46) 3178A.]

495. BUGARSKI, RANKO. Notes on the terminology of applied linguistics. *In* (pp. 1147–53) **26.**

496. BUTLER, CHRISTOPHER. Statistics in linguistics. Oxford: Blackwell, 1985. pp. x, 214.

497. CARPENTER, HUMPHREY. Sleuthing in the stacks: mysteries of the Bodleian. BkW, 12 Jan., 15.

498. COUTURE, BARBARA (ed.). Functional approaches to writing: research perspectives. London: Pinter. pp. xi, 271. (Open linguistics series.)

499. EDWARDS, PHILIP. The function of commentary. *In* (pp. 97–104) **44.**

500. HARBERT, EARL N.; REES, ROBERT A. (eds). Fifteen American authors before 1900: bibliographical essays on research and criticism. (Bibl. 1985, 401.) Rev. by David Timms in NQ (33:2) 276–7.

501. HJORT, ANNE METTE. The interests of critical editorial practice. Poetics (15:3) 259–77.

502. JANZEN, HENRY D. Preparing a diplomatic edition: Heywood's *The Escapes of Jupiter. In* (pp. 73–9) **44.**

503. MADDEN, LIONEL. Printed and on-line bibliographies for English literary studies: a decade of change. Library Review (35:4) 248–54.

504. MEYERS, JEFFREY. On editing collections of original essays. *See* **474.**

505. MORAN, MICHAEL G.; LUNSFORD, RONALD F. Research in composition and rhetoric: a bibliographic sourcebook. Westport, CT; London: Greenwood Press, 1984. pp. xviii, 501.

506. PICHT, HERIBERT; DRASKU, JENNIFER. Terminology: an introduction. Guildford: Univ. of Surrey, Dept of Linguistic and International Studies, 1985. pp. 265. (Dept of Linguistic and International Studies monographs, 2.)

507. POWELL, WALTER W.   Getting into print: the decision-making process in scholarly publishing. Chicago: Chicago UP, 1985. pp. xxxi, 260. Rev. by Herbert C. Morton in SchP (17:2) 189–92.

508. RENOUF, ANTOINETTE.   The elicitation of spoken English. *In* (pp. 177–97) **16.**

509. SCHNUCKER, ROBERT V.   The road of survival for journals in the humanities. SchP (17:4) 355–63.

510. SHAND, G. B.; SHADY, RAYMOND C. (eds).   Play-texts in old spelling: papers from the Glendon conference. *See* **44.**

511. TANSELLE, G. THOMAS.   Historicism and critical editing. *See* **339.**

512. WALKER, S.   Descriptive techniques for studying verbal graphic language. Unpub. doct. diss., Univ. of Reading, 1983.

513. WOLFE, GARY K.   Critical terms for science fiction and fantasy: a glossary and guide to scholarship. New York; London: Greenwood Press. pp. xxxvi, 162.

514. WOODS, ANTHONY; FLETCHER, PAUL; HUGHES, ARTHUR.   Statistics in language studies. Cambridge: CUP. pp. 350. (Cambridge textbooks in linguistics.)

515. ZITNER, S. P.   Excessive annotation, or piling Pelion on Parnassus. *In* (pp. 131–9) **44.**

LANGUAGE, LITERATURE, AND THE COMPUTER

516. ALSTON, R. C.   Searching ESTC online. Factotum Occasional Paper 1, 1982, 3–30.

517. —— SINGLETON, J. C.   Searching ESTC online. Factotum Occasional Paper 2, 1982, 3–19.

518. ALTENBERG, BENGT (ed.).   ICAME bibliography. ICAME News (10) 62–79.

519. —— ICAME 6th: the sixth International Conference on English Language Research on Computerized Corpora at Röstånga, Sweden, 19–22 May 1985. ICAME News (10) 10–61. (Abstracts of reports and papers.)

520. BAILEY, HERBERT S., JR.   On the future of scholarly communication. *See* **453.**

521. BARNHART, DAVID K.   Prizes and pitfalls of computerized searching for new words for dictionaries. Dic (7) 1985, 253–60.

522. BOENIG, ROBERT.   Computers and Old English: the IBM Quietwriter printer and medieval characters. OEN (19:2) 32–5.

523. BURROWS, J. F.   The reciprocities of style: literary criticism and literary statistics. EAS (39) 78–93.

524. BUTLER, CHRISTOPHER.   Computers in linguistics. Oxford: Blackwell, 1985. pp. ix, 266.

525. DEWEY, PATRICK R.   Interactive fiction: a checklist. AmLib (17:2) 132–7.

526. FERDINAND, C. Y.   Searching the ESTC: a review essay. AEB (8:4) 1984, 242–7.

527. GALLET, LILIANE.   La traduction assistée par ordinateur (TAO): réalisations, perspectives, conséquences: 'How will it affect my job?' *In* (pp. 621–35) **1.**

528. GEENS, DIRK.   Computers and language education: a case for cognitive learning. ITL (66) 1984, 49–60.

529. —— The role of computers in the making of a pedagogical dictionary. Rapport d'activités de l'Institut de Phonétique (20) 1985, 57–65.

530. GRISHMAN, RALPH.   Computational linguistics: an introduction. Cambridge: CUP. pp. vii, 409. (Studies in natural language processing.)

531. HABEL, CHRISTOPHER.   Stories – an artificial intelligence perspective (?). Poetics (15:1/2) 111–25.

532. HADDOCK, N. J.   Computing noun phrase reference. Edinburgh: University of Edinburgh, Department of Artificial Intelligence, 1985. pp. 29. (DAI working paper, 182.)

533. HIRST, GRAEME.   Semantic interpretation and the resolution of ambiguity. Cambridge: CUP. pp. xiv, 263. (Studies in natural language processing.)

534. HOLLAND, JOAN. The *Microfiche Concordance*: a lexicographer's tool. ANQ (24:7/8) 120–3. (*A Microfiche Concordance to Old English.*)

535. HUTCHINS, W. J. Machine translation: past, present, future. Chichester: Horwood. pp. 382. (Ellis Horwood series in computers and their applications.)

536. JASPAERT, LIEVEN. About the treatment of ambiguity in machine translation. ITL (64) 1984, 1–21.

537. JOHANSSON, STIG. Some observations on the order of adverbial particles and objects in the LOB Corpus. *In* (pp. 51–62) **43.**

538. KENNER, HUGH. Libraries and glowlamps: a strategy of reassurance. SchP (18:1) 17–22.

539. LINDSAY, D. Prosodic analysis by rule: final technical report. Keele: Dept of Communication and Neuroscience, Univ. of Keele, 1985. 24 leaves.

540. LINE, MAURICE B. The death of Procrustes? Structure, style, and sense. SchP (17:4) 291–301.

541. MADDEN, LIONEL. Printed and on-line bibliographies for English literary studies: a decade of change. *See* **503.**

542. MAY, JAMES E. On the inclusiveness of descriptive bibliographies: limitations of bibliographical catalogues like the ESTC. *See* **57.**

543. MOYNE, JOHN A. Understanding language: man or machine? New York; London: Plenum Press, 1985. pp. xvi, 357. (Foundations of computer science.)

544. NEVALAINEN, TERTTU; RISSANEN, MATTI. Do you support the *do*-support? Emphatic and non-emphatic *do* in affirmative statements in present-day spoken English. *In* (pp. 35–50) **43.**

545. NOËL, J.; JANSSEN, J.; MERGEAI, J.-P. Disambiguating definition language in two automatic dictionaries of English: outline of a computer-aided procedure. *In* (pp. 143–9) **12.**

546. RABEN, JOSEPH. Databases for the humanities. SchP (18:1) 23–8.

547. RANDALL, STARR D. The effect of editing and typesetting technology on the typographical error rate of selected newspapers. Unpub. doct. diss., Univ. of Utah. [Abstr. in DA (47) 695A.]

548. UNDERWOOD, JOHN H. Linguistics, computers and the language teacher: a communicative approach. Rowley, MA: Newbury House, 1984. pp. xv, 109. Rev. by R. L. Brandson in CJL (31:2) 160–3.

549. WANG, WILLIAM S. Y. (introd.). Language writing and the computer: readings from *Scientific American*. New York; Oxford: Freeman. pp. 124.

NEWSPAPERS AND OTHER PERIODICALS

550. ALEXANDER, J. H.   Literary criticism in the later *Noctes Ambrosianae*. YES (16) 17–31.

551. ALEXANDER, RICHARD J.   Article headings in *The Economist*: an analysis of puns, allusions and metaphors. AAA (11:2) 159–77.

552. ALLEN, FRANK.   *Dog River Review*. LMR (5:4) 12–14.

553. ALSOP, J. D.   The circulation of the *London Gazette*, 1717–19. JNPH (3:1) 23–6.

554. —— Joseph Addison's income from the *London Gazette*, 1717–1718. NQ (33:4) 491.

555. ANON.   50 years on. *See* **354.**

556. ASHLEY, PERRY J. (ed.).   American newspaper journalists, 1873–1900. Detroit, MI: Gale Research, 1983. pp. xiv, 392. (Dictionary of literary biography, 23.) Rev. by Sargent Bush, Jr, in YES (16) 344.

557. BAKER, WILLIAM.   *The Wind and the Rain* (1941–1951): the Cold War, politics, criticism, religion and poetry. Text & Context (1:1) 70–8.

558. BATTESTIN, MARTIN C.   Fielding's contributions to the *Universal Spectator* (1736–7). SP (83:1) 88–116.

559. BEARE, GERALDINE.   Indexing the *Strand Magazine*. JNPH (2:2) 20–5.

560. BEASLEY, CONGER, JR.   Hemingway and the *Kansas City Star*. SSMLN (16:1) 1–7.

561. BERGONZI, BERNARD.   *The Calendar of Modern Letters*. YES (16) 150–63.

562. BERRY, N.   *The Edinburgh Review* under Francis Jeffrey. Unpub. doct. diss., Univ. of Oxford, 1985.

563. BONE, MARTHA DENHAM.   Dorothy Parker and *New Yorker* satire. Unpub. doct. diss., Middle Tennessee State Univ., 1985. [Abstr. in DA (46) 2689A.]

564. BRAKE, LAUREL.   Literary criticism and the Victorian periodicals. YES (16) 92–116.

565. BROMWICH, DAVID.   Romantic poetry and the *Edinburgh* ordinances. YES (16) 1–16.

566. BROWN, LUCY.   Victorian news and newspapers. Oxford: Clarendon Press, 1985. pp. 303. Rev. by Richard Altick in TLS, 21 Feb., 185–6.

567. BROWN, MARY JANE.   English periodical criticism of the novel from 1845 to 1865: a search for goodness, truth, and beauty. Unpub. doct. diss., Univ. of Illinois at Urbana-Champaign. [Abstr. in DA (47) 907A.]

568. CAIRNS, SCOTT.   *The Virginia Quarterly Review*. LMR (5:1) 60–1.

569. CALDER, ANGUS.   Leads from Leeds. JCL (21:1) 9–11. (The origin of *The Journal of Commonwealth Literature*.)

570. CAMPION, DAN.   *The Paris Review*. LMR (5:1) 44–7.

571. CARTER, DAVID.   Coming home after the party: *Overland*'s first decade. Meanjin (44:4) 1985, 462–76.

572. CHAPPELL, FRED.   *The Southern Review*. LMR (5:4) 35–7.

573. CITINO, DAVID.   *Grand Street*. LMR (5:1) 20–5.

574. COHEN, JOHN.   *Reading Time* review: a content analysis. Reading Time (98) 13–18.

575. COHEN, RALPH.   The aims and roles of *New Literary History*. YES (16) 177–87.

576. COLEMAN, D. P.   The personal and intellectual background of Coleridge's periodical *The Friend* (1809–10), with particular reference to its moral and political preoccupations. Unpub. doct. diss., Univ. of Oxford. [Abstr. in IT (35) 545.]

577. COTSELL, MICHAEL.   'The Sensational Williams': a mutual friend in 1864. Dick (81:2) 1985, 79–85. (*All the Year Round*.)

578. COX, J. H.   'Carnation and colouring': sentimentalism in *The Universal Magazine of Knowledge and Pleasure*. Unpub. doct. diss., Univ. of Exeter, 1984. [Abstr. in IT (35) 46.]

579. CURTIS, MARY E.   Small failure, larger success: life history of a journal. SchP (17:3) 268–77. (*Language Learning and Communication*.)

580. DANKY, JAMES P. (ed.); HADY, MAUREEN E. (comp.); BOWLES, ANN (asst ed.).   Native American periodicals and newspapers, 1928–1982: bibliography, publishing record, and holdings. (Bibl. 1985, 466.) Rev. by Bill Katz in BB (43:2) 115–16.

581. DAVIE, DONALD.   Reflections on *PNR*. YES (16) 164–76.

582. DAVIES, JAMES A.   The effects of context: Carlyle and the *Examiner* in 1848. YES (16) 51–62.

583. DENMAN, PETER.   Ferguson and *Blackwood's*: the formative years. IUR (16) 141–58.

584. DICKINSON, DONALD C.   Paul Leicester Ford and *The Bibliographer*. ABC (7:4) 31–6.

585. DIXON, DIANA.   From instruction to amusement: attitudes of authority in children's periodicals before 1914. VPR (19:2) 63–7.

586. —— (comp.).   First annual review of work in newspaper history. JNPH (2:3) 52–6.

587. DOWLING, LINDA.   Letterpress and picture in the literary periodicals of the 1890s. *See* **70.**

588. DOXTATOR, ROBERT LUCAS.   James Stetson Metcalfe's signed criticism of the legitimate theatre in New York City: 1888–1927. Unpub. doct. diss., Univ. of Nebraska–Lincoln, 1985. [Abstr. in DA (46) 2132A.]

589. DOYLE, JAMES.   Canadian writers and American little magazines in the 1890's. CanL (110) 177–83.

590. DUEMER, JOSEPH.   *The Georgia Review*. LMR (5:1) 16–19.

591. ECKLEY, GRACE.   The entertaining *Nights* of Burton, Stead, and Joyce's Earwicker. JML (13:2) 339–44.

592. EDMUNDS, LINDSAY E.   *Spectrum.* LMR (5:3) 36–7.

593. ELLIS, FRANK H. (ed.).   Swift *vs* Mainwaring: *The Examiner* and *The Medley.* (Bibl. 1985, 473.) Rev. by J. A. Downie in Prose Studies (9:3) 103–4.

594. EPPERLY, ELIZABETH R.   Trollope and the young Austin Dobson. VPR (19:3) 90–9.

595. EVANS, JAMES E.   Mr Review on the 'glorious' *Tatler* and the 'inimitable' *Spectator.* JNPH (3:1) 2–9.

596. EVERMAN, WELCH D.   *2Plus2.* LMR (5:2) 43–6.

597. FENDER, STEPHEN.   *The New York Review of Books.* YES (16) 188–202.

598. FINCH, PETER.   Dwarf grapes? Planet (56) 89–98. (Small presses and little magazines, particularly in Wales.)

599. FIREOVED, JOSEPH.   Nathaniel Gardner and the *New-England Courant.* EAL (20:3) 1985/86, 214–35.

600. FRYCKSTEDT, MONICA.   *Douglas Jerrold's Shilling Magazine.* VPR (19:1) 2–27.

601. FRYCKSTEDT, MONICA CORREA.   Geraldine Jewsbury's *Athenaeum* reviews: a mirror of mid-Victorian attitudes to fiction. Uppsala: Acta Universitatis Upsaliensis; Stockholm: Almqvist & Wiksell. pp. 163. (Studia Anglistica Upsaliensia, 61.)

602. GEORGE, SHARON.   Margaret Fuller's *Dial* criticism: the merging of the Scottish common sense and Romantic traditions. ATQ (62) 17–28.

603. GERAETS, JOHN.   Kendrick Smithyman and Brasch's *Landfall.* Landfall (40:4) 443–57.

604. GINDIN, JAMES.   Roger Angell and the annals of baseball. MichQR (25:3) 568–81.

605. GINGOLD, ALFRED; BUSKIN, JOHN (eds).   Snooze, the best of our magazine. New York: Workman. pp. 272. (A parody of *The New Yorker.*) Rev. by Cyra McFadden in BW, 30 Nov., 7.

606. GLAZIER, LOSS PEQUEÑO.   *The Antigonish Review.* LMR (5:4) 6–8.

607. GLENDINNING, VICTORIA.   The book reviewer: the last amateur? EDH (44) 182–94.

608. GOULDEN, R. J.   No fleas on Curll. *See* **381.**

609. GRAUER, NEIL A.   Wits & sages. Baltimore, MD; London: Johns Hopkins UP, 1984. pp. ix, 268. (Interviews with US columnists.)

610. GURR, ANDREW.   *JCL* and the implied reader. JCL (21:1) 4–8.

611. HABICH, ROBERT D.   Transcendentalism and the *Western Messenger*: a history of the magazine and its contributors, 1835–1841. Rutherford, NJ: Fairleigh Dickinson UP, 1985. pp. 208. Rev. by Stephen Fender in TLS, 21 Feb., 182.

612. HALL, J. B.   *Antaeus.* LMR (5:1) 4–9.

613. HAMILTON, IAN (ed.).   The *New Review* anthology. London: Heinemann, 1985. pp. 320. Rev. by Ruth Pulik in UES (24:2) 54–5.

614. HANSEN, TOM.   *Coydog Review.* LMR (5:2) 3–7.

615. HANSON, JANELL.   *Piedmont Literary Review.* LMR (5:2) 29–31.

616. HARRIS, FRANCES. For *Arthur* read *Author*. Factotum (10) 1980, 14–16.

617. HAWLEY, JOHN C. Responses to Charles Kingsley's attack on political economy. VPR (19:4) 131–7.

618. HAWLEY, JOHN CHARLES. Charles Kingsley, rhetorical fiction, and the Victorian periodical press. Unpub. doct. diss., Univ. of Pennsylvania, 1985. [Abstr. in DA (46) 3725A.]

619. HENDERSON, ARCHIE. Pound's contributions to *L'Art libre* (1920). Paideuma (13:2) 1984, 271–83.

620. HENSON, GAIL. *Prairie Schooner*. LMR (5:1) 52–4.

621. HERTZ, ALAN. The Broad Church militant and Newman's humiliation of Charles Kingsley. VPR (19:4) 141–9.

622. HUMPHREY, CAROL SUE. 'This popular engine': an institutional study of New England newspapers, 1775–1789. Unpub. doct. diss., Univ. of North Carolina at Chapel Hill, 1985. [Abstr. in DA (46) 3843A.]

623. HYLAND, P. B. J. Richard Steele, the press and the Hanoverian succession, 1713–1716. Unpub. doct. diss., Univ. of Lancaster, 1984.

624. INGRAM, KEVIN. Rebel: the short life of Esmond Romilly. London: Weidenfeld and Nicolson, 1985. pp. xii, 252.

625. ITO, HIROYUKI. The language of *The Spectator*: as seen in the movement of English prose towards the rise of the novel. PoetT (23) 81–97.

626. JAWAD, A. S. Literary journalism in England and Egypt: a comparative study of the essay and the review. Unpub. doct. diss., City Univ., 1984. [Abstr. in IT (35) 539.]

627. JONES, CHARLOTTE D. The penny press and the origins of journalistic objectivity: the problem of authority in liberal America. Unpub. doct. diss., Univ. of Iowa, 1985. [Abstr. in DA (47) 700A–1A.]

628. KADAR, MARLENE. Partisan culture in the thirties: *Partisan Review*, the Surrealists and Leon Trotsky. CanRCL (13:3) 375–423.

629. KALLSEN, T. J. *Triquarterly*. LMR (5:1) 55–9.

630. KENT, CHRISTOPHER. More critics of drama, music and art. VPR (19:3) 99–105.

631. KIBLER, JAMES EVERETT, JR. *The Album* (1826): the significance of the recently discovered second volume. SB (39) 62–78.

632. KIRBY, DAVID. New magazines of 1985. LMR (5:2) 53–5.

633. KLUGER, RICHARD. The paper: the life and death of the *New York Herald Tribune*. New York: Knopf. pp. viii, 801. Rev. by Paul Gray in Time, 27 Oct., 96; by David Shaw in NYTB, 26 Oct., 13; by W. A. Swanberg in BW, 30 Nov., 6.

634. KNIGHT, CHARLES A. Bibliography and the shape of the literary periodical in the early eighteenth century. Library (8:3) 232–48.

635. KUNHARDT, PHILIP B. (ed.). *Life*: the first fifty years, 1936–1986. Boston, MA; Little Brown. pp. 319. Rev. by Jonathan Yardley in BkW, 23 Nov., 3–4.

636. LEVY, DAVID W. Herbert Croly of *The New Republic*: the life and thought of an American progressive. Guildford; Princeton, NJ: Princeton UP, 1985. pp. xvii, 335. Rev. by Hugh Brogan in TLS, 21 Feb., 182.

637. LITTLEFIELD, DANIEL F., JR; PARINS, JAMES W. American Indians and Alaska newspapers and periodicals, 1826–1924. (Bibl. 1985, 512.) Rev. by Bill Katz in BB (43:2) 118–19.

638. LONSDALE, ROGER. Goldsmith and the *Weekly Magazine*: the missing numbers. RES (37:146) 219–25.

639. LYNN, STEVEN. Johnson's *Rambler* and eighteenth-century rhetoric. ECS (19:4) 461–79.

640. McCANN, WESLEY. *Irish Booklore*: a retrospect. Linen Hall Review (3:1) 15.

641. McCORMICK, KATHLEEN. George Eliot's earliest prose: the Coventry *Herald* and the Coventry fiction. VPR (19:2) 57–62.

642. McDONALD, IVERACH. The history of *The Times*: vol. v, Struggles in war and peace 1939–1966. London: Times Books, 1984. pp. ii, 514.

643. McGHEE, FLORA ANN CALDWELL. Mississippi black newspapers: their history, content, and future. Unpub. doct. diss., Univ. of Southern Mississippi, 1985. [Abstr. in DA (47) 695A.]

644. McKINNON, BARRY. Interview with Brian Fawcett. ECanW (32) 122–33. (*Iron, NMFG*.)

645. MANNION, IRENE ELIZABETH. Criticism *con amore*: a study of *Blackwood's Magazine*, 1817–1834. Unpub. doct. diss., Univ. of California, Los Angeles, 1984. [Abstr. in DA (46) 3727A.]

646. MARKS, PATRICIA. American literary and drama reviews: an index to late nineteenth-century periodicals. Boston, MA: G. K. Hall, 1984. pp. xviii, 313. Rev. by Jerold J. Savory in VPR (19:2) 73.

647. —— Harriet Martineau: *Fraser's* 'Maid of [Dis]Honour'. VPR (19:1) 28–34.

648. MARTONE, MICHAEL. *Trivia*. LMR (5:4) 38–40.

649. MEZZINA, FRANCIS MARK. Frank Norris' *Wave* writings. Unpub. doct. diss., Florida State Univ., 1985. [Abstr. in DA (47) 179A.]

650. MILLER, KARL. The *London Review of Books*. YES (16) 203–12.

651. MILLS, TREVOR. Signatures in *The Patriot*, 1792–3. *See* **119.**

652. MOORE, CHARLES; HAWTREE, CHRISTOPHER (eds). 1936 as recorded by *The Spectator*. London: Joseph. pp. x, 337.

653. MORGAN, PETER F. Literary critics and reviewers in early nineteenth-century Britain. (Bibl. 1984, 625.) Rev. by Joanne Shattock in YES (16) 301–2.

654. MORRIS, A. J. L. A study of John St Loe Strachey's editorship of *The Spectator*, 1901–14. Unpub. doct. diss., Univ. of Cambridge. [Abstr. in IT (36) 14.]

655. MORVAN, ALAIN. Discours sur un exil intérieur: *The Jacobite's Journal* de Fielding. *In* (pp. 55–68) **35.**

656. MURPHY, SEAN. Burke and Lucas: an authorship problem re-examined. ECI (1) 143–56.

657. MYERSON, JOEL. New light on George Ripley and the *Harbinger's* New York years. *See* **415.**

658. NELSON, CAROLYN; SEECOMBE, M. Periodical publications,

1641–1700: a survey with illustrations. London: Bibliographical Soc. pp. xii, 113. (Occasional papers, 2.)

659. NEWSPAPER ARCHIVE DEVELOPMENTS. The *Times Literary Supplement* Index, 1902–1939. Reading: Newspaper Archive Developments, 1978. 2 vols. pp. xiii, 1782.

660. NIVEN, ALASTAIR. To what end? JCL (21:1) 11–13. (The function of *The Journal of Commonwealth Literature*.)

661. O'LEARY, PATRICK. Regency editor: life of John Scott. (Bibl. 1985, 527.) Rev. by J. H. Alexander in YES (16) 292–3.

662. OPPENLANDER, ELLA ANN. Dickens' *All the Year Round*: descriptive index and contributor list. Troy, NY: Whitston, 1984. pp. 752. Rev. by Andrew Sanders in Dick (82:3) 180–1.

663. PAGETTI, CARLO (ed.). *La Battaglia di Dorking*, tratto dal *Blackwood's Magazine*, Maggio 1871. Milan: Editrice Nord, 1985. pp. 161. Rev. by I. F. Clarke in SFS (13:1) 84–6.

664. PALMER, WILLIAM. History, tradition, and hubris: the baseball universe of Roger Angell. JPC (20:2) 17–27.

665. PARNELL, FRANK H.; ASHLEY, MIKE (comps); HAINING, PETER (introd.). Monthly terrors: an index to the weird fantasy magazines published in the United States and Great Britain. Westport, CT; London: Greenwood Press, 1985. pp. xxvii, 602. (Bibliographies and indexes in world literature, 4.)

666. PARRY, ANN. The Grove years, 1868–1883: a 'new look' for *Macmillan's Magazine*? VPR (19:4) 149–57.

667. PEATTIE, ROGER W. W. M. Rossetti's contributions to the *Edinburgh Weekly Review*. VPR (19:3) 108–10.

668. PITCHER, E. W. Eighteenth-century magazine serials: the 'Essays on Various Subjects' in the *London Magazine*. Library (8:4) 357–60.

669. —— Further remarks on arbitrary signatures in Smollett's *British Magazine* (1760–67). PBSA (80:1) 91–2.

670. —— Problems with eighteenth-century periodicals: *The Monthly Miscellany*. PBSA (80:2) 233–7.

671. —— Some contributions to eighteenth-century magazines by John Moir. NQ (33:1) 75–6.

672. —— Some puzzling reprintings of literary prose in the final years of the *Town and Country Magazine*. Library (8:2) 159–64.

673. PRATT, JUDITH STEVENS. The vaudeville criticism of Epes Winthrop Sargent, 1896–1910. Unpub. doct. diss., Univ. of Nebraska–Lincoln, 1985. [Abstr. in DA (46) 2859A.]

674. PRESCOTT, ANDREW. Some further letters to the *Tatler* and the *Spectator*. Factotum (14) 1982, 21–7.

675. PROPAS, SHARON W. William Michael Rossetti and *The Germ*. JPRS (6:2) 29–36.

676. RANDALL, STARR D. The effect of editing and typesetting technology on the typographical error rate of selected newspapers. *See* **547.**

677. RAVENSCROFT, ARTHUR. The origins. JCL (21:1) 2–4. (Of *The Journal of Commonwealth Literature*.)

678. REYNOLDS, BEN. *Real Fiction*. LMR (5:3) 31–2.

679. RIVERS, WILLIAM E. Nicholas Amhurst's *Terrae Filius* as background for Pope's satire of university education. PLL (22:2) 126–38.

680. RIZZO, BETTY. 'Innocent frauds': by Samuel Johnson. Library (8:3) 249–64.

681. ROBERSON, PATT FOSTER. A history of the *Hattiesburg American*. Unpub. doct. diss., Univ. of Southern Mississippi, 1985. [Abstr. in DA (47) 696A.]

682. ROGERS, PAT. The rise of the literary periodical. YES (16) 213–20 (review-article).

683. ROSTA, PAUL. The magazine that taught Faulkner, Fitzgerald, and Millay how to write. AH (37:1) 1985, 40–7.

684. RUGGIERI, HELEN. *Sphinx*. LMR (5:2) 41–2.

685. RUSHIN, PAT. *FM. Five*. LMR (5:2) 11–13.

686. SACHA, AMY HARDER. *Akwekon*. LMR (5:3) 3–5.

687. SAFFORD, DAN. *The North American Review*. LMR (5:1) 40–3.

688. SAVORY, JEROLD. Charles Kingsley in *Vanity Fair* and *Once a Week*. VPR (19:4) 137–40.

689. ―― MARKS, PATRICIA. The smiling Muse: Victoriana in the comic press. *See* **429**.

690. SCHLERET, JEAN-JACQUES. *Manhunt*, la revue de la seconde génération. Europe (62:664/65) 1984, 88–91.

691. SHARKEY, MICHAEL. A lost satire on the 1890's *Bulletin* writers and bohemians. ALS (12:4) 509–27.

692. SHATTOCK, JOANNE. Politics and literature: Macaulay, Brougham, and the *Edinburgh Review* under Napier. YES (16) 32–50.

693. SHERBO, ARTHUR. Gleanings from the *Scots Magazine* (1739–1800). SB (39) 210–19.

694. SHEVELOW, KATHRYN. The production of the female writing subject: letters to the *Athenian Mercury*. Genre (19:4) 385–407.

695. SMITH, R. T. *Amelia*. LMR (5:4) 3–5.

696. SPEER, LAUREL. *Cotton Boll/Atlanta Review*. LMR (5:3) 11–13.

697. SPICE, NICHOLAS (ed.). London reviews: a selection from the *London Review of Books* 1983–1985. London: Chatto & Windus, 1985. pp. vi, 222.

698. SPROTT, DUNCAN. 1784. London: Allen & Unwin. pp. 336. (Newspaper extracts from 1784.) Rev. by Edward Pearce in LRev, Apr. 1985, 35.

699. STEDMAN, JANE W. 'A peculiar sharp flavour': the contributions of Dr William Gilbert. VPR (19:2) 43–50.

700. STEFANILE, FELIX. *Mississippi Review*. LMR (5:1) 33–6.

701. STEPHENS, JOHN CALHOUN (ed.). The guardian. (Bibl. 1985, 547.) Rev. by Simon Varey in YES (16) 260–1.

702. STEWARD, D. E. *Frank*. LMR (5:4) 15–18.

703. STIEFVATER, P. M. *The Criterion*, 1922–1939: an inquest on the idea of a European review. Unpub. doct. diss., Univ. of Wales, Bangor, 1985. [Abstr. in IT (36) 475.]

704. SULLIVAN, ALVIN (ed.). British literary magazine: vol. 1, The Augustan age and the age of Johnson 1698–1788; vol. 2, The Romantic age 1789–1836. London: Greenwood Press, 1983. (Cf. bibl. 1985, 550; 551.) Rev. by Pat Rogers in YES (16) 213–20.

705. ——— British literary magazines: vol. 3, The Victorian and Edwardian age, 1837–1913. London: Greenwood Press, 1984. (Cf. bibl. 1985, 552.) Rev. by Bill Katz in BB (43:2) 119–20.

706. SULLIVAN, CHESTER. *The Painted Bride Quarterly.* LMR (5:4) 25–6.

707. SUTHERLAND, JAMES. The Restoration newspaper and its development. Cambridge: CUP. pp. ix, 262. Rev. by Pat Rogers in TLS, 12 Dec., 1396.

708. ——— The Restoration newspaper and its development. JNPH (3:1) 35–6.

709. SUTHERLAND, JOHN. *Cornhill's* sales and payments: the first decade. *See* **435.**

710. TAIT, JAMES A.; TAIT, HEATHER F. C. *The Bibliotheck:* an index to volumes 1–10 (1956–81). Edinburgh: Scottish Group of University, College, and Research Section, Library Assn, 1985. pp. iv, 41.

711. TALMADGE, JEFFREY D. *Salthouse.* LMR (5:3) 33–5.

712. TENER, ROBERT H. Breaking the code of anonymity: the case of the *Spectator,* 1861–1897. YES (16) 63–73.

713. THOVERON, GABRIEL. Quality/popular: intraduisibles en français? *In* (pp. 79–84) **12.**

714. TREGLOWN, JEREMY. Literary history and the *Lit. Supp.* YES (16) 132–49.

715. UFFELMAN, LARRY; SCOTT, PATRICK. Kingsley's serial novels: II, *The Water-Babies. See* **341.**

716. UFFELMAN, LARRY K. (ed.). Victorian periodicals, 1985: a checklist of scholarship and criticism. VPR (19:4) 160–4.

717. VANN, J. DON. Victorian novels in serial. New York: Modern Language Assn, 1985. pp. x, 181. Rev. by Rosemary T. VanArsdel in VPR (19:2) 78–9.

718. WAINWRIGHT, LOUDON. The great American magazine: an inside history of *Life.* New York: Knopf. pp. 443. Rev. by Lewis H. Lapham in NYTB, 16 Nov., 9; by Jonathan Yardley in BkW, 23 Nov., 3–4.

719. WEGNER, JURGEN. *Poetry Australia:* 21 years: 100 issues. *See* **443.**

720. WELLENS, OSCAR. John Payne Collier and the *British Lady's Magazine* (1815–1818): new attributions. NQ (32) 1985, 339–41.

721. WELLENS, OSKAR. Joseph Robertson: the Anti-Rowleian critic of the *Critical Review.* NM (87:4) 594–8.

722. WELLS, DANIEL A. Whitman allusions in *Harper's Monthly:* an annotated list of citations. WWQR (4:1) 16–23.

723. WHITE, BRUCE A. Elbert Hubbard and *The Philistine: a Periodical* *of Protest* (1895–1915): the muscular journalism of an American freethinker. VPR (19:3) 83–9.

724. WHITE, WILLIAM.   Ernest Bramah, Max Carrados, and *The News of the World.* BB (43:3) 189.

725. WHITEMAN, BRUCE.   *Here and Now*: a note and an index. CanP (18) 77–87.

726. WHITNEY, PATRICIA.   *En Masse*: an introduction and an index. CanP (19) 76–91.

727. WICKHAM, D. E. (ed.).   Letters to an editor: Montague Summers to C. K. Ogden. Edinburgh: Tragara Press. pp. 28.

728. WILLIAMSON, HENRY.   *The Weekly Despatch*: articles contributed by Henry Williamson in the years 1920–21. London: Henry Williamson Soc., 1983. pp. 54.

729. WILLIS, DONALD (ed.).   *Variety*'s complete science fiction reviews. New York; London: Garland, 1985. pp. xiv, 479.

730. WINKS, ROBIN W.   Canadian magazines. CanL (108) 94–103.

731. WOLFF, ROBERT LEE (comp.).   Nineteenth-century fiction: a bibliographical catalogue based on the collection formed by Robert Lee Wolff: vol. 5, Anonymous, pseudonymous, multiple-author fiction, annuals and periodicals, index. *See* **292.**

732. WOOD, J. L.   Defoe serialized. Factotum (19) 1984, 21–3.

733. —— Tommy Dishclout and Alexander Hogg. Factotum (11) 1981, 18–21. (*The New Spiritual Magazine.*)

734. WOODFIELD, MALCOLM.   Victorian weekly reviews and reviewing after 1860: R. H. Hutton and the *Spectator.* YES (16) 74–91.

735. YOUNG, CHRIS HIGGINS.   *The Nebraska Review.* LMR (5:2) 23–5.

THE ENGLISH LANGUAGE

GENERAL STUDIES

736. AARSLEFF, HANS. From Locke to Saussure: essays on the study of language and intellectual history. (Bibl. 1984, 658.) Rev. by Erik A. Hansen in EngS (67:1) 51–6.

737. AMOABENG, KWAKU. The English language in Ghana: a comprehensive, annotated bibliography. Unpub. doct. diss., State Univ. of New York at Stony Brook. [Abstr. in DA (47) 2148A.]

738. BUGARSKI, RANKO. Notes on the terminology of applied linguistics. *In* (pp. 1147–53) **26.**

739. BURCHFIELD, ROBERT. The English language. New York: OUP, 1985. (Cf. bibl. 1985, 597.) Rev. by David D. Eskey in MLJ (70:1) 89; by M. L. Samuels in NQ (33:2) 197–8; by Manfred Markus in AAA (11) 230–3.

740. BUTLER, CHRISTOPHER. Computers in linguistics. *See* **524.**

741. BUTTERFIELD, JEREMY (ed.). Language, mind and logic. Cambridge: CUP. pp. xi, 232.

742. CHOI, JUNE-YOUNG. Tongjae gwange. (Control relations.) JELL (31:4) 1985, 699–725.

743. CHOMSKY, NOAM. Changing perspectives on knowledge and use of language. LeuB (75) 1–71.

744. —— Knowledge of language: its nature, origin and use. London: Praeger; Westport, CT: Greenwood Press. pp.xxxii, 307. Rev. by Trevor Pateman in THES (708) 19.

745. CLUVER, A. D. DE V. Language variety. English Usage (17:2) 8–15.

746. COLLIN, FINN. Language and thought. Danish Yearbook of Philosophy (Copenhagen) (22) 3–36.

747. COUTURE, BARBARA (ed.). Functional approaches to writing: research perspectives. *See* **498.**

748. CRONKHITE, GARY. On the focus, scope, and coherence of the study of human symbolic activity. QJS (72:3) 231–46.

749. CRYSTAL, DAVID (ed.). Linguistic controversies: essays in linguistic theory and practice in honour of F. R. Palmer. (Bibl. 1982, 144.) Rev. by Barbara Korte in MLR (81:1) 154–5.

750. ESSER, JÜRGEN. Untersuchungen zum gesprochenen Englisch. Ein Beitrag zur strukturellen Pragmatik. (Bibl. 1985, 612.) Rev. by Elisabeth Wieser in AAA (11) 125–8.

751. FOULKES, A. P. Literature and propaganda. (Bibl. 1985, 616.) Rev. by André Boué in (38:4) 1985, 448–9.

752. FRIES, PETER HOWARD; FRIES, NANCY M. Toward an understanding of language: Charles Carpenter Fries in perspective. Amsterdam; Philadelphia, PA: Benjamins, 1985. pp. xvi, 384. (Amsterdam studies in the theory and history of linguistic science, 4.) (Current issues in linguistic theory, 40.)

753. George, Alexander.   Must the language of knowledge be used in explaining knowledge of language? Unpub. doct. diss., Harvard Univ. [Abstr. in DA (47) 2182A.]

754. Grandy, Richard E.; Warner, Richard (eds).   Philosophical grounds of rationality: intentions, categories, ends. Oxford: Clarendon Press. pp. vi, 500.

755. Greenbaum, Sidney; Leech, Geoffrey; Svartvik, Jan (eds). Studies in English linguistics for Randolph Quirk. (Bibl. 1982, 1049.) Rev. by Gunnel Tottie in SN (58:1) 115–23.

756. Greenberg, William J.   Aspects of the theory of singular reference: prolegomena to a dialectical logic of singular terms. New York; London: Garland, 1985. pp. xiv, 139. (Outstanding dissertations in linguistics.)

757. Haas, Mary R.   Lessons from American Indian linguistics. *In* (pp. 68–72) **38.**

758. Heller, Erich.   Notes on language, its deconstruction and on translating. *In* (pp. 1–11) **46.**

759. Henry, Desmond Paul.   That most subtle question (quaestio subtilissima): the metaphysical bearing of medieval and contemporary linguistic discipline. Manchester: Manchester UP, 1983. pp. xviii, 237. Rev. by Keith Arnold in CJL (31:1) 83–5.

760. Hrachovec, Herbert.   Irreconcilable similarities: man and semantic machines. Raritan (5:3) 103–17.

761. Kastovsky, Dieter; Szwedek, Aleksander (eds); Płocińska, Barbara (asst ed.).   Linguistics across historical and geographical boundaries in honour of Jacek Fisiak on the occasion of his fiftieth birthday: vol. 1, Linguistic theory and historical linguistics; vol. 2, Descriptive, contrastive and applied linguistics. *See* **26.**

762. Katzner, Kenneth.   The languages of the world. (Bibl. 1979, 1035a). London: Routledge & Kegan Paul. pp. 374. (Second ed.: first ed. 1977.)

763. Koerner, Konrad (ed.).   Edward Sapir: appraisals of his life and work. (Bibl. 1985, 1481.) Rev. by Regna Durnell in CJL (31:4) 373–7.

764. Krámský, Jiří.   The place of morphology in the system of language. *In* (pp. 9–12) **24.**

765. Kruhu Moderních Filologů.   Jubinlejní Ročenka Kruhu Moderních Filologů. (Jubilee anniversary report of the Czechoslovak Circle of Modern Philology.) *See* **24.**

766. Lamb, Sydney M.   On the aims of linguistics. *In* (pp. 1–11) **38.**

767. Lecercle, Jean-Jacques.   Philosophy through the looking-glass: language, nonsense and desire. London: Hutchinson, 1985. pp. 206.

768. Lewandowska-Tomaszczyk, Barbara.   Language universals, linguistic theory, and philosophy. *In* (pp. 77–84) **26.**

769. Lyons, John.   Language and linguistics: an introduction. (Bibl. 1985, 649.) Rev. by Raymond Hickey in Archiv (223:1) 129–32.

770. MacCabe, Colin.   Theoretical essays: film, linguistics, litera-ture. (Bibl. 1985, 9567.) Rev. by Christopher Butler in TLS, 14 Feb., 170.

771. McCrum, Robert; Cran, William; MacNeil, Robert.   The story of English. London: Faber & Faber; BBC Pubs; New York: Sifton–Viking Press. pp. 384. Rev. by Roy Harris in TLS, 26 Sept., 1062; by John Simon in BkW, 31 Aug., 5.

772. Martinich, A. P. (ed.).   The philosophy of language. New York; Oxford: OUP, 1085. pp. xi, 429.

773. Milroy, James; Milroy, Lesley.   Authority in language: investigating language prescription and standardisation. London: Routledge & Kegan Paul, 1985. pp. xiii, 189. (Language, education and society.)

774. Murphy, Peter T.   Language mastery, language mystery. Raritan (5:4) 127–45.

775. Newmeyer, Frederick J.   Has there been a 'Chomskyan revolution' in linguistics? Lang (62:1) 1–18.

776. Newspaper Archive Developments.   The *Times Literary Supple-ment* Index, 1902–1939. *See* **659.**

777. Nosek, Jiří.   Funkce a obsah v jazyce. (Function and content in language.) *In* (pp. 43–4) **4.**

778. —— Funkce a tvar v jazyce. (Function and form in language.) *In* (pp. 5–8) **24.**

779. Olorenshaw, Robert; Rogers, Patrick.   Les 100 pièges de l'anglais. Verviers, Belgium: Marabout, 1985. pp. 224. (Marabout service, 718).

780. Page, Norman (ed.).   The language of literature: a casebook. (Bibl. 1984, 803.) Rev. by J. Cresswell in NQ (33:1) 131–2.

781. Rastall, P. R.   Linguistic meta-theory: the formal and empiri-cal conditions of acceptability of linguistic theories and descriptions. Unpub. doct. diss., Univ. of St Andrews, 1984.

782. Robinson, Kimball L.   Will the real revised standard theory please stand up? JPhon (8:1) 1980, 53–62.

783. Rybacki, Karyn C.; Rybacki, Donald J.   Advocacy and opposition: an introduction to argumentation. Englewood Cliffs, NJ; London: Prentice–Hall. pp. xii, 222.

784. Sadrin, Anny.   Langage des origines, origines du langage dans *The Origin of Species*. CVE (23) 71–85.

785. Salverda, Renier.   Leading conceptions in linguistic theory. Dordrecht: Foris, 1985. pp. x, 157. (Geschiedenis van de taalkunde, 4.) Rev. by J. Kooij in ForumL (27:1) 76–9.

786. Société des Anglicistes de L'Enseignement Supérieur.   Actes du congrès de Poitiers. *See* **1.**

787. Steiner, George.   Real presence. Cambridge: CUP. pp. 24. (Leslie Stephen Memorial Lecture.)

788. Stewart, John.   Speech and human being: a complement to semiotics. QJS (72:1) 55–73.

789. STEYN, JACQUES.   Quo vadis linguistics – is there a future? SA Tydskrif vir Taalkunde/SA Journal of Linguistics (4:1) 56–70.
790. TABOSSI, P.   Interpreting words in context. Unpub. doct. diss., Univ. of Sussex, 1983.
791. TINDALE, CHRISTOPHER WILLIAM.   The speaking subject: speech acts, grammatology, and the phenomenology of speech. Unpub. doct. diss., Univ. of Waterloo. [Abstr. in DA (47) 1753A.]
792. TYDEMAN, WILLIAM (ed.).   The Welsh connection: essays by past and present members of the Department of English Language and Literature, University College of North Wales, Bangor. Llandysul: Gomer. pp. 211.
793. VERSCHUEREN, JEF.   Basic linguistic action verbs: a questionnaire. Antwerp: Universitaire Instelling, 1984, pp. 235. (Antwerp papers in linguistics, 37.)
794. WALKER, S.   Descriptive techniques for studying verbal graphic language. See **512.**
795. WATERS, T. R. W.   Sound and sense: the structure of language and our organization of experience. Unpub. doct. diss., Univ. of Exeter, 1983.
796. WELLS, G. A.   Herder's resistance to the idea that language is an invention. JEGP (85:2) 167–90.
797. WERTH, PAUL.   Focus, coherence, and emphasis. (Bibl. 1984, 854.) Rev. by Michael S. Rochemont in CJL (31:2) 189–93.
798. WOODS, ANTHONY; FLETCHER, PAUL; HUGHES, ARTHUR.   Statistics in language studies. See **514.**

GENERAL HISTORICAL STUDIES

799. AARSLEFF, HANS.   Joseph de Maistre and Victorian thought on the origin of language and civilization. In (pp. 96–108) **53.**
800. AUSTERLITZ, ROBERT.   Contrasting fact with fiction: the common denominator in internal reconstruction, with a bibliography. In (pp. 183–92) **26.**
801. BAMMESBERGER, ALFRED.   English etymology. Heidelberg: Winter, 1984. pp. 163. (Sprachwissenschaftliche Studienbucher, 1.) Rev. by Sheila M. Embleton in CJL (31:3) 303–6; by M. L. Samuels in NQ (33:2) 198–9.
802. BATELY, JANET.   Linguistic evidence as a guide to the authorship of Old English verse: a reappraisal, with special reference to *Beowulf. In* (pp. 409–31) **25.**
803. BENES, PETER; BENES, JANE MONTAGUE (eds).   American speech: 1600 to the present. Boston, MA: Boston Univ. Scholarly Pubs, 1985. pp. 114. (Dublin Seminar for New England Folklife, annual proceedings, 1983.) Rev. by J. L. Dillard in JAF (99) 347–50.
804. BERNDT, ROLF.   A history of the English language. (Bibl. 1985, 588.) Rev. by Gillis Kristensson in EngS (67:4) 378–9.
805. BIDDULPH, JOSEPH.   Gurt tots and tussicks: illuminating the oldest English of the South. Pontypridd: Languages Information Centre. pp. 28.

806. —— The languages of the old North: a portrait of the Northumbrian dialect of Early English & of the Celtic, Norse & other tongues once used in the North of England. Pontypridd: Languages Information Centre. pp. 24.

807. —— A shippen o'sheep: an introduction to the West Saxon of King Alfred's day. Pontypridd: Languages Information Centre. pp. 24.

808. BLAKE, NORMAN F. Jonathan Swift and the English language. Englisch Amerikanische Studien (Munster) (1) 106–19. (Irwin Ehrenpreis Memorial Lecture.)

809. BREKLE, HERBERT E. What is the history of linguistics and to what end is it studied? A didactic approach. In (pp. 1–10) **53.**

810. BYNON, THEODORA. August Schleicher: Indo-Europeanist and general linguist. In (pp. 129–49) **53.**

811. —— PALMER, F. R. (eds). Studies in the history of Western linguistics: in honour of R. H. Robins. See **53.**

812. CABLE, THOMAS. The rise of written standard English. In (pp. 75–94) ALDO SCAGLIONE, The emergence of national languages. Ravenna: Longo, 1984. pp. 233. (Speculum artium, 11.)

813. COLLINGE, NEVILLE E. The new historicism and its battles. FLH (7:1) 3–19.

814. DAVIES, ANNA MORPURGO. Karl Brugmann and late nineteenth-century linguistics. In (pp. 150–71) **53.**

815. EATON, ROGER, et al. (eds). Papers from the 4th international conference on English historical linguistics. Amsterdam, 10–13 April 1985. See **41.**

816. FISHER, JOHN H.; RICHARDSON, MALCOLM; FISHER, JANE L. (eds). An anthology of Chancery English. (Bibl. 1985, 702.) Rev. by Joseph P. Tuso in SCR (3:2) 103–4.

817. FISIAK, JACEK (ed.). Papers from the 6th International conference on historical linguistics. See **42.**

818. HAMMETT, I. M. Lord Monboddo's *Of the Origin and Progress of Language*: its sources, genesis and background, with special attention to the Advocates' Library. Unpub. doct. diss., Univ. of Edinburgh, 1985. [Abstr. in IT (35) 1486.]

819. HOENIGSWALD, HENRY M. Nineteenth-century linguistics on itself. In (pp. 172–88) **53.**

820. HYLDEGAARD HANSEN, BENTE. The historical implications of the Scandinavian linguistic element in English: a theoretical evaluation. NOWELE (4) 1984, 53–95.

821. KEYSER, SAMUEL JAY; O'NEIL, W. Rule generalization and optionality in language change. Dordrecht: Foris, 1985. pp. vii, 153. (Studies in generative grammar, 23.)

822. LAW, VIVIEN. Originality in the medieval normative tradition. In (pp. 43–55) **53.**

823. McCRUM, ROBERT. The English language: 1, The chaos of the ether; 2, Symptoms of the slang contagion; 3, The tract of corruption. Listener (116) 2 Oct., 10–12; 9 Oct., 14, 16; 16 Oct., 19–20.

824. —— Wonders of a living museum. Bulletin, 23/30 Dec., 172–4. (History of Australian English.)

825. McKusick, James C.   Coleridge's philosophy of language. New Haven, CT; London: Yale UP. pp. xiii, 175. (Yale studies in English, 195.) (Cf. bibl. 1985, 6674.)

826. McMurtry, Jo.   English language, English literature: the creation of an academic discipline. London: Mansell, 1985. pp. xi, 210.

827. Minagawa, Saburo; Takemae, Fumio.   Tudor Stuart cho eigo jiten. (A dictionary of Tudor and Stuart English.) Tokyo: Takemura Press. pp. 122.

828. Nagashima, Daisuke.   A note on Dr Johnson's *History of the English Language. In* (pp. 525–31) **26.**

829. Nielsen, Hans F.   Old English and continental Germanic languages. A survey of morphology and phonological interrelations. Innsbruck: Institut für Sprachwissenschaft, 1985. pp. 311. (Innsbrucker Beiträge zur Sprachwissenschaft, 33.)

830. Ó Mathúna, Sean P.   William Bathe, S.J., 1564–1614: a pioneer in linguistics. Amsterdam: Benjamins. pp. 211. (Amsterdam studies in the theory and history of linguistic science: 3, studies in the history of the language sciences, 37.)

831. Parks, Ward.   Flyting and fighting: pathways in the realization of the epic contest. Neophilologus (70:2) 292–306.

832. Percival, W. Keith.   Renaissance linguistics: the old and the new. *In* (pp. 56–68) **53.**

833. Richman, Gerald.   Artful slipping in Old English. Neophilologus (70:2) 278–91.

834. Salmon, Vivian.   Effort and achievement in seventeenth-century British linguistics. *In* (pp. 69–95) **53.**

835. Scheler, Manfred.   Shakespeares Englisch: eine sprachwissenschaftliche Einführung. Berlin; Bielefeld, W. Germany: Schmidt, 1982. pp. 171. (Grundlagen der Anglistik und Amerikanistik, 12.) Rev. by Heinz Reinhold in MLR (81:4) 984–5.

836. Toth, Karl.   AE *læ* 'Haupthaar'. Ang (104:1/2) 94–103

837. Voigts, Linda Ehrsam.   A handlist of Middle English in Harvard manuscripts. See **286.**

CURRENT LANGUAGE: GENERAL STUDIES

838. Butler, Christopher.   Statistics in linguistics. See **496.**

839. Copeland, James E. (ed.).   New directions in linguistics and semiotics. See **38.**

840. D'Agostino, Fred.   Chomsky's system of ideas. Oxford: Clarendon Press. pp. xii, 226. Rev. by Trevor Pateman in THES (708) 19.

841. Gottfried, Michael.   Cross-reference in a scientific sublanguage. Unpub. doct. diss., Univ. of Pennsylvania. [Abstr. in DA (47) 1306A.]

842. Greenbaum, Sidney (ed.).   The English language today. (Bibl. 1985, 620.) Rev. by Bernhard Kettemann in AAA (11) 227–9.

843. HANNAY, MIKE.   English comma placement: a functional view. DQR (16:4) 264–76.

844. LANGENDOEN, D. TERENCE; POSTAL, PAUL M.   The vastness of natural language. Oxford: Blackwell, 1984. pp. ix, 189. Rev. by Steven Lapointe in Linguistics and Philosophy (9:2) 225–43.

845. LEPSCHY, GIULIO.   European linguistics in the twentieth century. *In* (pp. 189–201) **53.**

846. NASH, WALTER.   English usage: a guide to first principles. London: Routledge & Kegan Paul. pp. xiii, 167. (Language, education and society.)

847. NICKEL, GERHARD; STALKER, JAMES C. (eds).   Problems of standardization and linguistic variation of present day English. Heidelberg: Groos. pp. 96. (Studies in descriptive linguistics, 15.)

848. PARKER, FRANK.   Linguistics for non-linguists. London: Taylor & Francis. pp. vii, 239.

849. PETERSON, SUSAN LYNN.   Sex-based differences in English argumentative text; a tagmemic sociolinguistic perspective. Unpub. doct. diss., Univ. of Texas at Arlington. [Abstr. in DA (47) 2146A.]

850. PHYTHIAN, B. A.   Good English. Sevenoaks: Teach Yourself, 1985. pp. 356. (Teach yourself books.)

851. POMPHREY, CATHY.   Language varieties and change. Cambridge: CUP, 1985. pp. 33. (Awareness of language.)

852. RICHARDS, JACK; PLATT, JOHN; WEBER, HEIDI.   Longman dictionary of applied linguistics. Harlow: Longman, 1985. pp. ix, 323.

853. STUBBS, MICHAEL.   Educational linguistics. Oxford: Blackwell. pp. 286. Rev. by Walter Nash in LRB (8:14) 26–7.

854. TODD, LORETO; HANCOCK, IAN.   International English usage. London: Croom Helm. pp. vii, 520.

855. VACHEK, JOSEF (ed.).   Praguiana: some basic and less known aspects of the Prague linguistic school. Amsterdam: Benjamins, 1983. (Cf. bibl. 1985, 689.) Rev. by François Chevillet in EA (38:4) 1985, 451–2.

856. WIERZBICKA, ANNA.   Metaphors linguists live by. PL (19:2) 287–313 (review-article).

VARIETIES OF ENGLISH

DIALECTS AND SPOKEN ENGLISH

General Dialect Studies

857. COLE, ROGER W. Literary representation of dialect: a theoretical approach to the artistic problem. USFLQ (24:3/4) 3–8, 48.

858. KACHRU, BRAJ B. The alchemy of English: the spread, functions and models of non-native Englishes. Oxford: Pergamon Inst. of English. pp. ix, 200. (English in the international context.)

859. TRUDGILL, PETER. Dialects in contact. Oxford: Blackwell. pp. 160. (Language in society, 10.) Rev. by J. C. Wells in THES (729) 16.

America

860. BARTELT, H. GUILLERMO. Tense/aspect variation in American Indian English. NJL (9) 47–53.

861. BENES, PETER; BENES, JANE MONTAGUE (eds). American speech: 1600 to the present. *See* **803.**

862. BIRNS, H. WILLIAM. Dialect in the Catskills: a study in language and culture. Unpub. doct. diss., Indiana Univ. of Pennsylvania. [Abstr. in DA (47) 2142A.]

863. CASSIDY, FREDERIC G. (ed.). Dictionary of American regional English: vol. 1, Introduction, A–C. (Bibl. 1985, 1383.) Rev. by Hugh Kenner in TLS, 9 May, 490–1.

864. DI PAOLO, MARIANNA. A study of double modals in Texas English. Unpub. doct. diss., Univ. of Texas at Austin. [Abstr. in DA (47) 2143A–4A.]

865. GINSBERG, ELAINE K. Virginia Woolf and the Americans. BRH (86:3) 1983/85, 347–59.

866. GOLD, DAVID L. Still more on the origin of the New York City English 'sliding pon(d)'. LeuB (75) 335–57.

867. GUSTAFSON, THOMAS B. Representative words: politics, literature and the American language, 1776–1865. Unpub. doct. diss., Stanford Univ. 2 vols. [Abstr. in DA (47) 2156A.]

868. HEDBERG, JOHANNES. The pronunciation of 'father' in American English – and 'rather' and 'lather'. MS (80) 297–8.

869. HORNBY, A. S. (ed.); RUSE, CHRISTINA A. (asst ed.). The Oxford paperback American dictionary. Oxford: OUP, 1983. pp. xxi, 714. (Oxford paperback reference.)

870. HORNBY, A. S.; HARRIS, DOLORES; STEWART, WILLIAM A. (eds). Oxford student's dictionary of American English. (Bibl. 1984, 1410.) Oxford: OUP. pp. 714. (Second ed.: first ed. 1983.)

871. KYTÖ, MERJA. *May* and *might* indicating 'epistemic possibility' in Early American English. *In* (pp. 131–42) **43.**

872. MACDONALD, MARGUERITE GOODRICH. Cuban-American English: the second generation in Miami. Unpub. doct. diss., Univ. of Florida, 1985. [Abstr. in DA (47) 520A.]

873. MILLER, MICHAEL T.   Virginia words: historical and geographical perspectives. *In* (pp. 11–21) **17.**

874. O'DWYER, B. T.   A study of attitudes, with specific reference to language attitudes among three Newfoundland dialects. Unpub. doct. diss., Univ. of Edinburgh, 1985. [Abstr. in IT (35) 1079.]

875. PENFIELD, JOYCE; ORNSTEIN-GALICIA, JACOB L.   Chicano English: an ethnic context dialect. Amsterdam; Philadelphia, PA: Benjamins, 1985, pp. 112. (Varieties of English around the world, general ser., 7.)

876. POULSEN, RICHARD C.   The mountain man vernacular: its historical roots, its linguistic nature, and its literary uses. New York: Lang, 1985. pp. 328. (American university studies: ser. 4, 22.) Rev. by J. L. Dillard in JAF (99) 347–50.

877. RALEY, PATTI L.; MURRAY, THOMAS E.   The language of handspinning. MJLF (12:2) 53–108.

878. SCHNEIDER, EDGAR W.   Regional variation in 19th century black English in the American South. *In* (pp. 467–87) **42.**

879. SIMPSON, DAVID.   The politics of American English, 1776–1850. New York; Oxford: OUP. pp. x, 301. Rev. by Richard Bridgman in AL (58:4) 623–4.

880. TAYLOR, HANNI ULRIKE.   Bidialectalism in a small liberal arts college. Unpub. doct. diss., Northern Illinois Univ. [Abstr. in DA (47) 2147A.]

881. TREMPER, ELLEN.   Black English in children's literature. LU (3:2) 1979/80, 105–24.

882. VIERECK, WOLFGANG.   On the origin and developments of American English. *In* (pp. 561–9) **42.**

883. WRIGHT, BARBARA HELEN WHITE.   Hypercorrections and dialect forms in the compositions of native born college students from Georgia. Unpub. doct. diss., City Univ. of New York, 1985. [Abstr. in DA (46) 3340A.]

The British Isles

884. ADAMS, G. B.   The English dialects of Ulster: an anthology of articles on Ulster speech. Ed. by MICHAEL BARRY and PHILIP TILLING. Holywood: Ulster Folk and Transport Museum. pp. xiv, 134.

885. ANTTILA, RAIMO.   An etymology for the aquatic '*acker/aiker*' in English, and other grains of truth? *In* (pp. 177–82) **26.**

886. AUSTIN, FRANCES O.   Relative *which* in late 18th century usage: the Clift family correspondence. *In* (pp. 15–29) **41.**

887. BAUER, GERO.   Medieval English scribal practice: some questions and some assumptions. *In* (pp. 199–210) **26.**

888. BEAL, JOAN C.   Lengthening of *a'* in Tyneside English. *In* (pp. 31–44) **41.**

889. BIDDULPH, JOSEPH.   A short grammar of Black Country. Pontypridd: Languages Information Centre. pp. 20.

890. CHESHIRE, J.   Grammatical variation in the English spoken in Reading, Berkshire. Unpub. doct. diss., Univ. of Reading, 1979.

891. CROWLEY, JOSEPH P.   The study of Old English dialects. EngS (67:2) 97–112.

892. DOBSON, BOB (ed.).   Woven in Lancashire: some Lancashire dialect poems. Blackpool: Landy, 1983. pp. 79.

893. DONALDSON, WILLIAM; YOUNG, DOUGLAS (eds).   Grampian hairst: an anthology of Northwest prose. Foreword by CUTHBERT GRAHAM; essay on Northeast Scots by DAVID MURISON. Aberdeen: Aberdeen UP, 1981. pp. xiv, 206.

894. DOUGLAS, S.   Links with Gaelic tradition found in the story traditions of Perthshire travelling people. Scottish Language (5) 15–22.

895. DOWNES, JOHN.   A dictionary of Devon dialect. Padstow: Tabb. pp. 97.

896. GINSBERG, ELAINE K.   Virginia Woolf and the Americans. See **865.**

897. GÓMEZ SOLIÑO, JOSÉ S.   La utilización humorística de rasgos dialectales en The Reeve's Tale y *The Second Shepherds' Play*: interpretación sociolingüística. (Humorous use of dialectal features in The Reeve's Tale and *The Second Shepherds' Play*: sociolinguistic implications.) *In* (pp. 285–7) ANA RÉGULO RODRÍGUEZ and MARÍA RÉGULO RODRÍGUEZ (eds), Serta gratulatoria in honorem Juan Régulo: vol. 1, Filología. La Laguna, Tenerife: Univ. de La Laguna, 1985. pp. 766.

898. HARRIS, J. K. M.   Linguistic change in a nonstandard dialect: phonological studies in the history of English in Ireland. Unpub. doct. diss., Univ. of Edinburgh, 1984.

899. HICKEY, RAYMOND.   Standard English, deviation and interference: a reply to Roger Lass. SAP (19) 11–14.

900. IHALAINEN, OSSI.   An enquiry into the nature of mixed grammars: two cases of grammatical variation in dialectal British English. *In* (pp. 371–9) **26.**

901. —— Synchronic variation and linguistic change: evidence from British English dialects. *In* (pp. 61–72) **41.**

902. KILLIAN, PATRICIA ANNE.   English in Ireland: an attitudinal study. Unpub. doct. diss., Univ. of Texas at Austin, 1985. [Abstr. in DA (46) 3018A.]

903. KIRK, JOHN M.; SANDERSON, STEWART; WIDDOWSON, J. D. A. (eds).   Studies in linguistic geography: the dialects of English in Britain and Ireland. London: Croom Helm, 1985. pp. xix, 186.

904. KORTLANDT, FREDERIK.   The origin of the Old English dialects. *In* (pp. 437–42) **26.**

905. KRISTENSSON, GILLIS.   A Middle English dialect boundary. *In* (pp. 443–57) **26.**

906. —— On voicing of initial fricatives in Middle English. SAP (19) 3–10.

907. LEEDS, WINIFRED.   Herefordshire speech: the southwest Midland dialect as spoken in Herefordshire and its environs. (Bibl. 1974, 1643.) Kimbolton: Arch, 1985. pp. 128. (Second ed.: first ed. 1974.)

908. LETLEY, A. E. C.   Literary uses of Scots dialect in certain nineteenth century novelists from John Galt to George Douglas Brown. Unpub. doct. diss., Univ. of London, Birkbeck Coll., 1983.

909. LETLEY, E.   'Revolution *there* as visible as anywhere else!': some literary uses of Scots in nineteenth-century fiction. Scottish Language (5) 30–8.

910. LORIMER, WILLIAM LAUGHTON (trans.).   The New Testament in Scots. Harmondsworth: Penguin, 1985. pp. xxv, 476. Rev. by W. S. Milne in Agenda (23:3/4) 46–50.

911. McCLURE, J. D.   What Scots owes to Gaelic. Scottish Language (5) 85–98.

912. McCLURE, J. DERRICK (ed.).   Scotland and the lowland tongue: studies in the language and literature of lowland Scotland, in honour of David D. Murison. (Bibl. 1985, 762.) Rev. by William Findlay in Cencrastus (23) 58–60.

913. MACLEOD, ISEABAIL.   Pocket guide to Scottish words. Glasgow: Drew. pp. 96.

914. MELCHERS, G.   Narrowing and extension of meaning in the Scandinavian-based vocabulary of Shetland dialect. Scottish Language (5) 110–19.

915. MIHASHI, ATUKO, *et al.*   Anglo-Irish gohou kaimei eno approach. (An approach to the analysis of the Anglo-Irish collocations.) Tokyo: Daigaku Shorin. pp. xiv, 316.

916. MILTON, C.   Hugh MacDiarmid and North-East Scots. Scottish Language (5) 39–47.

917. MUNRO, MICHAEL.   The patter: a guide to current Glasgow usage. Glasgow: Glasgow District Libraries, 1985. pp. 84.

918. NEWBROOK, M.   Sociolinguistic reflexes of dialect interference in West Wirral. Unpub. doct. diss., Univ. of Reading, 1982.

919. NICOLAISEN, W. F. H.   Gaelic place names in Scots. Scottish Language (5) 140–6.

920. NORTH, D. J.   Aspects of the phonology and agricultural terminology of the rural dialects of Surrey, Kent and Sussex. Unpub. doct. diss., Univ. of Leeds, 1982.

921. O BAOILL, DONALL P. (ed.).   Papers on Irish English. Dublin: Irish Assn for Applied Linguistics, 1985. pp. v, 78.

922. ONO, SHIGERU.   *Undergytan* as a 'Winchester' word. *In* (pp. 569–77) **26.**

923. PEPPER, JOHN.   Mandeer, it's magic! Belfast: Appletree. pp. 79.

924. PETYT, KEITH MALCOLM.   Dialect and accent in industrial West Yorkshire. Amsterdam; Philadelphia, PA: Benjamins, 1985. pp. 401. (Varieties of English around the world, general ser., 6.)

925. POUSSA, PATRICIA.   Historical implications of the distribution of the zero-pronoun relative clause in Modern English dialects: looking backwards towards OE from Map S5 of *The Linguistic Atlas of England*. *In* (pp. 99–117) **43.**

926. —— A note on the voicing of initial fricatives in Middle English. *In* (pp. 235–52) **41.**

927. PRICE, GLANVILLE.   The languages of Britain. (Bibl. 1984, 933.)

Rev. by François Chevillet in EA (38:3) 1985, 308–9; by Alan R. Thomas in AWR (82) 131–2.

928. RENDBOE, LAURITS.   How 'worn out' or 'corrupted' was Shetland Norn in its final stage? NOWELE (3) 1984, 53–88.

929. ROBINSON, MAIRI (ed.).   The concise Scots dictionary. (Bibl. 1985, 1417.) Rev. by Henry Hargreaves in AUR (51) 368–9; by Robert Burchfield in SLJ (supp. 24) 1–4.

930. ROMAINE, SUZANNE.   Syntactic variation and the acquisition of strategies of relativization in the language of Edinburgh school children. *In* (pp. 19–33) **43.**

931. SAMUELS, M. L.   The great Scandinavian belt. *In* (pp. 269–81) **41.**

932. SCHOOL BROADCASTING COUNCIL FOR SCOTLAND.   Scots fit? whit?: what?: Scots in the primary school. Edinburgh: School Broadcasting Council for Scotland, 1985. pp. 20.

933. SHEPHERD, V.   The circle of William Barnes's poetry: a discussion of the language and themes of his dialect poetry. Unpub. doct. diss., Univ. of Loughborough. [Abstr. in IT (35) 1493.]

934. SHUKEN, C.   Vowel systems in Hebridean English. Scottish Language (5) 131–9.

935. STEIN, DIETER.   Old English Northumbrian verb inflection revisited. *In* (pp. 637–50) **26.**

936. THOMSON, D. S.   Gaelic literary interactions with Scots and English work: a survey. Scottish Language (5) 1–14.

937. TRUDGILL, PETER (ed.).   Language in the British Isles. (Bibl. 1985, 776.) Rev. by François Chevillet in EA (38:3) 1985, 309–11; by Henry Rogers in CJL (31:2) 193–6; by František Vrhel in PP (29) 63–4.

938. VIERECK, WOLFGANG.   Dialectal speech areas in England: Orton's lexical evidence. *In* (pp. 725–40) **26.**

939. —— (ed.).   Focus on England and Wales. (Bibl. 1985, 779.) Rev. by Beat Glauser in AAA (11) 236–8.

940. WAKELIN, MARTYN F.   Discovering English dialects. (Bibl. 1978, 1290.) Aylesbury: Shire, 1985. pp. 63. (Discovering, 235.) (Third ed.: first ed. 1978.)

941. —— The *Exmoor Courtship* and *Exmoor Scolding*: an evaluation of two eighteenth-century dialect texts. *In* (pp. 741–51) **26.**

942. WALL, RICHARD.   An Anglo-Irish dialect glossary for Joyce's works. Gerrards Cross: Smythe. pp. 131.

943. WAUGH, D.   The transition from Gaelic to Scots or Scottish English in Caithness place-names. Scottish Language (5) 147–55.

944. WRIGHT, PETER.   The Lanky twang: how it is spoke. Lancaster: Dalesman. pp. 32.

Africa

945. AMOABENG, KWAKU.   The English language in Ghana: a comprehensive, annotated bibliography. *See* **737.**

946. AWONUSI, V. O.   Regional accents and internal variability in Nigerian English: a historical analysis. EngS (67:6) 555–60.

947. —— Sociolinguistic variation in Lagos English. Unpub. doct. diss., Univ. of London, University Coll., 1985. [Abstr. in IT (35) 534.]

948. BARNES, L. A.   South African Indian English. English Usage (17:2) 1–7.

949. BRANFORD, JEAN.   Some surprises from the corpus of the *Dictionary of South African English on Historical Principles.* Crux (20:4) 68–72.

950. CLUVER, A. D. DE V.   Code-switching. English Usage (17:1) 9–15.

951. DALPHINIS, MORGAN.   Caribbean and African languages: social history, language, literature and education. London: Karia, 1985. pp. xiv, 288.

952. HORNER, ROSEMARY H.   An analysis of Nigerian oral discourse within the context of an unscripted dramatic performance. Lore & Language (5:2) 47–62.

953. THOKA, THABANG.   Soweto is where it's at. English Usage (17:2) 16–22.

Australasia

954. BURCHFIELD, ROBERT (ed.).   The New Zealand pocket Oxford dictionary. Auckland: OUP. pp. xxiv, 901. Rev. by Forrest Scott in NZList, 26 Apr., 46.

955. GORDON, E.; MACLAGAN, M. A.   A study of the /iə/~/eə/ contrast in New Zealand English. New Zealand Speech-Language Therapists' Journal (40:2) 1985, 16–26.

956. HORVARTH, BARBARA M.   Variation in Australian English: the sociolects of Sydney. Cambridge; Melbourne: CUP, 1985. pp. xi, 200. (Cambridge studies in linguistics, 45.)

957. HUME, AMANDA.   F. W. C. Gerstäcker: an overlooked informant on language in mid-19th century Australia. AUMLA (66) 272–85.

958. LAWSON, ELIZABETH.   'Pinkie-plonk' in Australia: a lexical note. AUMLA (66) 286–8.

959. McCRUM, ROBERT.   Wonders of a living museum. *See* **824.**

960. MURRAY-SMITH, STEPHEN.   Right words: a guide to English usage in Australia. Melbourne: Penguin. pp. xiii, 361.

961. REID, TONY.   Separation and Kiwi standards. NZList, 3 May, 28–9.

962. WILKES, G. A.   Exploring Australian English. Sydney: Australian Broadcasting Corporation. pp. 96.

963. —— A spud by any other name. Bulletin, 23/30 Dec., 175–6. (Regional differences in Australian English.)

South Asia

964. AITCHISON, JEAN; AGNIHOTRI, RAMA KANT.   'I deny that I'm incapable of not working all night': divergence of negative structures in British and Indian English. *In* (pp. 3–14) **41.**

965. BURGESS, ANTHONY (introd.).   Hobson-Jobson: a glossary of colloquial Anglo-Indian words and phrases and of kindred terms, etymological, historical, geographical and discursive. By SIR HENRY YULE and A. C. BURNELL; revised ed. by WILLIAM CROOKE. London: Routledge & Kegan Paul, 1985. pp. xlviii, 1021. (Facsim. of second ed., 1903: first ed. 1886.)

966. KACHRU, BRAJ B.   The Indianization of English: the English language in India. New York; OUP, 1983. (Cf. bibl. 1984, 952.) Rev. by Peter Muhlhausler in NQ (33:2) 200–1.

Other Dialects

967. DALPHINIS, MORGAN.   Caribbean and African languages: social history, language, literature and education. *See* **951.**

968. EDWARDS, VIV.   Language in a black community. Clevedon: Multilingual Matters. pp. 169. (Multilingual matters, 24.)

969. MACDONALD, ALASDAIR A.   The Middle Scots expansion of *Iesu, nostra redemptio*, and a ghost in the Bannatyne manuscript. Neophilologus (70:3) 472–4.

970. POCHARD, J.-C.; DEVONISH, H.   Deixis in Caribbean English-lexicon creole: a description of 'a', 'da' and 'de'. Lingua (69) 105–20.

971. SEBBA, MARK; TATE, SHIRLEY.   You know what I mean: agreement marking in British black English. Journal of Pragmatics (10:2) 163–72.

Pidgins and Creoles

972. BATES-MIMS, MERELYN B.   *Chez les noirs*: a comparative-historical analysis of pidgin and creole languages. Unpub. doct. diss., Univ. of Cincinnati. [Abstr. in DA (47) 2142A.]

973. DEVONISH, HUBERT.   Language and liberation: Creole language politics in the Caribbean. London: Karia. pp. 157.

974. GÖRLACH, MANFRED.   Middle English – a creole? *In* (pp. 329–44) **26.**

975. HARRIS, JOHN.   Northern Territory pidgins and the origin of kriol. Canberra: Dept of Linguistics, Research School of Pacific Studies, Australian National Univ. pp. vii, 418. (Pacific linguistics, ser. C, 89.)

976. HOLM, J. (ed.).   Central American English. Heidelberg: Groos, 1983. pp. 184. (Variants of English around the world, text series, 2.) Rev. by Friedrich Wilhelm Gester in Archiv (222:2) 1985, 379–81.

977. KEPHART, RONALD F.   'It have more soft words': a study of creole English and reading in Carriacou, Grenada. Unpub. doct. diss., Univ. of Florida, 1985. [Abstr. in DA (47) 166A.]

978. LIPSKI, JOHN M.   Sobre el bilingüismo anglo-hispánico en Gibraltar. (On Anglo-Spanish bilingualism in Gibraltar.) NM (87:3) 414–27.

979. MUHLHAUSLER, PETER.   Pidgin and creole linguistics. Oxford: Blackwell. pp. 320. (Language in society, 11.)

980. SLEDGE, MAILANDE CHENEY.   The representation of the Gullah dialect in Francis Griswold's *A Sea Island Lady*. Unpub. doct. diss., Univ. of Alabama, 1985. [Abstr. in DA (46) 1917A.]

981. Todd, Loreto. The CM2 process: a selection of riddles in Cameroon Pidgin English. Lore & Language (5:2) 3–11.

Sociolinguistics

982. Anderson, A. Semantic and social-pragmatic aspects of meaning in task-oriented dialogue. Unpub. doct. diss., Univ. of Glasgow, 1983.

983. Anderson, Richard Henry. Social attitudes among Spanish-English speakers toward code-switching. Unpub. doct. diss., Univ. of Washington. [Abstr. in DA (47) 1304A.]

984. Awonusi, V. O. Sociolinguistic variation in Lagos English. See **947.**

985. Baker, Margaret P. Some functions of Mormon in-group language in creating and maintaining ethnic boundaries. Unpub. doct. diss., Arizona State Univ. [Abstr. in DA (47) 1304A.]

986. Black, John W., et al. The use of words in context: the vocabulary of college students. New York; London: Plenum, 1985. pp. xi, 263. (Cognition and language.)

987. Blake, Norman F. Jonathan Swift and the English language. See **808.**

988. Cluver, A. D. de V. Code-switching. See **950.**

989. Clyne, Michael G. Multilingual Australia: resources – needs – policies. Melbourne: River Seine, 1985. pp. 179.

990. Coates, Jennifer. Women, men, and language: a sociolinguistic account of sex differences in language. London: Longman. pp. 150. (Studies in language and linguistics.)

991. Cokely, Dennis Richard. Towards a sociolinguistic model of the interpreting process: focus on ASL and English. Unpub. doct. diss., Georgetown Univ., 1985. [Abstr. in DA (46) 3704A.]

992. Cook-Gumperz, Jenny (ed.). The social construction of literacy. Cambridge: CUP. pp. 330. (Studies in interactional sociolinguistics, 3.)

993. Corson, David. The lexical bar. See **1738.**

994. Craig, Holly, K.; Washington, Julie A. Children's turn-taking behaviours: sociolinguistic interactions. Journal of Pragmatics (10:2) 173–97.

995. Edwards, John. Language, society and identity. Oxford: Blackwell, in assn with Deutsch, 1985. pp. x, 245. (Language library.)

996. Etter-Lewis, Gwendolyn. Sociolinguistic patterns of code-switching in the language of preschool black children. Unpub. doct. diss., Univ. of Michigan, 1985. [Abstr. in DA (46) 1920A.]

997. Fisher, I. C. Linguistic indications of social class in the Victorian novel. Unpub. doct. diss., Univ. of Leicester, 1983.

998. Gilyard, R. Keith. Voicing myself; a study of sociolinguistic competence. Unpub. doct. diss., New York Univ., 1985. [Abstr. in DA (46) 3636A.]

999. Gumperz, John J.; Hymes, Dell (eds). Directions in

sociolinguistics: the ethnography of communication. Oxford: Blackwell. pp. x, 620.

1000. HEMPHILL, LOWRY ELIZABETH.   Context and conversational style: a reappraisal of social class differences in speech. Unpub. doct. diss., Harvard Univ. [Abstr. in DA (47) 2062A.]

1001. HICKEY, RAYMOND.   Standard English, deviation and interference: a reply to Roger Lass. *See* **899.**

1002. HILL, BEVERLY, *et al.*   Universals of linguistic politeness: quantitative evidence from Japanese and American English. Journal of Pragmatics (10:3) 347–71.

1003. HORNER, ROSEMARY H.   An analysis of Nigerian oral discourse within the context of an unscripted dramatic performance. *See* **952.**

1004. HORVARTH, BARBARA M.   Variation in Australian English: the sociolects of Sydney. *See* **956.**

1005. HOUSTON, ANN CELESTE.   Continuity and change in English morphology: the variable (ING). Unpub. doct. diss., Univ. of Pennsylvania, 1985. [Abstr. in DA (46) 1921A.]

1006. KANNAPELL, BARBARA MARIE.   Language choice reflects identity choice: a sociolinguistic study of deaf college students. Unpub. doct. diss., Georgetown Univ., 1985. [Abstr. in DA (47) 165A.]

1007. KELLER, ROBERT H.   Hostile language: bias in historical writing about American Indian resistance. JAC (9:4) 9–23.

1008. KNIGHT, STEPHEN; MUKHERJEE, S. N. (eds).   Words and worlds: studies in the social role of verbal culture. Sydney: Sydney Association for studies in society and culture, 1983. pp. 197, (plates) 4. (Sydney studies in society and culture, 1.)

1009. LEISI, ERNST.   Zum Thema sozio-kulturelle Semantik. PoetT (23) 116–34.

1010. LIPSKI, JOHN M.   Sobre el bilingüismo anglo-hispánico en Gibraltar. (On Anglo-Spanish bilingualism in Gibraltar.) *See* **978.**

1011. McDOUGALL, RUSSELL.   Opinion on location: regionalism in Australian and Canadian literature. True North/Down Under (Lantzville, B.C.) (4) 1985, 12–42.

1012. MISHRA, ARPITA.   Towards an analysis of conversation management: a cross-cultural perspective. Unpub. doct. diss., Univ. of California, Berkeley, 1985. [Abstr. in DA (46) 2680A.]

1013. MONTGOMERY, MARTIN.   An introduction to language and society. London: Methuen. pp. xxii, 211. (Studies in communication.)

1014. NELSON, EMMANUEL S.   Black America and the Australian Aboriginal literary consciousness. Westerly (30:4) 1985, 43–54.

1015. NEU, JOYCE.   A multivariate sociolinguistic analysis of the speech event negotiation. Unpub. doct. diss., Univ. of Southern California, 1985. [Abstr. in DA (46) 2283A.]

1016. NEWALL, VENETIA.   Folklore and male homosexuality. Folklore (97:2) 123–47. (Presidential Address to the Folklore Society.)

1017. NEWBROOK, M.   Sociolinguistic reflexes of dialect interference in West Wirral. *See* **918.**

1018. NICKEL, GERHARD; STALKER, JAMES C. (eds). Problems of standardization and linguistic variation of present day English. *See* **847.**

1019. NIGROSH, GALE HILARY. Audience in children's letter writing: a study of sociolinguistic development. Unpub. doct. diss., Brown Univ., 1985. [Abstr. in DA (46) 1923A.]

1020. NISHIMURA, MIWA. Intrasentential codeswitching in Japanese and English. Unpub. doct. diss., Univ. of Pennsylvania, 1985. [Abstr. in DA (47) 167A.]

1021. NORRIS, CHRISTOPHER. Suspended sentences: textual theory and the law. SoRA (18:2) 1985, 123–41.

1022. OMOLE, JAMES OLUKAYODE. A sociolinguistic analysis of Wole Soyinka's *The Interpreters*. Unpub. doct. diss., Univ. of Wisconsin–Milwaukee, 1985. [Abstr. in DA (46) 2283A.]

1023. PAIKEDAY, T. M. The native speaker is dead! Toronto; New York: Paikeday, 1985. pp. xiv, 109. Rev. by Paul Meara in MLR (81:4) 957–9.

1024. PENFIELD, JOYCE; ORNSTEIN-GALICIA, JACOB L. Chicano English: an ethnic context dialect. *See* **875.**

1025. PETERSON, SUSAN LYNN. Sex-based differences in English argumentative text; a tagmemic sociolinguistic perspective. *See* **849.**

1026. PHILLIPPS, K. C. Language and class in Victorian England. Oxford: Blackwell, 1985. pp. viii, 190. (Language library.) Rev. by Martha Vicinus in Lingua (69:3) 291–3.

1027. POMPHREY, CATHY. Language varieties and change. *See* **851.**

1028. ROMAINE, SUZANNE. The effects of language standardization on deletion rules: some comparative Germanic evidence from *t/d*-deletion. *In* (pp. 605–20) **26.**

1029. SCHIEFFELIN, BAMBI B.; OCHS, ELINOR (eds). Language socialization across cultures. Cambridge: CUP. pp. v, 274. (Studies in the social and cultural foundations of language, 3.)

1030. SEWELL, DAVID R. Varieties of language in the writings of Mark Twain. Unpub. doct. diss., Univ. of California, San Diego, 1984. [Abstr. in DA (46) 426A.]

1031. SIMPSON, P. A. The sociolinguistic analysis of literary dialogue, with specific reference to Flann O'Brien's *The Third Policeman*. Unpub. doct. diss., Ulster Polytechnic, 1984. [Abstr. in IT (35) 1079.]

1032. SKIPPER, JAMES K. Nicknames, coal miners and group solidarity. Names (34:2) 1984, 134–45.

1033. SMITH, OLIVIA. The politics of language, 1791–1819. (Bibl. 1985, 674; 879.) Rev. by Mark Philp in BJECS (9:2) 244–6: by P. M. S. Dawson in CritQ (27:2) 1985, 67–75; by Jon Klancher in HLQ (49:4) 409–14.

1034. 'SOURIS'. Nugae onomasticae III. Nomina (10) 149–61.

1035. SRIDHAR, KAMAL K. Sociolinguistic theory and non-native varieties of English. Lingua (68) 39–58.

1036. STEPHENS, DEBORAH ANNE. Linguistic aspects of code-switching among Spanish/English bilingual children. Unpub. doct. diss., Univ. of Arizona. [Abstr. in DA (47) 1308A–9A.]

1037. TAYLOR, HANNI ULRIKE. Bidialectalism in a small liberal arts college. *See* **880.**

1038. TURELL, MARÍA TERESA. La sociolingüística y los estudios ingleses. (Sociolinguistics and English studies.) RCEI (12) 35–53.

1039. WARDHAUGH, RONALD. An introduction to sociolinguistics. Oxford: Blackwell. pp. 384.

Ethnolinguistics and Anthropological Linguistics

1040. AITCHISON, JEAN; AGNIHOTRI, RAMA KANT. 'I deny that I'm incapable of not working all night': divergence of negative structures in British and Indian English. *In* (pp. 3–14) **41.**

1041. ALLAN, KEITH. Hearers, overhearers, and Clark & Carlson's informative analysis. Lang (62:3) 509–17.

1042. BAKER, CHARLOTTE PIERCE. Acquisition of /t,d/ deletion in vernacular black English: a study of head start preschoolers. Unpub. doct. diss., Temple Univ., 1985. [Abstr. in DA (46) 2280A.]

1043. BAKER, MARGARET P. Some functions of Mormon in-group language in creating and maintaining ethnic boundaries. *See* **985.**

1044. BAUGH, JOHN. Black street speech: its history, structure and survival. (Bibl. 1985, 895.) Rev. by Walter F. Edwards in Journal of Pragmatics (10:4) 503–6.

1045. BERGH, GUNNAR. The neuropsychological status of Swedish–English subsidiary bilinguals. Gothenburg: Acta Universitatis Gothoburgensis. pp. vi, 226. (Gothenburg studies in English, 61.) (Doct. diss., Gothenburg Univ.)

1046. BORDERS-SIMMONS, DENISE GLYN. Contextual variability and communicative competence: reference and cohesion strategies in narrative discourse by black working-class children. Unpub. doct. diss., Columbia Univ. Teachers College, 1985. [Abstr. in DA (47) 885A.]

1047. BROWN, PAULA. What do you call your pig? Who is your namesake? Names (34:4) 1984, 432–6.

1048. COLEMAN, CYNTHIA. Dominance patterns in the verbal interaction of black students at Frostburg State College. Unpub. doct. diss., Indiana Univ. of Pennsylvania, 1985. [Abstr. in DA (46) 3704A.]

1049. COLEMAN, MICHAEL C. Language, missionaries, and American Indians: the Presbyterian case (research report). Pubs of the Dept of English, Univ. of Turku (7) 1985, 27–35.

1050. CRAIG, HOLLY, K.; WASHINGTON, JULIE A. Children's turn-taking behaviours: sociolinguistic interactions. *See* **994.**

1051. D'AMICO-REISNER, LYNNE. An ethnolinguistic study of disapproval exchanges. Unpub. doct. diss., Univ. of Pennsylvania, 1985. [Abstr. in DA (46) 3704A.]

1052. DWIGHT, DEBRA MAYE. Analysis of pragmatic functions in the language of preschool black children. Unpub. doct. diss., Univ. of Alabama, 1985. [Abstr. in DA (46) 1856A–7A.]

1053. EDWARDS, VIV. Language in a black community. *See* **968.**

1054. FARHI, EMMANUELLE. Le yiddish, reflet de la conscience morale. *In* (pp. 129–42) **5.**

1055. GUMPERZ, JOHN J.; HYMES, DELL (eds). Directions in sociolinguistics: the ethnography of communication. *See* **999.**

1056. HILL, BEVERLY, *et al.* Universals of linguistic politeness: quantitative evidence from Japanese and American English. *See* **1002.**

1057. HIRVONEN, PEKKA. Investigating the language of Finnish Americans: an example of a departmental research project. Pubs of the Dept of English, Univ. of Turku (7) 1985, 65–75.

1058. HULTFORS, PÄR. Reactions to non-native English: native English-speakers' assessments of errors in the use of English made by non-native users of the language: 1. Acceptability and intelligibility. Stockholm: Almqvist & Wiksell. pp. xv, 246. (Stockholm studies in English, 67.) (Doct. diss., Stockholm Univ.)

1059. IHALAINEN, OSSI. Synchronic variation and linguistic change: evidence from British English dialects. *In* (pp. 61–72) **41.**

1060. KILLIAN, PATRICIA ANNE. English in Ireland: an attitudinal study. *See* **902.**

1061. KIM, KI-HONG. Expression of emotion between Americans and Koreans. CAE (19) 27–39.

1062. LEITNER, GERHARD. Gesprächsanalyse und Rundfunk-kommunikation: die Struktur englischer 'phone-ins'. Hildesheim: Olms, 1983. pp. 223. Rev. by Alwin Fill in AAA (11) 119–20.

1063. LINNARUD, MOIRA. Lexis in composition: a performance analysis of Swedish learners' written English. Malmö: Liber/Gleerup. pp. ix, 135. (Lund studies in English, 74.) (Doct. diss., Lund Univ.) Rev. by Hans Andersson in MS (80) 157–9.

1064. McHOUL, A. W. How texts talk: essay on reading and ethnomethodology. London; Boston, MA; Henley: Routledge & Kegan Paul, 1982. pp. xxii, 63. (International library of phenomenology and moral sciences.) Rev. by David Birch in MLR (81:1) 155–7.

1065. McKENNA, SHEILA CATHARINE. Ethnocultural differences in the use of spatial prepositions. Unpub. doct. diss., Columbia Univ., 1985. [Abstr. in DA (46) 2217A–18A.]

1066. MISHRA, ARPITA. Towards an analysis of conversation management: a cross-cultural perspective. *See* **1012.**

1067. MULLER, KURT E. Language competence: implications for national security. New York; London: Praeger. pp. xiii, 168. (Washington papers, 119.)

1068. NEU, JOYCE. A multivariate sociolinguistic analysis of the speech event negotiation. *See* **1015.**

1069. NEWALL, VENETIA. Folklore and male homosexuality. *See* **1016.**

1070. NILSEN, DON L. F. 'T'aint funny, McGee': the humor of put-downs and rejoinders. MFR (19:1) 1985, 37–44.

1071. O'DWYER, B. T. A study of attitudes, with specific reference to language attitudes among three Newfoundland dialects. *See* **874.**

1072. PARK, JONG-HO. Some linguistic and cultural differences between the Americans and the Koreans. Unpub. doct. diss., Hankuk Univ. of Foreign Studies, Seoul.

1073. Santraud, Jeanne-Marie; Saporta, Marc. Introduction à une étude du biculturalisme. *In* (pp. 3–10) **5.**

1074. —— (ed.). Les aspects littéraires du biculturalisme aux États-Unis. *See* **5.**

1075. Sebba, Mark; Tate, Shirley. You know what I mean: agreement marking in British black English. *See* **971.**

1076. Shuman, Amy. Storytelling rights: the uses of oral and written texts by urban adolescents. Cambridge: CUP. pp. ix, 227. (Cambridge studies in oral and literate culture, 11.)

1077. Vachek, Josef. An emotionally conditioned split of some personal names. *In* (pp. 693–700) **26.**

1078. Wale, William Martin. The interaction of an adult non-native speaker with adult and child native speakers: a naturalistic study. Unpub. doct. diss., Univ. of Texas at Austin, 1985. [Abstr. in DA (46) 3021A.]

1079. West, Thomas. Culture, cultures and bi-culturalism. *In* (pp. 159–69) **5.**

DISCOURSE ANALYSIS

1080. Aijmer, Karin.   Why is 'actually' so popular in spoken English? *In* (pp. 119–29) **16.**

1081. Barton, Ellen Lynn.   A theory of constituent structures and constituent utterances. Unpub. doct. diss., Northwestern Univ., 1985. [Abstr. in DA (46) 3334A.]

1082. Bateman, J. A.   Utterances in context: towards a systemic theory of the intersubjective achievement of discourse. Unpub. doct. diss., Univ. of Edinburgh. [Abstr. in IT (36) 902.]

1083. Biber, Douglas.   On the investigation of spoken/written differences. SL (40:1) 1–21.

1084. —— Spoken and written textual dimensions in English: resolving the contradictory findings. Lang (62:2) 384–414.

1085. Borders-Simmons, Denise Glyn.   Contextual variability and communicative competence: reference and cohesion strategies in narrative discourse by black working-class children. *See* **1046.**

1086. Borsch, Peter.   Agreement and anaphora: a study of the role of pronouns in syntax and discourse. New York: Academic Press, 1983. (Cf. bibl. 1985, 900.) Rev. by Margaret Stong-Jensen in CJL (31:4) 367–71.

1087. Boucher, Paul.   Time–space markers in oral discourse in English. *In* (pp. 235–46) **1.**

1088. Breivik, Leiv Egil.   Some remarks on cleft sentences in present-day English. *In* (pp. 815–26) **26.**

1089. Briscoe, E. J.   Towards an understanding of spoken sentence comprehension: the interactive determinism hypothesis. Unpub. doct. diss., Univ. of Cambridge, 1984. [Abstr. in IT (35) 534.]

1090. Brown, Gillian; Yule, George.   Discourse analysis. (Bibl. 1985, 902.) Rev. by Kay Wikberg in SL (40) 96–8.

1091. Buxton, H.   Rhythm and stress in speech. Unpub. doct. diss., Univ. of Cambridge, 1984.

1092. Carlson, Lauri.   Dialogue games: an approach to discourse analysis. Dordrecht: Reidel, 1983. (Cf. bibl. 1983, 821.) Rev. by László Imre Komlósi and László Tarnay in Journal of Pragmatics (10:2) 211–26.

1093. —— 'Well' in dialogue games: a discourse analysis of the interjection 'well' in idealized conversations. Amsterdam; Philadelphia, PA: Benjamins, 1984. pp. vii, 104. (Pragmatics and beyond, 5:5.)

1094. Chen, Ping.   Discourse and particle movement in English. SL (10:2) 79–95.

1095. Cook, Guy.   Problems and solutions in the transcription of context for discourse analysis. RANAM (19) 113–30.

1096. Cooper, Robin.   Tense and discourse location in situation semantics. Linguistics and Philosophy (9:1) 17–36.

1097. Coulthard, Malcolm.   An introduction to discourse analysis. (Bibl. 1977, 752.) London: Longman. pp. 224. (Applied linguistics and language study.) (Second ed.: first ed., 1977.)

1098. CROMBIE, WINIFRED.　Process and relation in discourse and language learning. Oxford: OUP, 1985. pp. xvii, 150.

1099. DE RYCKER, TEUN.　Imperative structures: form and function in conversational English. Antwerp: Universitaire Instelling, 1984. pp. 147.

1100. ERDMANN, PETER.　A note on reverse *wh*-clefts in English. *In* (pp. 851–8) **26.**

1101. EVANS, DAVID A.　Situations and speech acts: towards a formal semantics of discourse. New York; London: Garland, 1985. pp. vii, 211. (Outstanding dissertations in linguistics.) (Cf. bibl. 1982, 1027.)

1102. FIRBAS, JAN.　On the dynamics of written communication in the light of the theory of functional sentence perspective. *In* (pp. 40–71) CHARLES R. COOPER and SIDNEY GREENBAUM (eds), Studying writing: linguistic approaches. Beverly Hills, CA; London; New Delhi: Sage Pubs. pp. 272. (Written Communication Annual, 1.)

1103. FORNER, MONIKA.　My teacher in my house: discourse and syntax in caretaker–child interactions. Unpub. doct. diss., Univ. of Minnesota, 1985. [Abstr. in DA (46) 1921A.]

1104. GÜLICH, ELIZABETH; QUASTHOFF, UTA M.　Story-telling in conversation: cognitive and interactive aspects. Poetics (15:1/2) 217–41.

1105. HALLIDAY, M. A. K.　Linguistics in the university: the question of social accountability. *In* (pp. 51–67) **38.**

1106. HAMON, PHILIPPE.　Introduction à l'analyse du descriptif. Paris: Hachette, 1981. pp. 268. Rev. by Ross Chambers in RLC (58:3) 351–3.

1107. HARLEY, T. A.　Speech errors and models of planning discourse. Unpub. doct. diss., Univ. of Cambridge. [Abstr. in IT (36) 16.]

1108. HASAN, RUQAIYA (ed.).　Discourse on discourse: workshop reports from the Macquarie Workshop on Discourse Analysis, Feb. 21–25, 1983. Brisbane: Applied Linguistics Assn of Australia, 1985. pp. 112. (Occasional papers, 7.)

1109. HINRICHS, ERHARD.　Temporal anaphora in discourses of English. Linguistics and Philosophy (9:1) 63–82.

1110. HORVATH, JULIA; ROCHEMONT, MICHAEL.　Pronouns in discourse and sentence grammar. LI (17:4) 759–66.

1111. HWANG, SHICK-MO.　Oryu bunsuk e daehan jaego. (Some thoughts on error analysis.) JHY (7:3) 1985, 497–514.

1112. KIM, TAE-OK.　Si eui hyeongsanghwa gwajung gwa discourse analysis. (Poetic processes and discourse analysis.) JELL (31:4) 1985, 677–97.

1113. KOMLÓSI, LÁSZLÓ IMRE; TARNAY, LÁSZLÓ.　On Carlson's dialogue games. Journal of Pragmatics (10:2) 211–25 (review-article).

1114. LEITNER, GERHARD.　Gesprächsanalyse und Rundfunkkommunikation: die Struktur englischer 'phone-ins'. *See* **1062.**

1115. LINDE, CHARLOTTE.　Private stories in public discourse: narrative analysis in the social sciences. Poetics (15:1/2) 183–202.

1116. LONGACRE, ROBERT E.　Reshaping linguistics: context and content. *In* (pp. 79–95) **38.**

1117. MACDONELL, DIANE.   Theories of discourse: an introduction. Oxford: Blackwell. pp. 205.

1118. MALCOLM, KAREN RAE.   The dynamics of casual conversation: from the perspective of communication linguistics. Unpub. doct. diss., York Univ. Ont., 1985. [Abstr. in DA (46) 2282A.]

1119. MISHRA, ARPITA.   Towards an analysis of conversation management: a cross-cultural perspective. *See* **1012.**

1120. MODINI, PAUL.   A functional perspective on language. PP (29) 211–14.

1121. MOESCHLER, JACQUES.   Answers to questions about questions and answers. Journal of Pragmatics (10:2) 238–48 (review-article).

1122. MURRAY, D. K. C.   Language and interests. Unpub. doct. diss., Univ. of London, University Coll., 1985. [Abstr. in IT (35) 537.]

1123. MYERS, TERRY; BROWN, KEITH; McGONIGLE, BRENDAN (eds). Reasoning and discourse process. London: Academic Press. pp. xii, 295. (Cognitive science series.)

1124. NERBONNE, JOHN.   Reference time and time in narration. Linguistics and Philosophy (9:1) 83–95.

1125. NEVALAINEN, TERTTU.   Lexical variation of EModE exclusive adverbs: style switching or a change in progress?? *In* (pp. 179–94) **41.**

1126. —— RISSANEN, MATTI.   Do you support the *do*-support? Emphatic and non-emphatic *do* in affirmative statements in present-day spoken English. *In* (pp. 35–50) **43.**

1127. PEARSON, ELOISE.   Agreement/disagreement: an example of results of discourse analysis applied to the oral English classroom. ITL (74) 47–61.

1128. PETTINARI, CATHERINE JOHNSON.   Medical action into surgical text: a discourse analysis of the production and acquisition of a particular genre. Unpub. doct. diss., Univ. of Michigan, 1985. [Abstr. in DA (46) 3338A.]

1129. PICA, TERESA; DOUGHTY, CATHERINE; YOUNG, RICHARD. Making input comprehensible: do interactional modifications help? ITL (72) 1–25.

1130. PILCH, HERBERT.   The tag syntagm of spoken English. *In* (pp. 983–91) **26.**

1131. RAATH, J.; VAN DER WALT, P. J.; WEIDEMAN, A. J.   Continuity and discontinuity in talk: some brief notes on summonses. SA Tydskrif vir Taalkunde/SA Journal of Linguistics (4:4) 90–100.

1132. RENOUF, ANTOINETTE.   The elicitation of spoken English. *In* (pp. 177–97) **16.**

1133. ROOT, REBECCA LOUISE.   The semantics of anaphora in discourse. Unpub. doct. diss., Univ. of Texas at Austin. [Abstr. in DA (47) 1716A.]

1134. SCHIFFRIN, DEBORAH.   Functions of 'and' in discourse. Journal of Pragmatics (10:1) 41–66.

1135. SCHULZE, RAINER.   Strategic indeterminacy and face-work. SAP (19) 75–89.

1136. STEIN, DIETER. Discourse markers in Early Modern English. *In* (pp. 283–302) **41.**

1137. STOCKWELL, ROBERT P. Grammar as speaker's knowledge versus grammar as linguists' characterization of norms. *In* (pp. 125–33) **26.**

1138. STUBBS, MICHAEL. Discourse analysis: the sociolinguistic analysis of natural language. Chicago: Chicago UP, 1983. (Bibl. 1985, 919.) Rev. by Joseph F. Kess in CJL (31:1) 98–102.

1139. TOMLIN, RUSSELL S. The identification of foreground–background information in on-line oral descriptive discourse. PL (19:4) 465–94.

1140. TOTTIE, GUNNEL; BÄCKLUND, INGEGERD (eds). English in speech and writing: a symposium. *See* **16.**

1141. TRAPPES-LOMAX, H. R. N. Discourse, nominality and reference: a study in applied linguistics. Unpub. doct. diss., Univ. of Edinburgh, 1984.

1142. TROSBORG, ANNA. Apology strategies in native/non-native speakers of English. Dolphin (13) 44–64.

1143. —— Communicative competence. Dolphin (13) 7–17.

1144. VAN DIJK, TEUN A.; KINTSCH, WALTER. Strategies of discourse comprehension. (Bibl. 1985, 921.) Rev. by Hans Reichgelt in Journal of Semantics (4:3) 1985, 275–8.

1145. —— (ed.). Handbook of discourse analysis: vol. 1, Disciplines of discourse; vol. 2, Dimensions of discourse; vol. 3, Discourse and dialogue; vol. 4, Discourse analysis in society. Orlando, FL: Academic Press, 1985. pp. xvii, 302; xvii, 279; xix, 251; xvii, 228. Rev. by Joseph F. Kess in CJL (31:4) 386–96.

1146. VENTER, S. F.; WEIDEMAN, A. J. A measure of texture: cohesion in English drama dialogue and actual conversation. SA Tydskrif vir Taalkunde/SA Journal of Linguistics (4:2) 87–105.

1147. VENTOLA, EIJA. Text analysis in operation: a multilevel approach. Pubs of the Dept of English, Univ. of Turku (7) 1985, 329–57.

1148. VIITANEN, OUTI. On the position of 'only' in English conversation. *In* (pp. 165–75) **16.**

1149. WARNER, RICHARD G. Discourse connectives in English. New York; London: Garland, 1985. pp. vii, 193. (Outstanding dissertations in linguistics.) (Cf. bibl. 1980, 2229.)

1150. WATTS, RICHARD J. Relevance in conversational moves: a reappraisal of *well.* SAP (19) 37–59.

1151. WILLIS, J. D. The implications of discourse analysis for the teaching of oral communication. Unpub. doct. diss., Univ. of Birmingham, 1983/84.

1152. WIRTH, JESSICA R. (ed.). Beyond the sentence: discourse and sentential form. Ann Arbor, MI: Karoma, 1985. pp. viii, 144. Rev. by Gary D. Prideaux in CJL (31:2) 185–9.

1153. YOUNG, LYNNE. Static and dynamic discourse structure: an analysis within the framework of communication linguistics. ITL (72) 27–51.

STYLISTICS

STYLISTICS OF NON-LITERARY TEXTS

1154. ALEXANDER, RICHARD J.   Article headings in *The Economist*: an analysis of puns, allusions and metaphors. *See* **551.**

1155. ANSON, STAN.   Tabloid metaphor and broadsheet metonymy. SoRA (19:3) 250–67.

1156. ANTCZAK, FREDERICK J.   Thought and character: the rhetoric of democratic education. Ames: Iowa State UP, 1985. pp. viii, 242. Rev. by Donald M. Scott in JAH (73:2) 446–7.

1157. BETZ, RENEE REBETA.   A rhetorical community: a case study of 500 memoranda written by executives at a multi-national company. Unpub. doct. diss., Univ. of Illinois at Chicago. [Abstr. in DA (47) 890A.]

1158. BIBER, DOUGLAS.   Spoken and written textual dimensions in English: resolving the contradictory findings. *See* **1084.**

1159. BRUHN-JENSEN, KLAUS.   Making sense of the news: towards a theory and an empirical model of reception for the study of mass communication. Århus: Århus UP. pp. 392.

1160. ENKVIST, NILS ERIK.   Coherence, composition, and text linguistics. In (pp. 11–26) NILS ERIK ENKVIST (ed.), Coherence and composition: a symposium. Åbo: Åbo Akademi, 1985. pp. 134. (Meddelanden från Stiftelsen för Åbo Akademi forskningsinstitut, 101.)

1161. GARCIA, CARMEN MARIA.   Stylistic strategies in native and non-native English: how Venezuelans and Americans disagree, request and promise. Unpub. doct. diss., Georgetown Univ., 1985. [Abstr. in DA (46) 3705A.]

1162. GEIS, MICHAEL L.   The language of television advertising. (Bibl. 1983, 852.) Rev. by Eirlys E. Davies in Lingua (68:2/3) 257–63.

1163. GOODWIN, DAVID GORDON.   The rhetoric of British rhetorical handbooks (1758–1828) and Romantic modes of English epic poetry. Unpub. doct. diss., Univ. of Toronto. [Abstr. in DA (47) 2168A.]

1164. GOOSSENS, LOUIS.   What's in an advertising name? *In* (pp. 95–102) **12.**

1165. GRECIANO, GERTRUD.   Les 'opérations enfouies' du codage idiomatique. RANAM (19) 179–94.

1166. GREEN, JONATHON.   The slang thesaurus. London: Elm Tree. pp. xiv, 280. Rev. by Anthony Burgess in TLS, 5 Dec., 1373.

1167. HALLIDAY, M. A. K.   Linguistics in the university: the question of social accountability. *In* (pp. 51–67) **38.**

1168. HAMP, ERIC P.   Subject matter entails speech situation and style. PP (29) 109–10.

1169. HILTUNEN, RISTO.   On the syntax of sentence and clause in legal English. Pubs of the Dept of English, Univ. of Turku (7) 1985, 47–63.

1170. JAPP, PHYLLIS M.   Rhetoric and time: dimensions of temporality in theory and criticism. Unpub. doct. diss., Univ. of Nebraska–Lincoln. [Abstr. in DA (47) 1925A.]

1171. JOHANSSON, STIG.   Some observations on word frequencies in three corpora of present-day English texts. ITL (67/68) 1985, 117–26.

1172. KAHN, JOHN ELLISON (ed.).   The right word at the right time: a guide to the English language and how to use it. London; New York; Montreal: Readers Digest Assn, 1985. pp. 688.

1173. KEENE, NADENE ANN.   Male/female language: a stylistic analysis of freshman compositions. Unpub. doct. diss., Illinois State Univ., 1985. [Abstr. in DA (47) 451A.]

1174. KELLER, ROBERT H.   Hostile language: bias in historical writing about American Indian resistance. See **1007.**

1175. KELLY, D. ST L.   Legislative drafting and plain English. Adelaide Law Review (10:4) 409–26.

1176. KITMAN, MARVIN.   Blurring the type. NewL (69:6) 20–1.

1177. KOŠUKOVÁ, VIERA.   O niektorých charakteristických rysoch vojenskej odbornej terminológie v anglijskom jazyku. (On some characteristic features of [specialist] military terminology in English.) CJa (29) 255–8.

1178. LEHTO, LEENA.   Methodological aspects of legal translation. Pubs of the Dept of English, Univ. of Turku (7) 1985, 147–76.

1179. LEISI, ERNST.   Zum Thema sozio-kulturelle Semantik. See **1009.**

1180. LEISS, WILLIAM; KLINE, STEPHEN; JHALLY, SUT.   Social communication in advertising: persons, products and images of well-being. London: Methuen. pp. 327. Rev. by Jay Rosen in Listener, 27 Nov., 28–9.

1181. LEITNER, GERHARD.   Gesprächsanalyse und Rundfunkkommunikation: die Struktur englischer 'phone-ins'. See **1062.**

1182. LO BELLO, NINO.   Fractured English. English Usage (17:1) 16–22.

1183. McCORMACK, PEGGY.   The semiotics of economic language in James's fiction. AL (58:4) 540–56.

1184. McCRUM, ROBERT.   The English language: 1, The chaos of the ether; 2, Symptoms of the slang contagion; 3, The tract of corruption. See **823.**

1185. McKINLAY, JANE.   The writing of scholarly medical discussions. Pubs of the Dept of English, Univ. of Turku (7) 1985, 205–17.

1186. MORAN, MICHAEL G.; LUNSFORD, RONALD F.   Research in composition and rhetoric: a bibliographic sourcebook. See **505.**

1187. MURPHY, JAMES J. (ed.).   Renaissance eloquence: studies in the theory and practice of Renaissance rhetoric. (Bibl. 1985, 3549.) Rev. by David Marsh in JMH (58:1) 270–2.

1188. NELSON, JOHN S.; MEGILL, ALLAN.   Rhetoric of inquiry: projects and prospects. QJS (72:1) 20–37.

1189. NOËL, DIRK.   Towards a functional characterization of the news of the BBC World Service. Antwerp: Universitaire Instelling. pp. 236. (Antwerp Papers in Linguistics, 49.)

1190. OKBY, MAKMUD M.   Grammatical tension balancing and the

communicability of individual style: an interdisciplinary perspective.
FL (19:3/4) 1985, 499–522.

1191. PAPROTTÉ, WOLF; DIRVEN, RENÉ (eds).   The ubiquity of
metaphor: metaphor in language and thought. Amsterdam; Philadelphia, PA: Benjamins, 1985. pp. xix, 628. (Amsterdam studies in the
theory and history of linguistic science, 4.) (Current issues in linguistic
theory, 29.)

1192. PERKINS, C. D.   The language of the media: a critical and
stylistic analysis of some of the varieties and registers of English used in
the media. Unpub. doct. diss., Univ. of Wales, UWIST, 1983.

1193. PETERSON, SUSAN LYNN.   Sex-based differences in English
argumentative text; a tagmemic sociolinguistic perspective. *See* **849.**

1194. PUCI, JÁN.   K niektorým charakteristickým rysom termínu.
(On certain characteristic features of the technical term.) CJa (29)
208–11.

1195. RALEY, PATTI L.; MURRAY, THOMAS E.   The language of
handspinning. *See* **877.**

1196. REID, CHRISTOPHER.   Edmund Burke and the practice of
political writing. New York: St Martin's Press, 1985. (Cf. bibl. 1985,
1017.)

1197. ROY, SHARON SEILER.   Stylistic variation in the writing of a
group of computer professionals addressing different audiences. Unpub.
doct. diss., State Univ. of New York at Albany. [Abstr. in DA (47)
1310A.]

1198. SCHENKEL, DANIEL.   Are readability formulas reliable? Brussels
Preprints in Linguistics (8) 1983, 89–100.

1199. SIMPSON, DAVID.   The politics of American English, 1776–1850.
See **879.**

1200. SIPIORA, PHILLIP JOHN.   The rhetoric of ethnologic in Darwin,
Marx and Freud. Unpub. doct. diss., Univ. of Texas at Austin, 1985.
[Abstr. in DA (47) 523A.]

1201. SNELLINGS, COURTENAY MEADE.   A linguistic analysis of various verbal strategies in cross-examination. Unpub. doct. diss., Univ. of
Michigan, 1985. [Abstr. in DA (46) 3339A.]

1202. THOVERON, GABRIEL.   Quality/popular: intraduisibles en français? *In* (pp. 79–84) **12.**

1203. UFFEN, ELLEN SERLEN.   The rhetoric of rhetoric. CEAF
(16:2/3) 4–5.

1204. VANDENBERGEN, ANNE-MARIE.   Conjunction and continuity in
newspaper reports. *In* (pp. 85–94) **12.**

1205. VAN NOPPEN, J.-P.; DE JONGEN, R.   Metaphor – a bibliography
of post 1970 publications. Amsterdam; Philadelphia, PA: Benjamins,
1985. pp. x, 497. (Amsterdam studies in the theory and history of
linguistic science, 5.) (Library and information sources in linguistics,
17.)

1206. VAN NOPPEN, JEAN-PIERRE.   In and beyond the glossary, or on
making maps out of puzzles. *In* (pp. 165–74) **12.**

1207. —— Misreadings in theographic communication. Brussels Preprints in Linguistics (8) 1983, 71–88.

1208. van Peer, Willie. Stylistics and psychology: investigations of foregrounding. London: Croom Helm. pp. 220.

1209. Van Remortel, Marijke. Literalness and metaphorization: the case of 'turn'. Antwerp: Universitaire Instelling. pp. 130. (Antwerp papers in linguistics, 43.)

1210. Vick, Richard D. A comparison of selected stylistic features in technical and non-technical writing. Unpub. doct. diss., Drake Univ., 1985. [Abstr. in DA (47) 1717A.]

1211. Walter-Goldberg, Bettyruth. The jury summation as speech genre: an ethnographic study of what it means to those who use it. Unpub. doct. diss., Univ. of Pennsylvania, 1985. [Abstr. in DA (46) 3710A.]

1212. Young, Bob; Moody, Micky. The 'language of rock 'n' roll'. London: Sidgwick & Jackson, 1985. pp. 175.

LITERARY STYLISTICS AND POETICS

1213. Amos, Ashley Crandell. Linguistic means of determining the dates of Old English literary texts. (Bibl. 1985, 955.) Rev. by Thomas Cable in JEGP (85:1) 93–5.

1214. Azuike, M. N. Style, context and the written text: a linguistic examination of written English in Nigeria today. Unpub. doct. diss., Univ. of Exeter, 1984.

1215. Biber, Douglas. On the investigation of spoken/written differences. *See* **1083.**

1216. Cole, Roger W. Literary representation of dialect: a theoretical approach to the artistic problem. *See* **857.**

1217. Cousins, A. D. Oldham in defence of the Restoration: *Satires upon the Jesuits*. NM (87:1) 144–51.

1218. Cronan, Dennis. Alliterative rank in Old English poetry. SN (58:2) 145–58.

1219. Dewey, Patrick R. Interactive fiction: a checklist. *See* **525.**

1220. Dudman, V. H. Towards a theory of predication for English. Australian Journal of Linguistics (5:2) 1985, 143–96.

1221. Enkvist, Nils Erik. Coherence, composition, and text linguistics. *See* **1160.**

1222. Firbas, Jan. A case-study in the dynamics of written communication. *In* (pp. 859–76) **26.**

1223. Frieden, Ken. Genius and monologue. Ithaca, NY; London: Cornell UP, 1985. pp. 211.

1224. Götz, Dieter. Idioms and real texts. AAA (11:1) 83–93.

1225. Halliday, M. A. K. Linguistics in the university: the question of social accountability. *In* (pp. 51–67) **38.**

1226. Hussey, S. S. The literary language of Shakespeare. (Bibl. 1983, 1298.) Rev. by Jürgen Schäfer in MLR (81:4) 985–6.

1227. Ito, Hiroyuki. The language of *The Spectator*: as seen in the movement of English prose towards the rise of the novel. *See* **625.**

1228. KIM, TAE-OK. Munhak maeje rosuh eui eoneo: munhak text eui giho eoneohakjeok gochal. (Language as materials of literature: a semiolinguistic approach to the literary text.) JELL (32:4) 909–32.

1229. KRÁMSKÝ, JIŘÍ. The frequency of occurrence of personal pronouns in the style of fiction in modern English. Prague Studies in English (18) 1984, 37–45.

1230. —— Stylostatistical investigation of personal pronouns in modern English. SAP (18) 153–76.

1231. KRISTEVA, JULIA. Revolution in poetic language. (Bibl. 1985, 998.) Rev. by Donald Morton in WHR (40:1) 91–7.

1232. LEVERENZ, DAVID. The politics of Emerson's man-making words. PMLA (101:1) 38–56.

1233. MAHMOUD, MOHAMED A. W. A stylistic, sociolinguistic, and discourse analysis of linguistic naturalism in selected plays of Arthur Miller and Eugene O'Neill. Unpub. doct. diss., Univ. of Delaware, 1985. [Abstr. in DA (46) 3337A.]

1234. MATHIS, GILLES. Rhétorique(s) et stylistique(s). *In* (pp. 505–30) **1**.

1235. MONELL, SIV. The molecule strategy: a study of the description of character in *The Rainbow* by D. H. Lawrence. *In* (pp. 75–87) **43**.

1236. NEVALAINEN, TERTTU. Lexical variation of EModE exclusive adverbs: style switching or a change in progress? *In* (pp. 179–94) **41**.

1237. NEVANLINNA, SAARA. Variation in the syntactic structure of simile in OE prose. *In* (pp. 89–98) **43**.

1238. NOGUCHI, REI R. Linguistic description and literary interpretation. CLAJ (30:2) 171–83.

1239. PINTO, JULIO CÉSAR MACHADO. Temporal relations in the narrative: a semantico-semiotic approach. Unpub. doct. diss., Univ. of North Carolina at Chapel Hill, 1985. [Abstr. in DA (46) 3342A.]

1240. PLETT, HEINRICH F. Englische Rhetorik und Poetik 1479–1660. Eine systematische Bibliographie. Opladen: Westdeutscher, 1985. pp. xi, 456. (Forschungsberichte des Landes Nordrhein-Westfalen, 3201.) Rev. by Norbert Bachleitner in Spr (17) 309–11.

1241. RICHMAN, GERALD. Artful slipping in Old English. *See* **833**.

1242. ROSCOW, G. H. Syntax and style in Chaucer's poetry. (Bibl. 1984, 1112.) Rev. by Manfred Markus in Archiv (223:2) 394–8.

1243. SEIDEL, KATHRYN LEE. Emblems of anxiety: similes in *Huckleberry Finn*. Pubs of the Dept of English, Univ. of Turku (6) 1985, 131–44.

1244. SØRENSEN, KNUD. Charles Dickens, linguistic innovator. Århus: Arkona, 1985. pp. 176. (Acta Jutlandica, 61: Humanistisk ser., 58.) Rev. by K. C. Phillipps in EngS (67:3) 276–7.

1245. STANKIEWICZ, EDWARD. Linguistics, poetics, and the literary genres. *In* (pp. 155–78) **38**.

1246. STRAUCH, GÉRARD. Monologue intérieur et style indirect libre. *In* (pp. 531–53) **1**.

1247. TAMMI, PEKKA. Problems of Nabokov's poetics: a narratological analysis. Helsinki: Suomalainen Tiedeakatemia, 1985. pp. x, 390. (Annales Academiae Scientiarum Fennicae, ser. B, 231.) (Doct. diss.)

1248. van Noppen, J.-P.; de Jongen, R.   Metaphor – a bibliography of post 1970 publications. *See* **1207.**

1249. Wade, Sidney.   An analysis of the similes and their function in the characterization of the Green Knight. NM (87:3) 375–81.

1250. Wodak, Ruth.   Tales from the Vienna woods: sociolinguistic and psycholinguistic considerations of narrative analysis. Poetics (15:1/2) 153–82.

1251. Yu, Sung-Gon.   A linguistics analysis of poetic style with special reference to Emily Dickinson's poetry. Unpub. doct. diss., Hankuk Univ. of Foreign Studies (Seoul).

PSYCHOLOGY OF LANGUAGE

SOCIAL PSYCHOLOGY OF LANGUAGE

1252. BRISCOE, E. J.   Towards an understanding of spoken sentence comprehension: the interactive determinism hypothesis. *See* **1089.**

1253. COATES, JENNIFER.   Women, men, and language: a sociolinguistic account of sex differences in language. *See* **990.**

1254. COTTER, C. A.   Inference making processes in reading. Unpub. doct. diss., Univ. of Cambridge, 1983.

1255. FIRBAS, JAN.   On the dynamics of written communication in the light of the theory of functional sentence perspective. *See* **1102.**

1256. GILES, HOWARD; ST CLAIR, ROBERT N. (eds).   Recent advances in language, communication and social psychology. London: Erlbaum, 1985. pp. 303.

1257. KITTO, J. E.   Gender reference terms: a psychological perspective. Unpub. doct. diss., Univ. of Reading, 1985. [Abstr. in IT (35) 1487.]

1258. KNIGHT, STEPHEN; MUKHERJEE, S. N. (eds).   Words and worlds: studies in the social role of verbal culture. *See* **1008.**

1259. LANGUAGE AND GENDER WORKING PARTY.   Alice in genderland: reflections on language, power and control. Sheffield National Assn for the Teaching of English, 1985. pp. 108.

1260. NEU, JOYCE.   A multivariate sociolinguistic analysis of the speech event negotiation. *See* **1015.**

1261. OWEN, MARION.   Apologies and remedial interchanges: a study of language use in social interaction. (Bibl. 1985, 1037.) Rev. by Gaelan Dodds de Wolf in CJL (31:1) 86–7.

1262. REICHGELT, J. P. M.   Reference and quantification in the cognitive view of language. Unpub. doct. diss., Univ. of Edinburgh. [Abstr. in IT (36) 906.]

PSYCHOLINGUISTICS

1263. AITCHISON, JEAN.   The articulate mammal: an introduction to psycholinguistics. (Bibl. 1983, 798.) Rev. by Jelena Hlavsová in CJa (29) 225–6.

1264. BAŃCZEROWSKI, JERZY.   Glottotronics: an inevitable phase of linguistics (linguistic science fiction?). *In* (pp. 11–25) **26.**

1265. BAUM, SHARI R.   Syntactic processing in aphasia. Unpub. doct. diss., Brown Univ. [Abstr. in DA (47) 1712A.]

1266. BEHRENS, SUSAN JANET.   The role of the right hemisphere in the production of linguistic prosody: an acoustic analysis. Unpub. doct. diss., Brown Univ. [Abstr. in DA (47) 1712A.]

1267. BERGH, GUNNAR.   The neuropsychological status of Swedish–English subsidiary bilinguals. *See* **1045.**

1268. CHAFE, WALLACE.   Beyond Bartlett: narratives and remembering. Poetics (15:1/2) 139–51.

1269. CLOITRE, MARYLENE.   The effect of kind of anaphor on the accessibility of antecedent information. Unpub. doct. diss., Columbia Univ., 1985. [Abstr. in DA (47) 165A.]

1270. Cook, J. D.   The automatic encoding of meaning. Unpub. doct. diss., Univ. of Exeter, 1983.

1271. de Houwer, Annick.   Some features of the verb phrase in the speech of a three-year-old bilingual. Brussels Preprints in Linguistics (Special issue: *Linguistics in Belgium,* 7) 1985, 45–66.

1272. Donaldson, Morag L.   Children's explanations: a psycholinguistic study. Cambridge: CUP. pp. vii, 325.

1273. Ellis, Andrew W.; Beattie, Geoffrey.   The psychology of language and communication. London: Weidenfeld & Nicolson. pp. ix, 374. (Weidenfeld modern psychology.)

1274. Freeman, David Edward.   Use of pragmatic cohesion cues to resolve degrees of pronoun reference ambiguity in reading. Unpub. doct. diss., Univ. of Arizona. [Abstr. in DA (47) 1306A.]

1275. Garnham, Alan.   Psycholinguistics: central topics. London: Methuen, 1985. pp. 320.

1276. Harris, Margaret; Coltheart, Max.   Language processing in children and adults: an introduction. London: Routledge & Kegan Paul. pp. viii, 274.

1277. Hormann, Hans.; Innis, Robert E.   Meaning and context: an introduction to the psychology of language. Ed. by Robert E. Innis. New York; London: Plenum. pp. xiv, 294. (Cognition and language.)

1278. Hultfors, Pär.   Reactions to non-native English: native English-speakers' assessments of errors in the use of English made by non-native users of the language: 1. Acceptability and intelligibility. *See* **1058.**

1279. Klégr, Aleš.   Ke vztahu koordinace a asociace. (On coordination and association.) *In* (pp. 18–22) **24.**

1280. Lee, Soon-Sung.   The psycholinguistic nature of the reading process. ET (31) Feb., 199–212.

1281. Lewandowska, Barbara.   Cognitive basis for dynamic semantics. SAP (19) 107–17.

1282. McGregor, Graham (ed.).   Language for hearers. Oxford: Pergamon Press. pp. vii, 235. (Language and communication library, 8.)

1283. Matthews, Alison.   Pronoun resolution in two-clause sentences. Unpub. doct. diss., City Univ. of New York. [Abstr. in DA (47) 1308A.]

1284. Moyne, John A.   Understanding language: man or machine? *See* **543.**

1285. Paprotté, Wolf; Dirven, René (eds).   The ubiquity of metaphor: metaphor in language and thought. *See* **1191.**

1286. Rosenbaum, Bent; Sonne, Harly.   The language of psychosis. New York; London: New York UP. pp. xii, 141. (Psychoanalytic crosscurrents.)

1287. Shuman, Amy.   Storytelling rights: the uses of oral and written texts by urban adolescents. *See* **1076.**

1288. SPERBER, DAN; WILSON, DEIRDRE. Relevance: communication and cognition. Oxford: Blackwell. pp. viii, 279. Rev. by Paloma Tejada in RCEI (12) 183–4.

1289. TIRKKONEN-CONDIT, SONJA. Empirical studies in translation: textlinguistic and psycholinguistic perspectives. Joensuu, Finland: Univ. of Joensuu. pp. 61. (Faculty of Arts, studies in languages, 8.)

1290. TOMMOLA, JORMA. Measuring expectations in intensive listening. Pubs of the Dept of English, Univ. of Turku (7) 1985, 287–300.

1291. VANDERPLANK, ROBERT. Isochrony and intelligibility: two experiments on the perception of stress and rhythm and its role in understanding connected speech. Pubs of the Dept of English, Univ. of Turku (7) 1985, 301–28.

1292. WANG, WILLIAM S. Y. (introd.). Language writing and the computer: readings from *Scientific American. See* **549.**

1293. WHITEHEAD, E. L. Pronoun interpretation in reading. Unpub. doct. diss., CNAA, 1983.

1294. WODAK, RUTH. Tales from the Vienna woods: sociolinguistic and psycholinguistic considerations of narrative analysis. *See* **1250.**

1295. ZOHRAB, P. D. Verb-phrase anaphora: linguistics or cognitive science? SL (10:2) 425–42.

1296. ZUENGLER, JANE ELLEN. The effect of induced and perceived expertise on the language performance of native and nonnative speakers. Unpub. doct. diss., Columbia Univ. Teachers College, 1985. [Abstr. in DA (46) 2683A.]

LANGUAGE ACQUISITION AND DEVELOPMENT

1297. ANISFELD, MOSHE. Language development from birth to three. Hillsdale, NJ; London: Erlbaum, 1984. pp. xiv, 293. Rev. by Paul Rapier in CJL (31:3) 298–300.

1298. BAETENS BEARDSMORE, HUGO. Medium and message orientated communication compared with the BICS/CALP theory in bilingual education. *In* (pp. 191–9) **12.**

1299. BAKER, CHARLOTTE PIERCE. Acquisition of /t,d/ deletion in vernacular black English: a study of head start preschoolers. *See* **1042.**

1300. BERWICK, ROBERT C. The acquisition of syntactic knowledge. Cambridge, MA; London: MIT Press, 1985. pp. xii, 368. (MIT Press series in artificial intelligence, 16.) Rev. by Geoffrey Underwood in THES (710) 24.

1301. —— WEINBURG, AMY S. The grammatical basis of linguistic performance: language use and language acquisition. (Bibl. 1985, 1064.) Rev. by Susanne Carroll in CJL (31:2) 163–71.

1302. BRENER, R. Y. Children's acquisition of the deictic meaning of the third person pronouns of English. Unpub. doct. diss., Univ. of Hull. [Abstr. in IT (36) 466.]

1303. BROOKS, ELLEN J. Learning to read and write: the role of language acquisition and aesthetic development: a resource book. Introd. by MORTON BOTEL. New York; London: Garland. pp. xiv, 157. (Garland reference library of social science, 278.)

1304. Butters, Lesley Enid.   Linguistic and pragmatic factors in the acquisition of text competence. Unpub. doct. diss., McGill Univ., 1985. [Abstr. in DA (46) 3334A.]

1305. Coberly, Mary Schramm.   Initial and final consonant preferences across languages, in babbling, and in children's early speech. Unpub. doct. diss., Univ. of Colorado at Boulder, 1985. [Abstr. in DA (46) 2280A.]

1306. Coulomb, Claude.   Du linguistique à l'extra-linguistique. RANAM (19) 33–48.

1307. Crombie, Winifred.   Process and relation in discourse and language learning. *See* **1098.**

1308. Cruttenden, Alan.   Language in infancy and childhood: a linguistic introduction to language acquisition. Manchester: Manchester UP, 1985. pp. xiv, 193. (Second ed.: first ed. 1979.)

1309. Crystal, David.   Listen to your child: a parent's guide to children's language. Harmondsworth: Penguin. pp. 240.

1310. Cziko, Gary A.   Testing the language bioprogram hypothesis: a review of children's acquisition of articles. Lang (62:4) 878–98.

1311. de Houwer, Annick.   Some features of the verb phrase in the speech of a three-year-old bilingual. *See* **1271.**

1312. Demers, Patricia (ed.).   The creating word: papers from an international conference on the learning and teaching of English in the 1980s. Basingstoke: Macmillan. pp. viii, 215.

1313. Desclés, Jean-Pierre.   Archétypes cognitifs et représentations linguistiques. RANAM (19) 101–11.

1314. Donaldson, Morag L.   Children's explanations: a psycholinguistic study. *See* **1272.**

1315. Dubos, Ulrika.   Le recours à l'extralinguistique dans l'explication grammaticale. RANAM (19) 81–100.

1316. Eckman, Fred R.; Bell, Lawrence H.; Nelson, Diane (eds). Universals of second language acquisition. Rowley, MA: Newbury House, 1984. pp. xiv, 150. Rev. by Jana Vizmuller-Zocco in CJL (31:2) 196–8.

1317. Fletcher, Paul; Garman, Michael (eds).   Language acquisition: studies in first language development. Cambridge: CUP. pp. 625. (Second ed.: first ed. 1979.)

1318. Forner, Monika.   My teacher in my house: discourse and syntax in caretaker–child interactions. *See* **1103.**

1319. Geens, Dirk.   Computers and language education: a case for cognitive learning. *See* **528.**

1320. Higginson, Roy Patrick.   Fixing: assimilation in language acquisition. Unpub. doct. diss., Washington State Univ., 1985. [Abstr. in DA (46) 3335A.]

1321. Hyams, Nina M.   Language acquisition and the theory of parameters. Dordrecht; Lancaster: Reidel. pp. xiii, 186. (Studies in theoretical psycholinguistics.)

1322. Johnson Mills, Yvonne Latetia.   A study of language dominance across domains in bilingual children. Unpub. doct. diss., Howard Univ., 1985. [Abstr. in DA (46) 3018A.]

1323. KENNY, DENISE MARIE. The transition from prelinguistic to linguistic vocalizations. Unpub. doct. diss., Columbia Univ. Teachers College. [Abstr. in DA (47) 2141A.]

1324. LEE, DAVID. Language, children and society: an introduction to linguistics and language development. Brighton: Harvester Press. pp. xii, 222.

1325. LEE, ERIC J. Subsystems in the interlanguage lexicon. Rapport d'activités de l'Institut de Phonétique (20) 1985, 45–55.

1326. LOWENTHAL, F.; VANDAMME, F. (eds). Pragmatics and education. New York; London: Plenum. pp. viii, 343. (Language and language acquisition.)

1327. MACDONALD, C. A. Children's use and understanding of modal expressions. Unpub. doct. diss., Univ. of Edinburgh, 1983.

1328. MORGAN, JAMES L. From simple input to complex grammar. Cambridge, MA; London: MIT Press. pp. xii, 223.

1329. NIGROSH, GALE HILARY. Audience in children's letter writing: a study of sociolinguistic development. *See* **1019.**

1330. NYNS, ROLAND. Some notes on comprehension, theory and practice. Rapport d'activités de l'Institut de Phonétique (20) 1985, 73–93.

1331. PAIRA-PEMBERTON, JEAN. Coco-talk: the proper study of mankind. RANAM (19) 131–46.

1332. PINKER, STEVEN. Language learnability and language development. Cambridge, MA; London: Harvard UP, 1984. pp. xi, 435. (Cognitive science, 7.)

1333. RANDALL, JANET H. Morphological structure and language acquisition. New York; London: Garland, 1985. pp. 240. (Outstanding dissertations in linguistics.) (Cf. bibl. 1983, 2093.)

1334. REICH, PETER A. Language development. Englewood Cliffs, NJ; London: Prentice-Hall. pp. xii, 387.

1335. ROMAINE, SUZANNE. Syntactic variation and the acquisition of strategies of relativization in the language of Edinburgh school children. *In* (pp. 19–33) **43.**

1336. SCRIVEN, KAREN. The process of language acquisition: an investigation of issues in syntactic and semantic development. Unpub. doct. diss., Univ. of Iowa, 1985. [Abstr. in DA (46) 3019A.]

1337. STAFFORD, LAURA LYNNE. A comparison of maternal conversational interaction with twin and singleton children: implications for language acquisition. Unpub. doct. diss., Univ. of Texas at Austin, 1985. [Abstr. in DA (47) 346A.]

1338. STAIANO, ANTHONY VINCENT. Explorations in modality: the acquisition of 'may', 'can', and auxiliary 'is'. Unpub. doct. diss., Univ. of Kansas, 1985. [Abstr. in DA (46) 3020A.]

1339. STEDMON, J. A. Children's problems with plural references. Unpub. doct. diss., Univ. of Bristol, 1983.

1340. UNDERWOOD, JOHN H.   Linguistics, computers and the language teacher: a communicative approach. *See* **548.**

1341. WATSON, F. L.   Word age-of-acquisition effects in lexical processing. Unpub. doct. diss., Univ. of Aberdeen, 1985. [Abstr. in IT (35) 538.]

1342. WATTS, RICHARD J.   Generated or degenerate? Two forms of linguistic competence. *In* (pp. 157–73) **26.**

1343. WELLS, GORDON.   Language development in the pre-school years. Cambridge: CUP, 1985. pp. 484. (Language at home and at school, 2.)

PRAGMATICS

PRAGMATICS AND SPEECH ACT THEORY

1344. ATKINSON, J. MAXWELL; HERITAGE, JOHN (eds). Structures of social action: studies in conversation analysis. Cambridge: CUP, 1984. pp. xvi, 446. (Studies in emotion and social interaction.)

1345. BANGE, P. Towards a pragmatic analysis of narratives in literature. Poetics (15:1/2) 73–87.

1346. BAX, INGRID PUFAHL. How to assign work in an office: a comparison of spoken and written directives in American English. Journal of Pragmatics (10:6) 673–92.

1347. BLAIR, I. D. Situation semantics and its foundations. Unpub. doct. diss., Univ. of Edinburgh, 1985. [Abstr. in IT (35) 1077.]

1348. BLAND, SUSAN KESNER. The action nominal in English. Unpub. doct. diss., Cornell Univ., 1985. [Abstr. in DA (46) 1919A.]

1349. BRENER, R. Y. Children's acquisition of the deictic meaning of the third person pronouns of English. *See* **1302.**

1350. CARLSON, LAURI. Dialogue games: an approach to discourse analysis. *See* **1092.**

1351. CHAMONIKOLASOVÁ, JANA. Volné elementy v hovorové angličtině. (Free elements in colloquial English.) *In* (pp. 28–9) **4.**

1352. CHERRY, ROGER DENNIS. *Ethos* in written discourse: a study of literary and persuasive texts. Unpub. doct. diss., Univ. of Texas at Austin, 1985. [Abstr. in DA (46) 3015A.]

1353. CHIȚORAN, DUMITRU; CORNILESCU, ALEXANDRA. Elements of English sentence pragmatics. Bucharest: Bucharest Univ., 1985. pp. 370. Rev. by Ileana Baciu in AnUBLLS (35) 97–8.

1354. CHRZANOWSKA, ELŻBIETA. Factivity revisited. SAP(19) 129–41.

1355. DE RYCKER, TEUN. Imperative structures: form and function in conversational English. *See* **1099.**

1356. DOWTY, DAVID R. The effects of aspectual class on the temporal structure of discourse: semantics or pragmatics? Linguistics and Philosophy (9:1) 37–61.

1357. DUŠKOVÁ, LIBUŠE. Ke klasifikaci vedlejších vět uvozených jednoduchými a složenými relativy. (Classification of subordinate clauses introduced by simple and complex relatives.) *In* (pp. 20–1) **4.**

1358. DWIGHT, DEBRA MAYE. Analysis of pragmatic functions in the language of preschool black children. *See* **1052.**

1359. EGBE, D. I. An approach to the syntax and semantics of the imperative in English. Unpub. doct. diss., Univ. of Newcastle upon Tyne, 1985. [Abstr. in IT (36) 15.]

1360. ERMAN, BRITT. Some pragmatic expressions in English conversation. ('You know', 'you see', 'I mean'.) *In* (pp. 131–47) **16.**

1361. EVANS, DAVID A. Situations and speech acts: towards a formal semantics of discourse. *See* **1101.**

1362. FARWELL, DAVID LORING. The interpretation of functional relations. Unpub. doct. diss., Univ. of Illinois at Urbana-Champaign, 1985. [Abstr. in DA (46) 1920A.]

1363. FIRBAS, JAN.   Carriers of communicative dynamism. Prague Studies in English (18) 1984, 63–73.

1364. —— Ilustrace k pojetí jazyka jako sytému systémů. (Illustrations of the conception of language as a system of systems.) *In* (pp. 21–2) **4.**

1365. —— On the dynamics of written communication in the light of the theory of functional sentence perspective. *See* **1102.**

1366. —— A systemic view of functional sentence perspective. *In* (pp. 17–33) TEREZA DOBRZYŃSKA (ed.), Teoria tekstu. Wróclaw: Polish Academy of Sciences. pp. 148. (Ossolineum.)

1367. GARCIA, CARMEN MARIA.   Stylistic strategies in native and non-native English: how Venezuelans and Americans disagree, request and promise. *See* **1161.**

1368. GOLKOVÁ, EVA.   O funkci anglického prvního větného členu ve funkční větné perspektivě. (The function of the English first clause element in functional sentence perspective.) *In* (pp. 22–3) **4.**

1369. HÜBLER, AXEL.   Understatements and hedges in English. Philadelphia, PA: Benjamins, 1983. (Cf. bibl. 1984, 1760.) Rev. by Mark J. Stein in Journal of Pragmatics (10:6) 757–63.

1370. JAMES, FRANCIS.   Semantics and pragmatics of the word 'if'. Journal of Pragmatics (10:4) 453–80.

1371. JOLY, ANDRÉ.   Pour une analyse systématique des modalités non verbales de la communication. *In* (pp. 131–41) **12.**

1372. KASTOVSKY, DIETER.   Word-formation and pragmatics. WBEP (80) 63–78.

1373. KATO, KAZUO.   Another look at ellipsis: non-native recoverability of ellipsis and its implications for linguistic competence. Journal of Pragmatics (10:4) 415–54.

1374. KOMLÓSI, LÁSZLÓ IMRE; TARNAY, LÁSZLÓ.   On Carlson's dialogue games. *See* **1113.**

1375. KRYK, BARBARA.   How do indexicals fit into situations? On deixis in English and Polish. *In* (pp. 1289–1301) **26.**

1376. LEDDY, MICHAEL.   Origins of meaning: utterer, audience, speech-situation. Unpub. doct. diss., Boston College, 1985. [Abstr. in DA (46) 3341A.]

1377. LEE, WON-GOOG.   Youngeo eui bunryeolmun e daehan bunsuk. (A pragmatic analysis of English clefts.) UJH (28) Dec., 1985, 163–84.

1378. LEHTO, LEENA.   Methodological aspects of legal translation. *See* **1178.**

1379. LEITNER, GERHARD.   English traditional grammars in the nineteenth century. *In* (pp. 1333–55) **26.**

1380. LINDSEY, GEOFFREY ALAN.   Intonation and interrogation: tonal structure and the expression of a pragmatic function in English and other languages. Unpub. doct. diss., Univ. of California, Los Angeles, 1985. [Abstr. in DA (46) 2282A.]

1381. LOWENTHAL, F.; VANDAMME, F. (eds). Pragmatics and education. *See* **1326.**

1382. MALCOLM, KAREN RAE. The dynamics of casual conversation: from the perspective of communication linguistics. *See* **1118.**

1383. MILLER, SEUMAS RODERICK MACDONALD. Conventions and speech acts. Unpub. doct. diss., Univ. of Melbourne, 1985. [Abstr. in DA (47) 550A.]

1384. MISHRA, ARPITA. Towards an analysis of conversation management: a cross-cultural perspective. *See* **1012.**

1385. MODINI, PAUL. A functional perspective on language. *See* **1120.**

1386. MOESCHLER, JACQUES. Answers to questions about questions and answers. *See* **1121.**

1387. NISHIMURA, MIWA. Intrasentential codeswitching in Japanese and English. *See* **1020.**

1388. PHARIES, DAVID A. Charles S. Pierce and the linguistic sign. Amsterdam; Philadelphia, PA; Benjamins, 1985. pp. vi, 118. (Foundations of semiotics, 9.)

1389. PORTER, JOSEPH A. Pragmatics for criticism: two generations of speech act theory. Poetics (15:3) 243–57.

1390. PRATT, MARY LOUISE. Ideology and speech-act theory. PT (7:1) 59–72.

1391. PREISLER, BENT. Language function and modality: how to be tentative in English. Dolphin (13) 29–44.

1392. SACKS, HARVEY. Some considerations of a story told in ordinary conversations. Poetics (15:1/2) 127–38.

1393. SCHULZE, RAINER. Höflichkeit im Englischen. Zur linguistischen Beschreibung und Analyse von Alltagsgesprächen: mit einer Zusammenfassung in englische Sprache. Tübingen: Narr, 1985. pp. xvi, 279. (Cf. bibl. 1985, 1111.) Rev. by Wolfgang Grosser in AAA (11) 114–16.

1394. —— Strategic indeterminacy and face-work. *See* **1135.**

1395. SNELLINGS, COURTENAY MEADE. A linguistic analysis of various verbal strategies in cross-examination. *See* **1201.**

1396. TABAKOWSKA, ELŻBIETA. On the pragmatics of *the. In* (pp. 23–32) **17.**

1397. TROSBORG, ANNA. Apology strategies in native/non-native speakers of English. *See* **1142.**

1398. —— Communicative competence. *See* **1143.**

1399. TSOHATZIDIS, SAVAS L. Four types of counterexample to the latest test for perlocutionary act names. Linguistics and Philosophy (9:2) 219–23.

1400. WARD, GREGORY LOUIS. The semantics and pragmatics of preposing. Unpub. doct. diss., Univ. of Pennsylvania, 1985. [Abstr. in DA (46) 2284A.]

1401. WIERZBICKA, ANNA. A semantic metalanguage for the description and comparison of illocutionary meanings. Journal of Pragmatics (10:1) 67–107.

1402. YADUGIRI, M. A.   Some pragmatic implications of the use of 'yes' and 'no' in response to 'yes'–'no' questions. Journal of Pragmatics (10:2) 199–210.

1403. ZOHRAB, P. D.   Verb-phrase anaphora: linguistics or cognitive science? *See* **1295.**

PHONETICS AND PHONOLOGY

GENERAL STUDIES

1404. AKAMATSU, T. The theory of neutralization and the archiphoneme in functional phonology. Unpub. doct. diss., Univ. of Leeds, 1982.

1405. BECKMAN, MARY E. Stress and non-stress accent. Dordrecht: Foris. pp. xiii, 239. (Netherlands phonetic archives, 7.)

1406. BOLINGER, DWIGHT. Intonation and its parts: melody in spoken English. Stanford, CA: Stanford UP, 1985; London: Arnold. pp. xiii, 421. Rev. by David Crystal in TLS, 29 Aug., 949.

1407. BUXTON, H. Rhythm and stress in speech. *See* **1091.**

1408. CHURMA, DONALD G. Arguments from external evidence in phonology. New York; London: Garland, 1985. pp. ii, 123. (Outstanding dissertations in linguistics.) (Cf. bibl. 1980, 1642.)

1409. DONEGAN, PATRICIA J. On the natural phonology of vowels. New York; London: Garland, 1985. pp. vii, 273. (Outstanding dissertations in linguistics.) (Cf. bibl. 1979, 1445.)

1410. DRESSLER, WOLFGANG. Morphonology: the dynamics of derivation. Ann Arbor, MI: Karoma, 1985. pp. 439. Rev. by Rajendra Singh in CJL (13:4) 343–63.

1411. DURAND, JACQUES (ed.). Dependency and non-linear phonology. London: Croom Helm. pp. 336. (Croom Helm linguistics.)

1412. ELIASSON, STIG (ed.). Theoretical issues in contrastive phonology. Heidelberg: Groos, 1984. pp. 110. (Studies in descriptive linguistics, 13.) Rev. by P. Swiggers in ITL (70) 1985, 70–4.

1413. GUIERRE, LIONEL. Où en est l'accentuation du mot en anglais? *In* (pp. 273–83) **1.**

1414. HLADKÝ, JOSEF. Dělení slov a zvuková rovina. (Word-division and the phonic level of language.) *In* (pp. 26–7) **4.**

1415. KITIS, ELIZA. The relationship between systematic phonemics, phonological rules and systematic phonetics. Views on Language and Language Teaching (9:2) 24–30.

1416. LASS, ROGER. Phonology: an introduction to basic concepts. New York: CUP, 1984. (Cf. bibl. 1985, 1128.) Rev. by Jean-François Prunet in CJL (31:1) 102–7; by René Collier in LeuB (75:4) 527–30.

1417. MATSUSHITA, TOMONORI. Kyokussetsu doshi taikei no seizokusei to futomeika. (Continuity and opacity of ablaut in the English strong verbs.) SEL (63:1) 95–121.

1418. MATUZAKA, HIROSHI. Eigo onseigaku nyumon. (A guide to English phonetics.) Tokyo: Kenkyusha. pp. x, 188. (Guides to English language and literature.)

1419. MONAHAN, K. P. The theory of lexical phonology. Dordrecht; Leicester: Reidel. pp. xii, 219. (Studies in natural language and linguistic theory.)

1420. MUSTAPHA, H. An investigation of the plausibility of phonetic competence. Unpub. doct. diss., Univ. of Essex, 1984.

1421. PEDERSON, LEE.   A survey in deductive phonetics. ZDL (53:3) 289–309.

1422. PIGGOTT, GLYNE L.; SINGH, RAJENDRA.   The phonology of epenthetic segments. CJL (30:4) 1985, 415–51.

1423. POLDAUF, IVAN.   Germanic stress in English words. Prague Studies in English (18) 1984, 25–35.

1424. PULLEYBLANK, DOUGLAS.   Tone in lexical phonology. Dordrecht; Lancaster: Reidel. pp. xii, 249. (Studies in natural language and linguistic theory.)

1425. ROBERGE, PAUL T.   Grammatical prerequisites to phonological change? ZDL (52) 188–217.

1426. SINGH, RAJENDRA.   On finding a place for Trubetzkoy's brainchild. CJL (31:4) 343–63 (review-article).

1427. VACHEK, JOSEF.   A curious case of phonemic substitution. In (pp. 205–15) JACOB L. MEY (ed.), Language and discourse: test and protest. Amsterdam: Benjamins. pp. xiii, 611. (Linguistic and literary studies in Eastern Europe, 19.)

1428. VAN REENEN, PIET.   Phonetic feature definitions: their integration into phonology and their relation to speech. A case study of the feature NASAL. Dordrecht; Foris, 1982. pp. ix, 196. Rev. by René Collier in LeuB (75) 524–6.

1429. WILKENFELD, DEBORAH CEIL.   Encoding prosody in silent reading. Unpub. doct. diss., Univ. of Connecticut, 1985. [Abstr. in DA (46) 1927A.]

HISTORICAL PHONETICS AND HISTORICAL PHONOLOGY

1430. CHAPMAN, RAYMOND.   The treatment of sounds in language and literature. (Bibl. 1985, 1138.) Rev. by Andrew Welsh in ELN (23:3) 72–4; by Ronald R. Butters in SAQ (85:2) 208–9.

1431. CREEL, JAMES MELTON.   The phonetic play: *Pygmalion* from manuscript to first printing. See **303.**

1432. DANCHEV, ANDREI.   Interlanguage simplification in Middle English vowel phonology? In (pp. 239–52) **26.**

1433. DEPALMA, DONALD A.   *Česká přehláska* and the great English vowel shift: a comparative study. Unpub. doct. diss., Brown Univ. [Abstr. in DA (47) 1713A.]

1434. DRESHER, BEZALEL E.   Old English and the theory of phonology. New York; London: Garland, 1985. pp. xi, 272. (Outstanding dissertations in linguistics.) (Cf. bibl. 1978, 1460.)

1435. DUNCAN, EDWIN.   Chronological testing and the scansion of 'frea' in Old English poetry. NM (87:1) 92–101.

1436. GBUREK, HUBERT.   The vowel /a:/ in English. In (pp. 139–48) **42.**

1437. HICKEY, RAYMOND.   On syncope in Old English. In (pp. 359–66) **26.**

1438. —— Velar segments in Old English and Old Irish. In (pp. 267–79) **42.**

1439.   HOUSTON, ANN CELESTE.   Continuity and change in English morphology: the variable (ING). *See* **1005.**

1440.   HUBMAYER, KARL.   'Natürliche Diachronie': Untersuchungen zur phonetischen Motivation historischer phonologischer Prozesse im Englischen. Salzburg: Institut für Anglistik und Amerikanistik, Salzburg Univ. pp. 387. (Salzburger Studien zur Anglistik und Amerikanistik, 15.)

1441.   IKEGAMI, MASA.   Rhyme and pronunciation: some studies of English rhymes from *Kyng Alisaunder* to Skelton. Tokyo: Keio Tsushin, 1984. pp. xv, 406. (Cf. bibl. 1984, 1188.) Rev. by E. G. Stanley in NQ (33:4) 532–3.

1442.   KABELL, INGE; LAURIDSEN, HANNE.   Accent in English as described by the earliest Danish grammars of English. SAP (19) 15–27.

1443.   KEYSER, SAMUEL JAY; O'NEIL, WAYNE.   The simplification of the Old English strong nominal paradigms. *In* (pp. 85–107) **41.**

1444.   KING, ANNE.   The Ruthwell cross – a linguistic monument (runes as evidence for Old English). FLH (7:1) 43–79.

1445.   KRISTENSSON, GILLIS.   On voicing of initial fricatives in Middle English. *See* **906.**

1446.   LASS, ROGER; WRIGHT, SUSAN.   The South African chain shift: order out of chaos? *In* (pp. 137–61) **41.**

1447.   LUTZ, ANGELIKA.   The syllabic basis of word division in Old English manuscripts. EngS (67:3) 193–210.

1448.   MINKOVA, DONKA.   Of rhyme and reason: some foot-governed quantity changes in English. *In* (pp. 163–78) **41.**

1449.   NAKAO, TOSHIO.   Metathesis. *In* (pp. 547–56) **26.**

1450.   NIELSEN, HANS F.   Old English and continental Germanic languages. A survey of morphological and phonological interrelations. *See* **829.**

1451.   POUSSA, PATRICIA.   A note on the voicing of initial fricatives in Middle English. *In* (pp. 235–52) **41.**

1452.   ROMAINE, SUZANNE.   The effects of language standardization on deletion rules: some comparative Germanic evidence from *t/d*-deletion. *In* (pp. 605–20) **26.**

1453.   RUBACH, JERZY.   Degemination in Old English and the formal apparatus of generative phonology. *In* (pp. 621–35) **26.**

1454.   STOCKWELL, ROBERT P.   Assessment of alternative explanations of the Middle English phenomenon of high vowel lowering when lengthened in the open syllable. *In* (pp. 303–18) **41.**

1455.   SUPHI, M. S.   Non-linear analyses in English historical phonology. Unpub. doct. diss., Univ. of Edinburgh, 1985. [Abstr. in IT (35) 1487.]

1456.   WEŁNA, JERZY.   The Old English digraph <cg> again. *In* (pp. 753–62) **26.**

PHONETICS AND PHONOLOGY
OF CURRENT ENGLISH

1457.   ANDERSON, JOHN.   The English prosody /h/. *In* (pp. 799–809) **26.**

1458. ANDERSON, STEPHEN R.   Phonology in the twentieth century: theories of rules and theories of representations. Chicago; London: Chicago UP, 1985. pp. x, 373. Rev. by Douglas C. Walker in CJL (31:2) 199–201.

1459. BAILEY, CHARLES-JAMES N.   English phonetic transcription. Dallas, TX: Summer Inst. of Linguistics, 1985. pp. xxvi, 265. (Pubs. in linguistics, 74.) Rev. by Wolfgang Grosser in AAA (11) 116–19.

1460. BAKER, CHARLOTTE PIERCE.   Acquisition of /t,d/ deletion in vernacular black English: a study of head start preschoolers. *See* **1042.**

1461. BUCCELLATO, PATRICIA.   Différenciation vocalique, hiérarchie accentuelle en anglais et attribution du sens: similitude des réalisations. RANAM (19) 165–77.

1462. COBERLY, MARY SCHRAMM.   Initial and final consonant preferences across languages, in babbling, and in children's early speech. *See* **1305.**

1463. COUPER-KUHLEN, ELIZABETH.   An introduction to English prosody. London: Arnold. pp. 288.

1464. CRUTTENDEN, ALAN.   Intonation. Cambridge: CUP. pp. x, 290.

1465. CUNNINGHAM, U. M.   A linguistic theory of timing. Unpub. doct. diss., Univ. of Nottingham. [Abstr. in IT (36) 903.]

1466. DAVIS, STUART MICHAEL.   Topics in syllable geometry. Unpub. doct. diss., Univ. of Arizona, 1985. [Abstr. in DA (46) 2280A.]

1467. DIENSBERG, BERNHARD.   The phonology of modern French loanwords in present-day English. *In* (pp. 267–75) **26.**

1468. ECKMAN, FRED R.; MORAVCSIK, EDITH A.; WIRTH, JESSICA R. (eds).   Markedness: proceedings of the Twelfth Annual Linguistics Symposium of the University of Wisconsin–Milwaukee held March 11–12, 1983. New York; London: Plenum. pp. viii, 343.

1469. GBUREK, HUBERT.   The vowel /a:/ in English. *In* (pp. 139–48) **42.**

1470. GELUYKENS, RONALD.   'Questioning intonation': an empirical study into the prosodic feature 'rising intonation' and its relevance for the production and recognition of questions. Antwerp: Universitaire Instelling. pp. 101. (Antwerp papers in linguistics, 48.)

1471. GORDON, E.; MACLAGAN, M. A.   A study of the /iə/~/eə/ contrast in New Zealand English. *See* **955.**

1472. HAMMOND, MICHAEL.   The obligatory-branching parameter in metrical theory. Natural Language and Linguistic Theory (4:2) 185–228.

1473. HAN, GI-SUN.   Hyeongtaijeok saengsansung gwa eumwoonjeok tumyungsung. (Morphological productivity *vs* phonological transparency.) RRCNU (32) Dec., 7–12.

1474. HÂRȘAN, ELENA.   Practical guide to English phonetics. Bucharest: Academia de Studii Economice. pp. 145.

1475. HAYES, BRUCE.   A metrical theory of stress rules. New York; London: Garland, 1985. pp. vi, 212. (Outstanding dissertations in linguistics.)

1476. HEDBERG, JOHANNES.   The pronunciation of 'father' in American English – and 'rather' and 'lather'. *See* **868.**

1477. HENDERSON, LALITHA PAULIAH.   A phonological contrastive study of Tamil and English. Unpub. doct. diss., Victoria Univ., Toronto, 1984. [Abstr. in DA (46) 2281A.]

1478. HOEQUIST, CHARLES ERNEST, JR.   A comparative study of linguistic rhythm. Unpub. doct. diss., Yale Univ., 1985. [Abstr. in DA (46) 3335A.]

1479. JOHNS-LEWIS, CATHERINE (ed.).   Intonation in discourse. London: Croom Helm. pp. xxxvi, 302.

1480. JONGMAN, ALLARD.   Naturalness in phonetics: a study of context-dependency. Unpub. doct. diss., Brown Univ. [Abstr. in DA (47) 1715A.]

1481. KALACKAL, THOMAS.   A contrastive analysis of the phonological systems of English and Malayalam. Unpub. doct. diss., Northern Illinois Univ., 1985. [Abstr. in DA (46) 2679A.]

1482. KIM, SOON-TAEK.   Youngeo eui moeumgisul gwa geu munjejeom. (The description of English vowels and its problems.) JUJH (21) 1985, 73–82.

1483. KINGSTON, JOHN CLAYTON.   The phonetics and phonology of the timing of oral and glottal events. Unpub. doct. diss., Univ. of California, Berkeley, 1984. [Abstr. in DA (46) 2680A.]

1484. LASS, ROGER; WRIGHT, SUSAN.   The South African chain shift: order out of chaos? *In* (pp. 137–61) **41.**

1485. LEHISTE, ILSE.   The many linguistic functions of duration. *In* (pp. 96–122) **38.**

1486. LINDSAY, D.   Prosodic analysis by rule: final technical report. *See* **539.**

1487. LINDSEY, GEOFFREY ALAN.   Intonation and interrogation: tonal structure and the expression of a pragmatic function in English and other languages. *See* **1380.**

1488. LJOLJE, A.   Intonation and phonetic segmentation using hidden Markov models. Unpub. doct. diss., Univ. of Cambridge. [Abstr. in IT (36) 16.]

1489. LODGE, K. R.   Studies in the phonology of colloquial English. (Bibl. 1985, 1181.) Rev. by Marc Picard in CJL (31:4) 371–3.

1490. McCARTHY, JOHN J.   OCP effects: gemination and antigemination. LI (17:2) 207–63.

1491. NESPOR, MARINA; VOGEL, IRENE.   Prosodic phonology. Dordrecht: Foris. pp. xiv, 327. (Studies in generative grammar, 28.)

1492. NEVALAINEN, TERTTU; RISSANEN, MATTI.   Do you support the *do*-support? Emphatic and non-emphatic *do* in affirmative statements in present-day spoken English. *In* (pp. 35–50) **43.**

1493. PETRI, LUCREŢIA.   Intonaţie şi sens în limba engleză contemporană. (Intonation and meaning in contemporary English.) Bucharest: Bucharest Univ., 1985. pp. 24. (Summary of doct. diss.)

1494. —— Intonation and meaning in present-day English. Bucharest: Bucharest Univ. pp. 324.

1495. PULLEYBLANK, DOUGLAS.   Rule application on a noncyclic stratum. LI (17:3) 573–80.

1496. PULLUM, GEOFFREY K.; ZWICKY, ARNOLD M.   Phonological resolution of syntactic feature conflict. Lang (62:4) 751–73.

1497. PUPPEL, STANISŁAW.   Rhythm in stress-timed and syllable-timed languages: some general considerations. *In* (pp. 105–10) **26.**

1498. RINGO, CAROL CHAPIN.   The nature of change in phonological development: evidence from the acquisition of /s/ + stop and /s/ + nasal clusters. Unpub. doct. diss., Brown Univ., 1985. [Abstr. in DA (46) 1925A.]

1499. SCHEIN, BARRY; STERIADE, DONCA.   On geminates. LI (17:4) 691–744.

1500. SCHOUTEN, M. E. H.; REINDERS, J.; VAN ESSCHOTEN-ROELOFSEN, M.   De invloed van dialect – achtergrond op de uitspraak van het Engels. (The influence of dialect background on the pronunciation of English.) ForumL (27:3) 205–9.

1501. SELKIRK, ELIZABETH O.   Phonology and syntax: the relation between sound and structure. Cambridge, MA: MIT Press, 1984. pp. 476. Rev. by W. E. Cooper in SL (10:2) 235–41.

1502. SHUKEN, C.   Vowel systems in Hebridean English. *See* **934.**

1503. SPENCER, ANDREW.   Towards a theory of phonological development. Lingua (68) 3–38.

1504. SZWEDEK, ALEKSANDER.   Sentence stress and category membership. *In* (pp. 1051–61) **26.**

1505. TABOSSI, P.   Interpreting words in context. *See* **790.**

1506. TURNER, J. W.   Contextual variation and conservation: an illustration through effect. Unpub. doct. diss., Univ. of Sussex, 1984.

1507. VAN DER HULST, HARRY; SMITH, NORVAL (eds).   Advances in nonlinear phonology. Amsterdam; Philadelphia, PA: Benjamins, 1985. pp. vi, 396. (Linguistic models, 7.)

1508. ZWICKY, ARNOLD M.; ZWICKY, ELIZABETH D.   Imperfect puns, markedness and phonological similarity: with fronds like these, who needs anemones? FL (20:3/4) 493–503.

ORTHOGRAPHY

SPELLING, PUNCTUATION, HANDWRITING

1509. BAUER, GERO.   Medieval English scribal practice: some questions and some assumptions. *In* (pp. 199–210) **26.**

1510. BOURCIER, GEORGES.   L'orthographie de l'anglais: histoire et situation actuelle. Paris: Presses Universitaires de France, 1978. pp. 253.

1511. CLANTON, STACY M.   The 'number' of Sir Walter Ralegh's *Booke of the Ocean to Scinthia. See* **145.**

1512. DENEAU, DANIEL P.   Pointing theory and some Victorian practices. YREAL (4) 97–134. (The colon in *Jane Eyre, Vanity Fair, Bleak House* and *The Mill on the Floss.*)

1513. GARDINER-STALLAERT, NICOLE.   A fine point of difference. The use of the full stop at the end of verbless sentences in today's French and English formal expository critical texts. Langage et l'Homme (21:3) 209–16.

1514. GAUR, ALBERTINE.   A history of writing. New York: Scribner's, 1984. (Cf. bibl. 1985, 1204.) Rev. by Mark Van Stone in LQ (56:4) 422–4.

1515. HAMILTON, CHARLES.   In search of Shakespeare: a study of the poet's life and handwriting. San Diego, CA: Harcourt Brace Jovanovich, 1985; London: Hale. pp. 272. Rev. by Louis Marder in SNL (36:1) 12.

1516. HARRIS, ROY.   The origin of writing. London: Duckworth. pp. 184.

1517. HLADKÝ, JOSEF.   Dělení slov a zvuková rovina. (Word-division and the phonic level of language.) *In* (pp. 26–7) **4.**

1518. LEVINSON, JOAN PERSILY.   Punctuation and the orthographic sentence: a linguistic analysis. Unpub. doct. diss., City Univ. of New York, 1985. [Abstr. in DA (46) 3337A.]

1519. MACCABE, COLIN.   Righting English, or, Does spelling matter? London: Collins; Univ. of Strathclyde, 1984. pp. 7. (Collins English Dictionary annual lecture.)

1520. McLEOD, RANDALL.   Spellbound. *In* (pp. 81–96) **44.** (Renaissance typesetting problems.)

1521. MORTON, RICHARD.   How many revengers in *The Revengers Tragedy?* Archaic spellings and the modern annotator. *In* (pp. 113–22) **44.**

1522. NICKSON, M. A. E.   Sloane's codes: the solution to a mystery. *See* **265.**

1523. RONBERG, GERT.   The two manuscripts of *The Wars of Alexander*: a linguistic comparison. *See* **173.**

1524. SCHIPPER, WILLIAM.   Orthography and dialect in Cambridge University Library MS Ii.1.33. *See* **176.**

1525. TOON, THOMAS E.   Preliminaries to the linguistic analysis of the Old English glosses and glossaries. *In* (pp. 319–29) **41.**

LEXIS

VOCABULARY

General

See also under 'Single Words and Phrases', below.

1526. AKIMOTO, SANEHARU.   Eigo idiom no kenkyu. (A study of English idioms.) Tokyo: Shinozaki shorin. pp. vi, 186.

1527. BARNEY, STEPHEN.   Word-hoard: an introduction to Old English vocabulary. (Bibl. 1980, 1791.) New Haven, CT; London: Yale UP, 1985. pp. 96. (Yale language series.) (Second ed.: first ed. 1978.)

1528. BRANFORD, JEAN.   Some surprises from the corpus of the *Dictionary of South African English on Historical Principles*. See **949.**

1529. BRITTIN, NORMAN A.   From the 1940s to the 1980s: John D. MacDonald's increasing use of scatalogical language. Clues (7:1) 49–63.

1530. CARSTENSEN, BRODER.   Euro-English. *In* (pp. 827–35) **26.**

1531. CHASE, T. J. P.   A diachronic semantic classification of the English religious lexis. Unpub. doct. diss., Univ. of Glasgow, 1983.

1532. CLAIBORNE, ROBERT (introd.).   Word mysteries and histories: from quiche to humble pie. Boston, MA; Houghton Mifflin. pp. 308. (American Heritage dictionaries.) Rev. by Elizabeth Benedict in BW, 14 Dec., 14.

1533. DEKEYSER, XAVIER.   Romance loans in Middle English: a re-assessment. *In* (pp. 253–65) **26.**

1534. DIENSBERG, BERNHARD.   The phonology of modern French loanwords in present-day English. *In* (pp. 267–75) **26.**

1535. DIRVEN, RENÉ, *et al.*   The scene of linguistic action and its perspectivization by 'speak', 'talk', 'say' and 'tell'. (Bibl. 1984, 1245.) Rev. by Bob Rigter in LeuB (75:3) 417–27.

1536. DUNN, R. D.   Additions to OED from William Camden's *Remains* 1605, 1614, 1623. NQ (33:4) 451–60.

1537. GABRINER, P. J.   Antedatings, postdatings, and additions from Pope's translation of the *Iliad* for OED. NQ (33:1) 14–21.

1538. GEORGE, K. E. M.   Forenames as common nouns in English and French. SN (58:1) 39–45.

1539. GNEUSS, HELMUT.   Liturgical books in Anglo-Saxon England and their Old English terminology. *In* (pp. 91–141) **25.**

1540. GRAMBS, DAVID.   Longman companion dictionary: words about words. New York: McGraw–Hill, 1984; London: Routledge & Kegan Paul, 1985. pp. xix, 409.

1541. GREENBAUM, SIDNEY; WHITCUT, JANET (eds).   The complete plain words. By Sir ERNEST GOWERS. (BIBL. 1973, 1473.) London: HMSO. pp. vii, 288. (Third ed.: first ed. 1954.)

1542. GRIFFITHS, BILL.   The Old English alcoholic vocabulary: a re-examination. DUJ (78:2) 231–50.

1543. HOWARD, PHILIP.   A word in your ear. (Bibl. 1984, 1252.) Harmondsworth: Penguin, 1985. pp. 164. (Second ed.: first ed. 1983.)

1544. Iwasaki, Haruo. A few notes on the vocabulary of Laȝamon's *Brut*. PoetT (24) 1–15.

1545. Johansson, Stig. Some observations on word frequencies in three corpora of present-day English texts. *See* **1171.**

1546. Kahn, John. What's in a word? The fascinating stories behind some everyday words. London: Reader's Digest Assn, 1985. pp. 64.

1547. Kastovsky, Dieter. Word-formation and pragmatics. *See* **1372.**

1548. Kjellmer, Göran. Legible but not readable: on the semantics of English adjectives in '-able'. SN (58:1) 11–38.

1549. Krámský, Jiří. Synonyma v angličtině. (Synonyms in English.) CJa (29) parts 27–31: 260–3, 301–3, 396–9, 443–6; (30) part 32: 19–22.

1550. Lee, Eric J. Subsystems in the interlanguage lexicon. *See* **1325.**

1551. Linnarud, Moira. Lexis in composition: a performance analysis of Swedish learners' written English. *See* **1063.**

1552. Luschnig, C. A. E.; Luschnig, L. J. Etymidion: a students workbook for vocabulary building from Latin and Greek. Lanham, MD; London: UP of America, 1985. pp. v, 178.

1553. McConchie, R. W. Further additions to OED from John Cotta's *Ignorant Practisers of Physicke* (1612). NQ (33:4) 460–1.

1554. MacDonald, Alasdair A. The Middle Scots expansion of *Iesu, nostra redemptio*, and a ghost in the Bannatyne manuscript. *See* **969.**

1555. Magnusson, Ulf; Persson, Gunnar. Facets, phases and foci: studies in lexical relations in English. Umeå: Acta Universitatis Umensis; Stockholm: Almqvist & Wiksell. pp. v, 308. (Umeå studies in the humanities, 75.)

1556. O'Connor, Mark. The poetry of the North: finding the words. Westerly (31:1) 18–27.

1557. Phillips, Michael Joseph. Heart, mind, and soul in Old English: a semantic study. Unpub. doct. diss., Univ. of Illinois at Urbana-Champaign, 1985. [Abstr. in DA (46) 1925A.]

1558. Plank, Frans. The interpretation and development of form alternations conditioned across word boundaries: the case of *wife's*, *wives*, and *wives*'. *In* (pp. 205–33) **41.**

1559. Ross, Thomas W.; Brooks, Edward (eds). English glosses from British Library Additional Manuscript 37075. *See* **174.**

1560. Shapiro, Fred R. Neologisms in Coleridge's *Notebooks*. NQ (32) 1985, 346–7.

1561. —— Words for OED from De Quincey. ANQ (22) 1983, 49–50.

1562. Shaw, P. M. The major derivatives from geographical terms in English and German. Unpub. doct. diss., Univ. of Newcastle upon Tyne, 1983.

1563. Sørensen, Knud. Phrasal verb into noun. NM (87:2) 272–83.

1564. Spiegl, Fritz. The joy of words: 'a bedside book for English lovers'. London: Elm Tree. pp. xi, 223.

1565. STANLEY, E. G.   Notes on the text of the Old English *Genesis. In* (pp. 189–96) **36.**

1566. —— GRAY, DOUGLAS (eds).   Five hundred years of words and sounds: a festschrift for E. J. Dobson. (Bibl. 1984, 72.) Rev. by Nicholas Jacobs in MÆ (55:2) 273–4.

1567. SUNG, CHAN-KYUNG.   Jakpum eui jeoldaechi wa jung bu eui yeonghyang. (Value and direction of literary words.) JELL (32:4) 859–75.

1568. TERASAWA, YOSHIO.   Hebrew loan words in English. *In* (pp. 659–69) **26.**

1569. TZE, C.-W.   Towards an explication and description of synonymy in English. Unpub. doct. diss., Univ. of Edinburgh, 1983.

1570. VACHEK, JOSEF.   Some remarks on the English loans in Czech sports terminology. *In* (pp. 25–30) WOLFGANG VIERECK; WOLF-DIETRICH BALD (eds), English in contact with other languages. Budapest: Akadémiai Kiadó. pp. xix, 570. (B. Carstensen volume.)

1571. VORLAT, EMMA.   'Your marriage is going through a rocky patch': on idioms in the Lonely Hearts column. *In* (pp. 103–8) **12.**

SINGLE WORDS AND PHRASES

1572. *acker/aiker*] ANTTILA, RAIMO.   An etymology for the aquatic '*acker/aiker*' in English, and other grains of truth? *In* (pp. 177–82) **26.**

1573. *æpplede*] THOMPSON, PAULINE A.   Æpplede gold: an investigation of its semantic field. MedStud (48) 315–33.

1574. *also*] BOGUSŁAWSKI, ANDRZEJ.   'Also' from 'all so': on a set of particles in service of efficient communication. Journal of Pragmatics (10:5) 615–34.

1575. *and*] TRAUGOTT, ELIZABETH CLOSS.   On the origins of 'and' and 'but' connectives in English. SL (10:2) 137–50.

1576. *as*] DELECHELLE, GÉRARD.   La valeur causale de *as* et *with. In* (pp. 249–58) **1.**

1577. *Balkanize*] GOLD, DAVID L.   Offspring of English Balkanize. Names (34:2) 1984, 237–8.

1578. *bamboozled*] SIEBERT, DONALD T.   Bubbled, bamboozled, and *bit*: 'low bad' words in Johnson's *Dictionary*. SELit (26:3) 485–96.

1579. *be to*] VAN NOPPEN, JEAN-PIERRE.   'Be to' as an expression of futurity: human control only? Brussels Preprints in Linguistics (8) 1983, 52–8.

1580. *beam*] HAMP, ERIC P.   German *Baum*, English *beam. In* (pp. 345–6) **26.**

1581. *beorg*] GRIFFITH, F. M.   'Burh' and 'beorg' in Devon. Nomina (10) 93–103.

1582. *beorhhliðu*] HALL, J. R.   *Exodus* 449a: beorhhliðu. ANQ (22:7/8) 1984, 94–7.

1583. *bishop*] PITCHER, EDWARD W.   The gorge and the bishop: new information for the OED. ANQ (24:9/10) 152–3.

1584. *bit/bubbled*] SIEBERT, DONALD T.   Bubbled, bamboozled, and *bit*: 'low bad' words in Johnson's *Dictionary*. See **1578.**

1585. *but*] TRAUGOTT, ELIZABETH CLOSS. On the origins of 'and' and 'but' connectives in English. *See* **1575.**

1586. *carrageen*] BLISS, ANN. *Carrageen*. NQ (32) 1985, 382–4.

1587. *cruive*] DIETZ, KLAUS. Modern English *cruive* 'wicker salmon-trap'. *In* (pp. 277–91) **26.**

1588. *earme on eaxle*] LESTER, G. A. 'Earme on eaxle' (*Beowulf* 1117a). SN (58:2) 159–63.

1589. *'England expects...'*] OHLANDER, SÖLVE. Trafalgar revisited or my example – right or wrong! MS (80) 315–18.

1590. *England expects...*] RYNELL, ALARIK. 'England expects ...'. MS (80) 55–6.

1591. *-esque*] STEENBERGEN, G. JO. A contribution to etymology with special reference to the suffixes *-esque* and *-ish* in Germanic languages. Antwerp: Universitaire Instelling, 1982. pp. 27. (Antwerp papers in linguistics, 29.)

1592. *fægnige*] KIERNAN, KEVIN S. The lost letters of *Beowulf* 2253a. Neophilologus (70:4) 633–5.

1593. *fairy*] WILLIAMS, N. R. The semantics of the word 'fairy' in English between 1320 and 1829. Unpub. doct. diss., Univ. of Sheffield, 1984.

1594. *fals*] PETERS, HANS. Middle English 'fals'. Archiv (223:1) 120–5.

1595. *feormie*] KIERNAN, KEVIN S. The lost letters of *Beowulf* 2253a. *See* **1592.**

1596. *fiddler*] HEANEY, MICHAEL. Must every fiddler play a fiddle? REEDNewsletter (11:1) 10–11.

1597. *four (numeral) 4*] STILES, PATRICK V. The fate of the numeral '4' in Germanic (1). NOWELE (6) 1985, 81–104.

1598. *foxfire*] REA, JOHN A. Foxfire. ELN (24:2) 1–3.

1599. *frea*] DUNCAN, EDWIN. Chronological testing and the scansion of 'frea' in Old English poetry. *See* **1435.**

1600. *ganza*] WEEDON, MARGARET. 'Hawk', 'hand-saw', and 'ganza'? NQ (33:3) 356–7.

1601. *geflogen*] ONO, SHOKO. A note on a note: a grammatical remark. MESN (14) 4–5.

1602. *geflogen*] POPE, J. C. OE *geflogen*, ME *ihuld*: a second look at the 'tremulous' scribe's error. MESN (14) 3–4.

1603. *geflogen*] SCHIPPER, W. Response. MESN (14) 5–6.

1604. *gefrægnod*] BAMMESBERGER, ALFRED. On Old English *gefrægnod* in *Beowulf* 1333a. *In* (pp. 193–7) **26.**

1605. *gehedde*] POPE, JOHN C. *Beowulf* 505, 'gehedde', and the pretensions of Unferth. *In* (pp. 173–87) **36.**

1606. *gelendon mid aescum*] SCHENDL, HERBERT. 'Gelendon mid aescum': a problematic reading in Ælfric? WBEP (80) 217–20.

1607. *gentilesse*] ONO, MANA. Chaucer no Boece yakuni tsuite: 'gentilesse' wo chushin ni. (On Chaucer's translation of Boece: with special reference to 'gentilesse'.) StudME (1) 93–105.

1608. *gold*] THOMPSON, PAULINE A.   Æpplede gold: an investigation of its semantic field. *See* **1573.**

1609. *gorge*] PITCHER, EDWARD W.   The gorge and the bishop: new information for the OED. *See* **1583.**

1610. *hert-huntyng*] PRIOR, SANDRA PIERSON.   *Routhe* and *hert-huntyng* in the *Book of the Duchess*. JEGP (85:1) 4–19.

1611. *ihuld*] ONO, SHOKO.   A note on a note: a grammatical remark. *See* **1601.**

1612. *ihuld*] POPE, J. C.   OE *geflogen*, ME *ihuld*: a second look at the 'tremulous' scribe's error. *See* **1602.**

1613. *ihuld*] SCHIPPER, W.   Response. *See* **1603.**

1614. *indryhtu*] CROZIER, ALAN.   Old West Norse 'íþrótt' and Old English 'indryhtu'. SN (58:1) 3–10.

1615. *intellectual*] ALLEN, PETER.   The meanings of 'an intellectual': nineteenth- and twentieth-century English usage. UTQ (55:4) 342–58.

1616. *-ish*] STEENBERGEN, G. JO.   A contribution to etymology with special reference to the suffixes *-esque* and *-ish* in Germanic languages. *See* **1591.**

1617. *kynde*] WHITE, HUGH.   Langland's *Ymaginatif, kynde* and the *Benjamin Major*. MÆ (55:2) 241–8.

1618. *læ*] TOTH, KARL.   AE *læ* 'Haupthaar'. *See* **836.**

1619. *licere*] MATHESON, LISTER M.   *Licere*: a ghost word in the *Middle English Dictionary*. NQ (33:1) 9.

1620. *marketplace of ideas*] BOSMAJIAN, HAIG.   The metaphoric marketplace of ideas and the pig in the parlor. MidQ (26) Autumn 1984, 44–62.

1621. *marrow*] REA, JOANNE E.   Joyce and Rabelais: Mallow, marrow and Molly. Names (34:4) 1984, 430–1.

1622. *mere*] FRANK, ROBERTA.   'Mere' and 'sund': two sea-changes in *Beowulf*. *In* (pp. 153–72) **36.**

1623. *millennium*] KJELLMER, GÖRAN.   On the spelling of English 'millennium'. SN (58:2) 189–92.

1624. *moonshine*] PITCHER, E. W.   'Moonshine' 'illicit spirit' in OED. NQ (33:1) 21.

1625. **munddenn*] COATES, RICHARD.   Towards an explanation of the Kentish '-monden's. JEPNS (18) 40–7.

1626. *muster*] RYAN, J. S.   Soldier, sailor, convict, sheep: the 'chaining' of meaning of the noun and verb 'muster'. Working Papers in Language and Linguistics (Launceston, Tas.) (20) 37–46.

1627. *nathwæt*] RISSANEN, MATTI.   'Nathwæt' in the Exeter Book riddles. ANQ (24:7/8) 116–20.

1628. *(numeral) 4*] STILES, PATRICK V.   The fate of the numeral '4' in Germanic (1). *See* **1597.**

1629. *oferrswifenn*] MORRISON, STEPHEN.   Early Middle English 'oferrswifenn'. Archiv (223:1) 115–20.

1630. *ought (to)*] HARRIS, MARTIN.   English *ought (to)*. *In* (pp. 347–58) **26.**

1631. *pig in the parlor*] BOSMAJIAN, HAIG.   The metaphoric
marketplace of ideas and the pig in the parlor. *See* **1620.**

1632. *pinkie-plonk*] LAWSON, ELIZABETH.   'Pinkie-plonk' in Australia: a lexical note. *See* **958.**

1633. *quod*] PEVERETT, MICHAEL.   'Quod' and 'seide' in *Piers Plowman*. NM (87:1) 117–27.

1634. *routhe*] PRIOR, SANDRA PIERSON.   *Routhe* and *hert-huntyng* in the
Book of the Duchess. *See* **1610.**

1635. *say*] GOOSSENS, LOUIS.   'Say': a case of perspectivization on
the scene of linguistic action. Antwerp: Universitaire Instelling, 1982.
pp. 51. (Antwerp papers in linguistics, 25.)

1636. *Scotticism*] SHAPIRO, FRED R.   'Scotticism'. NQ (32) 1985, 210.

1637. *seide*] PEVERETT, MICHAEL.   'Quod' and 'seide' in *Piers Plowman*. *See* **1633.**

1638. *sliding pon(d)*] GOLD, DAVID L.   Still more on the origin of the
New York City English 'sliding pon(d)'. *See* **866.**

1639. *sum*] RISSANEN, MATTI.   'Sum' in Old English poetry. *In* (pp.
197–225) **36.**

1640. *sund*] FRANK, ROBERTA.   'Mere' and 'sund': two sea-changes
in *Beowulf*. *In* (pp. 153–72) **36.**

1641. *the*] DELMAS, CLAUDE.   Remarques à propos de *the*. *In* (pp.
259–70) **1.**

1642. *there*] KIM, YEON-SEUNG.   'There' gumun e euimi,
gineungjeok tucksung. (Semantic, functional characteristics of 'There'
sentences.) EngSt (10) 69–83.

1643. *þon*] ROBINSON, FRED C.   Literary dialect in *Maldon* and the
Casley transcript. ANQ (24:7/8) 103–4.

1644. *tooth*] LASS, ROGER.   Words without etyma: Germanic 'tooth'.
In (pp. 473–82) **26.**

1645. *turn*] VAN REMORTEL, MARIJKE.   Literalness and metaphorization: the case of 'turn'. *See* **1209.**

1646. *undergytan*] ONO, SHIGERU.   *Undergytan* as a 'Winchester'
word. *In* (pp. 569–77) **26.**

1647. *whittle*] MARKEY, T. L.   Anglo-Norse *thwaite* 'clearing', Engl.
whittle, and German *stossen*. IF (90) 1985, 209–12.

1648. *will*] STALLEY, R. F.   The will in Hume's *Treatise*. JHP (24:1)
41–53.

1649. *with*] DELECHELLE, GÉRARD.   La valeur causale de *as* et *with*.
In (pp. 249–58) **1.**

1650. *wyrd*] LOCHRIE, KARMA.   *Wyrd* and the limits of human
understanding: a thematic sequence in the Exeter Book. JEGP (85:3)
323–31.

NAMES
GENERAL

1651. BROWN, PAULA.   What do you call your pig? Who is your
namesake? *See* **1047.**

1652. BROWN, RUSSELL E.   Names and numbers in *The Adding Machine*. Names (34:3) 1984, 266–74.

1653. BROWNING, PETER.   Place names of the Sierra Nevada: from Abbot to Zumwalt. Berkeley, CA: Wilderness Press. pp. 257.

1654. CAMSELL, MARGARET.   Devon locative surnames in the fourteenth century. Nomina (10) 137–47.

1655. CLARK, C.; BATESON, M.   Bibliography. Nomina (10) 186–203.

1656. COLMAN, FRAN.   Numismatic evidence for onomastics. Nomina (10) 162–8 (review-article).

1657. DIETZ, KLAUS.   Modern English *cruive* 'wicker salmon-trap'. *In* (pp. 277–91) **26.**

1658. DILLARD, J. L.   Ethnic personal names – again? Names (34:4) 1984, 437–9.

1659. FRANCIS, WILLIAM A.   A conversation about names with novelist Vance Bourjaily. Names (34:4) 1984, 355–63.

1660. FRASER, IAN A.   Placenames of Scottish origin in Nova Scotia. Names (34:4) 1984, 364–72.

1661. FREEMAN, ANTHONY.   The moneyer and the mint in the reign of Edward the Confessor, 1042–1066. British Archaeological Reports: British ser. 145, parts 1 and 2. Oxford: B. A. R., 1985. pp. 582. Rev. by Fran Colman in Nomina (10) 178–80.

1662. FREEMAN, JOHN.   Some place-names of Archenfield and the Golden Valley recorded in the Balliol Herefordshire Domesday. Nomina (10) 61–77.

1663. GELLING, MARGARET.   Place-names in the landscape. (Bibl. 1985, 1334.) Rev. by Martyn Wakelin in MÆ (55:2) 274–5.

1664. GEORGE, K. E. M.   Forenames as common nouns in English and French. *See* **1538.**

1665. GOLD, DAVID.   How did biblical personal names come to designate wine bottles in English? Names (34:3) 1984, 351–3.

1666. HELLER, ERICH.   Notes on language, its deconstruction and on translating. *In* (pp. 1–11) **46.**

1667. HERRSCHER, WALTER.   Names in Donald Barthelme's short stories. Names (34:2) 1984, 125–33.

1668. INSLEY, J.   Scandinavian personal names in Norfolk. Unpub. doct. diss., Univ. of Nottingham, 1980.

1669. INSLEY, JOHN.   Toponymy and settlement in the North-West. Nomina (10) 169–76 (review-article).

1670. JENSEN, GILLIAN FELLOWS.   Scandinavian settlement names in the North-West. (Bibl. 1985, 1340.) Rev. by John Insley in Nomina (10) 169–76.

1671. KEATE, P. S.   Comments on the location of some of the forms in *PN Worcs* pp. 293–303. (Halesowen and its townships). JEPNS (18) 5–12.

1672. KENYON, DENISE.   Notes on Lancashire place-names: 1, The early names. JEPNS (18) 13–37.

1673. LASKER, G. W., *et al.*   Surnames and genetic structure.

Cambridge: CUP, 1985. pp. viii, 148. (Cambridge studies in biological anthropology 1.) Rev. by Cecily Clark in Nomina (10) 180–3.

1674. Lawson, Edwin D.; Roeder, Lynn M. Women's full first names, short names, and affectionate names: a semantic differential analysis. Names (34:2) 1984, 175–84.

1675. McArthur, Lewis L. Another approach to place-name classification. Names (34:2) 1984, 238–41.

1676. Mitchell, Jim. George Lewis I, King of England. Factotum (19) 1984, 18–21. (Double names.)

1677. Murray, Thomas E. Folk etymology in the streets of St Louis. Names (34:4) 1984, 373–82.

1678. Nicolaisen, W. F. H. Gaelic place names in Scots. See **919.**

1679. Owen, H. W. The place-names of the lordships of Ewloe and Hope, together with a dictionary of the elements. Unpub. doct. diss., Univ. of Wales, Bangor, 1983.

1680. Pineau, Lois Isabel. Russell's theory of ordinary names: a reinterpretation. Unpub. doct. diss., Univ. of Toronto, 1985. [Abstr. in DA (47) 935A–6A.]

1681. Scherr, Arthur. Change-of-name petitions of the New York courts: an untapped source in historical onomastics. Names (34:3) 1984, 284–302.

1682. Scherr, Jennifer. Names of springs and wells in Somerset. Nomina (10) 79–91.

1683. Scott, Forrest S. Personal names of students, and other Auckland onomastics. Te Reo (29) 257–300.

1684. Shaw, P. M. The major derivatives from geographical terms in English and German. See **1562.**

1685. Skipper, James K. Nicknames, coal miners and group solidarity. See **1032.**

1686. Smart, Veronica. Scandinavians, Celts, and Germans in Anglo-Saxon England: the evidence of moneyers' names. In (pp. 171–84) Mark Blackburn (ed.), Anglo-Saxon monetary history: essays in memory of Michael Dolley. Leicester: Leicester UP. pp. 366.

1687. Sockwell, Sandra McGrady. The place names of Colbert and Lauderdale counties, Alabama. Unpub. doct. diss., Univ. of Alabama, 1985. [Abstr. in DA (47) 890A.]

1688. 'Souris'. Nugae onomasticae III. See **1034.**

1689. Thorn, Frank. The identification of Domesday places in the south-western counties of England. Nomina (10) 41–59.

1690. Vachek, Josef. An emotionally conditioned split of some personal names. In (pp. 693–700) **26.**

1691. —— Notes on the use of capital graphemes in modern English and Czech. Prague Studies in English (18) 1984, 17–24.

1692. Waugh, D. The transition from Gaelic to Scots or Scottish English in Caithness place-names. See **943.**

1693. Waugh, D. J. The place-names of six parishes in Caithness, Scotland. Unpub. doct. diss., Univ. of Edinburgh, 1985. [Abstr. in IT (35) 1080.]

1694. WILSON, FREDERICK E.   Transcription of Afghan placenames to an English-style romanization. Names (34:2) 1984, 185–97.

SINGLE NAMES

1695. *Bassanio*] NATHAN, NORMAN.   Bassanio's name. ANQ (24:9/10) 129–31.

1696. *burh*] GRIFFITH, F. M.   'Burh' and 'beorg' in Devon. *See* **1581.**

1697. *Denali*] KARI, JAMES.   The Tenada–Denali–Mount McKinley controversy. Names (34:2) 1984, 241–3.

1698. *Dick Boulton*] WILHELM, ALBERT E.   Dick Boulton's name in *The Doctor and the Doctor's Wife*. Names (34:4) 1984, 423–5.

1699. *Dogberry*] COATES, RICHARD.   Dogberry and Verges as a pair in *Much Ado About Nothing*. Names (34:2) 1984, 236–7.

1700. *Euroclydon*] COONES, PAUL.   'Euroclydon': a Biblical place-name. JEPNS (18) 38–9.

1701. *Faulkner*] EMERSON, O. B.; HERMANN, JOHN P.   William Faulkner and the Faulkner family name. Names (34:3) 1984, 255–65.

1702. *Halley*] KRUCK, WILLIAM E.   The name of the comet. Names (34:3) 1984, 245–54.

1703. *-hām*] KENYON, DENISE.   The antiquity of '-hām' place-names in Lancashire and Cheshire. Nomina (10) 11–27.

1704. *Hell fer Sartain*] PENNELL, MELISSA McFARLAND.   Between Hell fer Sartain and Kingdom Come: John Fox, Jr's preservation of the masculine ethos. KFR (32:3/4) 130–6.

1705. *Jessica*] NATHAN, NORMAN.   Portia, Nerissa, and Jessica: their names. Names (34:4) 1984, 425–9.

1706. *Kingdom Come*] PENNELL, MELISSA McFARLAND.   Between Hell fer Sartain and Kingdom Come: John Fox, Jr's preservation of the masculine ethos. *See* **1704.**

1707. *Malkyn*] FLETCHER, ALAN J.   Line 30 of the Man of Law's Tale and the medieval Malkyn. ELN (24:2) 15–20.

1708. *Mallow*] REA, JOANNE E.   Joyce and Rabelais: Mallow, marrow and Molly. *See* **1621.**

1709. *Mendip*] COATES, RICHARD.   'Mendip'. Nomina (10) 5–9.

1710. *Miracle Mile*] GOLD, DAVID.   Miracle Mile. Names (34:2) 1984, 238.

1711. *Molly*] REA, JOANNE E.   Joyce and Rabelais: Mallow, marrow and Molly. *See* **1621.**

1712. *-monden*] COATES, RICHARD.   Towards an explanation of the Kentish '-monden's. *See* **1625.**

1713. *Mount McKinley*] KARI, JAMES.   The Tenada–Denali–Mount McKinley controversy. *See* **1697.**

1714. *Nerissa*] NATHAN, NORMAN.   Portia, Nerissa, and Jessica: their names. *See* **1705.**

1715. *Osric/Oswald*] NATHAN, NORMAN. Osric's name, and Oswald's. Names (34:2) 1984, 234–5.

1716. *Portia*] NATHAN, NORMAN.   Portia, Nerissa, and Jessica: their names. *See* **1705.**

1717.   *Scugger Ho*]   KRISTENSSON, GILLIS.   The place-name *Scugger Ho*
(Cumberland). NQ (33:1) 2–3.

1718.   *Stratford on Avon*]   MEL'NIKOVA, T. N.   K probleme lingvis-
ticheskogo statusa angliĭskikh toponimov tipa Stratford on Avon. (The
linguistic status of English place-names of the type 'Stratford on Avon'.)
VLU (1986:3) 115–16.

1719.   *Tenada*]   KARI, JAMES.   The Tenada–Denali–Mount McKinley
controversy. *See* **1697.**

1720.   *thwaite*]   MARKEY, T. L.   Anglo-Norse *thwaite* 'clearing', Engl.
whittle, and German *stossen*. *See* **1647.**

1721.   *Verges*]   COATES, RICHARD.   Dogberry and Verges as a pair in
Much Ado About Nothing. *See* **1699.**

1722.   *Weihnacht*]   WULFMAN, DAVID S.   Weihnacht and its variants
as personal and place names. Names (34:3) 1984, 340–1.

1723.   *Ymaginatif*]   WHITE, HUGH.   Langland's *Ymaginatif, kynde* and
the *Benjamin Major*. *See* **1617.**

DICTIONARIES, LEXICOLOGY, AND LEXICOGRAPHY

1724.   ABATE, FRANK R.   Dictionaries past and future: issues and
prospects. Dic (7) 1985, 270–83.

1725.   AITKEN, A. J.   The pronunciation entries for the CSD. Dic (7)
1985, 134–50.

1726.   ALLEN, R. E.   The Oxford spelling dictionary. Oxford: Clarendon Press. pp. xv, 299.

1727.   BALL, W. J.   Dictionary of link words in English discourse.
London: Macmillan. pp. vi, 154.

1728.   —— WOOD, F. T.   Dictionary of English grammar: based on
common errors. London: Macmillan. pp. 156.

1729.   BARNHART, DAVID K.   Prizes and pitfalls of computerized
searching for new words for dictionaries. *See* **521.**

1730.   BENSON, MORTON.   A combinatory dictionary of English. Dic
(7) 1985, 189–200.

1731.   —— BENSON, EVELYN; ILSON, ROBERT.   The BBI combinatory
dictionary of English: a guide to word combinations. Amsterdam;
Philadelphia, PA: Benjamins. pp. xxxvi, 286.

1732.   —— —— —— Lexicographic description of English. Amsterdam; Philadelphia, PA: Benjamins. pp. xiii, 288. (Studies in language,
companion ser., 14.)

1733.   BRANFORD, JEAN.   Some surprises from the corpus of the
Dictionary of South African English on Historical Principles. *See* **949.**

1734.   BURCHFIELD, R. W. (ed.).   A supplement to the Oxford English
dictionary: vol. 4, Se–Z. Oxford: Clarendon Press. pp. xxiii, 1454. Rev.
by Pat Rogers in TLS, 9 May, 487–8; by D. A. N. Jones in Listener,
12 June, 27–8.

1735.   BURCHFIELD, ROBERT (ed.).   The New Zealand pocket Oxford
dictionary. *See* **954.**

1736.   BURGESS, ANTHONY (introd.).   Hobson-Jobson: a glossary of colloquial Anglo-Indian words and phrases and of kindred terms, etymological, historical, geographical and discursive. By SIR HENRY YULE and A. C. BURNELL; revised ed. by WILLIAM CROOKE. *See* **965.**

1737. CASSIDY, FREDERIC G. (ed.).   Dictionary of American regional English: vol. 1, Introduction and A–C. (Bibl. 1985, 1383.) Rev. by Hugh Kenner in TLS, 9 May, 490–1; by T. K. Pratt in CJL (31:2) 179–85; by Lawrence S. Thompson in ANQ (24:9/10) 157–9; by Fred Strebeigh in Smithsonian (16:10) 154–5.

1738. CLAIBORNE, ROBERT (introd.).   Word mysteries and histories: from quiche to humble pie. *See* **1532.**

1739. COOPER, M. A.   A dictionary of lexical innovation in Early Modern English, 1500–1599. Unpub. doct. diss., Univ. of Newcastle upon Tyne, 1984. [Abstr. in IT (35) 535.]

1740. CORSON, DAVID.   The lexical bar. Oxford; Sydney: Pergamon Press, 1985. pp. x, 130.

1741. CRESSWELL, THOMAS; McDAVID, VIRGINIA.   The usage panel in *The American Heritage Dictionary*, second college edition. PL (19:1) 83–96.

1742. DAVIDSON, GEORGE W. (ed.).   Chambers pocket guide to good English. Edinburgh: Chambers, 1985. pp. viii, 132.

1743. DELBRIDGE, A. (gen. ed.).   Penguin Macquarie dictionary: the international dictionary for all Australians. Melbourne: Penguin in assn with Macquarie Library. pp. 752.

1744. DOLEZAL, FREDRIC.   Forgotten but important lexicographers. John Wilkins and William Lloyd: a modern approach to lexicography before Johnson. (Bibl. 1985, 1389.) Rev. by Joseph L. Subbiondo in Historiographia Linguistica (13:1) 92–8.

1745. —— John Wilkins' and William Lloyd's *Alphabetical Dictionary* (1668): towards a comprehensive, and systematically defined, lexicon. PL (19:1) 111–30.

1746. DOWNES, JOHN.   A dictionary of Devon dialect. *See* **895.**

1747. ECCLES, MARK.   Claudius Hollyband and the earliest French–English dictionaries. SP (83:1) 51–61.

1748. ESPY, WILLARD R.   Words to rhyme with: for poets and song writers: including a primer of prosody; a list of more than 80,000 words that rhyme; a glossary defining 9,000 of the more eccentric rhyming words; and a variety of exemplary verses, one of which does not rhyme at all. London: Macmillan. pp. xii, 656.

1749. FERGUSSON, ROSALIND (ed.).   The new Nuttall dictionary of English synonyms and antonyms. Harmondsworth: Viking Press. pp. 442. (Viking reference.)

1750. FIRNBERG, DAVID (comp.).   Cassell's spelling dictionary. (Bibl. 1976, 1718.) London: Cassell, 1985. pp. 278. (Second ed.: first ed. 1976, as *Cassell's New Spelling Dictionary*.)

1751. FRAWLEY, WILLIAM.   Intertextuality and the dictionary: toward a deconstructionist account of lexicography. Dic (7) 1985, 1–20.

1752. GEENS, DIRK.   The role of computers in the making of a pedagogical dictionary. *See* **529.**

1753. GLÄSER, ROSEMARIE. A plea for phraseo-stylistics. *In* (pp. 41–52) **26.**

1754. GOLD, DAVID L. The debate over 'Webster's Third' twenty-five years later: winnowing the chaff from the grain. Dic (7) 1985, 225–36.

1755. GRAMBS, DAVID. Longman companion dictionary: words about words. *See* **1540.**

1756. GREEN, JONATHON. The slang thesaurus. *See* **1166.**

1757. HANKS, PATRICK (ed.). Collins dictionary of the English language. (Bibl. 1979, 1729.) London: Collins. pp. xxvii, 1771. (Second ed.: first ed. 1979.)

1758. HAYWARD, ARTHUR L. (ed.). Cassell's concise English dictionary. London: Cassell, 1985. pp. 493. (Revised ed.: first ed. 1924.)

1759. HOAD, T. F. (ed.). The concise Oxford dictionary of English etymology. Oxford: OUP. pp. xvi, 552. Rev. by Erik Gunnemark in MS (80) 251–2.

1760. HOLLAND, JOAN. The *Microfiche Concordance*: a lexicographer's tool. *See* **534.**

1761. HORNBY, A. S.; HARRIS, DOLORES; STEWART, WILLIAM A. (eds). Oxford student's dictionary of American English. (Bibl. 1984, 1410.) *See* **870.**

1762. —— (ed.); RUSE, CHRISTINA A. (asst ed.). The Oxford paperback American dictionary. *See* **869.**

1763. ILSON, ROBERT (ed.). Lexicography: an emerging international profession. Manchester: Manchester UP. pp. xiv, 167. Rev. by Pat Rogers in TLS, 9 May, 487–8.

1764. JOST, DAVID. Survey of the reading program of the *Middle English Dictionary*. Dic (7) 1985, 201–13.

1765. —— LAPPERT, STEPHEN. A proposal for a textbook about the history and methodology of British and American lexicography. PL (19:1) 97–110.

1766. KAHN, JOHN ELLISON (ed.). The right word at the right time: a guide to the English language and how to use it. *See* **1172.**

1767. KIBBEE, DOUGLAS A. Progress in bilingual lexicography during the Renaissance. Dic (7) 1985, 21–31.

1768. KIPFER, BARBARA ANN. The declining role of the in-house dictionary staff. Dic (7) 1985, 237–45.

1769. LANDAU, SIDNEY I. The expression of changing social values in dictionaries. Dic (7) 1985, 261–9.

1770. LASS, ROGER. Words without etyma: Germanic 'tooth'. *In* (pp. 473–82) **26.**

1771. LAW, ALAN G.; SANDNESS, GLEN D. A microcomputer-based electronic dictionary for blind persons. Dic (7) 1985, 246–52.

1772. LEARMOUTH, TREVOR; MACWILLIAM, STUART (comps). Historic English dictionaries 1592–1899: a union catalogue of holdings in Exeter libraries. *See* **251.**

1773. LIPKA, LEONHARD. Semantic features and prototype theory in English lexicology. *In* (pp. 85–94) **26.**

1774. McArthur, Tom.   Worlds of reference: lexicography, learning and language from the clay tablet to the computer. Cambridge; New York: CUP. pp. ix, 230. Rev. by H. Stellingsma in ITL (74) 107–9.

1775. Macleod, Iseabail.   Pocket guide to Scottish words. *See* **913.**

1776. McLeod, William T. (ed.).   The Collins paperback English dictionary. London: Collins. pp. x, 1013.

1777. —— The Collins paperback thesaurus in A-to-Z form. London: Collins. pp. viii, 631.

1778. Mathews, M. M.   George Watson and the *Dictionary of American English.* Dic (7) 1985, 214–24.

1779. Minagawa, Saburo; Takemae, Fumio.   Tudor Stuart cho eigo jiten. (A dictionary of Tudor and Stuart English.) *See* **827.**

1780. Misenheimer, James B., Jr; O'Neill, Robert K.   The Cordell collection of dictionaries and Johnson's lexicographic presence; the love of books in two centuries. *See* **259.**

1781. Mort, Simon (ed.).   Longman Guardian new words. Harlow: Longman, pp. 219.

1782. Nagashima, Daisuke.   A note on Dr Johnson's *History of the English Language. In* (pp. 525–31) **26.**

1783. Noël, J.; Janssen, J.; Mergeai, J.-P.   Disambiguating definition language in two automatic dictionaries of English: outline of a computer-aided procedure. *In* (pp. 143–9) **12.**

1784. Reid, Tony.   Separation and Kiwi standards. *See* **961.**

1785. Robinson, Mairi.   The *Concise Scots Dictionary*: a final report. Dic (7) 1985, 112–33.

1786. Room, Adrian.   Dictionary of confusing words and meanings. London: Routledge & Kegan Paul, 1985. pp. 267. (Revision and consolidation of *Room's Dictionary of Confusibles* (bibl. 1979, 1755) and *Room's Dictionary of Distinguishables*, 1981.)

1787. —— Dictionary of translated names and titles. London: Routledge & Kegan Paul. pp. xviii, 460.

1788. —— Dictionary of true etymologies. London: Routledge & Kegan Paul. pp. 256.

1789. Saussy, George Stone, III.   The Penguin dictionary of curious and interesting words. New York: Facts on File, 1984; Harmondsworth: Penguin. pp. xii, 277.

1790. Schwarz, C. M.; Seaton, M. A. (eds).   Chambers concise usage dictionary. Edinburgh: Chambers, 1985. pp. 632.

1791. Stein, Gabriele.   Definitions and first person pronoun involvement in Thomas Elyot's *Dictionary. In* (pp. 1465–74) **26.**

1792. Strauss, Jürgen.   Concepts, fields, and 'non-basic' lexical items. *In* (pp. 135–44) **26.**

1793. Sundby, Bertil.   Towards a dictionary of English normative grammar. Dic (7) 1985, 151–88.

1794. Swannell, Julia (ed.).   The little Oxford dictionary of current English. Ed. by George Ostler. Oxford: Clarendon Press. pp. xiv, 688. (Sixth ed.: first ed. 1930.)

1795. Toon, Thomas E.   Preliminaries to the linguistic analysis of the Old English glosses and glossaries. *In* (pp. 319–29) **41.**

1796. Urdang, Laurence (ed.).   Longman synonym dictionary. Harlow: Longman. pp. ii, 1356.

1797. van Noppen, Jean-Pierre.   In and beyond the glossary, or on making maps out of puzzles. *In* (pp. 165–74) **12.**

1798. van Roey, Jacques.   Deceptive terminology for deceptive cognates. *In* (pp. 159–64) **12.**

1799. Viereck, Wolfgang.   Dialectal speech areas in England: Orton's lexical evidence. *In* (pp. 725–40) **26.**

1800. Wall, Richard.   An Anglo-Irish dialect glossary for Joyce's works. *See* **942.**

GRAMMAR

GENERAL

1801. ANDERSON, JOHN M.   Case grammar and the lexicon. Coleraine: New University of Ulster, 1984. pp. 123. (Occasional papers in linguistics and language learning, 10.)

1802. AOUN, JOSEPH.   A grammar of anaphora. Cambridge, MA; London: MIT Press, 1985. pp. vii, 190. (*Linguistic Inquiry* monographs, 11.)

1803. BALL, W. J.; WOOD, F. T.   Dictionary of English grammar: based on common errors. See **1728.**

1804. BARON, DENNIS E.   Grammar and gender. New Haven, CT; London: Yale UP. pp. ix, 249.

1805. BOWERS, JOHN S.   Grammatical relations. New York; London: Garland, 1985. pp. 812. (Outstanding dissertations in linguistics.)

1806. BURCHFIELD, ROBERT (introd.).   William Cobbett: *A Grammar of the English Language.* (Bibl. 1985, 1440.) Rev. by E. Pereira in UES (24:1) 39; by Vivian Salmon in NQ (33:2) 199–200.

1807. BURTON-ROBERTS, NOEL.   Utterance, relevance and problems with text grammar: review article. Australian Journal of Linguistics (5:2) 1985, 285–96.

1808. CHUNG, CHUNG-SEUNG.   Daemyoungsa joeum hyeonsang e gwanhan yeongu. (A study of the articulation of pronouns.) Unpub. doct. diss., Keimyung Univ. (Korea), 1985.

1809. CRAWLEY, R. A.   The effects of local and global factors on the comprehension of pronouns. Unpub. doct. diss., Univ. of Durham, 1985. [Abstr. in IT (35) 1077.]

1810. DIRVEN, RENÉ.   Definition of a pedagogical grammar, seen from a linguist's point of view. ITL (67/68) 1985, 43–67.

1811. GOOSSENS, LOUIS.   'Say': a case of perspectivization on the scene of linguistic action. See **1635.**

1812. GRIMSHAW, JANE B.   English *wh*-constructions and the theory of grammar. New York; London; Garland, 1985. pp. 239. (Outstanding dissertations in linguistics.) (Cf. bibl. 1978, 1688.)

1813. GUÉRON, J.; OBENAUER, H.-G.; POLLOCK, J. Y. (eds).   Grammatical representation. Dordrecht: Foris, 1985. pp. vi, 362. (Studies in generative grammar, 22.)

1814. HANSEN, ERIK; NIELSEN, HANS FREDE.   Irregularities in modern English. Odense: Odense UP. pp. 359.

1815. HAWKINS, JOHN A.   A comparative typology of English and German: unifying the contrasts. London: Croom Helm, 1985. pp. xiv, 244. Rev. by Christian Mair in AAA (11) 241–3.

1816. HERSKOVITS, ANNETTE.   Language and spatial cognition: an interdisciplinary study of the prepositions in English. Cambridge: CUP. pp. x, 208. (Studies in natural language processing.)

1817. IHALAINEN, OSSI.   An enquiry into the nature of mixed grammars: two cases of grammatical variation in dialectal British English. *In* (pp. 371–9) **26.**

1818. KEYSER, SAMUEL JAY; O'NEIL, W.   Rule generalization and optionality in language change. *See* **821.**

1819. KHAN, S. N.   Improved algorithms and methods for grammatical inference. Unpub. doct. diss., Univ. of Exeter, 1983.

1820. KIM, MIN-JOO.   Youngeo gyeok e gwanhan yeoksajeok gochal. (An historical study of case in English.) JELL (32:1) 154–77.

1821. LEE, BYUNG-CHOON.   Toward a unification of binding theory and empty category principle. BIHS (12) 343–73.

1822. LEE, KI-SUK.   Aspects of free relatives in English. JUJH (22) 277–303.

1823. LEHMANN, WINFRED P.   Mellow glory: see language steadily and see it whole. *In* (pp. 17–34) **38.**

1824. McLAUGHLIN, JOHN.   Old English syntax: a handbook. (Bibl. 1984, 1465.) Rev. by Marri Kilpiö in Spec (61:2) 442–4.

1825. PALMER, F. R.   Mood and modality. Cambridge: CUP. pp. xii, 243. (Cambridge textbooks in linguistics.)

1826. PARK, IN-WOONG.   On nominalization in English. BIHS (12) 325–42.

1827. PARK, JAE-DOO.   *Will* and *be going to* e daehayeo. (A study of the usage of 'will' and 'be going to'.) BIHS (12) 199–210.

1828. QUIRK, RANDOLPH.   Words at work: lectures on textual structure. Singapore: Singapore UP; Harlow: Longman. pp. 135.

1829. RADDEN, GÜNTER.   Looking back at case grammar. ITL (67/68) 1985, 185–99.

1830. SALKIE, R. M.   Auxiliaries and the nature of generalisations in grammatical theory. Unpub. doct. diss., Univ. of Cambridge, 1983.

1831. SHIN, GIL-SOON.   Youngeo busa yeongu. (A study of adverbs in the English language.) Unpub. doct. diss., Korea Univ.

1832. STOCKWELL, ROBERT P.   Grammar as speaker's knowledge versus grammar as linguists' characterization of norms. *In* (pp. 125–33) **26.**

1833. SUH, JUNG-IL.   On the presupposition of the factive verbs. JHY (7:3) 1985, 517–27.

1834. SUNDBY, BERTIL.   Towards a dictionary of English normative grammar. *See* **1793.**

1835. TOTTIE, GUNNEL; BÄCKLUND, INGEGERD (eds).   English in speech and writing: a symposium. *See* **16.**

1836. TRAUGOTT, ELIZABETH CLOSS (ed.).   On conditionals. Cambridge: CUP, pp. vi, 384.

1837. VAN RIEMSDIJK, HENK; WILLIAMS, EDWIN.   Introduction to the theory of grammar. Cambridge, MA; London: MIT Press. pp. xvi, 366. (Current studies in linguistics, 12.)

1838. VERMA, SHIVENDRA K.   A linguist's reflections on pedagogical grammar. ITL (69) 1985, 1–15.

1839. WERTH, PAUL.   A functional approach to presupposition:

pulling the plug on holes and filters. Belgian Journal of Linguistics (1) 239–79.

1840. WESTERGAARD, MARIT R.   Definite NP anaphora: a pragmatic approach. Oslo: Norwegian UP; Oxford: OUP. pp. 115.

1841. YANG, WOO-JIN.   GB iron gwa hapri jueui. (GB theory and rationalism.) JELL (31:4) 1985, 727–39.

GENERAL HISTORICAL STUDIES

1842. BAGHDIKIAN, SONIA.   'He did not seeke' or 'He seeketh not': are you a queen or a country woman? *In* (pp. 241–8) **12.**

1843. CABLE, THOMAS.   The rise of written standard English. *See* **812.**

1844. COVINGTON, MICHAEL A.   Grammatical theory in the Middle Ages. *In* (pp. 23–42) **53.**

1845. FRASER, THOMAS.   Did Old English have a middle voice? *In* (pp. 129–38) **42.**

1846. HATA, KOICHI.   Koeigo niokeru sonzai doshi no seiritsu nitsuite. (The formation of copula in Old English.) StudME (1) 39–51.

1847. HAUGLAND, KARI E.   DENG: a dictionary of English normative grammar 1700–1800. Three types of incongruence: 3, Co-occurrence. Bergen: Dept of English, Univ. of Bergen. pp. 74. (Linguistic project reports, 13.)

1848. IRVINE, MARTIN.   Bede the grammarian and the scope of grammatical studies in eighth-century Northumbria. ASE (15) 15–44.

1849. KABELL, INGE; LAURIDSEN, HANNE.   Accent in English as described by the earliest Danish grammars of English. *See* **1442.**

1850. KRZESZOWSKI, TOMASZ P.   An Elizabethan contrastive grammar of Spanish and French. *In* (pp. 1303–10) **26.**

1851. MATUNAMI, TAMOTU (ed.).   Eigo shi. (A history of English.) Tokyo: Taishukan. pp. xii, 184. (English language course, 1.)

1852. NAGUCKA, RUTA.   For a diachrony-in-synchrony analysis. *In* (pp. 395–407) **42.**

1853. OGURA, MICHIKO.   Old English 'impersonal' verbs and expressions. Copenhagen: Rosenkilde og Bagger. pp. 310. (Anglistica, 24.)

1854. SMITH, ROBIN D.   A syntactic quicksand: ellipsis in seventeenth and eighteenth-century English grammars. Delft: Eburon. pp. 415.

1855. TURNER, KATHLEEN.   Categorization, meaning, and change in the English modal system. Unpub. doct. diss., Univ. of Alabama, 1985. [Abstr. in DA (46) 1926A.]

1856. VAN ESSEN, A. J.   E. Kruisinga: a chapter in the history of linguistics in the Netherlands. (Bibl. 1984, 1544.) Rev. by F.G.A.M. Aarts in DQR (16:2) 153–4.

1857. WRIGHT, S. M.   Tense, aspect and text: processes of grammaticalization in the history of the English auxiliary. Unpub. doct. diss., Univ. of Cambridge. [Abstr. in IT (36) 908.]

HISTORICAL SYNTAX

1858. AIJMER, KARIN.   Polysemy, lexical variation and principles of semantic change: a study of the variation between *can* and *may* in Early Modern British English. *In* (pp. 143–70) **43.**

1859. ANDERSON, JOHN M. Old English morphology and the structure of noun phrases. FLH (7:1) 219–24.

1860. ARNAUD, RENÉ. Quelques observations quantitatives 'en temps réel' sur un changement: l'accroisement d'emploi de la forme progressive dans la 1re moitié du XIXe siècle. *In* (pp. 67–75) **1.**

1861. AUSTIN, FRANCES O. Relative *which* in late 18th century usage: the Clift family correspondence. *In* (pp. 15–29) **41.**

1862. BAGHDIKIAN, SONIA. Ambiguity on two levels: morphological and structural. Brussels Preprints in Linguistics (8) 1983, 42–61.

1863. —— 'He did not seeke' or 'he seeketh not': are you a queen or a country woman? Brussels Preprints in Linguistics (8) 1983, 26–41.

1864. —— Negation from the 14th to the 16th century. Brussels Preprints in Linguistics (8) 1983, 1–11.

1865. BREIVIK, LEIF EGIL. Variation in existential sentences in a synchronic-diachronic perspective. *In* (pp. 171–80) **43.**

1866. CAVANAUGH, D. The verb and particle collocation in Old English poetry: a descriptive analysis on the basis of syntax, metrical segmentation and stress. Unpub. doct. diss., Univ. of Oxford. [Abstr. in IT (35) 534.]

1867. CHEN, PING. Discourse and particle movement in English. *See* **1094.**

1868. DEKEYSER, XAVIER. English contact clauses revisited: a diachronic approach. FLH (7:1) 107–20.

1869. —— Relative markers in the Peterborough Chronicle: 1070–1154; or, linguistic change exemplified. FLH (7:1) 93–105.

1870. DENISON, DAVID. On word order in Old English. DQR (16:4) 277–95.

1871. —— The origins of periphrastic *do*: Ellegård and Visser reconsidered. *In* (pp. 45–60) **41.**

1872. DONNER, MORTON. The gerund in Middle English. EngS (67:5) 394–400.

1873. ENKVIST, NILS ERIK. More about the textual functions of the Old English adverbial *þa*. *In* (pp. 301–9) **26.**

1874. FISIAK, JACEK. Historical syntax. (Bibl. 1985, 1491.) Rev. by François Chevillet in EA (39:2) 195–7.

1875. FUJIWARA, HIROSHI. The relative clauses in *Beowulf*. *In* (pp. 311–16) **26.**

1876. GOOSSENS, LOUIS. Framing the linguistic action in Old and present-day English: OE *cwepan, secgan, sp(r)ecan* and present-day English *speak, talk, say* and *tell* compared. *In* (pp. 149–70) **42.**

1877. HAIMAN, JOHN (ed.). Iconicity in syntax: proceedings of a symposium on iconicity in syntax. Stanford, June 24–6, 1983. Amsterdam: Philadelphia, PA: Foris, 1983. pp. vi, 402. (Typological studies in language, 6.)

1878. HALL, MARGARET AUSTIN. Syntactic and semantic patterning with the verb 'be' in the older Germanic languages. Unpub. doct. diss., Univ. of California, Berkeley, 1985. [Abstr. in DA (47) 887A.]

1879. HANSEN, ERIK; NIELSEN, HANS FREDE. Irregularities in modern English. *See* **1814.**

1880. HARREL, PEGGY FERN. The syntax of the Blickling homilies: a structural analysis and a study of styles. Unpub. doct. diss., Univ. of Wisconsin–Madison, 1985. [Abstr. in DA (46) 3335A.]

1881. IKEGAMI, YOSHIHIKO. The drift toward agentivity and the development of the perfective use of *have* + pp. in English. *In* (pp. 381–6) **26.**

1882. IWASAKI, HARUO. Case and rhyme in Laȝamon's *Brut*. *In* (pp. 387–95) **26.**

1883. JACOBSEN, BENT. Existential 'there'. EngS (67:3) 250–62 (review-article).

1884. JOHANNESSON, NILS-LENNART. Variable subject deletion in Late Middle English topic constructions. *In* (pp. 119–29) **43.**

1885. KALDEWAIJ, JELLE. Structuralisme en transformationeel generatieve grammatica. (Structural and transformational generative grammar.) Dordrecht: Foris. pp. ix, 287. (Geschiedenis van de taal-kunde, 5.)

1886. KNIEZSA, VERONIKA. The progress of the expression of tem-poral relationships from Old English to Early Middle English. *In* (pp. 423–36) **26.**

1887. KOOPMAN, WILLEM F. Verb and particle combinations in Old and Middle English. *In* (pp. 109–21) **41.**

1888. KYTÖ, MERJA. *May* and *might* indicating 'epistemic possibility' in Early American English. *In* (pp. 131–42) **43.**

1889. LAGERQUIST, LINNEA M. The impersonal verb in context: Old English. *In* (pp. 123–36) **41.**

1890. MOESSNER, LILO. The English active verbal syntagm: a functional diachronic approach. FLH (7:1) 151–65.

1891. NAGUCKA, RUTA. Complementation in Ælfric's *Colloquy*. *In* (pp. 533–45) **26.**

1892. —— Remarks on complementation in Old English. *In* (pp. 195–204) **41.**

1893. NEVANLINNA, SAARA. Variation in the syntactic structure of simile in OE prose. *In* (pp. 89–98) **43.**

1894. NUNNALLY, THOMAS ERIE. The syntax of the genitive in Old, Middle, and early Modern English. Unpub. doct. diss., Univ. of Georgia, 1985. [Abstr. in DA (46) 2681A.]

1895. OGURA, MICHIKO. OE verbs of thinking. NM (87:3) 325–41.

1896. —— Old English 'impersonal periphrasis', or the construction 'copula+past participle' of 'impersonal' verbs. PoetT (23) 16–52.

1897. POUSSA, PATRICIA. Historical implications of the distribution of the zero-pronoun relative clause in Modern English dialects: looking backwards towards OE from Map S5 of *The Linguistic Atlas of England*. *In* (pp. 99–117) **43.**

1898. Rissanen, Matti. Expression of exclusiveness in Old English and the development of the adverb *only*. *In* (pp. 253–67) **41.**

1899. Rudanko, Juhani. Towards classifying verbs and adjectives governing the genitive in *Beowulf*. (Bibl. 1983, 1800, where scholar's forename incorrect).

1900. Smith, Robin D. A syntactic quicksand: ellipsis in seventeenth and eighteenth-century English grammars. *See* **1854.**

1901. Sørensen, Knud. Phrasal verb into noun. *See* **1563.**

1902. Spiller, Michael R. G. Pronouns in *Tam o' Shanter*. SLJ (13:1) 21–9.

1903. Stein, Dieter. Syntactic variation and change: the case of *do* in questions in Early Modern English. FLH (7:1) 121–49.

1904. Tieken-Boon van Ostade, Ingrid. Negative 'do' in eighteenth-century English: the power of prestige. DQR (16:4) 296–312.

1905. Travis, Lisa Demena. The role of INFL in word order change. *In* (pp. 331–41) **41.**

1906. van Kemenade, Ans. Old English infinitival complements and West-Germanic V-raising. *In* (pp. 73–84) **41.**

1907. Yerkes, David. Syntax and style in Old English: a comparison of the two versions of Wærferth's translation of Gregory's *Dialogues*. (Bibl. 1985, 1035.) Rev. by Peter S. Baker in MLR (81:2) 438–9.

1908. Yonekura, Hiroshi. The language of the Wycliffite Bible: the syntactic differences between the two versions. Tokyo: Aratake shippan, 1985. pp. xviii, 525. Rev. by Knud Sørensen in EngS (67:1) 78–80.

HISTORICAL MORPHOLOGY

1909. Anderson, John M. Old English morphology and the structure of noun phrases. *See* **1859.**

1910. Bochorishvili, N. K. O granit͡sakh slovoobrazovatel'nogo var'ironvanii͡a v angliĭskom i͡azyke XVI veka. (The limits of derivational variation in 16th century English.) NDFN (1986:1) 58–62.

1911. Bourcier, Georges. Remarques sur les dérivés chez Richard Rolle: où en est la morphologie? *In* (pp. 211–20) **26.**

1912. Colman, Fran. A *cæᵹ* to Old English syllable structure. *In* (pp. 225–30) **26.**

1913. Hansen, Erik; Nielsen, Hans Frede. Irregularities in modern English. *See* **1814.**

1914. Minkova, Donka. Of rhyme and reason: some foot-governed quantity changes in English. *In* (pp. 163–78) **41.**

1915. Nakao, Toshio. Metathesis. *In* (pp. 547–56) **26.**

1916. Nielsen, Hans F. Old English and continental Germanic languages. A survey of morphological and phonological interrelations. *See* **829.**

1917. Plank, Frans. The interpretation and development of form alternations conditioned across word boundaries: the case of *wife's*, *wives*, and *wives'*. *In* (pp. 205–33) **41.**

1918. Romaine, Suzanne. The effects of language standardization on deletion rules: some comparative Germanic evidence from *t/d*-deletion. *In* (pp. 605–20) **26.**

1919. —— Variability in word formation patterns and productivity in the history of English. *In* (pp. 451–65) **42.**

1920. RONBERG, GERT. The two manuscripts of *The Wars of Alexander*: a linguistic comparison. *See* **173.**

1921. STEIN, DIETER. Old English Northumbrian verb inflection revisited. *In* (pp. 637–50) **26.**

CURRENT ENGLISH GRAMMAR
GENERAL STUDIES

1922. AARTS, F. G. A. M. Dutch progress in English syntax: Zandvoort's *Handbook of English Grammar* and after. DQR (16:4) 249–63.

1923. ALBUYEH, ANN DAWSON. The constituent analysis theory of complexity. Unpub. doct. diss., Univ. of Wisconsin–Madison, 1985. [Abstr. in DA (47) 884A.]

1924. ASAKAWA, TERUO; KAMATA, SEIZABURO. Jodoshi. (Auxiliary verbs.) Tokyo: Taishukan. pp. viii, 232. (New English grammar, 4.)

1925. BARTON, ELLEN LYNN. A theory of constituent structures and constituent utterances. *See* **1081.**

1926. BLOCK, RUSSELL LLOYD. Revolution und Revision in der generativen Theoriebildung. Tübingen: Narr. pp. xiv, 266. (Studien zur englischen Grammatik, 3.)

1927. BOLTON, DAVID; OSCARSON, MATS; PETERSON, LENNART. Basic working grammar. Walton-on-Thames: Nelson. pp. x, 150.

1928. BOUCHER, PAUL. Time–space markers in oral discourse in English. *In* (pp. 235–46) **1.**

1929. BYRNE, FRANCIS. Evidence against grammars without empty categories. LI (17:4) 754–9.

1930. CHOI, KEY-SUN; KIM, GIL CHANG. Controlling of quantification rules in parsing of Montague grammar. PL (19:3) 315–50.

1931. COATES, JENNIFER. The semantics of the modal auxiliaries. (Bibl. 1984, 1573.) Rev. by Angela Downing in RCEI (12) 171–80.

1932. CORNISH, FRANCIS. Anaphoric relations in English and French: a discourse perspective. London: Croom Helm. pp. 242. (Croom Helm linguistic series.)

1933. COTTLE, BASIL. The language of literature: English grammar in action. London: Macmillan; New York: St Martin's Press, 1985. pp. vii, 158. Rev. by W. Hutchings in SCN (44:4) 65.

1934. CRUTTENDEN, A. The intonation of English sentences, with special reference to sentence adverbials. Unpub. doct. diss., Univ. of Manchester, 1981.

1935. DAHL, OSTEN. Tense and aspect systems. Oxford: Blackwell, 1985. pp. 240.

1936. DAVIDSEN-NIELSEN, NIELS. Har engelsk en fremtid?: betragtninger over futurum i engelsk og andre sprog. (Has English a future tense?: some notes on the future in English and other languages.) CEBAL (8) 27–44.

1937. DAVIES, EIRLYS. The English imperative. London: Croom Helm. pp. 275. (Croom Helm linguistics.)

1938. DE HACKBEIL, HANNA WALINSKA. The roots of phrase structure: the syntactic basis of English morphology. Unpub. doct. diss., Univ. of Washington. [Abstr. in DA (47) 1305A.]

1939. FREEMAN, DAVID EDWARD. Use of pragmatic cohesion cues to resolve degrees of pronoun reference ambiguity in reading. *See* **1274.**

1940. GARDNER, S. F. Parasyntax and the sentential level in axiomatic functionalism. Unpub. doct. diss., Univ. of St Andrews, 1985. [Abstr. in IT (35) 36–7.]

1941. GORGIS, D. T. The morphophonemics of the deverbal noun in modern standard Arabic and English. Unpub. doct. diss., Univ. of Manchester, 1982. [Abstr. in IT (35) 37.]

1942. HIETARANTA, PERTTI. A functional constraint on topicalization. SL (40:1) 40–7.

1943. HOCKETT, CHARLES F. The uniqueness fallacy. *In* (pp. 35–46) **38.**

1944. HORN, GEORGE M. The minimal distance principle revisited. *In* (pp. 909–34) **26.**

1945. HORVATH, JULIA; ROCHEMONT, MICHAEL. Pronouns in discourse and sentence grammar. *See* **1110.**

1946. JACOBSEN, BENT. Modern transformational grammar: with particular references to the theory of government and binding. Amsterdam; Oxford: North-Holland. pp. xv, 441. (North-Holland linguistic series, 53.)

1947. JOHNSEN, LARS. Om tællelighed på engelsk. (On the concept of countability in English.) CEBAL (8) 116–27.

1948. KJELLMER, GÖRAN. On 'pattern neatening' in the English pronominal system. SL (40:2) 149–60.

1949. KRULEE, GILBERT K. Two-level representations for natural language. PL (19:2) 205–86.

1950. LENSTRUP, RITA. Den reducerede engelske relativsætning kopieret i dansk oversættelse. (The reduced English relative clause imitated in Danish translation.) CEBAL (8) 163–203.

1951. McDANIEL, DANA S. Conditions on *wh*-chains. Unpub. doct. diss., City Univ. of New York. [Abstr. in DA (47) 888A.]

1952. McKENNA, SHEILA CATHARINE. Ethnocultural differences in the use of spatial prepositions. *See* **1065.**

1953. MACLEOD, C. Pronoun identification: the co-ordination of available information. Unpub. doct. diss., Univ. of Oxford, 1985.

1954. PARKER, FRANK; THORMEYER, JOHN. Analogizing from linguistics to folklore. Folklore (97:2) 148–85.

1955. PILCH, HERBERT. The tag syntagm of spoken English. *In* (pp. 983–91) **26.**

1956. POLAŃSKI, KAZIMIERZ. Some remarks on transformations. *In* (pp. 95–104) **26.**

1957. POSTAL, PAUL M.; PULLUM, GEOFFREY K. Misgovernment. LI (17:1) 104–10.

1958. QUIRK, RANDOLPH, *et al.* A comprehensive grammar of the English language. (Bibl. 1985, 1557.) Rev. by François Chevillet in EA (39:3) 327–9.

1959. EL-RAYYAN, MOHAMMAD RASHAD HAMD-ALLAH. Toward the construction of a temporal system for natural language in the light of the data of the Arabic and English languages. Unpub. doct. diss., Univ. of Pennsylvania. [Abstr. in DA (47) 1714A.]

1960. ROBERGE, PAUL T. Grammatical prerequisites to phonological change? *See* **1425.**

1961. ROOT, REBECCA LOUISE. The semantics of anaphora in discourse. *See* **1133.**

1962. SHAMSUDDIN. The time and tense relationship in English. Journal of Research (Humanities) (Multan) (1:1) 1984, 17–32.

1963. VALIN, ROBERT D., JR. An empty category as the subject of a tensed 's' in English. LI (17:3) 581–6.

CURRENT ENGLISH SYNTAX

1964. AARTS, FLOR; AARTS, JAN. English syntactic structures: functions and categories in sentence analysis. (Bibl. 1985, 1565.) Rev. by N. E. Osselton in EngS (67:1) 88–90.

1965. AIJMER, KARIN. Why is 'actually' so popular in spoken English? *In* (pp. 119–29) **16.**

1966. ALLAN, W. S. The role of the lexicon in syntactic change. Unpub. doct. diss., Univ. of Edinburgh, 1985. [Abstr. in IT (35) 1076.]

1967. ALLERTON, D. J. Valency and the English verb. New York: Academic Press, 1982. (Cf. bibl. 1983, 1897.) Rev. by Libuše Dušková in PP (29) 101–4; by Torban Thrane in SL (10:2) 485–91.

1968. ALTENBERG, BENGT. Contrastive linking in spoken and written English. *In* (pp. 13–40) **16.**

1969. ANDREWS, AVERY D., III. Studies in the syntax of relative and comparative clauses. New York; London: Garland, 1985. pp. 205. (Outstanding dissertations in linguistics.)

1970. AOUN, JOSEPH. Generalized binding: the syntax and logical form of WH interrogatives. Dordrecht: Foris. pp. viii, 173. (Studies in generative grammar, 26.)

1971. BÄCKLUND, INGEGERD. 'Beat until stiff': conjunction-headed abbreviated clauses in spoken and written English. *In* (pp. 41–55) **16.**

1972. BARSS, ANDREW; LASNIK, HOWARD. A note on anaphora and double objects. LI (17:2) 347–54.

1973. BAUM, SHARI R. Syntactic processing in aphasia. *See* **1265.**

1974. BÁZLIK, MIROSLAV. Akuzatívny objekt z hládiska valencie v porovnání s angličtinou. (The accusative object from the point of view of valency in comparison to English.) Jazykovedný časopis (Bratislava) (37) 39–45.

1975. BEESLEY, K. R. On the analysis of English adjectives in a Montague grammar. Unpub. doct. diss., Univ. of Edinburgh, 1983.

1976. BERWICK, ROBERT C. The acquisition of syntactic knowledge. *See* **1300.**

1977. BLAND, SUSAN KESNER. The action nominal in English. *See* **1348.**

1978. BOAS, HANS ULRICH. Formal versus explanatory generalizations in generative transformational grammar: an investigation into generative argumentation. (Bibl. 1984, 1495.) Rev. by R. Hendrich in Lingua (69:1/2) 165–72.

1979. BÖHMEROVÁ, ADELA. Neutralizácia negácie v angličtine a v slovenčine. (The neutralization of negation in English and in Slovak.) *In* (pp. 19–20) **4.**

1980. BORER, HAGIT. I-subjects. LI (17:3) 375–416.

1981. BOUCHARD, DENIS. Empty categories and the contraction debate. LI (17:1) 95–104.

1982. BREIVIK, LEIF EGIL. Existential 'there': a synchronic and diachronic study. (Bibl. 1985, 1578.) Rev. by Flor Aarts in SAP (19) 207–11; by Bent Jacobsen in EngS (67:3) 250–62; by R. S. Kirsner in LeuB (75:4) 531–9; by John Haiman in CJL (31:1) 88–91.

1983. —— Variation in existential sentences in a synchronic-diachronic perspective. *In* (pp. 171–80) **43.**

1984. BRODY, M. Conditions and NP-types. Unpub. doct. diss., Univ. of London, University Coll., 1984.

1985. BURTON-ROBERTS, NOEL. Analysing sentences: an introduction to English syntax. London: Longman. pp. viii, 265. (Learning about language.)

1986. CAMINERO, ROSARIO. WH Q movement in Spanish compared to WH movement in English. Unpub. doct. diss., Univ. of Pittsburgh, 1985. [Abstr. in DA (47) 1713A.]

1987. CANN, R. Features and morphology in generalized phrase structure grammar. Unpub. doct. diss., Univ. of Sussex, 1984.

1988. CARROLL, SUSANNE. Reflexives and the dependency relation 'R'. CJL (31:1) 1–43.

1989. CHAPPELL, HILARY. The 'get' passive revisited: a reply to Sussex (1982). PL (19:4) 413–24.

1990. CHEN, CHUNG-YU. On the physical modality of English verbs. PL (19:2) 131–54.

1991. CHOI, SOONJA. A cross-linguistic development study of negation in English, French and Korean. Unpub. doct. diss., State Univ. of New York at Buffalo. [Abstr. in DA (47) 2143A.]

1992. CHOMSKY, NOAM. Some concepts and consequences of the theory of government and binding. (Bibl. 1983, 1911.) Rev. by Marion Owen in MLR (81:3) 687–8.

1993. CLARK, ROBIN LEE. Boundaries and the treatment of control. Unpub. doct. diss., Univ. of California, Los Angeles, 1985. [Abstr. in DA (46) 3703A.]

1994. COMRIE, BERNARD. Tense in indirect speech. FL (20:3/4) 265–96.

1995. COOPER, ROBIN. Quantification and syntactic theory. Lancaster: Reidel, 1984. (Cf. bibl. 1985, 1585.) Rev. by Alice ter Meulen in SL (10:2) 493–500.

1996. CORNILESCU, ALEXANDRA.   On the syntax and semantics of free relative clauses in English and Romanian. *In* (pp. 1165–82) **26.**

1997. CULICOVER, PETER W.; WILKINS, WENDY.   Control, PRO, and the projection principle. Lang (62:1) 120–53.

1998. DAVIDSEN-NIELSEN, NIELS.   Modal verbs in English and Danish. *In* (pp. 1183–94) **26.**

1999. DAVIES, EIRLYS E.   English vocatives: a look at their function and form. SAP (19) 91–106.

2000. DAVIS, LORI J.   Remarks on the θ-criterion and case. LI (17:3) 564–8.

2001. DE RYCKER, TEUN.   The expanded form: a dynamic synchronic approach. Antwerp: Universitaire Instelling, 1982. pp. 138.

2002.   —— Imperative structures: form and function in conversational English. *See* **1099.**

2003. DESCLÉS, JEAN PIERRE; GUENTCHÉVA, ZLATKA; SHAUMYAN, SEBASTIAN.   Theoretical aspects of passivization in the framework of generative grammar. Amsterdam; Philadelphia, PA: Benjamins, 1985. pp. vi, 115. (Pragmatics and beyond, 6:1.)

2004. DI PAOLO, MARIANNA.   A study of double modals in Texas English. *See* **864.**

2005. DOMINICY, MARC.   Sur les emplois 'temporels' de *only*. *In* (pp. 211–17) **12.**

2006. DUŠKOVÁ, LIBUŠE.   On the nature of dependent *wh*-clauses. Prague Studies in English (18) 1984, 75–83.

2007.   —— On the type of definiteness expressed by the English possessives. PP (29) 197–207.

2008. EGBE, D. I.   An approach to the syntax and semantics of the imperative in English. *See* **1359.**

2009. EMONDS, JOSEPH E.   A unified theory of syntactic categories. Dordrecht: Foris, 1985. pp. 356. (Studies in generative grammar, 19.)

2010. ERDMANN, PETER.   Die 'for-to'-Konstruktion im britischen und amerikanischen Englisch. AAA (11:2) 139–58.

2011. ERTESCHIK-SHIR, NOMI.   *Wh*-questions and focus. Linguistics and Philosophy (9:2) 117–49.

2012. FITZPATRICK, EILEEN M.   Theme and case as determinants of the domain of movement. Unpub. doct. diss., New York Univ., 1985. [Abstr. in DA (46) 2281A.]

2013. FLYNN, MICHAEL J.   Structure building operations and word order. New York; London: Garland, 1985. pp. vii, 134. (Outstanding dissertations in linguistics.) (Cf. bibl. 1981, 1875.)

2014. FRENCH, ROBERT.   Control and thematic-government. Unpub. doct. diss., New York Univ., 1985. [Abstr. in DA (46) 2281A.]

2015. GELUYKENS, RONALD.   Focus phenomena in English: an empirical investigation into cleft and pseudo-cleft sentences. Antwerp: Universitaire Instelling, 1984. pp. 135. (Antwerp papers in linguistics, 38.)

2016. GLÄSER, ROSEMARIE.   A plea for phraseo-stylistics. *In* (pp. 41–52) **26.**

2017. GOOSSENS, LOUIS.   Framing the linguistic action in Old and present-day English: OE *cweþan, secgan, sp(r)ecan* and present-day English *speak, talk, say* and *tell* compared. *In* (pp. 149–70) **42.**

2018. —— 'Say': a case of perspectivization on the scene of linguistic action. *See* **1635.**

2019. GRIMSHAW, JANE. A morphosyntactic explanation for the mirror principle. LI (17:4) 745–9.

2020. —— Subjacency and the S/S' parameter. LI (17:2) 364–9.

2021. GRUIŢĂ, MARIANA. A contrastive syntax of English and Romanian: the compound and the complex sentence. Cluj-Napoca: Babeş-Bolyai UP, 1985. pp. 265.

2022. GUNNARSON, KJELL-ÅKE. Predicative structures and projections of lexical dependencies. LI (17:1) 13–47.

2023. GUSSENHOVEN, CAROLUS HENRICUS MARIA. On the grammar and semantics of sentence accents. (Bibl. 1984, 1603.) Rev. by M. G. Ashby in EngS (67:1) 87–8.

2024. HAEGEMAN, LILIANE. The present subjunctive in contemporary British English. SAP (19) 61–74.

2025. HAIMAN, JOHN. Natural syntax, iconicity and erosion. Cambridge: CUP, 1985. pp. viii, 285. (Cambridge studies in linguistics, 44.)

2026. HAJIČOVÁ, IVANA. Slovosledné pozice časových a místních určení. (The word-order of temporal and local adverbials.) *In* (pp. 24–5) **4.**

2027. HALLIDAY, M. A. K. It's a fixed word order language is English. ITL (67/68) 1985, 91–116.

2028. HARRIS, MARTIN. English *ought (to)*. *In* (pp. 347–58) **26.**

2029. HARRIS, MARTIN B. Aspects of subordination in English and other languages. BJRL (69:1) 195–209.

2030. HENY, FRANK; RICHARDS, BARRY (eds). Linguistic categories: auxiliaries and related puzzles: vol. 1, Categories; vol. 2, The scope, order and distribution of English auxiliary verbs. (Bibl. 1983, 1954.) Rev. by B. Rigter in Lingua (69:4) 355–82.

2031. HERMERÉN, LARS. Modalities in spoken and written English: an inventory of forms. *In* (pp. 57–91) **16.**

2032. HOLMBERG, ANDERS. Word order and sybtactic features in the Scandinavian languages and English. Stockholm: Stockholm Univ. pp. 254. (Doct. diss., Stockholm Univ.)

2033. HONG, SUNGSHIM. A and A' binding in Korean and English: government-binding parameters. Unpub. doct. diss., Univ. of Connecticut, 1985. [Abstr. in DA (46) 3336A.]

2034. HUBBARD, KATHERINE ELIZABETH. The syntax of English temporal constructions introduced by after, before, since, until, when, and while. Unpub. doct. diss., Univ. of Hawaii. [Abstr. in DA (47) 1715A.]

2035. JACOBSEN, BENT. Existential 'there'. *See* **1883.**

2036. JACOBSON, SVEN. Synonymy and hyponymy in syntactic variation. *In* (pp. 7–17) **43.**

2037. —— (ed.). Papers from the third Scandinavian symposium on syntactic variation, Stockholm, May 11–12, 1985. *See* **43.**

2038. JACOBSSON, BENGT.   Another look at negatively conditioned subject–operator inversion in English. SL (40:2) 161–85.

2039. JAEGGLI, OSVALDO A.   Arbitrary plural pronominals. Natural Language and Linguistic Theory (4:1) 43–76.

2040. —— Passive. LI (17:4) 587–622.

2041. JARVIS, DONALD K.   Some problems with noun number choice. SEEJ (30:2) 262–70.

2042. JOHANSSON, STIG.   Some observations on the order of adverbial particles and objects in the LOB Corpus. *In* (pp. 51–62) **43.**

2043. JONES, CHARLES FOSTER.   Syntax and thematics of infinitival adjuncts. Unpub. doct. diss., Univ. of Massachusetts, 1985. [Abstr. in DA (46) 3706A.]

2044. JØRGENSEN, ERIK.   The pattern 'in charge of' and its variants in contemporary English. EngS (67:4) 355–62.

2045. KAKIETEK, PIOTR.   Remarks on Lakoff's classification of verbs. *In* (pp. 935–45) **26.**

2046. KALLEN, J. L.   Linguistic fundamentals for Hiberno-English syntax. Unpub. doct. diss., Trinity Coll. Dublin, 1985/86. [Abstr. in IT (36) 904.]

2047. KATO, KAZUO.   Another look at ellipsis: non-native recoverability of ellipsis and its implications for linguistic competence. *See* **1373.**

2048. KILBY, DAVID.   Descriptive syntax and the English verb. (Bibl. 1984, 1620.) Rev. by Sheila M. Embleton in CJL (31:3) 306–8.

2049. KIM, YONG-SUK.   Licensing conditions on syntactic representation. Unpub. doct. diss., Kyunghee Univ. (Seoul.)

2050. KJELLMER, GÖRAN.   Help to/help ø revisited. EngS (66:2) 1985, 156–61.

2051. KNOWLES, JOHN.   The cleft sentence: a base-generated perspective. Lingua (69) 295–317.

2052. KOKTOVÁ, EVA.   Remarks on the semantics of sentence adverbials. Journal of Pragmatics (10:1) 27–40.

2053. KRÁMSKÝ, JIŘÍ.   Stylostatistical investigation of personal pronouns in modern English. *See* **1230.**

2054. LASNIK, HOWARD.   On accessibility. LI (17:1) 126–9.

2055. LEHRER, ADRIENNE.   English classifier constructions. Lingua (68) 109–48.

2056. LEVIN, BETH; RAPPAPORT, MALKA.   The formation of adjectival passives. LI (17:4) 623–61.

2057. LEVIN, NANCY S.; PRINCE, ELLEN F.   Gapping and causal implicature. PL (19:3) 351–64.

2058. LING, ÅGE.   The variant forms of 'aim to do' / 'aim at doing'. EngS (67:3) 263–8.

2059. LUMSDEN, M.   Syntactic and semantic properties of existential sentences. Unpub. doct. diss., Univ. of York, 1984.

2060. MCKINNON, M. L.   A procedural account of some English modals. Unpub. doct. diss., Univ. of Edinburgh, 1985. [Abstr. in IT (35) 1078.]

2061. MALLINSON, GRAHAM. Languages with and without extra-position. FL (20:1/2) 147–63.

2062. MANN, RICHARD PHILIP. A statistical survey of transitional device usage among writers of English as a second language and native writers of English. Unpub. doct. diss., Ohio State Univ. [Abstr. in DA (47) 1636A.]

2063. MARKOVÁ, MILENA. K poměru verbálních a nominálních rysů mezi češtinou a angličtinou z hlediska překladu. (The relation of verbal and nominal features in Czech and English.) *In* (pp. 39–40) **4.**

2064. —— On the relationship between gerund and verbal noun. PP (29) 83–91.

2065. MATTHEWS, ALISON. Pronoun resolution in two-clause sentences. *See* **1283.**

2066. MATTHEWS, P. H. Distributional syntax. *In* (pp. 245–77) **53.**

2067. MOON, KYUNG HWAN. A cross-linguistic approach to the syntax of verbs. Unpub. doct. diss., Univ. of Washington, 1985. [Abstr. in DA (46) 1922A.]

2068. MORRIS, R. Aspect, case and thematic structure in English. Unpub. doct. diss., Univ. of London (University Coll.), 1984.

2069. MUNSAT, STANLEY. *Wh*-complementizers. Linguistics and Philosophy (9:2) 191–217.

2070. NAKAJIMA, HEIZO. COMP as a SUBJECT. Linguistic Review (4) 1985, 121–52.

2071. NEVALAINEN, TERTTU; RISSANEN, MATTI. Do you support the *do*-support? Emphatic and non-emphatic *do* in affirmative statements in present-day spoken English. *In* (pp. 35–50) **43.**

2072. NEY, JAMES W. Semantic structures for the syntax of complements and auxiliaries in English. (Bibl. 1984, 1633.). Rev. by Brygida Rudzka-Ostyn in ITL (64) 1984, 94–101.

2073. NOSEK, JIŘÍ. Příslovečné určení v jednoduché větě: Přispěvek k soustavné syntaxi moderni angličtiny. (Adverbial modifier in a simple clause: a contribution to the systematic syntax of modern English.) JazA (23) 51–3.

2074. —— Semantic structure of attributes in modern English. Prague Studies in English (18) 1984, 47–61.

2075. O'GRADY, WILLIAM. In defence of general nativism. CJL (31:1) 45–53.

2076. OHLANDER, SÖLVE. Question-orientation versus answer-orientation in English interrogative clauses. *In* (pp. 963–82) **26.**

2077. PICKERING, MICHAEL. The geometry and logic of prepositional meaning. Pubs of the Dept of English, Univ. of Turku (6) 1985, 119–29.

2078. PINKHAM, JESSIE E. The formation of comparative clauses in French and English. New York; London: Garland, 1985. pp. xii, 162. (Outstanding dissertations in linguistics.) (Cf. bibl. 1982, 2255.)

2079. POUSSA, PATRICIA. Historical implications of the distribution of the zero-pronoun relative clause in Modern English dialects: looking backwards towards OE from Map S5 of *The Linguistic Atlas of England. In* (pp. 99–117) **43.**

2080. PREISLER, BENT. Language function and modality: how to be tentative in English. *See* **1391.**

2081. PULLUM, GEOFFREY K.; ZWICKY, ARNOLD M. Phonological resolution of syntactic feature conflict. *See* **1496.**

2082. PUTSEYS, YVAN. A modular approach to the grammar of English demonstrative determiners. ITL (67/68) 1985, 161–83.

2083. RANSOM, EVELYN N. Complementation: its meanings and forms. Amsterdam; Philadelphia, PA: Benjamins. pp. viii, 226. (Typological studies in language, 10.)

2084. REINHART, TANYA. Anaphora and semantic interpretation. (Bibl. 1985, 1646.) Rev. by Francis Cornish in Lingua (68) 241–56.

2085. RIGTER, BOB. Time intervals and identity relations across boundaries of intensional domains. Linguistics in the Netherlands (2:1) 199–208.

2086. —— TO and PRO. Linguistics in the Netherlands 1985, 157–65.

2087. ROCHEMONT, MICHAEL S. Focus in generative grammar. Amsterdam; Philadelphia, PA; Benjamins. pp. ix, 221. (Sigla, 4.)

2088. ROMAINE, SUZANNE. Syntactic variation and the acquisition of strategies of relativization in the language of Edinburgh school children. *In* (pp. 19–33) **43.**

2089. RUDANKO, JUHANI. On the syntax of pseudoclefts with VP focus in English. NM (87:2) 284–90.

2090. RUIN, INGER. About *today* and *tomorrow* in the past. *In* (pp. 63–73) **43.**

2091. SAFIR, KEN. Relative clauses in a theory of binding and levels. LI (17:4) 663–89.

2092. SELKIRK, ELIZABETH O. Phonology and syntax: the relation between sound and structure. *See* **1501.**

2093. SEPPÄNEN, AIMO. The syntax of 'seem' and 'appear' revisited. SL (40:1) 22–39.

2094. —— SEPPÄNEN, RUTH. Notes on quantifiers and definiteness in English. SN (58:2) 169–87.

2095. SICHELSCHMIDT, LORENZ. Optionality and choice in the analysis of adjective order: comments on Ney. SL (40) 135–48. (*Refers to* bibl. 1983, 1998.)

2096. SILIAKUS, H. J. Some syntactical features of linguistic texts. ITL (65) 1984, 57–77.

2097. SØRENSEN, KNUD. Phrasal verb into noun. *See* **1563.**

2098. STACZEK, JOHN J. The English pronominal reflexive: an aspect of usage variation. SAP (19) 119–28.

2099. STAŠKOVÁ, JAROSLAVA. K problematike vymedzenia významu anglických temporálnych predložiek. (Problems in defining meanings of English temporal prepositions.) *In* (pp. 60–1) **4.**

2100. STENSTRÖM, ANNA-BRITA. What does 'really' really do? Strategies in speech and writing. *In* (pp. 149–63) **16.**

2101. STUURMAN, FRITS. Phrase structure theory in generative grammar. Dordrecht: Foris, 1985. pp. 265. (Publications in language sciences, 20.)

2102. TAHAL, KAREL.   Nefinitní část průběhových tvarů anglického slovesa. (The non-finite part of English progressive verb forms.) CJa (30) 69–72.

2103. —— Průběhovost jako dějová fáze: Poznámky o průběhových tvarech anglického slovesa. (Progression as an action phase in the English verb.) CJa (30) 145–9.

2104. TÁRNYIKOVÁ, JARMILA.   Komunikativní přístup v syntaxi. (The communicative approach to syntax.) *In* (pp. 64) **4.**

2105. —— Sentence patterns in communication.   Germanica Olomucensia (6) 2–31.

2106. TOMLIN, RUSSELL S.   Basic word order: functional principles. London: Croom Helm. pp. 308.

2107. TOTTIE, GUNNEL.   The importance of being adverbial: adverbials of focusing and contingency in spoken and written English. *In* (pp. 93–118) **16.**

2108. TRAVIS, LISA DEMENA.   The role of INFL in word order change. *In* (pp. 331–41) **41.**

2109. TURBOVÁ, MILENA.   One type of semantico-syntactic variations of verbal lexemes. PP (29) 28–35.

2110. UTSCHIG, ANNE MARTINSON.   Main and subordinate clause word order. Unpub. doct. diss., Univ. of Minnesota, 1985. [Abstr. in DA (46) 3020A.]

2111. VANDENBERGEN, ANNE-MARIE.   Conjunction and continuity in newspaper reports. *In* (pp. 85–94) **12.**

2112. VAN NOPPEN, JEAN-PIERRE.   'Be to' as an expression of futurity: human control only? *See* **1579.**

2113. VAN OIRSOUW, ROBERT R.   Syntactic ambiguity: a systematic accident. *In* (pp. 145–55) **26.**

2114. VERHEIJEN, RON; BEUKEMA, FRITS.   Anaphora and free adjuncts: a GPSG account. FL (20:3/4) 393–412.

2115. VERMANT, STEFAN.   The English present perfect: a dynamic–synchronic approach. Antwerp: Universitaire Instelling, 1983. pp. 130. (Antwerp papers in linguistics, 32.)

2116. VIITANEN, OUTI.   On the position of 'only' in English conversation. *In* (pp. 165–75) **16.**

2117. WATERS, T. R. W.   Sound and sense: the structure of language and our organization of experience. *See* **795.**

2118. WATSON, GREER.   Pronouns and prepositional phrases. Unpub. doct. diss., Yale Univ., 1985. [Abstr. in DA (46) 3340A.]

2119. WEKKER, H. CHR.   Points of modern English syntax LXVIII. EngS (67:6) 561–4.

2120. WEKKER, HERMAN; HAEGEMAN, LILIANE.   A modern course in English syntax. London: Croom Helm, 1985. pp. 202.

2121. WELTE, WERNER.   On the meaning of the plural in English. AAA (11:1) 95–109.

2122. WHITNEY, ROSEMARIE.   The syntax and interpretation of $\bar{a}$-adjunctions. Linguistic Review (4) 1985, 251–60.

2123. WIESER, ELISABETH.   On the splitting in English of the 'of'-genitive. EngS (67:1) 57–71.

2124. WILLIAMS, EDWIN.   PRO and subject of NP. Natural Language and Linguistic Theory (3:3) 1985, 297–315.

2125. WILMET, MARC.   *A kiwi abounds in this area: note sur l'article 'indéfini générique'. *In* (pp. 219–26) **12.**

2126. ZABROCKI, TADEUSZ.   A processing explanation for a syntactic difference between English and Polish. *In* (pp. 1485–99) **26.**

2127. ZWANENBURG, WIECHER.   X-bar structure and argument structure in morphology. Linguistics in the Netherlands (2:1) 245–54.

CURRENT ENGLISH MORPHOLOGY

2128. ADAMCZEWSKI, HENRI.   Extra- et métalinguistique: la langue à la rencontre du réel. RANAM (19) 19–31.

2129. BRODOVICH, O. I.   Strukturnaîâ rol' sloga v angliĭskom îâzyke: dannye dialektov. (The structural role of the syllable in English: dialectal data.) VLU (1986:2) 69–78.

2130. BYBEE, JOAN L.   Morphology: a study of the relation between meaning and form. Amsterdam; Philadelphia, PA: Benjamins, 1985. pp. xii, 234. (Typological studies in language, 9.)

2131. CANN, R.   Features and morphology in generalized phrase structure grammar. *See* **1987.**

2132. CHO, CHUL-HYEON.   Youngeo dongsa hyeongsung bokhapeo eui saengsansung. (The productivity of verbal-nexus compounds in English.) IKY (55) 91–111.

2133. FUNK, WOLF-PETER.   Towards a definition of semantic constraints on negative prefixation in English and German. *In* (pp. 877–89) **26.**

2134. HAEGEMAN, LILIANE.   The present subjunctive in contemporary British English. *See* **2024.**

2135. HAN, GI-SUN.   Hyeongtaijeok saengsansung gwa eumwoonjeok tumyungsung. *See* **1473.**

2136. HOUSTON, ANN CELESTE.   Continuity and change in English morphology: the variable (ING). *See* **1005.**

2137. KOLESÁROVÁ, ALENA.   Problémy konverzie v angličtine. (Problems of English conversion.) CJa (29) 258–60.

2138. LIGHTNER, THEODORE M.   Introduction to English derivational morphology. Philadelphia, PA: Benjamins, 1983. (Cf. bibl. 1985, 1693.) Rev. by Laurie Bauer in SL (10:2) 223–31.

2139. METTINGER, ARTHUR.   Unendurable unpersons unmask unexampled untruths: remarks on the functions of negative prefixes in Orwell's *1984.* WBEP (80) 109–18.

2140. PULLEYBLANK, DOUGLAS.   Rule application on a noncyclic stratum. *See* **1495.**

2141. RANDALL, JANET H.   Morphological structure and language acquisition. *See* **1333.**

2142. ŘEŘICHA, VÁCLAV. Metodologické problémy analýzy anglických substantivních kompozit. (Problems of analysis of English nounal compounds.) *In* (pp. 57–8) **4.**

2143. —— The semantics of English deverbal compounds: the 'chewing-gum' type. Germanica Olomucensia (6) 33–42.

2144. SØRENSEN, KNUD. On countable and uncountable nouns in English. Dolphin (13) 17–29.

2145. SULEIMAN, M. Y. I. H. Trends in modern morphology: a critical study. Unpub. doct. diss., Univ. of St Andrews, 1984.

SEMANTICS

2146. AIJMER, KARIN. Polysemy, lexical variation and principles of semantic change: a study of the variation between *can* and *may* in Early Modern British English. *In* (pp. 143–70) **43.**

2147. —— Why is 'actually' so popular in spoken English? *In* (pp. 119–29) **16.**

2148. ALLAN, KEITH. Linguistic meaning. London: Routledge & Kegan Paul. 2 vols. pp. xxiii, 452; xi, 348.

2149. ALTENBERG, BENGT. Contrastive linking in spoken and written English. *In* (pp. 13–40) **16.**

2150. AOUN, JOSEPH. Generalized binding: the syntax and logical form of WH interrogatives. *See* **1970.**

2151. BACH, EMMON. The algebra of events. Linguistics and Philosophy (9:1) 5–16.

2152. BÄCKLUND, INGEGERD. 'Beat until stiff': conjunction-headed abbreviated clauses in spoken and written English. *In* (pp. 41–55) **16.**

2153. BĂNCILĂ, FLORICA. Remarks on the semantic representation of early English impersonal verbs. AnUBLLS (35) 77–80.

2154. BARCELONA SÁNCHEZ, ANTONIO. On the concept of depression in American English: a cognitive approach. RCEI (12) 7–33.

2155. BLAIR, I. D. Situation semantics and its foundations. *See* **1347.**

2156. BLEICH, DAVID. Intersubjective reading. NLH (17:3) 401–21.

2157. BLONSKY, MARSHALL (ed.). On signs: a semiotics reader. Oxford: Blackwell, 1985. pp. 356. Rev. by Christopher Norris in LRB (8:15) 15–16.

2158. BOGUSŁAWSKI, ANDRZEJ. 'Also' from 'all so': on a set of particles in service of efficient communication. *See* **1574.**

2159. BROWNE, ALLEN C. Univocal 'or' – again. LI (17:4) 751–4.

2160. BUNT, HARRY C. Mass terms and model-theoretic semantics. Cambridge: CUP, 1985. pp. xiii, 325. (Cambridge studies in linguistics, 42.)

2161. BYBEE, JOAN L. Morphology: a study of the relation between meaning and form. *See* **2130.**

2162. CHASE, T. J. P. A diachronic semantic classification of the English religious lexis. *See* **1531.**

2163. CHIŢORAN, DUMITRU. Metaphor in the English lexicon: the verb. *In* (pp. 837–49) **26.**

2164. COKELY, DENNIS RICHARD. Towards a sociolinguistic model of the interpreting process: focus on ASL and English. *See* **991.**

2165. COOPER, ROBIN. Tense and discourse location in situation semantics. *See* **1096.**

2166. COPELAND, JAMES E. (ed.). New directions in linguistics and semiotics. *See* **38.**

2167. CORNILESCU, ALEXANDRA. On the syntax and semantics of free relative clauses in English and Romanian. *In* (pp. 1165–82) **26.**

2168. CORNISH, FRANCIS. Anaphora and semantic interpretation. Lingua (68) 241–56 (review-article).

2169. CRESSWELL, M. J.   Adverbial modification: interval semantics and its rivals. Dordrecht; Lancaster: Reidel, 1985. pp. vii, 229. (Studies in linguistics and philosophy, 28.)

2170. CROSS, CHARLES B.   Jonathan Bennett on 'even if'. Linguistics and Philosophy (8:3) 1985, 353–7.

2171. CRUSE, D. A.   Lexical semantics. Cambridge: CUP. pp. 415. (Cambridge textbooks in linguistics.)

2172. CULLER, JONATHAN.   The pursuit of signs: semiotics, literature, deconstruction. (Bibl. 1985, 1733.) Rev. by Timothy J. Reiss in CanRCL (12:3) 1985, 422–32.

2173. DAVIES, EIRLYS E.   English vocatives: a look at their function and form. *See* **1999.**

2174. DECLERCK, RENAAT.   The manifold interpretations of generic sentences. Lingua (68) 149–88.

2175. DEELY, JOHN N.; POWEL, RALPH AUSTIN (eds).   Tractatus de signis: the semiotic of John Poinsot. Berkeley: California UP. pp. 607. Rev. by Thomas A. Sebeok in NYTB, 30 Mar., 15.

2176. DENISON, DAVID.   The origins of periphrastic *do*: Ellegård and Visser reconsidered. *In* (pp. 45–60) **41.**

2177. DESCLÉS, JEAN PIERRE; GUENTCHÉVA, ZLATKA; SHAUMYAN, SEBASTIAN.   Theoretical aspects of passivization in the framework of generative grammar. *See* **2003.**

2178. DOWTY, DAVID R.   The effects of aspectual class on the temporal structure of discourse: semantics or pragmatics? *See* **1356.**

2179. DUDMAN, V. H.   Towards a theory of predication for English. *See* **1220.**

2180. DUŠKOVÁ, LIBUŠE.   On the type of definiteness expressed by the English possessives. *See* **2007.**

2181. EGBE, D. I.   An approach to the syntax and semantics of the imperative in English. *See* **1359.**

2182. Entry cancelled.

2183. ERTESCHIK-SHIR, NOMI.   *Wh*-questions and focus. *See* **2011.**

2184. EVANS, JONATHAN D.; HELBO, ANDRÉ (eds).   Semiotics and international scholarship: towards a language of theory. Dordrecht; Boston, MA: Nijhoff. pp. xxii, 225. (NATO ASI, ser. D: Behavioural and social sciences, 33.)

2185. FAUCONNIER, GILLES.   Mental spaces: aspects of meaning construction in natural language. Cambridge, MA; London: MIT Press, 1985. pp. viii, 185. (Bradford book.)

2186. FERRIS, D. C.   The theory of grammar: the semantic study of a syntactic relation. Unpub. doct. diss., Univ. of Exeter, 1985. [Abstr. in IT (36) 466.]

2187. FILLMORE, CHARLES J.   Lexical semantics and text semantics. *In* (pp. 123–47) **38.**

2188. FREADMAN, ANNE; MORRIS, MEAGHAN.   Semiotics in Australia. *In* (pp. 1–17) THOMAS A. SEBEOK and JEAN UMIKER-SEBEOK (eds), The semiotic sphere. New York: Plenum Press. pp. xiii, 647.

2189. FUNK, WOLF-PETER.   Towards a definition of semantic constraints on negative prefixation in English and German. *In* (pp. 877–89) **26.**

2190. GATHERCOLE, VIRGINIA C.   Evaluating competing linguistic theories with child language data: the case of the mass-count distinction. Linguistics and Philosophy (9:2) 151–90.

2191. GAWRON, JEAN MARK.   Situations and prepositions. Linguistics and Philosophy (9:3) 327–82.

2192. —— Types, contents, and semantic objects. Linguistics and Philosophy (9:4) 427–76.

2193. GODDARD, CLIFF.   The natural semantics of 'too'. Journal of Pragmatics (10:5) 635–44.

2194. HADDOCK, N. J.   Computing noun phrase reference. *See* **532.**

2195. HAIJIMA, ICHIRO.   A study of industrial semantics. Tokyo: Senjo. pp. xiv, 178.

2196. HALL, MARGARET AUSTIN.   Syntactic and semantic patterning with the verb 'be' in the older Germanic languages. *See* **1878.**

2197. HAND, MICHAEL ROBERT.   Negation in English: an essay in game-theoretical semantics. Unpub. doct. diss., Florida State Univ., 1985. [Abstr. in DA (46) 2714A.]

2198. HANSEN, ERIK A.   John Locke and the semantic tradition. EngS (67:1) 51–6 (review-article).

2199. HERMERÉN, LARS.   Modalities in spoken and written English: an inventory of forms. *In* (pp. 57–91) **16.**

2200. HINRICHS, ERHARD WALTER.   A compositional semantics for Aktionsarten and NP reference in English. Unpub. doct. diss., Ohio State Univ., 1985. [Abstr. in DA (46) 2679A.]

2201. HINTIKKA, JAAKKO.   The semantics of 'a certain'. LI (17:2) 331–6.

2202. —— KULAS, JACK.   Anaphora and definite descriptions: two applications of game-theoretical semantics. Dordrecht; Lancaster: Reidel, 1985. pp. xii, 250. (Synthese language library, 26.)

2203. —— —— The game of language: studies in game-theoretical semantics and its applications. (Bibl. 1983, 2173.) Rev. by Jan Lemmens in Journal of Semantics (4:3) 1985, 265–70.

2204. HIRST, GRAEME.   Semantic interpretation and the resolution of ambiguity. *See* **533.**

2205. HOEPELMAN, JAAP.   Action, comparison and change: a study in the semantics of verbs. Tübingen: Niemeyer. pp. vi, 194. (Linguistische Arbeiten, 170.)

2206. HOLLAND, NORMAN N.   The miller's wife and the professors: questions about the transactive theory of reading. NLH (17:3) 423–47.

2207. INNIS, ROBERT E. (ed.).   Semiotics: an introductory anthology. Bloomington: Indiana UP, 1985; London: Hutchinson. pp. xvi, 331.

2208. JACKENDOFF, R. S.   Semantics and cognition. (Bibl. 1985, 1775.) Rev. by H. J. Verkuyl in Lingua (68:1) 59–90.

2209. JACOBSON, SVEN.   Synonymy and hyponymy in syntactic variation. *In* (pp. 7–17) **43.**

2210. —— (ed.).   Papers from the third Scandinavian symposium on syntactic variation, Stockholm, May 11–12, 1985. *See* **43.**

2211. JACOBSSON, BENGT.   Another look at negatively conditioned subject–operator inversion in English. *See* **2038.**

2212. JAEGGLI, OSVALDO A.   Arbitrary plural pronominals. *See* **2039.**

2213. JAMES, FRANCIS.   Semantics and pragmatics of the word 'if'. *See* **1370.**

2214. JOLY, ANDRÉ.   Pour une analyse systématique des modalités non verbales de la communication. *In* (pp. 131–41) **12.**

2215. JØRGENSEN, ERIK.   The pattern 'in charge of' and its variants in contemporary English. *See* **2044.**

2216. KAKIETEK, PIOTR.   Remarks on Lakoff's classification of verbs. *In* (pp. 935–45) **26.**

2217. KALDEWAIJ, JELLE.   Structuralisme en transformationeel generatieve grammatica. (Structural and transformational generative grammar.) *See* **1885.**

2218. KASTOVSKY, DIETER.   Diachronic word-formation in a functional perspective. *In* (pp. 409–21) **26.**

2219. KATO, KAZUO.   Another look at ellipsis: non-native recoverability of ellipsis and its implications for linguistic competence. *See* **1373.**

2220. —— Gradable gradability. EngS (67:2) 174–80.

2221. KEENAN, EDWARD L.; STAVI, JONATHAN.   A semantic characterization of natural language determiners. Linguistics and Philosophy (9:3) 253–326.

2222. KJELLMER, GÖRAN.   Legible but not readable: on the semantics of English adjectives in '-able'. *See* **1548.**

2223. KLEIN, EBERHARD.   Semantic and pragmatic indeterminacy in English non-finite verb complementation. (Bibl. 1985, 1783.) Rev. by Y. Putseys in SL (10:2) 516–19.

2224. KNITTLOVÁ, DAGMAR.   Connotation transfer: one of the central problems of translation linguistics. Germanica Olomucensia (6) 11–19.

2225. KOKTOVÁ, EVA.   Remarks on the semantics of sentence adverbials. *See* **2052.**

2226. KOPYTKO, ROMAN.   Verbs of sensory cognition: a semantic analysis of a lexical field in the lexicon of ME. SAF (19) 29–36.

2227. KRYK, BARBARA.   How do indexicals fit into situations? On deixis in English and Polish. *In* (pp. 1289–1301) **26.**

2228. KYTÖ, MERJA.   *May* and *might* indicating 'epistemic possibility' in Early American English. *In* (pp. 131–42) **43.**

2229. LANDMAN, FRED.   Towards a theory of information: the status of partial objects in semantics. Dordrecht: Foris, pp. xiv, 228. (Groningen–Amsterdam studies in semantics, 6.)

2230. —— VELTMAN, FRANK (eds).   Varieties of formal semantics. Proceedings of the fourth Amsterdam Colloquium, September, 1982. Dordrecht; Cinnaminson, NJ: Foris, 1984. pp. xii, 425. (Groningen–Amsterdam studies in semantics 3.) Rev. by Peter Rolf Lutzeier in Journal of Semantics (4:2) 1985, 193–9.

2231. LAWSON, EDWIN D.; ROEDER, LYNN M. Women's full first names, short names, and affectionate names: a semantic differential analysis. *See* **1674.**

2232. LEDDY, MICHAEL. Origins of meaning: utterer, audience, speech-situation. *See* **1376.**

2233. LEHRER, ADRIENNE. English classifier constructions. *See* **2055.**

2234. LEISI, ERNST. Zum Thema sozio-kulturelle Semantik. *See* **1009.**

2235. LEPPARD, D. G. An investigation into the theory and structure of metaphor, with special reference to Wordsworth and Yeats. Unpub. doct. diss., Univ. of Oxford, 1984.

2236. LESTER, B. Semantic structure and linguistic competence. Unpub. doct. diss., Univ. of Oxford, 1982.

2237. LeTOURNEAU, MARK STEPHEN. Semantic and textual conditions on noun phrase movement in English. Unpub. doct. diss., Purdue Univ. [Abstr. in DA (47) 2145A.]

2238. LEWANDOWSKA, BARBARA. Cognitive basis for dynamic semantics. *See* **1281.**

2239. LEWANDOWSKA-TOMASZCZYK, BARBARA. Language universals, linguistic theory, and philosophy. *In* (pp. 77–84) **26.**

2240. LIPKA, LEONHARD. Semantic features and prototype theory in English lexicology. *In* (pp. 85–94) **26.**

2241. LONGACRE, ROBERT E. Reshaping linguistics: context and content. *In* (pp. 79–95) **38.**

2242. LUDLOW, PETER JAY. The syntax and semantics of referential attitude reports. Unpub. doct. diss., Columbia Univ., 1985. [Abstr. in DA (47) 202A.]

2243. LUMSDEN, M. Syntactic and semantic properties of existential sentences. *See* **2059.**

2244. MACCORMAC, EARL R. A cognitive theory of metaphor. Cambridge, MA; London: MIT Press, 1985. pp. x, 254. (Bradford book.) Rev. by Frank Neussel in Lingua (70:1) 69–73.

2245. McCORMACK, PEGGY. The semiotics of economic language in James's fiction. *See* **1183.**

2246. McCOY, IWEN HUSEIN. Tense and aspect: a comparative study of meaning in English and Bahasa Indonesia. Unpub. doct. diss., Univ. of Texas at Austin, 1985. [Abstr. in DA (47) 452A.]

2247. MAGNUSSON, ULF; PERSSON, GUNNAR. Facets, phases and foci: studies in lexical relations in English. *See* **1555.**

2248. MARKEY, THOMAS L. Some verbal remarks. *In* (pp. 513–24) **26.**

2249. MATHIASSEN, LARS; ANDERSEN, PETER BØGH. Semiotics and informatics: the impact of computer based systems upon the professional language of nurses. Journal of Pragmatics (10:1) 1–26.

2250. MIALL, DAVID S. (ed.). Metaphor: problems and perspectives. (Bibl. 1983, 2209.) Rev. by Daniel O. Nathan in PhilL (10:1) 136–7.

2251. MIIRVET, ENÇ. Towards a referential analysis of temporal expressions. Linguistics and Philosophy (9:4) 405–26.

2252. MONELL, SIV. The molecule strategy: a study of the description of character in *The Rainbow* by D. H. Lawrence. *In* (pp. 75–87) **43.**

2253. MUNSAT, STANLEY. *Wh*-complementizers. *See* **2069.**

2254. NOSEK, JIŘÍ. Semantic structure of attributes in modern English. *See* **2074.**

2255. OGURA, MICHIKO. OE verbs of thinking. *See* **1895.**

2256. ORDOVER, STEPHANIE KATZ. Reflections of meaning theory. Unpub. doct. diss., Columbia Univ., 1985. [Abstr. in DA (47) 203A.]

2257. ORR, LEONARD. Intertextuality and the cultural text in recent semiotics. CE (48:8) 811–23.

2258. PAPROTTÉ, WOLF; DIRVEN, RENÉ (eds). The ubiquity of metaphor: metaphor in language and thought. *See* **1191.**

2259. PEPER, JÜRGEN. Die Metapher als Kulturfigur: ein literarästhetischer Beitrag zur Landes- und Kulturkunde. *In* (pp. 259–92) **15.**

2260. PETRIE, BRADFORD M. N. Semantics and physicalism. Unpub. doct. diss., Univ. of Michigan, 1985. [Abstr. in DA (46) 3377A.]

2261. PHARIES, DAVID A. Charles S. Pierce and the linguistic sign. *See* **1388.**

2262. PHILLIPS, MICHAEL JOSEPH. Heart, mind, and soul in Old English: a semantic study. *See* **1557.**

2263. PICKERING, MICHAEL. The geometry and logic of prepositional meaning. *See* **2077.**

2264. PINTO, JULIO CÉSAR MACHADO. Temporal relations in the narrative: a semantico-semiotic approach. *See* **1239.**

2265. POSNER, ROLAND. Semiotic paradoxes in language use, with particular reference to *Tristram Shandy*. Trans. by CHRISTIAN J. W. KLOESEL. ECent (20:2) 1979, 148–63.

2266. POST, MICHAŁ. A prototype approach to denominal adjectives. *In* (pp. 1003–13) **26.**

2267. POTTER, RICHARD C. The theory of self-appearing. PPR (46:4) 615–30.

2268. POWELL, M. J. The notion of literal meaning in contemporary linguistic semantics. Unpub. doct. diss., Univ. of Sussex, 1983.

2269. PREZIOSI, DONALD. Subjects + objects: the current state of visual semiotics. *In* (pp. 179–205) **38.**

2270. RANSOM, EVELYN N. Complementation: its meanings and forms. *See* **2083.**

2271. RAY, DAVID ARNOLD. Semantic order in Old English poetic variation. Unpub. doct. diss., Auburn Univ., 1985. [Abstr. in DA (46) 2701A.]

2272. REISS, TIMOTHY J. On exposition. CanRCL (12:3) 1985, 422–32 (review-article).

2273. ŘEŘICHA, VÁCLAV. The semantics of English deverbal compounds: the 'chewing-gum' type. *See* **2143.**

2274. RICHARD, MARK. Quotation, grammar, and opacity. Linguistics and Philosophy (9:3) 383–403.

2275. RISSANEN, MATTI. Expression of exclusiveness in Old English and the development of the adverb *only*. *In* (pp. 253–67) **41.**

2276. ROCHEMONT, MICHAEL S.   Focus in generative grammar. *See* **2087.**

2277. ROOM, ADRIAN.   Dictionary of true etymologies. *See* **1788.**

2278. ROOT, REBECCA LOUISE.   The semantics of anaphora in discourse. *See* **1133.**

2279. ROSS-GLASS, R. M.   A study of the implicit metaphors in selected fairy tales and their use in modern literature and the media. Unpub. doct. diss., Univ. of Leeds, 1982.

2280. RUIN, INGER.   About *today* and *tomorrow* in the past. *In* (pp. 63–73) **43.**

2281. RUSIECKI, JAN.   Adjectives and comparison in English: a semantic study. (Bibl. 1985, 1823.) Rev. by Ulf Teleman in NJL (9) 97–100.

2282. —— The semantics of antonymic pairs of adjectives: elicitation test evidence from English and Polish. *In* (pp. 1427–41) **26.**

2283. RUŽIČKOVÁ, EVA.   Verbonominálne konštrukcie a pomocné sloveso 'have'. (Verbo-nominal structures and the auxiliary 'have'.) *In* (pp. 56–7) **4.**

2284. SCHIFFRIN, DEBORAH.   Functions of 'and' in discourse. *See* **1134.**

2285. SCHMID, HERTA; VAN KESTEREN, ALOYSIUS (eds).   Semiotics of drama and theatre: new perspectives in the theory of drama and theatre. Amsterdam; Philadelphia, PA: Benjamins, 1984. pp. 584. Rev. by Jean Alter in PT (7:2) 355–9.

2286. SEBEOK, THOMAS A.   I think I am a verb: more contributions to the doctrine of signs. New York; London: Plenum. pp. xx, 245. (Topics in contemporary semiotics.)

2287. —— Symptom. *In* (pp. 211–30) **38.**

2288. SEILER, TH. B.; WANNEMACHER, W.   Concept development and the development of word meaning. Berlin; Heidelberg; New York: Springer, 1983. pp. xii, 348. Rev. by Adrienne Lehrer in SL (10:2) 256–64.

2289. SHAUMYAN, SEBASTIAN.   Semiotic laws in linguistics and natural science. *In* (pp. 231–57) **38.**

2290. SIMPKINS, SCOTT KEITH.   The semiotic dilemma of English Romantic poetry. Unpub. doct. diss., Univ. of Tulsa. [Abstr. in DA (47) 899A.]

2291. SLESS, DAVID.   In search of semiotics. London: Croom Helm, pp. 160.

2292. SMITH, CARLOTA.   A speaker-based approach to aspect. Linguistics and Philosophy (9:1) 97–115.

2293. SPENCE, N. C. W.   Ups & downs in semantics: an inaugural lecture. London: Bedford Coll., Univ. of London, 1982. pp. 20.

2294. STENSTRÖM, ANNA-BRITA.   What does 'really' really do? Strategies in speech and writing. *In* (pp. 149–63) **16.**

2295. STEWART, JOHN.   Speech and human being: a complement to semiotics. *See* **788.**

2296. STRAUSS, JÜRGEN. Concepts, fields, and 'non-basic' lexical items. *In* (pp. 135–44) **26.**

2297. SZWEDEK, ALEKSANDER. Sentence stress and category membership. *In* (pp. 1051–61) **26.**

2298. THORNE, JAMES P. *Because*. *In* (pp. 1063–6) **26.**

2299. THRANE, TORBEN. On delimiting the senses of near-synonyms in historical semantics: a case-study of adjectives of 'moral sufficiency' in the Old English *Andreas*. *In* (pp. 671–92) **26.**

2300. TIRRELL, M. LYNNE. Extending the metaphor: lessons for language. Unpub. doct. diss., Univ. of Pittsburgh. [Abstr. in DA (47) 2187A.]

2301. TODOROV, TZVETAN. Theories of the symbol. (Bibl. 1983, 2254.) Rev. by Charles Eric Reeves in PT (7:2) 341–9.

2302. TOTTIE, GUNNEL. The importance of being adverbial: adverbials of focusing and contingency in spoken and written English. *In* (pp. 93–118) **16.**

2303. TOUMAJIAN, T.-S. The semiotics of printed instructions (graphic signa). Unpub. doct. diss., Univ. of St Andrews. [Abstr. in IT (35) 1488.]

2304. TRAUGOTT, ELIZABETH CLOSS. Confrontation and association. *In* (pp. 515–26) **42.**

2305. —— On the origins of 'and' and 'but' connectives in English. *See* **1575.**

2306. TURBOVÁ, MILENA. Anglické překladové protějšky českého 'již/už'. (English equivalents of the Czech adverbs 'již/už'.) *In* (p. 65) **4.**

2307. VAN BENTHAM, JOHAN. Essays in logical semantics. Dordrecht: Reidel. pp. xi, 225. (Studies in linguistics and philosophy, 29.)

2308. —— TER MEULEN, ALICE. Generalized quantifiers in natural language. Dordrecht: Foris, 1985. pp. 169. (Groningen–Amsterdam studies in semantics, 4.)

2309. VAN DER AUWERA, JOHAN. The possibilities of *may* and *can*. *In* (pp. 1067–76) **26.**

2310. VAN NOPPEN, J.-P.; DE JONGEN, R. Metaphor – a bibliography of post 1970 publications. *See* **1207.**

2311. VAN OIRSOUW, ROBERT R. Syntactic ambiguity: a systematic accident. *In* (pp. 145–55) **26.**

2312. VERKUYL, H. J. On semantics without logic. Lingua (68) 59–90 (review-article).

2313. VIITANEN, OUTI. On the position of 'only' in English conversation. *In* (pp. 165–75) **16.**

2314. WAGNER, GEORG. Zur Semantik der kopulativen Verben des Englischen. Heidelberg: Groos. pp. vii, 300. (Sammlung Groos, 27.)

2315. WARD, GREGORY LOUIS. The semantics and pragmatics of preposing. *See* **1400.**

2316. WARREN, BEATRICE. Classifying adjectives. (Bibl. 1984, 1271.) Rev. by Yvan Putseys in ITL (71), 87–95.

2317. WESTNEY, PAUL. Notes on scales. Lingua (69) 333–54.

2318. WETTSTEIN, HOWARD.   Has semantics rested on a mistake? JP (83:4) 185–209.

2319. WHITNEY, ROSEMARIE.   The syntax and interpretation of *ā*-adjunctions. *See* **2122.**

2320. WIERZBICKA, ANNA.   Introduction. Journal of Pragmatics (10:5) 519–34. (A discussion of conversational opening gambits.)

2321. —— Precision in vagueness: the semantics of English 'approximatives'. Journal of Pragmatics (10:5) 597–614.

2322. —— A semantic metalanguage for the description and comparison of illocutionary meanings. *See* **1401.**

2323. —— What's in a noun? Or, how do nouns differ in meaning from adjectives? SL (10:2) 353-89.

2324. WOISETSCHLAEGER, ERICH F.   A semantic theory of the English auxiliary system. New York; London: Garland, 1985. pp. iii, 127. (Outstanding dissertations in linguistics.)

2325. WOLF, S. G.   The concept of semantics as a branch of inquiry in modern linguistics, with particular reference to Michel Bréal. Unpub. doct. diss., Univ. of Oxford. [Abstr. in IT (35) 538.]

2326. ZOHRAB, P. D.   Verb-phrase anaphora: linguistics or cognitive science? *See* **1295.**

TRANSLATION AND COMPARATIVE LINGUISTICS

2327. Baciu, Ileana.   Subject and *wh*-movement in English and Romanian. AnUBLLS (35) 72–6.

2328. Bald, Wolf-Dietrich.   Context in contrastive linguistics: *one* and *ein*. In (pp. 1117–32) **26.**

2329. Battarbee, Keith.   Trouble on the surface: on surface incompatibility and translation. Pubs of the Dept of English, Univ. of Turku (6) 1985, 7–16.

2330. Bowen, David.   The intercultural component in interpreter and translator training: a historical survey. Unpub. doct. diss., Georgetown Univ., 1985. [Abstr. in DA (47) 1222A.]

2331. Carstensen, Broder.   Euro-English. *In* (pp. 827–35) **26.**

2332. Choi, Soonja.   A cross-linguistic development study of negation in English, French and Korean. *See* **1991.**

2333. Comrie, Bernard.   Contrastive linguistics and language typology. *In* (pp. 1155–63) **26.**

2334. Cornilescu, Alexandra.   On the syntax and semantics of free relative clauses in English and Romanian. *In* (pp. 1165–82) **26.**

2335. Danchev, Andrei.   Interlanguage simplification in Middle English vowel phonology? *In* (pp. 239–52) **26.**

2336. Davidsen-Nielsen, Niels.   Modal verbs in English and Danish. *In* (pp. 1183–94) **26.**

2337. Debusscher, G.; van Noppen, J.-P. (eds).   Communiquer et traduire/communicating and translating: essays in honour of Jean Dierickx. *See* **12.**

2338. Dirven, René.   De invloed van het Engels op het Afrikaans. (The influence of English on Afrikaans.) SA Tydskrif vir Taalkunde/ SA Journal of Linguistics (4:4) 1–14.

2339. Dominicy, Marc.   Sur les emplois 'temporels' de *only*. *In* (pp. 211–17) **12.**

2340. Durmusoglu, G.   The notion of parallel texts and its place in contrastive and applied linguistics. Unpub. doct. diss., Univ. of Exeter, 1983.

2341. Fisiak, Jaček.   A note on the adaptation of English loanwords in Polish: verbs. ITL (67/68) 1985, 69–75.

2342. Fleksher, Luba Pasternak.   Russian/English contrastive text analysis: functional sentence perspective. Unpub. doct. diss., Columbia Univ. Teachers College. [Abstr. in DA (47) 1306A.]

2343. Funk, Wolf-Peter.   Towards a definition of semantic constraints on negative prefixation in English and German. *In* (pp. 877–89) **26.**

2344. Gallet, Liliane.   La traduction assistée par ordinateur (TAO): réalisations, perspectives, conséquences: 'How will it affect my job?' *In* (pp. 621–35) **1.**

2345. Garbagnati, Lucile.   Une traduction anesthésiante pour un texte subversif: Mark Twain: *The Adventures of Huckleberry Finn* (1884) traduit par W. L. Hughes, 1886. *In* (pp. 215–22) **1.**

2346. GARDINER-STALLAERT, NICOLE.   A fine point of difference. The use of the full stop at the end of verbless sentences in today's French and English formal expository critical texts. *See* **1513.**

2347. GLÄSER, ROSEMARIE.   A plea for phraseo-stylistics. *In* (pp. 41–52) **26.**

2348. GOFFIN, ROGER.   La science de la traduction 1955–1985: une tentative de bilan provisoire. *In* (pp. 27–36) **12.**

2349. GOGĂLNICEANU, CĂLINA LOUISA.   Gender and number in English and Romanian. Bucharest: Bucharest Univ., 1984. pp. 23. (Summary of doct. diss.)

2350. GRUIŢĂ, MARIANA.   A contrastive syntax of English and Romanian: the compound and the complex sentence. *See* **2021.**

2351. HAN, KYO-SOK.   Hangukeo e ggichin youngeo eui yeonghyeong. (A study of the influence of English on the Korean language.) JELL (32:4) 895–908.

2352. HAN, TAE-HO.   A study of the possibility of functional communicative translations: centred on the change of word-order and functional relation. ET (32) June, 105–31.

2353. HEIDELBERGER-LEONARD, IRÈNE.   Translation as the prime art of communication? A note on George Steiner's *After Babel*. *In* (pp. 19–25) **12.**

2354. HELLER, ERICH.   Notes on language, its deconstruction and on translating. *In* (pp. 1–11) **46.**

2355. HOUSE, JULIANE; BLUM-KULKA, SHOSHANA (eds).   Interlingual and intercultural communication: discourse and cognition in translation and second language studies. Tübingen: Narr. pp. 292. Rev. by Hans Lindquist in SL (40) 190–6.

2356. HUTCHINS, W. J.   Machine translation: past, present, future. *See* **535.**

2357. JASPAERT, LIEVEN.   About the treatment of ambiguity in machine translation. *See* **536.**

2358. KIRK, ROBERT.   Translation determined. Oxford: Clarendon Press. pp. 236.

2359. KRYK, BARBARA.   How do indexicals fit into situations? On deixis in English and Polish. *In* (pp. 1289–1301) **26.**

2360. KRZESZOWSKI, TOMASZ P.   An Elizabethan contrastive grammar of Spanish and French. *In* (pp. 1303–10) **26.**

2361. McCOY, IWEN HUSEIN.   Tense and aspect: a comparative study of meaning in English and Bahasa Indonesia. *See* **2246.**

2362. MOHAMED, MOHAMED ABDULLA.   Ellipsis: a contrastive study of Swahili and English discourse. Unpub. doct. diss., Columbia Univ. Teachers College. [Abstr. in DA (47) 2145A.]

2363. NÄSSLIN, SIV.   Restriction dans l'emploi de 'n'est-ce pas?': étude contrastive des 'tags' interrogatifs anglais at des expressions correspondantes en français et en suédois. Langage et l'Homme (21:2) 167–72.

2364. NISHIMURA, MIWA.   Intrasentential codeswitching in Japanese and English. *See* **1020.**

2365. PAOLUCCI, HENRY.   Italian and English 'models' for the modern vernacular literatures of India. *In* (pp. 209–31) ALDO SCAGLIONE, The emergence of national languages. Ravenna: Longo, 1984. pp. 233. (Speculum artium, 11.)

2366. ROMAINE, SUZANNE.   The effects of language standardization on deletion rules: some comparative Germanic evidence from *t/d*-deletion. *In* (pp. 605–20) **26.**

2367. RUSIECKI, JAN.   The semantics of antonymic pairs of adjectives: elicitation test evidence from English and Polish. *In* (pp. 1427–41) **26.**

2368. SUSSEX, ROLAND.   Paraphrase strategies and the teaching of translation. *In* (pp. 1475–83) **26.**

2369. TIRKKONEN-CONDIT, SONJA.   Empirical studies in translation: textlinguistic and psycholinguistic perspectives. *See* **1289.**

2370. TOMMOLA, JORMA.   Approaches to research on translation. Pubs of the Dept of English, Univ. of Turku (6) 1985, 159–87.

2371. VAN NOPPEN, JEAN-PIERRE.   La traduction de la métaphore et quelques hypothèses sur la mesure de l'equivalence. Brussels Preprints in Linguistics (8) 1983, 59–70.

2372. VAN ROEY, JACQUES.   Deceptive terminology for deceptive cognates. *In* (pp. 159–64) **12.**

2373. VASCONCELLOS, MURIEL HABEL DE.   Theme and focus: cross-language comparison via translations from extended discourse. Unpub. doct. diss., Georgetown Univ., 1985. [Abstr. in DA (46) 3710A.]

2374. VENUTI, LAWRENCE.   The translator's invisibility. Criticism (28:2) 179–212.

2375. VIRTANEN, TUIJA.   Aspects of adverbial cohesion in two genres of English and French. Pubs of the Dept of English, Univ. of Turku (6) 1985, 197–208.

2376. WHITBURN, M.   La chaînon manquant. *In* (pp. 55–63) **12.**

2377. WOLLIN, LARS; LINDQUIST, HANS (eds).   Translation studies in Scandinavia: proceedings from the Scandinavian Symposium on Translation Theory (SSOTT) II, Lund 14–15 June 1985. Lund: Gleerup. pp. 149. (Lund studies in English, 75.)

2378. ZABROCKI, TADEUSZ.   A processing explanation for a syntactic difference between English and Polish. *In* (pp. 1485–99) **26.**

TRADITIONAL CULTURE

FOLKLORE AND FOLKLIFE

GENERAL

2379. BRAMSBÄCK, BIRGIT. Folklore and W. B. Yeats: the function of folklore elements in three early plays. (Bibl. 1984, 1825.) Rev. by Dáithí O hÓgáin in IUR (16) 93–4.

2380. DORSON, RICHARD M. (ed.). Handbook of American folklore. (Bibl. 1984, 1828, where title incorrect.) Rev. by Eric Montenyohl in FF (19:1) 82–91.

2381. DUFF-COOPER, ANDREW. Andrew Lang: aspects of his work in relation to current social anthropology. Folklore (97:2) 186–205.

2382. FOLEY, JOHN MILES. Oral formulaic theory and research: an introduction and annotated bibliography. (Bibl. 1985, 1873.) Rev. by Franz H. Bäuml in Spec (61:3) 650–1.

2383. FUROMOTO, ATSUKO. America kokujin bungaku to folklore. (Black American literature and folklore.) Tokyo: Yamaguchi Press. pp. viii, 264.

2384. HELLER, ARNO. Literarische Landes- und Kulturkunde als kommunikativer Prozeß: ein amerikanistisches Beispiel. *In* (pp. 209–29) **15.**

2385. HORNADGE, BILL. Sydney or the Bush: the language of Australian folklore. *In* (pp. 243–51) KEITH HOLLINSHEAD (ed.), The possum stirs: conference proceedings of the Second National Folklore Conference. Sydney: Centre for Leisure and Tourism Studies. pp. 559.

2386. JOYNER, CHARLES. Reconsidering a relationship: folklore and history. KFR (32:1/2) 17–33.

2387. MENDOZA, KENNETH PAUL. Considering ethnopoetics: a translation theory for oral literature. Unpub. doct. diss., Univ. of California, San Diego, 1985. [Abstr. in DA (46) 2285A.]

2388. MOSELEY, MARY JEAN. American Indian oral tradition preservation, protection and public domain. Unpub. doct. diss., Univ. of North Dakota, 1985. [Abstr. in DA (46) 2694A.]

2389. OKEKE-EXIGBO, EMEKA. Paul Laurence Dunbar and the Afro-American folk tradition. Ob (6) Spring/Summer 1980, 63–74.

2390. PROPP, VLADIMIR. Theory and history of folklore. Ed. by ANATOLY LIBERMAN. Minneapolis: Minnesota UP, 1984. (Cf. bibl. 1985, 1882.) Rev. by Steven Swann Jones in JAF (99) 225–8.

2391. SEWARD, ADRIENNE LANIER. Early black film and folk tradition: an interpretive analysis of the use of folklore in selected all-black cast feature films. Unpub. doct. diss., Indiana Univ., 1985. [Abstr. in DA (46) 2775A.]

2392. SMITH, PAUL S. Tradition – a perspective: part IV, Variation on the prospective adopter's access to information. Lore & Language (5:1) 3–38.

AREA STUDIES AND COLLECTIONS
(MISCELLANEOUS)

2393. ABERNETHY, FRANCIS (ed.).   Sonovagun stew: a folklore miscellany. Dallas: Southern Methodist UP, 1985. pp. 183. Rev. by J. Kathleen Kell in ArizW (28:2) 162–3.

2394. ALEXANDER, MARGARET WALKER.   Black and white threads in Mississippi folk culture. MFR (19:1) 1985, 5–9.

2395. BAER, FLORENCE E.   Folklore and literature of the British Isles: an annotated bibliography. New York; London: Garland. pp. xxiv, 355. (Garland folklore bibliographies.)

2396. BLAEN, A.   A survey and analysis of some aspects of West Country folklore as found in selected writings of Eden Phillpotts, Thomas Hardy, John Cowper Powys, Arthur Quiller-Couch and Henry Williamson. Unpub. doct. diss., Univ. of Exeter, 1985. [Abstr. in IT (36) 472.]

2397. BOSWELL, GEORGE W.   North Mississippi contributions to Faulkner's fiction. MFR (20:1) 13–19.

2398. BUCHAN, DAVID (ed.).   Scottish tradition: a collection of Scottish folk literature. Boston, MA: Routledge & Kegan Paul, 1984. (Cf. bibl. 1985, 1890.) Rev. by Katherine Young in JAF (99) 341–2.

2399. CLEAVER, ALAN (ed.).   Mysteries, legends and traditions of Wycombe and its environs: to commemorate the 700th mayoral anniversary of High Wycombe. High Wycombe: Strange Pubs, 1985. pp. 48.

2400. GAUDET, MARCIA.   Tales from the levee: the folklore of St John the Baptist parish. Lafayette: Center for Louisiana Studies, Univ. of Southwestern Louisiana, 1984. pp. ix, 116. Rev. by David C. Estes in MFR (20:1) 29–31.

2401. HARTE, JEREMY.   Cuckoo pounds and singing barrows: the folklore of ancient sites in Dorset. Dorchester: Dorset Natural History & Archaeological Soc. pp. 102.

2402. MacCOLL, EWAN; SEEGER, PEGGY.   Till doomsday in the afternoon: the folklore of a family of Scots travellers, the Stewarts of Blairgowrie. Manchester: Manchester UP. pp. xi, 325.

2403. MAXTED, IAN.   . . . A most barbarous, dreadful, and shocking murder. . . . *See* **407.**

2404. NARVAEZ, PETER.   The folklore of 'old foolishness': Newfoundland media legends. CanL (108) 125–43.

2405. PALMER, ROY.   The folklore of Leicestershire and Rutland. Wymondham: Sycamore, 1985. pp. 288.

2406. RAVEN, JON.   Black Country and Staffordshire: stories, customs, superstitions, tales, legends and folklore. Wolverhampton: Broadside. pp. 140.

2407. WILLIAMS, JOHN RODGER.   Appalachian migrants in Cincinnati, Ohio: the role of folklore in the reinforcement of ethnic identity. Unpub. doct. diss., Indiana Univ., 1985. [Abstr. in DA (47) 624A.]

PROVERBS, PROVERBIAL EXPRESSIONS, RIDDLES, RHYMES, AND DITES

2408. Crane, Mary Thomas.   Proverbial and aphoristic sayings: sources of authority in the English Renaissance. Unpub. doct. diss., Harvard Univ. [Abstr. in DA (47) 2167A.]

2409. Daalder, Joost.   Wyatt's proverbial 'Though the wound be healed, yet a scar remains'. Archiv (223:2) 354–6.

2410. de Caro, F. A.   'A mystery is a muddle': gnomic expression in *A Passage to India*. MJLF (12:1) 15–23.

2411. Doctor, R.   The logic of riddles re-examined: an apologue to Maranda. Lore & Language (5:2) 13–33.

2412. Donaldson, Graham; Setterfield, Sue (comps).   Why do we say that? Newton Abbot: David & Charles. pp. 96.

2413. Doyle, Charles Clay.   Looking behind two proverbs of More. Moreana (23:91/92) 33–5.

2414. Dunn, R. D.   English proverbs from William Camden's *Remains Concerning Britain*. HLQ (49:3) 271–5.

2415. Edmunds, Susan.   The riddle ballad and the riddle. Lore & Language (5:2) 35–46.

2416. Fletcher, Alan J.   Line 30 of the Man of Law's Tale and the medieval Malkyn. *See* **1707.**

2417. Iles, Norman.   Who really killed Cock Robin? Nursery rhymes and carols restored to their original meanings. London: Hale. pp. 256.

2418. Murison, D.   Scots saws. Edinburgh: Thin; Mercat Press, 1981. pp. 92. Rev. by B. D. H. Miller in NQ (33:2) 219–20.

2419. Murray, Thomas E.   Folk etymology in the streets of St Louis. *See* **1677.**

2420. Nilsen, Don L. F.   'T'aint funny, McGee': the humor of put-downs and rejoinders. *See* **1070.**

2421. Raylor, Tim.   The source of 'He that fights and runs away'. NQ (33:4) 465–6.

2422. Reuter, O. R.   Proverbs, proverbial sentences and phrases in Thomas Deloney's works. Helsinki: Societias Scientiarum Fennica. pp. 146. (Commentationes humanarum litterarum, 79.)

2423. Slung, Michele (comp.).   Mother knows best: a timeless collection of maternal wisdom. London: Century. pp. 96.

2424. Todd, Loreto.   The CM2 process: a selection of riddles in Cameroon Pidgin English. *See* **981.**

2425. Weedon, Margaret.   'Hawk', 'hand-saw', and 'ganza'? *See* **1600.**

WRITTEN AND PRINTED MATERIALS, INSCRIPTIONS, EPITAPHS, GRAFFITI

2426. Creighton, Margaret Scott.   The private life of Jack Tar: sailors at sea in the nineteenth century. Unpub. doct. diss., Boston Univ., 1985. [Abstr. in DA (46) 2729A.]

2427. Duval, Gilles.   'History-histories': mémoire et création dans la littérature de colportage anglaise du 18e siècle. *In* (pp. 111–23) **34.**

SPOKEN NARRATIVE

2428. ANON. Stanley Robinson. Tocher (40) 170–224.

2429. BAGNALL, NORMA. The selchie in legend and literature. *In* (pp. 225–31) **28.**

2430. BALLARD, LINDA M. The concept of the 'character'. Lore & Language (5:1) 69–77.

2431. BARCHERS, SUZANNE INEZ. Hera transformed: female heroes in folk and fairy tales. Unpub. doct. diss., Univ. of Colorado at Boulder, 1985. [Abstr. in DA (46) 3124A.]

2432. BAUMAN, RICHARD. Story, performance and event: contextual studies of oral narratives. Cambridge: CUP. pp. x, 130. (Cambridge studies in oral and literate culture, 10.)

2433. BELLAMY, JOHN. Robin Hood: an historical enquiry. Bloomington: Indiana UP, 1985. (Cf. bibl. 1985, 1924.) Rev. by Michael Altschul in MedHum (14) 233–8.

2434. BOURKE, P. M. The treatment of myth and legend in the windows of St Neot's, Cornwall. Folklore (97:1) 63–9.

2435. BOWEN, BARBARA C. Renaissance collections of *facetiae*, 1499–1528: a new listing. RQ (39:2) 263–75.

2436. BRITAIN'S LITERARY HERITAGE. The Robert White Collection of Chapbooks from the University Library, Newcastle upon Tyne: a listing and guide to the Harvester microform. Brighton: Harvester Press, 1985. pp. 103. (Britian's literary heritage: popular literature in eighteenth and nineteenth century Britain.)

2437. BUMAND, GORDON. Focal problems: theory and support in stories and myths. High Wycombe: Leadership, 1985. pp. 252.

2438. CARLSON, PATRICIA ANN (ed.). Literature and lore of the sea. *See* **28.**

2439. CHANG, LINDA S. Brer Rabbit's Angolan cousin: politics and the adaptation of folk material. FF (19:1) 36–50.

2440. CLOT, S.; QUINEL, C.; DE MONTGON, A. Legends of Britain. Trans. by CAROLINE MOOREHEAD. London: Burke, 1983. pp. 189. (Myths and legends.) (New ed.: first ed. 1968.)

2441. COLLINS, ANDREW. London walkabout: a guide to discovering the myths and legends of ten sites in and around the City of London. Wickford: Earthquest, 1984. pp. 35.

2442. DAY, MARTIN S. The many meanings of myth. Lanham, MD: UP of America, 1984. pp. x, 564. Rev. by Mark E. Workman in JAF (99) 228–9.

2443. DIEPEVEEN, LEONARD. Folktales in the Harlem Renaissance. AL (58:1) 64–81.

2444. DILLON, MYLES (ed.). Irish sagas. Dublin: Mercier. pp. 175. (Thomas Davis lectures.)

2445. DIXON, GEOFFREY M. Folktales and legends of Kent. Peterborough: Minimax, 1984. pp. 64.

2446. DOUGLAS, S. Links with Gaelic tradition found in the story traditions of Perthshire travelling people. *See* **894.**

2447. FELLOWS, JENNIFER.   Sir Bevis of Hampton in popular tradition. Proceedings of the Hampshire Field Club and Archaeological Society (Gloucester) (42) 139–45.

2448. GODARD, BARBARA.   Tales within tales: Margaret Atwood's folk narratives. CanL (109) 57–84.

2449. GOSE, ELLIOT B., JR.   The world of the Irish wonder tale: an introduction to the study of fairy tales. Toronto: Toronto UP, 1985. pp. xxiv, 228. Rev. by Norman H. MacKenzie in CJIS (12:1) 106–8.

2450. GREENHILL, PAULINE JANE.   Contemporary folk poetry in southern Ontario. Unpub. doct. diss., Univ. of Texas at Austin, 1985. [Abstr. in DA (47) 623A.]

2451. HABTEYES, LOIS HASSELL.   'Tell me a story about long time': a study of the folkstory performance tradition in the United States Virgin Islands. Unpub. doct. diss., Univ. of Illinois at Urbana-Champaign, 1985. [Abstr. in DA (46) 3500A.]

2452. HALPERT, HERBERT; WIDDOWSON, J. D. A.   Folk-narrative performance and tape transcription: theory versus practice. Lore & Language (5:1) 39–50.

2453. HAMILTON, VIRGINIA.   The people could fly: American black folktales. New York: Knopf, 1985. pp. 178. Rev. by Floyd C. Dickman in OhioanaQ (29:2) 63–4.

2454. HART, SIDNEY (ed.).   One in specyal et al.: immortalizers of King Arthur. Presteigne: Three Golden Crowns, 1985. pp. viii, 145.

2455. HAVELOCK, ERIC A.   The muse learns to write: reflections on orality and literacy from antiquity to the present. New Haven, CT; London: Yale UP. pp. 144.

2456. HOLT, GEORGE.   Tales and tellers: storytelling in the South. SE (9:2) 1981, 25.

2457. HUGHES, MERION; EVANS, WAYNE.   Rumours and oddities from North Wales. Llanrwst: Gwasg Carreg Gwalch. pp. 79.

2458. INDYK, IVOR.   Some uses of myth in Australian literature. Australian Cultural History (Australian National Univ., Canberra) (5) 60–74.

2459. KASSER, STEPHEN JAY.   Speech into print: a structural account of Mark Twain's use of folklore. Unpub. doct. diss., Univ. of Pennsylvania, 1985. [Abstr. in DA (46) 2402A.]

2460. KELLY, EAMON.   According to custom: an evening of storytelling. Cork: Mercier. pp. 80.

2461. KNUTH, CAROLE BROWN.   From faller to phoenix: transformations in the verbal art of Clementina Todesco. ItalA (8:1) 36–43.

2462. LAMOINE, GEORGES.   *Richard II* and the myth of the Fisher King. CEl (30) 75–8.

2463. LINDAHL, CARL.   Psychic ambiguity at the legend core. JFR (23:1) 1–23.

2464. LOCHHEAD, MARION.   Edinburgh: lore and legend. London: Hale. pp. 224.

2465. LOFARO, MICHAEL A. (ed.).   Davy Crockett: the man, the legend, the legacy, 1786–1986. Knoxville: Tennessee UP, 1985. pp. xxiii, 203. Rev. by Karen Aubrey Ellstrom in MFR (20:1) 27–9.

2466. McDermitt, B. R. D. A comparison of a Scottish and American storyteller and their *Märchen* repertoires. Unpub. doct. diss., Univ. of Edinburgh. [Abstr. in IT (36) 909.]

2467. McLeish, Kenneth. Myths and folk stories of Britain and Ireland. Harlow: Longman. pp. 320.

2468. McNeil, W. K. (ed.). Ghost stories from the American South. Little Rock, AR: August House, 1985. pp. 170. Rev. by William B. McCarthy in SCR (3:4) 116–19; by Kim Burdick in JAF (99) 327–8.

2469. Marsden, Simon. The haunted realm: ghosts, witches and other strange tales of Britain. Introd. by Colin Wilson. Exeter: Webb & Bower. pp. 128.

2470. Matthews, John; Green, Marian. The Grail seeker's companion: a guide to the Grail quest in the Aquarian age. Wellingborough: Aquarian. pp. 208.

2471. Melani, Lilia. A child's psyche: recollections of fairy tales, myths and romances. LU (3:1) 1979, 14–27.

2472. Michaelis-Jena, Ruth. Eulenspiegel and Münchhausen: two German folk heroes. Folklore (97:1) 101–8.

2473. Mitchell, O. S. Tall tales in the fiction of W. O. Mitchell. CanL (108) 16–35.

2474. Morgan, Gareth. Rhyme in prose narrative: a precaution. Folklore (97:2) 219–21.

2475. Oxendine, Jill. Kathryn Windham: 'Something I wanted to tell you'. SE (9:2) 1981, 33–5.

2476. Parker, Frank; Thormeyer, John. Analogizing from linguistics to folklore. *See* **1954.**

2477. Patten, Bob; Patten, Jacqueline. Rab Channing: life and legends. Folklore (97:1) 56–62.

2478. Powell, Kirsten. Edward Burne-Jones and the legend of the briar rose. JPRS (6:2) 15–28.

2479. Price, Merlin. Folktales and legends of Gloucestershire. Peterborough: Minimax, 1984. pp. 64.

2480. Quinn, Bob. Atlantean. London: Quartet. pp. 184.

2481. Ranke, Kurt (ed.). Enzyklopädie des Märchens. Handwörterbuch zur historischen und vergleichenden Erzählforschung. Berlin: de Gruyter, 1979–85. 3 vols. pp. 1446; 1440; 228. Rev. by Heinz Rölleke in arcadia (21:1) 85–6.

2482. Ross-Glass, R. M. A study of the implicit metaphors in selected fairy tales and their use in modern literature and the media. *See* **2279.**

2483. Ruoff, A. LaVonne Brown. The survival of tradition: American Indian oral and written narratives. MassR (27:2) 274–93.

2484. Ryan, J. S. Perdurable story elements from Celtic folklore and mythology. Orana (21:3) 1985, 111–16.

2485. Scott, Bill. Complete book of Australian folklore. Sydney: Child & Henry. pp. 414.

2486. Secor, Robert.   The significance of Pennsylvania's eighteenth-century jest books. PMHB (110:2) 259–87.

2487. Shorrocks, G.   A note on the narrative of verbal conflict. Lore & Language (5:1) 87–93.

2488. Simpson, J. R.   King Arthur's enchanted sleep: early nineteenth century legends. Folklore (97:2) 206–9.

2489. Smith, Paul.   The book of nastier legends. London: Routledge & Kegan Paul. pp. 112.

2490. Steckmesser, Kent Ladd.   The 'good badman' in fact, film, and folklore. Claremont, CA: Regina, 1983. pp. vii, 161. Rev. by Richard W. Etulain in PacHR (55:2) 313–14.

2491. Tatar, Maria.   From nags to witches: stepmothers in the Grimms' fairy tales. *In* (pp. 28–41) **40.**

2492. Tatum, Stephen.   Inventing Billy the Kid: visions of the outlaw in America, 1881–1981. (Bibl. 1983, 2385.) Rev. by Robert Thacker in JCanStud (20:1) 1985, 161–9.

2493. Tobin, Niall (ed.).   The Irish reciter. Belfast: Blackstaff. pp. 136.

2494. von Franz, Marie-Louise.   Problems of the feminine in fairy-tales. Dallas, TX: Spring; Shaftesbury: Element, 1972. pp. 200.

2495. Wales, Tony.   Ballads, bands and bell-ringers: singers, musicians and story-tellers in old Sussex. Horsham: Field & Furrow, 1985. pp. 26. (Simple pleasures.)

2496. Walle, Alf H.   Devolution and evolution: hillbillies and cowboys as American savages. KFR (32:1/2) 58–68.

2497. Warner, Marina.   The Cinderella story. Listener (115) 23 Jan., 12–14.

2498. Webb, Barbara J.   Myth and history in the novels of Alejo Carpentier and Wilson Harris: theories of cultural transformation. Unpub. doct. diss., New York Univ., 1985. [Abstr. in DA (46) 3715A.]

2499. Wiltenburg, Joy Deborah.   Disorderly women and female power in the popular literature of early modern England and Germany. Unpub. doct. diss., Univ. of Virginia, 1984. [Abstr. in DA (46) 3133A–4A.]

2500. Wiltshire, Kathleen.   More ghosts and legends of the Wiltshire countryside. Ed. by Patricia M. C. Carrott. Melksham: Venton, 1984. pp. 166. (White Horse library.)

2501. Wooton, Anthony.   Animal folklore, myth and legend. Poole: Blandford. pp. 160.

2502. Wyatt, N.   Cain's wife. Folklore (97:1) 88–95; (97:2) 232.

2503. Zipes, Jack.   Fairy tales and the art of subversion: the classical genre for children and the process of civilization. (Bibl. 1985, 1980.) Rev. by Frank Bergmann in CanRCL (13:3) 481–2.

SONG AND MUSIC

2504. Andersen, Flemming G.; Holzapfel, Otto; Pettitt, Thomas.   The ballad as narrative: studies in the ballad tradition of

England, Scotland, Germany and Denmark. (Bibl. 1984, 1950.) Rev. by
B. D. H. Miller in NQ (33:2) 209–10.

2505. ANON.   Stanley Robinson. *See* **2428.**

2506. BOYES, GEORGINA (ed.).   The ballad today: proceedings of the
13th International Folk Ballad Conference, Centre for English Cultural
Tradition and Language, University of Sheffield, England, 18th–23rd
July 1982. Doncaster: January, 1985. pp. 111.

2507. BRENNAN, MICHAEL G.   Foxes and wolves in Elizabethan
episcopal propaganda. CEl (29) 83–6.

2508. BROWN, CHARLES T.   Music U.S.A.: America's country and
western tradition. Englewood Cliffs, NJ; London: Prentice-Hall.
pp. viii, 215.

2509. CARSON, CIARAN.   Pocket guide to Irish traditional music.
Belfast: Appletree. pp. 72.

2510. COOKE, PETER.   The fiddle tradition of the Shetland Isles.
Cambridge: CUP. pp. xii, 163. (Cambridge studies in ethno-
musicology.)

2511. DOBSON, BOB (ed.).   Woven in Lancashire: some Lancashire
dialect poems. *See* **892.**

2512. DOWNEY, JAMES C.   The American folk hymn in the British
Isles. MFR (19:2) 1985, 71–82.

2513. DRISKELL, GLENDA JOY.   Traditional black music and musicians in rural Alabama and northeast Mississippi, 1940–1982: an
ethnomusicological analysis. Unpub. doct. diss., Univ. of Alabama,
1985. [Abstr. in DA (46) 1860A.]

2514. DUGAW, DIANNE M.   Structural analysis of the female warrior
ballads: the landscape of a world turned upside down. JFR (23:1) 23–42.
(Broadside ballads.)

2515. EDMUNDS, S. C.   The English riddle ballads. Unpub. doct. diss.,
Univ. of Durham, 1985. [Abstr. in IT (35) 1082.]

2516. EDMUNDS, SUSAN.   The riddle ballad and the riddle. *See* **2415.**

2517. ELLIS, FRANK H.   Four new English broadsides. YLG (60:3/4)
111–18.

2518. FRANK, STUART M.   Ballads and songs of the whale-hunters,
1825–1895, from manuscripts in the Kendall Whaling Museum.
Unpub. doct. diss., Brown Univ., 1985. [Abstr. in DA (46) 1983A.]

2519. HARKER, D. I.; RUTHERFORD, F. (eds).   Songs from the
manuscript collection of John Bell. Durham: Surtees Society, 1985.
pp. xiv, 403. (Pubs. of the Surtees Soc., 196.)

2520. INBODEN, ROBIN LOUISE.   'The music in my heart I bore': the
ballad revival, Scott, and Wordsworth. Unpub. doct. diss., Cornell
Univ., 1985. [Abstr. in DA (46) 3040A.]

2521. KNAPMAN, ZINNIA.   A reappraisal of Percy's editing. FMJ (5:2)
202–14.

2522. LEHR, GENEVIEVE (ed.).   Come and I will sing you: a Newfoundland songbook. Toronto; London: Toronto UP, 1985. pp. xiv, 210.

2523. LEPOW, LAUREN.   'They that wad their true-love win': *Tam Lin*
and *Jane Eyre*. MSE (10:2) 1985, 110–26.

2524. MANN, DOUG.   Songs of the singing street. Edinburgh: Canongate, 1985. pp. 32.

2525. MILLER, TERRY E.   Folk music in America: a reference guide. New York; London: Garland. pp. xx, 424. (Garland reference library of the humanities, 496.)

2526. MUNRO, AILIE.   The folk music revival in Scotland. (Bibl. 1985, 1999.) Rev. by Thomas Crawford in SLJ (supp. 25) 29–32.

2527. NARVAEZ, PETER.   The protest songs of a labor union on strike against an American corporation in a Newfoundland company town: folkloristic analysis with special references to oral folk history. Unpub. doct. diss., Indiana Univ. [Abstr. in DA (47) 1441A–2A.]

2528. O'BRIEN, JANE.   The Grainger English folk song collection. Nedlands: Univ. of Western Australia, Dept of Music; Cambridge: Moore, 1985. pp. xv, 158. (Music monographs, 6.)

2529. OLSON, IAN A.   The influence of the Folk Song Society on the Greig–Duncan Folk Song Collection: methodology. FMJ (5:2) 176–201.

2530. PALMER, ROY.   Kidson's collecting. FMJ (5:2) 150–75.

2531. —— (ed.).   The Oxford book of sea songs. Oxford: OUP. pp. xxx, 343. Rev. by Hortense Wackett in Listener, 12 June, 25–6.

2532. RUSSELL, IAN (ed.).   Singer, song and scholar. Sheffield: Sheffield Academic Press. pp. 177.

2533. TUCKER, NICHOLAS.   Lullabies and child care: a historical perspective. *In* (pp. 17–27) **40.**

2534. WALES, TONY.   Ballads, bands and bell-ringers: singers, musicians and story-tellers in old Sussex. *See* **2495.**

2535. WEST, STEVE.   The devil visits the Delta: a view of his role in the blues. MFR (19:1) 1985, 11–23.

2536. WILTENBURG, JOY DEBORAH.   Disorderly women and female power in the popular literature of early modern England and Germany. *See* **2499.**

DANCE AND DRAMA

2537. ASAGBA, AUSTIN.   Roots of African drama: critical approaches and elements of continuity. Lore & Language (5:1) 51–67.

2538. CHANDLER, KEITH.   The archival morris films in the Vaughan Williams Memorial Library. Eynsham: Chandler, 1985. pp. 38. (Morris dancing in the South Midlands, 9.)

2539. HARROP, PETER.   Towards a morphology of the English folk play. Lore & Language (5:2) 63–99.

2540. HAYWARD, B. J.   Folk drama in Scotland. Unpub. doct. diss., Univ. of Glasgow, 1983.

2541. HEANEY, MICHAEL.   Must every fiddler play a fiddle? *See* **1596.**

2542. HELM, ALEX.   The English mummers' play. (Bibl. 1982, 2813.) Rev. by B. D. H. Miller in NQ (33:2) 218–19.

2543. —— Staffordshire folk drama. Ibstock: Guizer, 1984. pp. 72.

2544. HILLS, DAVID.   'Bushop Brian' and the dramatic entertainments of Cheshire. REEDNewsletter (11:1) 1–7.

2545. MILLINGTON, P. T. (comp.).   An interim list of Nottingham folk plays and related customs. Sheffield: Traditional Drama Research Group, 1984. pp. 42.

2546. PARRY, CAROLINE BALDERSTON.   'The Maypole is up, now give me the cup . . .'. REEDNewsletter (11:1) 7–9.

2547. ROUD, STEPHEN.   Mumming plays in Oxfordshire: an interim checklist. Sheffield: Traditional Drama Research Group, 1984. pp. 40.

2548. ROYAL SCOTTISH COUNTRY DANCE SOC.   The Inverclyde foursome: four Scottish country dances: to commemorate the Diamond Jubilee of the West Renfrewshire Branch of the Royal Scottish Country Dance Society 1925–1985. Greenock: Royal Scottish Country Dance Soc., 1985. pp. 8.

2549. SHIELDS, HUGH.   Oliver Goldsmith and popular song. Dublin: Folk Music Soc. of Ireland, 1985. pp. 11.

2550. YAXLEY, SUSAN (ed.).   Kemps nine daies wonder: performed in a daunce from London to Norwich: containing the pleasure, paines and kinde entertainment of William Kemp betweene London and that Citty in his late Morrice: wherein is somewhat set downe worth note; to reproove the slaunders spred of him; many things merry, nothing hurtfull. Dereham: Larks Press. 1985, pp. 32.

CUSTOM AND BELIEF

2551. BENNETT, GILLIAN.   Ghost and witch in the sixteenth and seventeenth centuries. Folklore (97:1) 3–14.

2552. BROOKS, JOHN.   Ghosts and witches of the Cotswolds. Norwich: Jarrold. pp. 144.

2553. BROWN, FRANCES.   Fairfield folk: a history of the British fairground and its people. Malvern: Malvern Publishing. pp. vi, 154.

2554. CLINCH, ROSEMARY.   Supernatural in Somerset. Bodmin: Bossiney. pp. 112.

2555. DINZELBACHER, PETER.   The way to the other world in medieval literature and art. Folklore (97:1) 70–87.

2556. DRURY, SUSAN M.   English love divinations using plants: an aspect. Folklore (97:2) 210–14.

2557. ELKINS, W. F.   William Lauron DeLaurence and Jamaican folk religion. Folklore (97:2) 215–18.

2558. HIRTH, ERIC.   Ghosts in Cornwall: a new look at hauntings in the south west. St Ives: St Ives. pp. 72.

2559. HURLEY, J. FINLEY.   Sorcery. Boston, MA; London: Routledge & Kegan Paul, 1985. pp. 232.

2560. JUDGE, ROY.   May morning and Magdalen College, Oxford. Folklore (97:1) 15–40.

2561. KERRIDGE, ROY.   Bizarre Britain: a calendar of eccentricity. Oxford: Blackwell, 1985. pp. xi, 210.

2562. LAFONTE, ANNE MARIE.   Herbal folklore. Bideford: Badger, 1984. pp. 86. (Devon's heritage.)

2563. LOCHHEAD, MARION.   Edinburgh: lore and legend. *See* **2464.**

2564. MENEFEE, SAMUEL PYEATT.   Wives for sale: an ethnographic study of British popular divorce. (Bibl. 1981, 2501.) Rev. by Valerie Shaw in MLR (81:1) 184–5.

2565. NEWALL, VENETIA.   Folklore and male homosexuality. *See* **1016.**

2566. OTTEN, CHARLOTTE F. (ed.).   A lycanthropy reader: werewolves in Western culture. New York: Syracuse UP. pp. xviii, 357.

2567. PEARSON, R. A.   More ghosts in and around Chesterfield. Chesterfield: Pearson. pp. 82.

2568. ST GEORGE, E. A.   Horse lore and magic: a study of horse, smith, iron and hero magic. London: Spook Enterprises, 1985. 15 leaves.

2569. SHEMANSKI, FRANCES.   A guide to fairs and festivals in the United States. Westport, CT; London: Greenwood Press, 1984. pp. viii, 339.

2570. SHUEL, BRIAN.   The National Trust guide to traditional customs of Britain. Exeter: Webb & Bower, 1985. pp. 208.

2571. SILVER, CAROLE.   On the origin of fairies: Victorians, Romantics, and folk belief. BIS (14) 141–56.

MATERIAL CULTURE, TECHNIQUES, AND OCCUPATIONS, FOLK ARTS AND CRAFTS

2572. GAILEY, ALAN.   Creating Ulster's Folk Museum. Ulster Folklife (32) 54–77.

2573. GOLDSACK, PAUL J.   Weatherwise: practical weather lore for sailors and outdoor people. Newton Abbot: David & Charles. pp. 160.

2574. RIKOON, JAMES SANFORD.   From flail to combine: folk culture and technological change in the rural Midwest. Unpub. doct. diss., Indiana Univ. [Abstr. in DA (47) 624A.]

CHILDREN'S TRADITIONS

2575. BROWN, MARC (comp.).   Hand rhymes. London: Collins, 1985. pp. 31.

2576. HILL, KAY.   Playing with words: the verbal folklore of Puerto Rican schoolchildren in a mainland setting. Unpub. doct. diss., Univ. of Connecticut, 1985. [Abstr. in DA (47) 623A–4A.]

2577. OPIE, IONA; OPIE, PETER.   The singing game. (Bibl. 1985, 2062.) Rev. by Brian Sutton-Smith in JAF (99) 239–40.

ENGLISH LITERATURE

GENERAL

GENERAL LITERARY STUDIES

2578. ADAMS, HAZARD. Philosophy of the literary symbolic. (Bibl. 1985, 2065.) Rev. by Shyamal Bagchee in MP (84:2) 239–41.

2579. ADAMS, PERCY G. Travel literature and the evolution of the novel. (Bibl. 1985, 2066.) Rev. by Jerry Beasley in ECent (27:1) 62–71; by I. S. MacLaren in UTQ (55:2) 1985/86, 204–9; by Angela Smallwood in NQ (33:2) 246–7.

2580. AITKEN, W. R. Scottish literature in English and Scots: a guide to information sources. (Bibl. 1985, 2068.) Rev. by J. H. Alexander in YES (16) 231–4.

2581. ALDRIDGE, A. OWEN. The interplay of history and literature. CLIO (11:3) 1982, 261–70.

2582. —— The re-emergence of world literature: a study of Asia and the West. Newark: Delaware UP; London: Assoc. UPs. pp. 228.

2583. ARMSTRONG, KAREN (ed.). Tongues of fire: an anthology of religious and poetic experience. Harmondsworth: Viking Press; Channel 4 TV, 1985. pp. 351.

2584. ATKINS, G. DOUGLAS. Reading deconstruction/deconstructive reading. (Bibl. 1985, 2073.) Rev. by Joseph A. Buttigieg in ECent (27:2) 182–8; by Raman Selden in MLR (81:3) 690–1.

2585. AVERINCEV, SERGEJ S. Das dauerhafte Erbe der Griechen: die rhetorische Grundeinstellung als Synthese des Traditionalismus und der Reflexion. *In* (pp. 267–71) **11.**

2586. EL-BAKRI, AHMAD. A linguistic approach to literary criticism. Arab Journal for the Humanities (5) Autumn 1985, 338–57.

2587. BALAKIAN, ANNA. Literature and literariness: introduction. CanRCL (13:2) 215–16. (Introduction to the 'The Specificity of the Literary Text: a Discussion'.) (*Refers to* **2623, 2650–1, 2727.**)

2588. BAŁUK-ULEWICZOWA, TERESA; KOROSADOWICZ, MARIA (eds). Proceedings of the third April Conference of University Teachers of English, Cracow 1984 (April 11–15). English language and literature: methods of teaching and research. *See* **17.**

2589. BARKER, FRANCIS, *et al.* (eds). Literature, politics and theory: papers from the Essex Conference 1976–84. *See* **29.**

2590. BASSNETT, SUZAN. Comparative literature and methodology. Degrés (Brussels) (14:46/47) i–i14.

2591. BAYM, NINA, *et al.* (eds). The Norton anthology of American literature. (Bibl. 1980, 2961.) New York; London: Norton, 1985. 2 vols. pp. xxxiv, 2535; xxxiv, 2652. (Second ed.: first ed. 1979.)

2592. BENTLEY, D. M. R. Boxing the compass: Ontario's geopoetics. CanP (18) v–xiii.

2593. BERTHOFF, WARNER. Literature and the continuances of virtue. Princeton, NJ; Guildford: Princeton UP. pp. xi, 293.

2594. BILTON, PETER, *et al.* (eds).   Essays in honour of Kristian Smidt. *See* **18**.

2595. BIRRELL, THOMAS ANTHONY.   Engels als vreemde letterkunde. (English as foreign literature.) Nijmegen: Katholieke Universiteit. pp. 12.

2596. BLACKHAM, H. J.   The fable as literature. (Bibl. 1985, 2086.) Rev. by J. Janisch in UES (24:2) 59–60; by T. A. Shippey in THES (706) 17.

2597. BLOOMFIELD, MORTON W. (ed.).   Allegory, myth, and symbol. (Bibl. 1983, 2487.) Rev. by T. A. Shippey in MLR (81:4) 967–9.

2598. BLYTHE, RONALD.   Divine landscapes. New York: Harcourt Brace Jovanovich; Harmondsworth: Viking Press. pp. 254. (Places of literary pilgrimage.) Rev. by Anthony Bailey in BkW, 12 Oct., 3, 13.

2599. BOLD, ALAN (ed.).   The sexual dimension in literature. (Bibl. 1983, 110.) Rev. by Jerry C. Beasley in MLR (81:4) 989–90.

2600. BONO, BARBARA J.   Literary transvaluation: from Vergilian epic to Shakespearean tragicomedy. (Bibl. 1985, 2089.) Rev. by John W. Velz in MP (84:1) 76–8.

2601. BOYLE, NICHOLAS; SWALES, MARTIN (eds).   Realism in European literature: essays in honour of J. P. Stern. *See* **46**.

2602. BRADBROOK, M. C.   Women and literature, 1779–1982. Introd. by INGA-STINA EWBANK. (Bibl. 1982, 2899.) Rev. by Rosemary Ashton in MLR (81:2) 456–7.

2603. BRADY, ANNE M.; CLEEVE, BRIAN.   A biographical dictionary of Irish writers. (Bibl. 1985, 2091.) Rev. by Peter Rowan in Linen Hall Review (3:1) 24–5.

2604. BRUMM, URSULA.   Recognizing a female aesthetic. EAL (20:3) 1985/86, 271–7 (review-article).

2605. BURR, NELSON R.   New Eden and new Babylon: religious thoughts of American authors: a bibliography: the Catholic heritage outside Roman allegiance. HMPEC (55:4) 329–41.

2606. CAMPBELL, FELICIA F.   The gambler as rebel and outsider. PhilP (32) 21–8.

2607. CARLSON, PATRICIA ANN (ed.).   Literature and lore of the sea. *See* **28**.

2608. CÉLIS, RAPHAËL (ed.).   Littérature et musique. Brussels: Facultés universitaires Saint-Louis, 1982. pp. 193. Rev. by Rodney Farnsworth in CanRCL (13:2) 282–5.

2609. CENTRE D'HISTOIRE DES IDEÉS DANS LES ILES BRITTANIQUES. Migrations: communications faites au colloque des 12 et 14 octobre 1985: mélanges offerts à Olivier Lutaud. *See* **35**.

2610. COLLIER, PETER.   The art of literary collaboration. BkW, 31 Aug., 4, 6.

2611. CONRAD, PETER.   The Everyman history of English literature. (Bibl. 1985, 2106.) Rev. by Sylvère Monod in EA (39:3) 317–18; by David Nokes in THES (698) 26.

2612. COTTLE, BASIL.   The language of literature: English grammar in action. *See* **1933**.

2613. Cross, Anthony. The Russian theme in English literature from the sixteenth century to 1980: an introductory survey and a bibliography. Oxford: Meeuws, 1985. pp. 280.

2614. Cunliffe, Marcus. The literature of the United States. New York: Viking Press; Harmondsworth: Penguin. pp. 512. (Fourth ed.: first ed. 1954.)

2615. Dabydeen, David (ed.). The black presence in English literature. Manchester: Manchester UP, 1985. pp. ix, 213. Rev. by Dennis Walden in TLS, 13 June, 663.

2616. Daiches, David. Literature and gentility in Scotland: the Alexander Lectures at the University of Toronto, 1980. (Bibl. 1985, 2109.) Rev. by J. H. Alexander in YES (16) 250–1.

2617. Datta, Kitty Scoular. Romanticism, religion and the self. Jadavpur University Essays and Studies (Calcutta) (4) 1984, 13–26.

2618. Daymond, Douglas M.; Monkman, Leslie G. (eds). Towards a Canadian literature: essays, editorials, and manifestos. Ottawa: Tecumseh, 1984. 2 vols. pp. 600. Rev. by Tracy Ware in DalR (65:4) 1985/86, 568–9; vol. 1 rev. by Germaine Warkentin in CanL (110) 109–11.

2619. Deane, Seamus. A short history of Irish literature. London: Hutchinson. pp. 282. Rev. by Patrick Parrinder in LRB (8:13) 16–17.

2620. Dearborn, Mary V. Pocahontas's daughters: gender and ethnicity in American culture. New York; Oxford: OUP. pp. 266.

2621. Delany, Sheila. Writing woman: women in literature medieval to modern. New York: Schocken, 1983. pp. vi, 218. Rev. by Lorrayne Y. Baird-Lange in SAC (8) 175–7.

2622. Dicks, Mark Jeffry. Reading irony. Unpub. doct. diss., Univ. of California, Santa Cruz, 1985. [Abstr. in DA (47) 1311A.]

2623. Dimić, Milan V. Opening a dialogue on Thomas Greene's literariness. CanRCL (13:2) 225–9.

2624. Di Pietro, Robert J.; Ifkovic, Edward (eds). Ethnic perspectives in American literature: selected essays on the European contribution. A source book. New York: Modern Language Association of America, 1983. pp. 333. Rev. by A. Owen Aldridge in CanRCL (13:2) 319–24.

2625. Donaldson, Ian. The rapes of Lucretia: a myth and its transformations. (Bibl. 1985, 2112.) Rev. by Martin Mueller in CanRCL (13:1) 117–19; by Brian Gibbons in ShS (37) 1984, 175–6.

2626. Drabble, Margaret (ed.). The Oxford companion to English literature. New York: OUP, 1985. (Cf. bibl. 1985, 2115.) Rev. by Arnold E. Davidson in CR (30:3) 416–17.

2627. Dunn, Robert P., *et al.* Bibliography. ChrisL (36:1) 51–71. (Items 8557-8658 in bibliography of works considered in a religious context.)

2628. Eade, J. C. The forgotten sky: a guide to astrology in English literature. (Bibl. 1985, 2119.) Rev. by Owen Gingerich in Spec (61:4) 922–3; by Robin Robbins in NQ (33:1) 101–3.

2629. Edel, Leon. Stuff of sleep and dreams: experiments in literary psychology. (Bibl. 1988, 2120.) Rev. by Veronica A. Makowsky in HJR (6:3) 1985, 204–5.

2630. EDGECOMBE, RODNEY.   Comic lessons. Theoria (67) 33–44.

2631. ELLIOTT, ROBERT C.   The literary persona. (Bibl. 1985, 2124.) Rev. by Harold Pagliaro in MLS (16:2) 91–3.

2632. ENRIGHT, D. J.   The alluring problem: an essay on irony. Oxford: OUP. pp. 178. Rev. by Christopher Ricks in LRB (8:21) 12–13; by David Nokes in Listener, 16 Oct., 24–5; by Hugh Kenner in TLS, 17 Oct., 1151–2.

2633. ERSKINE-HILL, HOWARD.   The Augustan idea in English literature. (Bibl. 1985, 2126.) Rev. by Robert James Merrett in Ariel (17:2) 85–9; by Howard D. Weinbrot in MP (83:3) 286–97; by Oliver Taplin in EC (36:1) 75–81.

2634. FARRELL, ELEANOR M.   'And clove the wind from unseen shores': the sea voyage motif in imaginative literature. Mythlore (12:3) 43–7, 60.

2635. FARRELL, THOMAS B.   Rhetorical resemblance: paradoxes of a practical art. QJS (72:1) 1–19.

2636. FEKETE, JOHN.   Literature and politics/literary politics. DalR (66:1/2) 45–86.

2637. FINLAYSON, IAIN.   Writers in Romney Marsh. (Pub. in USA as *The Sixth Continent: a Literary History of Romney Marsh.*) London: Severn House; New York: Atheneum. pp. 240. Rev. by Evelyn Toynton in NYTB, 23 Nov., 20.

2638. FRASER, JOHN.   The name of action: critical essays. (Bibl. 1985, 2133.) Rev. by Claude Rawson in LRB (8:2) 13–14.

2639. FREEDMAN, WILLIAM.   Some kinds of ironic blame-by-praise: an attempt to classify. CLQ (22:3) 138–52.

2640. FRIEDEN, KEN.   Genius and monologue. *See* **1223.**

2641. FROW, JOHN.   System and norm in literary evolution: for a Marxist literary history. CLIO (10:2) 1981, 153–81.

2642. FRYE, NORTHROP.   The great code: the Bible and literature. (Bibl. 1983, 2535.) Rev. by Gerald Gillespie in CL (38:3) 289–97.

2643. FURBANK, P. N.   On money in literature. Enc (67:4) 38–46.

2644. GABEL, GERNOT U.   Canadian literature: an index to theses accepted by Canadian universities, 1925–1980. Cologne: Gemini, 1984. pp. 157. Rev. in BB (43:3) 185.

2645. GARVEY, B. T.   Literature of utopia and dystopia. Unpub. doct. diss., Univ. of Bradford, 1985. [Abstr. in IT (35) 1489.]

2646. GILBERT, SANDRA M.; GUBAR, SUSAN (comps).   The Norton anthology of literature by women: the tradition in English. London: Norton, 1985. (Cf. bibl. 1985, 2137.)

2647. GOLDSTEIN, LAURENCE.   The flying machine and modern literature. Basingstoke: Macmillan. pp. xiv, 253.

2648. GOODMAN, AILENE S.   The extraordinary being: death and the mermaid in baroque literature. *In* (pp. 256–74) **28.**

2649. GREEN, J.   'A kind of another species': woman in Judeo-Christian tradition from the myth of the Fall to *Paradise Lost*. Unpub. doct. diss., Univ. of Sussex, 1983.

2650. GREENE, THOMAS M.   Closing remarks. CanRCL (13:2) 236–7. (Conclusion of 'The Specificity of the Literary Text: a Discussion'.)

2651. —— On the category of the literary. CanRCL (13:2) 217–24.

2652. GREER, GERMAINE.   The madwoman's underclothes: essays and occasional writings; 1968–85. London: Picador. pp. xxvii, 305.

2653. GRIFFIN, JASPAR.   The mirror of myth: classical themes & variations. London: Faber & Faber. pp. 144. (T. S. Eliot Memorial Lectures, 1984.)

2654. HAVELOCK, ERIC A.   The muse learns to write: reflections on orality and literacy from antiquity to the present. *See* **2455.**

2655. HAYNE, DAVID M.; SIROIS, ANTOINE; VIGNEAULT, JEAN (comps).   Preliminary bibliography of comparative Canadian literature (English-Canadian and French-Canadian): ninth supp., 1983–84; tenth supp., 1984–85. CanRCL (12:3) 1985, 462–8; (13:3) 450–7.

2656. HEDAYET, A. A. EL-A.   Cleopatra in English literature from Chaucer to Thomas May. Unpub. doct. diss., Univ. of Wales, Bangor, 1984. [Abstr. in IT (35) 43.]

2657. HIGH, PETER B.   An outline of American literature. Harlow: Longman. pp. 256.

2658. HJERETER, KATHLEEN G.   Doubly gifted: the author as visual artist. Foreword by JOHN UPDIKE. New York: Abrams. pp. 160. Rev. by Michael Patrick Hearn in ABC (7:9) 42–4.

2659. HOCHMAN, BARUCH.   Character in literature. Ithaca, NY; London: Cornell UP, 1985. pp. 204. Rev. by Steven Connor in Dick (82:2) 108–9.

2660. HOLDHEIM, W. WOLFGANG.   The hermeneutic mode: essays on time in literature and literary theory. (Bibl. 1985, 2548.) Rev. by John Goodlife in PhilL (10:1) 105–6.

2661. HUME, KATHRYN.   Fantasy and mimesis: responses to reality in western literature. (Bibl. 1985, 2162.) Rev. by Kathryn Sutherland in CritQ (28:4) 107–9; by Patrick Parrinder in MLR (81:3) 694–5.

2662. HUMM, PETER; STIGANT, PAUL; WIDDOWSON, PETER (eds).   Popular fictions: essays in literature and history. London: Methuen. pp. xiii, 224. (New accents.)

2663. IASAIL.   Bibliography bulletin for 1985. IUR (16) 180–233.

2664. JACK, R. D. S.   Scottish literature's debt to Italy. Edinburgh: Italian Inst. pp. vii, 86.

2665. JANOUŠEK, MIROSLAV.   Na okraj literárních jubileí: anglistika a amerikanistika. (Glosses on literary anniversaries 1987: English and American studies.) CJa (30) 153–60.

2666. JEFFARES, A. NORMAN.   Parameters of Irish literature in English: a lecture given at the Princess Grace Irish Library on Friday 25 April 1986 at 8.00 p.m. Gerrards Cross: Smythe. pp. 44. (Princess Grace Irish Library lectures, 1.)

2667. KAPLAN, CORA.   Sea changes: essays on culture and feminism. London: Verso. pp. 232. (Questions for feminism.)

2668. KARITA, MOTOJI.   Pocahontas to Matthiessen: America bungaku shiron. (Pocahontas to Matthiessen: an essay on American literature.) Tokyo: Yamaguchi Press. pp. 168.

2669. KASTOVSKY, DIETER; SZWEDEK, ALEKSANDER (eds); PŁOCIŃSKA, BARBARA (asst ed.).   Linguistics across historical and geographical boundaries in honour of Jacek Fisiak on the occasion of his fiftieth birthday: vol. 1, Linguistic theory and historical linguistics; vol. 2, Descriptive, contrastive and applied linguistics. *See* **26.**

2670. KAWASAKI, SUMIHIKO.   Igirisu bungakushi nyumon. (A guide to the history of English literature.) Tokyo: Kenkyusha Press. pp. vi, 190. (Guides to English language and literature.)

2671. KEHOE, MONIKA (ed.).   Historical, literary, and erotic aspects of lesbianism. New York; London: Harrington Park Press. pp. 182.

2672. KEITH, W. J.   Canadian literature in English. New York: Longman, 1985. (Cf. bibl. 1985, 2176.) Rev. by Tracy Ware in DalR (65:4) 1985/86, 569–73; by D. M. R. Bentley in CanP (18) 131–7; by George Woodcock in UTQ (55:3) 302–6; by Alan Lawson in CanL (110) 111–13.

2673. KELLIHER, HILTON; BROWN, SALLY.   English literary manuscripts. *See* **157.**

2674. KENNEDY, ALAN.   Criticism of value: response to John Fekete. DalR (66:1/2) 87–97.

2675. KILLEN, JOHN (ed.).   The Irish Christmas book. Belfast: Blackstaff, 1985. pp. ix, 180.

2676. —— The second Irish Christmas book. Belfast: Blackstaff. pp. 190.

2677. KIM, GLENN JOHN.   'This mad *instead*': studies in metaphor and literature. Unpub. doct. diss., Harvard Univ., 1985. [Abstr. in DA (46) 1928A.]

2678. KLÉGR, ALEŠ.   Konkordance k literárním dílům. (Concordances relating to literary works.) PP (29) 33–4.

2679. KONSTANTINOVIĆ, ZORAN; ANDERSON, WARREN; DIETZE, WALTER (eds).   Classical models in literature/Les modèles classiques dans les littératures/Klassische Modelle in der Literatur. Proceedings of the IXth Congress of the International Comparative Literature Association. *See* **11.**

2680. KRUHU MODERNÍCH FILOLOGŮ.   Jubinlejní Ročenka Kruhu Moderních Filologů. (Jubilee anniversary report of the Czechoslovak Circle of Modern Philology.) *See* **24.**

2681. KUNA, FRANZ; TSCHACHLER, HEINZ (eds).   Dialog der Texte: Literatur und Landeskunde. Beiträge zu Problemen einer integrativen Landes- und Kulturkunde des englischsprachigen Auslands. *See* **15.**

2682. KUYKENDALL, JOSEPH.   Darwin, the Bible, literature and consciousness. CAE (19) 501–7.

2683. LAWSON-PEEBLES, R.   Literature   and   landscape   in   the formative period of the United States. Unpub. doct. diss., Univ. of Oxford, 1983.

2684. LAYTON, LYNNE; SCHAPIRO, BARBARA ANN (eds). Narcissism and the text: studies in literature and the psychology of self. New York; London: New York UP. pp. xvi, 295. (Psychoanalytic crosscurrents.)

2685. LEE, ALVIN A. Towards a language of love and freedom: Frye deciphers *The Great Code*. ESCan (12:2) 124–37.

2686. LEE, DORIS DOUGLAS. Money in selected works of English literature: *c.* 700–1800. Unpub. doct. diss., Univ. of Kansas, 1985. [Abstr. in DA (47) 538A.]

2687. LERNER, LAURENCE. The literary imagination: essays on literature and society. (Bibl. 1984, 2172.) Rev. by Michael Wood in MLR (81:2) 428–9.

2688. LEVIȚCHI, LEON. Istoria literaturii engleze si americane: vol. 1. (A history of English and American literature: vol. 1.) Cluj-Napoca: Dacia, 1985. pp. 340.

2689. LEWIS, PETER (comp.). A fox-hunter's anthology. Woodbridge: Boydell, 1985. pp. xv, 364.

2690. LITTLEFIELD, DANIEL F., JR; PARINS, JAMES W. (eds). A biobibliography of native American writers, 1772–1924. (Bibl. 1982, 265.) Rev. by Bo Schöler in AIQ (10:4) 361–2.

2691. LOY, J. ROBERT. Attitudes toward authority in European literature to the eighteenth century. *In* (pp. 65–9) **11.**

2692. LUBKOLL, CHRISTINE. '. . . Und wär's ein Augenblick'. Der Sündenfall des Wissens und der Liebeslust in Faustdichtungen von der *Historia* bis zu Thomas Manns *Doktor Faustus*. Rheinfelden, W. Germany: Schäuble. pp. 345. (Deutsche und vergleichende Literaturwissenschaft, 9.)

2693. LUKACHER, NED. Primal scenes: literature, philosophy, psychoanalysis. Ithaca, NY; London: Cornell UP. pp. 342.

2694. LYONS, JOHN D.; NICHOLS, STEPHEN G., JR (eds). Mimesis: from mirror to method, Augustine to Descartes. (Bibl. 1983, 32.) Rev. by Michael G. Brennan in NQ (33:1) 99–100.

2695. MCDIARMID, M. P. The literature of 'ane symple land'. Scottish Language (5) 23–9.

2696. MCKINSEY, ELIZABETH. Niagara Falls: icon of the American sublime. Cambridge: CUP, 1985. pp. xvi, 332. (Cambridge studies in American literature and culture.)

2697. MACLAREN, I. S. The MacGregor syndrome; or, the survival of patterns of isolated butterflies on rocks in the haunted wilderness of the unnamed bush garden beyond the land itself. CanP (18) 118–30 (review-article).

2698. MACQUEEN, JOHN. Numerology: theory and outline history of a literary mode. (Bibl. 1985, 2201.) Rev. by John Took in MLR (81:4) 967; by Alexander Dunlop in RQ (39:2) 329–30.

2699. MCTAGGART, ARTHUR. The lies of literature. YYY (3) 1985, 209–31.

2700. Marino, Adrian.   Interpréter et/est moderniser les classiques. *In* (pp. 77–82) **11.**

2701. Mathias, Roland.   A ride through the wood: essays on Anglo-Welsh literature. Bridgend: Poetry Wales Press, 1985. pp. 320. Rev. by Raymond Stephens in AWR (83) 146–7; by Jeremy Hooker in Poetry Wales (21:4) 122–4.

2702. Meserole, Harrison T.; Rambeau, James M.   A select, annotated list of current articles on American literature. AL (58) 152–7, 316–23, 490–8, 690–6.

2703. Meynell, Hugo A.   The nature of aesthetic value. London: Macmillan. pp. vi, 158.

2704. Michael, Ian.   Epic to romance to novel: problems of genre identification. BJRL (68:2) 498–527.

2705. Miller, R. Baxter (ed.).   Black American literature and humanism. (Bibl. 1982, 3015.) Rev. by Kenneth Kinnamon in YES (16) 349–50.

2706. Minogue, S.   Language, truth and literature: an examination of some ways in which truth enters into literature, with special reference to the implications of the consequent moral dimension of literature for critical judgements about literature. Unpub. doct. diss., Univ. of Leicester, 1983.

2707. Mojtabai, Grace (A.G.).   To actualize the possible: the writer in the world. Nimrod (27:2) 1984, 56–9.

2708. Morvan, Alain (ed.).   Conformité et déviances. Lille: Lille iii UP, 1984. pp. 109. Rev. by Robert A. Day in EA (38:4) 1985, 447–8.

2709. Newspaper Archive Developments.   The *Times Literary Supplement* Index, 1902–1939. *See* **659.**

2710. Newton, K. M.   In defence of literary interpretation: theory and practice. Basingstoke: Macmillan. pp. 192.

2711. Olsen, Flemming.   Elements of textual analysis. Copenhagen: Gyldendal. pp. 166.

2712. Olsen, Stein Haugom.   The structure of literary understanding. (Bibl. 1981, 2663.) Rev. by K. K. Ruthven in AUMLA (65) 122–5.

2713. Otten, Charlotte F. (ed.).   A lycanthropy reader: werewolves in Western culture. *See* **2566.**

2714. Parkinson, Kathleen; Priestman, Martin (eds).   Peasants and countrymen in literature: a symposium organised by the English Department of the Roehampton Institute in February 1981. (Bibl. 1983, 101.) Rev. by Shelagh Hunter in YES (16) 309–10.

2715. Parks, Ward.   Flyting, sounding, debate: three verbal contest genres. PT (7:3) 439–58.

2716. Parrott, E. O. (ed.).   Imitations of immortality: a book of literary parodies. London: Viking Press. pp. xxiii, 383.

2717. Parsons, Nicholas.   The book of literary lists: a collection of annotated lists of fact, statistics and anecdote concerning books. *See* **420.**

2718. Paulin, Tom.   Ireland and the English crisis. (Bibl. 1985, 2221.) Rev. by Martin Mooney in Honest Ulsterman (80) 60–1; by Raymond Stephens in AWR (80) 124–9.

2719. PEDERSEN, VIGGO HJØRNAGER.   Engelsk litteratur i Danmark. (English literature in Denmark.) Odense: Odense UP. pp. 181.

2720. PLAISANT, MICHÈLE (ed.).   Les formes de l'arrivisme en Angleterre du XVIᵉ siècle à l'époque romantique. Lille: Lille III UP, 1984. pp. 288. Rev. by Robert Adams Day in EA (39:3) 322–4.

2721. POOLE, RICHARD (ed.).   Fiction as truth: selected literary writings by Richard Hughes. (Bibl. 1983, 2655.) Rev. by Jean Hamard in EA (38:4) 1985, 480.

2722. PRITCHETT, V. S.   A man of letters: selected essays. New York: Random House, 1985. (Cf. bibl. 1985, 2227.) Rev. by William Maxwell in NY, 9 June, 108–10; by Stephen Koch in BkW, 22 June, 3, 13.

2723. PROFUMO, DAVID; SWIFT, GRAHAM (eds).   The magic wheel: an anthology of fishing in literature. London: Heinemann. pp. 460.

2724. QUENNELL, PETER (ed. and adapt.).   An illustrated companion to world literature. By TORE ZETTERHOLM. London: Orbis. pp. 314. (Originally pub. in Swedish, 1981, as *Levande Litteratur: Från Gilgamesj till Bob Dylan.*)

2725. QUINTON, ANTHONY.   The divergence of the twain: poet's philosophy and philosopher's philosophy: a lecture delivered by Anthony Quinton to mark the official opening of the Centre for Research in Philosophy and Literature, University of Warwick, 8th October 1985. Coventry: Centre for Research in Philosophy and Literature, Univ. of Warwick, 1985. pp. 22.

2726. RAIMOND, JEAN.   La littérature anglaise. Paris: Presses Universitaires de France. pp. 128. (Que sais-je?)

2727. REYNOLDS, DAVID S.   Revising the American canon: the question of literariness. CanRCL (13:2) 230–5.

2728. ROBSON, W. W.   'The Definition of Literature', and other essays. (Bibl. 1984, 2210.) Rev. by Terry Eagleton in MLR (81:2) 428.

2729. —— A prologue to English literature. London: Batsford. pp. 254. Rev. by Philip Hobsbaum in THES (733) 20.

2730. ROCK, ROGER O.   The native American in American literature: a selectively annotated bibliography. Westport, CT: Greenwood Press, 1985. pp. 211. Rev. in BB (43:3) 186–7.

2731. ROGERS, PAT.   The rise of the literary periodical. *See* **682.**

2732. ROSS, MALCOLM.   The impossible sum of our traditions: reflections on Canadian literature. Toronto: McClelland & Stewart. pp. 211. Rev. by Patricia Koster in MalaR (77) 145.

2733. RUBIN, ABBA.   Images in transition: the English Jew in English literature. Westport, CT: Greenwood Press, 1984. pp. 157. (Contributions to the study of world literature, 4.)

2734. RUBIN, LOUIS D., JR (ed.).   The history of Southern literature. (Bibl. 1985, 2244.) Rev. by Victor A. Kramer in Cweal (113:7) 216–19: by Melvin J. Freedman in AL (58:3) 427–30.

2735. SALZMAN, JACK (ed.).   American studies: an annotated bibliography. Cambridge: CUP. 3 vols. pp. xii, 2058.

2736. —— The Cambridge handbook of American literature. Cambridge: CUP. pp. 286.

2737. SATO, TAISEI (comp.).   Bungaku ni okeru kodomo. (Children in literature.) Tokyo: Kasama Press. pp. 194.

2738. SCARBOROUGH, GEORGE.   Notes towards a supreme regionalism. SE (9:2) 1981, 41–2.

2739. SCHWENGER, PETER.   The flesh made word. DalR (65:2) 1985, 283–92.

2740. SEDGWICK, EVE KOSOFSKY.   Between men: English literature and male homosexual desire. New York; Guildford: Columbia UP, 1985. pp. x, 244. (Gender and culture.) Rev. by Peter Erickson in JEGP (85:3) 461–4; by C. Carroll Hollis in WWQR (3:4) 31–8; by Seymour Kleinberg in Review (8) 143–8.

2741. SELL, ROGER D.   The drama of fictionalized author and reader: a formalist obstacle to literary pragmatics. YREAL (4) 291–316.

2742. SHELL, MARC.   Money, language, and thought: literary and philosophic economies from the medieval to the modern age. (Bibl. 1985, 2254.) Rev. by Peter Haidu in CanRCL (13:3) 429–41; by G. Douglas Atkins in ECent (26:3) 1985, 297–305.

2743. SHUSTERMAN, RICHARD.   The object of literary criticism. Atlantic Highlands, NJ: Humanities Press, 1984. pp. 237. Rev. by Alec Hyslop in PhilL (10:1) 118–20; by Lorraine Kasprisin in JAE (20:3) 119–22.

2744. SMALLWOOD, P. J.   A concise chronology of English literature. London: Croom Helm, 1985. pp. 208.

2745. SMEED, J. W.   The Theophrastan 'character': the history of a literary genre. New York: OUP, 1985. (Cf. bibl. 1985, 2258.) Rev. by John Moore in SCN (44:3) 44–5.

2746. SOCIÉTÉ DES ANGLICISTES DE L'ENSEIGNEMENT SUPÉRIEUR. Actes du congrès de Poitiers. See **1.**

2747. SPENDER, DALE (ed.).   Feminist theorists: three centuries of women's intellectual traditions. (Pub. in USA as *Feminist Theorists: Three Centuries of Key Women Thinkers.*) See **20.**

2748. STALLYBRASS, PETER; WHITE, ALLON.   The politics and poetics of transgression. London: Methuen. pp. 280. (Taboo topics and works in literature.)

2749. STANZEL, FRANZ K.   National character as literary stereotype: an analysis of the image of Germany in English literature before 1800. Anglistik & Englischunterricht (29/30) 7–20.

2750. STECKMESSER, KENT LADD.   The 'good badman' in fact, film, and folklore. See **2490.**

2751. STEINER, GEORGE.   Real presence. See **787.**

2752. STEPHENS, MEIC (ed.).   Cydymaith i lenyddiaeth Cymru. [Cardiff]: Gwasg Prifysgol Cymru. pp. xiv, 622. Rev. by Rheinallt Llwyd in Poetry Wales (21:4) 125–9.

2753. —— The Oxford companion to the literature of Wales. Oxford: OUP. pp. xvii, 682. Rev. by A. M. Allchin in Planet (56) 99–101.

2754. STERN, JOSEF.   Metaphor as demonstrative. JP (82:12) 1985, 677–710.

2755. STEVICK, PHILIP. The world and the writer: a speculation on fame. SAQ (85:3) 239–51.

2756. STONEMAN, RICHARD (ed.). Daphne into laurel: translations of classical poetry from Chaucer to the present. (Bibl. 1983, 2699.) Rev. by David Hopkins in MLR (81:4) 972–3.

2757. TATLOW, ANTONY. Classical and radical organicism: towards a rhetoric of social gesture. *In* (pp. 83–8) **11.**

2758. THOMPSON, GEORGE A. J. Key sources in comparative and world literature: an annotated guide to reference materials. London: Lorrimer, 1982. (Cf. bibl. 1985, 2265.) Rev. by J. K. Wikeley in CanRCL (12:3) 1985, 471–3.

2759. THOMSON, D. S. Gaelic literary interactions with Scots and English work: a survey. *See* **936.**

2760. TIGGES, WIM. An anatomy of Nonsense. DQR (16:3) 162–85.

2761. TOMLINSON, T. B. Some styles of literary-historical scholarship: the case of Protestantism. Critical Review (28) 87–99 (review-article).

2762. TRUCHLAR, LEO (ed.). Für eine offene Literaturwissenschaft: Erkundungen und Erprobungen am Beispiel US-amerikanischer Texte/ Opening up literary criticism: essays on American prose and poetry. *See* **21.**

2763. TUCKER, E. F. J. Intruder into Eden: representations of the common lawyer in English literature, 1350–1750. (Bibl. 1985, 2270.) Rev. by Gary Schmidgall in JEGP (85:1) 108–10.

2764. TYDEMAN, WILLIAM (ed.). The Welsh connection: essays by past and present members of the Department of English Language and Literature, University College of North Wales, Bangor. *See* **792.**

2765. VALDÉS, MARIO J.; MILLER, OWEN (eds). Identity of the literary text. *See* **23.**

2766. VAN DYKE, CAROLYNN. The fiction of truth: structures of meaning in narrative and dramatic allegory. Ithaca, NY: Cornell UP, 1985. pp. 315. Rev. by Annabel Patterson in RQ (39:3) 541–4.

2767. VIZINCZEY, STEPHEN. Truth and lies in literature: essays and reviews. Sel. and introd. by CHRISTOPHER SINCLAIR-STEVENSON. London: Hamilton. pp. xi, 339.

2768. WAGNER, MARY ANN BLAKELY. A taxonomy for the study of satire in literary and pictorial art. Unpub. doct. diss., New York Univ., 1985. [Abstr. in DA (46) 2471A.]

2769. WARD, ROBERT E. A bio-bibliography of German-American writers, 1670–1970. White Plains, NY: Kraus, 1985. pp. 377. Rev. in BB (43:3) 187.

2770. WARE, TRACY. Notes on the literary histories of Canada. DalR (65:4) 1985/86, 566–76 (review-article).

2771. WATSON, RODERICK. The literature of Scotland. (Bibl. 1985, 2278.) Rev. by Fiona Stafford in NQ (33:2) 247–8; by Thomas Crawford in SLJ (supp. 25) 27–9.

2772. WEINER, ALAN R.; MEANS, SPENCER. Literary criticism index. (Bibl. 1985, 2283.) Rev. in BB (43:3) 187.

2773. WELLEK, RENÉ. 'The Attack on Literature', and other essays. (Bibl. 1985, 2284.) Rev. by Raman Selden in MLR (81:2) 419–21; by Stephen G. Nichols in CanRCL (13:3) 465–9.

2774. —— Literature, fiction and literariness. *In* (pp. 19–25) **11.**

2775. WHALLEY, GEORGE. Studies in literature and the humanities; innocence of intent. Ed. by BRIAN CRICK and JOHN FERNS. Basingstoke: Macmillan; Kingston, Ont.: McGill–Queen's UP, 1985. pp. x, 270. Rev. by Patricia Rae in DalR (65:2) 1985, 312–14.

2776. WHITEBROOK, M. F. Politics and literature: works of literature as models and depictions of political ideas. Unpub. doct. diss., Univ. of London, Birkbeck Coll., 1985.

2777. WOLFF, TATIANA (ed. and trans.). Pushkin on literature. Introd. by JOHN BAYLEY. London: Athlone Press. pp. xxxviii, 554. (Second ed.: first ed. 1971.)

2778. WRYCZA, P. J. Higher states of consciousness and literary creativity: the science of creative intelligence and its application to the work of some symbolist writers. Unpub. doct. diss., Univ. of East Anglia, 1982.

2779. ZACH, WOLFGANG. Das Stereotyp als literarische Norm. Zum dominanten Denkmodell des Klassizismus. *In* (pp. 97–113) G. BLAICHER (ed.), Erstarrtes Denken. Das Vorurteil und Stereotyp in der Literatur. Tübingen: Narr. pp. 372.

2780. ZACHARASIEWICZ, WALDEMAR. Das Bild Wiens und der Wiener im anglo-amerikanischen Schrifttums. Anglistik & Englisch-unterricht (29/30) 247–63.

2781. —— National stereotypes in literature in the English language: a review of research. YREAL (1) 1982, 75–120.

2782. ZELL, HANS M.; BUNDY, CAROL; COULON, VIRGINIA (eds). A new reader's guide to African literature. New York: Africana, 1983. (Cf. bibl. 1984, 250.)

2783. ZUNDEL, VERONICA (comp.). Eerdmans' book of Christian classics. Grand Rapids, MI: Eerdmans, 1985. pp. 125. Rev. by Elva McAllaster in ChrisL (35:4) 43–4.

DRAMA AND THE THEATRE

2784. BANKS, R. A. Drama and theatre arts. London: Hodder & Stoughton, 1985. pp. 384.

2785. BOOTH, MICHAEL R. Art and the classical actor: painting, sculpture, and the English stage. AUMLA (66) 260–71.

2786. BORDMAN, GERALD. American musical theatre: a chronicle. New York; Oxford: OUP. pp. viii, 787. (Second ed.: first ed. 1980.)

2787. BRYAN, GEORGE B. Stage lives: a bibliography and index to theatrical biographies in English. Westport, CT; London: Greenwood Press, 1985. pp. xvi, 368. (Bibliographies and indexes in the performing arts, 2.)

2788. COLE, SUSAN LETZLER. The absent one: mourning ritual, tragedy and the performance of ambiguity. University Park; London:

Pennsylvania State UP, 1985. pp. vi, 183. Rev. by W. B. Worthen in TJ (38:4) 504–5.

2789. Fitz-Simon, Christopher. The Irish Theatre. (Bibl. 1984, 2304.) Rev. by Patrick Rafroidi in Études irlandaises (9) 1984, 334.

2790. Greenwald, Michael L. New directions for the RSC. TS (31/32) 1984/85–1985/86, 5–14.

2791. Hartigan, Karelisa V. (ed.). To hold a mirror to nature: dramatic images and reflections. Washington, DC: UP of America, 1982. pp. viii, 164. (Univ. of Florida Dept of Classics, comparative drama conference papers, 1.) Rev. by Simon Williams in CanRCL (13:2) 296–8.

2792. Hartnoll, Phyllis. The theatre: a concise history. London: Thames & Hudson, 1985. pp. 288. (World of art.) (Second ed.: first pub. as *A Concise History of the Theatre*, 1968.)

2793. Hirst, David L. Tragicomedy. (Bibl. 1984, 2311.) Rev. by A. D. Nuttall in NQ (33:3) 412–13.

2794. Howard, Diana (comp.). Directory of theatre resources: a guide to research collections and information services. Kingswinford: Library Associations Information Services Group. pp.144. (Second ed.: first ed. 1980.)

2795. Kim, Woo-Tack. Youngguk heuigoksa. (The history of English drama.) Seoul: Eulyu. pp. 371.

2796. King, T. J. Shakespeare to Olivier: a great chain of acting, 1598–1935. NQ (33:3) 397–8.

2797. Leacroft, Helen; Leacroft, Richard. The theatre in Leicestershire: a history of entertainment in the county from the 15th century to the 1960s. Leicester: Leicestershire Libraries & Information Service. pp. 137.

2798. Mason, H. A. The tragic plane. (Bibl. 1985, 2317.) Rev. by John Gould in TLS, 5 Sept., 981.

2799. Miester, Charles W. Dramatic criticism: a history. Jefferson, NC; London: McFarland, 1985. pp. vii, 318.

2800. Mitchell, Mary Anne. The development of the mask as a critical tool for an examination of character and performer action. Unpub. doct. diss., Texas Tech Univ., 1985. [Abstr. in DA (47) 348A–9A.]

2801. Ortolani, Benito. International bibliography of the theatre, 1982. New York: Theatre Research Data Centre, Brooklyn Coll., 1985. pp. 185. Rev. by Felicia Hardison Londré in TJ (38:3) 381–2.

2802. O'Toole, L. M.; Shukman, A. (eds). Dramatic structure: poetic and cognitive semantics. Colchester: Department of Language and Linguistics, Univ. of Essex, 1979. pp. 96. (Russian poetics in translation, 6.)

2803. Owen, David. A history of the theatres and cinemas of Tameside. Manchester: Richardson, 1985. pp. 30.

2804. Palmer, D. J. (ed.). Comedy: developments in criticism. (Bibl. 1985, 2527.) Rev. by A. D. Nuttall in NQ (33:3) 413.

2805. Rayner, Alice A. Useful fictions: moral structure in British comedy from Shakespeare to Stoppard. Unpub. doct. diss., Univ. of California, Santa Barbara, 1985. [Abstr. in DA (46) 3043A.]

2806. REYNOLDS, PETER.   Drama: text into performance. Harmonds-worth: Penguin. pp. 107. (Penguin masterstudies.)

2807. RIEMER, SETH DANIEL.   National biases in French and English drama. Unpub. doct. diss., Cornell Univ., 1985. [Abstr. in DA (46) 2686A.]

2808. ROGERS, JEAN SCOTT.   Stage by stage: the making of the Theatre Museum. London: HMSO, 1985. pp. xvi, 72.

2809. ŠARČEVIĆ, SUSAN.   The classical hero and modern evolution. *In* (pp. 127–32) **11.**

2810. SCHMID, HERTA; VAN KESTEREN, ALOYSIUS (eds).   Semiotics of drama and theatre: new perspectives in the theory of drama and theatre. *See* **2285.**

2811. SOLHEIM, HELENE ELIZABETH.   Walter N. H. Harding and the Harding drama collection at the Bodleian Library, Oxford. *See* **281.**

2812. SÖRING, JÜRGEN.   Tragödie – Notwendigkeit und Zufall im Spannungsfeld tragischer Prozesse. Stuttgart: Klett–Cotta, 1982. pp. 398. Rev. by Roland Galle in arcadia (21:3) 302–4.

2813. STANLEY, KIMBERLY DIANE.   Language on holiday: twentieth-century literary critics define tragedy. Unpub. doct. diss., Univ. of Texas at Austin, 1985. [Abstr. in DA (47) 523A.]

2814. STATES, BERT O.   Great reckonings in little rooms: on the phenomenology of the theater. Berkeley; London: California UP, 1985. pp. 213. (Quantum book.)

2815. THIEL, GUDRUN.   The changing significance of the figure of death in various Everyman plays. Literator (7:1) 21–47.

2816. WATTS, MURRAY.   Christianity and the theatre. Edinburgh: Handsel Press. pp. 44.

2817. WICKHAM, GLYNNE.   A history of the theatre. Oxford: Phaidon; New York: CUP, 1985. pp. 264. Rev. by Peter Holland in TLS, 30 May 585; by Maarten A. Reilingh in TJ (38:4) 510–11.

2818. WIKANDER, MATTHEW H.   The play of truth and state: historical drama from Shakespeare to Brecht. Baltimore, MD: Johns Hopkins UP. pp. 287. Rev. by Lois Potter in THES (728) 18.

2819. YARROW, RALPH.   'Neutral' consciousness in the experience of theater. Mosaic (19:3) 1–14.

FICTION

2820. ABBOTT, H. PORTER.   Diary fiction: writing as action. (Bibl. 1985, 2328.) Rev. by Bernard Duyfhuizen in Novel (19:2) 174–8; by Janet Gurkin Altman in PT (7:3) 547–53; by Grahame Smith in JEGP (85:1) 92–3.

2821. AMOS, WILLIAM.   The originals: an A–Z of fiction's real-life characters. (Pub. in UK as *The Originals: Who's Really Who in Fiction.*) Boston, MA; Toronto: Little, Brown, 1985. (Cf. bibl. 1985, 2332.) Rev. by Wallace Jackson in SAQ (85:4) 414–16.

2822. BELL, MILLICENT. Narrative gaps/narrative meaning. Raritan (6:1) 84–102.

2823. BERRY, RALPH M. Telling the truth: facts, lies, and nonsense in the history of fiction. Unpub. doct. diss., Univ. of Iowa, 1985. [Abstr. in DA (47) 891A.]

2824. BONHEIM, HELMUT. How stories begin: devices of exposition in 600 English, American, and Canadian short stories. YREAL (1) 1982, 190–226.

2825. BURGESS, MOIRA (comp.). Scottish Fiction Reserve: directory of authors included in the scheme. *See* **202.**

2826. CARY, MEREDITH. Different drummers: a study of cultural alternatives in fiction. (Bibl. 1985, 2339.) Rev. by Diana Brydon in CanL (108) 160.

2827. CEBIK, L. B. Fictional narrative and truth: an epistemic analysis. (Bibl. 1985, 2340.) Rev. by Lorraine Foreman-Peck in JAE (20:3) 118–9; by Peter Lamarque in PhilL (10:1) 115–17.

2828. CHUNG, BYEONG-JO. Youngguk soseolsa. (The history of the English novel.) Seoul: Eulyu. pp. xi, 338.

2829. CURRIE, GREGORY. Works of fiction and illocutionary acts. PhilL (10:2) 304–7.

2830. CUSIN, MICHEL. D'un usage possible du schéma de Jakobson pour questionner les textes de fiction. *In* (pp. 115–20) **1.**

2831. DELANY, SHEILA. Journals and fiction. QQ (92:3) 1985, 457–64.

2832. EDEN, KATHY. Poetic and legal fiction in the Aristotelian tradition. Princeton, NJ; Guildford: Princeton UP. pp. 198.

2833. ERLICH, RICHARD D. 'That old white-bearded Satan' (or 'sympathy for the devil'): outsiders inside some fictive social worlds. PhilP (32) 1–14.

2834. ERMARTH, ELIZABETH DEEDS. Realism and consensus in the English novel. (Bibl. 1985, 2349.) Rev. by Steven Cohan in MLS (16:3) 345–50.

2835. FAIRBANKS, CAROL. Prairie women: images in American and Canadian fiction. New Haven, CT; London: Yale UP. pp. xi, 300.

2836. FLORA, JOSEPH M. The English short story. (Bibl. 1985, 2350.) Rev. by John V. Hagopian in SSF (23) 125–7; by Charles Bohner in DHLR (18:1) 1985/86, 88–90.

2837. GILLESPIE, GERALD. The incorporation of history as content and form: anticipations of the Romantic and modern novel. *In* (pp. 29–34) **19.**

2838. HARTWELL, DAVID. Age of wonders: exploring the world of science fiction. New York: Walker, 1984. pp. 205. Rev. by Linda Leith in SFS (13:1) 87–9.

2839. HUBIN, ALLEN J. Crime fiction, 1749–1980: a comprehensive bibliography. (Bibl. 1985, 2357.) Rev. by B. C. Bloomfield in Library (8:1) 96–8.

2840. JØRGENSEN, RAVN; SØRENSEN, KATHRINE. Pour une nouvelle typologie du roman. CEBAL (7) 1985, 83–101.

2841. KAUFFMAN, LINDA S.   Discourses of desire: gender, genre, and epistolary fictions. Ithaca, NY; London: Cornell UP. pp. 331.

2842. KAWIN, BRUCE F.   The mind of the novel: reflexive fiction and the ineffable. (Bibl. 1985, 2358.) Rev. by Helmut Bonheim in YES (16) 320–1.

2843. KIDUBUKA, F.   Narratology and the implied reader in the regional novel. Unpub. doct. diss., Univ. of Reading, 1985. [Abstr. in IT (35) 539.]

2844. KLEIN, HERBERT-GÜNTHER.   Der Romanbrief in der englischen Literatur vom 16. bis zum 18. Jahrhundert. Frankfurt: Lang. pp. 324. (Europäische Hochschulschriften, Reihe 14: Angelsächsische Sprache und Literatur, 154.)

2845. KLEIN, MICHAEL; PARKER, GILLIAN (eds).   The English novel and the movies. New York: Ungar; London: Lorrimer, 1981. pp. xi, 383. (Ungar film library.)

2846. KLOTZ, VOLKER.   Das europäische Kunstmärchen. Fünfundzwanzig Kapitel seiner Geschichte von der Renaissance bis zur Moderne. Stuttgart: Metzler, 1985. pp. 412.

2847. KNIGHT, STEPHEN.   Form and ideology in crime fiction. (Bibl. 1983, 2831.) Rev. by William W. Stowe in CanRCL (12:3) 1985, 438–40.

2848. KOIKE, SHIGERU, et al. (eds).   Igirisu, shosetu, hihyo: Aoki Yuzo sensei tuitou ronshu. (England, novels and criticism: essays in memory of Professor Yuzo Aoki.) Tokyo: Nan'undo. pp. 304.

2849. KONSTANTINOVIĆ, ZORAN; KUSHNER, EVA; KÖPECZI, BÉLA (eds).   Evolution of the novel/L'évolution du roman/Die Entwicklung des Romans. Proceedings of the IXth International Comparative Literature Association, Innsbruck 1979. *See* **19.**

2850. KUMSKOVA, E. I.   Amerikanskaîa romanticheskaîa povest'. (The American Romantic short story.) VMU (1986:5) 17–25.

2851. KUNA, FRANZ.   Dialog der Texte: Landeskunde als kultureller Prozess. *In* (pp. 425 41) **15.**

2852. LANSER, SUSAN SNIADER.   The narrative act: point of view in prose fiction. (Bibl. 1985, 2364.) Rev. by Uri Margolin in CanRCL (12:3) 1985, 498–503; by Steven Cohan in MLS (16:3) 345–50.

2853. LUBBERS, KLAUS.   Geschichte der irischen Erzählprosa: vol. 1, Von den Anfängen bis zum ausgehenden 19. Jahrhundert. Munich: Fink, 1985. pp. 266. Rev. by Heinz Kosok in IUR (16) 245–7.

2854. MCKENZIE, MALCOLM.   On the presentation of speech and thought in narrative fiction. Theoria (68) 37–48.

2855. MARTENS, LORNA.   The diary novel. Cambridge: CUP, 1985. pp. xi, 307. Rev. by Bernard Duyfhuizen in Novel (19:2) 174–8.

2856. MATARESE, SUSAN M.; SALMON, PAUL G.   Utopia and its malcontents: mechanisms of social control in the fictional state. MidQ (25) 1984, 268–82.

2857. MAYER, D. R.   American neighbourhood novel. Nagoya, Japan: Nagoya UP. pp. iv, 168.

2858. NEW, PETER.   Fiction and purpose in *Utopia, Rasselas, The Mill on the Floss,* and *Women in Love.* New York: St Martin's Press, 1985. (Cf.

bibl. 1985, 2374.) Rev. by Harry E. Shaw in JEGP (85:4) 567–9; by Andrew Sanders in Eng (35) 289–93.

2859. OTT, BILL. Forgotten fiction. AmLib (17:3) 166–7.

2860. PAVEL, THOMAS G. Fictional worlds. Cambridge, MA; London: Harvard UP. pp. viii, 178.

2861. PHILMUS, ROBERT M. Into the unknown: the evolution of science fiction from Francis Godwin to H. G. Wells. (Bibl. 1971, 2109.) Berkeley; London: California UP, 1983. pp. xviii, 174. (Second ed.: first ed. 1970.) Rev. by Patrick Parrinder in MLR (81:3) 695–6.

2862. PORTER, DENNIS. The pursuit of crime: art and ideology in detective fiction. (Bibl. 1984, 2374.) Rev. by William W. Stowe in CanRCL (12:3) 1985, 434–6.

2863. PRATT, ANNIS, et al. Archetypal patterns in women's fiction. (Bibl. 1983, 2852.) Rev. by Annegret J. Wiemer in CanRCL (12:3) 1985, 505–9; by Valerie Shaw in MLR (81:1) 185–6.

2864. QUERE, HENRI. Retour aux lieux familiers de la fiction: personnage, narration, description. In (pp. 125–35) **1.**

2865. RADFORD, JEAN (ed.). The progress of romance: the politics of popular fiction. See **45.**

2866. ROSEBURY, B. J. Art, affect and critical theory: the case of fiction. Unpub. doct. diss., Univ. of Kent, 1982.

2867. ROUSE, H. B. Genesis, mimesis and Clio: history and the novel – the novel as history. In (pp. 15–18) **19.**

2868. SAUERBERG, LARS OLE. Reading formula fiction: on absorption and identification. OL (40:4) 1985, 357–71.

2869. SEIDEL, KATHRYN LEE. The southern belle in the American novel. Tampa: South Florida UP, 1985. pp. 202. Rev. by Kathy Taylor in JMMLA (19:2) 43–8.

2870. SEIDEL, MICHAEL. Exile and the narrative imagination. New Haven, CT; London: Yale UP. pp. 256.

2871. SINGH, G. (ed.). Collected essays by Q. D. LEAVIS: vol. 1, *The Englishness of the English Novel.* (Bibl. 1985, 2382.) Rev. by John Halperin in NQ (33:3) 425–6.

2872. SOKOLOFF, JANICE M. The margin that remains: a study of aging in literature. Unpub. doct. diss., Univ. of Massachusetts, 1985. [Abstr. in DA (46) 3729A.]

2873. SPARSHOTT, FRANCIS. The case of the unreliable author. PhilL (10:2) 145–67.

2874. SPENDER, DALE. Mothers of the novel: 100 good women writers before Jane Austen. London: Pandora. pp. x, 357. Rev. by Pat Rogers in LRB (8:14) 11–13; by John Bayley in TLS, 27 June, 695–6.

2875. STRAUCH, GÉRARD. Monologue intérieur et style indirect libre. In (pp. 531–53) **1.**

2876. WATSON, RITCHIE DEVON, JR. The cavalier in Virginia fiction. Baton Rouge: Louisiana State UP, 1985. pp. viii, 298. Rev. by William L. Frank in AL (58:2) 302–3; by Robert Brinkmeyer in SAQ (85:4) 409–11.

2877. WILSON, ANNE. Magical thought in creative writing: the distinctive roles of fantasy and imagination in fiction. (Bibl. 1984, 2395.) Rev. by Claude Gavin in EA (38:4) 1985, 449–50.

2878. WOLFE, GARY K.   Critical terms for science fiction and fantasy: a glossary and guide to scholarship. *See* **513.**

LITERATURE FOR CHILDREN

2879. CARPENTER, HUMPHREY; PRICHARD, MARI.   The Oxford companion to children's literature. (Bibl. 1985, 2400.) Rev. by Brian Alderson in Library (8:2) 187–9.

2880. CARTER, CAROLYN.   Young people and books: a review of the research into young people's reading habits. Journal of Librarianship (18:1) 1–22.

2881. DeLUCA, GERALDINE; NATOV, RONI.   Comedy in children's literature. LU (1:1) 1977, 4–8.

2882. DEMERS, PATRICIA.   Holy Writ familiarized to juvenile conceptions. Cithara (25:2) 31–47.

2883. DUNHOUSE, MARY BETH (comp.).   International directory of children's literature. New York; Oxford: Facts on File. pp. 128.

2884. EDGAR, J.   Happy families. Yearbook of the Children's Literature Association (NZ) 1985, 15–20.

2885. FISHER, MARGERY.   Classics for children and young people. Stroud: Thimble. pp. 72. (Signal bookguide.)

2886. FOSTER-CARTER, O. V. E.   A structuralist analysis of racial bias in children's literature. Unpub. doct. diss., Univ. of Leeds, 1983.

2887. GILDERDALE, B.; KNIGHT, B.; BOWDEN, N.   Once upon a time (stories about the past). Yearbook of the Children's Literature Association (NZ) 1985, 30–47.

2888. HOFFELD, LAURA.   Where magic begins. LU (3:1) 1979, 4–13.

2889. KLEIN, GILLIAN.   Reading into racism: bias in children's literature and learning materials. London: Routledge & Kegan Paul, 1985. pp. 165. (Routledge education books.)

2890. KUZNETS, LOIS R.   Games of dark; psychofantasy in children's literature. LU (1:2) 1977, 17–24.

2891. MELANI, LILIA.   A child's psyche: recollections of fairy tales, myths and romances. *See* **2471.**

2892. POVSIC, FRANCIS.   Eastern Europe in children's literature: an annotated bibliography of English-language books. New York; London: Greenwood Press. pp. xxvi, 200. (Bibliographies and indexes in world literature, 8.)

2893. RYAN, J. S.   Perdurable story elements from Celtic folklore and mythology. *See* **2484.**

2894. SAXBY, MAURICE; WINCH, GORDON (eds).   Give them wings: the experience of children's literature. Melbourne: Macmillan, pp. xiv, 428.

2895. SEWELL, ELIZABETH.   Nonsense verse and the child. LU (4:2) 1980/81, 30–48.

2896. SMITH, JOSEPH H.; KERRIGAN, WILLIAM (eds).   Opening texts: psychoanalysis and the culture of the child. *See* **40.**

2897. STOTT, JON C. Midsummer night's dreams: fantasy and self-realization in children's fiction. LU (1:2) 1977, 25–39.

POETRY

2898. ABSE, DANNIE (ed.). Wales in verse. London: Secker & Warburg, 1983. pp. xiii, 91. Rev. by John Barnie in Poetry Wales (21:1) 141–3.

2899. ALEXANDER, HARRIET SEMMES (comp.). American and British poetry: a guide to the criticism, 1925–1978. Athens, OH: Swallow Press; Manchester: Manchester UP, 1984. pp. xi, 486.

2900. ARAI, AKIRA. Eishi kansho nyumon. (A guide to English poetry.) Tokyo: Kenkyusha. pp. vi, 158. (Guides to English language and literature.)

2901. ARMSTRONG, CHERRYL. Tracking the muse: the composing processes of poets. Unpub. doct. diss., Univ. of California, Santa Barbara, 1985. [Abstr. in DA (47) 1310A.]

2902. BLACK, JAMES D. Does a poem mean? Cresset (49:7) 11–13.

2903. BLESSINGTON, FRANCIS. On translating mediocrity: *Anacreontea* 3 and English poetry. CB (62:2) 21–6.

2904. BOLD, ALAN. Longman dictionary of poets: the lives and works of 1001 poets in the English language. Harlow: Longman, 1985. pp. 6, 314.

2905. —— (ed.). The poetry of motion: an anthology of sporting verse. Edinburgh: Mainstream. pp. 201.

2906. BOLLOBÁS, ENIKŐ. Tradition and innovation in American free verse: Whitman to Duncan. Budapest: Akadémiai Kiadó. pp. 328.

2907. BOOTH, STEPHEN. Poetic richness: a preliminary audit. PCP (19) 1984, 68–78.

2908. BURNETT, PAULA (ed.). The Penguin book of Caribbean verse: in English. Harmondworth: Penguin. pp. lxvi, 447. (Penguin poets.)

2909. CANTALUPO, CHARLES. Religio Poetae. Ren (36) 1984, 139–46.

2910. CHAMBERS, ROSS. Story and situation: narrative seduction and the power of fiction. (Bibl. 1985, 2341.) Rev. by Charles Bernheimer in CL (38:4) 372–4; by Ann Jefferson in MLR (81:1) 158–9.

2911. CROSSLEY-HOLLAND, KEVIN (ed.). The Oxford book of travel verse. Oxford: OUP. pp. 352.

2912. DAICHES, DAVID. God and the poets. (Bibl. 1985, 2439.) Rev. by Ross C. Murfin in JEGP (85:1) 131–4; by Herbert J. Levine in VQR (62:2) 366–9.

2913. DELAS, DANIEL. Vrai/faux/absurde: pour une approche pragmatique de la metaphore poétique. MP (83:3) 266–74.

2914. DOBSON, BOB (ed.). Woven in Lancashire: some Lancashire dialect poems. *See* **892.**

2915. DUBOIS, PAGE. History, rhetorical description and the epic from Homer to Spenser. (Bibl. 1984, 2457.) Rev. by Marilynn Desmond in CL (38:1) 96–8.

2916. DUNLOP, EILEEN; KAMM, ANTHONY (eds). The Scottish collection of verse to 1800. Glasgow: Drew, 1985. pp. 256.

2917. ENGLER, BALZ. Reading and listening: the modes of communicating poetry and their influence on the texts. (Bibl. 1982, 3390.) Rev. by David Birch in YES (16) 221.

2918. ERWIN, JOHN W. Lyric apocalypse: reconstruction in ancient and modern poetry. Chico, CA: Scholars Press, 1984. pp. 232. Rev. by Arthur W. Lynip in ChrisL (35:2) 53–4; by Walter E. Broman in PhilL (10:1) 99–101.

2919. EVERETT, BARBARA. Poets in their time: essays on English poetry from Donne to Larkin. London: Faber & Faber, pp. viii, 264. Rev. by Peter Porter in TLS, 26 Dec., 1441.

2920. FOLEY, BARBARA. Telling the truth: the theory and practice of documentary fiction. Ithaca, NY; London: Cornell UP. pp. 273.

2921. FRIED, DEBRA. Repetition, refrain, and epitaph. ELH (53:3) 615–32.

2922. GARLICK, RAYMOND; MATHIAS, ROLAND (eds). Anglo-Welsh poetry 1480–1980. (Bibl. 1984, 2256.) Rev. by Greg Hill in AWR (78) 1985, 72–4; by John Barnie in Poetry Wales (20:2) 1984, 85–94.

2923. GARRETT, JOHN. British poetry since the sixteenth-century: a student's guide. London: Macmillan. pp. 240.

2924. GELUYKENS, RONALD. 'Questioning intonation': an empirical study into the prosodic feature 'rising intonation' and its relevance for the production and recognition of questions. *See* **1470.**

2925. GIFFORD, HENRY. Poetry in a divided world. Cambridge: CUP. pp. 128. (Clark lectures, 1985.)

2926. HOLLANDER, JOHN. Vision and resonance: two senses of poetic form. New Haven, CT; London: Yale UP, 1985. pp. xiii, 322. (Second ed.; first ed. 1975.)

2927. HOŠEK, CHAVIVA; PARKER, PATRICIA (eds). Lyric poetry: beyond new criticism. Ithaca, NY: Cornell UP, 1985. pp. 375. Rev. by Joseph Adamson in ESCan (12:2) 250–4.

2928. JAMESON, MARY ANN. The year's work in Canadian poetry studies: 1985. CanP (18) 148–69.

2929. KELLOW, BRIAN; KRISAK, JOHN (eds). Drinkers' verse. London: Hutchinson. pp. x, 101.

2930. KERMODE, FRANK. The genesis of secrecy: on the interpretation of narrative. (Bibl. 1985, 2359.) Rev. by Gerald Gillespie in CL (38:3) 295–7.

2931. KINSELLA, THOMAS (ed.). The new Oxford book of Irish verse. Oxford: OUP. pp. xxx, 423. Rev. by James Simmons in Linen Hall Review (3:3) 8–9; by Patricia Craig in LRB (8:13) 17–18.

2932. LEVI, PETER. Visionary poets. Agenda (24:3) 27–50.

2933. LOGUE, CHRISTOPHER (ed.). Sweet and sour: an anthology of comic verse. London: Batsford, 1983. pp. 214.

2934. McFARLAND, THOMAS. Originality and imagination. (Bibl. 1985, 2466.) Rev. by Rudolf F. Storch in ELN (23:4) 58–60; by Daniel A. Dombrowski in PhilL (10:2) 341–2.

2935. MAHONEY, JOHN L. The whole internal universe: imitation and the new defense of poetry in British criticism, 1660–1830. New York:

Fordham UP, 1985. pp. x, 166. Rev. by Howard Erskine-Hill in TLS, 26 Dec., 1441.

2936. MARTINET, MARIE-MADELEINE. 'The sister arts' et le sens du temps. *In* (pp. 417–32) **1.**

2937. MATSUNAMI, TAMOTSU. To-in shi kara kyaku-in shi e. (From alliterative verse to end-rhyme.) StudME (1) 1–38.

2938. MORGAN, GARETH. Rhyme in prose narrative: a precaution. *See* **2474.**

2939. MURRAY, PATRICK (ed.). The deer's cry: a treasury of Irish religious verse. Dublin: Four Courts Press. pp. 295.

2940. NOBLE, JAMES. The four-stress hemistich in Laȝamon's *Brut*. NM (87:4) 545–9.

2941. PAULIN, TOM (ed.). The Faber book of political verse. London: Faber & Faber. pp. 481. Rev. by David Norbrook in LRB (8:10) 7–8; by Gerald Dawe in Honest Ulsterman (82) 68–71; by Dick Davis in Listener, 29 May, 24.

2942. PINTER, HAROLD; GODBERT, GEOFFREY; ASTBURY, ANTHONY (sels). 100 poems by 100 poets: an anthology. London: Methuen. pp. xiii, 177.

2943. PLETT, HEINRICH F. Englische Rhetorik und Poetik 1479–1660. Eine systematische Bibliographie. *See* **1240.**

2944. RHEE, WANG-JOO. Si eui bongil gwa jonjae eui jinri. (The essence of poetry and the truth of being.) UJH (29) 305–24.

2945. RICHARDS, BERNARD. Why are the images never appropriate all the way through? Listener (115) 16 Jan., 12–13. (Poetry on television.)

2946. RICKS, CHRISTOPHER. The force of poetry. (Bibl. 1985, 2472.) Rev. by Garrett Stewart in WHR (40:3) 261–71; by Marcia Leveson in UES (24:1) 66.

2947. ROBERTS, MARIE. British poets and secret societies. London: Croom Helm. pp. 181. (Smart, Burns, Shelley, Kipling, Yeats.)

2948. ROBERTS, PHILIP DAVIES. How poetry works: the elements of English poetry. Harmondsworth: Penguin. pp. 304. (Pelican books.)

2949. ROGERS, FRANKLIN R.; ROGERS, MARY ANN. Painting and poetry: form, metaphor, and the language of literature. Lewisburg, PA: Bucknell UP; London: Assoc. UPs, 1985. pp. 248.

2950. ROGERS, WILLIAM ELFORD. The three genres and the interpretation of lyric. (Bibl. 1985, 2475.) Rev. by E. D. Blodgett in CanRCL (13:2) 287–92.

2951. SACKS, PETER M. The English elegy: studies in the genre from Spenser to Yeats. (Bibl. 1985, 2476.) Rev. by G. W. Pigman, III, in RQ (39:3) 558–61.

2952. SERVOTTE, HERMAN. Language into meaning: a primer of poetry. Louvain: ACCO. pp. 93. (Argo studies, 2.) (Second ed.: first ed. 1980.)

2953. STORR, SHERMAN. Poetry and music: the artful twins. ERGS (43:4) 337–48.

2954. TANAKA, SEITARO. Gensho no machi eno tabi: eishi jyugo hen wo yomu. (A journey to the town of origin: readings of fifteen English poems.) Tokyo: Kokubunsya. pp. 264.

2955. WAIN, JOHN (ed.).   The Oxford library of English poetry. Oxford: OUP. 3 vols. pp. xx, 443; xiii, 511; xvi, 476.

2956. WILLIAMS, JOHN.   Reading poetry: a contextual introduction. London: Arnold, 1985. pp. x, 84. Rev. by W. D. Maxwell-Mahon in UES (24:1) 66–7.

2957. WOJCIK, JAN; FRONTAIN, RAYMOND-JEAN (eds).   Poetic prophecy in Western literature. Rutherford, NJ: Fairleigh Dickinson UP; London: Assoc. UPs, 1984. pp. 222.

2958. WOODS, SUSANNE.   Natural emphasis: English versification from Chaucer to Dryden. San Marino, CA: Huntington Library, 1985. pp. xiii, 310. Rev. by Peter Groves in RQ (39:3) 544–5; by Martin Elsky in GHJ (9:1) 1985, 42–5; by John Mulryan in Cithara (26:1) 54–5.

2959. YUN, SAM-HA.   Aeran si eui jeontong. (The tradition of Irish poetry.) JELL (32:1) 62–79.

PROSE

2960. AHRENDS, GÜNTER.   Sternes *Tristram Shandy* und der Literaturtyp der Anatomie. GRM (36:1) 16–31.

2961. BOLD, ALAN (ed.).   Drink to me only: the prose (and cons) of drinking. London: Clark, 1982. pp. 184.

2962. BRUCE, GEORGE; SCOTT, PAUL H. (eds).   A Scottish postbag: eight centuries of Scottish letters. Edinburgh: Chambers in assn with Saltire Soc. pp. xvii, 270.

2963. CHAPMAN, DAVID WAYNE.   The essay as a literary form. Unpub. doct. diss., Texas Christian Univ., 1985. [Abstr. in DA (46) 2683A.]

2964. DODD, PHILIP (ed.).   The art of travel: essays on travel writing. (Bibl. 1984, 58.) Rev. by Harold Beaver in YES (16) 221–3; by Jurgen Martini in Ariel (17:1) 104–6.

2965. GABEL, JOHN B.; WHEELER, CHARLES B.   The Bible as literature: an introduction. New York; Oxford: OUP. pp. xiv, 278. Rev. by Orval Wintermute in SAQ (85:4) 411–12.

2966. GAVRILIU, EUGENIA.   Observaţii asupra primelor contacte româneşti cu proza narativă engleză. (Remarks on the first contacts of Romanian literature with English narrative prose). AnUGSU (9) 16–18.

2967. RYKEN, LELAND (comp.).   The New Testament in literary criticism. New York: Ungar, 1984. pp. l, 349. Rev. by E. Lynn Harris in ChrisL (36:1) 37–9.

BIOGRAPHY AND AUTOBIOGRAPHY

2968. BATAILLE, GRETCHEN M.; SANDS, KATHLEEN MULLEN.   American Indian women: telling their lives. (Bibl. 1985, 2496.) Rev. by Valerie Sherer Mathes in PacHR (55:2) 306–7.

2969. BRADY, FRANK.   Fictional techniques in factual works. ECent (26:2) 1985, 158–70 (review-article).

2970. Coe, Richard N.   When the grass was taller: autobiography and the experience of childhood. London: Yale UP, 1984. (Cf. bibl. 1985, 2498.) Rev. by Susanna Egan in MP (84:1) 107–9.

2971. Culley, Margo (ed.).   A day at a time: the diary literature of American women from 1764 to the present. New York: Feminist Press, 1985. pp. 341. Rev. by Patricia Hampl in NYTB, 16 Mar., 19.

2972. Davis, Charles T.; Gates, Henry Louis, Jr (eds).   The slave's narrative. Oxford: OUP, 1985. pp. xxiv, 342.

2973. Eakin, Paul John.   Fictions in autobiography: studies in the art of self-invention. Princeton, NJ: Princeton UP, 1985. pp. x, 288. Rev. by James Olney in AL (58:4) 621–3; by Johnnie Gratton in PT (7:3) 565–7.

2974. Egan, Susanna.   Patterns of experience in autobiography. (Bibl. 1985, 2502.) Rev. by H. Porter Abbott in MLR (81:2) 421–3; by Andrew Brink in ESCan (12:2) 240–6.

2975. Epstein, Joseph.   Literary biography. NCrit (1:9) 1982/83, 27–37.

2976. Fleishman, Avrom.   Figures of autobiography: the language of self-writing in Victorian and modern England. (Bibl. 1985, 2503.) Rev. by Linda M. Shires in MLS (16:3) 351–5.

2977. Hassam, A. L.   Style and convention in the diary: an investigation with reference to the reader. Unpub. doct. diss., Univ. of Wales, Cardiff, 1984. [Abstr. in IT (35) 41.]

2978. Holmes, Richard.   Footsteps: adventures of a romantic biographer. New York: Sifton/Viking Press, 1985. (Cf. bibl. 1985, 2507.) Rev. by Leon Edel in BkW, 5 Jan., 5.

2979. Jones, Barry; Dixon, M. V.   The Macmillan dictionary of biography. Melbourne: Macmillan. pp. 917. (Second ed.: first ed. 1981.)

2980. Krupat, Arnold.   For those who come after: a study of native American autobiography. Berkeley; London: California UP, 1985. pp. xv, 167. Rev. by Janice Thaddeus in AL (58:3) 431–3.

2981. Lloyd, Genevieve.   The self as fiction: philosophy and autobiography. PhilL (10:2) 168–85.

2982. Lomask, Milton.   The biographer's craft. New York; London: Harper & Row. pp. ix, 194.

2983. Mallon, Thomas.   A book of one's own: people and their diaries. London: Picador, 1985. (Cf. bibl. 1985, 2513.) Rev. by Bernard Duyfhuizen in Novel (19:2) 172–4.

2984. Mandell, Nadine.   The illusion of subjectivity. PT (7:3) 527–45 (review-article).

2985. Nadel, Ira Bruce.   Biography: fiction, fact and form. (Bibl. 1985, 2516.) Rev. by Cherry Clayton in UES (24:1) 68–9; by Ben Jones in ESCan (12:4) 497–501.

2986. Picard, Hans Rudolf.   Das Tagebuch als Gattung zwischen Intimität und Öffentlichkeit. Archiv (223:1) 17–25.

2987. Siebenschuh, William R.   Fictional techniques and factual works. (Bibl. 1983, 3018.) Rev. by Frank Brady in ECent (26:2) 1985, 158–70.

2988. WEINTRAUB, STANLEY.   Reviewing literary biography: apprehending the *daimon*. UES (24:1) 18–23.

2989. WOODEN, WARREN W.   Sir Thomas Bodley's *Life of Himself* (1609) and the epideictic strategies of encomia. SP (83:1) 62–75.

RELATED STUDIES

2990. BASSETT, HELEN BARNES.   Literary places in and out of London: reached by public transport in a day. London: Threshold, 1985. pp. 128.

2991. BEAVER, HAROLD.   The great American masquerade. London: Vision Press; Totowa, NJ: Barnes & Noble, 1985. pp. 238. Rev. by William E. Lenz in AL (58:3) 430–1.

2992. BERMANT, CHAIM.   What's the joke? A study of Jewish humour through the ages. London: Weidenfeld & Nicolson. pp. vii, 259.

2993. BRUGIÈRE, BERNARD.   Qu'appelle-t-on aujourd'hui littérature apocalyptique? *In* (pp. 113–28) **2.**

2994. BULLOCK, ALAN.   The humanist tradition in the West. London: Thames & Hudson, 1985. pp. 208.

2995. COLE, GAROLD L.   Travels in America from the voyages of discovery to the present: an annotated bibliography of travel articles in periodicals, 1955–1980. Norman: Oklahoma UP, 1984. pp. 344. Rev. by Glenda Riley in CWH (32:4) 358–9.

2996. FOHR, S. D.   Adam and Eve: the spiritual symbolism of Genesis and Exodus. Lanham, MD; London: UP of America. pp. xiii, 147.

2997. FROST, DAVID; SHEA, MICHAEL.   The rich tide; men, women, ideas and their transatlantic impact. London: Collins. pp. 392.

2998. GAVRILIU, EUGENIA.   Observaţii asupra primelor contacte româneşti cu proza narativă engleză. (Remarks on the first contacts of Romanian literature with English narrative prose). *See* **2966.**

2999. GOODMAN, NELSON.   Of mind and other matters. Cambridge, MA; London: Harvard UP, 1984. pp. 210. Rev. by W. J. T. Mitchell in PT (7:1) 111–15.

3000. HONIG, EDWIN (ed.).   The poet's other voice: conversations on literary translation. Amherst: Massachusetts UP. pp. xiii, 218. Rev. by Charles Tomlinson in TLS, 21 Nov., 1296.

3001. HORDEN, PEREGRINE (ed.).   Freud and the humanities. London: Duckworth, 1985. pp. viii, 186.

3002. KELLY, JOAN.   Women, history, and theory: the essays of Joan Kelly. Chicago; London: Chicago UP, 1984. pp. xxvi, 163. (Women in culture and society.) Rev. by Susan Groag Bell in RQ (39:2) 284–6.

3003. KROEBER, KARL (ed.).   Traditional literatures of the American Indian: texts and interpretations. Lincoln: Nebraska UP, 1981. pp. 162. Rev. by Richard F. Fleck in AIQ (10:2) 167–9.

3004. KUKLICK, BRUCE.   Churchmen and philosophers: from Jonathan Edwards to John Dewey. New Haven, CT; London: Yale UP, 1985. pp. xx, 311. Rev. by Conrad Wright in NEQ (59:2) 291–4.

3005. McDOWELL, R. B.; WEBB, D. A.   Trinity College Dublin 1592–1952: an academic history. Cambridge; New York: CUP, 1982. pp. xxiv, 580. Rev. by J. C. Beckett in YES (16) 249–50.

3006. Mellinkoff, Ruth.　The mark of Cain. Berkeley: California UP, 1980. pp. 128. Rev. by Richard F. Hardin in CanRCL (12:3) 1985, 509–11.

3007. Mitchell, W. J. T.　How good is Nelson Goodman? PT (7:1) 111–15 (review-article).

3008. Mothersill, Mary.　Beauty restored. Oxford: Clarendon Press, 1984. pp. 438. Rev. by David Shusterman in PT (7:2) 327–8.

3009. Nussbaum, Martha C.　The fragility of goodness: luck and ethics in Greek tragedy and philosophy. Cambridge: CUP. pp. xvii, 544.

3010. Prior, Mary (ed.).　Women in English society 1500–1800. New York: Methuen, 1985. (Cf. bibl. 1985, 2528.) Rev. by Margaret J. M. Ezell in SCN (44:1/2) 15–16; by Merry E. Wiesner in SixCT (17:4) 559–60.

3011. Rissanen, Matti.　Middle English translations of Old English charters in the *Liber Monasterii de Hyda*: a case of historical error analysis. *In* (pp. 591–603) **26**.

3012. Schatzberg, Walter (ed.).　Relations of literature and science: a bibliography of scholarship, 1978–79. CLIO (10:1) 1980, 57–84.

3013. Shi, David E.　The simple life: plain living and high thinking in American culture. New York; Oxford: OUP, 1985. pp. viii, 332.

3014. Smith, Godfrey.　The English companion: an idiosyncratic A–Z of England and Englishness. London: Pavilion, 1984; Harmondsworth: Penguin, 1985. pp. 272.

3015. Stromberg, Roland N.　European intellectual history since 1789. (Bibl 1981, 5915.). Englewood Cliffs, NJ; London: Prentice-Hall. pp. x, 340. (Fourth ed.: first ed. 1966 pub. as *An Intellectual History of Modern Europe*.)

3016. Yamakawa, Kozo.　Daiju no shishin: eigungakusha to bijyutu hihyo. (The Tenth Muse: scholars of English literature and art criticism.) Kyoto: Appollon Press. pp. viii, 240.

LITERARY THEORY

This section is intended to cover general writings **about** literary history, criticism and critical theory. For general works **of** literary history and criticism, see under 'General Literary Studies'.

3017. Bassnett, Suzan.　Comparative literature and methodology. *See* **2590**.

3018. Beardsley, Monroe C.　Aesthetics: problems in the philosophy of criticism. (Bibl. 1961, 1437.) Indianapolis, IN: Hackett, 1981. pp. lxiv, 614. (Second ed.: first ed. 1958.) Rev. by Harold Osborne in JAE (20:1) 97–106.

3019. Curtis, Catherine Ann.　A study of conclusions in expository prose: professional writers versus textbook conventions. Unpub. doct. diss., Ohio State Univ., 1985. [Abstr. in DA (46) 3710A.]

3020. Dávidházi, Péter.　A filológia kihivása az amerikai kritikaelméletben. (A challenge to philology in American critical theory.) FK (30:4) 1984, 399–414.

3021. DEN HARTOG, DIRK. Is a humanist criticism still possible?: forum. Meridian (5:1) 63–79.

3022. DOBOZY, MARIA. Minstrel books: the legacy of Thomas Wright in German research. NM (87:4) 523–36.

3023. DYSERINCK, HUGO; FISCHER, MANFRED S. (eds). Internationale Bibliographie zu Geschichte und Theorie der Komparatistik. Stuttgart: Hiersemann, 1985. pp. xxx, 314.

3024. EAGLETON, TERRY. The function of criticism: from *The Spectator* to post-structuralism. (Bibl. 1985, 2539.) Rev. by Gary Wihl in SAQ (85:2) 199–202; by Richard Godden in PT (7:1) 147–56.

3025. —— Literary theory: an introduction. (Bibl. 1985, 2540.) Rev. by William E. Cain in CL (38:4) 362–6; by Don Bialostosky in Novel (19:2) 168–9.

3026. ELBRO, CARSTEN. The concept of time and literary criticism. OL (41:2) 97–118.

3027. FALCK, COLIN. Beyond theory. EC (36:1) 1–10.

3028. FLYNN, ELIZABETH A.; SCHWEICKART, PATROCINIO P. (eds). Gender and reading: essays on readers, texts, and contexts. Baltimore, MD; London: Johns Hopkins UP. pp. xxx, 306.

3029. FOUST, RONALD E. The rules of the game: a para-theory of literary theories. SCR (3:4) 5–14.

3030. FOWLER, ALASTAIR. Kinds of literature: an introduction to the theory of genres and modes. (Bibl. 1985, 2543.) Rev. by Melissa King in Journal of Literary Studies (2:1) 78–80.

3031. HAUSER, GERARD A. Introduction to rhetorical theory. New York; London: Harper & Row. pp. xi, 209.

3032. McGANN, JEROME J. The beauty of inflections: literary investigations in historical method and theory. (Bibl. 1985, 2553.) Rev. by William E. Cain in VQR (62:2) 336–43; by J. B. Hainsworth in NQ (33:4) 529–30; by John Lucas in TLS, 10 Oct., 1141; by Jack Stillinger in JEGP (85:4) 550–7.

3033. —— (ed.). Textual criticism and literary interpretation. Chicago; London: Chicago UP, 1985. pp. xi, 239. Rev. by Ruth Rosenburg in SCR (3:4) 119–21.

3034. MARGOLIN, URI. The doer and the dead: action as a basis for characterization in narrative. PT (7:2) 205–25.

3035. MIESTER, CHARLES W. Dramatic criticism: a history. *See* **2799.**

3036. NEWTON, K. M. In defence of literary interpretation: theory and practice. *See* **2710.**

3037. O'TOOLE, L. M.; SHUKMAN, A. (eds). Dramatic structure: poetic and cognitive semantics. *See* **2802.**

3038. PERRY, MENAHEM; STERNBERG, MEIR. The king through ironic eyes: biblical narrative and the literary reading process. PT (7:2) 275–322.

3039. PONS, XAVIER. The psychoanalytic approach to literature. Linq (14:1) 36–46.

3040. PRINCE, GERALD. Narratology: the form and functioning of narrative. (Bibl. 1985, 2557.) Rev. by Marie-Laure Ryan in CanRCL (13:1) 99–101; by Osamu Izumiya in MLR (81:3) 692–3.

3041. RADFORD, COLIN; MINOGUE, SALLY. The nature of criticism. (Bibl. 1981, 2949.) Rev. by Richard Shusterman in PT (7:2) 324–5.

3042. RAJAN, BALACHANDRA. The form of the unfinished: English poetics from Spenser to Pound. Princeton, NJ; Guildford: Princeton UP, 1985. pp. viii, 318.

3043. REEVES, CHARLES ERIC. The languages of convention: literature and consensus. PT (7:1) 3–28.

3044. RODWAY, ALLAN. The craft of criticism. (Bibl. 1983, 2920.) Rev. by Christopher Norris in MLR (81:2) 429–30.

3045. ROSSLYN, FELICITY. 'What then remains? Ourself'. CamQ (15) 164–7 (review-article).

3046. RYAN, RORY; RYAN, PAMELA. Articles on literary aesthetics, literary theory and critical methodology: a survey 1984/85. UES (24:2) 22–35.

3047. SAID, EDWARD W. The world, and text, and the critic. (Bibl. 1985, 2559.) Rev. by David Carroll in CL (38:2) 187–90.

3048. SHUSTERMAN, RICHARD. The object of literary criticism. *See* **2743.**

3049. SPARIOSU, MIHAI. Literature, mimesis and play: essays in literary theory. (Bibl. 1985, 2562.) Rev. by Matei Calinescu in CL (38:1) 87–90.

3050. STANZEL, F. K. A theory of narrative. (Bibl. 1984, 9646.) Rev. by Mieke Bal in PT (7:3) 555–7.

3051. STRAUCH, EDWARD H. Genre: kind, form or modulation? AJES (11) 1–17.

3052. SZONDI, PETER. *On Textual Understanding* and other essays. Trans. by HARVEY MENDELSOHN. Manchester: Manchester UP. pp. xxi, 224. (Theory and history of literature, 15.)

3053. TALLIS, RAYMOND. 'As if there could be such things as true stories'. CamQ (15) 95–106.

3054. TILGHMAN, B. R. But is it art? The value of art and the temptation of theory. Oxford: Blackwell, 1984. pp. xii, 193. (Values and philosophical inquiry.) Rev. by Alan Montefiore in NQ (33:2) 281–2.

3055. TODOROV, TZVETAN. Mikhail Bakhtin: the dialogical principle. (Bibl. 1985, 2564.) Rev. by Caryl Emerson in CL (38:4) 370–2.

3056. UHLIG, CLAUS. Theorie der Literaturhistorie: Prinzipien und Paradigmen. (Bibl. 1985, 2566.) Rev. by Kurt Otten in Archiv (222:2) 1985, 366–9.

3057. VANDER WEELE, MICHAEL. Hermeneutics and the classroom. CEAF (16:4/17:1) 1–6.

3058. VON HALLBERG, ROBERT (ed.). Canons. (Bibl. 1985, 2568.) Rev. by David E. Latané, Jr, in SoHR (20:2)) 175–81.

3059. WALTER, DONNA. The critics on criticism: a critical study. Ob (6) Winter 1980, 22–9.

3060. WATSON, GEORGE. The literary critics: a study of English descriptive criticism. (Bibl. 1973, 2507.) London: Hogarth Press. pp. 242. (Hogarth critics.) (Second ed.: first ed. 1973.)

3061. WHITE, HAYDEN.   Tropics of discourse: essays in cultural criticism. Baltimore, MD; London: Johns Hopkins UP, 1985. pp. 287. Rev. by Alan Durant in Prose Studies (9:3) 112–13.

3062. WILKES, G. A.   The writing of literary history. Notes and Furphies (Univ. of New England, Armidale, N.S.W.) (17) 3–8.

OLD ENGLISH

GENERAL AND ANONYMOUS

General Literary Studies; Editions and Studies of Anonymous Writings (except *Beowulf*)

3063. ACKER, PAUL. The going-out of the soul in *Blickling Homily* IV. ELN (23:4) 1–3.

3064. ANDERSON, EARL R. *The Battle of Maldon*: a reappraisal of possible sources, date, and theme. *In* (pp. 247–72) **36.**

3065. ANDERSON, JAMES E. Dual voices and the identity of speakers in the Exeter Book *Descent into Hell*. Neophilologus (70:4) 636–40.

3066. ANON. A bibliography of publications on medieval English language and literature in Japan from April 1983 to March 1985. MESN (special issue 1) 1–34.

3067. —— Manuscripts from Anglo-Saxon England: an exhibition in the University Library, Cambridge, to mark the Conference of the International Society of Anglo-Saxonists. Cambridge: Cambridge Univ. Library, 1985. pp. 29.

3068. ASSUNTO, KAREN KNAPP. The prosody of the 'Advent Lyrics'. Unpub. doct. diss., Univ. of Massachusetts. [Abstr. in DA (47) 895A.]

3069. BAUMLER, ELLEN R. Andrew in the city of the cannibals: a comparative study of the Latin, Greek, and Old English texts. Unpub. doct. diss., Univ. of Kansas, 1985. [Abstr. in DA (47) 525A.] (Legend of St Andrew.)

3070. BAZIRE, JOYCE; CROSS, JAMES E. (eds). Eleven Old English Rogationtide homilies. (Bibl. 1984, 2605.) Rev. by Celia Sisam in NQ (33:1) 96–7.

3071. BERKHOUT, CARL T. Old English bibliography 1985. OEN (19:2) 45–73.

3072. —— (comp.). Old English research in progress: 1985–1986. NM (87:3) 431–6.

3073. —— *et al.* Bibliography for 1985. ASE (15) 205–53.

3074. BJORK, ROBERT E. The Old English verse saints' lives: a study in direct discourse and the iconography of style. Toronto; London: Toronto UP, 1985. pp. x, 180. (McMaster Old English studies and texts, 4.)

3075. BLOOMFIELD, MORTON W. *Deor* revisited. *In* (pp. 273–82) **36.**

3076. BOENIG, ROBERT. Computers and Old English: the IBM Quietwriter printer and medieval characters. *See* **522.**

3077. BRADLEY, S. A. J. (ed.). Anglo-Saxon poetry: an anthology of Old English poems in prose translation, with introduction and headnotes. Melbourne; Toronto: Dent, 1982. (Bibl. 1985, 2592.) Rev. by N. F. Blake in MLR (81:2) 440–1.

3078. BRAGG, LOIS MARIAN. The lyric voice in Old English poetry. Unpub. doct. diss., State Univ. of New York at Buffalo, 1985. [Abstr. in DA (46) 1935A.]

3079. BRIDGES, MARGARET ENID. Generic contrast in Old English hagiographical poetry. (Bibl. 1984, 2615.) Rev. by Daniel G. Calder in Spec (61:3) 624–6.

3080. BROWN, GEORGE HARDIN.   Old English verse as a medium for Christian theology. *In* (pp. 15–28) **36.**

3081. BROWN, PHYLLIS RUGG; CRAMPTON, GEORGIA RONAN; ROBINSON, FRED C. (eds).   Modes of interpretation in Old English literature: essays in honour of Stanley B. Greenfield. *See* **36.**

3082. BUSSE, WILHELM.   Neo-exegetical criticism and Old English poetry: a critique of the typological and allegorical appropriation of medieval literature. YREAL (2) 1984, 1–54.

3083. CALDER, DANIEL G.   Figurative language and its contexts in *Andreas*: a study in medieval expressionism. *In* (pp. 115–36) **36.**

3084. CAVANAUGH, D.   The verb and particle collocation in Old English poetry: a descriptive analysis on the basis of syntax, metrical segmentation and stress. *See* **1866.**

3085. CAVILL, PAUL.   Notes on maxims in Old English narrative. NQ (33:2) 145–8.

3086. CHANCE, JANE.   Woman as hero in Old English literature. Syracuse, NY: Syracuse UP. pp. xvii, 155. Rev. by Allen J. Frantzen in ANQ (24:7/8) 124–6.

3087. CHASE, DENNIS.   *The Wife's Lament*: an eighth-century existential cry. USFLQ (24:3/4) 18–20.

3088. CHEREWATUK, KAREN.   Standing, turning, twisting, falling: posture and moral stance in *Genesis B*. NM (87:4) 537–44.

3089. CIGMAN, GLORIA (ed.).   Medieval sermon studies newsletter: 17 and 18. Coventry: English Dept, Univ. of Warwick. pp. 23; 23.

3090. CLAYTON, MARY.   Ælfric and 'Cogitis me'. NQ (33:2) 148–9.

3091. —— *Blickling Homily* XIII reconsidered. Leeds Studies in English (17) 25–40.

3092. —— Delivering the damned: a motif in OE homiletic prose. MÆ (55:1) 92–102.

3093. CLEMOES, PETER.   'Symbolic' language in Old English poetry. *In* (pp. 3–14) **36.**

3094. COCCHIARELLI, JOSEPH JOHN.   The Old English version of the enlarged Rule of Chrodegang. Unpub. doct. diss., Fordham Univ. [Abstr. in DA (47) 1331A.]

3095. COLMAN, FRAN.   A *cǣġ* to Old English syllable structure. *In* (pp. 225–30) **26.**

3096. COUTTS, CATHERINE (ed.).   International medieval bibliography. Publications of July–December 1985. Leeds: Leeds UP. pp. xlvii, 234.

3097. CRONAN, DENNIS JAMES.   Old English poetic simplexes. Unpub. doct. diss., Univ. of Minnesota. [Abstr. in DA (47) 2167A.]

3098. CROSS, J. E.   On the library of the Old English martyrologist. *In* (pp. 227–49) **25.**

3099. CROSS, JAMES E.   Identification: towards criticism. *In* (pp. 229–46) **36.**

3100. CROWLEY, JOSEPH P.   The study of Old English dialects. *See* **891.**

3101. DONOGHUE, DANIEL.   Word order and poetic style: auxiliary and verbal in *The Metres of Boethius*. ASE (15) 167–96.

3102. DUNCAN, EDWIN WILSON.   Stress, meter, and alliteration in Old English poetry. Unpub. doct. diss., Univ. of Texas at Austin, 1985. [Abstr. in DA (46) 3027A.]

3103. ENKVIST, NILS ERIK.   More about the textual functions of the Old English adverbial *þa*. *In* (pp. 301–9) **26.**

3104. FINLAY, ALISON.   The warrior Christ and the unarmed hero. *In* (pp. 19–29) **32.**

3105. FJALLDAL, MAGNUS.   The vocabulary of religious and secular rank in Anglo-Saxon poetry. Unpub. doct. diss., Harvard Univ., 1985. [Abstr. in DA (46) 1936A.]

3106. FRESE, DOLORES WARWICK.   Poetic prowess in *Brunanburh* and *Maldon*: winning, losing and literary outcome. *In* (pp. 83–99) **36.**

3107. GLEISSNER, REINHARD.   Die 'zweideutigen' altenglischen Rätsel des Exeter Book in ihrem zeitgenössischen Kontext. (Bibl. 1985, 2614.) Rev. by Peter Bierbaumer in AAA (11:2) 234–5.

3108. GNEUSS, HELMUT.   Liturgical books in Anglo-Saxon England and their Old English terminology. *In* (pp. 91–141) **25.**

3109. GODDEN, M. R.   Anglo-Saxon on the mind. *In* (pp. 271–98) **25.**

3110. GREENFIELD, STANLEY B.   *Wulf and Eadwacer*: all passion pent. ASE (15) 5–14.

3111. GRIFFITH, M. S.   The method of composition of Old English verse translation, with particular reference to *The Metres of Boethius*, *The Paris Psalter* and *Judgment Day* II. Unpub. doct. diss., Univ. of Oxford, 1984.

3112. GRIFFITHS, BILL.   The Old English alcoholic vocabulary: a re-examination. *See* **1542.**

3113. —— (trans.).   Guðlac B. Peterborough: Spectacular Diseases, 1985. pp. 38.

3114. HALL, J. R.   'Angels . . . and all the holy ones': *The Dream of the Rood* 153b–54a. ANQ (24:5/6) 65–8.

3115. —— Old English *Exodus* 399: 'Fyrst Ferhðbana' – once more. Archiv (222:2) 1985, 339–43.

3116. —— On the bibliographic unity of Bodleian MS Junius 11. *See* **153.**

3117. HARREL, PEGGY FERN.   The syntax of the Blickling homilies: a structural analysis and a study of styles. *See* **1880.**

3118. HECKELMAN, RONALD JOE.   'Promyse that is dette': toward a rhetoric and history of literary promising. Unpub. doct. diss., Claremont Graduate School, 1985. [Abstr. in DA (46) 3022A.]

3119. HICKEY, RAYMOND.   On syncope in Old English. *In* (pp. 359–66) **26.**

3120. HILL, JOYCE.   The Exeter Book and Lambeth Palace Library MS 149: a reconsideration. ANQ (24:7/8) 112–16.

3121. —— (ed.).   Old English minor heroic poems. (Bibl. 1984, 2673.) Rev. by D. G. Scragg in MÆ (55:2) 169–70.

3122. HILTON, CHADWICK B.   The Old English *Seasons for Fasting*: its place in the vernacular complaint tradition. Neophilologus (70:1) 155–9.

3123. HOLLAND, JOAN.   The *Microfiche Concordance*: a lexicographer's tool. See **534.**

3124. IRVING, EDWARD B., JR.   Crucifixion witnessed, or dramatic interaction in *The Dream of the Rood*. In (pp. 102–13) **36.**

3125. KAYLOR, NOEL HAROLD, JR.   The medieval translations of Boethius' *Consolation of Philosophy* in England, France, and Germany: an analysis and annotated bibliography. Unpub. doct. diss., Vanderbilt Univ., 1985. [Abstr. in DA (47) 524A.]

3126. KEYNES, SIMON.   King Athelstan's books. In (pp. 143–201) **25.**

3127. KLINCK, ANNE L.   A damaged passage in the Old English *Ruin*. SN (58:2) 165–8.

3128. —— Growth and decay in *The Riming Poem*, lines 51–54. ELN (23:3) 1–3.

3129. KNIEZSA, VERONIKA.   The progress of the expression of temporal relationships from Old English to Early Middle English. In (pp. 423–36) **26.**

3130. KORHAMMER, MICHAEL.   The orientation system in the Old English *Orosius*: shifted or not? In (pp. 251–69) **25.**

3131. KORTLANDT, FREDERIK.   The origin of the Old English dialects. In (pp. 437–42) **26.**

3132. KOSSICK, S. G.   Gnomic verse and Old English riddles. UES (24:2) 1–6.

3133. KOTZOR, GÜNTER (ed.).   Das altenglische Martyrologium. (Bibl. 1984, 2648.) Rev. by D. W. Rollason in YES (16) 223–4.

3134. LANGEFELD, BRIGITTE.   A third Old English translation of part of Gregory's *Dialogues*, this time embedded in the Rule of Chrodegang. ASE (15) 197–204.

3135. LANGUAGES INFORMATION CENTRE.   Guide to Anglo-Saxon poetry: with reference to other early Germanic languages (a résumé of alliterative metres). Pontypridd: Languages Information Centre, 1985. 4 leaves.

3136. LAPIDGE, MICHAEL.   Surviving booklists from Anglo-Saxon England. In (pp. 33–89) **25.**

3137. —— GNEUSS, HELMUT (eds).   Learning and literature in Anglo-Saxon England: studies presented to Peter Clemoes on the occasion of his sixty-fifth birthday. See **25.**

3138. LOCHRIE, KARMA.   Anglo-Saxon morning sickness. Neophilologus (70:2) 316–18.

3139. —— The structure and wisdom of *Judgment Day 1*. NM (87:2) 201–10.

3140. —— *Wyrd* and the limits of human understanding: a thematic sequence in the Exeter Book. See **1650.**

3141. LOGARBO, MONA LYNN.   The body and soul as kinsmen: an explanation of the theology of the Anglo-Saxon body–soul theme in terms of an underlying Anglo-Saxon spirituality of kinship. Unpub. doct. diss., Fordham Univ. [Abstr. in DA (47) 1315A.]

3142. LUND, NIELS (ed.).   Two voyagers at the court of King Alfred: the ventures of Ohthere and Wulfstan together with the description of northern Europe from the OE Orosius. Trans. by CHRISTINE E. FELL. York: Sessions, 1984. pp. 71.

3143. MACRAE-GIBSON, O. D.   The metrical entities of Old English. NM (87:1) 59–91.

3144. MAGENNIS, HUGH.   Contrasting features in the non-Ælfrician lives in the Old English *Lives of Saints*. Ang (104:3/4) 316–48.

3145. —— The exegesis of inebriation: treading carefully in Old English. ELN (23:3) 3–6.

3146. —— 'Monig oft gesæt': some images of sitting in Old English poetry. Neophilologus (70:3) 442–52.

3147. —— Water–wine miracles in Anglo-Saxon saints' lives. ELN (23:3) 7–9.

3148. MATSUNAMI, TAMOTSU.   To-in shi kara kyaku-in shi e. See **2937**.

3149. MELLINKOFF, RUTH.   Serpent imagery in the illustrated Old English Hexateuch. *In* (pp. 51–64) **36**.

3150. NELSON, MARIE.   *The Battle of Maldon* and *Juliana*: the language of confrontation. *In* (pp. 137–50) **36**.

3151. NICHOLS, STEPHEN G., JR.   Romanesque signs: early medieval narrative and iconography. (Bibl. 1985, 2650.) Rev. by June Hall Martin McCash in CL (38:2) 195–7.

3152. OHLGREN, THOMAS H.   London, British Library MS Harley 603, fol. 12. See **169**.

3153. PHILLIPS, MICHAEL JOSEPH.   Heart, mind, and soul in Old English: a semantic study. See **1557**.

3154. RANKIN, SUSAN.   The liturgical background of the Old English Advent lyrics: a reappraisal. *In* (pp. 317–40) **25**.

3155. RAY, DAVID ARNOLD.   Semantic order in Old English poetic variation. See **2271**.

3156. RENOIR, ALAIN.   Old English formulas and themes as tools for contextual interpretation. *In* (pp. 65–79) **36**.

3157. RISSANEN, MATTI.   Middle English translations of Old English charters in the *Liber Monasterii de Hyda*: a case of historical error analysis. *In* (pp. 591–603) **26**.

3158. —— 'Nathwæt' in the Exeter Book riddles. See **1627**.

3159. —— 'Sum' in Old English poetry. *In* (pp. 197–225) **36**.

3160. RIZZO, TANIA.   Sources for Medieval Studies in the libraries of the Claremont Colleges. Chronica (39) 17–19.

3161. ROBINSON, FRED C.   Literary dialect in *Maldon* and the Casley transcript. See **1643**.

3162. RUBACH, JERZY.   Degemination in Old English and the formal apparatus of generative phonology. *In* (pp. 621–35) **26**.

3163. SCRAGG, D. G.   *The Devil's Account of the Next World* revisited. ANQ (24:7/8) 107–10. (BL MS Cotton Tiberius A. iii.)

3164. —— The homilies of the Blickling manuscript. *In* (pp. 299–316) **25.**

3165. SMITH, AILSA STEWART.   Non-aristocratic poetry: the world beyond *Beowulf. In* (pp. 44–9) RICHARD WHITAKER and EDGARD SIENAERT (eds), Oral tradition and literacy: changing visions of the world. Durban: Natal University Oral Documentation and Research Centre. pp. xiv, 302.

3166. STANLEY, E. G.   *The Judgement of the Damned* (from Cambridge, Corpus Christi College 201 and other manuscripts), and the definition of Old English verse. *In* (pp. 363–91) **25.**

3167. —— Notes on the text of the Old English *Genesis. In* (pp. 189–96) **36.**

3168. STEIN, DIETER.   Old English Northumbrian verb inflection revisited. *In* (pp. 637–50) **26.**

3169. SUZUKI, SEIICHI.   Syllable theory and Old English verse: a preliminary observation. *In* (pp. 651–7) **26.**

3170. SZARMACH, PAUL E.   British Library, Cotton Vespasian D.vi. fol. 62v. *See* **185.**

3171. —— Two notes on the Vercelli Homilies. ELN (24:2) 3–7.

3172. —— (ed.).   Studies in earlier Old English prose. Albany: New York State UP, 1985. pp. vi, 420. Rev. in ANQ (24:7/8) 123–4.

3173. THRANE, TORBEN.   On delimiting the senses of near-synonyms in historical semantics: a case-study of adjectives of 'moral sufficiency' in the Old English *Andreas. In* (pp. 671–92) **26.**

3174. TRAHERN, JOSEPH B., JR (ed.).   Year's work in Old English studies 1985. OEN (20:1) 35–165.

3175. TURNER, KANDY MORROW.   A study of *The Rhyming Poem*: text, interpretation, and Christian context. Unpub. doct. diss., North Texas State Univ. [Abstr. in DA (47) 1340A.]

3176. TURVILLE-PETRE, JOAN (ed.).   The Old English *Exodus*: text, translation, and commentary, by J. R. R. TOLKIEN. (Bibl. 1984, 2666.) Rev. by N. F. Blake in MLR (81:2) 439–40.

3177. VALENTINE, VIRGINIA.   Offa's *The Battle of Maldon.* Exp (44:3) 5–7.

3178. VON ERTZDORFF, XENJA; WYNN, MARIANNE (eds).   Liebe – Ehe – Ehebruch in der Literatur des Mittelalters. Giessen: Schmitz, 1984. pp. 173. (Beiträge zur deutschen Philologie, 58.)

3179. WALL, JOHN.   Penance as poetry in the late fourteenth century. *In* (pp. 179–91) **32.**

3180. WALSH, RICHARD J.   International medieval bibliography: publications of January–June 1985. Leeds: Univ. of Leeds. pp. xlvii, 243.

3181. WEŁNA, JERZY.   The Old English digraph <cg> again. *In* (pp. 753–62) **26.**

3182. YERKES, DAVID (ed.).   The Old English *Life of Machutus.* Buffalo, NY: Toronto UP, 1984. (Cf. bibl. 1985, 2680.) Rev. by Peter J. Lucas in MÆ (55:2) 267–9; by T. F. Hoad in NQ (33:2) 204–8.

3183. ZETTERSTEN, ARNE. Old and Middle English studies in the Nordic countries. MESN (15) 3–10.

Related Studies

3184. ALBRECTSEN, ERLING (ed.). *Asserius, de rebus gestis Ælfredi* og *Chronicon Æthelweardi*: to tidlige engelske krøniker. (*Asserius, de rebus gestis Ælfredi* and *Chronicon Æthelweardi*: two early English chronicles.) Odense: Odense UP. pp. 125.

3185. BERSCHIN, W. (ed.). Lateinische Dichtungen des X. und XI. Jahrhunderts. Festgabe für Walter Bulst zum 80. Geburtstag. Heidelberg: Schneider, 1981. pp. 309. Rev. by Peter Godman in MÆ (55:1) 131.

3186. BLAIR, PETER HUNTER. Whitby as a centre of learning in the seventh century. *In* (pp. 3–32) **25.**

3187. BONNER, GERALD. Bede and his legacy. DUJ (78:2) 219–30.

3188. BROWN, MICHELLE P. Paris, Bibliothèque Nationale, lat. 10861 and the scriptorium of Christ Church, Canterbury. *See* **143.**

3189. CAMPBELL, JAMES; JOHN, ERIC; WORMALD, PATRICK. The Anglo-Saxons. Oxford: Phaidon, 1982. pp. 272.

3190. CLOVER, CAROL J. Maiden warriors and other sons. JEGP (85:1) 35–49.

3191. —— LINDOW, JOHN (eds). Old Norse–Icelandic literature: a critical guide. Ithaca, NY; London: Cornell UP, 1985. pp. 387. (Islandica, 45.)

3192. CONTAMINE, PHILIPPE. War in the Middle Ages. Trans. by MICHAEL JONES. Oxford: Blackwell, 1984. pp. xvi, 387. Rev. by Christopher Allmand in MÆ (55:1) 125–6.

3193. COOK, WILLIAM R.; HERZMAN, RONALD B. The medieval world view: an introduction. (Bibl. 1985, 2974.) Rev. by G. R. Evans in MÆ (55:1) 119–20.

3194. DENG-SU, I. L'opera agiografica di Alcuino. (Bibl. 1985, 2691.) Rev. by John J. Contreni in Spec (61:2) 427–8.

3195. DEROLEZ, R. Runes and magic. ANQ (24:7/8) 96–102.

3196. DOYLE, EDWARD GERARD (ed.). Sedulius Scottus: *On Christian Rulers* and *The Poems*. (Bibl. 1985, 2693.) Rev. by Jan Ziolkowski in Spec (61:2) 465–6.

3197. DUMVILLE, DAVID (ed.). The *Historica Brittonum* 3: the Vatican recension. Cambridge: Brewer, 1985. pp. xx, 122. Rev. by J. D. Burnley in EngS (67:5) 450–1.

3198. —— KEYNES, SIMON (gen. eds). The Anglo-Saxon chronicle, a collaborative edition: vol. 4, MS B.: a semi-diplomatic edition with introduction and indices. Ed. by SIMON TAYLOR. (Bibl. 1984, 2695.) Rev. by Mark Griffith in MÆ (55:2) 271.

3199. DUMVILLE, DAVID N. The West Saxon genealogical regnal list: manuscripts and texts. *See* **149.**

3200. FARRELL, ROBERT T. News and notes on archaeology. OEN (19:2) 36–40.

3201. FLORI, JEAN. L'idéologie du glaive: préhistoire de la chevalerie.

Geneva: Droz, 1983. pp. viii, 205. (Travaux d'histoire éthico-politique, 33.) Rev. by Maurice Keen in MÆ (55:1) 118–19.

3202. GATCH, M. McC.   The Office in late Anglo-Saxon monasticism. *In* (pp. 341–62) **25.**

3203. HILL, THOMAS D.   Odin, Rinda and Thaney, the mother of St Kentigern. MÆ (55:2) 230–7.

3204. IRVINE, MARTIN.   Bede the grammarian and the scope of grammatical studies in eighth-century Northumbria. *See* **1848.**

3205. KALINKE, MARIANNE E.; MITCHELL, P. M.   Bibliography of Old Norse-Icelandic romances. Ithaca, NY: Cornell UP, 1985. pp. xii, 140. (Islandica, 46.) Rev. by Jürg Glauser in JEGP (85:3) 437–41.

3206. KING, ANNE.   The Ruthwell cross – a linguistic monument (runes as evidence for Old English). *See* **1444.**

3207. LAPIDGE, MICHAEL.   Litanies of the saints in Anglo-Saxon manuscripts: a preliminary list. *See* **160.**

3208. —— The school of Theodore and Hadrian. ASE (15) 45–72.

3209. —— SHARPE, RICHARD.   A bibliography of Celtic-Latin literature 400–1200. Dublin: Royal Irish Academy, 1985. pp. xxii, 361. (Royal Irish dictionary of medieval Latin from Celtic sources, ancillary pubs, 1.)

3210. LENDINARA, PATRIZIA.   The third book of the *Bella Parisiacae Urbis* by Abbo of Saint-Germain-des-Prés and its Old English gloss. ASE (15) 73–89.

3211. MERTENS, VOLKER; MÜLLER, ULRICH (eds).   Epische Stoffe des Mittelalters. Stuttgart: Kröner, 1984. pp. x, 529. (Kröners Taschenausgabe, 483.) Rev. by Marianne E. Kalinke in JEGP (85:1) 70–1.

3212. NÍ CHATHÁIN, PRÓINSÉAS.   Sir Samuel Ferguson and the ogham inscriptions. IUR (16) 159–69.

3213. OWEN-CROCKER, GALE R.   Dress in Anglo-Saxon England. Manchester: Manchester UP. pp. xii, 241.

3214. PENNICK, NIGEL.   Runestaves and oghams. Cambridge: Runestaff. pp. 25. (Second ed.: first ed., as *Ogham and Runic*, 1979.)

3215. SAUER, HANS (ed.).   Theodulfi Capitula in England: die altenglischen Übersetzungen zusammen mit dem lateinischen Text. (Bibl. 1979, 3331.) Rev. by David N. Dumville in Archiv (223:2) 388–92.

3216. SCHACH, PAUL.   Instant saga style: the evidence of the manuscripts. *See* **175.**

3217. SIMS-WILLIAMS, PATRICK.   Thoughts on Ephrem the Syrian in Anglo-Saxon England. *In* (pp. 205–26) **25.**

AUTHORS

Ælfric

3218. BENDER-DAVIS, JEANNINE M.   Ælfric's techniques of translation and adaptation as seen in the composition of his Old English *Latin Grammar*. Unpub. doct. diss., Pennsylvania State Univ., 1985. [Abstr. in DA (47) 170A.]

3219. CLAYTON, MARY.   Ælfric and the nativity of the Blessed Virgin Mary. Ang (104:3/4) 286–315.

3220. —— Delivering the damned: a motif in OE homiletic prose. *See* **3092.**

3221. LEINBAUGH, THEODORE H. A damaged passage in Ælfric's *De creatore et creatura*: methods of recovery. *See* **162.**

3222. —— The sources for Ælfric's Easter sermon: the history of the controversy and a new source. NQ (33:3) 294–311.

3223. MAGENNIS, HUGH. Contrasting features in the non-Ælfrician lives in the Old English *Lives of Saints*. *See* **3144.**

3224. NAGUCKA, RUTA. Complementation in *Ælfric's Colloquy*. *In* (pp. 533–45) **26.**

3225. NEVANLINNA, SAARA. Variation in the syntactic structure of simile in OE prose. *In* (pp. 89–98) **43.**

3226. SCHENDL, HERBERT. 'Gelendon mid aescum': a problematic reading in Ælfric? *See* **1606.**

3227. TKACZ, CATHERINE BROWN. The topos of tormentor tormented in Ælfric's *Passio Sancti Vincentii Martyris*. BSUF (25:2) 1984, 3–13.

3228. TRAHERN, JOSEPH B., JR. Ælfric: more sources for two homilies. ANQ (24:7/8) 110–11.

Aldhelm

3229. WIELAND, GERNOT. Aldhelm's *De octo vitiis principalibus* and Prudentius' *Psychomachia*. MÆ (55:1) 85–92.

Alfred

3230. GNEUSS, HELMUT. King Alfred and the history of Anglo-Saxon libraries. *In* (pp. 29–49) **36.**

3231. LUND, NIELS (ed.). Two voyagers at the court of King Alfred: the ventures of Ohthere and Wulfstan together with the description of northern Europe from the OE Orosius. Trans. by CHRISTINE E. FELL. *See* **3142.**

3232. NEVANLINNA, SAARA. Variation in the syntactic structure of simile in OE prose. *In* (pp. 89–98) **43.**

Cædmon

3233. HALL, J. R. The Conybeare *Cædmon*: a turning point in the history of Old English scholarship. *See* **310.**

Cynewulf

3234. NELSON, MARIE. *The Battle of Maldon* and *Juliana*: the language of confrontation. *In* (pp. 137–50) **36.**

3235. SWENSON, KAREN. 'Wapentake': a realistic detail in Cynewulf's *Juliana*. NQ (33:1) 3–6.

Wulfstan

3236. LAGERQUIST, LINNEA M. The impersonal verb in context: Old English. *In* (pp. 123–36) **41.**

3237. SWANTON, MICHAEL (trans. and ed.). Three lives of the last Englishmen. New York; London: Garland, 1984. pp. xxx, 156. (Library of medieval literature, ser. B, 10.) (BL MS Harley 3776, fols 1–24; Peterborough Cathedral MS 1, fols 320–39; BL MS Cotton Claudius Av, fols 160ᵛ–98.) Rev. by J. D. A. Ogilvy in ELN (23:3) 64–5.

BEOWULF

3238. BAMMESBERGER, ALFRED. On Old English *gefrægnod* in *Beowulf* 1333a. *In* (pp. 193–7) **26.**

3239. BATELY, JANET. Linguistic evidence as a guide to the authorship of Old English verse: a reappraisal, with special reference to *Beowulf*. *In* (pp. 409–31) **25.**

3240. BELLMAN, JAMES FREDRICK, JR. The institutional environment of *Beowulf*. Unpub. doct. diss., Univ. of Nebraska–Lincoln, 1985. [Abstr. in DA (46) 3026A.]

3241. BERKHOUT, CARL T.; MEDINE, RENÉE. *Beowulf* 770a: 'reþe renweardas'. NQ (33:4) 433–4.

3242. BESSINGER, JESS B., JR; YEAGER, ROBERT F. (eds). Approaches to teaching *Beowulf*. New York: Modern Language Assn of America, 1984. pp. xvii, 214. (Approaches to teaching masterpieces of world literature.) Rev. by Peter J. Lucas in NQ (33:1) 94.

3243. BRAEGER, PETER C. Connotations of (*Earm*) *Sceapen*: *Beowulf* ll. 2228–2229 and the shape-shifting dragon. ELit (13:2) 327–30.

3244. CASSIDY, FREDERIC G. Knowledge of *Beowulf* in its own time. YREAL (1) 1982, 1–12.

3245. CLEMOES, PETER. 'Symbolic' language in Old English poetry. *In* (pp. 3–14) **36.**

3246. CRONAN, DENNIS. Alliterative rank in Old English poetry. *See* **1218.**

3247. DALDORPH, BRIAN. 'Mar-Peace' ally: Unferð in *Beowulf*. MSE (10:3) 143–60.

3248. DAMICO, HELEN. Beowulf's Wealhtheow and the valkyrie tradition. (Bibl. 1985, 2738.) Rev. by Joseph Harris in Spec (61:2) 400–3; by Daniel G. Calder in JEGP (85:3) 441–3; by John Himes in NQ (33:1) 94–6.

3249. —— *Þrymskviða* and Beowulf's second fight: the dressing of the hero in parody. SS (58:4) 407–28.

3250. DEROLEZ, R. Focus on *Beowulf*: variation or meaning. *In* (pp. 9–16) **18.**

3251. FARRELL, ELEANOR. The epic hero and society: Cuchulainn, Beowulf and Roland. Mythlore (13:1) 25–8, 50.

3252. FOLEY, JOHN MILES. Narrativity in *Beowulf*, the Odyssey, and the Serbo-Croatian 'return song'. *In* (pp. 295–301) **11.**

3253. FRANK, ROBERTA. 'Mere' and 'sund': two sea-changes in *Beowulf*. *In* (pp. 153–72) **36.**

3254. FUJIWARA, HIROSHI. The relative clauses in *Beowulf*. *In* (pp. 311–16) **26.**

3255. GREENFIELD, STANLEY B. Beowulf and the judgement of the righteous. *In* (pp. 393–407) **25.**

3256. HALE, STEVEN LEE. Embedded narratives in the *Iliad*, *Beowulf*, and *The Song of Roland*: text and context. Unpub. doct. diss., Univ. of Georgia, 1985. [Abstr. in DA (47) 171A.]

3257. HALL, MARGARET AUSTIN. Syntactic and semantic patterning with the verb 'be' in the older Germanic languages. *See* **1878.**

3258. HARUTA, SETSUKO. The women in *Bēowulf.* PoetT (23) 1–15.

3259. HIGLEY, SARAH LYNN. 'Aldor on ofre' or the reluctant hart: a study of liminality in *Beowulf.* NM (87:3) 342–53.

3260. HUPPÉ, BERNARD F. The hero in the earthly city: a reading of *Beowulf.* Binghamton: New York State UP, 1984. pp. x, 201. (Medieval and Renaissance texts and studies, 33). Rev. by Edward B. Irving, Jr, in Spec (61:3) 668–70.

3261. KIERNAN, KEVIN S. The lost letters of *Beowulf* 2253a. *See* **1592.**

3262. —— Madden, Thorkelin, and MS Vitellius/Vespasian A xv. *See* **159.**

3263. KROGH, BODIL. 'Heorot revisited': håbløshed og heltemod i: brugen af *Beowulf* som litteratur og i litteratur i det 20 årh. med hovedvægt på J. R. R. Tolkiens forfatterskab. ('Heorot revisited': despair and valour: the use of *Beowulf* as literature and in literature in the 20th century, with special reference to J. R. R. Tolkien's writing.) Odense: Udgivelsesudvalget Odense Universitet. pp. 139.

3264. KROLL, NORMA. *Beowulf*: the hero as keeper of human polity. MP (84:2) 117–29.

3265. LESTER, G. A. 'Earme on eaxle' (*Beowulf* 1117a). *See* **1588.**

3266. LOCHRIE, KARMA. Anglo-Saxon morning sickness. *See* **3138.**

3267. NILES, JOHN D. *Beowulf*: the poem and its tradition. (Bibl. 1985, 2749.) Rev. by Stanley B. Greenfield in CL (38:1) 98–100; by Margaret E. Goldsmith in MÆ (55:2) 166–7; by Howell Chickering in Spec (61:1) 186–9.

3268. PARKS, WARD. Flyting and fighting: pathways in the realization of the epic contest. *See* **831.**

3269. —— Flyting, sounding, debate: three verbal contest genres. *See* **2715.**

3270. POPE, JOHN C. *Beowulf* 505, 'gehedde', and the pretensions of Unferth. *In* (pp. 173–87) **36.**

3271. RAY, DAVID ARNOLD. Semantic order in Old English poetic variation. *See* **2271.**

3272. ROBERTS, GILDAS. *Beowulf*: new translation into modern English verse. St Johns, Nfld.: Breakwater, 1984. pp. xii, 100. Rev. by M. C. Seymour in EngS (67:4) 364; by E. G. Stanley in NQ (33:1) 96.

3273. ROBINSON, FRED C. *Beowulf* and the appositive style. Knoxville: Tennessee UP, 1985. pp. ix, 106. (Hodges Lectures.) Rev. by Roberta Frank in Spec (61:4) 992–4; by Joyce Hill in NQ (33:4) 530–1; by M. C. Seymour in EngS (67:4) 363–4.

3274. STANLEY, E. G. Rudolf von Raumer: long sentences in *Beowulf* and the influence of Christianity on Germanic style. NQ (33:4) 434–8.

3275. SUZUKI, SEIICHI. Syllable theory and Old English verse: a preliminary observation. *In* (pp. 651–7) **26.**

3276. TAYLOR, PAUL BEEKMAN. The traditional language of treasure in *Beowulf.* JEGP (85:2) 191–205.

3277. TEMPLE, MARY KAY.   *Beowulf* 1258–1266: Grendel's lady-mother. ELN (23:3) 10–15.

3278. THUNDY, ZACHARIAS P.   *Beowulf*: date and authorship. NM (87:1) 102–16.

3279. TRIPP, RAYMOND P., JR.   *Beowulf* 1314a: the hero as *alfwalda* 'ruler of elves'. Neophilologus (70:4) 630–2.

3280. —— More about the fight with the dragon. *Beowulf* 2208b–3182. (Bibl. 1985, 2758.) Rev. by Rolf H. Bremmer, Jr, in EngS (67:4) 364–6.

3281. WAHBAH, MAJDĪ.   Malḥamat Bīwulf wa-makānatuhā min al-adab al-Awrubī. (The epic of *Beowulf* and its place in European literature.) ʿĀlam al-Fikr (16) 1985, 209–26.

3282. WEINSTOCK, HORST.   Comment on 'Knowledge of *Beowulf* in Its Own Time' by Professor Frederic G. Cassidy. YREAL (1) 1982, 13–25. (*Refers to* **3244**.)

MIDDLE ENGLISH
AND FIFTEENTH CENTURY

GENERAL AND ANONYMOUS

General Literary Studies;
Editions and Studies of Anonymous Writings
(except Drama and the Gawain Poet)

3283. ACKERMAN, ROBERT W.; DAHOOD, ROGER (eds). Ancrene Riwle: introduction and part I. Binghamton, NY: Center for Medieval and Early Renaissance Studies, 1984. pp. 110. (Medieval and Renaissance texts and studies.) Rev. by B. S. Lee in UCTSE (15) 66–70.

3284. AERS, DAVID (ed.). Medieval literature: criticism, ideology and history. See **33**.

3285. ALEXANDER, J. J. G. (gen. ed.). A survey of manuscripts illuminated in the British Isles: vol. 5, Gothic manuscripts 1285–1385, by LUCY FREEMAN SANDLER, 1, Text and illustrations; 2 Catalogue. See **137**.

3286. ANDREW, MALCOLM (ed.). Two Early Renaissance bird poems: *The Harmony of Birds, The Parliament of Birds*. Washington, DC: Folger Shakespeare Library; London; Toronto: Assoc. UPs. 1984. pp. 113. Rev. by John Norton-Smith in NQ (33:4) 533–4.

3287. ANON. A bibliography of publications on medieval English language and literature in Japan from April 1983 to March 1985. See **3066**.

3288. ARN, MARY-JO; WIRTJES, HANNEKE; JENSEN, HANS (eds). Historical and editorial studies in medieval and early modern English for Johan Gerritsen. (Bibl. 1985, 23.) Rev. by J. G. Riewald in EngS (67:1) 83–6, by A. S. G. Edwards in Library (8:2) 179–81.

3289. BARBER, RICHARD. King Arthur: hero and legend. (Bibl. 1974, 4106.) Woodbridge: Boydell. pp. 256. (Third ed.: first ed. 1974.)

3290. BARRETT, ALEXANDRA (ed.). *The Book of Tribulation*, ed. from MS Bodley 423. Heidelberg: Winter, 1983. pp. 174. (Middle English texts, 15.) Rev. by Bella Millett in MÆ (55:1) 132.

3291. BAUER, GERO. Medieval English scribal practice: some questions and some assumptions. *In* (pp. 199–210) **26**.

3292. BEADLE, RICHARD; GRIFFITHS, JEREMY (eds). St John's College, Cambridge, MS L. 1.: a facsimile. (Bibl. 1985, 2772.) Rev. by Edward Wilson in MÆ (55:2) 279–81.

3293. BENNETT, J. A. W. Middle English Literature. Ed. and completed by DOUGLAS GRAY. Oxford: Clarendon Press. pp. xi, 496. (Oxford history of English literature, 1:2.)

3294. BENSON, LARRY D. (ed.). King Arthur's death: the Middle English stanzaic *Morte Arthur* and alliterative *Morte Arthure*. Exeter: Exeter UP. pp. xxxvi, 257.

3295. BISHOP, IAN. Lapidary formulas as topics of invention – from Thomas of Hales to Henryson. RES (37:148) 469–77.

3296. BJELLAND, KAREN THERESA. The voice-address structure of the *South English Legendary*. Unpub. doct. diss., Catholic Univ. of America. [Abstr. in DA (47) 1315A.]

3297. BLAKE, NORMAN.   Critical approaches to medieval devotional prose. AAS (6:2) 131–47.

3298. BOFFEY, J.   The manuscript context of English courtly love lyrics, *c*. 1450–1530. *See* **140.**

3299. BOFFEY, JULIA.   Manuscripts of English courtly love lyrics in the later Middle Ages. *See* **141.**

3300. BOITANI, PIERO; TORTI, ANNA (eds).   Medieval and pseudo-medieval literature: the J. A. W. Bennett Memorial Lectures, Perugia, 1982–3. (Bibl. 1985, 32.) Rev. by J. D. Burnley in MLR (81:3) 696–7.

3301. BOLLARD, J. K.   Sovereignty and the loathly lady in English, Welsh and Irish. Leeds Studies in English (17) 41–59.

3302. BOLTON, W. F.   Middle English in the law reports and records of 11–13 Richard II. ELN (24:1) 1–8.

3303. BOONE, LAUREL.   The relationship between *The Owl and the Nightingale* and the Marie de France's *Lais* and *Fables*. ESCan (11:2) 1985, 157–77.

3304. BRADY, BRIGID.   Language and form in fourteenth-century English vision literature. Unpub. doct. diss., Rutgers Univ., 1985. [Abstr. in DA (46) 1935A.]

3305. BRAY, J. R.   The legend of St Katherine in later Middle English literature. Unpub. doct. diss., Univ. of London, Birkbeck Coll., 1984. [Abstr. in IT (35) 541–2.]

3306. BREWER, DEREK.   The place of medieval literature in English studies. *In* (pp. 679–94) **1.**

3307. BROWNLEE, KEVIN; BROWNLEE, MARINA SCORDILIS (eds). Romance: generic transformation from Chrétien de Troyes to Cervantes. Hanover, NH; London: New England UP, 1985. pp. viii, 293.

3308. BRYCE, DEREK.   The mystical way and the Arthurian quest. Lampeter: Llanerch. pp. 160.

3309. BUNT, GERRIT HENDRIK VOLKEN.   William of Palerne: an alliterative romance, re-edited from MS King's College Cambridge 13. (Bibl. 1985, 2784.) Rev. by J. D. Burnley in EngS (67:4) 368–9.

3310. BURNLEY, J. D.   Curial prose in England. Spec (61:3) 593–614.

3311. BURNS, E. JANE.   Arthurian fictions: rereading the Vulgate cycle. Columbus: Ohio State UP for Miami Univ., 1985. pp. 208. Rev. by Robert S. Sturges in RR (77:4) 452–5.

3312. BURROW, J. A.   The ages of man: a study in medieval writing and thought. Oxford: Clarendon Press. pp. x, 211. Rev. by John Marenbon in THES (717) 18.

3313. —— Essays on medieval literature. New York: OUP, 1984. (Cf. bibl. 1985, 2785.) Rev. by Joerg O. Fichte in SAC (8) 170–2; by Robert B. Burlin in Spec (61:3) 630–1; by A. V. C. Schmidt in MÆ (55:1) 134–5.

3314. —— Medieval writers and their work: Middle English literature and its background, 1100–1500. (Bibl. 1984, 2782.) Rev. by Derek Pearsall in MLR (81:1) 164–5.

3315. CARPENTER, C. T. An edition of the Lent and Palm Sunday sermons contained in the fifteenth-century translation of the late twelfth-century Latin *Filius matris* cycle. Unpub. doct. diss., Univ. of London, Bedford Coll., 1984.

3316. CARRUTHERS, MARY J.; KIRK, ELIZABETH D. (eds). Acts of interpretation: the text and its contexts, 700–1600. Essays on medieval and Renaissance literature in honor of E. Talbot Donaldson. (Bibl. 1984, 55.) Rev. by Derek Pearsall in MLR (81:4) 969–72.

3317. CIGMAN, GLORIA (ed.). Medieval sermon studies newsletter: 17 and 18. *See* **3089.**

3318. COOKE, W. G. Notes on the alliterative *Morte Arthure*. EngS (67:4) 304–7.

3319. COOKE, WILLIAM G. *The Tournament of Tottenham*: an alliterative poem and an Exeter performance. REEDNewsletter (11:2) 1–3.

3320. COUTTS, CATHERINE (ed.). International medieval bibliography. Publications of July–December 1985. *See* **3096.**

3321. DAHOOD, ROGER (ed.). The avowing of King Arthur. (Bibl. 1985, 2791.) Rev. by Ralph Hanna, III, in Spec (61:1) 132–4; by J. A. Burrow in NQ (33:2) 217–18.

3322. DEAN, CHRISTOPHER. Sir Gawain in the alliterative *Morte Arthure*. PLL (22:2) 115–25.

3323. DEKEYSER, XAVIER. Romance loans in Middle English: a re-assessment. *In* (pp. 253–65) **26.**

3324. DESMOND, MARILYNN ROBIN. 'I wol now singen, yif I kan': the *Aeneid* in medieval French and English narrative. Unpub. doct. diss., Univ. of California, Berkeley, 1985. [Abstr. in DA (46) 2687A.]

3325. DESPRES, DENISE LOUISE. Franciscan spirituality: vision and the authority of Scripture. Unpub. doct. diss., Indiana Univ., 1985. [Abstr. in DA (46) 3026A.]

3326. DOVE, MARY. The perfect age of man's life. Cambridge: CUP. pp. 189.

3327. DUGGAN, HOYT N. Alliterative patterning as a basis for emendation in Middle English alliterative poetry. SAC (8) 73–105.

3328. —— The shape of the B-verse in Middle English alliterative poetry. Spec (61:3) 564–92.

3329. EADIE, J. The authorship of *The Owl and the Nightingale*: a reappraisal. EngS (67:6) 471–7.

3330. EDWARDS, A. S. G. (ed.). Middle English prose: a critical guide to major authors and genres. (Bibl. 1985, 2798.) Rev. by Sarah M. Horrall in ESCan (12:3) 336–9; by Albert E. Hartung in Spec (61:3) 644–6.

3331. FARHAN, I. H. The influence of Averroistic thought on English literature during the Middle Ages and the Renaissance. Unpub. doct. diss., Univ. of Birmingham, 1983/84.

3332. FEIN, SUSANNA GREER. The Middle English alliterative tradition of the allegorical *chanson d'aventure*: a critical edition of *De Tribus*

Regibus Mortuis, Somer Soneday, The Foure Leues of the Trewlufe, and *Death and Liffe.* Unpub. doct. diss., Harvard Univ., 1985. [Abstr. in DA (47) 173A.]

3333. FELLOWS, JENNIFER.   Sir Bevis of Hampton in popular tradition. *See* **2447.**

3334. FEWSTER, C. S.   Narrative transformations of past and present in Middle English romance: *Guy of Warwick, Amis and Amiloun* and the *Squyr of Lowe Degre.* Unpub. doct. diss., Univ. of Liverpool, 1984. [Abstr. in IT (35) 542.]

3335. FLETCHER, ALAN J.   The sermon booklets of Friar Nicholas Philip. MÆ (55:2) 188–202.

3336. FLINT, MICHAEL.   Character and characterization in some Middle English Arthurian romances. Unpub. doct. diss., Univ. of Auckland.

3337. FOWLER, DAVID C.   The Bible in Middle English literature. (Bibl. 1985, 2803.) Rev. by David L. Jeffrey in ESCan (12:4) 452–4, by G. H. Russell in SAC (8) 185–8, by Phillip C. Broadman in ChrisL (35:2) 37–8.

3338. FRANKLIN, MICHAEL J.   'Fyngres heo haþ feir to folde': trothplight in some of the love lyrics of MS Harley 2253. MÆ (55:2) 176–87.

3339. FURROW, MELISSA M. (ed.).   Ten fifteenth-century comic poems. New York; London: Garland, 1985. pp. xviii, 500. (Garland medieval texts, 13.)

3340. GANIM, JOHN M.   Style and consciousness in Middle English narrative. (Bibl. 1985, 2807.) Rev. by Helen Cooper in MÆ (55:2) 278–9.

3341. GEE, ELIZABETH.   A miracle of Saint Kenelm in MS Douce 368. NQ (33:2) 149–54.

3342. GELLRICH, JESSE.   The argument of the book: medieval writing and modern theory. CLIO (10:3) 1981, 245–63.

3343. GELLRICH, JESSE M.   The idea of the book in the Middle Ages: language, theory, mythology, and fiction. Ithaca, NY; London: Cornell UP, 1985. pp. 292. Rev. by Stephen G. Nichols in MedHum (14) 199–205; by Marci L. Colish in CLIO (15:1) 1985, 83–6.

3344. GLASSCOE, MARION.   *The Fair Maid of Ribblesdale:* content and context. NM (87:4) 555–7.

3345. —— (ed.).   The medieval mystical tradition in England: papers read at Dartington Hall, July 1984. (Bibl. 1985, 33.) Rev. by Denise L. Despres in SAC (8) 191–3.

3346. GÖLLER, KARL-HEINZ (ed.).   Spätmittelalterliche Artusliteratur. Paderborn: Schöningh, 1984. pp. 160. (Beiträge zur englischen und amerikanischen Literatur, 3.)

3347. GÖRLACH, MANFRED.   Middle English – a creole? *In* (pp. 329–44) **26.**

3348. GRABES, HERBERT.   The mutable glass: mirror-imagery in titles and texts of the Middle Ages and English Renaissance. (Bibl. 1983,

3433.) Rev. by A. J. Minnis in MÆ (55:1) 120–3; by Brian Gibbons in ShS (37) 1984, 187–8.

3349. GRAY, DOUGLAS (ed.).   The Oxford book of late medieval verse and prose. (Bibl. 1985, 2815.) Rev. by N. F. Blake in EngS (67:1) 73–5.

3350. —— STANLEY, E. G. (eds).   Middle English studies presented to Norman Davis in honour of his seventieth birthday. (Bibl. 1985, 2816.) Rev. by Hiroyuki Matsumoto in SAC (8) 193–4.

3351. GRENNEN, JOSEPH E.   *We Ben Chapmen.* Exp (44:3) 3–5.

3352. GRIFFITHS, JEREMY.   'The culture of the court, the culture of the country'. MESN (14) 1–3.

3353. GROUT, P. B., *et al.* (eds).   The legend of Arthur in the Middle Ages: studies presented to A. H. Diverres by colleagues, pupils and friends. (Bibl. 1984, 2820.) Rev. by Rosemary Morris in MÆ (55:2) 304–6.

3354. HAMEL, MARY (ed.).   *Morte Arthure*: a critical edition. New York; London: Garland, 1984. pp. xi, 546. (Garland medieval texts, 9.)

3355. HANNA, RALPH, III.   The Index of Middle English prose: handlist 1, A handlist of manuscripts containing Middle English prose in the Henry E. Huntington Library. (Bibl. 1984, 192.) Rev. by C. Paul Christianson in SAC (8) 196–200; by E. G. Stanley in NQ (33:1) 97–8.

3356. HARKIN, S. D.   An edition of *The Owl and the Nightingale*. Unpub. doct. diss., Univ. of Wales, UWIST, 1985. [Abstr. in IT (36) 468.]

3357. HARRINGTON, DAVID V.   The Harley lyric *Wynter Wakeneth Al My Care.* Exp (44:2) 3–4.

3358. HART, SIDNEY (ed.).   One in specyal et al.: immortalizers of King Arthur. *See* **2454.**

3359. HARVEY, CAROL J.   The Anglo-Norman courtly lyric. JRMMRA (7) 27–40.

3360. HECKELMAN, RONALD JOE.   'Promyse that is dette': toward a rhetoric and history of literary promising. *See* **3118.**

3361. HENRY, AVRIL.   *Pe Pilgrimage of pe Lyfe of pe Manhode*: the large design, with special reference to Books 2–4. NM (87:2) 229–36.

3362. —— The structure of Book 1 of *Pe Pilgrimage of pe Lyfe of pe Manhode.* NM (87:1) 128–41.

3363. —— (ed.).   The mirour of mans saluacioune: a Middle English translation of *Speculum humanae salvationis*: a critical edition of the fifteenth-century manuscript illustrated from Der Spiegel der menschen Behältnis, Speyer, Drach, *c.* 1475. Aldershot: Scolar Press. pp. 347.

3364. HILL, BETTY.   *Sir Orfeo* 241–56, 102–12. NQ (33:1)13–14.

3365. HILL, THOMAS.   Androgyny and conversion in the Middle English lyric: *In the Vaile of Restles Mynd.* ELH (53:3) 459–70.

3366. HIRSH, JOHN C. (ed.).   *Barlam and Iosaphat*: a Middle English life of Buddha. London: Early English Text Soc.; OUP. pp. xi, 224. (EETS, 290.) (MS Peterhouse 257.)

3367. HORNER, PATRICK J. (comp.).   The index of Middle English prose: handlist 3, A handlist of manuscripts containing Middle English prose in the Digby Collection, Bodleian Library Oxford. *See* **156.**

3368. HYDE, THOMAS.   The poetic theology of love: Cupid in

Renaissance literature. Newark: Delaware UP; London: Assoc. UPs. pp. 212.

3369. JACKSON, W. T. H. (ed.). The interpretation of medieval lyric poetry. (Bibl. 1982, 3734.) Rev. by Elizabeth Wilson Poe in RPh (40:2) 274–8.

3370. JONES, F.   A note on *Harley Lyrics* 7. NM (87:1) 142–3.

3371. JONES, MEREDITH JOY.   The Harley lyrics in context: the structure and organization of MS Harley 2253. Unpub. doct. diss., Univ. of Michigan, 1985. [Abstr. in DA (46) 3347A.]

3372. JOST, DAVID.   Survey of the reading program of the *Middle English Dictionary. See* **1764.**

3373. KANE, GEORGE.   Some fourteenth-century 'political' poems. *In* (pp. 82–91) **32.**

3374. KANE, HAROLD (ed.).   The prickynge of love. Atlantic Highlands, NJ: Humanities Press, 1983. (Cf. bibl. 1984, 2835.) Rev. by Sarah M. Horrall in SAC (8) 211–13; by Joyce Bazire in MÆ (55:2) 294–5.

3375. KAYLOR, NOEL HAROLD, JR.   The medieval translations of Boethius' *Consolation of Philosophy* in England, France, and Germany: an analysis and annotated bibliography. *See* **3125.**

3376. KEISER, GEORGE R.   The Middle English *Treatyse of Fysshynge wyth an Angle* and the gentle reader. YLG (61:1/2) 22–48.

3377. KELLY, H. A.   The non-tragedy of Arthur. *In* (pp. 92–114) **32.**

3378. KER, N. R.   Books, collectors and libraries: studies in the medieval heritage. Ed. by ANDREW G. WATSON. *See* **245.**

3379. KIKUCHI, KIYOAKI.   Repetition in *The Owl and the Nightingale.* SEL (English number) 17–38.

3380. KINDRICK, ROBERT L.   Politics and poetry at the court of James III. SSL (19) 1984, 40–55.

3381. KNIEZSA, VERONIKA.   The progress of the expression of temporal relationships from Old English to Early Middle English. *In* (pp. 423–36) **26.**

3382. KNIGHT, STEPHEN.   The social function of the Middle English romances. *In* (pp. 99–122) **33.**

3383. KRATZMANN, GREGORY (ed.).   *Colkelbie Sow* and *The Talis of the Fyve Bestes.* (Bibl. 1984, 2843.) Rev. by Sally Mapstone in MÆ (55:2) 301.

3384. —— SIMPSON, JAMES (eds).   Medieval English religious and ethical literature: essays in honour of G. H. Russell. *See* **32.**

3385. KRISTENSSON, GILLIS.   A Middle English dialect boundary. *In* (pp. 443–57) **26.**

3386. LACY, NORRIS J. (ed.); ASHE, GEOFFREY (assoc. ed.).   The Arthurian encyclopedia. New York; London: Garland. pp. xxxvii, 649. (Garland reference library of the humanities, 585.)

3387. LAWTON, DAVID A. (ed.).   *Joseph of Arimathea*: a critical edition. New York; London: Garland, 1983. pp. liv, 72. (Garland medieval texts, 5.) Rev. by Jerry L. Ball in SAC (8) 220–2.

3388. LAWTON, L. S.   Text and image in late medieval English vernacular literary manuscripts. *See* **161.**

3389.   LEES, ROSEMARY ANN.   The negative language of the Dionysian school of mystical theology: an approach to *The Cloud of Unknowing*. (Bibl. 1985, 2841.) Rev. by J. P. H. Clark in MÆ (55:2) 292–4.

3390.   LESTER, G. A.   The index of Middle English prose: handlist 2, A handlist of manuscripts containing Middle English prose in the John Rylands University Library of Manchester and Chetham's Library, Manchester. Woodbridge; Dover, NH: Boydell & Brewer, 1985. pp. xvi, 112. Rev. by C. Paul Christianson in SAC (8) 196–200; by E. G. Stanley in NQ (33:1) 97–8.

3391.   LEWIS, R. E.; BLAKE, N. F.; EDWARDS, A. S. G.   Index of printed Middle English prose. New York; London: Garland, 1985. pp. xxxiii, 362. (Garland reference library of the humanities, 537.)

3392.   LOPEZ, LONGINO LUIS.   The rhetoric of reward in Middle English alliterative dream poetry. Unpub. doct. diss., Univ. of New Mexico, 1985. [Abstr. in DA (46) 1937A.]

3393.   McALINDON, THOMAS.   The medieval assimilation of Greek romance: a chapter in the history of a narrative type. YREAL (3) 1985, 24–56.

3394.   McDONALD, CRAIG.   *The Thre Prestis of Peblis* and *The Meroure of Wyssdome*: a possible relationship. SSL (17) 1982, 153–64.

3395.   McMAHON, KATHERINE G.   The *South English Legendary*: an investigation and a critical edition of the lives of Agnes, Scholastica, and Juliana. Unpub. doct. diss., Northern Illinois Univ., 1985. [Abstr. in DA (46) 2688A.]

3396.   McSPARRAN, FRANCES (ed.).   Octavian. London: Early English Text Society; OUP. pp. 244. (Early English Text Society, 289.)

3397.   MATSUNAMI, TAMOTSU.   To-in shi kara kyaku-in shi e. *See* **2937.**

3398.   MEALE, C. M.   The social and literary contexts of a late medieval manuscript: a study of BL MS Harley 2252 and its owner John Colyns. *See* **165.**

3399.   MINNIS, A. J.   Medieval theory of authorship: scholastic literary attitudes in the later Middle Ages. (Bibl. 1985, 2848.) Rev. by Janet Coleman in YES (16) 224–6; by C. David Benson in ELN (23:4) 74–5; by Stephen G. Nichols in MedHum (14) 199–205.

3400.   MOORE, J. K. (ed.).   Selected Middle English lyrics. Wellington: English Dept, Victoria Univ., 1985. pp. vi, 377.

3401.   MORRIS, TONI JEAN BURNS.   The development of English prose style and the fourteenth-century English mystics. Unpub. doct. diss., Kent State Univ., 1985. [Abstr. in DA (47) 189A.]

3402.   MUELLER, JANEL H.   The native tongue and the word: developments in English prose style 1380–1580. (Bibl. 1985, 2852.) Rev. by P. J. C. Field in Prose Studies (9:1) 73–5; by David M. Zesmer in ChrisL (35:4) 58–60; by Annabel Patterson in JEGP (85:1) 104–6.

3403.   NEVANLINNA, SAARA (ed.).   The Northern Homily Cycle: the expanded version in MSS Harley 4196 and Cotton Tiberius E vii: III, From the Fifth to the Twenty-Fifth Sunday after Trinity. Helsinki: Société Néophilologique, 1984. pp. 304. (Mémoires de la Société Néophilologique de Helsinki, 43.)

3404. NICHOLS, STEPHEN.   The book and the author in the Middle Ages: two recent studies. MedHum (14) 199–205 (review-article).

3405. NIXON, INGEBORG (ed.).   Thomas of Erceldoune. (Bibl. 1985, 2855.) Rev. by Alasdair A. MacDonald in EngS (67:2) 184–6.

3406. NOVAK, MARIAN HARRISON.   Saints' lives and legends and their influence on early English and continental literature. Unpub. doct. diss., Washington State Univ., 1985. [Abstr. in DA (47) 1723A.]

3407. O'BRIEN, S. M.   An edition of seven homilies from Lambeth Palace Library MS 487. Unpub. doct. diss., Univ. of Oxford. [Abstr. in IT (35) 542.]

3408. O'MARA, VERONICA M.   A Middle English versified penance composed of popular prayer tags. NQ (33:4) 449–50.

3409. PAYNE, ROBERTA LOUISE.   The influence of Dante on medieval English dream visions. Unpub. doct. diss., Univ. of Denver, 1985. [Abstr. in DA (46) 2688A.]

3410. PORTER, E.   The conduct of war as reflected in certain Middle English romances, with special reference to the alliterative *Morte Arthure*. Unpub. doct. diss., Queen's Univ., Belfast, 1984.

3411. PRICE, JOCELYN.   'Inner' and 'outer': conceptualizing the body in *Ancrene Wisse* and Aelred's *De institutis inclusarum*. *In* (pp. 192–208) **32.**

3412. QUINN, WILLIAM A.   Pagan parallels in the Prologue to *St Erkenwald*. Archiv (223:2) 350–3.

3413. RANSOM, DANIEL.   Poets at play: irony and parody in the Harley Lyrics. Norman, OK: Pilgrim, 1985. pp. xxx, 160. Rev. by Theo Stemmler in SAC (8) 233–6.

3414. REISS, EDMUND; REISS, LOUISE HORNER; TAYLOR, BEVERLY.   Arthurian legend and literature, an annotated bibliography: vol. 1, The Middle Ages. New York; London: Garland, 1984. pp. xvii, 467. (Garland reference library of the humanities, 415.) Rev. by Valerie M. Lagorio in Spec (61:4) 991–2; by Blake Lee Spahr in RPh (40:1) 123–6.

3415. RISSANEN, MATTI.   Middle English translations of Old English charters in the *Liber Monasterii de Hyda*: a case of historical error analysis. *In* (pp. 591–603) **26.**

3416. RIZZO, TANIA.   Sources for Medieval Studies in the libraries of the Claremont Colleges. *See* **3160.**

3417. RONBERG, GERT.   The two manuscripts of *The Wars of Alexander*: a linguistic comparison. *See* **173.**

3418. ROONEY, A.   Hunting in Middle English literature, 1300–1500. Unpub. doct. diss., Univ. of Cambridge. [Abstr. in IT (35) 1491.]

3419. Ross, D. J. A.   Studies in the Alexander Romance. London: Pindar, 1985. pp. 403.

3420. Ross, THOMAS W.; BROOKS, EDWARD (eds).   English glosses from British Library Additional Manuscript 37075. *See* **174.**

3421. SALTER, ELIZABETH.   Fourteenth century English poetry: contexts and readings. Ed. by DEREK PEARSALL and NICOLETTE ZEEMAN. (Cf. bibl. 1984, 2898, where title incorrect.) Rev. by John C. Hirsch in MÆ (55:2) 291–2.

3422. SCHEPS, WALTER; LOONEY, J. ANNA.   Middle Scots poets: a reference guide to James I of Scotland, Robert Henryson, William Dunbar, and Gavin Douglas. Boston, MA: G. K. Hall. pp. xvi, 292. Rev. by Priscilla Bawcutt in SLJ (supp. 25) 1–2.

3423. SCHIPPER, WILLIAM. Orthography and dialect in Cambridge University Library MS Ii.1.33. *See* **176.**

3424. SHUTT, TIMOTHY BAKER. *Logos* and *physis* – the word in the world: poetic uses of the stars during the Middle Ages and the Renaissance. Unpub. doct. diss., Univ. of Virginia, 1984. [Abstr. in DA (46) 1937A.]

3425. SIGAL, GALE. Aurora's ascent: conflict and desire in the medieval dawn-song. Unpub. doct. diss., City Univ. of New York, 1985. [Abstr. in DA (46) 3348A.]

3426. SKUBIKOWSKI, KATHLEEN M. A readers' edition of *Cursor Mundi*. Unpub. doct. diss., Indiana Univ., 1985. [Abstr. in DA (46) 3028A.]

3427. SPACKMAN, A. A critical edition of *The Court of Love*. Unpub. doct. diss., Univ. of Dundee, 1983.

3428. SPEARING, A. C. Medieval to Renaissance in English poetry. (Bibl. 1985, 2881.) Rev. by Tony Davenport in Eng (35) 159–64.

3429. SPENCER, HELEN L. The fortunes of a Lollard sermon-cycle in the later fifteenth century. MedStud (48) 352–96.

3430. STIELSTRA, DIANE. The portrayal of consciousness in medieval romance. Unpub. doct. diss., Indiana Univ., 1985. [Abstr. in DA (46) 3715A.]

3431. SZITTYA, PENN R. The antifraternal tradition in medieval literature. Princeton, NJ; Guildford: Princeton UP. pp. xvi, 316.

3432. TARVERS, JOSEPHINE KOSTER. The language of prayer in Middle English, 1200–1400. Unpub. doct. diss., Univ. of North Carolina at Chapel Hill, 1985. [Abstr. in DA (46) 3363A.]

3433. TAVORMINA, M. TERESA. A liturgical allusion in the *Scottish Legendary*: the largesse of St Lawrence. NQ (33:2) 154–7.

3434. THOMPSON, J. J. Robert Thornton and his book producing activities: aspects of the transmission of certain late medieval texts in the light of their present context in Thornton's manuscripts. *See* **186.**

3435. TORKAR, ROLAND. Cotton Vitellius A. xv (pt.1) and the *Legend of St Thomas*. EngS (67:4) 290–303.

3436. TORRES, HECTOR AVALOS. Bilingualism in medieval England: the Old French and Middle English versions of the *Ancrene Wisse*. Unpub. doct. diss., Univ. of Texas at Austin. [Abstr. in DA (47) 1716A–17A.]

3437. TRIGG, STEPHANIE. Israel Gollancz's *Wynnere and Wastoure*: political satire or editorial politics? *In* (pp. 115–27) **32.**

3438. VANEMAN, KAREN HASLANGER. Interpreting the Middle English romance: the audience in *Of Arthour and of Merlin*. Unpub. doct. diss., Wayne State Univ. [Abstr. in DA (47) 1316A.]

3439. VICARI, PATRICIA. *Sparagmos*: Orpheus among the Christians. *In* (pp. 63–83) JOHN WARDEN (ed.), Orpheus: the metamorphoses of a myth. Toronto: Toronto UP, 1982. pp. xiii, 238.

3440. VITTO, CINDY LYNN.   The virtuous pagan in Middle English literature. Unpub. doct. diss., Rice Univ., 1985. [Abstr. in DA (46) 1937A.]

3441. VON ERTZDORFF, XENJA; WYNN, MARIANNE (eds).   Liebe – Ehe – Ehebruch in der Literatur des Mittelalters. *See* **3178.**

3442. WALSH, RICHARD J.   International medieval bibliography: publications of January–June 1985. *See* **3180.**

3443. WATKINS, LOUISE WEBBER.   'Swiche cursed stories': incest in the Middle English romances. Unpub. doct. diss., Vanderbilt Univ. [Abstr. in DA (47) 1316A.]

3444. WHATLEY, GORDON.   Heathens and saints: *St Erkenwald* in its legendary context. Spec (61) 330–63.

3445. WHITE, H. R. B.   Nature and the natural man in some medieval English writers. Unpub. doct. diss., Univ. of Oxford. [Abstr. in IT (35) 542.]

3446. WILHELM, JAMES (ed.).   The romance of Arthur: vol. 2. New York; London: Garland. pp. 271.

3447. WILHELM, JAMES J.; GROSS, LAILA ZAMUELIS (eds).   The romance of Arthur. (Bibl. 1985, 2894.) Rev. by Blake Lee Spahr in RPh (39:4) 501–3.

3448. WILSON, KATHARINA M.   'Pig-in-a-poke': the topos of open-eyed spouse selection. CLS (23:3) 181–94. (Misogyny in medieval literature.)

3449. WINTERS, MARGARET (ed.).   *The Romance of Hunbaut*: an Arthurian poem of the thirteenth century. (Bibl. 1984, 2931.) Rev. by Gerald S. Giauque in Spec (61:4) 1012–13.

3450. WOLFZETTEL, FRIEDRICH (ed.).   Artusrittertum im späten Mittelalter. Ethos und Ideologie. Giessen: Schmitz, 1984. pp. 203. (Beiträge zur deutschen Philologie, 57.) Rev. by Volker Mertens in GRM (32) 232–7.

3451. ZETTERSTEN, ARNE.   Old and Middle English studies in the Nordic countries. *See* **3183.**

Drama

3452. ASHLEY, KATHLEEN M.   The resurrection of Lazarus in the late medieval English and French cycle drama. PLL (22:3) 227–44.

3453. BEADLE, RICHARD (ed.).   The York plays. (Bibl. 1985, 2902.) Rev. by O. S. Pickering in Archiv (222:2) 1985, 391–4.

3454. —— KING, PAMELA M. (eds).   York mystery plays: a selection in modern spelling. (Bibl. 1984, 3007.) Rev. by Meg Twycross in NQ (33:3) 404–5; by Darryll Grantley in SAC (8) 164–6.

3455. CAWLEY, A. C.   The Towneley *Processus Talentorum*: a survey and interpretation. Leeds Studies in English (17) 131–9.

3456. —— STEVENS, MARTIN (eds).   The Towneley *Processus Talentorum*: text and commentary. Leeds Studies in English (17) 105–30.

3457. CHURCH, JO HALL.   Discourse theory and deconstruction: the rhetoric of the York Cycle passion plays. Unpub. doct. diss., Texas Woman's Univ., 1985. [Abstr. in DA (46) 3357A.]

3458. Cooke, William G.   *The Tournament of Tottenham*: an alliterative poem and an Exeter performance. *See* **3319.**

3459. Cramer, James Douglas.   Theophany in the English Corpus Christi play. Unpub. doct. diss., Univ. of Michigan. [Abstr. in DA (47) 1928A.]

3460. Davidson, Clifford.   From creation to doom: the York cycle of mystery plays. (Bibl. 1985, 2909a.) Rev. by Richard Beadle in MÆ (55:2) 299.

3461. —— The lost Coventry Drapers' play of doomsday and its inconographic context. Leeds Studies in English (17) 141–58.

3462. Drumbl, Johann.   *Quem Quaeritis*: teatro sacro dell'alto medioevo. Rome: Bulzoni, 1981. pp. 401. Rev. by Anselme Davril in CompDr (20:1) 65–75.

3463. Fletcher, Alan J.   'Fart prycke in cule': a late-Elizabethan analogue from Ireland. METh (8:2) 134–9.

3464. Gash, Anthony.   Carnival against Lent: the ambivalence of medieval drama. *In* (pp. 74–98) **33.**

3465. Gómez Soliño, José S.   La utilización humorística de rasgos dialectales en The Reeve's Tale y *The Second Shepherds' Play*: interpretación sociolingüística. (Humorous use of dialectal features in The Reeve's Tale and *The Second Shepherds' Play*: sociolinguistic implications.) *See* **897.**

3466. Grantley, D. R.   A critical edition of the play of Mary Magdalene from Bodley MS Digby 133. Unpub. doct. diss., Univ. of London, Birkbeck Coll., 1983.

3467. Hanks, D. Thomas, Jr.   'Quicke Bookis' – the Corpus Christi drama and English children in the Middle Ages. JPC (19:4) 63–73.

3468. Happé, Peter (ed.).   Medieval English drama: a casebook. London: Macmillan, 1984. pp. 222. (Casebooks.)

3469. Higgins, Anne Thorn.   Time and the English Corpus Christi drama. Unpub. doct. diss., Yale Univ., 1985. [Abstr. in DA (46) 3358A.]

3470. Hildahl, Frances Erdey.   Dramaturgy and philosophy in *The Castle of Perseverance*: the issues of authority, power, and influence. Unpub. doct. diss., Univ. of Rochester, 1985. [Abstr. in DA (46) 3358A.]

3471. Homan, Richard L.   Devotional themes in the violence and humor of the *Play of the Sacrament*. CompDr (20:4) 327–40.

3472. Lancashire, Ian.   Dramatic texts and records of Britain: a chronological topography to 1558. Buffalo, NY; London: Toronto UP, 1984. (Cf. bibl. 1985, 2921.) Rev. by Gail McMurray Gibson in SAC (8) 215–19; by Kathleen M. Ashley in JEGP (85:1) 106–8.

3473. Lester, Geoffrey.   Holy Week processions in Seville. METh (8:2) 103–18.

3474. Levey, David.   The structure of *The Castle of Perseverance*. Literator (7:1) 48–57.

3475. Lumiansky, R. M.; Mills, David (eds).   The Chester mystery cycle: essays and documents. (Bibl. 1985, 2923.) Rev. by Richard Beadle in MÆ (55:2) 296–8.

3476. —— —— The Chester mystery cycle: vol. 2, Commentary and glossary. London: Early English Text Society; OUP. pp. xx, 465. (EETS, 8.)

3477. McDONALD, PETER. The Towneley cycle at Toronto. METh (8:1) 51–60.

3478. McRAE, MURDO WILLIAM. Everyman's last rites and the digression on priesthood. CLit (13:3) 305–9.

3479. MEREDITH, PETER; TAILBY, JOHN E. (eds). The staging of religious drama in the later Middle Ages: texts and documents in English translation. (Bibl. 1983, 3662.) Rev. by Helen Phillips in MÆ (55:2) 295–6; by G. A. Lester in EngS (67:4) 366–7.

3480. —— TYDEMAN, WILLIAM; RAMSAY, KEITH. Acting medieval plays. Lincoln: Honywood, 1985. pp. 56.

3481. MILLS, DAVID. *The Towneley Plays* or *The Towneley Cycle?* Leeds Studies in English (ns 17) 95–104.

3482. NICHOLS, ANN ELJENHOLM. Costume in the Moralities: the evidence of East Anglian art. CompDr (20:4) 305–14.

3483. PICKERING, KENNETH; WOOD, KEVIN; DART, PHILIP (adapters). The Mysteries at Canterbury cathedral. Ed. by SHIRLEY BENNETTS. Worthing: Churchman. pp. xii, 196.

3484. POTTER, ROBERT. The *Ordo Virtutum*: ancestor of the English Moralities? CompDr (20:3) 201–10.

3485. RICHARDS, DOUGLAS WILLIAM. Preachers and players: the contest between agents of sermon and game in the moral drama from *Mankind* to *Like Will to Like*. Unpub. doct. diss., Univ. of Rochester. [Abstr. in DA (47) 1337A.]

3486. TYDEMAN, WILLIAM. English medieval theatre, 1400–1500. London: Routledge & Kegan Paul. pp. 256. (Theatre production studies.) Rev. by Pamela M. King in THES (698) 26.

3487. VINCE, RONALD W. Ancient and medieval theatre; a historiographical handbook. (Bibl. 1985, 2939.) Rev. by Alan Woods in TS (30) 1983/84, 84.

Related Studies

3488. ALFORD, JOHN A.; SENIFF, DENNIS P. (eds). Literature and law in the Middle Ages: a bibliography of scholarship. (Bibl. 1985, 2946.) Rev. by Milija N. Pavlović in MLR (81:3) 697–700.

3489. ALLARD, GUY-H. (ed.). Jean Scot écrivain; actes du 4e colloque international 1983. Paris: Vrin; Bellarmin. pp. 368.

3490. ALTSCHUL, MICHAEL. Later medieval and Renaissance England: new perspectives on old issues. MedHum (14) 233–8 (review-article).

3491. ANDERSEN, LISE PRÆSTGAARD (ed.). Partalopa saga. Copenhagen: Reitzels, 1983. pp. ciii, 201. (Editiones Arnamagnænæ, ser. B, 28.) Rev. by Constance B. Hieatt in JEGP (85:1) 84–6.

3492. ANDREWS, KENNETH R. Trade, plunder and settlement: maritime enterprise and the genesis of the British Empire, 1480–1630. Cambridge: CUP, 1984. pp. x, 394. Rev. by Michael Altschul in MedHum (14) 233–8.

3493. Aston, T. H. (gen. ed.).   The history of the University of Oxford; vol. 1, The early Oxford schools. Ed. by J. I. Catto: asst ed. Ralph Evans. (Bibl. 1984, 2965.) Rev. by V. H. H. Green in MÆ (55:2) 275–8.

3494. Backhouse, Janet.   Books of hours. *See* **138.**

3495. Berschin, W. (ed.).   Lateinische Dichtungen des X und XI Jahrhunderts. Festgabe für Walter Bulst zum 80. Geburtstag. *See* **3185.**

3496. Boulton, Maureen Barry McCann (ed.).   The Old French *Evangile de l'Enfance.* Toronto: Pontifical Institute of Medieval Studies, 1984. pp. ix, 116. (Studies and texts, 70.) Rev. by Keith Busby in MÆ (55:2) 313–14.

3497. Bourke, P. M.   The treatment of myth and legend in the windows of St Neot's, Cornwall. *See* **2434.**

3498. Braswell, Laurel.   The moon and medicine in Chaucer's time. SAC (8) 145–56.

3499. Braswell, Mary Flowers.   Sin, the lady and the law: the English noblewoman in the late Middle Ages. MedHum (14) 81–101.

3500. Brown, Elizabeth A. R.   Georges Duby and the three orders. Viator (17) 51–64.

3501. Brownlee, Kevin.   Poetic identity in Guillaume de Machaut. Madison: Wisconsin UP, 1984. pp. x, 268. Rev. by C. R. Attwood in MÆ (55:2) 321–2; by Don A. Monson in MLR (81:2) 477–8; by André Crépin in SAC (8) 168–70.

3502. Brundage, James A.   'Allas! that evere love was synne': sex and medieval canon law. CathHR (72:1) 1–13.

3503. Bryant, Geoffrey F.   Domesday Book: how to read it and what its text means: the example of Waltham, Lincolnshire and district. Grimsby: Waltham Branch, Workers' Educational Assn, 1985. pp. 111.

3504. Buschinger, Danielle; Crépin, André (eds).   Comique, satire et parodie dans la tradition renardienne et les fabliaux: actes du colloque des 15 et 16 janvier, 1983. (Bibl. 1985, 2968.) Rev. by Roy J. Pearcy in Spec (61:1) 124–6.

3505. Bynum, Caroline Walker.   Fast, feast, and flesh: the religious significance of food to medieval women. Representations (11) 1985, 1–25.

3506. Cadden, Joan.   Medieval scientific and medical views of sexuality: questions of propriety. MedHum (14) 157–71.

3507. Chibnall, Marjorie.   Anglo-Norman England 1066–1166. Oxford: Blackwell. pp. 240.

3508. Colish, Marcia L.   The mirror of language: a study in the medieval theory of knowledge. (Bibl. 1985, 2973.) Rev. by James Simpson in MÆ (55:2) 123–5.

3509. Contamine, Philippe.   War in the Middle Ages. Trans. by Michael Jones. *See* **3192.**

3510. Dales, Richard C.   Robert Grosseteste's place in medieval discussions of the eternity of the world. Spec (61:3) 544–63.

3511. Davidson, Herbert A.   Averroes on the material intellect. Viator (17) 91–137.

3512. DAY, MILDRED LEAKE (ed.).   The rise of Gawain, nephew of Arthur. New York; London: Garland, 1984. pp. xliii, 131. (Garland library of medieval literature, A/15.) Rev. by Keith Busby in Spec (61:4) 913–15.

3513. DEMBOWSKI, PETER F.   Jean Froissart and his *Meliador*: context, craft and sense. Lexington, KY: French Forum, 1983. pp. 196. (Edward C. Armstrong monographs on medieval literature, 2.) Rev. by Ruth Morse in MÆ (55:2) 316–17.

3514. DOBOZY, MARIA.   Minstrel books: the legacy of Thomas Wright in German research. *See* **3022.**

3515. DRONKE, PETER.   Dante and medieval Latin traditions. Cambridge: CUP. pp. xiii, 153.

3516. —— Women writers of the Middle Ages: a critical study of texts from Perpetua (†203) to Marguerite Porete (†1310). (Bibl. 1985, 2982.) Rev. by Daniel Sheerin in SAC (8) 180–3; by Joan M. Ferrante in RQ (39:1) 67–9.

3517. DUFOURNET, JEAN (ed.).   Approches du Lancelot en prose. Paris: Librairie Honoré Champion, 1984. pp. 196. (Collection Unichamp.) Rev. by Elspeth Kennedy in MÆ (55:2) 311–12.

3518. EASTING, ROBERT.   Owein at Patrick's purgatory. MÆ (55:2) 159–75.

3519. FARMER, SHARON.   Persuasive voices: clerical images of medieval wives. Spec (61:3) 517–43.

3520. FLEMING, JOHN V.   Reason and the lover. (Bibl. 1985, 2989.) Rev. by C. H. L. Bodenham in MÆ (55:1) 145–7.

3521. FLORI, JEAN.   L'idéologie du glaive: préhistoire de la chevalerie. *See* **3201.**

3522. GAUNT, SIMON.   Did Marcabru know the Tristan legend? MÆ (55:1) 108–13.

3523. GIES, FRANCES.   The knight in history. New York: Harper & Row, 1984; London: Hale. pp. 256.

3524. GILLINGHAM, JOHN; HOLT, J. C. (eds).   War and government in the Middle Ages: essays in honour of J. O. Prestwich. Totowa NJ: Barnes & Noble, 1984. pp. xi, 198. Rev. by Michael Altschul in MedHum (14) 233–8.

3525. GLENDINNING, ROBERT.   Pyramus and Thisbe in the medieval classroom. Spec (61) 51–78.

3526. GRAFTON, ANTHONY; JARDINE, LISA.   From Humanism to the humanities: education and the liberal arts in fifteenth- and sixteenth-century Europe. London: Duckworth. pp. xvi, 224.

3527. HANSEN, WILLIAM F.   Saxo Grammaticus and the life of Hamlet: a translation, history, and commentary. (Bibl. 1983, 3611.) Rev. by Heather O. Donoghue in MÆ (55:2) 341; by John Reibetanz in RenR (9:4) 1985, 284–6.

3528. HIEATT, CONSTANCE B.; JONES, ROBIN F.   Two Anglo-Norman culinary collections edited from British Library manuscripts, Additional 32084 and Royal 12.C.xii. *See* **155.**

3529.   HILL, THOMAS D.   Odin, Rinda and Thaney, the mother of St Kentigern. *See* **3203.**

3530.   HOULBROOKE, RALPH A.   The English family 1450–1700. White Plains, NY: Longman, 1984. pp. 272. Rev. by Sherrin Marshall in SixCT (17:3) 380.

3531.   HULT, DAVID F.   Lancelot's two steps: a problem in textual criticism. *See* **313.**

3532.   —— Self-fulfilling prophecies: readership and authority in the first *Roman de la Rose.* Cambridge: CUP. pp. xx, 450.

3533.   HUNT, R. W.   The schools and the cloister: the life and writings of Alexander Nequam (1157–1217). Oxford: Clarendon Press; New York: OUP, 1984. pp. xiii, 165. Rev. by A. G. Rigg in Spec (61:3) 666–8.

3534.   ILLINGWORTH, R. N.   The structure of the Anglo-Norman *Voyage of St Brendan* by Benedeit. MÆ (55:2) 217–29.

3535.   KALINKE, MARIANNE E.; MITCHELL, P. M.   Bibliography of Old Norse-Icelandic romances. *See* **3205.**

3536.   KIBLER, WILLIAM W. (ed.).   The knight with the lion, or, Yvain: (Le chevalier au lion). New York; London: Garland, 1985. pp. xl, 331. (Garland library of medieval literature ser. A, 48.)

3537.   KIECKHEFER, RICHARD.   Unquiet souls: fourteenth-century saints and their religious milieu. (Bibl. 1985, 3004.) Rev. by Marianne E. Kalinke in JEGP (85:1) 96–7.

3538.   KITTLESON, JAMES M.; TRANSUE, PAMELA J. (eds).   Rebirth, reform, and resilience: universities in transition, 1300–1700. Columbus: Ohio State UP, 1984. pp. 368. Rev. by C. B. Schmitt in RQ (39:1) 76–8.

3539.   KOHL, STEPHAN.   Das englische Spätmittelalter. Kulturelle Normen, Lebenspraxis, Texte. Tübingen: Niemeyer. pp. viii, 270. (Studien zur englischen Philologie, Neue Folge, 24.)

3540.   KROLL, JEROME; BACHRACH, BERNARD.   Sin and the etiology of disease in pre-crusade Europe. JHM (41:4) 395–414.

3541.   KROLL, RENATE.   Der narrative Lai als eigenständige Gattung in der Literatur des Mittelalters. Zum Strukturprinzip der 'Aventure' in den Lais. Tübingen: Niemeyer, 1984. pp. vii, 234. (Beihefte zur Zeitschrift für romanische Philologie, 201.) Rev. by Karen Pratt in MÆ (55:2) 309–10.

3542.   LAPIDGE, MICHAEL; SHARPE, RICHARD.   A bibliography of Celtic-Latin literature 400–1200. *See* **3209.**

3543.   LECOUTEUX, CLAUDE.   Fantômes et revenants au moyen âge. Paris: Imago. pp. 253.

3544.   LESTER, G. A.   The *Mystère d'Adam* and English pictorial iconography. Lore & Language (5:1) 79–85.

3545.   LÖFFLER, CHRISTA MARIA.   The voyage to the otherworld island in early Irish literature (Bibl. 1984, 2943.) Rev. by J. E. Caerwyn Williams in MÆ (55:1) 127–8.

3546.   MERTENS, VOLKER; MÜLLER, ULRICH (eds).   Epische Stoffe des Mittelalters. *See* **3211.**

3547.   MIQUET, J. (ed.).   *Fierabras*: roman en prose de la fin du XIVe siècle; publié d'après les manuscrits fonds français 4969 et 2172 de la

Bibliothèque Nationale à Paris. Ottawa: Éditions de l'Université d'Ottawa, 1983 pp. 210. Rev. by M. J. Ailes in MÆ (55:1) 317–18.

3548. Moi, Toril.   Desire in language: Andreas Capellanus and the controversy of courtly love. *In* (pp. 11–33) **33.**

3549. Moran, J. Ann Hoeppner.   The growth of English schooling, 1340–1548: learning, literature, and laicization in pre-Reformation York diocese. (Bibl. 1985, 3016.) Rev. by Malcolm C. Burson in Spec (61:4) 971–3.

3550. Muir, Lynette.   Literature and society in medieval France: the mirror and the image 1100–1500. London: Macmillan, 1985. pp. 224. (New studies in medieval history.)

3551. Muscatine, Charles.   The Old French fabliaux. New Haven, CT; London: Yale UP. pp. xii, 219.

3552. Noble, Peter S.; Paterson, Linda M. (eds).   Chrétien de Troyes and the Troubadours: essays in memory of the late Leslie Topsfield. (Bibl. 1985, 3019.) Rev. by Sarah Kay in MÆ (55:1) 144–5.

3553. Norton, Christopher; Park, David (eds).   Cistercian art and architecture in the British Isles. Cambridge: CUP. pp. x, 453, (plates) 190.

3554. Ólason, Vésteinn.   The traditional ballads of Iceland: historical studies. Reykjavík: Stofnun Árna Magnússonar, 1982. pp. 418. Rev. by Patricia Conroy in JEGP (85:1) 86–7.

3555. Orme, Nicholas.   From childhood to chivalry: the education of English kings and aristocracy (1066–1530). New York: Methuen, 1984. (Cf. bibl. 1985, 3022.) Rev. by Elaine Clark in Spec (61:4) 977–9.

3556. Palmer, R. Barton (ed.).   Guillaume de Machaut: *The Judgment of the King of Bohemia* (*Le Jugement dou Roy de Behaingne*). (Bibl. 1985, 3024.) Rev. by Angela Dzelzainis in MÆ (55:2) 322–3.

3557. Paterson, Linda.   Tournaments and knightly sports in twelfth- and thirteenth-century Occitania. MÆ (55:1) 72–84.

3558. Pereiah, Alan R. (trans.).   Paulus Venetus: *Logica Parva*: a translation of the 1472 edition. Munich; Vienna: Philosophia; Washington, DC.: Catholic Univ. of America, 1984. pp. 375. Rev. by William E. McMahon in Spec (61:4) 979–81.

3559. Reames, Sherry L.   The *Legenda aurea*: a reexamination of its paradoxical history. Princeton, NJ: Princeton UP, 1985. pp. 321. Rev. by Eugene F. Rice, Jr, in RQ (39:2) 279–82.

3560. Rejhon, Annalee C.   *Cân Rolant*: the medieval Welsh version of the *Song of Roland*. Berkeley: California UP, 1984. pp. x, 264. (Univ. of California pubs in modern philology, 113.) Rev. by Ceridwen Lloyd-Morgan in MÆ (55:1) 147–8.

3561. Ribard, Jacques.   Le moyen âge: littérature et symbolisme. Paris: Champion, 1984. pp. 168. Rev. by Keith Busby in MÆ (55:1) 138–9.

3562. Rollason, D. W. (ed.).   Goscelin of Canterbury's account of the translation and miracles of St Mildrith (*BHL* 5961/4): an edition with notes. MedStud (48) 139–210.

3563. Russell, Jeffrey Burton.   Lucifer: the devil in the Middle

Ages. (Bibl. 1985, 3034.) Rev. by Allan E. Bernstein in Spec (61:4) 994–7.

3564. SANDQVIST, SVEN.   Notes textuelles sur le *Roman de Tristan* de Beroul. Lund: Gleerup, 1984. pp. 169. (Études Romanes de Lund, 39.) Rev. by Stewart Gregory in MÆ (55:2) 310–11.

3565. SAUL, NIGEL.   Scenes from provincial life: knightly families in Sussex 1280–1400. Oxford: Clarendon Press. pp. 300.

3566. SCARISBRICK, J. J.   The Reformation and the English people. Oxford: Blackwell, 1984. pp. viii, 203. Rev. by Michael Altschul in MedHum (14) 233–8.

3567. SCHACH, PAUL.   Instant saga style: the evidence of the manuscripts. *See* **175.**

3568. SHORT, IAN (ed.).   Medieval French textual studies in memory of T. B. W. Reid. (Bibl. 1985, 3038.) Rev. by A. J. Holden in MÆ (55:1) 139–42.

3569. SINCLAIR, K. V.   The Anglo-Norman miracles of the foundation of the hospital of St John in Jerusalem. MÆ (55:1) 102–8.

3570. SOUTHERN, R. W.   Robert Grosseteste: the growth of an English mind in medieval Europe. Oxford: Clarendon Press. pp. 300.

3571. SWANTON, MICHAEL (trans. and ed.).   Three lives of the last Englishmen. *See* **3237.**

3572. TAYLOR, JANE H. M. (ed.).   *Dies illa*: death in the Middle Ages. Proceedings of the 1983 Manchester Colloquium. Liverpool: Cairns, 1984. pp. 223. (Vinaver studies in French, 1.) Rev. by Peter S. Noble in MÆ (55:1) 129.

3573. TOWNSEND, DAVID.   Robert Grosseteste and Walter of Wimborne. MÆ (55:1) 113–17.

3574. VERBEKE, GERARD.   The presence of stoicism in medieval thought. (Bibl. 1984, 2999.) Rev. by Armand Maurer in JHP (24:2) 264–6.

3575. WALLACE, KATHRYN YOUNG (ed.).   *La Estoire de Seint Aedward le Rei*: attributed to Matthew Paris. London: Anglo-Norman Text Soc., 1983. pp. l, 181. (Anglo-Norman texts, 41.) Rev. by Brian J. Levy in MÆ (55:2) 272–3.

3576. WEISHEIPL, JAMES A.   Nature and motion in the Middle Ages. Ed. by WILLIAM E. CARROLL. Washington, DC: Catholic UP of America, 1985. pp. xii, 292.

3577. WEISS, JUDITH.   The date of the Anglo-Norman *Boeve de Haumtone*. MÆ (55:2) 237–41.

3578. WILLIMAN, DANIEL (ed.).   The Black Death: the impact of the fourteenth century plague. Papers of the eleventh Annual Conference of the Center for Medieval and Early Renaissance Studies. Binghamton, NY: Center for Medieval and Early Renaissance Studies, 1982. pp. 159. (Medieval and Renaissance Texts and Studies, 13.) Rev. by Glending Olson in SAC (8) 264–6.

3579. WOOD, REGA; GÁL, GEDEON; GREEN, R. (eds).   Generalibus inceptoris Guillelmi de Ockham: '*Quaestiones in Librum Quartum*

Sententiarum (reportatio)'. (Bibl. 1985, 2711.) Rev. by Williell R. Thomson in Spec (61:2) 483–4.

3580. WRIGHT, NEIL (ed.).   The *Historia regum Britannie* of Geoffrey of Monmouth: 1, Bern, Burgerbibliothek, MS 568. Cambridge: Brewer, 1985. pp. lxv, 174. Rev. by J. D. Burnley in EngS (67:5) 450–1.

AUTHORS
(except Chaucer and the Gawain Poet)
John Capgrave

3581. SEYMOUR, M. C.   The manuscripts of John Capgrave's English works. *See* **178.**

William Caxton

3582. BLAKE, N. F.   William Caxton: a bibliographical guide. New York; London: Garland, 1985. pp. x, 227. (Garland reference library of the humanities, 524.)

3583. HAMER, R.   Jean Golein's *Festes nouvelles*: a Caxton source. MÆ (55:2) 254–60.

3584. NEEDHAM, PAUL.   The printer & the pardoner: an unrecorded indulgence printed by William Caxton for the Hospital of St Mary Rounceval, Charing Cross. Washington, DC: Library of Congress. pp. 101. Rev. by Martha Driver in ABC (7:9) 44–6.

3585. SMITH, JEREMY J.   Some spellings in Caxton's Malory. PoetT (24) 58–63.

3586. SPISAK, JAMES W. (ed.).   Caxton's Malory: a new edition of Sir Thomas Malory's *Le Morte Darthur*, based on the Pierpont Morgan copy of William Caxton's edition of 1483. (Bibl. 1985, 3064.) Rev. by J. M. Cowen in MÆ (55:2) 303–4; by Tsuyoshi Mukai in SEL (English number) 85–99.

Charles of Orleans

3587. YENAL, EDITH.   Charles d'Orléans: a bibliography of primary and secondary sources. New York: Aris Press, 1984. pp. 103. Rev. by Mary-Jo Arn in EngS (67:1) 75–8.

Colman (d. 1113)

3588. SWANTON, MICHAEL (trans. and ed.).   Three lives of the last Englishmen. *See* **3237.**

Gavin Douglas

3589. AMSLER, MARK E.   The quest for the present tense: the poet and the dreamer in Douglas' *The Palice of Honour*. SSL (17) 1982, 186–208.

3590. PARKINSON, DAVID.   Mobbing scenes in Middle Scots verse: Holland, Douglas, Dunbar. JEGP (85:4) 494–509.

William Dunbar

3591. BAWCUTT, PRISCILLA.   Dunbar and an epigram. SLJ (13:2) 16–19.

3592. FINKELSTEIN, RICHARD.   Amplification in William Dunbar's aureate poetry. SLJ (13:2) 5–15.

3593. HAMBLIN, MARY ELIZABETH.   Dunbar's style. Unpub. doct. diss., Emory Univ., 1985. [Abstr. in DA (47) 173A.]

3594. KING, PAMELA M.   Dunbar's *The Golden Targe*: a Chaucerian masque. SSL (19) 1984, 115–31.
3595. PARKINSON, DAVID.   Mobbing scenes in Middle Scots verse: Holland, Douglas, Dunbar. *See* **3590.**

John Gower

3596. GITTES, KATHARINE S.   Ulysses in Gower's *Confessio Amantis*: the Christian soul as silent rhetorician. ELN (24:2) 7–14.
3597. MINNIS, A. J. (ed.).   Gower's *Confessio Amantis*: responses and reassessments. (Bibl. 1985, 3076.) Rev. by Hugh White in MÆ (55:2) 289–90.
3598. NICHOLSON, PETER.   The 'confession' in Gower's *Confessio Amantis*. SN (58:2) 193–204.
3599. RUNACRES, C. A. J.   Moral judgement and the individual in John Gower's *Confessio Amantis*. Unpub. doct. diss., Univ. of Bristol, 1985. [Abstr. in IT (36) 910.]
3600. SMITH, J. J.   Studies in the language of some manuscripts of Gower's *Confessio Amantis*. Unpub. doct. diss., Univ. of Glasgow, 1985. [Abstr. in IT (36) 469.]
3601. WICKERT, MARIA.   Studies in John Gower. (Bibl. 1983, 3707.) Rev. by R. F. Yeager in MLR (81:1) 166–7.
3602. WRIGHT, STEPHEN K.   Gower's Geta and the sin of supplantation. NM (87:2) 211–17.

Thomas de Hales

3603. BISHOP, IAN.   Lapidary formulas as topics of invention – from Thomas of Hales to Henryson. *See* **3295.**

Robert Henryson

3604. BISHOP, IAN.   Lapidary formulas as topics of invention – from Thomas of Hales to Henryson. *See* **3295.**
3605. DUNCAN, F. M. M.   Robert Henryson: a critical and biographical study. Unpub. doct. diss., Univ. of Aberdeen, 1983.
3606. McDIARMID, MATTHEW P.   Robert Henryson. (Bibl. 1983, 3711.) Rev. by J. H. Alexander in YES (16) 231–4.
3607. MURPHY, COLETTE.   Henryson's mice: three animals of style. PoetT (23) 53–73.
3608. POWELL, MARIANNE.   *Fabula docet*: studies in the background and interpretation of Henryson's *Morall Fabillis*. (Bibl. 1985, 3090.) Rev. by Sally Mapstone in MÆ (55:2) 300.

Thomas Hoccleve

3609. TORTI, ANNA.   Mirroring in Hoccleve's *Regement of Princes*. PoetT (24) 39–57.

Richard Holland

3610. PARKINSON, DAVID.   Mobbing scenes in Middle Scots verse: Holland, Douglas, Dunbar. *See* **3590.**
3611. RIDDY, FELICITY J.   Dating *The Buke of the Howlat*. RES (37:145) 1–10.

Margery Kempe

3612. BECKWITH, SARAH.   A very material mysticism: the medieval mysticism of Margery Kempe. *In* (pp. 34–57) **33.**

William Langland
3613. AERS, DAVID.   Reflections on the 'allegory of the theologians', ideology and *Piers Plowman. In* (pp. 58–73) **33.**

3614. ALLEN, JUDSON BOYCE.   Langland's reading and writing: *detractor* and the pardon passus. Spec (59) 1984, 342–62.

3615. BARR, HELEN.   The use of Latin quotations in *Piers Plowman* with special reference to Passus XVIII of the 'B' text. NQ (33:4) 440–8.

3616. DONALDSON, E. TALBOT.   Long Will's apology: a translation. *In* (pp. 30–4) **32.**

3617. DOYLE, A. I.   Remarks on surviving manuscripts of *Piers Plowman. In* (pp. 35–48) **32.**

3618. ECONOMOU, GEORGE D.   The vision's aftermath in *Piers Plowman*: the poetics of the Middle English dream-vision. Genre (18:4) 1985, 313–21.

3619. FINLAY, ALISON.   The warrior Christ and the unarmed hero. *In* (pp. 19–29) **32.**

3620. FREDELL, JOEL WILLIS.   Medieval portraiture and the roots of late gothic aesthetics. Unpub. doct. diss., Indiana Univ., 1985. [Abstr. in DA (47) 895A.]

3621. GRAY, N. J.   A study of *Piers Plowman* in relation to the medieval penitential tradition. Unpub. doct. diss., Univ. of Cambridge, 1984. [Abstr. in IT (35) 542.]

3622. GRAY, NICK.   The clemency of cobblers: a reading of Glutton's confession in *Piers Plowman*. Leeds Studies in English (17) 61–75.

3623. —— Langland's quotations from the penitential tradition. MP (84:1) 53–60.

3624. GRIFFITHS, LAVINIA.   Personification in *Piers Plowman*. Cambridge: Brewer; Dover, NH: Boydell & Brewer, 1985. pp. 230. (*Piers Plowman* studies, 3.) Rev. by Elizabeth D. Kirk in SAC (8) 195–6.

3625. HUGHES, M. E. J.   Modes of satire in medieval literature, with special reference to *Piers Plowman*. Unpub. doct. diss., Univ. of Cambridge. [Abstr. in IT (36) 469.]

3626. KERBY-FULTON, K. E.   The voice of honest indignation: a study of reformist apocalypticism in relation to *Piers Plowman*. Unpub. doct. diss., Univ. of York. [Abstr. in IT (36) 469.]

3627. NORTON-SMITH, JOHN.   William Langland. (Bibl. 1985, 3123.) Rev. by John A. Alford in Spec (61:1) 192–5.

3628. PHILLIPS, J. C.   Style and meaning in *Piers Plowman*. Unpub. doct. diss., Univ. of York. [Abstr. in IT (35) 1083.]

3629. SAITO, TOMOKO.   Piers the Plowman: *Petrus, id est, Christus* saiko. (Piers the Plowman: a second thought on *Petrus, id est, Christus*.) StudME (1) 107–21.

3630. SCHMIDT, A. V. C.   The inner dreams in *Piers Plowman*. MÆ (55:1) 24–40.

3631. SIMPSON, JAMES.   'Et vidit deus cogitaciones eorum': a parallel instance and possible source for Langland's use of a Biblical formula at *Piers Plowman* B.XV.200a. NQ (33:1) 9–13.

3632. —— From reason to affective knowledge: modes of thought and poetic form in *Piers Plowman*. MÆ (55:1) 1–23.

3633. —— The role of *scientia* in *Piers Plowman*. *In* (pp. 49–65) **32**.

3634. —— The transformation of meaning: a figure of thought in *Piers Plowman*. RES (37:146) 161–83.

3635. STOKES, MYRA. Justice and mercy in *Piers Plowman*: a reading of the B text Visio. Canberra: Croom Helm, 1984. (Cf. bibl. 1984, 3127.) Rev. by Anna Baldwin in MÆ (55:2) 290–1; by A. V. C. Schmidt in NQ (33:2) 211–12.

3636. SWANSON, R. N. Langland and the priest's title. NQ (33:4) 438–40.

3637. THORNE, J. R.; UHART, MARIE-CLAIRE. Robert Crowley's *Piers Plowman*. MÆ (55:2) 248–54.

3638. WALDRON, R. A. Langland's originality: the Christ-knight and the Harrowing of Hell. *In* (pp. 66–81) **32**.

3639. WHITE, HUGH. Langland's *Ymaginatif, kynde* and the *Benjamin Major*. *See* **1617**.

Layamon

3640. IWASAKI, HARUO. Case and rhyme in Laȝamon's *Brut*. *In* (pp. 387–95) **26**.

3641. —— A few notes on the vocabulary of Laȝamon's *Brut*. *See* **1544**.

3642. LE SAUX, FRANÇOISE. Laȝamon's Welsh sources. EngS (67:5) 385–93.

3643. NOBLE, JAMES. The four-stress hemistich in Laȝamon's *Brut*. *See* **2940**.

Leofric of Bourne

3644. SWANTON, MICHAEL (trans. and ed.). Three lives of the last Englishmen. *See* **3237**.

Nicholas Love

3645. JOHNSON, I. R. The Latin source of Nicholas Love's *Mirrour of the Blessed Lyf of Jesu Christ*: a reconsideration. NQ (33:2) 157–60.

John Lydgate

3646. EBIN, LOIS A. John Lydgate. Boston, MA: G. K. Hall, 1985. pp. vii, 163. (Twayne's English authors, 407.) Rev. by A. S. G. Edwards in SAC (8) 183–5.

3647. EDWARDS, A. S. G. Lydgate's use of Chaucer: structure, strategy and style. RCEI (10) 175–82.

3648. MOSSER, DANIEL W. The two scribes of the Cardigan manuscript and the 'evidence' of scribal supervision and shop production. *See* **167**.

Richard Maidstone

3649. EDDEN, VALERIE. Richard Maidstone's *Penitential Psalms*. Leeds Studies in English (17) 77–94.

Sir Thomas Malory

3650. ANDERSON, EARL R. Malory's 'Fair maid of Ascolat'. NM (87:2) 237–54.

3651. CLOUGH, ANDREA. Malory's *Morte Darthur*: the 'hoole book'. MedHum (14) 139–56.

3652. LEMMEDU, BEVERLY.   Knighthood in the *Morte Darthur*. Cambridge: Brewer, 1985. pp. ix, 394. (Arthurian studies, 11.)

3653. McCARTHY, TERENCE.   Private worlds in *Le Morte Darthur*. EA (39:1) 3–14.

3654. MORSE, MARGARET LOUISE.   Love's governance versus the king's: the transformation of the cart episode. Unpub. doct. diss., Univ. of North Carolina at Chapel Hill, 1985. [Abstr. in DA (47) 172A.]

3655. ROSS, MEREDITH JANE.   The sublime to the ridiculous: the restructuring of Arthurian materials in selected modern novels. Unpub. doct. diss., Univ. of Wisconsin–Madison, 1985. [Abstr. in DA (46) 3717A.]

3656. SANDERS, ARNOLD ALLEN, JR.   'Hyd wythyn the bodye': the narrative logic of Sir Thomas Malory. Unpub. doct. diss., Brown Univ. [Abstr. in DA (47) 1736A.]

3657. SMITH, JEREMY J.   Some spellings in Caxton's Malory. *See* **3585.**

3658. WHITAKER, MURIEL.   Arthur's kingdom of adventure; the world of Malory's *Morte Darthur*. (Bibl. 1984, 3149.) Rev. by J. D. Burnley in EngS (67:1) 81–2; by P. J. C. Field in MÆ (55:2) 304; by Maureen Halsall in ESCan (12:1) 101–5.

3659. WYATT, JAMES LEO.   The ways of worship: motif patterns in Sir Thomas Malory's *Tale of Gareth*. Unpub. doct. diss., Univ. of Kentucky. [Abstr. in DA (47) 918A.]

Sir John Mandeville

3660. MANUEL CUENCA, CARMEN.   Elementos fantásticos en *Los viajes de Juan de Mandeville*. (Fantastic elements in *The Travels of Sir John Mandeville*.) Atlantis (8) 20–35.

Robert Mannyng

3661. SMALLWOOD, T. M.   Another example of the double-copying of a passage of Middle English. *See* **181.**

3662. SULLENS, IDELLE (ed.).   Robert Mannyng of Brunne: *Handlyng Synne*. Binghamton, NY: Center for Medieval and Early Renaissance Studies, 1983. pp. xlvi, 382. (Medieval and Renaissance texts and studies, 14.) Rev. by B. S. Lee in UCTSE (15) 70–1; by Judith Weiss in MÆ (55:1) 132–4; by O. S. Pickering in NQ (33:2) 210–11.

Henry Medwall

3663. CRUPI, CHARLES W.   Christian doctrine in Henry Medwall's *Nature*. Ren (34:2) 1982, 100–12.

3664. FLETCHER, ALAN J.   'Fart prycke in cule': a late-Elizabethan analogue from Ireland. *See* **3463.**

The Paston Family

3665. LESTER, G. A.   Sir John Paston's *Grete Boke*: a descriptive catalogue, with an introduction, of British Library MS Lansdowne 285. (Bibl. 1985, 3157.) Rev. by P. R. Robinson in SAC (8) 222–4.

John Purvey

3666. YONEKURA, HIROSHI.   John Purvey's version of the Wycliffite Bible: a reconsideration of his translation method. StudME (1) 67–91.

Richard Rolle

3667. BOURCIER, GEORGES.   Remarques sur les dérivés chez Richard Rolle: où en est la morphologie? *In* (pp. 211–20) **26.**

John Wyclif

3668. HUDSON, ANNE (ed.).   English Wycliffite sermons: vol. 1. (Bibl. 1985, 143.) Rev. by John A. Alford in MP (84:1) 67–9.

3669. KENNY, ANTHONY.   Wyclif. Oxford; New York: OUP, 1985. pp. ix, 115. Rev. by Anthony Tuck in SAC (8) 213–15; by Michael Altschul in MedHum (14) 233–8; by A. S. McGrade in RQ (39:3) 514–15.

3670. VON NOLCKEN, CHRISTINA.   An unremarked group of Wycliffite sermons in Latin. MP (83:3) 233–49.

3671. YONEKURA, HIROSHI.   The language of the Wycliffite Bible: the syntactic differences between the two versions. *See* **1908.**

GEOFFREY CHAUCER

General Studies,
and Works other than *The Canterbury Tales* and
Troilus and Criseyde

3672. AERS, DAVID.   Chaucer. Brighton: Harvester Press. pp. xi, 121. (Harvester new readings.) Rev. by Stanley Hussey in THES (721) 16.

3673. BAGHDIKIAN, SONIA.   Ambiguity on two levels: morphological and structural. *See* **1862.**

3674. BAIRD-LANGE, LORRAYNE Y.; BOWERS, BEGE.   An annotated Chaucer bibliography, 1984. SAC (8) 279–336.

3675. BIRNEY, EARLE.   Essays on Chaucerian irony. Ed., with an essay on irony, by BERYL ROWLAND. Toronto; Buffalo, NY; London: Toronto UP, 1985. pp. xxx, 162. Rev. by Bernard O'Donoghue in THES (704) 20.

3676. BLAKE, N. F.   *The Book of the Duchess* again. EngS (67:2) 122–5.

3677. BOITANI, PIERO; MANN, JILL (eds).   The Cambridge Chaucer companion. Cambridge: CUP. pp. 274.

3678. BOWERS, BEGE K. (comp.).   Chaucer research in progress: 1985–1986. NM (87:3) 437–55.

3679. BREWER, DEREK.   An introduction to Chaucer. (Bibl. 1985, 3180.) Rev. by C. Joy Watkin in CritQ (28:4) 97–8.

3680. BUCKLER, PATRICIA PRANDINI.   The fourteenth century environment of discourse: rhetoric and imagination in Chaucer's audience. Unpub. doct. diss., Univ. of Louisville. [Abstr. in DA (47) 2153A.]

3681. BUCKMASTER, ELIZABETH.   Meditation and memory in Chaucer's *House of Fame*. MLS (16:3) 279–87.

3682. BURNLEY, DAVID.   Courtly speech in Chaucer. PoetT (24) 16–38.

3683. —— A guide to Chaucer's language. (Bibl. 1985, 3182.) Rev. by E. Guy in Ariel (17:2) 79–81.

3684. —— Some terminology of perception in the *Book of the Duchess*. ELN (23:3) 15–22.

3685. BURNLEY, J. D.   Chaucer's landscape and the philosophers' tradition. (Bibl. 1983, 3803.) Rev. by Rita Copeland in RPh (40:1) 135–8.

3686. —— Curial prose in England. *See* **3310.**

3687. CORMAN, CATHERINE TALMAGE.   'Whereas a man may have noon audience, noght helpeth it to tellen his sentence': rhetorical process in Chaucer's poetry. Unpub. doct. diss., Univ. of California, Los Angeles, 1985. [Abstr. in DA (47) 173A.]

3688. DESMOND, MARILYNN.   Chaucer's *Aeneid*: 'the naked text in English'. PCP (19) 1984, 62–7. (*Dido*.)

3689. DE WEEVER, JACQUELINE.   Chaucer's moon: Cinthia, Diana, Latona, Lucina, Prosperpina. Names (34:2) 1984, 154–74.

3690. DONALDSON, E. TALBOT.   The swan at the well: Shakespeare reading Chaucer. (Bibl. 1985, 3189.) Rev. by Derek Pearsall in ELN (24:2) 69–71; by A. C. Spearing in RQ (39:4) 804–6; by S. G. Kossick in UES (24:1) 31–2; by Morton W. Bloomfield in SAC (8) 177–9.

3691. DUȚESCU, DAN (trans. and ed.).   Legenda femeilor cinstitie și alte poeme. (*The Legend of Good Women* and other poems.) Bucharest: Cartea Românească. pp. 448.

3692. EDWARDS, A. S. G.   Chaucer's *House of Fame*. Exp (44:2) 4–5.

3693. —— Lydgate's use of Chaucer: structure, strategy and style. *See* **3647.**

3694. FERSTER, JUDITH.   Chaucer on interpretation. Cambridge: CUP, 1985. pp. x, 194. Rev. by Ruth A. Cameron in ChrisL (36:1) 29–30; by Stanley Hussey in THES (721) 16; by C. Joy Watkin in CritQ (28:4) 104; by A. C. Spearing in EC (86:1) 68–75.

3695. FINLAYSON, JOHN.   Seeing, hearing and knowing in *The House of Fame*. SN (58:1) 47–57.

3696. FYLER, JOHN M.   '"Cloude", – and al that y of spak': *The House of Fame*, v. 978. NM (87:4) 565–8.

3697. GILLMEISTER, HEINER.   Chaucer's conversion: allegorical thought in medieval literature. (Bibl. 1985, 3197.) Rev. by James Dean in Spec (61:1) 151–3; by Russell Hope Robbins in SAC (8) 188–91.

3698. HARDMAN, PHILLIPA.   Chaucer's Muses and his 'Art Poetical'. RES (37:148) 478–94.

3699. HEFFERNAN, CAROL FALVO.   That dog again: *melancholia canina* and Chaucer's *Book of the Duchess*. MP (84:2) 185–90.

3700. HERMANN, JOHN P.; BURKE, JOHN J. (eds).   Signs and symbols in Chaucer's poetry. (Bibl. 1984, 3188.) Rev. by John M. Fyler in YES (16) 230–1.

3701. HOLLAND, NORMAN N.   The miller's wife and the professors: questions about the transactive theory of reading. *See* **2206.**

3702. JEFFREY, DAVID LYLE (ed.).   Chaucer and scriptural tradition. (Bibl. 1985, 3202.) Rev. by David C. Fowler in SAC (8) 203–9; by M. Teresa Tavormina in JEGP (85:1) 99–102.

3703. KANE, GEORGE.   Chaucer. New York: OUP, 1984. (Cf. bibl.

1985, 3204.) Rev. by Donald R. Howard in SAC (8) 209–10; by C. Joy Watkin in CritQ (28:4) 96–7; by Paul G. Ruggiers in Spec (61:4) 945–6.

3704. KAYLOR, NOEL HAROLD, JR. The medieval translations of Boethius' *Consolation of Philosophy* in England, France, and Germany: an analysis and annotated bibliography. *See* **3125.**

3705. KING, PAMELA M. Dunbar's *The Golden Targe*: a Chaucerian masque. *See* **3594.**

3706. KNIGHT, STEPHEN. Geoffrey Chaucer. Oxford: Blackwell. pp. x, 173. (Rereading literature.) Rev. by Pamela M. King in THES (728) 18.

3707. LAWTON, DAVID. Chaucer's narrators. Woodbridge: Boydell & Brewer. pp. 166. Rev. by Bernard O'Donoghue in THES (704) 20; by C. Joy Watkin in CritQ (28:4) 102–4.

3708. LEYERLE, JOHN; QUICK, ANNE. Chaucer, a bibliographical introduction. Toronto; London: Toronto UP. pp. xx, 321. (Toronto medieval bibliographies, 10.)

3709. LYNCH, ANDREW. 'Taking keep' of the *Book of the Duchess. In* (pp. 167–78) **32.**

3710. MACHAN, TIM WILLIAM. Techniques of translation: Chaucer's *Boece.* Norman, OK: Pilgrim, 1985. pp. ix, 163. Rev. by A. J. Minnis in SAC (8) 225–9.

3711. MEHL, DIETER. Geoffrey Chaucer: an introduction to his narrative poetry. Cambridge: CUP. pp. 256.

3712. MINNIS, A. J. Chaucer and pagan antiquity. (Bibl. 1985, 3213.) Rev. by John M. Fyler in MLR (81:3) 704–6.

3713. MOSS, R. Burlesque rhetoric in Chaucer, Nashe and Sterne. Unpub. doct. diss., Univ. of Sussex, 1982.

3714. MOSSER, DANIEL WAYNE. The Cardigan Chaucer manuscript and the process of fifteenth-century book production. *See* **168.**

3715. ONO, MANA. Chaucer no Boece yakuni tsuite: 'gentilesse' wo chushin ni. *See* **1607.**

3716. PEARSALL, DEREK. Chaucer's poetry and its modern commentators: the necessity of history. *In* (pp. 123–47) **33.**

3717. PHILLIPS, HELEN. *The Book of the Duchess*, lines 31–96: are they a forgery? EngS (67:2) 113–21.

3718. —— (ed.). The Book of the Duchess. (Bibl. 1985, 3218.) Rev. by A. Inskip Dickerson in Spec (61:1) 128–30.

3719. PRIOR, SANDRA PIERSON. *Routhe* and *hert-huntyng* in the *Book of the Duchess. See* **1610.**

3720. RUGGIERS, PAUL G. (ed.). Editing Chaucer: the great tradition. (Bibl. 1985, 3222.) Rev. by N. F. Blake in MLR (81:4) 975–6; by George R. Keiser in JEGP (85:1) 251–3; by A. I. Doyle in Spec (61:3) 700–4; by John H. Fisher in SAC (8) 239–41.

3721. SANDVED, ARTHUR O. Introduction to Chaucerian English. Cambridge: Brewer; Dover, NH: Boydell & Brewer, 1985. pp. x, 107. (Chaucer studies, 11.) Rev. by Roger Lass in NM (87:4) 599–605; by N. F. Blake in SAC (8) 241–5.

3722. SCHLESS, HOWARD H. Chaucer and Dante: a revaluation.

(Bibl. 1985, 3223.) Rev. by Winthrop Wetherbee in MP (83:4) 419–20; by Daniel J. Ransom in CanRCL (12:3) 514–17; by N. R. Havely in Spec (61:4) 997–9; by Janet L. Smarr in JEGP (85:1) 97–9; by David Wallace in SAC (8) 245–9; by C. Joy Watkin in CritQ (28:4) 100–1.

3723. SEYMOUR, M. C.   Chaucer's *Legend of Good Women*: two fallacies. RES (37:148) 528–34.

3724. SHOAF, RICHARD ALLEN.   Dante, Chaucer, and the currency of the word: money, images, and reference in late medieval poetry. (Bibl. 1985, 3226.) Rev. by Alfred David in Spec (61:2) 468–70; by Joan Ferrante in RPh (39:3) 393–6.

3725. SIMPSON, JAMES.   Dante's 'astripetam aquilam' and the theme of poetic discretion in the *House of Fame*. EAS (39) 1–18.

3726. SKLUTE, LARRY.   Virtue of necessity: inconclusiveness and narrative form in Chaucer's poetry. Columbus: Ohio State UP, 1984. pp. vii, 160. Rev. by Robert M. Jordan in SAC (8) 251–4; by R. A. Shoaf in JEGP (85:3) 443–5.

3727. STEVENSON, BARBARA JEAN.   Chaucer's disputed authorship of *The Equatorie of the Planetis*. Unpub. doct. diss., Georgia State Univ., Coll. of Arts and Sciences. [Abstr. in DA (47) 896A.]

3728. TRAVERSI, DEREK.   The literary imagination: studies in Dante, Chaucer, and Shakespeare. Newark, NJ: Delaware UP, 1982. (Cf. bibl. 1984, 3225.) Rev. by Charles Garton in MLR (81:3) 703–4.

3729. WALLACE, DAVID.   Chaucer and the early writings of Boccaccio. Woodbridge; Dover, NH: Boydell & Brewer, 1985. pp. xii, 209. (Chaucer studies, 12.) Rev. by B. A. Windeatt in SAC (8) 254–7; by Piero Boitani in NQ (33:2) 213–14.

3730. WEISS, ALEXANDER.   Chaucer's native heritage. (Bibl. 1985, 3235.) Rev. by George Kane in Spec (61:4) 1011–12; by N. F. Blake in EngS (67:1) 72–3; by Thomas Hahn in SAC (8) 258–60.

3731. WRIGHT, CONSTANCE S.   Lines 880–886 in Chaucer's 'Legend of Thisbe' in *The Legend of Good Women*. ANQ (24:5/6) 68–9.

The Canterbury Tales

3732. ALEXANDER, MICHAEL.   *The Miller's Tale* by Geoffrey Chaucer. Basingstoke: Macmillan. pp. 96. (Macmillan master guides.)

3733. BAKER, DONALD C.   William Thynne's printing of the Squire's Tale: manuscript and printer's copy. *See* **87.**

3734. BESSERMAN, LAWRENCE.   Girdles, belts, and cords: a leitmotif in Chaucer's General Prologue. PLL (22:3) 322–5.

3735. BLAKE, N. F.   The textual tradition of *The Canterbury Tales*. (Bibl. 1985, 3243.) Rev. by Stephen Knight in AUMLA (166) 311–13; by Andrew Wawn in TLS, 28 Nov., 1356.

3736. —— (ed.).   *The Canterbury Tales*, ed. from the Hengwrt manuscript. (Bibl. 1985, 3244.) Rev. by Manfred Görlach in Archiv (223:1) 159–61.

3737. BOLLARD, J. K.   Sovereignty and the loathly lady in English, Welsh and Irish. *See* **3301.**

3738. BURNLEY, J. D. Christine de Pizan and the so-called *style clergial*. MLR (81:1) 1–6.

3739. BURROW, J. A. Chaucer's Canterbury pilgrimage. EC (36:2) 97–119. (F. W. Bateson Memorial Lecture.)

3740. CHMAITELLI, NANCY ADELYNE. The theme of synagogue, ecclesia, and the Whore of Babylon in the visual arts and in the poetry of Dante and Chaucer: a background study for Chaucer's Wife of Bath. Unpub. doct. diss., Rice Univ. [Abstr. in DA (47) 1722A–3A.]

3741. CONNER, EDWIN LEE. The Squire's Tale and its teller: medieval tradition and Chaucer's artistry of allusion. Unpub. doct. diss., Vanderbilt Univ., 1985. [Abstr. in DA (47) 534A.]

3742. COOK, JON. Carnival and *The Canterbury Tales*: 'only equals may laugh' (Herzen). *In* (pp. 169–91) **33.**

3743. COOPER, HELEN. The structure of *The Canterbury Tales*. (Bibl. 1985, 3252.) Rev. by Derek Pearsall in MÆ (55:2) 284–5; by D. C. Baker in ELN (23:4) 57–8.

3744. CURTIS, PENELOPE. Some discarnational impulses in the *Canterbury Tales*. *In* (pp. 128–45) **32.**

3745. DISBROW, SARAH. The Wife of Bath's old wives' tale. SAC (8) 59–71.

3746. ELLIOTT, RALPH W. V. Chaucer's clerical voices. *In* (pp. 146–55) **32.**

3747. ELLIS, ROGER. Patterns of religious narrative in the *Canterbury Tales*. London: Croom Helm. pp. 316. Rev. by Pamela M. King in THES (728) 18.

3748. FERSTER, JUDITH. Interpretation and imitation in Chaucer's Franklin's Tale. *In* (pp. 148–68) **33.**

3749. FLETCHER, ALAN J. Line 30 of the Man of Law's Tale and the medieval Malkyn. *See* **1707.**

3750. FRADENBURG, LOUISE O. The Wife of Bath's passing fancy. SAC (8) 31–58.

3751. FREDELL, JOEL WILLIS. Medieval portraiture and the roots of late gothic aesthetics. *See* **3620.**

3752. GLOVER, KYLE STEPHEN. Chaucer's concept of 'compaignye': a study of covenants in *The Canterbury Tales*. Unpub. doct. diss., Univ. of Missouri–Columbia, 1985. [Abstr. in DA (46) 3346A.]

3753. GÓMEZ SOLIÑO, JOSÉ S. La utilización humorística de rasgos dialectales en The Reeve's Tale y *The Second Shepherds' Play*: interpretación sociolingüística. (Humorous use of dialectal features in The Reeve's Tale and *The Second Shepherds' Play*: sociolinguistic implications.) *See* **897.**

3754. GREEN, DONALD C. The semantics of power: 'maistrie' and 'soveraynetee' in *The Canterbury Tales*. MP (84:1) 18–23.

3755. GRENNEN, JOSEPH E. The Wife of Bath and the scholastic concept of 'operatio'. JRMMRA (97) 41–8.

3756. HALLIBURTON, THOMAS LAUGHLIN. Why do English professors say such crazy things about the *Canterbury Tales*?: an investigation of the rhetoric, logic, method, and history of academic exegesis of Chaucer's

Tales in America, 1900–1984. Unpub. doct. diss., Univ. of Texas at Austin, 1985. [Abstr. in DA (46) 3027A.]

3757. HORVATH, RICHARD P.   A critical interpretation of *Canterbury Tales* B² 3981. ELN (24:1) 8–12.

3758. KIM, SHIN-GON.   Junggi youngeo eohwi eui igil yoso e gwanhan yeongu: *Canterbury Tales* eui General Prologue reul jungsim euro. (A study of heterogeneous elements: Middle English words used in the General Prologue of *The Canterbury Tales*.) Unpub. doct. diss., Yeungnam Univ. (Korea).

3759. KNIGHT, STEPHEN.   Chaucer's religious Canterbury Tales. *In* (pp. 156–66) **32.**

3760. KOLVE, V. A.   Chaucer and the imagery of narrative: the first five *Canterbury Tales*. (Bibl. 1985, 3279.) Rev. by Charles Muscatine in Spec (61:3) 674–6; by James I. Wimsatt in SAQ (85:1) 98–101; by Seth Lerer in MP (84:1) 64–7; by Helen Cooper in MÆ (55:2) 286–9; by C. Joy Watkin in CritQ (28:4) 99–100.

3761. KUPERSMITH, WILLIAM.   Chaucer's Physician's Tale and the Tenth Satire of Juvenal. ELN (24:2) 20–3.

3762. LAWLER, TRAUGOTT.   The one and the many in the *Canterbury Tales*. (Bibl. 1983, 3876.) Rev. by Helen Cooper in MÆ (55:2) 285–6.

3763. LEE, B. S.   Chaucer's handling of a medieval feminist hierarchy. UES (24:1) 1–6.

3764. LOMPERIS, LINDA SUSAN.   Poetry of authority and the authority of poetry in *The Canterbury Tales*. Unpub. doct. diss., Cornell Univ., 1985. [Abstr. in DA (46) 2688A.]

3765. McALINDON, T.   Cosmology, contrariety and the Knight's Tale. MÆ (55:1) 41–57.

3766. McCLELLAN, WILLIAM T.   Dialogic discourse in the Clerk's Tale. Unpub. doct. diss., City Univ. of New York, 1985. [Abstr. in DA (46) 3361A.]

3767. MOSSER, DANIEL W.   The two scribes of the Cardigan manuscript and the 'evidence' of scribal supervision and shop production. *See* **167.**

3768. NOLAN, BARBARA.   'A poet ther was': Chaucer's voices in the General Prologue to *The Canterbury Tales*. PMLA (101:2) 154–69.

3769. OLSON, PAUL A.   *The Canterbury Tales* and the good society. Princeton, NJ; Guildford: Princeton UP. pp. xix, 323.

3770. PEARSALL, DEREK.   *The Canterbury Tales*. Sydney: Allen & Unwin, 1985. (Cf. bibl. 1985, 3291.) Rev. by Paul G. Ruggiers in Spec (61:4) 981–2; by Stephen Knight in AUMLA (66) 311–13; by C. Joy Watkin in CritQ (28:4) 98–9; by David Aers in Eng (35) 268–73.

3771. RAMSEY, R. VANCE.   Paleography and scribes of shared training. *See* **170.**

3772. REX, RICHARD.   Old French bacon and the Wife of Bath. MSE (10:2) 1985, 132–7.

3773. —— Pastiche as irony in the Prioress's Prologue and Tale. SSF (23:1) 1–8.

3774. —— Wild horses, justice, and charity in the Prioress's Tale. PLL (22:4) 339–51.

3775. RUDAT, WOLFGANG E. H.   Milton and The Miller's Tale: Chaucerian allusions in *Paradise Lost*. Euphorion (80:4) 417–26.

3776. RUGGIERS, PAUL G.; BAKER, DONALD C. (gen. eds).   A variorum edition of the works of Geoffrey Chaucer: vol. 2: part 9, The Nun's Priest's Tale. Ed. by DEREK PEARSALL. (Bibl. 1985, 3297.) Rev. by Ralph Hanna, III, in AEB (8:3) 1984, 184–97; by M. C. Seymour in EngS (67:2) 186–7.

3777. SAMSON, A. R.   Chaucer's moral vocabulary: meaning and ironic form in the *Canterbury Tales*. Unpub. doct. diss., Univ. of Wales, Swansea, 1983.

3778. SCHLESINGER, GEORGE.   A tale of two cuckolds. DUJ (79:1) 51–8.

3779. SEAMAN, DAVID M.   'The wordes of the Frankeleyn to the Squier': an interpretation. ELN (24:1) 12–18.

3780. SMITH, MACKLIN.   'Or I wol caste a ston.' SAC (8) 3–30.

3781. STOCK, LORRAINE KOCHANSKE.   The two Mayings in Chaucer's Knight's Tale: convention and invention. JEGP (85:2) 206–21.

3782. VON ERTZDORFF, XENJA; WYNN, MARIANNE (eds).   Liebe – Ehe – Ehebruch in der Literatur des Mittelalters. *See* **3178.**

3783. WENZEL, SEIGFRIED (ed.).   Summa virtutum de remediis anime. Athens: Georgia UP, 1984. pp. ix, 373. (Chaucer Library.) Rev. by T. P. Dolan in SAC (8) 260–3; by Anne Hudson in NQ (33:2) 215–17.

Troilus and Criseyde

3784. ANDERSON, DAVID.   Cassandra's analogy: *Troilus* v. 1450–1521. HUSL (13:1) 1985, 1–17.

3785. ASAKAWA, JUNKO.   'Here bygynneth game': *Troilus and Criseyde* no katarino kozo. ('Here bygynneth game': the narrative structure of *Troilus and Criseyde*.) SEL (63:1) 3–12.

3786. BRONSON, LARRY.   The 'sodeyn Diomede' – Chaucer's composite portrait. BSUF (25:2) 1984, 14–19.

3787. CLOGAN, PAUL M.   Criseyde's book of the romance of Thebes. HUSL (13:1) 1985, 18–28.

3788. EVANS, MURRAY J.   'Making strange': the narrator (?), the ending (?), and Chaucer's *Troilus*. NM (87:2) 218–28.

3789. GRENNEN, JOSEPH E.   Aristotelian ideas in Chaucer's *Troilus*: a preliminary study. MedHum (14) 125–38.

3790. GUTHRIE, STEVEN R.   Chaucer's French pentameter. Unpub. doct. diss., Brown Univ., 1985. [Abstr. in DA (46) 2289A.]

3791. LEVINE, ROBERT.   Restraining ambiguities in Chaucer's *Troilus and Criseyde*. NM (87:4) 558–64.

3792. MACK, MARY F.   Lovesickness in *Troilus*. PCP (19) 1984, 55–61.

3793. MANZALAOUI, MAHMOUD.   Swooning lovers: a theme in Arab and European romance. CompCrit (8) 71–90.

3794. MARESCA, THOMAS E.   Three English epics: studies of *Troilus* *and Criseyde, The Faerie Queene,* and *Paradise Lost.* (Bibl. 1984, 3303.) Rev. by Thomas H. Cain in CLIO (11:1) 1981, 88–91.

3795. MÜLLER-OBERHÄUSER, GABRIELE.   Dialogsteuerung und Handlungsmotivierung in Chaucers *Troilus and Criseyde.* Frankfurt: Lang. pp. 579. (Europäische Hochschulschriften: Reihe 14, Angelsächsische Sprache und Literatur, 158.)

3796. SANDERLIN, GEORGE.   In defense of Criseyde. USFLQ (24:3/4) 47–8.

3797. SIGAL, GALE.   Aurora's ascent: conflict and desire in the medieval dawn-song. *See* **3425.**

3798. SLOCUM, SALLY K.   Criseyde among the Greeks. NM (87:3) 365–74.

3799. STIELSTRA, DIANE.   The portrayal of consciousness in medieval romance. *See* **3430.**

3800. WEJKSNORA, LOUISE R.   Classical gods and Christian God: religious allusions and the moral of Chaucer's *Troilus and Criseyde.* Unpub. doct. diss., City Univ. of New York. [Abstr. in DA (47) 1317A.]

3801. WETHERBEE, WINTHROP.   Chaucer and the poets: an essay on *Troilus and Criseyde.* (Bibl. 1985, 3322.) Rev. by Jonathan Beck in Spec (61:3) 716–21; by R. A. Shoaf in JEGP (85:1) 102–4; by Paul G. Ruggiers in CanRCL (12:3) 1985, 511–14; by C. Joy Watkin in CritQ (28:4) 101–2; by N. F. Blake in MLR (81:4) 976–7.

3802. WINDEATT, B. A. (ed.).   *Troilus and Criseyde*: a new edition of *The Book of Troilus.* (Bibl. 1985, 3324.) Rev. by C. David Benson in SAC (8) 266–70; by N. F. Blake in MLR (81:4) 974–5; by Derek Pearsall in MÆ (55:2) 281–4; by Donald C. Baker in ELN (23:3) 65–8; by Anne Hudson in NQ (33:2) 214–15; by Philip Horne in CamQ (15:2) 120–6.

3803. WOOD, CHAUNCEY.   The elements of Chaucer's *Troilus.* (Bibl. 1985, 3325.) Rev. by Melissa Furrow in DalR (65:2) 1985, 317–19; by A. V. C. Schmidt in MÆ (55:1) 135–7.

THE GAWAIN POET

3804. BERGNER, H.   The two courts: two modes of existence in *Sir Gawain and the Green Knight.* EngS (67:5) 401–16.

3805. BESSERMAN, LAWRENCE.   The idea of the Green Knight. ELH (53:2) 219–39.

3806. BLANCH, ROBERT J.   *Sir Gawain and the Green Knight*: a reference guide. (Bibl. 1985, 3331.) Rev. by G. C. Britton in NQ (33:2) 212–13.

3807. —— WASSERMAN, JULIAN N.   To 'ouertake your wylle': volition and obligation in *Sir Gawain and the Green Knight.* Neophilologus (70:1) 119–29.

3808. BOGDANOS, THEODORE.   *Pearl*: image of the ineffable: a study in medieval poetic symbolism. (Bibl. 1985, 3332.) Rev. by J. Angela Carson in SAC (8) 166–8.

3809. CLARK, S. L.; WASSERMAN, JULIAN N.   The passing of the seasons and the apocalyptic in *Sir Gawain and the Green Knight.* SCR (3:1) 3–22.

3810. CRONAN, DENNIS.   Alliterative rank in Old English poetry. *See* **1218.**

3811. EADIE, J.   A new source for the Green Knight. NM (87:4) 569–77.

3812. FIELD, ROSALIND.   The Heavenly Jerusalem in *Pearl*. MLR (81:1) 7–17.

3813. GREEN, RICHARD FIRTH.   Sir Gawain and the *sacra cintola*. ESCan (11:1) 1985, 1–11.

3814. JOHNSON, LYNN STALEY.   The voice of the Gawain-poet. (Bibl. 1985, 3344.) Rev. by Robert J. Blanch in Spec (61:4) 942–5.

3815. JONASSEN, FREDERICK B.   Elements from the traditional drama of England in *Sir Gawain and the Green Knight*. Viator (17) 221–54.

3816. KOWALIK, BARBARA.   Artistry and Christianity in *Pearl*. YREAL (4) 1–34.

3817. LUCAS, PETER J.   Hautdesert in *Sir Gawain and the Green Knight*. Neophilologus (70:2) 319–20.

3818. MANES, CHRISTOPH.   A plum for the *Pearl*-poet. ELN (23:4) 4–6.

3819. MANN, JILL.   Price and value in *Sir Gawain and the Green Knight*. EC (36:4) 294–318.

3820. NEWMAN, BARBARA FLORENCE.   Sin, judgment, and grace in the works of the *Gawain*-poet. Unpub. doct. diss., Cornell Univ., 1985. 2 vols. [Abstr. in DA (46) 3027A.]

3821. NICHOLLS, J. W.   The matter of courtesy: a study of medieval courtesy books and the *Gawain* poet. Cambridge; Dover, NH: Brewer, 1985. pp. x, 241. Rev. by Renate Haas in SAC (8) 231–3.

3822. ——— The matter of courtesy: a study of medieval courtesy books and the *Gawain*-poet. Unpub. doct. diss., Univ. of Cambridge, 1983.

3823. PRIOR, SANDRA PIERSON.   *Patience* – beyond apocalypse. MP (83:4) 337–48.

3824. ROGERS, SYLVIA PETERS.   Geometrical structures in *Sir Gawain and the Green Knight*. Unpub. doct. diss., Stanford Univ. [Abstr. in DA (47) 525A.]

3825. SHICHTMAN, MARTIN B.   *Sir Gawain and the Green Knight*: a lesson in the terror of history. PLL (22:1) 3–15.

3826. SHOAF, R. A.   The poem as green girdle: commercium in *Sir Gawain and the Green Knight*. Gainesville: Florida UP, 1984. pp. xi, 105. (Humanities monographs, 55.) Rev. by William F. Pollard in SAC (8) 249–51.

3827. SILVERSTEIN, THEODORE (ed.).   *Sir Gawain and the Green Knight*: a new critical edition. (Bibl. 1985, 3351.) Rev. by Basil Cottle in JEGP (85:2) 253–6; by Malcolm Andrew in Spec (61:2) 470–2; by Ronald Waldron in NQ (33:1) 98–9.

3828. WADE, SIDNEY.   An analysis of the similes and their function in the characterization of the Green Knight. *See* **1249.**

3829. WOLFZETTEL, FRIEDRICH (ed.).   Artusrittertum im späten Mittelalter. Ethos und Ideologie. *See* **3450.**

SIXTEENTH CENTURY

GENERAL

General Literary Studies

3830. ANDERSON, JUDITH H.   Biographical truth: the representation of historical persons in Tudor–Stuart writing. (Bibl. 1985, 3355.) Rev. by Jonquil Bevan in NQ (33:1) 103.

3831. BERKOWITZ, STEVEN BENNETT.   A critical edition of George Buchanan's *Baptistes* and of the anonymous *Tyrannicall-Government Anatomized*. Unpub. doct. diss., Harvard Univ. [Abstr. in DA (47) 2166A.]

3832. BONHEIM, HELMUT.   Why the West created the South American 'savage'. Listener (116) 18/25 Dec., 34–5.

3833. BRADBROOK, M. C.   The artist and society in Shakespeare's England. Introd. by BRIAN VICKERS. Brighton: Harvester Press; Totowa, NJ: Barnes & Noble, 1982. pp. x, 176. (Collected papers of Muriel Bradbrook, 1.) Rev. by Rosalind Miles in MLR (81:4) 978–9; by Brian Gibbons in SLS (37) 1984, 184.

3834. BRIGGS, JULIA.   This stage-play world: English literature and its background, 1580–1625. (Bibl. 1985, 3359.) Rev. by Lois Potter in ShS (37) 1984, 188–9.

3835. BROWNLEE, KEVIN; BROWNLEE, MARINA SCORDILIS (eds). Romance: generic transformation from Chrétien de Troyes to Cervantes. *See* **3307.**

3836. CHAUDHURI, S.   Some aspects of Renaissance pastoral and its English developments. Unpub. doct. diss., Univ. of Oxford, 1981.

3837. COWAN, IAN B.; SHAW, DUNCAN (eds).   The Renaissance and Reformation in Scotland: essays in honour of Gordon Donaldson. Edinburgh: Scottish Academic Press, 1983. pp. 261.

3838. DATTA, KITTY.   Modes of singularity in Renaissance literature. Jadavpur University Essays and Studies (Calcutta) (3) 1981, 49–62.

3839. DEES, JEROME S.   Recent studies in the English emblem. ELR (16:3) 391–420.

3840. DIEHL, HUSTON.   Graven images: Protestant emblem books in England. RQ (39:1) 49–66.

3841. DONKER, MARJORIE; MULDROW, GEORGE M.   Dictionary of literary rhetorical conventions of the English Renaissance. (Bibl. 1983, 3954.) Rev. by Peter Mack in MLR (81:4) 973–4.

3842. ESTRIN, BARBARA L.   The raven and the lark: lost children in literature of the English Renaissance. Lewisburg, PA: Bucknell UP; London: Assoc. UPs, 1985. pp. 228. Rev. by Henry D. Janzen in UWR (19:2) 78–80.

3843. FARNSWORTH, JANE ELIZABETH.   Intimate relationships between women in English Renaissance literature, 1558–1642. Unpub. doct. diss., Queen's Univ. at Kingston, 1985. [Abstr. in DA (46) 2299A.]

3844. FERGUSON, MOIRA.   First feminists: British women writers,

1578–1799. Bloomington: Indiana UP, 1985. pp. 461. Rev. by Linda Austin in SCN (44:1/2) 14–15.

3845. GOLDBERG, JONATHAN.   Voice terminal echo: postmodernism and English Renaissance texts. New York; London: Methuen. pp. 194. Rev. by Sheila T. Cavanagh in GHJ (9:1) 1985, 46–50; by Leah S. Marcus in Criticism (28:4) 459–63.

3846. GREENBLATT, STEPHEN (ed.).   The power of forms in the English Renaissance. (Bibl. 1985, 3369.) Rev. by Lois Potter in ShS (37) 1984, 193–4.

3847. HANNAY, MARGARET PATTERSON (ed.).   Silent but for the word: Tudor women as patrons, translators, and writers of religious works. *See* **52.**

3848. HECKELMAN, RONALD JOE.   'Promyse that is dette': toward a rhetoric and history of literary promising. *See* **3118.**

3849. HECKSHER, WILLIAM S.   Art and literature: studies in relationship. Baden Baden: Koerner; Durham, NC: Duke UP, 1985. pp. 528. (Saecula spiritalia, 17.) Rev. by Harriette Andreadis in SCN (44:4) 57–9.

3850. HELGERSON, RICHARD.   The land speaks: cartography, chorography, and subversion in Renaissance England. Representations (16) 51–85.

3851. —— Recent studies in the English Renaissance. SELit (26:1) 145–99.

3852. HOWARD, JEAN E.   The new historicism in Renaissance studies. ELR (16:1) 13–43.

3853. HYDE, THOMAS.   The poetic theology of love: Cupid in Renaissance literature. *See* **3368.**

3854. LANHAM, RICHARD A.   The motives of eloquence: literary rhetoric in the Renaissance. (Bibl. 1982, 4146.) Rev. by Paul Ramsey in RenR (9:3) 1985, 223–6.

3855. MONTROSE, LOUIS.   Renaissance literary studies and the subject of history. ELR (16:1) 5–12.

3856. PATRIDES, C. A.   Premises and motifs in Renaissance thought and literature. (Bibl. 1985, 3381.) Rev. by Gordon Campbell in MLR (81:2) 441–2.

3857. PATTERSON, ANNABEL.   Censorship and interpretation: the conditions of writing and reading in early modern England. Madison: Wisconsin UP, 1984. pp. ix, 283. Rev. by Blair Worden in NQ (33:2) 220–1; by Ronald H. Fritze in SixCT (17:1) 112–13; by Philip Edwards in RQ (39:2) 325–8.

3858. PEYRE, YVES.   Mythes de renaissance. *In* (pp. 67–93) **37.**

3859. QUINT, DAVID.   Origin and originality in Renaissance literature: versions of the source. (Bibl. 1985, 3384.) Rev. by Wayne A. Rebhorn in CL (38:4) 384–6; by Philip R. Berk in RenR (9:4) 1985, 278–80.

3860. RICHMOND, HUGH M.   Puritans and libertines: Anglo–French literary relations in the Reformation. (Bibl. 1984, 3376.) Rev. by David

Scott Kastan and Nancy J. Vickers in CL (38:2) 197–201; by Lois Potter in ShS (36) 1983, 176.

3861. SCHOENBAUM, S.   Shakespeare and others. (Bibl. 1985, 3451.) Rev. by A. R. Braunmuller in Library (8:2) 177–8.

3862. SHARPE, KEVIN.   The politics of literature in Renaissance England. Hist (71) 235–47 (review-article).

3863. VENET, GISÈLE.   Temps mythiques et temps tragique: du Moyen Age au Baroque. *In* (pp. 11–24) **2.**

3864. WALLER, GARY F.   Struggling into discourse: the emergence of Renaissance women's writing. *In* (pp. 238–56) **52.**

3865. WATTERSON, WILLIAM COLLINS.   Elizabethan pastoral satire. Unpub. doct. diss., Brown Univ., 1976. [Abstr. in DA (46) 2703A.]

3866. WOODBRIDGE, LINDA.   Women and the English Renaissance: literature and the nature of womankind, 1540–1620. (Bibl. 1985, 3392.) Rev. by Ronald B. Bond in Ariel (17:2) 81–5; by Ian Sowton in ESCan (12:3) 340–6.

Drama and the Theatre

3867. AGNEW, JEAN-CHRISTOPHE.   Worlds apart: the market and the theater in Anglo-American thought, 1550–1750. Cambridge: CUP. pp. xvi, 262.

3868. ATKINSON, DAVID.   Marriage under compulsion in English Renaissance drama. EngS (67:6) 483–504.

3869. BELSEY, CATHERINE.   The subject of tragedy: identity and difference in Renaissance drama. (Bibl. 1985, 3398.) Rev. by Andrew Gurr in LRB (8:2) 20, 22; by M. H. Simpson in UES (24:2) 40–2; by Marina Warner in TLS, 26 May, 539.

3870. BENSEL-MEYERS, LINDA DIANE.   A 'figure cut in alabaster': the paradoxical widow of Renaissance drama. Unpub. doct. diss., Univ. of Oregon, 1985. [Abstr. in DA (46) 1945A.]

3871. BENTLEY, GERALD EADES.   The profession of player in Shakespeare's time, 1590–1642. (Bibl. 1985, 3399.) Rev. by Andrew Gurr in MP (83:4) 428–30; by Niels Bugge Hansen in CLIO (15:1) 1985, 89–91.

3872. BERGERON, DAVID M.   The Bible in English Renaissance pageants. CompDr (20:2) 160–70.

3873. —— (ed.).   Pageantry in the Shakespearean theater. Athens: Georgia UP, 1985. pp. vii, 251. Rev. by Maurice Charney in SAQ (85:4) 401–2.

3874. BOND, DAVID.   On playing musidors. NQ (33:4) 469–71. (*Mucedorus and Amadine.*)

3875. BOTTOMS, J. F.   The development and influence of the English court entertainment in the sixteenth century. Unpub. doct. diss., Univ. of Sheffield, 1984.

3876. BRADEN, GORDON.   Renaissance tragedy and Senecan tradition: anger's privilege. New Haven, CT; London: Yale UP, 1985. pp. xii, 260. Rev. by Anna Lydia Motto and John R. Clark in CJ (81:2) 176–8; by John Mulryan in Cithara (25:2) 79–80; by Geoffrey Aggeler in WHR

(40:4) 383–6; by Katharine Eisman Maus in RQ (39:2) 330–3; by Peter Conrad in TLS, 14 Mar., 279–80.

3877. BRADFORD, ALAN T. Use and uniformity in Elizabethan architecture and drama. JDJ (5:1/2) 27–61.

3878. BRISTOL, MICHAEL D. Carnival and theater: plebeian culture and the structure of authority in Renaissance England. (Bibl. 1985, 3403.) Rev. by Nicholas Grene in THES (698) 27; by John Wilders in TLS, 18 July, 790; by Viviana Comensoli in RenR (10:4) 384–6.

3879. BRYANT, J. C. Tudor drama and religious controversy. Macon, GA: Mercer UP, 1984. pp. x, 165. Rev. by David Norbrook in NQ (33:4) 543.

3880. CAREY, ANNA KIRWAN STECK. 'Less than a man': the child actors and tragic satire. Unpub. doct. diss., Univ. of Cincinnati. [Abstr. in DA (47) 908A.]

3881. CAWLEY, A. C.; GAINES, BARRY (eds). A Yorkshire tragedy. Manchester: Manchester UP. pp. x, 192. (Revels plays.)

3882. CHUTER, D. M. Finance and financiers in the Elizabethan drama: a critical and historical study. Unpub. doct. diss., Univ. of London (King's Coll.), 1984.

3883. COHEN, WALTER. Drama of a nation: public theater in Renaissance England and Spain. Ithaca, NY; London: Cornell UP, 1985. pp. 416. Rev. by Leo Salingar in RQ (39:4) 812–16; by John Wilders in TLS, 18 July, 790.

3884. COLTHORPE, MARION. Anti-Catholic masques performed before Queen Elizabeth I. NQ (33:3) 316–18.

3885. —— Pageants before Queen Elizabeth I at Coventry in 1566. NQ (32) 1985, 458–60.

3886. COOK, ANN JENNALIE. The privileged playgoers of Shakespeare's London, 1576–1642. (Bibl. 1985, 3409.) Rev. by Lois Potter in ShS (36) 1983, 179.

3887. COOK, JUDITH. At the sign of the swan: an introduction to Shakespeare's contemporaries. Introd. by TREVOR NUNN. London: Harrap, pp. 207.

3888. DEAN, PAUL. *The Tragedy of Tiberius* (1607): debts to Shakespeare. NQ (31:2) 1984, 213–14.

3889. DESSEN, ALAN C. Elizabethan stage conventions and modern interpreters. (Bibl. 1985, 3412.) Rev. by Lois Potter in NQ (33:4) 543–4; by Donald Gwynn Watson in Review (8) 63–6; by Howard C. Cole in JEGP (85:2) 260–3; by Richard Jacobs in Eng (35) 164–73.

3890. FOAKES, R. A. Illustrations of the English stage: 1580–1642. Stanford, CA: Stanford UP, 1985. (Cf. bibl. 1985, 3414.) Rev. by Richard Studing in SCN (44:3) 36–8; by Judith Milhous in TJ (38:1) 115–16; by David Mann in Library (8:1) 87–90.

3891. FREY, CHARLES. Recent studies in Elizabethan and Jacobean drama. SELit (26:2) 345–402.

3892. GAIR, W. REAVLEY. The Children of Paul's: the story of a theatre company, 1553–1608. (Bibl. 1985, 3416, where scholar's initial omitted.) Rev. by Lois Potter in ShS (37) 1984, 197.

3893. GERRITSEN, JOHAN.   De Witt, van Buchell, the Swan and the Globe: some notes. *In* (pp. 29–46) **18.**

3894. GIBBONS, BRIAN (ed.).   Elizabethan and Jacobean comedies. (Bibl. 1984, 3385.) Rev. by Nigel Brooks in NQ (33:3) 412.

3895. ⸺ Elizabethan and Jacobean tragedies. (Bibl. 1984, 3386.) Rev. by T. W. Craik in NQ (33:1) 110.

3896. GOLDBERG, DENA.   *Appius and Virginia*: a story of rape and tyranny – two Renaissance versions. DalR (66:1/2) 98–106.

3897. GRISWOLD, WENDY.   Renaissance revivals: city comedy and revenge tragedy in the London theatre 1576–1980. Chicago; London: Chicago UP. pp. ix, 288.

3898. HATTAWAY, MICHAEL.   Elizabethan popular theatre: plays in performance. (Bibl. 1985, 3422.) Rev. by Brian Gibbons in ShS (37) 1984, 183–4; by Jay L. Halio in MLR (81:3) 715–16.

3899. HILLS, DAVID.   'Bushop Brian' and the dramatic entertainments of Cheshire. *See* **2544.**

3900. HODGES, C. WALTER; SCHOENBAUM, S.; LEONE, LEONARD (eds). The third Globe: symposium for the reconstruction of the Globe Playhouse, Wayne State University, 1979. Detroit, MI: Wayne State UP, 1981. pp. 267. Rev. by Lois Potter in ShS (36) 1983, 178–9.

3901. HOLLAND, PETER.   Style at the Swan. EC (36:3) 193–209.

3902. HYLAND, PETER.   Disguise and Renaissance tragedy. UTQ (55:2) 1985/86, 161–71.

3903. KIEFER, FREDERICK.   Fortune and Elizabethan tragedy. (Bibl. 1985, 3427.) Rev. by John Margeson in MP (83:3) 307–10.

3904. LEGGATT, ALEXANDER.   *Arden of Faversham*. ShS (36) 1983, 121–33.

3905. LEVIN, RICHARD.   Performance-critics *vs* close readers in the study of English Renaissance drama. MLR (81:3) 545–59.

3906. LEVINE, LAURA.   Men in women's clothing: anti-theatricality and effeminization from 1579–1642. Criticism (28:2) 121–43.

3907. LIMON, JERZY.   Gentlemen of a company: English players in central and eastern Europe 1590–1660. (Bibl. 1985, 3430.) Rev. by Richard Paul Knowles in SCN (44:3) 38–40.

3908. LOMAX, M. A.   The traditions behind the staging of selected adult company drama, *c.* 1607–14. Unpub. doct. diss., Univ. of York, 1983.

3909. McALINDON, T.   English Renaissance tragedy. Basingstoke: Macmillan. pp. xiii, 269.

3910. MacINTYRE, JEAN.   Conventions of costume change in Elizabethan plays. ExRC (12) 105–14.

3911. MAGUIN, JEAN-MARIE.   Strategies for the page and strategies for the stage: some interludes of image and language basic to the production of meaning. CEl (29) 39–51. (*Gorboduc, Hamlet.*)

3912. MAGUIRE, LAURIE E.   John Holland and *John of Bordeaux*. NQ (33:3) 327–33.

3913. MEYER, VERNE ALLYN.   The relationship between prominent themes in John Calvin's theology and common arguments in the

'Puritan' critique of English theatre from 1577 to 1633. Unpub. doct. diss., Univ. of Minnesota, 1985. [Abstr. in DA (46) 2858A.]

3914. MROCZKOWSKA-BRAND, KATARZYNA.   Overt theatricality and the *theatrum mundi* metaphor in Spanish and English drama, 1570–1640. Unpub. doct. diss., Univ. of Rochester, 1985. [Abstr. in DA (46) 3025A.]

3915. ORLIN, LENA COWEN.   Man's house as his castle in Elizabethan domestic tragedy. Unpub. doct. diss., Univ. of North Carolina at Chapel Hill, 1985. [Abstr. in DA (46) 3362A.]

3916. PAUL, DAVID.   The Bard and company. NCrit (1:9) 1982/83, 8–26.

3917. RAMEL, JACQUES.   Méta-diégèse et extra-diégèse dans le théâtre élisabéthain. *In* (pp. 341–56) **1.**

3918. RASMUSSEN, ERIC.   The implications of past tense verbs in early Elizabethan dumb shows. EngS (67:5) 417–19.

3919. REISS, TIMOTHY J.   Tragedy and truth: studies in the development of a Renaissance and neoclassical discourse. (Bibl. 1983, 4040.) Rev. by Gerald Gillespie in CanRCL (13:1) 120–5.

3920. REYNOLDS, JAMES A.   Repentance and retribution in early English drama. Salzburg: Institut für Anglistik und Amerikanistik, Salzburg Univ., 1982. pp. vii, 116. (Salzburg studies in English: Jacobean drama studies, 96.) Rev. by Lois Potter in ShS (36) 1983, 177.

3921. RICHARDS, DOUGLAS WILLIAM.   Preachers and players: the contest between agents of sermon and game in the moral drama from *Mankind* to *Like Will to Like. See* **3485.**

3922. RONAN, CLIFFORD J.   *Selimus* and the blinding of Gloster. NQ (33:3) 360–1.

3923. ROWAN, D. F.   The quest for Shakespeare's Globe. UTQ (55:4) 424–8 (review-article).

3924. ROZETT, MARTHA TUCK.   The doctrine of election and the emergence of Elizabethan tragedy. (Bibl. 1985, 3449.) Rev. by Robert Y. Turner in RQ (39:4) 808–10.

3925. SALOMON, BROWNELL.   Critical analyses in English Renaissance drama: a bibliographic guide. (Bibl. 1980, 308.) New York; London: Garland, 1985. pp. xviii, 198. (Garland reference library of the humanities, 588.) (Second ed.: first ed. 1979.) Rev. by Barbara Cohen-Stratyner in TJ (38:4) 497–8.

3926. SAMS, ERIC (ed.).   Shakespeare's lost play: *Edmund Ironside.* London: Fourth Estate. pp. 400. Rev. by Andrew Gurr in LRB (8:2) 20, 22; by Richard Proudfoot in THES (712) 18.

3927. SCHRICKX, WILLEM.   'Pickleherring' and English actors in Germany. ShS (36) 1983, 135–47.

3928. SHAND, G. B.; SHADY, RAYMOND C. (eds).   Play-texts in old spelling: papers from the Glendon conference. *See* **44.**

3929. SHEPHERD, SIMON.   Marlowe and the politics of Elizabethan theatre. Brighton: Harvester Press. pp. xix, 231. Rev. by Julia Briggs in THES (723) 18.

3930. SPINRAD, PHOEBE S.   Memento mockery: some skulls on the Renaissance stage. ExRC (10) 1984, 1–11.

3931. STEVENS, DAVID.   English Rennaissance theatre history: a reference guide. (Bibl. 1985, 3456.) Rev. by Thomas Manning in TS (30) 1983/84, 77–8; by R. L. Smallwood in MLR (81:3) 716–17.

3932. STREITBERGER, W. R.   William Cornish and the players of the chapel. METh (8:1) 3–20.

3933. THOMSON, PETER.   Shakespeare's theatre. (Bibl. 1984, 3449.) Rev. by David George in TS (30) 1983/84, 74–6; by Donald Gwynne Watson in Review (8) 59–77; by Lois Potter in ShS (37) 1984, 195.

3934. TYDEMAN, WILLIAM.   The image of the city in English Renaissance drama. EAS (38) 1985, 29–44.

3935. WEIMANN, ROBERT.   History and the issue of authority in representation: the Elizabethan theater and the Reformation. NLH (17:3) 449–76.

3936. WHITE, E. N.   People and places: the social and topographical context of drama in York, 1554–1609. Unpub. doct. diss., Univ. of Leeds, 1984. [Abstr. in IT (36) 902.]

3937. WHITE, R. S.   The rise and fall of an Elizabethan fashion: love letters in romance and Shakespearean comedy. CEl (30) 35–47.

3938. WHITE, W. W. P.   Calvinism and English stage, with special reference to the period 1547–1576. Unpub. doct. diss., Univ. of Bristol, 1983.

3939. WHITWORTH, CHARLES WALTERS (ed.).   Three sixteenth-century comedies. (Bibl. 1984, 3390.) Rev. by Nigel Brooks in NQ (33:3) 411–12.

3940. WILKS, J. S.   'A thousand several tongues': the idea of conscience in Tudor and Jacobean drama. Unpub. doct. diss., Univ. of Birmingham, 1983/84.

Fiction

3941. BLAIM, ARTUR.   Early English utopian fiction. Lublin, Poland: Uniwersytet Marii Curie-Skłodowskiej, 1984. pp. 133.

3942. GILLESPIE, GERALD.   Erring and wayfaring in baroque fiction. RLC (58:3) 1984, 277–99.

3943. MICHAELIS-JENA, RUTH.   Eulenspiegel and Münchhausen: two German folk heroes. *See* **2472.**

3944. SALZMAN, PAUL.   English prose fiction 1558–1700: a critical history. (Bibl. 1985, 3465.) Rev. by W. R. Owens in NQ (33:4) 538–9; by John J. O'Connor in RQ (39:1) 130–2; by Randolph P. Almasy in SixCT (17:4) 561–2.

3945. WHITE, R. S.   The rise and fall of an Elizabethan fashion: love letters in romance and Shakespearean comedy. *See* **3937.**

Poetry

3946. ANDREW, MALCOLM (ed.).   Two Early Renaissance bird poems: *The Harmony of Birds, The Parliament of Birds. See* **3286.**

3947. CLARKE, JOSEPH KELLY.   The *praeceptor amoris* in English

Renaissance lyric poetry: one aspect of the poet's voice. Unpub. doct. diss., North Texas State Univ., 1985. [Abstr. in DA (47) 187A.]

3948. CONRAN, TONY. 'Ye Bryttish poets . . .': some observations on early Anglo-Welsh poetry. AWR (84) 8–18.

3949. COOK, ELIZABETH. Seeing through words: the scope of late Renaissance poetry. New Haven, CT; London: Yale UP. pp. 192. Rev. by Gerald Hammond in THES (721) 16.

3950. DOUGHTIE, EDWARD (ed.). *Liber Lilliati*: Elizabethan verse and song (Bodleian MS Rawlinson poetry 148). Newark: Delaware UP; London: Assoc. UPs, 1985. pp. 232. Rev. by Steven May in SixCT (17:1) 118; by Katherine Duncan-Jones in TLS, 21 Feb., 228.

3951. FARMER, NORMAN K. Poets and the visual arts in Renaissance England. (Bibl. 1985, 3470.) Rev. by Jonathan B. Riess in SixCT (17:1) 123–4.

3952. FUMERTON, PATRICIA. Exchanging gifts: the Elizabethan currency of children and poetry. ELH (53:2) 241–78.

3953. —— 'Secret' arts: Elizabethan miniatures and sonnets. Representations (15) 57–97.

3954. GILMAN, ERNEST B. Iconoclasm and poetry in the English Reformation: down went Dagon. Chicago; London: Chicago UP. pp. xi, 227.

3955. GREENE, THOMAS M. Light in Troy: imitation and discovery in Renaissance poetry. (Bibl. 1985, 3473.) Rev. by Martin Mueller in CanRCL (13:3) 484–7.

3956. HULSE, CLARK. Metamorphic verse: the Elizabethan minor epic. (Bibl. 1984, 3469.) Rev. by Thomas M. Greene in MLR (81:4) 979–80.

3957. HUTTON, JAMES. Themes of peace in Renaissance poetry. Ed. by RITA GUERLAC. London: Cornell UP, 1984. (Cf. bibl. 1985, 3476.) Rev. by John M. Steadman in CL (38:4) 382–4; by Barbara C. Ewell in JEGP (85:4) 559–61.

3958. JORGENS, ELISE BICKFORD. The well-tun'd word: musical interpretations of English poetry, 1597–1651. (Bibl. 1985, 3479.) Rev. by F. W. Sternfeld in RQ (39:1) 132–4.

3959. LOW, ANTHONY. The georgic revolution. Princeton, NJ; Guildford: Princeton UP, 1985. pp. xii, 369. Rev. by Terry Comito in RQ(39:3) 535–9.

3960. MCFARLANE, IAN D. The Renaissance epitaph. MLR (81:4) xxv–xxxv. (Presidential Address to the Modern Humanities Research Assn.)

3961. MACK, MAYNARD; LORD, GEORGE DEFOREST (eds). Poetic traditions of the English Renaissance. (Bibl. 1985, 3481.) Rev. by Brian Gibbons in ShS (37) 1984–5.

3962. MARTINES, LAURO. Society and history in English Renaissance verse. (Bibl. 1985, 3482.) Rev. by John E. Van Domelen in SCN (44:1/2) 13–14; by Christopher Wortham in AUMLA (66) 301–3; by George Parfitt in NQ (33:4) 541–3.

3963. MARTZ, LOUIS L. English religious poetry, from Renaissance to Baroque. ExRC (11) 1985, 1–28.

3964. MERRIX, ROBERT P. The vale of lillies and the bower of bliss: soft-core pornography in Elizabethan poetry. JPC (19:4) 3–7, 11–16.

3965. MIROLLO, JAMES V.   Mannerism and Renaissance poetry: concept, mode, inner design. New Haven, CT: Yale UP, 1984. pp. xv, 225. Rev. by Murray Roston in JEGP (85:2) 256–8; by Lucy Gent in RQ (39:3) 545–8.

3966. NORBROOK, DAVID.   Poetry and politics in the English Renaissance. Boston, MA; Melbourne: Routledge & Kegan Paul. (Bibl. 1985, 3483.) Rev. by John N. King in HLQ (49:3) 277–80; by Christopher Hill in NQ (33:2) 226–7.

3967. OTTEN, CHARLOTTE F.   'Environ'd with eternity': God, poems, and plants in sixteenth and seventeenth century England. Lawrence, KS: Coronado Press, 1985. pp. xix, 198. Rev. by William C. Johnson in SixCT (17:4) 539; by Kathleen M. Swain in ELN (24:1) 100–2; by John E. van Domelen in SCN (44:4) 71–2; by Jeannine Bohlmeyer in ChrisL (35:3) 23–4.

3968. PEARCY, LEE T.   The mediated muse: English translations of Ovid 1560–1700. (Bibl. 1985, 3485.) Rev. by Frank T. Coulson in Manuscripta (30:1) 73–5; by James Egan in SCN (44:3) 43–4.

3969. PIGMAN, G. W., III.   Grief and English Renaissance elegy. Cambridge, MA: Harvard UP, 1985. (Cf. bibl. 1985, 3486.) Rev. by Celeste Schenck in SixCT (17:4) 528–9; by Achsah Guibbory in RQ (39:2) 384–6.

3970. RASPA, ANTHONY.   The emotive image: Jesuit poetics in the English Renaissance. (Bibl. 1985, 3488.) Rev. by Thomas P. Roche, Jr, in GHJ (9:1) 1985, 51–7; by David R. Shore in ESCan (12:4) 455–9.

3971. ROBINSON, LILLIAN S.   Monstrous regiment: the lady knight in sixteenth-century epic. New York; London: Garland, 1985. pp. v, 412. (Garland publications in comparative literature.)

3972. SCHLEINER, LOUISE.   The living lyre in English verse from Elizabeth through the Restoration. (Bibl. 1985, 3489.) Rev. by Derek Attridge in RQ (39:1) 134–6; by Alan Shaw in MichQR (25:4) 754–9; by Hallett Smith in JEGP (85:2) 271–2.

3973. —— Recent studies in poetry and music of the English Renaissance. ELR (16:1) 253–68.

3974. SHUTT, TIMOTHY BAKER.   *Logos* and *physis* – the word in the world: poetic uses of the stars during the Middle Ages and the Renaissance. *See* **3424.**

3975. SMITH, A. J.   The metaphysics of love: studies in Renaissance love poetry from Dante to Milton. (Bibl. 1985, 3491.) Rev. by Michael G. Brennan in NQ (33:4) 537–8; by Jonathan F. S. Post in RQ (39:3) 539–41.

3976. STEPHEN, JILL ELLEN.   The poetry of *Tottel's Miscellany*: its rhetorical context and place in the development of some aspects of sixteenth-century lyric style. Unpub. doct. diss., New York Univ. [Abstr. in DA (47) 1339A.]

3977. VAN, DAVID.   The dichotomous imagination: a study of English companion poems, 1596–1630. Unpub. doct. diss., Drew Univ. [Abstr. in DA (47) 1737A.]

3978. VENET, GISÈLE.   Mémoire et création dans la poétique baroque. *In* (pp. 137–46) **34.**

3979. WALLER, GARY F.   English poetry of the sixteenth century. London: Longman. pp. xiv, 315. (Longman literature in English.)

3980. WIDDICOMBE, KAREN ELIZABETH.   'The worth of my untutored lines': a study of *Lucrece* and the erotic narrative verse of the 1590's. Unpub. doct. diss., Univ. of Toronto. [Abstr. in DA (47) 2172A.]

3981. WILLIAMS, FRANKLIN B., JR (ed.).   The Gardyners passetaunce: (*c.* 1512). With notes on the two unique editions in Westminster Abbey Library, descriptions of the bindings in which they were preserved and the other items found in these bindings, by HOWARD M. NIXON. *See* **63.**

3982. WYNNE-DAVIES, M.   A study of Arthurian poetry in the English Renaissance from Spenser to Dryden. Unpub. doct. diss., Univ. of London, Royal Holloway Coll., 1985. [Abstr. in IT (35) 1491.]

3983. ZIM, R.   A study of metrical versions of the Psalms in English, 1530–1601. Unpub. doct. diss., Univ. of Leeds, 1984.

Prose

3984. BASKERVILLE, E. J.   Some lost works of propaganda and polemic from the Marian period. Library (8:1) 47–52.

3985. BRUBACHER, DEMAS.   Epideictic rhetoric in the works of John Colet. Unpub. doct. diss., Memphis State Univ., 1984. [Abstr. in DA (45) 2555A.]

3986. CRANE, MARY THOMAS.   Proverbial and aphoristic sayings: sources of authority in the English Renaissance. *See* **2408.**

3987. FEDDERSON, KIM MURRAY.   The rhetoric of the Elizabethan sermon. Unpub. doct. diss., York Univ. (Canada), 1985. [Abstr. in DA (47) 187A.]

3988. KRETZOI, CHARLOTTE.   Changes in the meaning and function of plain style. *In* (pp. 249–53) **11.**

3989. KRZESZOWSKI, TOMASZ P.   An Elizabethan contrastive grammar of Spanish and French. *In* (pp. 1303–10) **26.**

3990. MACLACHLAN, HUGH.   The death of Guyon and the *Elizabethan Book of Homilies*. Spenser Studies (4) 1983, 93–114.

3991. STEIN, DIETER.   Discourse markers in Early Modern English. *In* (pp. 283–302) **41.**

3992. TAYLOR, ANTHONY BRIAN.   Marlowe and *The Mirror for Magistrates*. NQ (33:3) 336–7.

3993. WAAGE, FREDERICK O.   Meg and Mall: two Renaissance London heroines. JPC (20:1) 105–17.

3994. WHITE, R. S.   The rise and fall of an Elizabethan fashion: love letters in romance and Shakespearean comedy. *See* **3937.**

3995. WILSON, K. J.   Incomplete fictions: the formation of English Renaissance dialogue. Washington, DC: Catholic UP of America, 1985. pp. 198. Rev. by Thomas F. Mayer in SixCT (17:4) 506–7; by Janel M. Mueller in RQ (39:2) 336–9.

3996. Entry cancelled.

Related Studies

3997. ANDREWS, KENNETH R.   Trade, plunder and settlement: maritime enterprise and the genesis of the British Empire, 1480–1630. *See* **3492.**

3998. BEIER, A. L. Masterless men: the vagrancy problem in England, 1560–1640. London: Methuen, 1985. pp. 233. Rev. by Peter Hyland in SCN (44:3) 47.

3999. BENTLEY, JERRY H. Humanists and holy writ: New Testament scholarship in the Renaissance. (Bibl. 1985, 3499.) Rev. by Daniel Bornstein in RenR (9:3) 1985, 220–2.

4000. BOOY, D. G. The morality of learning and the concept of the poet: a study of the debate on the purpose, role and scope of human learning in England in the late sixteenth and early seventeenth centuries, with particular reference to Samuel Daniel and Fulke Greville. Unpub. doct. diss., Univ. of London (Royal Holloway Coll.), 1984.

4001. CARRIVE, LUCIEN. Le royaume de Dieu, l'apocalypse et le millenium dans le protestantisme anglais classique. *In* (pp. 31–46) **2.**

4002. COLTHORPE, MARION. A 'prorogued' Elizabethan tournament. REEDNewsletter (11:2) 3–6. (*Refers to* **3319.**)

4003. COOGAN, ROBERT. The Pharisee against the Hellenist: Edward Lee versus Erasmus. RQ (39:3) 476–506.

4004. DiMATTEO, ANTHONY JOSEPH. A select anthology of Renaissance mythography. Unpub. doct. diss., City Univ. of New York. [Abstr. in DA (47) 897A.]

4005. DOWLING, MARIA. Humanism in the age of Henry VIII. London: Croom Helm. pp. 283.

4006. GRAFTON, ANTHONY; JARDINE, LISA. From Humanism to the humanities: education and the liberal arts in fifteenth- and sixteenth-century Europe. *See* **3526.**

4007. GRANT, PATRICK. Literature and the discovery of method in the English Renaissance. (Bibl. 1985, 3547.) Rev. by Graham Parry in THES (688) 17.

4008. GRAY, DOUGLAS. Books of comfort. *In* (pp. 209–21) **32.**

4009. GREENBLATT, STEPHEN. Psychoanalysis and Renaissance culture. *In* (pp. 210–24) **27.**

4010. GROSS, HARVEY. Technique and *épistémè*: John Dowland's *Can She Excuse My Wrongs*. BRH (86:3) 1983/85, 318–34.

4011. HALLEY, JANET E. Heresy, orthodoxy, and the politics of religious discourse: the case of the English Family of Love. Representations (15) 98–120.

4012. HAYES, T. WILSON. The peaceful apocalypse: Familism and literacy in sixteenth-century England. SixCT (17:2) 131–43.

4013. HENDERSON, KATHERINE USHER; McMANUS, BARBARA F. Half humankind: contexts and texts of the controversy about women in England, 1540–1640. Urbana: Illinois UP, 1985. pp. 390. Rev. by Linda Austin in SCN (44:1/2) 14–15.

4014. HOLECZEK, HEINZ (ed.). Erasmus Deutsch: vol. 1. Stuttgart: Frommann–Holzboog, 1983. pp. 339. Rev. by Peter G. Bietenholz in RQ (39:2) 297–9.

4015. HOLMES, PETER. Resistance and compromise: the political thought of the Elizabethan Catholics. Cambridge; New York: CUP, 1982. pp. viii, 357. Rev. by Raymond A. Anselment in YES (16) 234–6.

4016. HOULBROOKE, RALPH A. The English family 1450–1700. *See* **3530.**

4017. JAMES, MERVYN. Society, politics and culture: studies in early modern England. Cambridge: CUP. pp. vii, 485. (Past and present pubs.) (1485–1642.)

4018. KAHN, VICTORIA. Humanism and the resistance to theory. *In* (pp. 373–96) **27.**

4019. —— Rhetoric, prudence, and skepticism in the Renaissance. Ithaca, NY: Cornell UP, 1985. pp. 243. Rev. by Joel B. Altman in RQ (39:2) 314–17.

4020. KENNEDY, WILLIAM J. Jacopo Sannazaro and the uses of pastoral. Hanover, NH: New England UP, 1983. pp. viii, 238. Rev. by Fred J. Nichols in CL (38:4) 386–8.

4021. KING, JOHN N. Patronage and piety: the influence of Catherine Parr. *In* (pp. 43–60) **52.**

4022. KITTLESON, JAMES M.; TRANSUE, PAMELA J. (eds). Rebirth, reform, and resilience: universities in transition, 1300–1700. *See* **3538.**

4023. KLAITS, JOSEPH. Servants of Satan: the age of the witchhunts. Bloomington: Indiana UP. pp. 212. Rev. by Donald C. Nugent in SixCT (17:4) 560–1.

4024. KRATZMANN, GREGORY. *The Dialoges of Creatures Moralysed*: a sixteenth-century medieval book of ethics. *In* (pp. 222–32) **32.**

4025. LAKE, PETER. Moderate Puritans and the Elizabethan church. Cambridge; New York: CUP, 1982. pp. viii, 357. Rev. by Raymond A. Anselment in YES (16) 234–6.

4026. LAMB, MARY ELLEN. The Cooke sisters: attitudes towards learned women in the Renaissance. *In* (pp. 107–25) **52.**

4027. LEVIN, CAROLE. Lady Jane Grey: protestant queen and martyr. *In* (pp. 92–106) **52.**

4028. MANLEY, LAWRENCE (ed.). London in the age of Shakespeare: an anthology. London: Croom Helm. pp. 288.

4029. MARTINET, MARIE-MADELEINE. Iconologie élisabéthaine du temps mythique: l'homme au bord du jardin et la tour de feu. *In* (pp. 25–30) **2.**

4030. MENDYK, STAN. Early British chorography. SixCT (17:4) 459–81.

4031. MILLER, HELEN. Henry VIII and the English nobility. Oxford: Blackwell. pp. vi, 286.

4032. MONSARRAT, GILLES D. Light from the porch: stoicism and English Renaissance literature. (Bibl. 1985, 3525.) Rev. by Michael G. Brennan in NQ (33:2) 231–2.

4033. ORRÙ, MARCO. Anomy and reason in the English Renaissance. JHI (47:2) 177–96.

4034. PALMER, ALAN; PALMER, VERONICA. Who's who in

Shakespeare's England. (Bibl. 1985, 3528.) Rev. by E. W. Ives in YES (16) 240–2; by Lois Potter in ShS (36) 1983, 174.

4035. PRESCOTT, ANNE LAKE.   The Pearl of the Valois and Elizabeth I: Marguerite de Navarre's *Miroir* and Tudor England. *In* (pp. 61–76) **52.**

4036. PRIMUS, JOHN H.   The Dedham Sabbath debate: more light on English Sabbatarianism. SixCT (17:1) 87–102.

4037. QUINN, DAVID BEERS.   Set fair for Roanoke: voyages and colonies, 1584–1606. Chapel Hill: North Carolina UP, 1985. pp. 467. Rev. by Virginia DeJohn Anderson in RQ (39:2) 304–6.

4038. RUMMEL, ERIKA.   Erasmus as a translator of the classics. Toronto: Toronto UP, 1985. pp. 182. Rev. by J. K. Sowards in RQ (39:2) 295–7.

4039. SCARISBRICK, J. J.   The Reformation and the English people. *See* **3566.**

4040. SCHMITT, CHARLES B.   John Case and Aristotelianism in Renaissance England. (Bibl. 1985, 3533.) Rev. by B. C. Southgate in JHP (24:1) 124–5; by Noel Malcolm in NQ (33:1) 104.

4041. SHIRLEY, JOHN W.; HOENIGER, F. DAVID (eds).   Science and the arts in the Renaissance. Washington, DC: Folger Shakespeare Library, 1985. pp. 220. Rev. by Laurinda S. Dixon in RenR (10:4) 386–8.

4042. SIDER, ROBERT D. (ed.).   Collected works of Erasmus: vol. 42, New Testament scholarship: paraphrases on Romans and Galatians. Trans. and notes by JOHN P. PAYNE, ALBERT RABIL, JR, and WARREN S. SMITH, JR. Toronto; London: Toronto UP, 1984. pp. xxxviii, 192.

4043. SMITH, LACEY BALDWIN.   Treason in Tudor England: politics and paranoia. London: Cape. pp. 320.

4044. STRONG, ROY.   Henry, Prince of Wales: and England's lost renaissance. London: Thames & Hudson. pp. 264.

4045. THORNE, J. R.; UHART, MARIE-CLAIRE.   Robert Crowley's *Piers Plowman. See* **3637.**

4046. TRINKAUS, CHARLES.   The scope of Renaissance Humanism. (Bibl. 1985, 3538.) Rev. by John D'Amico in RenR (9:4) 1985, 281–3.

4047. VICKERS, BRIAN.   Valla's ambivalent praise of pleasure: rhetoric in the service of Christianity. Viator (17) 271–319.

4048. —— (ed.).   Occult and scientific mentalities in the Renaissance. (Bibl. 1985, 3539.) Rev. by Thomas H. Jobe in SixCT (17:1) 113–15; by Frank L. Borchardt in RQ (39:1) 73–6.

4049. WAYNE, VALERIE.   Some sad sentence: Vives' *Instruction of a Christian Woman. In* (pp. 15–29) **52.**

4050. WHIGHAM, FRANK.   Ambition and privilege: the social tropes of Elizabethan courtesy theory. (Bibl. 1985, 3391.) Rev. by Ann Thompson in Prose Studies (9:1) 75–6.

4051. ZARET, DAVID.   The heavenly contract: ideology and organization in pre-revolutionary Puritanism. Chicago: Chicago UP, 1985. pp. 214. Rev. by Norman L. Jones in SixCT (17:4) 517–18; by Christian R. Davis in SCN (44:4) 69–70.

Literary Theory

This section is intended to contain studies **about** the literary theory, literary historiography, literary criticism, etc., produced *in* the sixteenth century. For modern works **of** literary history and criticism dealing generally with this period, see under 'Sixteenth Century: General Literary Studies'.

4052. CREWE, JONATHAN. Hidden designs: the critical profession and Renaissance literature. New York; London: Methuen. pp. viii, 181.

4053. DERRICK, THOMAS J. (ed.). The arte of rhetorique. (Bibl. 1985, 3545.) Rev. by Gerald Morgan in MLR (81:4) 977–8.

4054. PLETT, HEINRICH F. Englische Rhetorik und Poetik 1479–1660. Eine systematische Bibliographie. *See* **1240.**

AUTHORS
Roger Ascham

4055. WILSON, K. J. Incomplete fictions: the formation of English Renaissance dialogue. *See* **3995.**

Anne Askew

4056. BEILIN, ELAINE V. Anne Askew's self-portrait in the *Examinations. In* (pp. 77-91) **52.**

John Bale

4057. PINEAS, RAINER. John Bale on Thomas More. Moreana (23:90) 77–8.

Lodowick Bryskett

4058. TROMLY, FREDERIC B. Lodowick Bryskett's elegies on Sidney in Spenser's *Astrophel* volume. RES (37:147) 384–8.

George Buchanan

4059. BERKOWITZ, STEVEN BENNETT. A critical edition of George Buchanan's *Baptistes* and of the anonymous *Tyrannicall-Government Anatomized. See* **3831.**

William Camden

4060. DUNN, R. D. English proverbs from William Camden's *Remains Concerning Britain. See* **2414.**

4061. —— Fragment of an unpublished essay on printing by William Camden. *See* **150.**

4062. —— (ed.). Remains concerning Britain. Toronto; Buffalo, NY; London: Toronto UP, 1984. pp. l, 576. Rev. by Richard L. DeMolen in SixCT (16) 1985, 536–7; by Bryce Lyon in Spec (61:3) 632–3; by F. J. Levy in RQ (39:1) 128–30; by David Norbrook in NQ (33:4) 546–7; by James P. Carley in RenR (9:4) 1985, 308–9.

John Colet

4063. TRAPP, J. B. An English late-medieval cleric and Italian thought: the case of John Colet, Dean of St Paul's (1467–1519). *In* (pp. 233–50) **32.**

Sir John Davies (1569–1626)

4064. COLTHORPE, MARION. Sir John Davies and an Elizabethan court entertainment. NQ (33:3) 373–4.

4065. HILLER, GEOFFREY G. Allusions to Spenser by John Davies and Sir John Davies. NQ (33:3) 394–5.

4066. KLEMP, P. J.   Fulke Greville and Sir John Davies: a reference guide. Boston, MA: G. K. Hall, 1985. pp. 128. Rev. by Sara Jayne Steen in SCN (44:3) 43.

Thomas Deloney

4067. DEVINE, PAUL.   Unity and meaning in Thomas Deloney's *Thomas of Reading*. NM (87:4) 578–93.

4068. REUTER, O. R.   Proverbs, proverbial sentences and phrases in Thomas Deloney's works. *See* **2422.**

4069. —— Some notes on Thomas Deloney's indebtedness to Shakespeare. NM (87:2) 255–61.

Richard Edwards

4070. GUINLE, FRANCIS.   Concerning a source of Richard Edwards' *Damon and Pithias*. CEl (30) 71–2.

Sir Thomas Elyot

4071. STEIN, GABRIELE.   Definitions and first person pronoun involvement in Thomas Elyot's *Dictionary*. *In* (pp. 1465–74) **26.**

4072. WILSON, K. J.   Incomplete fictions: the formation of English Renaissance dialogue. *See* **3995.**

John Fisher

4073. MURPHY, CLARE MARIE.   Saint John Fisher and the Field of the Cloth of Gold. Moreana (23:89) 5–13.

Abraham Fraunce

4074. TAYLOR, ANTHONY BRIAN.   Abraham Fraunce's debts to Arthur Golding in *Amintas Dale*. NQ (33:3) 333–6.

4075. —— 'O brave new world': Abraham Fraunce and *The Tempest*. ELN (23:4) 18–23.

Thomas Garter

4076. HAPPÉ, PETER.   Aspects of dramatic technique in Thomas Garter's *Susanna*. METh (8:1) 61–3.

4077. HORNER, OLGA.   Susanna's double life. METh (8:1) 76–102.

4078. MILLS, DAVID.   The Comedy of Virtuous and Godly Susanna. METh (8:1) 67–71. (Review of performance by Joculatores Lancastrienses.)

George Gascoigne

4079. STEPHENS, JOHN.   George Gascoigne's *Posies* and the persona in sixteenth-century poetry. Neophilologus (70:1) 130–41.

4080. WILLIAMS, NANCY.   The eight parts of a theme in *Gascoigne's Memories:* III. SP (83:2) 117–37.

Arthur Golding

4081. TAYLOR, ANTHONY BRIAN.   Abraham Fraunce's debts to Arthur Golding in *Amintas Dale*. *See* **4074.**

4082. —— Debts to Golding in Spenser's minor poems. NQ (33:3) 345–7.

4083. —— George Sandys and Arthur Golding. NQ (33:3) 387–91.

4084. —— Spenser and Golding: further debts in *The Faerie Queene*. NQ (33:3) 342–5.

Barnabe Googe

4085. BECKWITH, MARC.   Barnabe Googe's *Zodiake of Life*: a translation reconsidered. JRMMRA (7) 97–107.

Robert Greene

4086. MAGUIRE, LAURIE E. John Holland and *John of Bordeaux*. *See* **3912.**

4087. PAROTTI, PHILLIP. Having it both ways: Renaissance traditions in Robert Greene's *Mars and Venus*. ExRC (12) 46–56.

4088. RONAN, CLIFFORD J. *Selimus* and the blinding of Gloster. *See* **3922.**

4089. SONDERGARD, SID. Bruno's dialogue war on pedantry: an Elizabethan dramatic motif. Unpub. doct. diss., Univ. of Southern California. [Abstr. in DA (47) 539A.]

4090. STEIN, DIETER. Discourse markers in Early Modern English. *In* (pp. 283–302) **41.**

John Hall

4091. ZIM, RIVKAH. The Maidstone Burghmote and John Hall's *Courte of Vertue* (1565). NQ (33:3) 320–7.

Henry Hare

4092. McCABE, RICHARD A. Meditation, pilgrimage, and paradise: the literary career of Henry Hare, second Lord Coleraine. Library (8:1) 59–67. (Re-attribution of works credited to Hugh Hare.)

Sir John Harington (1561–1612)

4093. CRAIG, D. H. Sir John Harington. Boston, MA: G. K. Hall, 1985. pp. 168. (Twayne's English authors, 386.) Rev. by T. G. A. Nelson in AUMLA (65) 105–8.

4094. NELSON, T. G. A. Sir John Harington and the Renaissance debate over allegory. SP (82:3) 1985, 359–79.

Stephen Hawes

4095. EDWARDS, A. S. G. William Walter and Hawes's *Pastime of Pleasure*. NQ (33:4) 450–1.

4096. LERER, SETH. The rhetoric of fame: Stephen Hawes's aureate diction. Spenser Studies (5) 1984, 169–84.

Richard Hooker

4097. FAULKNER, ROBERT K. Richard Hooker and the politics of a Christian England. (Bibl. 1982, 4301.) Rev. by Mark R. Shaw in SixCT (17:3) 370–1.

4098. McCABE, RICHARD A. Richard Hooker's polemic rhetoric. Long Room (31) 7–17.

Will Kemp

4099. YAXLEY, SUSAN (ed.). Kemps nine daies wonder: performed in a daunce from London to Norwich: containing the pleasure, paines and kinde entertainment of William Kemp betweene London and that Citty in his late Morrice: wherein is somewhat set downe worth note; to reproove the slaunders spred of him; many things merry, nothing hurtfull. *See* **2550.**

Thomas Kyd

4100. DAALDER, JOOST. The role of 'Senex' in Kyd's *The Spanish Tragedy*. CompDr (20:3) 247–60.

4101. JOY, SUSAN E. The Kyd/Marlowe connection. NQ (33:3) 338–9.

4102. MIOLA, ROBERT S.   Another Senecan echo in Kyd's *The Spanish Tragedy*. NQ (33:3) 337.

John Leland

4103. CARLEY, JAMES P.   John Leland and the contents of English pre-dissolution libraries: Glastonbury Abbey. *See* **144.**

4104. —— John Leland in Paris: the evidence of his poetry. SP (83:1) 1–50.

Thomas Lodge

4105. CUVELIER, ÉLIANE.   Thomas Lodge: témoin de son temps. Paris: Didier, 1984. pp. 574. Rev. by Arthur F. Kinney in RQ (39:4) 794–6.

4106. FALKE, ANNE.   The 'Marguerite' and the 'Margarita' in Thomas Lodge's *A Margarite of America*. Neophilologus (70:1) 142–54.

4107. GENTILI, VANNA.   Thomas Lodge's *Wounds of Civil War*: an assessment of context, sources and structure. YREAL (2) 1984, 119–64.

John Lyly

4108. HODGES, DEVON L.   Renaissance fictions of anatomy. Amherst: Massachusetts UP, 1985. pp. xii, 153. Rev by Robert Boenig in SCN (44:4) 57; by Graham Parry in THES (688) 17; by David Novarr in RQ (39:2) 339–43.

4109. SCRAGG, LEAH.   The metamorphosis of *Gallathea*: a study in creative adaptation. Washington, DC: UP of America, 1982. pp. viii, 141. Rev. by Lois Potter in ShS (37) 1984, 191–2.

Christopher Marlowe

4110. BECKERMAN, BERNARD.   Scene patterns in *Doctor Faustus* and *Richard III*. *In* (pp. 31–41) **50.**

4111. BENSTON, KIMBERLY W.   The shaping of the Marlovian sublime. Unpub. doct. diss., Yale Univ., 1982. [Abstr. in DA (46) 3373A–4A.]

4112. BOCCIA, MICHAEL.   Faustus unbound: a reconsideration of the fate of Faustus in Christopher Marlowe's *Doctor Faustus*. USFLQ (25:1/2) 8–12.

4113. BROWN, JOHN RUSSELL (ed.).   *Tamburlaine the Great, Edward the Second* and *The Jew of Malta*: a casebook. (Bibl. 1982, 4319.) Rev. by T. W. Craik in YES (16) 239–40.

4114. BURNETT, MARK THORNTON.   Two notes on metre and rhyme in *Doctor Faustus*. NQ (33:3) 337–8.

4115. CHEUNG, KING KOK.   The woe and wonder of despair: a study of Doctor Faustus, Macbeth, and Satan. Unpub. doct. diss., Univ. of California, Berkeley, 1984. [Abstr. in DA (46) 987A.]

4116. COVELLA, FRANCIS DOLORES.   The choral nexus in *Doctor Faustus*. SELit (26:2) 201–15.

4117. CUNNINGHAM, KAREN JEAN.   The spectacle of the self: language and embodiment in Marlowe. Unpub. doct. diss., Univ. of California, Santa Barbara, 1985. [Abstr. in DA (47) 1331A.]

4118. DANSON, LAWRENCE.   Continuity and character in Shakespeare and Marlowe. SELit (26:2) 217–34.

4119. ERIKSEN, ROY T.   Marlowe's Petrarch: *In morte di madonna Laura.*
CEl (29) 13–25.

4120. HJORT, ANNE METTE.   The interests of critical editorial
practice. *See* **501.**

4121. JOBE, DON.   Marlowe's *Dr Faustus.* Exp (44:3) 12–14.

4122. JOY, SUSAN E.   The Kyd/Marlowe connection. *See* **4101.**

4123. KEEFER, MICHAEL H.   Misreading Faustus misreading: the
question of context. DalR (65:4) 1985/86, 511–33.

4124. LEONARD, JAMES S.   Melville's Ahab as Marlovian hero. ATQ
(62) 47–58.

4125. MACINTYRE, JEAN.   *Doctor Faustus* and the later Shakespeare.
CEl (29) 27–37. (*Troilus and Cressida, King Lear, Macbeth.*)

4126. ORMEROD, DAVID; WORTHAM, CHRISTOPHER (eds).   *Dr Faustus:*
the A-text. (Bibl. 1985, 3608.) Rev. by J. S. Ryan in AUMLA (66)
316–18.

4127. PINCISS, GERALD.   Christopher Marlowe. New York: Ungar,
1975; London: Lorrimer, 1985. pp. 138. (World dramatists.)

4128. PISTOTNIK, V.   Marlowe in performance: professional productions on the British stage, 1960–1982. Unpub. doct. diss., Univ. of
Birmingham, 1983/84.

4129. SHEPHERD, SIMON.   Marlowe and the politics of Elizabethan
theatre. *See* **3929.**

4130. SOKOLOVA, BOIKA.   Renaissance aesthetics and Marlowe's
Faustus. In (pp. 127–35) **17.**

4131. SONDERGARD, SID.   Bruno's dialogue war on pedantry: an
Elizabethan dramatic motif. *See* **4089.**

4132. TAKEMOTO, YUKIHIRO.   Minshubon *Faust Hakushi* to *Faustus
Hakushi:* kyokun kara monogatari e. (*Doctor Faust* and *Doctor Faustus:*
from examples to history.) SEL (63:1) 29–40.

4133. TAYLOR, ANTHONY BRIAN.   Marlowe and *The Mirror for Magistrates. See* **3992.**

4134. TETZELI VON ROSADOR, K.   'Supernatural soliciting': temptation and imagination in *Doctor Faustus* and *Macbeth. In* (pp. 42–59) **50.**

4135. VON BRENTANO, ALISA R.   Marlowe and Melville. Unpub. doct.
diss., Univ. of Tennessee, 1985. [Abstr. in DA (46) 2687A.]

4136. WYMER, ROWLAND.   'When I behold the heavens': a reading of
Doctor Faustus. EngS (67:6) 505–10.

'Martin Marprelate'

4137. APPLETON, ELIZABETH.   Oxford's role in the Marprelate
controversy. SNL (36:1) 10.

Francis Merbury

4138. SCOLNICOV, HANNA.   To understand a parable: the mimetic
mode of *The Marriage of Wit and Wisdom.* CEl (29) 1–11.

Sir Thomas More

4139. BAUMANN, UWE.   Die Antike in den Epigrammen und Briefen
Sir Thomas Mores. Zurich: Schoningh, 1984. (Cf. bibl. 1985, 3617.)
Rev. by R. J. Schoeck in RQ (39:4) 760–2.

4140. Billingsley, Dale B.   The editorial design of the 1557 *English Works. See* **91.**

4141. Chené, Adèle.   La proximité et la distance dans l'*Utopie* de Thomas More. RenR (10:3) 277–88.

4142. Doyle, Charles Clay.   Looking behind two proverbs of More. *See* **2413.**

4143. Foley, Stephen Merriam; Miller, Clarence H. (eds).   The complete works of St Thomas More: vol. 11, *The Answer to a Poisoned Book.* New Haven, CT; London: Yale UP, 1985. pp. xcii, 424.

4144. Fox, Alistair.   Thomas More: history and providence. (Bibl. 1985, 3624.) Rev. by Calvin A. Pater in JMH (58:2) 531–3.

4145. Gabrieli, Vittorio.   *Sir Thomas More*: sources, characters, ideas. Moreana (23:90) 17–43.

4146. Gogan, Brian.   The common corps of Christendom: ecclesiological themes in the writings of Sir Thomas More. (Bibl. 1984, 3622a.) Rev. by Calvin A. Pater in JMH (58:2) 531–3, by André Godin in Moreana (23:89) 81–8.

4147. Kendall, Angela J.   Thomas More, Richard Fox and the manor of Temple Guyting in 1515. Moreana (23:91/92) 5–10.

4148. Kendrick, Christopher.   More's *Utopia* and uneven development. Boundary 2 (13:2/3) 1985, 233–66.

4149. Kuon, Peter.   Utopischer Entwurf und fiktionale Vermittlung. Studien zum Gattungswandel der literarischen Utopie zwischen Humanismus und Frühaufklärung. Heidelberg: Winter. pp. 536. (Studia romanica, 66.)

4150. Logan, George M.   The meaning of Thomas More's *Utopia.* (Bibl. 1985, 3631.) Rev. by Calvin A. Pater in JMH (58:2) 531–3.

4151. Marc'hador, Germain.   Thomas More vu par l'*Hispanidad.* Moreana (23:91/92) 113–18.

4152. Marius, Richard.   Thomas More: a biography. (Bibl. 1985, 3634.) Rev. by Thurman L. Smith in SixCT (17:4) 550–2.

4153. Marmion, John P.   'The controversial Sir Thomas More.' Moreana (23:90) 57–9.

4154. Pineas, Rainer.   John Bale on Thomas More. *See* **4057.**

4155. Pitcher, Edward W. R.   'To die laughing': Poe's allusion to Sir Thomas More in *The Assignation.* SSF (23:2) 197–200.

4156. Rousseau, Marie-Claude.   Non sum Oedipus sed Morus. Moreana (23:91/92) 173–87.

4157. Rude, Donald W.   Two unreported references to Sir Thomas More. Moreana (23:91/92) 83–4.

4158. Samaan, Angele Botros.   Death and the death-penalty in More's *Utopia* and some utopian novels. Moreana (23:90) 5–15. (*Erewhon, The Fixed Period, News from Nowhere, Brave New World, Nineteen Eighty-Four.*)

4159. Sawada, Paul Akio.   Was More a Utopian or a Realpolitiker? Moreana (23:91/92) 21–9.

4160. Schirmer, Ruth; Schirmer, Walter F. (sels and trans).

Thomas Morus Lebenszeugnis in Briefen. Heidelberg: Schneider, 1984. pp. 207.

4161. SCHOECK, R. J.   Telling More from Erasmus: an 'essai' in Renaissance humanism. Moreana (23:91/92) 11–19.

4162. SMITH, CONSTANCE.   Charles Dickens on More. Moreana (23:91/92) 37–8.

4163. TELLE, EMILE V.   Edmund Lodge on John and Thomas More (1795). Moreana (23:89) 93–6.

4164. VAN DER BLOM, NICOLAS.   La démission de More selon Érasme (d'après Allen X., lettres 2735, 2750 et 2780). Moreana (23:89) 29–34.

4165. VASQUÉ, FRANÇOIS.   Thomas More s'est-il suicidé? Moreana (23:91/92) 119–20.

4166. WEGEMER, GERARD B.   The literary and philosophic design of Thomas More's *Utopia*. Unpub. doct. diss., Univ. of Notre Dame. [Abstr. in DA (47) 917A.]

4167. WILSON, K. J.   Incomplete fictions: the formation of English Renaissance dialogue. *See* **3995.**

4168. WINKLER, GERHARD B.   Cönobium, Religion und Toleranz. Oder: wie christlich sind Thomas Mores Utopier? WBEP (80) 277–86.

Richard Mulcaster

4169. BREITENBERG, MARK.   '. . . the hole matter opened': iconic representation and interpretation in *The Quenes Majesties Passage*. Criticism (28:1) 1–25.

Thomas Nashe

4170. CREWE, JONATHAN V.   Unredeemed rhetoric: Thomas Nashe and the scandal of authorship. (Bibl. 1985, 3649.) Rev. by Paul Ramsey in RenR (9:3) 1985, 223–6.

4171. HODGES, DEVON L.   Renaissance fictions of anatomy. *See* **4108.**

4172. HUTSON, L. M.   Thomas Nashe's literary exploitation of festive wit in its social context. Unpub. doct. diss., Univ. of Oxford, 1983.

4173. MOSS, R.   Burlesque rhetoric in Chaucer, Nashe and Sterne. *See* **3713.**

4174. TOBIN, J. J. M.   Nashe and *Measure for Measure*. NQ (33:3) 360.

4175. WEIMANN, ROBERT.   Fictionality and the rise of realism: Rabelais and Nashe. *In* (pp. 139–43) **19.**

Thomas Norton

4176. RASMUSSEN, ERIC.   The implications of past tense verbs in early Elizabethan dumb shows. *See* **3918.**

Edward de Vere, Earl of Oxford

4177. APPLETON, ELIZABETH.   Oxford's role in the Marprelate controversy. *See* **4137.**

4178. CYR, GORDON C.   The 'burden of proof' falls on all of us. SNL (36:2) 31.

4179. —— Macbeth and the holes in the Stratfordian chronology. SNL (36:4) 56.

4180. —— The Stratfordians' own case against their candidate. SNL (36:3) 40.

4181. CYR, HELEN W.   Lord Oxford said it first. SNL (36:1) 11.

4182. Fowler, William Plumer.   Shakespeare revealed in Oxford's letters. SNL (36:3) 40.

4183. Marder, Louis.   Oxford as author? SNL (36:4) 57.

4184. Sweet, George Elliott.   Seven for Shakespeare. SNL (36:2) 28–9.

George Peele

4185. Aspöck, Ingeborg M.   'The herald of his age.' Zum dramatischen Werk des Elisabethaners George Peele. Unpub. doct. diss., Univ. of Salzburg, 1985.

4186. Edwards, Philip.   'Seeing is believing': action and narration in *The Old Wives Tale* and *The Winter's Tale. In* (pp. 79–93) **50.**

4187. Nellis, Marilyn K.   Peele's *Edward I.* Exp (44:2) 5–7.

Mary Herbert, Countess of Pembroke

4188. Bornstein, Diane.   The style of the Countess of Pembroke's translation of Philippe de Mornay's *Discours de la vie et de la mort. In* (pp. 126–34) **52.**

4189. Fisken, Beth Wynne.   Mary Sidney's *Psalmes*: education and wisdom. *In* (pp. 166–83) **52.**

4190. Hannay, Margaret P.   'Doo what men may sing': Mary Sidney and the tradition of admonitory dedication. *In* (pp. 149–65) **52.**

George Puttenham

4191. Attridge, Derek.   Puttenham's perplexity: nature, art, and the supplement in Renaissance poetic theory. *In* (pp. 257–79) **27.**

4192. Crewe, Jonathan V.   The hegemonic theater of George Puttenham. ELR (16:1) 71–85.

Richard Rainolde

4193. Ronan, Clifford J.   Daniel, Rainolde, Demosthenes, and the degree speech of Shakespeare's Ulysses. RenR (9:2) 1985, 111–18.

Sir Walter Ralegh

4194. Bendarz, James P.   Ralegh in Spenser's historical allegory. Spenser Studies (4) 1983, 49–70.

4195. Clanton, Stacy M.   The 'number' of Sir Walter Ralegh's *Booke of the Ocean to Scinthia. See* **145.**

4196. Drummond, C. Q.   Style in Ralegh's short poems. SCR (3:1) 23–36.

4197. Hammond, Gerald (ed.).   Sir Walter Ralegh: selected writings. (Bibl. 1985, 3659.) Rev. by John Gouws in NQ (33:3) 410–11.

4198. Rudick, Michael.   The text of Ralegh's lyric, *What Is Our Life?* SP (83:1) 76–87.

Margaret More Roper

4199. Verbrugge, Rita.   Margaret More Roper's personal expression in the *Devout Treatise upon the Pater Noster. In* (pp. 30–42) **52.**

Thomas Sackville

4200. Rasmussen, Eric.   The implications of past tense verbs in early Elizabethan dumb shows. *See* **3918.**

Reginald Scot

4201. West, Robert H.   Reginald Scot and Renaissance writings on witchcraft. Boston, MA: G. K. Hall, 1984. pp. 142. (Twayne's English authors, 385.) Rev. by Wayne Shumaker in RQ (39:2) 323–5.

Sir Philip Sidney

4202. BISWAS, D. C.   Shakespeare's conception of a courtier. Jadavpur University Essays and Studies (Calcutta) (4) 1984, 44–52.

4203. BOGDAN, DEANNE.   Sidney's defence of Plato and the 'lying' Greek poets: the argument from hypothesis. CML (7:1) 43–55.

4204. CRAFT, WILLIAM.   The discovery of delight in Sydney's *New Arcadia*. RenP 1–10.

4205. DRENNAN, WILLIAM R.   'Or know your strengths': Sidney's attitude toward rebellion in *Ister Banke*. NQ (33:3) 339–40.

4206. —— Sidney's debt to Machiavelli: a new look. JRMMRA (7) 83–96.

4207. DROMODE, GRIGORE; MUGURE, MIHAELA.   Ecouri ale gîndirii renascentiste în poezia lui Philip Sidney. (Echoes of Renaissance thought in Philip Sidney's poetry.) Steaua (37:10) 30.

4208. FERRY, ANNE.   The 'inward' language: sonnets of Wyatt, Sidney, Shakespeare, Donne. (Bibl. 1985, 3669.) Rev. by John H. Ottenhoff in SCN (44:1/2) 10–12.

4209. GOUWS, JOHN (ed.).   The prose works of Fulke Greville, Lord Brooke. Oxford: Clarendon Press. pp. lxvii, 279. Rev. by Blair Worden in LRB (8:12) 19–20, 22; by A. G. Voss in UES (24:2) 37–8; by H. R. Woudhuysen in TLS, 15 Aug., 895.

4210. GREENFIELD, THELMA N.   The eye of judgment: reading the *New Arcadia*. (Bibl. 1985, 3671.) Rev. by Katherine Duncan-Jones in YES (16) 236–8.

4211. HOGAN, PATRICK G., JR.   *The Arcadia*: from Sidney's prose to Shirley's drama. ExRC (12) 36–45.

4212. LEVAO, RONALD.   Renaissance minds and their fictions: Cusanus, Sidney, Shakespeare. Berkeley; London: California UP, 1985. pp. xxiv, 446. (Cf. bibl. 1979, 4264.) Rev. by Florence Mcgee in SCN (44:3) 42; by Raymond B. Waddington in RQ (39:4) 791–3.

4213. LINDHEIM, NANCY.   The structures of Sidney's *Arcadia*. (Bibl. 1985, 3675.) Rev. by Katherine Duncan-Jones in MLR (81:4) 981–3.

4214. MANGANARO, ELISE SALEM.   Plato and Aristotle in Sidney's poetics: theory and practice. Unpub. doct. diss., Univ. of North Carolina at Chapel Hill, 1985. [Abstr. in DA (46) 3360A.]

4215. PARKINSON, E. MALCOLM.   Sidney's portrayal of mounted combat with lances. Spenser Studies (5) 1984, 231–51.

4216. ROCHE, THOMAS P., JR.   Autobiographical elements in Sidney's *Astrophil and Stella*. Spenser Studies (5) 1984, 209–29.

4217. SIEMIRADZKI, M. A.   Context and character in Sidney's *Arcadia*s. Unpub. doct. diss., Univ. of York. [Abstr. in IT (35) 1083.]

4218. SIMON, ELLIOTT M.   Sidney's *Old Arcadia*: in praise of folly. SixCT (17:3) 285–302.

4219. SUTTON, JOHN L., JR.   A historical source for the rebellion of the commons in Sidney's *Arcadia*. ELN (23:4) 6–11.

4220. TROMLY, FREDERIC B.   Lodowick Bryskett's elegies on Sidney in Spenser's *Astrophel* volume. *See* **4058.**

4221. TUCKER, ELLEN DEITZ.   Friendly rivalry in Philip Sidney's *Arcadia.* Unpub. doct. diss., Claremont Graduate School, 1985. [Abstr. in DA (46) 2304A.]

4222. VOSS, A. E.   The 'right poet' in *Astrophil and Stella.* UES (24:2) 7–10.

4223. WALLER, GARY F.; MOORE, MICHAEL D. (eds).   Sir Philip Sidney and the interpretation of Renaissance culture: the poet in his time and in ours: a collection of critical and scholarly essays. (Bibl. 1984, 3704.) Rev. by Katherine Duncan-Jones in NQ (33:2) 221.

4224. WOODHUYSEN, H. R.   *Astrophel and Stella* 75: a 'new' text. RES (37:147) 388–92.

John Skelton

4225. HALPERN, RICHARD.   John Skelton and the poetics of primitive accumulation. *In* (pp. 225–56) **27.**

4226. SCATTERGOOD, JOHN.   Skelton and traditional satire: *Ware the Hauke.* MÆ (55:2) 203–16.

4227. —— (ed.).   The complete English poems. (Bibl. 1983, 4258.) Rev. by B. O'Donoghue in MÆ (55:2) 301–3.

4228. SCHIBANOFF, SUSAN.   Taking Jane's cue: *Phyllyp Sparowe* as a primer for women readers. PMLA (101:5) 832–47.

4229. SHARRATT, BERNARD.   John Skelton: finding a voice – notes after Bakhtin. *In* (pp. 192–222) **33.**

Robert Southwell

4230. OXLEY, B. W.   The poetry of an artificial man: a study of the Latin and English verse of Robert Southwell. Unpub. doct. diss., Univ. of St Andrews, 1985. [Abstr. in IT (35) 44.]

4231. WINTER, DEBORAH KATHLEEN.   The image of the archetypal 'burning babe' in metaphysical poetry and art. Unpub. doct. diss., Univ. of Miami, 1985. [Abstr. in DA (46) 1954A.]

4232. YOSHIDA, SACHIKO.   Southwell to Crashaw. (Southwell and Crashaw.) Kyoto: Appollon Press. pp. xii, 304.

Edmund Spenser

4233. BEECHER, DONALD.   Spenser's Redcrosse Knight and his encounter with Despair: some aspects of the 'Elizabethan malady'. CEl (30) 1–15.

4234. BENDARZ, JAMES P.   Ralegh in Spenser's historical allegory. *See* **4194.**

4235. BIEMAN, ELIZABETH.   'Sometimes I . . . mask in myrth lyke to a Comedy': Spenser's *Amoretti.* Spenser Studies (4) 1983, 131–41.

4236. BOCHORISHVILI, N. K.   Slovo v poèzii Edmunda Spensera. (The word in Spenser's poetry.) VMU (1986:4) 43–8.

4237. BORRIS, K. H.   A commentary on Book Six of Spenser's *The Faerie Queene.* Unpub. doct. diss., Univ. of Edinburgh. [Abstr. in IT (36) 910.]

4238. BRADY, CIARAN.   Spenser's Irish crisis: humanism and experience in the 1590s. Past and Present (111) 17–49.

4239. BRENNAN, MICHAEL G. Foxes and wolves in Elizabethan episcopal propaganda. *See* **2507.**

4240. BROWN, MARIANNE. Spenserian technique: *The Shepheardes Calender.* YREAL (2) 1984, 54–118.

4241. CALDWELL, ELLEN CASHWELL. The breach of time: history and violence in the *Aeneid, The Faerie Queene,* and *2 Henry VI.* Unpub. doct. diss., Univ. of North Carolina at Chapel Hill. [Abstr. in DA (47) 1719A.]

4242. CHENEY, DONALD. Spenser's fortieth birthday and related fictions. Spenser Studies (4) 1983, 3–31.

4243. CRAIG, JOANNE. The queen, her handmaid, and Spenser's career. ESCan (12:3) 255–68.

4244. DASENBROCK, REED WAY. Escaping the squire's double bind in Books III and IV of *The Faerie Queene.* SELit (26:1) 25–45.

4245. DAVIES, R. 'Femina Christiana' and the triumph of 'caritas': humanist influence upon the presentation of Spenser's Britomart. Unpub. doct. diss., Univ. of Wales, Cardiff, 1983.

4246. DAVIES, STEVIE. The idea of woman in Renaissance literature: the feminine reclaimed. Brighton: Harvester Press. pp. xi, 273. Rev. by S. J. Wiseman in THES (715) 17.

4247. DeNEEF, A. LEIGH. Spenser and the motives of metaphor. (Bibl. 1984, 3726.) Rev. by Gerald Morgan in MLR (81:4) 980–1.

4248. DUNDAS, JUDITH. The spider and the bee: the artistry of Spenser's *Faerie Queene.* Urbana: Illinois UP, 1985. pp. 232. Rev. by Donald Cheney in RQ (39:4) 798–81; by L. S. Young in SCN (44:3) 40–2.

4249. ERIKSEN, ROY TOMMY. A mannerist topos in Spenser and Shakespeare. *In* (pp. 17–28) **18.**

4250. FUMERTON, PATRICIA. Exchanging gifts: the Elizabethan currency of children and poetry. *See* **3952.**

4251. GAFFNEY, C. *Colin Clouts Come Home Againe.* Unpub. doct. diss., Univ. of Edinburgh, 1983.

4252. GARDNER, PHILIP ALAN TENNANT. The banquet of the word: Biblical authority and interpretation in Spenser and the Fletchers. Unpub. doct. diss., Univ. of Toronto, 1985. [Abstr. in DA (47) 909A.]

4253. GLECKNER, ROBERT F. Blake and Spenser. Baltimore, MD; London: Johns Hopkins UP, 1985. pp. xi, 403. Rev. by Irene Tayler in RQ (39:4) 802–3.

4254. GOLD, EVA. Lyric fictions in *The Faerie Queene* and three Shakespearean plays. Unpub. doct. diss., Indiana Univ. [Abstr. in DA (47) 1734A.]

4255. GOLDBERG, JONATHAN. Endlesse works: Spenser and the structures of discourse. (Bibl. 1985, 3706.) Rev. by G. L. Teskey in RenR (9:2) 1985, 121–9.

4256. GREENFIELD, SAYRE NELSON. Glances at faerie landscape: setting and the structures of Spenser's *The Faerie Queene.* Unpub. doct. diss., Univ. of Pennsylvania, 1985. [Abstr. in DA (46) 2300A.]

4257. GROSS, KENNETH. Spenserian poetics: idolatry, iconoclasm, and magic. Ithaca, NY; London: Cornell UP, 1985. pp. 271. Rev. by Jonathan Goldberg in Criticism (28:3) 341–3.

4258. GUILLORY, JOHN.   Poetic authority: Spenser, Milton, and literary history. (Bibl. 1985, 3709.) Rev. by Richard S. Ide in Review (7) 1985, 101–5.

4259. HELGERSON, RICHARD.   Self-crowned laureates: Spenser, Jonson, Milton and the literary system. (Bibl. 1984, 3735.) Rev. by Richard S. Ide in Review (7) 1985, 97–101; by Alan F. Nagel in PT (7:3) 588–90.

4260. HILLER, GEOFFREY G.   Allusions to Spenser by John Davies and Sir John Davies. *See* **4065.**

4261. HUME, ANTHEA.   Edmund Spenser: Protestant poet. (Bibl. 1985, 3713.) Rev. by Alastair Fowler in CamQ (15:1) 64–9.

4262. KILLMAN, ROBIN RENEE.   Reflections of the Pléiade aesthetic in Edmund Spenser's minor poems. Unpub. doct. diss., Univ. of Tennessee, 1985. [Abstr. in DA (47) 538A.]

4263. KOMURASAKI, SHIGENORI.   *Yousei no Jo-ou* dai 5kan ni okeru karada no imagery. (Body imagery in *The Faerie Queene*, Book v.) SEL (63:1) 13–28.

4264. KRIER, THERESA M.   'All suddenly abasht she chaunged hew': abashedness in *The Faerie Queene*. MP (84:2) 130–43.

4265. LEAVELL, LINDA.   And yet another ring of echoes in Spenser's *Epithalamion*. SCR (3:2) 14–26.

4266. LOEWENSTEIN, JOSEPH.   Echo's ring: Orpheus and Spenser's career. ELR (16:2) 287–302.

4267. LOMAX, MARION.   *The Faerie Queene* and the Book of Revelation as sources for spectacle in *The Second Maiden's Tragedy*. NQ (33:3) 378–9.

4268. MacLACHLAN, HUGH.   The death of Guyon and the *Elizabethan Book of Homilies*. *See* **3990.**

4269. McLEAN, GEORGE EDWARD.   Spenser's territorial history: Book v of the *Faerie Queene* and *A View of the Present State of Ireland*. Unpub. doct. diss., Univ. of Arizona. [Abstr. in DA (47) 1335A.]

4270. MANNING, R. J.   Deuicefull sights: Spenser's emblematic practice in *The Faerie Queene*, v. 1–3. Spenser Studies (5) 1984, 65–89.

4271. MEYER, RUSSELL J.   'Fixt in heauens hight': Spenser, astronomy, and the date of the *Cantos of Mutabilitie*. Spenser Studies (4) 1983, 115–29.

4272. MILLER, DAVID LEE.   Spenser's poetics: the poem's two bodies. PMLA (101:2) 170–85.

4273. MILLER, JACQUELINE T.   The omission in Red Cross Knight's story: narrative inconsistencies in *The Faerie Queene*. ELH (53:2) 279–88.

4274. MONTROSE, LOUIS ADRIAN.   The Elizabethan subject and the Spenserian text. *In* (pp. 303–40) **27.**

4275. MORGAN, GERALD.   Holiness as the first of Spenser's Aristotelian moral virtues. MLR (81:4) 817–37.

4276. —— The idea of temperance in the second book of *The Faerie Queene*. RES (37:145) 11–39.

4277. OATES, MARY I.   *Fowre Hymnes*: Spenser's retractations of Paradise. Spenser Studies (4) 1983, 143–69.

4278. ORAM, WILLIAM A.   Elizabethan fact and Spenserian fiction. Spenser Studies (4) 1983, 33–47.

4279. PATTERSON, ANNABEL.   Re-opening the green cabinet: Clément Marot and Edmund Spenser. ELR (16:1) 44–70.

4280. QUILLIGAN, MAUREEN.   Milton's Spenser: the politics of reading. (Bibl. 1985, 3727.) Rev. by Barbara K. Lewalski in RQ (39:2) 353–6.

4281. QUITSLUND, JON A.   Spenser and the patroness of the *Fowre Hymnes*: 'Ornaments of all true love and beautie'. *In* (pp. 184–202) **52.**

4282. RINALDI, M. T.   Woman in the Renaissance: Ariosto's *Orlando Furioso* and Spenser's *The Faerie Queene*. Unpub. doct. diss., Univ. of Lancaster, 1983.

4283. ROCHE, THOMAS P., JR.   The menace of Despair and Arthur's vision, *Faerie Queene*, I, 9. Spenser Studies (4) 1983, 71–92.

4284. SILCOX, MARY VERA.   'Such subtile craft': the role of the poet–speaker in Daniel's *Delia*, Spenser's *Amoretti*, and Drayton's *Idea*. Unpub. doct. diss., Queen's Univ. at Kingston, 1985. [Abstr. in DA (46) 2303A.]

4285. STILLMAN, CAROL A.   Politics, precedence, and the order of the dedicatory sonnets in *The Faerie Queene*. Spenser Studies (5) 1984, 143–8.

4286. TAYLOR, ANTHONY BRIAN.   Debts to Golding in Spenser's minor poems. *See* **4082.**

4287. —— Spenser and Golding: further debts in *The Faerie Queene*. *See* **4084.**

4288. TESKEY, GORDON.   From allegory to dialectic: imagining error in Spenser and Milton. PMLA (101:1) 9–23.

4289. TROMLY, FREDERIC B.   Lodowick Bryskett's elegies on Sidney in Spenser's *Astrophel* volume. *See* **4058.**

4290. TUNG, MASON.   Spenser's 'emblematic' imagery: a study of emblematics. Spenser Studies (5) 1984, 185–207.

4291. VECCHI, LINDA MARY.   The poetic unity of Edmund Spenser's *Complaints*. Unpub. doct. diss., Univ. of Western Ontario. [Abstr. in DA (47) 1737A.]

4292. VICARI, PATRICIA.   The triumph of art, the triumph of death: Orpheus in Spenser and Milton. *In* (pp. 207–30) JOHN WARDEN (ed.), Orpheus: the metamorphoses of a myth. Toronto: Toronto UP, 1982. pp. xiii, 238.

4293. VINK, DONALD JAMES.   Freud and Spenser: a dream poetic: an isomorphic comparison of Freud's *The Interpretation of Dreams* and Spenser's *The Faerie Queene* emphasizing Books II and VI. Unpub. doct. diss., Tulane Univ., 1985. [Abstr. in DA (47) 191A.]

4294. WALLACE, LAURIE ANN.   The Renaissance transformation of Eve. Unpub. doct. diss., Texas Christian Univ., 1985. [Abstr. in DA (46) 3364A.]

4295. WALLS, KATHRYN.   Abessa and the Lion: *The Faerie Queene*, I.3. 1–12. Spenser Studies (5) 1984, 3–30.

4296. WEATHERBY, HAROLD L.   The old theology: Spenser's Dame Nature and the transfiguration. Spenser Studies (5) 1984, 113–42.

4297. WILSON, ROBERT R.   Narrative allusiveness: the interplay of stories in two Renaissance writers, Spenser and Cervantes. ESCan (12:2) 138–62.

4298. WOODBRIDGE, L.   Amoret and Belphoebe: fairy tale and myth. NQ (33:3) 340–2.

Henry Howard, Earl of Surrey

4299. HARDISON, O. B.   Tudor Humanism and Surrey's translation of the *Aeneid*. SP (83:3) 237–60.

Chidiock Tichborne

4300. HIRSCH, RICHARD S. M. (ed.).   The works of Chidiock Tichborne. ELR (16:2) 303–18.

Richard Tottel

4301. STEPHEN, JILL ELLEN.   The poetry of *Tottel's Miscellany*: its rhetorical context and place in the development of some aspects of sixteenth-century lyric style. *See* **3976.**

George Turberville

4302. GREENHUT, DEBORAH SCHNEIDER.   Feminine rhetorical culture: Tudor adaptations of Ovid's *Heroides*. Unpub. doct. diss., Rutgers Univ., 1985. [Abstr. in DA (46) 1948A.]

William Tyndale

4303. ALLEN, WARD S.   The testing of Tyndale's Bible. Moreana (23:91/92) 51–8.

4304. ANDERSON, MARVIN W.   William Tyndale (d. 1536): a martyr for all seasons. SixCT (17:3) 331–51.

4305. BOEHRER, BRUCE.   Tyndale's *The Practyse of Prelates*: Reformation doctrine and the royal supremacy. RenR (10:3) 257–76.

Nicholas Udall

4306. NORLAND, HOWARD B.   *Roister Doister* and the 'regularizing' of English comedy. Genre (18:4) 1985, 323–34.

William Walter

4307. EDWARDS, A. S. G.   William Walter and Hawes's *Pastime of Pleasure*. *See* **4095.**

Thomas Wilson

4308. CRAFTON, JOHN MICHAEL.   A critical old-spelling edition of Thomas Wilson's *The Arte of Rhetorique* (1553). Unpub. doct. diss., Univ. of Tennessee, 1985. 2 vols. [Abstr. in DA (46) 2698A.]

Sir Thomas Wyatt

4309. DAALDER, JOOST.   Recovering the text of Wyatt's *Disdain Me Not without Desert*. *See* **304.**

4310. —— Text and meaning of Wyatt's *Like as the Byrde in the Cage Enclosed*. ELN (24:2) 24–33.

4311. —— Wyatt's *Defamed Guiltiness by Silence Unkept*. Exp (44:3) 7–10.

4312. —— Wyatt's proverbial 'Though the wound be healed, yet a scar remains'. *See* **2409.**

4313. MASON, H. A.   Wyatt among the Muses. NQ (33:3) 311–12.

4314. —— (ed.).   Sir Thomas Wyatt: a literary portrait: selected poems. Bristol: Bristol Classical. pp. 354.

WILLIAM SHAKESPEARE
Editions and Textual Criticism

4315.   ALLEN, MICHAEL J. B.; MUIR, KENNETH (eds).   Shakespeare's plays in quarto: a facsimile edition of copies primarily from the Henry E. Huntington Library. (Bibl. 1985, 3752.) Rev. by Paul Bertram in RQ (39:1) 137–8; by MacDonald P. Jackson in ShS (37) 1984, 211–12.

4316.   BEVINGTON, DAVID.   Editorial indications of stage business in old-spelling editions. *In* (pp. 105–12) **44.**

4317.   BINNS, J. W.   Shakespeare's Latin citations: the editorial problem. ShS (35) 1982, 119–28.

4318.   BLAYNEY, PETER W. M.   The texts of *King Lear* and their origins: vol. 1, Nicholas Okes and the First Quarto. (Bibl. 1985, 3754.) Rev. by MacDonald P. Jackson in ShS (37) 1984, 210–11.

4319.   COOKSON, LINDA (ed.).   Macbeth. Harlow: Longman. pp. xx, 262. (Longman study texts.)

4320.   CORBALLIS, RICHARD.   Copy-text for Theobald's *Shakespeare*. Library (8:2) 156–9.

4321.   EDWARDS, PHILIP (ed.).   Hamlet, Prince of Denmark. (Bibl. 1985, 3759.) Rev. by Dieter Mehl in SJW 217–20; by Peter Conrad in TLS, 14 Mar., 279–80.

4322.   EVANS, G. BLAKEMORE (ed.).   Romeo and Juliet. (Bibl. 1984, 3789.) Rev. by Dieter Mehl in SJW 211–12; by Katherine Duncan-Jones in NQ (33:2) 223–4.

4323.   FOAKES, R. A. (ed.).   A midsummer night's dream. (Bibl. 1985, 3761.) Rev. by Dieter Mehl in SJW 213–14.

4324.   FRASER, RUSSELL (ed.).   All's well that ends well. Cambridge: CUP, 1985. pp. xiii, 154. (New Cambridge Shakespeare.)

4325.   GAINES, BARRY.   Textual apparatus – rationale and audience. *In* (pp. 65–71) **44.**

4326.   GANZEL, DEWEY.   Fortune and men's eyes: the career of John Payne Collier. (Bibl. 1985, 3762.) Rev. by MacDonald P. Jackson in ShS (37) 1984, 217.

4327.   GURR, ANDREW (ed.).   King Richard II. (Bibl. 1985, 3764.) Rev. by Dieter Mehl in SJW 215–16.

4328.   HAMMOND, ANTONY (ed.).   Richard III. (Bibl. 1982, 4495.) Rev. by Erik Frykman in Samlaren (107) 127–9 (in Swedish); by George Walton Williams in ShS (36) 1983, 184.

4329.   HUMPHREYS, A. R. (ed.).   Much ado about nothing. (Bibl. 1985, 3766.) Rev. by George Walton Williams in ShS (36) 1983, 186.

4330.   HUMPHREYS, ARTHUR (ed.).   Julius Caesar. Oxford: Clarendon Press. (Cf. bibl. 1984, 3793.) Rev. by W. P. Williams in NQ (33:1) 105–6.

4331.   JENKINS, HAROLD (ed.).   Hamlet. (Bibl. 1984, 3794.) Rev. by Erik Frykman in Samlaren (107) 127–9 (in Swedish); by G. Blakemore

Evans in MLR (81:3) 710–12; by George Walton Williams in ShS (36) 1983, 181–2.

4332. KERRIGAN, JOHN (ed.).   Love's labour's lost. Harmondsworth: Penguin, 1982. pp. 259. (New Penguin Shakespeare.) Rev. by George Walton Williams in ShS (36) 1983, 186–8.

4333. KLEIN, HOLGER M. (ed.).   Hamlet. Stuttgart: Reclam, 1984. 2 vols. pp. 372; 687. Rev. by Brigitte Leuschner in SJO (122) 199–201.

4334. LEVIȚCHI, LEON D.; ȘTEFĂNESCU-DRĂGĂNEȘTI, VIRGIL (eds). Opere complete: vol. 4 (Complete works: vol. 4.); Henry al IV-lea, partea a II-a (2 Henry IV), Mult zgomot pentru nimic (Much ado about nothing) trans. by LEON LEVIȚCHI; Henric al V-lea (Henry V) trans. by ION VINEA; Nevestele vesele din Windsor (The merry wives of Windsor) trans. by VLAICU BIRNA. Bucharest: Univers, 1982. pp. 560.

4335. —— —— Opere complete: vol. 5. (Complete works: vol. 5.); Iulius Cezar (Julius Caesar) trans. by TUDOR VIANU; Cum vă place (All's well that ends well) trans. by VIRGIL TEODORESCU; A două-sprezecea noapte (Twelfth Night) trans. by MIHNEA GHEORGHIU; Hamlet, trans. by LEON D. LEVIȚCHI and DAN DUȚESCU. Bucharest: Univers. pp. 496.

4336. McAVOY, WILLIAM C. (comp.).   *Twelfth Night, or What You Will*: a bibliography to supplement the new variorum edition of 1901. New York: Modern Language Assn of America, 1984. pp. vi, 57. Rev. by Jeanne Addison Roberts in AEB (8:4) 1984, 264–7.

4337. MEHL, DIETER.   The New Cambridge Shakespeare. SJW 208–19 (review-article).

4338. MORRIS, BRIAN (ed.).   The taming of the shrew. (Bibl. 1985, 3773.) Rev. by G. Blakemore Evans in MLR (81:1) 167–70; by George Walton Williams in ShS (36) 1983, 184–6.

4339. MUIR, KENNETH (ed.).   Troilus and Cressida. (Bibl. 1985, 3774.) Rev. by MacDonald P. Jackson in ShS (37) 1984, 205–8.

4340. ODUARAN, AKPOFURE.   The first 'collected edition' of Shake-speare: a study of Nicholas Rowe's edition of 1709. Unpub. doct. diss., Univ. of New Brunswick, 1984. [Abstr. in DA (46) 2301A.]

4341. OLIVER, H. J. (ed.).   The taming of the shrew. (Bibl. 1985, 3775, where scholar's second initial incorrect.) Rev. by MacDonald P. Jackson in ShS (37) 1984, 203–5.

4342. ORGEL, STEPHEN (ed.).   The tempest. Oxford: OUP. pp. 272. (Oxford Shakespeare.)

4343. PALMER, KENNETH (ed.).   Troilus and Cressida. (Bibl. 1985, 3776.) Rev. by MacDonald P. Jackson in ShS (37) 1984, 205–8.

4344. RASMUSSEN, ERIC.   The relevance of cast-off copy in deter-mining the nature of omissions: Q2 Hamlet. *See* **125.**

4345. ROWSE, A. L. (ed.).   *All's Well That Ends Well*; *Henry the Fifth*; *Macbeth*; *King Richard the Third*; *The Taming of the Shrew*: modern text with introduction. Lanham, MD; London: UP of America, 1985. pp. 645. (Contemporary Shakespeare, 3.)

4346. SALGĀDO, GĀMINI; SALGĀDO, FENELLA (eds).   The merchant of

Venice. Introd. by DAVID SUCHET. Harlow: Longman. pp. xvii, 276. (Longman study texts.)

4347. SAMS, ERIC (ed.).   Shakespeare's lost play: *Edmund Ironside*. See **3926.**

4348. SANDERS, NORMAN (ed.).   Henry VI. (Bibl. 1981, 4441–3.) Rev. by George Walton Williams in ShS (36) 1983, 182–4.

4349. —— Othello. New York: CUP, 1984. (Cf. bibl. 1984, 3802.) Rev. by Dieter Mehl in SJW 209–11; by Katherine Duncan-Jones in NQ (33:2) 224–5; by E. A. J. Honigmann in MLR (81:3) 709.

4350. TAYLOR, GARY.   Inventing Shakespeare. SJW 26–44.

4351. —— The transmission of *Pericles*. PBSA (80:2) 193–217.

4352. —— (ed.).   Henry V. (Bibl. 1985, 3783.) Rev. by MacDonald P. Jackson in ShS (37) 1984, 202–3.

4353. THOMPSON, ANN (ed.).   The taming of the shrew. (Bibl. 1984, 3805.) Rev. by Dieter Mehl in SJW 212–13; by Eric Sams in NQ (33:2) 222–3; by E. A. J. Honigmann in MLR (81:3) 708–9.

4354. TRUSSLER, SIMON (notes).   The two noble kinsmen. London: Methuen; Royal Shakespeare Company. pp. 84. (Swan Theatre plays.)

4355. WAITH, EUGENE M. (ed.).   Titus Andronicus. (Bibl. 1984, 3806.) Rev. by W. P. Williams in NQ (33:1) 105–6.

4356. WELLS, STANLEY.   Re-editing Shakespeare for the modern reader. (Bibl. 1985, 3784.) Rev. by Philip C. McGuire in CR (30:2) 423–5; by Paul Bertram in ELN (23:3) 69–71; by Philip Edwards in AEB (8:4) 1984, 260–3; by Leah Scragg in CritQ (28:3) 103–8.

4357. —— (ed.).   Shakespeare's *Sonnets* and *A Lover's Complaint*. Oxford: Clarendon Press, 1985. pp. v, 201.

4358. —— TAYLOR, GARY (gen. eds).   The complete works: William Shakespeare. Introds by STANLEY WELLS. Oxford: Clarendon Press. pp. xlvii, 1432. Rev. by Muriel Bradbook in Listener, 6 Nov., 24; by Elizabeth Ward in BkW, 21 Dec., 6.

4359. —— —— William Shakespeare: the complete works. Introds by STANLEY WELLS; essay on Shakespeare's spelling and punctuation by VIVIAN SALMON. Oxford: Clarendon Press. pp. lxiii, 1456. (Original spelling ed.)

4360. WERSTINE, PAUL.   The editorial usefulness of printing house and compositor studies. *In* (pp. 35–64) **44.**

4361. WILLIAMS, GEORGE WALTON.   The year's contributions to Shakespearian study: 3, Textual studies. ShS (35) 1982, 179–91.

4362. WILSON, RODERICK (ed.).   King Lear. London: Macmillan. pp. 122. (Macmillan modern Shakespeare.)

4363. —— *Macbeth*: complete and unabridged. London: Macmillan. pp. 94. (Macmillan modern Shakespeare.)

4364. —— The merchant of Venice. London: Macmillan. pp. 123. (Macmillan modern Shakespeare.)

4365. WOODSON, WILLIAM C.   Isaac Reed's 1785 Variorum Shakespeare, SB (39) 220–9.

General Scholarship and Criticism
4366. ADAMSON, W.D.   The calumny pattern in Shakespeare. YREAL (4) 35–66.

4367. AKISHIMA, YURIKO.   Shakespeare siki igirisu shindan. (A Shakespearian diagnosis of England.) Tokyo: Asahi Shinbun. pp. 214.

4368. ALVIS, JOHN; WEST, THOMAS G. (eds).   Shakespeare as political thinker. (Bibl. 1985, 3791.) Rev. by Brian Gibbons in ShS (36) 1983, 164.

4369. ANZAI, TETUO.   Shakespeare and Montaigne reconsidered. Tokyo: Renaissance Inst. pp. iv, 96.

4370. AOYAMA, SEIKO.   Shakespeare to London. (Shakespeare and London.) Tokyo: Sincho sha. pp. 198.

4371. APPLETON, ELIZABETH.   Oxford's role in the Marprelate controversy. *See* **4137.**

4372. AQUINO, DEBORAH T. CURREN.   The sense of an ending in Shakespeare's early comedies. JRMMRA (7) 109–21.

4373. ASTINGTON, JOHN H.   Eye and hand on Shakespeare's stage. RenR (10:1) 109–21.

4374. AL-AYECH, ADIB ABDUL R.   Originalitatea interpretarii scenice a operei shakesperiene in tarile arabe si in Romania. (Staggering originality: Shakespeare's works in the Arab countries and Romania.) Unpub. doct. diss., Bucharest Univ., 1985.

4375. —— Shakespeare în România şi în tările arabe. (Shakespeare in Romania and the Arab world.) Bucharest: Bucharest Univ. pp. 21. (Summary of doct. diss.)

4376. BAMBER, LINDA.   Comic women, tragic men: a study of gender and genre in Shakespeare. (Cf. bibl. 1985, 3795.) Rev. by Nancy Cotton in TS (30) 1983/84, 72–4; by Burton Hatlen in Review (8) 251–5.

4377. BARBER, C. L.; WHEELER, RICHARD P.   The whole journey: Shakespeare's power of development. Berkeley; London: California UP. pp. xxix, 354.

4378. BARG, MIHAIL.   Shakespeare és a törtenelem. (Shakespeare and history.) Trans. (from Russian) by ÉVA RADNÓCKI. (Cf. bibl. 1981, 4455.) Budapest: Gondolat. pp. 299.

4379. BARTON, ANNE.   'Enter mariners, wet': realism in Shakespeare's last plays. *In* (pp. 28–49) **46.**

4380. BATE, A. J.   Studies in Shakespeare and the English Romantic imagination. Unpub. doct. diss., Univ. of Cambridge, 1984.

4381. BATE, JONATHAN.   Shakespeare and the English Romantic imagination. Oxford: Clarendon Press. pp. 320. Rev. by Terence Dawson in NC (2) 127–32; by Ian Scott-Kilvert in THES (730) 22.

4382. —— Shakespearean allusion in English caricature in the age of Gillray. *See* **65.**

4383. BAUMGART, WOLFGANG.   Die Krone. SJW 101–18.

4384. BECKETT, RUTH.   Another Shakespearean influence in *Waverley*. ScottN (9) 2–7.

4385. BEINER, G.   The form of Shakespearean comedy: an analysis, with special reference to *The Comedy of Errors, Love's Labour's Lost, The Two Gentlemen of Verona, The Taming of the Shrew* and *A Midsummer Night's Dream*. Unpub. doct. diss., Univ. of Manchester, 1978.

4386. BERCE, SANDA. Imagini concettiste la Shakespeare şi Keats. (Conceits in Shakespeare and Keats.) StUCNPhil (30) 1985, 42–53.

4387. BERGERON, DAVID M. Shakespeare's romances and the royal family. Lawrence: Kansas UP, 1985. pp. 257. Rev. by E. A. J. Honigmann in RQ (39:3) 561–3; by Diane M. Ross in SixCT (17:1) 119–20; by Thomas L. Berger in SAQ (84:5) 402–3.

4388. —— (ed.). Pageantry in the Shakespearean theater. *See* **3873.**

4389. BERRY, RALPH. Shakespeare and the awareness of the audience. New York: St Martin's Press, 1985. (Cf. bibl. 1985, 3805.) Rev. by John Russell Brown in TJ (38:2) 242–3.

4390. BERTRAM, PAUL. White spaces in Shakespeare. (Bibl. 1985, 3807.) Rev. by George Williams in ShS (36) 1983, 188–9.

4391. BEVINGTON, DAVID. Action is eloquence: Shakespeare's language of gesture. (Bibl. 1985, 3808.) Rev. by Donald Gwynn Watson in Review (8) 59–77; by Richard Jacobs in Eng (35) 164–73.

4392. BIRRINGER, JOHANNES. Rhapsodies of words: 'trapicality' in Shakespeare's theater. NLH (17:3) 496–510.

4393. BLANPIED, JOHN W. Time and the artist in Shakespeare's English histories. (Bibl. 1985, 3810.) Rev. by Edward W. Tayler in RQ (39:1) 145–7.

4394. BLIGH, JOHN. Shakespearian character study to 1800. ShS (37) 1984, 141–53.

4395. BRADBROOK, MURIEL. Social nuances in Shakespeare's early comedies. *In* (pp. 1–8) **18.**

4396. BRADBURY, MALCOLM; PALMER, DAVID (gen. eds). Shakespearian tragedy. London: Arnold, 1984. pp. 185. (Stratford-upon-Avon studies, 20.) Rev. by P. van Schaik in UES (24:1) 32–3; by Leah Scragg in CritQ (28:3) 105–8.

4397. BRENNAN, ANTHONY. Shakespeare's dramatic structures. London: Routledge & Kegan Paul. pp. 164. Rev. by Lois Potter in THES (717) 17.

4398. BRISSENDEN, ALAN. Shakespeare and the dance. (Bibl. 1985, 3815.) Rev. by Brian Gibbons in ShS (36) 1983, 161.

4399. BROCKBANK, PHILIP. Blood and wine, tragic ritual from Aeschylus to Soyinka. ShS (36) 1983, 11–19.

4400. BROLLEY, JOHN E. Qualifying Shakespeare's handwriting as proof of authenticity. SNL (36:3) 38.

4401. BRÖNNIMANN, WERNER. Shakespeare's tragic practice. EngS (67:3) 211–15 (review-article).

4402. BROWN, JOHN RUSSELL. Discovering Shakespeare: a new guide to the plays. (Bibl. 1985, 3816.) Rev. by Brian Gibbons in ShS (36) 1983, 157–9.

4403. BULMAN, JAMES C. Bond, Shakespeare, and the absurd. ModDr (29:1) 60–70.

4404. —— The heroic idiom of Shakespearean tragedy. Newark: Delaware UP; London: Assoc. UPs, 1985. pp. 254.

4405. CANTACUZINO, I. I.   Aspecte medicale în opera lui Shakespeare. (Medical aspects of Shakespeare's work.) *In* (pp. 151–60) G. BRĂTESCU (ed.), Retrospective medicale: studii, note şi documente. (Medical retrospective: studies, notes and documents.) Bucharest: Editura medicală, 1985. pp. 792.

4406. CARLIN, PATRICIA L.   The Shakespearean response to mortality: overcoming death in history, comedy and tragedy. Unpub. doct. diss., Princeton Univ. [Abstr. in DA (47) 2166A.]

4407. CARROLL, WILLIAM C.   The metamorphoses of Shakespearean comedy. (Bibl. 1985, 3823.) Rev. by Robert N. Watson in RQ (39:3) 565–7.

4408. CARTELLI, THOMAS.   Ideology and subversion in the Shakespearean set speech. ELH (53:1) 1–25.

4409. CHENG, VINCENT JOHN.   Shakespeare and Joyce: a study of *Finnegans Wake*. (Bibl. 1984, 3829.) Rev. by Utz Riese in SJO (122) 221–3.

4410. CLARK, SANDRA (ed.).   Hutchinson Shakespeare dictionary: an A–Z guide to Shakespeare's plays, characters and contemporaries. London: Hutchinson. pp. 291.

4411. COHEN, WALTER.   Shakespeares Realität und Shakespeares Realismus: Neue politische Interpretationen. SJO (122) 59–64.

4412. COLOŞENCO, MIRCEA.   Barbu traducînd din Shakespeare şi Baudelaire. (Ion Barbu's translations of Shakespeare and Baudelaire.) Manuscriptum (17:3) 123–7.

4413. CONLEY, TIMOTHY KEVIN.   Resounding fury: Faulkner's Shakespeare, Shakespeare's Faulkner. *In* (pp. 83–124) **51.**

4414. CORODI, VASILE.   Şt. O. Iosif traducător al lui Shakespeare. (Şt. O. Iosif, translator of Shakespeare's works.) Manuscriptum (17:4) 140–9.

4415. COTSELL, MICHAEL.   'The Sensational Williams': a mutual friend in 1864. *See* **577.**

4416. COURSEN, H. R.   The compensatory psyche: a Jungian approach to Shakespeare. Lanham, MD; London: UP of America. pp. 240.

4417. COX, C. B.; PALMER D. J. (eds).   Shakespeare's wide and universal stage. (Bibl. 1984, 3834.) Rev. by R. S. White in NQ (33:1) 107–8.

4418. COX, CATHERINE IRENE.   The antic death: restoration and Shakespeare's comic–tragic synthesis. Unpub. doct. diss., Univ. of Florida, 1985. [Abstr. in DA (46) 2698A.]

4419. CYR, GORDON C.   The 'burden of proof' falls on all of us. *See* **4178.**

4420. —— The Stratfordians' own case against their candidate. *See* **4180.**

4421. CYR, HELEN W.   Lord Oxford said it first. *See* **4181.**

4422. CZACH, CORNELIA.   Die Logik der Phantasie. Shakespeares

Spätstücke *Pericles, Cymbeline, The Winter's Tale* und *The Tempest*. Frankfurt: Lang. pp. 212. (Arbeiten zur Ästhetik, Didaktik, Literatur- und Sprachwissenschaft, 11.)

4423. DANDO, JOEL ALLAN. The poet as critic: Byron in his letters and journals. Case studies of Shakespeare and Johnson. Unpub. doct. diss., Harvard Univ., 1985. [Abstr. in DA (46) 1947A.]

4424. DANSON, LAWRENCE. Continuity and character in Shakespeare and Marlowe. *See* **4118.**

4425. DASH, IRENE G. Wooing, wedding, and power: women in Shakespeare's plays. (Bibl. 1985, 3839.) Rev. by Burton Hatlen in Review (8) 247–9.

4426. DAVIES, STEVIE. The idea of woman in Renaissance literature: the feminine reclaimed. *See* **4246.**

4427. DAVIS, J. MADISON. Walker Percy's *Lancelot*: the Shakespearean threads. *In* (pp. 159–72) **51.**

4428. D'IAKONOVA, N. Shekspir i angliĭskaia literatura XX veka. (Shakespeare and twentieth century English literature.) VLit (1986:10) 67–93.

4429. DOLLIMORE, JONATHAN. Radical tragedy: religion, ideology, and power in the drama of Shakespeare and his contemporaries. (Bibl. 1985, 3843.) Rev. by Richard Waswo in CLIO (14:3) 1985, 331–5; by Mary Beth Rose in Review (7) 1985, 21–8; by Roy Battenhouse in ChrisL (35:2) 35–6; by Jonathan Goldberg in MP (84:1) 71–5.

4430. —— SINFIELD, ALAN (eds). Political Shakespeare: new essays in cultural materialism. (Bibl. 1985, 43.) Rev. by Nigel Smith in Eng (35) 57–66; by Claudette Hoover in QQ (93:2) 421–3; by Philip C. McGuire in TJ (38:4) 501–2; by Paul N. Seigel in CLIO (15:1) 1985, 86–9; by Günter Walch in SJO (122) 202–6; by Eric Anderson in Listener (115) 23 Jan., 30.

4431. DONALDSON, IAN (ed.). Jonson and Shakespeare. Atlantic Highlands, NJ: Humanities Press, 1983. (Bibl. 1985, 3846.) Rev. by Judd Arnold in SCN (44:3) 35–6.

4432. DRAKAKIS, JOHN (ed.). Alternative Shakespeares. New York: Methuen, 1985. (Cf. bibl. 1985, 3848.) Rev. by Ralph Berry in QQ (93:2) 423–5; by Nigel Smith in Eng (35) 57–66.

4433. DREHER, DIANE ELIZABETH. Domination and defiance: fathers and daughters in Shakespeare. Lexington: Kentucky UP, 1985. pp. xii, 209. Rev. by Phyllis Rackin in TJ (38:4) 498–9.

4434. EAGLESON, ROBERT D. (ed.). A Shakespeare glossary. By C. T. ONIONS. Oxford: Clarendon Press. pp. xvii, 326. (Third ed.: first ed. 1911.)

4435. EAGLETON, TERRY. William Shakespeare. Oxford: Blackwell. pp. 135. (Rereading literature.) Rev. by René Weis in THES (698) 23; by Andrew Rissick in NewSt (111:1869) 26–7.

4436. EDWARDS, PHILIP. Shakespeare: a writer's progress. Oxford: OUP. pp. vi, 204. (OPUS.) Rev. by René Weis in THES (698) 23; by Andrew Gurr in LRB (8:2) 20, 22.

4437. ÉGRI, PÉTER. The shadow of Shakespeare across the Atlantic:

the Shakespearean tradition in early American tragedy. ActLitH (28:3/4) 345–63.

4438. ELAM, KEIR. Shakespeare's universe of discourse: language-games in the comedies. New York: CUP, 1984. (Cf. bibl. 1984, 3848.) Rev. by W. Thomas MacCary in JEGP (85:4) 561–3; by Bridget Gellert Lyons in Raritan (5:4) 147–54; by Richard P. Wheeler in RQ (39:1) 141–5; by A. Lynne Magnusson in RenR (10:2) 229–32.

4439. ERICKSON, PETER. Patriarchal structures in Shakespeare's drama. (Bibl. 1985, 3851.) Rev. by Phyllis Rackin in TJ (38:4) 499; by Burton Hatlen in Review (8) 355–62.

4440. ERIKSEN, ROY TOMMY. A mannerist topos in Spenser and Shakespeare. *In* (pp. 17–28) **18.**

4441. EVANS, BERTRAND. Shakespeare's tragic practice. (Bibl. 1984, 3852.) Rev. by Werner Brönnimann in EngS (67:3) 211–15.

4442. EVANS, MALCOLM. Signifying nothing: truth's true contents in Shakespeare's text. Brighton: Harvester Press. pp. x, 291.

4443. FAAS, EKBERT. Shakespeare's poetics. Cambridge: CUP. pp. xxiv, 283. Rev. by Gerald Hammond in THES (701) 21.

4444. FABINY, TIBOR (ed.). Shakespeare and the emblem: studies in Renaissance inconography and inconology. Szeged, Hungary: Attila Jozsef UP, 1984. pp. 481. Rev. by Ellen M. Caldwell in Cithara (25:2) 78–9.

4445. FLY, RICHARD. The evolution of Shakespearean metadrama: Abel, Burckhardt, and Calderwood. CompDr (20:2) 124–39.

4446. FOSTER, DONALD WAYNE. Elegy by W. S.: a study in attribution. Unpub. doct. diss., Univ. of California, Santa Barbara, 1985. [Abstr. in DA (47) 1332A.]

4447. FOWLER, WILLIAM PLUMER. Shakespeare revealed in Oxford's letters. *See* **4182.**

4448. FOX, LEVI. The Shakespeare book. Norwich: Jarrold; Shakespeare Birthplace Trust, 1985. pp. 32.

4449. FRENCH, MARILYN. Shakespeare's division of experience. (Bibl. 1985, 3859.) Rev. by Burton Hatlen in Review (8) 249–51; by Brian Gibbons in ShS (37) 1984, 179–80.

4450. FRENCH, TITA. A rhetoric of comedy: essays on language as a theme in Shakespeare's comedies. Unpub. doct. diss., Texas Christian Univ., 1985. [Abstr. in DA (46) 2699A.]

4451. FRIEDLANDER, DOUGLAS RICHARD. Shakespeare's functional characters. Unpub. doct. diss., State Univ. of New York at Stony Brook, 1985. [Abstr. in DA (47) 535A.]

4452. FRYE, NORTHROP. Northrop Frye on Shakespeare. New Haven, CT: Yale UP. pp. 186. Rev. by Kenneth Muir in THES (732) 18; by S. Schoenbaum in NYTB, 30 Nov., 15.

4453. FRYKMAN, ERIK. Shakespeare. Stockholm: Norstedt. pp. 309. Rev. by Hans Andersson in MS (80) 143–5.

4454. FUJITA, MINORU. Pageantry and spectacle in Shakespeare. Tokyo: Renaissance Inst., Sophia Univ., 1982. pp. v, 161. Rev. by Lois Potter in ShS (37) 1984, 192–3.

4455. GALLAGHER, PATRICIA M. LOUISE. Book by the Bard: a study of four musical comedies adapted from the plays of Shakespeare. Unpub doct. diss., Univ. of Missouri–Columbia, 1985. [Abstr. in DA (47) 347A.]

4456. GARBER, MARJORIE. Coming of age in Shakespeare. (Bibl. 1985, 3862.) Rev. by Brian Gibbons in ShS (37) 1984, 178–9.

4457. GENZEL, HANS-JOCHEN. Die Oper und Shakespeare. Bemerkungen und Beispiele zur Adaption. SJO (122) 159–76.

4458. GHEORGHIU, MIHNEA. Ziua lui Shakespeare. (Shakespeare's birthday.) RomLit, 24 Apr., 20–1

4459. GOLDMAN, MICHAEL. Acting and action in Shakespearean tragedy. (Bibl. 1985, 4043.) Rev. by Richard Jacobs in Eng (35) 164–73; by Sidney Homan in JEGP (85:2) 263–6.

4460. GOY-BLANQUET, DOMINIQUE. Des histoires tristes. *In* (pp. 31–49) **37.**

4461. GRAY, J. C. (ed.). Mirror up to Shakespeare: essays in honour of G. A. Hibbard. (Bibl. 1985, 35.) Rev. by Roger Lewis in NQ (33:2) 225–6.

4462. GREENMAN, DAVID. Women, men, and spirituality in Shakespearean romance. Thought (61:242) 360–9.

4463. GREER, GERMAINE. Shakespeare. Oxford: OUP. pp. 136. (Past masters.) Rev. by S. G. Kossick in UES (24:2) 38–9; by John Bayley in Listener, 20 Mar., 27–8.

4464. GRIFFITHS, TREVOR R.; JOSCELYNE, TREVOR A. Longman guide to Shakespeare quotations. Harlow: Longman, 1985. pp. 667.

4465. HABICHT, WERNER. How German is Shakespeare in Germany? Recent trends in criticism and performance in West Germany. ShS (37) 1984, 155–62.

4466. —— Rollentheorie und Shakespeare-Interpretation. WBEP (80) 51–62.

4467. HALE, JOHN K. Can the *Poetics* of Aristotle aid the interpretation of Shakespeare's comedies? Antichthon (Sydney) (19) 1985, 16–31.

4468. HAMILTON, CHARLES. In search of Shakespeare: a study of the poet's life and handwriting. *See* **1515.**

4469. —— A letter in Shakespeare's hand. SNL (36:3) 37.

4470. HAMMERSCHMIDT-HUMMEL, HILDEGARD. Shakespeare in der Bildkunst – Arbeiten an einem Projekt. SJW 138–46.

4471. HANNA, SARA. Shakespeare's Greek plays. Unpub. doct. diss., Indiana Univ., 1985. [Abstr. in DA (46) 3040A.]

4472. HART, B. Shakespeare and the idea of metamorphosis. Unpub. doct. diss., Univ. of Kent, 1983.

4473. HARTWIG, JOAN. Shakespeare's analogical scene: parody as structural syntax. (Bibl. 1985, 3875.) Rev. by Leah Scragg in CritQ (28:3) 105–8; by J. L. Styan in JEGP (85:1) 118–21; by John Drakakis in NQ (33:1) 106–7.

4474. HATLEN, BURTON. Five feminist studies of Shakespeare. Review (8) 241–64 (review-article).

4475. HAWKES, TERENCE. That Shakespeherian rag: essays on a critical process. London: Methuen. pp. 200.

4476. HAWKINS, HARRIETT. The devil's party: critical counter-interpretations of Shakespearian drama. (Bibl. 1985, 3877.) Rev. by Maurice Charney in RQ (39:4) 810–12; by Hilary Semple in Journal of Literary Studies (2:1) 80–2.

4477. —— The year's contributions to Shakespearian study: 1, Critical studies. ShS (35) 1982, 153–73.

4478. HAYS, MICHAEL. On Maeterlinck reading Shakespeare. ModDr (29:1) 49–59.

4479. HEILMAN, ROBERT B. (ed.). Shakespeare: the tragedies: new perspectives. (Bibl. 1985, 3880.) Rev. by R. S. White in NQ (33:4) 545.

4480. HENNING, HANS. Schillers Shakespeare-Rezeption. SJO (122) 110–28.

4481. HILL, JAMES L. 'What, are they children?': Shakespeare's tragic women and the boy actors. SELit (26:2) 235–58.

4482. HIRSH, JAMES E. The structure of Shakespearean scenes. (Bibl. 1985, 3884.) Rev. by Brian Gibbons in ShS (36) 1983, 160–1.

4483. HODGES, DEVON L. Renaissance fictions of anatomy. *See* **4108.**

4484. HOLBROOK, DAVID. The crow of Avon? Shakespeare, sex and Ted Hughes. CamQ (15) 1–12.

4485. HOLDSWORTH, R. V. Sexual allusions in *Love's Labour's Lost, The Merry Wives of Windsor, Othello, The Winter's Tale*, and *The Two Noble Kinsmen*. NQ (33:3) 351–3.

4486. HOMAN, SIDNEY. When the theater turns to itself: the aesthetic metaphor in Shakespeare. (Bibl. 1985, 3887.) Rev. by Brian Gibbons in ShS (36) 1983, 162.

4487. HONIGMANN, E. A. J. Shakespeare's impact on his contemporaries. (Bibl. 1985, 3890.) Rev. by Lois Potter in ShS (36) 1983, 173.

4488. —— (ed.). Shakespeare and his contemporaries: essays in comparison. *See* **50.**

4489. HOWARD, JEAN E. Shakespeare's art of orchestration: stage technique and audience response. Urbana: Illinois UP, 1984. pp. x, 212. Rev. by Paul Gaudet in TJ (38:1) 116–17; by Ralph Berry in JEGP (85:1) 121–3; by Maurice Charney in RQ (39:3) 563–4.

4490. HUNTER, GEORGE K. Bourgeois comedy: Shakespeare and Dekker. *In* (pp. 1–15) **50.**

4491. IBRAHIM, G. A.-N. T. Patterns and themes in Shakespeare's early comedies. Unpub. doct. diss., Univ. of Glasgow, 1983.

4492. JAGENDORF, ZVI. The happy end of comedy: Jonson, Molière and Shakespeare. Newark: Delaware UP; London: Assoc. UPs, 1984. pp. 177.

4493. JOLLY, JAMES LESTER, JR. American operas based on the plays of William Shakespeare, 1948–1976. Unpub. doct. diss., Louisiana State Univ. and Agricultural and Mechanical College, 1985. [Abstr. in DA (47) 706A.]

4494. JONES-DAVIES, M. T. (ed.). Mythe et histoire. Société Française Shakespeare, actes du congrès, 1983. *See* **37.**

4495. KENDALL, GILLIAN MURRAY. Shakespeare's romances and the quest for secular immortality. Unpub. doct. diss., Harvard Univ. [Abstr. in DA (47) 2168A.]

4496. KHAN, MAQBOOL H. E. E. Stoll and the Bradleyan tragedies. AJES (11) 167–87.

4497. KIM, WOO-TACK. Metatheatre wa Shakespeare. (Shakespeare and metatheatre.) JELL (32:4) 667–92.

4498. KIRSCH, ARTHUR. Shakespeare and the experience of love. (Bibl. 1985, 3904.) Rev. by Brian Gibbons in ShS (37) 1984, 176–8; by Maqbool Hasan Khan in AJES (11) 113–20.

4499. KOGAN, L. M. Un scriitor de geniu văzut de un filozof de geniu – Shakespeare și Hegel. (A writer of genius noticed by a philosopher of genius – Shakespeare and Hegel.) Forum (28:6) 40–50.

4500. KOLIN, PHILIP C. (ed.). Shakespeare and Southern writers: a study in influence. See **51.**

4501. KOMOROWSKI, JAROSŁAW. Shakespeare w Wilnie, 1786–1864. (Shakespeare in Vilna, 1786–1864.) Pamiętnik Teatralny (Warsaw) (35:2/3) 181–200.

4502. KRANZ, DAVID L. Shakespeare's new idea of Rome. *In* (pp. 371–80) **49.**

4503. KUJAWIŃSKA-COURTNEY, KRYSTYNA. Wpływ współczesnej Szekspirowi cenzury na jego sztuki o historii Anglii. (The influence of contemporary censorship on Shakespeare's English history plays.) Pamiętnik Teatralny (Warsaw) (35:4) 507–15.

4504. KWON, SAE-HO. Shakespeare haesuk e gwanhan wisang. (Topology and the interpretation of Shakespeare.) YYY (3) 1985, 25–51.

4505. KWON, SEI-HO. John Falstaff eui humor. (On Falstaff's humour.) JHY (7:3) 1985, 561–79.

4506. LANDON, ANTONY. Total Shakespeare: the vision of George Wilson Knight. Pubs of the Dept of English, Univ. of Turku (6) 1985, 73–83.

4507. LANIER, GREGORY WARREN. The development of Shakespeare's tragicomic romances. Unpub. doct. diss., Univ. of Michigan. [Abstr. in DA (47) 912A.]

4508. LEGGATT, ALEXANDER. Shakespeare and the actor's body. RenR (10:1) 95–107.

4509. LEVAO, RONALD. Renaissance minds and their fictions: Cusanus, Sidney, Shakespeare. See **4212.**

4510. LEVIN, RICHARD A. Love and society in Shakespearean comedy: a study of dramatic form and content. Newark: Delaware UP; London: Assoc. UPs, 1985. pp. 203.

4511. LYONS, BRIDGET GELLERT. Shakespeare's wordplay. Raritan (5:4) 147–54 (review-article).

4512. MacCARY, W. THOMAS. Friends and lovers: the phenomenology of desire in Shakespeare's comedy. (Bibl. 1985, 3921.) Rev. by Marianne Novy in PQ (65:2) 278–80; by Coppélia Kahn in RQ (39:2) 243–6.

4513. McGuire, Philip C. Speechless dialect: Shakespeare's open silences. Berkeley; London: California UP, 1985. pp. xxvii, 191.

4514. MacIntyre, Jean. *Doctor Faustus* and the later Shakespeare. *See* **4125.**

4515. McLeish, Kenneth. Longman guide to Shakespeare's characters: a who's who of Shakespeare. Harlow: Longman, 1985. pp. 264.

4516. McRoberts, J. Paul. Shakespeare and the medieval tradition: an annotated bibliography. New York; London: Garland, 1985. pp. xxix, 256. Rev. by Barbara Cohen-Stratyner in TJ (38:4) 496–7.

4517. Manea, Aureliu. Spectacole imaginare. (Fancied shows.) Cluj-Napoca: Dacia. pp. 160.

4518. Manlove, Colin N. The gap in Shakespeare: the motif of division from *Richard II* to *The Tempest*. (Bibl. 1985, 3925.) Rev. by Brian Gibbons in ShS (36) 1983, 163–4.

4519. Marder, Louis. Eric Sams and *Edmund Ironside*. SNL (36:1) 1, 19.

4520. —— A new Shakespeare residence: the Cheshire Cheese? SNL (36:1) 1, 7.

4521. —— Oxford as author? *See* **4183.**

4522. —— Pforzheimer Shakespeareana sold to University of Texas–Austin. *See* **255.**

4523. —— Shakespeare's data bank makes slow but steady progress. SNL (36:1) 1–2.

4524. —— Shakespeare's residence at the Cheshire Cheese. SNL (36:3) 36.

4525. —— *Shall I die* continues to live. SNL (36:1) 4, 6.

4526. —— *Shall I die* is not dead yet; miscellaneous arguments. SNL (36:2) 26.

4527. Marienstras, Richard. New perspectives on the Shakespearean world. (Bibl. 1985, 3928.) Rev. by René Weis in THES (688) 17.

4528. Marsden, Jean Inger. The re-imagined text: Shakespeare, adaptation, and theory in the Restoration and eighteenth century. Unpub. doct. diss., Harvard Univ. [Abstr. in DA (47) 2169A.]

4529. Martinet, Marie-Madeleine. Les mythes historiques chez Shakespeare: rumeur ou silence? *In* (pp. 21–9) **37.**

4530. Matumoto, Hiroshi. Shakespeare no zentaizo: kamen to sugao no aida. (Between the mask and the true face: a study of Shakespeare.) Tokyo: Kenkyusha. pp. 248.

4531. Mead, Stephen X. Shakespeare's concept of chastity: a study of the problem plays. Unpub. doct. diss., Indiana Univ. [Abstr. in DA (47) 1735A.]

4532. Mehl, Dieter. Shakespeare's tragedies: an introduction. Cambridge: CUP. pp. x, 272. (Trans. of **4533.**)

4533. —— Die Tragödien Shakespeares: eine Einführung. (Bibl. 1985, 3929.) Rev. by Kurt Otten in Archiv (223:2) 166–9.

4534. Metz, G. Harold. *Wonne* is 'lost, quite lost'. MLS (16:2) 3–12.

4535. Miola, Robert S. Shakespeare's Rome. (Bibl. 1985, 3931.)

Rev. by Mary Beth Rose in Review (7) 1985, 36–8; by A. A. Ansari in AJES (11) 232–8.

4536. MIRIYA, SAZBURO. Nihon ni okeru Shakespeare. (Shakespeare in Japan.) Tokyo: Yashio Press. pp. 202.

4537. MOON, SANG-DEUK. Shakespeare eui ambivalence. (Shakespeare's use of ambivalence.) JELL (32:4) 647–66.

4538. MORISSEY, WILL. Shakespeare and his Roman plays: studies by Cantor, Platt, and Blits. IJPP (14:1) 115–33 (review-article).

4539. MORRIS, HARRY. Last things in Shakespeare. Tallahassee: Florida State UP. pp. xii, 348. Rev. by Roy Battenhouse in SAQ (85:4) 416–18.

4540. MUIR, KENNETH. Shakespeare: contrasts and controversies. (Bibl. 1985, 3933.) Rev. by Leah Scragg in CritQ (28:3) 105–8; by John Pitcher in TLS, 18 July, 790.

4541. —— (sel.). Interpretations of Shakespeare: British Academy Shakespeare lectures. (Bibl. 1985, 3935.) Rev. by R. S. White in NQ (33:4) 545–6; by Leah Scragg in CritQ (28:3) 102–8; by Mary-Helen Simpson in UES (24:1) 33.

4542. MURPHY, CHRISTINA. The artistic design of societal commitment: Shakespeare and the poetry of Henry Timrod. *In* (pp. 29–47) **51.**

4543. NAKAGAWA, HAJIME. Zoku Shakespeare geki no doke. (Fools in Shakespeare: part 2.) Kyoto: Appollon Press. pp. 230. (*See also* bibl. 1979, 4459.)

4544. NEELY, CAROL THOMAS. Broken nuptials in Shakespeare's plays. New Haven, CT; London: Yale UP, 1985. pp. xi, 261. Rev. by Ann Thompson in THES (703) 18; by Jimmy L. Williams I in SCR (3:2) 105–6.

4545. NICULESCU, LUMINITSA. Shakespeare and alchemy: let us not admit impediments. YREAL (2) 1984, 165–98.

4546. NOVY, MARIANNE L. Love's argument: gender relations in Shakespeare. (Bibl. 1985, 3943.) Rev. by Burton Hatlen in Review (8) 253–64; by Catherine Belsey in RQ (39:4) 806–8.

4547. NUTTALL, A. D. A new mimesis: Shakespeare and the representation of reality. (Bibl. 1985, 3944.) Rev. by Warwick Slinn in AUMLA (64) 1985, 238–47.

4548. ORRELL, JOHN. The quest for Shakespeare's Globe. (Bibl. 1985, 3948.) Rev. by William H. Allison in Review (7) 1985, 153–61; by David Stevens in TS (30) 1983/84, 76–7; by D. F. Rowan in UTQ (55:4) 424–8; by Lois Potter in ShS (37) 1984, 195–6.

4549. PARKER, G. F. Johnson's criticism of Shakespeare. Unpub. doct. diss., Univ. of Cambridge, 1985. [Abstr. in IT (35) 47.]

4550. PARKER, PATRICIA. Deferral, dilation, différance: Shakespeare, Cervantes, Jonson. *In* (pp. 182–209) **27.**

4551. —— HARTMAN, GEOFFREY (eds). Shakespeare and the question of theory. London: Methuen, 1985. pp. xiii, 335. Rev. by Ann Thompson in THES (703) 18; by Hilary Semple in Journal of Literary Studies (2:2) 71–6.

4552. PAUL, DAVID. The Bard and company. *See* **3916.**

4553. Peyre, Yves. Mythes de renaissance. *In* (pp. 67–93) **37.**

4554. Pirie, David B. (ed.). Essays on Shakespeare. Cambridge: CUP. pp. ix, 246. Rev. by Ann Pasternak Slater in TLS, 14 Nov., 1271–2; by Frank Kermode in LRB (8:20) 8–10; by Kenneth Muir in THES (732) 18.

4555. Platt, Michael. Rome and Romans according to Shakespeare. (Bibl. 1985, 3938.) Rev. by Will Morrisey in IJPP (14:1) 115–33.

4556. Porter, Joseph A. Pragmatics for criticism: two generations of speech act theory. *See* **1389.**

4557. Pye, Christopher Lucian. Mock sovereignty: theatricality and power in Shakespeare's history plays. Unpub. doct. diss., Cornell Univ., 1985. [Abstr. in DA (46) 1952A.]

4558. Ramsey, P. A. (ed.). Rome in the Renaissance: the city and the myth. Papers of the thirteenth Annual Conference of the Center for Medieval and Early Renaissance Studies. *See* **49.**

4559. Reed, Robert Rentoul, Jr. Crime and God's judgment in Shakespeare. (Bibl. 1985, 3960.) Rev. by Mary Beth Rose in Review (7) 1985, 33–4; by Virginia M. Vaughan in MLS (16:4) 86–8.

4560. Reuter, O. R. Some notes on Thomas Deloney's indebtedness to Shakespeare. *See* **4069.**

4561. Rhome, Frances Dodson. Shakespeare's comic women: or Jill had trouble with Jack! BSUF (25:2) 1984, 20–8.

4562. Richardson, Thomas J. Is Shakespeare dead? Mark Twain's irreverent question. *In* (pp. 63–82) **51.**

4563. Rodetis, George A. Delacroix and Shakespeare: a struggle between form and imagination. JAE (20:1) 27–39.

4564. Rose, Mary Beth. Moral-historical-critical-poststructural: approaches and assumptions in recent Shakespearean scholarship. Review (7) 1985, 19–41 (review-article).

4565. Rovine, Harvey. Shakespeare's silent characters. Unpub. doct. diss., Univ. of Illinois at Urbana-Champaign, 1985. [Abstr. in DA (46) 3197A.]

4566. Rowan, Stephen Charles. A dancing of attitudes: Burke's rhetoric on Shakespeare. Unpub. doct. diss., Univ. of British Columbia, 1985. [Abstr. in DA (47) 1338A.]

4567. Rowse, A. L. Further light on Shakespeare. Spect (256:8233) 39–41.

4568. Rubinstein, Frankie. Shakespeare's dream-stuff: a forerunner of Freud's *Dream Material*. AI (43:4) 335–55.

4569. Rude, Donald W. Two echoes of Shakespeare in popular seventeenth-century literature. NQ (33:4) 480.

4570. Sahel, Pierre. Le pensée politique dans les drames historiques de Shakespeare. Paris: Didier, 1984. pp. v, 660. Rev. by M. C. Bradbrook in EA (39:2) 204–5.

4571. Sales, Roger (ed.). Shakespeare in perspective: vol. 2. London: Ariel, 1985. pp. 333.

4572. Salgādo, Gāmini. The year's contributions to Shakespearian study: 2, Shakespeare's life, times and stage. ShS (35) 1982, 174–9.

4573. SALINGAR, LEO.   Dramatic form in Shakespeare and the Jacobeans. Cambridge: CUP. pp. x, 292. Rev. by Lois Potter in THES (717) 17.

4574. SANDLER, ROBERT (ed.).   Northrop Frye on Shakespeare. New Haven, CT; London: Yale UP. pp. vi, 186.

4575. SANIEWSKI, URSULA.   Die Abschiedsszenen in Shakespeare's Komödien. Rheinfelden, W. Germany: Schäuble. pp. x, 220. (Anglistik, 1.)

4576. SCHABERT, INA.   Shakespeare als politischer Philosoph: Sein Werk und die Schule von Leo Strauss. SJW 7–25.

4577. SCHELER, MANFRED.   Shakespeares Englisch: eine sprachwissenschaftliche Einführung. See **835.**

4578. SCHOENBAUM, SAMUEL.   William Shakespeare: records and images. (Bibl. 1982, 4643.) Rev. by E. W. Ives in YES (16) 240–2.

4579. SCHWANBOM, PER.   Shakespeare i teori och praktik. (Shakespeare in theory and practice.) Horisont (33:1) 39–44.

4580. SCRAGG, LEAH.   Deconstructing Shakespeare? CritQ (28:3) 102–8 (review-article).

4581. —— The metamorphosis of *Gallathea*: a study in creative adaptation. See **4109.**

4582. SEN GUPTA, S. C.   A Shakespeare manual. (Bibl. 1985, 3980.) Rev. by Leah Scragg in CritQ (28:3) 103–8.

4583. SHAW, GARY HOWARD.   Gracing monsters: a study of Shakespeare's last plays. Unpub. doct. diss., Univ. of Virginia, 1984. [Abstr. in DA (46) 2702A.]

4584. SIEGEL, PAUL N.   Kelly and Tillyard. CLIO (10:1) 1980, 88–91.

4585. SIEMON, JAMES R.   Shakespeare iconoclasm. Berkeley: California UP, 1984. pp. 307. Rev. by Jean E. Howard in RQ (39:1) 138–41.

4586. SIMMONS, J. L.   Shakespeare and the antique Romans. *In* (pp. 77–92) **49.**

4587. SINGH, SARUP.   Family relationships in Shakespeare and the Restoration comedy of manners. (Bibl. 1985, 3984.) Rev. by Mary Beth Rose in Review (7) 1985, 38–40.

4588. SLATER, ANN PASTERNAK.   Shakespeare the director. (Bibl. 1985, 3985.) Rev. by Alan C. Dessen in MLR (81:3) 712–14; by Brian Gibbons in ShS (37) 1984, 181–2.

4589. SLIGHTS, CAMILLE WELLS.   The casuistical tradition in Shakespeare, Donne, Herbert, and Milton. (Bibl. 1985, 3986.) Rev. by Brian Gibbons in ShS (36) 1983, 162–3.

4590. SLIGHTS, WILLIAM W. E.   Nature's originals: value in Shakespearian pastoral. ShS (37) 1984, 69–74.

4591. SLINN, WARWICK.   Hard and soft formalism: what ever happened to mimesis? A review of A. D. Nuttall, *A New Mimesis: Shakespeare and the Representation of Reality.* AUMLA (64) 1985, 238–47 (review-article).

4592. SMALLWOOD, P. J. (ed.).   Johnson's preface to Shakespeare: a facsimile of the 1778 edition. Bristol: Bristol Classical, 1985. pp. 212.

4593. SMIDT, KRISTIAN.   Unconformities in Shakespeare's early comedies. Basingstoke: Macmillan. pp. 240. Rev. by Ann Thompson in THES (738) 18.

4594. SNYDER, SUSAN.   Auden, Shakespeare, and the defence of poetry. ShS (36) 1983, 29–37.

4595. SONDERGARD, SID.   Bruno's dialogue war on pedantry: an Elizabethan dramatic motif. *See* **4089.**

4596. SOYINKA, WOLE.   Shakespeare and the living dramatist. ShS (36) 1983, 1–10.

4597. STEVENS, PAUL.   Imagination and the presence of Shakespeare in *Paradise Lost*. Madison: Wisconsin UP. pp. ix, 270. Rev. by Lucy Newlyn in TLS, 8 Aug., 871.

4598. SUHAMY, HENRI.   Shakespeare historien: propagateur de mythes, ou recenseur sceptique? *In* (pp. 9–19) **37.**

4599. SUMMERS, JOSEPH H.   Dreams of love and power: on Shakespeare's plays. Oxford; New York: Clarendon Press, 1984. pp. xi, 161. Rev. by Leah Scragg in CritQ (28:3) 105–8; by Donald Gwynn Watson in Review (8) 71–2; by Marianne Novy in JEGP (85:4) 564–5; by Robert Ornstein in ELN (23:4) 67–8.

4600. SUTHERLAND, JEAN MURRAY.   Shakespeare and Seneca: a symbolic language for tragedy. Unpub. doct. diss., Univ. of Colorado at Boulder, 1985. [Abstr. in DA (46) 3044A.]

4601. TAYLOR, GARY.   Moment by moment by Shakespeare. (Bibl. 1985, 3997.) Rev. by Lois Potter in THES (688) 17.

4602. TAYLOR, MARK.   Shakespeare's darker purpose: a question of incest. (Bibl. 1983, 4514.) Rev. by Larry S. Champion in MLR (81:4) 986–7.

4603. TENNENHOUSE, LEONARD.   Power on display: the politics of Shakespeare's genres. New York; London: Methuen. pp. 250. Rev. by Nicholas Grene in THES (737) 16.

4604. TERRIS, OLWEN (ed.).   Shakespeare: a list of audio-visual materials available in the UK. London: British Universities Film & Video Council. pp. 72.

4605. THAYER, C. G.   Shakespearean politics: government and misgovernment in the great histories. (Bibl. 1985, 4001.) Rev. by Mary Beth Rose in Review (7) 1985, 34–6.

4606. TOMLINSON, M. A.   Authority and dissidence in Shakespeare's history plays and tragedies. Unpub. doct. diss., Univ. of Cambridge, 1984.

4607. TROUSDALE, MARION.   Shakespeare and the rhetoricians. (Bibl. 1985, 4003.) Rev. by Nancy Lindheim in MLR (81:4) 983–4; by Brian Gibbons in ShS (37) 1984, 180–1.

4608. TUNNICLIFFE, C.   A study of Christian and pagan warrior heroes in Shakespeare's tragedies, with special reference to the influence of earlier English drama and classical literature on the heroic idea in Shakespeare. Unpub. doct. diss., Univ. of London (Bedford Coll.), 1984.

4609. UPHAUS, ROBERT W.   Beyond tragedy: structure and

experience in Shakespeare's romances. (Bibl. 1983, 4517.) Rev. by R. A. Foakes in YES (16) 242–3.

4610. VAN DEN BERG, KENT T.   Playhouse and cosmos: Shakespearean theater as metaphor. Newark: Delaware UP, 1985. pp. 192. Rev. by Arthur F. Kinney in HLQ (49:3) 283–6.

4611. VERCH, MARIA.   Die Brontës und Shakespeare. Archiv (223:1) 45–63.

4612. VICKERS, BRIAN.   Rites of passage in Shakespeare's prose. SJW 45–67.

4613. WATSON, CHARLES S.   Simms's use of Shakespearean characters. *In* (pp. 13–28) **51.**

4614. WATSON, DONALD GWYNN.   Shakespeare and the stage. Review (8) 59–77.

4615. WATSON, ROBERT N.   Shakespeare and the hazards of ambition. (Bibl. 1985, 4014.) Rev. by James Fitzmaurice in SixCT (17:3) 382–3.

4616. WELLS, ROBIN HEADLAM.   Shakespeare, politics and the state. London: Macmillan. pp. 150. (Context and commentary.)

4617. WELLS, STANLEY.   Shakespeare in Hazlitt's theatre criticism. ShS (35) 1982, 43–55.

4618. —— Shakespeare scholarship and the modern theatre. BJRL (69:1) 276–93.

4619. —— (ed.).   The Cambridge companion to Shakespeare studies. Cambridge: CUP. pp. 353.

4620. WESTLUND, JOSEPH.   Shakespeare's reparative comedies: a psychoanalytic view of the middle plays. (Bibl. 1985, 4018.) Rev. by Robert N. Watson in MP (84:2) 216–19.

4621. WHEELER, RICHARD P.   Shakespeare's development and the problem comedies: turn and counter-turn. (Bibl. 1985, 4019.) Rev. by F. W. Brownlow in MLR (81:1) 170–1.

4622. WHITE, R. S.   Criticism of the comedies up to *The Merchant of Venice*: 1953–82. ShS (37) 1984, 1–11.

4623. —— Innocent victims: poetic injustice in Shakespearean tragedy. (Bibl. 1984, 3973.) London: Athlone Press. pp. 149. (Second ed.: first ed. 1982.) Rev. by René J. A. Weis in THES (724) 20.

4624. —— 'Let wonder seem familiar': endings in Shakespeare's romance vision. (Bibl. 1985, 4020.) Rev. by M. H. Simpson in UES (24:2) 39–40.

4625. —— The rise and fall of an Elizabethan fashion: love letters in romance and Shakespearean comedy. *See* **3937.**

4626. WILLIS, PAUL JONATHAN.   The forest in Shakespeare: setting as character. Unpub. doct. diss., Washington State Univ., 1985. [Abstr. in DA (47) 918A.]

4627. WILSON, R. F.   Echo and Narcissus: the Shakespearian construction of reality. Unpub. doct. diss., Univ. of York, 1985.

4628. WINCHELL, MARK ROYDEN.   Renaissance men: Shakespeare's influence on Robert Penn Warren. *In* (pp. 137–58) **51.**

4629. YOUNG, THOMAS DANIEL.   Lanier and Shakespeare. *In* (pp. 49–61) **51.**

Productions

4630. ADLING, WILFRIED.   Theaterrezeption in der Veränderung. SJO (122) 15–20.

4631. BARTHOLOMEUSZ, DENNIS.   Shakespeare on the Melbourne stage, 1843–61. ShS (35) 1982, 31–41.

4632. BARTON, JOHN.   Playing Shakespeare. (Bibl. 1984, 3979.) Rev. by Donald Gwynn Watson in Review (8) 68–9.

4633. BERRY, RALPH.   Changing styles in Shakespeare. (Bibl. 1983, 4541.) Rev. by Brian Gibbons in ShS (36) 1983, 159–60.

4634. —— Komisarjevsky at Stratford-upon-Avon. ShS (36) 1983, 73–84.

4635. BIRKETT, J.   *Cymbeline* in the twentieth century: a study of major British productions. Unpub. doct. diss., Univ. of Birmingham, 1983/84.

4636. BOLTZ, INGEBORG; JAUSLIN, CHRISTIAN.   Verzeichnis der Shakespeare-Inszenierungen und Bibliographie der Kritiken, Spielzeit 1984/85. SJW 177–97.

4637. BOOTH, MICHAEL R.   The Meininger company and English Shakespeare. ShS (35) 1982, 13–20.

4638. BROCKBANK, PHILIP (ed.).   Players of Shakespeare: essays in Shakespearean performance by twelve players with the Royal Shakespeare Company. (Bibl. 1985, 4032.) Rev. by Donald Gwynn Watson in Review (8) 69–70.

4639. BULMAN, JAMES C.   *As You Like It* and the perils of pastoral. SFN (11:1) 9.

4640. CARLSON, MARVIN.   The Italian Shakespearians: performances by Ristori, Salvini, and Rossi in England and America. Washington, DC: Folger Shakespeare Library; London: Assoc. UPs, 1985. pp. 224. (Folger books.) Rev. by Daniel J. Watermeier in TJ (38:4) 499–501; by Christopher Smith in NC (2) 141–7.

4641. CHARNEY, MAURICE.   Is Shakespeare suitable for television? SFN (10:2) 1–2.

4642. CLAYTON, THOMAS.   Theatrical Shakespearegresses at the Guthrie and elsewhere: notes on 'legitimate production'. NLH (17:3) 511–38.

4643. COOK, HARDY M.   Two Lears for television: an exploration of televisual strategies. LitFQ (14:4) 179–86.

4644. COURSEN, H. R.   A German *Hamlet*. SFN (11:1) 4.

4645. DESSEN, ALAN C.   Shakespeare's scripts and the modern director. ShS (36) 1983, 57–64.

4646. —— The supernatural on television. SFN (11:1) 1, 8.

4647. DE VIGNY, ALFRED.   Desdemona's handkerchief on the French stage: 'preface of 1839 to *Le More de Venise*', 'letter to Lord *** on the opening night of 24 October 1829 and on a system of dramatic composition'. Trans. by ROSANNA WARREN. CompCrit (8) 231–50.

4648. DONALDSON, PETER S.   Liz White's black *Othello*. SFN (11:1) 5, 10.

4649. DRAPER, R. P.   *The Winter's Tale*: text and performançe. Basingstoke: Macmillan, 1985. pp. 80. (Text and performance.)

4650. DRESSLER, ROLAND. Zwischen Fachurteil und Laienverstand. Aus einer theatersoziologischen Untersuchung zur Klassikrezeption. SJO (122) 21–5.

4651. EDWARDS, IFOR. Lady Helena Faucit Martin (1817–1898): Shakespearean actress. Wrexham: Edwards, 1985. pp. 25.

4652. EVANS, PETER. 'To the oak, to the oak!': the finale of *The Merry Wives of Windsor*. TN (40:3) 106–14.

4653. FOULKES, RICHARD. Shakespeare and the Victorian stage. Cambridge: CUP. pp. xii, 456. Rev. by Ian Clarke in NC (2) 133–40.

4654. FRIDÉN, ANN. 'He shall live a man forbid': Ingmar Bergman's *Macbeth*. ShS (36) 1983, 65–73.

4655. —— *Macbeth* in the Swedish theatre 1838–1968. Malmö: Liber. pp. 318. (Doct. diss., Gothenburg Univ.)

4656. GIBSON, PHILLIP JAY. A stage mirror of *Richard II*: Shakespeare's play as produced at Stratford-upon-Avon. Unpub. doct. diss., Univ. of Tennessee. [Abstr. in DA (47) 910A.]

4657. GREENWALD, MICHAEL L. Directions by indirections: John Barton of the Royal Shakespeare Company. Newark: Delaware UP; London: Assoc. UPs, 1985. pp. 317.

4658. GURY, JACQUES. Shakespeare, du Globe au petit écran, en passant par Drury Lane: *Romeo and Juliet*, 1595 – 1748 – 1978. *In* (pp. 327–31) **1.**

4659. HABICHT, WERNER. How German is Shakespeare in Germany? Recent trends in criticism and performance in West Germany. *See* **4465.**

4660. HALL, H. GASTON. French Hamlets. NC (2) 42–57.

4661. HARING-SMITH, TORI. From farce to metadrama: a stage history of *The Taming of the Shrew*, 1594–1983. Westport, CT; London: Greenwood Press, 1985. pp. x, 280. (Contributions in drama and theatre studies, 16.)

4662. HARPER, WENDY ROGERS. Polanski *vs* Welles on *Macbeth*: character or fate? LitFQ (14:4) 203–10.

4663. HILL, JAMES L. 'What, are they children?': Shakespeare's tragic women and the boy actors. *See* **4481.**

4664. HOLLAND, PETER. Style at the Swan. *See* **3901.**

4665. HOLMBERG, ARTHUR. Another opening, another show? AR (44:2) 220–30.

4666. JACKSON, RUSSELL. Before the Shakespeare revolution: developments in the study of nineteenth-century Shakespearian production. ShS (35) 1982, 1–12.

4667. JAUSLIN, CHRISTIAN. Bühnenbericht 1984/85. SJW 155–76.

4668. JORGENS, JACK. Kurosawa's *Ran*: a samurai *Lear*. SFN (10:2) 1, 4.

4669. JOYCE, ELIZABETH. From prince to punk: student reception and the English *Hamlet* of the mid-century. NC (2) 31–41.

4670. KACHUR, BARBARA ANNE. Herbert Beerbohm Tree: Shakespearean actor–manager. Unpub. doct. diss., Ohio State Univ. [Abstr. in DA (47) 1532A.]

4671. Keyn, Ulf.   Erfahrungen mit Theaterarbeit – Wirklichkeit und Wirkung. SJO (122) 7–14.

4672. Kimbrough, R. Alan.   Olivier's *Lear* and the limits of video. SFN (11:1) 6.

4673. Komorowski, Jarosław.   Pierwszy polski *Ryszard III*. (The first performance of *Richard III* in Poland.) Pamiętnik Teatralny (Warsaw) (35:1) 13–15.

4674. Komsar, Mohammed.   Deleuze on theatre: a case study of Carmelo Benes' *Richard III*. TJ (38:1) 19–33.

4675. Kuckhoff, Armin-Gerd.   Der ganze Shakespeare? SJO (122) 26–35.

4676. —— Shakespeare auf den Bühnen der DDR im Jahre 1984. SJO (122) 177–91.

4677. Leiter, Samuel L. (ed.); Brown, Langdon, et al. (assoc. eds). Shakespeare around the globe: a guide to notable postwar revivals. New York; London: Greenwood Press. pp. xiii, 972.

4678. Manheim, Michael.   The history play and film and TV. SFN (11:1) 6.

4679. Marder, Louis.   Shakespeare on the modern stage. SNL (36:4) 50.

4680. Moore, Don D.   Three stage versions of *Measure for Measure*'s duke: the providential, the pathetic, the personable. ExRC (12) 58–67.

4681. Olivier, Laurence.   Henry V. London: Lorrimer, 1984. pp. 93. (Classic film scripts.)

4682. Paker, Saliha.   *Hamlet* in Turkey. NC (2) 89–105.

4683. Pantůčková, Lidmila.   Několik poznámek k Nerudově vztahu k Shakespearovi. (Jan Neruda's relationship to Shakespeare.) *In* (pp. 54–7) **24.**

4684. Pursell, Michael.   Artifice and authenticity in Zeffirelli's *Romeo and Juliet*. LitFQ (14:4) 173–8.

4685. Raby, Peter.   'Fair Ophelia': a life of Harriet Smithson Berlioz. Cambridge: CUP, 1982. pp. xiii, 216. (Shakespearean actress who married Berlioz.) Rev. by Lois Potter in ShS (37) 1984, 200–1.

4686. Rothwell, Kenneth S.   *A Midsummer Night's Dream*. SFN (10:2) 5–6.

4687. —— Shakespeare all over: a Brazilian *Romeo and Juliet*. SFN (11:1) 7.

4688. Senelick, Laurence.   Gordon Craig's Moscow *Hamlet*, a reconstruction. (Bibl. 1983, 4613.) Rev. by Lois Potter in ShS (37) 1984, 201; by James H. Butler in TS (28/29) 1981/82–1982/83, 106–8.

4689. Shaw, William P.   Violence and vision in Polanski's *Macbeth* and Brook's *Lear*. LitFQ (14:4) 211–13.

4690. Shrimpton, Nicholas.   Shakespeare performances in Stratford-upon-Avon and London, 1981–2. ShS (36) 1983, 149–55.

4691. —— Shakespeare performances in Stratford-upon-Avon and London, 1982–3. ShS (37) 1984, 163–73.

4692. Smith, Brian.   The Dream in High Park. CanTR (47) 29–37.

4693. TEAGUE, FRANCES.   The Alabama Shakespeare festival. SoQ (19:2) 1981, 43–53.

4694. WARREN, ROGER.   Interpretations of Shakespearian comedy, 1981. ShS (35) 1982, 141–52.

4695. WESTLEY, MARGARET GRACE.   A stage history of *Troilus and Cressida*. Unpub. doct. diss., Univ. of Toronto, 1985. [Abstr. in DA (47) 715A.]

4696. WILLIAMS, SIMON.   The 'great quest' arrives: early German Hamlets. TJ (38:3) 291–308.

4697. —— Shakespeare at the Burgtheater: from Heinrich Anschütz to Josef Kainz. ShS (35) 1982, 21–9.

4698. WILLSON, ROBERT F., JR.   A double life: *Othello* as *film noir* thriller. SFN (11:1) 3, 10.

4699. WOOD, ROBERT E.   Cooling the comedy: television as a medium for Shakespeare's *Comedy of Errors*. LitFQ (14:4) 195–202.

Separate Works

See also under 'Editions' and 'Productions', above.

All's Well That Ends Well

4700. COHEN, EILEEN Z.   'Virtue is bold': the bed-trick and characterization in *All's Well That Ends Well* and *Measure for Measure*. PQ (65:2) 171–86.

4701. COLE, HOWARD C.   The *All's Well* story from Boccaccio to Shakespeare. (Bibl. 1985, 4097.) Rev. by Jonas Barish in YES (16) 227–30; by Lois Potter in ShS (36) 1983, 176–7.

4702. DANNREUTHER, DAPHNE DAVIS.   Shakespeare's 'fantastical trick': a reader-response approach to the problem comedies. Unpub. doct. diss., Middle Tennessee State Univ. [Abstr. in DA (47) 1733A.]

4703. DESMET, CHRISTY.   Speaking sensibly: feminine rhetoric in *Measure for Measure* and *All's Well That Ends Well*. RenP, 43–51.

4704. HARRINGTON, DAVID V.   Shakespeare's generosity: problems in forgiving Bertram. SJO (122) 91–6.

4705. PARKER, R. B.   War and sex in *All's Well That Ends Well*. ShS (37) 1984, 99–113.

Antony and Cleopatra

4706. BARROLL, J. LEEDS.   Shakespearean tragedy: genre, tradition, and change in *Antony and Cleopatra*. Washington, DC: Folger Shakespeare Library; London: Assoc. UPs, 1984. pp. 309. Rev. by W. L. Godshalk in JEGP (85:3) 445–7.

4707. BROCKBANK, J. P.   Myth and history in Shakespeare's Rome. *In* (pp. 95–111) **37.**

4708. CANTOR, PAUL A.   Shakespeare's Rome: Republic and Empire. (Bibl. 1979, 4375.) Rev. by Will Morrisey in IJPP (14:1) 115–33.

4709. CARDUCCI, JANE SHOOK.   'Our hearts you see not': Shakespeare's Roman men. Unpub. doct. diss., Univ. of Nevada, Reno, 1985. [Abstr. in DA (46) 1946A.]

4710. DAÑOBEITIA FERNÁNDEZ, MARÍA LUISA.   Cleopatra's role-taking: a study of *Antony and Cleopatra*. RCEI (12) 55–73.

4711. DURBACH, ERROL.   *Antony and Cleopatra* and *Rosmersholm*: 'third empire' love tragedies. CompDr (20:1) 1–16.

4712. HILL, JAMES L.   The marriage of true bodies: myth and metamorphosis in *Antony and Cleopatra*. YREAL (2) 1984, 211–37.

4713. HUZAR, ELEANOR G.   Mark Antony: marriages and careers. CJ (81:2) 97–111.

4714. MOSELEY, C. W. R. D.   Cleopatra's prudence: three notes on the use of emblems in *Antony and Cleopatra*. SJW 119–37.

4715. SIMARD, RODNEY.   Source and *Antony and Cleopatra*: Shakespeare's adaptation of Plutarch's Octavia. SJO (122) 65–74.

4716. VERMA, RAJIVA.   Winners and losers: a study of *Macbeth* and *Antony and Cleopatra*. MLR (81:4) 838–52.

4717. WORTHEN, W. B.   The weight of Antony: staging 'character' in *Antony and Cleopatra*. SELit (26:2) 295–308.

4718. YOON, CHUNG-EUN.   'Let Rome in Tiber melt': *Antony and Cleopatra* e natanan sarang. (The love of *Antony and Cleopatra*.) JELL (32:4) 719–39.

As You Like It

4719. DALEY, A. STUART.   To moralize a spectacle: *As You Like It*, Act 2, scene 1. PQ (65:2) 147–70.

4720. PARSONS, R. D.   Touchstone's butterwomen. NQ (33:3) 356.

4721. WILCHER, ROBERT.   The art of the comic duologue in three plays by Shakespeare. ShS (35) 1982, 87–100.

The Comedy of Errors

4722. SLIGHTS, CAMILLE WELLS.   Time's debt to season: *The Comedy of Errors*, IV.ii.58. ELN (24:1) 22–5.

4723. TETZELI VON ROSADOR, K.   Plotting the early comedies: *The Comedy of Errors*, *Love's Labour's Lost*, *The Two Gentlemen of Verona*. ShS (37) 1984, 13–22.

4724. WELLS, STANLEY.   Reunion scenes in *The Comedy of Errors* and *Twelfth Night*. WBEP (80) 267–76.

Coriolanus

4725. ALVIS, JOHN.   Coriolanus and Aristotle's magnanimous man reconsidered. IJPP (7:4) 1978, 4–28.

4726. BROCKBANK, J. P.   Myth and history in Shakespeare's Rome. *In* (pp. 95–111) **37.**

4727. BUTLER, GUY.   William Fulbecke: a new Shakespeare source? NQ (33:3) 363–5.

4728. CARDUCCI, JANE SHOOK.   'Our hearts you see not': Shakespeare's Roman men. *See* **4709.**

4729. DAVIES, OLIVER FORD.   The Roman plays: an actor's view. *In* (pp. 157–67) **37.**

4730. GARNER, L.   Shakespeare's materialist drama: text as history in

1 Henry VI and *Coriolanus*. Unpub. doct. diss., Univ. of East Anglia, 1984. [Abstr. in IT (36) 469.]

4731. Yi, Duck-Soo. Biyoungungjeok sahoe insik gwa gojeonjoek bigeuk eui hangae: *Coriolanus* eui bigeukjoek galdeung yangsang. (Non-heroic social concept and the limitation of classical tragedy: modes of tragic conflict in *Coriolanus*.) YYY (4) 51–97.

Cymbeline

4732. Fitts, William David. *Cymbeline* and the woman in the wilderness: the twelfth chapter of the Apocalypse as a source study. Unpub. doct. diss., Texas A&M Univ., 1985. [Abstr. in DA (46) 3039A.]

4733. Frost, David L. 'Mouldy tales': the context of Shakespeare's *Cymbeline*. EAS (39) 19–38.

4734. Marshall, Cynthia Ann. Last things and last plays: eschatology in Shakespeare's romances. Unpub. doct. diss., Univ. of Virginia. [Abstr. in DA (47) 2169A.]

4735. Nudd, Rosemary. Coming to life: the four last plays of Shakespeare as beginning and end of drama. Unpub. doct. diss., Vanderbilt Univ., 1985. [Abstr. in DA (46) 2301A.]

4736. Taylor, Michael. The pastoral reckoning in *Cymbeline*. ShS (36) 1983, 97–106.

Hamlet

4737. Abedi, Razi. *Hamlet* and 19th century sensibility. Journal of Research (Humanities) (Multan) (1:1) 1984, 33–46.

4738. Abiteboul, Maurice. *Hamlet* aujourd'hui: du drame élisabéthain au roman policier moderne. Caliban (23) 27–40.

4739. Adams, Richard. Polonius: did Dover Wilson miss a trick? EDH (44) 24–45.

4740. Biswas, D. C. Shakespeare's conception of a courtier. *See* **4202.**

4741. Blythe, David-Everett. Shakespeare's *Hamlet*. Exp (44:2) 9–10.

4742. Bonnefoy, Yves. Readiness, ripeness: *Hamlet, Lear*. NLH (17:3) 477–91.

4743. Brennan, Anthony S. *Hamlet*: how to shoot an arrow over the house and hurt your brother. MidQ (23:1) 1981, 9–25.

4744. Calderwood, James L. To be and not to be: negation and metadrama in *Hamlet*. (Bibl. 1985, 4125.) Rev. by Mary Beth Rose in Review (7) 1985, 31–3.

4745. Cox, Catherine I. Saturnalian sacrifice: comic-tragic blending in *Hamlet*. ExRC (12) 87–104.

4746. Dodsworth, Martin; Knights, L. C. (introd.). Hamlet closely observed. (Bibl. 1985, 4127.) Rev. by Peter Conrad in TLS, 14 Mar., 279–80.

4747. Eames, S. The Shakespearean cliff: madness and dramatic imagination in *Hamlet* and *King Lear*. Unpub. doct. diss., Univ. of Sussex, 1983.

4748. EDWARDS, PHILIP.   Tragic balance in *Hamlet*. ShS (36) 1983, 43–52.

4749. EVANS, G. BLAKEMORE.   Two notes on *Hamlet*. MLR (81:1) 34–6.

4750. FRYE, ROLAND MUSHAT.   The Renaissance Hamlet: issues and response in 1600. (Bibl. 1985, 4129a.) Rev. by R. A. Foakes in MP (84:1) 69–71; by Roy Battenhouse in CLIO (14:3) 1985, 335–8.

4751. GIRARD, RENÉ.   Hamlet's dull revenge. *In* (pp. 280–302) **27.**

4752. GOLOMB, HARAI.   *Hamlet* in Chekhov's major plays: some perspectives of literary allusion and literary translation. NC (2) 69–88.

4753. HABICHT, WERNER.   Hamlet's prophetic soul: an obscured myth? *In* (pp. 113–26) **37.**

4754. HARDY, BARBARA.   The figure of narration in *Hamlet*. DQR (16:1) 2–15.

4755. HIBBARD, G. R.   Common errors and unusual spellings in *Hamlet* Q2 and F. RES (37:145) 55–61.

4756. JOSE, NICHOLAS.   Hamlet, Marvell and the times. Critical Review (28), 47–62.

4757. KÉRY, LÁSZLÓ.   Hamlet és az öngyilkosság. (Hamlet and suicide.) Nagyvilág (31:11) 1708–15.

4758. KHAN, MAQBOOL H.   The fare in *Hamlet*. AJES (11) 33–42.

4759. KIM, WOO-TACK.   Shakespeare wa post-modernism: *Hamlet* wa *Rosenkrantz and Guildenstern Are Dead* eui daebi reul tonghan Shakespeare eui hyeondaesung yeongu. (Shakespeare and post-modernism: a study of Shakespeare's modernity through the contrastive analysis of *Hamlet* and *Rosencrantz and Guildenstern Are Dead*.) IKS (15) 41–58.

4760. KLEIN, H. M.   'Rightly to be great': *Hamlet*, IV.iv.53–6. NQ (33:3) 357–8.

4761. KLEIN, HOLGER.   Receiving *Hamlet* reception. NC (2) 5–13.

4762. LANG, BEREL.   Hamlet's grandmother and other literary facts. AR (44:2) 167–75.

4763. LETHBRIDGE, ROBERT.   Bourget, Maupassant and *Hamlet*. NC (2) 58–68.

4764. LEVENSON, JILL L.   *Hamlet* andante/*Hamlet* allegro: Tom Stoppard's two versions. ShS (36) 1983, 21–8.

4765. LORANT, ANDRÉ.   Oedipus, Hamlet and Don Carlos: fathers and sons in dramatic literature. Neohelicon (12:2) 1985, 115–48.

4766. LU, GU-SUN.   Hamlet across space and time. ShS (36) 1983, 53–6.

4767. MARHOLD, HARTMUT.   Shakespeare im 'Konsequenten Naturalismus'. SJO (122) 129–51.

4768. MASLEN, ELIZABETH.   Scenes unseen in *Hamlet*. *See* **80.**

4769. MILLER, ANTHONY.   Hamlet II.ii/III.iv: mirrors of revenge. Sydney Studies in English (11) 1985/86, 3–22.

4770. —— A reminiscence of Erasmus in *Hamlet*, III.ii.92–95. ELN (24:1) 19–22.

4771. MUIR, KENNETH.   William Shakespeare: *King Lear*. Harmondsworth: Penguin. pp. 122. (Penguin masterstudies.)

4772. MÜLLER-SCHWEFE, GERHARD. Corpus Hamleticum: Shakespeares *Hamlet* in Wandel der Medien. Tübingen: Francke. pp. 300. Rev. by Julian Hilton in NC (2) 148–55.

4773. NATHAN, NORMAN. Osric's name, and Oswald's. *See* **1715.**

4774. NATOLI, JOSEPH. Dimensions of consciousness in *Hamlet.* Mosaic (19:1) 91–8.

4775. O'MEARA, J. P. The unseen grief: a critical view of tragic visionary imagination in Shakespeare's *Richard II*, with further reference to *Hamlet.* Unpub. doct. diss., Univ. of East Anglia, 1983. [Abstr. in IT (36) 470.]

4776. PALMER, CHRISTOPHER. The mysteriousness of Hamlet. Meridian (5:1) 3–14.

4777. POTTER, A. M. A confrontation with the text: approaches to the problem of teaching *Hamlet.* Crux (20:1) 19–36.

4778. PRICE, JOSEPH G. (ed.). *Hamlet*: critical essays. New York; London: Garland. pp. xviii, 516.

4779. ROSE, JACQUELINE. Hamlet – the Mona Lisa of literature. CritQ (28:1/2) 35–49.

4780. SJÖGREN, GUNNAR. Hamlet the Dane: ten essays. (Bibl. 1983, 4681.) Rev. by Lois Potter in ShS (37) 1984, 198.

4781. SRIGLEY, MICHAEL. Hamlet's prophetic soul. SN (58:2) 205–14.

4782. TUREK, CHARLES. Shakespeare's *Hamlet.* Exp (44:2) 8–9.

4783. WEEDON, MARGARET. 'Hawk', 'hand-saw', and 'ganza'? *See* **1600.**

4784. WILCHER, ROBERT. The art of the comic duologue in three plays by Shakespeare. *See* **4721.**

Henry IV

4785. ABRAMS, RICHARD. Rumor's reign in *2 Henry IV*: the scope of personification. ELR (16:3) 467–95.

4786. BAKER, CHRISTOPHER. The Christian context of Falstaff's finer end'. ExRC (12) 68–86.

4787. BEVINGTON, DAVID (ed.). *Henry the Fourth, parts I and II*: critical essays. New York; London: Garland. pp. xxii, 457. (Shakespeare criticism, 5.)

4788. HUNT, MAURICE. Time and timelessness in *1 Henry IV.* ExRC (10) 1984, 56–66.

4789. JACKSON, MacD. P. The manuscript copy for the quarto (1598) of Shakespeare's *1 Henry IV.* NQ (33:3) 353–4.

4790. MELCHIORI, GIORGIO. Reconstructing the ur-*Henry IV. In* (pp. 59–77) **18.**

4791. —— Sir John Umfrevile in *Henry IV*, Part 2, i.i.161–79. YREAL (2) 1984, 199–209.

4792. SIDER, JOHN W. Falstaff's broken voice. ShS (37) 1984, 85–8.

4793. VECCHIO, MONICA JOAN. Sovereign reality: time and necessity in the political world of Shakespeare's mature history plays, with bibliographical analysis. Unpub. doct. diss., Fordham Univ., 1985. [Abstr. in DA (46) 2305A.]

Henry V

4794. ANDREWS, MICHAEL CAMERON. Fluellen; or Speedwell. NQ (33:3) 354–6.

4795. BROWN, KEITH. Historical context and *Henry V*. CEl (29) 77–81.

4796. PLATT, MICHAEL. Falstaff in the valley of the shadow of death. IJPP (8:1) 1979, 5–29.

4797. SORGE, THOMAS. Der Widerspruch in *Heinrich V*. SJO (122) 47–58.

4798. TAYLOR, MARK. Imitation and perspective in *Henry V*. CLIO (16:1) 35–47.

4799. VECCHIO, MONICA JOAN. Sovereign reality: time and necessity in the political world of Shakespeare's mature history plays, with bibliographical analysis. See **4793.**

4800. WALCH, GÜNTER. Tudor-Legende und Geschichtsbewegung in *The Life of King Henry V*: Zur Rezeptionslenkung durch den Chorus. SJO (122) 36–46.

4801. WHALLON, WILLIAM. Bilingual wordplay on 'neck' and 'chin'. SNL (36:3) 39.

Henry VI

4802. CALDWELL, ELLEN CASHWELL. The breach of time: history and violence in the *Aeneid*, *The Faerie Queene*, and *2 Henry VI*. See **4241.**

4803. GARNER, L. Shakespeare's materialist drama: text as history in *1 Henry VI* and *Coriolanus*. See **4730.**

4804. MONTGOMERY, W. L. *The Contention between York and Lancaster*: a critical edition. Unpub. doct. diss., Univ. of Oxford. [Abstr. in IT (35) 543.]

4805. SAHEL, PIERRE. *Henri VI*: le mythe contre l'histoire. *In* (pp. 51–66) **37.**

4806. WARREN, ROGER. 'Contrarieties agree': an aspect of dramatic technique in *Henry VI*. ShS (37) 1984, 75–83.

Henry VIII

4807. BOWERS, RICK. Shakespeare's *Henry VIII*. ii.i.62–68, 124–31. Exp (44:2) 10–12.

Julius Caesar

4808. BLITS, JAN H. The end of the ancient republic: essays on *Julius Caesar*. Durham, NC: Carolina Academic Press, 1982. pp. 95. Rev. by Will Morrisey in IJPP (14:1) 115–33.

4809. BROCKBANK, J. P. Myth and history in Shakespeare's Rome. *In* (pp. 95–111) **37.**

4810. CARDUCCI, JANE SHOOK. 'Our hearts you see not': Shakespeare's Roman men. See **4709.**

4811. DAVIES, OLIVER FORD.   The Roman plays: an actor's view. *In* (pp. 157–67) **37.**

4812. ELLOWAY, DAVID.   *Julius Caesar* by William Shakespeare. Introd. by HAROLD BROOKS. Basingstoke: Macmillan. pp. viii, 88. (Macmillan master guides.)

4813. FLEISSNER, R. F.   That philosophy in *Julius Caesar* again. Archiv (222:2) 1985, 344–5.

4814. GORECKI, JOHN E.   An echo of *Julius Caesar* in *Paradise Lost*. NQ (33:1) 36.

4815. PECHTER, EDWARD.   *Julius Caesar* and *Sejanus*: Roman politics, inner selves and the powers of the theatre. *In* (pp. 60–78) **50.**

4816. TAKADA, SHIGEKI.   Calls and silence: style of distance in *Julius Caesar*. SStudT (23) 1984/85, 1–37.

King Lear

4817. BARNES, HAZEL E.   Flaubert and Sartre on madness in *King Lear*. PhilL (10:2) 211–21.

4818. BONNEFOY, YVES.   Readiness, ripeness: *Hamlet, Lear*. *See* **4742.**

4819. BOOTH, STEPHEN.   *King Lear, Macbeth*, indefinition, and tragedy. (Bibl. 1985, 3812.) Rev. by Mary Beth Rose in Review (7) 1985, 28–31; by Russell Frazer in MP (83:4) 423–8.

4820. BROWNING, ANDREW HOLT.   *King Lear* and the development of Shakespeare's romances. Unpub. doct. diss., Univ. of Virginia, 1985. [Abstr. in DA (46) 3038A.]

4821. BUTLER, F. G.   Blessing and cursing in *King Lear*. UES (24:1) 7–11.

4822. —— Who are King Lear's philosophers? An answer, with some help from Erasmus. EngS (67:6) 511–24.

4823. BUTLER, GUY.   William Fulbecke: a new Shakespeare source? *See* **4727.**

4824. CANDIDO, JOSEPH.   Lear's 'Yeas' and 'Nays'. ELN (23:4) 16–18.

4825. CASEY, FRANCIS.   *King Lear* by William Shakespeare. Introd. by HAROLD BROOKS. Basingstoke: Macmillan, pp. viii, 96. (Macmillan master guides.)

4826. CHOI, YOUNG.   Edward Bond's *Lear*: a modern Shakespeare offshoot. JELL (31:4) 1985, 659–76.

4827. COATES, JOHN.   'Poor Tom' and the spiritual journey in *King Lear*. DUJ (79:1) 7–14.

4828. COTNER, THOMAS EWING, III.   Shakespeare's use of animal imagery for characterization and psychological development in two selected tragedies: *Othello* and *King Lear*. Unpub. doct. diss., Univ. of Texas at Austin. [Abstr. in DA (47) 1733A.]

4829. DANSON, LAWRENCE (ed.).   On *King Lear*. Guildford: Princeton UP, 1981. (Bibl. 1985, 4193.) Rev. by F. David Hoeniger in MLR (81:2) 442–4.

4830. EAMES, S.   The Shakespearean cliff: madness and dramatic imagination in *Hamlet* and *King Lear*. *See* **4747.**

4831. FLAHIFF, F. T. Lear's map. CEl (30) 17–33.

4832. GAISER, GOTTLIEB. The Fool's prophecy as a key to his function in *King Lear*. Ang (104:1/2) 115–17.

4833. GOLD, ELISE M. *King Lear* and aesthetic tyranny in Shelley's *The Cenci, Swellfoot the Tyrant*, and *The Witch of Atlas*. ELN (24:1) 58–70.

4834. KOSSICK, S. G. *King Lear*: the closing scenes. Crux (20:2) 54–63.

4835. MURPHY, JOHN L. Darkness and devils: exorcism and *King Lear*. Athens: Ohio UP, 1984. pp. xii, 267. Rev. by F. W. Brownlow in PQ (65:1) 131–3.

4836. OLSSON, Y. B. Edmund and Lear (a study in the structure of *King Lear*). DUJ (78:2) 251–8.

4837. RONAN, CLIFFORD J. *Selimus* and the blinding of Gloster. See **3922.**

4838. SIMPSON, DAVID. Great things of us forgot: seeing *Lear* better. CritQ (28:1/2) 15–31.

4839. TAYLOR, GARY; WARREN, MICHAEL (eds). The division of the kingdoms: Shakespeare's two versions of *King Lear*. (Bibl. 1985, 4206.) Rev. by MacDonald P. Jackson in ShS (37) 1984, 208–10.

4840. USMANI, Z. A. *King Lear*: nothing and the thing itself. AJES (11) 43–74.

4841. VISWANATHAN, S. 'This same learned Theban': *King Lear*, III.iv.161. NQ (33:3) 362–3.

4842. WAWRYTKO, SANDRA A. Meaning as merging: the hermeneutics of reinterpreting *King Lear* in the light of *Hsiao-Ching*. PEW (36:4) 393–408.

4843. WEIS, RENÉ J. A. Dissent and moral primitivism in *King Lear*. Eng (35) 197–218.

4844. WEST, GILIAN. 'My father, poorly led'? A suggested emendation to King Lear, IV.i.10. ELN (23:3) 22–3.

4845. WILLIAMS, GEORGE WALTON. Petitionary prayer in *King Lear*. SAQ (85:4) 360–73.

4846. WITTREICH, JOSEPH. 'Image of that horror': history, prophecy and apocalypse in *King Lear*. (Bibl. 1985, 4212, where title incorrect.) Rev. by John Reibetanz in UTQ (55:4) 428–32; by Rene E. Fortin in JEGP (85:3) 448–50.

A Lover's Complaint

4847. KERRIGAN, JOHN (ed.). The sonnets; and A lover's complaint. London: Viking Press. pp. 458. (New Penguin Shakespeare.) Rev. by Barbara Everett in LRB (8:22) 7–10.

Love's Labour's Lost

4848. BEINER, G. Endgame in *Love's Labour's Lost*. Ang (103:1/2) 1985, 48–70.

4849. GOLD, EVA. Lyric fictions in *The Faerie Queene* and three Shakespearean plays. See **4254.**

4850. GORZKOWSKA, REGINA. *Love's Labour's Lost* as a love debate:

consideration of the ending. Zagadnienia Rodzajów Literackich (Lódź) (27:2) 57–61.

4851. GRAZIANI, RENÉ. M. Marcadé and the Dance of Death: *Love's Labour's Lost*, v.ii. 705–11. RES (37:147) 392–5.

4852. GREENE, THOMAS M. The vulnerable text: essays on Renaissance literature. New York; Guildford: New York UP. pp. xx, 254.

4853. TETZELI VON ROSADOR, K. Plotting the early comedies: *The Comedy of Errors, Love's Labour's Lost, The Two Gentlemen of Verona.* See **4723.**

4854. WATT, R. J. C. Armado's 'fadge not' in *Love's Labour's Lost*: the case against emendation. NQ (33:3) 349–50.

4855. WHITE, R. S. Muscovites in *Love's Labour's Lost.* NQ (33:3) 350.

Macbeth

4856. BOOTH, STEPHEN. *King Lear, Macbeth*, indefinition, and tragedy. See **4819.**

4857. BROWN, JOHN RUSSELL (ed.). Focus on *Macbeth*. Boston, MA: Routledge & Kegan Paul, 1982. (Cf. bibl. 1985, 4222.) Rev. by Brian Gibbons in ShS (37) 1984, 184.

4858. CALDERWOOD, JAMES L. If it were done: Macbeth and tragic action. Amherst: Massachusetts UP. pp. xvii, 156.

4859. CHEUNG, KING KOK. The woe and wonder of despair: a study of Doctor Faustus, Macbeth, and Satan. See **4115.**

4860. CLARK, ARTHUR MELVILLE. Murder under trust; or the topical *Macbeth*, and other Jacobean matters. (Bibl. 1985, 4223.) Rev. by Lois Potter in ShS (36) 1983, 174.

4861. CYR, GORDON C. Macbeth and the holes in the Stratfordian chronology. See **4179.**

4862. FOSTER, DONALD W. Macbeth's war on time. ELR (16:3) 319–42.

4863. HAMILTON, SUSANNA. 'The charm's wound up': reference back in *Macbeth*. Eng (35) 113–19.

4864. LIM, C. S. Dr Johnson's quotation from *Macbeth*. NQ (33:4) 518.

4865. PANAGHIS, APHRODITE M. *Macbeth*: an essay. Parousia (4) 105–17.

4866. RUDE, DONALD W. A possible source for Shakespeare's *Macbeth*, v.i.217–219. ANQ (24:9/10) 131–2.

4867. SINFIELD, ALAN. *Macbeth*: history, ideology and intellectuals. CritQ (28:1/2) 63–77.

4868. SÖRING, JÜRGEN. Tragödie – Notwendigkeit und Zufall im Spannungsfeld tragischer Prozesse. See **2812.**

4869. TETZELI VON ROSADOR, K. 'Supernatural soliciting': temptation and imagination in *Doctor Faustus* and *Macbeth*. In (pp. 42–59) **50.**

4870. VERMA, RAJIVA. Winners and losers: a study of *Macbeth* and *Antony and Cleopatra*. See **4716.**

4871. VICKERS, MICHAEL. A source in Plutarch's *Life of Pelopidas* for Lady Macbeth. NQ (33:3) 365–7.

4872. WESTERWEEL, BART. Macbeth, time and prudence. DQR (16:4) 313–25.

4873. WILLBERN, DAVID. Phantasmagoric *Macbeth*. ELR (16:3) 520–49.

4874. WILSON, G. R. The poisoned chalice and the blasphemed babe: Macbeth's Black Mass. AJES (11) 121–41.

4875. ZEONG, YUN-SHIG. Shakespeare and Milton: a poetic approach through Aristotle's *Poetics* and Longinus' *The Sublime*: *Macbeth* and *Paradise Lost*. Unpub. doct. diss., Univ. of Arkansas, 1984. [Abstr. in DA (46) 3729A.]

Measure for Measure

4876. AHN, WOOKYU. Shakespeare eui icheok bocheok, *Measure for Measure* e gwanhan bipyeong deul. (Criticisms of Shakespeare's *Measure for Measure*: with special reference to interpretations of the Duke.) CAE (19) 237–52.

4877. BAWCUTT, N. W. 'He who the sword of heaven will bear': the Duke versus Angelo in *Measure for Measure*. ShS (37) 1984, 89–97.

4878. BENTLEY, GREGORY WAYNE. Shakespeare and the new disease: the dramatic function of syphilis in *Troilus and Cressida*, *Measure for Measure* and *Timon of Athens*. Unpub. doct. diss., Univ. of California, Davis, 1985. [Abstr. in DA (47) 534A.]

4879. BROWN, CAROLYN E. Erotic religious flagellation and Shakespeare's *Measure for Measure*. ELR (16:1) 139–65.

4880. —— *Measure for Measure*: Isabella's beating fantasies. AI (43:1) 67–80.

4881. BURNS-HARPER, CAROLYN. 'A looker-on here in Vienna': *Measure for Measure* as paradigm of contraries. Unpub. doct. diss., Univ. of Colorado at Boulder. [Abstr. in DA (47) 1927A.]

4882. COHEN, EILEEN Z. 'Virtue is bold': the bed-trick and characterization in *All's Well That Ends Well* and *Measure for Measure*. See **4700.**

4883. DANNREUTHER, DAPHNE DAVIS. Shakespeare's 'fantastical trick': a reader-response approach to the problem comedies. See **4702.**

4884. DEBAX, JEAN-PAUL. Ironie et cruauté dans *Measure for Measure*. In (pp. 471–88) **1.**

4885. DESMET, CHRISTY. Speaking sensibly: feminine rhetoric in *Measure for Measure* and *All's Well That Ends Well*. See **4703.**

4886. HAMMOND, PAUL. The argument of *Measure for Measure*. ELR (16:3) 496–519.

4887. LILLY, MARK. *Measure for Measure* by William Shakespeare. Introd. by HAROLD BROOKS. Basingstoke: Macmillan. pp. 96. (Macmillan master guides.)

4888. MEHL, DIETER. Corruption, retribution and justice in *Measure for Measure* and *The Revenger's Tragedy*. In (pp. 114–28) **50.**

4889. NICHOLLS, GRAHAM. Measure for measure. Basingstoke: Macmillan. pp. 94. (Text and performance.)

4890. ROSS, CHERYL LYNN. The plague and the figures of power:

authority and subversion in English Renaissance drama. Unpub. doct. diss., Stanford Univ., 1985. [Abstr. in DA (46) 2303A.]

4891. SEIGEL, CATHARINE F. Hands off the hothouses: Shakespeare's advice to the King. JPC (20:1) 81–8.

4892. TOBIN, J. J. M. Nashe and *Measure for Measure*. See **4174**.

The Merchant of Venice

4893. ANSARI, A. A. *The Merchant of Venice*: an existential comedy. AJES (11) 18–32.

4894. BRADSHAW, GRAHAM. *The Merchant of Venice*: does Jessica lie? Meridian (5:2) 99–108.

4895. DRAUDT, MANFRED. The unity of *The Merchant of Venice*. WBEP (80) 5–26.

4896. DREXLER, R. D. Note on *Bleak House* and *The Merchant of Venice*. Dick (82:3) 149–50.

4897. ERLICH, BRUCE. Queenly shadows: on mediation in two comedies. ShS (35) 1982, 65–77.

4898. GAUDET, PAUL. Lorenzo's 'infidel': the staging of difference in *The Merchant of Venice*. TJ (38:3) 275–90.

4899. GEARY, KEITH. The nature of Portia's victory: turning to men in *The Merchant of Venice*. ShS (37) 1984, 55–68.

4900. HORN, R. L. *The Merchant of Venice* (III.ii.84): Bassanio's 'stayers of sand'. ANQ (24:5/6) 69–70.

4901. NATHAN, NORMAN. Bassanio's name. See **1695**.

4902. —— Portia, Nerissa, and Jessica: their names. See **1705**.

4903. RASMUSSEN, ERIC. Shakespeare's *The Merchant of Venice*, III.ii.63–68. Exp (44:2) 12–13.

4904. SHARP, RONALD A. Gift exchange and the economies of spirit in *The Merchant of Venice*. MP (83:3) 250–65.

4905. WHEELER, THOMAS. *The Merchant of Venice*: an annotated bibliography. New York; London: Garland, 1985. pp. xxii, 386. (Garland Shakespeare bibliographies, 9.) (Garland reference library of the humanities, 423.)

The Merry Wives of Windsor

4906. SIDER, JOHN W. Falstaff's broken voice. See **4792**.

A Midsummer Night's Dream

4907. BEINER, G. Comedy as heuristic fiction: *A Midsummer Night's Dream* in the context of Shakespearean comedy. YREAL (3) 1985, 57–110.

4908. BIJVOET, MARIA CHRISTINA. *Liebestod*: the meaning and function of the double love-death in major interpretations of four Western legends. Unpub. doct. diss., Univ. of Illinois at Urbana-Champaign, 1985. [Abstr. in DA (46) 1931A.]

4909. CARROLL, D. ALLEN. *A Midsummer Night's Dream*: an annotated bibliography. New York; London: Garland. pp. xxxvii, 641. (Garland

Shakespeare bibliographies, 12.) (Garland reference library of the humanities, 440.)

4910. ERLICH, BRUCE.   Queenly shadows: on mediation in two comedies. *See* **4897.**

4911. GARLICK, KENNETH.   Illustrations to *A Midsummer Night's Dream* before 1920. *See* **74.**

4912. HODGDON, BARBARA.   Gaining a father: the role of Egeus in the Quarto and the Folio. RES (37:148) 534–42.

4913. HORN, R. L.   A note on Duke Theseus. SN (58:1) 67–9.

4914. HUNT, MAURICE.   Individuation in *A Midsummer Night's Dream*. SCR (3:2) 1–13.

4915. LEINWAND, THEODORE B.   'I believe we must leave the killing out': deference and accommodation in *A Midsummer Night's Dream*. RenP 11–30.

4916. MICHAEL, NANCY CAROLYN.   Amateur theatricals and professional playwriting: the relationship between *Peter Squentz* and *A Midsummer Night's Dream*. CLS (23:3) 195–204.

4917. RHOADS, DIANA AKERS.   Shakespeare's defense of poetry: *A Midsummer Night's Dream* and *The Tempest*. Lanham, MD; London: UP of America, 1985. pp. vii, 255.

4918. SASAKI, MICHIRU.   The metamorphoses of the moon: folk belief in lunar influence on life and the symbolic scheme of *A Midsummer Night's Dream*. SStudT (23) 1984/85, 59–93.

4919. SCHALKWYK, DAVID.   The role of imagination in *A Midsummer Night's Dream*. Theoria (66) 51–65.

4920. STANSBURY, JOAN.   Characterization of the four young lovers in *A Midsummer Night's Dream*. ShS (35) 1982, 57–63.

Much Ado About Nothing

4921. COATES, RICHARD.   Dogberry and Verges as a pair in *Much Ado About Nothing*. *See* **1699.**

4922. COOK, CAROL.   'The sign and semblance of her honor': reading gender difference in *Much Ado About Nothing*. PMLA (101:2) 186–202.

4923. SARKAR, SHYAMAL KUMAR.   The structure of *Much Ado About Nothing*. SStudT (23) 1984/85, 39–58.

4924. ZIMMERMANN, HEINZ.   Prinzipien des dramatischen Rhythmus in *Much Ado About Nothing*: Reflexionen über Möglichkeiten und Grenzen einer temporalen Dramenanalyse. SJW 68–87.

Othello

4925. CARDULLO, BERT.   Three notes on drama. USFLQ (24:1/2) 1985, 12, 34.

4926. COTNER, THOMAS EWING, III.   Shakespeare's use of animal imagery for characterization and psychological development in two selected tragedies: *Othello* and *King Lear*. *See* **4828.**

4927. ELLIOTT, M. S.   Shakespeare's invention of Othello: an enquiry into lexicon and syntax. Unpub. doct. diss., Univ. of London (Queen Mary Coll.), 1985. [Abstr. in IT (35) 542–3.]

4928. EVERETT, BARBARA. 'Spanish' Othello: the making of Shakespeare's Moor. ShS (35) 1982, 101–12.

4929. —— Two damned cruces: *Othello* and *Twelfth Night*. RES (37:146) 184–97.

4930. FOAKES, R. A. The descent of Iago: satire, Ben Jonson, and Shakespeare's *Othello*. *In* (pp. 16–30) **50.**

4931. LEE, DAE-SUK. *Othello*: gujojeok image yeongu. (Dual aspects of structural images in *Othello*.) JELL (32:2) 205–18.

4932. NEILL, MICHAEL. Changing places in *Othello*. ShS (37) 1984, 115–31.

4933. ORKIN, MARTIN. Civility and the English colonial enterprise: notes on Shakespeare's *Othello*. Theoria (68) 1–14.

4934. SMITH, DANNY LEROY. Certainty and the marriage of minds: epistemology made human in *Othello*. Unpub. doct. diss., Univ. of Dallas. [Abstr. in DA (47) 190A.]

4935. TEAGUE, FRANCES. *Othello* and New Comedy. CompDr (20:1) 54–64.

4936. YI, DUCK-SOO. Migaein eui sarang gwa munmyungin eui jeungo: *Othello* eui bigeukjeok galdeung yangsang. (Love of the barbarian and hatred of the civilized: modes of tragic conflict in *Othello*.) JHY (8:1) 171–228.

Pericles

4937. DAVIES, H. NEVILLE. *Pericles* and the Sherley brothers. *In* (pp. 94–113) **50.**

4938. DESAI, R. W. Stevens' *Peter Quince at the Clavier* and *Pericles*. ELN (23:3) 57–60.

4939. DICKEY, STEPHEN. Language and role in *Pericles*. ELR (16:3) 550–66.

4940. HUNT, MAURICE. A looking glass for *Pericles*. ELit (13:1) 3–11.

4941. MARSHALL, CYNTHIA ANN. Last things and last plays: eschatology in Shakespeare's romances. *See* **4734.**

4942. NUDD, ROSEMARY. Coming to life: the four last plays of Shakespeare as beginning and end of drama. *See* **4735.**

The Phoenix and the Turtle

4943. BILTON, PETER. Graves on lovers, and Shakespeare at a lovers' funeral. ShS (36) 1983, 39–42.

The Rape of Lucrece

4944. DUBROW, HEATHER. The rape of Clio: attitudes to history in Shakespeare's *Lucrece*. ELR (16:3) 425–41.

4945. FRENCH, TITA. A 'badge of fame': Shakespeare's rhetorical Lucrece. ExRC (10) 1984, 97–106.

4946. WIDDICOMBE, KAREN ELIZABETH. 'The worth of my untutored lines': a study of *Lucrece* and the erotic narrative verse of the 1590's. *See* **3980.**

Richard II

4947. GOLD, EVA. Lyric fictions in *The Faerie Queene* and three Shakespearean plays. *See* **4254.**

4948. LAMOINE, GEORGES. *Richard II* and the myth of the Fisher King. *See* **2462.**

4949. LEGGATT, ALEXANDER. A double reign: *Richard II* and *Perkin Warbeck. In* (pp. 129–39) **50.**

4950. O'MEARA, J. P. The unseen grief: a critical view of tragic visionary imagination in Shakespeare's *Richard II*, with further reference to *Hamlet. See* **4775.**

4951. REYNOLDS, JAMES A. Repentance and retribution in early English drama. *See* **3920.**

4952. VECCHIO, MONICA JOÀN. Sovereign reality: time and necessity in the political world of Shakespeare's mature history plays, with bibliographical analysis. *See* **4793.**

Richard III

4953. BECKERMAN, BERNARD. Scene patterns in *Doctor Faustus* and *Richard III. In* (pp. 31–41) **50.**

4954. DEAN, PAUL. *The Tragedy of Tiberius* (1607): debts to Shakespeare. *See* **3888.**

4955. ENDEL, PEGGY GOODMAN. Profane icon: the throne scene of Shakespeare's *Richard III*. CompDr (20:2) 115–23.

4956. HABICHT, WERNER. Rhythmen der Szenenfolge in *Richard III*. SJW 88–100.

4957. MOORE, JAMES A. *Richard III*: an annotated bibliography. New York; London: Garland. pp. li, 867. (Garland Shakespeare bibliographies, 11.) (Garland reference library of the humanities, 425.) (Cf. bibl. 1983, 4784.)

4958. URKOWITZ, STEVEN. Reconsidering the relationship of quarto and folio texts of *Richard III*. ELR (16:3) 442–66.

Romeo and Juliet

4959. BIJVOET, MARIA CHRISTINA. *Liebestod*: the meaning and function of the double love-death in major interpretations of four Western legends. *See* **4908.**

4960. COLACO, JILL. The window scenes in *Romeo and Juliet* and folk songs of the night visit. SP (83:2) 138–57.

4961. GOLD, EVA. Lyric fictions in *The Faerie Queene* and three Shakespearean plays. *See* **4254.**

4962. MOSES, JUDITH A. Love imagined. Unpub. doct. diss., State Univ. of New York at Buffalo. [Abstr. in DA (47) 2151A.] (*Romeo and Juliet, Samson Agonistes*, and *Jane Eyre*.)

4963. STAMM, R. The first meeting of the lovers in Shakespeare's *Romeo and Juliet*. EngS (67:1) 2–13.

4964. STAMM, RUDOLF. The orchard scene (II.ii) in Shakespeare's *Romeo and Juliet* revisited: a study in dramatic configuration. WBEP (80) 237–48.

4965. —— The second orchard scene in Shakespeare's *Romeo and Juliet*. *In* (pp. 110–21) **18.**

The Sonnets

4966. DONOGHUE, DENIS. Shakespeare in the sonnets. Raritan (6:1) 123–37 (review-article).

4967. EASTHOPE, ANTONY. Same text, different readings: Shakespeare's Sonnet 94. CritQ (28:1/2) 53–60.

4968. FINEMAN, JOEL. Shakespeare's perjured eye: the invention of poetic subjectivity in the sonnets. Berkeley; London: California UP. pp. ix, 365. Rev. by Denis Donoghue in Raritan (6:1) 123–37.

4969. GREENE, THOMAS M. The vulnerable text: essays on Renaissance literature. *See* **4852.**

4970. GUTHRIE, STEVEN R. Chaucer's French pentameter. *See* **3790.**

4971. HARDER, KELSIE B. Southern formalism at Shakespeare: Ransom on the Sonnets. *In* (pp. 125–36) **51.**

4972. KERRIGAN, JOHN (ed.). The sonnets; and A lover's complaint. *See* **4847.**

4973. PEQUIGNEY, JOSEPH. Such is my love: a study of Shakespeare's sonnets. Chicago; London: Chicago UP, 1985. pp. ix, 249. Rev. by Andrew Gurr in LRB (8:2) 20, 22; by Denis Donoghue in Raritan (6:1) 123–37.

4974. SWEET, GEORGE ELLIOTT. Seven for Shakespeare. *See* **4184.**

The Taming of the Shrew

4975. COLLINS, KATHLEEN RETTIG. Shakespeare's *Taming of the Shrew*: a structural and theatrical analysis. Unpub. doct. diss., Univ. of North Dakota, 1985. [Abstr. in DA (46) 2698A.]

4976. DANIELL, DAVID. The good marriage of Katherine and Petruchio. ShS (37) 1984, 23–31.

4977. KEHLER, DOROTHEA. Echoes of the induction in *The Taming of the Shrew*. RenP 31–42.

4978. NEWMAN, KAREN. Renaissance family politics and Shakespeare's *The Taming of the Shrew*. ELR (16:1) 86–100.

4979. SACCIO, PETER. Shrewd and kindly farce. ShS (37) 1984, 33–40.

The Tempest

4980. BELTON, ELLEN R. 'When no man was his own': magic and self-discovery in *The Tempest*. UTQ (55:2) 1985/86, 127–40.

4981. CLAYTON, M. G. 'Tempests, and such like drolleries': Jonson, Shakespeare and the figure of Vergil. Unpub. doct. diss., Univ. of Cambridge. [Abstr. in IT (35) 1083.]

4982. DELBAERE-GARANT, JEANNE. Prospero to-day: maguś, monster or patriarch? *In* (pp. 293–302) **12.**

4983. EDDY, YVONNE MARIE SHIKANY. The tempest trope in William Shakespeare's *The Tempest*. Unpub. doct. diss., Purdue Univ., 1985. [Abstr. in DA (47) 187A.]

4984. GIBIŃSKA, MARTA. 'Travellers ne'er did lie, though fools at home condemn 'em': some remarks on the dramatic presentation of romance material in *The Tempest*. *In* (pp. 115–26) **17**.

4985. GILLIES, JOHN. Shakespeare's Virginian masque. ELH (53:4) 673–707.

4986. HILLMAN, RICHARD. *The Tempest* as romance and anti-romance. UTQ (55:2) 1985/86, 141–60.

4987. JOLLY, ROSLYN. Transformations of Caliban and Ariel: imagination and language in David Malouf, Margaret Atwood and Seamus Heaney. WLWE (26:2) 295–330.

4988. JOWETT, JOHN. New created creatures: Ralph Crane and the stage directions in *The Tempest*. ShS (36) 1983, 107–20.

4989. KOMAROWA, VALENTINA P. Das Problem der Gesellschaftsform in Montaignes *Essays* und Shakespeares *Sturm*. Trans. by MARLIES JUHNKE. SJO (122) 75–90.

4990. LOUGHREY, BRYAN; TAYLOR, NEIL. Ferdinand and Miranda at chess. ShS (35) 1982, 113–18.

4991. LUCAZEAU, MICHEL. Y a-t-il une source patristique de *La Tempête*? Compte rendu d'enquête. *In* (pp. 30–45) **35**.

4992. MARSHALL, CYNTHIA ANN. Last things and last plays: eschatology in Shakespeare's romances. *See* **4734**.

4993. NUDD, ROSEMARY. Coming to life: the four last plays of Shakespeare as beginning and end of drama. *See* **4735**.

4994. PITTOCK, MALCOLM. Widow Dido. NQ (33:3) 368–9.

4995. REESE, M. M. Masters and men: some reflections on *The Tempest*. AJES (11) 162–6.

4996. RHOADS, DIANA AKERS. Shakespeare's defense of poetry: *A Midsummer Night's Dream* and *The Tempest*. *See* **4917**.

4997. SCHEVILL, JAMES. The scientist on the stage: Shakespeare's *The Tempest* and Brecht's *Galileo*. SJO (122) 152–8.

4998. SCHMIDGALL, GARY. The discovery at chess in *The Tempest*. ELN (23:4) 11–16.

4999. SHAKMAN, MICHAEL L. *The Tempest*. AI (43:1) 81–96.

5000. TAYLOR, ANTHONY BRIAN. 'O brave new world': Abraham Fraunce and *The Tempest*. *See* **4075**.

5001. WRIGHT, ROSEMARY. Prospero's lime tree and the pursuit of 'vanitas'. ShS (37) 1984, 133–40.

Sir Thomas More

5002. GABRIELI, VITTORIO. *Sir Thomas More*: sources, characters, ideas. *See* **4145**.

Timon of Athens

5003. ANSARI, A. A. The protagonist's dilemma in *Timon of Athens*. AJES (11) 142–61.

5004. BENTLEY, GREGORY WAYNE. Shakespeare and the new disease: the dramatic function of syphilis in *Troilus and Cressida*, *Measure for Measure* and *Timon of Athens*. *See* **4878**.

5005. HOLDSWORTH, R. V. Middleton and Shakespeare: the case for

Middleton's hand in *Timon of Athens*. Unpub. doct. diss., Univ. of Manchester, 1982.

5006. RUSZKIEWICZ, JOHN J.   *Timon of Athens*: an annotated bibliography. New York; London: Garland. pp. xxvii, 274. (Garland Shakespeare bibliographies, 10.) (Garland reference library of the humanities, 388.)

5007. WALLACE, JOHN M.   *Timon of Athens* and the three Graces: Shakespeare's Senecan study. MP (83:4) 349–63.

5008. YI, DUCK-SOO.   Isangjeok ingan eui molrak gwa bigeuk eui hangae: *Timon of Athens* eui galdeung yangsang. (The failure of an ideal man and the limitation of tragedy: modes of tragic conflict in *Timon of Athens*.) YYY (3) 1985, 155–207.

Titus Andronicus

5009. CARDUCCI, JANE SHOOK.   'Our hearts you see not': Shakespeare's Roman men. *See* **4709.**

5010. GONZÁLEZ, JOSÉ MANUEL.   El tema de la venganza en *Titus Andronicus* o el sinsentido trágico del existir. (The theme of revenge in *Titus Andronicus* or the tragic senselessness of existence.) RCEI (12) 123–35.

5011. PAXTON, NANCY L.   Daughters of Lucrece: Shakespeare's response to Ovid in *Titus Andronicus*. *In* (pp. 217–24) **11.**

5012. SUHAMY, HENRI.   À propos d'une phrase de Muriel Bradbrook: rhétorique et cruauté dans *Titus Andronicus*. *In* (pp. 489–98) **1.**

Troilus and Cressida

5013. ADAMSON, JANE.   Drama in the wind: entertaining ideas in *Troilus and Cressida*. Critical Review (27) 1985, 3–17.

5014. BENTLEY, GREGORY WAYNE.   Shakespeare and the new disease: the dramatic function of syphilis in *Troilus and Cressida*, *Measure for Measure* and *Timon of Athens*. *See* **4878.**

5015. COOK, CAROL.   Unbodied figures of desire. TJ (38:1) 34–52.

5016. DANNREUTHER, DAPHNE DAVIS.   Shakespeare's 'fantastical trick': a reader-response approach to the problem comedies. *See* **4702.**

5017. DUSINBERRE, JULIET.   *Troilus and Cressida* and the definition of beauty. ShS (36) 1983, 85–95.

5018. ELDRIDGE, ELAINE.   Moral order in Shakespeare's *Troilus and Cressida*: the case of the Trojans. Ang (104:1/2) 33–44.

5019. LEE, KYUNG-SHIK.   F *Troilus* eui inswae byeonchick e daehan seogihakjeok gochal. (Bibliographical explanation of printing irregularities in F *Troilus*.) *See* **111.**

5020. REINERT, OTTO.   The unmended gear: the 'problem' in *Troilus and Cressida*. *In* (pp. 90–103) **18.**

5021. RONAN, CLIFFORD J.   Daniel, Rainolde, Demosthenes, and the degree speech of Shakespeare's Ulysses. *See* **4193.**

5022. VELZ, JOHN W.   An early allusion to *Troilus and Cressida*. NQ (33:3) 358–60.

5023. VOSS, A. E.   Tragedy and history: the case of *Troilus and Cressida*. UCTSE (16) 1–11.

Twelfth Night

5024. EVERETT, BARBARA.   Two damned cruces: *Othello* and *Twelfth Night. See* **4929.**

5025. FREUND, ELIZABETH.   *Twelfth Night* and the tyranny of interpretation. ELH (53:3) 471–89.

5026. FULLER, ROY.   *Twelfth Night*: a personal view. Edinburgh: Tragara Press 1985. pp. 25. (Limited ed.)

5027. PAFFORD, J. H. P.   Pigrogromitus: *Twelfth Night*, II.iii.23. NQ (33:3) 358.

5028. WELLS, STANLEY.   Reunion scenes in *The Comedy of Errors* and *Twelfth Night. See* **4724.**

5029. —— (ed.).   *Twelfth Night*: critical essays. New York; London: Garland. pp. 312. (Shakespearean criticism, 3.)

5030. WIKANDER, MATTHEW H.   As secret as maidenhead: the profession of the boy-actress in *Twelfth Night*. CompDr (20:4) 349–63.

5031. WILCHER, ROBERT.   The art of the comic duologue in three plays by Shakespeare. *See* **4721.**

5032. YEARLING, ELIZABETH M.   Language, theme, and character in *Twelfth Night*. ShS (35) 1982, 79–86.

The Two Gentlemen of Verona

5033. TETZELI VON ROSADOR, K.   Plotting the early comedies: *The Comedy of Errors, Love's Labour's Lost, The Two Gentlemen of Verona. See* **4723.**

The Winter's Tale

5034. BERKELEY, DAVID S.; KARIMIPOUR, ZAHRA.   Blood-consciousness as a theme in *The Winter's Tale*. ExRC (11) 1985, 89–98.

5035. DRAPER, R. P.   *The Winter's Tale*: text and performance. *See* **4649.**

5036. EDWARDS, PHILIP.   'Seeing is believing': action and narration in *The Old Wives Tale* and *The Winter's Tale. In* (pp. 79–93) **50.**

5037. GASPAR, JULIA; WILLIAMS, CAROLYN.   The meaning of the name 'Hermione'. NQ (33:3) 367.

5038. GRANTLEY, DARRYLL.   *The Winter's Tale* and early religious drama. CompDr (20:1) 17–37.

5039. LANDE, MAYDEE G.   *The Winter's Tale*: a question of motive. AI (43:1) 51–65.

5040. McCANDLESS, DAVID FOLEY.   *The Winter's Tale*: summary and summit of Shakespeare's canon. Unpub. doct. diss., Stanford Univ. [Abstr. in DA (47) 348A.]

5041. MARSHALL, CYNTHIA ANN.   Last things and last plays: eschatology in Shakespeare's romances. *See* **4734.**

5042. NUDD, ROSEMARY.   Coming to life: the four last plays of Shakespeare as beginning and end of drama. *See* **4735.**

5043. SAHEL, PIERRE.   Le spectateur de la fin du *Conte d'hiver. In* (pp. 357–68) **1.**

SEVENTEENTH CENTURY

GENERAL

General Literary Studies

5044. ALDRIDGE, A. OWEN. Early American literature: a comparatist approach. (Bibl. 1985, 4359.) Rev. by Charlotte Kretzoi in CanRCL (12:3) 1985, 525–9; by J. A. Leo Lemay in ECent (26:1) 1985, 101–4.

5045. ARAKELIAN, PAUL G. The myth of a Restoration style shift. ECent (20:3) 1979, 227–45.

5046. BONHEIM, HELMUT. Why the West created the South American 'savage'. See **3832.**

5047. BOZEMAN, THEODORE DWIGHT. The Puritans' *Errand into the Wilderness* reconsidered. NEQ (59:2) 231–51.

5048. BRADBROOK, M. C. The artist and society in Shakespeare's England. Introd. by BRIAN VICKERS. See **3833.**

5049. BRAVERMAN, RICHARD LEWIS. Capital relations and English literature, 1660–1730. Unpub. doct. diss., Columbia Univ., 1985. [Abstr. in DA (47) 186A.]

5050. CHILDS, F. A. Prescriptions for manners in English courtesy literature, 1690–1760, and their social implications. Unpub. doct. diss., Univ. of Oxford, 1984.

5051. CRIST, TIMOTHY J. (ed.) Short-title catalogue of books printed in England, Scotland, Ireland, Wales, and British America and of English books printed in other countries, 1641–1700: vol. 2. E2927–O1000. By DONALD WING. (Bibl. 1982, 215.) (Second ed.: first ed. 1948.) Rev. by Alexandra Mason in PBSA (80:2) 255–62.

5052. DAMROSCH, LEOPOLD, JR. God's plot and man's stories: studies in the fictional imagination from Milton to Fielding. Chicago; London: Chicago UP, 1985. pp. ix, 343. Rev. by Isabel Rivers in THES (706) 17.

5053. DATTA, KITTY. Modes of singularity in Renaissance literature. See **3838.**

5054. DEES, JEROME S. Recent studies in the English emblem. See **3839.**

5055. DIEHL, HUSTON. Graven images: Protestant emblem books in England. See **3840.**

5056. FARNSWORTH, JANE ELIZABETH. Intimate relationships between women in English Renaissance literature, 1558–1642. See **3843.**

5057. FERGUSON, MOIRA. First feminists: British women writers, 1578–1799. See **3844.**

5058. GOLDBERG, JONATHAN. Voice terminal echo: postmodernism and English Renaissance texts. See **3845.**

5059. HECKSHER, WILLIAM S. Art and literature: studies in relationship. See **3849.**

5060. HELGERSON, RICHARD. The land speaks: cartography, chorography, and subversion in Renaissance England. See **3850.**

5061. —— Recent studies in the English Renaissance. See **3851.**

5062. HILL, CHRISTOPHER.   Literature and the English Revolution. Seventeenth Century (1:1) 15–30.

5063. HÖLTGEN, KARL JOSEF.   Aspects of the emblem: studies in the English emblem tradition and the European context. With a foreword by SIR ROY STRONG. Kassel: Reichenberger. pp. 204. (Problemata semiotica, 2.) Rev. by Alan R. Young in DalR (65:4) 1985/86, 598–601.

5064. HOWARD, JEAN E.   The new historicism in Renaissance studies. *See* **3852.**

5065. IRONS, GLENWOOD HENRY.   From monolithic authority to omniscient authorship in 17th century English literature and culture. Unpub. doct. diss., State Univ. of New York at Buffalo, 1985. [Abstr. in DA (46) 1949A.]

5066. JANSSENS, G. A. M.; AARTS, F. G. A. M. (eds).   Studies in seventeenth-century English literature, history and bibliography: Festschrift for Professor T. A. Birrell on the occasion of his sixtieth birthday. (Bibl. 1985, 4379.) Rev. by Dominic Baker-Smith in Neophilologus (70:3) 462–8.

5067. KENNY, VIRGINIA C.   The country-house ethos in English literature 1688–1750: themes of personal retreat and national expansion. (Bibl. 1985, 4382.) Rev. by Peter Dixon in BJECS (9:2) 270–1.

5068. KENSHUR, OSCAR.   Open form and the shape of ideas: literary structures as representations of philosophical concept in the seventeenth and eighteenth centuries. Lewisburg, PA: Bucknell UP; London: Assoc. UPs. pp. 140.

5069. KLEIN, JÜRGEN.   Astronomie und Anthropozentrik. Die Copernicanische Wende bei John Donne, John Milton und den Cambridge Platonists. Frankfurt; Berne; New York: Lang. pp. 353. (Aspekte der englischen Giestes- und Kulturgeschichte, 6.).

5070. KOLODNY, ANNETTE.   The land before her: fantasy and experience of the American frontiers, 1630–1860. (Bibl. 1985, 4384.) Rev. by Ursula Brumm in EAL (20:3) 1985/86, 271–7.

5071. KORSHIN, PAUL J.   Typologies in England 1650–1820. (Bibl. 1985, 4385.) Rev. by G. S. Rousseau in JEGP (85:1) 125–8.

5072. LEWIS, MARY JANE.   A sweet sacrifice: civil war in New England. Unpub. doct. diss., State Univ. of New York at Binghamton. [Abstr. in DA (47) 530A.]

5073. MONTROSE, LOUIS.   Renaissance literary studies and the subject of history. *See* **3855.**

5074. MYERS, WILLIAM (ed.).   Restoration and revolution. London; Sydney; Dover, NH: Croom Helm. pp. 248. Rev. by N. H. Keeble in THES (693) 16.

5075. NUSSBAUM, FELICITY A.   The brink of all we hate: English satires on women, 1660–1750. (Bibl. 1985, 4394.) Rev. by Kate Flint in BJECS (9:2) 261–2; by Laurie A. Finke in ECent (27:3) 287–92; by Carol Houlihan Flynn in SAQ (85:1) 101–2; by Isobel Grundy in NQ (33:1) 110–11.

5076. PARRY, GRAHAM.   The golden age restor'd: the culture of the

Stuart court, 1603–42. New York: St Martin's Press. (Cf. bibl. 1982, 5062.) Rev. by Sara Jayne Steen in SCN (44:4) 59–60.

5077. PATTERSON, ANNABEL.   Censorship and interpretation: the conditions of writing and reading in early modern England. *See* **3857.**

5078. PEYRE, YVES.   Mythes de renaissance. *In* (pp. 67–93) **37.**

5079. RAMSEY, P. A. (ed.).   Rome in the Renaissance: the city and the myth. Papers of the thirteenth Annual Conference of the Center for Medieval and Early Renaissance Studies. *See* **49.**

5080. ROUSSEL, ROY.   The conversation of the sexes: seduction and equality in selected seventeenth- and eighteenth-century texts. New York; Oxford: OUP. pp. 178.

5081. SALMON, VIVIAN.   Effort and achievement in seventeenth-century British linguistics. *In* (pp. 69–95) **53.**

5082. SHARPE, KEVIN.   The politics of literature in Renaissance England. *See* **3862.**

5083. SMITH, N. S.   'The interior word': aspects of the use of language and rhetoric in radical Puritan and sectarian literature, *c.*1640–*c.*1660. Unpub. doct. diss., Univ. of Oxford, 1985. [Abstr. in IT (35) 544.]

5084. SOCIÉTÉ D'ÉTUDES ANGLO-AMÉRICAINES DES XVIIe ET XVIIIe SIÈCLES.   Maître et serviteur dans le monde anglo-américain des XVIIe et XVIIIe siècles. Actes du Colloque 1985. *See* **30.**

5085. SOCIÉTÉ D'ÉTUDES ANGLO-AMÉRICAINES DES XVIIe ET XVIIIe SIÈCLES.   Mémoire et création dans le monde anglo-américain aux XVIIe et XVIIIe siècles: Actes du Colloque tenu à Paris les 21 et 22 octobre 1983. *See* **34.**

5086. STOCK, R. D.   The holy and the daemonic from Sir Thomas Browne to William Blake. Guildford: Princeton UP, 1982. (Cf. bibl. 1985, 4402.) Rev. by D. R. M. Wilkinson in YES (16) 286–8.

5087. TAYLOR, J. A.   The literary presentation of James I and Charles I, with special reference to the period *c.* 1614–1630. Unpub. doct. diss., Univ. of Oxford, 1985. [Abstr. in IT (35) 543.]

5088. TODD, JANET (ed.).   A dictionary of British and American women writers 1660–1800. Totowa, NJ: Rowman & Allanheld, 1985. (Cf. bibl. 1985, 4405.) Rev. by Jayne K. Kribbs in AL (58:1) 122–4; by Helen Wilcox in BJECS (9:2) 249–51.

5089. TRUBOWITZ, RACHEL.   The past in the present: T. S. Eliot's idea of the seventeenth century. Unpub. doct. diss., Columbia Univ., 1985. [Abstr. in DA (46) 3363A.]

5090. VAUGHTER, PAUL H.   Ways to embarrass a bishop, being a discourse on anti-Episcopal satires in the *Thomason Tracts*. JPC (20:1) 69–79.

5091. VON FRANK, ALBERT J.   The sacred game: provincialism and frontier consciousness in American literature, 1630–1860. New York: CUP, 1985. pp. viii, 188. Rev. by Andrew Delbanco in SAF (14:2) 243–5; by Jerome Loving in SCR (3:2) 109–10.

5092. WALLACE, JOHN M. (ed.).   The golden and the brazen world: papers in literature and history, 1650–1800. Berkeley; London: California UP, 1985. pp. xiii, 213. (UCLA, 10.)

5093. WALLER, GARY F.   Struggling into discourse: the emergence of Renaissance women's writing. *In* (pp. 238–56) **52.**

5094. WITHERSPOON, ALEXANDER M.; WARNKE, FRANK J. (eds). Seventeenth-century prose and poetry. San Diego, CA; London: Harcourt Brace Jovanovich, 1982. pp. xxvi, 1124. (Second ed.: first ed. 1963.)

Drama and the Theatre

5095. AGNEW, JEAN-CHRISTOPHE.   Worlds apart: the market and the theater in Anglo-American thought, 1550–1750. *See* **3867.**

5096. ALTIERI, JOANNE.   The theatre of praise: the panegyric tradition in seventeenth-century English drama. Newark: Delaware UP; London: Assoc. UPs. pp. 240.

5097. ATKINSON, D. G.   Marriage and domestic tradition in Jacobean tragedy: a study of selected plays. Unpub. doct. diss., Univ. of London, Birkbeck Coll., 1985.

5098. ATKINSON, DAVID.   Marriage under compulsion in English Renaissance drama. *See* **3868.**

5099. BEALE, PETER.   The burning of the Globe. TLS, 20 June, 689–90.

5100. BENSEL-MEYERS, LINDA DIANE.   A 'figure cut in alabaster': the paradoxical widow of Renaissance drama. *See* **3870.**

5101. BERGERON, DAVID M.   The Bible in English Renaissance pageants. *See* **3872.**

5102. BOTICA, A.   Audience, playhouse and play in Restoration theatre. Unpub. doct. diss., Univ. of Oxford. [Abstr. in IT (35) 532–3.]

5103. BRUNKHORST, MARTIN.   Drama und Theater der Restaurationszeit. Heidelberg: Winter, 1985. pp. 232. (Forum Anglistik.)

5104. BUTLER, MARTIN.   Theatre and crisis, 1632–1642. (Bibl. 1985, 4427.) Rev. by Lee Bliss in RQ (39:2) 349–51.

5105. CAREY, ANNA KIRWAN STECK.   'Less than a man': the child actors and tragic satire. *See* **3880.**

5106. COOK, JUDITH.   At the sign of the swan: an introduction to Shakespeare's contemporaries. Introd. by TREVOR NUNN. *See* **3887.**

5107. CORBIN, PETER; SEDGE, DOUGLAS (eds).   Three Jacobean witchcraft plays. Manchester: Manchester UP. pp. xii, 259. (Revels plays companion library.) (*Sophonisba, The Witch, The Witch of Edmonton.*)

5108. DANCHIN, PIERRE (ed.).   The prologues and epilogues of the Restoration 1660–1700: part II, 1677–1690. Nancy: Nancy UP, 1984. 2 vols. pp. xxxvi, 411; ii, 446. Rev. by A. H. Scouten in EA (38:4) 1985, 460–1.

5109. DEAN, CHRISTOPHER.   The Simpson players' tour of North Yorkshire in 1616. NQ (33:3) 381.

5110. DE MOURGUES, ODETTE.   Love in Molière and in Restoration comedy: literature or sociology? Seventeenth Century (1:1) 57–67.

5111. EATON, SARA JOAN.   The rhetoric of sexual revenge in Jacobean drama. Unpub. doct. diss., Univ. of Minnesota, 1985. [Abstr. in DA (46) 3724A.]

5112. FINKELPEARL, PHILIP J. 'The comedians' liberty': censorship of the Jacobean stage reconsidered. ELR (16:1) 123–38.

5113. FREER, COBURN. The poetics of Jacobean drama. (Bibl. 1985, 4431.) Rev. by Lois Potter in ShS (36) 1983, 180.

5114. FREY, CHARLES. Recent studies in Elizabethan and Jacobean drama. *See* **3891.**

5115. FROST, C. M. The problem of evil in Jacobean drama: studies in the theological assumptions of select Jacobean dramatists. Unpub. doct. diss., Univ. of Cambridge.

5116. GAINES, BARRY. Textual apparatus – rationale and audience. *In* (pp. 65–71) **44.**

5117. GRISWOLD, WENDY. Renaissance revivals: city comedy and revenge tragedy in the London theatre 1576–1980. *See* **3897.**

5118. HIGHFILL, PHILIP H., JR; BURNIM, KALMAN A.; LANGHANS, EDWARD A. A biographical dictionary of actors, actresses, musicians, dancers, managers, and other stage personnel in London, 1660–1800: vol. 7, Habgood to Houbert; vol. 8, Hough to Keyse; vol. 9, Kickill to Machin; vol. 10, M'Intosh to Nash. Carbondale; Edwardsville: Southern Illinois UP, 1982–84. pp. vi, 436; vi, 448; vi, 409; vi, 425. Rev. by Stanley Wells in MLR (81:2) 435–6.

5119. HODGES, C. WALTER; SCHOENBAUM, S.; LEONE, LEONARD (eds). The third Globe: symposium for the reconstruction of the Globe Playhouse, Wayne State University, 1979. *See* **3900.**

5120. HOLLAND, PETER. Style at the Swan. *See* **3901.**

5121. HUGHES, DEREK. Providential justice and English comedy, 1660–1700: a review of the external evidence. MLR (81:2) 273–92.

5122. HYLAND, PETER. Disguise and Renaissance tragedy. *See* **3902.**

5123. JONES, ROBERT. Engagement with knavery. Durham, NC: Duke UP. pp. 177. Rev. by James P. Barry in OhioanaQ (29:3) 124–5.

5124. KENDALL, KATHRYN McQUEEN. Theatre, society, and women playwrights in London from 1695 through the Queen Anne era. Unpub. doct. diss., Univ. of Texas at Austin. [Abstr. in DA (47) 1532A.]

5125. KENNY, SHIRLEY STRUM (ed.). British theatre and the other arts, 1660–1800. (Bibl. 1985, 12.) Rev. by Peter Lewis in BJECS (9:2) 264–7.

5126. KLINGLER, HELMUT. 'Tragedy' 1660–1737: terminology and genre. WBEP (80) 79–92.

5127. KRANTZ, SUSAN ELLEN. The first Fortune: the plays and the playhouse. Unpub. doct. diss., Tulane Univ., 1985. [Abstr. in DA (47) 189A.]

5128. LEINWAND, THEODORE B. London triumphing: the Jacobean Lord Mayor's show. CLIO (11:2) 137–53.

5129. LEVIN, RICHARD. Performance-critics *vs* close readers in the study of English Renaissance drama. *See* **3905.**

5130. LEVINE, LAURA. Men in women's clothing: anti-theatricality and effeminization from 1579–1642. *See* **3906.**

5131. LIMON, JERZY. Dangerous matter: English drama and politics in 1623/24. Cambridge: CUP. pp. 174.

5132. LOMAX, MARION. *The Faerie Queene* and the Book of Revelation as sources for spectacle in *The Second Maiden's Tragedy*. *See* **4267.**

5133. McALINDON, T. English Renaissance tragedy. *See* **3909.**

5134. MAGER, DONALD N. At the outer edge of resemblance: systems of signification in plays and courtly music during the reign of Charles I. Unpub. doct. diss., Wayne State Univ. [Abstr. in DA (47) 1335A.]

5135. MAGUIRE, LAURIE E. A stage property in *A Larum for London*. NQ (33:3) 371–3.

5136. MARSDEN, JEAN INGER. The re-imagined text: Shakespeare, adaptation, and theory in the Restoration and eighteenth century. *See* **4528.**

5137. MEYER, VERNE ALLYN. The relationship between prominent themes in John Calvin's theology and common arguments in the 'Puritan' critique of English theatre from 1577 to 1633. *See* **3913.**

5138. MILHOUS, JUDITH; HUME, ROBERT D. Producible interpretation: eight English plays, 1675–1707. Carbondale: Southern Illinois UP, 1985. pp. xv, 336. (*The Country Wife, All for Love, The Spanish Fryar, Venice Preserv'd, Amphitryon, The Wives Excuse, Love for Love, The Beaux' Stratagem.*) Rev. by Jack Vaughn in TJ (38:1) 117–18.

5139. MORTON, RICHARD. How many revengers in *The Revengers Tragedy*? Archaic spellings and the modern annotator. *In* (pp. 113–22) **44.**

5140. MROCZKOWSKA-BRAND, KATARZYNA. Overt theatricality and the *theatrum mundi* metaphor in Spanish and English drama, 1570–1640. *See* **3914.**

5141. NORBROOK, DAVID. *The Masque of Truth*: court entertainments and international protestant politics in the early Stuart period. Seventeenth Century (1:2) 81–110.

5142. ORRELL, JOHN. The theatre at Christ Church, Oxford, in 1605. ShS (35) 1982, 129–40.

5143. POSS, RICHARD LEE. The myth of Venice in English drama of the seventeenth century. Unpub. doct. diss., Univ. of Georgia. [Abstr. in DA (47) 2170A.]

5144. POWELL, JOCELYN. Restoration theatre production. (Bibl. 1985, 4460.) Rev. by Edward Burns in BJECS (9:2) 263–4.

5145. RAMEL, JACQUES. Méta-diégèse et extra-diégèse dans le théâtre élisabéthain. *In* (pp. 341–56) **1.**

5146. REYNOLDS, JAMES A. Repentance and retribution in early English drama. *See* **3920.**

5147. SALINGAR, LEO. Dramatic form in Shakespeare and the Jacobeans. *See* **4573.**

5148. SCHOENBAUM, S. Old-spelling editions: the state of the art. *In* (pp. 9–26) **44.**

5149. SCHRICKX, WILLEM. 'Pickleherring' and English actors in Germany. *See* **3927.**

5150. SHAND, G. B.; SHADY, RAYMOND C. (eds). Play-texts in old spelling: papers from the Glendon conference. *See* **44.**

5151. SHELLEY, PAULA DIANE. The use of dance in Jacobean drama to develop character. Unpub. doct. diss., Univ. of California, Los Angeles, 1985. [Abstr. in DA (46) 3538A.]

5152. SHEPHERD, SIMON. Amazons and warrior women: varieties of feminism in seventeenth-century drama. (Bibl. 1984, 4469.) Rev. by Douglas Brooks-Davies in YES (16) 264–8.

5153. SPINRAD, PHOEBE S. Memento mockery: some skulls on the Renaissance stage. *See* **3930.**

5154. STAGG, LOUIS CHARLES. The figurative language of the tragedies of Shakespeare's chief 17th-century contemporaries. (Bibl. 1985, 4464.) Rev. by Lois Potter in ShS (36) 1983, 174.

5155. STYAN, J. L. Restoration comedy in performance. Cambridge: CUP. pp. 400.

5156. THOMPSON, PEGGY. Radical individualism in seventeenth-century drama. Unpub. doct. diss., Indiana Univ., 1985. [Abstr. in DA (46) 2703A.]

5157. TURNER, ROBERT KEAN. Accidental evils. *In* (pp. 27–33) **44.**

5158. TYDEMAN, WILLIAM. The image of the city in English Renaissance drama. *See* **3934.**

5159. WERSTINE, PAUL. The editorial usefulness of printing house and compositor studies. *In* (pp. 35–64) **44.**

5160. WHITE, E. N. People and places: the social and topographical context of drama in York, 1554–1609. *See* **3936.**

5161. WILKS, J. S. 'A thousand several tongues': the idea of conscience in Tudor and Jacobean drama. *See* **3940.**

5162. WYMER, ROWLAND. Suicide and despair in the Jacobean drama. Brighton: Harvester Press. pp. xiii, 193. Rev. by Philip Edwards in THES (698) 26.

Fiction

5163. DAVIS, LENNARD J. Factual fictions: the origins of the English novel. (Bibl. 1985, 4475.) Rev. by Jerry Beasley in ECent (27:1) 62–71.

5164. GILLESPIE, GERALD. Erring and wayfaring in baroque fiction. *See* **3942.**

5165. KNIGHT, DAVID. Science fiction of the seventeenth century. Seventeenth Century (1:1) 69–79.

5166. MCDERMOTT, HUBERT. *Vertue Rewarded*: the first Anglo-Irish novel. Studies (75:298) 177–85.

5167. SPENCER, JANE. The rise of the woman novelist: from Aphra Behn to Jane Austen. Oxford: Blackwell. pp. 256. Rev. by Anthony Kearney in THES (723) 18.

Poetry

5168. BRADEN, GORDON. Beyond frustration: Petrarchan laurels in the seventeenth century. SELit (26:1) 5–23.

5169. BRADFORD, R. W. An investigation of theories of prosody and poetic form in the Restoration and eighteenth century, with special reference to blank verse. Unpub. doct. diss., Univ. of Oxford, 1983.

5170. BROWNE, R.   A George for an Oliver. Factotum (8) 1980, 14–17. (Eulogy to Cromwell rewritten to suit George I.)

5171. CLARKE, JOSEPH KELLY.   The *praeceptor amoris* in English Renaissance lyric poetry: one aspect of the poet's voice. *See* **3947.**

5172. DIME, GREGORY T.   The difference between 'strong lines' and 'metaphysical poetry'. SELit (26:1) 47–57.

5173. DOODY, MARGARET ANNE.   The daring muse: Augustan poetry reconsidered. (Bibl. 1985, 5226.) Rev. by Francis Doherty in BJECS (9:2) 251–2; by Howard Erskine-Hill in TLS, 14 Mar., 280.

5174. FOWLER, ALASTAIR.   Country House poems: the politics of a genre. Seventeenth Century (1:1) 1–14.

5175. GILMAN, ERNEST B.   Iconoclasm and poetry in the English Reformation: down went Dagon. *See* **3954.**

5176. GREENWOOD, D. S.   The seventeenth-century English poetic biblical paraphrase: practitioners, texts and contexts. Unpub. doct. diss., Univ. of Cambridge, 1985. [Abstr. in IT (35) 45.]

5177. KNAPP, STEVEN.   Personification and the sublime: Milton to Coleridge. Cambridge, MA; London: Harvard UP, 1985. pp. 178. Rev. by Rosemary Ashton in TLS, 19 Sept., 1035–6.

5178. LINDEN, STANTON J.   Mystical alchemy, eschatology, and seventeenth-century religious poetry. PCP (19) 1984, 79–88.

5179. LOW, ANTHONY.   The georgic revolution. *See* **3959.**

5180. McFARLANE, IAN D.   The Renaissance epitaph. *See* **3960.**

5181. MARTZ, LOUIS L.   English religious poetry, from Renaissance to Baroque. *See* **3963.**

5182. MESEROLE, HARRISON T. (ed.).   American poetry of the seventeenth century. University Park: Pennsylvania State UP, 1985. pp. xxvi, 576. Rev. by Larry A. Carlson in ChrisL (36:1) 30–1.

5183. MIROLLO, JAMES V.   Mannerism and Renaissance poetry: concept, mode, inner design. *See* **3965.**

5184. OTTEN, CHARLOTTE F.   'Environ'd with eternity': God, poems, and plants in sixteenth and seventeenth century England. *See* **3967.**

5185. PETILLON, PIERRE.   *Day of Doom*: la rhétorique de la fin des temps dans la Nouvelle Angleterre du XVIIe siècle. *In* (pp. 63–75) **2.**

5186. RAY, ROBERT H.   Unrecorded seventeenth-century allusions to Donne. NQ (33:4) 464–5.

5187. SCHLEINER, LOUISE.   Recent studies in poetry and music of the English Renaissance. *See* **3973.**

5188. SCODEL, JOSHUA KEITH.   Lapidary texts: the English poetic epitaph from Jonson to Pope. Unpub. doct. diss., Yale Univ., 1985. [Abstr. in DA (47) 1339A.]

5189. SLOANE, MARY COLE.   The visual in metaphysical poetry. (Bibl. 1982, 5138.) Rev. by Paulina Palmer in YES (16) 247–8.

5190. STOCKDALE-KLAUS, LISA FLORENCE.   Criteria for evaluating the English neoclassical imitation of classical and foreign verse satire, 1600–1750. Unpub. doct. diss., Vanderbilt Univ., 1985. [Abstr. in DA (46) 2288A.]

5191. VAN, DAVID. The dichotomous imagination: a study of English companion poems, 1596–1630. *See* **3977.**

5192. VAN EMDEN, JOAN. The metaphysical poets. Basingstoke: Macmillan. pp. viii, 96. (Macmillan master series.)

5193. VAN HOOK, J. W. 'Concupiscence of witt': the metaphysical conceit in baroque poetics. MP (84:1) 24–38.

5194. VENET, GISÈLE. Mémoire et création dans la poétique baroque. *In* (pp. 137–46) **34.**

5195. WOOD, N. P. The decline of the neo-classical pastoral, 1680–1730: a study in Theocritean and Virgilian influence. Unpub. doct. diss., Univ. of Durham, 1984.

5196. WYNNE-DAVIES, M. A study of Arthurian poetry in the English Renaissance from Spenser to Dryden. *See* **3982.**

5197. ZIM, R. A study of metrical versions of the Psalms in English, 1530–1601. *See* **3983.**

Prose

5198. BRAUNMULLER, A. R. (ed.). A seventeenth-century letter-book: a facsimile edition of Folger MS. V.a.321. (Bibl. 1984, 4507.) Rev. by Katherine Duncan-Jones in NQ (33:1) 108–9.

5199. CHARD, C. R. Horror and terror in literature of the Grand Tour, and in the gothic novel. Unpub. doct. diss., Univ. of Cambridge, 1985. [Abstr. in IT (35) 544.]

5200. CRANE, MARY THOMAS. Proverbial and aphoristic sayings: sources of authority in the English Renaissance. *See* **2408.**

5201. DAY, JAMES FREDERICK. Venal heralds and mushroom gentlemen: seventeenth-century character books and the sale of honor. Unpub. doct. diss., Duke Univ., 1985. [Abstr. in DA (46) 2298A.]

5202. FIREOVED, JOSEPH D. An anthology of colonial sermons. Unpub. doct. diss., Univ. of Delaware, 1985. [Abstr. in DA (47) 529A.]

5203. KRETZOI, CHARLOTTE. Changes in the meaning and function of plain style. *In* (pp. 249–53) **11.**

5204. REEDY, GÉRARD. The Bible and reason: Anglicans and scripture in late seventeenth-century England. Philadelphia: Pennsylvania UP, 1985. pp. 184. Rev. by Donald R. Dickson in SCN (44:4) 66–8.

5205. SHEVELOW, KATHRYN. The production of the female writing subject: letters to the *Athenian Mercury*. *See* **694.**

5206. SKERPAN, ELIZABETH P. Rhetorical genres and the *Eikon Basilike*. ExRC (11) 1985, 99–111.

5207. STAFFORD, NORA MCGHEE. Some elements of style in the religious prose of William Bates. Unpub. doct. disc., Baylor Univ., 1985. [Abstr. in DA (46) 2304A.]

5208. SUTLIFF, KRISTENE GAIL. The influence of the Royal Society on the prose style of Joseph Glanvill. Unpub. doct. diss., Oklahoma State Univ., 1985. [Abstr. in DA (47) 916A.]

5209. VAN DELFT, LOUIS. La notion de 'caractère' âl'âge classique. *In* (pp. 59–63) **11.**

Biography and Autobiography

5210. BATTESTIN, MARTIN C. (ed.). British novelists, 1660–1800: 1, A–L; 2, M–Z. Detroit, MI: Gale Research, 1985. pp. xviii, 325; xii, 372. (Dictionary of literary biography, 39.) Rev. by Peter Sabor in QQ (93:4) 907–10.

5211. PERRY, DENNIS R. Autobiographical structures in seventeenth-century Puritan histories. Unpub. doct. diss., Univ. of Wisconsin–Madison. [Abstr. in DA (47) 2161A.]

Related Studies

5212. ANDREWS, KENNETH R. Trade, plunder and settlement: maritime enterprise and the genesis of the British Empire, 1480–1630. *See* **3492.**

5213. BEIER, A. L. Masterless men: the vagrancy problem in England, 1560–1640. *See* **3998.**

5214. BIRNBAUM, G. Servants in England and America in the 17th century: the beginnings of slavery. *In* (pp. 45–64) **30.**

5215. CARRIVE, LUCIEN. Le royaume de Dieu, l'apocalypse et le millenium dans le protestantisme anglais classique. *In* (pp. 31–46) **2.**

5216. CHU, JONATHAN M. Neighbors, friends or madmen: the Puritan adjustment to Quakerism in seventeenth-century Massachusetts Bay. Westport, CT; London: Greenwood Press, 1985. pp. xiii, 205. (Contributions to the study of religion, 14.)

5217. COHEN, CHARLES LLOYD. God's caress: the psychology of Puritan religious experience. New York; Oxford: OUP. pp. xiv, 310.

5218. DALY, PETER M.; VALERI-TOMASZUK, PAOLA. Andrew Willet, England's first religious emblem writer. RenR (10:2) 181–200.

5219. DANNENFELDT, KARL H. Sleep: theory and practice in the late Renaissance. JHM (41:4) 415–41.

5220. DiMATTEO, ANTHONY JOSEPH. A select anthology of Renaissance mythography. *See* **4004.**

5221. DUFFY, EAMON. The godly and the multitude in Stuart England. Seventeenth Century (1:1) 31–55.

5222. FRASER, ANTONIA. The weaker vessel. (Bibl. 1984, 4523.) Rev. by Phyllis Mack in RQ (39:1) 149–51.

5223. HALLI, ROBERT W., JR. Quack: the writings and career of Francis Anthony. RenP 97–110.

5224. HENDERSON, KATHERINE USHER; McMANUS, BARBARA F. Half humankind: contexts and texts of the controversy about women in England, 1540–1640. *See* **4013.**

5225. HILL, CHRISTOPHER. The collected essays of Christopher Hill: vol. 2, Religion and politics and 17th century England; vol. 3, People and ideas in 17th century England. Brighton: Harvester Press. pp. xi, 356; xi, 340.

5226. HOULBROOKE, RALPH A. The English family 1450–1700. *See* **3530.**

5227. HUTTON, RONALD. The Restoration: a political and religious history of England and Wales 1658–1667. Oxford: Clarendon Press, 1985. pp. 379. Rev. by J. V. Guerinot in SCN (44:3) 46–7.

5228.   JACOB, JAMES R.   Henry Stubbs, radical Protestantism and the early Enlightenment. Cambridge: CUP, 1983. pp. 222. Rev. by Richard H. Popkin in JHP (24:2) 270–3.

5229.   JAMES, MERVYN.   Society, politics and culture: studies in early modern England. *See* **4017.**

5230.   JENNINGS, HUMPHREY (comp.); JENNINGS, MARY-LOU; MADGE, CHARLES (eds).   Pandaemonium, 1660–1886: the coming of the machine as seen by contemporary observers. London: Deutsch, 1985. pp. xxxviii, 276.

5231.   KITTLESON, JAMES M.; TRANSUE, PAMELA J. (eds).   Rebirth, reform, and resilience: universities in transition, 1300–1700. *See* **3538.**

5232.   KLAITS, JOSEPH.   Servants of Satan: the age of the witchhunts. *See* **4023.**

5233.   KNOESPEL, KENNETH J.   From poetry to history: Ovid's *Metamorphoses* and seventeenth-century historiography. RenP 111–21.

5234.   LEITES, EDMUND.   The Puritan conscience and modern sexuality. New Haven, CT; London: Yale UP. pp. xi, 208.

5235.   MARTINET, MARIE-MADELEINE.   Les espaces de la mémoire créatrice en Angleterre aux XVIIe et XVIIIe siècles. *In* (pp. 59–74) **34.**

5236.   MENHENNET, ALAN.   Grimmelshausen, the picaresque, and the large loose baggy monster. Seventeenth Century (1:2) 111–26.

5237.   MONTGOMERY, MICHAEL S. (comp.).   American Puritan studies: an annotated bibliography of dissertations, 1882–1981. Westport, CT; London: Greenwood Press, 1984. pp. xxii, 419. (Bibliographies and indexes in American history, 1.) Rev. in BB (43:3) 186.

5238.   ORRÙ, MARCO.   Anomy and reason in the English Renaissance. *See* **4033.**

5239.   PEARSON, DAVID.   A note on the authorship of Thomas Morton's *Catholike Appeale.* NQ (33:3) 377.

5240.   QUINN, DAVID BEERS.   Set fair for Roanoke: voyages and colonies, 1584–1606. *See* **4037.**

5241.   REAY, BARRY.   The Quakers and the English Revolution. New York: St Martin's Press, 1985. pp. 184. Rev. by Christian R. Davis in SCN (44:4) 68–9.

5242.   ROGERS, NORMA PRICHARD.   John Sherman: Puritan and Cambridge Platonist. Unpub. doct. diss., Univ. of Mississippi. [Abstr. in DA (47) 1338A.]

5243.   ROUX, LOUIS.   Les artistes et leurs protecteurs en Angleterre au 17e siècle. *In* (pp. 5–30) **30.**

5244.   ROWSE, A. L.   Reflections on the Puritan revolution. London: Methuen. pp. 256.

5245.   SEAVER, PAUL S.   Wallington's world: a puritan artisan in seventeenth-century London. Stanford, CT: Stanford UP, 1985. pp. 258. Rev. by Donald R. Dickson in SCN (44:4) 70–1.

5246.   SHAPIRO, BARBARA J.   Probability and certainty in seventeenth-century England: a study of the relationship between natural science, religion, history, law, and literature. (Bibl. 1984, 4413.) Rev. by Richard H. Popkin in JHP (24:3) 416–18.

5247. STOUT, HARRY S.   The New England soul: preaching and religious culture in colonial New England. New York; Oxford: OUP. pp. xii, 398.

5248. TEAGUE, FRANCES.   New light on Bathsua Makin. SCN (44:1/2) 16.(Writer on female education.)

5249. UNDERDOWN, DAVID.   Revel, riot, and rebellion: popular politics and culture in England 1603–1660. Oxford: Clarendon Press, 1985; New York: OUP. pp. xii, 324.

5250. VERDEIL, MARIE-HÉLÈNE.   La dynastie Winthrop: 'Covenant' et relations sociales en Nouvelle-Angleterre au 17e siècle. *In* (pp. 31–43) **30.**

5251. WEAVER, JOHN DAVID.   Franz Daniel Pastorius (1651–c.1720): early life in Germany with glimpses of his removal to Pennsylvania. Unpub. doct. diss., Univ. of California, Davis, 1985. [Abstr. in DA (47) 903A.]

Literary Theory

This section is intended to contain studies **about** the literary theory, literary historiography, literary criticism, etc., produced *in* the seventeenth century. For modern works **of** literary history and criticism dealing generally with this period, see under 'Seventeenth Century: General Literary Studies'.

5252. CREWE, JONATHAN.   Hidden designs: the critical profession and Renaissance literature. *See* **4052.**

5253. DAALDER, JOOST.   Herbert's 'poetic theory'. GHJ (9:2) 17–34.

5254. JOHNSON, ANTHONY.   'Angles', 'squares', or 'roundes': Ben Jonson and the Palladian aesthetic. Pubs of the Dept of English, Univ. of Turku (7) 1985, 77–101.

5255. METER, J. H.   The literary theories of Daniel Heinsius: a study of the development and background of his views on literary theory and criticism during the period from 1602 to 1612. (Bibl. 1985, 4545.) Rev. by O. B. Hardison, Jr in RQ (39:2) 299–302.

5256. PONSFORD, M. J.   The poetry of Thomas Traherne in relation to the thought and poetics of his period. Unpub. doct. diss., Univ. of Newcastle upon Tyne, 1984.

5257. ZACH, WOLFGANG.   Das Stereotyp als literarische Norm. Zum dominanten Denkmodell des Klassizismus. *See* **2779.**

AUTHORS

John Abbott ('John' or 'Augustine Rivers', 'John Ashton')
5258. JORDAN, RICHARD D.   John Abbott's 1647 *Paradise Lost.* MQ (20:2) 48–51.

Richard Allestree
5259. THOMAS, JOHN A.   A moral voice for the Restoration lady: a comparative view of Allestree and Vives. JRMMRA (7) 123–42.

Lancelot Andrewes
5260. DESMOND, JOHN.   Walker Percy and T. S. Eliot: the Lancelot Andrewes connection. SoR (22:3) 465–77.

Walter Aston
5261. KAY, DENNIS.   Poems by Sir Walter Aston, and a date for the Donne/Goodyer verse epistle 'Alternis Vicibus'. RES (37:146) 198–210.

John Aubrey
5262. NICHOLSON, OLIVER.   Iamblichus in John Aubrey's *Miscellanies*. NQ (33:4) 481–2.

Francis Bacon
5263. FATTORI, MARTA (ed.).   Francis Bacon, Seminario Internazionale. Rome: Ateneo, 1984. pp. 327. Rev. by Marie-Thérèse Belin in Revue Internationale de Philosophie (40:4) 453–5.

5264. HODGES, DEVON L.   Renaissance fictions of anatomy. *See* **4108.**

5265. KIERNAN, MICHAEL (ed.).   The Essayes, or Counsel, Civill and Morall. Oxford: Clarendon Press; Cambridge, MA: Harvard UP, 1985. pp. xlix, 339. Rev. by F. J. Levy in RQ (39:4) 796–8.

5266. LE DOEUFF, MICHÈLE.   L'homme et la nature dans les jardins de la science. Revue Internationale de Philosophie (40:4) 359–77.

5267. LEVY, F. J.   Francis Bacon and the style of politics. ELR (16:1) 101–22.

5268. LLASERA, MARGARET.   Art, artifice and the artificial in the works of Francis Bacon. BSEAA (22) 7–18.

5269. MALHERBE, MICHEL.   L'induction des notions chez Francis Bacon. Revue Internationale de Philosophie (40:4) 427–45.

5270. PAULSON, RONALD.   Francis Bacon in retrospect. Raritan (5:3) 1–25.

5271. PITCHER, JOHN (ed.).   The essays. Harmondsworth: Penguin, 1985. pp. 287. (Penguin classics.)

5272. POUSSEUR, JEAN-MARIE.   De l'interprétation: une logique pour l'invention. Revue Internationale de Philosophie (40:4) 378–98.

5273. REES, GRAHAM.   Mathematics and Francis Bacon's natural philosophy. Revue Internationale de Philosophie (40:4) 399–426.

5274. —— UPTON, CHRISTOPHER (eds).   Francis Bacon's natural philosophy: a new source: a transcription of manuscript Hardwick 72A. Chalfont St Giles: British Soc. for the History of Science, 1984. pp. 197. (BSHS monographs, 5.)

5275. ROWLAND, IRENE (ed.).   Francis Bacon's personal life-story: vol. 1, The age of Elizabeth. (Bibl. 1949, 2301); vol. 2, The age of James. By ALFRED DODD. (Vol. 2 originally ed. by EDWARD D. JOHNSON.) London: Rider. 2 vols in 1. pp. 580. (Vol. 1, second ed.: first ed. 1949.)

5276. WEINBERGER, JERRY.   Science, faith, and politics: Francis Bacon and the utopian roots of the modern age: a commentary on Bacon's *Advancement of Learning*. Ithaca, NY; London: Cornell UP, 1985. pp. 342.

5277. WHITNEY, CHARLES.   Francis Bacon and modernity. New Haven, CT; London: Yale UP. pp. vii, 240.

John Banks

5278. KOTAB, A. Y.   A critical edition of four tragedies by John Banks. Unpub. doct. diss., Univ. of Leeds, 1982.

Robert Baron

5279. MAULE, J. F.   Robert Baron's *Cyprian Academy* (1647). NQ (33:3) 393–4.

Richard Baxter

5280. HASKIN, DAYTON.   Baxter's quest for origins: novelty and originality in the autobiography. ECent (21:2) 1980, 145–61.

5281. KEEBLE, N. H.   The autobiographer as apologist: *Reliquiae Baxterianae* (1696). Prose Studies (9:2) 105–19.

Beaumont and Fletcher

5282. BOWERS, FREDSON (gen. ed.).   The dramatic works in the Beaumont and Fletcher canon: vol. 6, *Wit without Money*, ed. by HANS WALTER GABLER, *The Pilgrim*, ed. by CYRUS HOY, *The Wild Goose Chase*, ed. by FREDSON BOWERS, *A Wife for a Month*, ed. by ROBERT KEAN TURNER, *Rule a Wife and Have a Wife*, ed. by GEORGE WALTON WILLIAMS. Cambridge: CUP, 1985. pp. vii, 605. Rev. by Katherine Duncan-Jones in TLS, 20 Sept. 1985, 1034.

5283. FARABAUGH, ROBIN INGRAHAM.   Artists for their time: dialectic and cultural change in the works of Beaumont and Fletcher. Unpub. doct. diss., Cornell Univ., 1985. [Abstr. in DA (46) 2699A.]

Francis Beaumont

5284. DEGYANSKY, BARBARA KNIGHT.   A reconsideration: George and Nell of *The Knight of the Burning Pestle*. ELN (23:3) 27–32.

Aphra Behn

5285. BEHRMANN, ALFRED.   Aphra Behn's *The Emperor of the Moon*: anatomy of a 'European' comic play. YREAL (2) 1984, 239–74.

5286. DeRITTER, JONES.   The Gypsy, *The Rover*, and the Wanderer: Aphra Behn's revision of Thomas Killigrew. Restoration (10:2) 82–92.

5287. DHUICQ, BERNARD.   *Oroonoko*: expérience et création. *In* (pp. 41–8) **34.**

5288. GOREAU, ANGELINE.   Aphra Behn: a scandal to modesty (*ca.*1640–1689). *In* (pp. 8–27) **20.**

5289. HERSEY, WILLIAM ROBERT.   A critical old-spelling edition of Aphra Behn's *The City Heiress*. Unpub. doct. diss., Univ. of New Hampshire, 1985. [Abstr. in DA (46) 3040A.]

5290. O'DONNELL, MARY ANN (comp.).   Aphra Behn: an annotated bibliography of primary and secondary sources. New York; London: Garland. pp. xix, 557. (Garland reference library of the humanities, 505.)

5291. TRUSSLER, SIMON (notes).   An adaptation of *The Rover (The Banished Cavaliers)*. London: Methuen. pp. 72. (Swan Theatre plays.)

Edward Benlowes

5292. MORTON, GERALD W.   An interesting Benlowes allusion. NQ (33:3) 392.

Sir Thomas Bodley

5293. WOODEN, WARREN W.   Sir Thomas Bodley's *Life of Himself* (1609) and the epideictic strategies of encomia. *See* **2989.**

William Bosworth

5294. RIDDELL, JAMES A.   The life of William Bosworth. HLQ (49:2) 165–74.

Anne Bradstreet

5295. BUCHANAN, JANE BRITTON.   Poetic identity in the New World: Anne Bradstreet, Emily Dickinson, and Derek Walcott. Unpub. doct. diss., Tufts Univ., 1985. [Abstr. in DA (46) 3031A.]

5296. MARTIN, WENDY.   An American triptych: Anne Bradstreet, Emily Dickinson, Adrienne Rich. (Bibl. 1985, 4571.) Rev. by Ursula Brumm in EAL (20:3) 1985/86, 271–7; by Claire Keyes in Legacy (3:1) 74–6.

Alexander Brome

5297. DUBINSKI, ROMAN R. (ed.).   Poems. (Bibl. 1985, 4573.) Rev. by Raymond A. Anselment in RenR (9:4) 1985, 275–8.

Richard Brome

5298. CUTTS, JOHN.   Original music for two Caroline plays – Richard Brome's *The English Moor; or the Mock-Marriage* and James Shirley's *The Gentlemen of Venice*. NQ (33:1) 21–5.

5299. SESSA, JACQUELINE.   *Les Antipodes* de Richard Brome, comédie anglaise et comédie européenne. *In* (pp. 223–30) **1.**

Sir Thomas Browne

5300. DATTA, KITTY SCOULAR.   Sir Thomas Browne and *Vox Norwici*. NQ (33:4) 461.

5301. MORRIS, G. C. R.   Sir Thomas Browne's daughters, 'cosen Barker' and the Cottrells. NQ (33:4) 472–9.

5302. PATRIDES, C. A. (ed.).   Approaches to Sir Thomas Browne: the Ann Arbor tercentary lectures and essays. (Bibl. 1985, 4579.) Rev. by Jonathan Post in YES (16) 251–3.

5303. REGAN, P. J.   Tall, opaque words: diction and rhetoric in the works of Sir Thomas Browne. Unpub. doct. diss., Univ. of Newcastle upon Tyne. [Abstr. in IT (36) 20.]

5304. SINGER, THOMAS CONWAY.   Sir Thomas Browne and 'the hieroglyphical schools of the Egyptians': a study of the Renaissance search for the natural language of the world. Unpub. doct. diss., Columbia Univ., 1985. [Abstr. in DA (46) 2304A.]

George Villiers, Second Duke of Buckingham

5305. FOWLER, JAMES.   Catiline quoted in *The Chances*. NQ (33:4) 467–9.

5306. PHIPPS, CHRISTINE (ed.).   Buckingham: public and private man: the prose, poems and commonplace book of George Villiers, second Duke of Buckingham (1628–1687). New York; London: Garland, 1985. pp. xvii, 346. (Renaissance imagination, 13.)

John Bunyan

5307. BACKSCHEIDER, PAULA R.   A being more intense: a study of the prose works of Bunyan, Swift, and Defoe. New York: AMS Press, 1984. pp. xxi, 222.

5308. CAMÉE, JEAN-FRANÇOIS.   Mémoire et création: de *Grace Abounding* au *Pilgrim's Progress*. *In* (pp. 99–109) **34.**

5309. LACASSAGNE, CLAUDE-LAURENCE. *Grace Abounding*...: la narration et la grâce. *In* (pp. 89–97) **34.**

5310. LUXON, THOMAS HYATT. The pilgrim's passive progress: Luther and Bunyan on talking and doing, word and way. ELH (53:1) 73–98.

5311. OWENS, W. R. A critical edition of John Bunyan's posthumously published treatise *Of Antichrist, and his Ruine* (1692). Unpub. doct. diss., Open Univ., 1984.

5312. —— The date of Bunyan's treatise *Of Antichrist*. Seventeenth Century (1:2) 153–7.

5313. ROSENWASSER, DAVID. The idea of enclosure: prisons and havens at the rise of the novel. Unpub. doct. diss., Univ. of Virginia, 1985. [Abstr. in DA (46) 3728A.]

5314. SAMS, HORACE, JR. Temptation in imaginative literature of Milton and Bunyan: two faces of the Puritan persona. Unpub. doct. diss., Univ. of South Florida, 1985. [Abstr. in DA (46) 3043A.]

5315. SHARROCK, ROGER (gen. ed.). Good news for the vilest of men; The advocateship of Jesus Christ. Ed. by RICHARD L. GREAVES. Oxford: Clarendon Press, 1985. pp. xliii, 231. (Miscellaneous works of John Bunyan, 11.) Rev. by Jacques B. H. Alblas in EngS (67:5) 453–4.

5316. SIM, S. D. Dialogues with closure: ideology and identity in the fiction of Dent, Bunyan and Defoe. Unpub. doct. diss., Univ. of Manchester, 1983. [Abstr. in IT (35) 45–6.]

5317. THICKSTUN, MARGARET OLOFSON. From Christiana to Standfast: subsuming the feminine in *The Pilgrim's Progress*. SELit (26:3) 439–53.

Robert Burton

5318. HODGES, DEVON L. Renaissance fictions of anatomy. *See* **4108.**

Samuel Butler (1613–1680)

5319. COPE, KEVIN L. The conquest of truth: Wycherley, Rochester, Butler, and Dryden and the Restoration critique of satire. Restoration (10:1) 19–40.

Thomas Campion

5320. LINDLEY, DAVID. Thomas Campion. Leiden: Brill. pp. x, 242. (Medieval and Renaissance authors, 7.)

Thomas Carew

5321. ALTIERI, JOANNE. Responses to a waning mythology in Carew's political poetry. SELit (26:1) 107–24.

5322. HANNAFORD, RENÉE. Self-presentation in Carew's *To A. L. Perswasions to Love*. SELit (26:1) 97–106.

Lady Elizabeth Carey

5323. HOLDSWORTH, R. V. Middleton and *The Tragedy of Mariam*. NQ (33:3) 379–80.

James Carkesse

5324. MARTIN, PHILIP W. Lucid intervals: Dryden, Carkesse, and Wordsworth. NQ (33:1) 42–4.

Elizabeth Cary, Viscountess Falkland

5325. FISCHER, SANDRA K. Elizabeth Cary and tyranny, domestic and religious. *In* (pp. 225–37) **52.**

John Caryll
5326. TAYLOR, RICHARD C.   The originality of John Caryll's *Sir Saloman*. CompDr (20:3) 261–9.
George Chapman
5327. CLARK, MICHAEL EUGENE.   George Chapman and Ben Jonson: a conflict in theory. Unpub. doct. diss., Univ. of Michigan. [Abstr. in DA (47) 712A.]
5328. CUMMINGS, L. A.   A new basis for the hand of George Chapman: the 1577 *Real Iamblichus* volume. ExRC (11) 1985, 120–7.
5329. FLORBY, GUNILLA.   The painful passage to virtue: a study of George Chapman's *The Tragedy of Bussy d'Ambois* and *The Revenge of Bussy d'Ambois*. (Bibl. 1984, 4592.) Rev. by A. R. Braunmuller in YES (16) 238–9.
5330. MANNING, JOHN.   The eagle and the dove: Chapman and Donne's *The Canonization*. NQ (33:3) 347–8.
5331. MARGESON, JOHN.   Chapman's experiments with tragic form. *In* (pp. 47–58) **18.**
5332. TRICOMI, A. H.   Philip, Earl of Pembroke, and the analogical way of reading political tragedy. JEGP (85:3) 332–45.
Edward Hyde, Earl of Clarendon
5333. BROWNLEY, MARTINE WATSON.   Clarendon and the rhetoric of historical form. Philadelphia: Pennsylvania UP, 1985. pp. 239. Rev. by Annabel Patterson in WHR (40:4) 380–2; by Timothy W. Crusius in SCN (44:3) 48–9.
5334. —— Clarendon, Gibbon, and the art of historical portraiture. ELN (24:1) 49–58.
Sir Aston Cokayne
5335. SHAW, CATHERINE M. (ed.).   The obstinate lady. New York; London: Garland. pp. xcix, 141. (Renaissance imagination, 17.)
William Congreve
5336. KROLL, RICHARD W.   Discourse and power in *The Way of the World*. ELH (53:4) 727–58.
Charles Cotton
5337. HARTLE, P. N.   Defoe and *The Wonders of the Peake*: the place of Cotton's poem in *A Tour thro' the Whole Island of Great Britain*. EngS (67:5) 420–31.
5338. HARTLE, PAUL.   The source of Roxana's song. NQ (33:1) 46.
John Cotton
5339. DELAMOTTE, EUGENIA.   John Cotton and the rhetoric of grace. EAL (21:1) 49–74.
Abraham Cowley
5340. GREEN, MARY ELIZABETH.   The poet in Solomon's house: Abraham Cowley as Baconian apostle. Restoration (10:2) 68–75.
5341. LÖFFLER, ARNO.   'A hard and nice subject': Zur Problematick der Selbstdarstellung in Cowleys Essay *Of My Self*. Ang (104:3/4) 349–68.
Richard Crashaw
5342. FABRY, FRANK.   Richard Crashaw and the art of allusion: pastoral in *A Hymn to . . . Sainte Teresa*. ELR (16:3) 373–82.

5343. HEALY, T. F. Richard Crashaw: poetry and Anglicanism at Cambridge in the early seventeenth century. Unpub. doct. diss., Univ. of London, Queen Mary Coll., 1983.

5344. ROBERTS, JOHN R. Richard Crashaw: annotated bibliography of criticism, 1632–1980. (Bibl. 1985, 4620, where scholar's initial incorrect.) Rev. by Paul A. Parrish in SCN (44:1/2) 12–13.

5345. YOSHIDA, SACHIKO. Southwell to Crashaw. (Southwell and Crashaw.) *See* **4232.**

5346. YOUNG, R. V. Richard Crashaw and the Spanish Golden Age. (Bibl. 1985, 4623.) Rev. by Gerald Hammond in MLR (81:3) 719–20.

Samuel Daniel

5347. BOOY, D. G. The morality of learning and the concept of the poet: a study of the debate on the purpose, role and scope of human learning in England in the late sixteenth and early seventeenth centuries, with particular reference to Samuel Daniel and Fulke Greville. *See* **4000.**

5348. DAVIS, DICK. Samuel Daniel: a neglected Elizabethan poet. EDH (44) 1–23.

5349. RONAN, CLIFFORD J. Daniel, Rainolde, Demosthenes, and the degree speech of Shakespeare's Ulysses. *See* **4193.**

5350. SILCOX, MARY VERA. 'Such subtile craft': the role of the poet–speaker in Daniel's *Delia*, Spenser's *Amoretti*, and Drayton's *Idea*. *See* **4284.**

Sir William D'Avenant

5351. GELLERT, JAMES. The sources of Davenant's *The Law Against Lovers*. *See* **309.**

John Davies (1625–1693)

5352. HILLER, GEOFFREY G. Allusions to Spenser by John Davies and Sir John Davies. *See* **4065.**

John Day

5353. DAVIES, H. NEVILLE. *Pericles* and the Sherley brothers. *In* (pp. 94–113) **50.**

Thomas Dekker

5354. COMENSOLI, VIVIANA. Challenging the homiletic tradition: the domestic drama of Thomas Dekker, 1599–1621. Unpub. doct. diss., Univ. of British Columbia, 1985. [Abstr. in DA (47) 1331A.]

5355. HUNTER, GEORGE K. Bourgeois comedy: Shakespeare and Dekker. *In* (pp. 1–15) **50.**

5356. ROSS, CHERYL LYNN. The plague and the figures of power: authority and subversion in English Renaissance drama. *See* **4890.**

5357. SCHAFER, ELIZABETH. The ring story in *Northward Ho*, 1.i.: an English source. NQ (33:3) 374–5.

5358. WAAGE, FREDERICK O. Meg and Mall: two Renaissance London heroines. *See* **3993.**

Sir John Denham

5359. RADCLIFFE, DAVID HILL. 'These delights from several causes move': heterogeneity and genre in *Coopers Hill*. PLL (22:4) 352–71.

5360. TASCH, PETER A. Dryden and Denham. NQ (33:1) 44.

John Donne

5361. ANTHONY, J. PHILLIP.   Donne's *The Relique*. Exp (44:2) 13–15.

5362. BAUMLIN, JAMES S.   Donne as imitative poet: the evidence of *Satyre II*. ExRC (11) 1985, 29–42.

5363. —— Donne's problems and the Neo-Latin tradition. Neolatin Bulletin (El Cajon, CA) (3:1) 1985, 1–4.

5364. CERASANO, S. P.   The Dean of St Paul's at court. NQ (33:3) 385–6.

5365. DOCHERTY, THOMAS.   John Donne, undone. London: Methuen. pp. 253.

5366. DUBINSKI, ROMAN.   Donne's *Holy Sonnets* and the seven penitential Psalms. RenR (10:2) 201–16.

5367. ELMIMIAN, ISAAC.   The dedicatory letter as a rhetorical device: the example of Donne. CML (6:2) 127–36.

5368. EVETT, DAVID.   Donne's poems and the five styles of Renascence art. JDJ (5:1/2) 101–31.

5369. FELPERIN, HOWARD.   Canonical texts and non canonical interpretations: the neohistoricist rereading of Donne. SoRA (18:3) 1985, 235–50.

5370. GILMAN, ERNEST B.   'To adore, or scorne an image': Donne and the iconoclastic controversy. JDJ (5:1/2) 63–100.

5371. GLASER, JOE.   *Goodfriday, 1613*: a soul's form. CLit (13:2) 168–76.

5372. GRANQVIST, RAOUL.   Edmund Gosse: the reluctant critic of John Donne. NM (87:2) 262–71.

5373. —— The reception of Edmund Gosse's *Life of John Donne* (1899). EngS (67:6) 525–38.

5374. HARLAND, PAUL W.   Dramatic technique and personae in Donne's sermons. ELH (53:4) 709–26.

5375. HÖLTGEN, KARL JOSEF.   Aspects of the emblem: studies in the English emblem tradition and the European context. With a foreword by SIR ROY STRONG. *See* **5063.**

5376. KAY, DENNIS.   Poems by Sir Walter Aston, and a date for the Donne/Goodyer verse epistle 'Alternis Vicibus'. *See* **5261.**

5377. KIM, MYONG-OK.   Eliot eui Donne bipyeong gwa Donne si eui hyeondaesung. (Eliot's criticism of Donne and the modernity of Donne's poetry.) JELL (32:3) 387–406.

5378. KIM, YOUNG HO.   Baroque elements in Donne's poetry. Pegasus (8) 1985, 5–19.

5379. KLEIN, JÜRGEN.   Astronomie und Anthropozentrik. Die Copernicanische Wende bei John Donne, John Milton und den Cambridge Platonists. *See* **5069.**

5380. LAPORTE, VALERIE DOROTHY.   John Donne and the esoteric tradition. Unpub. doct. diss., Columbia Univ. [Abstr. in DA (47) 913A.]

5381. LLASERA, MARGARET.   'Howerely in Inconstancee': transience and transformation in the poetry of John Donne. BSEAA (23) 39–56.

5382. ——John Donne, *Poems*: bibliographie sélective et critique. BSEAA (23) 7–16.

5383. LUCAS, PATRICIA DIANE.   Sea-voyage imagery in the poetry of John Donne. Unpub. doct. diss., Case Western Reserve Univ., 1985. [Abstr. in DA (46) 2700A.]

5384. McGERR, ROSEMARIE POTZ.   Donne's 'Blest Hermaphrodite' and the *Poetria nova*. NQ (33:3) 349.

5385. MANN, LINDSAY A.   Sacred and profane love in Donne. DalR (65:4) 1985/86, 534–50.

5386. MANNING, JOHN.   The eagle and the dove: Chapman and Donne's *The Canonization. See* **5330.**

5387. MAROTTI, ARTHUR F.   John Donne, coterie poet. Madison; London: Wisconsin UP. pp. xviii, 369. Rev. by Arthur F. Kinney in CR (30:4) 538–9; by Graham Parry in THES (717) 17.

5388. OUKUMA, SAKAE.   Donne, emblem, manierisumu: chiki no kansatu. (Donne, emblem, mannerism: the observation of wit.) Tokyo: Hakuoh-sha. pp. xiv, 332.

5389. PEARSON, DAVID.   An unrecorded book from the library of John Donne. *See* **271.**

5390. PINNINGTON, A. J.   Reformation themes and tensions in John Donne's *Divine Poems*. Unpub. doct. diss., Univ. of Sussex, 1983.

5391. PRITCHARD, R. E.   Donne's angels in the corners. NQ (33:3) 348–9.

5392. RAY, ROBERT H.   Unrecorded seventeenth-century allusions to Donne. *See* **5186.**

5393. ROBERTS, JOHN R.   John Donne: an annotated bibliography of modern criticism, 1968–1978. (Bibl. 1985, 4660.) Rev. by William White in BB (43:1) 59.

5394. SALOMON, WILLIS ANTHONY.   The uses of situation: John Donne's *Songs and Sonets*. Unpub. doct. diss., Univ. of California, Berkeley, 1985. [Abstr. in DA (47) 915A.]

5395. SELLIN, PAUL R.   John Donne and 'Calvinist' views of grace. (Bibl. 1985, 4661.) Rev. by Terry G. Sherwood in RenR (9:3) 1985, 231–2.

5396. SHAW, ROBERT B.   The call of God: the theme of vocation in the poetry of Donne and Herbert. (Bibl. 1985, 4663.) Rev. by Paulina Palmer in YES (16) 247–8.

5397. SHERWOOD, TERRY G.   Fulfilling the circle: a study of John Donne's thought. (Bibl. 1985, 4664.). Rev. by Jeanne Shami in RenR (9:4) 1985, 296–9; by Mark Roberts in NQ (33:2) 227–9; by David R. Shore in ESCan (12:4) 459–62.

5398. SLOANE, THOMAS O.   Donne, Milton, and the end of Humanist rhetoric. (Bibl. 1985, 4666.) Rev. by Arthur F. Kinney in JEGP (85:3) 450–4; by Barbara K. Lewalski in ChrisL (35:4) 42–3.

5399. WALKER, JULIA M.   The visual paradigm of *The Good-Morrow*: Donne's cosmographical glasse. RES (37:145) 61–5.

Michael Drayton

5400. GREENHUT, DEBORAH SCHNEIDER.   Feminine rhetorical culture: Tudor adaptations of Ovid's *Heroides. See* **4302.**

5401. Silcox, Mary Vera. 'Such subtile craft': the role of the poet–speaker in Daniel's *Delia*, Spenser's *Amoretti*, and Drayton's *Idea*. *See* **4284.**

John Dryden

5402. Armistead, J. M. Egypt in the Restoration: a perspective on *All for Love*. PLL (22:2) 139–53.

5403. —— The occultism of Dryden's 'American' plays in context. Seventeenth Century (1:2) 127–52.

5404. Bates, Richard. Dryden, Boccaccio, and Montaigne. NQ (33:1) 44.

5405. Bywaters, David. Dryden and the Revolution of 1688: political parallel in *Don Sebastian*. JEGP (85:3) 346–65.

5406. Cope, Kevin L. The conquest of truth: Wycherley, Rochester, Butler, and Dryden and the Restoration critique of satire. *See* **5319.**

5407. Cordner, Michael. Dryden's *Astraea Redux* and Fanshawe's *Ode*. NQ (31:3) 1984, 341–2.

5408. Corse, Douglas Taylor. Arms and the man: a study of Dryden's *Aeneid*. Unpub. doct. diss., Univ. of Florida, 1985. [Abstr. in DA (47) 187A.]

5409. Donaldson, Ian. Fathers and sons: Jonson, Dryden and *MacFlecknoe*. SoRA (18:3) 1985, 314–27.

5410. Foxton, Rosemary. Delariviere Manley and 'Astrea's vacant throne'. NQ (33:1) 41–2.

5411. Fujimura, Thomas H. Dryden's changing political views. Restoration (10:2) 93–104.

5412. Gardiner, Anne Barbeau. A Jacobite song by John Dryden. YLG (61:1/2) 49–54.

5413. —— The roots of authority: fidelity to inherited laws in Dryden's *The Hind and the Panther*. CLIO (11:1) 1981, 15–28.

5414. Genster, Julia Ann. 'These veracious pages': the epistle and its audiences from Dryden to Austen. Unpub. doct. diss., Univ. of California, Berkeley, 1985. [Abstr. in DA (47) 910A.]

5415. Gill, R. B. Dryden, Pope, and the person in personal satire. ELit (13:2) 219–20.

5416. Gilmore, Sue Chaney. The Aeneas analogy: a study of the Aeneas tradition in the works of Dryden, Hardy, and Tate. Unpub. doct. diss., Vanderbilt Univ., 1985. [Abstr. in DA (46) 2287A.]

5417. Graver, Bruce E. Wordsworth and the language of epic: the translation of the *Aeneid*. SP (83:3) 261–85.

5418. Harth, Phillip; Fisher, Alan; Cohen, Ralph. New homage to John Dryden. Los Angeles: William Andrews Clark Memorial Library, 1983. pp. 88. Rev. in SCN (44:1/2) 4–5.

5419. Hees, Edwin. Dryden's Jacobitism: 'that hard necessity'. ESA (29:2) 77–86.

5420. Hinnant, Charles H. Dryden's definition of a play in *An Essay of Dramatic Poesy*: a structuralist approach. StudECC (15) 161–72.

5421. Hopkins, David. John Dryden. Cambridge: CUP. pp. 224. (British and Irish authors.) Rev. by David Nokes in TLS, 8 Aug., 871.

5422. LINDSAY, W. A.   Dryden and Juvenal. Unpub. doct. diss., Trinity Coll. Dublin, 1982/83.

5423. MARTIN, PHILIP W.   Lucid intervals: Dryden, Carkesse, and Wordsworth. *See* **5324.**

5424. MONTI-POUAGARE, STALO.   The achievement of suspense in a group of Oedipus plays. Unpub. doct. diss., Pennsylvania State Univ. [Abstr. in DA (47) 1314A.]

5425. NOVAK, MAXIMILLIAN E.; GUFFEY, GEORGE R. (eds).   The works of John Dryden: vol. 13, Plays: *All for Love, Oedipus, Troilus and Cressida.* Berkeley: California UP, 1985. pp. 651. Rev. by J. V. Guerinot in SCN (44:1/2) 1–3.

5426. POYET, ALBERT.   Poésie et théâtralité dans *All for Love* de John Dryden. *In* (pp. 111–22) **30.**

5427. —— Stratégies argumentatives et ambiguïtés poétiques dans la deuxième partie de *The Hind and the Panther.* BSEAA (22) 29–46.

5428. REEDY, GERARD.   The Bible and reason: Anglicans and scripture in late seventeenth-century England. *See* **5204.**

5429. REVERAND, CEDRIC D.   Double, double Dryden. ECent (27:2) 188–93 (review-article).

5430. —— Dryden's final poetic mode: *To the Dutchess of Ormond* and *Fables.* ECent (26:1) 1985, 3–21.

5431. RUDDICK, WILLIAM.   Scott and Johnson as biographers of Dryden. NRam (25) 1984, 19–26.

5432. SALVAGGIO, RUTH.   Dryden's dualities. (Bibl. 1985, 4708.) Rev. by Cedric D. Reverand in ECent (27:2) 188–93.

5433. SELDEN, RAMAN.   Absalom and Achitophel. Harmondsworth: Penguin. pp.112. (Penguin masterstudies.)

5434. SHADDY, VIRGINIA M.   L'influence française et le rôle de Dryden dans l'évolution des idées générales et de la rhetorique en occident. Lille: Atelier National de Reproduction des Thèses, 1983. pp. 1008.

5435. SHERBO, ARTHUR.   Dryden and the fourth Earl of Lauderdale. SB (39) 199–210.

5436. SLOMAN, JUDITH.   Dryden: the poetics of translation. Ed. by ANNE MCWHIR. (Bibl. 1985, 4715.) Rev. by Stuart Gillespie in CamQ (15) 261–8; by Thomas H. Fujimura in JEGP (85:3) 454–6; by Ann Messenger in Ariel (17:3) 118–19.

5437. TASCH, PETER A.   Dryden and Denham. *See* **5360.**

5438. —— Pope and Dryden on shutting doors. NQ (33:4) 499–500.

5439. THOMAS, W. K.   The crafting of *Absalom and Achitophel*: Dryden's 'pen for a party'. (Bibl. 1982, 5345.) Rev. by David Wykes in NQ (33:4) 550–2.

5440. VACHÉ, JEAN.   'The numbers of poetry and vocal music' in *King Arthur*: the internal evidence. CEl (30) 59–70.

5441. VANCE, JOHN A.   Antony bound: fragmentation and insecurity in *All for Love.* SELit (26:3) 421–38.

5442. VILIKOVSKÝ, JÁN. John Dryden, jeho teória a prax vnitroliterárného prekladu. (John Dryden, his theory and practice of internal translation.) *In* (pp. 68) **4.**

5443. ZWICKER, STEVEN N. Politics and language in Dryden's poetry: the arts of disguise. (Bibl. 1985, 4720.) Rev. by J. V. Guerinot in SCN (44:1/2); by A. E. Wallace Maurer in SAQ (85:2) 213–14; by Annabel Patterson in MP (83:4) 432–4; by Thomas H. Fujimura in JEGP (85:1) 129–31; by Irène Simon in EngS (67:3) 273–5.

John Eachard

5444. KRAMER, ROBERTA. John Eachard's *The Grounds & Occasions of the Contempt of the Clergy and Religion Enquired into in a Letter Written to R. L.* Unpub. doct. diss., City Univ. of New York. [Abstr. in DA (47) 912A.]

John Eliot

5445. COGLEY, RICHARD W. John Eliot and the origins of the American Indians. EAL (21:3) 1986/87, 210–25.

Sir George Etherege

5446. RIGAUD, NADIA. L'évolution des relations entre maîtres et serviteurs dans le théâtre d'Etherege. *In* (pp. 87–95) **30.**

5447. WESS, ROBERT. Utopian rhetoric in *The Man of Mode.* ECent (27:2) 141–61.

John Evelyn

5448. BOWLE, JOHN (ed.). The diary of John Evelyn. New York: OUP, 1983. (Cf. bibl. 1983, 5197.) Rev. by Jeanne K. Welcher in SCN (44:1/2) 18–19.

5449. ROSTENBERG, LEONA. Restoration bibliography: the diaries of John Evelyn, Samuel Pepys, and Robert Hooke: 1, John Evelyn. ABC (7:7) 21–8.

Mildmay Fane

5450. MORTON, GERALD W. An interesting Benlowes allusion. *See* **5292.**

Sir Richard Fanshawe

5451. CORDNER, MICHAEL. Dryden's *Astraea Redux* and Fanshawe's *Ode. See* **5407.**

5452. DAVIDSON, P. R. K. An edition of the poems of Sir Richard Fanshawe. Unpub. doct. diss., Univ. of Cambridge. [Abstr. in IT (36) 910.]

Owen Felltham

5453. PEBWORTH, TED-LARRY. An Anglican family worship service of the Interregnum: a canceled early text and a new edition of Owen Felltham's *A Form of Prayer.* ELR (16:1) 206–33.

Richard Flecknoe

5454. RUDE, DONALD W. Two echoes of Shakespeare in popular seventeenth-century literature. *See* **4569.**

Giles Fletcher, the Younger

5455. GARDNER, PHILIP ALAN TENNANT. The banquet of the word: Biblical authority and interpretation in Spenser and the Fletchers. *See* **4252.**

John Fletcher

5456. BLAU, HERBERT.   The absolved riddle: sovereign pleasure and the baroque subject in the tragedies of John Fletcher. NLH (17:3) 539–54.

5457. FOWLER, JAMES.   Catiline quoted in *The Chances*. *See* **5305.**

5458. PÁLFFY, ISTVÁN.   Theater und Aussenpolitik im England der Stuarts. Zu *The Tragedy of Sir John van Olden Barnavelt* von John Fletcher und Philip Massinger. SJO (122) 97–109.

5459. TRUSSLER, SIMON (notes).   The two noble kinsmen. *See* **4354.**

Phineas Fletcher

5460. GARDNER, PHILIP ALAN TENNANT.   The banquet of the word: Biblical authority and interpretation in Spenser and the Fletchers. *See* **4252.**

John Ford

5461. BLACKBURN, JOHN MEREDITH.   An old-spelling, critical edition of John Ford's *The Lover's Melancholy*. Unpub. doct. diss., Univ. of Tennessee. [Abstr. in DA (47) 906A.]

5462. GIBSON, COLIN (ed.).   The selected plays of John Ford. Cambridge: CUP. pp. xiv, 470. (Plays by Renaissance and Restoration dramatists.) (*Broken Heart*, *'Tis Pity She's a Whore*, *Perkin Warbeck*.)

5463. HART, DOMINICK J. (ed.).   *The Fancies, Chast and Nobles*: a critical edition. New York; London: Garland, 1985. pp. ix, 300. (Renaissance imagination, 12.)

5464. LEGGATT, ALEXANDER.   A double reign: *Richard II* and *Perkin Warbeck*. *In* (pp. 129–39) **50.**

5465. PADHI, S.   A critical old-spelling edition of *The Spanish Gipsie* by Middleton, Rowley (and possibly Ford). Unpub. doct. diss., Univ. of Oxford, 1985. [Abstr. in IT (35) 44–5.]

5466. SPINRAD, PHOEBE S.   Ceremonies of complement: the symbolic marriage in Ford's *The Broken Heart*. PQ (65:1) 23–37.

Sir Henry Goodyer

5467. KAY, DENNIS.   Poems by Sir Walter Aston, and a date for the Donne/Goodyer verse epistle 'Alternis Vicibus'. *See* **5261.**

Fulke Greville, Lord Brooke

5468. BOOY, D. G.   The morality of learning and the concept of the poet: a study of the debate on the purpose, role and scope of human learning in England in the late sixteenth and early seventeenth centuries, with particular reference to Samuel Daniel and Fulke Greville. *See* **4000.**

5469. GOODMAN, JEFFREY A.   Meaning in context: Fulke Greville's *Sonnet* LXXX. ELR (16:3) 360–72.

5470. GOUWS, JOHN (ed.).   The prose works of Fulke Greville, Lord Brooke. *See* **4209.**

5471. KLEMP, P. J.   Fulke Greville and Sir John Davies: a reference guide. *See* **4066.**

Joseph Hall

5472. ASTBURY, RAYMOND.   An echo of Varro in Joseph Hall's *Virgidemiae*. NQ (33:3) 369–70.

5473. GOTTLIEB, SIDNEY. Sterne's Slawkenbergius and Joseph Hall. CEl (30) 79–80.

George Herbert

5474. BENET, DIANA. Secretary of praise: the poetic vocation of George Herbert. (Bibl. 1985, 4748.) Rev. by Daniel W. Doerksen in RenR (9:4) 1985, 305–8.

5475. BIENZ, JOHN. Images and ceremonial in *The Temple*: Herbert's solution to a Reformation controversy. SELit (26:1) 73–95.

5476. BLAU, RIVKAH TEITZ. Various praise: Psalms in *The Temple, Paradise Lost*, and *Samson Agonistes*. Unpub. doct. diss., Columbia Univ., 1983. [Abstr. in DA (46) 2297A.]

5477. BLOCK, CHANA. Spelling the word: George Herbert and the Bible. (Bibl. 1985, 4751.) Rev. by Mary Ellen Rickey in RQ (39:2) 351–3; by Noel J. Kinnamon in ChrisL (35:2) 47–9; by Coburn Freer in GHJ (9:1) 1985, 33–6; by John Drury in TLS, 28 Feb., 228.

5478. BONNELL, WILLIAM. The eucharistic substance of George Herbert's *Prayer (1)*. GHJ (9:2) 35–47.

5479. DAALDER, JOOST. Herbert's 'poetic theory'. *See* **5253.**

5480. DINSHAW, F. E. The intellectual background to George Herbert's *The Temple*. Unpub. doct. diss., Univ. of Oxford, 1983.

5481. FLESCH, WILLIAM BENJAMIN. The disconsolate: the poetry of irreparable loss. Unpub. doct. diss., Cornell Univ. [Abstr. in DA (47) 535A.]

5482. GOTTLIEB, SIDNEY. Eliot's *The Death of Saint Narcissus* and Herbert's *Affliction (1)*. GHJ (9:2) 55–8.

5483. HAMMOND, GERALD. 'Poor dust should lie still low': George Herbert and Henry Vaughan. Eng (35) 1–22.

5484. HOVEY, KENNETH ALAN. Holy war and civil peace: George Herbert's Jacobean politics. ExRC (11) 1985, 112–19.

5485. JUDGE, JEANNIE SARGENT. 'The Sonne of Man': George Herbert and the Incarnation. Unpub. doct. diss., Boston Univ. [Abstr. in DA (46) 3726A.]

5486. LEE, KEUN-SUP. *The Temple* eui gujo e gwanhan yeongu. (On the structure of *The Temple*.) JELL (32:4) 569–602.

5487. LULL, JANIS. George Herbert's revisions in *The Church* and the carnality of *Love (III)*. GHJ (9:1) 1985, 1–16.

5488. MALPEZZI, FRANCES M. Herbert's *The Thanksgiving* in context. Ren (34:3) 1982, 185–95.

5489. MARTZ, LOUIS (ed.). George Herbert and Henry Vaughan. Oxford: OUP. pp. xxxi, 569. (Oxford authors.)

5490. MARX, MICHAEL STEVEN. 'The church with psalms must shout': the influence of the Psalms on George Herbert's *The Church*. Unpub. doct. diss., Univ. of Michigan, 1985. [Abstr. in DA (46) 3361A.]

5491. MUSTAZZA, LEONARD. Herbert's *The Forerunners*. Exp (44:3) 21–3.

5492. NARDO, ANNA K. George Herbert pulling for Prime. SCR (3:4) 28–42.

5493. NEEDS, L. D. Proving one God, one harmonic: the persona of

George Herbert's *The Temple* and its poetic legacy. Unpub. doct. diss., Univ. of York, 1984.

5494. RAY, ROBERT H. The Herbert allusion book: allusions to George Herbert in the seventeenth century. SP (83:4) iii–ix, 1–182.

5495. —— Herbert's seventeenth-century reputation: a summary and new considerations. GHJ (9:2) 1–15.

5496. RENAUX, SIGRID. George Herbert's *The Windows* illuminated: a critical approach. GHJ (9:1) 1985, 26–32.

5497. ROSTON, MURRAY. Herbert and mannerism. JDJ (5:1/2) 133–67.

5498. SCHOENFELDT, MICHAEL CARL. 'The distance of the meek': George Herbert and his God. Unpub. doct. diss., Univ. of California, Berkeley, 1985. [Abstr. in DA (46) 2701A.]

5499. SHAWCROSS, JOHN T. Two Herbert allusions. GHJ (9:2) 57–8.

5500. SPENCE, MARTIN. Herbert's *Employment II*. Exp (44:3) 18–21.

5501. STEVENS, RALPH STODDARD, III. Grief and praise: George Herbert's rhetoric of devotion. Unpub. doct. diss., Univ. of Washington. [Abstr. in DA (47) 1339A.]

5502. STRIER, RICHARD. Love known: theology and experience in George Herbert's poetry. (Bibl. 1985, 4770.) Rev. by Daniel W. Doerksen in RenR (9:4) 1985, 305–8.

5503. THORPE, DOUGLAS. 'Delight into sacrifice:' resting in Herbert's *Temple*. SELit (26:1) 59–72.

5504. VEITH, GENE EDWARD, JR. Reformation spirituality: the religion of George Herbert. Lewisburg, PA: Bucknell UP; London: Assoc. UPs, 1985. pp. 289. Rev. by John H. Ottenhoff in GHJ (9:1) 1985, 37–41; by John Drury in TLS, 28 Feb., 228.

5505. WADDINGTON, RAYMOND B. The title image of Herbert's *The Pulley*. GHJ (9:2) 49–53.

5506. WATSON, THOMAS RAMEY. God's geometry: motion in the English poetry of George Herbert. GHJ (9:1) 1985, 17–25.

5507. WESTERWEEL, BART. Patterns and patterning: a study of four poems by George Herbert. (Bibl. 1985, 4772.) Rev. by Sidney Gottlieb in RQ (39:4) 816–18; by Fram Dinshaw in NQ (33:2) 232–3.

5508. WHITLOCK, BAIRD W. The sacramental poetry of George Herbert. SCR (3:1) 37–49.

5509. WILCOX, H. E. 'Something understood': the reputation and influence of George Herbert to 1715. Unpub. doct. diss., Univ. of Oxford, 1984.

Robert Herrick

5510. COIRO, ANN BAYNES. 'Let poets feed on aire': Herrick's mocking epigrams. RenP 83–95.

5511. —— Robert Herrick's *Hesperides* and the epigram book tradition. Unpub. doct. diss., Univ. of Maryland, 1985. [Abstr. in DA (47) 1331A.]

5512. STALLYBRASS, PETER. 'Wee feaste in our defense': patrician carnival in early modern England and Robert Herrick's *Hesperides*. ELR (16:1) 234–52.

Thomas Heywood

5513. BAINES, BARBARA J.   Thomas Heywood. Boston, MA: G. K. Hall, 1984. pp. 178. (Twayne's English authors, 388.) Rev. by Don J. McDermott in SCN (44:1/2) 17–18.

5514. BERGERON, DAVID M. (ed.).   Thomas Heywood's pageants: a critical edition. New York; London: Garland. pp. vii, 147. (Renaissance imagination, 16.)

5515. BROMLEY, LAURA G.   Domestic conduct in *A Woman Killed with Kindness*. SELit (26:2) 259–76.

5516. HENDERSON, DIANA E.   Many mansions: reconstructing *A Woman Killed with Kindness*. SELit (26:2) 277–94.

5517. JANZEN, HENRY D.   Preparing a diplomatic edition: Heywood's *The Escapes of Jupiter*. In (pp. 73–9) **44.**

5518. SCOBIE, BRIAN W. M. (ed.).   A woman killed with kindness. (Bibl. 1985, 4785.) Rev. by David Atkinson in CEl (30) 117–23.

Thomas Hobbes

5519. CANTALUPO, CHARLES.   How to be a literary reader of Hobbes's most famous chapter. Prose Studies (9:2) 67–79.

5520. DALSGÅRD-HANSEN, POVL.   Hobbes' system med særlig henblik på nominalismen. (Hobbes' system with special reference to nominalism.) Philosophia (Univ. of Aarhus) (13) 161–78.

5521. HANSEN, KLAUS.   Thomas Hobbes' menneskesyn: mennesket som genstand og ophav: sprog, fornuft, tro. (Thomas Hobbes' view of man: man as object and source: language, reason, faith.) Philosophia (Univ. of Aarhus) (13) 136–60.

5522. HARTLE, P. N.   Defoe and *The Wonders of the Peake*: the place of Cotton's poem in *A Tour thro' the Whole Island of Great Britain*. See **5337.**

5523. JONES, HAROLD WHITMORE.   Thomas Hobbes vs Thomas White. Chester: Jones. pp. 84.

5524. LESSAY, FRANCK.   L'état de nature selon Hobbes: point de départ ou point de dépassement de l'histoire. In (pp. 3–14) **34.**

5525. —— Naissance de la république hobbienne: les lieux de l'artifice. CEl (30) 49–58.

5526. MATHIE, WILLIAM.   Reason and rhetoric in Hobbes's *Leviathan*. IJPP (14:2/3) 281–98.

5527. SCHOFIELD, CHARLES MALCOLM.   Argument and unity in the political and moral teachings of Thomas Hobbes's *Leviathan*. Unpub. doct. diss., Univ. of Missouri–Columbia, 1985. [Abstr. in DA (47) 551A.]

5528. STOFFELL, BRIAN FREDERICK.   Commonwealth and civility: a study of Thomas Hobbes. Unpub. doct. diss., Univ. of British Columbia, 1985. [Abstr. in DA (47) 1357A.]

5529. TRICAUD, FRANÇOIS.   Remarques sur le poids du passé et le pouvoir d'innover selon Hobbes et selon Hume. In (pp. 15–21) **34.**

5530. WILSON, JOHN J.   Reason and obligation in *Leviathan*. IJPP (8:1) 1979, 30–57.

Nicholas Hookes

5531. RAY, ROBERT H.   Unrecorded seventeenth-century allusions to Donne. *See* **5186.**

James I and VI, King of England and Scotland

5532. AKRIGG, G. P. V. (ed.).   Letters of King James VI & I. (Bibl. 1985, 4796.) Rev. by Allan Pritchard in ESCan (12:1) 105–8.

5533. CRAIGIE, JAMES; LAW, ALEXANDER (eds).   Minor prose works of King James I and VI. (Bibl. 1985, 4797.) Rev. by Matthew P. McDiarmid in SLJ (supp. 25) 3–5.

5534. YAMADA, AKIHIRO.   The printing of King James I's *The True Lawe of Free Monarchies* with special reference to the 1603 editions. *See* **135.**

Robert Johnson

5535. RUDE, DONALD W.   Two unreported references to Sir Thomas More. *See* **4157.**

Ben Jonson

5536. AYRES, PHILIP J.   The nature of Jonson's Roman history. ELR (16:1) 166–81.

5537. BARTON, ANNE.   Ben Jonson, dramatist. New York; Melbourne: CUP, 1984. (Cf. bibl. 1985, 4801.) Rev. by George Parfitt in NQ (33:2) 229–30; by Alastair Fowler in Review (8) 93–9; by C. G. Thayer in ELN (23:4) 68–9.

5538. BONNEAU, DANIELLE.   Maîtres et serviteurs dans les comédies de Ben Jonson. *In* (pp. 65–85) **30.**

5539. BRADY, JENNIFER.   Jonson's elegies of the plague years. DalR (65:2) 1985, 208–30.

5540. BROCK, D. HEYWARD.   A Ben Jonson companion. (Bibl. 1984, 4848, where scholar's forename misspelt.) Rev. by Lois Potter in ShS (37) 1984, 189.

5541. CLARK, MICHAEL EUGENE.   George Chapman and Ben Jonson: a conflict in theory. *See* **5327.**

5542. CLAYTON, M. G.   'Tempests, and such like drolleries': Jonson, Shakespeare and the figure of Vergil. *See* **4981.**

5543. DER, DON W.   Jonson's *On My First Sonne*. Exp (44:2) 16–18.

5544. DONALDSON, IAN.   Fathers and sons: Jonson, Dryden and *MacFlecknoe*. *See* **5409.**

5545. —— Jonson's magic houses. EAS (39) 39–61.

5546. —— (ed.).   Ben Jonson. Oxford: OUP, 1985. pp. xx, 787. (Oxford authors.) Rev. by A. J. Smith in TLS, 11 July, 765.

5547. DUTTON, RICHARD.   Ben Jonson: to the first folio. (Bibl. 1985, 4810.) Rev. by Sara van den Berg in RQ (39:2) 346–9.

5548. —— (ed.).   *Epigrams* and *The Forest*. (Bibl. 1985, 4811.) Rev. by Peter Hyland in NQ (33:3) 413–14.

5549. EVANS, ROBERT C.   Jonson's *Epitaph on the Countess of Shrewsbury*. Exp (44:3) 15–17.

5550. —— Strategic debris: Jonson's satires on Inigo Jones in the context of Renaissance patronage. RenP 69–81.

5551. FALLON, J. L.   Jonson's Ananias. Exp (44:2) 15–16.

5552. FOAKES, R. A. The descent of Iago: satire, Ben Jonson, and Shakespeare's *Othello*. *In* (pp. 16–30) **50.**

5553. FOWLER, ALASTAIR. Ben Jonson, realist. Review (8) 93–9 (review-article).

5554. FOWLER, JAMES. Catiline quoted in *The Chances*. *See* **5305.**

5555. GREENE, THOMAS M. The vulnerable text: essays on Renaissance literature. *See* **4852.**

5556. HEES, EDWIN. Unity of vision in Ben Jonson's tragedies and masques. Theoria (67) 21–32.

5557. HYLAND, PETER. 'The wild Anarchie of Drinke': Ben Jonson and alcohol. Mosaic (19:3) 25–33.

5558. JAGENDORF, ZVI. The happy end of comedy: Jonson, Molière and Shakespeare. *See* **4492.**

5559. JENSEN, EJNER J. Ben Jonson's comedies on the modern stage. Ann Arbor, MI: UMI Research Press; Epping: Bowker, 1985. pp. viii, 158. (Theater and dramatic studies, 27.)

5560. JOHNSON, ANTHONY. 'Angles', 'squares', or 'roundes': Ben Jonson and the Palladian aesthetic. *See* **5254.**

5561. —— Ben Jonson: an ungathered allusion. NQ (33:3) 384–5.

5562. JUDKINS, DAVID C. The nondramatic works of Ben Jonson: a reference guide. Boston, MA: G. K. Hall, 1982. pp. xx, 260. Rev. by Alexander Leggatt in YES (16) 245–7.

5563. JUNEJA, RENU. Audience manipulation in Jonson's comedies. BSUF (25:2) 1984, 29–41.

5564. LANIER, DOUGLAS M. Brainchildren: self-representation and patriarchy in Ben Jonson's early works. RenP 53–68.

5565. LAWRY, J. S. *Catiline* and 'the sight of Rome in us'. *In* (pp. 395–407) **49.**

5566. LEE, JONGSOOK. Ben Jonson's poesis: a literary dialectic of ideal and history. Unpub. doct. diss., Univ. of Minnesota, 1985. [Abstr. in DA (46) 3041A.]

5567. —— Who is Cecilia, what was she? Cecilia Bulstrode and Jonson's epideictics. JEGP (85:1) 20–34.

5568. LEGGATT, ALEXANDER. Ben Jonson: his vision and his art. (Bibl. 1984, 4865.) Rev. by Ian Donaldson in YES (16) 244–5.

5569. LEHRMAN, WALTER D.; SARAFINSKI, DOLORES J.; SAVAGE, ELIZABETH. The plays of Ben Jonson, a reference guide. (Bibl, 1983, 5294.) Rev. by Ian Donaldson in YES (16) 244–5.

5570. LINDLEY, DAVID. Embarrassing Ben: the masques for Frances Howard. ELR (16:3) 343–59.

5571. LOEWENSTEIN, JOSEPH. The Jonsonian corpulence; or, the poet as mouthpiece. ELH (53:3) 491–518.

5572. —— Responsive readings: versions of Echo in pastoral, epic, and the Jonsonian masque. (Bibl. 1985, 4825.) Rev. by Michael G. Brennan in NQ (33:2) 230–1.

5573. LUKACS, BARBARA ANN. Ben Jonson: a study of the four late plays. Unpub. doct. diss., Drew Univ. [Abstr. in DA (47) 1735A.] (*The Devil is an Ass, The Staple of News, The New Inn, The Magnetic Lady*.)

5574. Maus, Katharine Eisaman.   Ben Jonson and the Roman frame of mind. (Bibl. 1985, 4829.) Rev. by David McPherson in PQ (65:2) 281–4; by Robert S. Miola in AJP (107:3) 446–8.

5575. Miles, Rosalind.   Ben Jonson: his life and work. London: Routledge & Kegan Paul. pp. xi, 320.

5576. Murray, Timothy.   From foul sheets to legitimate model: antitheater, text, Ben Jonson. NLH (14:3) 1983, 641–4.

5577. Parker, Patricia.   Deferral, dilation, différance: Shakespeare, Cervantes, Jonson. In (pp. 182–209) **27.**

5578. Patterson, Annabel.   'Roman-cast similitude': Ben Jonson and the English use of Roman history. In (pp. 381–94) **49.**

5579. Peacock, Alan J.   Ben Jonson, Celia, and Ovid. NQ (33:3) 381–4.

5580. ——— Ben Jonson: superannuated lover. EA (39:3) 308–16.

5581. Pechter, Edward.   *Julius Caesar* and *Sejanus*: Roman politics, inner selves and the powers of the theatre. In (pp. 60–78) **50.**

5582. Peterson, Richard S.   Icon and mystery in Jonson's *Masque of Beutie.* JDJ (5:1/2) 169–99.

5583. Pironon, Jean.   Le thème de *La foire* de Ben Jonson à Defoe: changements de mentalité et typologie jungienne. In (pp. 433–44) **1.**

5584. Riddell, James A.   Variant title-pages of the 1616 Jonson folio. *See* **127.**

5585. Ross, Cheryl Lynn.   The plague and the figures of power: authority and subversion in English Renaissance drama. *See* **4890.**

5586. Rydlewska, Julita.   *Epicoene* and the craft of comedy. SAP (18) 223–30.

5587. Sellin, Paul R.   The politics of Ben Jonson's *Newes from the New World Discover'd in the Moone.* Viator (17) 321–37.

5588. Sweeney, John Gordon, iii.   Jonson and the psychology of public theater: 'To coin the spirit, spend the soul'. (Bibl. 1985, 4836.) Rev. by Katharine Eisaman Maus in WHR (40:3) 272–5; by David McPherson in PQ (65:2) 281–4.

5589. Trussler, Simon (ed.).   Bartholomew Fair. London: Methuen. pp. xli, 154. (Methuen student eds.)

5590. ——— (notes).   *Every Man in his Humour*: a programme/text with commentary. London: Methuen; Royal Shakespeare Company. pp. 76. (Swan theatre plays.)

5591. Wayne, Don E.   Penshurst: the semiotics of place and the poetics of history. (Bibl. 1985, 4837.) Rev. by Stuart M. Kurland in MP (84:2) 219–22.

5592. Womack, Peter.   Ben Jonson. Oxford: Blackwell. pp. 192. (Rereading literature.)

John Josselyn

5593. Lindholdt, Paul Jeffrey.   A critical edition of John Josselyn's 1674 *Account of Two Voyages to New-England.* Unpub. doct. diss., Pennsylvania State Univ., 1985. [Abstr. in DA (46) 2693A.]

Thomas Killigrew
5594. DeRitter, Jones. The Gypsy, *The Rover*, and the Wanderer: Aphra Behn's revision of Thomas Killigrew. *See* **5286.**

5595. Lough, J.; Crane, D. E. L. Thomas Killigrew and the possessed nuns of Loudon: the text of a letter of 1635. DUJ (78:2) 259–68.

Sir William Killigrew
5596. Vander Motten, J. P. Another annotated copy of Sir William Killigrew's *Four New Playes* (1666). *See* **342.**

5597. —— An unnoticed Restoration epilogue. EngS (67:4) 308–10.

Sir William Kingsmill
5598. Eames, John. Sir William Kingsmill (1613–1661) and his poetry. EngS (67:2) 126–55.

Emilia Lanier
5599. Lewalski, Barbara K. Of God and good women: the poems of Aemilia Lanyer. *In* (pp. 203–24) **52.**

Nathaniel Lee
5600. Brown, Richard E. Nathaniel Lee's political dramas, 1679–1683. Restoration (10:1) 41–52.

5601. Monti-Pouagare, Stalo. The achievement of suspense in a group of Oedipus plays. *See* **5424.**

John Locke
5602. Ashcraft, Richard. Revolutionary politics and Locke's *Two Treatises of Government*. Princeton, NJ; Guildford: Princeton UP. pp. xxii, 613.

5603. Attig, John C. (comp.). The works of John Locke: a comprehensive bibliography from the seventeenth century to the present. Westport, CT: Greenwood Press, 1985. pp. xx, 185. (Bibliographies and indexes in philosophy, 1.) Rev. by Jean S. Yolton in Library (8:4) 381–2.

5604. Brantley, Richard E. Locke, Wesley, and the method of English Romanticism. (Bibl. 1985, 4841.) Rev. by Howard H. Hinkel in ChrisL (35:4) 37–9; by Richard Fadem in PhilL (10:1) 120–1.

5605. Braverman, Richard. Locke, Defoe, and the politics of childhood. ELN (24:1) 36–48.

5606. Clark, S. H. Blake's *Milton* and the response to Locke in the poetry of sensibility. Unpub. doct. diss., Univ. of Cambridge. [Abstr. in IT (35) 1085.]

5607. Colman, John. John Locke's moral philosophy. (Bibl. 1983, 5323.) Rev. by Carole Stewart in JHP (24:1) 127–9.

5608. Dunn, John. Locke. New York: OUP, 1984. (Bibl. 1985, 4843.) Rev. by James Egan in SCN (44:1/2) 20–1.

5609. Ferreira, M. Jamie. Locke's 'constructive skepticism' – a reappraisal. JHP (24:2) 211–22.

5610. Hansen, Erik A. John Locke and the semantic tradition. *See* **2198.**

5611. Jolley, Nicholas. Leibniz and Locke: a study of the *New*

Essays on Human Understanding. New York: OUP, 1984. (Cf. bibl. 1984, 4900.) Rev. by G. A. J. Rogers in JHP (24:4) 556–8.

5612. McLaverty, James. From definition to explanation: Locke's influence on Johnson's dictionary. JHI (47:3) 377–94.

5613. Tarcov, Nathan. Locke's education for liberty. Chicago: Chicago UP, 1984. pp. viii, 272. Rev. by Mark Goldie in JMH (58:1) 300–1.

5614. Woodhouse, R. S. Locke. Minneapolis: Minnesota UP, 1983. pp. 198.

5615. Yolton, John W. Locke: an introduction. Oxford: Blackwell, 1985. pp. xii, 162. Rev. by R. W. Dyson in BJECS (9:2) 246–7.

John Marston

5616. Chauchaix, J. Histoire et mythe dans la *Sophonisbe* de J. Marston. *In* (pp. 127–45) **37.**

5617. Horne, R. C. Voices of alienation: the moral significance of Marston's satiric strategy. MLR (81:1) 18–33.

5618. Jackson, MacDonald P.; Neill, Michael (eds). The selected plays of John Marston. Cambridge: CUP. pp. xvi, 266. (Plays by Renaissance and Restoration dramatists.) (*Antonio and Mellida, Antonio's Revenge, The Malcontent, The Dutch Courtesan, Sophonisba.*)

5619. Ono, Yoshiko. Marston no tragical satire: *Antonio's Revenge* ni okeru 'revenger' kosatu. (Tragical satire in Marston: a reflection on the 'revenger' in *Antonio's Revenge*.) SEL (63:2) 315–30.

Andrew Marvell

5620. Alpers, Paul. Convening and convention in pastoral poetry. NLH (14:2) 1983, 277–304.

5621. Burke, Richard C. Marvell's nymph and man's uses of nature. ExRC (10) 1984, 80–91.

5622. Chernaik, Warren L. The poet's time: politics and religion in the work of Andrew Marvell. (Bibl. 1985, 4896.) Rev. by Peter L. Rudnytsky in RQ (39:3) 572–4; by Elizabeth Jackson in UES (24:1) 33–4.

5623. Chibnall, Jennifer. Something to the purpose: Marvell's rhetorical strategy in *The Rehearsal Transpros'd* (1672). Prose Studies (9:2) 80–104.

5624. Crane, David. Marvell and Milton on Cromwell. NQ (33:4) 464.

5625. Cummings, Robert. The 'moe of dust' in Marvell's *Upon Appleton House*. ELN (24:1) 25–7.

5626. Davidson, Peter. An early echo of poems by Marvell. NQ (33:1) 41.

5627. Jose, Nicholas. Hamlet, Marvell and the times. *See* **4756.**

5628. Kerrigan, William. Marvell and nymphets. Greyfriar (27) 3–21.

5629. Klause, John. The unfortunate fall: theodicy and the moral imagination of Andrew Marvell. (Bibl. 1985, 4861.) Rev. by Nigel Smith in NQ (33:4) 550.

5630. LARSON, CHARLES. Marvell's Richard Cromwell: 'he, vertue dead, Revives'. Mosaic (19:2) 57–67.

5631. LORD, GEORGE deF. (ed.). Andrew Marvell: complete poetry. London: Dent, 1984. pp. xl, 275. (Everyman Library.) Rev. by E. E. Duncan-Jones in NQ (33:2) 234.

5632. MAULE, JEREMY. Marvell's Hastings elegy – a supplementary note. RES (37:147) 395–9.

5633. MULDROW, GEORGE M. The forty lines of Andrew Marvell's *On a Drop of Dew*. ELN (23:3) 23–7.

5634. NUTTALL, A. D. Ovid immoralised: the method of wit in Marvell's *The Garden. In* (pp. 79–89) **18.**

5635. PITTOCK, MURRAY. Falcon and falconer: *The Second Coming* and Marvell's *Horatian Ode*. IUR (16) 175–9.

5636. PITTOCK, MURRAY G. H. Samuel Richardson: a note from Marvell. NQ (33:4) 513.

5637. READINGS, W. J. The Restoration and the fall of language: the search for meaning in the poetry of Marvell and Milton. Unpub. doct. diss., Univ. of Oxford, 1985. [Abstr. in IT (35) 45.]

5638. STOCKER, MARGARITA. Apocalyptic Marvell: the Second Coming in seventeenth-century poetry. Brighton: Harvester Press. pp. xv, 381. Rev. by Warren Chernaik in THES (733) 20.

5639. —— Thematic indication in the translation of Marvell's Latin poetry: *Ingelo*. NQ (33:1) 31–2.

5640. SZILAGYI, STEPHEN. Credible praise: Marvell's dilemma in his elegy on Oliver Cromwell. MLS (16:3) 109–21.

5641. WILCHER, ROBERT. Andrew Marvell. (Bibl. 1985, 4869.) Rev. by Alan Rudrum in TLS, 28 Feb., 228.

5642. —— (ed.). Andrew Marvell: selected poetry and prose. London: Methuen. pp. ix, 292. (Methuen English texts.)

5643. YOUNG, R. V. Andrew Marvell and the devotional tradition. Ren (38:4) 204–27.

Philip Massinger

5644. GARRETT, M. Philip Massinger's attitude to spectacle. Unpub. doct. diss., Univ. of Oxford, 1983.

5645. LAWLESS, DONALD S. On the date of Massinger's *The Maid of Honour*. NQ (33:3) 391–2.

5646. PÁLFFY, ISTVÁN. Theater und Aussenpolitik im England der Stuarts. Zu *The Tragedy of Sir John van Olden Barnavelt* von John Fletcher und Philip Massinger. *See* **5458.**

Cotton Mather

5647. BREITWIESER, MITCHELL ROBERT. Benjamin Franklin: the price of representative personality. Cambridge: CUP, 1985. pp. x, 309. Rev. by J. A. Leo Lemay in AL (58:1) 127–9.

5648. JESKE, JEFFREY. Cotton Mather: physico-theologian. JHI (47:4) 583–94.

5649. WHITE, EUGENE E. Cotton Mather's *A Companion for Communicants* and rhetorical genre. SSJ (51:4) 326–43.

Thomas Middleton

5650. BROMHAM, A. A.   The tragedy of peace: political meaning in *Women Beware Women*. SELit (26:2) 309–29.

5651. BROMHAM, TONY.   *The Changeling* by Thomas Middleton and William Rowley. Basingstoke: Macmillan. pp. ix, 85. (Macmillan master guides.)

5652. GUNDY, D. C.   Tourneur's *The Revenger's Tragedy* II.ii.216–18. Exp (44:3) 11–12.

5653. HOLDSWORTH, R. V.   Middleton and Shakespeare: the case for Middleton's hand in *Timon of Athens*. *See* **5005.**

5654. —— Middleton and *The Tragedy of Mariam*. *See* **5323.**

5655. JACKSON, MACD. P. (introd.).   *The Revenger's Tragedy*: a facsimile of the 1607/8 quarto, attributed to Thomas Middleton. Rutherford, NJ: Fairleigh Dickinson UPs; London: Assoc. UP, 1984. pp. 114. Rev. by T. W. Craik in NQ (33:1) 109–10.

5656. KAPLAN, JOEL H.   Thomas Middleton's epitaph on the death of Richard Burbage, and John Payne Collier. PBSA (80:2) 225–32.

5657. KISTNER, A. L.; KISTNER, M. K.   Heirs and identity: the bases of social order in *Michaelmas Term*. MLS (16:4) 61–71.

5658. KOWSAR, MOHAMMAD.   Middleton and Rowley's *The Changeling*: the besieged temple. Criticism (28:2) 145–64.

5659. LEVINE, ROBERT T.   Middleton's *The Widow*. Exp. (44:2) 18–20.

5660. LIMON, JERZY.   The 'missing source' for Middleton's *A Game at Chess* (v. iii. 141–7) found. NQ (33:3) 386–7.

5661. MEHL, DIETER.   Corruption, retribution and justice in *Measure for Measure* and *The Revenger's Tragedy*. In (pp. 114–28) **50.**

5662. MULHOLLAND, PAUL.   Thomas Middleton's *The Two Gates of Salvation* (1609): an instance of running-title rotation. *See* **121.**

5663. PADHI, S.   A critical old-spelling edition of *The Spanish Gipsie* by Middleton, Rowley (and possibly Ford). *See* **5465.**

5664. ROBERTS, MARILYN.   The structural technique of Thomas Middleton. Unpub. doct. diss., Columbia Univ., 1984. [Abstr. in DA (47) 915A.]

5665. ROSS, CHERYL LYNN.   The plague and the figures of power: authority and subversion in English Renaissance drama. *See* **4890.**

5666. SCHRICKX, WILLEM.   *The Revenger's Tragedy* and its contemporary Dutch adaptation by Theodore Rodenburg. *In* (pp. 104–9) **18.**

5667. THOMSON, LESLIE.   'Enter above': the staging of *Women Beware Women*. SELit (26:2) 331–43.

5668. WAAGE, FREDERICK O.   Meg and Mall: two Renaissance London heroines. *See* **3993.**

5669. YACHNIN, PAUL.   The significance of two allusions in Middleton's *Phoenix*. NQ (33:3) 375–7.

John Milton

5670. ANDERSON, DOUGLAS.   Unfallen marriage and the fallen imagination in *Paradise Lost*. SELit (26:1) 125–44.

5671. ANON.   Milton bookplate. *See* **191.**

5672. —— (ed.).   Milton shi to shiso: Ochi Fumio hakushi kijyu kinen ronbunshu. (The poetry and ideas of Milton: essays presented to Dr Fumio Ochi on his seventy-seventh birthday.) Tokyo: Yamaguchi Press. pp. viii, 430.

5673. BATE, JONATHAN.   *Kubla Khan* and *At A Solemn Music*. ELN (24:1) 71–3.

5674. BAUMAN, MICHAEL E.   Heresy in paradise and the ghosts of readers past. CLAJ (30:1) 59–68.

5675. BECKWITH, MARC.   *Comus* and the *Zodiacus Vitae*. MQ (20:4) 145–7.

5676. BERKELEY, DAVID S.; KHODDAM, SALWA.   Rejoinder to N. Flinker's *Biblical Samson: More about the Hero* (MQ (19:1) 1985, 10–20). MQ (20:2) 54.

5677. BIDNEY, MARTIN.   *Christabel* as dark double of *Comus*. SP (83:2) 182–200.

5678. BLAKEMORE, STEVEN.   Language and logos in *Paradise Lost*. SoHR (20:4) 325–40.

5679. —— Pandemonium and Babel: architectural hierarchy in *Paradise Lost*. MQ (20:4) 142–5.

5680. BLAU, RIVKAH TEITZ.   Various praise: Psalms in *The Temple*, *Paradise Lost*, and *Samson Agonistes*. See **5476.**

5681. BLESSINGTON, FRANCIS C.   The portrait in the spoon: George Eliot's Casaubon and John Milton. MQ (20:1) 29–31.

5682. BLONDEL, JACQUES.   Milton et l'actualité: les *Milton Studies* (1981–1984). EA (39:3) 294–301 (review-article).

5683. BOND, W. H.   Thomas Hollis and Baron's Milton: a strange device. See **93.**

5684. BROWN, CEDRIC C.   John Milton's aristocratic entertainments. pp. xii, 210. (Cf. bibl. 1985, 4905, where pagination incorrect.) Rev. by David A. Lowenstein in SCN (44:3) 33–4; by Lucy Newlyn in TLS, 8 Aug., 871; by R. D. Bedford in THES (704) 20.

5685. —— Milton's 'Arcades' in the Trinity Manuscript. RES (37:148) 542–9.

5686. BROWN, MARY RUTH.   *Paradise Lost* and John 15: Eve, the branch and the church. MQ (20:4) 127–31.

5687. BUDICK, SANFORD.   The dividing Muse: images of sacred disjunction in Milton's poetry. (Bibl. 1985, 4907.) Rev. by Archie Burnett in NQ (33:4) 547–8; by Mary Ann Radzinowicz in JEGP (85:2) 267–9; by Eugenie R. Freed in UES (24:1) 36–7.

5688. BURNETT, ARCHIE.   Milton's style: the shorter poems, *Paradise Regained*, and *Samson Agonistes*. (Bibl. 1985, 4908.) Rev. by Mary Ann Radzinowicz in MLR (81:1) 171–2.

5689. CANAVAN, FRANCIS.   John Milton and freedom of expression. IJPP (7:3) 1978, 50–65.

5690. CHEUNG, KING KOK.   The woe and wonder of despair: a study of Doctor Faustus, Macbeth, and Satan. See **4115.**

5691. CHOE, OK-YOUNG.   *Paradise Lost* e geuryeojin Milton eui Satan yeongu. (A study of Milton's Satan in *Paradise Lost*.) JELL (32:2) 219–35.

5692. CHRISTOPHER, GEORGIA B.   Milton and the science of the saints. Guildford: Princeton UP, 1982. (Cf. bibl. 1985, 4912.) Rev. by Archie Burnett in YES (16) 253–4.

5693. COOMBS, JAMES H.   Wordsworth and Milton: prophet–poets. Unpub. doct. diss., Brown Univ., 1985. [Abstr. in DA (46) 1946A.]

5694. CRANE, DAVID.   Marvell and Milton on Cromwell. *See* **5624.**

5695. DAHIYAT, EID A.   Milton and Franklin. EAL (21:1) 44–8.

5696. DANIEL, CLAY.   Astraea, the golden scales, and the scorpion: Milton's heavenly reflection of the scene in Eden. MQ (20:3) 92–8.

5697. DANIELSON, DENNIS RICHARD.   Milton's good God: a study in literary theodicy. (Bibl. 1985, 4916.) Rev. by Roger Lejosne in MLR (81:3) 717–18.

5698. DAVIES, DAVID; DOWLING, PAUL.   'Shrewd books, with dangerous Frontispices': *Areopagitica*'s motto. MQ (20:2) 33–7.

5699. DAVIES, S.   Images of kingship in John Milton's *Paradise Lost*. Unpub. doct. diss., Univ. of Manchester, 1978. [Abstr. in IT (35) 543.]

5700. DAVIES, STEVIE.   The idea of woman in Renaissance literature: the feminine reclaimed. *See* **4246.**

5701. DAVIS, PATRICIA ELIZABETH.   Covenant and the 'Crowne of Life': a figural tapestry in *Paradise Lost*. MStud (22) 141–50.

5702. DAVIS, ROBERT LEIGH.   That two-handed engine and the consolation of *Lycidas*. MQ (20:2) 44–8.

5703. DuROCHER, RICHARD J.   Milton and Ovid. Ithaca, NY; London: Cornell UP, 1985. (Cf. bibl. 1983, 5408.) Rev. by Jonathan Bate in THES (693) 16; by Lucy Newlyn in TLS, 8 Aug., 871.

5704. DZELZAINIS, M. M.   The ideological context of John Milton's *History of Britain*. Unpub. doct. diss., Univ. of Cambridge, 1984.

5705. EDMUNDSON, MARK WRIGHT.   Towards reading Freud: moments of self-representation in Milton, Wordsworth, Keats, Emerson, Whitman and Sigmund Freud. Unpub. doct. diss., Yale Univ., 1985. [Abstr. in DA (46) 3357A.]

5706. ELLRODT, ROBERT.   Milton et la vision édénique. *In* (pp. 47–62) **2.**

5707. ENTZMINGER, ROBERT L.   Divine word: Milton and the redemption of language. Pittsburgh, PA: Duquesne UP, 1985. pp. 188. Rev. by Jacqueline T. Miller in RQ (39:3) 567–9.

5708. FALLON, ROBERT THOMAS.   Captain or colonel: the soldier in Milton's life and art. Columbia: Missouri UP, 1984. pp. x, 272. Rev. by Hugh M. Richmond in JEGP (85:4) 565–7; by Jacki DiSalvo in ANQ (24:5/6) 91–2.

5709. FALLON, STEPHEN MICHAEL.   'Degrees of substance': Milton's spirit world and seventeenth-century philosophy. Unpub. doct. diss., Univ. of Virginia, 1985. [Abstr. in DA (47) 535A.]

5710. FAULDS, JOSEPH MERKLE.   The Son and Satan in *Paradise Lost*: an inquiry into the poetic theodicy of John Milton in the Western tradition. Unpub. doct. diss., Univ. of Dallas. [Abstr. in DA (47) 909A.]

5711. FLEMING, RAY. 'Sublime and pure thoughts, without transgression': the Dantean influence in Milton's *Donna leggiadra*. MQ (20:2) 38–44.

5712. FLESCH, WILLIAM BENJAMIN. The disconsolate: the poetry of irreparable loss. *See* **5481.**

5713. FREEMAN, JAMES A.; LOW, ANTHONY (eds). Urbane Milton: the Latin poetry. (Bibl. 1985, 4933.) Rev. by Archie Burnett in NQ (33:3) 416.

5714. FULLER, ELIZABETH ELY. Milton's kinesthetic vision in *Paradise Lost*. (Bibl. 1985, 4934.) Rev. by Diana Benet in MQ (20:3) 110–11.

5715. GAGEN, JEAN. Did Milton nod? MQ (20:1) 17–22.

5716. GAST, MARLENE. Wordsworth and Milton: varieties of connection. Unpub. doct. diss., Boston College, 1985. [Abstr. in DA (46) 2299A.]

5717. GORECKI, JOHN E. An echo of *Julius Caesar* in *Paradise Lost*. *See* **4814.**

5718. GOTTLIEB, SIDNEY. Milton's land-ships and John Wilkins. MP (84:1) 60–2.

5719. GREEN, A. L. Milton's Eve and Ovid's *Metamorphoses*. Unpub. doct. diss., Univ. of Durham, 1985. [Abstr. in IT (35) 1084.]

5720. GREEN, J. 'A kind of another species': woman in Judeo-Christian tradition from the myth of the Fall to *Paradise Lost*. *See* **2649.**

5721. GREGORY, E. R. Milton and the Camenae. ExRC (12) 1–18.

5722. GRIFFIN, DUSTIN. Milton and the decline of epic in the eighteenth century. NLH (14:1) 1982, 143–54.

5723. GRIFFIN, DUSTIN H. Regaining paradise: Milton and the eighteenth century. Cambridge: CUP. pp. ix, 299. Rev. by Lucy Newlyn in TLS, 8 Aug., 871; by James Sambrook in THES (717) 17.

5724. HAMMOND, GERALD. Milton's *On Shakespeare*. SoHR (20:2) 115–24.

5725. HARADA, JUN. Toward *Paradise Lost*: temptation and antichrist in the English revolution. MStud (22) 45–77.

5726. HARRIS, N. Milton's 'Sataneid': the poet and the devil in *Paradise Lost*. A study of Milton's use in *Paradise Lost* of Dante's *Divina Commedia* and of three Italian Renaissance chivalric epics . . . Unpub. doct. diss., Univ. of Leicester. [Abstr. in IT (36) 911.]

5727. HILL, CHRISTOPHER. The experience of defeat: Milton and some contemporaries. New York: Viking Penguin, 1984. (Cf. bibl. 1984, 5054.) Rev. by Perez Zagorin in JMH (58:2) 549–51.

5728. HINZ, E. J.; TEUNISSEN, J. J. Milton, Whitman, Wolfe and Laurence: *The Stone Angel* as elegy. DalR (65:4) 1985/86, 474–91.

5729. HOAGWOOD, TERENCE ALLAN. Shelley, Milton, and the poetics of ideological transformation: *Paradise Lost* and the prologue to *Hellas*. RPP (10:2) 25–48.

5730. HOGAN, PATRICK COLM. Lapsarian Odysseus: Joyce, Milton, and the structure of *Ulysses*. JJQ (24:1) 55–72.

5731. HUNTER, WILLIAM B., JR. Milton's *Comus*: family piece. (Bibl. 1985, 4950). Rev. by Paul Stevens in RenR (9:4) 1985, 302–5.

5732. IDE, RICHARD S.   Five versions of Milton at Horton. Review (7) 1985, 89–111 (review-article).

5733. JACOBSON, HOWARD.   Milton's Harapha. ANQ (24:5/6) 70–1.

5734. JAMESON, FREDRIC.   Religion and ideology: a political reading of *Paradise Lost. In* (pp. 35–56) **29.**

5735. JONES, EDWARD JOHN.   Milton's sonnets: the critical comment, 1900–1985. Unpub. doct. diss., Ohio Univ., 1985. [Abstr. in DA (47) 912A.]

5736. KATES, JUDITH A.   Tasso and Milton: the problem of Christian epic. (Bibl. 1985, 4955.) Rev. by Charles Stanley Ross in MP (83:3) 305–7.

5737. KELLER, EVE.   Tetragrammic numbers: gematria and the line total of the 1674 *Paradise Lost.* MQ (20:1) 23–5.

5738. KELLEY, MAURICE (ed.).   The complete prose works of John Milton: vol. 8, 1666–1682. (Bibl. 1984, 5066.) Rev. by Gordon Campbell in MLR (81:2) 444–5.

5739. KERRIGAN, WILLIAM.   The irrational coherence of *Samson Agonistes.* MStud (22) 217–32.

5740. —— The sacred complex: on the psychogenesis of *Paradise Lost.* (Bibl. 1985, 4957.) Rev. by Richard S. Ide in Review (7) 1985, 105–11.

5741. —— BRADEN, GORDON.   Milton's coy Eve: *Paradise Lost* and Renaissance love poetry. ELH (53:1) 27–51.

5742. KILBORN, JUDITH MARGARET.   Presence and absence: goodness and evil in *Paradise Lost.* Unpub. doct. diss., Purdue Univ., 1985. [Abstr. in DA (46) 3360A.]

5743. KLEIN, JÜRGEN.   Astronomie und Anthropozentrik. Die Copernicanische Wende bei John Donne, John Milton und den Cambridge Platonists. *See* **5069.**

5744. KNEALE, DOUGLAS.   Milton, Wordsworth, and the 'joint labourers' of *The Prelude.* ESCan (12:1) 37–54.

5745. KNOESPEL, KENNETH J.   The limits of allegory: textual expansion of Narcissus in *Paradise Lost.* MStud (22) 79–99.

5746. KRANIDAS, THOMAS.   Milton on teachers and teaching. MQ (20:1) 26–9.

5747. LABRIOLA, ALBERT C.   'God speaks': Milton's dialogue in heaven and the tradition of divine deliberation. Cithara (25:2) 5–30.

5748. LEONARD, J. K.   Names and naming in *Paradise Lost.* Unpub. doct. diss., Univ. of Cambridge, 1985. [Abstr. in IT (35) 543–4.]

5749. LEWALSKI, BARBARA KIEFER.   *Paradise Lost* and the rhetoric of literary forms. Guildford: Princeton UP, 1985. (Cf. bibl. 1985, 4967.) Rev. by Lucy Newlyn in TLS, 8 Aug., 871; by Michael Lieb in MP (84:2) 225–8; by Joseph Wittreich in RQ (39:3) 569–72; by Chris Kendrick in Criticism (28:2) 213–16.

5750. LIEB, MICHAEL.   'Hate in heav'n': Milton and the *odium dei.* ELH (53:3) 519–39.

5751. LOCHMAN, DANIEL T.   'If there be aught of presage': Milton's Samson as riddler and prophet. MStud (22) 195–216.

5752. LUXTON, ANDREA THOMASING JOY.   Milton's hermeneutics: an intertextual study of the Epistle to the Hebrews and *Paradise Lost.* Unpub. doct. diss., Catholic Univ. of America. [Abstr. in DA (47) 1334A.]

5753. McCOLLEY, DIANE. Subsequent or precedent? Eve as Milton's defense of poesie. MQ (20:4) 132–6.

5754. McCORD, CLARE FINLEY. 'Various style': Milton's interpolated sonnets and their tradition. Unpub. doct. diss., Case Western Reserve Univ., 1985. [Abstr. in DA (46) 3727A.]

5755. MacCULLUM, HUGH. Milton and the sons of God: the divine image in Milton's epic poetry. Toronto; London: Toronto UP. pp. x, 325.

5756. McGUIRE, MARYANN CALE. Milton's Puritan masque. (Bibl. 1985, 4974.) Rev. by Richard S. Ide in Review (7) 1985, 93–7.

5757. MARCUSE, MICHAEL J. The Lauder controversy and the Jacobite cause. Studies in Burke and his Time (18:1) 1977, 27–47.

5758. MARKS, HERBERT JOSEPH. The language of Adam: Biblical naming and poetic etymology. Unpub. doct. diss., Yale Univ., 1985. [Abstr. in DA (47) 1311A.]

5759. MÁRQUEZ SÁNCHEZ, REUBEN, JR. 'The worst of superstitions': Milton's *Of True Religion* and the issue of religious tolerance. Prose Studies (9:3) 21–38.

5760. MARTINDALE, CHARLES. John Milton and the transformation of ancient epic. London: Croom Helm. pp. 239. Rev. by Paul Hammond in THES (724) 20.

5761. MATHIS, GILLES. Mémoire et création dans *Le Paradis perdu. In* (pp. 147–67) **34.**

5762. MAULE, JEREMY. Milton's 'three and twentieth year' again. NQ (33:1) 32–3.

5763. MERRILL, THOMAS. Epic God-talk: *Paradise Lost* and the grammar of religious language. Jefferson, NC; London: McFarland. pp. vii, 132.

5764. MILLER, LEO. Milton's *Apology.* Exp (44:2) 20–1.

5765. —— Milton's *Defensio* ordered wholesale for the States of Holland. *See* **409.**

5766. —— Two Milton state letters: new dates and new insights. NQ (33:4) 461–4.

5767. MOHANTY, CHRISTINE ANN. Water imagery in the poetry of John Milton: death and regeneration. Unpub. doct. diss., State Univ. of New York at Stony Brook. [Abstr. in DA (47) 1736A.]

5768. MOSES, JUDITH A. Love imagined. *See* **4962.**

5769. MOYLES, R. G. The text of *Paradise Lost*: a study in editorial procedure. (Bibl. 1985, 4980.) Rev. by Claud A. Thompson in ESCan (12:3) 346–50.

5770. MUSTAZZA, LEONARD. 'To hear new utterance flow': language before the fall in *Paradise Lost.* CLAJ (30:2) 184–209.

5771. —— Vonnegut's Tralfamadore and Milton's Eden. ELit (13:2) 299–312.

5772. NALINI, JAIN.   Echoes of Milton in Johnson's *Irene*. ANQ (24:9/10) 134–6.

5773. NYQUIST, MARY.   Textual overlapping and Dalilah's harlotlap. *In* (pp. 341–72) **27.**

5774. OBERTINO, JAMES.   Milton's use of Aquinas in *Comus*. MStud (22) 21–43.

5775. OCHI, FUMIO.   Waga Milton tanbou: kenkyu to zuisou. (My search for Milton: studies and essays.) Tokyo: Sion-sha. pp. vi, 236.

5776. OSLER, ALAN.   John Marchant's lectures on *Paradise Lost*. MQ (20:2) 52–3.

5777. PHELAN, HERBERT J.   What is the persona doing in *L'Allegro* and *Il Penseroso*? MStud (22) 3–20.

5778. POTTER, LOIS.   A preface to Milton. (Bibl. 1972, 5149.) Harlow: Longman. pp. x, 182. (Second ed.: first ed. 1971.)

5779. READINGS, W. J.   The Restoration and the fall of language: the search for meaning in the poetry of Marvell and Milton. *See* **5637.**

5780. REVARD, STELLA P.   *L'Allegro* and *Il Penseroso*: classical tradition and Renaissance mythography. PMLA (101:3) 338–50.

5781. —— Milton and Classical Rome: the political context of *Paradise Regained*. *In* (pp. 411–19) **49.**

5782. RUDAT, WOLFGANG E. H.   Milton and The Miller's Tale: Chaucerian allusions in *Paradise Lost*. *See* **3775.**

5783. RUMRICH, JOHN PETER.   Mead and Milton. MQ (20:4) 136–41.

5784. SAMMONS, TODD H.   'As the vine curls her tendrils': marriage topos and erotic countertopos in *Paradise Lost*. MQ (20:4) 117–27.

5785. SAMS, HORACE, JR.   Temptation in imaginative literature of Milton and Bunyan: two faces of the Puritan persona. *See* **5314.**

5786. SARKAR, MALABIKA.   The quest for paradise: Milton and the Romantics. Jadavpur University Essays and Studies (Calcutta) (4) 1984, 53–63.

5787. SCHAAR, CLAES.   'The full voic'd quire below': vertical context systems in *Paradise Lost*. (Bibl. 1985, 4995.) Rev. by John Steadman in YES (16) 254–5.

5788. SCHERER, BARRYMORE LAURENCE.   Let there be light! Opera News, 1 Mar., 10–13.

5789. SCHINDLER, WALTER.   Voice and crisis: invocation in Milton's poetry. Hamden, CT: Archon; Shoe String Press, 1984. pp. 130. Rev. by Thomas Kranidas in RQ (39:1) 148–9; by James Egan in SCN (44:3) 34–5.

5790. SERPELL, MICHAEL.   Milton's 'blind mouths'. BC (35:2) 199–213.

5791. SHAWCROSS, JOHN T.   Further remarks on Milton's influence: Shelley and Shaw. MQ (20:3) 85–92.

5792. SHIRATORI, MASATAKA.   Milton kenkyu noto. (Milton studies.) Tokyo: Yumi Press. pp. 144.

5793. SHOAF, R. A.   Milton: poet of duality: a study of semiosis in the poetry and the prose. New Haven, CT: Yale UP, 1985. pp. xiv, 225. Rev.

by Lucy Newlyn in TLS, 8 Aug., 871; by Lorraine Chaskalson in UES (24:1) 34–5; by Chris Kendrick in Criticism (28:2) 213–16.

5794. SHULLENBERGER, WILLIAM. Wrestling with the angel: *Paradise Lost* and feminist criticism. MQ (20:3) 69–85.

5795. SIMS, JAMES H.; RYKEN, LELAND (eds). Milton and scriptural tradition: the Bible into poetry. (Bibl. 1985, 5001.) Rev. by John B. Gabel in SAQ (85:1) 106–7; by Archie Burnett in NQ (33:3) 416–17.

5796. SMITH, JULIA J. Milton and death. DUJ (79:1) 15–22.

5797. SNIDER, ALVIN. The self-mirroring mind in Milton and Traherne. UTQ (55:4) 313–27.

5798. SONG, HONG-HAN. Milton's prophetic view of history in *Paradise Lost*. Pegasus (8) 1985, 34–52.

5799. STEADMAN, JOHN M. The hill and the labyrinth: discourse and certitude in Milton and his near-contemporaries. (Bibl. 1985, 5003.) Rev by Heather Ross Asals in RQ (39:2) 356–8; by James Egan in SCN (44:1/2) 6–7; by Alvin Snider in MP (84:1) 82–5; by Archie Burnett in NQ (33:4) 548–9; by Frank L. Huntley in JEGP (85:2) 269–70.

5800. STEVENS, PAUL. Imagination and the presence of Shakespeare in *Paradise Lost*. *See* **4597.**

5801. STOLLMAN, SAMUEL S. Satan, Sin, and Death: a Mosaic trio in *Paradise Lost*. MStud (22) 101–20.

5802. STRASSER, GERHARD FRIEDRICH. The iconography of war in d'Aubigné, Gryphius, and Milton. Unpub. doct. diss., Brown Univ., 1974. [Abstr. in DA (46) 2690A.]

5803. SWAIN, KATHLEEN M. Some Dante and Milton analogues. Ren (37) 1984, 43–51.

5804. SWISS, MARGO. Crisis of conscience: a theological context for Milton's *How Soon Hath Time*. MQ (20:3) 98–103.

5805. TATUM, JAMES. Apollonius of Rhodes and the resourceless hero of *Paradise Regained*. MStud (22) 255–70.

5806. TEAGUE, ANTHONY G. The fall of Satan and Harrowing of Hell: literary preludes to Milton. JELL (32:3) 407–30.

5807. TEAGUE, FRANCES. Milton and the pygmies. MQ (20:1) 31–2.

5808. TESKEY, GORDON. From allegory to dialectic: imagining error in Spenser and Milton. *See* **4288.**

5809. —— Milton's choice of subject in the context of Renaissance critical theory. ELH (53:1) 53–72.

5810. THORNE-THOMSEN, SARA. Milton's 'advent'rous song': lyric genres in *Paradise Lost*. Unpub. doct. diss., Brown Univ., 1985. [Abstr. in DA (46) 1953A.]

5811. TIPPENS, DARRYL. The kenotic experience of *Samson Agonistes*. MStud (22) 173–94.

5812. TRAVERS, MICHAEL ERNEST. The devotional experience in Milton's poetry. Unpub. doct. diss., Michigan State Univ., 1985. [Abstr. in DA (46) 1954A.]

5813. TREIP, MINDELE ANNE. *Comus* as 'Progress'. MQ (20:1) 1–13.

5814. TSUJI, HIROKO. The 'tragic notes' and the language of *Paradise Lost*, Book IX. SEL (63:1) 41–59.

5815. Vicari, Patricia.   The triumph of art, the triumph of death: Orpheus in Spenser and Milton. *See* **4292.**

5816. Walker, Julia M.   'For each seem'd either': free will and predestination in *Paradise Lost.* MQ (20:1) 13–16.

5817. Wallace, Laurie Ann.   The Renaissance transformation of Eve. *See* **4294.**

5818. Watson, Thomas Ramey.   Milton's pyramids. ANQ (24:9/10) 132–4.

5819. Weber, Burton J.   The schematic design of the *Samson* middle. MStud (22) 233–54.

5820. Weiland, Kurt F.   Michaelmas and Milton's Ludlow maske: the influence of the Christian services. MSE (10:3) 197–206.

5821. Wentersdorf, Karl P.   Allusion and theme in the third movement of Milton's *Lycidas.* MP (83:3) 275–9.

5822. Werman, Golda.   Repentance in *Paradise Lost.* MStud (22) 121–39.

5823. Wilding, Michael.   Milton's *Areopagitica*: liberty for the sects. Prose Studies (9:2) 7–38.

5824. Wilson, A. N.   The life of John Milton. (Bibl. 1984, 5174.) Rev. by Richard S. Ide in Review (7) 1985, 89–93.

5825. Wittreich, Joseph.   Interpreting *Samson Agonistes.* Princeton, NJ; Guildford: Princeton UP. pp. xxx, 394.

5826. Yoon, Kee-Ho.   Satan eui myosa e natanan Milton eui hyeonsilgwan. (Milton's view of reality in *Paradise Lost.*) RRCNU (32) Dec., 69–80.

5827. Zeong, Yun-Shig.   Shakespeare and Milton: a poetic approach through Aristotle's *Poetics* and Longinus' *The Sublime*: *Macbeth* and *Paradise Lost. See* **4875.**

5828. —— Sihak mit shinhakjeok cheukmyeon esuh gochalhan bigeukjeok yoin gwa geu hyogwa: Milton eui *Paradise Lost* rcul jungsim euro. (An approach to tragic causes and effects: Milton's *Paradise Lost* and Aristotle's *Poetics.*) JELL (32:1) 3–21.

Henry More

5829. Henry, John.   A Cambridge Platonist's materialism: Henry More and the concept of soul. JWCI (49) 172–95.

Thomas Morton

5830. Sternberg, Paul R.   The publication of Thomas Morton's *New English Canaan* reconsidered. *See* **433.**

Dudley North, Fourth Baron North

5831. Randall, Dale B. J. (ed.).   Gentle flame: the life and verse of Dudley, Fourth Lord North (1602–1677). (Bibl. 1985, 5018.) Rev. by Jenijoy La Belle in JEGP (85:1) 123–4.

John Oldham

5832. Cousins, A. D.   Oldham in defence of the Restoration: *Satires upon the Jesuits. See* **1217.**

'Orinda' (Katherine Philips)

5833. Brashear, Lucy.   The 'Matchless Orinda's' missing sister: Mrs C. P. Restoration (10:2) 76–81.

5834. LIMBERT, CLAUDIA (ed.). Two poems and a prose receipt: the unpublished juvenilia of Katherine Philips (text). ELR (16:2) 383–90.

Thomas Otway

5835. AIKINS, JANET E. A plot discover'd; or, the uses of *Venice Preserv'd* within *Clarissa*. UTQ (55:3) 219–34.

5836. MUNNS, JESSICA. Does Otway praise Rochester in *The Poet's Complaint?* NQ (33:1) 40–1.

5837. SOLOMON, HARRY M. The rhetoric of 'redressing grievances': court propaganda as the hermeneutical key to *Venice Preserv'd*. ELH (53:2) 289–310.

Richard Overton

5838. SMITH, NIGEL. Richard Overton's Marpriest tracts: towards a history of Leveller style. Prose Studies (9:2) 39–66.

John Paulet, Marquis of Winchester

5839. MABER, R. G. Pierre le Moyne's encomium of Margaret Roper, translated by John Paulet, Marquis of Winchester (1652). Moreana (23:90) 47–52. (Includes facsim.)

Henry Peacham the Younger

5840. YOUNG, A. R. Henry Peacham, Ripa's *Iconologia*, and Vasari's lives. RenR (9:3) 1985, 177–88.

William Penn

5841. FROST, J. WILLIAM. William Penn's experiment in the wilderness: promise and legend. PMHB (107:4) 1983, 577–605.

Samuel Pepys

5842. DELAFORCE, PATRICK. Pepys in love: Elizabeth's story. London: Bishopsgate. pp. 248.

5843. EDWARDS, A. S. G. (introd.). Manuscript Pepys 2006: a facsimile: Magdalene College Cambridge. Norman, OK: Pilgrim; Woodbridge: Boydell & Brewer, 1985. pp. xxxii, unnumbered leaves. Rev. by N. F. Blake in EngS (67:6) 565–6.

5844. LANOIX, LOUIS. Samuel Pepys: le serviteur et le maître. *In* (pp. 165–79) **30.**

5845. LATHAM, ROBERT (ed.). The shorter Pepys. Berkeley: California UP; London: Bell & Hyman, 1985. pp. 1096. Rev. in BW, 23 Feb., 42.

5846. ROSTENBERG, LEONA. A look at Pepys. ABC (7:10) 17–24.

Alexander Radcliffe

5847. ROBINSON, KEN. The authorship of *Ovidius Exulans* (1673). NQ (33:1) 36–7.

Thomas Randolph

5848. BORIAS, GEORGES. Randolph's *Praeludium*: an edited transcription, comprising a short introductory note. CEl (29) 53–76.

John Wilmot, Earl of Rochester

5849. COPE, KEVIN L. The conquest of truth: Wycherley, Rochester, Butler, and Dryden and the Restoration critique of satire. *See* **5319.**

5850. LOVE, HAROLD. The text of Rochester's *Upon Nothing*. *See* **320.**

5851. MANNING, GILLIAN. Rochester and *Much A-do about Nothing*. NQ (33:4) 479–80.

5852. —— Some quotations from Rochester in Charles Blount's *Philostratus*. NQ (33:1) 38–40.

5853. MUNNS, JESSICA.   Does Otway praise Rochester in *The Poet's Complaint? See* **5836.**

5854. RUSSELL, FORD.   Satiric perspective in Rochester's *A Satyr against Reason and Mankind*. PLL (22:1) 245–53.

5855. WALKER, KEITH (ed.).   The poems of John Wilmot, Earl of Rochester. (Bibl. 1985, 5040.) Rev. by D. J. Womersley in NQ (33:2) 236–8; by Irène Simon in EngS (67:3) 270–2; by John H. O'Neill in HLQ (49:3) 280–3; by Ken Robinson in MLR (81:4) 988–9.

William Rowley

5856. BROMHAM, TONY.   *The Changeling* by Thomas Middleton and William Rowley. *See* **5651.**

5857. DARBY, T. L.   A critical, old-spelling edition of *A New Wonder, a Woman Never Vext*, by William Rowley. Unpub. doct. diss., Univ. of London (King's Coll.), 1983.

5858. DARBY, TRUDI.   Rowley's hand in collaboration. *See* **97.**

5859. DAVIES, H. NEVILLE.   *Pericles* and the Sherley brothers. *In* (pp. 94–113) **50.**

5860. KOWSAR, MOHAMMAD.   Middleton and Rowley's *The Changeling*: the besieged temple. *See* **5658.**

5861. PADHI, S.   A critical old-spelling edition of *The Spanish Gipsie* by Middleton, Rowley (and possibly Ford). *See* **5465.**

Thomas Salusbury

5862. GAIR, REAVLEY.   In search of 'the mustie fopperies of antiquity'. *In* (pp. 123–30) **44.**

5863. —— Royalist view of Parliament in 1642. DalR (66:1/2) 107–17.

George Sandys

5864. HAYNES, JONATHAN.   The humanist as traveler: George Sandys's *Relation of a Journey begun An Dom. 1610*. Rutherford, NJ: Fairleigh Dickinson UP; London: Assoc. UPs. pp. 159.

5865. TAYLOR, ANTHONY BRIAN.   George Sandys and Arthur Golding. *See* **4083.**

Daniel Scargill

5866. DAVIDSON, PETER.   An early echo of poems by Marvell. *See* **5626.**

Samuel Sewall

5867. ROSENWALD, LAWRENCE.   Sewall's *Diary* and the margins of Puritan literature. AL (58:3) 325–41.

James Shirley

5868. CUTTS, JOHN.   Original music for two Caroline plays – Richard Brome's *The English Moor; or the Mock-Marriage* and James Shirley's *The Gentlemen of Venice*. *See* **5298.**

5869. HOGAN, PATRICK G., JR.   *The Arcadia*: from Sidney's prose to Shirley's drama. *See* **4211.**

5870. LUCOW, BEN.   James Shirley. (Bibl. 1984, 5221.) Rev. by Georges Bas in EA (38:4) 1985, 457–8.

5871. VENUTI, LAWRENCE.   The politics of allusion: the gentry and Shirley's *The Triumph of Peace*. ELR (16:1) 182–205.

5872. WALKER, K. P.   James Shirley, *The Dukes Mistris*: an old-spelling edition. Unpub. doct. diss., Univ. of Edinburgh. [Abstr. in IT (36) 910.]

5873. WALKER, KIM.   Press variants and proof correction in Shirley's *The Dukes Mistris* (1638). See **130.**

5874. YEARLING, E. M. (ed.).   The cardinal. Manchester: Manchester UP. pp. x, 166. (Revels plays.)

John Smith

5875. BARBOUR, PHILIP L. (ed.).   The complete works of Captain John Smith (1580–1631) in three volumes. Chapel Hill: North Carolina UP for Inst. of Early American History and Culture, Williamsburg, VA. pp. lxxii, 448; xii, 488; xi, 513. Rev. by Warren M. Billings in JAH (73:3) 715–17.

5876. GURA, PHILIP F.   John who? Captain John Smith and early American literature. EAL (21:3) 1986/87, 260–7 (review-article).

Thomas Southerne

5877. BOWEN, E. K.   Thomas Southerne's *Sir Thomas Love*: a critical edition. Unpub. doct. diss., Univ. of Stirling, 1985. [Abstr. in IT (35) 1083.]

William Strachey

5878. FOSTER, DONALD WAYNE.   Elegy by W. S.: a study in attribution. See **4446.**

Joseph Swetham

5879. VAN HEERTUM, CISCA.   An eighteenth-century edition of Joseph Swetham's *The Araignment of Lewd, Idle, Froward and Unconstant Women*. Factotum (21) 1985, 9.

Edward Taylor

5880. PATTERSON, J. DANIEL.   A critical edition of Edward Taylor's *Gods Determinations*. Unpub. doct. diss., Kent State Univ., 1985. [Abstr. in DA (47) 181A.]

5881. ROWE, KAREN E.   Saint and singer: Edward Taylor's typology and the poetics of meditation. Cambridge; New York: CUP. pp. xviii, 341. (Cambridge studies in American literature and culture.)

5882. SCHULDINER, MICHAEL.   The Christian hero and the classical journey in Edward Taylor's *Preparatory Meditations. First Series*. HLQ (49:2) 113–32.

5883. WAINWRIGHT, JANA DIANE.   Edward Taylor studies from 1971–1984: an analysis and annotated bibliography. Unpub. doct. diss., Texas A&M Univ., 1985. [Abstr. in DA (46) 3037A.]

Sir William Temple

5884. MOLITOR, HELEN O'BRIEN.   Sir William Temple, Meric Casaubon, and Swift's *Mechanical Operation of the Spirit*. NQ (33:4) 484–5.

John Toland

5885. DANIEL, STEPHEN H.   John Toland: his methods, manners, and mind. Montreal: McGill–Queen's UP, 1984. pp. 248. Rev. by Ezra Talmor in JHP (24:4) 562–4.

Cyril Tourneur

5886. GUNDY, D. C.   Tourneur's *The Revenger's Tragedy* II.ii.216–18. *See* **5652.**

5887. JACKSON, MacD. P. (introd.).   *The Revenger's Tragedy*: a facsimile of the 1607/8 quarto, attributed to Thomas Middleton. *See* **5655.**

5888. MEHL, DIETER.   Corruption, retribution and justice in *Measure for Measure* and *The Revenger's Tragedy*. *In* (pp. 114–28) **50.**

5889. SCHRICKX, WILLEM.   *The Revenger's Tragedy* and its contemporary Dutch adaptation by Theodore Rodenburg. *In* (pp. 104–9) **18.**

Aurelian Townshend

5890. KAPLAN, JOEL H.   A Man of Canada, 1635. CanL (110) 191–2.

Thomas Traherne

5891. PONSFORD, M. J.   The poetry of Thomas Traherne in relation to the thought and poetics of his period. *See* **5256.**

5892. REHKOPF, DON.   Thomas Traherne: a visionary for the laboratory. ChCen (103:23) 693–4.

5893. ROSS, J. C. B.   The placing of Thomas Traherne: a study of the several seventeenth-century contexts of his thought and style. Unpub. doct. diss., Univ. of Cambridge, 1984.

5894. SMITH, JULIA J.   Thomas and Philip Traherne. NQ (33:1) 25–31.

5895. SNIDER, ALVIN.   The self-mirroring mind in Milton and Traherne. *See* **5797.**

Sir Thomas Urquhart

5896. CRAIK, R. J.   A critical study of the works of Sir Thomas Urquhart of Cromarty. Unpub. doct. diss., Univ. of Southampton, 1984.

5897. JACK, R. D. S.; LYALL, R. (eds).   The jewel. (Bibl. 1985, 5076.) Rev. by David Norbrook in NQ (33:4) 549.

Sir John Vanbrugh

5898. HUGHES, DEREK.   Cibber and Vanbrugh: language, place, and social order in *Love's Last Shift*. CompDr (20:4) 287–304.

Henry Vaughan

5899. CONRAN, TONY.   'Ye Bryttish poets . . .': some observations on early Anglo-Welsh poetry. *See* **3948.**

5900. DICKSON, DONALD R.   Vaughan's *The Water-fall* and Protestant meditation. ExRC (10) 1984, 28–40.

5901. HAMMOND, GERALD.   'Poor dust should lie still low': George Herbert and Henry Vaughan. *See* **5483.**

5902. MARTZ, LOUIS (ed.).   George Herbert and Henry Vaughan. *See* **5489.**

5903. RUDRUM, ALAN.   Henry Vaughan. (Bibl. 1982, 5701.) Rev. by Paulina Palmer in YES (16) 247–8.

5904. THOMAS, NOEL KENNEDY.   Henry Vaughan: poet of revelation. Worthing: Churchman, 1985. pp. 196.

5905. WATSON, G. J.   Eschatology in the work of Henry Vaughan. Unpub. doct. diss., Univ. of Reading, 1983.

5906. WATSON, GRAEME J. Political change and continuity of vision in Henry Vaughan's *Daphnis: an Elegiac Eclogue*. SP (83:2) 158–81.
5907. —— The temple in *The Night*: Henry Vaughan and the collapse of the Established Church. MP (84:2) 144–61.

Thomas Vaughan

5908. RUDRUM, ALAN (ed.). The works of Thomas Vaughan. (Bibl. 1985, 5087.) Rev. by Michael H. Keefer in ESCan (12:1) 108–14; by Oliver Johnson in NQ (33:2) 234–5.

John Webster

5909. GOLDBERG, DENA. *Appius and Virginia*: a story of rape and tyranny – two Renaissance versions. See **3896.**
5910. HAMMOND, ANTONY. *The White Devil* in Nicholas Okes's Shop. See **103.**
5911. MOORE, DON D. (ed.). Webster: the critical heritage. (Bibl. 1985, 5101.) Rev. by Lois Potter in ShS (36) 1983, 174–5.
5912. PROUDFOOT, RICHARD. A Jacobean dramatic fragment. TLS, 13 June, 651.
5913. SCHAFER, ELIZABETH. The ring story in *Northward Ho*, 1.i.: an English source. See **5357.**
5914. WAAGE, FREDERICK O. *The White Devil* dicover'd: backgrounds and foregrounds to Webster's tragedy. New York: Lang, 1984. pp. 185. Rev. by Peter Hyland in SCN (44:1/2) 16–17.

Michael Wigglesworth

5915. PETILLON, PIERRE. *Day of Doom*: la rhétorique de la fin des temps dans la Nouvelle Angleterre du XVIIe siècle. *In* (pp. 63–75) **2.**

George Wilkins

5916. DAVIES, H. NEVILLE. *Pericles* and the Sherley brothers. *In* (pp. 94–113) **50.**

John Wilkins

5917. DOLEZAL, FREDRIC. John Wilkins' and William Lloyd's *Alphabetical Dictionary* (1668): towards a comprehensive, and systematically defined, lexicon. See **1745.**
5918. GOTTLIEB, SIDNEY. Milton's land-ships and John Wilkins. See **5718.**

William Winstanley

5919. RUDE, DONALD W. Two echoes of Shakespeare in popular seventeenth-century literature. See **4569.**

John Winthrop the Elder

5920. LEWIS, MARY JANE. A sweet sacrifice: civil war in New England. See **5072.**

William Wycherley

5921. COPE, KEVIN L. The conquest of truth: Wycherley, Rochester, Butler, and Dryden and the Restoration critique of satire. See **5319.**
5922. PAYNE, DEBORAH C. Reading the signs in *The Country Wife*. SELit (26:3) 403–19.

EIGHTEENTH CENTURY

GENERAL

General Literary Studies

5923. ADAMS, PERCY. Perception and the eighteenth-century traveller. ECent (26:2) 1985, 139–57.

5924. ALLEN, ROBERT R.; KORSHIN, PAUL J. (eds). The eighteenth century: a current bibliography: ns 5, for 1979. New York: AMS Press, 1983. pp. xiv, 643. Rev. by A. J. Sambrook in MLR (81:2) 424–6.

5925. ALSTON, R. C. Searching ESTC online. *See* **516.**

5926. —— SINGLETON, J. C. Searching ESTC online. *See* **517.**

5927. ARAKELIAN, PAUL G. The myth of a Restoration style shift. *See* **5045.**

5928. ATKINS, G. DOUGLAS. The money of stories of money. ECent (26:3) 1985, 297–305 (review-article).

5929. BARRELL, JOHN. English literature in history, 1730–80: an equal, wide survey. (Bibl. 1984, 5290.) Rev. by Isaac Kramnick in ECent (26:2) 1985, 186–92.

5930. BATE, JONATHAN. Shakespearean allusion in English caricature in the age of Gillray. *See* **65.**

5931. BATTESTIN, MARTIN C. The providence of wit: aspects of form in Augustan literature and arts. New York: OUP, 1974. pp. 331. (Cf. bibl. 1977, 4992.) Rev. by Ronald Paulson in Studies in Burke and his Time (Texas Tech Univ., Lubbock, TX) (17:3) 1976, 234–40.

5932. BECHLER, R. Lovelace progenitor: a study of the eighteenth-century villain. Unpub. doct. diss., Univ. of Cambridge.

5933. BELSEY, CATHERINE. The Romantic construction of the unconscious. *In* (pp. 57–76) **29.**

5934. BERTELSEN, LANCE. The Nonsense Club: literature and popular culture, 1749–1764. Oxford: Clarendon Press. pp. 304.

5935. BOGEL, FREDRIC V. Literature and insubstantiality in later eighteenth-century England. (Bibl. 1985, 5114.) Rev. by Stephen Cox in ECent (27:3) 299–304; by Leopold Damrosch, Jr, in Review (7) 1985, 57–64; by John A. Dussinger in JEGP (85:3) 456–9; by Serge Soupel in EA (38:4) 1985, 465; by Francis Doherty in BJECS (9:1) 98–9.

5936. BORCK, JIM SPRINGER (ed.). The eighteenth century: a current bibliography: ns 6, for 1980. New York: AMS Press, 1984. pp. xii, 643. Rev. by A. J. Sambrook in MLR (81:2) 424–6.

5937. BOZEMAN, THEODORE DWIGHT. The Puritans' *Errand into the Wilderness* reconsidered. *See* **5047.**

5938. BRAVERMAN, RICHARD LEWIS. Capital relations and English literature, 1660–1730. *See* **5049.**

5939. BRITAIN'S LITERARY HERITAGE. The Robert White Collection of Chapbooks from the University Library, Newcastle upon Tyne: a listing and guide to the Harvester microform. *See* **2436.**

5940. BROWN, LAURA. Contemporary theory and the defense of eighteenth-century studies: Brian McCrea, G. S. Rousseau, and Melvyn New. ECent (26:3) 1985, 281–95.

5941. BUELL, LAWRENCE.   New England literary culture: from revolution through renaissance. Cambridge: CUP. pp. xii, 513. (Cambridge studies in American literature and culture.)

5942. BURNS, JAMES.   From 'polite learning' to 'useful knowledge'. HT (36) Apr., 21–9.

5943. BURR, NELSON R.   New Eden and new Babylon: religious thoughts of American authors: a bibliography: the optimistic reaction to Puritanism. HMPEC (55:1) 57–77.

5944. CHILDS, F. A.   Prescriptions for manners in English courtesy literature, 1690–1760, and their social implications. *See* **5050.**

5945. CLARK, ANNA.   The politics of seduction in English popular culture, 1748–1848. *In* (pp. 47–70) **45.**

5946. COLE, RICHARD CARGILL.   Irish booksellers and English writers 1740–1800. *See* **363.**

5947. COPLEY, STEPHEN (ed.).   Literature and the social order in eighteenth-century England. (Bibl. 1985, 5120, where 'ed.' not noted.) Rev. by Stuart Sim in BJECS (9:1) 97–8; by Leslie Mitchell in NQ (33:1) 118.

5948. COX, STEPHEN.   What was distinctive about the later eighteenth century? ECent (27:3) 299–304 (review-article).

5949. DAMROSCH, LEOPOLD, JR.   God's plot and man's stories: studies in the fictional imagination from Milton to Fielding. *See* **5052.**

5950. —— Looking for coherence in the later eighteenth century. Review (7) 1985, 57–64 (review-article).

5951. DAY, WILLIAM PATRICK.   In the circles of fear and desire: a study of gothic fantasy. (Bibl. 1985, 5122.) Rev. by John C. Hawley in ChrisL (35:4) 36–7; by Patrick Brantlinger in Criticism (28:2) 220–2; by Valerie Shaw in THES (697) 17.

5952. DE BOLLA, PETER.   Marxism, ideology, and false scholarship: a reply to G. S. Rousseau. ECent (27:1) 52–61.

5953. DOLLE, RAYMOND FRANCIS.   Treasure quests in New World literature. Unpub. doct. diss., Pennsylvania State Univ., 1985. [Abstr. in DA (46) 2691A.]

5954. DOYLE, JAMES.   North of America: images of Canada in the literature of the United States 1775–1900. (Bibl. 1985, 5123.) Rev. by Russell Brown in QQ (93:4) 897–9.

5955. EDDY, R.   Mysticism in eighteenth-century English literature. Unpub. doct. diss., Univ. of Durham, 1983.

5956. FERGUSON, MOIRA.   First feminists: British women writers, 1578–1799. *See* **3844.**

5957. FERGUSON, ROBERT A.   Law and letters in American culture. (Bibl. 1985, 5125.) Rev. by Lawrence M. Friedman in JAH (73:1) 166–7.

5958. FRANK, FREDERICK S.   Guide to the gothic: an annotated bibliography of criticism. (Bibl. 1984, 5310.) Rev. in BB (43:3) 185.

5959. GLOCK, WALDO SUMNER.   Eighteenth-century English literary

studies: a bibliography. (Bibl. 1985, 5129.) Rev. in BB (43:3) 185–6; by
A. J. Sambrook in MLR (81:2) 424–6.

5960. GOODWIN, KEN LESLIE.   A history of Australian literature.
Basingstoke: Macmillan. pp. ix, 322. (Macmillan history of literature.)

5961. GUSTAFSON, THOMAS B.   Representative words: politics,
literature and the American language, 1776–1865. *See* **867.**

5962. HÖFELE, ANDREAS.   Die Originalität der Fälschung: Zur Funktion des literarischen Betrugs in England 1750–1800. PoetA (18:1/2)
75–95.

5963. HORNE, COLIN J.   The classical temper in Britain: origins and
components. *In* (pp. 62–75) JOHN HARDY and ANDREW MCCREDIE
(eds), The classical temper in western Europe. Melbourne: OUP, 1984.
pp. 120.

5964. HUNDERT, E. J.   A satire of self-disclosure: from Hegel through
Rameau to the Augustans. JHI (47:2) 235–48.

5965. JORDANOVA, L. J. (ed.);   WILLIAMS, RAYMOND (introd.).
Languages of nature: critical essays on science and literature. London:
Free Association Books. pp. 351.

5966. KENSHUR, OSCAR.   Open form and the shape of ideas: literary
structures as representations of philosophical concept in the seventeenth
and eighteenth centuries. *See* **5068.**

5967. KORSHIN, PAUL J.   Recent studies in the Restoration and
eighteenth century. SELit (26:3) 537–87.

5968. —— ALLEN, ROBERT R. (eds).   Greene centennial studies:
essays presented to Donald Greene in the centennial year of the
University of Southern California. (Bibl. 1985, 22.) Rev. by Harlan W.
Hamilton in SAQ (85:4) 396–9.

5969. —— (gen. ed.).   The eighteenth century: a current bibliography: ns. 5, for 1979. New York: AMS Press, 1983. pp. xiv, 643. Rev.
by Robert Van Dusen in MLS (16:3) 325–7.

5970. KRAMNICK, ISAAC.   English literature in history. ECent (26:2)
1985, 186–92 (review-article).

5971. KROPF, C. R.   Unity and the study of eighteenth-century
literature. ECent (21:1) 1980, 25–40.

5972. LEMAY, J. A. LEO.   American literatures. ECent (26:1) 1985,
101–4.

5973. LUCAS, JOHN.   Romantic to modern literature: essays and ideas
of culture, 1750–1900. New York: Barnes & Noble, 1982. (Cf. bibl. 1983,
5650.) Rev. by Terry Eagleton in YES (16) 273–4.

5974. MACPHERSON, JAY.   The spirit of solitude: conventions and
continuities in late romance. (Bibl. 1985, 5141.) Rev. by Lorraine Weir
in CL (38:1) 102–3.

5975. MACQUEEN, JOHN.   The Enlightenment and Scottish literature:
vol. 1, Progress and poetry. (Bibl. 1983, 5654.) Rev. by J. H. Alexander
in YES (16) 231–4.

5976. MEAD, JOAN TYLER.   'Spare me a few minutes I have Something to Say': poetry in manuscripts of sailing ships. *In* (pp. 23–31) **28.**

5977. MEEHAN, MICHAEL.   Liberty and poetics in eighteenth century

England. London; Sydney: Croom Helm. pp. 190. Rev. by A. J. Sambrook in THES (703) 18.

5978. MITCHELL, ADRIAN.   No new thing: the concept of novelty and early Australian writing. *In* (pp. 52–63) **31.**

5979. MORRIS, K. L.   Religious medievalism: aspects of the medieval church in later eighteenth century and nineteenth century English literature. Unpub. doct. diss., Univ. of Hull, 1982.

5980. MULLAN, J. D.   Sentiment and sociability: a study of English sentimental literature of the eighteenth century. Unpub. doct. diss., Univ. of Cambridge, 1985.

5981. PATEY, DOUGLAS LANE.   Probability and literary form: philosophic theory and literary practice in the Augustan age. (Bibl. 1984, 5333.) Rev. by Alain Morvan in EA (38:4) 1985, 462–3; by James L. Battersby in MP (84:1) 85–92; by Marion Hobson in NQ (33:2) 243–4; by John A. Dussinger in JEGP (8:3) 456–9; by Richard W. F. Kroll in BJECS (9:2) 252–3.

5982. PROSTKO, JACK.   Instructive and delightful talk: conversation and eighteenth-century English literature. Unpub. doct. diss., Stanford Univ., 1985. [Abstr. in DA (46) 2302A.]

5983. RAESIDE, J. M.   Self-consciousness in the works of certain major French and English authors in the first half of the eighteenth century. Unpub. doct. diss., Univ. of Oxford, 1984.

5984. RAFROIDI, PATRICK.   The year's work in Irish-English literature Autumn 1985–Autumn 1986. Études irlandaises (11) 195–215.

5985. RAVEN, J. R.   English popular literature and the image of business, 1760–1790. *See* **425.**

5986. RAWSON, CLAUDE.   Order from confusion sprung: studies in eighteenth-century literature from Swift to Cowper. (Bibl. 1985, 5148.) Rev. by Denis Donoghue in LRB (8:2) 11–12; by Penelope Wilson in THES (694) 21.

5987. ROGERS, KATHARINE M.   Feminism in eighteenth-century England. (Bibl. 1985, 5149.) Rev. by Douglas Brooks-Davies in YES (16) 264–8; by Susan Staves in ECent (26:2) 1985, 170–6.

5988. ROGERS, PAT.   Eighteenth-century encounters: studies in literature and society in the age of Walpole. (Bibl. 1985, 5150.) Rev. by Denis Donoghue in LRB (8:2) 11–12.

5989. —— Literature and popular culture in eighteenth-century England. (Bibl. 1985, 5151.) Rev. by Denis Donoghue in LRB (8:2) 11–12.

5990. ROUSSEL, ROY.   The conversation of the sexes: seduction and equality in selected seventeenth- and eighteenth-century texts. *See* **5080.**

5991. SALES, ROGER.   Closer to home: writers and places in England, 1780–1830. Cambridge, MA; London: Harvard UP. pp. 153.

5992. —— English literature in history, 1780–1830: pastoral and politics. (Bibl. 1984, 5340.) Rev. by Philip Cox in KSR (1) 91–6.

5993. SAMBROOK, JAMES.   The eighteenth century: the intellectual and cultural context of English literature, 1700–1789. London: Longman.

pp. 290. (Longman literature in English.) Rev. by Pat Rogers in LRB (8:19) 20–1; by Brean S. Hammond in THES (724) 20.

5994. SARGENT, MARK L.   Rekindled fires: Jamestown and Plymouth in American literature, 1765–1863. Unpub. doct. diss., Claremont Graduate School, 1985. [Abstr. in DA (46) 2694A.]

5995. SIMPSON, K. G.   The Protean Scot: multiple voice in eighteenth-century Scottish literature. Unpub. doct. diss., Univ. of Strathclyde, 1984.

5996. SITTER, JOHN.   Literary loneliness in mid-eighteenth-century England. (Bibl. 1985, 5155.) Rev. by Joan H. Pittock in BJECS (9:1) 96–7.

5997. SMITH, MARGARET M.; BOUMELHA, PENNY.   Index of English literary manuscripts: vol. 3, 1700–1800: part 1, Addison–Fielding. *See* **182.**

5998. SOCIÉTÉ D'ÉTUDES ANGLO-AMÉRICAINES DES XVIIe ET XVIIIe SIÈCLES.   Maître et serviteur dans le monde anglo-américain des XVIIe et XVIIIe siècles. Actes du Colloque 1985. *See* **30.**

5999. SOCIÉTÉ D'ÉTUDES ANGLO-AMÉRICAINES DES XVIIe ET XVIIIe SIÈCLES.   Mémoire et création dans le monde anglo-américain aux XVIIe et XVIIIe siècles: Actes du Colloque tenu à Paris les 21 et 22 octobre 1983. *See* **34.**

6000. SPACKS, PATRICIA MEYER; CARNOCHAN, W. B.   A distant prospect: eighteenth-century views of childhood. Papers read at a Clark Library seminar 13 October 1979. Los Angeles, CA: William Andrews Clark Memorial Library, 1982. pp. vi, 50. Rev. by A. J. Sambrook in YES (16) 255–6.

6001. SPECK, W. A.   Society and literature in England, 1700–60. (Bibl. 1985, 5156.) Rev. by J. C. D. Clark in JMH (58:3) 713–15.

6002. STAVES, SUSAN.   Eighteenth-century feminism. ECent (26:2) 1985, 170–6 (review-article).

6003. THORSLEV, PETER L., JR.   Romantic contraries: freedom *versus* destiny. (Bibl. 1985, 5161.) Rev. by Donald H. Reiman in RPP (10:2) 65–9.

6004. TUVESON, ERNEST LEE.   The avatars of thrice great Hermes: an approach to Romanticism. (Bibl. 1985, 5241.) Rev. by Richard Gravil in MLR (81:3) 722–4.

6005. VON FRANK, ALBERT J.   The sacred game: provincialism and frontier consciousness in American literature, 1630–1860. *See* **5091.**

6006. WARNER, MICHAEL DAVID.   The letters of the Republic: literature and print in republican America. *See* **442.**

6007. WEBB, TIMOTHY (ed.).   English Romantic Hellenism, 1700–1824. (Bibl. 1985, 5165.) Rev. by Charles Martindale in MLR (81:1) 175–6.

6008. WEINBROT, HOWARD D.   The emperor's old toga: Augustanism and the scholarship of nostalgia. MP (83:3) 286–97 (review-article).

6009. WENDORF, RICHARD (ed.).   Articulate images: the sister arts from Hogarth to Tennyson. (Bibl. 1985, 5168.) Rev. by Bruce Redford in MP (83:3) 316–18; by Stephen Leo Carr in ECent (26:2) 1985, 203–8.

6010. WILDE, WILLIAM H.; HOOTON, JOY; ANDREWS, BARRY.   The Oxford companion to Australian literature. Melbourne; Oxford: OUP, 1985. pp. x, 760. Rev. by A. D. Hope in LRB (8:15) 10–11.

6011. WOMACK, P.   Improvement and romance: the Scottish Highlands in British writing after the Forty-Five. Unpub. doct. diss., Univ. of Edinburgh, 1985. [Abstr. in IT (35) 1085.]

Drama and the Theatre

6012. AGNEW, JEAN-CHRISTOPHE.   Worlds apart: the market and the theater in Anglo-American thought, 1550–1750. *See* **3867.**

6013. BARNES, J. P.   Exuberance and restriction in English drama, 1725–1741. Unpub. doct. diss., Univ. of Wales, Swansea, 1983.

6014. BOTICA, A.   Audience, playhouse and play in Restoration theatre. *See* **5102.**

6015. FREEMAN, TERENCE M.   With arched brow and leering eye: the resurgence of satiric drama in the British theatre of the third quarter of the eighteenth century. Unpub. doct. diss., Univ. of Pennsylvania, 1985. [Abstr. in DA (46) 2299A.]

6016. GOULDEN, R. J.   Margate entertainments. Factotum (15) 1982, 16–18. (Theatre bills.)

6017. HEROU, JOSETTE.   Jeux de l'âme et du corps sur la scène comique en Angleterre au XVIIIe siècle. *In* (pp. 87–98) **14.**

6018. —— Maîtres et valets dans la comédie anglaise du 18e siècle: ambiguïtés et inversions. *In* (pp. 97–110) **30.**

6019. HIGHFILL, PHILIP H., JR; BURNIM, KALMAN A.; LANGHANS, EDWARD A.   A biographical dictionary of actors, actresses, musicians, dancers, managers, and other stage personnel in London, 1660–1800: vol. 7, Habgood to Houbert; vol. 8, Hough to Keyse; vol. 9, Kickill to Machin; vol. 10, M'Intosh to Nash. *See* **5118.**

6020. KENDALL, KATHRYN MCQUEEN.   Theatre, society, and women playwrights in London from 1695 through the Queen Anne era. *See* **5124.**

6021. KENNY, SHIRLEY STRUM (ed.).   The performers and their plays. New York; London: Garland, 1982. pp. 600, in various pagings. (Eighteenth-century English drama.)

6022. KLINGLER, HELMUT.   'Tragedy' 1660–1737: terminology and genre. *See* **5126.**

6023. KNOTT, DAVID.   William Garner of Margate, librarian and actor. Factotum (16) 1983, 16–18.

6024. LIESENFELD, VINCENT J.   The Licensing Act of 1737. (Bibl. 1985, 5182.) Rev. by Robert D. Hume in MP (83:3) 313–16.

6025. MARSDEN, JEAN INGER.   The re-imagined text: Shakespeare, adaptation, and theory in the Restoration and eighteenth century. *See* **4528.**

6026. MILHOUS, JUDITH; HUME, ROBERT D.   Producible interpretation: eight English plays, 1675–1707. *See* **5138.**

6027. —— —— (eds).   Vice-Chamberlain Coke's theatrical papers,

1706–1715. (Bibl. 1985, 5183.) Rev. by Charles H. Shattuck in YES (16) 258–9; by Phyllis T. Dirks in TS (28/29) 1981/82–1982/83, 101–2.

6028.   MOHR, HANS-ULRICH.   Lillos *The London Merchant* – ein 'bürgerliches' Trauerspiel? GRM (36:3) 267–88.

6029.   RALPH, RICHARD.   The life and works of John Weaver: an account of his life and theatrical productions, with an annotated reprint of his complete publications. London: Dance Books, 1985. pp. xii, 1075.

6030.   RANGER, P. V.   Terror and pity reign in every breast: gothic drama in the London patent theatres 1750–1820. Unpub. doct. diss., Univ. of Southampton, 1984.

6031.   RITCHEY, DAVID.   A guide to the Baltimore stage in the eighteenth century: a history and day book calendar. (Bibl. 1983, 5702.) Rev. by Gerald Kahan in TS (28/29) 1981/82–1982/83, 111–12.

6032.   ROSENFELD, SYBIL.   The Georgian theatre of Richmond, Yorkshire and its circuit. (Bibl. 1985, 5187.) Rev. by Marion Jones in NQ (33:2) 246.

6033.   STONE, GEORGE WINCHESTER, JR (ed.).   The stage and the page: London's 'whole show' in the eighteenth-century theatre. (Bibl. 1985, 5190.) Rev. by Harold Love in YES (16) 256-8.

6034.   TROOST, LINDA VERONIKA.   The rise of English comic opera: 1762–1800. Unpub. doct. diss., Univ. of Pennsylvania, 1985. [Abstr. in DA (46) 2304A.]

Fiction

6035.   ALDISS, BRIAN W.; WINGROVE, DAVID.   Trillion year spree: the history of science fiction. London: Gollancz. pp. 511. Rev. by John Clute in TLS, 31 Oct., 1223.

6036.   ANDRIANO, JOSEPH DOMINIC.   Our ladies of darkness: Jungian readings of the female daimon in gothic fiction. Unpub. doct. diss., Washington State Univ. [Abstr. in DA (47) 2150A.]

6037.   BAILEY, JUTTA M.   A study of women characters in selected novels of women writers of the Romantic period. Unpub. doct diss., Univ. of Arkansas, 1985. [Abstr. in DA (46) 3024A.]

6038.   BALL, ROLAND C.   The new forms of the novel in the period of Romanticism. *In* (pp. 155–60) **19.**

6039.   BARKER, GERARD A.   Grandison's heirs: the paragon's progress in the late eighteenth-century novel. Newark, NJ: Delaware UP; London: Assoc. UPs, 1985. pp. 187.

6040.   BARTOLOMEO, JOSEPH FRANCIS.   A poetics of fiction: eighteenth-century foundations. Unpub. doct. diss., Harvard Univ. [Abstr. in DA (47) 2165A.]

6041.   BEASLEY, JERRY C.   Facts about fiction: two new books on the early history of the novel. ECent (27:1) 62–71 (review-article).

6042.   —— Novels of the 1740s. (Bibl. 1985, 5196.) Rev. by Osamu Izumiya in YES (16) 272–3.

6043.   BOUCÉ, PAUL-GABRIEL (ed.).   Sexuality in eighteenth-century Britain. (Bibl. 1985, 5198.) Rev. by Jerry C. Beasley in MLR (81:4) 990–2.

6044. CARTER, MARGARET LOUISE. 'Fiend, spectre, or delusion?':
narrative doubt and the supernatural in gothic fiction. Unpub. doct.
diss., Univ. of California, Irvine. [Abstr. in DA (47) 908A.]
6045. CASTLE, TERRY. Masquerade and civilisation: the carnival-
esque in eighteenth-century English culture and fiction. London:
Methuen. pp. x, 395.
6046. CHARD, C. R. Horror and terror in literature of the Grand
Tour, and in the gothic novel. *See* **5199.**
6047. COX, J. H. 'Carnation and colouring': sentimentalism in *The
Universal Magazine of Knowledge and Pleasure. See* **578.**
6048. FLANDERS, WALLACE AUSTIN. Structures of experience:
history, society, and personal life in the eighteenth-century British
novel. (Bibl. 1985, 5203.) Rev. by Ira Konigsberg in MLS (16:3) 363–7.
6049. FOSTER, JAMES OTIS. Puritanism, character, and narrative in
the eighteenth-century English novel. Unpub. doct. diss., Univ. of
Virginia. [Abstr. in DA (47) 1733A.]
6050. FURST, LILIAN R. Fictions of romantic irony in European
narrative 1760–1857. Cambridge MA: Harvard UP, 1984. (Bibl. 1985,
5204.) Rev. by Logan Spiers in EngS (67:6) 572–4; by Stuart M. Sperry
in JEGP (85:1) 134–5.
6051. GRANT, RENA JANE. From Clarissa to Lady Chatterley:
character in the British novel. Unpub. doct. diss., Yale Univ., 1985.
[Abstr. in DA (47) 1334A.]
6052. GREGORY, P. The popular fiction of the eighteenth-century
commercial circulating libraries. *See* **228.**
6053. GRENIER, CECILIA MARIE. Martyrs, mystics and madwomen:
images of the nun in selected fiction, 1780–1840. Unpub. doct. diss.,
State Univ. of New York at Binghamton. [Abstr. in DA (47) 524A.]
6054. HAHN, H. GEORGE; BEHM, CARL, III. The eighteenth-century
British novel and its background: an annotated bibliography and guide
to topics. Metuchen, NJ; London: Scarecrow Press, 1985. pp. ix, 392.
Rev. in BB (43:3) 186.
6055. JONES, JOSEPH; JONES, JOHANNA. Canadian fiction. Boston,
MA: G. K. Hall, 1981. pp. 180. (Twayne's world authors, 630.) Rev. by
David Staines in MLR (80:2) 450–1.
6056. KINKEAD-WEEKES, MARK. Dr Johnson on the rise of the novel.
NRam (24) 1983, 28–9.
6057. KNIGHT, CHARLES A. Satire and conversation: the logic of
interpretation. ECent (26:3) 1985, 239–61.
6058. KONIGSBERG, IRA. Narrative technique in the English novel:
Defoe to Austen. Hamden, CT: Archon. Rev. by Anthony Kearney in
THES (698) 25.
6059. LANGBAUER, LAURIE. Empty constructions: women and
romance in the English novel. Unpub. doct. diss., Cornell Univ., 1985.
[Abstr. in DA (46) 2700A.]
6060. LÉVY, MAURICE. Le roman gothique, genre anglais. Europe
(62:659) 1984, 5–13.
6061. MACEY, SAMUEL L. Money and the novel: mercenary

motivation in Defoe and his immediate successors. (Bibl. 1985, 5441.) Rev. by Maximillian E. Novak in MLR (81:2) 448–9; by G. Douglas Atkins in ECent (26:3) 1985, 297–305.

6062. MILLER, NANCY K.   The heroine's text: readings in the French and English novel, 1722–1782. (Bibl. 1983, 5723.) Rev. by Roseann Runte in CanRCL (12:3) 1985, 537–9; by John C. O'Neal in ECL (10:2) 87–97.

6063. MORVAN, ALAIN.   La tolérance dans le roman anglais de 1726 à 1771. (Bibl. 1984, 5383.) Rev. by Ian Campbell Ross in EA (38:4) 1985, 463–5.

6064. O'NEAL, JOHN C.   Review essay: eighteenth-century female protagonists and the dialectics of desire. ECL (10:2) 87–97.

6065. POPKIN, SUSAN MARSHA.   The aesthetics of narrative self-consciousness in eighteenth-century fiction, biography, and history: a study of the narrator and the reader. Unpub. doct. diss., New York Univ. [Abstr. in DA (47) 1337A.]

6066. REITZ, ANN L.   Sawbones to savior to cynic: the doctor's relation to society in English fiction of the eighteenth, nineteenth, and twentieth centuries. Unpub. doct. diss., Univ. of Cincinnati, 1985. [Abstr. in DA (46) 2701A.]

6067. ROSS, IAN CAMPBELL.   Rewriting Irish literary history: the case of the Irish novel. EA (39:4) 385–9.

6068. SAMUELS, SHIRLEY.   The family, the state, and the novel in the early Republic. AmQ (38:3) 381–95.

6069. SCHEUERMANN, MONA.   Social protest in the eighteenth-century English novel. Columbus: Ohio State UP, 1985. pp. 247.

6070. SHROFF, HOMAI J.   The eighteenth-century novel: the idea of the gentleman. (Bibl. 1985, 5216.) Rev. by A. F. T. Lurcock in NQ (33:2) 245.

6071. SMITH, GRAHAME.   The novel and society: Defoe to George Eliot. Totowa, NJ: Barnes & Noble, 1984. (Cf. bibl. 1984, 5392.) Rev. by Robert C. Schweik in JEGP (85:3) 459–61.

6072. SPENCER, JANE.   The rise of the woman novelist: from Aphra Behn to Jane Austen. *See* **5167.**

6073. TODD, JANET.   Women's friendship in literature. (Bibl. 1984, 5395.) Rev. by John C. O'Neal in ECL (10:2) 87–97.

6074. TOMPKINS, JANE P.   Sensational designs: the cultural work of American fiction, 1790–1860. (Bibl. 1985, 5219.) Rev. by Emily Stipes Watts in CR (30:3) 415–16; by Carl Brucker in SCR (3:4) 106–9; by Julian Moynahan in TLS, 14 Feb., 170; by Terence Martin in AL (58:4) 626–8; by Lora Romero in WHR (40:4) 373–6.

6075. VIROLLE, ROLAND.   Madame de Genlis, mercier de Compiègne: gothique anglais ou gothique allemand? Europe (62:659) 1984, 29–38.

6076. WARD, PATRICIA A.   Medievalism in the Romantic novel. *In* (pp. 35–9) **19.**

Literature for Children

6077. BALIBAR, RENÉE.   National language, education, literature. *In* (pp. 126–47) **29.**

6078. FEARN, M.   Childhood and the image of the child in English children's literature, 1760–1830. Unpub. doct. diss., Univ. of Loughborough, 1984. [Abstr. in IT (35) 46.]

6079. JOHN RYLANDS UNIVERSITY LIBRARY OF MANCHESTER.   Children's books of yesterday: a survey of 200 years of children's reading: an exhibition in the Deansgate Building, Winter 1985. *See* **242.**

6080. PICKERING, SAMUEL, JR.   Allegory and the first school stories. *In* (pp. 42–68) **40.**

6081. SUMMERFIELD, GEOFFREY.   Fantasy and reason: children's literature in the eighteenth century. Athens: Georgia UP, 1985. (Cf. bibl. 1985, 5223.) Rev. by Winfred Kaminski in LU (10) 167–70; by Janet Todd in BJECS (9:2) 276–7.

6082. WATTERS, DAVID H.   'I spake as a child': authority, metaphor and *The New-England Primer*. EAL (20:3) 1985/86, 193–213.

Poetry

6083. ARNOLD, R. A.   The English hymn in the eighteenth century: an historical and critical study. Unpub. doct. diss., Univ. of Edinburgh, 1983.

6084. BARRY, K. M.   Language, music and the sign: a study in aesthetics, poetics and poetic practice from Collins to Coleridge. Unpub. doct. diss., Univ. of Cambridge. [Abstr. in IT (36) 20.]

6085. BRADFORD, R. W.   An investigation of theories of prosody and poetic form in the Restoration and eighteenth century, with special reference to blank verse. *See* **5169.**

6086. BROWNE, R.   A George for an Oliver. *See* **5170.**

6087. CLARK, S. H.   Blake's *Milton* and the response to Locke in the poetry of sensibility. *See* **5606.**

6088. DOODY, MARGARET ANNE.   The daring muse: Augustan poetry reconsidered. *See* **5173.**

6089. FORSTER, HAROLD.   Poems autographed by the author. Factotum (6) 1979, 12–14.

6090. —— Poems autographed by the author – further notes. Factotum (9) 1980, 10–11.

6091. FOXON, DAVID.   Poems autographed by the author. Factotum (8) 1980, 21–3.

6092. FRAISTAT, NEIL.   The poem and the book: interpreting collections of Romantic poetry. (Bibl. 1985, 5229.) Rev. by Charles E. Lloyd in ANQ (24:9/10) 160.

6093. GOODWIN, DAVID GORDON.   The rhetoric of British rhetorical handbooks (1758–1828) and Romantic modes of English epic poetry. *See* **1163.**

6094. GOULDEN, R. J.   The authorship of Foxon's P1138. Factotum (5) 1979, 14–15.

6095. GRIFFIN, DUSTIN.   Milton and the decline of epic in the eighteenth century. *See* **5722.**

6096. GRIFFIN, DUSTIN H.   Regaining paradise: Milton and the eighteenth century. *See* **5723.**

6097. HARRISON, FRANK LL.   Music, poetry and polity in the age of Swift. ECI (1) 37–63.

6098. HOROWITZ, K. J.   Poets and epitaphs in the eighteenth and early nineteenth centuries: Pope to Wordsworth. Unpub. doct. diss., Univ. of Cambridge, 1985. [Abstr. in IT (35) 544.]

6099. IREYS, VIRGINIA FOOTE.   Pastoral heroines in eighteenth-century English poetry. Unpub. doct. diss., Univ. of California, Berkeley, 1985. [Abstr. in DA (47) 911A.]

6100. KINSLEY, WILLIAM.   'Allusion' in the eighteenth century: the disinherited critic. *In* (pp. 23–45) ROBERT JAMES MERRETT (ed.)., Man and nature: proceedings of the Canadian Society for Eighteenth-Century Studies: vol. 3. Edmonton, Alta.: Academic Printing & Publishing, 1984. pp. xii, 162.

6101. KNAPP, STEVEN.   Personification and the sublime: Milton to Coleridge. *See* **5177.**

6102. LONSDALE, ROGER.   The new Oxford book of eighteenth century verse. (Bibl. 1985, 5232.) Rev. by Craig Raine in LRev, Feb. 1985, 6–8.

6103. MARSHALL, MADELEINE FORELL; TODD, JANET.   English congregational hymns in the eighteenth century. (Cf. bibl. 1984, 5404, where first scholar's surname omitted.) Rev. by W. Hutchings in MLR (81:2) 445–6.

6104. PRESTON, CATHY LYNN MAKIN.   The ballad tradition and the making of meaning. Unpub. doct. diss., Univ. of Colorado at Boulder. [Abstr. in DA (47) 2171A.]

6105. RIEHLE, WOLFGANG.   The fragment in English Romantic poetry. *In* (pp. 133–8) **11.**

6106. SAMPSON, H. GRANT.   The physico-theological epic in the later eighteenth century. *In* (pp. 49–60) ROGER L. EMERSON, WILLIAM KINGSLEY, and WALTER MOSER (eds), Man and nature: proceedings of the Canadian Society for Eighteenth-Century Studies: vol. 2. Montreal: Canadian Society for Eighteenth-Century Studies, 1984. pp. xi, 156.

6107. SCHULZ, MAX F.   Paradise preserved: recreations of Eden in eighteenth- and nineteenth-century England. Cambridge: CUP, 1985. pp. xviii, 384. Rev. by J. R. Watson in THES (699) 17.

6108. SCODEL, JOSHUA KEITH.   Lapidary texts: the English poetic epitaph from Jonson to Pope. *See* **5188.**

6109. SEYMOUR, BARBARA JEAN.   A radiant trail: the extension of the conceit through eighteenth-century English poetry. Unpub. doct. diss., Univ. of Oregon, 1985. [Abstr. in DA (47) 190A.]

6110. SHIELDS, DAVID S.   Mental nocturnes: night thoughts on man and nature in the poetry of eighteenth-century America. PMHB (110:2) 237–58.

6111. SIMPKINS, SCOTT KEITH.   The semiotic dilemma of English Romantic poetry. *See* **2290.**

6112. STOCKDALE-KLAUS, LISA FLORENCE.   Criteria for evaluating the English neoclassical imitation of classical and foreign verse satire, 1600–1750. *See* **5190.**

6113. VOGLER, THOMAS A.   The tropology of silence in eighteenth-century English blank verse. ECent (26:3) 1985, 211–37.

6114. WHITELEY, P.   'These happy studies of our prime': Mark Akenside's *The Pleasures of Imagination* and 'the pleasures of the imagination' and their relation to the poetry of the eighteenth century. Unpub. doct. diss., Univ. of Manchester, 1981.

6115. WILLIAMS, ANNE.   Prophetic strain: the greater lyric in the eighteenth century. (Bibl. 1985, 5245.) Rev. by Douglas Brooks-Davies in BJECS (9:2) 258–9.

6116. WOOD, N. P.   The decline of the neo-classical pastoral, 1680–1730: a study in Theocritean and Virgilian influence. *See* **5195.**

Prose

6117. BROWNE, RON.   Humbugs and waggeries. Factotum (22) 20–2.

6118. BUTLER, MARILYN (ed.).   Burke, Paine, Godwin, and the Revolution controversy. (Bibl. 1985, 5247.) Rev. by Mark Philip in BJECS (9:2) 244–6.

6119. CHARD, C. R.   Horror and terror in literature of the Grand Tour, and in the gothic novel. *See* **5199.**

6120. FERGUSON, ROBERT A.   'We hold these truths': strategies of control in the literature of the Founders. *In* (pp. 1–28) **47.**

6121. FIREOVED, JOSEPH D.   An anthology of colonial sermons. *See* **5202.**

6122. GREENFIELD, BRUCE ROBERT.   The rhetoric of discovery: British and American exploration narratives, 1760–1845 and American renaissance writing. Unpub. doct. diss., Columbia Univ., 1985. [Abstr. in DA (46) 2293A.]

6123. PITCHER, E. W.   Some puzzling reprintings of literary prose in the final years of the *Town and Country Magazine*. *See* **672.**

6124. POSSIN, HANS-JOACHIM.   Englische Reiseliteratur des 18. Jahrhunderts. Ang (103:1/2) 1985, 96–108.

6125. REDFORD, BRUCE.   The converse of the pen: acts of intimacy in the eighteenth-century familiar letter. Chicago; London: Chicago UP. pp. ix, 252.

6126. SECOR, ROBERT.   The significance of Pennsylvania's eighteenth-century jest books. *See* **2486.**

6127. STEPHAN, SANDRA WHITE.   'Solid sense and elegant expression': the rhetorical backgrounds of the eighteenth-century essay. Unpub. doct. diss., Tulane Univ., 1985. [Abstr. in DA (47) 191A.]

6128. VAN DELFT, LOUIS.   La notion de 'caractère' á l'âge classique. *In* (pp. 59–63) **11.**

6129. WAKELIN, MARTYN F. The *Exmoor Courtship* and *Exmoor Scolding*: an evaluation of two eighteenth-century dialect texts. *In* (pp. 741–51) **26.**

Biography and Autobiography

6130. ERTL, HEIMO. 'The manner wherein God has dealt with my soul': Methodistische *Lives* im 18. Jahrhundert. Ang (104:1/2) 63–93.
6131. POPKIN, SUSAN MARSHA. The aesthetics of narrative self-consciousness in eighteenth-century fiction, biography, and history: a study of the narrator and the reader. *See* **6065.**

Related Studies

6132. BARIDON, MICHEL. Jardins et paysages: existe-t-il un style anglais? Dix-huitième siècle (18) 427–46.
6133. BARRELL, JOHN. The political theory of painting from Reynolds to Hazlitt: 'the body of the public'. New Haven, CT; London: Yale UP. pp. viii, 366. Rev. by Marina Warner in Independent, 20 Nov., 11.
6134. BLOCH, RUTH H. Visionary republic: millennial themes in American thought, 1756–1800. Cambridge: CUP, 1985. pp. xvi, 291. (Cf. bibl. 1981, 5899.)
6135. BLONDEL, MADELEINE. Deux ecclésiastiques anglais et leurs domestiques au 18e siècle. *In* (pp. 181–96) **30.**
6136. BRUNETEAU, CLAUDE. La maladie anglaise. *In* (pp. 11–24) **14.**
6137. CALDWELL, RONALD J. The era of the French Revolution: a bibliography of the history of Western civilization 1789–1799. New York; London: Garland, 1985. 2 vols. pp. 1299. (Garland reference library of social science, 284.)
6138. CARR, STEPHEN LEO. Unarticulated questions. ECent (26:2) 1985, 203–8 (review-article).
6139. CARRÉ, JACQUES. Architecture et société britanniques au XVIIIe siècle: pour une problématique. *In* (pp. 7–19) **1.**
6140. CHITNIS, ANAND C. The Scottish Enlightenment and early Victorian English society. London: Croom Helm. pp. vi, 201.
6141. COHEN, RALPH (ed.). Studies in eighteenth-century British art and aesthetics. Berkeley; London: California UP, 1985. pp. x, 244. (Clark Library pubs, UCLA, 9.)
6142. COUNTRYMAN, EDWARD. The people's American Revolution. London: British Assn for American Studies, 1983. pp. 47. (BAAS pamphlets in American studies, 13.)
6143. DAICHES, DAVID; JONES, PETER; JONES, JEAN (eds). A hotbed of genius: the Scottish Enlightenment 1730–1790. Edinburgh: Edinburgh UP. pp. xi, 160.
6144. DAVIES, HUNTER. The grand tour. London: Hamilton. pp. 224.
6145. DESFOND, HÉLÈNE. Tyburn chez Mandeville et Fielding, ou le corps exemplaire du pendu. *In* (pp. 61–70) **14.**
6146. DIMIĆ, MILAN V. Vampiromania in the eighteenth century: the other side of Enlightenment. *In* (pp. 1–22) ROBERT JAMES MERRETT (ed.), Man and nature: proceedings of the Canadian Society for

Eighteenth-Century Studies: vol. 3. Edmonton, Alta.: Academic Printing & Publishing, 1984. pp. xii, 162.

6147. DUTRUCH, SUZANNE.   Henry et John Fielding magistrates: âme de la ville et corps de la police. *In* (pp. 71–86) **14.**

6148. FRUCHTMAN, JACK, JR.   The apocalyptic politics of Richard Price and Joseph Priestley: a study in late eighteenth-century English millennialism. Philadelphia, PA: American Philosophical Soc., 1983. pp. 125. Rev. by Arthur H. Williamson in JHP (24:3) 418–20.

6149. HARLAN, DAVID.   A world of double visions and second thoughts: Jonathan Dickinson's 'Display of God's special grace'. EAL (21:2) 118–30.

6150. HILL, BRIDGET (comp.).   Eighteenth-century women: an anthology. London: Allen & Unwin, 1984. pp. ix, 271. Rev. by Margarette Smith in BJECS (9:1) 95–6.

6151. IKIN, BRIDGET.   The re-talesman of Grub Street. Factotum (5) 1979, 27–30. (Hack's advertisement.)

6152. JENNINGS, HUMPHREY (comp.); JENNINGS, MARY-LOU; MADGE, CHARLES (eds).   Pandaemonium, 1660–1886: the coming of the machine as seen by contemporary observers. *See* **5230.**

6153. JOHNSON, E. D. H.   Paintings of the British social scene from Hogarth to Sickert. New York: Rizzoli; London: Weidenfeld & Nicolson. pp. 287. Rev. by Gerald Weales in Smithsonian (17:8) 210–11.

6154. JOUVE, MICHEL.   Corps difformes et âmes perverses: quelques réflexions sur la pratique de la caricature. *In* (pp. 111–20) **14.**

6155. LACROIX, JEAN-MICHEL.   La publicité des produits pharmaceutiques dans la presse anglaise du XVIIIe siècle. *In* (pp. 37–50) **14.**

6156. LAMOINE, GEORGES.   L'âme et le corps en prison au XVIIIe siècle. *In* (pp. 51–60) **14.**

6157. LEITES, EDMUND.   The Puritan conscience and modern sexuality. *See* **5234.**

6158. MARTINET, MARIE-MADELEINE.   Les espaces de la mémoire créatrice en Angleterre aux XVIIe et XVIIIe siècles. *In* (pp. 59–74) **34.**

6159. MITCHELL, BRIGITTE.   Le corps et l'âme du Révérend John Penrose. *In* (pp. 25–36) **14.**

6160. MONTGOMERY, MICHAEL S. (comp.).   American Puritan studies: an annotated bibliography of dissertations, 1882–1981. *See* **5237.**

6161. MORROW, NANCY V.   The problem of slavery in the polemic literature of the American Enlightenment. EAL (20:3) 1985/86, 236–55.

6162. MUSSELWHITE, DAVID.   The trial of Warren Hastings. *In* (pp. 77–103) **29.**

6163. ROSS, IAN.   Adam Smith as rhetorician. *In* (pp. 61–74) ROGER L. EMERSON, WILLIAM KINSLEY, and WALTER MOSER (eds), Man and nature: proceedings of the Canadian Society for Eighteenth-Century Studies: vol. 2. Montreal: Canadian Society for Eighteenth-Century Studies, 1984. pp. xi, 156.

6164. SCHIEBINGER, LONDA.   Skeletons in the closet: the first illustrations of the female skeleton in eighteenth-century anatomy. Representations (14) 42–82.

6165. SHER, RICHARD B.   Church and university in the Scottish Enlightenment: the moderate literati of Edinburgh. Princeton, NJ: Princeton UP; Edinburgh: Edinburgh UP, 1985. pp. xix, 389.

6166. SOLKIN, DAVID H.   Portraiture in motion: Edward Penny's *Marquis of Granby* and the creation of a public for English art. HLQ (49:1) 1–23.

6167. SPROTT, DUNCAN.   1784. *See* **698.**

6168. STOUT, HARRY S.   The New England soul: preaching and religious culture in colonial New England. *See* **5247.**

6169. TURNER, PATRICIA ANN.   Tampered truths: a rhetorical analysis of antebellum slave narratives. Unpub. doct. diss., Univ. of California, Berkeley, 1985. [Abstr. in DA (47) 1025A.]

6170. TURNER, ROGER.   Capability Brown: and the eighteenth-century English landscape. London: Weidenfeld & Nicolson, 1985. pp. 204.

6171. VAN LANINGHAM, KATHY MANDRELL.   *The Memoirs of Count de Gramont*: a new translation and annotation. Unpub. doct. diss., Univ. of Arkansas, 1985. [Abstr. in DA (47) 1737A.]

6172. YAZAWA, MELVIN.   From colonies to commonwealth: familial ideology and the beginnings of the American republic. Baltimore, MD; London: Johns Hopkins UP, 1985. pp. ix, 261. (New studies in American intellectual and cultural history.)

Literary Theory

This section is intended to contain studies **about** the literary theory, literary historiography, literary criticsm, etc., produced *in* the eighteenth century. For modern works **of** literary history and criticism dealing generally with this period, see under 'Eighteenth Century: General Literary Studies'.

6173. BARONE, DENNIS.   James Logan and Gilbert Tennent: enlightened classicist versus awakened evangelist. EAL (21:2) 103–17.

6174. COHEN, MURRAY.   Eighteenth-century English literature and modern critical methodologies. ECent (20:1) 1979, 5–23.

6175. KINSLEY, WILLIAM.   'Allusion' in the eighteenth century: the disinherited critic. *See* **6100.**

6176. MARSHALL, DONALD G.   The history of eighteenth-century criticism and modern hermeneutical philosophy: the example of Richard Hurd. ECent (21:3) 1980, 198–211.

6177. SMITH, DEBRA MORRIS.   The idea of inspiration in eighteenth-century literary theory. SAQ (85:2) 183–91.

6178. TODD, JANET.   Sensibility: an introduction. London: Methuen. pp. 169.

6179. ULMAN, HOWARD LEWIS, III.   Thought and language in George Campbell's *The Philosophy of Rhetoric*. Unpub. doct. diss., Pennsylvania State Univ., 1985. [Abstr. in DA (47) 163A.]

6180.   ZACH, WOLFGANG.   Das Stereotyp als literarische Norm. Zum dominanten Denkmodell des Klassizismus. *See* **2779.**

AUTHORS
Joseph Addison

6181.   ALSOP, J. D.   Joseph Addison's income from the *London Gazette*, 1717–1718. *See* **554.**

6182.   EVANS, JAMES E.   Mr Review on the 'glorious' *Tatler* and the 'inimitable' *Spectator*. *See* **595.**

6183.   GAMEZ, LUIS RENE.   The 'angel' image in Addison's *The Campaign*. NQ (33:4) 486–9.

6184.   KNIGHT, CHARLES A.   Bibliography and the shape of the literary periodical in the early eighteenth century. *See* **634.**

6185.   LOCKWOOD, THOMAS.   An Addison borrowing from Molière. RLC (59:4) 425–6.

6186.   LOUGH, JOHN.   Two more British travellers in the France of Louis XIV. Seventeenth Century (1:2) 159–75.

6187.   OTTEN, ROBERT M.   Joseph Addison. Boston, MA: G. K. Hall, 1982. pp. xiv, 182. (Twayne's English authors, 338.) Rev. by Alba Graziano in YES (16) 261–2.

6188.   PRESCOTT, ANDREW.   Some further letters to the *Tatler* and the *Spectator*. *See* **674.**

John Aikin

6189.   PLANK, JEFFREY.   John Aikin on science and poetry. Studies in Burke and his Time (18:3) 1977, 167–78.

Mark Akenside

6190.   DIX, R. C.   A critical introduction to Akenside's *The Pleasures of (the) Imagination*. Unpub. doct. diss. Univ. of Oxford, 1983.

6191.   DIX, ROBIN.   The composition of Akenside's *The Pleasures of the Imagination* (1772). NQ (33:4) 521–3.

6192.   JUMP, HARRIET.   Akenside's other epistle. NQ (33:4) 508–12.

6193.   WHITELEY, P.   'These happy studies of our prime': Mark Akenside's *The Pleasures of Imagination* and 'the pleasures of the imagination' and their relation to the poetry of the eighteenth century. *See* **6114.**

Nicholas Amhurst

6194.   RIVERS, WILLIAM E.   Nicholas Amhurst's *Terrae Filius* as background for Pope's satire of university education. *See* **679.**

Mary Astell

6195.   HILL, BRIDGET (ed.).   The first English feminist: *Reflections upon Marriage* and other writings by Mary Astell. Aldershot: Gower/Temple Smith. pp. 244.

6196.   KINNAIRD, JOAN K.   Mary Astell: inspired by ideas (1668–1731). *In* (pp. 28–39) **20.**

6197.   PERRY, RUTH.   The celebrated Mary Astell: an early English feminist. Chicago; London: Chicago UP. pp. xiv, 549. (Women in culture and society.)

Robert Bage
6198. FAULKNER, PETER (ed.). Hermsprong, or, Man as he is not. (Bibl. 1985, 5295.) Rev. by T. W. Craik in BJECS (9:2) 270.

Joel Barlow
6199. CAMFIELD, GREGG. Joel Barlow's dialectic of progress. EAL (21:2) 131–43.

James Beattie
6200. KING, EVERARD H. Wordsworth and Beattie's *Minstrel*: the progress of poetic autobiography. YREAL (3) 1985, 131–62.

William Beckford
6201. C., C. W. (ed.). A dialogue in the shades: Rare doings at Roxburghe Hall. Ipswich: Cox, 1985. pp. 213. (Facsim. of ed. pub. London, 1819.)
6202. MAVOR, ELIZABETH (ed.). The grand tour of William Beckford: selections from *Dreams, Waking Thoughts and Incidents*. Harmondsworth: Penguin. pp. 161. (Penguin travel library.)

Richard Bentley
6203. JESTIN, LOFTUS HUGH DUDLEY. Richard Bentley the Younger (1708–1782): a critical biography. Unpub. doct. diss., Yale Univ., 1985. 2 vols. [Abstr. in DA (46) 3359A.]

George Berkeley
6204. BERMAN, DAVID. Berkeley's *Siris* and the 'whisky patriots'. ECI (1) 200–3.
6205. —— (ed.). George Berkeley: essays and replies. Dublin: Irish Academic Press, 1985. pp. 171.
6206. DUPAS, JEAN-CLAUDE. Le visible et l'invisible chez Berkeley. Études irlandaises (11) (SOFEIR supp.) 45–56.
6207. FLAGE, DANIEL E. Berkeley on abstraction. JHP (24:4) 483–501.
6208. KEARNEY, RICHARD. Berkeley and the Irish mind. Études irlandaises (11) (SOFEIR supp.) 27–43.
6209. KELLY, PATRICK. Berkeley and Ireland. Études irlandaises (11) (SOFEIR supp.) 7–25.
6210. PITCHER, GEORGE. Berkeley on the perception of objects. JHP (24:1) 99–105.
6211. RABATÉ, JEAN-MICHEL. Berkeley entre Joyce et Beckett. Études irlandaises (11) (SOFEIR supp.) 57–76.

William Blake
6212. ADAMS, HAZARD. The dizziness of freedom; or, why I read William Blake. CE (48:5) 431–43.
6213. AUBREY, BRYAN. Watchman of eternity: Blake's debt to Jacob Boehme. Lanham, MD; London: UP of America. pp. xiii, 193.
6214. BARIDON, MICHEL. '"Copy for ever" is my rule': Blake lecteur de Reynolds dans le débat sur memoire et création. *In* (pp. 75–87) **34.**
6215. BATE, JONATHAN. Shakespeare and the English Romantic imagination. *See* **4381.**
6216. BEHRENDT, STEPHEN C. 'The consequence of high powers': Blake, Shelley, and prophecy's public dimension. PLL (22:3) 254–75.

6217. —— 'This accursed family': Blake's *America* and the American Revolution. ECent (27:1) 26–51.

6218. BENTLEY, G. E., JR.   The way of a papermaker with a poet: Joshua Gilpin, William Blake, and the arts in 1796. NQ (33:1) 80–4.

6219. —— The way of a papermaker with a poet: Joshua Gilpin, William Blake, and the arts in 1796: a postscript. NQ (33:4) 525.

6220. —— William Blake, musician. RCEI (12) 147–51.

6221. BIDNEY, MARTIN.   Solomon and Pharaoh's daughter: Blake's response to Wordsworth's prospectus to *The Recluse*. JEGP (85:4) 532–49.

6222. BILLIGHEIMER, RACHEL V.   The dance as vision in Blake and Yeats. UES (24:2) 11–16.

6223. —— The eighth eye: prophetic vision in Blake's poetry and design. CLQ (22:2) 93–110.

6224. BINDMAN, DAVID.   William Blake and popular religious imagery. Burlington Magazine (128) 712–17.

6225. BORKOWSKA, EWA.   Iconography and iconology: a study of William Blake's illuminated poetry. KN (33) 165–74.

6226. BRACHER, MARK.   'Being form'd'; thinking through Blake's *Milton*. Barrytown, NY: Station Hill Press, 1985. pp. xvi, 288. Rev. by Nelson Hilton in RPP (10:1) 67–70.

6227. CLARK, S. H.   Blake's *Milton* and the response to Locke in the poetry of sensibility. *See* **5606.**

6228. DÎRLĂU, ANDREI.   Metapoesis la Blake şi Eminescu. (Metapoesis in the works of Blake and Eminescu.) Amfiteatru (20:6) 8.

6229. ELLIS, HELEN.   Blake's 'Bible of Hell': *Visions of the Daughters of Albion* and the Song of Solomon. ESCan (12:1) 23–36.

6230. ESSICK, ROBERT N.   Variation, accident, and intention in William Blake's *The Book of Urizen*. SB (39) 230–5.

6231. FERBER, MICHAEL.   The social vision of William Blake. (Bibl. 1985, 5323.) Rev. by Jenijoy La Belle in RPP (10:1) 63–6; by Karen Shabetai in Criticism (28:3) 343–6.

6232. FURIA, PHILIP.   Pound and Blake on Hell. Paideuma (10:3) 1981, 599–601.

6233. GARDNER, STANLEY.   Blake's *Innocence and Experience* retraced. London: Athlone Press. pp. 211.

6234. GEORGE, DIANA HUME.   Reading Isaiah and Ezekiel through Blake. NOR (13:3) 12–21.

6235. GLAUSSER, WAYNE.   A note on the twenty years of Blake's Spectre. ELN (24:2) 43–4.

6236. GLECKNER, ROBERT F.   Blake and Spenser. *See* **4253.**

6237. GLEN, HEATHER.   Vision and disenchantment: Blake's *Songs* and Wordsworth's *Lyrical Ballads*. (Bibl. 1985, 5327.) Rev. by François Piquet in EA (38:4) 1985, 465–6.

6238. GODARD, JERRY CARIS.   Mental forms creating: William Blake anticipates Freud, Jung, and Rank. Lanham, MD; London: UP of America, 1985. pp. 173.

6239. GOURLAY, ALEXANDER S.   Blake's sisters: a critical edition, with commentary, of *The Book of Thel* and *Visions of the Daughters of Albion*. Unpub. doct. diss., Univ. of Iowa, 1985. [Abstr. in DA (46) 2699A.]

6240. GRECO, NORMA A.   Mother figures in Blake's *Songs of Innocence* and the female will. RPP (10:1) 1–15.

6241. GRESHAM, GWENDOLYN HOLLOWAY PARHAM.   The voice of honest indignation: William Blake's critique of the polity, liturgy, ethics, and theology of the Church of England. Unpub. doct. diss., Univ. of Arkansas, 1985. [Abstr. in DA (46) 3040A.]

6242. GROSS, DAVID.   Infinite indignation: teaching, dialectical vision, and Blake's *Marriage of Heaven and Hell*. CE (48:2) 175–86.

6243. —— 'Mind-forg'd manacles': hegemony and counter-hegemony in Blake. ECent (27:1) 3–25.

6244. HAMPSEY, JOHN.   *Tiriel* revisited: the case of problem children. Greyfriar (27) 31–48.

6245. HILTON, NELSON.   Blake in the chains of being. ECent (21:3) 1980, 212–35.

6246. —— The heavy metal of Blake's language. NOR (13:3) 34–9.

6247. —— Literal imagination: Blake's vision of words. (Bibl. 1985, 5332.) Rev. by David Fuller in BJECS (9:2) 269–70.

6248. HIMY, ARMAND.   Blake et l'apocalyptique dans *Jérusalem*. *In* (pp. 131–47) **2.**

6249. HIRST, DESIRÉE.   The theosophical preoccupations of Blake and Yeats. AJES (11) 209–31.

6250. HOLMES, JOHN R.   William Blake's place in the mystical tradition. Unpub. doct. diss., Kent State Univ., 1985. [Abstr. in DA (47) 188A.]

6251. HOWARD, JOHN.   Infernal poetics: poetic structures in Blake's Lambeth prophecies. Rutherford, NJ: Fairleigh Dickinson UP; London: Assoc. UPs, 1984. pp. 259.

6252. HUH, BONG-WHA.   William Blake eui poetic mysticism. (Blake's poetic mysticism.) Unpub. doct. diss., Keimyung Univ. (Korea).

6253. IMAIZUMI, YOKO.   Brotherhood in Blake: psychology and poetics. Unpub. doct. diss., Yale Univ., 1985. [Abstr. in DA (46) 3359A.]

6254. —— Onna ga shouchou suru seishin sayou: Blake no *Jerusalem*. (Psychic operations symbolized by the female in Blake's *Jerusalem*.) SEL (63:2) 241–56.

6255. KAMUSIKIRI, SANDRA DARLENE.   'A building of magnificence': Blake's major prophecies and eighteenth-century conceptions of the human sublime. Unpub. doct. diss., Univ. of California, Riverside, 1985. [Abstr. in DA (46) 3726A.]

6256. KANG, YOP.   *Songs of Innocence* and *Of Experience* eui seosi: geu yeeonjajeok sunggyeok. (Prophetic character of Blake's introductions to the *Songs*.) UJH (28) 1985, 145–62.

6257. LEE, JUDITH.   Scornful beauty: a note on Blake and Ariosto. ELN (23:4) 35–8.

6258. LEONARD, GARRY MARTIN.   William Blake's 'vegetable existence' and James Joyce's 'moral paralysis': the relationship between

Blake's Romantic philosophy and Joyce's thematic concerns in *Dubliners* and *A Portrait of the Artist as a Young Man*. Unpub. doct. diss., Univ. of Florida, 1985. [Abstr. in DA (47) 1319A.]

6259. LINCOLN, ANDREW.   Blake and the natural history of creation. EAS (39) 94–103.

6260. LISTER, RAYMOND.   The paintings of William Blake. Cambridge: CUP. pp. 176, (plates) 75.

6261. LUSSIER, MARK.   'Vortext' as philosopher's stone: Blake's textual mirrors and the transformation of audience. NOR (13:3) 40–50.

6262. MCARTHUR, MURRAY GILCHRIST.   Language and history in Blake's *Milton* and Joyce's *Ulysses*. Unpub. doct. diss., Univ. of Western Ontario, 1985. [Abstr. in DA (46) 2689A.]

6263. MCCORD, JAMES.   Mixed motives and deadly acts: historical and dramatic character in William Blake's *King Edward the Third*. ECS (19:4) 480–501.

6264. —— West of Atlantis: William Blake's unromantic view of the American war. CR (30:3) 383–99.

6265. MARVEL, LAURA.   Blake and Yeats: visions of apocalypse. CLit (13:1) 95–105.

6266. MILLER, DAN.   Blake's allusions: *Jerusalem* 86. NOR (13:3) 22–33.

6267. NANAVUTTY, PILOO.   'The River of Oblivion'. AJES (11) 93–7.

6268. PALEY, MORTON D.   The continuing city: William Blake's *Jerusalem*. (Bibl. 1985, 5350.) Rev. by Mary Lynn Johnson in JEGP (85:2) 275–8.

6269. —— PHILLIPS, MICHAEL (eds).   William Blake: essays in honour of Sir Geoffrey Keynes. (Bibl. 1975, 6394.) Rev. by Leonard M. Trawick in Studies in Burke and his Time (Texas Tech Univ., Lubbock, TX) (17:2) 1976, 156–9.

6270. PORTER, PETER (sel. and introd.).   William Blake. Oxford: OUP. pp. 61. (Illustrated poets.)

6271. PUNTER, D. G.   Blake and dialectic. Unpub. doct. diss., Univ. of Cambridge, 1984.

6272. PUNTER, DAVID.   Blake, Hegel and dialectic. (Bibl. 1985, 5353.) Rev. by Stephen Prickett in MLR (81:1) 159–60.

6273. —— Blake, trauma and the female. NLH (15) 1984, 475–90.

6274. RAINE, KATHLEEN.   The city in William Blake. AJES (11) 75–92.

6275. —— The sleep of Albion. AJES (11) 188–208.

6276. —— The sleep of Albion. MichQR (25:4) 684–98.

6277. REISNER, M. E.   William Blake and Westminster Abbey. *In* (pp. 185–98) ROGER L. EMERSON, GILLES GIRARD, and ROSEANN RUNTE (eds), Man and nature: proceedings of the Canadian Society for Eighteenth-Century Studies: vol. 1. London, Ont.: Univ. of Western Ontario, 1982. pp. xvi, 224. Rev. by Robert James Merrett in CanRCL (13:1) 125–8.

6278. RIEHL, JOE.   Gnosticism in Blake's *I Saw a Chapel All of Gold*. NOR (13:3) 6–11.

6279. ROBINSON, DOUGLAS. Joan of Orc: a reading of Twain's French fantasy through Blake's *America: a Prophesy*. AmSS (18) 15–26.

6280. SŁAWEK, TADEUSZ. The outline shadow: phenomenology, grammatology, Blake. Katowice: Uniwersytet Śląski 1985. pp. 159. (Prace naukowe Universytetu Śląskiego w Katowicach, 727.)

6281. STIEG, ELIZABETH JOY. William Blake and the prophetic tradition. Unpub. doct. diss., Univ. of Toronto, 1985. [Abstr. in DA (47) 916A.]

6282. TAKANO, MASAO. Kansei no utage: Keats, Wordsworth, Blake. (A feast of sensibility: Keats, Wordsworth, Blake.) Tokyo: Shinozaki Shorin Press. pp. 258.

6283. TANNENBAUM, LESLIE. Biblical tradition in Blake's early prophecies: the great code of art. (Bibl. 1985, 5360.) Rev. by D. R. M. Wilkinson in YES (16) 286–8.

6284. THINÈS, GEORGES. Blake et Faust. Brussels: Centre international d'études poétiques. pp. 41. (Courrier du Centre international d'études poétiques, 171.)

6285. —— William Blake et Arthur Rimbaud: deux visions de l'infernal. BALLF (44:1) 12–27.

6286. VOGLER, THOMAS A. Intertextual signifiers and the Blake of that already. RPP (9:1) 1985, 1–33.

6287. WEBSTER, BRENDA S. Blake's prophetic psychology. (Bibl. 1985, 5365.) Rev. by François Piquet in EA (38:4) 1985, 466–7.

6288. WELCH, DENNIS M. Imitation in Blake's *Night Thoughts* illustrations. *See* **85.**

6289. WITKE, JOANNE. William Blake's epic: imagination unbound. London: Croom Helm. pp. viii, 231.

6290. WYLER, S. William Blake and the prophetic tradition. Unpub. doct. diss., Univ. of Oxford, 1985. [Abstr. in IT (35) 50.]

James Boaden

6291. COHAN, STEVEN (ed.). The plays of James Boaden. New York; London: Garland, 1980. (Eighteenth-century English drama, 5.) (Facsims of texts pub. 1793–1803; pp. lxx, and pagination of individual items.)

Henry St John, Viscount Bolingbroke

6292. BLACK, JEREMY. Bolingbroke's attack on Pope: a lawyer's comment. NQ (33:4) 513–14.

6293. CLINGHAM, G. J. Bolingbroke's copy of Pope's *Works 1717–1735* in Tonbridge School library. *See* **210.**

6294. WOOD, J. L. The Craftsman and Miss Gumley's bum. Factotum (8) 1980, 25–7; (9) 1980, 24.

James Boswell

6295. BRADY, FRANK. Fictional techniques in factual works. *See* **2969.**

6296. —— James Boswell: the later years, 1769–95. Toronto: McGraw-Hill, 1984. (Bibl. 1985, 5369.) Rev. by Oliver W. Ferguson in SAQ (85:4) 399–400; by David Crane in BJECS (9:2) 247–8; by Isobel

Grundy in MLR (81:2) 453–5; by Thomas Crawford in SLJ (supp. 25) 13–17.

6297. BUCHANAN, DAVID.   The treasure of Auchinleck: the story of the Boswell papers. (Bibl. 1980, 6583.) Rev. by Donald Greene in Studies in Burke and his Time (Texas Tech Univ., Lubbock, TX) (18:2) 1977, 114–27.

6298. CARRINGTON, DOROTHY.   Boswell's Corsica. EDH (44) 46–62.

6299. GREENE, DONALD.   A bear by the tail: the genesis of the Boswell industry. Studies in Burke and his Time (Texas Tech Univ., Lubbock, TX) (18:2) 1977, 114–27 (review-article).

6300. HILLYARD, BRIAN.   Boswell's *Account of Corsica*. Factotum (18) 1984, 16–18.

6301. HOOK, DAVID.   Mr Boswell's books and the Inquisition. *See* **235.**

6302. LUSTIG, IRMA S.   Boswell without Johnson: the years after. NRam (26) 1985/86, 36–8.

6303. —— POTTLE, FREDERICK A. (eds).   Boswell: the applause of the jury, 1782–1785. (Bibl. 1985, 5374.) Rev. by William C. Dowling in YES (16) 285–6.

6304. —— —— Boswell: the English experiment: 1785–1789. London: Heinemann. pp. xxii, 332. (Yale editions of the private papers of James Boswell.)

6305. McFARLAND, RONALD E.   Considering Boswell's poetry. NRam (23) 1982, 30–40.

6306. STEWART, CHARLOTTE A.   The life of a Johnson collection. *See* **283.**

6307. TURNBULL, GORDON.   Criminal biographer: Boswell and Margaret Caroline Rudd. SELit (26:3) 511–35.

Samuel Boyse

6308. SHERBO, A.   Three letters of Samuel Boyse and a poem by Cowper (?). NQ (33:1) 78–80.

Frances Brooke

6309. EDWARDS, MARY JANE (ed.).   The history of Emily Montague. Ottawa: Carleton UP, 1985. pp. lxxi, 459. (Centre for Editing Early Canadian Texts, 1.) Rev. by Tracy Ware in CanL (110) 114–15; by Clara Thomas in QQ (93:3) 659–60.

Henry Brooke

6310. SMITH, HELEN.   Little John Good and *Jack the Giant Queller*. Factotum (5) 1979, 13–14.

John Brown

6311. EDDY, DONALD D.   John Brown, *Essays on the Characteristics*. *See* **99.**

Edmund Burke

6312. BERNSEN, MICHAEL.   Die Revolution des Stils: Stil und Stilbegriff in Edmund Burkes *Reflections on the Revolution in France*. PoetA (18:1/2) 117–39.

6313. KRAMNICK, ISAAC.   The rage of Edmund Burke. (Bibl. 1977, 5317.) Rev. by Lawrence Lipking in ECent (20:1) 1979, 65–81.

6314. Murphy, Sean.   Burke and Lucas: an authorship problem re-examined. *See* **656.**

6315. Poupko, Chana Kasachkoff.   Parallels in Burke's *Reflections* and the Old Testament on the idea of community. Studies in Burke and his Time (Texas Tech Univ., Lubbock, TX) (17:2) 1976, 119–25.

6316. Rashid, Salim.   Economists and the age of chivalry: notes on a passage in Burke's *Reflections*. ECS (20:1) 56–61.

6317. Ritchie, Daniel E. C.   Edmund Burke's nineteenth-century literary significance in England. Unpub. doct. diss., Rutgers Univ. 1985. [Abstr. in DA (46) 1953A.]

6318. Todd, William B.   A bibliography of Edmund Burke. Godalming: St Paul's Bibliographies, 1982. pp. 316. (Second ed.: first ed. 1964.) Rev. by F. P. Lock in YES (16) 278–9.

6319. Wells, G. A.   Burke on ideas, words and imagination. BJECS (9:1) 45–51.

Fanny Burney

6320. Epstein, Julia.   Writing the unspeakable: Fanny Burney's mastectomy and the fictive body. Representations (16) 131–66.

6321. Epstein, Julia L.   Fanny Burney's epistolary voices. ECent (27:2) 162–79.

6322. Simons, Judy (introd.).   Cecilia, or, Memoirs of an heiress. London: Virago Press. pp. xiii, 919. (Virago modern classics, 213.)

6323. Straub, Kristina.   Fanny Burney's *Evelina* and the 'gulphs, pits, and precipices' of eighteenth-century female life. ECent (27:3) 230–46.

6324. —— Women's pastimes and the ambiguity of female self-identification in Fanny Burney's *Evelina*. ECL (10:2) 58–72.

Robert Burns

6325. Brown, Mary Ellen.   Burns and tradition. (Bibl. 1985, 5390.) Rev. by Kenneth A. Thigpen in JAF (99) 489–90; by Christopher MacLachlan in SLJ (supp. 35) 11–12.

6326. Bryson, Frank.   Tam o Shanter. Glasgow: Scotsoun Productions, 1985. (Cassette with accompanying text in Scotscrieve, read by Frank Bryson of Kilwinning.) Rev. by J. Derrick McClure in SLJ (supp. 24) 4–6.

6327. Carnochan, W. B.   The moral sentiment of *To a Louse*. SSL (17) 1982, 245–8.

6328. Crawford, Thomas.   Burns and Tolstoy. SLJ (13:1) 51–64.

6329. Grimble, Ian.   Robert Burns. Twickenham: Hamlyn. pp. 128.

6330. Groves, David.   James Hogg: verses for Burns and Byron. NQ (33:2) 161–3.

6331. Hempstead, James L.   Captain Richard Brown. BurnsC (11) 88–92.

6332. Jack, R. D. S.; Noble, Andrew (eds).   The art of Robert Burns. (Bibl. 1985, 5394.) Rev. by David W. Lindsay in YES (16) 288–9.

6333. Jackson, Alan D.   D. H. Lawrence, 'physical consciousness' and Robert Burns. SLJ (13:1) 65–76.

6334. LAMONT-BROWN, RAYMOND.   Robert Burns and the assasssins.
BurnsC (11) 50–3.

6335. LIDDLE, I. A.   The personal and literary reputation of Robert
Burns, 1786–1896. Unpub. doct. diss., Univ. of Wales, Aberystwyth,
1984. [Abstr. in IT (35) 544.]

6336. LOW, DONALD A.   Burns's *Epistle to a Tiviotdale Farmer's Wife.*
SLJ (13:1) 47–50.

6337. —— Robert Burns. Edinburgh: Scottish Academic Press.
pp. 144. (Scottish writers, 8.)

6338. —— (ed.).   The Kilmarnock poems. (Bibl. 1985, 5395.) Rev.
by David Groves in NQ (33:4) 555; by Christopher MacLachlan in SLJ
(supp. 25) 10–11.

6339. MCGUIRK, CAROL.   Robert Burns and the sentimental era.
(Bibl. 1985, 5397.) Rev. by Cynthia L. Caywood in SAQ (85:4) 408–9;
by Ian Campbell in RPP (10:1) 61–2; by K. G. Simpson in AUMLA
(66) 294–8.

6340. MACLACHLAN, CHRISTOPHER.   Point of view in some poems of
Burns. SLJ (13:1) 5–20.

6341. MACLAINE, ALLAN H.   Burlesque as a satiric method in the
poems and songs of Burns. SLJ (13:1) 30–46.

6342. M[ACKAY], J. A.   The complete works of Robert Burns: a new
edition. BurnsC (11) 14–16.

6343. ROY, G. Ross.   The '1827' edition of Robert Burns's *Merry
Muses of Caledonia.* BurnsC (11) 32–45.

6344. —— Robert Burns: editions and critical works 1968–1982. SSL
(19) 1984, 216–51.

6345. —— (ed.).   The letters of Roberts Burns: vol. 1, 1780–1789;
vol. 2, 1790–1796. Ed. by J. DE LANCEY FERGUSON. Oxford: Clarendon
Press, 1985. 2 vols. pp. 493; 521. (Second ed.: first ed. 1931.) Rev. by
K. G. Simpson in SLJ (supp. 25) 6–10; by Douglas Dunn in TLS,
25 July, 803–4; by Andrew Noble in THES (701) 21.

6346. SPILLER, MICHAEL R. G.   Pronouns in *Tam o' Shanter. See* **1902.**

6347. STRANGE, WILLIAM C.   The fire argument in *The Jolly Beggars*
and *The Cotter's Saturday Night.* SSL (17) 1982, 209–17.

Susanna Centlivre

6348. FRUSHELL, RICHARD C.   Marriage and marrying in Susanna
Centlivre's plays. PLL (22:1) 16–38.

Richard Challoner

6349. BROWNE, R. K.   Richard Challoner 1691–1781. Factotum (12)
1981, 17–22.

Thomas Chatterton

6350. CRUMP, M. J.   Chatterton's Rowley poems: an unnoticed
cancel. *See* **96.**

6351. HAYWOOD, I.   The making of history: a study of the literary
forgeries of James Macpherson and Thomas Chatterton in relation to
eighteenth century ideas of history and fiction. Unpub. doct. diss., Univ.
of London (University Coll.), 1983.

6352. Höfele, Andreas.   Die Originalität der Fälschung: Zur Funktion des literarischen Betrugs in England 1750–1800. See **5962**.

6353. Wellens, Oskar.   Joseph Robertson: the Anti-Rowleian critic of the *Critical Review*. See **721**.

Philip Dormer Stanhope, Earl of Chesterfield

6354. Black, Jeremy.   Reflections on Chesterfield. NQ (33:1) 74–5.

Charles Churchill

6355. Bulckaen-Messina, Denise.   Jeu des acteurs et reflets de l'âme dans la *Rosciade* (1761) de Charles Churchill. *In* (pp. 99–110) **14**.

Colley Cibber

6356. Hughes, Derek.   Cibber and Vanbrugh: language, place, and social order in *Love's Last Shift*. See **5898**.

6357. Koon, Helene.   Colley Cibber: a biography. Lexington: Kentucky UP. pp. xi, 242. Rev. by Pat Rogers in TLS, 18 July, 789.

John Cleland

6358. Houston, Joann.   Finding meaning: a discussion of pornography and eroticism in John Cleland's *Memoirs of a Woman of Pleasure* and some parallels between Matthew G. Lewis' *The Monk*. Unpub. doct. diss., Florida State Univ., 1985. [Abstr. in DA (47) 188a.]

6359. Sabor, Peter.   The censor censured: expurgating *Memoirs of a Woman of Pleasure*. ECL (9:3) 1985, 192–201.

6360. —— (ed.).   Memoirs of a woman of pleasure. (Bibl. 1985, 5412.) Rev. by Peter Wagner in BJECS (9:2) 274–5.

6361. Wagner, Peter.   The assertion of body and instinct: John Cleland's *Memoirs of a Woman of Pleasure. In* (pp. 139–56) **14**.

6362. —— (ed.).   Fanny Hill, or, Memoirs of a woman of pleasure. Harmondsworth: Penguin, 1985. pp. 233. (Penguin classics.)

George Colman the Younger

6363. Sutcliffe, Barry (ed.).   Plays by George Colman the Younger and Thomas Morton. (Bibl. 1984, 5626.) Rev. by Edward Burns in BJECS (9:1) 110–11.

Robert Colvill

6364. Cole, Richard C.   Robert Colvill's *Savannah*. SSL (17) 1982, 81–98.

Matthew Concanen

6365. Gerrard, Christine.   *An Ode on the Times*: the political fortunes of James Sterling and Matthew Concanen. NQ (33:4) 502–4.

William Cowper

6366. Anderson, David R.   Landscape and theodicy in Pope, Thomson, and Cowper. ELit (13:1) 13–27.

6367. Hopkins, K. V. J.   William Cowper as an evangelical poet. Unpub. doct. diss., Univ. of Hull. 1984.

6368. King, James.   William Cowper: a biography. Durham, NC: Duke UP. pp. 340. Rev. by W. B. Carnochan in TLS, 11 July, 765.

6369. —— Ryskamp, Charles (eds).   The letters and prose writings of William Cowper: vol. 5, Prose 1756–*c.* 1799 and cumulative index. Oxford: Clarendon Press. pp. xxvi, 246.

6370. Newey, Vincent.   Cowper's poetry: a critical study and reassessment. (Bibl. 1985, 5418.) Rev. by A. J. Sambrook in YES (16) 279–80.

6371. SHERBO, A.   Three letters of Samuel Boyse and a poem by Cowper (?). *See* **6308.**

6372. TY, ELEANOR.   Cowper's *Connoisseur* 138 and Samuel Johnson. NQ (33:1) 63:4.

6373. WATSON, J. R.   Cowper's *Olney Hymns*. EAS (38) 1985, 45–65.

George Crabbe

6374. FAULKNER, THOMAS C. (ed.); BLAIR, RHONDA L. (asst ed.). Selected letters and journals of George Crabbe. New York: OUP, 1985. pp. xlvii, 441. (Cf. bibl. 1985, 5421, where title and pagination incorrect.) Rev. by Marilyn Butler in TLS, 3 Jan., 3–4; by Irène Simon in EngS (67:6) 570–1.

6375. KLEIN, JO.   Closely observed pains. British Medical Journal (London) (293) 1611–13.

6376. POSTER, JEM (ed.).   Selected poetry. Manchester: Carcanet Press; MidNAG. pp. 168.

'J. Hector St John de Crèvecœur'
(Michel-Guillaume Jean de Crèvecœur)

6377. CHEVIGNARD, BERNARD.   Mémoire et création dans les *Letters from an American Farmer* de St John de Crèvecœur. *In* (pp. 125–35) **34.**

6378. GERBAUD, COLETTE.   Terre et culture: un pionnier. Saint Jean de Crèvecœur et divers aspects du phénomène culturel. *In* (pp. 11–30) **5.**

6379. PÜTZ, MANFRED.   Dramatic elements and the problem of literary mediation in the works of Hector St John de Crèvecœur. YREAL (3) 1985, 111–30.

Erasmus Darwin

6380. GOLD, KAREN.   Evolution of the Romantic poets (by a space scientist): Karen Gold talks to Desmond King-Hele, critic and scientist. THES (698) 12.

6381. KING-HELE, DESMOND.   Erasmus Darwin and the Romantic poets. London: Macmillan. pp. vii, 294. Rev. by Joseph Bristow in THES (709) 20; by Gillian Beer in TLS, 19 Sept., 1036.

Daniel Defoe

6382. ALAM, FAKRUL.   Daniel Defoe as a colonial propagandist. Unpub. doct. diss., Univ. of British Columbia, 1984. [Abstr. in DA (46) 3723A.]

6383. BACKSCHEIDER, PAULA R.   A being more intense: a study of the prose works of Bunyan, Swift, and Defoe. *See* **5307.**

6384. —— Cross-purposes: Defoe's *History of the Union*. CLIO (11:2) 1982, 165–86.

6385. —— The genesis of *Roxana*. ECent (27:3) 211–29.

6386. BASTIAN, F.   Defoe in France in 1725? NQ (33:4) 491–5.

6387. BELL, IAN A.   Defoe's fiction. (Bibl. 1985, 5431.) Rev. by W. R. Owens in EngS (67:6) 567–8; by John Richetti in TLS, 18 Apr., 428.

6388. BIRDSALL, VIRGINIA OGDEN.   Defoe's perpetual seekers: a study of the major fiction. Lewisburg, PA: Bucknell UP; London: Assoc. UPs, 1985. pp. 203. Rev. by John Richetti in TLS, 18 Apr., 428.

6389. BOARDMAN, MICHAEL M.   Defoe and the uses of narrative. (Bibl. 1985, 5434.) Rev. by Everett Zimmerman in MLR (81:2) 446–7; by Lennard Davis in ECent (27:2) 193–205.

6390. BRAVERMAN, RICHARD.   Locke, Defoe, and the politics of childhood. *See* **5605.**

6391. CRUISE, JAMES JOSEPH.   Governing scripture: authority and the early English novel. Unpub. doct. diss., Univ. of Pennsylvania, 1985. [Abstr. in DA (46) 2298A.]

6392. DANON, RUTH.   Work in the English novel: the myth of vocation. London: Croom Helm, 1985. pp. 214. Rev. by Kathryn Sutherland in CritQ (28:4) 110–11.

6393. DAVIS, LENNARD J.   Fiction and theory: three books on Defoe. ECent (27:2) 193–205 (review-article).

6394. DAY, ROBERT ADAMS.   Speech acts, orality, and the epistolary novel. ECent (21:3) 1980, 187–97.

6395. DOWNIE, J. A.   Defoe's *Shortest Way with the Dissenters*: irony, intention and reader-response. Prose Studies (9:2) 120–39.

6396. DU SORBIER, FRANÇOISE.   A la recherche de la femme perdue: Moll Flanders et Roxana. *In* (pp. 121–30) **14.**

6397. EVANS, JAMES E.   Mr Review on the 'glorious' *Tatler* and the 'inimitable' *Spectator*. *See* **595.**

6398. FURBANK, P. N.; OWENS, W. R.   Defoe and the 'improvisatory' sentence. EngS (67:2) 157–66.

6399. —— What if Defoe did not write the *History of the Wars of Charles XII?* PBSA (80:3) 333–47.

6400. HALIMI, SUZY.   Defoe au service de Guillaume III. *In* (pp. 123–32) **30.**

6401. HARTLE, P. N.   Defoe and *The Wonders of the Peake*: the place of Cotton's poem in *A Tour thro' the Whole Island of Great Britain*. *See* **5337.**

6402. HARTLE, PAUL.   The source of Roxana's song. *See* **5338.**

6403. HASKELL, ROSEMARY ANNE.   The antagonistic structure of the colonial experience in five novels of Daniel Defoe: a question of struggle and identity. Unpub. doct. diss., Univ. of North Carolina at Chapel Hill, 1985. [Abstr. in DA (47) 188A.]

6404. KIM, SUNG-KYOON.   *Roxana* neun wansung doen soseol inga? (Did Defoe complete *Roxana*?) JELL (32:4) 783–803.

6405. LAMOINE, GEORGES.   Le *True Born Englishman*: à la recherche de ses ancêtres. *In* (pp. 46–54) **35.**

6406. LAURENCE, ANNE.   Daniel Defoe and imprisonment for debt. Text & Context (1:1) 59–69.

6407. LAWSON, JACQUELINE ELAINE.   'Ill-govern'd families': domestic misconduct in the novels of Defoe, Richardson, and Fielding. Unpub. doct. diss., Brown Univ., 1985. [Abstr. in DA (47) 1735A.]

6408. MERRETT, ROBERT JAMES.   The traditional and progressive aspects of Daniel Defoe's ideas about sex, family, and marriage. ESCan (12:1) 1–22.

6409. NEMOIANU, VIRGIL.   Picaresque retreat: from Xenophon's *Anabasis* to Defoe's *Singleton*. CLS (23:2) 91–102.

6410. NOVAK, MAXIMILLIAN E. Realism, myth, and history in Defoe's fiction. (Bibl. 1985, 5446.) Rev. by Lennard Bavis in ECent (27:2) 193–205.

6411. OWENS, W. R.; FURBANK, P. N. Defoe and the Dutch Alliance: some attributions examined. BJECS (9:2) 169–82.

6412. —— —— Defoe and imprisonment for debt: some attributions reviewed. RES (37:148) 495–502.

6413. —— —— A KWIC concordance to Daniel Defoe's *Moll Flanders*. New York; London: Garland, 1985. pp. ix, 1111. (Garland reference library of the humanities, 620.)

6414. PIRONON, JEAN. Le thème de *La foire* de Ben Jonson à Defoe: changements de mentalité et typologie jungienne. In (pp. 433–44) **1.**

6415. RALIAN, ANTOANETA (trans. and ed.). Jurnal din anul ciumei. (Journal of the plague year.) Bucharest: Univers, 1985. pp. 256.

6416. ROSENWASSER, DAVID. The idea of enclosure: prisons and havens at the rise of the novel. *See* **5313.**

6417. SCHONHORN, MANUEL. Defoe, political parties, and the monarch. StudECC (15) 187–97.

6418. —— Defoe's poetry in *Robinson Crusoe*. NQ (33:1) 45–6.

6419. SHIMADA, TAKAU. A possible source for *The Consolidator*. NQ (33:1) 45.

6420. —— Possible sources for *Serious Reflections of Robinson Crusoe*. RES (37:146) 211–15.

6421. SILL, GEOFFREY M. Defoe and the idea of fiction, 1713–1719. (Bibl. 1985, 5450.) Rev. by Lennard Davis in ECent (27:2) 193–205.

6422. SIM, S. D. Dialogues with closure: ideology and identity in the fiction of Dent, Bunyan and Defoe. *See* **5316.**

6423. SOUILLER, DIDIER. Le récit picaresque. Littératures (14) 13–26.

6424. WOOD, J. L. Defoe serialized. *See* **732.**

John Dennis

6425. WHEELER, DAVID M. John Dennis and the religious sublime. CLAJ (30:2) 210–18.

Timothy Dwight

6426. CLARK, GREGORY DALLAN. Timothy Dwight's *Travels in New England and New York* and the rhetoric of Puritan public discourse. Unpub. doct. diss., Rensselaer Polytechnic Institute, 1985. [Abstr. in DA (46) 3032A.]

Jonathan Edwards

6427. DE PROSPO, R. C. Theism in the discourse of Jonathan Edwards. Newark: Delaware UP, 1985. pp. 292. Rev. by Stephen J. Stein in JAH (73:2) 454–5.

6428. GUELZO, ALLEN CARL. The unanswered question: the legacy of Jonathan Edwards's *Freedom of the Will* in early American religious philosophy. Unpub. doct. diss., Univ. of Pennsylvania. [Abstr. in DA (47) 1354A.]

6429. HEIMERT, ALAN. The Yale Edwards. EAL (20:3) 1985/86, 256–70 (review-article).

6430. Miller, Perry; Smith, John E. (gen. eds). The works of Jonathan Edwards: vols 1–7. (Bibl. 1980, 6685; 1985, 5464). Rev. by Alan Heimert in EAL (20:3) 1985/86, 256–70.

6431. Osburg, Barbara Jean. The development of metaphor in the sermons of Jonathan Edwards: the individual reflection of an historical progress. Unpub. doct. diss., Saint Louis Univ., 1984. [Abstr. in DA (46) 1943A.]

6432. Pettit, Norman. Prelude to mission: Brainerd's expulsion from Yale. NEQ (59:1) 28–50.

6433. Storms, C. Samuel. Tragedy in Eden: original sin in the theology of Jonathan Edwards. Lanham, MD; London: UP of America, 1985. pp. xii, 316.

6434. Yarbrough, Stephen R. Jonathan Edwards on rhetorical authority. JHI (47:3) 395–408.

George Farquhar

6435. Dixon, Peter (ed.). The recruiting officer. Manchester: Manchester UP. pp. 200. (Revels plays.)

Elizabeth Graeme Ferguson

6436. Slotten, Martha C. Elizabeth Graeme Ferguson: a poet in 'the Athens of North America'. PMHB (108) 1984, 259–88.

Robert Fergusson

6437. Daiches, David. Robert Fergusson. (Bibl. 1983, 6084.) Rev. by J. H. Alexander in YES (16) 231–4.

6438. Freeman, F. W. Robert Fergusson and the Scots humanist compromise. (Bibl. 1985, 5469.) Rev. by William Findlay in Cencrastus (23) 57–8.

6439. O'Brien, Jerry. The Sonsie muse: the satiric use of neo-classical diction in the poems of Robert Fergusson. SSL (19) 1984, 165–76.

Henry Fielding

6440. Abdel-Latif, S. M. Some aspects of the language and style of Henry Fielding's novels. Unpub. doct. diss., Univ. of Sheffield, 1984. [Abstr. in IT (35) 46.]

6441. Amory, Hugh. The evidence of things not seen: concealed proofs of Fielding's Juvenal. *See* **297.**

6442. Battestin, Martin C. Fielding's contributions to the *Universal Spectator* (1736–7). *See* **558.**

6443. Benedict, Barbara MacVean. The tensions of realism: oppositions of perception in some novels of Fielding and Austen. Unpub. doct. diss., Univ. of California, Berkeley, 1985. [Abstr. in DA (47) 906A.]

6444. Burling, William J. Henry Fielding and the 'William Hint' letter: a reconsideration. NQ (33:4) 498–9.

6445. Cleary, Thomas R. Henry Fielding: political writer. (Bibl. 1985, 5475.) Rev. by James Gray in ESCan (12:4) 468–76; by Pat Rogers in NQ (33:4) 552–3.

6446. Cruise, James Joseph. Governing scripture: authority and the early English novel. *See* **6391.**

6447. DAY, ROBERT ADAMS. Speech acts, orality, and the epistolary novel. *See* **6394.**

6448. KRAFT, QUENTIN G. Narrative transformation in *Tom Jones*: an episode in the emergence of the English novel. ECent (26:1) 1985, 23–45.

6449. LAWSON, JACQUELINE ELAINE. 'Ill-govern'd families': domestic misconduct in the novels of Defoe, Richardson, and Fielding. *See* **6407.**

6450. MADELIN, HERVÉ. Henry Fielding and Jacques Esprit. YREAL (1) 1982, 27–74.

6451. MORVAN, ALAIN. Discours sur un exil intérieur: *The Jacobite's Journal* de Fielding. *In* (pp. 55–68) **35.**

6452. MYER, VALERIE GROSVENOR. His virtue square: a note on *Tom Jones*. NQ (33:1) 58.

6453. PROBYN, CLIVE T. James Harris to Parson Adams in Germany: some light on Fielding's Salisbury set. PQ (64) 1985, 130–9.

6454. REYNOLDS, R. C. Johnson on Fielding. CLit (13:2) 157–67.

6455. SIMPSON, K. G. (ed.). Henry Fielding: justice observed. London: Vision Press; Totowa, NJ: Barnes & Noble, 1985. pp. 205. (Critical studies.) Rev. by David McNeil in DalR (65:2) 1985, 310–12.

6456. TRAINER, CHARLES R. Fielding's novels: the transformation of drama. Greyfriar (27) 22–30.

6457. TRIFU, SEVER. Satiră la Fielding şi Swift. (Satire in Fielding's and Swift's works.) Tribuna, 6 Nov., 10.

6458. VAREY, SIMON. Henry Fielding. Cambridge: CUP. pp. 168. (British and Irish authors.)

6459. WERKMÄSTER, JOHAN. Den symmetriska romanen: en studie i Henry Fieldings *Tom Jones*. (The symmetrical novel: a study of Henry Fielding's *Tom Jones*.) Horisont (33:2) 36–43.

George Flint

6460. GOULDEN, R. J. The authorship of Foxon's P1138. *See* **6094.**

Samuel Foote

6461. HIND, CHARLES. News of the trade. *See* **389.**

6462. TAYLOR, GEORGE (ed.). Plays by Samuel Foote and Arthur Murphy. (Bibl. 1985, 5502.) Rev. by Edward Burns in BJECS (9:1) 110–1; by Brean S. Hammond in NQ (33:1) 119–20.

Martha Fowke ('Maria Sansom', 'Mrs S-N-M', 'Clio', 'Mira')

6463. DAVIS, KAREN E. Martha Fowke: 'A lady once too well known'. ELN (23:3) 32–6.

Benjamin Franklin

6464. BARONE, DENNIS. A note on Benjamin Franklin's English grammar. ELN (23:4) 31–3.

6465. BREITWIESER, MITCHELL ROBERT. Benjamin Franklin: the price of representative personality. *See* **5647.**

6466. CLARK, MICHAEL. Benjamin Franklin and Cooper's *The Pioneers*. ELN (24:1) 73–8.

6467. DAHIYAT, EID A. Milton and Franklin. *See* **5695.**

6468. DAUBER, KENNETH. Benjamin Franklin and the idea of authorship. Criticism (28:3) 255–86.

6469. FERGUSON, ROBERT A.   'We hold these truths': strategies of control in the literature of the Founders. *In* (pp. 1–28) **47.**

6470. GRIFFITH, JOHN.   Franklin for the many and the few. EAL (21:2) 166–72 (review-article).

6471. LARSON, DAVID M.   Benevolent persuasions: the art of Benjamin Franklin's philanthropic papers. PMHB (110:2) 197–217.

6472. LEMAY, J. A. LEO.   The canon of Benjamin Franklin, 1722–1776: new attributions and reconsiderations. Newark: Delaware UP; London: Assoc. UPs. pp. 162. Rev. by John Griffith in EAL (21:2) 166–72.

6473. LOOBY, CHRISTOPHER.   'The affairs of the Revolution occasion'd the interruption': writing, revolution, deferral, and conciliation in Franklin's *Autobiography*. AmQ (38:1) 72–96.

6474. MACHOR, JAMES L.   The urban idyll of the new Republic: moral geography and the mythic hero of Franklin's *Autobiography*. PMHB (110:2) 219–35.

6475. SILVERMAN, KENNETH (ed.).   *Autobiography* and other writings. New York; Harmondsworth: Penguin. pp. xxii, 270. (Penguin classics.)

6476. SULLIVAN, PATRICK.   Benjamin Franklin, the inveterate (and crafty) public instructor: instruction on two levels in *The Way to Wealth*. EAL (21:3) 1986/87, 248–59.

6477. WARNER, MICHAEL.   Franklin and the letters of the republic. Representations (16) 110–30.

6478. WILLCOX, WILLIAM B. (ed.);   ARNOLD, DOUGLAS M. (assoc. ed.).   The papers of Benjamin Franklin: vol. 25, October 1, 1777 through February 28, 1788. New Haven, CT; London: Yale UP. pp. lxv, 779.

Philip Freneau

6479. SHIELDS, DAVID S.   Mental nocturnes: night thoughts on man and nature in the poetry of eighteenth-century America. *See* **6110.**

Edward Fryer

6480. JEFCOATE, GRAHAM.   Edward Fryer, M.D.: an English gentlemen and his circle in Göttingen, 1785–90. Factotum (18) 1984, 28–35.

Nathaniel Gardner

6481. FIREOVED, JOSEPH.   Nathaniel Gardner and the *New-England Courant*. *See* **599.**

David Garrick

6482. DIRCKS, PHYLLIS T.   David Garrick. Boston, MA: G. K. Hall, 1985. pp. 152. (Twayne's English authors, 403.) Rev. by Joseph R. Roach in TJ (38:1) 120.

6483. JENKINS, ELIZABETH.   Dr Johnson and David Garrick. NRam (23) 1982, 20–1.

6484. KENDALL, ALAN.   David Garrick: a biography. London: Harrap, 1985. pp. 224.

John Gay

6485. FERDINAND, C.   The illustrated pirate. *See* **376.**

6486. FULLER, JOHN (ed.).   Dramatic works. London; New York:

OUP, 1983. (Bibl. 1985, 5517.) Rev. by C. J. Rawson in MLR (81:3) 720; by Patricia Meyer Spacks in PLL (22:1) 100–4.

6487. LOUGHREY, BRYAN; TREADWELL, T. O. (eds). The beggar's opera. Harmondsworth: Penguin. pp. 122. (Penguin classics.)

6488. SPACKS, PATRICIA MEYER. John Gay's *Dramatic Works*. PLL (22:1) 100–4 (review-article).

6489. TEMPERLEY, NICHOLAS. Film forum: *The Beggar's Opera* (1953 and 1983). ECL (10:2) 109–17.

Edward Gibbon

6490. BROWNLEY, MARTINE WATSON. Clarendon, Gibbon, and the art of historical portraiture. *See* **5334.**

6491. CRADDOCK, PATRICIA B. Young Edward Gibbon: gentleman of letters. (Bibl. 1985, 5521.) Rev. by Rachel Trickett in YES (16) 282–5.

6492. EPSTEIN, WILLIAM H. Professing Gibbon: the autobiographical profession of literary study. ECent (27:2) 115–40.

6493. LEVINE, JOSEPH M. Edward Gibbon and the quarrel between the ancients and the moderns. ECent (26:1) 1985, 47–62.

6494. PORTER, ROY. Gibbon, the secular scholar. HT (36) Sept., 46–51.

William Gilpin

6495. PIGRAME, STELLA. Gilpin and the picturesque. NRam (24) 1983, 3–16.

William Godwin

6496. CRONIN, RICHARD. Carps and *Caleb Williams*. KSR (1) 35–48.

6497. GIRARD, GAÏD. Maîtres et serviteurs dans *Caleb Williams*: passage du témoin et figures du double. *In* (pp. 197–209) **30.**

6498. JONES, CHRIS. Godwin to Mary: the first letter. KSR (1) 61–74.

6499. KELLY, GARY. 'The solitary life': autobiography in Rousseau and Godwin. *In* (pp. 93–101) ROGER L. EMERSON, GILLES GIRARD, and ROSEANN RUNTE (eds), Man and nature: proceedings of the Canadian Society for Eighteenth-Century Studies: vol. 1. London, Ont.: Univ. of Western Ontario, 1982. pp. xvi, 224. Rev. by Robert James Merrett in CanRCL (13:1) 125–8.

6500. KLAUS, H. GUSTAV. William Godwins *Things as They Are*. Sozialgeschichte im Roman. GRM (36:4) 399–413.

6501. MARSHALL, PETER H. William Godwin. (Bibl. 1985, 5522a.) Rev. by Serge Soupel in EA (38:4) 1985, 468–9; by Seamus Deane in KSR (1) 85–90; by David McCracken in MP (84:1) 99–101.

6502. PHILIP, M. F. E. William Godwin's *Political Justice*: 1788–1800. Unpub. doct. diss., Univ. of Oxford, 1983.

6503. PHILP, MARK. Godwin's *Political Justice*. London: Duckworth. pp. x, 278.

Oliver Goldsmith

6504. DIXON, PETER. 'On Torno's Cliffs': Goldsmith and Regnard. NQ (33:1) 73–4.

6505. DIXSAUT, JEAN. Les plaisirs de l'équivoque dans *The Vicar of Wakefield*: 'something applicable to both sides'. BSEAA (23) 57–64.

6506. DUSSINGER, JOHN A. Philanthropy and the selfish reader in

Goldsmith's *Life of Nash*. Studies in Burke and his Time (Texas Tech Univ., Lubbock, TX) (19:3) 1978, 197–207.

6507. GERI, CARL (introd.). The history of Little Goody Two-Shoes. Guildford: Genesis, 1985. pp. xxviii, 156.

6508. HARP, RICHARD L. New perspectives for Goldsmith's biography. ECent (21:2) 1980, 162–75.

6509. LONSDALE, ROGER. Goldsmith and the *Weekly Magazine*: the missing numbers. *See* **638.**

6510. MADELIN, HERVÉ. *The Vicar of Wakefield* et l'apologétique des Augustéens. EA (39:3) 257–67.

6511. RAFROIDI, PATRICK. Goldsmith ou la géographie du cœur. Études irlandaises (9) 1984, 97–105.

6512. SCHÖTT, ROLAND. Miljövårdskämpe eller bakåtsträvare?: ett tolkningsförsök av Goldsmiths *Deserted Village*. (An environmental protectionist or a reactionary?: an essay in interpretation of Goldsmith's *Deserted Village*.) Artes (12:1) 74–88.

6513. SHIELDS, HUGH. Oliver Goldsmith and popular song. *See* **2549.**

6514. SOUPEL, SERGE. Oliver Goldsmith (1730?–1774), *The Vicar of Wakefield* (1766): bibliographie sélective et critique. BSEAA (23) 17–24.

6515. SWARBRICK, ANDREW (ed.). The art of Oliver Goldsmith. Totowa, NJ: Barnes & Noble, 1984. (Cf. bibl. 1985, 5529.) Rev. by W. B. Hutchings in BJECS (9:1) 106–8; by Valerie Grosvenor Myer in NQ (33:2) 239–40.

6516. WOODS, SAMUEL H. The Goldsmith 'problem'. Studies in Burke and his Time (Texas Tech Univ., Lubbock, TX) (19:1) 1978, 47–60.

6517. —— Images of the orient: Goldsmith and the Philosophes. StudECC (15) 257–70.

6518. WOODS, SAMUEL H., JR. Oliver Goldsmith: a reference guide. Boston, MA: G. K. Hall, 1982. pp xxiii, 208. Rev. by Peter Dixon in YES (16) 277–8.

6519. ZONG-QI, CAI. Structural antitheses in Goldsmith's *The Deserted Village*. PLL (22:3) 326–30.

James Grainger

6520. REID, HUGH. A note on James Grainger's *Ode to Solitude*. NQ (33:4) 518.

George Granville, Baron Lansdowne

6521. TODD, DENNIS. An echo of Granville in Pope's *Dunciad* I, 202. NQ (33:4) 512–13.

Richard Graves

6522. TRACY, CLARENCE. Richard Graves (1715–1804): the sprightly author of *The Spiritual Quixote*. NRam (24) 1983, 17–25.

Thomas Gray

6523. EDGECOMBE, R. S. Diction and allusion in two early Odes by Gray. DUJ (79:1) 31–6.

6524. ELLIOTT, ROGER. The bard as moping owl. CamQ (15) 207–15.

6525. JACKSON, WALLACE. Thomas Gray: drowning in human voices. Criticism (28:4) 361–77.

Eliza Haywood

6526. SPENDER, DALE (introd.). The history of Miss Betsy Thought-less. London: Pandora. pp. xii, 594. (Mothers of the novel.)

Samuel Hearne

6527. GREENFIELD, BRUCE. The idea of discovery as a source of narrative structure in Samuel Hearne's *Journey to the Northern Ocean*. EAL (21:3) 1986/87, 189–209.

Robert Heron

6528. LAMONT-BROWN, RAYMOND. Robert Burns and the assasssins. *See* **6334.**

James Hervey

6529. SOUPEL, SERGE. Visions édéniques et visions apocalyptiques chez James Hervey (1714–1758.) *In* (pp. 77–87) **2.**

Lord Hervey

6530. PAVLOPOULOS, FRANÇOISE. Mémoire, *Mémoires* et création chez Lord Hervey. *In* (pp. 49–58) **34.**

6531. PEEREBOOM, J. J. Hervey and the facts as he saw them. DQR (16:4) 326–40.

John Hill

6532. ROUSSEAU, G. S. Seven new Hill letters. EA (39:2) 174–87.

6533. ——— (ed.). The letters and papers of Sir John Hill, 1714–1775. (Bibl. 1984, 5742.) Rev. by Hugh Ormsby-Lennon in YES (16) 270–2.

Francis Hoffman

6534. HARRIS, FRANCES. Political verse by Francis Hoffman. *See* **387.**

John Home

6535. ELLENBERGER, GARY N. The life and literature of John Home. Unpub. doct. diss., Univ. of Utah. [Abstr. in DA (47) 21A.]

6536. MALEK, JAMES S. (ed.). The plays of John Home. New York; London: Garland, 1980. (Eighteenth-century English drama, 22.) (Facsims of texts pub. 1757–78; pp. xliii, and pagination of individual items.)

David Hume

6537. BOX, MARK. An illusion in Hume's *An Enquiry Concerning the Principles of Morals* identified. NQ (33:1) 60–1.

6538. SHAPIRO, GARY. The man of letters and the author of nature: Hume on philosophical discourse. ECent (26:2) 1985, 115–37.

6539. SIEBERT, DONALD T. David Hume's last words: the importance of *My Own Life*. SSL (19) 1984, 132–47.

6540. STALLEY, R. F. The will in Hume's *Treatise. See* **1648.**

6541. TRICAUD, FRANÇOIS. Remarques sur le poids du passé et le pouvoir d'innover selon Hobbes et selon Hume. *In* (pp. 15–21) **34.**

6542. TWEYMAN, STANLEY. Scepticism and belief in Hume's *Dialogues Concerning Natural Religion*. Dordrecht; Lancaster: Nijhoff. pp. xv, 167. (International archives of the history of ideas, 106.)

6543. VANCE, JOHN A. Johnson and Hume: of like historical minds. StudECC (15) 241–56.

6544. Womersley, David.   Hume and Mary Shelley. NQ (33:2) 164–5.

6545. Wright, John P.   The sceptical realism of David Hume. (Bibl. 1985, 5544.) Rev. by James King in JHP (24:2) 275–8.

Richard Hurd

6546. Marshall, Donald G.   The history of eighteenth-century criticism and modern hermeneutical philosophy: the example of Richard Hurd. *See* **6176.**

Thomas Jefferson

6547. Ferguson, Robert A.   'We hold these truths': strategies of control in the literature of the Founders. *In* (pp. 1–28) **47.**

Soame Jenyns

6548. Rompkey, Ronald.   A draft of Soame Jenyns's *Free Inquiry into the Nature and Origin of Evil* (1757). NQ (33:4) 518–21.

6549. —— Soame Jenyns. Boston, MA: G. K. Hall, 1984. pp. xv, 184. (Twayne's English authors, 391.) Rev. by Jeremy Black in NQ (33:2) 242–3.

Robert Jephson

6550. Nelson, Bonnie.   Much ado about something: *The Law of Lombardy* and the 'Othello play' phenomenon. SN (58:1) 71–83.

Dr Samuel Johnson

6551. Alexander, David.   Doctor Johnson and his contemporaries. University of York, Heslington Hall, 15 October–9 November 1984: a guide to the exhibition. York: Visual Arts Soc., Univ. of York, 1984. pp. ii, 21.

6552. Alkon, Paul; Folkenflik, Robert.   Samuel Johnson: pictures and words. Papers presented at a Clark Library seminar, 23 October, 1982. Los Angeles, CA: William Andrews Clark Memorial Library, Univ. of California, 1984. pp. xi, 118.

6553. Bartolomeo, Joseph F.   Johnson, Richardson, and the audience for fiction. NQ (33:4) 517.

6554. Bate, Jonathan.   Johnson and Shakespeare. NRam (26) 1985/86, 11–13.

6555. Battersby, James L.   Samuel Johnson's enthusiasm for history. Review (8) 157–88 (review-article).

6556. Birmingham Public Libraries.   Dr Samuel Johnson 1709–1784, a bicentenary exhibition: Central Library, Chamberlain Square. Birmingham: Birmingham Public Libraries, 1984. pp. 15.

6557. Brack, O. M., Jr.   Samuel Johnson and the epitaph on a duckling. BkIA (45) 62–79.

6558. Chadwick, Owen.   The religion of Samuel Johnson. YLG (60:3/4) 119–36.

6559. Chapin, Chester.   Samuel Johnson and the Scottish common sense school. ECent (20:1) 1979, 50–64.

6560. Clingham, G. J.   'The inequalities of memory': Johnson's epitaphs on Hogarth. Eng (35) 221–32.

6561. —— A note on Johnson's use of two Restoration poems in his

Drury Lane *Prologue*. NRam (26) 1985/86, 45. (Garrick's inaugural prologue as actor-manager.)

6562. COLLINGS, FRANK. Dr Johnson and his medical advisers. NRam (25) 1984, 3–18.

6563. COOK, DONALD N. The history of Dr Johnson's summer-house. NRam (24) 1983, 49–58.

6564. CURLEY, THOMAS M. Johnson and the geographical revolution: *A Journey to the Western Islands of Scotland*. Studies in Burke and his Time (Texas Tech Univ., Lubbock, TX) (17:3) 1976, 180–98.

6565. DAMROSCH, LEOPOLD, JR. Samuel Johnson and reader-response criticism. ECent (21:2) 1980, 91–108.

6566. DANDO, JOEL ALLAN. The poet as critic: Byron in his letters and journals. Case studies of Shakespeare and Johnson. *See* **4423.**

6567. DEMARIA, ROBERT, JR. Johnson's *Dictionary* and the language of learning. Oxford: Clarendon Press. pp. xii, 303. Rev. by Frank Stack in THES (731) 15.

6568. DITCHFIELD, G. M. Dr Johnson and the Dissenters. BJRL (68:2) 373–409.

6569. —— Dr Johnson and the Dissenters. NRam (26) 1985/86, 5–7.

6570. DOMNARSKI, WILLIAM. Samuel Johnson and the law. NRam (23) 1982, 2–10.

6571. DONALDSON, IAN. Samuel Johnson and the art of observation. ELH (53:4) 779–99.

6572. DOWNIE, J. A. Swift and Johnson: the problems of the life of Swift. NRam (24) 1983, 26–7.

6573. ELLIS, FRANK H. (introd.). Essay on the stile of Doctor Samuel Johnson (1787). By Robert Burrowes. Los Angeles, CA: William Andrews Clark Memorial Library, 1984. pp. xxii, 29. (Augustan Repr. Soc., 229.) Rev. by G. J. Clingham in BJECS (9:2) 248–9.

6574. ENGELL, JAMES. Johnson inhibited. HLB (33:3) 1985, 292–302.

6575. FLEEMAN, J. D. Dr Johnson and 'Miss Fordice'. NQ (33:1) 59–60.

6576. —— A preliminary handlist of copies of books associated with Dr Samuel Johnson. (Bibl. 1984, 5777.) Rev. by David Wheeler in BJECS (9:2) 254–6.

6577. —— (ed.). A journey to the Western Islands of Scotland. Oxford: Clarendon Press, 1985. pp. lx, 371. Rev. by Mervyn Jannetta in Library (8:3) 284–5.

6578. GOLD, JOEL J. John Wilkes and the writings of 'pensioner Johnson'. Studies in Burke and his Time (Texas Tech Univ., Lubbock, TX) (18:2) 1977, 85–98.

6579. GRAY, JAMES. *Auctor* et *auctoritas*: Dr Johnson's views on the authority of authorship. ESCan (12:3) 269–84.

6580. GREENE, DONALD (ed.). Samuel Johnson. New York: OUP, 1984. (Cf. bibl. 1984, 5779.) Rev. by David Wheeler in BJECS (9:2) 254–6; by A. F. T. Lurcock in NQ (32:2) 240–1; by G. J. Clingham in CamQ (15:1) 77–84.

6581. GRIFFIN, ROBERT JOHN. Samuel Johnson and the act of reflection. Unpub. doct. diss., Yale Univ., 1985. [Abstr. in DA (46) 3358A.]

6582. GRUNDY, ISOBEL.   Samuel Johnson and the scale of greatness. Leicester: Leicester UP. pp. 288. Rev. by David Nokes in THES (713) 19.

6583. —— The stability of truth. NRam (25) 1984, 35–44.

6584. —— (ed.).   Samuel Johnson: new critical essays. Totowa, NJ: Barnes & Noble, 1984. (Cf. bibl. 1985, 5568.) Rev. by James Gray in DalR (65:2) 1985, 300–7; by David Wheeler in BJECS (9:2) 254–6; by A. F. T. Lurcock in NQ (33:4) 553–4.

6585. HARDY, JOHN.   Samuel Johnson's literary criticism. EAS (39) 62–77.

6586. HARRIS, JOCELYN.   Samuel Johnson, Samuel Richardson, and the dial-plate. BJECS (9:2) 157–63.

6587. HENSON, E.   Samuel Johnson and the romance of chivalry. Unpub. doct. diss., Univ. of Leicester, 1983.

6588. HUDSON, N. J.   Studies in the moral and religious thought of Johnson. Unpub. doct. diss., Univ. of Oxford, 1984.

6589. HUNDLEY, PATRICK D.   Dr Johnson's theory of autobiography. NRam (23) 1982, 11–16.

6590. INGRAMS, RICHARD (ed.).   Dr Johnson by Mrs Thrale: the 'anecdotes' of Mrs Piozzi in their original form. London: Chatto & Windus, 1984. pp. xvii, 136.

6591. JACK, IAN.   Johnson and autobiography. NRam (23) 1982, 28–9.

6592. JAIN, N. J.   Johnson as a critic of poetic language. Unpub. doct. diss., Univ. of Oxford, 1983.

6593. JEMIELITY, THOMAS.   Samuel Johnson, *The Vanity of Human Wishes*, and biographical criticism. StudECC (15) 227–39.

6594. JENKINS, ELIZABETH.   Dr Johnson and David Garrick. *See* **6483.**

6595. KERSLAKE, JOHN.   Portraits of Johnson. NRam (25) 1984, 32–4.

6596. KIM, MOON-SOO.   Johnson munhak e itseosuh eui botong saramdeul e daehan gwansim: *Life of Savage* reul choolbaljom euro hayeo. (Johnson's concern for the common people: with special reference to the *Life of Savage*.) EngSt (10) 51–67.

6597. KINKEAD-WEEKES, MARK.   Dr Johnson on the rise of the novel. *See* **6056.**

6598. LAWSON, TOM O.   Pope's *An Essay on Man* and Samuel Johnson's duplicitous reaction to it. JELL (32:3) 431–44.

6599. LEVINSON, HARRY NORMAN.   Another look at Johnson's apprai- sal of Swift. EA (39:4) 438–43.

6600. LIM, C. S.   Dr Johnson's quotation from *Macbeth. See* **4864.**

6601. LIVINGSTON, CHELLA COURINGTON.   Samuel Johnson's literary treatment of women. Unpub. doct. diss., Univ. of South Carolina, 1985. [Abstr. in DA (46) 3041A.]

6602. LUSTIG, IRMA S.   Boswell without Johnson: the years after. *See* **6302.**

6603. LYNN, STEVEN.   Johnson's *Rambler* and eighteenth-century rhetoric. *See* **639.**

6604. McHENRY, LAWRENCE C., JR.   Dr Samuel Johnson's head-tilt – a hitherto unrecognized example of ivth cranial nerve palsy. Neurology (Minneapolis) (33:4, suppl. 2) 1983, 230.

6605. MacINERY, JOHN.   Johnson and the art of translation. NRam (23) 1982, 19–20.

6606. McLAVERTY, JAMES.   From definition to explanation: Locke's influence on Johnson's dictionary. *See* **5612.**

6607. MARCUSE, MICHAEL J.   The Lauder controversy and the Jacobite cause. *See* **5757.**

6608. MISENHEIMER, JAMES B., JR.   Johnson and the critic as idealist: some reflections on famous passages from his criticism. NRam (26) 1985/86, 16–33.

6609. —— O'NEILL, ROBERT K.   The Cordell collection of dictionaries and Johnson's lexicographic presence; the love of books in two centuries. *See* **259.**

6610. MUIRHEAD, JOHN.   A model for Johnson's Polyphilus. NQ (33:4) 514–17.

6611. NAGASHIMA, DAISUKE.   A note on Dr Johnson's *History of the English Language*. *In* (pp. 525–31) **26.**

6612. NALINI, JAIN.   Echoes of Milton in Johnson's *Irene*. *See* **5772.**

6613. NOKES, DAVID.   Johnson and Swift. NRam (26) 1985/86, 35–6.

6614. PAGE, K. A. J.   Samuel Johnson's *Rasselas* and its intellectual background. Unpub. doct. diss., Univ. of London, Birkbeck Coll., 1984.

6615. PARKER, G. F.   Johnson's criticism of Shakespeare. *See* **4549.**

6616. PATEY, DOUGLAS LANE.   Johnson's refutation of Berkeley: kicking the stone again. JHI (47:1) 139–45.

6617. PERKINS, DAVID.   Johnson and modern poetry. HLB (33:3) 1985, 303–12.

6618. POTKAY, ADAM.   Johnson and the terms of succession. SELit (26:3) 497–509.

6619. PRIMER, IRWIN.   Tracking a source for Johnson's *Life of Pope*. YLG (61:1/2) 55–60.

6620. REILMAN, JAMES E.   Dr Johnson and the law: an Enlightenment view. NRam (26) 1985/86, 9–11.

6621. REYNOLDS, R. C.   Johnson on Fielding. *See* **6454.**

6622. RICKS, CHRISTOPHER.   Dr Johnson and the Falkland Islands. NRam (26) 1985/86, 13–15.

6623. RIZZO, BETTY.   'Innocent frauds': by Samuel Johnson. *See* **680.**

6624. ROGERS, J. W. P.   Dr Johnson and the English eccentrics. NRam (26) 1985/86, 5–7.

6625. RUDD, NIALL.   Cicero's *De Senectute* and *The Vanity of Human Wishes*. NQ (33:1) 59.

6626. RUDDICK, WILLIAM.   Scott and Johnson as biographers of Dryden. *See* **5431.**

6627. SHARMA, A. B.   Dr Johnson: an economic perspective. Unpub. doct. diss., Univ. of Aberdeen, 1983.

6628. Siebenschuh, William R.   On the locus of faith in Johnson's sermons. Studies in Burke and his Time (Texas Tech Univ., Lubbock, TX) (17:2) 1976, 103–17.

6629. Siebert, Donald T.   *Bubbled, bamboozled,* and *bit:* 'low bad' words in Johnson's *Dictionary. See* **1578.**

6630. Sisk, John P.   Doctor Johnson kicks a stone. PhilL (10:1) 65–75.

6631. Smallwood, P. J. (ed.).   Johnson's preface to Shakespeare: a facsimile of the 1778 edition. *See* **4592.**

6632. Smith, Joseph H.   Samuel Johnson and stories of childhood. Thought (61:240) 105–17.

6633. Stewart, Charlotte A.   The life of a Johnson collection. *See* **283.**

6634. Stock, R. D.   Samuel Johnson and neoclassical dramatic theory: the intellectual context of the *Preface to Shakespeare.* (Bibl. 1975, 6766.) Rev. by P. T. Dircks in Studies in Burke and his Time (Texas Tech Univ., Lubbock, TX) (17:1) 1976, 61–4.

6635. Taylor, Charlotte.   Random thoughts on *Rasselas.* NRam (23) 1982, 22–4.

6636. Ty, Eleanor.   Cowper's *Connoisseur* 138 and Samuel Johnson. *See* **6372.**

6637. Uphaus, Robert W.   The 'equipoise' of Johnson's *Life of Savage.* Studies in Burke and his Time (Texas Tech Univ., Lubbock, TX) (17:1) 1976, 43–54.

6638. Vance, John A.   Johnson and Hume: of like historical minds. *See* **6543.**

6639. —— Samuel Johnson and the sense of history. (Bibl. 1985, 5597.) Rev. by John J. Burke in CLIO (14:3) 1985, 346–9; by Richard B. Schwartz in SAQ (85:3) 314–15; by G. J. Clingham in EC (36:3) 255–63; by James L. Battersby in Review (8) 157–88.

6640. Vaughn, Anthony.   Strangled with a bowstring: a clear case of character assassination. NRam (23) 1982, 21–2.

6641. Venturo, David Francis.   Johnson the poet. Unpub. doct. diss., Harvard Univ. [Abstr. in DA (47) 2172A.]

6642. Wharton, T. F.   Samuel Johnson and the theme of hope. (Bibl. 1985, 5602a.) Rev. by Joan H. Pittock in BJECS (9:1) 105–6.

6643. Wilson, Ross.   The enigma of port and Dr Johnson. NRam (25) 1984, 30–2.

6644. Young, Gary Ramsey.   The controversy surrounding Samuel Johnson's late conversion. Unpub. doct. diss., Univ. of Texas at Arlington, 1985. [Abstr. in DA (47) 918A.]

Samuel Johnson (of Cheshire)

6645. Rudolph, Valerie C. (ed.).   The plays of Samuel Johnson of Cheshire. New York; London: Garland, 1980. (Eighteenth-century English drama, 25.) (Facsims of texts pub. 1729–32; transcripts of MSS; pp. xxi, and pagination of individual items.)

Sir William Jones

6646. Cannon, Garland.   The construction of the European image of the Orient: a bicentenary reappraisal of Sir William Jones as poet and translator. CompCrit (8) 166–88.

'Junius'

6647. CORDASCO, FRANCESCO. Political poems compiled by Junius (1772): a further note. NQ (33:4) 523.

6648. —— An unrecorded Bensley edition of Junius. NQ (33:1) 84.

6649. LINDSAY, DAVID W. Junius and the Grafton administration, 1768–1770. Prose Studies (9:2) 160–76.

Hugh Kelly

6650. BATAILLE, ROBERT R. Hugh Kelly (1739–1777): a bibliography. BB (43:4) 228–34.

6651. CARVER, LARRY (ed.); GROSS, MARY J. H. (textual notes). The plays of Hugh Kelly. New York; London: Garland, 1980. (Eighteenth-century English drama, 26.) (Facsims of texts pub. 1768–75; transcript of MS; pp. lvi, and pagination of individual items.)

Richard Payne Knight

6652. ERDMAN, DAVID V. Grub Street behind the skirts of Margaret Nicholson. Factotum (11) 1981, 25–7.

William Lauder

6653. MARCUSE, MICHAEL J. The Lauder controversy and the Jacobite cause. See **5757.**

Richard Lee

6654. DOUGLAS, JANE. Citizen Lee and the Tree of Liberty. See **367.**

Charlotte Lennox

6655. LÖFFLER, ARNO. Die wahnsinnige Heldin: Charlotte Lennox' *The Female Quixote*. AAA (11:2) 63–81.

6656. SHULMAN, SANDRA (introd.). The female Quixote, or, The adventures of Arabella. London: Pandora. pp. xv, 423. (Mothers of the novel.)

M. G. Lewis

6657. ABENSOUR, LILIANE. Limites-non frontières d'une œuvre: *Le Moine* de M. G. Lewis. Europe (62:659) 1984, 13–18.

6658. ARNAUD, PIERRE. Au service de Lucifer: le diable, la magie et le pacte dans *Le Moine* de M. G. Lewis. *In* (pp. 133–51) **30.**

6659. FAURE, ALAIN. Du simple au double: du *Moine* de M. G. Lewis aux *Élixirs du diable* de E. T. A. Hoffmann. Europe (62:659) 1984, 54–62.

6660. FIEROBE, CLAUDE. La topographie romanesque de M. G. Lewis dans *The Monk*. EA (39:1) 15–25.

6661. HOUSTON, JOANN. Finding meaning: a discussion of pornography and eroticism in John Cleland's *Memoirs of a Woman of Pleasure* and some parallels between Matthew G. Lewis' *The Monk. See* **6358.**

6662. SCHORK, R. J. Lewis' *The Monk*. Exp (44:3) 26–9.

George Lillo

6663. MOHR, HANS-ULRICH. Lillos *The London Merchant* – ein 'bürgerliches' Trauerspiel? *See* **6028.**

Edmund Lodge

6664. TELLE, EMILE V. Edmund Lodge on John and Thomas More (1795). *See* **4163.**

James Macpherson

6665. GASKILL, HOWARD. 'Ossian' Macpherson: towards a rehabilitation. CompCrit (8), 113–48.

6666. HAYWOOD, I. The making of history: a study of the literary forgeries of James Macpherson and Thomas Chatterton in relation to eighteenth century ideas of history and fiction. *See* **6351.**

6667. HÖFELE, ANDREAS. Die Originalität der Fälschung: Zur Funktion des literarischen Betrugs in England 1750–1800. *See* **5962.**

6668. MURPHY, PETER T. Fool's gold: the Highland treasures of Macpherson's Ossian. ELH (53:3) 567–91.

6669. SHEN, RICHARD B. 'Those Scotch imposters and their cabal': Ossian and the Scottish Enlightenment. *In* (pp. 55–63) ROGER L. EMERSON, GILLES GIRARD, and ROSEANN RUNTE (eds), Man and nature: proceedings of the Canadian Society for Eighteenth-century Studies: vol. 1. London, Ont.: Univ. of Western Ontario, 1982. pp. xvi, 224. Rev. by Robert James Merrett in CanRCL (13:1) 125–8.

Samuel Madden

6670. ALKON, PAUL. Samuel Madden's *Memoirs of the Twentieth Century.* SFS (12:2) 1985, 184–201.

Arthur Mainwaring

6671. HARRIS, FRANCES. For *Arthur* read *Author. See* **616.**

6672. —— Jacob Tonson and the *Advice to the Electors of Great Britain. See* **385.**

6673. —— Robert Walpole, Arthur Mainwaring, and the *Letter to a Friend Concerning the Publick Debts.* Factotum (11) 1981, 22–3.

David Mallet

6674. NUSSBAUM, FELICITY A. (ed.). The plays of David Mallet. New York; London: Garland, 1980. pp. 500. (Eighteenth-century English drama, 28.) (Facsims of texts pub. 1731–63; pp. xliii, and pagination of individual items.)

Bernard Mandeville

6675. DANIEL, STEPHEN H. Myth and rationality in Mandeville. JHI (47:4) 595–609.

Mary de la Rivière Manley

6676. ANON. Sunderland v. Manley. Factotum (21) 1985, 22–3.

6677. FOXTON, ROSEMARY. Delariviere Manley and 'Astrea's vacant throne'. *See* **5410.**

6678. MORGAN, FIDELIS (ed.). A woman of no character: an autobiography of Mrs Manley. London: Faber & Faber. pp. 176.

John Marchant

6679. OSLER, ALAN. John Marchant's lectures on *Paradise Lost. See* **5776.**

John Moir

6680. PITCHER, E. W. Some contributions to eighteenth-century magazines by John Moir. *See* **671.**

James Burnett, Lord Monboddo

6681. BROWN, IAIN GORDON. A character of Lord Monboddo. NQ (33:4) 523–4.

6682. HAMMETT, I. M. Lord Monboddo's *Of the Origin and Progress of Language*: its sources, genesis and background, with special attention to the Advocates' Library. *See* **818.**

Lady Mary Wortley Montagu

6683. GRUNDY, ISOBEL. Further retrospect. Factotum (10) 1980, 16–17.

6684. RUBENSTEIN, JILL. Women's biography as a family affair: Lady Louisa Stuart's 'Biographical Anecdotes' of Lady Mary Wortley Montagu. Prose Studies (9:1) 1–21.

Edward Moore

6685. AMBERG, ANTHONY. Moore's *Gamester* on the London stage, 1771–1871. TN (40:2) 55–60.

Hannah More ('Z')

6686. WOOD, LAURENCE. The monster gin. Factotum (4) 1978, 11.

Arthur Murphy

6687. SCHWARTZ, RICHARD B. (ed.). The plays of Arthur Murphy. New York; London: Garland, 1979. 4 vols. (Eighteenth-century English drama, 30.) (Facsims of texts pub. 1786–98; pp. xxx, and pagination of individual items.)

Peter Newby

6688. WHITEHEAD, MAURICE (ed.). Peter Newby: 18th century Lancashire recusant poet: with a selection of his poetry. Lancaster: Centre for North-West Regional Studies, Univ. of Lancaster, 1980. pp. 44. (Occasional papers, 7.)

Roger North

6689. COCHRANE, HAMILTON EDWARDS. Roger North's *Lives of the Norths*: a critical study. Unpub. doct. diss., Univ. of Minnesota, 1985. [Abstr. in DA (46) 1946A.]

6690. MILLARD, PETER (ed.). *General Preface* and *Life of Dr John North*. (Bibl. 1985, 5626.) Rev. by Patricia Köster in ESCan (12:4) 462–8.

John Boyle, Fifth Earl of Orrery

6691. ELIAS, A. C., JR. Lord Orrery's copy of *Memoirs of the Life and Writings of Swift* (1751). *See* **214.**

Thomas Paine

6692. POWELL, DAVID. Tom Paine: the greatest exile. New York: St Martin's Press, 1985. (Cf. bibl. 1985, 5630.) Rev. by Daryl E. Jones in AL (58:4) 624–6.

Thomas Percy

6693. BROOKS, CLEANTH; FALCONER, A. F. (gen. eds). The Percy letters: vol. 8, The correspondence of Thomas Percy and John Pinkerton. Ed. by HARRIET HARVEY WOOD. New Haven, CT; London: Yale UP, 1985. pp. xl, 124.

6694. KNAPMAN, ZINNIA. A reappraisal of Percy's editing. *See* **2521.**

Hester Lynch Piozzi (Mrs Thrale)

6695. BROWNLEY, MARTINE WATSON. A note on Gabriel Pozzi and his wife's writing. NRam (25) 1984, 45–7.

6696. INGRAMS, RICHARD (ed.). Dr Johnson by Mrs Thrale: the 'anecdotes' of Mrs Piozzi in their original form. *See* **6590.**

6697. McCarthy, William.   Hester Thrale Piozzi: portrait of a literary woman. Chapel Hill: North Carolina UP. pp. 306. Rev. by David Nokes in TLS, 18 Apr., 414.

Alexander Pope

6698. Alkalay-Gut, Karen.   Women in a trap: Pope and Ovid in *Eloisa to Abelard*. CLit (13:3) 272–84.

6699. Anderson, David R.   Landscape and theodicy in Pope, Thomson, and Cowper. *See* **6366.**

6700. Black, Jeremy.   Bolingbroke's attack on Pope: a lawyer's comment. *See* **6292.**

6701. Brooks-Davies, Douglas.   Pope's *Dunciad* and the queen of night: a study in emotional Jacobitism. Manchester: Manchester UP, 1985. pp. ix, 190.

6702. Brown, Laura.   Alexander Pope. (Bibl. 1985, 5639.) Rev. by Felicity Rosslyn in CamQ (15:2) 166; by Catherine Koralek in Eng (35) 293–7.

6703. Cartwright, Graham.   Pope's books: a postscript to Mack. *See* **209.**

6704. Clingham, G. J.   Bolingbroke's copy of Pope's *Works 1717–1735* in Tonbridge School library. *See* **210.**

6705. Cowler, Rosemary (ed.).   The prose works of Alexander Pope: vol. 2, The major works, 1725–1744. Oxford: Blackwell; Hamden, CT: Archon. pp. xv, 529. Rev. by Robert Halsband in NYTB, 5 Oct., 20.

6706. Fairer, David.   Pope's imagination. (Bibl. 1985, 5646.) Rev. by Nigel Wood in BJECS (9:2) 277–9.

6707. Ferguson, Rebecca.   The unbalanced mind: Pope and the rule of passion. Brighton: Harvester Press. pp. 224.

6708. Gabriner, P. J.   Antedatings, postdatings, and additions from Pope's translation of the *Iliad* for OED. *See* **1537.**

6709. Genster, Julia Ann.   'These veracious pages': the epistle and its audiences from Dryden to Austen. *See* **5414.**

6710. Gill, R. B.   Dryden, Pope, and the person in personal satire. *See* **5415.**

6711. Hahn, H. George.   Broadsides on the Thames: the social context of *The Rape of the Lock*, II, 47–52. Ang (104:1/2) 118–21.

6712. Hammond, Brean S.   Pope. Brighton: Harvester Press. pp. xi, 218. (Harvester new readings.) Rev. by David Nokes in THES (726) 18.

6713. Ingram, Allan.   Intricate laughter in the satire of Swift and Pope. London: Macmillan. pp. x, 206. Rev. by Frank Stack in THES (715) 17.

6714. Jackson, Wallace.   Pope and the character of good sense. ECent (27:3) 293–8 (review-article).

6715. —— Vision and re-vision in Alexander Pope. (Bibl. 1985, 5652.) Rev. by David Fairer in BJECS (9:1) 103–4.

6716. Jannetta, Mervyn.   Alexander Pope: a new issue traced and another concealed edition. Factotum (2) 1978, 13–15.

6717. Jones, W. L.   The contemporary context of Alexander Pope's correspondence. Unpub. doct. diss., Univ. of Edinburgh, 1984.

6718. LANOIX, LOUIS. Pope, poëte des lumières. *In* (pp. 153–64) **30.**

6719. LAWSON, TOM O. Pope's *An Essay on Man* and Samuel Johnson's duplicitous reaction to it. *See* **6598.**

6720. MACK, MAYNARD. Alexander Pope: a life. (Bibl. 1985, 5655.) Rev. by Christopher Ricks in Enc (66:1) 38–41; by Denis Donoghue in BkW, 9 Feb., 1, 8–9; by John Wain in NYTB, 2 Mar., 11; by R. I. Ferguson in UES (24:2) 42–4.

6721. —— (ed.). The last and greatest art: some unpublished poetical manuscripts of Alexander Pope. Toronto: Assoc. UPs, 1984. (Cf. bibl. 1985, 5658.) Rev. by Pat Rogers in MLR (81:3) 721–2; by Brean S. Hammond in BJECS (9:1) 102–3.

6722. MARTIN, PETER. Pursuing innocent pleasures: the gardening world of Alexander Pope. (Bibl. 1985, 5659.) Rev. by Vincent Carretta in PQ (65:2) 285–7.

6723. MORRIS, DAVID. Alexander Pope: the genius of sense. (Bibl. 1985, 5660.) Rev. by Wallace Jackson in ECent (27:3) 293–8; by Peter Thorpe in SoHR (20:1) 72–4; by Nigel Wood in BJECS (9:2) 277–9.

6724. NICHOL, D. W. Pope, Warburton and the Kemptons: problems of literary legacy (with a book-trade correspondence). *See* **416.**

6725. NICHOL, DONALD W. Piracy of Pope's Homer. *See* **417.**

6726. PATEY, DOUGLAS LANE. Art and integrity: concepts of self in Alexander Pope and Edward Young. MP (83:4) 364–78.

6727. —— 'Love deny'd': Pope and the allegory of despair. ECS (20:1) 34–55.

6728. PLOWDEN, G. F. C. Pope on classic ground. (Bibl. 1985, 5662.) Rev. by David Nokes in BJECS (9:1) 104–5.

6729. POLLAK, ELLEN. The poetics of sexual myth: gender and ideology in the verse of Swift and Pope. Chicago: Chicago UP. Rev. by Brean S. Hammond in THES (693) 16.

6730. RIVERS, WILLIAM E. Nicholas Amhurst's *Terrae Filius* as background for Pope's satire of university education. *See* **679.**

6731. ROSSLYN, FELICITY. 'The dear ideas': Pope on passion. CamQ (15) 216–28.

6732. RUMBOLD, V. Pope and the gothic past. Unpub. doct. diss., Univ. of Cambridge, 1984.

6733. SHANKMAN, STEVEN. Pope's *Iliad*: Homer in the age of passion. (Bibl. 1985, 5668.) Rev. by Ronald L. Bogue in CL (38:3) 299–301.

6734. SONG, NAK-HUN. Alexander Pope si e banyoung daen isung mit bi-isung eui gaenyeom e gwanhayeo. (On the idea of reason and non-reason as reflected in Pope's poetry). EngSt (10) 17–38.

6735. STACK, FRANK. Pope and Horace: studies in imitation. (Bibl. 1985, 5670.) Rev. by Pat Rogers in TLS, 11 July, 765.

6736. SZILAGYI, STEPHEN. Pope's *Two or Three*. Exp (44:3) 23–6.

6737. TASCH, PETER A. Pope and Dryden on shutting doors. *See* **5438.**

6738. TODD, DENNIS. An echo of Granville in Pope's *Dunciad* 1, 202. *See* **6521.**

6739. WILLIAMS, ROBERT W. Fate and the narrative of *The Rape of the Lock*. Sydney Studies in English (11) 1985/86, 23–30.

6740. —— A poem is a speaking picture: Pope and iconography. Sydney Studies in English (12) 21–35.

6741. WILSON, PENELOPE. Feminism and the Augustans: some readings and problems. CritQ (28:1/2) 80–92.

Ann Radcliffe

6742. CHARD, CHLOE (ed.). The romance of the forest. Oxford: OUP. pp. 400. (World's classics.)

6743. KAMIO, MITUO. Yureijo no uchi to soto: Radcliffe *Udolpho no shinpi*. (Outside and inside the haunted castle: Radcliffe's *Mysteries of Udolpho*.) SEL (63:1) 61–74.

6744. LONDON, APRIL. Ann Radcliffe in context: marking the boundaries of *The Mysteries of Udolpho*. ECL (10:1) 35–47.

James Ralph

6745. SHIELDS, DAVID S. Mental nocturnes: night thoughts on man and nature in the poetry of eighteenth-century America. *See* **6110.**

Allan Ramsay

6746. BROWN, IAIN GORDON. 'Superfyn poetry nae doubt?': advice to Allan Ramsay, and a criticism of *The Gentle Shepherd*. Bibliotheck (13:2) 33–41.

Rudolf Erich Raspe

6747. MICHAELIS-JENA, RUTH. Eulenspiegel and Münchhausen: two German folk heroes. *See* **2472.**

George Richards

6748. LEARY, LEWIS. George Richards: 'The best poet America ever produced'. EAL (20:3) 1985/86, 131–55.

Samuel Richardson

6749. AIKINS, JANET E. A plot discover'd; or, the uses of *Venice Preserv'd* within *Clarissa*. *See* **5835.**

6750. ANDON-MILLIGAN, LILLIAN HILJA. Samuel Richardson's *Clarissa*: more room for raillery. Unpub. doct. diss., Univ. of California, Irvine. [Abstr. in DA (47) 905A.]

6751. BARTOLOMEO, JOSEPH F. Johnson, Richardson, and the audience for fiction. *See* **6553.**

6752. BERTOLINO, JANE VICTORIA. Richardson's and Goldoni's *Pamela*: similarities and variations. Unpub. doct. diss., Rutgers Univ. [Abstr. in DA (47) 893A.]

6753. CASTLE, TERRY. Clarissa's ciphers: meaning and disruption in Richardson's *Clarissa*. (Bibl. 1985, 5691.) Rev. by William Beatty Warner in ECent (26:1) 1985, 73–94; by Douglas Brooks-Davies in YES (16) 264–8.

6754. CRUISE, JAMES JOSEPH. Governing scripture: authority and the early English novel. *See* **6391.**

6755. CUMMINGS, KATHERINE M. Reconstructing 'life with father': the daughter's novel seduction. Unpub. doct. diss., Univ. of Wisconsin–Madison, 1985. [Abstr. in DA (46) 3345A.]

6756. DAPHINOFF, DIMITER. Samuel Richardsons *Clarissa*. Text,

Rezeption und Interpretation. Berne: Francke. pp. 323. (Schweizer anglistische Arbeiten, 108.)

6757. —— (ed.). An alternative ending to Richardson's *Clarissa*. (Bibl. 1984, 5658.) Rev. by Jocelyn Harris in YES (16) 268–70.

6758. DAY, ROBERT ADAMS. Speech acts, orality, and the epistolary novel. *See* **6394.**

6759. DIXSAUT, JEAN. 'Uncommon gradations': l'amour, le corps et l'âme dans *Pamela. In* (pp. 131–8) **14.**

6760. EAGLETON, TERRY. The rape of Clarissa: writing, sexuality and class struggle in Samuel Richardson. (Bibl. 1985, 5696.) Rev. by Ian Donaldson in YES (16) 262–4.

6761. FLYNN, CAROL HOULIHAN. Samuel Richardson: a man of letters. (Bibl. 1984, 5906.) Rev. by Jocelyn Harris in YES (16) 268–70.

6762. FRAIL, ROBERT JOHN. The British connection: the Abbé Prévost and the translations of the novels of Samuel Richardson. Unpub. doct. diss., Columbia Univ., 1985. [Abstr. in DA (47) 170A.]

6763. GENSTER, JULIA ANN. 'These veracious pages': the epistle and its audiences from Dryden to Austen. *See* **5414.**

6764. GOLDBERG, RITA. Sex and Enlightenment: women in Richardson and Diderot. (Cf. bibl. 1984, 5908 when scholar's forename incorrect.) Rev. by Margarette Smith in BJECS (9:1) 95–6; by John C. O'Neal in ECL (10:2) 87–97.

6765. GREENE, MILDRED SARAH E. 'A chimera of her own creating': love and fantasy in Madame de Lafayette's *Princesse de Clèves* and Richardson's *Clarissa*. RMRLL (40:4) 221–32.

6766. GWILLIAM, TASSIE. 'Like Tiresias': metamorphosis and gender in *Clarissa*. Novel (19:2) 101–17.

6767. GWILLIAM, TASSIE KATHERINE. Samuel Richardson's fictions of gender. Unpub. doct. diss., Cornell Univ., 1985. [Abstr. in DA (46) 2700A.]

6768. HALLDÉN, RUTH. Den moderna romanens fader: om Samuel Richardsons författarskap. (The father of the modern novel: on Samuel Richardson's work.) Artes (12:1) 89–99.

6769. HARRIS, JOCELYN. Samuel Johnson, Samuel Richardson, and the dial-plate. *See* **6586.**

6770. HILLIARD, RAYMOND F. *Pamela*: autonomy, subordination, and the 'state of childhood'. SP(83:2) 201–17.

6771. KIM, SANG-HEE. *Pamela* eui gujo. (The structure of *Pamela*.) JHY (8:1) 75–97.

6772. LAWSON, JACQUELINE ELAINE. 'Ill-govern'd families': domestic misconduct in the novels of Defoe, Richardson, and Fielding. *See* **6407.**

6773. LAWSON, TOM O. Character influence: Samuel Richardson's *Sir Charles Grandison* and its influence upon the main character in George Eliot's *The Mill on the Floss*. IKY (55) 159–85.

6774. LEITES, EDMUND. The Puritan conscience and modern sexuality. *See* **5234.**

6775. MCDERMOTT, HUBERT. *Vertue Rewarded*: the first Anglo-Irish novel. *See* **5166.**

6776. PITTOCK, MURRAY G. H.   Samuel Richardson: a note from Marvell. *See* **5636.**

6777. RINEHART, HOLLIS.   *Clarissa* and the concept of tragedy: the death of Lovelace. *In* (pp. 37–47) ROGER L. EMERSON, WILLIAM KINSLEY, and WALTER MOSER (eds), Man and nature: proceedings of the Canadian Society for Eighteenth-Century Studies: vol. 2. Montreal: Canadian Society for Eighteenth-Century Studies, 1984. pp. xi, 156.

6778. ROGERS, KATHARINE M.   Creative variation: *Clarissa* and *Les Liaisons dangereuses*. CL (38:1) 36–52.

6779. ROSENWASSER, DAVID.   The idea of enclosure: prisons and havens at the rise of the novel. *See* **5313.**

6780. SCHMITZ, GÖTZ.   'Such visionary stuff': Träume und Einbildungen in Samuel Richardsons *Clarissa*. Ang (104:1/2) 45–62.

6781. SMITH, SARAH W. R.   Samuel Richardson: a reference guide. Boston, MA: G. K. Hall, 1984. pp. xxxi, 425. Rev. by W. R. Owens in NQ (33:1) 118–19.

6782. STEVENSON, JOHN ALLEN.   'A geometry of his own': Richardson and the marriage-ending. SELit (26:3) 469–83.

6783. TENER, ROBERT H.   The authorship of a neglected appraisal of *Clarissa*. ELN (24:2) 58–66.

6784. TIERNEY, JAMES E.   More on George Faulkner and the London book trade. *See* **438.**

6785. WARNER, WILLIAM BEATTY.   Redeeming interpretation. ECent (26:1) 1985, 73–94 (review-article).

6786. WEHRS, DONALD R.   Irony, storytelling, and the conflict of interpretations in *Clarissa*. ELH (53:4) 759–77.

6787. ZOMCHICK, JOHN P.   Tame spirits, brave fellows, and the web of law: Robert Lovelace's legalistic conscience. ELH (53:1) 99–120.

Joseph Ritson

6788. SIMPSON, ROGER.   A source for Peacock's *The Misfortunes of Elphin*. NQ (33:2) 165–6.

William Robertson

6789. SMITTEN, JEFFREY.   Robertson's *History of Scotland*: narrative structure and the sense of reality. CLIO (11:1) 1981, 29–47.

Richard Rolt

6790. BLACK, JEREMY.   Richard Rolt, 'Patriot' historian. Factotum (16) 1983, 19–23.

Nicholas Rowe

6791. ARMISTEAD, J. M.   Calista and the 'equal empire' of her 'sacred sex'. StudECC (15) 173–85.

6792. MILHOUS, JUDITH.   The first production of Rowe's *Jane Shore*. TJ (38:3) 309–21.

Susanna Rowson

6793. PIACENTINO, EDWARD J.   Susanna Haswell Rowson: a bibliography of first editions of primary works and secondary sources. BB (43:1) 13–16.

Richard Savage

6794. UPHAUS, ROBERT W.   The 'equipoise' of Johnson's *Life of Savage*. *See* **6637.**

Sarah Scott

6795. SPENCER, JANE (introd.).   A description of Millenium Hall and the country adjacent. London: Virago Press. pp. xvi, 207. (Virago modern classics, 214.)

Anthony Ashley Cooper, Third Earl of Shaftesbury

6796. EDDY, DONALD D.   John Brown, *Essays on the Characteristics*. See **99.**

6797. ENDOU, KENICHI.   Shaftesbury no shigakuni shimeru sukou no ichi. (The place of 'the sublime' in Shaftesburian poetics.) SEL (63:2) 227–39.

6798. INGLESFIELD, ROBERT.   Shaftesbury's influence on Thomson's *Seasons*. BJECS (9:2) 141–56.

6799. METZ, KARL H.   'The social chain of being'. Zum Topos des sozialen Konservativismus und zur Entstehung des Gedankens der sozialen Verantwortung im Grossbritannien der industriellen Revolution. Archiv für Kulturgeschichte (68:1) 151–83.

William Shenstone

6800. CALHOUN, RANDALL LEE.   William Shenstone's aesthetic theory and poetry. Unpub. doct. diss., Ball State Univ., 1985. [Abstr. in DA (47) 907A.]

Frances Sheridan

6801. HOGAN, ROBERT; BEASLEY, JERRY C. (eds).   The plays of Frances Sheridan. Newark: Delaware UP; London; Toronto: Assoc. UPs, 1984. pp. 209. Rev. by Christopher Murray in ECI (1) 214–15.

Richard Brinsley Sheridan

6802. CAMÉE, JEAN-FRANÇOIS.   La critique des conventions théâtrales dans *The Critic* de Sheridan. *In* (pp. 317–26) **1.**

6803. DAVISON, PETER (ed.).   Sheridan: comedies: *The Rivals, A Trip to Scarborough, The School for Scandal, The Critic*: a casebook. Basingstoke: Macmillan. pp. 223. (Casebook series.) Rev. by T. O. Treadwell in TLS, 18 July, 789.

6804. LEFANU, WILLIAM (ed.).   Betsy Sheridan's journal. Oxford; New York: OUP. pp. xii, 223.

6805. MORWOOD, JAMES.   The life and works of Richard Brinsley Sheridan. Edinburgh: Scottish Academic Press, 1985. pp. viii, 200. Rev. by T. O. Treadwell in TLS, 18 July, 789.

6806. ROWE, JEREMY.   *The Rivals* by Richard Sheridan. Basingstoke: Macmillan. pp. viii, 88. (Macmillan master guides.)

Thomas Sheridan

6807. HERNLUND, PATRICIA.   A new work by Thomas Sheridan. See **388.**

Christopher Smart

6808. BOOTH, MARK W.   Song form and the mind in Christopher Smart's later poetry. StudECC (15) 211–25.

6809. GOODSON, P. R.   The significance of music in the life and religious poetry of Christopher Smart. Unpub. doct. diss., Univ. of Edinburgh. [Abstr. in IT (36) 911.]

6810. KATZ, ADELAIDE E.   The alphabet of redemption in

15

Christopher Smart's *Jubilate Agno*. Unpub. doct. diss., Columbia Univ., 1984. [Abstr. in DA (47) 189A.]

6811. PITCHER, E. W.   Additions to *Christopher Smart: An Annotated Bibliography 1743–1983* (1984): the 'General Publications' lists. ANQ (24:5/6) 71–2.

6812. RIZZO, BETTY.   'The Bite' – Kitty Smart to Henry Fox. RES (37:146) 215–19.

6813. WALSH, MARCUS.   Smart's pillars and the Hutchinsonians. NQ (33:1) 67–70.

6814. —— WILLIAMSON, KARINA (eds).   The poetical works of Christopher Smart: vol. 2, Religious poetry 1763–1771. (Bibl. 1985, 5720.) Rev. by Claude Rawson in BJECS (9:1) 108–9.

Tobias Smollett

6815. BOLD, ALAN (ed.).   Smollett: author of the first distinction. Totowa, NJ: Barnes & Noble, 1982. (Cf. bibl. 1983, 6361.) Rev. by G. S. Rousseau in YES (16) 275–7.

6816. CARGILL, MARY TERRELL.   Images of the eighteenth-century city: Bath, London, and Edinburgh in *Humphry Clinker*. Unpub. doct. diss., Univ. of Mississippi. [Abstr. in DA (47) 1330A.]

6817. HILLYARD, BRIAN.   The fingerprint in practice. *See* **56.**

6818. KELLEY, ROBERT E.   From letter to 'Letter': Smollett's *Travels*. SSL (20) 1985, 101–22.

6819. PITCHER, E. W.   Further remarks on arbitrary signatures in Smollett's *British Magazine* (1760–67). *See* **669.**

6820. —— On the attribution to Smollett of *The Unfortunate Lovers*. NQ (33:4) 521.

6821. ROUSSEAU, G. S.   Tobias Smollett: essays of two decades. (Bibl. 1985, 5726.) Rev. by John Valdimir Price in YES (16) 274–5.

6822. SHIMADA, TAKAU.   Kaempfer's *The History of Japan* as a most possible source for Smollett's *Atom*. NQ (33:1) 70–3.

6823. —— Key to the Japanese names in *The History and Adventures of an Atom*. ELN (23:4) 24–31.

Sir Richard Steele

6824. BLACK, JEREMY.   Laying up rights with providence: an unpublished letter of Sir Richard Steele. NQ (33:4) 490–1.

6825. DAMMERS, RICHARD H.   Richard Steele. (Cf. bibl. 1985, 5729, where author's surname incorrect.) Rev. by Alba Graziano in YES (16) 261–2.

6826. EVANS, JAMES E.   Mr Review on the 'glorious' *Tatler* and the 'inimitable' *Spectator*. *See* **595.**

6827. GRUNDY, ISOBEL.   Further retrospect. *See* **6683.**

6828. HYLAND, P. B. J.   Richard Steele, the press and the Hanoverian succession, 1713–1716. *See* **623.**

6829. KNIGHT, CHARLES A.   Bibliography and the shape of the literary periodical in the early eighteenth century. *See* **634.**

6830. PRESCOTT, ANDREW.   Some further letters to the *Tatler* and the *Spectator*. *See* **674.**

6831. ROEDEL, HARLAN DEAN.   The fine gentleman in the works of

Richard Steele. Unpub. doct. diss., Univ. of Kansas, 1985. [Abstr. in DA (46) 3043A.]

James Sterling

6832. GERRARD, CHRISTINE. *An Ode on the Times*: the political fortunes of James Sterling and Matthew Concanen. *See* **6365.**

Laurence Sterne

6833. AHRENDS, GÜNTER. Sternes *Tristram Shandy* und der Literaturtyp der Anatomie. *See* **2960.**

6834. ALSOP, D. K. A stylistic analysis of *Tristram Shandy*, with consideration of some influences upon Sterne's writing. Unpub. doct. diss., Univ. of London, Westfield Coll. [Abstr. in IT (36) 470.]

6835. BRACK, O. M., JR. A book for a parlour-window. Review (8) 273–301 (review-article).

6836. BROWNE, RONALD. 'Curious cuts'. *See* **67.**

6837. BRÜCKMANN, PATRICIA. Addendum to 'Mr Shandy's hip' (23:9/10). ANQ (24:5/6) 71.

6838. BYRD, MAX. Tristram Shandy. (Bibl. 1985, 5733.) Rev. by Valerie Grosvenor Myer in NQ (33:3) 421.

6839. CALDWELL, ROY CHANDLER, JR. Ludic narrative in the novel: *Projet pour une révolution à New York*; *Das Schloss*; *Tristram Shandy*. Unpub. doct. diss., Univ. of North Carolina at Chapel Hill, 1985. [Abstr. in DA (47) 170A.]

6840. CASH, ARTHUR H. Laurence Sterne: the later years. London: Methuen. pp. xxiv, 390.

6841. CONRAD, PETER. Shandyism: the character of romantic irony. (Bibl. 1982, 6459.) Rev. by Arthur H. Cash in ECent (20:3) 1979, 277–83.

6842. CRUISE, JAMES JOSEPH. Governing scripture: authority and the early English novel. *See* **6391.**

6843. DENIZOT, PAUL. Yorick et la quête du bonheur, ou les équivoques ludiques du corps et de l'âme. *In* (pp. 157–66) **14.**

6844. GOTTLIEB, SIDNEY. Sterne's Slawkenbergius and Joseph Hall. *See* **5473.**

6845. IKIN, BRIDGET. A Sterne warning: false imprints and piracies in the 1780's. *See* **391.**

6846. LAMPKIN, FRANCES LORETTA MURRELL. Metaphor, motif, and the moment: form and human relationships in Laurence Sterne's *Tristram Shandy*, James Joyce's *Ulysses*, and John Barth's *Lost in the Funhouse*. Unpub. doct. diss., Texas A & M Univ., 1985. 2 vols. [Abstr. in DA (47) 172A.]

6847. MARSH, CHARLES WILLIAM, JR. The anatomy of *Tristram Shandy*. Unpub. doct. diss., Univ. of Kansas, 1985. [Abstr. in DA (47) 538A.]

6848. MENGEL, EWALD. Formen und Funktionen des *wit* in Laurence Sternes *Tristram Shandy*. Archiv (223:2) 269–82.

6849. MITROI, MIHAI (trans. and ed.). O calatorie sentimentala; Jurnalul pentru Eliza. (A sentimental journey; Journal to Eliza.)

Bucharest: Univers. pp. 207. Rev. by Rodica Mihăilă in AnUBLLS (35) 104.

6850. MOGLEN, HELENE.   The philosophical irony of Laurence Sterne. (Bibl. 1976, 6751.) Rev. by Arthur H. Cash in ECent (2:3) 1979, 277–83.

6851. MONKMAN, KENNETH (ed.).   Sterne's memoirs: a hitherto unrecorded holograph now brought to light in facsimile. Coxwold: Laurence Sterne Trust; Cambridge: Heffers, 1985. pp. xxxii, 16.

6852. MOSS, R.   Burlesque rhetoric in Chaucer, Nashe and Sterne. *See* **3713.**

6853. MYER, VALERIE GROSVENOR (ed.).   Laurence Sterne: riddles and mysteries. (Bibl. 1985, 5739.) Rev. by Fred Price in BJECS (9:1) 101–2; by I. M. Grundy in NQ (33:3) 422–3.

6854. NEW, MELVYN.   Whim-whams and flim-flams: the Oxford University Press edition of *Tristram Shandy*. Review (7) 1985, 1–18 (review-article).

6855. —— (gen. ed.).   The life and opinions of Tristram Shandy, gentleman: vols 1–2, Text, ed. by MELVYN NEW and JOAN NEW; vol. 3, Notes, ed. by MELVYN NEW, RICHARD A. DAVIES, and W. G. DAY. Gainesville: Florida UP, 1978; 1984. vols 1–2, pp. 966; vol. 3, pp. 572. Rev. by O. M. Brack, Jr, in Review (8) 273–301, by John A. Dussinger in JEGP (85:2) 249–51.

6856. OSLAND, DIANNE.   Life, and the opinions of Tom Collins. Southerly (45:2) 1985, 227–42.

6857. POSNER, ROLAND.   Semiotic paradoxes in language use, with particular reference to *Tristram Shandy*. Trans. by CHRISTIAN J. W. KLOESEL. *See* **2265.**

6858. ROSS, IAN CAMPBELL (ed.).   The life and opinions of Tristram Shandy, gentleman. (Bibl. 1985, 5744.) Rev. by Melvyn New in Review (7) 1985, 1–18.

6859. SWEARINGEN, JAMES E.   Reflexivity in *Tristram Shandy*: an essay in phenomenological criticism. (Bibl. 1980, 7036.) Rev. by Arthur H. Cash in ECent (20:3) 1979, 277–83.

6860. TINKLER-VILLANI, VALERIA.   The life of Tristram: Sterne's sacred bawdy. DQR (16:2) 82–96.

6861. UHLIG, CLAUS.   Wissen und Meinen bei Sterne: Zur literarischen Epistemologie in *Tristram Shandy*. Ang (104:3/4) 369–96.

6862. ZWANEVELD, AGNES M.   *Tristram Shandy* in Nederland. (*Tristram Shandy* in the Netherlands.) De Gids (149:6) 513–24.

George Alexander Stevens

6863. KAHAN, GERALD.   George Alexander Stevens and *The Lecture on Heads*. (Bibl. 1985, 5748.) Rev. by Peter Wagner in BJECS (9:2) 262–3.

Solomon Stoddard

6864. GURA, PHILIP F.   Solomon Stoddard's irreverent way. EAL (21:1) 29–43.

Joseph Strutt

6865. HOUGH, B. L.   A consideration of the antiquarian and literary works of Joseph Strutt, with a transcript of a hitherto unedited manuscript novel. Unpub. doct. diss., Univ. of London (Queen Mary Coll.), 1984.

Jonathan Swift

6866. AHRENDS, GÜNTER. Sternes *Tristram Shandy* und der Literaturtyp der Anatomie. *See* **2960.**

6867. BACKSCHEIDER, PAULA R. A being more intense: a study of the prose works of Bunyan, Swift, and Defoe. *See* **5307.**

6868. BARNES, FORRESTINE SEIFERTH. Tonal modulations as related to characterizations in Swift's poetry. Unpub. doct. diss., Howard Univ., 1985. [Abstr. in DA (46) 3038A.]

6869. BLAKE, NORMAN F. Jonathan Swift and the English language. *See* **808.**

6870. COLEBOURNE, BRYAN. Some notes on Sir Harold Williams' edition of Swift's *Poems*. Linen Hall Review (3:2) [misnumbered 3:3] 18–19.

6871. CRAVEN, KENNETH. *A Tale of a Tub* and the 1697 Dublin controversy. ECI (1) 97–110.

6872. DEANE, SEAMUS. Swift and the Anglo-Irish intellect. ECI (1) 9–22.

6873. DOLL, DAN. The word and the thing in Swift's prose. StudECC (15) 199–210.

6874. DOWNIE, J. A. Jonathan Swift: political writer. (Bibl. 1985, 5757.) Rev. by Simon Varey in BJECS (9:1) 93–4.

6875. —— Swift and Johnson: the problems of the life of Swift. *See* **6572.**

6876. EHRENPREIS, IRVIN. Swift: the man, his work, and the age: vol. 3, Dean Swift. Cambridge, MA: Harvard UP, 1983. (Bibl. 1985, 5758.) Rev. by John Irwin Fischer in ECent (27:1) 71–80; by James Sutherland in NQ (33:1) 111–12.

6877. EILON, D. Private spirit: a moral and political theme in Swift's prose. Unpub. doct. diss., Univ. of Cambridge. [Abstr. in IT (35) 1492.]

6878. ELIAS, A. C., JR. Lord Orrery's copy of *Memoirs of the Life and Writings of Swift* (1751). *See* **214.**

6879. —— Swift at Moor Park: problems in biography and criticism. (Bibl. 1985, 5764.) Rev. by Edward J. Rielly in MLS (16:3) 316–18.

6880. FABRICANT, CAROLE. Swift's landscape. (Bibl. 1985, 5766.) Rev. by D. J. Womersley in NQ (33:1) 113–14.

6881. FISCHER, JOHN IRWIN. Dividing to conquer: the achievement of Irvin Ehrenpreis's *Swift: The Man, His Works, and The Age*. ECent (27:1) 71–80 (review-article).

6882. —— The government's response to Swift's *An Epistle to a Lady*. PQ (65:1) 39–59.

6883. FOX, CHRISTOPHER. The myth of Narcissus in Swift's *Travels*. ECS (20:1) 17–33.

6884. HIGGINS, IAN. Possible 'hints' for *Gulliver's Travels* in the *Voyages* of Jan Huygen van Linschoten. NQ (33:1) 47–50.

6885. INGRAM, ALLAN. Intricate laughter in the satire of Swift and Pope. *See* **6713.**

6886. LEVINSON, HARRY NORMAN.   Another look at Johnson's appraisal of Swift. *See* **6599.**

6887. LOCK, F. P.   Swift's Tory politics. (Bibl. 1985, 5777.) Rev. by
James Sutherland in NQ (33:1) 112.

6888. McCANN, WESLEY.   Swift at Tollymore Park. *See* **252.**

6889. McMINN, JOSEPH.   Swift and George Faulkner, 'Prince of
Dublin Printers'. *See* **404.**

6890. McWHIR, ANNE.   *Animal religiosum* and the witches in *A Voyage to
the Houyhnhnms*. ESCan (12:4) 375–86.

6891. MADOFF, MARK.   Gulliver shifts for himself. *In* (pp. 47–62)
ROBERT JAMES MERRETT (ed.), Man and nature: proceedings of the
Canadian Society for Eighteenth-Century Studies: vol. 3. Edmonton,
Alta.: Academic Printing & Publishing, 1984. pp. xii, 162.

6892. MOLITOR, HELEN O'BRIEN.   Sir William Temple, Meric
Casaubon, and Swift's *Mechanical Operation of the Spirit*. *See* **5884.**

6893. MOORE, LESLIE.   'Instructive trees': Swift's *Broom-stick*, Boyle's
Reflections, and satiric figuration. ECS (19:3) 313–32.

6894. NEMAN, BETH S.   A modest proposal for testing *A Voyage to the
Country of the Houyhnhnms* for dramatic irony. ELN (24:2) 37–43.

6895. NOKES, DAVID.   Johnson and Swift. *See* **6613.**

6896. —— Jonathan Swift, a hypocrite reversed: a critical biography.
New York: OUP, 1985. (Cf. bibl. 1985, 5788.) Rev. by Alan Harrison in
ECI (1) 211–12 (in Gaelic); by Keith Walker in TLS, 24 Jan., 84; by
Brean S. Hammond in BJECS (9:2) 267–8.

6897. Ó HÁINLE, C. G.   Neighbors in eighteenth century Dublin:
Jonathan Swift and Seán Ó Neachtain. Éire-Ireland (21:4) 106–21.

6898. PASSMANN, DIRK.   Jean de Thevenot and burials in Lilliput. NQ
(33:1) 50–1.

6899. PASSMANN, DIRK F.   Chinese transport in *A Tale of a Tub*. NQ
(33:4) 482–4.

6900. PEAKE, CHARLES.   Jonathan Swift and the art of raillery: a
lecture given at the Princess Grace Irish Library on Wednesday
15 October 1986: together with notes on Irish writers associated with
Swift. Gerrards Cross: Smythe, 1986. pp. 40. (Princess Grace Irish
Library lectures, 3.)

6901. PETERSON, LELAND D.   Problems of authenticity and text in
three early poems attributed to Swift. HLB (33:4) 1985, 404–24.

6902. POLLAK, ELLEN.   The poetics of sexual myth: gender and
ideology in the verse of Swift and Pope. *See* **6729.**

6903. PROBYN, CLIVE.   Swift's *Verses on the Death of Dr Swift*: the notes.
SB (39) 47–61.

6904. RAWSON, CLAUDE (ed.).   The character of Swift's satire: a
revised focus. (Bibl. 1985, 5795.) Rev. by Max Byrd in MLR (81:2)
449–51; by Peter Dixon in NQ (33:1) 115–16.

6905. REAL, HERMANN J.; VIENKEN, HEINZ J.   The Blessed Virgin's
milk powderized. NQ (33:1) 63.

6906. —— —— Child-killing and child-selling once again: a new
source for Swift's *A Modest Proposal*. NQ (33:1) 53–4.

6907. —— —— 'I knew and could distinguish those two heroes at first sight': Homer and Aristotle in Glubbdubdrib. NQ (33:1) 51–3.

6908. —— —— Psychoanalytical criticism and Swift: the history of a failure. ECI (1) 127–41.

6909. —— —— Swift's *A Description of the Morning*, lines 9–10. NQ (33:1) 47.

6910. —— —— Swift's *Verses Wrote in a Lady's Ivory Table-book*. BJECS (9:2) 165–7.

6911. —— —— What's in a name: Pedro de Mendez again. ANQ (24:9/10) 136–42.

6912. —— —— (eds). Proceedings of the first Münster symposium on Jonathan Swift. Munich: Fink, 1985. pp. 396, (plates) 22. Rev. by Ian Campbell Ross in ECI (1) 212–13.

6913. RICHARDSON, J. A. The effect of Swift's satire. Unpub. doct. diss., Univ. of Manchester, 1983. [Abstr. in IT (35) 47.]

6914. RODINO, RICHARD H. Swift studies, 1965–1980: an annotated bibliography. (Bibl. 1984, 6027.) Rev. by D. J. Womersley in NQ (33:1) 114–15.

6915. ROGERS, PAT (ed.). The complete poems. (Bibl. 1985, 5802.) Rev. by Donald C. Mell, Jr, in MLR (81:1) 172–5.

6916. ROSS, ANGUS; WOOLLEY, DAVID (eds). Jonathan Swift. (Bibl. 1985, 5803.) Rev. by John Valdimir Price in NQ (33:2) 238–9.

6917. —— —— *A Tale of a Tub* and other works. Oxford: OUP. pp. xxviii, 237. (World's classics.)

6918. SCOTT, JOHN WALTER. Swift and the grotesque: to vex rather than divert. Unpub. doct. diss., Univ. of Arkansas, 1985. [Abstr. in DA (46) 3044A.]

6919. SHERBO, ARTHUR. Swift's abuse of poetic diction. CLit (13:2) 141–56.

6920. SMITH, MARGARETTE. 'In the case of David': Swift's *Drapier's Letters*. Prose Studies (9:2) 140–59.

6921. THOMPSON, PAUL V.; THOMPSON, DOROTHY JAY (eds). The account books of Jonathan Swift. (Bibl. 1985, 5809.) Rev. by J. A. Downie in BJECS (9:2) 268; by Jenny Mezciems in NQ (33:1) 112–13.

6922. TRIFU, SEVER. Satiră la Fielding şi Swift. See **6457.**

6923. TURNER, PAUL (ed.). Gulliver's travels. Oxford: OUP. pp. xli, 379. (World's classics.)

6924. VEITH, DAVID M. (ed.). Essential articles for the study of Jonathan Swift's poetry. Hamden, CT: Archon, 1985. pp. xii, 345. Rev. by Pat Rogers in BJECS (9:2) 260.

6925. WILSON, PENELOPE. Feminism and the Augustans: some readings and problems. See **6741.**

6926. WOOD, NIGEL. Swift. Brighton: Harvester Press. pp. xiv, 153. (Harvester new readings.) Rev. by David Nokes in THES (726) 18.

6927. WYRICK, DEBORAH BAKER. Jonathan Swift and the vested word. Unpub. doct. diss., Duke Univ., 1985. [Abstr. in DA (47) 1341A.]

Lewis Theobald

6928. CORBALLIS, RICHARD.   Copy-text for Theobald's *Shakespeare*. *See* **4320.**

Edward Thompson

6929. PARKE, CATHERINE N. (ed.).   The plays of Edward Thompson. New York; London: Garland, 1980. (Eighteenth-century English drama, 34.) (Facsim of texts pub. 1775–76; transcripts of MSS; pp. xix, and pagination of individual items.)

James Thomson

6930. ANDERSON, DAVID R.   Landscape and theodicy in Pope, Thomson, and Cowper. *See* **6366.**

6931. COHEN, MICHAEL.   The Whig sublime and James Thomson. ELN (24:1) 27–35.

6932. INGLESFIELD, ROBERT.   Shaftesbury's influence on Thomson's *Seasons. See* **6798.**

6933. SAMBROOK, JAMES (ed.).   *Liberty, The Castle of Indolence,* and other poems. Oxford: Clarendon Press. pp. x, 420. (Oxford English texts.)

6934. SCOTT, MARY JANE; SCOTT, PATRICK.   The manuscript of James Thomson's *Scots Elegy*. SSL (17) 1982, 135–44.

Royall Tyler

6935. CARSON, ADA LOU.   Thomas Pickman Tyler's *Memoirs of Royall Tyler*: an annotated edition. Unpub. doct. diss., Univ. of Minnesota, 1985. [Abstr. in DA (46) 3031A.]

6936. PRESSMAN, RICHARD S.   Class positioning and Shays' Rebellion: resolving the contradictions of *The Contrast*. EAL (21:2) 87–102.

Horace Walpole

6937. BROOKE, JOHN (ed.).   Memoirs of King George II. New Haven, CT; London: Yale UP, 1985. 3 vols. pp. xxxii, 248; ix, 295; ix, 291. (Yale edition of Horace Walpole's memoirs.)

6938. DRALLE, LEWIS A.   The daily hum of the eighteenth century. Studies in Burke and his Time (Texas Tech Univ., Lubbock, TX) (17:2) 1976, 127–38 (review-article).

6939. JESTIN, CATHERINE T.   Notes by 'A curious gentleman'. *See* **241.**

6940. LEWIS, W. S. (gen. ed.).   The Yale edition of Horace Walpole's correspondence: vols 25–7, 35–9. (Bibl. 1972, 6191; 1974, 7489, 7490; 1975, 7059). Rev. by Lewis A. Dralle in Studies in Burke and his Time (Texas Tech Univ., Lubbock, TX) (17:2) 1976, 127–38.

6941. SABOR, PETER.   Horace Walpole: a reference guide. Boston, MA: G. K. Hall, 1984. pp. xxvii, 270. Rev. by Jeremy Black in NQ (33:2) 241–2.

6942. —— Review essay: Horace Walpole's *Correspondence*, 'A Mighty Maze but not without a Plan'. ECL (10:2) 98–108.

William Warburton

6943. NICHOL, D. W.   Pope, Warburton and the Kemptons: problems of literary legacy (with a book-trade correspondence). *See* **416.**

Jane Warton

6944. REID, HUGH.   Jenny: the fourth Warton. NQ (33:1) 84–92.

Joseph Warton

6945. LE PREVOST, CHRISTINA. More unacknowledged verse by Joseph Warton. RES (37:147) 317–47.

6946. VANCE, JOHN A. Joseph and Thomas Warton. (Bibl. 1985, 5824.) Rev. by Hugh Reid in NQ (33:3) 417–18.

Isaac Watts

6947. BROOKS, G. P. Mental improvement and vital piety: Isaac Watts and the benefits of astronomical study. DalR (65:4) 1985/86, 551–64.

Phillis Wheatley

6948. ISANI, MUKHTAR ALI. *An Elegy on Leaving. . .* : a new poem by Phillis Wheatley. AL (58:4) 609–13.

6949. JORDAN, JUNE. The difficult miracle of black poetry in America or something like a sonnet for Phillis Wheatley. MassR (27:2) 252–62.

6950. O'NEALE, SONDRA. A slave's subtle war: Phillis Wheatley's use of Biblical myth and symbol. EAL (21:2) 144–65.

Gilbert White

6951. MABEY, RICHARD. Gilbert White: a biography of the author of *The Natural History of Selborne*. London: Century. pp. ix, 239. Rev. by Eric Christiansen in Independent, 18 Dec., 10.

Paul Whitehead

6952. CARRETTA, VINCENT (introd.). Satires written by Mr Whitehead. Los Angeles, CA: William Andrews Clark Memorial Library, 1984. pp. xiv, 52. (Augustan Reprint Soc., 223.) Rev. by Alain Morvan in EA (38:4) 1985, 461–2.

John Wilkes

6953. STOCKDALE, ERIC. John Almon and the state-prisoner. See **434.**

John Wolcot ('Peter Pindar')

6954. IKIN, BRIDGET. Peter Pindar and the pirates. See **390.**

Mary Wollstonecraft

6955. BRODY, MIRIAM. Mary Wollstonecraft: sexuality and women's rights (1759–1797). *In* (pp. 40–59) **20.**

6956. DUHET, PAULE-MARIE. Bonheur et douleur dans *Elements of Morality for the Use of Children* (1790–1791) de Mary Wollstonecraft. *In* (pp. 167–76) **14.**

6957. —— Mary Wollstonecraft, *A Vindication of the Rights of Woman* (1792): bibliographie sélective et critique. BSEAA (23) 25–36.

6958. GURALNICK, ELISSA S. Radical politics in Mary Wollstonecraft's *A Vindication of the Rights of Woman*. Studies in Burke and his Time (Texas Tech Univ., Lubbock, TX) (18:3) 1977, 155–66.

6959. HARASYM, S. D. Ideology and self; a theoretical discussion of the 'self' in Mary Wollstonecraft's fiction. ESCan (12:2) 163–77.

6960. JONES, CHRIS. Godwin to Mary: the first letter. See **6498.**

6961. MORVAN, ALAIN. Passion et idéologie dans les romans de Mary Wollstonecraft. BSEAA (23) 65–78.

6962. POOVEY, MARY. The proper lady and the woman writer: ideology as style in the works of Mary Wollstonecraft, Mary Shelley, and

Jane Austen. (Bibl. 1985, 5832.) Rev. by Judith Wilt in MP (83:4) 434–7; by James Thompson in Review (8) 27–9.

Sir Nathaniel William Wraxall

6963. JANES, REGINA.   Sir Nathaniel William Wraxall: agent for Paul Benfield. NQ (33:1) 76–8.

George Wright ('Bob Short, Jr')

6964. PITCHER, E. W.   New facts on George Wright's eighteenth-century miscellaneous publications. PBSA (80:2) 237–40.

Ann Yearsley

6965. FERGUSON, MOIRA.   Resistance and power in the life and writings of Ann Yearsley. ECent (27:3) 247–68.

Edward Young

6966. BROWN, STEPHEN NEAL.   Edward Young: an eighteenth-century literary career. Unpub. doct. diss., Univ. of Virginia, 1985. [Abstr. in DA (47) 1733A.]

6967. CHIBKA, ROBERT L.   The stranger within Young's *Conjectures.* ELH (53:3) 541–65.

6968. CORNFORD, S. W.   A critical edition of Edward Young's *Night Thoughts.* Unpub. doct. diss., Univ. of Cambridge. [Abstr. in IT (36) 20.]

6969. FORSTER, HAROLD.   Edward Young: the poet of the *Night Thoughts*, 1683–1765. Alburgh: Erskine Press. pp. xiii, 434. Rev. by Jonathan Keates in Independent, 18 Dec., 10.

6970. —— The sea-pieces of Edward Young. Factotum (9) 1980, 8–10.

6971. PATEY, DOUGLAS LANE.   Art and integrity: concepts of self in Alexander Pope and Edward Young. *See* **6726.**

6972. TASCH, PETER A.   The first edition of Young's *Vindication of Providence.* NQ (33:4) 495–7.

6973. WELCH, DENNIS M.   Imitation in Blake's *Night Thoughts* illustrations. *See* **85.**

NINETEENTH CENTURY

GENERAL

General Literary Studies

6974. ALTICK, RICHARD D. Nineteenth-century best-sellers: a third list. *See* **353.**

6975. ASHLEY, PERRY J. (ed.). American newspaper journalists, 1873–1900. *See* **556.**

6976. BARNES, JOHN. 'Through clear Australian eyes': landscape and identity in Australian writing. *In* (pp. 86–104) **31.**

6977. BATE, A. J. Studies in Shakespeare and the English Romantic imagination. *See* **4380.**

6978. BEALE, DONALD A. 'Striving with systems': Romanticism and the current critical scene. Theoria (66) 13–28.

6979. BEASECKER, ROBERT; PADY, DONALD (eds). Annual bibliography of Midwestern literature: 1984. Midamerica (13) 148–65.

6980. BELSEY, CATHERINE. The Romantic construction of the unconscious. *In* (pp. 57–76) **29.**

6981. BERCOVITCH, SACVAN. The problem of ideology in American literary history. CI (12:4) 631–53.

6982. —— (ed.). Reconstructing American literary history. *See* **47.**

6983. —— JEHLEN, MYRA (eds). Ideology and classic American literature. Cambridge: CUP. pp. xii, 451. (Cambridge studies in American literature and culture.)

6984. BERTHOLD, DENNIS. Cape Horn passages: literary conventions and nautical realities. *In* (pp. 40–50) **28.**

6985. BLAEN, A. A survey and analysis of some aspects of West Country folklore as found in selected writings of Eden Phillpotts, Thomas Hardy, John Cowper Powys, Arthur Quiller-Couch and Henry Williamson. *See* **2396.**

6986. BLAKE, KATHLEEN. Love and the woman question in Victorian literature: the art of self-postponement. (Bibl. 1984, 6101.) Rev. by Mary Burgan in JEGP (85:2) 278–82.

6987. BRAKE, LAUREL. Literary criticism and the Victorian periodicals. *See* **564.**

6988. BRITAIN'S LITERARY HERITAGE. The Robert White Collection of Chapbooks from the University Library, Newcastle upon Tyne: a listing and guide to the Harvester microform. *See* **2436.**

6989. BUELL, LAWRENCE. New England literary culture: from revolution through renaissance. *See* **5941.**

6990. —— The New England Renaissance and American literary ethnocentrism. Prospects (10) 1985, 409–22.

6991. BURNS, JAMES. From 'polite learning' to 'useful knowledge'. *See* **5942.**

6992. BURR, NELSON R. New Eden and new Babylon: religious thoughts of American authors: a bibliography: religious naturalism: the religious mysticism of nature. HMPEC (55:2) 137–63.

6993. ——— New Eden and new Babylon: religious thoughts of American authors: a bibliography: the optimistic reaction to Puritanism. *See* **5943.**

6994. CHAPMAN, RAYMOND.   The sense of the past in Victorian literature. New York: St Martin's Press; London: Croom Helm. pp. 212. Rev. by Jerome H. Buckley in CLIO (16:1) 81–4; by Donald Hawes in THES (720) 15.

6995. CHAPPLE, J. A. V.   Science and literature in the nineteenth century. London: Macmillan. pp. xi, 192. (Context and commentary.)

6996. CHASE, CYNTHIA.   Decomposing figures: rhetorical readings in the Romantic tradition. Baltimore, MD; London: Johns Hopkins UP. pp. ix, 234.

6997. CHITTICK, KATHRYN.   Literature and politics in 1833. DalR (66:1/2) 118–29.

6998. CLARK, ANNA.   The politics of seduction in English popular culture, 1748–1848. *In* (pp. 47–70) **45.**

6999. CLARK, WILLIAM BEDFORD; TURNER, W. CRAIG (eds).   Critical essays on American humor. Boston, MA: G. K. Hall, 1984. pp. viii, 232. (Critical essays on American literature.) Rev. by John Lang in SCR (3:1) 96–8; by Louis J. Budd in SAF (14:1) 115–17.

7000. CLEMENTS, PATRICIA.   Baudelaire and the English tradition. Princeton, NJ: Princeton UP, 1985. pp. x, 442. Rev. by Robert Gibson in THES (710) 23.

7001. CNUDDE-KNOWLAND, A.   Maurice Maeterlinck and English and Anglo-Irish literature: a study of parallels and influences. Unpub. doct. diss., Univ. of Oxford, 1984.

7002. COALE, SAMUEL.   The heart of darkness in the American romance. Pakistan Journal of American Studies (Islamabad) (4:2) 15–25.

7003. COLLINS, ROBERT A.; PEARCE, HOWARD D. (eds).   The scope of the fantastic: selected essays from the First International Conference on the Fantastic in Literature and Film. Westport, CT; London: Greenwood Press, 1985. pp. xii, 295. (Contributions to the study of science fiction and fantasy, 10.)

7004. COMANZO, CHRISTIAN.   Mythe solaire, héros solaire. CVE (23) 35–46.

7005. CONNOLLY, CYRIL.   100 key books of the modern movement from England, France and America 1880–1950. London: Allison & Busby. pp. 160. (Prev. pub. as *The Modern Movement*, 1965.)

7006. COSSLETT, TESS.   The 'scientific movement' and Victorian literature. (Bibl. 1984, 6114.) Rev. by Rosemary Ashton in MLR (81:2) 455–6.

7007. CROSS, NIGEL.   The common writer: life in nineteenth-century Grub Street. (Bibl. 1985, 5854.) Rev. by Diana Dixon in JNPH (2:2) 38–40; by Louis James in VPR (19:4) 59; by Dennis Walder in THES (691) 19; by Stephen Gill in Dick (82:2) 110–11; by Richard Altick in LRB (8:11) 16–17; by Alan Bell in TLS, 14 Feb., 171.

7008. CULLER, A. DWIGHT.   The Victorian mirror of history. New

Haven, CT; London: Yale UP. pp. xii, 320. Rev. by George H. Ford in ELN (24:2) 82–3.

7009. DALSIMER, KATHERINE. Female adolescence: psychoanalytic reflections on works of literature. New Haven, CT; London: Yale UP. pp. 149.

7010. DARBY, ROBERT. The fall of fortress criticism. Overland (102) 6–15 (review-article). (Guides to Australian literature.)

7011. DAVIES, BARRIE. *Dulce* vs. *utile*: the Kevin O'Brien syndrome in New Brunswick literature. StudCanL (11:2) 161–7.

7012. DEACON, RICHARD. The Cambridge Apostles; a history of Cambridge University's elite intellectual secret society. London: Royce, 1985. pp. x, 214. Rev. by Mark Le Fanu in Listener, 20 Feb., 27.

7013. DEANE, SEAMUS. Celtic revivals: essays in modern Irish literature, 1880–1980. (Bibl. 1985, 5857.) Rev. by James Simmons in Honest Ulsterman (81) 85, 89–96.

7014. DOCKER, JOHN. Antipodean literature: a world upside down? Overland (103) 48–56.

7015. DOLLE, RAYMOND FRANCIS. Treasure quests in New World literature. *See* **5953.**

7016. DOWLING, LINDA. Language and decadence in Victorian *fin de siècle*. Princeton, NJ; Guildford: Princeton UP. pp. xvi, 294.

7017. EADEN, P. R.; MORES, F. H. (eds). Mapped but not known: the Australian landscape of the imagination. Essays and poems presented to Brian Elliott, 11 April 1985. *See* **31.**

7018. EAVES, MORRIS; FISCHER, MICHAEL (eds). Romanticism and contemporary criticism. Ithaca, NY; London: Cornell UP. pp. 246.

7019. EDMUNDSON, MARK WRIGHT. Towards reading Freud: moments of self-representation in Milton, Wordsworth, Keats, Emerson, Whitman and Sigmund Freud. *See* **5705.**

7020. ENGELBERG, KARSTEN (ed.). The Romantic heritage: a collection of critical essays. Copenhagen: Copenhagen UP, 1983. pp. 229. Rev. by Jean Raimond in EA (38:4) 1985, 468.

7021. ERDMAN, DAVID V. (ed.); DENDLE, BRIAN J. (asst ed.). The Romantic movement: a selective and critical bibliography for 1984. New York; London: Garland, 1985. pp. xxviii, 456. (Garland reference library of the humanities, 219.)

7022. FISHER, MARVIN. Continuities: essays and ideas in American literature. Lanham, MD; London: UP of America. pp. xii, 158.

7023. FISHER, PHILIP. Appearing and disappearing in public: social space in late-nineteenth-century literature and culture. *In* (pp. 155–88) **47.**

7024. FOULKE, ROBERT. The literature of voyaging. *In* (pp. 1–13) **28.**

7025. FRASER, HILARY. Beauty and belief: aesthetics and religion in Victorian literature. Cambridge: CUP. pp. xii, 287. Rev. by John Beer in THES (713) 19.

7026. FRASER, JOHN. America and the patterns of chivalry. (Bibl. 1984, 6131.) Rev. by Edward Wagenknecht in YES (16) 315–16.

7027. FRIEDMAN, DONALD FLANELL. The Symbolist dead city: a landscape of poesis. Unpub. doct. diss., New York Univ., 1985. [Abstr. in DA (47) 171A.]

7028. GATES, HENRY LOUIS, JR.   James Gronniosaw and the trope of the talking book. SoR (22:2) 253–72.

7029. GÉRARD, ALBERT.   Essais d'histoire littéraire africaine. Paris: Agence de coopération culturelle et technique, 1984. pp. 248.

7030. GILMORE, MICHAEL T.   American Romanticism and the marketplace. HLQ (49:4) 414–19.

7031. —— American romanticism and the marketplace. Chicago; London: Chicago UP, 1985. pp. ix, 177. Rev. by Nina Baym in JEGP (85:4) 600–2; by Agnes M. Donohue in CLIO (16:1) 89–92; by Carl Brucker in SCR (3:4) 106–9; by Elizabeth A. Meese in Criticism (28:2) 216–20; by Joel Myerson in NEQ (59:2) 308–10; by William H. Shurr in AL (58:2) 282–4; by Robert D. Habich in JAH (73:1) 187–9.

7032. GOLDEN, CATHERINE JEAN.   The Victorian illustrated book: authors who composed with graphic images and words. See **75.**

7033. GOODWIN, KEN LESLIE.   A history of Australian literature. See **5960.**

7034. GRAY, RICHARD.   Writing the South: ideas of an American region. Cambridge: CUP. pp. xiv, 333. (Cambridge studies in American literature and culture.) Rev. by Paul Binding in Listener, 25 Sept., 21–2.

7035. GUSTAFSON, THOMAS B.   Representative words: politics, literature and the American language, 1776–1865. See **867.**

7036. HEADON, DAVID.   Eccentrics, explorers and evangelists: a camel ride through the literature of the Northern Territory: part 1, Eccentrics and explorers. Westerly (31:1) 45–54.

7037. —— Reworking the convict tradition: Brother Jonathan and the off scourings of England in penal Australia. Australasian Journal of American Studies (Melbourne) (3:2) 1984, 3–17.

7038. HEDIN, RAYMOND.   Muffled voices: the American slave narrative. CLIO (10:2) 1981, 129–42.

7039. HESELTINE, HARRY.   The uncertain self: essays in Australian literature and criticism. Melbourne: OUP. pp. 222.

7040. HIMMELFARB, GERTRUDE.   From Clapham to Bloomsbury: a genealogy of morals. Commentary (79:2) 1985, 36–45.

7041. HÖLTGEN, KARL JOSEF.   Aspects of the emblem: studies in the English emblem tradition and the European context. With a foreword by SIR ROY STRONG. See **5063.**

7042. HOLTON, ROBERT.   'A true bond of unity': popular education and the foundation of the discipline of English literature in England. DalR (66:1/2) 31–44.

7043. HOMANS, MARGARET.   Bearing the word: language and female experience in nineteenth-century women's writing. Chicago; London: Chicago UP. pp. xiv, 326. (Women in culture and society.)

7044. HOWE, IRVING.   The American newness: culture and politics in the age of Emerson. Cambridge, MA: Harvard UP. pp. 99. Rev. by Benjamin DeMott in NYTB, 29 June, 17; by Robert Coles in NEQ (59:4) 564–6; by Stanley T. Gutman in AL (58:4) 631–3.

7045. HUMPHRIES, JEFFERSON.   Metamorphoses of the raven: literary overdeterminedness in France and the South since Poe. (Bibl. 1985, 5880.) Rev. by Burton R. Pollin in AL (58:3) 435–7.

7046. HUNTER, LYNETTE.   Rhetorical stance in modern literature: allegories of love and death. New York: St Martin's Press, 1984. (Cf. bibl. 1985, 5882.) Rev. by Deanne Bogdan in JAE (20:2) 111–13.

7047. IKIN, VAN; WALKER, BRENDA.   Annual bibliography of Commonwealth literature 1984: Australia (with Papua New Guinea). JCom Lit (20:2) 1985, 19–41.

7048. JAMES, TREVOR.   English literature from the Third World. Harlow: Longman. pp. 207. (York handbooks.)

7049. JAY, PAUL.   Being in the text: self-representation from Wordsworth to Roland Barthes. (Bibl. 1985, 5886.) Rev. by Raymond E. Fitch in JEGP (85:1) 136–9; by Jane Marie Todd in CL (38:3) 298–9; by H. Porter Abbott in PT (7:3) 569–71.

7050. JOLLIFFE, JOHN W. (introd.)   Nineteenth-century short title catalogue: series 1, phase 1, 1801–1815: vol. 1, A–C. (Bibl. 1984, 132.) Rev. by Patricia Fleming in VPR (19:2) 68–9.

7051. JORDANOVA, L. J. (ed.); WILLIAMS, RAYMOND (introd.). Languages of nature: critical essays on science and literature. See **5965.**

7052. KAMUF, PEGGY.   Monumental de-facement: on Paul de Man's *The Rhetoric of Romanticism.* CL (38:4) 319–28.

7053. KASER, DAVID.   Books and libraries in camp and battle: the Civil War experience. See **244.**

7054. KEEN, J. M.   The Perseus and Pygmalion legends in later nineteenth-century literature and art, with special reference to the influence of Ovid's *Metamorphoses.* Unpub. doct. diss., Univ. of Southampton, 1983.

7055. KIMBLE, MARY ELLEN.   Literary presentations of pioneer women in Kansas and neighboring states. KQ (18:3) 105–20.

7056. KOLIN, PHILIP C. (ed.).   Shakespeare and Southern writers: a study in influence. See **51.**

7057. KOPPELMAN, CONSTANCE ELEANORE.   Nature in art and culture: the Tile Club artists, 1870–1900. Unpub. doct. diss., State Univ. of New York at Stony Brook, 1985. [Abstr. in DA (46) 1720A.]

7058. KÜHNELT, HARRO H.   Österreich-England/Amerika. Abhandlungen zur Literatur-Geschichte. Ed. by SYLVIA M. PATSCH. Vienna: Brandstätter. pp. 295.

7059. LAMB, W. KAYE.   Seventy-Five Years of Canadian Bibliography: bibliographical studies in reprint. PBSC (24) 1985, 73–85.

7060. LANG, PETER CHRISTIAN.   Literarischer Unsinn im späten 19. und frühen 20. Jahrhundert: systematische Begründung und historische Rekonstruktion. Frankfurt: Lang, 1982. pp. 170. (Beiträge zur neueren literatur, 8.) Rev. by Armin Arnold in CanRCL (13:2) 311–13.

7061. LIBERMAN, SERGE.   Creative writing by Jews in Australia. Outrider (Indooroopilly, Qld) (1:2) 1984, 187–205.

7062. LIMERICK, PATRICIA NELSON.   Desert passages: encounters with the American deserts. Albuquerque: New Mexico UP, 1985. pp. 218. Rev. by Donald Worster in ArizW (28:2) 167–9.

7063. LUCAS, JOHN.   Moderns and contemporaries; novelists, poets, critics. (Bibl. 1985, 5899.) Rev. by Philip Hobsbaum in THES (708) 18; by David Sexton in TLS 9 May, 506.

7064. MACDONALD, MARY LU.   The natural world in early nineteenth-century Canadian literature. CanL (111) 48–65.

7065. MACDONALD, MARY LUCINDA.   Literature and society in the Canadas, 1830–1850. Unpub. doct. diss., Carleton Univ., 1984. [Abstr. in DA (47) 1851A.]

7066. McDOUGALL, RUSSELL.   Opinion on location: regionalism in Australian and Canadian literature. *See* **1011.**

7067. McGANN, JEROME J.   The romantic ideology: a critical investigation. (Bibl. 1985, 5904.) Rev. by Roger Lundin in ChrisL (35:2) 52–3; by Lilian R. Furst in CanRCL (13:2) 301–3; by Bradford K. Mudge in MLS (16:4) 79–80.

7068. McGREGOR, GAILE.   The Wacousta syndrome: explorations in the Canadian langscape. Toronto; Buffalo, NY; London: Toronto UP, 1985. pp. viii, 473. Rev. by Tracy Ware in DalR (65:4) 1985/86, 573–5; by I. S. MacLaren in CanP (18) 118–30; by Mary Lu MacDonald in CanL (111) 173–5; by Michael Hurley in QQ (93:3) 665–7; by Mark Williams in Landfall (40:3) 338–49 (with reply by Gaile McGregor (40:4) 519–26 and rejoinder by Mark Williams (40:4) 526–7).

7069. McKENZIE, D. F.   Oral culture, literacy and print in early New Zealand: the Treaty of Waitangi. Wellington: Victoria UP, 1985. pp. 47. Rev. by Gregory Palmer in TLS, 24 Oct., 1203.

7070. MAHARG, P. A.   Models of the self: a study of selfhood in nine late nineteenth century authors. Unpub. doct. diss., Univ. of Edinburgh, 1984.

7071. MARKS, PATRICIA.   American literary and drama reviews: an index to late nineteenth-century periodicals. *See* **646.**

7072. MARSH, JAN.   The Pre-Raphaelite sisterhood. New York: St Martin's Press, 1985. pp. viii, 408. Rev. by Barbara J. Dunlap in VPR (19:3) 117–19.

7073. MARTIN, STODDARD.   Art, Messianism and crime: a study of antinomianism in modern literature and lives. Basingstoke: Macmillan, 1985. pp. 218.

7074. MEAD, JOAN TYLER.   'Spare me a few minutes I have Something to Say': poetry in manuscripts of sailing ships. *In* (pp. 23–31) **28.**

7075. MEISEL, MARTIN.   Realizations: narrative, pictorial, and theatrical arts in nineteenth-century England. (Bibl. 1985, 5907.) Rev. by George Levine in MP (84:2) 233–5.

7076. —— Seeing it feelingly: Victorian symbolism and narrative art. HLQ (49:1) 67–92.

7077. MENDILOW, JONATHAN.   The Romantic tradition in British political thought. London: Croom Helm. pp. 267. Rev. by Philip Dodd in THES (694) 21.

7078. MILLER, KARL.   Doubles: studies in literary history. (Bibl.

1985, 5912.) Rev. by John Batchelor in Eng (35) 85–8; by Derek Russell Davis in EC (36:1) 89–94; by R. Baird Shuman in SSF (23) 134–5.

7079. MITCHELL, ADRIAN.   No new thing: the concept of novelty and early Australian writing. *In* (pp. 52–63) **31.**

7080. MONSMAN, GERALD.   Recent studies in the nineteenth century. SELit (26:4) 777–828.

7081. MORGAN, JANET (comp.).   Victorian literature at St Deiniol's Library: a bibliography of poetry, plays and fiction. 1837–1901. *See* **262.**

7082. MORGAN, PATRICK.   The literature of Gippsland. Westerly (31:1) 28–44.

7083. —— The literature of Gippsland: the social and historical context of early writings, with bibliography. Churchill, Vic.: Gippsland Inst. of Advanced Education. pp. 50.

7084. MORRIS, K. L.   Religious medievalism: aspects of the medieval church in later eighteenth century and nineteenth century English literature. *See* **5979.**

7085. MORTON, PETER.   The vital science: biology and the literary imagination, 1860–1900. (Bibl. 1985, 5913.) Rev. by Julia L. Epstein in CLIO (15:1) 1985, 100–2.

7086. MYERSON, JOEL (ed.).   The Transcendentalists: a review of research and criticism. (Bibl. 1985, 5914.) Rev. by Norman Schwenk in NQ (33:4) 569–70; by Sanford E. Marovitz in BB (43:3) 183–5.

7087. NATHAN, RHODA B. (ed.).   Nineteenth-century women writers of the English-speaking world. New York; London: Greenwood Press. pp. xiv, 275. (Contributions in women's studies, 69.)

7088. NESTOR, P. A.   Female friendships and communities: a study of women writers, 1840–1880. Unpub. doct. diss., Univ. of Oxford, 1982.

7089. NICHOLS, BROOKS ASHTON.   The poetics of epiphany: nineteenth-century origins of the modern literary 'moment'. Unpub. doct. diss., Univ. of Virginia, 1984. [Abstr. in DA (46) 1951A.]

7090. OBEIDAT, MARWAN MOHAMMAD.   The Muslim East in American literature: the formation of an image. Unpub. doct. diss., Indiana Univ., 1985. [Abstr. in DA (47) 531A.]

7091. OH, MOON-KIL.   Nangmanjueui wa byeonhwa eui genyeom. (Romanticism and the concept of change.) JELL (31:4) 1985, 591–610.

7092. PANTŮČKOVÁ, LIDMILA.   Několik poznámek ke vztahu Jana Nerudy k americké literatuře. (Notes on the relation of Jan Neruda to American literature.) *In* (pp. 44–5) **4.**

7093. PIZER, DONALD.   Realism and naturalism in nineteenth-century American literature. (Bibl. 1967, 5345.) Carbondale: Southern Illinois UP, 1984. pp. xiv, 227. (Second ed.; first ed. 1966.) Rev. by Earl N. Harbert in SAF (13) 1985, 112–13; by George Hendrick in ALR (18) 1985, 291–3; by Stephen C. Brennan in SCR (3:1) 94–6.

7094. POSTLETHWAITE, DIANA.   Making it whole: a Victorian circle and the shape of their world. Columbus: Ohio State UP, 1984. pp. xx, 282. Rev. by John R. Reed in JEGP (85:4) 574–5.

7095. POSTON, LAWRENCE.   Poetry as pure act: a Coleridgean ideal in early Victorian England. MP (84:2) 162–84.

7096. PRECOSKY, DON.   Seven myths about Canadian literature. StudCanL (11:1) 86–95.

7097. RAFROIDI, PATRICK.   The year's work in Irish-English literature Autumn 1985–Autumn 1986. *See* **5984.**

7098. RATHFORK, JOHN.   The failure of Southwest regionalism. SDR (19:4) 1982, 85–99.

7099. REED, ARDEN (ed.).   Romanticism and language. (Bibl. 1985, 44.) Rev. by Mark Storey in Eng (35) 67–73; by Stuart Peterfreund in JEGP (85:3) 464–7.

7100. RICE, MICHAEL.   British views of the Boers. Standpunte (39:1) 39–56.

7101. RICHARDS, THOMAS KARR.   Large promises: a literary history of English advertising, 1887–1914. Unpub. doct. diss., Stanford Univ. [Abstr. in DA (47) 2171A.]

7102. RIEWALD, J. G.; BAKKER, J.   The critical reception of American literature in the Netherlands 1824–1900: a documentary conspectus from contemporary periodicals. Amsterdam: Rodopi, 1982. pp. 349. (Costerus, 33.) Rev. by Harold Beaver in YES (16) 310–11.

7103. ROBBINS, J. ALBERT (ed.).   American literary scholarship: an annual, 1980. Durham, NC; Duke UP, 1982. pp. xx, 625. Rev. by Edward Gallafont in YES (16) 314–5.

7104. ROBINSON, FRED MILLER (postscr.).   Victoria Earle Matthews: *The Value of Race Literature* (1895). MassR (27:2) 169–91.

7105. ROONEY, CHARLES J., JR.   Dreams and visions: a study of American utopias, 1865–1917. (Bibl. 1985, 5925.) Rev. by Kenneth M. Roemer in AL (58:1) 132–4.

7106. ROSENBAUM, BARBARA; WHITE, PAMELA (comps).   Index of English literary manuscripts: vol. 4, 1800–1900: part 1, Arnold–Gissing. (Bibl. 1983, 246.) Rev. by Joanne Shattock in YES (16) 299–301.

7107. ROSS, BRUCE CLUNIES.   Landscape and the Australian imagination. *In* (pp. 224–43) **31.**

7108. SALES, ROGER.   Closer to home: writers and places in England, 1780–1830. *See* **5991.**

7109. SARGENT, MARK L.   Rekindled fires: Jamestown and Plymouth in American literature, 1765–1863. *See* **5994.**

7110. SAUER, LISELOTTE.   Marionetten, Maschinen, Automaten. Der künstliche Mensch in der deutschen und englischen Romantik. Bonn: Bouvier, 1983. pp. 513. Rev. by Lilian R. Furst in arcadia (21:3) 323–4.

7111. SAVORY, JEROLD; MARKS, PATRICIA.   The smiling Muse: Victoriana in the comic press. *See* **429.**

7112. SCANLON, TONY.   Eccentrics, explorers and evangelists: a camel ride through the literature of Northern Territory: part 2, Evangelists: the Aborigines in missionary literature. Westerly (31:1) 55–63.

7113. SCHUELLER, MALINI JOHAR.   The mono-dialogic narrative in America. Unpub. doct. diss., Purdue Univ. [Abstr. in DA (47) 2161A.]

7114. SIEBERS, TOBIN.   The Romantic fantastic. (Bibl. 1985, 5934.) Rev. by Frederick Burwick in RPP (10:2) 71–6.

7115. SIMONS, KENT STEVEN.   Taming the powers of the air: science, pseudoscience, and religion in nineteenth-century American literature. Unpub. doct. diss., Emory Univ., 1985. [Abstr. in DA (47) 183A.]

7116. SIMPSON, J. R. King Arthur's enchanted sleep: early nineteenth century legends. *See* **2488.**

7117. SINGH, AMRITJIT; VERMA, RAJIVA; JOSHI, IRENE M. (eds). Indian literature in English, 1827–1979: a guide to information sources. (Bibl. 1983, 255.) Rev. by Prabhu S. Guptara in YES (16) 311–13.

7118. SOLLORS, WERNER. 'Never was born': the mulatto, an American tragedy. MassR (27:2) 293–316.

7119. SPENGEMANN, WILLIAM C. American writers and English literature. ELH (52:1) 1985, 209–38.

7120. SPRINGER, HASKELL. Call them all Ishmael? Fact and form in some nineteenth-century sea narratives. *In* (pp. 14–22) **28.**

7121. STOICULESCU, MIRA; BOTTEZ, MONICA; CONSTANTINESCU, AURELIA (eds). An anthology of English literature: the Victorian age. Bucharest: Bucharest Univ., 1985. pp. 519.

7122. SUTHERLAND, JOHN. *Cornhill's* sales and payments: the first decade. *See* **435.**

7123. SWANICK, ERIC L. New Brunswick literature and the pursuit of bibliography. *See* **58.**

7124. SWINDELLS, J. Gender, class and labour in Victorian writing. Unpub. doct. diss., Univ. of Cambridge, 1985. [Abstr. in IT (35) 546.]

7125. SWINDELLS, JULIA. Victorian writing and working women. Oxford: Polity Press, 1985. pp. 240. (Feminist perspectives.) Rev. by John Lucas in THES (722) 15; by Kathryn Sutherland in CritQ (28:4) 113.

7126. TAKAHASHI, YASUNARI. Ecstasy no keifu. (The tradition of ecstasy.) Tokyo: Chikuma. pp. xxiv, 306.

7127. TAYLOR, BEVERLY; BREWER, ELISABETH. The return of King Arthur: British and American literature since 1800. Totowa, NJ: Barnes & Noble, 1983. (Cf. bibl. 1983, 6600.) Rev. by E. D. Mackerness in NQ (32:3) 1985, 421–2; by Donald Gray in JEGP (84:2) 1985, 275–8.

7128. TENER, ROBERT H. Breaking the code of anonymity: the case of the *Spectator*, 1861–1897. *See* **712.**

7129. TOTH, EMILY (ed.). Regionalism and the female imagination. New York: Human Sciences Press, 1985. pp. 205. Rev. by Susan Koppelman in CR (30:3) 427–8.

7130. TURNER, GRAEME. National fictions: literature, film and the construction of Australian narrative. Sydney: Allen & Unwin. pp. vii, 156. (Australian cultural studies.)

7131. TURTON, L. G. Turgenev and the context of English literature, 1850–1900. Unpub. doct. diss., Univ. of Warwick, 1984. [Abstr. in IT (35) 547.]

7132. UFFELMAN, LARRY K. (ed.). Victorian periodicals, 1985: a checklist of scholarship and criticism. *See* **715.**

7133. VANCE, NORMAN. The sinews of the spirit: the ideal of Christian manliness in Victorian literature and religious thought. (Bibl. 1985, 5949.) Rev. by David Newsome in TLS, 8 Aug., 856.

7134. VAN LEEUWEN, HENDRIK.   The liaison of visual and written Nonsense. *See* **84.**

7135. VEYRIRAS, PAUL.   Sainte Elisabeth de Hongrie héroïne victorienne? CVE (23) 3–15.

7136. VON FRANK, ALBERT J.   The sacred game: provincialism and frontier consciousness in American literature, 1630–1860. *See* **5091.**

7137. WECKER, CHRISTOPH (ed.).   American–German literary interrelations in the nineteenth century. Munich: Fink, 1983. pp. 173. (American studies, 55.) Rev. by Eva-Marie Kröller in CanRCL (13:2) 309–10.

7138. WEISBUCH, ROBERT.   Atlantic double-cross: American literature and British influence in the age of Emerson. Chicago; London: Chicago UP. pp. xxiii, 334.

7139. WILDE, WILLIAM H.; HOOTON, JOY; ANDREWS, BARRY.   The Oxford companion to Australian literature. *See* **6010.**

7140. WILLSON, LAWRENCE.   American letters ii. SewR (94:1) 131–42 (review-article).

7141. WOLF, BRYAN JAY.   Romantic re-vision: culture and consciousness in nineteenth-century American painting and literature. (Bibl. 1985, 5962.) Rev. by David C. Miller in MLS (16:4) 72–4.

7142. WOODFIELD, MALCOLM.   Victorian weekly reviews and reviewing after 1860: R. H. Hutton and the *Spectator*. *See* **734.**

7143. WOODRESS, JAMES (ed.).   American literary scholarship: an annual, 1979. (Bibl. 1983, 274.) Rev. by Edward Gallafont in YES (16) 314–15.

7144. WYATT, DAVID.   The fall into Eden: landscape and imagination in California. Cambridge: CUP. pp. xviii, 280. (Cambridge studies in American literature and culture.)

7145. YARWOOD, VAUGHAN.   The use of paradigm: classical models of Empire in early New Zealand writing. JNZL (4) 10–20.

Drama and the Theatre

7146. ABEL, CHARLES DOUGLAS.   The acting of Edmund Kean, tragedian. Unpub. doct. diss., Univ. of Toronto, 1985. [Abstr. in DA (46) 2485A.]

7147. BAINS, YASHDIP SINGH.   Popular-priced stock companies and their repertory in Montreal and Toronto in the 1890s. CanD (12:2) 332–41.

7148. CAVE, RICHARD ALLEN.   Romantic drama in performance. *In* (pp. 79–104) **48.**

7149. —— (ed.).   The Romantic theatre: a symposium. *See* **48.**

7150. COOLEY, EDNA HAMMER.   Women in American theatre, 1850–1870: a study in professional equity. Unpub. doct. diss., Univ. of Maryland. [Abstr. in DA (47) 1927A–8A.]

7151. COREN, MICHAEL.   Theatre Royal: 100 years of Stratford East. London: Quartet, 1984. pp. 115.

7152. DAVIS, TRACY C.   Does the theatre make for good? Actresses' purity and temptation in the Victorian era. QQ (93:1) 33–49.

7153.   DÉDÉYAN, CHARLES.   Le drame romantique en Europe: France – Angleterre – Allemagne – Italie – Espagne – Russie. Paris: Société d'Édition d'Enseignement Supérieur, 1982. pp. 408. Rev. by Anna M. Whittmann in CanRCL (13:1) 145–7.

7154.   DOXTATOR, ROBERT LUCAS.   James Stetson Metcalfe's signed criticism of the legitimate theatre in New York City: 1888–1927. *See* **588.**

7155.   DUNN, SHEILA.   The theatres of Bromley: a century of theatre in Bromley. London: Lanthorn, 1984. pp. 81.

7156.   EDWARDS, IFOR.   Lady Helena Faucit Martin (1817–1898): Shakespearean actress. *See* **4651.**

7157.   ÉGRI, PÉTER.   The shadow of Shakespeare across the Atlantic: the Shakespearean tradition in early American tragedy. *See* **4437.**

7158.   FLYNN, JOYCE.   Melting plots: patterns of racial and ethnic amalgamation in American drama before Eugene O'Neill. AmQ (38:3) 417–38.

7159.   FLYNN, JOYCE ANNE.   Ethnicity after sea-change: the Irish dramatic tradition in nineteenth century American drama. Unpub. doct. diss., Harvard Univ., 1985. [Abstr. in DA (47) 21A.]

7160.   FOULKES, RICHARD.   Shakespeare and the Victorian stage. *See* **4653.**

7161.   FRASER, KATHLEEN DORIS JANE.   Theatrical touring in late nineteenth-century Canada: Iva Van Cortland and the Tavernier Company, 1877–1896. Unpub. doct. diss., Univ. of Western Ontario, 1985. [Abstr. in DA (46) 2858A.]

7162.   GEE, CHRISTINA; KNIGHT, JUDITH.   Bibliography. (Byron, Coleridge, Keats, Shelley, Wordsworth.) *In* (pp. 113–26) **48.**

7163.   GOLDHURST, WILLIAM.   Cheers! tears! and laughter: popular drama in 1883. JPC (19:4) 85–93.

7164.   HARRIS, LAURILYN J.   'In truth she has good cause for spleen': Madame Vestris' American tour. TS (28/29) 1981/82, 1982/83, 41–58.

7165.   HEWISON, ROBERT.   Footlights! A hundred years of Cambridge comedy. (Bibl. 1983, 6648.) Rev. by Arvid F. Sponberg in TJ (38:2) 248–9.

7166.   JOHNSON, CLAUDIA D.; JOHNSON, VERNON E.   Nineteenth-century theatrical memoirs. (Bibl. 1984, 6267.) Rev. in BB (43:4) 264.

7167.   KAUFMAN, RHODA HELFMAN.   The Yiddish theatre in New York, 1880–1920: a secular revival. TS (30) 1983/84, 57–61.

7168.   KENT, CHRISTOPHER.   More critics of drama, music and art. *See* **630.**

7169.   LYNES, RUSSELL.   The lively audience: a social history of the visual and performing arts in America, 1890–1950. New York; London: Harper & Row, 1985. pp. x, 489. (New American nation.)

7170.   McARTHUR, BENJAMIN.   Actors and American culture, 1880–1920. Philadelphia, PA: Temple UP, 1984. pp. xiv, 289. Rev. by Tice L. Miller in TJ (38:2) 237–8.

7171.   McLENNAN, KATHLEEN ANN.   American domestic drama 1870 to 1910: individualism and the crisis of community. Unpub. doct. diss., Univ. of Wisconsin–Madison, 1985. [Abstr. in DA (46) 2858A.]

7172. MARKS, PATRICIA.   American literary and drama reviews: an index to late nineteenth-century periodicals. *See* **646.**

7173. MAXWELL, D. E. S.   A critical history of modern Irish drama, 1891–1980. (Bibl. 1985, 5995.) Rev. by Stephen Watt in JEGP (85:4) 583–6; by Seamus Deane in CJIS (12:1) 95–7; by Patrick Diskin in NQ (33:2) 273–4.

7174. MILLER, JAMES.   The magic curtain: the story of theatre in Inverness. Inverness: Friends of Eden Court. pp. 60.

7175. MURPHY, BRENDA.   Literary stepchildren: nineteenth-century dramatists. Review (8) 197–204 (review-article).

7176. NEIL, JANET SNYDER.   Masks and headgear in native American ritual/theatre on the northwest coast. TJ (38:4) 453–62.

7177. OFFORD, JOHN.   The theatres of Portsmouth. Horndean: Milestone, 1983. pp. 72. (Down Memory Lane.)

7178. O'NEILL, PATRICK B.   *Fitzallan.* CanD (12:2) 372–4.

7179. PICK, JOHN.   The West End: mismanagement and snobbery. Eastbourne: Offord, 1983. pp. 215. (City arts.)

7180. PRATT, JUDITH STEVENS.   The vaudeville criticism of Epes Winthrop Sargent, 1896–1910. *See* **673.**

7181. RABY, PETER.   'Fair Ophelia': a life of Harriet Smithson Berlioz. *See* **4685.**

7182. RANGER, P. V.   Terror and pity reign in every breast: gothic drama in the London patent theatres 1750–1820. *See* **6030.**

7183. RICHARDSON, ALAN TURNER.   A mental theater: poetic drama and consciousness in the Romantic age. Unpub. doct. diss., Harvard Univ., 1985. [Abstr. in DA (46) 1952A.]

7184. SANDERSON, MICHAEL.   From Irving to Olivier: a social history of the acting profession in England, 1880–1983. New York: St Martin's Press, 1984. (Cf. bibl. 1985, 6001.) Rev. by Jon Beryl in TJ (38:2) 238–9.

7185. SCHMIDT, JOHANN N.   Ästhetik des Melodramas. Studien zu einem Genre des populären Theaters im England des 19. Jahrhunderts. Heidelberg: Winter. pp. 408. (Britannica et Americana: Folge 3, 7.)

7186. SEKINE, MASARU (ed.).   Irish writers and the theatre. Gerrards Cross: Smythe. pp. viii, 246. (Irish literary studies, 23.)

7187. SMITH, MARY ELIZABETH.   Three political dramas from New Brunswick. CanD (12:1) 144–8. (*The Triumph of Intrigue, Measure by Measure, Done in Darkness.*)

7188. SMITH, SUSAN VALERIA HARRIS.   Masks in modern drama. Berkeley; London: California UP, 1984. pp. xi, 237.

7189. TERFLOTH, JOHN H.   Johann Adam Breysig: pioneer of the panorama stage design and the box set, 1808. TS (30) 1983/84, 5–15.

7190. WEBB, TIMOTHY.   The Romantic poet and the stage: a short, sad, history. *In* (pp. 9–46) **48.**

7191. WILLIAMS, ARTHUR E.   Charles Kean the director. TS (28/29) 1981–82/1982–83, 73–84.

7192. WOODFIELD, JAMES.   English theatre in transition, 1881–1914. Totowa, NJ: Barnes & Noble, 1984. (Cf. bibl. 1984, 6281.) Rev. by Robert G. Laurence in ESCan (12:4) 484–7.

Fiction

7193. ALDISS, BRIAN W.; WINGROVE, DAVID. Trillion year spree: the history of science fiction. *See* **6035.**

7194. ALEXANDER, LYNN MAE. The forgotten icon: the seamstress in Victorian fiction. Unpub. doct. diss., Univ. of Tulsa. [Abstr. in DA (47) 1329A.]

7195. ANDERSON, C. E. The representation of women in Scottish fiction: character and symbol. Unpub. doct. diss., Univ. of Edinburgh, 1985. [Abstr. in IT (35) 1085.]

7196. ANDRIANO, JOSEPH DOMINIC. Our ladies of darkness: Jungian readings of the female daimon in gothic fiction. *See* **6036.**

7197. ASKWITH, BETTY. After Jane Austen: some nineteenth-century lady novelists. EDH (44) 106–24.

7198. AUERBACH, NINA. Romantic imprisonment: women and other glorified outcasts. New York; Guildford: Columbia UP. pp. xxiv, 315. (Gender and culture.) Rev. by Marcia Gordon in Novel (19:3) 278–82; by Tony Tanner in THES (700) 15.

7199. BAILEY, JUTTA M. A study of women characters in selected novels of women writers of the Romantic period. *See* **6037.**

7200. BAINBRIDGE, WILLIAM SIMS. Dimensions of science fiction. Cambridge, MA; London: Harvard UP. pp. 278.

7201. BALL, ROLAND C. The new forms of the novel in the period of Romanticism. *In* (pp. 155–60) **19.**

7202. BAYER-BERENBAUM, LINDA. The gothic imagination: expansion in gothic literature and art. Rutherford, NJ: Fairleigh Dickinson UP; London; Toronto: Assoc. UPs, 1982. pp. 155. Rev. by Maria Teresa Chialant in YES (16) 308–9.

7203. BAYM, NINA. Novels, readers, and reviewers: responses to fiction in antebellum America. (Bibl. 1985, 6015.) Rev. by Alfred Habegger in JEGP (85:3) 472–4.

7204. BENDIXEN, ALFRED. It was a mess! How Henry James and others actually wrote a novel. NYTB, 27 Apr., 3.

7205. BLAKE, A. J. Fiction as history: an examination of the ideological content of the 19th century novel of manners, with a case study of the portrayal of the ruling class in Anthony Trollope's novels. Unpub. doct. diss., CNAA, 1985. [Abstr. in IT (36) 470.]

7206. BLUM, JOANNE DANIELLE. Defying the constraints of gender: the male/female double of women's fiction. Unpub. doct. diss., Ohio State Univ. [Abstr. in DA (47) 2154A.]

7207. BRADBURY, RAY (introd.); HAINING, PETER (comp.). Tales of dungeons and dragons. London: Century. pp. xx, 406. (Century fantasy and SF.)

7208. BREEN, JON L. Novel verdicts: a guide to courtroom fiction. Metuchen, NJ; London: Scarecrow Press, 1984. pp. xii, 266.

7209. BREMNER, S. The fiction of time-travel in the nineteenth-century. Unpub. doct. diss., Univ. of Manchester, 1983.

7210. BROOKS, PETER. Reading the plot: design and intention in narrative. (Bibl. 1985, 6025.) Rev. by Peter K. Garrett in JEGP (85:1) 87–9; by Mieke Bal in PT (7:3) 557–64.

7211. BROWN, MARY JANE.   English periodical criticism of the novel from 1845 to 1865: a search for goodness, truth, and beauty. *See* **567.**

7212. BRUFFEE, KENNETH A.   Elegiac romance: cultural change and loss of the hero in modern fiction. (Bibl. 1985, 8926.) Rev. by Patricia Merivale in CL (38:4) 391–4.

7213. BURGESS, MOIRA.   The Glasgow novel: a survey and bibliography. Motherwell: Scottish Library Assn; Glasgow District Libraries. pp. 123. (Second ed.: first ed. 1973.)

7214. BURT, JOHN.   Romance, character and the bounds of sense (II). Raritan (5:3) 48–60.

7215. CAHALAN, JAMES M.   Great hatred, little room: the Irish historical novel. (Bibl. 1985, 6028.) Rev. by Patrick Rafroidi in Études irlandaises (9) 1984, 334–5.

7216. CAMPBELL, PAUL.   Respectable little green men. Linen Hall Review (3:1) 4–5.

7217. CARTER, MARGARET LOUISE.   'Fiend, spectre, or delusion?': narrative doubt and the supernatural in gothic fiction. *See* **6044.**

7218. CAWTHRA, G. M.   Developments in fictional prose from the late Victorian to the early modern period. Unpub. doct. diss., Univ. of Sheffield, 1984. [Abstr. in IT (35) 48.]

7219. CHAINEY, GRAHAM.   From Boniface to Porterhouse: Cambridge in fiction. Cambridge Review (107:2290) 20–3.

7220. CLARESON, THOMAS D.   Science fiction in America, 1870s–1930s: an annotated bibliography of primary sources. Westport, CT; London: Greenwood Press, 1984. pp. xiv, 305. (Bibliographies and indexes in American literature, 1.) Rev. by Donald M. Hassler in BB (43:4) 260–1.

7221. COALE, SAMUEL CHASE.   In Hawthorne's shadow: American romance from Melville to Mailer. Lexington: Kentucky UP, 1985. pp. ix, 245. Rev. by Elizabeth Ammons in AL (58:4) 630–1; by Andrew Noble in THES (710) 25.

7222. COGAN, FRANCES B.   Weak fathers and other beasts: an examination of the American male in domestic novels, 1850–1870. AmS (25) Fall 1984, 5–20.

7223. COX, MICHAEL; GILBERT, R. W. (sels).   The Oxford book of English ghost stories. Oxford: OUP. pp. 544.

7224. CURRENT GARCÍA, EUGENE.   The American short story before 1850. (Bibl. 1985, 6039.) Rev. by Robert F. Marler in AL (58:3) 433–5.

7225. DALESKI, H. M.   The divided heroine: a recurrent pattern in six English novels. (Bibl. 1985, 6041.) Rev. by Diane S. Bonds in DHLR (18:1) 1985/86, 90–1; by Mary Burgan in JEGP (85:2) 278–82.

7226. DENEAU, DANIEL P.   Pointing theory and some Victorian practices. *See* **1512.**

7227. DICKSTEIN, MORRIS.   Popular fiction and critical values: the novel as a challenge to literary history. *In* (pp. 29–66) **47.**

7228. DIEDRICH, MARIA. The cry of the women: Die Arbeiterdarstellungen frühviktorianischer Romanschriftstellerinnen. Ang (104:3/4) 397–422.

7229. DILLER, HANS-JURGEN. The image of the Middle Ages in nineteenth-century scholarship and fiction. *In* (pp. 147–58) **17.**

7230. DOBRINER, JILL. Bound by expansion: 19th-century American fiction and social change. Unpub. doct. diss., Brandeis Univ. [Abstr. in DA (47) 177A.]

7231. DOBRZYCKA, IRENA. Literature for the masses and the rise of the English social novel. *In* (pp. 459–63) **19.**

7232. ELIOT, SIMON. Public libraries and popular authors, 1883–1912. *See* **215.**

7233. ENGEL, ELLIOT; KING, MARGARET F. The Victorian novel before Victoria: British fiction during the reign of William IV, 1830–1837. (Bibl. 1985, 6047.) Rev. by K. E. Batley in UES (24:1) 39–40; by Roger Day in Dick (82:1) 54–5.

7234. FADEL, Y. The concept of gentility in the Victorian novel. Unpub. doct. diss., Univ. of Leicester, 1984.

7235. FICK, THOMAS HALE. An American dialectic: power and innocence from Cooper to Kosinski. Unpub. doct. diss., Indiana Univ., 1985. [Abstr. in DA (46) 3033A.]

7236. FINDLAY, L. M. 'Raly it's give me such a turn': responding to the reflexive in the nineteenth-century novel. ESCan (12:2) 192–209.

7237. FISHER, I. C. Linguistic indications of social class in the Victorian novel. *See* **997.**

7238. FISHER, PHILIP. Hard facts: setting and form in the American novel. (Bibl. 1985, 6707.) Rev. by Melissa King in UES (24:2) 61–2.

7239. FLINT, KATE. The woman reader and the opiate of fiction: 1855–1870. *In* (pp. 46–61) **39.**

7240. GALLAGHER, CATHERINE. The industrial reformation of English fiction: social discourse and narrative form, 1832–1867. Chicago; London: Chicago UP, 1985. pp. xv, 320. Rev. by Brian Harrison in LRB (8:11) 17–19; by John P. McGowan in SoHR (20:2) 171–3; by Leonée Ormond in THES (690) 17; by Jeremy Hawthorn in Eng (35) 273–8; by Sarah Webster Goodwin in CLIO (16:1) 87–9; by John Kucich in Criticism (28:2) 347–50.

7241. GARROD, C. M. Individuation of middle class women in British fiction, 1848–1914. Unpub. doct. diss., Univ. of London (Bedford Coll.), 1984.

7242. GEE, R. The teacher in the novel: a study of three Victorian novelists. Unpub. doct. diss., Univ. of Exeter, 1983.

7243. GERLACH, JOHN. Toward the end: closure and structure in the American short story. (Bibl. 1985, 6056.) Rev. by Leonard Butts in SSF (23) 135–6.

7244. GILEAD, SARAH. Liminality, anti-liminality, and the Victorian novel. ELH (53:1) 183–97.

7245. GILMOUR, ROBIN. The novel in the Victorian age: a modern introduction. London: Arnold. pp. 256. Rev. by Adrian Poole in THES (733) 20.

7246. GITTER, ELISABETH G.   The Victorian literary kiss. BIS (13) 1985, 165–80.

7247. GOOD, HOWARD.   Acquainted with the night: the image of journalists in American fiction, 1890–1930. Metuchen, NJ; London: Scarecrow Press. pp. xii, 130.

7248. GRANT, RENA JANE.   From Clarissa to Lady Chatterley: character in the British novel. *See* **6051.**

7249. GREENFIELD, BRUCE ROBERT.   The rhetoric of discovery: British and American exploration narratives, 1760–1845 and American renaissance writing. *See* **6122.**

7250. GRENIER, CECILIA MARIE.   Martyrs, mystics and madwomen: images of the nun in selected fiction, 1780–1840. *See* **6053.**

7251. GRIBBLE, JENNIFER.   The Lady of Shalott in the Victorian novel. Salem, NH: Salem House, 1983. (Cf. bibl. 1984, 6324.) Rev. by F. S. Schwarzbach in HJR (7:1) 1985, 51–2.

7252. GROSS, KONRAD.   Arbeit als literarisches Problem. Studien zum Verhältnis von Roman und Gesellschaft in der viktorianischen Zeit. Würzburg: Königshausen & Neumann, 1982. pp. 380.

7253. GROSS, LOUIS S.   The transformed land: studies in American gothic narrative. Unpub. doct. diss., Univ. of Pennsylvania. [Abstr. in DA (47) 1323A.]

7254. HABEGGER, ALFRED.   Gender, fantasy and realism in American literature. (Bibl. 1984, 2124.) Rev. by Brenda Murphy in MLS (16:4) 81–5.

7255. HAINING, PETER (ed.).   Vampire: chilling tales of the undead. London: Allen; Severn House, 1985. pp. 239.

7256. HAIT, ELIZABETH ANNE.   The city of Paris: a shape and a shaping force in selected nineteenth-century British fiction. Unpub. doct. diss., Univ. of Tennessee, 1985. [Abstr. in DA (47) 536A.]

7257. HAMILTON, C. S.   American dreaming: the American adventure formula in the western and hard-boiled detective novel, 1890–1940. Unpub. doct. diss., Univ. of Sussex, 1983.

7258. HANSON, CLARE.   Short stories and short fictions, 1880–1980. New York: St Martin's Press, 1985. (Cf. bibl. 1985, 6066.) Rev. by Ronald L. Johnson in WHR (40:2) 174–7.

7259. HARDY, BARBARA.   Forms of feeling in Victorian fiction. (Bibl. 1985, 6067.) Rev. by Lars Hartveit in EngS (67:1) 86–7; by Roger Day in Dick (82:1) 53–4; by Patrick Swinden in NQ (33:2) 260–2; by John Bayley in LRev, Mar. 1985, 12–14.

7260. HARPHAM, GEOFFREY GALT.   On the grotesque: strategies of contradiction in art and literature. (Bibl. 1985, 6068.) Rev. by Donald W. Crawford in JAE (20:2) 119–20.

7261. HAWTHORN, JEREMY (ed.).   The nineteenth-century British novel. *See* **39.**

7262. HERGENHAN, LAURIE.   Unnatural lives: studies in Australian fiction about the convicts, from James Tucker to Patrick White. (Bibl. 1984, 6328.) Rev. by Terry Goldie in Ariel (17:1) 102–4.

7263. —— (ed.). The Australian short story: an anthology from the 1890s to the 1980s. St Lucia; London: Queensland UP. pp. xxiv, 329. (Portable Australian authors.)

7264. HERMANN, ELISABETH. Opfer der Geschichte. Die Darstellung der nordamerikanischen Indianer im Werk James Fenimore Coopers und seiner Zeitgenossen. Frankfurt: Lang. pp. 266. (Europäische Hochschulschriften: Reihe 14, Angelsächsische Sprache und Literatur, 157.)

7265. HERZOG, KRISTIN. Women, ethnics, and exotics: images of power in mid-nineteenth century fiction. (Bibl. 1985, 6072, where title incomplete.) Rev. by Elizabeth Ammons in SAF (14:2) 239–41.

7266. HOCHMAN, BARUCH. The test of character: from the Victorian novel to the modern. Rutherford, NJ: Fairleigh Dickinson UP, 1983. pp. 224. Rev. by George Otte in DHLR (18:1) 1985/86, 94–6.

7267. HOLUBETZ, MARGARETE. Death-bed scenes in Victorian fiction. EngS (67:1) 14–34.

7268. HOVANEC, EVELYN. Reader's guide to coal mining fiction and selected prose narratives. BB (43:3) 159–71.

7269. HOWARD, JUNE. Form and history in American literary naturalism. Chapel Hill: North Carolina UP, 1985. pp. xii, 207. Rev. by Vincent Fitzpatrick in AL (58:4) 644–7.

7270. HUNTER, SHELAGH. Victorian idyllic fiction: pastoral strategies. (Bibl. 1985, 6074.) Rev. by C. H. Muller in UES (24:1) 40–1.

7271. HURST, MARY JANE GAINES. The voice of the child in American literature: linguistic approaches to fictional child language. Unpub. doct. diss., Univ. of Maryland. [Abstr. in DA (47) 2158A.]

7272. JAMES, EDWARD. The Anglo–Irish disagreement: past Irish futures. Linen Hall Review (3:4) 5–8.

7273. JAŘAB, JOSEF. Early Afro-American fiction. Germanica Olomucensia (6) 51–68.

7274. JOHNSON, DEBORAH MEEM. The inner epic tradition in nineteenth-century novels by women. Unpub. doct. diss., State Univ. of New York at Stony Brook, 1985. [Abstr. in DA (47) 898A.]

7275. JOHNSON, PATRICIA. The role of the middle-class woman in the mid-nineteenth-century British industrial novel. Unpub. doct. diss., Univ. of Minnesota, 1985. [Abstr. in DA (46) 3041A.]

7276. JONES, JOSEPH; JONES, JOHANNA. Canadian fiction. *See* **6055.**

7277. JOSEPH, GERHARD. Framing Caws. Review (8) 189–95 (review-article).

7278. KEEPING, CHARLES (ed.). Charles Keeping's book of classic ghost stories. London: Blackie. pp. 142.

7279. KERR, HOWARD; CROWLEY, JOHN W.; CROW, CHARLES L. (eds). The haunted dusk: American supernatural fiction 1820–1920. (Bibl. 1985, 6078.) Rev. by David Mogen in HJR (6:3) 1985, 206–7.

7280. KESSLER, CAROL FARLEY (ed.). Daring to dream: utopian stories by United States women, 1836–1919. (Bibl. 1985, 6079.) Rev. by Susan Gubar in SFS (13:1) 79–83.

7281. KESTNER, JOSEPH.   Protest and reform: the British social narrative by women, 1827–1867. Madison: Wisconsin UP, 1985. (Cf. bibl. 1985, 6080.) Rev. by Patrick Brantlinger in JEGP (85:4) 575–7; by Leohee Ormond in THES (690) 17; by Kathryn Sutherland in CritQ (28:4) 111–12.

7282. KILROY, JAMES F. (ed.).   The Irish short story: a critical history. (Bibl. 1985, 28.) Rev. by James M. Cahalan in Éire–Ireland (21:4) 154–8; by Patrick Diskin in NQ (33:2) 274–5.

7283. KINNEY, JAMES L.   Amalgamation! Race, sex, and rhetoric in the nineteenth-century American novel. Westport, CT: Greenwood Press, 1985. pp. 259. (Contributions in Afro-American and African studies, 90.) Rev. by Chapel Petty Schmitt in ALR (19:1) 82–3; by Donald B. Gibson in JAH (73:1) 188–9.

7284. KLAUS, H. GUSTAV (ed.).   The socialist novel in Britain: towards the recovery of a tradition. (Bibl. 1983, 113.) Rev. by Michael Wilding in YES (16) 347–8.

7285. KLOOSTER, DAVID J.   The art of the present moment: studies in the American short story. Unpub. doct. diss., Boston College, 1985. [Abstr. in DA (46) 3352A.]

7286. KONIGSBERG, IRA.   Narrative technique in the English novel: Defoe to Austen. *See* **6058.**

7287. KOWALEWSKI, MICHAEL JOHN.   Violence and verbal form in American fiction. Unpub. doct. diss., Rutgers Univ. [Abstr. in DA (47) 2159A.]

7288. KURAMOCHI, HARUMI.   Jukyu seiki eikoku shosetu: josei to kekkon. (Nineteenth-century English novels: women and marriage.) Tokyo: Arateke. pp. vi, 252.

7289. LANGBAUER, LAURIE.   Empty constructions: women and romance in the English novel. *See* **6059.**

7290. LASCELLES, MARY.   The story-teller retrieves the past: historical fiction and fictitious history in the art of Scott, Stevenson, Kipling, and some others. (Bibl. 1983, 6548.) Rev. by S. Wiqar Husain in AJES (11) 109–13.

7291. LEDGERWOOD, MIKLE DAVE.   The images of the Indian in four New-World literatures. Unpub. doct. diss., Univ. of North Carolina at Chapel Hill, 1985. [Abstr. in DA (46) 3346A.]

7292. LEE, A. ROBERT (ed.).   The nineteenth-century American short story. London: Vision Press. pp. 196. (Critical studies.)

7293. LENAR, FAYE MERTINE.   The emergence of the passionate woman in American fiction, 1850–1920. Unpub. doct. diss., Syracuse Univ., 1985. [Abstr. in DA (46) 2693A.]

7294. LETLEY, A. E. C.   Literary uses of Scots dialect in certain nineteenth century novelists from John Galt to George Douglas Brown. *See* **908.**

7295. LETLEY, E.   'Revolution *there* as visible as anywhere else!': some literary uses of Scots in nineteenth-century fiction. *See* **909.**

7296. LEVINE, GEORGE.   The realistic imagination: English fiction from Frankenstein to Lady Chatterley. (Bibl. 1985, 6089.) Rev. by Pierre Coustillas in EA (38:4) 1985, 474–5.

7297. LOESBERG, JONATHAN.   The ideology of narrative form in sensation fiction. Representations (13) 115–38.

7298. LUBBERS, KLAUS.   Emancipatory women in late nineteenth-century Anglo-Irish fiction: a note on the emergence of a motif. CJIS (12:1) 53–8.

7299. LUKACS, PAUL BRADDOCK.   Against the current: a historical perspective in ante-bellum American fiction. Unpub. doct. diss., Johns Hopkins Univ. [Abstr. in DA (47) 530A.]

7300. McADAMS, RUTH ANN.   The Shakers in American fiction. Unpub. doct. diss., Texas Christian Univ., 1985. [Abstr. in DA (46) 1942A.]

7301. McKAY, JANET HOLGREN.   Narration and discourse in American realistic fiction. (Bibl. 1984, 6355.) Rev. by Brenda Murphy in MLS (16:4) 81–5.

7302. McLAVERTY, JAMES.   Authorial revision. Review (8) 119–38 (review-article).

7303. MacMILLAN, CARRIE.   Seaward vision and sense of place: the Maritime novel, 1880–1920. StudCanL (11:1) 19–37.

7304. MADDEN-SIMPSON, JANET (ed.).   Woman's part: an anthology of short fiction by and about Irish women 1890–1960. Dublin: Arlen House; London; New York: Boyars, 1984. pp. 223. Rev. by Patrick Rafroidi in Études irlandaises (9) 1984, 335.

7305. MAILLOUX, STEVEN.   Interpretive conventions: the reader in the study of American fiction. (Bibl. 1984, 6358.) Rev. by Robert Crosman in CL (38:1) 85–6.

7306. MANDEL, ERNEST.   Delightful murder: a social history of the crime story. Minneapolis: Minnesota UP, 1984. pp. 152. Rev. by Thomas E. Lewis in JMMLA (19:2) 39–43.

7307. MANNING, S. L.   The nature of provincialism: some nineteenth-century Scottish and American fiction. Unpub. doct. diss., Univ. of Cambridge. [Abstr. in IT (35) 1081.]

7308. MARSHALL, TOM.   Re-visioning: comedy and history in the Canadian novel. QQ (93:1) 52–65.

7309. MATTHEWS, BRIAN ERNEST.   Romantics and mavericks: the Australian short story. Townsville, Qld.: Foundation for Australian Literary Studies. pp. 48. (Monograph/Foundation for Australian Literary Studies, 14.)

7310. MENENDEZ, ALBERT J.   Civil War novels: an annotated bibliography. New York; London: Garland. pp. xii, 174. (Garland reference library of the humanities, 700.)

7311. —— The subject is murder: a selective subject guide to mystery fiction. New York; London: Garland. pp. 332. (Garland reference library of the humanities, 627.)

7312. MILLER, DANNY LESTER.   Images of women in southern

Appalachian mountain literature. Unpub. doct. diss., Univ. of Cincinnati, 1985. [Abstr. in DA (47) 180A.]

7313. MILLER, J. HILLIS.   Fiction and repetition: seven English novels. (Bibl. 1985, 6105.) Rev. by John Preston in YES (16) 319–20.

7314. MILLER, JANE.   Women writing about men. London: Virago Press. pp. viii, 311. Rev. by Anita Susan Grossman in TLS, 26 Sept., 1077; by S. G. Kossick in UES (24:2) 62–3; by Elaine Showalter in LRB (8:5) 8–9; by Clare Hanson in THES (700) 15.

7315. MILNE, GORDON.   Ports of call: a study of the American nautical novel. Lanham, MD; London: UP of America. pp. ix, 120.

7316. MONNET, S. A.   The Jew and the nineteenth-century novel (1860–1900). Unpub. doct. diss., Univ. of Reading, 1983.

7317. MUKHERJEE, MEENAKSHI.   Realism and reality: the novel and society in India. Delhi; Oxford: OUP, 1985. pp. ix, 218.

7318. MÜLLENBROCK, HEINZ-JOACHIM.   James Fenimore Coopers *Leatherstocking Tales* und die Anfänge des historischen Romans in Amerika. PoetA (18:3/4) 288–304.

7319. MÜLLER, WOLFGANG G.   The erudite detective: a tradition in English and American detective fiction. Spr (17) 245–62.

7320. NADEL, IRA B.; FREDEMAN, WILLIAM H. (eds).   Victorian novelists after 1885. Detroit, MI: Gale Research, 1983. pp. x, 392. (Dictionary of literary biography, 18.) Rev. by J. G. Watson in NQ (33:2) 262–4.

7321. NATARAJAN, N.   The witty woman in nineteenth century English comic fiction. Unpub. doct. diss., Univ. of Aberdeen, 1983.

7322. OLSON, CHRISTOPHER PETER.   Narrational and temporal form in the nineteenth- and twentieth-century novel. Unpub. doct. diss., Northwestern Univ., 1985. [Abstr. in DA (46) 2290A.]

7323. OREL, HAROLD.   The Victorian short story: development and triumph of a literary genre. Cambridge: CUP. pp. x, 213. Rev. by Michael Wheeler in THES (726) 18.

7324. ORTIZ, GLORIA MONSERRATE.   The dandy and the *señorito*: eros and social class in the nineteenth century novel. Unpub. doct. diss., Harvard Univ., 1985. [Abstr. in DA (47) 172A.]

7325. PALMER, JERRY.   Thrillers: genesis and structure of a popular genre. (Bibl. 1980, 7395.) Rev. by William W. Stowe in CanRCL (12:3) 1985, 440–1.

7326. PARKER, HERSHEL.   Flawed texts and verbal icons: literary authority in American fiction. (Bibl. 1985, 6116.) Rev. by Louis A. Renza in ELN (23:4) 70–3; by Tracy Ware in CanL (110) 113–14; by James McLaverty in Review (8) 119–38; by James L. W. West, III, in JEGP (85:4) 588–90.

7327. PEYTON, RICHARD (ed.).   Deadly odds: crime and mystery stories of the turf. London: Souvenir. pp. 366.

7328. PFAELZER, JEAN.   The utopian novel in America, 1886–1896: the politics of form. (Bibl. 1985, 6119.) Rev. by Kenneth M. Roemer in AL (58:1) 132–4.

7329. PLATZ, NORBERT H. Die Beeinflussung des Lesers. Untersuchungen zum pragmatischen Wirkungspotential viktorianischer Romane zwischen 1844 und 1872. Tübingen: Niemeyer. pp. xi, 358. (Buchreihe der Anglia, 25.)

7330. PONS, XAVIER. The psychoanalytic approach to literature. *See* **3039.**

7331. POWELL, PHILIP E. Tyger burning bright: the French Revolution and historical imagination. Unpub. doct. diss., New York Univ., 1985. [Abstr. in DA (46) 3715A.]

7332. QUALLS, BARRY V. The secular pilgrims of Victorian fiction: the novel as book of life. (Bibl. 1985, 6123.) Rev. by Sheila M. Smith in MLR (81:2) 457–8.

7333. RALPH, PHYLLIS C. Transformations: fairy tales, adolescence, and the novel of female development in Victorian fiction. Unpub. doct. diss., Univ. of Kansas, 1985. [Abstr. in DA (46) 3042A.]

7334. REITZ, ANN L. Sawbones to savior to cynic: the doctor's relation to society in English fiction of the eighteenth, nineteenth, and twentieth centuries. *See* **6066.**

7335. ROBINSON, DOUGLAS. American apocalypses: the image of the end of the world in American literature. Baltimore, MD; London: Johns Hopkins UP, 1985. pp. xviii, 283. Rev. by Christopher Wilson in AL (58:4) 671–2; by Lewis F. Archer in ChrisL (35:3) 32–4.

7336. ROWLAND, DIANE BAKER. Sisterhood and social conscience: the emergence and evolution of the feminist New Woman in selected American fiction, 1864–1933. Unpub. doct. diss., Univ. of Miami, 1985. [Abstr. in DA (46) 2294A.]

7337. RUSSELL, NORMAN. The novelist and mammon: literary responses to the world of commerce in the nineteenth century. Oxford: Clarendon Press. pp. x, 226. Rev. by David Grylls in TLS, 26 Sept., 1078.

7338. SEGAL, HOWARD P. Technological utopianism in American culture. Chicago: Chicago UP, 1985. pp. x, 301. Rev. by Jean Christie in PMHB (110:2) 312–14.

7339. SHAPIRO, ANN R. A separate sphere: the woman question in selected fiction by nineteenth-century American women, 1852–1899. Unpub. doct. diss., New York Univ., 1985. [Abstr. in DA (46) 2294A.]

7340. SHAW, HARRY E. The forms of historical fiction: Sir Walter Scott and his successors. (Bibl. 1985, 6134.) Rev. by Daniel Whitmore in MP (84:1) 94–9; by Kenneth M. Sroka in SLJ (supp. 24) 7–9; by Joseph W. Turner in CLIO (15:1) 1985, 91–3.

7341. SINGH, G. (ed.). Collected essays by Q. D. LEAVIS: vol. 2, The American novel and reflections on the European novel. (Bibl. 1985, 6135.) Rev. by John Halperin in NQ (33:3) 426–7.

7342. SMALL, IAN. Annotating 'hard' nineteenth century novels. EC (36:4) 281–93.

7343. SMITH, PETER. Public and private value: studies in the nineteenth-century novel. (Bibl. 1984, 6400.) Rev. by Doris Feldmann in Archiv (223:2) 413–15; by Cicely Palser Havely in NQ (33:1) 120–1.

7344. SPENCER, JANE.   The rise of the woman novelist: from Aphra Behn to Jane Austen. *See* **5167.**

7345. STEPTO, ROBERT B.   Distrust of the reader in Afro-American narratives. *In* (pp. 300–22) **47.**

7346. STEWART, GARRETT.   Death sentence: styles of dying in British fiction. (Bibl. 1985, 2384.) Rev. by David Suchoff in WHR (40:1) 89–91.

7347. STRYCHACZ, THOMAS FRANK.   Challenging mass culture: American writers and literary authority, 1880–1940. Unpub. doct. diss., Princeton Univ. [Abstr. in DA (47) 2162A.]

7348. SUCHOFF, DAVID BRUCE.   Reciprocal testimonies: conservatism and change in the novel. Unpub. doct. diss., Univ. of California, Berkeley, 1985. [Abstr. in DA (46) 2690A.]

7349. SULLIVAN, SHERRY.   Indians in American fiction, 1820–1850: an ethnohistorical perspective. CLIO (15:3) 239–57.

7350. SUTHERLAND, JOHN.   Henry Colburn, publisher. *See* **436.**

7351. TETZELI VON ROSADOR, KURT.   Gems and jewellery in Victorian fiction. YREAL (2) 1984, 275–317.

7352. THOMPSON, RAYMOND H.   The return from Avalon: a study of the Arthurian legend in modern fiction. London: Greenwood Press, 1985. (Contributions to the study of science fiction and fantasy, 14.) (Cf. bibl. 1985, 9178.)

7353. THORNTON, LAWRENCE.   Unbodied hope: narcissim and the modern novel. Lewisburg, PA: Bucknell UP; London: Assoc. UPs, 1984. pp. 223.

7354. TIFFIN, CHRIS.   Nationalism, landscape, and class in Anglo-Australian fiction. Ariel (17:1) 17–32.

7355. TSENG, SEN-YEE.   Bibliolatry: books and reading as a convention in selected Victorian novels. Unpub. doct. diss., Kent State Univ., 1985. [Abstr. in DA (47) 191A.]

7356. VANN, J. DON.   Victorian novels in serial. *See* **717.**

7357. VAREILLE, JEAN-CLAUDE.   Culture savante et culture populaire: brèves remarques à propos des horizons idéologiques, des structures, et de la littérarité du roman policier. Caliban (23) 5–19.

7358. VERNON, JOHN.   Money and fiction: literary realism in the nineteenth and early twentieth centuries. London: Cornell UP, 1984. (Cf. bibl. 1985, 6154.) Rev. by Steven Connor in Dick (82:2) 108–9; by Kathryn Sutherland in CritQ (28:4) 109–10.

7359. VERZEA, ILEANA.   The reception of the English historical novel in Romania. *In* (pp. 103–7) **19.**

7360. WAGAR, W. WARREN.   Terminal visions: the literature of last things. (Bibl. 1984, 6414.) Rev. by David Ketterer in CanRCL (13:3) 492–5.

7361. WALLE, ALF H.   Devolution and evolution: hillbillies and cowboys as American savages. *See* **2496.**

7362. WARD, PATRICIA A.   Medievalism in the Romantic novel. *In* (pp. 35–9) **19.**

7363. WEINSTEIN, PHILIP M.   The semantics of desire: changing models of identity from Dickens to Joyce. (Bibl. 1985, 6158.) Rev. by Ross Chambers in JEGP (85:1) 144–5.

7364. WEISS, DANIEL.   The critic agonistes: psychology, myth, and the art of fiction. Ed. by ERIC SOLOMON and STEPHEN ARKIN. Seattle; London: Washington UP, 1985. pp. xii, 270. Rev. by Frank R. Cunningham in AL (58:2) 295–7; by Jefferson Hunter in NER (9:2) 242–9.

7365. WILKES, J. C.   The treatment of the recent past in nineteenth-century fiction, with particular reference to George Eliot. Unpub. doct. diss., Univ. of Oxford, 1983.

7366. WILLARD, NANCY.   High talk in the starlit wood: on spirits and stories. MichQR (25:1) 81–95.

7367. WILLIAMS, RAYMOND.   Forms of English fiction in 1848. *In* (pp. 1–16) **29.**

7368. WOLFF, ROBERT LEE (comp.).   Nineteenth-century fiction: a bibliographical catalogue based on the collection formed by Robert Lee Wolff: vol. 5, Anonymous, pseudonymous, multiple-author fiction, annuals and periodicals, index. *See* **292.**

7369. ZATLIN, LINDA GERTNER.   The nineteenth-century Anglo-Jewish novel. Boston, MA: G. K. Hall, 1981. pp. 157. (Twayne's English authors, 295.) Rev. by Max F. Schulz in MLR (81:1) 181–2.

Literature for Children

7370. CARPENTER, HUMPHREY.   Secret gardens: the golden age of children's literature. (Bibl. 1985, 6170.) Rev. by Catherine Sheldrick Ross in LQ (56:3) 352–7; by Michael Patrick Hearn in ABC (7:2) 37–40; by Penelope Lively in LRev, Aug. 1985, 36–7.

7371. DIXON, DIANA.   From instruction to amusement: attitudes of authority in children's periodicals before 1914. *See* **585.**

7372. ENGEN, RODNEY K.   The myth of Kate Greenaway. *See* **72.**

7373. FEARN, M.   Childhood and the image of the child in English children's literature, 1760–1830. *See* **6078.**

7374. GOLDMAN, IRENE CAROLYN.   Captains of industry and their mates: a new look at the American business novel from Howells to Dreiser. Unpub. doct. diss., Boston Univ. [Abstr. in DA (47) 1323A.]

7375. HONIG, EDITH LAZAROS.   A quiet rebellion: the portrait of the female in Victorian children's fantasy. Unpub. doct. diss., Fordham Univ., 1985. [Abstr. in DA (46) 2300A.]

7376. JARMAN, DAVID; VAN OSS, CELIA.   Childhood's pattern. London: Firethorn, 1985. pp. xiv, 210.

7377. JOHN RYLANDS UNIVERSITY LIBRARY OF MANCHESTER.   Children's books of yesterday: a survey of 200 years of children's reading: an exhibition in the Deansgate Building, Winter 1985. *See* **242.**

7378. LaCAMPAGNE, ROBERT J.   From Huck to Holden to Dinky Hocker: current humor in the American adolescent novel. LU (1:1) 1977, 62–71.

7379. PFLIEGER, PAT.   A reference guide to modern fantasy for children. Westport, CT; London: Greenwood Press, 1984. pp. xvii, 690.

7380. PICKERING, SAMUEL, JR. Allegory and the first school stories. *In* (pp. 42–68) **40.**

Poetry

7381. ALTON, R. E. 'The Barberry Tree': three 'blithesome blossoms'. An editorial note. RES (37:147) 348.

7382. BARRY, K. M. Language, music and the sign: a study in aesthetics, poetics and poetic practice from Collins to Coleridge. *See* **6084.**

7383. BATE, JONATHAN. Shakespeare and the English Romantic imagination. *See* **4381.**

7384. BEER, JOHN. Who wrote *The Barberry Tree?* RES (37:147) 349–59.

7385. BROMWICH, DAVID. Romantic poetry and the *Edinburgh* ordinances. *See* **565.**

7386. CHAPMAN, MICHAEL (ed.). The Paperbook of South African English poetry. Johannesburg: Donker. pp. 318.

7387. CHATTERJEE, SATI. Art and inspiration: the continuing debate. Jadavpur University Essays and Studies (Calcutta) (4) 1984, 1–12.

7388. CHATTERJEE, VISVANATH. The name and nature of Romanticism. Jadavpur University Essays and Studies (Calcutta) (4) 1984, 146–52.

7389. CHAUDHURI, SUKANTA. Romanticism and the pastoral tradition. Jadavpur University Essays and Studies (Calcutta) (4) 1984, 27–43.

7390. CLARIDGE, LAURA P. Discourse of desire: the paradox of Romantic poetry. Unpub. doct. diss., Univ. of Maryland, 1985. [Abstr. in DA (47) 1330A.]

7391. COATES, PAUL. Words after speech: a comparative study of Romanticism and symbolism. Basingstoke: Macmillan. pp. xii, 215.

7392. CURRAN, STUART. Poetic form and British Romanticism. New York; Oxford: OUP. pp. ix, 265.

7393. DE MAN, PAUL. The rhetoric of Romanticism. (Bibl. 1985, 6186.) Rev. by Northrop Frye in TLS, 17 Jan., 51; by Mark Storey in Eng (35) 67–73; by Paul Hamilton in LRev, Aug. 1985, 29–30; by Lillian R. Furst in JEGP (85:1) 90–2; by David Simpson in SAQ (85:2) 202–4.

7394. DOYLE, JAMES. The Confederation poets and American publishers. *See* **368.**

7395. DYSON, A. E. (ed.). Poetry criticism and practice: developments since the symbolists: a casebook. London: Macmillan. pp. 217. (Casebook series.)

7396. ERICKSON, LEE. The poets' corner: the impact of technological changes in printing on English poetry, 1800–1850. *See* **100.**

7397. FINCH, G. J. Romantic poetry and the limits of explication. Ariel (16:1) 1985, 27–42.

7398. FLEISHMAN, AVROM. Notes for a history of Victorian poetic genres. Genre (18:4) 1985, 363–74.

7399. FREDEMAN, WILLIAM E.; NADEL, IRA B. (eds). Victorian poets after 1850. Detroit, MI: Gale Research, 1985. pp. xvi, 437. (Dictionary of literary biography, 35.) Rev. by Bernard Richards in NQ (33:4) 560–1.

7400. —— —— (eds). Victorian poets before 1850. Detroit, MI: Gale Research, 1984. pp. xvi, 417. (Dictionary of literary biography, 32.) Rev. by Bernard Richards in NQ (33:4) 560–1.

7401. GITTER, ELISABETH G. The Victorian literary kiss. *See* **7246.**

7402. GOODWIN, DAVID GORDON. The rhetoric of British rhetorical handbooks (1758–1828) and Romantic modes of English epic poetry. *See* **1163.**

7403. HARVEY, GEOFFREY. The Romantic tradition in modern English poetry: rhetoric and experience. Basingstoke: Macmillan. pp. xi, 134. (Wordsworth, Hardy, Betjeman, Larkin.)

7404. HOFFPAUIR, RICHARD. Romantic fallacies. New York; Berne; Frankfurt: Lang. pp. xxix, 189. Rev. by Ronald Tetreault in DalR (65:4) 1985/86, 601–3.

7405. HOROWITZ, K. J. Poets and epitaphs in the eighteenth and early nineteenth centuries: Pope to Wordsworth. *See* **6098.**

7406. KNAPP, STEVEN. Personification and the sublime: Milton to Coleridge. *See* **5177.**

7407. KODAMA, SANEHIDE. American poetry and Japanese culture. Hamden, CT: Archon, 1984. pp. xi, 264. Rev. by Don L. Cook in AL (58:1) 134–6.

7408. KRAMER, LAWRENCE. Music and poetry: the nineteenth century and after. (Bibl. 1985, 6194.) Rev. by Mortimer H. Frank in JEGP (85:4) 590–3.

7409. LEE, A. ROBERT (ed.). Nineteenth-century American poetry. London: Vision Press, 1985. pp. 224. (Critical studies.)

7410. LENTRICCHIA, FRANK. On the ideologies of poetic modernism, 1980–1913: the example of William James. *In* (pp. 220–49) **47.**

7411. LEVINE, RHONDA JOY. The grammatical architectonics of Romantic discourse: deictics and figure in Romantic lyrics. Unpub. doct. diss., Univ. of California, San Diego, 1985. [Abstr. in DA (46) 1950A.]

7412. LUCAS, JOHN. Modern English poetry: from Hardy to Hughes: a critical survey. London: Batsford. pp. 218.

7413. MAYS, J. C. C. The authorship of 'The Barberry Tree'. RES (37:147) 360–70.

7414. METZGER, LORE. One foot in Eden: modes of pastoral in Romantic poetry. Chapel Hill: North Carolina UP. pp. xix, 274. Rev. by Tim Chilcott in THES (723) 18.

7415. MILLER, J. HILLIS. The linguistic moment: from Wordsworth to Stevens. (Bibl. 1985, 6197.) Rev. by Michael Fischer in JEGP (85:4) 572–4.

7416. MURRAY, LES A. (ed.). The new Oxford book of Australian verse. Melbourne; Oxford: OUP. pp. xxv, 399.

7417. OAKES, KAREN KILCUP. Reading the feminine: gender gestures in poetic voice. Unpub. doct. diss., Brandeis Univ. [Abstr. in DA (47) 531A.]

7418. PRESTON, CATHY LYNN MAKIN. The ballad tradition and the making of meaning. *See* **6104.**

7419. PROCHÁZKA, MARTIN. K problému tvůrčí metody v poezii a estetice anglického romantismu. (Problems of creative methods in poetry and the aesthetics of English Romanticism.). *In* (pp. 55–6) **4.**

7420. RAIZIS, M. BYRON. From Caucasus to Pittsburgh: the Prometheus theme in British and American poetry. Athens: Gnosis, 1985. pp. xvi, 290.

7421. RICHARDSON, ALAN TURNER. A mental theater: poetic drama and consciousness in the Romantic age. *See* **7183.**

7422. RIEHLE, WOLFGANG. The fragment in English Romantic poetry. *In* (pp. 133–8) **11.**

7423. SARKAR, MALABIKA. The quest for paradise: Milton and the Romantics. *See* **5786.**

7424. SCHAPIRO, BARBARA A. The Romantic mother: narcissistic patterns in Romantic poetry. (Bibl. 1985, 6200.) Rev. by Linda M. Shires in MLS (16:3) 351–5.

7425. SCHOR, ESTHER HELEN. Romantic elegy: the consolations of transcendence in England and America. Unpub. doct. diss., Yale Univ., 1985. [Abstr. in DA (47) 1338A.]

7426. SCHULZ, MAX F. Paradise preserved: recreations of Eden in eighteenth- and nineteenth-century England. *See* **6107.**

7427. SEEBER, HANS ULRICH. The English pastoral in the nineteenth century. YREAL (4) 67–96.

7428. SHARKEY, MICHAEL. A lost satire on the 1890's *Bulletin* writers and bohemians. *See* **691.**

7429. SIMPKINS, SCOTT KEITH. The semiotic dilemma of English Romantic poetry. *See* **2290.**

7430. SIMPSON, J. R. King Arthur's enchanted sleep: early nineteenth century legends. *See* **2488.**

7431. SIMPSON, ROGER. Epics in the Romantic period. NQ (33:2) 160–1.

7432. STARZYK, LAWRENCE. The reflex of the living image in the poet's mind: Victorian mirror poetry. JPRS (7:1) 34–43.

7433. WALLACE, RONALD. God be with the clown: humor in American poetry. (Bibl. 1985, 6211.) Rev. by Ed Folsom in WWQR (3:3) 36–8.

7434. WATERSTON, ELIZABETH. Regions and eras in Ontario poetry. CanP (18) 1–10.

7435. WEBB, TIMOTHY. The Romantic poet and the stage: a short, sad, history. *In* (pp. 9–46) **48.**

7436. WESLING, DONALD. The new poetries: poetic form since Coleridge and Wordsworth. Lewisburg, PA: Bucknell UP; London: Assoc. UPs, 1985. pp. 228.

7437. WORDSWORTH, JONATHAN. 'The Barberry Tree' revisited. RES (37:147) 371–7.

7438. York, R. A.   The poem as utterance. London: Methuen. pp. 214.

Prose

7439. Bailey, Brigitte Gabcke.   Pictures of Italy: American aesthetic response and the development of the nineteenth-century American travel sketch. Unpub. doct. diss., Harvard Univ., 1985. [Abstr. in DA (47) 175a.]

7440. Donaldson, William; Young, Douglas (eds).   Grampian hairst: an anthology of Northwest prose. Foreword by Cuthbert Graham; essay on Northeast Scots by David Murison. *See* **893.**

7441. Greenfield, Bruce Robert.   The rhetoric of discovery: British and American exploration narratives, 1760–1845 and American renaissance writing. *See* **6122.**

7442. Nabholtz, John R.   'My reader my fellow-labourer': a study of English Romantic prose. Columbia: Missouri UP, 1985. pp. viii, 134.

7443. Newsome, David.   The emotive nature of Victorian prose. EDH (44) 195–208.

7444. Wasko, Jean Kay.   The familiar letter as a literary genre in the nineteenth-century. Unpub. doct. diss., Saint Louis Univ., 1984. [Abstr. in DA (46) 1954a.]

Biography and Autobiography

7445. Buckley, Jerome Hamilton.   The turning key: autobiography and the subjective impulse since 1800. (Bibl. 1984, 6107.) Rev. by Raymond E. Fitch in JEGP (85:1) 136–9; by Ira B. Nadel in Prose Studies (9:1) 85–6.

7446. Burdett, Susan.   From memory to imagination: from a poetics of memory to a poetics of the imagination. Unpub. doct. diss., Univ. of California, Davis, 1985. [Abstr. in DA (46) 1946a.]

7447. Cockshut, A. O. J.   The art of autobiography in 19th and 20th century England. (Bibl. 1985, 6230.) Rev. by Susanna Egan in MP (84:1) 107–9; by Cherry Clayton in UES (24:1) 68–9.

7448. Davis, Christian R.   The rhetoric of nineteenth-century American evangelical autobiography. Unpub. doct. diss., Pennsylvania State Univ., 1985. [Abstr. in DA (46) 2691a.]

7449. Landow, George P.   Approaches to Victorian autobiography. (Bibl. 1984, 2525.) Rev. by William A. Madden in CLIO (11:1) 1981, 101–4.

7450. Palmer, Alan.   Napoleon's earliest English biographers. EDH (44) 86–105.

7451. Peterson, Linda H.   Victorian autobiography: the tradition of self-interpretation. New Haven, CT; London: Yale UP. pp. ix, 228. Rev. by Catherine Harland in QQ (93:4) 902–3; by Philip Dodd in THES (710) 22.

7452. Sanders, Valerie.   'Absolutely an act of duty': choice of profession in autobiographies by Victorian women. Prose Studies (9:3) 54–70. (Fanny Kemble, Harriet Martineau, Margaret Oliphant, Elizabeth M. Sewell.)

Related Studies

7453. AARSLEFF, HANS. Joseph de Maistre and Victorian thought on the origin of language and civilization. *In* (pp. 96–108) **53.**

7454. BARRELL, JOHN. The political theory of painting from Reynolds to Hazlitt: 'the body of the public'. *See* **6133.**

7455. BARTRAM, M. Venetian Renaissance painting: the literary response in the nineteenth century. Unpub. doct. diss., Univ. of Reading, 1982.

7456. BERLIN, IRA, *et al.* (eds). Freedom: a documentary history of emancipation 1861–1867: selected from the holdings of the National Archives of the United States: vol. 1, The destruction of slavery. Cambridge: CUP, 1985. pp. xxxviii, 852.

7457. BINSTOCK, L. R. A study of music in Victorian prose. Unpub. doct. diss., Univ. of Oxford, 1985. [Abstr. in IT (35) 545.]

7458. BOURNE, J. M. Patronage and society in nineteenth-century England. London: Arnold. pp. 288.

7459. BRITAIN, IAN. Fabianism and culture: a study in British socialism and the arts, *c.* 1884–1918. (Bibl. 1985, 6240.) Rev. by John Stokes in YES (16) 345–6.

7460. CARR, STEPHEN LEO. Unarticulated questions. *See* **6138.**

7461. CHITNIS, ANAND C. The Scottish Enlightenment and early Victorian English society. *See* **6140.**

7462. COLLS, ROBERT; DODD, PHILIP (eds). Englishness: politics and culture 1880–1920. London: Croom Helm. pp. 378.

7463. COOPER, EMMANUEL. The sexual perspective: homosexuality and art in the last 100 years in the West. London: Routledge & Kegan Paul. pp. xx, 324.

7464. COWEN, ANNE; COWEN, ROGER. Victorian Jews through British eyes. Oxford: OUP. pp. xxvii, 196. (Littman library of Jewish civilization.)

7465. COWLING, MAURICE. Religion and public doctrine in modern England: vol. 2, Assaults. Cambridge: CUP, 1985. pp. xxvii, 375. Rev. by Shirley Robin Letwin in Listener, 23 Jan., 29–30.

7466. CREIGHTON, MARGARET SCOTT. The private life of Jack Tar: sailors at sea in the nineteenth century. *See* **2426.**

7467. DEARBORN, MARY V. Pocahontas revisited: gender and ethnicity in American culture from the Civil War to the present. Unpub. doct. diss., Columbia Univ., 1984. [Abstr. in DA (47) 900A.]

7468. DEIS, ELIZABETH J.; FRYE, LOWELL T. 'London or else the back-woods': some British views of America in the 1830s. SAQ (85:4) 374–87.

7469. DENVIR, BERNARD. The late Victorians: art, design and society, 1852–1910. London: Longman. pp. 269. (Documentary history of taste in Britain.)

7470. ELLIS, ALEC. Educating our masters: influences on the growth of literacy in Victorian working class children. Aldershot: Gower, 1985. pp. vii, 209.

7471. ESCARBELT, BERNARD. 'Un peuple de *paysans*': difficultés de terminologie dans l'étude de l'Irlande au début du XIXe siècle. *In* (pp. 155–65) **1.**

7472. FRYKMAN, ERIK. *Punch* cartoons and the Victorian lower classes. *In* (pp. 174–80) **18.**

7473. FULMER, HAL W. Mythic imagery and Irish nationalism: Henry Grattan against union, 1800. WJSC (50:2) 144–57.

7474. GAY, PETER. The bourgeois experience: Victoria to Freud: vol. 2, The tender passion. New York; Oxford: OUP. pp. viii, 490. Rev. by Peter Kemp in Listener, 19 June, 25–6.

7475. GOLBY, J. M. (ed.). Culture and society in Britain 1850–1890: a source book of contemporary writings. Oxford: OUP. pp. 320.

7476. GREENWOOD, JAMES. The wilds of London. New York; London: Garland, 1985. pp. viii, 364. (Facsim. of ed. pub. London 1874.) (Rise of urban Britain.)

7477. GRÜNZWEIG, WALTER. Niemals verging sein deutsches Herz: Charles Sealsfield in der Literaturkritik der NS-Zeit. Österreich in Geschichte und Literatur (Graz) (30:1) 40–61.

7478. HAMBURGER, LOTTE; HAMBURGER, JOSEPH. Troubled lives: John and Sarah Austin. Toronto: Toronto UP, 1984. pp. xv, 261. Rev. by Martin L. Friedland in MillNL (21:2) 16–17.

7479. HAPKE, LAURA. Down there on a visit: late-nineteenth century guidebooks to the city. JPC (20:2) 41–55.

7480. HARRIS, JACK T. The true Pre-Raphaelite [W.H.H.]. JPRS (7:1) 29–33.

7481. HERSTEIN, SHEILA R. A mid-Victorian feminist, Barbara Leigh Smith Bodichon. New Haven, CT; London: Yale UP, 1985. pp. xiv, 205.

7482. HUMPHREY, RICHARD. The historical novel as philosophy of history: three German contributions: Alexis, Fontane, Döblin. London: Inst. of Germanic Studies, Univ. of London. pp. x, 1975. (Bithell series of dissertations, 10.)

7483. JEFFREY, REBECCA A. W. H. Deverell: some observations and a checklist. JPRS (6:2) 83–93.

7484. JENNINGS, HUMPHREY (comp.); JENNINGS, MARY-LOU; MADGE, CHARLES (eds). Pandaemonium, 1660–1886: the coming of the machine as seen by contemporary observers. *See* **5230.**

7485. JOHANNSEN, ROBERT W. To the halls of the Montezumas: the Mexican war in the American imagination. New York; Oxford: OUP, 1985. pp. xi, 363.

7486. JOHNSON, E. D. H. Paintings of the British social scene from Hogarth to Sickert. *See* **6153.**

7487. KEARNEY, ANTHONY. The louse on the locks of literature: John Churton Collins. Edinburgh: Scottish Academic Press. pp. xii, 185. Rev. by Donald Hawes in THES (732) 18.

7488. LEVINE, PHILIPPA. The amateur and the professional: antiquarians, historians and archaeologists in Victorian England, 1838–1886. Cambridge: CUP. pp. 220.

7489. MACKENZIE, JOHN M. (ed.). Imperialism and popular culture. Manchester: Manchester UP. pp. 264.

7490. MCMURTRY, JO. English language, English literature: the creation of an academic discipline. *See* **826.**

7491. MARCUS, STEVEN. Freud and the culture of psychoanalysis: studies in the transition from Victorian humanism to modernity. (Bibl. 1984, 6513.) Rev. by Frank McCombie in NQ (33:1) 132.

7492. MORRIS, R. J. (ed.). Class, power and social structure in British nineteenth-century towns. Leicester: Leicester UP. pp. 240. (Themes in urban history.)

7493. NEMOIANU, VIRGIL. The taming of Romanticism: European literature and the age of Biedermeier. (Bibl. 1985, 6260.) Rev. by Theodore Ziolkowski in CanRCL (13:3) 488–92.

7494. NORD, DEBORAH EPSTEIN. The apprenticeship of Beatrice Webb. London: Macmillan, 1985. pp. x, 294. Rev. by Patrick Parrinder in Prose Studies (9:3) 107–10.

7495. O'BRIEN, MICHAEL (ed.). All clever men, who make their way: critical discourse in the Old South. Fayetteville: Arkansas UP, 1982. pp. 456. Rev. by I. B. Holley, Jr, in SAQ (83:4) 1984, 473–5.

7496. ØVERLAND, ORM. Norwegian-American theater and drama 1865–1885. *In* (pp. 189–200) **18.**

7497. POOVEY, MARY. 'Scenes of an indelicate character': the medical 'treatment' of Victorian women. Representations (14) 137–68.

7498. RUSSELL, CHARLES. Poets, prophets and revolutionaries: the literary avant-garde from Rimbaud through postmodernism. Oxford: OUP, 1985. pp. xi, 303.

7499. SHAW, DONALD. 'American-ness' in Spanish American literature. CompCrit (8) 213–27.

7500. SHEFER, ELAINE. The nun and the convent in Pre-Raphaelite art. JPRS (6:2) 70–82.

7501. SILVER, CAROLE. On the origin of fairies: Victorians, Romantics, and folk belief. *See* **2571.**

7502. SLOTKIN, RICHARD. The fatal environment: the myth of the frontier in the age of industrialization. New York: Atheneum, 1985. pp. xiii, 636. Rev. by David W. Noble in PacHR (55:3) 473–4.

7503. SOLLORS, WERNER. A critique of pure pluralism. *In* (pp. 250–79) **47.**

7504. SPIESS, REINHARD F. Rezeptionstheorie und historischer Roman. Zum Beispiel: Charles Sealsfields historisches Nordamerika. *In* (pp. 97–102) **19.**

7505. STEVENSON, LOUISE L. Scholarly means to evangelical ends: the New Haven scholars and the transformation of higher learning in America, 1830–1890. Baltimore, MD; London: Johns Hopkins UP. pp. 221. (New studies in American intellectual and cultural history.)

7506. TURNER, FRANK M. The Greek heritage in Victorian Britain. (Bibl. 1983, 6932.) Rev. by Pierre Fontaney in EA (38:4) 1985, 472–3.

7507. TURNER, PATRICIA ANN. Tampered truths: a rhetorical analysis of antebellum slave narratives. *See* **6169.**

7508. VOGELER, MARTHA S. Frederic Harrison: the vocations of a positivist. Oxford: Clarendon Press; New York: OUP, 1984. pp. xviii, 493.

7509. VON ARX, JEFFREY PAUL. Progress and pessimism: religion, politics and history in late nineteenth century Britain. Cambridge, MA; London: Harvard UP, 1985. pp. x., 233. (Harvard historical studies, 104.)

7510. WATERS, M. D. The garden in Victorian literature. Unpub. doct. diss., Univ. of Kent, 1985. [Abstr. in IT (36) 471.]

7511. WOODFIELD, M. J. R. H. Hutton, critic and theologian: a study of the writings of R. H. Hutton on Newman, Arnold, Tennyson, Wordsworth and George Eliot. Unpub. doct. diss., Univ. of Cambridge, 1985.

7512. WRIGHT, T. R. The religion of humanity: the impact of Comtean positivism on Victorian Britain. Cambridge: CUP. pp. xiii, 306.

7513. YELLING, J. A. Slums and slum clearance in Victorian London. London: Allen & Unwin. pp. x, 160. (London research series in geography, 10.)

7514. YOUNG, ROBERT M. Darwin's metaphor: nature's place in Victorian culture. Cambridge: CUP, 1985. pp. xvii, 341.

Literary Theory

This section is intended to contain studies **about** the literary theory, literary historiography, literary criticism, etc., produced *in* the nineteenth century. For modern works **of** literary history and criticism dealing generally with this period, see under 'Nineteenth Century: General Literary Studies'.

7515. ALI, MUHSIN JASSIN. Scheherezade in England: a study of nineteenth-century English criticism of *The Arabian Nights*. (Bibl. 1983, 6834.) Rev. by Mahmoud Manzalaoui in YES (16) 334–5.

7516. CHRIST, CAROL T. Victorian and modern poetics. (Bibl. 1985, 6278.) Rev. by Ashton Nichols in SoHR (20:1) 80–2; by David G. Riede in JEGP (85:1) 140–2.

7517. EIGNER, EDWIN M.; WORTH, GEORGE J. (eds). Victorian criticism of the novel. Cambridge: CUP, 1985. pp. vi, 258. Rev. by Aidan Day in THES (691) 19; by Penny Boumelha in TLS, 10 Oct., 1141.

7518. FITE, DAVID. Harold Bloom: the rhetoric of romantic vision. Amherst: Massachusetts UP, 1985. pp. xiv, 230. Rev. by Rupert Christiansen in THES (701) 21.

7519. FROW, JOHN. Marxism and literary history. Oxford: Blackwell. pp. 352.

7520. HANDWERK, GARY J. Irony and ethics in narrative: from Schlegel to Lacan. New Haven, CT; London: Yale UP, 1985. pp. ix, 231.

7521. HORSTMANN, ULRICH. Ästhetizismus und Dekadenz. Zum Paradigmakonflikt in der englischen Literaturtheorie des späten

neunzehnten Jahrhunderts. (Bibl. 1984, 6428.) Rev. by Claus Daufen-
bach in arcadia (21:1) 105–11.

7522. McFarland, Thomas.   Imagination and its cognates: supplementary considerations. SLI (19:2) 35–50.

7523. Mannion, Irene Elizabeth.   Criticism *con amore*: a study of
Blackwood's Magazine, 1817–1834. *See* **645.**

7524. Mortier, Roland.   Cent ans de littérature comparée: l'acquis,
les perspectives. *In* (pp. 11–17) **11.**

7525. O'Hara, Daniel T.   The romance of interpretation: visionary
criticism from Pater to de Man. New York; Guildford: Columbia UP,
1985. pp. x, 256. Rev. by Paul A. Bové in DalR (65:4) 1985/86, 594–7.

7526. Schwarz, Daniel R.   The humanistic heritage: critical theories of the English novel from James to Hillis Miller. London:
Macmillan. pp. viii, 282. Rev. by Rupert Christiansen in THES (720)
15.

7527. Sypher, Wylie.   A Modernist lexicon. SewR (94:3) 497–503
(review-article.)

7528. Todd, Janet.   Sensibility: an introduction. *See* **6178.**

7529. Wilkie, Brian.   The Romantic ideal of unity. SLI (19:2) 5–21.

AUTHORS

Henry Adams

7530. Carney, Raymond.   The imagination in ascendance: Henry
Adams' *Mont Saint Michel and Chartres*. SoR (22:3) 506–31.

7531. Kronick, Joseph G.   The limits of contradiction: irony and
history in Hegel and Henry Adams. CLIO (15:4) 391–410.

7532. Mellard, James M.   The problem of knowledge and *The
Education of Henry Adams*. SCR (3:2) 55–68.

7533. Podhoretz, Norman.   Henry Adams: the 'powerless' intellectual in America. NCrit (1:10) 1982/83, 6–15.

7534. Sommer, Robert Francis.   The masks of Henry Adams.
Unpub. doct. diss., Duke Univ., 1985. [Abstr. in DA (46) 2294A.]

Louisa M. Alcott

7535. Carpenter, Lynette.   'Did they never see anyone angry
before?': the sexual politics of self-control in Alcott's *A Whisper in the
Dark*. Legacy (3:2) 31–41.

7536. Goldman, Suzy.   Louisa May Alcott: the separation between
art and family. LU (1:2) 1977, 91–7.

7537. Moyle, Geraldine.   The tenth muse lately sprung up in the
marketplace: women and professional authorship in nineteenth-century
America. Unpub. doct. diss., Univ. of California, Los Angeles, 1985.
[Abstr. in DA (47) 332A.]

7538. Myerson, Joel; Shealy, Daniel.   Louisa May Alcott on
vacation: four uncollected letters. RALS (14:1/2) 1984, 113–41.

7539. —— —— Louisa May Alcott's *A Wail*: an unrecorded satire of
the Concord authors. PBSA (80:1) 93–9.

7540. —— —— (eds).   Three contemporary accounts of Louisa May
Alcott, with glimpses of other Concord notables. NEQ (59:1) 109–22.

7541. SHEALY, DANIEL LESTER. The author-publisher relationships of Louisa May Alcott. Unpub. doct. diss., Univ. of South Carolina, 1985. [Abstr. in DA (46) 3721A.]

7542. STRICKLAND, CHARLES. Victorian domesticity: families in the life and art of Louisa May Alcott. University: Alabama UP, 1985. pp. xv, 198. Rev. by Larry A. Carlson in AL (58:4) 635–6.

7543. ZEHR, JANET SUSAN. Louisa May Alcott and the female fairy tale. Unpub. doct. diss., Univ. of Illinois at Urbana-Champaign, 1985. [Abstr. in DA (46) 3355A.]

William Alexander

7544. DONALDSON, WILLIAM (introd.). The Laird of Drammochdyle and his contemporaries, or, Random sketches done in outline with a burnt stick. Aberdeen: Aberdeen UP. pp. 160.

Horatio Alger, Jr

7545. BODE, CARL (ed.). *Ragged Dick* and *Struggling Upward.* New York; Harmondsworth: Penguin, 1985. pp. xxii, 280. (Penguin American library.)

7546. SCHARNHORST, GARY; BALES, JACK. The lost life of Horatio Alger, Jr. (Bibl. 1985, 6302, where first scholar's name misspelt.) Rev. by Adrienne Siegel in JAH (72:4) 958; by Steven Allaback in ALR (19:1) 91–2; Raymond H. Robinson in NEQ (59:1) 135–7.

William Allingham

7547. HUSNI, SAMIRA. William Allingham: cold words hiding life in their veins. JPRS (6:2) 60–9.

'F. Anstey' (T. A. Guthrie)

7548. HAMPSON, ROBERT G. Conrad, Guthrie, and *The Arabian Nights.* Conradiana (18:2) 141–3.

William Archer

7549. POSTLEWAIT, THOMAS. Prophet of the new drama: William Archer and the Ibsen campaign. Westport, CT: Greenwood Press. pp. xx, 190. Rev. by Yvonne Shafer in TJ (38:4) 507–8.

Matthew Arnold

7550. ALLOTT, MIRIAM; SUPER, ROBERT H. (eds). Matthew Arnold. Oxford: OUP. pp. xxxi, 616. (Oxford authors.)

7551. APROBERTS, RUTH. Arnold and God. (Bibl. 1985, 6305.) Rev. by David J. DeLaura in Review (7) 1985, 119–44.

7552. BROWNSTEIN, RACHAEL M. Representing the self: Arnold and Brontë on Rachael. BIS (13) 1985, 1–24.

7553. BUCKLER, WILLIAM E. On the poetry of Matthew Arnold: essays in critical reconstruction. (Bibl. 1985, 6308.) Rev. by Clyde de L. Ryals in MLR (81:2) 460–2.

7554. DELAURA, DAVID J. Ruth apRoberts, Matthew Arnold, and God. Review (7) 1985, 119–44 (review-article).

7555. GIDDINGS, ROBERT (ed.). Matthew Arnold: between two worlds. London: Vision Press. pp. 207. (Critical studies.)

7556. HARRINGTON, DAVID V. Buried passion in Matthew Arnold's *Tristram and Iseult.* Arnoldian (13:1) 1985/86, 23–30.

7557. HARRIS, TERRY G. Reconstructing Christianity: Matthew

Arnold's religious essays, Christian Romanticism, and the Church of England. Unpub. doct. diss., Univ. of Missouri–Columbia, 1985. [Abstr. in DA (46) 3358A.]

7558. HONAN, PARK. Matthew Arnold: a life. (Bibl. 1985, 6317.) Rev. by Sir Roy Shaw in JAE (20:1) 121–4.

7559. KIJINSKI, JOHN L. Values, assumptions, and persuasion in the literary criticism of Arnold, Pater, and Wilde. Unpub. doct. diss., Univ. of Wisconsin–Madison, 1985. [Abstr. in DA (46) 3360A.]

7560. LESSA, RICHARD. Arnold's *Thyrsis*; the pastoral elegy and the true poet. DUJ (79:1) 37–44.

7561. MANSELL, DARREL. Matthew Arnold's *The Study of Poetry* in its original context. MP (83:3) 279–85.

7562. NEIMAN, FRASER. A note on Arnold scholarship: Spring 1985–Spring 1986. Arnoldian (13:2) 44–52.

7563. SCOTT, NATHAN A., JR. The poetics of belief: studies in Coleridge, Arnold, Pater, Santayana, Stevens, and Heidegger. Chapel Hill: North Carolina UP, 1985. pp. 250. Rev. by Nelvin Vos in ChrisL (35:4) 49–50.

7564. SHARPE, WILLIAM. Confronting the unpoetical city: Arnold, Clough, and Baudelaire. Arnoldian (13:1) 1985/86, 10–22.

7565. STARZYK, LAWRENCE J. 'The Worthies began a revolution': Browning, Mill, Arnold and the poetics of self-acquaintance. Arnoldian (13:2) 10–27.

7566. STEDMAN, JANE W. Some unpublished letters of Matthew Arnold to Richard D'Oyly Carte. Arnoldian (13:2) 1–9.

7567. TAYLOR, M. The idea of knowledge in the development of cultural criticism in the 19th century, with particular reference to Carlyle, Ruskin and Arnold. Unpub. doct. diss., Univ. of London, Birkbeck Coll. [Abstr. in IT (36) 22.]

7568. UHLIG, CLAUS. Conceptual architecture in nineteenth-century writing. CLS (23:3) 218–33.

7569. —— Literature, philosophy, religion: on conceptual architecture in some Victorian writers. YREAL (3) 1985, 163–84.

7570. WHEELER, SAUNDRA SEGAN. Matthew Arnold and the young writer. Unpub. doct. diss., New York Univ., 1985. [Abstr. in DA (46) 3729A.]

7571. YOON, JI-KWAN. Inmunjueui jeongshin eui hyeondaejeok euimi: Matthew Arnold reul eotuochae bol gutinga. (Liberal humanism at the present time: Arnold's contemporary meaning.) EngSt (10) 95–108.

Jane Austen

7572. BARFOOT, CEDRIC CHARLES. The thread of connection: aspects of fate in the novels of Jane Austen and others. (Bibl. 1984, 6567.) Rev. by Joan H. Pittock in YES (16) 296–7.

7573. BARKER, A. D. Women and independence in the nineteenth-century novel: a study of Austen, Trollope and James. Unpub. doct. diss., Univ. of St Andrews, 1985. [Abstr. in IT (35) 48.]

7574. BENEDICT, BARBARA MacVEAN. The tensions of realism:

oppositions of perception in some novels of Fielding and Austen. *See* **6443**.

7575. BOREN, LYNDA S.   The performing self: psychodrama in Austen, James and Woolf. CR (30:1) 1–24.

7576. BOUMAN, ANDREW A.   Of Jane Austen and inclusiveness: the case for quotas in the new Lutheran Church. Cresset (49:3) 6–12. (Sin in *Sense and Sensibility*.)

7577. BURROWS, J. F.   The reciprocities of style: literary criticism and literary statistics. *See* **523**.

7578. CREESE, RICHARD.   Austen's *Emma*. Exp (44:2) 21–3.

7579. DAVIES, J. M. Q.   *Emma* as charade and the education of the reader. PQ (65:2) 231–42.

7580. ERICKSON, JOYCE QUIRING.   Public and private in Jane Austen's novels. MidQ (25) 1984, 201–19.

7581. GENSTER, JULIA ANN.   'These veracious pages': the epistle and its audiences from Dryden to Austen. *See* **5414**.

7582. GILSON, DAVID.   A bibliography of Jane Austen. (Bibl. 1984, 6578.) Rev. by Brian Southam in YES (16) 293–6.

7583. GREY, J. DAVID (ed.).   The Jane Austen handbook: with a dictionary of Jane Austen's life and works. London: Athlone Press. pp. xi, 511. Rev. by Brigid Brophy in TLS, 14 Nov., 1284.

7584. HALPERIN, JOHN.   The life of Jane Austen. (Bibl. 1985, 6357.) Rev. by Park Honan in BJECS (9:1) 99–101; by Carolyn Heilbrun in Novel (19:2) 183–5; by Karen B. Mann in SAQ (85:3) 301–3; by Robert W. Rogers in JEGP (85:4) 569–71; by James Thompson in Review (8) 26–7.

7585. HARDY, JOHN.   Jane Austen's heroines: intimacy in human relationships. (Bibl. 1985, 6359.) Rev. by John C. Hawley in ChrisL (35:2) 46–7.

7586. HEYNS, MICHIEL.   Shock and horror: the moral vocabulary of *Mansfield Park*. ESA (29:1) 1–18.

7587. JONES, KATHLEEN ANNE.   Jane Austen's fictional parents. Unpub. doct. diss., Univ. of North Carolina at Chapel Hill, 1985. [Abstr. in DA (46) 3360A.]

7588. KAUFMANN, DAVID.   Closure in *Mansfield Park* and the sanctity of the family. PQ (65:2) 211–29.

7589. KEARNEY, J. A.   A comparative study in the novels of Jane Austen and George Eliot: reason and feeling as components of moral choice. Unpub. doct. diss., Univ. of York. [Abstr. in IT (35) 1086.]

7590. KIRKHAM, MARGARET.   Jane Austen: feminism and fiction. (Bibl. 1985, 6363.) Rev. by James Thompson in Review (8) 24–6; by Frederick M. Keener in YES (16) 297–8.

7591. LANE, MAGGIE.   Jane Austen's England. London: Hale. pp. 224.

7592. LEWIS, LISA A. F.   Kipling's Jane: some echoes of Austen. ELT (29:1) 76–82.

7593. LITVAK, JOSEPH.   The infection of acting: theatricals and theatricality in *Mansfield Park*. ELH (53:2) 331–55.

7594. McDonagh, Oliver.   The church in *Mansfield Park*: a serious call? Sydney Studies in English (12) 101–13.

7595. Meyers, Kate Beaird.   Jane Austen's use of literary allusion in the Sotherton episode of *Mansfield Park*. PLL (22:1) 96–9.

7596. Meyersohn, Marylea.   The uses of conversation in Jane Austen: the social contexts of speech. Unpub. doct. diss., Columbia Univ. [Abstr. in DA (47) 914A.]

7597. Monaghan, David (ed.).   Jane Austen in a social context. (Bibl. 1984, 6594.) Rev. by James Thompson in Review (8) 29.

7598. Moon, Hak-Sook.   Jane Austen eui doduckgwan: gyeolhon eul tonghae bon sahoe jowha. (Morality in Jane Austen's novels: marriage and social harmony.) Unpub. doct. diss., Yeungnam Univ., Korea.

7599. Moon, Woo-Sang.   *Pride and Prejudice* e gwanhayeo. (On *Pride and Prejudice*.) EngSt (10) 1–16.

7600. Mooneyham, Laura G.   The rhetoric of education in Jane Austen's novels. Unpub. doct. diss., Vanderbilt Univ., 1985. [Abstr. in DA (47) 538A.]

7601. Naono, Yuko.   Jane Austen no shōsetsu: onna shujinko wo megutte. (The novels of Jane Austen: a study of the female protagonists.) Tokyo: Kaibunsha. pp. 244.

7602. Olsen, Stein Haugom.   Appreciating *Pride and Prejudice*. In (pp. viii, 1–14) **39.**

7603. Pennala, Judy L.   The thematic and structural use of time in the novels of Jane Austen. Unpub. doct. diss., Georgia State Univ., College of Arts and Sciences, 1985. [Abstr. in DA (46) 2302A.]

7604. Pettingell, Phoebe.   Jane and the Janeites. NewL (69:16) 14–15.

7605. Ronen, Ruth.   Space in fiction. PT (7:3) 421–38.

7606. Smith, Johanna Mary.   Domestic passion: sister-brother incest in four nineteenth-century novels. Unpub. doct. diss., Claremont Graduate School, 1985. [Abstr. in DA (46) 2702A.]

7607. Smith, Leroy W.   Jane Austen and the drama of woman. (Bibl. 1984, 6611.) Rev. by Park Honan in BJECS (9:1) 99–101; by James Thompson in Review (8) 24–7.

7608. Southam, B. C. (ed.).   The Watsons: a fragment. Orig. ed. by R. W. Chapman. London: Athlone Press, 1985. pp. viii, 164. (Jane Austen library, 4.) (Second ed.: first ed. 1927.)

7609. Stéphane, Nelly.   Une parodie du roman noir: *Northanger Abbey* de Jane Austen. Europe (62:659) 1984, 19–28.

7610. Tanner, Tony.   Jane Austen. London: Macmillan. pp. 320.

7611. Thompson, James.   Jane Austen and history. Review (8) 21–32 (review-article).

7612. ——Jane Austen and the limits of language. JEGP (85:4) 510–31.

7613. Todd, Janet (ed.).   Jane Austen: new perspectives. (Bibl. 1985, 6388.) Rev. by James Thompson in Review (8) 29.

7614. Williams, Michael.   Jane Austen: six novels and their methods. Basingstoke: Macmillan. pp. viii, 214. Rev. by Brigid Brophy in TLS, 14 Nov., 1284.

7615. WILTSHIRE, JOHN.   The world of *Emma*. Critical Review (27) 1985, 84–97 (review-article).

Anna Laetitia Barbauld

7616. BALIBAR, RENÉE.   National language, education, literature. *In* (pp. 126–47) **29.**

William Barnes

7617. CHEDZOY, ALAN.   William Barnes: a life of the Dorset poet. Wimborne, Dorset: Dovecote Press. pp. 192. Rev. by C. H. Sisson in TLS, 20 June, 676.

7618. JONES, BERNARD.   William Barnes' *Guide to Dorchester. See* **109.**

7619. SHEPHERD, V.   The circle of William Barnes's poetry: a discussion of the language and themes of his dialect poetry. *See* **933.**

Bernard Barton

7620. BURNESS, EDWINA.   Charles Lamb, Bernard Barton and the Quakers. CLB (53) 148–54.

Pakenham Thomas Beatty

7621. BEATTY, C. J. P.   Victor Hugo, Swinburne, and an Irish poet. *In* (pp. 134–44) **18.**

Thomas Lovell Beddoes

7622. MAYS, J. C. C.   The authorship of 'The Barberry Tree'. *See* **7413.**

Ambrose Bierce

7623. DAVIDSON, CATHY N.   The experimental fictions of Ambrose Bierce: structuring the ineffable. (Bibl. 1985, 6411.) Rev. in OhioanaQ (29:1) 32–3; by Barton Levi St Armand in SSF (23) 119–23.

Elizabeth Bisland (Elizabeth Bisland Wetmore)

7624. WILLIAMS, SUSAN MILLAR.   *'L'Enfant terrible'?* Elizabeth Bisland and the South. SoR (22:4) 680–96.

Wilfrid Scawen Blunt

7625. FAULKNER, PETER (ed.).   Jane Morris to Wilfrid Scawen Blunt: the letters of Jane Morris to Wilfrid Scawen Blunt together with extracts from Blunt's diaries. Exeter: Exeter UP. pp. xii, 140.

7626. TIDRICK, KATHRYN.   Heart-beguiling Araby. Cambridge; New York: CUP, 1981. pp. xii, 244. Rev. by Mahmoud Manzalaoui in YES (16) 334–5.

George Henry Boker

7627. TANNE, STEPHEN LEONARD.   My complex case: the sonnet sequences of George Henry Boker. Unpub. doct. diss., State Univ. of New York at Stony Brook. [Abstr. in DA (47) 1327A.]

George Borrow

7628. COLLIE, MICHAEL.   George Borrow, eccentric. (Bibl. 1984, 6640.) Rev. by Heinz Reinhold in YES (16) 316–18.

7629. —— FRASER, ANGUS.   George Borrow: a bibliographical study. (Bibl. 1985, 6416.) Rev. by J. F. Fuggles in Library (8:2) 186–7.

7630. RIDLER, A. M.   George Borrow as a linguist: images and contexts. Unpub. doct. diss., CNAA, 1983.

7631. WILLIAMS, H. M.   A study of George Borrow's travel writings and autobiographical fiction, with special reference to romance and the picaresque. Unpub. doct. diss., Univ. of Wales, Aberystwyth, 1984. [Abstr. in IT (36) 22.]

Dion Boucicault

7632. DAVIS, JIM.   The importance of being Caleb: the influence of Boucicault's *Dot* on the comic styles of J. L. Toole and Joseph Jefferson. Dick (82:1) 27–32.

7633. MURPHY, BRENDA.   Literary stepchildren: nineteenth-century dramatists. *See* **7175.**

7634. SMITH, JAMES L. (ed.).   London assurance. London: Black; New York: Norton, 1984. pp. xlvii, 137. (New mermaids.) Rev. by Ronald W. Strang in NQ (33:3) 419.

7635. THOMSON, PETER (ed.).   Plays. (Bibl. 1985, 6419.) Rev. by Brenda Murphy in Review (8) 197–204.

Hjalmar Hjorth Boyesen

7636. SEYERSTED, PER.   From Norwegian romantic to American realist: studies in the life and writings of Hjalmar Hjorth Boyesen. (Bibl. 1985, 6420.) Rev. by Orm Øverland in EngS (67:4) 374–6.

Charlotte Mary Brame ('Bertha M. Clay')

7637. DROZDZ, GREGORY.   Charlotte Mary Brame: Hinckley's forgotten daughter. London: Drozdz, 1984. pp. 39.

The Brontës

7638. ANON. (ed.).   A day at Howarth: a reminiscence by the Rev. Thomas Akroyd. BST (19) 49–54.

7639. CHITHAM, EDWARD.   The Brontës' Irish background. New York: St. Martin's Press; London: Macmillan. pp. x. 168.

7640. —— WINNIFRITH, TOM (eds).   Selected Brontë poems. Oxford: Blackwell, 1985. pp. xxxi, 262. Rev. by Christine Alexander in AUMLA (66) 303–7.

7641. DUTHIE, ENID L.   The Brontës and nature. London: Macmillan. pp. 240.

7642. GROVE, ROBIN.   The Brontës: self devouring. Critical Review (28), 70–86.

7643. KLAUS, MEREDITH McSWEENEY.   A Brontë reading list, 1986. BST (19) 83–9.

7644. LYON, KIM.   The Dentdale Brontë trail. Dent: Lyon Equipment, 1985. pp. 32.

7645. PRENTIS, B. L.   The Brontë sisters and George Eliot: aspects of their intellectual and literary relationship. Unpub. doct. diss., Univ. of Wales, Swansea, 1984. [Abstr. in IT (35) 546.]

7646. QUARM, JOAN.   Purified by woe – on faith and suffering. BST (19) 17–26.

7647. REES, JOAN.   Profligate son: Branwell Brontë and his sister. London: Hale. pp. 208.

7648. SULLIVAN, SHEILA.　Studying the Brontës. Harlow: Longman. pp. 151. (York handbooks.)

7649. TILLOTSON, KATHLEEN.　'Back to the beginning of this century'. BST (19) 3–17.

7650. VERCH, MARIA.　Die Brontës und Shakespeare. *See* **4611.**

7651. WILKS, BRIAN (ed.).　The illustrated Brontës of Haworth: scenes and characters from the lives and writings of the Brontë sisters. London: Collins. pp. 224. (Willow books.)

Anne Brontë

7652. JACOBS, N. M.　Gender and layered narrative in *Wuthering Heights* and *The Tenant of Wildfell Hall*. JNT (16:3) 204–19.

7653. PATTERSON, SALLY.　Before their time: an examination of the role of women in society as portrayed by Charlotte Brontë in *Jane Eyre* and *Villette* and Anne Brontë in *Agnes Grey* and *The Tenant of Wildfield Hall*. BST (19) 55–9.

Branwell Brontë

7654. FRASER, REBECCA.　Mrs Robinson and Branwell Brontë: some mistaken evidence. BST (19) 29–31.

Charlotte Brontë

7655. ALEXANDER, CHRISTINE (ed.).　An edition of the early writings of Charlotte Brontë: vol. 1, *The Glass Town Saga: 1826–1832*. Oxford: Blackwell. pp. xxiv, 383.

7656. ANON.　'Innocent and un-Londony': impressions of Charlotte Brontë. BST (19) 44–9.

7657. BARKER, JULIET R. V.　Charlotte Brontë's photograph. BST (19) 27–8.

7658. —— Subdued expectations: Charlotte Brontë's marriage settlement. BST (19) 33–9.

7659. BARNARD, ROBERT.　Charlotte Brontë's unfinished novels. *In* (pp. 122–33) **18.**

7660. BROWNSTEIN, RACHAEL M.　Representing the self: Arnold and Brontë on Rachael. *See* **7552.**

7661. BUTLER, JANET.　Charlotte Brontë's *Professor*. Exp (44:3) 35–7.

7662. CHASE, KAREN.　Eros and psyche: the representation of personality in Charlotte Brontë, Charles Dickens and George Eliot. (Bibl. 1985, 6444.) Rev. by Penny Boumelha in Eng (35) 78–82.

7663. CHILDERS, MARY.　Narrating structures of opportunity. Genre (19:4) 447–69.

7664. CLARK-BEATTIE, ROSEMARY.　Fables of rebellion: anti-Catholicism and the structure of *Villette*. ELH (53:4) 821–47.

7665. CODACCIONI, MARIE-JOSÉ.　L'autre vie de Bertha Rochester. *In* (pp. 107–14) **1.**

7666. CRUMP, R. W.　Charlotte and Emily Brontë, 1846–1915: a reference guide. (Bibl. 1985, 6446.) Rev. by T. J. Winnifrith in YES (16) 326–7.

7667. GRIGORESCU, DAN (ed.).　Shirley. Trans. by DUMITRU MAZILU. Bucharest: Minerva. 2 vols. pp. xxxv, 396; 416.

7668. KING, JEANETTE. Jane Eyre. Milton Keynes: Open UP. pp. 128. (Open guides to literature.)

7669. LEAVIS, L. R. David Copperfield and Jane Eyre. EngS (67:2) 167–73.

7670. LEMON, CHARLES (ed.). A leaf from an unopened volume, or, The manuscript of an unfortunate author: an Angrian story. Haworth: Brontë Soc. pp. xvi, 66.

7671. LEPOW, LAUREN. 'They that wad their true-love win': Tam Lin and Jane Eyre. See **2523.**

7672. LINTOTT, S. The roar the other side of silence: Charlotte Brontë, George Eliot and the literary consequences of women's passivity. Unpub. doct. diss., Univ. of Kent, 1983.

7673. MAYNARD, JOHN. Charlotte Brontë and sexuality. (Bibl. 1985, 6461.) Rev. by Martha Vicinus in Criticism (28:3) 350–2; by A. T. Cosslett in NQ (33:2) 251; by Penny Boumelha in Eng (35) 78–85.

7674. MERRETT, ROBERT JAMES. The conduct of a spiritual autobiography in Jane Eyre. Ren (37:1) 1984, 2–15.

7675. MOSES, JUDITH A. Love imagined. See **4962.**

7676. NESTOR, PAULINE. Female friendships and communities: Charlotte Bronte, George Eliot, Elizabeth Gaskell. Oxford: Clarendon Press, 1985. pp. 220. Rev. by Marion Shaw in BST (19) 62–3; by John Lucas in THES (722) 15.

7677. NEUFELDT, VICTOR A. (ed.). The poems of Charlotte Brontë: a new text and commentary. New York; London: Garland, 1985. pp. xlvii, 497. (Garland English texts, 9.) Rev. by Margaret Smith in BST (19) 59–61.

7678. PATTERSON, SALLY. Before their time: an examination of the role of women in society as portrayed by Charlotte Brontë in Jane Eyre and Villette and Anne Brontë in Agnes Grey and The Tenant of Wildfield Hall. See **7653.**

7679. PICKREL, PAUL. Jane Eyre: the apocalypse of the body. ELH (53:1) 165–82.

7680. ROSENGARTEN, HERBERT; SMITH, MARGARET (eds). Villette. New York: OUP, 1984. (Cf. bibl. 1985, 6467.) Rev. by Janet Butler in JEGP (85:4) 577–9; by Karen MacLeod Hewitt in NQ (33:2) 250–1.

7681. WINNIFRITH, TOM (ed.). The poems of Charlotte Brontë: a new annotated and enlarged edition of the Shakespeare Head Brontë. (Bibl. 1985, 6472.) Rev. by W. A. Craik in NQ (33:4) 558–9.

7682. YAEGER, PATRICIA S. Honey-mad women: Charlotte Brontë's bilingual heroines. BIS (14) 11–35.

Emily Brontë

7683. BAL, MIEKE; VAN ZOEST, AART. Structure narrative et signification: le cas de Wuthering Heights. In (pp. 317–27) **19.**

7684. BARCLAY, JANET M. Emily Brontë criticism 1900–1982: an annotated check-list. Westport, CT: Meckler, 1984. pp. 162. Rev. by Sue Hanson in BB (43:3) 181–2.

7685. BURNS, MARJORIE. 'This shattered prison': versions of Eden in Wuthering Heights. In (pp. 30–45) **39.**

7686. CHITHAM, E. H.   The poems of Emily Brontë: a new text edited from the manuscripts, with full transcriptions and commentary. Unpub. doct. diss., Univ. of Sheffield, 1984.

7687. CLAYBOROUGH, ARTHUR.   Arnold Kettle and *Wuthering Heights*: the anatomy of an argument. *In* (pp. 146–56) **18.**

7688. FLINTOFF, EVERARD.   The geography of *Wuthering Heights*. DUJ (78:2) 277–88.

7689. HOLDERNESS, GRAHAM.   Wuthering Heights. pp. 99. (Bibl. 1985, 6481, where pagination incorrect.) Rev. by Arthur Pollard in BST (19) 61–2.

7690. HOMANS, MARGARET.   Women writers and poetic identity: Dorothy Wordsworth, Emily Brontë, and Emily Dickinson. (Bibl. 1984, 6686.) Rev. by Anne K. Mellor in RPP (10:1) 77–8.

7691. JACOBS, N. M.   Gender and layered narrative in *Wuthering Heights* and *The Tenant of Wildfell Hall. See* **7652.**

7692. KAVANAGH, JAMES H.   Emily Brontë. (Bibl. 1985, 6482.) Rev. by Catherine Koralek in Eng (35) 293–7; by Felicity Rosslyn in CamQ (15:2) 164–7; by Tom Winnifrith in NQ (33:4) 559.

7693. KOVEL, JOEL.   Heathcliff's quest: unconscious themes in *Wuthering Heights*. HUSL (13:1) 1985, 29–42.

7694. LEVY, ANITA.   The history of desire in *Wuthering Heights*. Genre (19:4) 409–30.

7695. MUIR, STUART.   The grotesque in first-person narration: psychoanalysis and narratology. Unpub. doct. diss., Princeton Univ. [Abstr. in DA (47) 2152A.]

7696. PARKER, PATRICIA.   The (self-) identity of the literary text: property, propriety, proper place, and proper name in *Wuthering Heights*. *In* (pp. 92–116) **23.**

7697. PLUMLY, STANLEY.   The abrupt edge. OhioR (37) 15–32. (Writers' treatment of death.)

7698. SMITH, JOHANNA MARY.   Domestic passion: sister-brother incest in four nineteenth-century novels. *See* **7606.**

Lord Brougham

7699. SHATTOCK, JOANNE.   Politics and literature: Macaulay, Brougham, and the *Edinburgh Review* under Napier. *See* **692.**

Charles Brockden Brown

7700. BERTHOLD, DENNIS.   Desacralizing the American gothic: an iconographic approach to *Edgar Huntly*. SAF (14:2) 127–38.

7701. MOSES, RICHARD P.   The Quakerism of Charles Brockden Brown. QH (75:1) 12–25.

7702. PRIBEK, THOMAS.   A note on 'depravity' in *Wieland*. PQ (64) 1985, 273–80.

7703. VOLOSHIN, BEVERLY R.   *Wieland*: 'accounting for appearances'. NEQ (59:3) 341–58.

George Douglas Brown ('George Douglas', 'Kennedy King')

7704. SOMMERS, JEFFREY.   Notes and documents. SSL (19) 1984, 252–8.

Thomas Edward Brown
7705. SUTTON, MAX KEITH.   How listeners shape stories: a model for readers in Brown's *Fo'c's'le Yarns*. JNT (16:2) 117–30.

The Brownings
7706. KELLEY, PHILIP; HUDSON, RONALD (eds).   The Brownings' correspondence: vol. 1, September 1809–December 1826; vol. 2, January 1827–December 1831. (Bibl. 1985, 6505.) Rev. by Philip Drew in MLR (81:2) 459–60.

7707. MUNICH, ADRIENNE AUSLANDER; GARRISON, VIRGINIA; RAILEY, KEVIN.   Robert and Elizabeth Barrett Browning: an annotated bibliography for 1983. BIS (13) 1985, 201–12.

7708. —— RAILEY, KEVIN.   Robert and Elizabeth Barrett Browning: an annotated bibliography for 1984. BIS (14) 157–70.

Elizabeth Barrett Browning
7709. DAVID, DEIRDRE.   'Art's a service': social wound, sexual politics, and *Aurora Leigh*. BIS (13) 1985, 113–36.

7710. LEIGHTON, ANGELA.   Elizabeth Barrett Browning. Brighton: Harvester Press. pp. xiii, 179. (Key women writers.)

7711. MERMIN, DOROTHY.   Barrett Browning's stories. BIS (13) 1985, 99–112.

7712. —— The damsel, the knight, and the Victorian woman poet. CI (13:1) 64–80.

7713. —— Elizabeth Barrett Browning through 1844: becoming a woman poet. SELit (26:4) 713–36.

7714. SHARP, PHILLIP DAVID.   Poetry in process: Elizabeth Barrett Browning and the sonnets notebook. Unpub. doct. diss., Louisiana State Univ. and Agricultural and Mechanical College, 1985. [Abstr. in DA (47) 916A.]

7715. STONE, MARJORIE.   Cursing as one of the fine arts: Elizabeth Barrett Browning's political poems. DalR (66:1/2) 155–73.

Robert Browning
7716. BARENT, RAE M.   Some existential aspects in the poetry of Robert Browning. Unpub. doct. diss., Duquesne Univ. [Abstr. in DA (47) 1330A.]

7717. BORNSTEIN, GEORGE.   'What porridge had John Keats?': Pound's *L'Art* and Browning's 'popularity'. Paideuma (10:2) 1981, 303–6.

7718. BRADY, ANN P.   The metaphysics of pornography in *The Ring and the Book*. BIS (13) 1985, 137–64.

7719. CALCRAFT, M. B. M.   Robert Browning's *Pacchiarotto* volume: a reinterpretation and reassessment. Unpub. doct. diss., Univ. of Southampton, 1985. [Abstr. in IT (36) 20.]

7720. EDWARDS, SUZANNE.   Robert Browning's *Saul*: Pre-Raphaelite painting in verse. JPRS (6:2) 53–9.

7721. ERICKSON, LEE.   Robert Browning: his poetry and his audience. (Bibl. 1985, 6511.) Rev. by W. David Shaw in MP (84:1) 101–4.

7722. HAIGWOOD, LAURA E.   Gender-to-gender anxiety and influence in Robert Browning's *Men and Women*. BIS (14) 97–118.

7723. JACK, IAN; SMITH, MARGARET (eds).   The poetical works of Robert Browning: vol. 2, *Strafford*; *Sordello*. (Bibl. 1985, 6518.) Rev. by Philip Drew in YES (16) 324–5.

7724. JACOBS, GERALDINE.   Parent-child relationships in Browning's *The Ring and the Book*. Unpub. doct. diss., Univ. of Detroit, 1985. [Abstr. in DA (46) 3359A.]

7725. KORG, JACOB.   Browning and Italy. (Bibl. 1985, 6520.) Rev. by John Maynard in Review (7) 1985, 297–304.

7726. MAYNARD, JOHN.   How substantial was Browning? Review (7) 1985, 297–304 (review-article).

7727–8. Entries cancelled.

7729. O'NEILL, PATRICIA.   Pedigree of self-making: Shelley's influence on Browning and Hardy. Unpub. doct. diss., Northwestern Univ. [Abstr. in DA (47) 2170A.]

7730. POSNOCK, ROSS.   Henry James and the problem of Robert Browning. (Bibl. 1985, 6524.) Rev. by Boyd Litzinger in Cithara (26:1) 55–7; by Adeline R. Tintner in SAQ (85:4) 403–5; by Philip Sharp in HJR (7:1) 1985, 52–3.

7731. RYALS, CLYDE DE L.   Becoming Browning: the poems and plays of Robert Browning, 1833–1846. Columbus: Ohio State UP, 1983. pp. x, 292. Rev. by John Woolford in NQ (33:4) 561–2; by John Maynard in Review (7) 1985, 297–304.

7732. SLINN, E. WARWICK.   Browning and the fictions of identity. Totowa, NJ: Barnes & Noble, 1982. (Cf. bibl. 1983, 7181.) Rev. by Barbara Arnett Melchiori in YES (16) 325–6.

7733. SPECK, GORDON R.   *The Noble Bachelor* and Browning's duchess. BSJ (35:1) 1985, 35–7.

7734. STARZYK, LAWRENCE J.   'The Worthies began a revolution': Browning, Mill, Arnold and the poetics of self-acquaintance. *See* **7565.**

7735. SURTEES, VIRGINIA.   Browning's *Last Duchess*. LRB (8:17) 17–18.

7736. THOMAS, DONALD.   Robert Browning: a life within life. (Bibl. 1983, 7182.) Rev. by Linda A. Rubel in MLS (16:3) 318–20.

7737. WEISSMANN, JUDITH.   Women without meaning: Browning's feminism. MidQ (23:2) 1982, 200–14.

Mary Brunton

7738. MAITLAND, SARA (introd.).   Self-control: a novel. London: Pandora. pp. 437. (Mothers of the novel.)

7739. WELDON, FAY (introd.).   Discipline. London: Pandora. pp. 375. (Mothers of the novel.)

Daniel Bryan

7740. STUDER, WAYNE MALCOLM.   The frustrated muse: the life and works of Daniel Bryan, *c.* 1790–1866. Unpub. doct. diss., Univ. of Minnesota, 1984. [Abstr. in DA 3641A.]

William Cullen Bryant

7741. OLSON, STEVE. A perverted poetics: Bryant's and Emerson's concern for a developing American literature. ATQ (61) 15–22.

7742. PORTER, DANIEL R. The Knickerbockers and the historic site in New York State. NYH (64) 1983, 35–50.

Edward Bulwer-Lytton (Lord Lytton)

7743. CRAGG, WILLIAM E. Bulwer's *Godolphin*: the metamorphosis of the fashionable novel. SELit (26:4) 675–90.

7744. DAVIS, GLENDA MANNING. *On Art in Fiction*: a study of Bulwer-Lytton's theory in practice. Unpub. doct. diss., Howard Univ., 1985. [Abstr. in DA (46) 3039A.]

7745. STEPHENS, JOHN RUSSELL. E. Bulwer-Lytton: a misattributed article identified. NQ (33:2) 161.

Edward Burne-Jones

7746. PFORDRESHER, JOHN. Edward Burne-Jones' gothic romance: *A Story of the North*. Archiv (223:2) 283–96.

7747. —— 'The vocabulary of the unconscious': Burne-Jones's first story. Mosaic (19:1) 57–72. (*The Cousins.*)

Sir Richard Burton

7748. ECKLEY, GRACE. The entertaining *Nights* of Burton, Stead, and Joyce's Earwicker. *See* **591.**

7749. GOURNAY, JEAN-FRANÇOIS. L'appel du Proche-Orient: Richard Francis Burton et son temps 1821–1890. (Bibl. 1984, 6761.) Rev. by Peter Marshall in EA (38:4) 1985, 473–4.

7750. TIDRICK, KATHRYN. Heart-beguiling Araby. *See* **7626.**

Adam Hood Burwell

7751. MACDONALD, MARY LU (ed.). 'New' poems of Adam Hood Burwell. CanP (18) 99–117.

Horace Bushnell

7752. KRAMER, MICHAEL P. Horace Bushnell's philosophy on language considered as a mode of cultural criticism. AmQ (38:4) 573–90.

Samuel Butler

7753. BREUER, HANS-PETER; HOWARD, DANIEL F. (eds). Erewhon, or, Over the range. (Bibl. 1984, 6763.) Rev. by Roger Robinson in JNZL (4) 83–5.

7754. JOLICŒUR, CLAUDE. Mythologie chrétienne et structure narrative dans *The Way of All Flesh* de Samuel Butler. *In* (pp. 91–101) **1.**

7755. JONES, HENRY FESTING (ed.). The notebooks of Samuel Butler. London: Hogarth Press, 1985. pp. 438. (Lives and letters.)

7756. NORRMAN, RALF. Samuel Butler and the meaning of chiasmus. London: Macmillan. pp. ix, 315.

George Gordon Noel, Lord Byron

7757. BAKER, MARK. Byron *epistolaris*. Unpub. doct. diss., Columbia Univ., 1985. [Abstr. in DA (46) 2296A.]

7758. BANTAŞ, ANDREI. Opere: vol. 1. (Works: vol. 1.) Bucharest: Univers, 1985. pp. 508. Rev. by Andrei Bantaş in RomLit, 30 Jan., 20.

7759. BARKER-BENFIELD, B. C. The honeymoon of Joseph and

Henrietta Chichester, with Daniel Roberts' memories of Byron and Shelley. BLR (12:2) 119–41.

7760. BEATY, FREDERICK L.   Byron the satirist. DeKalb: Northern Illinois UP, 1985. pp. 236. Rev. by Clement T. Goode in ELN (24:2) 71–3.

7761. BIELAWSKI, LARRY.   Emerson and Byron. ATQ (62) 59–62.

7762. BLAICHER, GÜNTHER.   Wilhelm Müller and the political reception of Byron in nineteenth-century Germany. Archiv (223:1) 1–16.

7763. BOYES, MEGAN.   Queen of a fantastic realm. Derby: Tatler. pp. 117. (Byron's relationship with Mary Ann Chaworth.)

7764. BREWER, WILLIAM DEAN.   The 'war of earthly minds': Julian versus Maddalo in the poetry of Shelley and Byron. Unpub. doct. diss., Univ. of Virginia, 1985. [Abstr. in DA (47) 1732A.]

7765. CORBETT, M. J.   Lord Byron's dramas: their cultural context and influence. Unpub. doct. diss., CNAA, 1985. [Abstr. in IT (36) 470.]

7766. CROMPTON, LOUIS.   Byron and Greek love: homophobia in 19th-century England. Berkeley: California UP, 1985. (Cf. bibl. 1985, 6553.) Rev. by Seymour Kleinberg in Review (8) 139–43.

7767. DANDO, JOEL ALLAN.   The poet as critic: Byron in his letters and journals. Case studies of Shakespeare and Johnson. See **4423.**

7768. ELLEDGE, W. PAUL.   Byron's Harold at sea. PLL (22:2) 154–64.

7769. FREEMAN, JOHN.   'Paradise of exiles': the Shelley–Byron conference in Pisa. KSR (1) 1–14.

7770. GOLDBERG, LEONARD S.   Center and circumference in Byron's *Lara*. SELit (26:4) 655–73.

7771. GRAHAM, PETER.   A 'polished horde': the great world in *Don Juan*. BRH (86:3) 1983/85, 255–69.

7772. GRAHAM, PETER W. (ed.).   Byron's bulldog: the letters of John Cam Hobhouse to Lord Byron. (Bibl. 1985, 6556.) Rev. by Robert F. Gleckner in SAQ (85:2) 209–12.

7773. GRIGORESCU, DAN; POP, LIA-MARIA (eds).   Opere. (Works.) Vol. 1, trans. by AUREL COVACI, PETRE SOLOMON, and VIRGIL TEODORESCU; vol. 2, trans. by ȘTEFAN AVĂDANEI *et al.* Bucharest: Univers, 1985. pp. 511; 576.

7774. GROVES, DAVID.   James Hogg: verses for Burns and Byron. See **6330.**

7775. HILL, JAMES L.   Experiments in the narrative of consciousness: Byron, Wordsworth, and *Childe Harold*, cantos 3 and 4. ELH (53:1) 121–40.

7776. HOFFMEISTER, GERHART.   Byron und der europäische Byronismus. (Bibl. 1984, 6781.) Rev. by Rolf P. Lessenich in Archiv (223:1) 170–3.

7777. KNIGHT, CHARLES A.   Satire and conversation: the logic of interpretation. See **6057.**

7778. KOPRINCE, SUSAN.   The clue from *Manfred* in *Daisy Miller*. AQ (42) 293–304.

7779. LACROIX, JEAN.   Récrire l'épopée au XIX-ème siècle par la voix d'un mythe moderne: Byron. CREL (3) 1985, 57–76.

7780. LEHMANN, JOHN. Three literary friendships: Byron & Shelley, Rimbaud & Verlaine, Robert Frost & Edward Thomas. London: Quartet, 1983. pp. 184.

7781. McDONALD, SHEILA J. The impact of libertinism on Byron's *Don Juan*. BRH (86:3) 1983/85, 291–317.

7782. McGANN, JEROME J. (ed.). Byron. Oxford: OUP. pp. xxviii, 1080. (Oxford authors.)

7783. —— The complete poetical works: vol. 4. Oxford: Clarendon Press. pp. xxi, 568.

7784. —— The complete poetical works: vol. 5, *Don Juan*. Oxford: Clarendon Press. pp. xxiv, 771.

7785. MARCHAND, LESLIE A. (ed.). Byron's letters and journals: vol. 12, 'The trouble of an index'; anthology of memorable passages and index to the eleven volumes. (Bibl. 1982, 7251.) (*See also* bibl. 1984, 6790 for other vols.) Rev. by Andrew Nicholson in YES (16) 302–4.

7786. MARTIN, PHILIP W. Byron: a poet before his public. (Bibl. 1984, 6791.) Rev. by Philip Healy in KSR (1) 78–84.

7787. MELCHIORI, GIORGIO. The dramas of Byron. *In* (pp. 47–60) **48.**

7788. MOOG-GRÜNEWALD, MARIA. Tassos Leid. Zum Ursprung moderner Dichtung. Arcadia (21:2) 113–28.

7789. NICHOLSON, J. A. L. Poetry and action in Byron's development. Unpub. doct. diss., Univ. of Warwick, 1983.

7790. OUEIJAN, NAJI BOULOS. A compendium of eastern elements in Byron's oriental tales. Unpub. doct. diss., Baylor Univ., 1985. [Abstr. in DA (46) 2302A.]

7791. PROCHÁZKA, MARTIN. Byronismus a problémy české máchovské recepce. (Byronism and its reception in Czech romantic literature.) Česká literatura (Prague) (34) 1–23.

7792. —— Máchova poezie a problém Byronova vlivu: pokus o funkcionální analýzu. (K. H. Mácha's poetry and the problem of Lord Byron's influence.) *In* (pp. 187–207) PAVEL VAŠÁK (ed.), Prostor Máchova díla. Prague: Československý spisovatel. pp. 281.

7793. RAIZIS, MARIOS BYRON. Lord Byron and Greek Orthodoxy. Balkan Studies (27:1) 51–66.

7794. RITT, NIKOLAUS Byron and his contemporary reception in Vienna. WBEP (80) 187–200.

7795. ROBINSON, CHARLES E. (ed.). Lord Byron and his contemporaries. (Bibl. 1985, 6573.) Rev. by Andrew Nicholson in YES (16) 305–6.

7796. RUDOLF, ANTHONY. Byron's *Darkness*: lost summer and nuclear winter. London: Menard, 1984. pp. 15.

7797. SCHWEIZER, HAROLD. Ambition and vocation in Lord Byron's *Childe Harold's Pilgrimage*. AAA (11:2) 179–93.

7798. SELAIHA, N. M. K. Byron's plays: structure and irony: a re-assessment in the context of modernism. Unpub. doct. diss., Univ. of Exeter, 1984.

7799. SHARP, MICHAEL STEWART. 'Freedom's battle': war and revolution in Byron's major poetry. Unpub. doct. diss., Univ. of Wisconsin–Madison, 1985. [Abstr. in DA (46) 3728A.]

7800. STOREY, MARK. Byron and the eye of appetite. London: Macmillan. pp. 76. Rev. by P. W. Martin in THES (757) 16.

7801. SULLIVAN, ERNEST W., II. A fragment of a possible Byron poem in manuscript. *See* **184.**

7802. VITAL, ANTHONY PAUL. Lord Byron's embarrassment: poesy and the feminine. BRH (86:3) 1983/85, 269–80.

William Carleton

7803. HAYLEY, BARBARA. A bibliography of the writings of William Carleton. Gerrards Cross: Smythe, 1985. pp. 241.

7804. WATERS, MAUREEN. William Carleton: the writer as witness. Études irlandaises (11) 51–63.

Thomas Carlyle

7805. BAKER, LEE C. R. The open secret of *Sartor Resartus*: Carlyle's method of converting his reader. SP (83:2) 218–35.

7806. BRIDGMAN, RICHARD. From Greenough to 'Nowhere': Emerson's *English Traits*. NEQ (59:4) 469–85.

7807. CAMPBELL, IAN. More conversations with Carlyle: the Monckton Milnes diaries, 2. Prose Studies (9:1) 22–9.

7808. —— Thomas Carlyle in 1981. SSL (17) 1982, 242–5.

7809. CATE, GEORGE ALLAN (ed.). The correspondence of Thomas Carlyle and John Ruskin. (Bibl. 1983, 7235.) Rev. by Rodger L. Tarr in Review (7) 1985, 243–6.

7810. DAVIES, JAMES A. The effects of context: Carlyle and the *Examiner* in 1848. *See* **582.**

7811. FINDLAY, L. M. 'Maternity must forth': the poetics and politics of gender in Carlyle's *French Revolution*. DalR (66:1/2) 130–54.

7812. —— Paul de Man, Thomas Carlyle, and *The Rhetoric of Temporality*. DalR (65:2) 1985, 159–81.

7813. FRYKMAN, ERIK. Carlyle's reception and influence in Sweden. SSL (19) 1984, 17–39.

7814. GOLDBERG, MICHAEL K.; SIEGEL, JULES P. (eds). Carlyle's *Latter-Day Pamphlets*. Ottawa: Canadian Federation for the Humanities, 1983. pp. 594. Rev. by Rodger L. Tarr in Review (7) 1985, 240–3.

7815. HARRIS, KENNETH MARC. Reason and understanding reconsidered: Coleridge, Carlyle, and Emerson. ELit (13:2) 263–81.

7816. JUCKETT, ELIZABETH COX. The art of the tightrope dancer: Thackeray's response to Carlyle. Unpub. doct. diss., Univ. of Pennsylvania. [Abstr. in DA (47) 1734A.]

7817. KAPLAN, FRED. Thomas Carlyle: a biography. (Bibl. 1985, 6602.) Rev. by James R. Kincaid in MLS (16:3) 375–7; by Frank M. Turner in JMH (58:1) 303–5; by Rodger L. Tarr in Review (7) 1985, 247–58.

7818. LLOYD, TOM. Madame Roland and Schiller's aesthetics: Carlyle's *The French Revolution*. Prose Studies (9:3) 39–53.

7819. Entry cancelled.

7820. METZ, KARL H. 'The social chain of being'. Zum Topos des sozialen Konservativismus und zur Entstehung des Gedankens der sozialen Verantwortung im Grossbritannien der industriellen Revolution. *See* **6799**.

7821. RENNER, STANLEY. *Sartor Resartus* retailored? Conrad's *Lord Jim* and the peril of idealism. YREAL (3) 1985, 185–222.

7822. ROSENBERG, JOHN D. Carlyle and the burden of history. Cambridge, MA: Harvard UP; Oxford: Clarendon Press, 1985. pp. x, 209.

7823. SANDERS, CHARLES RICHARD. A brief history of the 'Duke–Edinburgh Edition of the Carlyle Letters'. *See* **480**.

7824. SORENSEN, D. R. Thomas Carlyle's method of epic and prophetic history, 1820–1837. Unpub. doct. diss., Univ. of Oxford, 1983.

7825. TARR, RODGER L. Truth and fiction: Carlyle edited and re-edited. Review (7) 1985, 239–58 (review-article).

7826. TAYLOR, M. The idea of knowledge in the development of cultural criticism in the 19th century, with particular reference to Carlyle, Ruskin and Arnold. *See* **7567**.

7827. TIMKO, MICHAEL. Gods of the lower world: romantic egoists and Carlylean heroes. BIS (14) 125–40.

7828. UHLIG, CLAUS. Conceptual architecture in nineteenth-century writing. *See* **7568**.

7829. —— Literature, philosophy, religion: on conceptual architecture in some Victorian writers. *See* **7569**.

7830. VANDEN BOSSCHE, CHRIS R. Carlyle, career, and genre. Arnoldian (13:2) 28–43.

7831. —— Desire and deferral of closure in Carlyle's *Sartor Resartus* and *The French Revolution*. JNT (16:1) 72–8.

7832. VIJN, J. P. Carlyle and Jean Paul, their spiritual optics. (Bibl. 1985, 6607.) Rev. by Frederick Burwick in CL (38:2) 203–5.

Edward Carpenter

7833. BEITH, GILBERT (introd.). Towards democracy: complete edition in four parts. London: GMP, 1985. pp. 416. (Gay modern classics.)

7834. BROWN, A. D. A consideration of some parallels in the personal and social ideals of E. M. Forster and Edward Carpenter. Unpub. doct. diss., Univ. of Wales, Bangor, 1983.

7835. RAHMAN, TARIQ. Edward Carpenter and E. M. Forster. DUJ (79:1) 59–69.

Joseph Comyns Carr

7836. POULSON, CHRISTINE. Costume designs by Burne-Jones for Irving's production of *King Arthur*. Burlington Magazine (128:994) 18–24.

'Lewis Carroll' (Charles Lutwidge Dodgson)

7837. ASH, RUSSELL (introd.). Alice's adventure under ground. London: Pavilion. pp. 20, unnumbered facsim. Rev. by M. C. in Junior Bookshelf (50:2) 58.

7838. CLARK, BEVERLY LYON. The mirror worlds of Carroll,

Nabokov, and Pynchon: fantasy in the 1860s and 1960s. VNRN (3) 1979, 24–6.

7839. COHEN, MORTON N.   Another wonderland: Lewis Carroll's *The Nursery Alice*. LU (7/8) 1983/84, 120–6.

7840. GOODACRE, SELWYN H.; KINCAID, JAMES R. (eds).   Alice's adventures in Wonderland. (Bibl. 1983, 7257.) Rev. by Peter Heath in AEB (8:3) 1984, 204–11.

7841. KLOTZ, VOLKER.   Das europäische Kunstmärchen. Fünfundzwanzig Kapitel seiner Geschichte von der Renaissance bis zur Moderne. *See* **2846.**

7842. MADDEN, WILLIAM A.   Framing the Alices. PMLA (101:3) 362–73.

7843. NATOV, RONI.   The persistence of Alice. LU (3:1) 1979, 38–61.

7844. PRESTON, MICHAEL J.   A concordance to the verse of Lewis Carroll. New York; London: Garland, 1985. pp. xx, 344. (Garland reference library of the humanities, 485.)

7845. —— (ed.).   A KWIC concordance to Lewis Carroll's *Alice's Adventures in Wonderland* and *Through the Looking-glass*. Introd. by JAMES R. KINCAID. New York; London: Garland. pp. xxix, 628. (Garland reference library of the humanities, 676.)

7846. ROTHER, CAROLE.   Lewis Carroll's lesson: coping with fears of personal destruction. PCP (19) 1984, 89–94.

7847. SIBLEY, BRIAN (postscr.).   Alice's adventures in Wonderland. London: Methuen, pp. 158.

7848. STEIG, MICHAEL.   Alice as self and other: experiences of reading *Alice's Adventures in Wonderland*. ESCan (12:2) 178–91.

7849. WATSON, GEORGE.   Tory Alice. ASch (55) 543–52.

7850. ZADWORNA-FJELLESTAD, DANUTA.   *Alice's Adventures in Wonderland* and *Gravity's Rainbow*: a study in duplex fiction. Stockholm: Almqvist & Wiksell. pp. v, 123. (Stockholm studies in English, 68.) (Doct. diss. Stockholm Univ.)

Madison Cawein

7851. SCOTT, ROBERT IAN.   T. S. Eliot and the original *Waste Land*. UWR (19:2) 61–4.

Sir George Tomkyns Chesney

7852. PAGETTI, CARLO (ed.).   *La Battaglia di Dorking*, tratto dal *Blackwood's Magazine*, Maggio 1871. *See* **663.**

Charles W. Chesnutt

7853. FERGUSON, SALLYANN H.   Chesnutt's *The Conjuror's Revenge*: the economics of direct confrontation. Ob (7) Summer/Winter 1981, 37–42.

7854. FRAIMAN, SUSAN.   Mother–daughter romance in Charles W. Chesnutt's *Her Virginia Mammy*. SSF (22) 1985, 443–8.

7855. LUPOLD, HARRY FORREST.   Charles W. Chesnutt: a black writer caught in two worlds. OhioanaQ (29:1) 4–7.

Kate Chopin

7856. BARDOT, JEAN.   L'influence française dans la vie et l'œuvre de Kate Chopin. *In* (pp. 31–46) **5.**

7857. BONNER, THOMAS, JR.   Christianity and Catholicism in the fiction of Kate Chopin. SoQ (20:2) 1982, 118–25.

7858. MAHLENDORF, URSULA R.   The wellsprings of literary creation: an analysis of male and female 'artist stories' from the German Romantics to American writers of the present. Columbia, SC: Camden, 1985. pp. xx, 292. (Studies in German literature, linguistics and culture, 18.) Rev. by Lee B. Jennings in JEGP (85:4) 635–6.

7859. MITSUTANI, MARGARET.   Kate Chopin's *The Awakening*: the narcissism of Edna Pontellier. SEL (English number) 3–15.

7860. MOSELEY, MERRITT.   Chopin and mysticism. SoS (25:4) 367–74.

7861. NYE, LORRAINE M.   Four birth dates for Kate Chopin. SoS (25:4) 375–6.

7862. SKAGGS, PEGGY.   Kate Chopin. Boston, MA: G. K. Hall, 1985. pp. 130. (Twayne's US authors, 485.) Rev. by Andrea Hammer in ALR (19:1) 80–2.

7863. TAYLOR, H.   Gender, race and region: a study of three postbellum women writers of Louisana: Grace King, Ruth McEnery Stuart and Kate Chopin. Unpub. doct. diss., Univ. of Sussex, 1984.

John Clare

7864. BROWNLOW, TIMOTHY.   John Clare and picturesque landscape. (Bibl. 1985, 6630.) Rev. by John Dixon Hunt in BJECS (9:2) 257–8.

7865. CHILCOTT, TIM.   'A real world & doubting mind': a critical study of the poetry of John Clare. (Bibl. 1985, 6632.) Rev. by Edward Storey in JCSJ (5) 47–9.

7866. COUNSEL, JUNE.   Coming to Clare. JCSJ (5) 5–8.

7867. CROSSAN, GREG.   The nine *Lives* of John Clare. JCSJ (5) 37–46.

7868. —— Some fugitive John Clare items, 1820–1977. NQ (33:2) 167–70.

7869. ESTERMANN, BARBARA.   John Clare: an annotated primary and secondary bibliography. New York; London: Garland, 1985. pp. xxvii, 303. (Garland reference library of the humanities, 581.) (Cf. bibl. 1985, 6634.)

7870. GILLIN, RICHARD L.   Minute particulars and imaginative forms. JCSJ (5) 22–9.

7871. LINES, RODNEY.   John Clare and herbal medicine. JCSJ (5) 16–21.

7872. LUCAS, JOHN.   *The Flitting*. JCSJ (5) 9–13.

7873. ROBINSON, ERIC; POWELL, DAVID (eds).   John Clare. (Bibl. 1985, 6642.) Rev. by Bernard Beatty in BJECS (9:1) 109–10.

7874. —— —— (eds); GRAINGER, MARGARET (assoc. ed.).   The later poems of John Clare, 1837–1864. New York: OUP, 1984. (Cf. bibl. 1984, 6860.) Rev. by P. M. S. Dawson in MLR (81:1) 178–80; by Lynne Pearce in NQ (33:1) 122–3.

7875. SPENCER, C. M.   Artifice in the poetry of John Clare: a study of formal devices and their reception by the reader. Unpub. doct. diss., Univ. of Wales, Cardiff, 1984. [Abstr. in IT (36) 21.]

7876. STOREY, MARK (ed.).   The letters of John Clare. Oxford:

Clarendon Press, 1985. pp. xliii, 705. Rev. by Tim Chilcott in THES (706) 17; by Tom Paulin in TLS, 20 June, 675–6; by Peter Morgan in EngS (67:6) 568–70; by R. K. R. Thornton in JCSJ (5) 50–2.

7877. THORNTON, R. K. R.   The nature of *The Parish*. JCSJ (5) 30–5.

7878. WILLIAMS, MERRYN; WILLIAMS, RAYMOND (eds).   John Clare: selected poetry and prose. London: Methuen. pp. viii, 252. (Methuen English texts.)

Marcus Clarke

7879. McDONALD, AVIS G.   Rufus Dawes and changing narrative perspectives in *His Natural Life*. ALS (12:3) 347–58 (review-article).

7880. WILDING, MICHAEL.   'Weird melancholy': inner and outer landscapes in Marcus Clarke's stories. *In* (pp. 128–45) **31.**

Arthur Hugh Clough

7881. JOHNSON, ROBERT.   Modern Mr Clough. Arnoldian (13:1) 1985/86, 1–9.

7882. SHARPE, WILLIAM.   Confronting the unpoetical city: Arnold, Clough, and Baudelaire. *See* **7564.**

William Cobbett

7883. AARTS, F. G. A. M.   William Cobbett: Radical, reactionary and poor man's grammarian. Neophilologus (70:4) 603–14.

7884. SPATER, GEORGE.   William Cobbett: the poor man's friend. (Bibl. 1985, 6650.) Rev. by A. J. Sambrook in YES (16) 281–2.

Samuel Taylor Coleridge

7885. AVIS, PAUL.   Coleridge on Luther. CLB (56) 249–55.

7886. BANERJEE, JIBON KRISHNA.   Moral concerns in the dramatic works of Wordsworth, Coleridge and Southey. Jadavpur University Essays and Studies (Calcutta) (4) 1984, 74–9.

7887. BARTH, J. ROBERT.   Theological implications of Coleridge's theory of imagination. SLI (19:2) 23–33.

7888. BATE, JONATHAN.   *Kubla Khan* and *At A Solemn Music. See* **5673.**

7889. BEER, JOHN.   Coleridge, Hazlitt, and *Christabel*. RES (37:145) 40–54.

7890. —— Coleridge's originality as a critic of Shakespeare. SLI (19:2) 51–69.

7891. —— Did Lamb understand Coleridge? CLB (56) 232–49.

7892. —— Who wrote *The Barberry Tree*? *See* **7384.**

7893. BIDNEY, MARTIN.   *Christabel* as dark double of *Comus. See* **5677.**

7894. BROOKS, LINDA MARIE.   'Salto mortale': the negative sublime in Schiller and Coleridge. Unpub. doct. diss., Univ. of California, Los Angeles, 1985. [Abstr. in DA (46) 1938A.]

7895. BURWICK, FREDERICK.   Coleridge's *Limbo* and *Ne Plus Ultra*: the multeity of intertextuality. RPP (9:1) 1985, 35–45.

7896. BYGRAVE, S. J.   'Egotism' as a romantic concept in Coleridge. Unpub. doct. diss., Univ. of Cambridge, 1983.

7897. BYGRAVE, STEPHEN.   Coleridge and the self: Romantic egotism. Basingstoke: Macmillan. pp. xiii, 235. (Macmillan studies in Romanticism.) Rev. by Paul Hamilton in THES (713) 19.

7898. CHAI, LEON CHRISTOPHER.   Melville and European Romanticism: studies on Melville's relations to major European Romantic writers. Unpub. doct. diss., Univ. of Virginia, 1984. [Abstr. in DA (46) 1941A.]

7899. CHRISTENSEN, JEROME.   'Like a guilty thing surprised': deconstruction, Coleridge, and the apostasy of criticism. CI (12:4) 769–87.

7900. CHRISTIE, W. H.   Francis Jeffrey, Samuel Taylor Coleridge's *Biographia Literaria* and the contemporary criticism of William Wordsworth. Unpub. doct. diss., Univ. of Oxford, 1982.

7901. COLEMAN, D. P.   The personal and intellectual background of Coleridge's periodical *The Friend* (1809–10), with particular reference to its moral and political preoccupations. *See* **576.**

7902. EILENBERG, SUSAN RUTH.   Strange power of speech: usurping voices in Wordsworth and Coleridge. Unpub. doct. diss., Yale Univ., 1985. [Abstr. in DA (46) 3357A.]

7903. ENGELL, JAMES; BATE, W. JACKSON (eds).   Biographia Literaria. (Bibl. 1985, 6661.) Rev. by Thomas McFarland in MP (83:4) 405–13.

7904. FARNESS, JAY.   Strange contraries in familiar Coleridge. ELit (13:2) 231–45.

7905. FERRIS, DAVID SAMUEL.   Transfigurations. Unpub. doct. diss., State Univ. of New York at Buffalo, 1985. [Abstr. in DA (46) 1947A.]

7906. FRUMAN, NORMAN.   *Ozymandias* and the reconciliation of opposites. SLI (19:2) 71–87.

7907. GATTA, JOHN, JR.   Coleridge's *Fears in Solitude* and the prospects of social redemption. Cithara (26:1) 36–43.

7908. GRAVIL, RICHARD; NEWLYN, LUCY; ROE, NICHOLAS (eds).   Coleridge's imagination: essays in memory of Pete Laver. Cambridge: CUP, 1985. pp. 280.

7909. HAMLIN, CYRUS.   The faults of vision: identity and poetry (a dialogue of voices, with an essay on *Kubla Khan*). *In* (pp. 119–45) **23.**

7910. HARDING, ANTHONY JOHN.   Coleridge and the inspired word. Kingston, Ont.: McGill–Queen's UP, 1985. pp. xiv, 187. Rev. by Rosemary Ashton in TLS, 19 Sept., 1035–6; by Robert N. Essick in RPP (10:1) 71–5.

7911. HARRIS, KENNETH MARC.   Reason and understanding reconsidered: Coleridge, Carlyle, and Emerson. *See* **7815.**

7912. HEFFERNAN, JAMES A. W.   The re-creation of landscape: a study of Wordsworth, Coleridge, Constable and Turner. (Bibl. 1985, 6665.) Rev. by Andrew Graham-Dixon in LRev, Aug., 1985, 30–1; by Anne K. Mellor in RPP (10:2) 83–4; by John E. Jordan in Review (8) 55–7.

7913. JACKSON, H. J.   'Turning and turning': Coleridge on our knowledge of the external world. PMLA (101:5) 848–56.

7914. —— (ed.).   Samuel Taylor Coleridge. Oxford: OUP, 1985. pp. xviii, 733. (Oxford authors.) Rev. by Rosemary Ashton in TLS, 19 Sept., 1035–6.

7915. JASPER, DAVID.   Coleridge as poet and religious thinker:

inspiration and revelation. Allison Park, PA; Pickwick Pubs, 1985. (Cf. bibl. 1985, 6668.) Rev. by Steve H. Cook in ChrisL (35:3) 25–7.

7916. —— (ed.). The interpretation of belief: Coleridge, Schleiermacher and Romanticism. London: Macmillan. pp. ix, 192.

7917. KIM, CHUNG-GUN. Coleridge eui bangbeobron. (Coleridge on method.) JELL (32:4) 877–93.

7918. KITSON, P. J. The seventeenth century influence on the early religious and political thought of S. T. Coleridge, 1790–1804. Unpub. doct. diss., Univ. of Hull, 1984.

7919. KITSON, PETER. Coleridge's anecdote of John Thelwall. NQ (32) 1985, 345.

7920. LEFEBURE, MOLLY. The bondage of love: a life of Mrs Samuel Taylor Coleridge. London: Gollancz. pp. 287. Rev. by Norman Fruman in TLS, 22 Aug., 910–11.

7921. LEVERE, TREVOR H. Poetry realized in nature: Samuel Taylor Coleridge and early nineteenth-century science. (Bibl. 1985, 6671.) Rev. by Stuart M. Tave in MLR (81:1) 177–8.

7922. LEVY, DAVID. S. T. Coleridge's replies to Adam Smith's 'Pernicious opinion': a study in hermetic social engineering. IJPP (14:1) 89–114.

7923. LUTHER, SUSAN MILITZER. 'The hidden fire': Samuel Taylor Coleridge and the Daughters of Memory. Unpub. doct. diss., Vanderbilt Univ. [Abstr. in DA (47) 1735A.]

7924. McKUSICK, JAMES C. Coleridge's philosophy of language. *See* **825.**

7925. METZ, KARL H. 'The social chain of being'. Zum Topos des sozialen Konservativismus und zur Entstehung des Gedankens der sozialen Verantwortung im Grossbritannien der industriellen Revolution. *See* **6799.**

7926. MODIANO, RAIMONDA. Coleridge and the concept of nature. (Bibl. 1985, 6679.) Rev. by Paul Hamilton in THES (713) 19; by Rosemary Ashton in TLS, 19 Sept., 1035–6.

7927. MOON, KENNETH. Lowry's *Under the Volcano* and Coleridge's *Kubla Khan.* Exp (44:2) 44–7.

7928. MORÈRE, PIERRE. Mémoire et création dans les Préfaces des *Lyrical Ballads*: l'héritage du dix-huitième siècle. *In* (pp. 23–39) **34.**

7929. MORROW, JOHN. The national church in Coleridge's *Church and State*: a response to Allen. JHI (47:4) 640–52. (*Refers to* bibl. 1985, 6651.)

7930. MUDGE, BRADFORD K. The politics of autobiography in the *Biographia Literaria.* SCR (3:2) 27–45.

7931. NEWLYN, L. A. The myth of loss: echo, allusion and interconnection in the poetry of Wordsworth and Coleridge, 1797–1807. Unpub. doct. diss., Univ. of Oxford, 1983.

7932. NEWLYN, LUCY. Coleridge, Wordsworth and the language of allusion. Oxford: Clarendon Press. pp. 220. (Oxford English monographs.) Rev. by John Beer in THES (713) 19; by Rosemary Ashton in TLS, 19 Sept., 1035–6.

7933. —— Parodic allusion: Coleridge and the 'Nehemiah Higginbottom' sonnets, 1797. CLB (56) 255–9.

7934. ROE, N. H.   Wordsworth, Coleridge and the French Revolution, 1789–1795. Unpub. doct. diss., Univ. of Oxford, 1985.

7935. RZEPKA, CHARLES J.   Christabel's 'wandering mother' and the discourse of the self: a Lacanian reading of repressed narration. RPP (10:1) 17–43.

7936. —— The self as mind: vision and identity in Wordsworth, Coleridge and Keats. Cambridge, MA; London: Harvard UP. pp. viii, 286.

7937. SATO, TOSHIHIKO.   *Nightingales*: Coleridge's challenge to a future poet and Keats's probable reply. University of Saga Studies in English (Japan) (13) 1985, 11–24.

7938. SCOTT, NATHAN A., JR.   The poetics of belief: studies in Coleridge, Arnold, Pater, Santayana, Stevens, and Heidegger. *See* **7563.**

7939. SHAPIRO, FRED R.   Neologisms in Coleridge's *Notebooks*. *See* **1560.**

7940. SIMONS, JOHN.   Coleridge and the sublime: *This Lime-Tree Bower My Prison*. CLB (56) 260–3.

7941. STELZER, SKAIDRITE DOKS.   Coleridge and the sublime: a true language. Unpub. doct. diss., Kent State Univ., 1985. [Abstr. in DA (47) 191A.]

7942. VLASOPOLOS, ANCA.   The symbolic method of Coleridge, Baudelaire, and Yeats. (Bibl. 1984, 6921.) Rev. by Barbara Hall in RPP (10:2) 77–81; by Hazard Adams in MLS (16:4) 93–4.

7943. WALLEN, MARTIN JAMES.   The voices of revision in *The Ancient Mariner*, 1798–1828. Unpub. doct. diss., Vanderbilt Univ., 1985. [Abstr. in DA (46) 2305A.]

7944. WATSON, KENNETH VANCE.   Coleridge's marginal dialectics. Unpub. doct. diss., Duke Univ., 1985. [Abstr. in DA (46) 2703A.]

7945. WILKIE, BRIAN.   The Romantic ideal of unity. *See* **7529.**

7946. WYLIE, I. M.   The influence of natural philosophy on the early thought of Coleridge, with particular reference to *Religious Musings*. Unpub. doct. diss., Univ. of Oxford, 1985. [Abstr. in IT (35) 547.]

7947. YAMADA, YUTAKA.   Shijin Coleridge. (The poet Coleridge.) Tokyo: Yamaguchi Press. pp. viii, 518.

J. P. Collier

7948. KAPLAN, JOEL H.   Thomas Middleton's epitaph on the death of Richard Burbage, and John Payne Collier. *See* **5656.**

7949. WELLENS, OSCAR.   John Payne Collier and the *British Lady's Magazine* (1815–1818): new attributions. *See* **720.**

Mortimer Collins

7950. LEFANU, WILLIAM.   J. Sheridan LeFanu. NQ (33:2) 172. (Re-attribution of articles.)

Wilkie Collins

7951. BLAIN, VIRGINIA (ed.).   No name. Oxford: OUP. pp. 504. (World's classics.)

7952. LONOFF, SUE.   Wilkie Collins and his Victorian readers: a study in the rhetoric of authorship. (Bibl. 1985, 6701.) Rev. by Sheila M. Smith in MLR (81:2) 457–8.

7953. MILLER, D. A. 'Cage aux folles': sensation and gender in Wilkie Collins's *The Woman in White*. In (pp. 94–124) **39.**

7954. —— *Cage aux folles*: sensation and gender in Wilkie Collins's *The Woman in White*. Representations (14) 107–36.

J. Fenimore Cooper

7955. ADAMS, CHARLES HANSFORD. 'The guardian of the law': authority and identity in James Fenimore Cooper. Unpub. doct. diss., Univ. of Virginia, 1985. [Abstr. in DA (46) 3030A.]

7956. ANDERSON, DOUGLAS. Cooper's improbable pictures in *The Pioneers*. SAF (14:1) 35–48.

7957. BLAKEMORE, STEVEN. Language and world in *The Pathfinder*. MLS (16:3) 237–46.

7958. CLARK, MICHAEL. Benjamin Franklin and Cooper's *The Pioneers. See* **6466.**

7959. —— Caves, houses, and temples in James Fenimore Cooper's *The Pioneers*. MLS (16:3) 227–36.

7960. CLARK, ROBERT (ed.). James Fenimore Cooper: new critical essays. London: Vision Press, 1985. pp. 208. (Critical studies.) Rev. by Brian Lee in TLS, 27 June, 704; by Andrew Hook in THES (705) 21.

7961. ERWIN, ROBERT. The first of the Mohicans. AR (44:2) 149–60.

7962. HANSEN, KLAUS PETER. Die retrospektive Mentalität: Europäische Kulturkritik und amerikanische Kultur. (Bibl. 1985, 6709.) Rev. by Walter Grünzweig in AAA (11) 250–2.

7963. HERMANN, ELISABETH. Opfer der Geschichte. Die Darstellung der nordamerikanischen Indianer im Werk James Fenimore Coopers und seiner Zeitgenossen. *See* **7264.**

7964. HUGHES, JAMES M. Inner and outer seas in Dickinson, Dana, Cooper and Roberts. In (pp. 202–11) **28.**

7965. MADISON, ROBERT D. Cooper's *The Wind-And-Wing* and the concept of the Byronic pirate. In (pp. 119–32) **28.**

7966. MÜLLENBROCK, HEINZ-JOACHIM. James Fenimore Coopers *Leatherstocking Tales* und die Anfänge des historischen Romans in Amerika. *See* **7318.**

7967. NEVIUS, BLAKE, et al. (eds). The leatherstocking tales: vol. 1, *The Pioneers, The Last of the Mohicans, The Prairie*; vol. 2, *The Pathfinder, The Deerslayer*. New York: Library of America; Cambridge: CUP, 1985. pp. 1347; 1051. (Literary classics of the United States.) Rev. by Tony Tanner in THES (735) 18.

7968. PARKER, R. N. The notion of the outsider in the writings of Cooper, Hawthorne, Twain and Faulkner. Unpub. doct. diss., Univ. of Wales, Swansea, 1984. [Abstr. in IT (36) 24.]

7969. PORTER, DANIEL R. The Knickerbockers and the historic site in New York State. *See* **7742.**

7970. RINGE, DONALD A. The source for an incident in Cooper's *The Redskins*. ELN (24:2) 66–8.

7971. SELLEY, APRIL. 'I have been, and ever shall be, your friend':
Star Trek, The Deerslayer and the American romance. JPC (20:1) 89–104.
7972. SHILLINGLAW, SUSAN GRACE. The art of Cooper's landscapes:
identity, theme, and structure in the Leatherstocking tales. Unpub.
doct. diss., Univ. of North Carolina at Chapel Hill, 1985. [Abstr. in DA
(46) 3354A.]
7973. SLOTKIN, RICHARD (introd.). The last of the Mohicans.
Harmondsworth: Penguin. pp. xxvii, 352. (Penguin classics.)
7974. WALLACE, JAMES D. Early Cooper and his audience. New
York; Guildford: Columbia UP. pp. xi, 230. Rev. by Michael T. Gilmore
in AL (58:3) 437–8; by Andrew Hook in THES (705) 21; by Brian Lee in
TLS, 27 June, 704.
7975. —— Early Cooper and his audience. Unpub. doct. diss.,
Columbia Univ., 1983. [Abstr. in DA (47) 184A.]

John Corry

7976. PITCHER, E. W. The miscellaneous works of John Corry
(1760?–1825?). PBSA (80:1) 83–90.

Stephen Crane

7977. BAUM, ROSALIE MURPHY. Alcoholism and family abuse in
Maggie and *The Bluest Eye.* Mosaic (19:3) 91–105.
7978. GRMELA, JOSEF. Několik poznámek k interpretaci Maggie, dítě
ulice Stephena Cranea. (Notes on the interpretation of Stephen Crane's
Maggie.) *In* (pp. 23–4) **4.**
7979. MARÍN MADRAZO, PILAR. The meaning of Henry Fleming's
initiation in the complete *The Red Badge of Courage.* RCEI (12) 75–87.
7980. MITCHELL, LEE CLARK (ed.). New essays on *The Red Badge of
Courage.* Cambridge: CUP. pp. x, 150. (American novel.)
7981. MONTEIRO, GEORGE. Crane's coxcomb. MFS (31:2) 1985,
295–305.
7982. —— Stephen Crane, dramatist. ALR (19:1) 42–51.
7983. SEDYCIAS, JOAO A. Crane, Azevedo, and Gamboa: a comparative study. Unpub. doct. diss., State Univ. of New York at Buffalo, 1985.
[Abstr. in DA (46) 3026A.]
7984. SHAW, MARY ANN. Crane's concept of heroism: satire in the
war stories of Stephen Crane. Unpub. doct. diss., Texas A&M Univ.,
1985. [Abstr. in DA (47) 182A.]
7985. SMITH, JOYCE CALDWELL. The comic image in the fiction of
Stephen Crane. Unpub. doct. diss., Georgia State Univ., College of Arts
and Sciences, 1985. [Abstr. in DA (46) 3036A.]
7985a. STAPE, J. H. The date and writing of Conrad's *Stephen Crane:
A Note Without Dates.* NQ (33:2) 184–5.

Aleister Crowley

7986. BOOTH, MARTIN (ed.). Selected poems. Wellingborough:
Aquarium. pp. 192.

Allan Cunningham

7987. POLLIN, BURTON R. Traces in *Annabel Lee* of Allan Cunningham's poem. ANQ (22) 1984, 133–5.

Robert Curzon (1810–1873)

7988. FRASER, IAN H. C. The heir of Parham: Robert Curzon, 14th
Baron Zouche. *See* **219.**

Augustin Daly

7989. MURPHY, BRENDA. Literary stepchildren: nineteenth-century dramatists. *See* **7175.**

7990. WILMETH, DON B.; CULLEN, ROSEMARY (eds). Plays by Augustin Daly. (Bibl. 1984, 6966.) Rev. by Brenda Murphy in Review (8) 197–204.

Richard Henry Dana

7991. HUGHES, JAMES M. Inner and outer seas in Dickinson, Dana, Cooper and Roberts. *In* (pp. 202–11) **28.**

George Darley

7992. LANGE, D. J. An edition of the poems of George Darley. Unpub. doct. diss., Univ. of Cambridge, 1983.

Charles Darwin

7993. AIRAUDI, JESSE T. A slumber sealed: science and idealism in Darwin's *Autobiography.* SCR (2:2) 1985, 38–48.

7994. ALLAND, ALEXANDER (comp.). Human nature: Darwin's view. New York; Guildford: Columbia UP, 1985. pp. x, 242.

7995. JARRATT, SUSAN CAROLE FUNDERBURGH. A Victorian sophistic: the rhetoric of knowledge in Darwin, Newman, and Pater. Unpub. doct. diss., Univ. of Texas at Austin, 1985. [Abstr. in DA (46) 3041A.]

7996. KUYKENDALL, JOSEPH. Darwin, the Bible, literature and consciousness. *See* **2682.**

7997. NORRIS, MARGOT. Beasts of the modern imagination: Darwin, Nietzsche, Kafka, Ernst, and Lawrence. Baltimore, MD; London: Johns Hopkins UP, 1985. pp. xii, 265. Rev. by Daniel Dervin in Cithara (26:1) 57–60; by Irving Massey in Criticism (28:2) 230–2.

7998. SADRIN, ANNY. Langage des origines, origines du langage dans *The Origin of Species. See* **784.**

7999. SIPIORA, PHILLIP JOHN. The rhetoric of ethnologic in Darwin, Marx and Freud. *See* **1200.**

Thomas De Quincey

8000. MAY, CLAIRE BEASLEY. Fall and redemption: a mythic interpretation of Thomas De Quincey's imaginative prose. Unpub. doct. diss., Univ. of Georgia, 1985. [Abstr. in DA (46) 1951A.]

8001. SHAPIRO, FRED R. Words for OED from De Quincey. *See* **1561.**

8002. SNYDER, ROBERT LANCE. De Quincey's literature of power: a mythic paradigm. SELit (26:4) 691–711.

8003. WINBERG, CHRISTINE. Imagining Wordsworth: De Quincey and the art of biography. UCTSE (16) 12–23.

Charles Dickens

8004. ADRIAN, ARTHUR A. Dickens and the parent–child relationship. (Bibl. 1985, 6754.) Rev. by Peter Preston in NQ (33:2) 253–4; by Sara Hudson in SoHR (20:1) 74–5.

8005. BARCLAY, DEAN ARNE. Enormous tradition: literary allusions in Thackeray and Dickens. Unpub. doct. diss., Harvard Univ. [Abstr. in DA (47) 906A.]

8006. BASU, S. Charles Dickens as an historical novelist, with special reference to *Barnaby Rudge*. Unpub. doct. diss., Univ. of London (External), 1985. [Abstr. in IT (35) 1492.]

8007. BEN-EPHRAIM, GAVRIEL.   The imagination and its vicissitudes in *Great Expectations*. HUSL (13:1) 1985, 43–62.

8008. BIRD, TOBY ANNE.   Dickens and the tradition of comedy: a study of *Pickwick Papers* and *Our Mutual Friend*. Unpub. doct. diss., City Univ. of New York, 1985. [Abstr. in DA (46) 3356A.]

8009. BOCK, CAROL A.   Violence and the fictional modes of *Nicholas Nickleby*. MSE (10:2) 1985, 87–101.

8010. BOTTEZ, MONICA.   Aspects of the Victorian novel: recurrent images in Charles Dickens's works. Bucharest: Bucharest Univ., 1985. pp. 276.

8011. BRADSHAW, STEVE.   A preposterous way of death? Listener (115) 16 Jan., 7–8. (On spontaneous human combustion.)

8012. BRATTIN, JOEL J.   Reading between the lines: interpreting Dickens's later manuscripts. *See* **300.**

8013. BUTTS, DENNIS.   *Bleak House* by Charles Dickens. London: Macmillan. pp. viii, 96. (Macmillan master guides.)

8014. COATS, DARYL R.   'The devil is loose in London somewhere': five supernatural figures in the works of Charles Dickens. Unpub. doct. diss., Univ. of Mississippi. [Abstr. in DA (47) 1330A.]

8015. COBBAN, ALEX.   Charles Dickens and Christmas customs. Brentwood: Discovering London. pp. 28.

8016. COHN, ALAN M.; COLLINS, K. K.   The cumulated Dickens checklist, 1970–1979. Troy, NY: Whitston, 1982. pp. vi, 391. Rev. by Sylvère Monod in YES (16) 321–2; by Peter Preston in NQ (33:2) 254–5.

8017. COLLINS, NORMAN (introd.).   David Copperfield. London: Grafton. pp. 828.

8018. CONNOR, STEVEN.   Charles Dickens. (Bibl. 1985, 6783.) Rev. by Catherine Koralek in Eng (35) 293–7; by Felicity Rosslyn in CamQ (15) 164–7; by Dennis Walder in THES (698) 24.

8019. COTSELL, MICHAEL.   The companion to *Our Mutual Friend*. London: Allen & Unwin. pp. xvi, 316. (Dickens companions, 1.) Rev. by Michael Slater in THES (735) 18.

8020. —— 'The Sensational Williams': a mutual friend in 1864. *See* **577.**

8021. CRAWFORD, IAIN.   Sex and seriousness in *David Copperfield*. JNT (16:1) 41–54.

8022. CUMMINGS, KATHERINE M.   Reconstructing 'life with father': the daughter's novel seduction. *See* **6755.**

8023. DALDRY, G.   Charles Dickens and the form of the novel: 'fiction' and 'narrative' in Dickens' work. Unpub. doct. diss., Univ. of Liverpool. [Abstr. in IT (35) 1492.]

8024. DANON, RUTH.   Work in the English novel: the myth of vocation. *See* **6392.**

8025. DAVIS, JIM.   The importance of being Caleb: the influence of Boucicault's *Dot* on the comic styles of J. L. Toole and Joseph Jefferson. *See* **7632.**

8026. DAVIS, PAUL. Imaging *Oliver Twist*: Hogarth, illustration, and the part of darkness. *See* **69.**

8027. DE GUILLEBON, BRIGITTE. Problématique du personnage chez Dickens. *In* (pp. 121–4) **1.**

8028. DENMAN, PETER. Krook's death and Dickens's authorities. Dick (82:3) 131–41.

8029. DIERKS, KARIN. Handlungsstrukturen im Werk von Charles Dickens. Göttingen: Vanderhoeck & Ruprecht, 1982. pp. 395. (Palaestra, Untersuchungen aus der Deutschen und Englischen Philologie und Literaturgeschichte, 275.) Rev. by Heinz Reinhold in YES (16) 323–4.

8030. DOWLING, CONSTANCE. Cervantes, Dickens, and the world of the juvenile criminal. Dick (82:3) 151–7.

8031. DREXLER, R. D. Note on *Bleak House* and *The Merchant of Venice*. *See* **4896.**

8032. ERICSSON, CATARINA. A child is a child, you know: the inversion of father and daughter in Dickens's novels. Stockholm: Almqvist & Wiksell. pp. v, 94. (Doct. diss., Stockholm Univ.) (Stockholm studies in English, 66.)

8033. FEDERICO, ANNETTE R. 'Some wasting fire within her': unfolding feminism in four novels by Dickens. MSE (10:3) 161–83.

8034. FIEDLER, LESLIE A. *Martin Chuzzlewit* – a great bad book. DQR (16:1) 16–21.

8035. FIELDING, K. J. Studying Charles Dickens. Harlow: Longman. pp. 135. (York handbooks.)

8036. FLEISSNER, R. F. The Harvard affair 'proves' a Holmes connection with *Edwin Drood*. Clues (7:2) 109–13.

8037. FLINT, KATE. Dickens. Brighton: Harvester Press. pp. xi, 159. Rev. by Dennis Walder in THES (720) 15.

8038. FOOR, SHEILA MARIE. Dickens's 'walls of words' in *Bleak House*. Unpub. doct. diss., Ohio State Univ., 1985. [Abstr. in DA (46) 3725A.]

8039. FORD, GEORGE H. Openers and overtures in Dickens' novels: 'In my beginning is my end'. Mosaic (19:1) 1–14.

8040. FORSYTE, CHARLES. The Sapsea fragment – fragment of what? Dick (82:1) 12–26.

8041. FRANK, LAWRENCE. Charles Dickens and the Romantic self. (Bibl. 1985, 6807.) Rev. by Charmazel Dudt in ChrisL (35:2) 41–2.

8042. GIDDINGS, ROBERT (ed.). The changing world of Charles Dickens. (Bibl. 1985, 6814.) Rev. by Peter Preston in NQ (33:2) 252–3.

8043. GOLDING, ROBERT. Idiolects in Dickens: the major techniques and chronological development. Basingstoke: Macmillan, 1985. pp. vii, 255. Rev. by Norman Page in Dick (82:1) 52–3; by Dennis Walder in THES (648) 24.

8044. GOTTFRIED, BARBARA. Sexual and textual politics in *Bleak House*: expanding the parameters of feminist readings. Unpub. doct. diss., Univ. of California, Santa Cruz, 1985. [Abstr. in DA (46) 1948A.]

8045. HARA, EIICHI. Stories present and absent in *Great Expectations*. ELH (53:3) 593–614.

8046. HEWETT, EDWARD; AXTON, W. F. Convivial Dickens: the drinks of Dickens and his times. Athens: Ohio UP, 1983. pp. xvi, 191. Rev. by Peter Preston in NQ (33:2) 254.

8047. HOEFNAGEL, DICK. An early hint of *Great Expectations*. Dick (82:2) 83–4.

8048. HOPKINS, DEWI. Micawber lives. Liverpool: Gild of St George. pp. 12. (Gild of St George pamphlet.)

8049. HOUGH, GRAHAM. Language and reality in *Bleak House*. *In* (pp. 50–67) **46.**

8050. INGHAM, PATRICIA. Dialect as 'realism': *Hard Times* and the industrial novel. RES (37:148), 518–27.

8051. JACOBSON, WENDY S. The companion to *The Mystery of Edwin Drood*. London: Allen & Unwin. pp. 209. (Dickens companions, 2.) Rev. by Michael Slater in THES (735) 18.

8052. JAFFE, AUDREY. 'Never be safe but in hiding': omniscience and curiosity in *The Old Curiosity Shop*. Novel (19:2) 118–34.

8053. JAFFE, AUDREY ANNE. 'Vanishing points': the Dickens narrator and the fantasy of omniscience. Unpub. doct. diss., Univ. of California, Berkeley, 1985. [Abstr. in DA (47) 912A.]

8054. JAHN, KAREN FROST. Providence in the Victorian novel: *Bleak House*, *Middlemarch*, and *The Mayor of Casterbridge* examined for their aesthetic realization of Providence. Unpub. doct. diss., Univ. of Detroit, 1981. [Abstr. in DA (47) 537A.]

8055. JUSTIN, HENRI. *The Signalman*'s signal-man. Journal of the Short Story in English (7) 9–16.

8056. KAPLAN, FRED (introd.). Charles Dickens' book of memoranda: a photographic and typographic facsimile of the notebook begun in January 1855. (Bibl. 1983, 7456.) Rev. by Richard J. Dunn in MLS (16:2) 80–2; by Andrew Sanders in Dick (82:3) 180–1.

8057. KEITT, DIANE. Charles Dickens and Robert Seymour: the battle of wills. *See* **79.**

8058. KELLY, MARY ANN. From nightmare to reverie: continuity in *Our Mutual Friend*. DUJ (79:1) 45–50.

8059. KINSLEY, JAMES (ed.). The Pickwick papers. Oxford: Clarendon Press. pp. 600.

8060. LANGBAUER, LAURIE. Dickens's streetwalkers: women and the form of romance. ELH (53:2) 411–31.

8061. LARSON, JANET L. Dickens and the broken scripture. Athens: Georgia UP, 1985. pp. xvi, 364. Rev. by Sylvère Monod in EA (39:4) 467–8.

8062. LAURENCE, DAN H.; QUINN, MARTIN (eds). Shaw on Dickens. New York: Ungar, 1985. pp. 196. Rev. by Gladys M. Crane in TJ (38:4) 511.

8063. LEAVIS, L. R. *David Copperfield* and *Jane Eyre*. *See* **7669.**

8064. LIGHTMAN, NAOMI. The 'Vulcanic dialect' of *Great Expectations*. Dick (82:1) 33–8.

8065. LUND, MICHAEL. Literary pieces and whole audiences: *Denis Duval*, *Edwin Drood*, and *The Landleaguers*. Criticism (28:1) 27–49.

8066. LYNCH, TONY. Dickens's England: a travellers' companion. London: Batsford. pp. 200.

8067. McCALLUM, LAUREN. Narrative structures and meaning in Dickens' *Little Dorrit*. Unpub. doct. diss., Univ. of Montreal. [Abstr. in DA (47) 2170A.]

8068. McFARLANE, J. J. Artist into text: nineteenth-century expressions of self in crisis, being a study of three novels of the 1860s in England and France: *Our Mutual Friend, L'Éducation sentimentale* and *Dominique*. Unpub. doct. diss., Univ. of York, 1984.

8069. MacKAY, CAROL HANBERY. The letter-writer and the text in *Martin Chuzzlewit*. SELit (26:4) 737–58.

8070. MacLAINE, ALLAN H. Melville's 'sequel' to *Bartleby the Scrivener* and Dickens' *Story of the Bagman's Uncle* in *Pickwick Papers*: an unnoticed link. ATQ (60) 37–42.

8071. McLEOD, CAROL. Canadian notes: Francis Dickens of the North West Mounted Police. Dick (82:3) 142–8. (Dickens's son.)

8072. MAGNET, MYRON. Dickens and the social order. Philadelphia: Pennsylvania UP, 1985. pp. 266. Rev. by Robert Alter in Commentary (81:4) 72–4; by Richard T. Gaughan in Novel (19:2) 189–92; by Alexander Welsh in CLIO (16:1) 84–7; by L. R. Leavis in ModAge (30:3/4) 299–303; by David Parker in Dick (82:2) 103–6.

8073. MONOD, SYLVÈRE. Martin Chuzzlewit. (Bibl. 1985, 6868.) Rev. by Jeremy Hawthorn in Eng (35) 273–8.

8074. MOTT, G. I wallow in words: Dickens, journalism and public affairs, 1831–1838. Unpub. doct. diss., Univ. of Leicester, 1984.

8075. OPPENLANDER, ELLA ANN. Dickens' *All the Year Round*: descriptive index and contributor list. *See* **662.**

8076. PAGE, H. M. Charles Dickens, *Little Dorrit*. Harmondsworth: Penguin. pp. 136. (Penguin masterstudies.)

8077. PAROISSIEN, DAVID (ed.). Selected letters of Charles Dickens. Boston, MA: G. K. Hall, 1985. (Cf. bibl. 1985, 6876.) Rev. by Dennis Walder in THES (698) 24; by Eileen Power in Dick (82:3) 181–3.

8078. PHILIP, NEIL; NEUBURG, VICTOR (eds). *A December Vision*: his social journalism. London: Collins. pp. 160.

8079. PIKE, BURTON. The myth of the city in the novel. *In* (pp. 421–4) **19.**

8080. PURTON, V. Loathsome flowers: Dickens and the sentimentalist tradition. Unpub. doct. diss., Univ. of East Anglia, 1982.

8081. RAINA, BADRI N. Dickens and the dialectic of growth. Madison: Wisconsin UP. pp. xiii, 172. Rev. by Jeremy Hawthorn in Eng (35) 273–8.

8082. ROSENFELT, ZELL BERMAN. Charles Dickens: attitudes toward artists. Unpub. doct. diss., George Washington Univ. [Abstr. in DA (47) 915A.]

8083. SAYWOOD, BARRIE. *Martin Chuzzlewit*: language as disguise. Dick (82:2) 86–97.

8084. SCHLICKE, PAUL. Dickens and popular entertainment. London:

Allen & Unwin, 1985. pp. xiv, 288. Rev. by Mary McGowan in Dick (82:2) 101–3; by Dennis Walder in THES (698) 24.

8085. SELL, ROGER D.   Dickens and the new historicism: the polyvocal audience and discourse of *Dombey and Son*. *In* (pp. 62–79) **39.**

8086. SMITH, CONSTANCE.   Charles Dickens on More. *See* **4162.**

8087. SØRENSEN, KNUD.   Charles Dickens, linguistic innovator. *See* **1244.**

8088. STONE, HARRY (ed.); BLOCK, IRVING (ill.).   George Silverman's explanation. Northridge: California State Univ., Santa Susana Press, 1984. pp. 44. (Limited ed.) Rev. by Michael Slater in Dick (82:2) 106–8.

8089. STYCZYNSKA, ADELA.   The shifting point of view in the narrative design of *Little Dorrit*. Dick (82:1) 39–51.

8090. SWANN, CHARLES.   Dickens, Ruskin and the city: parallels or influence? Dick (82:2) 67–81.

8091. TAMBLING, JEREMY.   Prison-bound: Dickens and Foucault. EC (36:1) 11–31.

8092. THOMAS, RONALD R.   Dickens's sublime artifact. BIS (14) 71–95.

8093. TILLOTSON, KATHLEEN.   March 1846, 'at Sixes and sevens'; a new letter. Dick (82:2) 98–9.

8094. TREMPER, ELLEN.   Commitment and escape: the fairy tales of Thackeray, Dickens, and Wilde. LU (2:1) 1978, 38–47.

8095. VEREŞ, GRIGORE.   Charles Dickens. (Bibl. 1984, 7080.) Rev. by Avădanei Ştefan in AnUILit (32) 97–8.

8096. WALLIS, BRUCE L.   Dickens' *Hard Times*. Exp (44:2) 26–7.

8097. WORTH, GEORGE J.   *Great Expectations*: an annotated bibliography. New York; London: Garland. pp. xxii, 346. (Garland Dickens bibliographies, 5.) (Garland reference library of the humanities, 555.)

8098. YOSHIDA, TAKAO.   Dickens no tanoshimi. (The joy of Dickens.) Tokyo: Kogaku Press. pp. viii, 212.

Emily Dickinson

8099. AGRAWAL, ABHA.   Emily Dickinson: search for self. New Delhi: Young Asia, 1977. pp. 207. Rev. by Frederick L. Morey in DS (57) 10–13.

8100. ALLEN, MICHAEL.   Emily Dickinson as an American provincial poet. Brighton: British Assn for American Studies, 1985. pp. 55. (BAAS pamphlets in American studies, 14.)

8101. ARNDT, MURRAY D.   Emily Dickinson and the limits of language. DS (57) 19–27.

8102. BAKKER, J.   Emily Dickinson's secret. DQR (16:4) 341–50.

8103. BEAMAN, DARLENE SUZETTE.   'A thorn-choked garden plot': women's place in Emily Dickinson and Christina Rossetti. Unpub. doct. diss., Rice Univ. [Abstr. in DA (47) 1732A.]

8104. BENFEY, CHRISTOPHER E. G.   Emily Dickinson and the problem of others. (Bibl. 1985, 6912.) Rev. by Joanne Feit Diehl in WHR (40:3) 281–3.

8105. BRUMM, ANNA-MARIE.   Religion and the poet: Emily Dickinson and Annette von Droste-Huelshoff. DS (59) 21–38.

8106. BUCHANAN, JANE BRITTON.   Poetic identity in the New World: Anne Bradstreet, Emily Dickinson, and Derek Walcott. *See* **5295.**

8107. BURBICK, JOHN.   Emily Dickinson and the economics of desire. AL (58:3) 361–78.

8108. BYERS, JOHN R., JR.   The possible background of three Dickinson poems. DS (57) 35–8.

8109. CARTON, EVAN.   The rhetoric of American romance: dialectic and identity in Emerson, Dickinson, Poe, and Hawthorne. Baltimore, MD; London: Johns Hopkins UP, 1985. pp.288.

8110. DELPHY, FRANÇOISE.   Emily Dickinson. (Bibl. 1984, 7099.) Rev. by David Porter in EA (39:4) 480–1.

8111. DERRICK, PAUL SCOTT.   Emily Dickinson, Martin Heidegger and the poetry of dread. WHR (40:1) 27–38.

8112. DICKENSON, DONNA.   Emily Dickinson. Leamington Spa: Berg, 1985. pp. 132. (Berg women's series.)

8113. DOBSON, JOANNE.   'The invisible lady': Emily Dickinson and conventions of the female self. Legacy (3:1) 41–55.

8114. EBERWEIN, JANE DONAHUE.   Dickinson: strategies of limitation. (Bibl. 1985, 6924, where scholar's second name misspelt.) Rev. by Joan Burbick in AL (58:4) 636–8; by Ruth Miller in MichQR (25:4) 760–3; by Ann Cory Bretz in ChrisL (35:3) 23–5; by Alice Hall Petry in Legacy (3:1) 72–4.

8115. GILBERT, SANDRA M.   The American sexual poetics of Walt Whitman and Emily Dickinson. *In* (pp. 123–54) **47.**

8116. HAGENBÜCHLE, ROLAND.   Signs and process: the concept of language in Emerson and Dickinson. DS (58) 59–88.

8117. HANSON, CHARLES D.   Dickinson's *Victory Comes Late*. Exp (44:2) 30–2.

8118. HUGHES, GERTRUDE REIF.   Subverting the cult of domesticity: Emily Dickinson's critique of women's work. Legacy (3:1) 17–28.

8119. HUGHES, JAMES M.   Inner and outer seas in Dickinson, Dana, Cooper and Roberts. *In* (pp. 202–11) **28.**

8120. JAŘAB, JOSEF.   The gradual advent of Emily Dickinson. *In* (pp. 46–51) **24.**

8121. JOHNSON, GREG.   Emily Dickinson: perception and the poet's quest. University: Alabama UP, 1985. pp. 231. Rev. by Alice Hall Petry in Legacy (3:1) 72–4.

8122. JUHASZ, SUZANNE.   Writing doubly: Emily Dickinson and female experience. Legacy (3:1) 5–15.

8123. KJAER, NIELS.   Emily Dickinson in Denmark. DS (59) 45–6.

8124. —— The poet of the moment: Emily Dickinson and Soren Kierkegaard. DS (59) 46–9.

8125. LEONARD, DOUGLAS NOVICH.   Pictureless trope: a Dickinson experiment. DS (57) 28–34.

8126. LILIENDAHL, ANN.   Emily Dickinson in Europe: her literary reputation in selected countries. (Bibl. 1985, 6934.) Rev. by Frederick L. Morey in DS (59) 14–20.

8127. LINDBERG-SEYERSTED, BRITA.   Gender and women's literature:

thoughts on a relationship illustrated by the cases of Emily Dickinson and Sylvia Plath. AmSS (18) 1–14.

8128. LINK, FRANZ H.   Zwei amerikanische Dichterinnen: Emily Dickinson und Hilda Doolittle. Berlin: Duncker & Humblot, 1979. pp. 110. Rev. by Frederick L. Morey in DS (59) 44.

8129. LOVING, JEROME.   Emily Dickinson: the poet as experienced virgin. Review (7) 1985, 145–51 (review-article).

8130. LOVING, JEROME M.   Emily Dickinson: the poet on the second story. Cambridge: CUP. pp. xv, 128. (Cambridge studies in American literature and culture.)

8131. MCNEIL, HELEN.   Emily Dickinson. London: Virago Press. pp. xvi, 208. (Virago pioneers.)

8132. MILLER, CRISTANNE.   'A letter is a joy of earth': Dickinson's communication with the world. Legacy (3:1) 29–39.

8133. MILLER, RUTH.   On the track of Emily Dickinson. MichQR (25:4) 760–70 (review-article).

8134. MILLS, ELIZABETH MCGEACHY.   Wording the unspeakable: Emily Dickinson and A. R. Ammons. Unpub. doct. diss., Univ. of North Carolina at Chapel Hill, 1985. [Abstr. in DA (47) 902A.]

8135. MONTEIRO, GEORGE.   Emily Dickinson's missing correspondence: a new letter by Lavinia. RALS (14:1/2) 1984, 167–8.

8136. MOORE, GEOFFREY (ed.).   Emily Dickinson. Oxford: OUP. pp. 60. (Illustrated poets.)

8137. MOREY, FREDERICK L.   Dickinson – Kant: the first critique. DS (60) 1–70.

8138. —— Emily Dickinson as a modern. DS (58) 19–22.

8139. —— Placing Emily Dickinson in a school. DS (58) 4–8.

8140. —— The poetry levels of Emily Dickinson. DS (58) 9–18.

8141. MUNK, LINDA JOY.   Nanzia Nunzio, Queen Mab, and Lenore: three aspects of Dickinson. Unpub. doct. diss., Univ. of Toronto, 1985. [Abstr. in DA (47) 902A.]

8142. NEWMAN, ROBERT D.   Emily Dickinson's influence on Roethke's *In Evening Air*. DS (57) 28–40.

8143. OTOMO, TAKESHI (ed.).   Nihonni okeru Emily Dickinson shoshi. (A bibliography of Emily Dickinson in Japan.) Tokyo: Senshu UP. pp. iv, 248.

8144. PERKINSON, GRACE.   Latin scholars at the academy: a monograph on an Emily Dickinson textbook. Deer Isle, ME: Skyefield Press. pp. 12. Rev. by Mary Lewis Chapman in DS (59) 13.

8145. PETTINGELL, PHOEBE.   Small worlds. NewL (69:18) 14–15.

8146. POLLAK, VIVIAN R.   Dickinson: the anxiety of gender. (Bibl. 1985, 6943.) Rev. by David Porter in Legacy (3:1) 76–7; by Jerome Loving in Review (7) 1985, 145–51.

8147. ROBINSON, FRED MILLER.   Strategies of smallness: Wallace Stevens and Emily Dickinson. WSJ (10:1) 27–35.

8148. ROBINSON, JOHN.   Emily Dickinson: looking to Canaan. London: Faber & Faber. pp. 191. (Faber student guides.)

8149. ST ARMAND, BARTON LEVI.   Emily Dickinson and her culture:

the soul's society. (Bibl. 1985, 6946.) Rev. by Ruth Miller in MichQR (25:4) 766–70; by Cristanne Miller in ELN (24:2) 78–81; by Frederick L. Morey in DS (57) 3–9; by Joan Burbick in Legacy (3:1) 69–70.

8150. SHURR, WILLIAM H.   The marriage of Emily Dickinson: a study of the fascicles. (Bibl. 1985, 6948.) Rev. by Jerome Loving in Review (7) 1985, 145–51.

8151. SINGLEY, CAROL J.   Reaching lonely heights: Sarah Jewett, Emily Dickinson, and female initiation. CLQ (22:1) 75–82.

8152. SMITH, MARTHA NELL.   'Rowing in Eden': gender and the poetics of Emily Dickinson. Unpub. doct. diss., Rutgers Univ., 1985. [Abstr. in DA (47) 183A.]

8153. WHITE, WILLIAM.   Emily Dickinson: a current bibliography. DS (57) 41–5; (59) 1–13.

8154. WOLFF, CYNTHIA GRIFFIN.   Emily Dickinson. New York: Knopf. pp. 641. Rev. by Elizabeth Frank in NYTB, 23 Nov., 7; by James R. Mellow in BkW, 23 Nov., 1–2; by Liz Rosenberg in BW, 14 Dec., 1, 4.

8155. WOLOSKY, SHIRA.   Emily Dickinson: a voice of war. (Bibl. 1985, 6956.) Rev. by Beverly R. Valoshin in AL (58:3) 446–7; by Ruth Miller in MichQR (25:4) 763–6; by Frederick L. Morey in DS(57) 14–16; by Joan Burbick in Legacy (3:1) 70–1.

8156. YU, SUNG-GON.   A linguistics analysis of poetic style with special reference to Emily Dickinson's poetry. *See* **1251.**

8157. YUKMAN, CLAUDIA.   Speaking to strangers: Dickinson's and Whitman's poetics of historical presence. Unpub. doct. diss., Brandeis Univ. [Abstr. in DA (47) 184A.]

Benjamin Disraeli

8158. GOLDMAN, D.   The technique and development of Disraeli's novels. Unpub. doct. diss., Univ. of Keele, 1979.

8159. HAYES, M. J.   Duty to self and society in the early writings of Benjamin Disraeli. Unpub. doct. diss., Univ. of London, External, 1984. [Abstr. in IT (35) 1086.]

8160. MOSLEY, CHARLES.   Disraeli's invention: the political novel. Enc (66:1) 46–53.

Austin Dobson

8161. EPPERLY, ELIZABETH R.   Trollope and the young Austin Dobson. *See* **594.**

Charles M. Doughty

8162. TIDRICK, KATHRYN.   Heart-beguiling Araby. *See* **7626.**

Frederick Douglass

8163. BLASSINGAME, JOHN W. (gen. ed.).; FULKERSON, GERALD (textual ed.).   The Frederick Douglass papers, series 1: Speeches, debates and interviews: vol. 3, 1855–63. New Haven, CT; London: Yale UP, 1985. pp. xxxvi, 679.

8164. HOWARD-PITNEY, DAVID.   The enduring black jeremiad: the American jeremiad and black protest rhetoric, from Frederick Douglass to W. E. B. DuBois, 1841–1919. AmQ (38:3) 481–92.

8165. MACKETHAN, LUCINDA H.   From fugitive slave to man of letters: the conversion of Frederick Douglass. JNT (16:1) 55–71.

8166. SUNDQUIST, ERIC J.   Frederick Douglass: literacy and paternalism. Raritan (6:2) 108–24.

Sir Arthur Conan Doyle

8167. ASIMOV, ISAAC; GREENBERG, MARTIN HENRY; WAUGH, CHARLES G. (eds).   Sherlock Holmes through time and space. New York: Bluejay, 1984; London: Severn House, 1985. pp. 355.

8168. COX, DON RICHARD.   Arthur Conan Doyle. New York: Ungar, 1985. pp. vii, 251.

8169. CYPSER, DARLENE.   Barker, the hated rival. BSJ (35:4) 1985, 211–12. (*The Retired Colourman.*)

8170. DAHLINGER, S. E.   In search of the Agra treasure (or gelt by association). BSJ (36:4) 217–9. (*The Sign of Four.*)

8171. ECO, UMBERTO; SEBEOK, THOMAS A. (eds).   The sign of three: Dupin, Holmes, Peirce. Bloomington: Indiana UP, 1984. pp. xi, 236. Rev. by J. Gerald Kennedy in PhilL (10:1) 122–3.

8172. EYLES, ALLEN.   Sherlock Holmes: a centenary celebration. London: Murray, pp. 144.

8173. FLEISSNER, R. F.   The Harvard affair 'proves' a Holmes connection with *Edwin Drood. See* **8036.**

8174. FLEISSNER, ROBERT F.   An exegesis of Sherlock Holmes's 'faith'. BSJ (36:4) 207–10.

8175. GALBO, THOMAS S.   The first adventure of *The Blue Carbuncle.* BSJ (36:4) 203–6.

8176. GIBSON, JOHN MICHAEL; GREEN, RICHARD LANCELYN (eds). The unknown Conan Doyle: letters to the press. London: Secker & Warburg. pp. 377. Rev. in Edinburgh Review (74) 166–7; by J. I. M. Stewart in LRB (8:10) 13–14; by Hugh Greene in Listener, 27 Feb., 23–4.

8177. GREEN, RICHARD LANCELYN (ed.).   The Sherlock Holmes letters. London: Secker & Warburg. pp. 266.

8178. —— (sel.).   Letters to Sherlock Holmes. Harmondsworth: Penguin, 1985. pp. 234.

8179. —— GIBSON, JOHN MICHAEL.   A bibliography of A. Conan Doyle. (Bibl. 1984, 7169.) Rev. by J. G. Watson in NQ (33:2) 258–60.

8180. HAINING, PETER (sel. and introd.).   Sherlock Holmes and the devil's foot: further cases of the world's most famous detective. London: Severn House. pp. 117.

8181. HAMMER, DAVID L.   Sherlock Holmes: secret agent. BSJ (36:4) 231–4.

8182. HARDWICK, MICHAEL.   The complete guide to Sherlock Holmes. London: Weidenfeld & Nicolson. pp. 255.

8183. HERZINGER, KIM.   Inside and outside Sherlock Holmes: a rhapsody. Shen (36:3) 91–109.

8184. REDMOND, DONALD A.   Ship ahoy, Captain Basil. BSJ (36:4) 223–30.

8185. ROSENBERG, SAMUEL.   Conan Doyle et James Joyce. Trans. by GÉRARD-GEORGES LEMAIRE. Europe (62:657/58) 1984, 106–9.

8186. RUSSELL, WILLIAM L.   *The Adventure of the Priory School*: its Biblical genesis. BSJ (36:4) 211–15.

8187. SHREFFLER, PHILIP A.   On writing the Sherlockian paper. BSJ (36:1) 37–41.

8188. SPECK, GORDON R.   *The Noble Bachelor* and Browning's duchess. *See* **7733.**

8189. STREBEIGH, FRED.   To his modern fans, Sherlock is still worth a close look. Smithsonian (17:9) 60–6, 68.

8190. Entry cancelled.

Sara Jeannette Duncan

8191. DEAN, MISAO.   A note on *Cousin Cinderella* and *Roderick Hudson*. StudCanL (11:1) 96–8.

8192. FOWLER, MARIAN.   Redney: a life of Sara Jeannette Duncan. (Bibl. 1985, 7007.) Rev. by Judith Skelton Grant in ESCan (12:1) 114–18.

8193. MORTON, ELIZABETH.   Religion in Elgin: a re-evaluation of the subplot of *The Imperialist* by Sara Jeannette Duncan. StudCanL (11:1) 99–107.

Maria Edgeworth

8194. BOUR, ISABELLE.   Une autre écriture: les contes moraux de Maria Edgeworth. EA (39:2) 129–38.

8195. FIGES, EVA (introd.).   Belinda. London: Pandora. pp. xi, 434. (Mothers of the novel.)

8196. —— Patronage. London: Pandora. pp. 631. (Mothers of the novel.)

8197. MORTIMER, ANTHONY.   *Castle Rackrent* and its historical contexts. Études irlandaises (9) 1984, 107–23.

8198. TOPLISS, I. E.   The novels of Maria Edgeworth: Enlightenment and tutelage. Unpub. doct. diss., Univ. of Cambridge, 1985. [Abstr. in IT (35) 547.]

'George Eliot' (Mary Ann Evans)

8199. ANDRES, S. P.   Images at an exhibition: an organic theory of imagery in *Middlemarch* and *The Portrait of a Lady*. Unpub. doct. diss., Univ. of Edinburgh, 1985. [Abstr. in IT (35) 1488.]

8200. BEER, GILLIAN.   George Eliot. Brighton: Harvester Press. pp. xii, 246. (Key women writers.) Rev. by Kathryn Sutherland in CritQ (28:4) 112–13; by Valerie Shaw in THES (722) 15; by Rosemary Ashton in LRB (8:14) 13–14.

8201. BENNETT, BRUCE.   Catherine Spence, George Eliot and the contexts of literary possibility. JCL (21:1) 202–10.

8202. BERKELEY, LINDA EILEEN.   George Eliot: towards a complex realism. Unpub. doct. diss., Columbia Univ., 1984. [Abstr. in DA (47) 2166A.]

8203. BERMEJO GARCÍA, FUENCISLA.   Otras notas al diálogo de la primera novela de George Eliot. (Further notes on the dialogue in George Eliot's first novel.) Atlantis (8) 37–52.

8204. BLESSINGTON, FRANCIS C.   The portrait in the spoon: George Eliot's Casaubon and John Milton. *See* **5681.**

8205. BOLTON, FRANCES.   George Eliot and Italian Renaissance painting. *In* (pp. 159–67) **17.**

8206. CAHILL, AUDREY F.   Why not write in the first person? Why use complex plots? Some thoughts on George Eliot's theory and practice. Theoria (68) 15–23.

8207. CARROLL, DAVID (ed.).   Middlemarch. Oxford: Clarendon Press. pp. lxxxv, 825. (Clarendon edition of the novels of George Eliot.)

8208. CAVELL, RICHARD ANTHONY.   *Sub voce*: voice and the poetics of indirection in Flaubert, George Eliot and Verga. Unpub. doct. diss., Univ. of Toronto. [Abstr. in DA (47) 2150A.]

8209. CHO, CHUNG-HO.   *Daniel Deronda*: yeosung eui chamhim. (*Daniel Deronda*: the real power of woman.) JELL (32:4) 805–14.

8210. COSTABILE, RITA MARY.   Moral authority: George Eliot's politics. Unpub. doct. diss., Columbia Univ., 1985. [Abstr. in DA (46) 2298A.]

8211. DEERY, PATRICIA.   Margaret Fuller and Dorothea Brooke. RES (36:143) 1985, 379–85.

8212. DENTITH, SIMON.   George Eliot. Brighton: Harvester. pp. x, 150. (Harvester new readings.)

8213. EASSON, ANGUS.   Statesman, dwarf and weaver: Wordsworth and nineteenth-century narrative. *In* (pp. 16–29) **39.**

8214. ERMARTH, ELIZABETH DEEDS.   'Th'observed of all observers': George Eliot's narrator and Shakespeare's audience. *In* (pp. 126–40) **39.**

8215. FELTES, N. N.   One round of a long ladder: gender, profession, and the production of *Middlemarch*. ESCan (12:2) 210–28.

8216. FOLTINEK, HERBERT.   George Eliot. Darmstadt: Wissenschaftliche Buchgesellschaft, 1982. pp. vi, 158. (Erträge der Forschung, 182.) Rev. by Rosemary Ashton in MLR (81:2) 457.

8217. FREADMAN, RICHARD.   Eliot, James and the fictional self: a study in character and narration. Basingstoke: Macmillan. pp. 224.

8218. GOLDFARB, RUSSELL M.   Rosamond Vincy of *Middlemarch*. CLAJ (30:1) 83–99.

8219. GRAVER, SUZANNE.   George Eliot and community: a study in social theory and fictional form. (Bibl. 1985, 7035.) Rev. by Mark Halliday in MP (84:2) 228–32; by Carol A. Martin in VPR (19:3) 112–13; by Thomas A. Langford in ChrisL (35:2) 51–2.

8220. GRAY, B. M.   The listening faculty: studies in George Eliot's use of music, voice and natural sound. Unpub. doct. diss., Univ. of London (Birkbeck Coll.) [Abstr. in IT (36) 21.]

8221. HAIGHT, GORDON S. (ed.).   Selections from George Eliot's letters. London: Yale UP, 1985. pp. x, 567. (Cf. bibl. 1985, 7037.) Rev. in QQ (93:1) 222–3; by Wendy W. Fairey in VQR (62) 396–7; by Sara Hudson in SoHR (20:1) 76–8; by John Bayley in LRev, July 1985, 5–8.

8222. HANDLEY, GRAHAM (ed.).   Daniel Deronda. (Bibl. 1985, 7038.)

Rev. by Alan W. Bellringer in EngS (67:5) 462–3; by Valerie Grosvenor Myer in NQ (33:2) 255–6.

8223. HOWARD, C. F. With a single drop of ink for a mirror: George Eliot's developing ideas of representation in the realistic novel. Unpub. doct. diss., Univ. of York, 1985.

8224. JAHN, KAREN FROST. Providence in the Victorian novel: *Bleak House*, *Middlemarch*, and *The Mayor of Casterbridge* examined for their aesthetic realization of Providence. *See* **8054.**

8225. KEARNEY, J. A. A comparative study in the novels of Jane Austen and George Eliot: reason and feeling as components of moral choice. *See* **7589.**

8226. KELLY, MARGUERITE ANNE. George Eliot and philanthropy. Unpub. doct. diss., Univ. of Pittsburgh, 1985. [Abstr. in DA (46) 2301A.]

8227. KHWAJA, WAQAS AHMAD. An approach to *Middlemarch*. Cactus (Lahore) 1985, 90–112.

8228. KIDD, MILLIE MARIE. George Eliot's use of irony. Unpub. doct. diss., Univ. of Illinois at Urbana-Champaign, 1985. [Abstr. in DA (46) 1950A.]

8229. LAWSON, TOM O. Character influence: Samuel Richardson's *Sir Charles Grandison* and its influence upon the main character in George Eliot's *The Mill on the Floss*. *See* **6773.**

8230. LEAVIS, L. R. George Eliot's creative mind: *Felix Holt* as the turning point of her art. EngS (67:4) 311–26.

8231. LEE, KYUNG-SOON. George Eliot eui soseol e itseosuh eui dodeukjeok sangsangryeok. (Moralistic imagination in George Eliot's novels.) Unpub. doct. diss., Chonnan National Univ. (Korea.)

8232. LENIHAN, PATRICIA DIANE. Regionalism in the fictional debuts of Trollope, Gaskell, and Eliot. Unpub. doct. diss., Catholic Univ. of America. [Abstr. in DA (47) 1334A.]

8233. LINTOTT, S. The roar the other side of silence: Charlotte Brontë, George Eliot and the literary consequences of women's passivity. *See* **7672.**

8234. McCORMICK, KATHLEEN. George Eliot's earliest prose: the Coventry *Herald* and the Coventry fiction. *See* **641.**

8235. McSWEENEY, KERRY. The ending of *The Mill on the Floss*. ESCan (12:1) 55–68.

8236. —— (ed.). Middlemarch. Boston, MA: Allen & Unwin, 1984. (Bibl. 1985, 7054.) Rev. by Robert O'Kell in ESCan (12:4) 477–80; by Michael Wheeler in NQ (33:2) 256–7.

8237. MALMGREN, CARL D. Reading authorial narration: the example of *The Mill on the Floss*. *See* **10857.**

8238. MASSARDIER-KENNEY, FRANCOISE. A study of women in four realist writers: Sand, Flaubert, Eliot and James. Unpub.. doct. diss., Kent State Univ. [Abstr. in DA (47) 1721A.]

8239. NESTOR, PAULINE. Female friendships and communities: Charlotte Bronte, George Eliot, Elizabeth Gaskell. *See* **7676.**

8240. NOBLE, THOMAS A. (ed.). Scenes of clerical life. Oxford:

Clarendon Press, 1985. pp. xl, 334. (Cf. bibl. 1985, 7061, where pagination incorrect.) Rev. by Alan W. Bellringer in EngS (67:5) 462–3.

8241. PACE, TIMOTHY.   Silence in the courtroom: George Eliot and the language of morality in *Adam Bede*. ELit (13) 43–55.

8242. PRENTIS, B. L.   The Brontë sisters and George Eliot: aspects of their intellectual and literary relationship. *See* **7645.**

8243. REID, J. M.   Creative affinities: George Eliot's early experiments in fiction, 1857–1863. Unpub. doct. diss., Univ. of London (Birkbeck Coll.), 1985. [Abstr. in IT (35) 546.]

8244. ROBICHEAU, JOAN MARGARET.   George Henry Lewes, George Eliot and Anthony Trollope: experiments in realism. Unpub. doct. diss., Univ. of Toronto. [Abstr. in DA (47) 2171A.]

8245. SCHLESINGER, GEORGE.   A tale of two cuckolds. *See* **3778.**

8246. SHUTTLEWORTH, SALLY.   George Eliot and nineteenth-century science: the make-believe of a beginning. (Bibl. 1985, 7068.) Rev. by Kurt Tetzeli von Rosador in Archiv (223:2) 415–18.

8247. SMITH, JOHANNA MARY.   Domestic passion: sister-brother incest in four nineteenth-century novels. *See* **7606.**

8248. STASSIJNS, MACHTELD LUCIA.   'By force of art': the place of melodrama in George Eliot's early fiction. Unpub. doct. diss., Queen's Univ. at Kingston, 1985. [Abstr. in DA (46) 3349A.]

8249. THOMAS, JEANIE GAYLE.   Reading *Middlemarch*: reclaiming the middle distance. Unpub. doct. diss., Univ. of Washington, 1985. [Abstr. in DA (46) 1953A.]

8250. WARHOL, ROBYN R.   Toward a theory of the engaging narrator: earnest interventions in Gaskell, Stowe, and Eliot. PMLA (101:5) 811–18.

8251. WELSH, ALEXANDER.   George Eliot and blackmail. Cambridge, MA: Harvard UP, 1985. pp. xi, 388. Rev. by Thomas Vargish in CLIO (16:1) 92–4; by Rosemary Ashton in LRB (8:14) 13–14; by A. O. J. Cockshut in EC (36:4) 342–7.

8252. WHEELER, HELEN.   *The Mill on the Floss* by George Eliot. Basingstoke: Macmillan, pp. viii, 88. (Macmillan master guides.)

8253. WILKES, G. A.   *The Mill on the Floss* as moral fable? Sydney Studies in English (11) 1985–86, 69–82.

8254. WILKES, J. C.   The treatment of the recent past in nineteenth-century fiction, with particular reference to George Eliot. *See* **7365.**

8255. WOLFF, MICHAEL.   George Eliot, other-wise Marian Evans. BIS (13) 1985, 25–44.

8256. ZIM, RIVKAH.   Awakened perceptions in *Daniel Deronda*. EC (36:3) 210–34.

Ralph Waldo Emerson

8256a. ACHARYA, S.   Emerson and India. Unpub. doct. diss., Univ. of Oxford, 1983.

8257. ADDISON, ELIZABETH HODNETT.   Emerson, Quakerism, and an American aesthetic. Unpub. doct. diss., Duke Univ., 1985. [Abstr. in DA (47) 1320A.]

8258. BIELAWSKI, LARRY.   Emerson and Byron. *See* **7761.**

8259. BISHOP, JONATHAN. Emerson and Christianity. Ren (38:3) 183–200.

8260. BRIDGMAN, RICHARD. From Greenough to 'Nowhere': Emerson's *English Traits. See* **7806.**

8261. BURKHOLDER, ROBERT E. Emerson, Kneeland, and the Divinity School Address. AL (58:1) 1–14.

8262. CALLENS, JOHAN. Memories of the sea in Shepard's Illinois. ModDr (29:3) 403–15.

8263. CAMERON, SHARON. Representing grief: Emerson's 'experience'. Representations (15) 15–41.

8264. CARAFIOL, PETER. Reading Emerson: writing history. CR (30:4) 431–51.

8265. CARLET, YVES. La religion transcendantale et la nouvelle Amérique. *In* (pp. 23–36) **1.**

8266. CARTON, EVAN. The rhetoric of American romance: dialectic and identity in Emerson, Dickinson, Poe, and Hawthorne. *See* **8109.**

8267. CASTELAZ, DONALD RICHARD. Fire under the Andes: Emerson's philosophy of composition. Unpub. doct. diss., Univ. of Wisconsin–Milwaukee, 1985. [Abstr. in DA (46) 2298A.]

8268. CHANG, CHUNG-NAM. Henry David Thoreau wa Ralph Waldo Emerson eui jayeonkwan bigyo. (A comparative study on the viewpoint of nature of H. D. Thoreau and R. W. Emerson.) IKS (15) 59–75.

8269. CHANG, YOUNG-HEE. Journeys between the real and the ideal. Unpub. doct. diss., State Univ. of New York at Albany, 1985. [Abstr. in DA (46) 3032A.]

8270. CHMAJ, BETTY E. The journey and the mirror: Emerson and the American arts. Prospects (10) 1985, 353–408.

8271. COTKIN, GEORGE. Ralph Waldo Emerson and William James as public philosophers. Historian (49:1) 49–63.

8272. DAMERON, J. LASLEY. Emerson's *Each and All* and Goethe's *Eins und Alles.* EngS (67:4) 327–30.

8273. DILLMAN, RICHARD. Tom Outland: Emerson's American scholar in *The Professor's House.* MidQ (25) 1984, 375–85.

8274. DUNN, ELIZABETH SUE. 'A deranged balance': Emerson's creator in the finite. Unpub. doct. diss., Univ. of North Carolina at Chapel Hill, 1985. [Abstr. in DA (46) 3350A.]

8275. GRANT, JAMES DICKINSON. Ralph Waldo Emerson and John Dewey: a study of intellectual continuities and influence. Unpub. doct. diss., Harvard Univ., 1985. [Abstr. in DA (46) 2318A–19A.]

8276. HAGENBÜCHLE, ROLAND. Signs and process: the concept of language in Emerson and Dickinson. *See* **8116.**

8277. HANSON, VIRGINIA; PEDERSEN, CLARENCE (comps). The sage from Concord: the essence of Ralph Waldo Emerson. Wheaton, IL; London: Theosophical Pub. House, 1985. pp. xiii, 127.

8278. HARRIS, KENNETH MARC. Reason and understanding reconsidered: Coleridge, Carlyle, and Emerson. *See* **7815.**

8279. HERNDON, JERRY A. Emerson's *Nature* and Whitman's *Song of Myself.* YREAL (4) 195–232.

8280. HODDER, ALAN DONALDSON. Emerson's rhetoric of revelation: *Nature*, the reader, and the apocalypse within. Unpub. doct. diss., Harvard Univ. [Abstr. in DA (47) 2157A.]

8281. HOWE, IRVING. The American newness: culture and politics in the age of Emerson. *See* **7044.**

8282. HOWES, GEOFFREY CHANDLER. Robert Musil and the legacy of Ralph Waldo Emerson. Unpub. doct. diss., Univ. of Michigan, 1985. [Abstr. in DA (46) 3364A.]

8283. LEVERENZ, DAVID. The politics of Emerson's man-making words. *See* **1232.**

8284. MARTIN, JOHN. 'This is the ship of pearl . . .'. BkIA (45) 17–25.

8285. NEUFELDT, LEONARD N.; BARR, CHRISTOPHER. 'I shall write like a Latin Father': Emerson's *Circles.* NEQ (59:1) 92–108.

8286. O'BRIEN, MICHAEL (ed.). All clever men, who make their way: critical discourse in the Old South. *See* **7495.**

8287. OLSON, STEVE. A perverted poetics: Bryant's and Emerson's concern for a developing American literature. *See* **7741.**

8288. PACKER, BARBARA. Origin and authority: Emerson and the Higher Criticism. *In* (pp. 67–92) **47.**

8289. PETRY, ALICE HALL. The meeting of the twain: Emerson's *Hamatreya.* ELN (23:3) 47–51.

8290. POIRIER, RICHARD. The question of genius. Raritan (5:4) 77–104.

8291. PÜTZ, MANFRED (trans. and ed.); KRIEGER, GOTTFRIED (trans. and notes). Ralph Waldo Emerson. Die Natur. Ausgewählte Essays. Stuttgart: Reclam, 1982. pp. 280. Rev. by Gudrum M. Grabher in AAA (11) 129–31.

8292. ROBINSON, DAVID. The legacy of Emerson's Journals. RALS (13:1) 1983, 1–9.

8293. SHARMA, L. N. Ralph Waldo Emerson and Advaita Vedanta. Unpub. doct. diss., Univ. of Lancaster, 1983.

8294. SHIMKIN, DAVID. Emerson's playful habit of mind. ATQ (62) 3–16.

8295. SHUBIK, VALERIE REID. Willa Cather: an Emersonian angle of vision. Unpub. doct. diss., Univ. of Nebraska–Lincoln, 1985. [Abstr. in DA (46) 3721A.]

8296. STRELOW, MICHAEL. Emerson abroad and at home: the making of the paradigm in *Essays, First Series.* ATQ (59) 43–52.

8297. VAN LEER, DAVID. Emerson's epistemology: the argument of the essays. Cambridge: CUP. pp. xviii, 282.

8298. WARNER, NICHOLAS O. God's wine and devil's wine: the idea of intoxication in Emerson. Mosaic (19:3) 55–68.

8299. YANG, JAMES MIN-CHING. Emerson as a biographer. Unpub. doct. diss., Indiana Univ., 1985. [Abstr. in DA (46) 2695A.]

8300. YARBROUGH, STEPHEN R. From the vice of intimacy to the vice of habit: the theories of friendship in Emerson and Thoreau. TJQ (13:3/4) 1981, 63–72.

Sir Samuel Ferguson

8301. DENMAN, PETER. Ferguson and *Blackwood's*: the formative years. *See* **583.**

8302. Ní CHATHÁIN, PRÓINSÉAS. Sir Samuel Ferguson and the ogham inscriptions. *See* **3212.**

8303. Ó DÚILL, GRÉAGÓIR. Sir Samuel Ferguson, administrator and archivist. IUR (16) 117–40.

8304. READE, P. F. Samuel Ferguson and the idea of an Irish national literature, 1830–1850. Unpub. doct. diss., Univ. of Kent, 1983.

Susan Ferrier

8305. ASHTON, ROSEMARY (introd.). Marriage. London: Virago Press. pp. xvi, 513. Rev. by Jean Ann Scott Miller in SLJ (supp. 25) 17–18.

8306. CULLINAN, MARY. Susan Ferrier. Boston, MA: G. K. Hall, 1984. pp. xii (unnumbered), 135. (Twayne's English authors, 392.) Rev. by W. A. Craik in SLJ (supp. 24) 13–15.

James T. Fields

8307. SHEALY, DANIEL. 'Poor Jimmy's knock': a letter on the death of James T. Fields. NHR (12:2) 15–17.

Jane Findlater and Mary Findlater

8308. BINDING, PAUL (introd.). Crossriggs. London: Virago Press. pp. xiv, 380. (Virago modern classics, 203.) Rev. by Jean Ann Scott Miller in SLJ (supp. 25) 18.

Clyde Fitch

8309. HELLIE, THOMAS LOWELL. Clyde Fitch: playwright of New York's leisure class. Unpub. doct. diss., Univ. of Missouri–Columbia, 1985. [Abstr. in DA (47) 713A.]

Edward Fitzgerald

8310. TERHUNE, ALFRED MCKINLEY; TERHUNE, ANNABELLE BURDICK (eds). The letters of Edward FitzGerald. (Bibl. 1984, 7282.) Rev. by Peter Morgan in MLS (16:4) 75–7.

Mary Hallock Foote

8311. GRAULICH, MELODY. Mary Hallock Foote. Legacy (3:2) 43–52.

Paul Leicester Ford

8312. DICKINSON, DONALD C. Paul Leicester Ford and *The Bibliographer*. *See* **584.**

Harold Frederic

8313. DONALDSON, SCOTT (introd.). The damnation of Theron Ware, or, Illumination. New York; Harmondsworth: Penguin. pp. xxx, 346. (Penguin classics.)

8314. OEHLSCHLAEGER, FRITZ. Passion, authority, and faith in *The Damnation of Theron Ware*. AL (58:2) 238–55.

Mary E. Wilkins Freeman

8315. BARNES, MARY HANFORD. Realism in the early works of Mary E. Wilkins Freeman. Unpub. doct. diss., Arizona State Univ. [Abstr. in DA (47) 1725A.]

8316. BRESSLER, CHARLES EDWARD. The uncollected short stories of

Mary E. Wilkins Freeman. Unpub. doct. diss., Univ. of Georgia, 1985. [Abstr. in DA (47) 528A.]

8317. DONOVAN, JOSEPHINE.   Silence or capitulation: prepatriarchal 'mothers' gardens' in Jewett and Freeman. SSF (23:1) 43–8.

8318. KENDRICK, BRENT L. (ed.).   The infant sphinx: collected letters of Mary E. Wilkins Freeman. Metuchen, NJ: Scarecrow Press, 1985. pp. xv, 587. (Cf. bibl. 1982, 7767.) Rev. by Robert M. Luscher in AL (58:1) 125–7.

Margaret Fuller

8319. CHEVIGNY, BELL GALE.   To the edges of ideology: Margaret Fuller's centrifugal evolution. AmQ (38:2) 173–201.

8320. DEERY, PATRICIA.   Margaret Fuller and Dorothea Brooke. *See* **8211.**

8321. GEORGE, SHARON.   Margaret Fuller's *Dial* criticism: the merging of the Scottish common sense and Romantic traditions. *See* **602.**

8322. HABICH, ROBERT D.   Margaret Fuller's journal for October 1842. HLB (33:3) 1985, 280–91.

8323. URBANSKI, MARIE MITCHELL OLSEN.   Margaret Fuller: feminist writer and revolutionary (1810–1850). *In* (pp. 75–89) **20.**

John Galt

8324. GORDON, IAN A. (ed.).   The entail: or the lairds of Grippy. Oxford: OUP, 1984. pp. xxii, 414. (World's classics.) Rev. by T. W. Craik in BJECS (9:1) 112.

8325. GRAHAM, ROBERT J.   John Galt's *Bogle Corbet*: a parable of progress. SLJ (13:2) 31–47.

8326. SCOTT, P. H.   John Galt. Edinburgh: Scottish Academic Press, 1985. pp. 130. (Scottish writers, 5.)

8327. WATERSTON, ELIZABETH.   John Galt: reappraisals. Guelph, Ont.: Guelph UP, 1985. pp. 128. Rev. by A. A. den Otter in CanL (109) 139–40.

8328. WILSON, PATRICIA J.   John Galt at work: comments on the MS of *Ringan Gilhaize*. SSL (20) 1985, 160–76.

8329. —— (ed.).   Ringen Gilhaize or, The Covenanters. (Bibl. 1985, 7147.) Rev. by Charles Swann in NQ (33:4) 556–7.

John Gamble

8330. O'BRIEN, GEORGE.   The first Ulster author: John Gamble 1770–1831. Éire–Ireland (21:3) 131–41.

Elizabeth Cleghorn Gaskell

8331. BRODETSKY, TESSA.   Elizabeth Gaskell. Leamington Spa: Berg. pp. 113. (Berg women's series.)

8332. BUCHANAN, LAURIE E.   Contradicting the ideal: the heroines in the novels of Elizabeth Gaskell. Unpub. doct. diss., Bowling Green State Univ., 1985. [Abstr. in DA (47) 186A.]

8333. COLLIN, DOROTHY W.   The composition and publication of Elizabeth Gaskell's *Cranford*. *See* **364.**

8334. HOWELL, MARY LOU BROOKS.   The heart of Elizabeth Gaskell: the Unitarian spirit. Unpub. doct. diss., Texas Woman's Univ., 1985. [Abstr. in DA (46) 1949A.]

8335. KIM, SUN-HEE. Elizabeth Gaskell eui jakpumron mit *Wives and Daughters* e natanan dodeuksung. (Elizabeth Gaskell's art and moral purpose in *Wives and Daughters*.) JUJH (22) 197–214.

8336. LENIHAN, PATRICIA DIANE. Regionalism in the fictional debuts of Trollope, Gaskell, and Eliot. *See* **8232.**

8337. NESTOR, PAULINE. Female friendships and communities: Charlotte Bronte, George Eliot, Elizabeth Gaskell. *See* **7676.**

8338. REDDY, MAUREEN TERESA. Elizabeth Gaskell's short fiction. Unpub. doct. diss., Univ. of Minnesota, 1985. [Abstr. in DA (46) 1952A.]

8339. SCHOR, HILARY MARGO. Scheherezade in the market place: Elizabeth Gaskell and the fiction of transformation. Unpub. doct. diss., Stanford Univ. [Abstr. in DA (47) 2171A.]

8340. WARHOL, ROBYN R. Toward a theory of the engaging narrator: earnest interventions in Gaskell, Stowe, and Eliot. *See* **8250.**

W. S. Gilbert

8341. SIR ARTHUR SULLIVAN SOCIETY. *The Sorcerer* and *Trial by Jury*: a booklet to commemorate the centenary of the first revival, 11 October 1884. Saffron Walden: Sir Arthur Sullivan Soc., 1984. pp. 58.

8342. CARDULLO, BERT. The art and business of W. S. Gilbert's *Engaged*. ModDr (28:3) 1985, 462–73.

8343. EDEN, DAVID. Gilbert and Sullivan: the creative conflict. Rutherford, NJ: Fairleigh Dickinson UP; London: Assoc. UPs. pp. 224.

8344. HIGGINS, REGINA KIRBY. Victorian laughter: the comic operas of Gilbert and Sullivan. Unpub. doct. diss., Indiana Univ., 1985. [Abstr. in DA (46) 2700A.]

8345. NEWMAN, JAY. The Gilbertianism of *Patience*. DalR (65:2) 1985, 263–82.

8346. ROWELL, GEORGE (ed.). Plays by W. S. Gilbert: *The Palace of Truth, Sweethearts, Princess Toto, Engaged, Rosencrantz and Guildenstern.* Cambridge; New York: CUP, 1982. pp. x, 189. Rev. by Michael R. Booth in YES (16) 335–6.

William Gilbert

8347. STEDMAN, JANE W. 'A peculiar sharp flavour': the contributions of Dr William Gilbert. *See* **699.**

George Gissing

8348. COLLIE, MICHAEL. George Gissing: a bibliographical study. Winchester: St Paul's Bibliographies, 1985. pp. 167. Rev. by Brian Lake in BC (35:3) 385–6. (Revised and expanded ed.: first ed. 1975.)

8349. COUSTILLAS, PIERRE. Some personal observations on realism and idealism in *New Grub Street*. CVE (24) 63–78.

8350. —— BROOK, CLIFFORD (eds). A life's morning. (Cf. bibl. 1985, 7165, where second scholar's name omitted.) Rev. by Sylvère Monod in EA (39:2) 227–9.

8351. —— (ed.). Workers in the dawn. pp. cii, 374, 436. (Cf. bibl. 1985, 7166, where pagination incorrect.) Rev. by Sylvère Monod in EA (39:2) 227–9.

8352. GREENSLADE, W. P. The concept of degeneration, 1880–1910, with particular reference to the work of Thomas Hardy, George Gissing and H. G. Wells. Unpub. doct. diss., Univ. of Warwick, 1982.

8353. GRYLLS, DAVID. The paradox of Gissing. London: Allen & Unwin. pp. xi, 350.

8354. —— Realism and romantic convention in Gissing. CVE (24) 79–93.

8355. HALPERIN, JOHN (introd.). The emancipated. London: Hogarth Press, 1985. pp. viii, 456.

8356. —— Will Warburton: romance of real life. London: Hogarth Press, 1985. pp. 332.

8357. HULL, G. W. The concept of the artist in the work of George Gissing. Unpub. doct. diss., Univ. of Wales, Bangor, 1984. [Abstr. in IT (35) 49.]

8358. KORG, JACOB. Realism as discovery in the novels of George Gissing. CVE (24) 95–107.

8359. SELIG, ROBERT L. A further Gissing attribution from the *Chicago Post*. PBSA (80:1) 100–4.

8360. SLOAN, J. Culture and circumstance: a study of George Gissing's fiction in its ideological context. Unpub. doct. diss., Univ. of Oxford, 1983.

8361. STEPPUTAT, J. Introversion and extroversion in certain late Victorian writers. Unpub. doct. diss., Univ. of St Andrews, 1985. [Abstr. in IT (35) 50.]

8362. STOENESCU, STEFAN (ed.). Thyrza. Trans. by BIANCA ZAMFI-RESCU. Bucharest: Univers, 1985. pp. 606.

8363. TINDALL, GILLIAN (introd.). Born in exile. London: Hogarth Press, 1985. pp. 506.

8364. TURTON, L. G. Turgenev and the context of English literature, 1850–1900. *See* **7131.**

Lucie Duff Gordon

8365. GENDRON, CHARISSE. Lucie Duff Gordon's *Letters from Egypt*. Ariel (17:2) 49–61.

8366–7. Entries cancelled.

Robert Gowan

8368. SMITH, MARY ELIZABETH. Three political dramas from New Brunswick. *See* **7187.**

John Gray

8369. HEALY, PHILIP (ed.). Park: a fantastic story. Manchester: Carcanet Press, 1984. pp. 125.

Anna Katharine Green

8370. MAIDA, PATRICIA D. Anna Katharine Green. Legacy (3:2) 53–9.

Kate Greenaway

8371. ENGEN, RODNEY K. The myth of Kate Greenaway. *See* **72.**

Gavin Greig

8372. DONALDSON, WILLIAM (introd.). Logie o' Buchan: an Aberdeenshire pastoral. Aberdeen: Bisset, 1985. pp. x, 319. (Aberdeenshire classics.) Rev. by Ian A. Olson in AUR (51) 371–2; by the same in SLJ (supp. 25) 22–4.

Sir Henry Rider Haggard

8373. HAULE, JAMES M. *She* and the moral dilemma of Elizabeth Bowen. CLQ (22:4) 205–14.

8374. VOGELSBERGER, HARTWIG A. *King Romance* – Rider Haggard's achievement. Unpub. doct. diss., Univ. of Salzburg, 1984.

Sarah Josepha Hale

8375. MOYLE, GERALDINE. The tenth muse lately sprung up in the marketplace: women and professional authorship in nineteenth-century America. *See* **7537.**

Thomas Hardy

8376. ARKANS, NORMAN. Hardy's novel impression-pictures. CLQ (22:3) 153–64.

8377. BADAWI, M. Thomas Hardy and the meaning of freedom. Unpub. doct. diss., Univ. of St Andrews, 1985. [Abstr. in IT (35) 47–8.]

8378. BALL, DAVID. Hardy's experimental fiction. Eng (35) 27–36.

8379. BJÖRK, LENNART A. (ed.). The literary notebooks of Thomas Hardy. New York: New York UP, 1985. (Cf. bibl. 1985, 7191.) Rev. by Dale Kramer in Review (8) 1–19.

8380. BOETTCHER, RALPH CARL. The romantic past: primitivism and some novels by Thomas Hardy, D. H. Lawrence, and Robert Graves. Unpub. doct. diss., Columbia Univ. [Abstr. in DA (47) 906A.]

8381. BOUMELHA, PENNY. Thomas Hardy and women: sexual ideology and narrative form. Totowa, NJ: Barnes & Noble, 1982. (Bibl. 1984, 7352.) Rev. by Valerie Shaw in MLR (81:1) 186.

8382. BULLEN, J. B. The expressive eye: fiction and perception in the work of Thomas Hardy. Oxford: Clarendon Press. pp. 280. Rev. by Richard H. Taylor in THES (715) 17.

8383. CLARK, R. A. Lyric form in the poetry of Thomas Hardy. Unpub. doct. diss., Univ. of Lancaster, 1983.

8384. CRICK, BRIAN. Love and the intellectual: *A Pair of Blue Eyes.* Retford: Brynmill, 1985. pp. 42. (Gadfly literary supplement.)

8385. DANON, RUTH. Work in the English novel: the myth of vocation. *See* **6392.**

8386. DAVE, JAGDISH CHANDRA. The human predicament in Hardy's novels. Introd. by LANCE ST JOHN BUTLER. London: Macmillan, 1985. pp. xii, 215. (Macmillan Hardy studies.)

8387. EBBATSON, ROGER (ed.). A pair of blue eyes. Harmondsworth: Penguin. pp. 479. (Penguin classics.)

8388. ELLIOTT, RALPH W. V. Thomas Hardy's English. (Bibl. 1985, 7203.) Rev. by David Levey in UES (24:1) 42.

8389. ESCURET, ANNIE. *A Pair of Blue Eyes*: la mer et la falaise. CVE (23) 111–31.

8390. FAUROT, MARGARET RANDOLPH.   The topographical imagination: vision and recantation in the poetry of Thomas Hardy. Unpub. doct. diss., Univ. of California, Santa Cruz, 1985. [Abstr. in DA (47) 909A.]

8391. FRANK, LINDA PINSKER.   Bovarysm, its concept and application to literature: Stendhal, Flaubert, Hardy, Alas, and Lewis. Unpub. doct. diss., Purdue Univ., 1985. [Abstr. in DA (46) 1931A.]

8392. GARCES, J. P.   La mer dans les romans de Thomas Hardy. CVE (23) 99–109.

8393. GATRELL, SIMON (ed.).   *The Return of the Native*: a facsimile of the manuscript with related materials. New York; London: Garland. pp. xx, 493. (Thomas Hardy archive, 2.)

8394. —— *Tess of the d'Urbervilles*: a facsimile of the manuscript with related materials. New York; London: Garland. 2 vols. pp. xix, 373; 310. (Thomas Hardy archive, 1.)

8395. —— Under the greenwood tree. Oxford: OUP, 1985. pp. xxxiii, 218. (World's classics.)

8396. GIBSON, JAMES.   *Tess of the d'Urbervilles* by Thomas Hardy. Basingstoke: Macmillan. pp. x. 85. (Macmillan master guides.)

8397. GILMORE, SUE CHANEY.   The Aeneas analogy: a study of the Aeneas tradition in the works of Dryden, Hardy, and Tate. *See* **5416.**

8398. GREENSLADE, W. P.   The concept of degeneration, 1880–1910, with particular reference to the work of Thomas Hardy, George Gissing and H. G. Wells. *See* **8352.**

8399. HANDS, T.   The ecclesiastical background to the novels of Thomas Hardy. Unpub. doct. diss., Univ. of Oxford, 1984.

8400. HEROLD, JOHN C.   Thomas Hardy's last four novels: a selectivist approach. Unpub. doct. diss., State Univ. of New York at Buffalo. [Abstr. in DA (47) 537A.]

8401. HETHERINGTON, T. B.   A critical edition of Thomas Hardy's novel *The Well-Beloved*. Unpub. doct. diss., Univ. of Kent, 1983.

8402. HETHERINGTON, TOM (ed.).   The well-beloved. Oxford: OUP. pp. 336. (World's classics.)

8403. HUGHES, J. D.   A comparative study of the nature and development of narrative style in the fiction of Thomas Hardy (with special reference to *Desperate Remedies* and *Jude the Obscure*). Unpub. doct. diss., Univ. of Oxford, 1985. [Abstr. in IT (35) 49.]

8404. HYNES, SAMUEL (ed.).   The complete poetical works of Thomas Hardy. Oxford: Clarendon Press. (Vol. 1, bibl. 1985, 7217; vol. 2, bibl. 1984, 7377, where publisher incorrect; vol. 3, bibl. 1985, 7218, where publisher incorrect.) Rev. in QQ (93:2) 459; by Joan Grundy in MLR (81:3) 727–9.

8405. —— Thomas Hardy. (Bibl. 1985, 7219.) Rev. in QQ (93:2) 459.

8406. INGHAM, PATRICIA (ed.).   Jude the obscure. Oxford: OUP, 1985. pp. xxxix, 451. (World's classics.)

8407. JAHN, KAREN FROST.   Providence in the Victorian novel: *Bleak House*, *Middlemarch*, and *The Mayor of Casterbridge* examined for their aesthetic realization of Providence. *See* **8054.**

8408. JEWELL, JOHN ROBERT. Searching for the city of light: homelessness in Thomas Hardy's modern novels. Unpub. doct. diss., Kent State Univ., 1985. [Abstr. in DA (47) 188A.]

8409. JOHNSON, BRUCE. True correspondence: a phenomenology of Thomas Hardy's novels. (Bibl. 1985, 7221.) Rev. by Pierre Coustillas in EA (39:1) 105–6.

8410. JONES, T. A critical edition of Thomas Hardy's *The Mayor of Casterbridge*, collating all relevant manuscripts and authorial printed texts and recording substantive and accidental variants. Unpub. doct. diss., Univ. of Exeter, 1983.

8411. KIM, CHUL-SOO. Thomas Hardy soseol eui bigeukjeok yoin. (The tragic elements in Thomas Hardy's novels.) Unpub. doct. diss., Busan National Univ. (Korea).

8412. KRAMER, DALE. Using Hardy's notebooks. Review (8) 1–19 (review-article).

8413. LOCK, CHARLES. *The Darkling Thrush* and the habit of singing. EC (36:2) 120–41.

8414. LOTHE, JAKOB. Hardy's authorial narrative method in *Tess of the d'Urbervilles. In* (pp. 156–70) **39.**

8415. LOWMAN, R. J. Thomas Hardy and the rural question. Unpub. doct. diss., Univ. of Southampton, 1983.

8416. MAY, CHARLES E. The magic of metaphor in *The Return of the Native.* CLQ (22:2) 111–18.

8417. MILLER, J. HILLIS. Topography and tropography in Thomas Hardy's *In Front of the Landscape. In* (pp. 73–91) **23.**

8418. MITCHELL, P. E. The shorter poems of Thomas Hardy: a critical study. Unpub. doct. diss., Univ. of Cambridge, 1984.

8419. MOXHAM, R. J. Time and individuation in works by Sophocles, Thomas Hardy and Julio Cortázar. Unpub. doct. diss., Univ. of Manchester, 1982. [Abstr. in IT (35) 41.]

8420. ODA, MINORU. Foreign correspondence: news from Japan. ELT (26:4) 1983, 228–30. (Hardy scholarship in Japan.)

8421. —— Foreign correspondence on recent Hardy scholarship in Japan: bibliographical commentary III. ELT (29:4) 379–85.

8422. —— Foreign report: recent work on Hardy in Japan. ELT (28:2) 1985, 182–7.

8423. O'NEILL, PATRICIA. Pedigree of self-making: Shelley's influence on Browning and Hardy. *See* **7729.**

8424. PAULIN, TOM. Thomas Hardy: the poetry of perception. (Bibl. 1978, 7326.) London: Macmillan. pp. x, 225. (Second ed.: first ed. 1975.)

8425. PONSFORD, MICHAEL. Thomas Hardy's control of sympathy in *Tess of the d'Urbervilles.* MidQ (274) 487–503.

8426. POPPLEWELL, LAWRENCE (ed.). An origin for the native. Bournemouth: Melledgen. pp. 36.

8427. PURDY, RICHARD LITTLE; MILLGATE, MICHAEL (eds). The collected letters of Thomas Hardy: vol. 5, 1914–1919. (Bibl. 1985, 7240.) Rev. by Merryn Williams in NQ (33:4) 562–3.

8428. RABBETTS, J. The ache of modernism: a comparative study of the novels of Thomas Hardy and William Faulkner. Unpub. doct. diss., Univ. of Essex, 1984.

8429. Rose, Beatrix Astrid Bloem.   Spatial configurations in three novels: *Jude the Obscure*, *The Castle*, and *Het Zwarte Licht*. Unpub. doct. diss., Purdue Univ., 1985. [Abstr. in DA (46) 1934A.]

8430. Runcie, Catherine.   On figurative language: a reading of Shelley's, Hardy's and Hughes's skylark poems. AUMLA (66) 205–17.

8431. Schork, R. J.   A Virgilian allusion in Hardy's *Desperate Remedies*. ANQ (24:9/10) 145–6.

8432. Schur, Owen Marius.   Developments and transformations of pastoral melancholy in some poems of Keats, Tennyson, and Hardy. Unpub. doct. diss., Yale Univ., 1985. [Abstr. in DA (47) 1338A.]

8433. Steele, Bruce (ed.).   'Study of Thomas Hardy' and other essays. By D. H. Lawrence. Introd. by Melvyn Bragg. London: Grafton. pp. xi, 194. (Cf. bibl. 1985, 7245.)

8434. Taylor, Richard H. (ed.).   Emma Hardy diaries. Ashington: Mid Northumberland Arts Group, 1985. pp. 216. (Facsims.)

8435. Thomas, J. E.   Social conditioning versus biological determinism: a study of the women characters in the 'minor' novels of Thomas Hardy. Unpub. doct. diss., Univ. of Hull, 1985. [Abstr. in IT (35) 50.]

8436. Vaché, Jean.   *Tess of the d'Urbervilles*, de la ballade à l'opéra. EA (39:1) 37–49.

8437. Wickens, G. Glen.   Victorian theories of language and *Tess of the d'Urbervilles*. Mosaic (19:1) 99–115.

8438. Wittenberg, Judith Bryant.   Angles of vision and questions of gender in *Far from the Madding Crowd*. CR (30:1) 25–40.

Frances Ellen Watkins Harper

8439. Fryar, Lillie B.   The aesthetics of language: Harper, Hurston and Morrison. Unpub. doct. diss., State Univ. of New York at Buffalo. [Abstr. in DA (47) 529A.]

Charles Harpur

8440. Ackland, Michael.   Charles Harpur and his editors. *See* **349.**

8441. —— Plot and counter plot in Charles Harpur's *The Bushrangers*. Australasian Drama Studies (St Lucia, Qld) (8) 49–61 (review-article).

8442. Perkins, Elizabeth.   Rhetoric and the man: Charles Harpur and the call to armed rebellion. Age Monthly Review (Melbourne) Sept., 14–17.

Joel Chandler Harris

8443. Chang, Linda S.   Brer Rabbit's Angolan cousin: politics and the adaptation of folk material. *See* **2439.**

8444. Keenan, Hugh T.   Twisted tales: propaganda in the Tar-Baby stories. SoQ (22:2) 1984, 54–69.

8445. Montenyohl, Eric L.   Joel Chandler Harris's revision of Uncle Remus: the first revision of *A Story of the War*. ALR (19:1) 65–72.

8446. Walker, Alice.   Uncle Remus, no friend of mine. SE (9:2) 1981, 29–31.

John Harris

8447. THOMAS, CHARLES. John Harris of Bolenowe, poet and preacher, 1820–1884: a tribute: a lecture delivered at the Royal Institution of Cornwall, Truro, Monday 19th March 1984. Truro: Cornish Methodist Historical Assn, 1984. pp. 24.

Nathaniel Hawthorne

8448. BAUER, DALE MARIE. The failure of community: women and resistance in Hawthorne's, James's, and Wharton's novels. Unpub. doct. diss., Univ. of California, Irvine, 1985. [Abstr. in DA (46) 3718A.]

8449. BECKER, ALLIENNE R. *Alice Doane's Appeal*: a literary double of Hoffman's *Die Elixiere des Teufels*. CLS (23:1) 1–11.

8450. BENSICK, CAROL MARIE. La nouvelle Beatrice: Renaissance and romance in *Rappaccini's Daughter*. (Bibl. 1985, 7267.) Rev. by Margaret Hallissy in SSF (23) 133–4; by Claudia D. Johnson in AL (58:1) 129–30.

8451. BORDHEAD, RICHARD H. The school of Hawthorne. New York; Oxford: OUP. pp x, 254.

8452. BRAND, DANA. The panoramic spectator in America: a rereading of some of Hawthorne's sketches. ATQ (59) 5–18.

8453. BUDICK, E. MILLER. The world as specter: Hawthorne's historical art. PMLA (101:2) 218–32.

8454. BURNS, JEROME EDWARD. Social and personal transformation through relationships in the major romances of Nathaniel Hawthorne. Unpub. doct. diss., Marquette Univ., 1985. [Abstr. in DA (46) 3031A.]

8455. BUSH, SARGENT, JR. Hawthorne's domestic quest: narratives of the 1830's. BkIA (45) 38–49.

8456. CAPPELLO, MARY. *Rappaccini's Daughter* as translation. PQ (65:2) 263–77.

8457. CAREY, NORMAN E. The integration of allegory into narrative structure in Hawthorne's writing. Unpub. doct. diss., Univ. of Pennsylvania, 1985. [Abstr. in DA (46) 3718A.]

8458. CARTON, EVAN. The rhetoric of American romance: dialectic and identity in Emerson, Dickinson, Poe, and Hawthorne. *See* **8109.**

8459. CHRISTOPHERSEN, BILL. *Young Goodman Brown* as historical allegory: a lexical link. SSF (23:2) 202–4.

8460. COHEN, HAZEL. The rupture of relations: revolution and romance in Hawthorne's *My Kinsmen, Major Molineux*. ESA (29:1) 19–30.

8461. COLACURCIO, MICHAEL J. The province of piety: moral history in Hawthorne's early tales. (Bibl. 1985, 7277.) Rev. by Nina Baym in JEGP (85:1) 150–2.

8462. —— (ed.). New essays on *The Scarlet Letter*. Cambridge: CUP, 1985. pp. viii, 164. (American novel.)

8463. COWLES, DAVID L. A profane tragedy: Dante in Hawthorne's *Rappaccini's Daughter*. ATQ (60) 5–24.

8464. CUDDY, LOIS A. Mother–daughter identification in *The Scarlet Letter*. Mosaic (19:2) 101–15.

8465. DANIEL, CLAY. *The Scarlet Letter*: Hawthorne, Freud, and the Transcendentalists. ATQ (61) 23–36.

8466. DONOHUE, AGNES MCNEILL.   Hawthorne: Calvin's ironic step-child. (Bibl. 1985, 7281.) Rev. by Kathleen Verduin in NEQ (59:1) 149–52; by David O. Tomlinson in AL (58:1) 143–5; by Nina Baym in JEGP (85:2) 288–90.

8467. ELLIS, WILLIAM NEAL.   The ambiguous method: an analysis of the structures of *The Scarlet Letter*. Unpub. doct. diss., Univ. of Colorado at Boulder, 1985. [Abstr. in DA (46) 2293A.]

8468. FERRARO, WILLIAM M.   An interpretation of Hawthorne and the American character. SAQ (85:2) 165–75.

8469. FITZGERALD, EDWARD F.   'At once merry and bitter': the relation of comic incongruity to character and theme in the works of Nathaniel Hawthorne. Unpub. doct. diss., New York Univ., 1985. [Abstr. in DA (46) 2293A.]

8470. GARAVAGLIA, JAMES M.   Hawthorne's crowded fiction. Unpub. doct. diss., Wayne State Univ. [Abstr. in DA (47) 1323A.]

8471. GOLLIN, RITA K.   Portraits of Nathaniel Hawthorne. (Bibl. 1985, 7293.) Rev. by Joseph Kestner in PLL (22:2) 221–3.

8472. GRAHAM, DOROTHY BETH HARBIN.   The archetypes of individuation in Nathaniel Hawthorne's life, the major romances, and *Rappaccini's Daughter*. Unpub. doct. diss., Georgia State Univ., College of Arts and Sciences, 1985. [Abstr. in DA (46) 3033A.]

8473. HUDGINS, ANDREW.   Landscape and movement in *The Scarlet Letter*. SDR (19:4) 1982, 5–17.

8474. IDOL, JOHN L., JR.   A show of hands in *The Artist of the Beautiful*. SSF (22) 1985, 455–60.

8475. JONES, BUFORD.   Current Hawthorne bibliography. NHR (12:1) 22–3; (12:2) 22–7.

8476. JOSEPH, SISTER.   Rose of all the Hawthornes. NHR (12:1) 12–13.

8477. KESTNER, JOSEPH.   Hawthorne's portraits. PLL (22:2) 221–3 (review-article).

8478. KIM, SUK-HYEON.   *The Scarlet Letter* a natanan Hawthorne eui yesuljeok gibeob gwa yulijeok, gamsangjeok hosoryeok e gwanhan yeongu. (Hawthorne's artistic technique and the appeal to morals and the emotions in *The Scarlet Letter*.) Unpub. doct. diss., Keimyung Univ. (Korea), 1985.

8479. LEWIS, ANN CLIFFORD.   Hawthorne's insulated men and women. Unpub. doct. diss., Univ. of Denver, 1985. [Abstr. in DA (46) 2693A.]

8480. MCKIBBEN, KARAN.   Hawthorne's quarrel with scribbling women and art. Unpub. doct. diss., Univ. of California, Riverside, 1985. [Abstr. in DA (46) 1942A.]

8481. MARTIN, TERENCE.   Septimius Felton and Septimius Norton: matters of history and immortality. NHR (12:1) 1–4.

8482. MAYS, JAMES O'DONALD.   Hawthorne and the Roebuck Hotel. NHR (12:1) 15.

8483. —— Mr Hawthorne goes to England: the adventures of a reluctant diplomat. (Bibl. 1984, 7487.) Rev. by Keith Carabine in NQ (33:1) 134–5.

8484. MILLER, EDWIN HAVILAND. Hawthorne at the Salem Custom-house. NHR (12:1) 15–16.

8485. MIZRUCHI, SUSAN LAURA. The power of historical knowledge: narrating the past in Hawthorne, James, and Dreiser. Unpub. doct. diss., Princeton Univ., 1985. [Abstr. in DA (46) 3035A.]

8486. MONTEIRO, GEORGE. *Grandfather's Chair* in the Arundel Library. NHR (12:1) 16.

8487. —— Hawthorne's summer romance. DQR (16:2) 97–108.

8488. O'BRIEN, MICHAEL (ed.). All clever men, who make their way: critical discourse in the Old South. See **7495.**

8489. OLANDER, KAREN A. The Hawthorne–James relation: from *The Scarlet Letter* to *The Golden Bowl*. Unpub. doct. diss., Univ. of North Carolina at Chapel Hill, 1985. [Abstr. in DA (47) 180A.]

8490. PARK, IK-TU. Hawthorne in Korean perspective, 1953–1985. NHR (12:2) 11–13.

8491. PARKER, R. N. The notion of the outsider in the writings of Cooper, Hawthorne, Twain and Faulkner. See **7968.**

8492. PASS, OLIVIA McNEELY. Hawthorne's complex vision: the growth of a new consciousness as revealed by the female characters in the four major novels. Unpub. doct. diss., Univ. of Southwestern Louisiana, 1985. [Abstr. in DA (47) 181A.]

8493. PFISTER, JOEL. Hawthorne and the history of personal life. Unpub. doct. diss., Yale Univ., 1985. [Abstr. in DA (47) 1730A.]

8494. PONDER, MELINDA. Hawthorne and Raymond, Maine. NHR (12:2) 4–10.

8495. PRIBEK, THOMAS. Dr Clarke in Nathaniel Hawthorne's *Lady Eleanore's Mantle*: a note on source and significance. MSE (10:2) 1985, 127–31.

8496. —— Hawthorne's Blackstone. ANQ (24:9/10) 142–4.

8497. RICHARDS, JEFFREY H. Hawthorne's posturing observer: the case of *Sights from a Steeple*. ATQ (59) 35–42.

8498. ROBINSON, DANNY LEE. 'An image of an image': the shape of Hawthorne biography, 1840–1904. Unpub. doct. diss., Duke Univ., 1985. [Abstr. in DA (47) 182A.]

8499. ROZAKIS, LAURIE N. Another possible source for Hawthorne's Hester Prynne. ATQ (59) 63–72.

8500. RUST, RICHARD D. 'I seek for truth': Hawthorne's use of the talisman. NHR (12:1) 5–7.

8501. SHEALY, DANIEL. 'Poor Jimmy's knock': a letter on the death of James T. Fields. See **8307.**

8502. STRYCHACZ, THOMAS F. Coverdale and women: feverish fantasies in *The Blithedale Romance*. ATQ (62) 29–46.

8503. SUTHERLAND, JUDITH L. The problematic fictions of Poe, James, and Hawthorne. (Bibl. 1985, 7334.) Rev. by J. Gerald Kennedy in AL (58:2) 288–9.

8504. TENBRUNSEL, WILLIAM JAMES. Nathaniel Hawthorne and the authority of tradition. Unpub. doct. diss., Rutgers Univ. [Abstr. in DA (47) 2162A.]

8505. Timms, D.   Europe and European realism in the works of Hawthorne and James, from *The Marble Faun* to *The Portrait of a Lady*. Unpub. doct. diss., Univ. of Manchester, 1985. [Abstr. in IT (36) 476.]

8506. Tóth, Csaba.   Hawthorne in Hungary. NHR (12:1) 7–9.

8507. Tritt, Michael.   *Young Goodman Brown* and the psychology of projection. SSF (23:1) 113–17.

8508. Valenti, Patricia Dunlavy.   The frozen art or the ethereal domain: Hawthorne's concept of sculpture. SSF (22) 1985, 323–30.

8509. Wallace, James D.   Immortality in Hawthorne's *Septimius Felton*. SAF (14:1) 19–33.

8510. Whelan, Robert Emmet.   God as artist in *The Marble Faun*. Ren (34:3) 1982, 144–60.

8511. Woodson, Thomas.   A new installment of Hawthorne's *Spectator*. NHR (12:2) 1–3.

8512. —— Smith, L. Neal; Pearson, Norman Holmes (eds).   The centenary edition of the works of Nathaniel Hawthorne: vol. 15, The letters, 1813–1843; vol. 16, The letters, 1843–1853. Columbus: Ohio State UP, 1984. pp. xvii, 795; xiii, 775. Rev. by Richard Harter Fogle in AL (58:3) 441–3; by John L. Idol, Jr, in JEGP (85:4) 586–8.

8513. Wyatt, Jennifer Fugett.   Portraits of Hester Prynne. Unpub. doct. diss., Univ. of Washington, 1985. [Abstr. in DA (46) 1944A.]

8514. Young, Philip.   Hawthorne's secret: an un-told tale. (Bibl. 1985, 7338.) Rev. by John Seelye in SAQ (85:3) 311–13.

8515. Youra, Steven J.   'The fatal hand': a sign of confusion in Hawthorne's *The Birth-Mark*. ATQ (60) 43–52.

8516. Zapf, Hubert.   The poetological theme in Hawthorne's *Blithdale Romance*. ATQ (60) 73–82.

William Hazlitt

8517. Beer, John.   Coleridge, Hazlitt, and *Christabel*. See **7889.**

8518. Bromwich, David.   Hazlitt: the mind of a critic. (Bibl. 1985, 7340.) Rev. by Jeffrey C. Robinson in Review (7) 1985, 72–6; by Maria Del Sapio in YES (16) 298–9.

8519. Kinnaird, John.   William Hazlitt: critic of power. (Bibl. 1981, 7879.) Rev. by Jeffrey C. Robinson in Review (7) 1985, 65–76.

8520. Neve, Michael (introd.).   Liber amoris, or, The new Pygmalion. London: Hogarth Press, 1985. pp. xii, 287. (Lives and letters.)

8521. Read, R.   The evocative genre of art criticism: a study of descriptive prose in the works of Hazlitt, Ruskin, Pater and Adrian Stokes. Unpub. doct. diss., Univ. of Reading, 1982.

8522. Robinson, Jeffrey C.   Romanticism through the mind of Hazlitt. Review (7) 1985, 65–76 (review-article).

8523. Wells, Stanley.   Shakespeare in Hazlitt's theatre criticism. See **4617.**

Lafcadio Hearn

8524. Lamoine, Bernadette.   Lafcadio Hearn et la mer. CVE (23) 157–76.

8525. WILLIAMS, SUSAN MILLAR. *'L'Enfant terrible'?* Elizabeth Bisland and the South. *See* **7624.**

W. E. Henley

8526. GLINES, ELSA F. 'My dear Miss Page' and 'Demon Harry': some early letters of W. E. Henley. HLQ (49:4) 325–55.

8527. NEWTON, JOY. The sculptor and the poet: Auguste Rodin and William Ernest Henley. Laurels (57) Fall, 103–21.

James A. Herne

8528. McCONACHIE, BRUCE A. Herne's *Shore Acres* and the family in the tradition of the Irish-American theatre. TS (30) 1983/84, 17–28.

Ella Higginson

8529. KOERT, DOROTHY. The lyric singer: a biography of Ella Higginson. Bellingham, WA: Center for Pacific Northwest Studies, Western Washington Univ., 1985. pp. vi, 155. Rev. by Karen Anderson in PacNQ (77:2) 73.

Thomas Hill (1807–1860)

8530. MULLALY, EDWARD. Thomas Hill: the Fredericton years. StudCanL (11:2) 190–205.

James Hogg

8531. BLIGH, JOHN. The doctrinal premises of Hogg's *Confessions of a Justified Sinner.* SSL (19) 1984, 148–64.

8532. GROVES, DAVID. A fragment of a ballad by James Hogg. Bibliotheck (13:2) 42–5.

8533. —— James Hogg: verses for Burns and Byron. *See* **6330.**

8534. —— *A Vision* by James Hogg. NQ (33:2) 164.

8535. —— (ed.). Selected poems and songs. Edinburgh: Scottish Academic Press. pp. xxxiii, 232.

8536. —— Tales of love and mystery. Edinburgh: Canongate, 1985. pp. 216. Rev. by Gillian H. Hughes in SLJ (supp. 24) 10–11.

8537. MACK, D. S. Editing James Hogg: some textual and bibliographical problems in Hogg's prose work. Unpub. doct. diss., Univ. of Stirling, 1984. [Abstr. in IT (35) 1086.]

8538. MACLEOD, INNES (ed.). Statistics of Selkirkshire (1832). Glasgow: Dept of Adult and Continuing Education, 1984. pp. iv, 12 leaves. (Scottish local history texts, 3.)

8539. MASSIE, ALLAN. James Hogg and Sir Walter Scott: a study in friendship. EDH (44) 63–85.

8540. STEEL, JUDY (ed.). A shepherd's delight: a James Hogg anthology. Edinburgh: Canongate, 1985. pp. 160.

Marietta Holley

8541. WINTER, KATE H. Marietta Holley: life with 'Josiah Allen's wife'. (Bibl. 1985, 7364.) Rev. by Jack Vanderhoof in NYH (67:2) 250–1.

Oliver Wendell Holmes

8542. MARTIN, JOHN. 'This is the ship of pearl . . .'. *See* **8284.**

Thomas Hood

8543. COWAN, S. A. An allusion to Thomas Hood's *Mermaid of Margate* in T. S. Eliot's *Waste Land.* ANQ (24:5/6) 75–7.

Gerard Manley Hopkins
8544. DOWNES, DAVID ANTHONY.   Hopkins' sanctifying imagination. Lanham, MD; London: UP of America, 1985. pp. 129.

8545. FRANK, ELLEN EVE.   Literary architecture: essays toward a tradition: Walter Pater, Gerard Manley Hopkins, Marcel Proust, Henry James. (Bibl. 1982, 8021.) Rev. by Jean-Georges Ritz in EA (38:4) 1985, 448.

8546. FREDERICK, DOUGLAS.   The prose style of landscape description in the journals of Gerard Manley Hopkins. Unpub. doct. diss., Catholic Univ. of America. [Abstr. in DA (47) 1333A.]

8547. GRAHAM, CARLA J.   Counter stress: the response of the artist to Christ in the poetry of Gerard Manley Hopkins. Unpub. doct. diss., Southern Illinois Univ. at Carbondale, 1985. [Abstr. in DA (46) 3039A.]

8548. KIM, YOUNG-NAM.   G. M. Hopkins eui sieo yeongu: *The Windhover* reul jungsim euro. (Inscape and language in Hopkins's poetry: *The Windhover.*) RRCNU (31) June, 31–42.

8549. KOH, JUNGJA.   Gerard Manley Hopkins eui siron yeongu: sijeok inscape reul jungsim euro. (Gerard Manley Hopkins's poetic inscape.) JELL (32:1) 46–59.

8550. McDERMOTT, L. E.   *Pied Beauty*: Hopkins's poetic art. Crux (20:2) 18–22.

8551. MacKENZIE, NORMAN H.   Hopkins and Horace – a new discovery. ELN (23:3) 41–2.

8552. MANION, CLARE DUNSFORD.   Gerard Manley Hopkins: the poet as species. Unpub. doct. diss., Boston Univ., 1985. [Abstr. in DA (46) 3361A.]

8553. MOLLOY, SHAUN.   The ardour of Gerard Manley Hopkins. KN (33) 149–53.

8554. NORTH, JOHN S.; MOORE, MICHAEL D. (eds).   Vital candle: Victorian and modern bearings in Gerard Manley Hopkins. Waterloo, Ont.: Waterloo UP, 1984. pp. viii, 155. Rev. by David A. Kent in ESCan (12:4) 481–4; by Jerome Bump in ChrisL (34:4) 1985, 61–2.

8555. ONG, WALTER J.   Hopkins, the self and God. Toronto; London: Toronto UP. pp. viii, 180.

8555a. ORSINI, DANIEL J.   Hopkins' monastic sonnets: a revaluation. SoCR (16:2) 1984, 104–13.

8556. PHILLIPS, CATHERINE (ed.).   Gerard Manley Hopkins. Oxford: OUP, pp. xlii, 429. (Oxford authors.)

8557. RICHARDS, BERNARD.   Why are the images never appropriate all the way through? *See* **2945.**

8558. SMITH, LYLE H., JR.   Beyond the romantic sublime: Gerard Manley Hopkins. Ren (34:3) 1982, 173–84.

8559. SMITH, WILLIAM STALLINGS.   The poetry of Gerard Manley Hopkins: a continuity of the Romantic tradition. Unpub. doct. diss., Duquesne Univ., 1985. [Abstr. in DA (46) 2702A.]

George Moses Horton
8560. O'NEALE, SONDRA.   Roots of our literary culture: George Moses Horton and biblical protest. Ob (7) Summer/Winter 1981, 18–28.

W. D. Howells
8561. ARMS, GEORGE.   A sidelight on Howells. ALR (19:1) 73–7.

8562. CADY, EDWIN H. Young Howells and John Brown: episodes in a radical education. Columbus: Ohio State UP, 1985. pp. xii, 116. Rev. by Alfred Habegger in NEQ (59) 294–8; by Everett Carter in ALR (19:1) 86–8; by Don E. Weaver in OhioanaQ (29:1) 31; by Brian Morton in TLS, 1 Aug., 838.

8563. COWARD, NANCY POTTS. Mothers and sons in the fiction of Mark Twain, William Dean Howells, and Henry James. Unpub. doct. diss., Univ. of North Carolina at Chapel Hill. [Abstr. in DA (47) 1727A.]

8564. CROWLEY, JOHN W. The black heart's truth: the early career of W. D. Howells. Chapel Hill: North Carolina UP, 1985. pp. xv, 192. Rev. by Brian Morton in TLS, 1 Aug., 838; by Kenneth E. Eble in AL (58:3) 447–9; by Alfred Habegger in NEQ (59) 294–8; by Kermit Vanderbilt in ALR (19:1) 89–91.

8565. —— Winifred Howells and the economy of pain. OldN (10) 1984, 41–75.

8566. DAUGHERTY, SARAH B. Howells, Tolstoy, and the limits of realism: the case of *Annie Kilburn*. ALR (19:1) 21–41.

8567. DOOLEY, PATRICK K. Moral purpose in Howells' realism. AmS (25) Fall 1984, 75–7.

8568. EBLE, KENNETH E. Howells and Twain: being and staying friends. OldN (10) 1984, 91–100.

8569. —— Old Clemens and W. D. H.: the story of a remarkable friendship. Baton Rouge: Louisiana State UP, 1985. pp. xii, 242. Rev. by Howard G. Baetzhold in NEQ (59:4) 604–7; by Don E. Weaver in Ohioana Q (29:3) 122–3; by Carl Bude in NYTB, 5 Jan., 18.

8570. ELLER, JONATHAN ROBERT. A critical edition of W. D. Howells' *My Literary Passions*. Unpub. doct. diss., Indiana Univ., 1985. [Abstr. in DA (47) 1727A.]

8571. FREEDMAN, JONATHAN ERNST. 'The quickened consciousness': aestheticism in Howells and James. Unpub. doct. diss., Yale Univ., 1984. [Abstr. in DA (46) 2290A.]

8572. GIRGUS, SAM B. The new age of narcissism: the sexual politics of Howells' *A Modern Instance*. Mosaic (19:1) 33–44.

8573. JACKSON, FLEDA BROWN. A sermon without exegesis: the achievement of stasis in *The Rise of Silas Lapham*. JNT (16:2) 131–47.

8574. KAPLAN, AMY. 'The knowledge of the line': realism in Howells' *A Hazard of New Fortunes*. PMLA (101:1) 69–81.

8575. KHANTAVICHIAN, SANGUANSRI. The significance of the imagery of home in the work of W. D. Howells. Unpub. doct. diss., Tulane Univ., 1985. [Abstr. in DA (47) 529A.]

8576. LOVE, GLEN A. *The Landlord at Lion's Head*: Howells and 'the riddle of the painful earth'. OldN (10) 1984, 107–25.

8577. MONTANYE, ELIZABETH ANNE. Behind the convention of the open ending in Henry James and William Dean Howells. Unpub. doct. diss., Indiana Univ., 1985. [Abstr. in DA (47) 531A.]

8578. MONTEIRO, GEORGE. William Dean Howells: two notes. RALS (13:2) 1983, 215–17.

8579. MURPHY, JAMES L.   The poet's friend? A jab at the youthful William Dean Howells. OhioanaQ (29:3) 92–5.

8580. PAYNE, ALMA J.   The Ohio world of William Dean Howells – ever distant, ever near. OldN (10) 1984, 127–37.

8581. PORTE, JOEL.   Manners, morals, and mince pie: Howells' America revisited. Prospects (10) 1985, 443–60.

8582. REITT, BARBARA BLACK.   Modernization and the emerging book editor, 1865–1895: William Dean Howells as bench mark in a world of change. *See* **426.**

8583. SANJEK, DAVID LOUIS RUSSELL.   The humiliation of memory: a study of William Dean Howells' autobiographical prose. Unpub. doct. diss., Washington Univ., 1985. [Abstr. in DA (46) 3036A.]

8584. SORURY, MORTEZA.   'The riddle of the painful earth': pragmatism and morality in the novels of William Dean Howells. Unpub. doct. diss., Indiana Univ. [Abstr. in DA (47) 1730A.]

8585. WASSERSTROM, WILLIAM.   Howells and the high cost of junk. OldN (10) 1984, 77–90.

8586. WORTHAM, THOMAS (ed.).   'The real diary of a boy': Howells in Ohio, 1852–1853. OldN (10) 1984, 3–40.

Elbert Hubbard

8587. WHITE, BRUCE A.   Elbert Hubbard and *The Philistine: a Periodical of Protest* (1895–1915): the muscular journalism of an American freethinker. *See* **723.**

Thomas Hughes

8588. PICKERING, SAMUEL, JR.   The 'race of real children' and beyond in *Tom Brown's School Days*. Arnoldian (11:2) 1984, 36–46.

Fergus Hume

8589. KNIGHT, STEPHEN (introd.).   Madame Midas. London: Hogarth Press, 1985. pp. 282.

8590. —— The mystery of a hansom cab. London: Hogarth Press, 1985. pp. 224.

Leigh Hunt

8591. BLAINEY, ANN.   Immortal boy: a portrait of Leigh Hunt. Sydney: Croom Helm, 1985. (Cf. bibl. 1985, 7400.) Rev. by William St. Clair in TLS, 18 Apr., 428.

8592. CHENEY, DAVID R.   Leigh Hunt and the Dashwood annuity. BkIA (45) 50–61.

8593. DUNLAP, RHODES (introd.).   *Captain Sword and Captain Pen*: an anti-war poem first published in 1835 here reproduced in facsimile to mark the bicentennial of the author's birth. Iowa City: Friends of the Univ. of Iowa Libraries, 1984. pp. vi, 31, viii, 112, (plates) 7. Rev. by Raymond N. MacKenzie in VPR (18:4) 1985, 160–1.

8594. McCOWN, ROBERT A.   The life & times of Leigh Hunt: papers delivered at a symposium at the University of Iowa, April 13, 1984. Iowa City: Friends of the University of Iowa Libraries, 1985. pp. 108. Rev. by William St Clair in TLS, 18 Apr., 428.

8595. STAM, DAVID H.   The doors and windows of the library: Leigh Hunt and special collections. *See* **282.**

8596. WALTMAN, JOHN L.; MCDANIEL, GERALD G. Leigh Hunt: a comprehensive bibliography. New York: Garland. pp. xxv, 273. Rev. by William St Clair in TLS, 18 Apr., 428.

Richard Holt Hutton

8597. TENER, ROBERT H. The authorship of a neglected appraisal of *Clarissa. See* **6783.**

8598. WOODFIELD, MALCOLM. R. H. Hutton: critic and theologian: the writings of R. H. Hutton on Newman, Arnold, Tennyson, Wordsworth and George Eliot. Oxford: Clarendon Press. pp. x, 225.

Washington Irving

8599. AYLESWORTH, JOHN ROBERT. Specimens of taste for our maturer age: neoclassicism as realized in America in selected works of Horatio Greenough and Washington Irving. Unpub. doct. diss., Ohio Univ., 1985. [Abstr. in DA (46) 1760A–1A.]

8600. BRODWIN, STANLEY (ed.). The Old and New World Romanticism of Washington Irving. Introd. by WILLIAM L. HEDGES. New York; London: Greenwood Press. pp. vi, 195. (Prepared under the auspices of Hofstra Univ.)

8601. COHEN, DAVID S. Washington Irving's *Guests from Gibbet Island*. NJH (104:1/2) 70–83.

8602. DAIGREPONT, LLOYD M. *Rip Van Winkle* and the gnostic vision of history. CLIO (15:1) 1985, 47–59.

8603. FUNK, ELISABETH PALING. Washington Irving and his Dutch-American heritage as seen in *A History of New York*, *The Sketch Book*, *Bracebridge Hall*, and *Tales of a Traveller*. Unpub. doct. diss., Fordham Univ. [Abstr. in DA (47) 1322A.]

8604. KLEINFIELD, HERBERT L. (gen. ed.). The complete works of Washington Irving: vols 19–21, *Life of George Washington*. Ed. by ALLEN GUTTMANN and JAMES A. SAPPENFIELD. Boston, MA: G. K. Hall, 1982. 5 vols in 3. pp. xlvi, 716; xvi, 342; xviii, 552. Rev. by J. A. Leo Lemay in MLR (81:3) 725–6.

8605. PANCOST, DAVID W. How Washington Irving published *The Sketch Book* in England. *See* **418.**

8606. PAPINCHAK, ROBERT ALLAN. *The Little Man in Black*: the narrative mode of America's first short story. SSF (22) 1985, 195–201.

8607. PORTER, DANIEL R. The Knickerbockers and the historic site in New York State. *See* **7742.**

8608. RUBIN-DORSKY, JEFFREY. Washington Irving and the genesis of the fictional sketch. EAL (21:3) 1986/87, 226–47.

8609. —— Washington Irving: sketches of anxiety. AL (58:4) 499–522.

Helen Hunt Jackson

8610. FRIEND, RUTH ELLEN. Helen Hunt Jackson: a critical study. Unpub. doct. diss., Kent State Univ., 1985. [Abstr. in DA (47) 177A.]

8611. WHITAKER, ROSEMARY. Helen Hunt Jackson. Legacy (3:1) 56–62.

Harriet Jacobs

8612. BRAXTON, JOANNE M. Harriet Jacobs' *Incidents in the Life of a*

Slave Girl: the re-definition of the slave narrative genre. MassR (27:2) 379–87.

Henry James

8613.   ALLEN, ELIZABETH.   A woman's place in the novels of Henry James. New York: St Martin's Press, 1984. pp. vii, 223. Rev. by Penny Boumelha in JEGP (85:2) 290–1.

8614.   ANDRES, S. P.   Images at an exhibition: an organic theory of imagery in *Middlemarch* and *The Portrait of a Lady. See* **8199.**

8615.   ANESKO, MICHAEL.   'Friction with the market': Henry James and the profession of authorship. New York; Oxford: OUP. pp. xii, 258.

8616.   ARCHER, BARBARA CLARK.   Speech, manners, and society in Henry James. Unpub. doct. diss., Columbia Univ., 1985. [Abstr. in DA (46) 2292A.]

8617.   ARMSTRONG, PAUL B.   The phenomenology of Henry James. (Bibl. 1985, 7421.) Rev. by Donna Przybylowicz in HJR (7:1) 1985, 48–9; by Ruth Bernard Yeazell in Review (7) 1985, 49–55.

8618.   AZIZ, MAQBOOL (ed.).   The tales of Henry James: vol. 3, 1875–1879. (Bibl. 1985, 7423.) Rev. by Dieter Mehl in Archiv (222:1) 1985, 128–31.

8619.   BAMBROUGH, RENFORD.   Ounces of example: Henry James, philosopher. *In* (pp. 169–82) **46.**

8620.   BARKER, A. D.   Women and independence in the nineteenth-century novel: a study of Austen, Trollope and James. *See* **7573.**

8621.   BARTON JOHNSON, D.   A Henry James parody in *Ada*. VNRN (3) 1979, 33–4.

8622.   BAUER, DALE MARIE.   The failure of community: women and resistance in Hawthorne's, James's, and Wharton's novels. *See* **8448.**

8623.   BELL, IAN F. A. (ed.).   Henry James: fiction as history. (Bibl. 1985, 7425.) Rev. by Ross Posnock in Criticism (28:2) 222–6.

8624.   BELL, MILLICENT.   The critical James. SewR (94:1) 148–59 (review-article).

8625.   BELLRINGER, ALAN W.   The ambassadors. Boston, MA; Sydney: Allen & Unwin, 1984. (Cf. bibl. 1985, 7427.) Rev. by Roger Card in NQ (33:2) 277–8.

8626.   BENERT, ANNETTE LARSON.   Monsters, bagmen, and little old ladies: Henry James and the unmaking of America. AQ (42:4) 331–43.

8627.   BERKSON, DOROTHY.   Why does she marry Osmond? The education of Isabel Archer. ATQ (60) 53–72.

8628.   BISHOP, GEORGE JONATHAN.   When the master relents: the neglected short fictions of Henry James. Unpub. doct. diss., State Univ. of New York at Buffalo, 1985. [Abstr. in DA (46) 3031A.]

8629.   BLACKALL, JEAN FRANTZ.   Henry and Edith: *The Velvet Glove* as an 'in' joke. HJR (7:1) 1985, 21–5.

8630.   BOONE, JOSEPH A.   Modernist manoeuvrings in the marriage plot: breaking ideologies of gender and genre in James's *The Golden Bowl*. PMLA (101:3) 374–88.

8631.   BOREN, LYNDA S.   The performing self: psychodrama in Austen, James and Woolf. *See* **7575.**

8632. Brown, Clarence A. *The Sacred Fount*: a study in art and value. Ren (34:2) 1982, 67–80.

8633. Buitenhuis, Peter. Americans in European gardens. HJR (7:2/3) 124–30.

8634. Burlui, Irina. Henry James în contemporaneitate. (Henry James today.) Cronica (21:51) 8.

8635. Butler, Christopher (ed.). The ambassadors. Oxford: OUP, 1985. pp. xlvii, 450. (World's classics.)

8636. Caramello, Charles. Reading Gertrude Stein reading Henry James, or Eros is Eros is Eros is Eros. HJR (6:3) 1985, 182–203.

8637. Carton, Evan. Henry James the critic. Raritan (5:3) 118–36 (review-article).

8638. Charvet, B. R. The ideal of freedom and its contradictions in the novels and tales of Henry James. Unpub. doct. diss., Univ. of London, Birkbeck Coll., 1983.

8639. Childress, Ron. James's *Daisy Miller*. Exp (44:2) 24–5.

8640. Choi, Kyong Do. Don eui dodeukjoek euimi: *Gwibuin eui Chosang*. (Money and morality in *The Portrait of a Lady*.) JHY (8:1) 251–70.

8641. —— Money and pragmatic morality in Henry James. Unpub. doct. diss., Univ. of Nebraska–Lincoln, 1985. [Abstr. in DA (46) 3718A.]

8642. —— *The Portrait of a Lady* esuh eui don eui doducksung. (*The Portrait of a Lady*: money and morality.) JELL (32:3) 445–59.

8643. Clements, A. G. A study of 'the possible other case' in Henry James's later novels and stories. Unpub. doct. diss., Univ. of Wales, Bangor, 1985. [Abstr. in IT (36) 23.]

8644. Cohen, Paula Marantz. Freud's *Dora* and James's *Turn of the Screw*: two treatments of the female 'case'. Criticism (28:1) 73–87.

8645. Coon, Anne Christine. Widows, spinsters and lovers: the controlling female figure in the fiction of Henry James. Unpub. doct. diss., State Univ. of New York at Buffalo. [Abstr. in DA (47) 1321A.]

8646. Coroneos, C. The modern novella: James, Conrad and Lawrence. Unpub. doct. diss., Univ. of Oxford, 1984.

8647. Coward, Nancy Potts. Mothers and sons in the fiction of Mark Twain, William Dean Howells, and Henry James. *See* **8563.**

8648. Cox, James M. The memoirs of Henry James: self-interest as autobiography. SoR (22:2) 231–51.

8649. Dean, Misao. A note on *Cousin Cinderella* and *Roderick Hudson*. *See* **8191.**

8650. Dipiero, W. S. William James and Henry James. Tri-Quarterly (67) 93–107.

8651. Djwa, Sandra. *Ut pictura poesis*: the making of a lady. HJR (7:2/3) 72–85.

8652. Dorsey, Laurens, M. 'Something like the old dream of the secret life': Henry James's imaginative vision and Romantic inheritance, with special attention to the opening paragraphs of his preface to *The Spoils of Poynton*. HJR (7:1) 1985, 13–20.

8653. EAKIN, PAUL JOHN. Fictions in autobiography: studies in the art of self-invention. *See* **2973.**

8654. EDEL, LEON. Henry James: a life. (Bibl. 1985, 7446.) Rev. by Martha Banta in AL (58:4) 639–43.

8655. —— The myth of America in *The Portrait of a Lady*. HJR (7:2/3) 8–17.

8656. —— (ed.). Henry James: Letters: vol. 4, 1895–1916. (Bibl. 1985, 7448.) Rev. by Edward Wagenknecht in MLR (81:3) 729–30; by Philip Horne in CamQ (15:2) 126–41; by Tamara Follini in EC (36:1) 81–8.

8657. —— Literary criticism. (Bibl. 1985, 7451.) Rev. by Michael Wood in LRB (8:10) 12–13.

8658. —— LAURENCE, DAN H. A bibliography of Henry James. (Bibl. 1985, 7449.) Rev. by Alan W. Bellringer in YES (16) 336–8.

8659. —— POWERS, LYALL H. (eds). The complete notebooks of Henry James. Oxford: OUP. pp. 633. Rev. by Louis Auchincloss in BkW, 28 Dec., 1, 8.

8660. —— TINTNER, ADELINE. The private life of Peter Quin(t): origins of *The Turn of the Screw*. HJR (7:1) 1985, 2–4.

8661. ENGELBERG, EDWARD. The displaced cathedral in Flaubert, James, Lawrence and Kafka. Arcadia (21:3) 245–62.

8662. ESCH, DEBORAH LEE. The senses of the past: the rhetoric of temporality in Henry James. Unpub. doct. diss., Yale Univ., 1985. [Abstr. in DA (47) 1313A–14A.]

8663. EVANS, CHRISTINE ANN. The darkening medium: speech and silence in the works of Theodor Fontane, Henry James and Marcel Proust. Unpub. doct. diss., Harvard Univ., 1985. [Abstr. in DA (47) 170A.]

8664. FAULKNER, PETER (ed.). A Modernist reader: Modernism in England 1910–1930. London: Batsford. pp. 171.

8665. FISCHER, SANDRA K. Isabel Archer and the enclosed chamber: a phenomenological reading. HJR (7:2/3) 48–58.

8666. FOGEL, DANIEL MARK. Framing James' *Portrait*: an introduction. HJR (7:2/3) 1–6.

8667. FOLLINI, T. L. 'Hero and historian': the autobiographical writings of Henry James. Unpub. doct. diss., Univ. of Cambridge, 1985. [Abstr. in IT (35) 55.]

8668. FOLLINI, TAMARA (introd.). Italian hours. London: Century. pp. xix, 376. (Century travellers.)

8669. FOWLER, VICTORIA C. Henry James's American girl: the embroidery on the canvas. (Bibl. 1985, 7457.) Rev. by Judith E. Funston in CR (30:1) 121–3.

8670. FREADMAN, RICHARD. Eliot, James and the fictional self: a study in character and narration. *See* **8217.**

8671. FREEDMAN, JONATHAN ERNST. 'The quickened consciousness': aestheticism in Howells and James. *See* **8571.**

8672. FRUG, JERRY. Henry James, Lee Marvin and the Law. NYTB 16 Feb., 1.

8673. GARDINER, PATRICK. Professor Nussbaum on *The Golden Bowl*. NLH (15:1) 1983, 179–84.

8674. GARGANO, JAMES W. Imagery as action in *The Beast in the Jungle*. AQ (42:4) 351–67.

8675. GILMORE, MICHAEL T. The commodity world of *The Portrait of a Lady*. NEQ (59:1) 51–74.

8676. GOETZ, WILLIAM R. Henry James and the darkest abyss of romance. Baton Rouge: Louisiana State UP. pp. 215. Rev. by Nicola Bradbury in TLS, 26 Sept., 1078.

8677. GOLOVACHEVA, I. V. Avtorskiĭ zamysel povesti Genri Dzheĭmsa *Povrot vinta*. (Authorial design in Henry James' *The Turn of the Screw*.) VLU (1986:4) 46–50.

8678. GRIBBLE, JENNIFER. Value in *The Golden Bowl*. Critical Review (27) 1985, 50–65 (review-article).

8679. GUNTER, SUSAN ELIZABETH. The influence of Turgenev's heroines on the women of Henry James's 1880's novels. Unpub. doct. diss., Univ. of South Carolina. [Abstr. in DA (47) 1324A.]

8680. HABEGGER, ALFRED. Henry James's rewriting of Minny Temple's letters. AL (58:2) 159–80.

8681. HALPERIN, JOHN. Elizabeth Bowen and Henry James. HJR (7:1) 1985, 45–7.

8682. HORNE, F. P. A textual and critical study of the New York Edition of the novels and tales of Henry James. Unpub. doct. diss., Univ. of Cambridge, 1984. [Abstr. in IT (35) 56.]

8683. HUBNER, P. Henry James et *La Scène américaine* (1907): le drame transatlantique des cultures. *In* (pp. 79–96) **5.**

8684. HUTCHINSON, STUART. Henry James: an American as Modernist. (Bibl. 1985, 7472.) Rev. by Ruth Bernard Yeazell in Review (7) 1985, 43–7.

8685. HYNES, JOSEPH. The fading figure in the worn carpet. AQ (42:4) 321–30.

8686. IAN, MARCIA. Consecrated diplomacy and the concretion of self. HJR (7:1) 1985, 27–33.

8687. JACKSON, BRENDAN. A reluctant American: Ezra Pound's response to Whitman, Whistler and Henry James. Paideuma (11:2) 1982, 326–34.

8688. JACOBSON, MARCIA. Henry James and the mass market. (Bibl. 1985, 7474.) Rev. by William Veeder in HJR (7:1) 1985, 50–1.

8689. JONES, VIVIEN. James the critic. New York: St Martin's Press, 1985. (Cf. bibl. 1985, 7476.) Rev. by Catherine B. Cox in AL (58:2) 273–4.

8690. JURISH, ALICE EILEEN. And what is fate but love? A study of marriage and passion in the works of Henry James. Unpub. doct. diss., Univ. of California, Davis, 1985. [Abstr. in DA (47) 1324A.]

8691. KERMODE, FRANK (ed.). *The Figure in the Carpet*, and other stories. Harmondsworth: Penguin. pp. 453. (Penguin classics.)

8692. KIM, YONG-CHOL. Henry James eui *The Aspern Papers*: nouvelle soseoljeok teuksung eul jungsim euro. (Henry James's *The Aspern Papers*: a study of its nouvelle qualities.) JELL (32:4) 815–29.

8693. KIMMEY, JOHN.   James's London tales of the 1880s. HJR (8:1) 37–46.

8694. KNOX, MELISSA.   'Beltraffio': Henry James' secrecy. AI (43:3) 211–27.

8695. KOPRINCE, SUSAN.   The clue from *Manfred* in *Daisy Miller*. *See* **7778.**

8696. KROOK, DOROTHEA.   Isabel Archer figures in some early stories of Henry James. HJR (7:2/3) 131–9.

8697. LEEMING, DAVID ADAMS.   An interview with James Baldwin on Henry James. HJR (8:1) 47–56.

8698. LEVIN, HARRY (ed.).   The ambassadors. Harmondsworth: Penguin. pp. 517. (Penguin classics.)

8699. LUBIN, DAVID M.   Act of portrayal: Eakins, Sargent, James. Hew Haven, CT; London: Yale UP, 1985. pp. xiii, 189. (Yale publications in the history of art, 32.) (Cf. bibl. 1984, 7700.) Rev. by Marianna Torgovnick in AL (58:4) 643–4.

8700. LYON, J. M.   Thought and the novel: James, Conrad and Lawrence. Unpub. doct. diss., Univ. of Cambridge, 1985.

8701. McCORMACK, PEGGY.   The semiotics of economic language in James's fiction. *See* **1183.**

8702. MACNAUGHTON, W. R.   In defense of James's *The Tragic Muse*. HJR (7:1) 1985, 5–12.

8703. MAINI, DARSHAN SINGH.   The politics of Henry James. HJR (6:3) 1985, 158–71.

8704. MARGOLIS, ANNE T.   Henry James and the problem of audience: an international act. Ann Arbor, MI: UMI Research Press, 1985. pp. xvii, 249. (Cf. bibl. 1981, 8008.) Rev. by Marcia Jacobson in AL (58:4) 638–9.

8705. MARTIN, ROBERT K.   The sorrows of young Roderick: Wertherism in *Roderick Hudson*. ESCan (12:4) 387–95.

8706. MARTIN, W. R.; OBER, WARREN U.   Refurbishing James's *A Light Man*. AQ (42:4) 305–14.

8707. MASSARDIER-KENNEY, FRANCOISE.   A study of women in four realist writers: Sand, Flaubert, Eliot and James. *See* **8238.**

8708. MAUFORT, MARC.   Communication as translation of the self: Jamesian inner monologue in O'Neill's *Strange Interlude* (1927). *In* (pp. 319–28) **12.**

8709. MAYER, CHARLES W.   Drabble and James: *A Voyage to Cythera* and *In the Cage*. SSF (21) 1984, 57–63.

8710. MEDINA, ANGELA.   Edwardian couples: aesthetics and moral experience in *The Golden Bowl*. NLH (15:1) 1983, 51–71.

8711. MEHL, DIETER.   Editing a 'constantly revising author'. Archiv (222:1) 1985, 128–36 (review-article).

8712. MILLIGAN, IAN.   Some misprints in *The Awkward Age*. NQ (33:2) 177–8.

8713. MIZRUCHI, SUSAN LAURA. The power of historical knowledge: narrating the past in Hawthorne, James, and Dreiser. *See* **8485.**

8714. MONTANYE, ELIZABETH ANNE. Behind the convention of the open ending in Henry James and William Dean Howells. *See* **8577.**

8715. MOON, MICHAEL. Sexuality and visual terrorism in *The Wings of the Dove*. Criticism (28:4) 427–43.

8716. MOORE, GEOFFREY (ed.); CRICK, PATRICIA(notes). Daisy Miller. Harmondsworth: Penguin. pp.126. (Penguin classics.)

8717. MURPHY, PATRICK D. Illumination and affection in the parallel plots of *The Rich Boy* and *The Beast in the Jungle*. PLL (22:4) 406–16.

8718. NASSAR, EUGENE PAUL. Essays critical and metacritical. (Bibl. 1985, 7493.) Rev. by Ewa Thompson in ModAge (30:3/4) 326–8.

8719. NIES, FREDERICK JAMES. Revision of *The Princess Casamassima*. Unpub. doct. diss., Univ. of South Carolina, 1985. [Abstr. in DA (46) 3035A.]

8720. NUSSBAUM, MARTHA CRAVEN. Flawed crystals: James's *The Golden Bowl* and literature as moral philosophy. NLH (15:1) 1983, 25–50.

8721. —— Reply to Richard Wollheim, Patrick Gardiner, and Hilary Putnam. NLH (15:1) 1983, 201–8.

8722. OAKS, SUSAN JEAN. Henry James and nineteenth-century psychology: empirical self-knowledge in *The Bostonians*, *The Princess Casamassima*, and *The Tragic Muse*. Unpub. doct. diss., New York Univ. [Abstr. in DA (47) 1325A.]

8723. OLANDER, KAREN A. The Hawthorne–James relation: from *The Scarlet Letter* to *The Golden Bowl*. *See* **8489.**

8724. PERRY, MENAHEM; STERNBERG, MEIR. The king through ironic eyes: biblical narrative and the literary reading process. *See* **3038.**

8725. POWERS, LYALL. Visions and revisions. HJR (7:2/3) 105–16.

8726. POWERS, LYALL H. Thornton Wilder as literary cubist: an acknowledged debt to Henry James. HJR (7:1) 1985, 34–44.

8727. PUTNAM, HILARY. Taking rules seriously: a response to Martha Nussbaum. NLH (15:1) 1983, 193–200.

8728. PUTT, S. GORLEY. A preface to Henry James. Harlow: Longman. pp. 224. (Preface books.)

8729. —— (ed.). *An International Episode* and other stories. Harmondsworth: Penguin, 1985. pp. 238. (Penguin classics.) (*An International Episode, The Pension Beaurepas, Lady Barberina*.)

8730. RAMRAS-RAUCH, GILA. The protagonist in transition: studies in modern fiction. (Bibl. 1983, 8099.) Rev. by Holger A. Pausch in CanRCL (13:1) 155–7.

8731. RENNER, STANLEY. 'Why can't they tell you why?': a clarifying echo of *The Turn of the Screw*. SAF (14:2) 205–13.

8732. RICHMOND, MARION. The early critical reception of *The Portrait of a Lady*. HJR (7:2/3) 158–63.

8733. —— Henry James's *The Portrait of a Lady*: a bibliography of primary material and annotated criticism. HJR (7:2/3) 164–95.

8734. RIVKIN, JULIE.   The logic of delegation in *The Ambassadors*. PMLA (101:5) 819–31.

8735. ROWE, JOHN CARLOS.   The theoretical dimensions of Henry James. London: Methuen, 1985. pp. xv, 288. (Cf. bibl. 1985, 7504.) Rev. by Patrick Parrinder in THES (705) 22; by Ross Posnock in Criticism (28:2) 222–6.

8736. SABISTON, ELIZABETH.   Isabel Archer: the architecture of consciousness and the international theme. HJR (7:2/3) 29–47.

8737. SCHARNHORST, GARY.   Henry James and the Reverend William Rounseville Alger. HJR (8:1) 71–5.

8738. SECOR, ROBERT.   Henry James and Violet Hunt, the 'improper person of Babylon'. JML (13:1) 3–36.

8739. SEED, DAVID.   Completing the picture: deduction and creation in Henry James's *The Sacred Fount*. EA (39:3) 268–80.

8740. —— Social irony and melodrama in Henry James's *The Other House*. DUJ (79:1) 71–7.

8741. SHELSTON, ALAN (ed.).   Henry James: *Washington Square* and *The Portrait of a Lady*: a casebook. (Bibl. 1984, 7741.) Rev. by Charles Lock in NQ (33:1) 136.

8742. SNAPE, R.   The nature and implications of wealth in the writings of Henry James. Unpub. doct. diss., Univ. of Manchester, 1981.

8743. SPECTOR, CHERYL ANN.   Henry James and the light of allusion. Unpub. doct. diss., Cornell Univ. [Abstr. in DA (47) 532A.]

8744. STAFFORD, WILLIAM T.   The enigma of Serena Merle. HJR (7:2/3) 117–23.

8745. —— (ed.).   Novels 1881–1886: *Washington Square, The Portrait of a Lady, The Bostonians*. New York: Library of America; Cambridge: CUP, 1985. pp. 1249.

8746. STOWE, WILLIAM W.   Balzac, James, and the realistic novel. (Bibl. 1985, 7513.) Rev. by Ruth Bernard Yeazell in Review (7) 1985, 47–9.

8747. STOWELL, H. PETER.   Impressionism in James's late stories. RLC (58:1) 1984, 27–36.

8748. TANNER, TONY.   Henry James: the writer and his work. Amherst: Massachusetts UP, 1985. pp. x, 142. Rev. by Patrick Parrinder in THES (705) 22; by Charles Higgins in AL (58:3) 449–51; by Nina Baym in NEQ (59:1) 138–41; by George Bishop in Criticism (28:3) 352–3.

8749. TIMMS, D.   Europe and European realism in the works of Hawthorne and James, from *The Marble Faun* to *The Portrait of a Lady*. See **8505**.

8750. TINTNER, ADELINE.   Hogarth's *Marriage à la Mode* and Henry James's *A London Life*: versions of the English rococo. JPRS (17:1) 69–89.

8751. TINTNER, ADELINE R.   James discovers Jan Vermeer of Delft. HJR (8:1) 57–70.

8752. —— The museum world of Henry James. Ann Arbor, MI: UMI

Research Press. pp. xxviii, 390. Rev. by Nicola Bradbury in TLS, 26 Sept., 1078.

8753. TORGOVNIK, MARIANNA.   The visual arts, pictorialism and the novel: James, Lawrence, and Woolf. Princeton, NJ: Princeton UP, 1985. pp. xii, 267. Rev. by Nicola Bradbury in EC (36:4) 347–52.

8754. TORSNEY, CHERYL.   The political context of *The Portrait of a Lady*. HJR (7:2/3) 86–104.

8755. TURTON, L. G.   Turgenev and the context of English literature, 1850–1900. *See* **7131.**

8756. VEEDER, WILLIAM.   Image as argument: Henry James and the style of criticism. HJR (6:3) 1985, 172–81.

8757. WAGENKNECHT, EDWARD.   The tales of Henry James. New York: Ungar; London: Lorrimer, 1984. pp. vi, 266. (Literature and life.) Rev. by James W. Gargano in SSF (23:1) 128–31.

8758. WEBSTER, D.   Representing the economy and the economies of representation: readings in the fiction and criticism of Henry James. Unpub. doct. diss., Univ. of Warwick, 1984. [Abstr. in IT (35) 550.]

8759. WESTERVELT, L. A.   The individual and the form: Maggie Verver's tactics in *The Golden Bowl*. Ren (36) 1984, 146–59.

8760. WHITE, ROBERT.   Love, marriage, and divorce: the matter of sexuality in *The Portrait of a Lady*. HJR (7:2/3) 59–71.

8761. WIESENFARTH, JOSEPH.   A woman in *The Portrait of a Lady*. HJR (7:2/3) 18–28.

8762. WILLIAMS, M. A.   Being and seeing: a phenomenological study of the later novels of Henry James. Unpub. doct. diss., Univ. of Sheffield, 1983.

8763. WOLLHEIM, RICHARD.   Flawed crystals: James's *The Golden Bowl* and the plausibility of literature as moral philosophy. NLH (15:1) 1983, 185–92.

8764. YEAZELL, RUTH BERNARD.   Subject and object in Henry James. Review (7) 1985, 43–55 (review-article).

Henry James, Sr

8765. BROWN, STEVEN ELLIOTT.   The works of Henry James, Sr: a bibliography. BB (43:1) 23–9.

8766. HABEGGER, ALFRED.   The lessons of the father: Henry James, Sr, on sexual difference. HJR (8:1) 1–36.

William James

8767. BIRD, GRAHAM.   William James. London: Routledge & Kegan Paul. pp. vi, 221. (Arguments of the philosophers.)

8768. COTKIN, GEORGE.   Ralph Waldo Emerson and William James as public philosophers. *See* **8271.**

8769. DIPIERO, W. S.   William James and Henry James. *See* **8650.**

8770. HASSAN, IHAB.   Imagination and belief: Wallace Stevens and William James in our clime. WSJ (10:1) 3–8.

8771. LENTRICCHIA, FRANK.   On the ideologies of poetic modernism, 1980–1913: the example of William James. *In* (pp. 220–49) **47.**

8772. MYERS, GERALD E.   William James: his life and thought. New Haven, CT; London: Yale UP. pp. xxi, 682.

8773. SHAW, W. DAVID. The poetics of pragmatism: Robert Frost and William James. NEQ (59:2) 159–88.

8774. SUTTON, WALTER. Coherence in Pound's *Cantos* and William James's pluralistic universe. Paideuma (15:1) 7–21.

Anna Brownell Jameson

8775. YORK, LORRAINE M. 'Sublime desolation': European art and Jameson's perceptions of Canada. Mosaic (19:2) 43–56.

Richard Jefferies

8776. BLENCH, J. W. The influence of Richard Jefferies upon Henry Williamson, part 1. DUJ (79:1) 79–89.

Francis Jeffrey

8777. BERRY, N. *The Edinburgh Review* under Francis Jeffrey. *See* **562.**

8778. CHRISTIE, W. H. Francis Jeffrey, Samuel Taylor Coleridge's *Biographia Literaria* and the contemporary criticism of William Wordsworth. *See* **7900.**

8779. MORGAN, PETER. Francis Jeffrey as epistolary critic. SSL (17) 1982, 116–34.

8780. MORGAN, PETER F. (ed.). Jeffrey's criticism: a selection. (Bibl. 1985, 7539.) Rev. by J. H. Alexander in YES (16) 292–3.

John Edward Jenkins

8781. POYNTING, JEREMY. John Edward Jenkins and the Imperial conscience. JCL (21:1) 211–21.

Douglas Jerrold

8782. FRYCKSTEDT, MONICA. *Douglas Jerrold's Shilling Magazine.* *See* **600.**

Sarah Orne Jewett

8783. AMMONS, ELIZABETH. The shape of violence in Jewett's *A White Heron.* CLQ (22:1) 6–16.

8784. BUSCH, BEVERLEY GAIL. The nature and extent of the influence of Sarah Orne Jewett on Willa Sibert Cather. Unpub. doct. diss., Drew Univ. [Abstr. in DA (47) 1726A.]

8785. DONOVAN, JOSEPHINE. Nan Prince and the golden apples. CLQ (22:1) 17–27.

8786. —— Silence or capitulation: prepatriarchal 'mothers' gardens' in Jewett and Freeman. *See* **8317.**

8787. HOHMANN, MARTI. Sarah Orne Jewett to Lillian M. Munger: twenty-three letters. CLQ (22:1) 28–35.

8788. MOBLEY, MARILYN E. Rituals of flight and return: the ironic journeys of Sarah Orne Jewett's female characters. CLQ (22:1) 36–42.

8789. NAGEL, GWEN L. 'This prim corner of land where she was queen': Sarah Orne Jewett's New England gardens. CLQ (22:1) 43–62.

8790. RENZA, LOUIS A. *A White Heron* and the question of minor literature. (Bibl. 1985, 7546.) Rev. by John E. Bassett in Criticism (28:4) 474–6.

8791. SHERMAN, SARAH W. Victorians and the matriarchal mythology: a source for Mrs Todd. CLQ (22:1) 63–74.

8792. SINGLEY, CAROL J. Reaching lonely heights: Sarah Jewett, Emily Dickinson, and female initiation. *See* **8151.**

Geraldine Jewsbury

8793. FRYCKSTEDT, MONICA CORREA. Geraldine Jewsbury's *Athenaeum* reviews: a mirror of mid-Victorian attitudes to fiction. *See* **601**.

Lionel Johnson

8794. PITTOCK, MURRAY G. H. A new letter from Lionel Johnson. ELT (29:3) 309–10.

John Keats

8795. ASKE, MARTIN. Keats and Hellenism: an essay. New York: CUP, 1985. (Cf. bibl. 1985, 7550.) Rev. by Penelope Wilson in THES (706) 17.

8796. AUSTIN, ALLEN C. Toward resolving Keats' Grecian Urn Ode. Neophilologus (70:4) 615–29.

8797. BAHTI, TIMOTHY. Ambiguity and indeterminacy: the juncture. CL (38:3) 209–23.

8798. BAKER, JEFFREY. John Keats and symbolism. Brighton: Harvester Press. pp. 211.

8799. BAKER, JOHN MILTON, JR. Myth and poetic statement: the myth as function of discursive temporality in texts of Hölderlin, Keats and Wordsworth. Unpub. doct. diss., Brown Univ., 1985. [Abstr. in DA (46) 3024A.]

8800. BEN-PORAT, ZIVA. Represented reality and literary models: European Autumn on Israeli soil. PT (7:1) 29–58.

8801. BERCE, SANDA. Imagini concettiste la Shakespeare și Keats. *See* **4386**.

8802. ELLIOTT, NATHANIEL Y. Keats's *To Solitude*. Exp (44:3) 29–31.

8803. GOELLNICHT, DONALD C. The poet–physician: Keats and medical science. Pittsburgh, PA: Pittsburgh UP, 1984. pp. xii, 291. Rev. by T. J. Murray in DalR (65:4) 1985/86, 603–6; by Anthony J. Harding in ESCan (12:3) 357—60; by Robert Gittings in KSR (1) 75–7.

8804. GRIGELY, J. C. Keats and fame. Unpub. doct. diss., Univ. of Oxford, 1984.

8805. HOPKINS, BROOKE. Keats' *Ode on a Grecian Urn*: the use of the world. AI (43:2) 121–31.

8806. KIRCHHOFF, FREDERICK. Keats's nightingale, the process of writing, and the self of the poet. ELit (13:1) 29–41.

8807. KNIGHT, CHARLES A. Satire and conversation: the logic of interpretation. *See* **6057**.

8808. LAU, BETH. Keats's eagles and the creative process. RPP (10:2) 49–63.

8809. LEE, CHONG-HO. Keats si eui yeongu: sangsangryeok euroseo eui yeosung wonri. (The fabric of love and death: evolution of the feminine principle in the poems of John Keats.) Seoul: Seoul National UP. pp. 277. (Cf. bibl. 1984, 7827.)

8810. LITTLE, G. L. 'Do I wake or sleep?': Keats's *Ode to a Nightingale*. Sydney Studies in English (11) 1985/86, 40–50.

8811. O'ROURKE, JAMES L. Persona and voice in the odes of Keats. Unpub. doct. diss., Univ. of Washington, 1985. [Abstr. in DA (46) 3727A.]

8812. PÉTER, ÁGNES. The romantics and the symbolist movement: an analysis of Keats' *Ode to Psyche*. ActLitH (28:1/2) 55–63.

8813. PLUMLY, STANLEY. The abrupt edge. *See* **7697.**

8814. REED, THOMAS ANDREW. Keats and the politics of poetry. Unpub. doct. diss., Princeton Univ., 1985. [Abstr. in DA (47) 539A.]

8815. RZEPKA, CHARLES J. The self as mind: vision and identity in Wordsworth, Coleridge and Keats. *See* **7936.**

8816. SATO, TOSHIHIKO. Extemporization and elaboration: Keats's *Faery's Court* and *La Belle Dame*. Hiroshima Studies in English Language and Literature (29) 1985, 1–20.

8817. —— Keats's *To Autumn*: a new reading. Essays in English Romanticism: the tenth anniversary issue of the Japan Assn of English Romanticism (Tokyo) 1985, 544–54. (In Japanese.)

8818. —— *Nightingales*: Coleridge's challenge to a future poet and Keats's probable reply. *See* **7937.**

8819. SCHUR, OWEN MARIUS. Developments and transformations of pastoral melancholy in some poems of Keats, Tennyson, and Hardy. *See* **8432.**

8820. SHEPKO, CAROL WHITEHOUSE. 'The shore of tangled wonder': apprehensions of space in Keats's poetry. Unpub. doct. diss., City Univ. of New York. [Abstr. in DA (47) 1339A.]

8821. TAKANO, MASAO. Kansei no utage: Keats, Wordsworth, Blake. (A feast of sensibility: Keats, Wordsworth, Blake.) *See* **6282.**

8822. VANTINE, DIANE L. Imagination and myths in John Keats's poetry. Unpub. doct. diss., Univ. of Denver, 1985. [Abstr. in DA (46) 2703A.]

8823. VAN TUYL, JOANNE. The aesthetic immediacy of selected lyric poems of Keats, Fet and Verlaine. Unpub. doct. diss., Univ. of North Carolina at Chapel Hill. [Abstr. in DA (47) 1722A.]

8824. VENDLER, HELEN. The odes of John Keats. (Bibl. 1985, 7587.) Rev. by Stuart M. Sperry in MLS (16:3) 342–4; by Robert M. Ryan in MP (83:3) 319–21.

8825. WALDOFF, LEON. Keats and the silent work of imagination. Urbana; Chicago: Illinois UP, 1985. pp. xv, 215. Rev. by Barbara Schapiro in ELN (24:2) 74–6.

8826. WATKINS, DANIEL P. A reassessment of Keats' *Otho the Great*. CLIO (16:1) 49–66.

8827. WILKES, JOANNE. Keats's silent historian: the *Ode on a Grecian Urn*. Sydney Studies in English (12) 56–63.

8828. YAMAUCHI, MASAKAZU. Keats kenkyu: monogatari shi wo chushin ni. (A study of Keats: with special reference to his narrative poetry.) Osaka: Osaka Kyoiku Tosho. pp. x, 328.

John Keble

8829. GALLIMORE, EDITH ANGELA. John Keble's poetic theory and practice. Unpub. doct. diss., Univ. of Toronto, 1985. [Abstr. in DA (46) 2699A.]

8830. MOBERLY, P. J. Charlotte Mary Yonge's Anglicanism: an examination of John Keble's influence on her literary development and achievement. Unpub. doct. diss., Univ. of London, King's Coll. [Abstr. in IT (36) 21.]

Henry Kendall

8831. DINGLEY, R. J. The track to Ogygia: a note on Henry Kendall. Southerly (46:3) 352–9.

Grace King

8832. PIACENTINO, EDWARD J. The enigma of black identity in Grace King's *Joe*. SoLJ (19:1) 56–67.

8833. TAYLOR, H. Gender, race and region: a study of three postbellum women writers of Louisiana: Grace King, Ruth McEnery Stuart and Kate Chopin. *See* **7863.**

8834. WILLIAMS, CAROL ANNE. A Southern writer's retrospective: betrayal, rage, and survival in the Reconstruction fiction of Grace King. Unpub. doct. diss., Texas A&M Univ. [Abstr. in DA (47) 1328A.]

Charles Kingsley

8835. HAWLEY, JOHN C. Responses to Charles Kingsley's attack on political economy. *See* **617.**

8836. Entry cancelled.

8837. HAWLEY, JOHN CHARLES. Charles Kingsley, rhetorical fiction, and the Victorian periodical press. *See* **618.**

8838. HERTZ, ALAN. The Broad Church militant and Newman's humiliation of Charles Kingsley. *See* **621.**

8839. ISON, MARY M. Things nobody even heard of: Jessie Willcox Smith draws the water-babies. *See* **78.**

8840. MULLER, CHARLES H. Spiritual evolution and muscular theology: lessons from Kingsley's natural theology. UCTSE (16) 24–34.

8841. —— *The Water Babies* – moral lessons for children. UES (24:1) 12–17.

8842. SAVORY, JEROLD. Charles Kingsley in *Vanity Fair* and *Once a Week*. *See* **688.**

8843. UFFELMAN, LARRY; SCOTT, PATRICK. Kingsley's serial novels: 2, *The Water-Babies*. VPR (19:4) 122–31.

8844. —— —— Kingsley's serial novels: II, *The Water-Babies*. *See* **341.**

8845. VEYRIRAS, PAUL. Sainte Elisabeth de Hongrie héroïne victorienne? *See* **7135.**

8846–7. Entries cancelled.

William Kirby

8848. HATCH, RONALD. Narrative development in the Canadian historical novel. CanL (110) 79–96.

Caroline M. Kirkland

8849. ROBERTS, AUDREY. Caroline M. Kirkland: additions to the canon. BRH (86:3) 1983/85, 338–46.

Charles Lamb

8850. BEER, JOHN. Did Lamb understand Coleridge? *See* **7891.**

8851. BURNESS, EDWINA. Charles Lamb, Bernard Barton and the Quakers. *See* **7620.**

8852. McMULLIN, B. J. A case for 'columniation'. *See* **115.**

8853. MISENHEIMER, JAMES B., JR. Aesthetic universality: the nostalgia of Elia 150 years after. CLB (53) 128–41.

8854. MONSMAN, GERALD. Confessions of a prosaic dreamer: Charles Lamb's art of autobiography. Durham, NC: Duke UP, 1984. pp. viii, 165. Rev. by Fred V. Randel in JEGP (85:2) 272–5; by James A. Davies in Prose Studies (9:3) 104–5; by Stanley Jones in NQ (33:4) 557–8.

8855. SIMPSON, DAVID. What bothered Charles Lamb about *Poor Susan*? SELit (26:4) 589–612.

8856. WATSON, J. R. Lamb and food. CLB (54) 160–75.

Letitia Elizabeth Landon (L.E.L.)

8857. RENALDS, BRENDA HART. Letitia Elizabeth Landon: a literary life. Unpub. doct. diss., Univ. of South Carolina, 1985. [Abstr. in DA (46) 3043A.]

Andrew Lang

8858. COMANZO, CHRISTIAN. Mythe solaire, héros solaire. *See* **7004.**

8859. CRAWFORD, ROBERT. Pater's *Renaissance*, Andrew Lang, and anthropological romanticism. ELH (53:4) 849–79.

8860. DUFF-COOPER, ANDREW. Andrew Lang: aspects of his work in relation to current social anthropology. *See* **2381.**

Sidney Lanier

8861. GABIN, JANE S. A living minstrelsy: the poetry and music of Sidney Lanier. Macon, GA: Mercer UP, 1985. pp. viii, 181. Rev. by Anne E. Rowe in AL (58:2) 307–8; by Alan Pope in ALR (19:1) 85–6.

8862. YOUNG, THOMAS DANIEL. Lanier and Shakespeare. *In* (pp. 49–61) **51.**

8863. Entry cancelled.

Edward Lear

8864. COLLEY, ANN. Edward Lear and the Pre-Raphaelite impossibility: reflections on the Lear exhibit: the national academy of design, New York, September 10 – November 3, 1985. JPRS (7:1) 44–9.

8865. HEARN, MICHAEL PATRICK. How pleasant is it to know Mr Lear? ABC (7:1) 21–7.

8866. TIGGES, WIM. The limerick: the sonnet of Nonsense? DQR (16:3) 220–36.

Sheridan Le Fanu

8867. HALL, WAYNE. Le Fanu's house by the marketplace. Éire–Ireland (21:1) 55–72.

8868. LEFANU, WILLIAM. J. Sheridan LeFanu. *See* **7950.**

8869. LOZES, JEAN. Le mode fantastique chez Joseph Sheridan Le Fanu. Études irlandaises (9) 1984, 57–66.

8870. McCormack, W. J. (introd.). Borrhomeo the astrologer: a monkish tale. Edinburgh: Tragara Press, 1985. pp. 35.

8871. Zeender, Marie-Noelle. Miroir de l'âme irlandaise: aspects du fantastique chez Le Fanu, chez Wilde et chez Stoker. Études irlandaises (9) 1984, 67–80.

Hugh Legaré

8872. O'Brien, Michael. A character of Hugh Legaré. Knoxville: Tennessee UP, 1985. pp. xiii, 357. Rev. by George Walton Williams in AL (58:4) 633–5.

G. H. Lewes

8873. Robicheau, Joan Margaret. George Henry Lewes, George Eliot and Anthony Trollope: experiments in realism. See **8244.**

Henry Wadsworth Longfellow

8874. Tucker, Edward L. The shaping of Longfellow's *John Endicott*: a textual history including two early versions. Charlottesville: Virginia UP, 1985. pp. liii, 192. Rev. by T. D. Seymour Bassett in NEQ (59:3) 449–52.

James Russell Lowell

8875. Royot, Daniel. James Russell Lowell: un humoriste Yankee face au Sud et à l'esclavage. EA (39:1) 26–36.

Thomas Babington, Lord Macaulay

8876. Pollard, Arthur. Paternalism and liberty: Tory Southey and Whig Macaulay. *In* (pp. 181–8) **18.**

8877. Prickett, Stephen. Macaulay's vision of 1930: Wordsworth and the battle for the wilderness. EAS (39) 104–17.

8878. Shattock, Joanne. Politics and literature: Macaulay, Brougham, and the *Edinburgh Review* under Napier. See **692.**

George MacDonald

8879. Broome, F. H. The science-fantasy of George MacDonald. Unpub. doct. diss., Univ. of Edinburgh. [Abstr. in IT (36) 912.]

8880. Hein, Rolland. The harmony within: the spiritual vision of George MacDonald. (Bibl. 1984, 7904.) Rev. by David S. Robb in Ariel (17:1) 98–101.

8881. Holbrook, David (introd.). Phantastes. (Bibl. 1983, 8259.) Rev. by M. H. Parkinson in NQ (33:1) 127.

8882. King, Don. The childlike in George MacDonald and C. S. Lewis. Mythlore (12:4) 17–22, 26.

8883. Manlove, Colin. The circle of the imagination: George MacDonald's *Phantastes* and *Lilith*. SSL (17) 1982, 55–80.

8884. Phillips, Michael (ed.). The fisherman's lady. Basingstoke: Pickering. pp. 268.

8885. —— The marquis' secret. Basingstoke: Pickering. pp. 228.

8886. Robb, David S. George MacDonald's Scottish novels: three notes. NQ (33:2) 174–7.

8887. Sutherland, Elizabeth (ed.). The gold key and the green life: some fantasies and Celtic tales. London: Constable. pp. 222.

8888. Triggs, Kathy. The stars and stillness: a portrait of George MacDonald. Cambridge: Lutterworth. pp. vii, 182.

Archibald Maclaren

8889. CHRISTIAN, JOHN (introd.).   The fairy family: a series of ballads and metrical tales illustrating the fairy faith of Europe. Illus. by EDWARD BURNE JONES. London: Dalrymple, 1985. pp. lii, 195. (Limited ed. of 500 copies.)

'Fiona MacLeod' (William Sharp)

8890. SUTHERLAND, ELIZABETH (ed.).   The gold key and the green life: some fantasies and Celtic tales. *See* **8887.**

James Clarence Mangan

8891. LLOYD, DAVID.   James Clarence Mangan's oriental translations and the question of origins. CL (38:1) 20–35.

8892. SHANNON-MANGAN, ELLEN.   A letter and a poem: a new source for the life of Mangan. Éire–Ireland (21:1) 6–15.

Captain Frederick Marryat

8893. BROSSE, MONIQUE.   Vrais ou faux gémeaux: Frederick Marryat et Édouard Corbière. *In* (pp. 205–13) **1.**

James Marsh

8894. CONSER, WALTER H., JR (ed.).   James Marsh and the Germans. NEQ (59:2) 259–66.

Harriet Martineau

8895. MARKS, PATRICIA.   Harriet Martineau: *Fraser's* 'Maid of [Dis]Honour'. *See* **647.**

8896. SANDERS, VALERIE.   Reason over passion: Harriet Martineau and the Victorian novel. Brighton: Harvester Press. pp. xv, 236.

8897. WEINER, GABY.   Harriet Martineau: a reassessment (1802–1876). *In* (pp. 60–74) **20.**

C. R. Maturin

8898. FIEROBE, CLAUDE.   C. R. Maturin: nationalisme et fantastique. Études irlandaises (9) 1984, 43–55.

8899. MUIR, STUART.   The grotesque in first-person narration: psychoanalysis and narratology. *See* **7695.**

Henry Mayhew

8900. CANNING, JOHN (ed.); BRIGGS, ASA (introd.).   The illustrated Mayhew's London: the classic account of London street life and characters in the time of Charles Dickens and Queen Victoria. London: Weidenfeld & Nicolson. pp. 264.

Herman Melville

8901. BOUBEL, KAREN BRANDSER.   The conflict of good and evil: a musical and dramatic study of Britten's *Billy Budd*. Unpub. doct. diss., Univ. of Wisconsin–Madison, 1985. [Abstr. in DA (46) 2119A.]

8902. BRODHEAD, RICHARD (ed.).   New essays on *Moby Dick*. Cambridge: CUP. pp. viii, 184. (American novel.)

8903. BRYANT, JOHN.   Allegory and breakdown in *The Confidence-Man*: Melville's comedy of doubt. PQ (65:1) 113–30.

8904. —— (ed.).   A companion to Melville studies. New York; London: Greenwood Press. pp. xxvii, 906.

8905. BUSCH, FREDERICK.   Melville's mail. IowaR (16:2) 150–63.

8906. CHAI, LEON CHRISTOPHER. Melville and European Romanticism: studies on Melville's relations to major European Romantic writers. *See* **7898.**

8907. CHANG, YOUNG-HEE. Journeys between the real and the ideal. *See* **8269.**

8908. CLAREY, JOELLYN. D. H. Lawrence's *Moby-Dick*: a textual note. *See* **302.**

8909. COFFLER, GAIL H. (comp.). Melville's classical allusions: a comprehensive index and glossary. Westport, CT; London: Greenwood Press, 1985. pp. xiv, 153.

8910. COWAN, BAINARD. Exiled waters: *Moby-Dick* and the crisis of allegory. (Bibl. 1985, 7654.) Rev. by Harold Beaver in YES (16) 332–3.

8911. DE GRAZIA, EMILIO. A coming indistinctly into view: a familiar review of *Moby-Dick*. *In* (pp. 133–42) **28.**

8912. DE PAUL, STEPHEN. The documentary fiction of Melville's *Omoo*: the crossed grammars of acculturation. Criticism (28:1) 51–72.

8913. DIETRICHSON, JAN W. Herman Melville in literary history. *In* (pp. 157–73) **18.**

8914. DILLINGHAM, WILLIAM B. Melville's later novels. Athens: Georgia UP. pp. xii, 430. Rev. by R. Bruce Bickley, Jr, in AL (58:4) 628–30.

8915. DUBAN, JAMES. 'This "all" feeling': Melville, Norton, and Schleiermacher. ELN (23:4) 38–42.

8916. DUNPHY, MARK RAYMOND. Double consciousness in Melville's middle novels. Unpub. doct. diss., Univ. of Tulsa, 1985. [Abstr. in DA (46) 2290A.]

8917. DURER, CHRISTOPHER S. Melville's 'synthesizing' narrator, *Mardi*, Fichte, and the 'Frühromantiker'. RPP (10:1) 45–60.

8918. FISCHER, JOHN DAVID. Inside narratives: Melville and the crisis of originality. Unpub. doct. diss., Princeton Univ., 1985. [Abstr. in DA (46) 3033A.]

8919. GALLAGHER, SUSAN VANZANTEN. Jack Blunt and his dream book. AL (58:4) 614–19.

8920. HELLENBRAND, HAROLD. Behind closed doors: Ishmael's dreams and hypnagogic trances in *Moby Dick*. ATQ (61) 47–56.

8921. HILBERT, BETSY. The truth of the thing: nonfiction in *Moby-Dick*. CE (48:8) 824–31.

8922. HORSLEY-MEACHAM, GLORIA. Melville's dark satyr unmasked. ELN (23:3) 43–7.

8923. IM, HEON-KEE. Melville eui juyo soseol yeongu: juyo inmuldeul eui sungsuhjeok jomyeong. (A study of Melville's major novels: with biblical interpretations of heroes.) Unpub. doct. diss., Chungnam National Univ., Korea.

8924. JAWORSKI, PHILIPPE. Melville, le désert et l'empire. Paris: Presses de l'École Normale Supérieure. pp. 366.

8925. KARDUX, JOHANNA CORNELIA. The improper self: identity and writing in Melville's early work. Unpub. doct. diss., Cornell Univ., 1985. [Abstr. in DA (46) 2692A.]

8926. LAMB, ROBERT PAUL. The place of *The Confidence-Man* in Melville's career. SoR (22:3) 489–505.

8927. LEONARD, JAMES S. Melville's Ahab as Marlovian hero. *See* **4124.**

8928. MacLAINE, ALLAN H. Melville's 'sequel' to *Bartleby the Scrivener* and Dickens' *Story of the Bagman's Uncle* in *Pickwick Papers*: an unnoticed link. *See* **8070.**

8929. MARTIN, ROBERT K. Hero, captain, and stranger: male friendship, social critique, and literary form in the sea novels of Herman Melville. Chapel Hill: North Carolina UP. pp. xvi, 139. Rev. by John W. Crowley in NEQ (59:3) 441–4.

8930. —— Saving Captain Vere: *Billy Budd* from Melville's novella to Britten's opera. SSF (23:1) 49–56.

8931. MAUFORT, MARC. Visions of the American experience: the O'Neill–Melville connection. Unpub. doct. diss., Université Libre de Bruxelles.

8932. O'BRIEN, ELLEN J. That 'insular Tahiti': Melville's truth-seeker and the sea. *In* (pp. 193–201) **28.**

8933. PARK, YOUNG-UI. Herman Melville eui yeongu: dongyangjeok gwanjeom eseo. (A study of Herman Melville from the oriental point of view.) Seoul: Hansin Munwhasa, pp. 123. (Doct. diss., Jeonbuk National Univ., Korea.)

8934. —— Herman Melville yeongu: dongyangjeok gwanjeom eseo. (The oriental interpretation of Herman Melville.) Unpub. doct. diss., Chungnam National Univ, Korea.

8935. PATTON, MARILYN. The hidden artist and the art of hiding in *Moby Dick*. ATQ (59) 19–34.

8936. PERCY, WALKER. Herman Melville. NCrit (2:3) 1983/84, 39–42.

8937. POWELL, WILLIAM GREGORY. The plurality of the whale: Aristotelean, deconstruction, and reader response readings of *Moby-Dick*. Unpub. doct. diss., Florida State Univ., 1985. [Abstr. in DA (46) 2694A.]

8938. PRIBEK, THOMAS. Melville's copyists: the 'Bar-tenders' of Wall Street. PLL (22:2) 176–86.

8939. —— The 'safe' man of Wall Street: characterizing Melville's lawyer. SSF (23:2) 191–5.

8940. RIDDLE, MARY-MADELEINE GINA. Herman Melville's *Piazza Tales*: a prophetic vision. Gothenburg: Acta Universitatis Gothoburgensis, 1985. pp. 166. (Gothenburg studies in English, 55.) Rev. by Erik Kielland-Lund in Edda (86) 381–2. (Cf. bibl. 1984, 7964.)

8941. ROGIN, MICHAEL PAUL. Subversive genealogy: the politics and art of Herman Melville. (Bibl. 1985, 7700.) Rev. by John Franzosa in Criticism (28:1) 112–14.

8942. RORIPAUGH, ROBERT. Melville's *Typee* and frontier travel literature of the 1830's and 1840's. SDR (19:4) 1982, 46–64.

8943. ROSENBLUM, JOSEPH. A cock fight between Melville and Thoreau. SSF (23:2) 159–67.

8944. SARBU, ALADÁR.   Melville, our contemporary. ActLitH (27:3/4) 1985, 295–306.

8945. SCORZA, THOMAS J.   In the time before steamships: *Billy Budd*, the limits of politics, and modernity. (Bibl. 1981, 8232.) Rev. by Will Morrisey in IJPP (8:2/3) 1980, 223–34.

8946. —— Tragedy in the state of nature: Melville's *Typee*. IJPP (8:1) 1979, 103–20.

8947. SIEDLECKI, PETER A.   Herman Melville and his untrustworthy metaphor. *In* (pp. 170–9) **17.**

8948. SLOUKA, MARK Z.   Herman Melville's journey to *The Piazza*. ATQ (61) 3–14.

8949. SMITH, JOHANNA MARY.   Domestic passion: sister-brother incest in four nineteenth-century novels. *See* **7606.**

8950. STEIN, SUZANNE HELENE.   The pusher and the sufferer: an unsentimental reading of *Moby-Dick*. Unpub. doct. diss., Rutgers Univ. [Abstr. in DA (47) 183A.]

8951. SUNDQUIST, ERIC J.   *Benito Cereno* and New World slavery. *In* (pp. 93–122) **47.**

8952. TOLCHIN, NEAL.   Primal ground: mourning, gender and creativity in the art of Herman Melville. Unpub. doct. diss., Rutgers Univ. [Abstr. in DA (47) 2163A.]

8953. UJHÁZY, MÁRIA.   Herman Melville's world of whaling. (Bibl. 1984, 7979.) Rev. by Harold Beaver in YES (16) 331–2.

8954. VON BRENTANO, ALISA R.   Marlowe and Melville. *See* **4135.**

8955. WEGENER, LARRY EDWARD (ed.).   A concordance to Herman Melville's *Pierre, or, The Ambiguities*: in two volumes. New York; London: Garland, 1985. pp. xx, 1561. (Garland reference library of the humanities, 592.)

8956. WILLIAMS, MARK.   'Design of darkness': the religious and political heresies of Captain Ahab and Johann Voss. Australasian Journal of American Studies (Melbourne) (5:1) 24–40.

8957. WIXON, RICHARD L.   Herman Melville: critic of America and harbinger of ecological crisis. *In* (pp. 143–53) **28.**

8958. YAGI, TOSHIO.   *Hakugei* kaitai. (Deconstructing *Moby-Dick*.) Tokyo: Kenkyusha Press. pp. x, 162.

George Meredith

8959. BEER, GILLIAN; HARRIS, MARGARET (eds).   The notebooks of George Meredith. Salzburg: Institut für Anglistik und Amerikanistik, Salzburg Univ., 1983. pp. xiii, 216. (Salzburg studies in English literature: Romantic reassessment, 73:2.) Rev. by P. D. Edwards in AUMLA (65) 103–5.

8960. DEIS, ELIZABETH JANE.   Marriage as aesthetic, social, and philosophical ideal in the novels of George Meredith: a developmental study. Unpub. doct. diss., Duke Univ., 1985. [Abstr. in DA (47) 1332A.]

8961. HARRIS, MARGARET.   The topicality of *Beauchamp's Career*. YREAL (4) 135–94.

8962. MCMASTER, GRAHAM.   *Harry Richmond*: Meredith's unwritten attack on Victorian legitimacy. PoetT (24) 64–85.

8963. OGUNSANWO, OLATUBOSUN.   George Meredith and F. Scott Fitzgerald: literary affinities, narrative indirectness and realism. *In* (pp. 245–8) **19.**

8964. RALIAN, ANTOANETA (ed. and trans.).   Unul dintre cuceritorii nostri. (One of our conquerors.) Bucharest: Minerva. 2 vols: pp. xlx, 254; 319.

8965. SHAHEEN, MOHAMMAD.   Meredith to Evans and Thomson. *See* **430.**

8966. WILLIAMS, CAROLYN.   Unbroken patternes: gender, culture, and voice in *The Egoist.* BIS (13) 1985, 45–70.

John Stuart Mill

8967. ARSCOTT, A. J.   Mill's alleged advocacy of centralization. MillNL (21:2) 2–5.

8968. BERGER, FRED R.   Mill's concept of happiness. IJPP (7:3) 1978, 95–117.

8969. GHOSH, TAPAN KUMAR.   The culture of the feeling: a study of Wordsworth and Mill. Jadavpur University Essays and Studies (Calcutta) (4) 1984, 106–15.

8970. GLASSMAN, PETER.   J. S. Mill: the evolution of a genius. Gainesville: Florida UP, 1985. pp. 195.

8971. HIMMELFARB, GERTRUDE (ed.).   On liberty. Harmondsworth: Penguin, 1982. pp. 186. (Penguin classics.)

8972. LONOFF, SUE.   Cultivated feminism: Mill and *The Subjection of Women.* PQ (65:1) 79–102.

8973. QUINCY, KEITH.   Samuel Bailey and Mill's defence of freedom of discussion. MillNL (21:1) 4–18.

8974. REES, JOHN.   John Stuart Mill's *On Liberty*: constructed from published and unpublished sources by G. L. WILLIAMS. Oxford: Clarendon, 1985. pp. xi, 210. Rev. by C. L. Ten in MillNL (21:2) 17–21.

8975. ROBSON, ANN P.; ROBSON, JOHN M. (eds).   Newspaper writings. Toronto: Toronto UP; London: Routledge & Kegan Paul. 4 vols. pp. cxvii, 1526. (Collected works of John Stuart Mill, 22–5.)

8976. ROBSON, JOHN M. (ed.); CAIRNS, JOHN C. (introd.).   Essays on French history and historians. Toronto: Toronto UP; London: Routledge & Kegan Paul, 1985. pp. cxix, 517. (Collected works of John Stuart Mill, 20.) Rev. by Chris Jones in Prose Studies (9:3) 105–7.

8977. —— STILLINGER, JACK (eds).   *Autobiography*, and literary essays. (Bibl. 1984, 8002.) Rev. by Neville Masterman in MLR (81:3) 726–7.

8978. SCHRAM, GLENN N.   John Stuart Mill and pornography. Cresset (49:5) 24–5.

8979. SEMMEL, BERNARD.   John Stuart Mill and the pursuit of virtue. (Bibl. 1985, 7730.) Rev. by Robert W. Hoag in JHP (24:3) 421–3.

8980. STARZYK, LAWRENCE J.   'The Worthies began a revolution': Browning, Mill, Arnold and the poetics of self-acquaintance. *See* **7565.**

Richard Monckton Milnes

8981. CAMPBELL, IAN.   More conversations with Carlyle: the Monckton Milnes diaries, 2. *See* **7807.**

Mary Russell Mitford

8982. MOORE, J. The making of Mary Russell Mitford's *Our Village*. Unpub. doct. diss., Univ. of Liverpool, 1984. [Abstr. in IT (35) 49–50.]

Susanna Moodie

8983. BALLSTADT, CARL. Secure in conscious worth: Susanna Moodie and the Rebellion of 1837. CanP (18) 88–98.

8984. —— HOPKINS, ELIZABETH; PETERMAN, MICHAEL (eds). Susanna Moodie: letters of a lifetime. Toronto: Toronto UP, 1985. pp. x, 390. Rev. by George Woodcock in CanL (109) 101–3; by Clara Thomas in QQ (93:3) 660–1.

Lady Morgan (Sydney Owenson)

8985. BROPHY, BRIGID (introd.). The wild Irish girl. London: Pandora. pp. xi, 255. (Mothers of the novel.)

8985a. RAMADAN, S. M. Y. Sydney Owenson (Lady Morgan): a study of her life and works. Unpub. doct. diss., Trinity Coll. Dublin, 1983/84.

William Morris

8986. BANHAM, JOANNA; HARRIS, JENNIFER (eds). William Morris and the Middle Ages: a collection of essays: together with a catalogue of works exhibited at the Whitworth Art Gallery, 28 September– 8 December 1984. (Bibl. 1985, 7743, where first scholar's forename incorrect.) Rev. by Joseph R. Dunlap in ABC (7:2) 40–5.

8987. BOOS, FLORENCE S. Sexual polarities in *The Defence of Guenevere*. BIS (13) 1985, 181–200.

8988. CRANNY-FRANCIS, A. William Morris' *News from Nowhere*: the propaganda of desire. Unpub. doct. diss., Univ. of East Anglia, 1983.

8989. FAULKNER, PETER (ed.). Jane Morris to Wilfrid Scawen Blunt: the letters of Jane Morris to Wilfrid Scawen Blunt together with extracts from Blunt's diaries. *See* **7625.**

8990. HUNT, STEPHEN. An Icelandic source for an incident in William Morris's *Glittering Plain*. NQ (33:2) 172.

8991. KELVIN, NORMAN (ed.). The collected letters of William Morris: vol. 1, 1848–80. (Bibl. 1985, 7748.) Rev. by Frederick Kirchhoff in MLS (16:3) 358–63; by Joan Rees in MLR (81:1) 182–4.

8992. MARSH, JAN. Jane and May Morris: a biographical story 1839–1938. London: Pandora. pp. 330.

8993. MILLER, SUSAN FISHER. Hopes and fears for the tower: William Morris's spirit at Yeats's Ballylee. Éire–Ireland (21:2) 43–56.

8994. SILVER, CAROLE. The romance of William Morris. Athens: Ohio UP, 1982. pp. xviii, 233. Rev. by Frederick Kirchhoff in MLS (16:3) 358–63.

8995. SKOBLOW, JEFFREY DAVID. Forgetting and remembering: William Morris and *The Earthly Paradise*. Unpub. doct. diss., Johns Hopkins Univ. [Abstr. in DA (46) 3363A.]

8996. STERNBERG, ELLEN W. Verbal and visual seduction in *The Defence of Guenevere*. JPRS (6:2) 45–52.

8997. TIMO, H. A. A church without God: a study of the prose romances and unfinished novel of William Morris. Unpub. doct. diss., Univ. of Nottingham, 1980.

'Petroleum V. Nasby' (D. R. Locke)

8998. GROSH, RONALD M.   Civil War politics in the novels of David Ross Locke. Midamerica (13) 19–30.

Alice Dunbar Nelson

8999. HULL, GLORIA T. (ed.).   Give us each day: the diary of Alice Dunbar Nelson. New York: Norton, 1984. pp. 480. Rev. by Michelle Cliff in BSch (16:5) 1985, 56.

John Henry Newman

9000. GRIFFIN, JOHN R.   Newman and William Palmer: a note on the *Apologia*. ELN (24:2) 33–6.

9001. HERTZ, ALAN.   The Broad Church militant and Newman's humiliation of Charles Kingsley. *See* **621.**

9002. HILL, ALAN G. (ed.).   Loss and gain: the story of a convert. Oxford: OUP. pp. xxv, 317.

9003. JARRATT, SUSAN CAROLE FUNDERBURGH.   A Victorian sophistic: the rhetoric of knowledge in Darwin, Newman, and Pater. *See* **7995.**

9004. SCHMIDT, PAUL HENRY.   Newman and post-modernism: a study of Newman's prose non-fiction and its relation to poststructuralist literary theory. Unpub. doct. diss., Univ. of Minnesota, 1985. [Abstr. in DA (46) 3028A.]

9005. TRACEY, GERARD (ed.).   The letters and diaries of John Henry Newman: vol. 6, The *via media* and Froude's *Remains*, January 1837 to December 1838. (Bibl. 1985, 7762.) Rev. by Clyde de L. Ryals in MLR (81:1) 180–1.

9006. WAKEFIELD, GORDON S.   Kindly light: meditations on Newman's poem. London: Epworth, 1984. pp. xiii, 72.

9007. WINTERTON, GREGORY (introd.).   The dream of Gerontius. London: Mowbray. pp. xx, 55. (Mowbray's popular Christian paperbacks.)

Mary Gove Nichols

9008. MYERSON, JOEL.   Mary Gove Nichols' *Mary Lydon*: a forgotten reform novel. AL (58:4) 523–39.

William Douglas O'Connor

9009. FREEDMAN, FLORENCE BERNSTEIN.   William Douglas O'Connor: Walt Whitman's chosen knight. Athens: Ohio UP, 1985. pp. xiv, 368. Rev. by Kenneth M. Price in AL (58:3) 444–5; by Roger Asselineau in WWQR (3:4) 39–40.

Margaret Oliphant

9010. CLARKE, J. S.   The novels of Margaret Oliphant. Unpub. doct. diss., Univ. of Leicester, 1983.

9011. FITZGERALD, PENELOPE (introd.).   The rector; The doctor's family. London: Virago Press. pp. xvi, 192. (Chronicles of Carlingford.) (Virago modern classics, 227.)

9012. —— Salem Chapel. London: Virago Press. pp. xiii, 461. (Chronicles of Carlingford.) (Virago modern classics, 228.)

9013. GRAY, MARGARET K. (ed.). Selected short stories of the supernatural. Edinburgh: Scottish Academic Press, 1985. pp. xiv, 256. (Assn for Scottish Literary Studies, 15.)

9014. HAYTHORNTHWAITE, J. A. The proceeds of literature: a study of some aspects of the publication and reception of the writings of Mrs Margaret Oliphant. Unpub. doct. diss., Univ. of Strathclyde, 1983.

9015. RUBIK, MARGARETE. The return of the convict in Mrs Oliphant's *The Son of his Father*. WBEP (80) 201–15.

9016. WILLIAMS, MERRYN. Margaret Oliphant: a critical biography. Basingstoke: Macmillan. pp. 176. Rev. by Rosemary Dinnage in TLS, 26 Dec., 1443.

9017. —— (ed.). *The Doctor's Family* and other stories. Oxford: OUP. pp. 224. (World's classics.)

Amelia Opie

9018. WINTERSTON, JEANETTE (introd.). Adeline Mowbray, or, The mother and daughter. London: Pandora. pp. viii, 275. (Mothers of the novel.)

'Oliver Optic' (William Taylor Adams)

9019. JONES, DOLORES BLYTHE. An 'Oliver Optic' checklist: an annotated catalog index to the series, nonseries stories and magazine publications of William Taylor Adams. Westport, CT; London: Greenwood Press, 1985. pp. xvii, 181. (Bibliographies and indexes in American literature, 4.)

9020. Entry cancelled.

Thomas Nelson Page

9021. BARGAINNIER, EARL F. *Red Rock*: a reappraisal. SoQ (22:2) 1984, 44–53.

Francis Turner Palgrave

9022. NELSON, MEGAN JANE. Francis Turner Palgrave and *The Golden Treasury*. Unpub. doct. diss., Univ. of British Columbia, 1985. [Abstr. in DA (47) 1336A.]

9023. PEARCE, BRIAN LOUIS (ed.). Palgrave: selected poems. London: Brentham, 1985. pp. vi, 64.

William Gifford Palgrave

9024. TIDRICK, KATHRYN. Heart-beguiling Araby. *See* **7626.**

Francis Parkman

9025. COUPER, RICHARD W. Francis who? Thoughts on Parkman and New York State. NYH (64) 1983, 280–95.

9026. TOWNSEND, KIM. Francis Parkman and the male tradition. AmQ (38:1) 97–113.

Walter Pater

9027. BLOCK, ED, JR. Walter Pater, Arthur Symons, W. B. Yeats, and the fortunes of the literary portrait. SELit (26:4) 759–76.

9028. BUCKLER, WILLIAM E. (ed.). Walter Pater: three major texts. New York; London: New York UP. pp. viii, 550. (*Renaissance, Appreciations, Imaginary Portraits.*)

9029. CRAWFORD, ROBERT. Pater's *Renaissance*, Andrew Lang, and anthropological romanticism. *See* **8859.**

9030. ITO, ISAO. Pater: bi no tankyu. (Pater: in quest of beauty.) Tokyo: Nagata Press. pp. 246.

9031. JARRATT, SUSAN CAROLE FUNDERBURGH. A Victorian sophistic: the rhetoric of knowledge in Darwin, Newman, and Pater. *See* **7995.**

9032. KEEFE, ROBERT. *Apollo in Picardy*: Pater's monk and Ruskin's madness. ELT (29:4) 361–70.

9033. KIJINSKI, JOHN L. Values, assumptions, and persuasion in the literary criticism of Arnold, Pater, and Wilde. *See* **7559.**

9034. KUDO, YOSHIMI. Walter Pater kenkyu. (A study of Walter Pater.) Tokyo: Nan'undo. pp. 374. (Revised ed.)

9035. LOSEY, JAY B. Epiphany in Pater's portraits. ELT (29:3) 297–308.

9036. PHILLIPS, ADAM (ed.). The Renaissance: studies in art and poetry. Oxford: OUP. pp. 192. (World's classics.)

9037. READ, R. The evocative genre of art criticism: a study of descriptive prose in the works of Hazlitt, Ruskin, Pater and Adrian Stokes. *See* **8521.**

9038. SCOTT, NATHAN A., JR. Pater's imperative – to dwell poetically. NLH (15:1) 1983, 93–118.

9039. —— The poetics of belief: studies in Coleridge, Arnold, Pater, Santayana, Stevens, and Heidegger. *See* **7563.**

9040. SMALL, IAN. Annotating 'hard' nineteenth century novels. *See* **7342.**

9041. —— (ed.). Marius the Epicurean: his sensations and ideas. Oxford: OUP. pp. xxx, 292. (World's classics.)

9042. UHLIG, CLAUS. Literature, philosophy, religion: on conceptual architecture in some Victorian writers. *See* **7569.**

Elizabeth Palmer Peabody

9043. RONDA, BRUCE A. (ed.). Letters of Elizabeth Palmer Peabody: American renaissance woman. (Bibl. 1985, 7782.) Rev. by Robert N. Hudspeth in CR (30:1) 114–16.

Thomas Love Peacock

9044. BACHINGER, K. E. How Sherwood Forest became the valley of many-colored grass: Peacock's *Maid Marian* as a source for Poe's *Eleonora*. ANQ (24:5/6) 72–5.

9045. BACHINGER, KATRINA E. Poe's Folio Club: a pun on Peacock's Folliott. NQ (31) 1984, 66.

9046. BURNS, BRYAN. The classicism of Peacock's *Gryll Grange*. KSMB (36) 1985, 89–101.

9047. BUTLER, MARILYN. Druids, bards and twice-born Bacchus: Peacock's engagement with primitive mythology. KSMB (36) 1985, 57–76.

9048. DAWSON, CARL. Peacock's comedy: a retrospective glance. KSMB (36) 1985, 102–13.

9049. JOUKOVSKY, NICHOLAS A. Peacock before *Headlong Hall*: a new look at his early years. KSMB (36) 1985, 1–40.

9050. MADDEN, LIONEL. 'Terrestrial paradise': the Welsh dimension in Peacock's life and work. KSMB (36) 1985, 41–56.

9051. MILLS, HOWARD. The dirty boots of the bourgeoisie: Peacock on music. KSMB (36) 1985, 77–88.

9052. MULVIHILL, JAMES. A Tookean presence in Peacock's *Melincourt*. EngS (67:3) 216–20.

9053. SIMPSON, ROGER. A source for Peacock's *The Misfortunes of Elphin*. See **6788**.

Elizabeth Stuart Phelps ('H. Trusta')

9054. FETTERLEY, JUDITH. 'Checkmate': Elizabeth Stuart Phelps's *The Silent Partner*. Legacy (3:2) 17–29.

Sir Arthur Wing Pinero

9055. ROWELL, GEORGE (ed.). Plays. Cambridge: CUP. pp. 303. (British and American playwrights 1750–1920.) (*The Schoolmistress, The Second Mrs Tanqueray, Trelawny of the 'Wells', The Thunderbolt*.)

James Robinson Planché

9056. ROY, DONALD (ed.). Play by James Robinson Planché. Cambridge: CUP. pp. xi, 241. (British and American playwrights 1750–1920.)

Edgar Allan Poe

9057. AHN, IMSOO. Edgar Allan Poe eui jakpum e natanan double image. (Poe's double image.) JELL (32:1) 23–43. (Refers to *William Wilson, The Fall of the House of Usher*, and *The Cask of Amontillado*.)

9058. BACHINGER, K. E. How Sherwood Forest became the valley of many-colored grass: Peacock's *Maid Marian* as a source for Poe's *Eleonora*. See **9044**.

9059. BACHINGER, KATRINA E. Poe's Folio Club: a pun on Peacock's Folliott. See **9045**.

9060. BOHM, ARND. A German source for Edgar Allan Poe's *The Raven*. CLS (23:4) 310–23.

9061. CARTON, EVAN. The rhetoric of American romance: dialectic and identity in Emerson, Dickinson, Poe, and Hawthorne. See **8109**.

9062. COTRĂU, LIVIU. The fantastic fiction of Edgar Allan Poe. Unpub. doct. diss., Bucharest Univ., 1985.

9063. —— Proza fantastică a lui Edgar Allan Poe. (The fantastic fiction of Edgar Allan Poe.) Bucharest: Bucharest Univ. pp. 25. (Summary of doct. diss.)

9064. DE GRAZIA, EMILIO. Poe's other beautiful woman. *In* (pp. 176–84) **28**.

9065. ECO, UMBERTO; SEBEOK, THOMAS A. (eds). The sign of three: Dupin, Holmes, Peirce. See **8171**.

9066. FISHER, BENJAMIN FRANKLIN, IV. The flights of a good man's mind: gothic fantasy in Poe's *The Assignation*. MLS (16:3) 27–34.

9067. FUKUCHI, CURTIS KEN. Poe's 'plot of God'. Unpub. doct. diss., Harvard Univ. [Abstr. in DA (47) 2156A.]

9068. GOLDHURST, WILLIAM.   Self-reflective fiction by Poe: three tales. MLS (16:3) 4–14.

9069. HOWES, CRAIG.   *The Fall of the House of Usher* and elegiac romance. SoLJ (19:1) 68–78.

9070. ITO, SHOKO.   Arnheim eno michi: Edgar Allan Poe no bungaku. (The road to Arnheim: the literature of Edgar Allan Poe.) Tokyo: Kirihara. pp. viii. 262.

9071. JHANG, GAP-SANG.   E. A. Poe eui danpeon soseolgwan: iron gwa shiljae. (Poe's short stories: theory and praxis.) Unpub. doct. diss., Kyungpook National Univ. (Korea).

9072. KIRKHAM, E. BRUCE.   Poe's Amontillado, one more time. ANQ (24:9/10) 144–5.

9073. KNAPP, BETTINA L.   Edgar Allan Poe. New York: Ungar, 1984. pp. 233. Rev. by Benjamin Franklin Fisher, IV, in AL (58:1) 141–2.

9074. LEVINE, SUSAN; LEVINE, STUART.   'How-to' satire: Cervantes, Marryat, Poe. MLS (16:3) 15–26.

9075. LJUNGQUIST, KENT.   The grand and the fair: Poe's landscape aesthetics and pictorial techniques. Potomac, MD: Scripta Humanistica, 1984. pp. x, 216. Rev. by Patrick F. Quinn in AL (58:2) 286–8.

9076. MATHESON, T. J.   Poe's *The Black Cat* as a critique of temperance literature. Mosaic (19:3) 69–81.

9077. MONTEIRO, GEORGE.   The poem as felony. AR (44:2) 209–19.

9078. MONTGOMERY, MARION.   Why Poe drank liquor. (Bibl. 1985, 7803.) Rev. by T. H. Pickett in SoHR (20:2) 201–3.

9079. MUIR, STUART.   The grotesque in first-person narration: psychoanalysis and narratology. *See* **7695.**

9080. ODIN, JAISHREE.   Suggestiveness – Poe's writings from the perspective of Indian *Rasa* theory. CLS (23:4) 297–309.

9081. PITCHER, EDWARD W. R.   'To die laughing': Poe's allusion to Sir Thomas More in *The Assignation. See* **4155.**

9082. POLLIN, BURTON R.   Traces in *Annabel Lee* of Allan Cunningham's poem. *See* **7987.**

9083. POUNDS, WAYNE.   Paul Bowles and Edgar Allan Poe: the disintegration of the personality. TCL (32:3/4) 424–39.

9084. RICHARD, CLAUDE.   Destin, design, dasein: Lacan, Derrida and *The Purloined Letter.* IowaR (12:4) 1981, 1–11.

9085. ROBBINS, J. ALBERT.   A new manuscript of Poe's *For Annie. See* **329.**

9086. ROBINSON, DOUGLAS.   Trapped in the text: *The Pit and the Pendulum.* Journal of the Short Story in English (7) 63–75.

9087. SAUNDERS, JUDITH P.   'If this I saw': optic dilemmas in Poe's writings. ATQ (62) 63–72.

9088. SKAGGS, MERRILL MAGUIRE.   Poe's longing for a bi-cameral mind. SoQ (19:2) 1981, 54–64.

9089. SOWE, GORA.   From Plato to Coleridge: the influence of the Platonic tradition on Poe's critical essays, tales, and poems. Unpub. doct. diss., Oklahoma State Univ., 1985. [Abstr. in DA (47) 902A.]

9090. UBA, GEORGE R.   Malady and motive: medical history and *The Fall of the House of Usher*. SAQ (85:1) 10–22.

9091. UCHIDA, ICHIGORO.   Edgar Allan Poe to seikimatu no illustration. *See* **83.**

9092. WALKER, I. M. (ed.).   Edgar Allan Poe: the critical heritage. London: Routledge & Kegan Paul. pp. xvii, 419.

9093. WILLIAMS, MICHAEL JOHN STUART.   'The charnel character to the figure': language and interpretation in the fiction of Edgar Allan Poe. Unpub. doct. diss., Washington State Univ., 1985. [Abstr. in DA (46) 3354A.]

9094. ZANGER, JULES.   Poe's endless voyage: *The Narrative of Arthur Gordon Pym*. PLL (22:3) 276–83.

Charles Reade

9095. ELLIOTT, J. M.   A comparative study of the dramatic and narrative versions of Charles Reade's *It Is Never Too Late to Mend*. Unpub. doct. diss., Univ. of London, Royal Holloway Coll., 1984.

9096. HAMMET, MICHAEL (ed.).   Plays by Charles Reade. Cambridge: CUP. pp. xi, 170. (British and American playwrights 1750–1920.) *(Masks and Faces, The Courier of Lyons, It is Never too Late to Mend.)*

John Hamilton Reynolds

9097. JONES, LEONIDAS.   The life of John Hamilton Reynolds. (Bibl. 1985, 7825.) Rev. by L. M. Findlay in NQ (33:2) 249–50.

John Richardson

9098. MCGREGOR, GAILE.   The Wacousta syndrome: explorations in the Canadian langscape. *See* **7068.**

Anne Thackeray Ritchie

9099. SHANKMAN, LILLIAN F.   Some unpublished letters and journals of Anne Thackeray Ritchie and her family and friends: an annotated edition, with a comprehensive introduction. Unpub. doct. diss., New York Univ., 1985. [Abstr. in DA (46) 3044A.]

'Pearl Rivers' (Mrs Eliza Jane (Poitevant) Nicholson)

9100. HOLDITCH, W. KENNETH.   The singing heart: a study of the life and work of Pearl Rivers. SoQ (20:2) 1982, 87–117.

Sir Charles G. D. Roberts

9101. ADAMS, JOHN COLDWELL.   Sir Charles God Damn: the life of Sir Charles G. D. Roberts. Toronto: Toronto UP, 1984. pp. x, 236. Rev. by Tracey Ware in CanP (19) 117–19; by Bryan N. S. Gooch in MalaR (77) 143–4.

9102. PACEY, DESMOND (ed.).   The collected poems of Sir Charles G. D. Roberts: a critical edition. Wolfville, N.S.: Wombat, 1985. pp. xxxii, 672. Rev. by Ed Jewinski in CanP (19) 105–8.

9103. SKALA, DIANA.   A letter from Sir Charles G. D. Roberts (a personal memoir). StudCanL (11:2) 270–82.

E. P. Roe

9104. CAREY, GLENN O.   Edward Payson Roe. Boston, MA: G. K. Hall, 1985. pp. xvi, 117. (Twayne's US authors. 480.) Rev. by Martin J. Fertig in ALR (19:1) 78–80.

William Roscoe
9105. HURST, CLIVE.   The Dunston collection. *See* **239.**

Christina Rossetti
9106. BEAMAN, DARLENE SUZETTE.   'A thorn-choked garden plot': women's place in Emily Dickinson and Christina Rossetti. *See* **8103.**

9107. DOUBLEDAY, JAMES F.   Rossetti's *A Birthday.* Exp (44:2) 29–30.

9108. MERMIN, DOROTHY.   The damsel, the knight, and the Victorian woman poet. *See* **7710.**

9109. PORTER, PETER (sel. and introd.).   Christina Rossetti. Oxford: OUP. pp. 59. (Illustrated poets.)

9110. SMITH, GROVER.   Ford Madox Ford and the Christina Rossetti influence. ELT (29:3) 287–96.

9111. WATSON, JEANIE.   'Eat me, drink me, love me': the dilemma of sisterly-sacrifice. JPRS (7:1) 50–62.

Dante Gabriel Rossetti
9112. MARSH, JAN.   Jane and May Morris: a biographical story 1839–1938. *See* **8992.**

9113. PEATTIE, ROGER W.   Ruskin's August 1870 letter to D. G. Rossetti. NQ (33:2) 173–4.

9114. RIEDE, DAVID G.   Dante Gabriel Rossetti and the limits of Victorian vision. (Bibl. 1985, 7844.) Rev. by Richard L. Stein in CL (38:2) 207–8.

William Michael Rossetti
9115. PEATTIE, ROGER W.   W. M. Rossetti's contributions to the *Edinburgh Weekly Review. See* **667.**

9116. —— Whitman, Charles Aldrich and W. M. Rossetti in 1885: background to the Whitman subscription. *See* **272.**

9117. PROPAS, SHARON W.   William Michael Rossetti and *The Germ. See* **675.**

Josiah Royce
9118. MICHAELS, WALTER BENN.   Corporate fiction: Norris, Royce, and Arthur Machen. *In* (pp. 189–219) **47.**

John Ruskin
9119. AUSTIN, LINDA M.   The art of absence in *The Stones of Venice.* JPRS (6:2) 1–14.

9120. —— Ruskin and Rose at play with words. Criticism (28:4) 409–25.

9121. AUSTIN, LINDA MARILYN.   John Ruskin in the landscape of fiction. Unpub. doct. diss., Univ. of Rochester. [Abstr. in DA (47) 905A.]

9122. BRADLEY, J. L. (ed.).   Ruskin: the critical heritage. (Bibl. 1985, 7852.) Rev. by Gary Wihl in MP (83:4) 438–41.

9123. BRADLEY, LESLIE JOHN ALEXANDER.   Ruskin and Italy. Unpub. doct. diss., Univ. of Massachusetts. [Abstr. in DA (47) 907A.]

9124. CASILLO, ROBERT.   The meaning of Venetian history in Ruskin and Pound. UTQ (55:3) 235–60.

9125. —— The stone alive: Adrian Stokes and John Ruskin. JPRS (7:1) 1–28.

9126. FELLOWS, JAY.   Ruskin's maze: mastery and madness in his art. (Bibl. 1985, 7856.) Rev. by Pierre Fontaney in EA (38:4) 1985, 473.

9127. FINLEY, C. STEPHEN.   Ruskin's apocalypse. Arnoldian (13:1) 33–41 (review-article).

9128. —— The structure of Ruskin's *Fors Clavigera*. Prose Studies (9:3) 71–85.

9129. FITCH, RAYMOND E.   The poison sky: myth and apocalypse in Ruskin. (Bibl. 1985, 7858.) Rev. by C. Stephen Finley in Arnoldian (13:1) 1985/86, 33–41; by Malcolm Hardman in YES (16) 328–31.

9130. FRENCH, R. L.   The significance of personal elements in Ruskin's rhetoric. Unpub. doct. diss., Univ. of Loughborough, 1982. [Abstr. in IT (35) 48.]

9131. HARDMAN, MALCOLM.   Ruskin and Bradford: an experiment in Victorian cultural history. Manchester: Manchester UP. pp. viii, 408.

9132. HELSINGER, ELIZABETH K.   Ruskin and the art of the beholder. (Bibl. 1985, 7859.) Rev. by Malcolm Hardman in YES (16) 328–31.

9133. HOLLAND, MERIDEL.   John Ruskin's lectionary. See **234.**

9134. KEEFE, ROBERT.   *Apollo in Picardy*: Pater's monk and Ruskin's madness. See **9032.**

9135. MOORE, JOHN DAVID.   Prelection, prophecy, and persuasion: the rhetorical development of John Ruskin as a Victorian sage. Unpub. doct. diss., Univ. of Washington, 1985. [Abstr. in DA (46) 1951A.]

9136. PEATTIE, ROGER W.   Ruskin's August 1870 letter to D. G. Rossetti. See **9113.**

9137. READ, R.   The evocative genre of art criticism: a study of descriptive prose in the works of Hazlitt, Ruskin, Pater and Adrian Stokes. See **8521.**

9138. RHODES, ROBERT; JANIK, DEL IVAN (eds).   Studies in Ruskin: essays in honor of Van Akin Burd. (Bibl. 1985, 7871.) Rev. by Malcolm Hardman in YES (16) 328–31.

9139. ROBERTS, BARBARA A.   Ruskin's voice of authority. Unpub. doct. diss., Univ. of Alabama, 1985. [Abstr. in DA (46) 3362A.]

9140. ROGAL, OWEN SHANE.   Formal necessities and furious temptations in John Ruskin's *Modern Painters*. Unpub. doct. diss., Rutgers Univ. [Abstr. in DA (47) 190A.]

9141. SAWYER, PAUL L.   Ruskin's poetic argument: the design of the major works. Ithaca, NY: Cornell UP, 1985. pp. 336. Rev. by Norman Vance in QQ (93:1) 199–201; by Wendell Stacy Johnson in ELN (24:2) 76–8.

9142. SECOR, ROBERT.   John Ruskin and Alfred Hunt: new letters and the record of a friendship. (Bibl. 1984, 8142.) Rev. by Malcolm Hardman in YES (16) 328–31.

9143. SPEAR, JEFFREY L.   Dreams of an English Eden: Ruskin and his tradition in social criticism. (Bibl. 1985, 6604.) Rev. by Samuel L. Chell in CLIO (14:3) 1985, 329–31; by Dinah Birch in NQ (33:2) 258; by Raymond E. Fitch in JEGP (85:2) 285–7.

9144. SWANN, CHARLES.   Dickens, Ruskin and the city: parallels or influence? See **8090.**

9145. TAYLOR, M. The idea of knowledge in the development of cultural criticism in the 19th century, with particular reference to Carlyle, Ruskin and Arnold. *See* **7567.**

9146. UNRAU, JOHN. Ruskin and St Mark's. New York: Thames & Hudson, 1984. (Cf. bibl. 1984, 8145.) Rev. by Mary Ann Stankiewicz in JAE (20:3) 117–18.

9147. WIHL, GARY. Ruskin and the rhetoric of infallibility. London: Yale UP, 1985. (Cf. bibl. 1985, 7874.)

9148. WITEMEYER, HUGH. *Of Kings' Treasuries*: Pound's allusion to Ruskin in *Hugh Selwyn Mauberley*. Paideuma (15:1) 23–31.

Charles Sangster

9149. TIERNEY, FRANK M. (ed.). *The St Lawrence and the Saguenay* and other poems. (Bibl. 1985, 7876.) Rev. by W. J. Keith in ECanW (33) 175–80; by Laurel Boone in CanL (110) 128–9.

Olive Schreiner

9150. CHILDERS, MARY. Narrating structures of opportunity. *See* **7663.**

9151. COETZEE, J. M. Farm novel and *Plaasroman* in South Africa. EngA (13:2) 1–19.

9151a. LENTA, MARGARET. Independence as the creative choice in two South African fictions. Ariel (17:1) 35–52.

9152. PIENAAR, JOHAN. *The Story of an African Farm*: the opportunity for study across the media. Crux (20:1) 47–51.

9153. STANLEY, LIZ. Olive Schreiner: new women, free women, all women (1855–1920). *In* (pp. 229–43) **20.**

Michael Scott

9154. MILLIGAN, IAN. Richard Hughes and Michael Scott: a further source for *A High Wind in Jamaica*. NQ (33:2) 192–3.

Sir Walter Scott

9155. ALEXANDER, J. H. Scott's *The Chase* and Wordsworth's *Hart-Leap Well*. ScottN (9) 10–13.

9156. ANDERSON, JAMES. 'Sir Walter Scott and History', with other papers. (Bibl. 1985, 7886.) Rev. by Charles Dédéyan in EA (38:4) 1985, 469–70.

9157. BARRETT, DEBORAH J. Balfour of Burley: the evil energy in Scott's *Old Mortality*. SSL (17) 1982, 248–53.

9158. BECKETT, RUTH. Another Shakespearean influence in *Waverley*. *See* **4384.**

9159. BEIDERWELL, BRUCE. The reasoning of those times: Scott's *Waverley* and the problems of punishment. CLIO (15:1) 1985, 15–30.

9160. BEIDERWELL, BRUCE JOHN. Civil punishment in the Waverley novels. Unpub. doct. diss., Univ. of California, Los Angeles, 1985. [Abstr. in DA (46) 3723A.]

9161. CRAWFORD, THOMAS. Walter Scott. (Bibl. 1984, 8171.) Rev. by J. H. Alexander in YES (16) 231–4.

9162. DRYDEN, EDGAR A. *Waverley* and American romance: the thematics of a form. Genre (18:4) 1985, 335–61.

9163. EASSON, ANGUS. Statesman, dwarf and weaver: Wordsworth and nineteenth-century narrative. *In* (pp. 16–29) **39.**

9164. GARSIDE, P. D.   Dating *Waverley*'s early chapters. Bibliotheck (13:3) 61–81.

9165. —— Scott's first *Letter on Reform*: an edited version. ScottN (8) 2–14.

9166. GARSIDE, PETER.   Scott as a political journalist. RES (37:148) 503–17.

9167. GARSIDE, PETER DIGNUS.   Union and *The Bride of Lammermoor*. SSL (19) 1984, 72–93.

9168. GROVES, DAVID.   *Lines Addressed to Miss Jarman, of the Theatre-Royal*: a poem by Walter Scott. ScottN (9) 13–14.

9169. HARKIN, PATRICIA.   The fop, the fairy, and the genres of Scott's *Monastery*. SSL (19) 1984, 177–93.

9170. HEWITT, DAVID.   The Magnum Opus and the Pforzheimer manuscripts. *See* **231.**

9171. —— The new Edinburgh Edition of the Waverley Novels. *See* **468.**

9172. HOLLINGWORTH, BRIAN.   The tragedy of Lucy Ashton, the bride of Lammermoor. SSL (19) 1984, 94–105.

9173. HURST, CLIVE.   The Dunston collection. *See* **239.**

9174. HUSSEIN, H. Y.   The historical novels of Walter Scott and Najīb Mahfūz: a comparative study. Unpub. doct. diss., Univ. of Edinburgh, 1985. [Abstr. in IT (35) 1080.]

9175. INBODEN, ROBIN LOUISE.   'The music in my heart I bore': the ballad revival, Scott, and Wordsworth. *See* **2520.**

9176. KERR, JAMES.   Scott's fable of regeneration: *The Heart of Midlothian*. ELH (53:4) 801–20.

9177. KERR, JAMES P.   Fiction against history: the uses of romance in the Waverley novels. Unpub. doct. diss., Rutgers Univ. [Abstr. in DA (47) 2169A.]

9178. MACARIE, MANUELA.   Alexandru Odobescu şi Walter Scott. (Alexander Odobescu and Sir Walter Scott.) ConvLit (42:11) 11.

9179. MCMASTER, GRAHAM.   Scott and society. New York: CUP, 1981. (Cf. bibl. 1985, 7931.) Rev. by Peter Garside in YES (16) 290–2.

9180. MASSIE, ALAN.   James Hogg and Sir Walter Scott: a study in friendship. *See* **8539.**

9181. MILLGATE, JANE.   Walter Scott: the making of a novelist. Toronto: Toronto UP, 1984. (Bibl. 1985, 7935.) Rev. by Daniel Whitmore in MP (84:1) 94–9; by David S. Robb in NQ (33:4) 554–5.

9182. MITCHELL, JEROME.   Scott holdings in the Library at Schloss Corvey. *See* **260.**

9183. MÜLLENBROCK, HEINZ-JOACHIM.   James Fenimore Coopers *Leatherstocking Tales* und die Anfänge des historischen Romans in Amerika. *See* **7318.**

9184. NATIONAL LIBRARY OF SCOTLAND.   Sir Walter Scott's Magnum Opus and the Pforzheimer manuscripts: essays to commemorate the acquisition of two great collections by the National Library of Scotland. Edinburgh: National Library of Scotland. pp. 27.

9185. Ross, Marlon B.   Scott's chivalric pose: the function of metrical romance in the Romantic period. Genre (19:3) 267–97.

9186. Ruddick, William.   Scott and Johnson as biographers of Dryden. *See* **5431.**

9187. —— Scott in the Trossachs. ScottN (9) 15.

9188. Sutherland, Kathryn.   Travel books, fishing manuals, and Scott's *Redgauntlet.* SLJ (13:2) 20–30.

9189. Tait, Margaret.   *The Surgeon's Daughter*: possible sources? ScottN (9) 7–10.

9190. Whitmore, Daniel.   Bibliolatry and the rule of the Word: a study of Scott's *Old Mortality.* PQ (65:2) 243–62.

9191. Wilt, Judith.   Secret leaves: the novels of Walter Scott. Chicago; London: Chicago UP, 1985. pp. vii, 231.

Charles Sealsfield

9192. Grünzweig, Walter.   Überlegungen zum Verhältnis von Literaturstudium und Landeskunde am Beispiel der Romane Charles Sealsfields. *In* (pp. 315–34) **15.**

Mary Shelley

9193. Aldiss, Brian (introd.).   The last man. London: Hogarth Press, 1985. pp. 342.

9194. Banerji, Krishna.   Enlightenment and romanticism in the gothic: a study of Mary Shelley's *Frankenstein.* Jadavpur University Essays and Studies (Calcutta) (4) 1984, 95–105.

9195. Birkett, Julian.   The monster lives on. Listener (116) 23 Oct., 8, 11.

9196. Hammond, Ray.   The modern Frankenstein: fiction becomes fact. Poole: Blandford Press. pp. 200.

9197. Hindle, Maurice (ed.).   Frankenstein. Harmondsworth: Penguin, 1985. pp. 265. (Penguin classics.)

9198. Newman, Beth.   Narratives of seduction and the seductions of narrative: the frame structure of *Frankenstein.* ELH (53:1) 141–63.

9199. Scrivener, Michael.   *Frankenstein*'s ghost story: the last Jacobin novel. Genre (19:3) 299–318.

9200. Vasbinder, Samuel Holmes.   Scientific attitudes in Mary Shelley's *Frankenstein.* (Bibl. 1985, 7979.) Rev. by David Ketterer in SFS (13:3) 395–7.

9201. Veeder, William.   Mary Shelley and Frankenstein: the fate of androgyny. London: Chicago UP. pp. ix, 277. Rev. by Jane Aaron in THES (704) 20.

9202. —— The negative Oedipus: father, *Frankenstein,* and the Shelleys. CI (12:2) 365–90.

9203. Womersley, David.   Hume and Mary Shelley. *See* **6544.**

Percy Bysshe Shelley

9204. Barker-Benfield, B. C.   The honeymoon of Joseph and Henrietta Chichester, with Daniel Roberts' memories of Byron and Shelley. *See* **7759.**

9205. Behrendt, Stephen C.   'The consequence of high powers': Blake, Shelley, and prophecy's public dimension. *See* **6216.**

9206. BEN-PORAT, ZIVA. Represented reality and literary models: European Autumn on Israeli soil. *See* **8800.**

9207. BLANK, G. K.   Shelley and the problem of Wordsworth's influence. Unpub. doct. diss., Univ. of Southampton, 1984.

9208. ——— Shelley's Wordsworth: the desiccated celandine. ESA (29:2) 87–96.

9209. BREWER, WILLIAM DEAN.   The 'war of earthly minds': Julian versus Maddalo in the poetry of Shelley and Byron. *See* **7764.**

9210. BRINKLEY, ROBERT A.   On the composition of *Mont Blanc*: staging a Wordsworthian scene. ELN (24:2) 45–57.

9211. CASON, ROBERT ERNST.   Shelley, Pindar, and the ideology of the ode. Unpub. doct. diss., Southern Illinois Univ. at Carbondale, 1985. [Abstr. in DA (46) 3039A.]

9212. CAVE, RICHARD ALLEN.   *The Cenci* in performance. KSMB (36) 1985, 114–18.

9213. CHAI, LEON CHRISTOPHER.   Melville and European Romanticism: studies on Melville's relations to major European Romantic writers. *See* **7898.**

9214. CHATTERJEE, VISVANATH.   Shelley's *Adonais*: a romantic transmutation of the elegiac tradition. Jadavpur University Essays and Studies (Calcutta) (4) 1984, 80–94.

9215. CLARK, T. J. A.   Shelley: introspection, sensibility and the theme of the mind's lack of power. Unpub. doct. diss., Univ. of Oxford, 1984.

9216. CROOK, N.; GUITON, D.   Shelley's venomed melody. Cambridge: CUP. pp. xii, 273. Rev. by Martin Priestman in THES (730) 22.

9217. CROOK, NORA.   Shelley and the solar microscope. KSR (1) 49–59.

9218. CRUCEFIX, M. J.   The development of Shelley's conception of language. Unpub. doct. diss., Univ. of Oxford, 1985. [Abstr. in IT (35) 545.]

9219. CURRAN, STUART.   Shelleyan drama. *In* (pp. 61–77) **48.**

9220. DAWSON, P. M. S.   'A sort of natural magic': Shelley and animal magnetism. KSR (1) 15–34.

9221. DOOLAN, PAUL M.   Shelley en Prometheus. (Shelley and Prometheus.) De Gids (149:1) 22–32.

9222. ENGELBERG, K.   An annotated bibliography of criticism of P. B. Shelley's life and poetry, 1822–1860, with special reference to biographical events significant in the creation of the Shelley myth. Unpub. doct. diss., Univ. of Oxford, 1983.

9223. ESSICK, ROBERT N.   'A shadow of some golden dream': Shelley's language in *Epipsychidion*. PLL (22:2) 165–75.

9224. FAULK, RONALD HUGH.   Shelley's theory of language. Unpub. doct. diss., Northwestern Univ. [Abstr. in DA (47) 909A.]

9225. FLESCH, WILLIAM BENJAMIN.   The disconsolate: the poetry of irreparable loss. *See* **5481.**

9226. FREEMAN, JOHN.   'Paradise of exiles': the Shelley–Byron conference in Pisa. *See* **7769.**

9227. FRIEDERICH, REINHARD H.   The apocalyptic mode and Shelley's *Ode to the West Wind*. Ren (36) 1984, 168–70.

9228. GOLD, ELISE M.   *King Lear* and aesthetic tyranny in Shelley's *The Cenci, Swellfoot the Tyrant*, and *The Witch of Atlas. See* **4833.**

9229. HARDY, JOHN; BROWN, NICHOLAS.   Shelley's 'Dome of many-coloured glass'. Sydney Studies in English (11) 1985/86, 103–6.

9230. HOAGWOOD, TERENCE ALLAN.   Shelley, Milton, and the poetics of ideological transformation: *Paradise Lost* and the prologue to *Hellas. See* **5729.**

9231. HOULIHAN, JAMES WILLIAM.   Lyrico-narrative in Pindar and Shelley. Unpub. doct. diss., Univ. of California, Santa Barbara, 1985. [Abstr. in DA (46) 3345A.]

9232. KEACH, WILLIAM.   Shelley's style. (Bibl. 1985, 8000.) Rev. by Stephen C. Behrendt in PQ (65:1) 134–6; by Paul Hamilton in LRev, Aug. 1985, 29–30; by Frederick Kirchhoff in ELN (24:1) 102–3; by Lucy Newlyn in EC (36:3) 263–8;

9233. KLOPPER, DIRK.   Repetition and death in Shelley's *Epipsychidion*: a post-structuralist reading. Journal of Literary Studies (2:2) 57–64.

9234. LEHMANN, JOHN.   Three literary friendships: Byron & Shelley, Rimbaud & Verlaine, Robert Frost & Edward Thomas. *See* **7780.**

9235. OGLE, ROBERT B.   Shelley's whirlwind imagery in *Prometheus Unbound*: a segment of its evolution. ELN (23:3) 36–41.

9236. O'NEILL, PATRICIA.   Pedigree of self-making: Shelley's influence on Browning and Hardy. *See* **7729.**

9237. RÁCZ, ISTVÁN.   Shelley's reception in Hungary. HSE (18) 1985, 59–69.

9238. REIMAN, DONALD H. (ed.).   Percy Bysshe Shelley: vol. 2, *The Mask of Anarchy. See* **171.**

9239. —— Percy Bysshe Shelley: vol. 3, *Hellas: a Lyrical Drama*: a facsimile of the press-copy transcript, and fair-copy transcripts of *Written on Hearing the News of the Death of Napoleon* and *Letters to Maria Gisborne*, as well as a fragment of the press-copy transcript of *Lines Written Among the Euganean Hills*: all in the Henry E. Huntington Library. *See* **172.**

9240. RIEDER, JOHN.   Description of a struggle: Shelley's radicalism on Wordsworth's terrain. Boundary 2 (13:2/3) 1985, 267–87.

9241. RUNCIE, CATHERINE.   On figurative language: a reading of Shelley's, Hardy's and Hughes's skylark poems. *See* **8430.**

9242. SAKAGUCHI, SHUSAKU.   Shelley no sekai shi to kaikaku no rhetoric. (The world of Shelley: his poetry and the rhetoric of innovation.) Tokyo: Kinseido. pp. 250.

9243. SCRIVENER, MICHAEL HENRY.   Radical Shelley: the philosophical anarchism and utopian thought of Percy Bysshe Shelley. (Bibl. 1985, 8006.) Rev. by P.M.S. Dawson in YES (16) 306–8.

9244. SHAWCROSS, JOHN T.   Further remarks on Milton's influence: Shelley and Shaw. *See* **5791.**

9245. TRAYIANNOUDI, P.   Shelley's myth as a displaced mode of representation: *Alastor, Epipsychidion, Adonais, Prometheus Unbound.* Unpub. doct. diss., Univ. of Essex, 1984.

9246. WELBURN, ANDREW J. Power and self-consciousness in the poetry of Shelley. Basingstoke: Macmillan. pp. xiv, 234. (Macmillan studies in Romanticism.)

William Gilmore Simms

9247. MERIWETHER, JAMES B. Simms' 'sharp snaffles' and 'baldhead Bill Bauldy': two views of men – and of women. SoCR (16:2) 1984, 66–71.

9248. WATSON, CHARLES S. Simms's use of Shakespearean characters. *In* (pp. 13–28) **51.**

Joshua Slocum

9249. BERTHOLD, DENNIS. Deeper surroundings: the presence of *Walden* in Slocum's *Sailing Alone Around the World. In* (pp. 161–75) **28.**

Robert Southey

9250. BANERJEE, JIBON KRISHNA. Moral concerns in the dramatic works of Wordsworth, Coleridge and Southey. *See* **7886.**

9251. METZ, KARL H. 'The social chain of being'. Zum Topos des sozialen Konservativismus und zur Entstehung des Gedankens der sozialen Verantwortung im Grossbritannien der industriellen Revolution. *See* **6799.**

9252. POLLARD, ARTHUR. Paternalism and liberty: Tory Southey and Whig Macaulay. *In* (pp. 181–8) **18.**

9253. STEEL, JOHN (ed.). Mr Rowlandson's England. Woodbridge: Antique Collectors' Club, 1985. pp. 201.

E. D. E. N. Southworth

9254. DOBSON, JOANNE. The hidden hand: subversion of cultural ideology in three mid-nineteenth-century American women's novels. AmQ (38:2) 223–42.

9255. MOYLE, GERALDINE. The tenth muse lately sprung up in the marketplace: women and professional authorship in nineteenth-century America. *See* **7537.**

C. H. Spence

9256. BENNETT, BRUCE. Catherine Spence, George Eliot and the contexts of literary possibility. *See* **8201.**

9257. MAGAREY, SUSAN. Unbridling the tongues of women: a biography of Catherine Helen Spence. Sydney: Hale & Iremonger, 1985. pp. 240.

E. C. Stedman

9258. CULBERTSON, STEVEN LEE. Edmund Clarence Stedman: a critical reassessment. Unpub. doct. diss., Bowling Green State Univ., 1985. [Abstr. in DA (47) 176A.]

Robert Louis Stevenson

9259. CLUNAS, A. B. 'Out of my country and myself I go': a critical examination of the fiction of Robert Louis Stevenson. Unpub. doct. diss., Univ. of Stirling, 1983.

9260. DESEBROCK, JEAN (introd.). Picturesque old Edinburgh. Edinburgh: Albyn Press, 1983. pp. 96.

9261. GELDER, K.   The short stories of Robert Louis Stevenson. Unpub. doct. diss., Univ. of Stirling, 1985. [Abstr. in IT (35) 1085.]

9262. HAMMOND, J. R.   A Robert Louis Stevenson companion: a guide to the novels, essays and short stories. London: Macmillan, 1984. pp. x, 252. Rev. by C. H. Muller in UES (24:1) 41–2.

9263. HEATH, STEPHEN.   Psychopathia sexualis: Stevenson's *Strange Case*. CritQ (28:1/2) 93–108.

9264. HILLIER, ROBERT IRWIN.   The South Seas fiction of Robert Louis Stevenson. Unpub. doct. diss., Univ. of New Hampshire, 1985. [Abstr. in DA (47) 537A.]

9265. JACKSON, DAVID H.   The Stanford *Falesá* and textual scholarship. Review (8) 79–92 (review-article).

9266. LETLEY, EMMA (ed.).   *Kidnapped* and *Catriona*. Oxford: OUP. pp. 496. (World's classics.)

9267. LUKENS, REBECCA.   Stevenson's *Garden*: verse is verse. LU (4:2) 1980/81, 49–55.

9268. MAHMOUD, M. M.   Travel and adventure in the works of Robert Louis Stevenson. Unpub. doct. diss., Univ. of Glasgow, 1984.

9269. MASSIE, ALLAN (introd.).   *Moral Emblems* and other poems. Edinburgh: Polygon. pp. viii, 75.

9270. NEILLANDS, ROBIN (introd.).   Travels with a donkey in the Cevennes. London: Chatto & Windus. pp. 128.

9271. NOBLE, ANDREW (ed.).   From the Clyde to California: Robert Louis Stevenson's emigrant journey. Aberdeen: Aberdeen UP, 1985. pp. x, 291. (*The Amateur Emigrant, The Old and New Pacific Capitals, The Silverado Squatters*.) Rev. by Kenneth Gelder in SLJ (supp. 25) 20–2.

9272. NORQUAY, GLENDA.   Moral absolutism in the novels of Robert Louis Stevenson, Robin Jenkins and Muriel Spark: challenges to realism. Unpub. doct. diss., Univ. of Edinburgh, 1985. [Abstr. in IT (35) 1087.]

9273. STEPPUTAT, J.   Introversion and extroversion in certain late Victorian writers. *See* **8361.**

9274. THOMAS, RONALD R.   In the company of strangers: absent voices in Stevenson's *Dr Jekyll and Mr Hyde* and Beckett's *Company*. MFS (32:2) 157–73.

9275. WATSON, RODERICK (introd.).   *Strange Case of Dr Jekyll and Mr Hyde*: a centenary edition. Edinburgh: Canongate. pp. 148.

'Joachim Hayward Stocqueler' (J. H. Siddons)

9276. LOHRLI, ANNE.   The urbane Mr Stocqueler. NQ (33:2) 170–2.

Bram Stoker

9277. DALBY, RICHARD (introd.).   The dualists, or, The death doom of the double born. Edinburgh: Tragara Press. pp. 29.

9278. FINNÉ, JACQUES.   Bibliographie de Dracula. Paris: Age d'homme. pp. 215. (Contemporains.)

9279. PERRY, DENNIS R.   Whitman's influence on Stoker's *Dracula*. WWQR (3:3) 29–35.

9280. PHILLIPS, ROBERT; RIEGER, BRANIMIR.   The agony and the ecstasy: a Jungian analysis of two vampire novels, Meredith Ann

Pierce's *The Darkangel* and Bram Stoker's *Dracula*. PhilP (31) 1985, 10–19.

9281. ZEENDER, MARIE-NOELLE. Miroir de l'âme irlandaise: aspects du fantastique chez Le Fanu, chez Wilde et chez Stoker. *See* **8871.**

Harriet Beecher Stowe

9282. AMMONS, ELIZABETH. *Uncle Tom's Cabin* and American culture. Legacy (3:2) 60–1 (review-article).

9283. GOSSETT, THOMAS F. *Uncle Tom's Cabin* and American culture. (Bibl. 1985, 8038.) Rev. by Elizabeth Ammons in Legacy (3:2) 60–1; by James D. Wallace in NEQ (59:2) 305–8; by Gerald T. Burns in AL (58:2) 299–301; by John C. Inscoe in NCHR (63:2) 267; by Lucinda H. MacKethan in GaHQ (70:2) 345–7.

9284. SUNDQUIST, ERIC J. (ed.). New essays on *Uncle Tom's Cabin*. Cambridge: CUP. pp. viii, 200. (American novel.)

9285. WARHOL, ROBYN R. Poetics and persuasion: *Uncle Tom's Cabin* as a Realist novel. ELit (13:2) 283–97.

9286. —— Toward a theory of the engaging narrator: earnest interventions in Gaskell, Stowe, and Eliot. *See* **8250.**

Lady Louisa Stuart

9287. RUBENSTEIN, JILL. Women's biography as a family affair: Lady Louisa Stuart's 'Biographical Anecdotes' of Lady Mary Wortley Montagu. *See* **6684.**

9288. —— (ed.). Memoire of Frances, Lady Douglas. Edinburgh: Scottish Academic Press, 1985. pp. xxi, 106. Rev. by W. A. Craik in SLJ (supp. 24) 12–13.

Ruth McEnery Stuart

9289. TAYLOR, H. Gender, race and region: a study of three postbellum women writers of Louisana: Grace King, Ruth McEnery Stuart and Kate Chopin. *See* **7863.**

Algernon Charles Swinburne

9290. BEATTY, C. J. P. Victor Hugo, Swinburne, and an Irish poet. *In* (pp. 134–44) **18.**

9291. HOLT, TERRENCE EDWARD. 'Clothed with derision': myth as parody in the poetry of Algernon Charles Swinburne. Unpub. doct. diss., Cornell Univ., 1985. [Abstr. in DA (46) 1949A.]

9292. LOUIS, MARGOT KATHLEEN. Swinburne and his gods: the roots and growth of an agnostic poetry. Unpub. doct. diss., Univ. of Toronto, 1985. [Abstr. in DA (47) 913A.]

9293. WILLIAMS, KATHERINE. 'Some new-born': Renaissance forms in Swinburne's lyrics. Unpub. doct. diss., City Univ. of New York. [Abstr. in DA (47) 917A.]

Arthur Symons

9294. BECKSON, KARL. Arthur Symons on John Millington Synge: a previously unpublished memoir. Éire–Ireland (21:4) 77–80.

9295. BLOCK, ED, JR. Walter Pater, Arthur Symons, W. B. Yeats, and the fortunes of the literary portrait. *See* **9027.**

9296. LEIGH, JOHN. Arthur Symons and the evolution of Pound's concepts of absolute rhythm and precision. Paideuma (15:1) 55–9.

9297. MARKERT, L. W.   Arthur Symons: critic of the seven arts. Unpub. doct. diss., Univ. of Oxford, 1985. [Abstr. in IT (35) 52.]

9298. Entry cancelled.

Bayard Taylor

9299. AL-SHAIKH-ALI, A. S.   Bayard Taylor and his contemporaries: the Near East in nineteenth century American poetry. Unpub. doct. diss., Univ. of Manchester, 1983. [Abstr. in IT (36) 476.]

Tom Taylor

9300. RAY, REBECCA LEA.   A stage history of Tom Taylor's *Our American Cousin*. Unpub. doct. diss., New York Univ., 1985. [Abstr. in DA (46) 2133A.]

Alfred, Lord Tennyson

9301. ALBRIGHT, DANIEL.   Tennyson: the Muses' tug of war. Charlottesville: Virginia UP. pp. 256. Rev. by A. S. Byatt in TLS, 14 Nov., 1274.

9302. BEETZ, KIRK H.   Tennyson: a bibliography, 1827–1982. Metuchen, NJ: Scarecrow Press, 1984. pp. vi, 528. (Scarecrow author bibliographies, 68.) Rev. in BB (43:4) 263; by P. G. Scott in Review (8) 101–17.

9303. BELCHER, MARGARET.   A forgotten poem by Tennyson? TRB (4:5) 217–19.

9304. BRUNNER, LARRY.   'Let them take example': failed asceticism in Tennyson's *St Simeon Stylites*. ChrisL (35:2) 17–31.

9305. COLLEY, ANN.   Edward Lear and the Pre-Raphaelite impossibility: reflections on the Lear exhibit: the national academy of design, New York, September 10 – November 3, 1985. *See* **8864.**

9306. COLLEY, ANN C.   Tennyson and madness. (Bibl. 1985, 8061.) Rev. by Herbert F. Tucker in MP (83:3) 321–5.

9307. COLLINS, PHILIP.   Tennyson, poet of Lincolnshire. Lincoln: Tennyson Soc., 1984, pp. 20. (Tennyson Soc. occasional papers, 6.)

9308. DAY, A.   The sceptical strain: readings in Tennyson's poetry, 1829–1855. Unpub. doct. diss., Univ. of Leicester, 1983.

9309. ENGLISH, J. S.   The postcard world of Tennyson. Lincoln: Lincolnshire Recreational Services Library Dept, 1984. pp. 37.

9310. FOLTINEK, HERBERT.   'Theirs not to reason why': Alfred Lord Tennyson on the human condition. WBEP (80) 27–38.

9311. FULWEILER, HOWARD W.   Tennyson's *The Holy Grail*: the representation of representation. Ren (38:3) 144–59.

9312. GARDNER, TRACI.   Tennyson's *Locksley Hall*. Exp (44:2) 23–4.

9313. GRASSO, ANTHONY ROBERT.   The epistemology and structure of Tennyson's *In Memoriam*: a study of poetic development. Unpub. doct. diss., Univ. of Toronto, 1985. [Abstr. in DA (47) 910A.]

9314. GRAY, J. E.   Thro' the vision of the night: a study of source, evolution and structure in Tennyson's *Idylls of the King*. (Bibl. 1985, 8285.) Rev. by P. J. C. Field in MÆ (55:2) 306.

9315. HAIR, DONALD. Tennyson's faith: a re-examination. UTQ (55:2) 1985/86, 185–203.

9316. KENNEDY, JUDITH E. Tennyson and the *Zeitgeist: In Memoriam* in relation to nineteenth-century idealism. Unpub. doct. diss., New York Univ., 1985. [Abstr. in DA (46) 3726A.]

9317. KNIES, E. A. Tennyson at Aldworth: the diary of James Henry Mangles. Athens: Ohio UP, 1984. pp. xviii, 155. Rev. by Susan Shatto in NQ (33:2) 257.

9318. KOLB, JACK. Charles Astor Bristed, Harry Hallam and Tennyson's *Timbuctoo*. TRB (4:5) 197–210.

9319. PATTISON, ROBERT. Tennyson and tradition. (Bibl. 1984, 8296.) Rev. by John R. Reed in CLIO (11:1) 1981, 97–101.

9320. PELTASON, TIMOTHY. Reading *In Memoriam*. Princeton, NJ; Guildford: Princeton UP, 1985. pp. xii, 181. (Princeton essays in literature.) Rev. by A. S. Byatt in TLS, 14 Nov., 1274; by Joseph Bristow in Eng (35) 279–84; by Elaine Jordan in EC (36:3) 268–75.

9321. PLATIZKY, ROGER S. Madness and method in Tennyson's poetry. Unpub. doct. diss., Rutgers Univ., 1985. [Abstr. in DA (46) 1951A.]

9322. POSTON, LAWRENCE. Victorian elegiac stanzas: more on the Tennyson–Trench relationship. PQ (64:2) 1985, 279–89.

9323. SAKELLIOU-SCHULTZ, LIANA. Tennyson's Lotos: the place where life hides away. Parousia (4) 135–45.

9324. SCHUR, OWEN MARIUS. Developments and transformations of pastoral melancholy in some poems of Keats, Tennyson, and Hardy. *See* **8432.**

9325. SCOTT, P. G. 'No such scarecrows in your father's time': a new Tennyson bibliography. Review (8) 101–17 (review-article).

9326. SHATTO, SUSAN (ed.). Tennyson's *Maud*: a definitive edition. London: Athlone Press. pp. xxi, 296. Rev. by A. S. Byatt in TLS, 14 Nov., 1274; by Norman Page in TRB (4:5) 222–4.

9327. —— SHAW, MARION (eds). In memoriam. (Bibl. 1985, 8074.) Rev. by Kerry McSweeney in YES (16) 318–19; by Norman Page in TRB (4:5) 220–2.

9328. SINFIELD, ALAN. Alfred Tennyson. Oxford: Blackwell. pp. x, 202. (Re-reading literature.) Rev. by Joseph Bristow in Eng (35) 279–84; by Aidan Day in THES (709) 20; by A. S. Byatt in TLS, 14 Nov., 1274.

9329. STURMAN, CHRISTOPHER. Tennyson's 'Balloon Stanzas' re-considered. TRB (4:5) 211–16.

9330. THOMSON, ALASTAIR W. The poetry of Tennyson. London: Routledge & Kegan Paul. pp. x, 278. Rev. by Aidan Day in THES (734) 20.

9331. WARD, GEOFFREY. Dying to write: Maurice Blanchot and Tennyson's *Tithonus*. CI (12:4) 672–87.

9332. WILLIAMS, W. E. (sel.); CALDER, JENNI (introd.). Tennyson: poems. Harmondsworth: Penguin, 1985. pp. 233. (Penguin poetry library.)

William Makepeace Thackeray

9333. BARCLAY, DEAN ARNE. Enormous tradition: literary allusions in Thackeray and Dickens. *See* **8005.**

9334. CASE, CAROL ANN. Class consciousness in Thackeray's *Vanity Fair.* Unpub. doct. diss., Univ. of Houston. [Abstr. in DA (47) 2167A.]

9335. CHASE, KAREN. The kindness of consanguinity: family history in *Henry Esmond.* MLS (16:3) 213–26.

9336. CLARKE, MICAEL M. Virginia Woolf's Thackerayan heritage. ThN (20) 1984, 4–5.

9337. ELKINS, WILLIAM R. Thackeray's *Vanity Fair.* Exp (44:3) 31–5.

9338. FITZGERALD, MARY KATERI. William Makepeace Thackeray's writings about Ireland and the Irish; the uses of stereotype. Unpub. doct. diss., Univ. of Connecticut, 1985. [Abstr. in DA (46) 1947A.]

9339. GOULD, CAROL GRANT. Thackeray and the death of innocence in Victorian fiction. Unpub. doct. diss., New York Univ. [Abstr. in DA (47) 1333A.]

9340. JUCKETT, ELIZABETH COX. The art of the tightrope dancer: Thackeray's response to Carlyle. *See* **7816.**

9341. LUND, MICHAEL. Literary pieces and whole audiences: *Denis Duval, Edwin Drood,* and *The Landleaguers. See* **8065.**

9342. ORAM, RICHARD W. William Gordon McCabe and Thackeray. ThN (20) 1984, 3–4.

9343. RIGNALL, J. M. Thackeray's *Henry Esmond* and the struggle against the power of time. *In* (pp. 80–93) **39.**

9344. SUTHERLAND, JOHN. The genesis of Thackeray's *Denis Duval.* RES (37:146) 226–33.

9345. —— Thackeray and France, 1842. NQ (33:2) 166–7.

9346. TREMPER, ELLEN. Commitment and escape: the fairy tales of Thackeray, Dickens, and Wilde. *See* **8094.**

9347. VASCILESCU-POTLOG, RUXANDRA (trans. and ed.). Peripeţiile lui Philip în drumul său prin lume arătînd cine l-a jefuit, cine l-a ajutat şi cine nu l-a băgat în seamă. (The adventures of Philip.) Bucharest: Univers. pp. 640.

John Thelwall ('John Beaufort')

9348. KITSON, PETER. Coleridge's anecdote of John Thelwall. *See* **7919.**

Berte Thomas

9349. WEISS, RUDOLF. The Barker inheritance. Berte Thomas and Harley Granville-Barker: *The Family of the Oldroyds.* WBEP (80) 249–65.

James Thompson ('B.V.')

9350. SHAHEEN, MOHAMMAD. Meredith to Evans and Thomson. *See* **430.**

Henry David Thoreau

9351. ATON, JIM. Stalking Henry Thoreau: an interview with Walter Harding. SDR (22:4) 1984, 47–60.

9352. BAKER, LARRY. *The Ponds* as linkage. TJQ (13:1/2) 1981, 21–6.

9353. BERTHOLD, DENNIS. Deeper surroundings: the presence of *Walden* in Slocum's *Sailing Alone Around the World. In* (pp. 161–75) **28.**

9354. Bonner, Willard H. (ed.). Harp on the shore: Thoreau and the sea. Completed by George R. Levine. Albany: New York State UP, 1985. pp. vii, 129. Rev. by Donald Yannella in AL (58:3) 438–40.

9355. Cameron, Sharon. Writing nature: Henry Thoreau's *Journal*. New York; Oxford: OUP, 1985. pp. x, 173. Rev. by Kevin Van Anglen in AL(58:3) 440–1; by Richard Bridgman in NEQ (59:3) 431–4; by Stephen Tatum in WHR (40:4) 376–80; by Denis Donoghue in TLS, 25 Apr., 435.

9356. Carlet, Yves. Thoreau et le temps retrouvé: *A Week on the Concord and Merrimack Rivers. In* (pp. 149–71) **2.**

9357. Chang, Chung-Nam. Henry David Thoreau wa Ralph Waldo Emerson eui jayeonkwan bigyo. *See* **8268.**

9358. Chang, Young-Hee. Journeys between the real and the ideal. *See* **8269.**

9359. Clark, Daniel S. The West Branch revisited. TJQ (13:3/4) 1981, 38–45.

9360. Dillman, Richard H. Thoreau's Harvard education in rhetoric and composition, 1833–1837. TJQ (13:3/4) 1981, 47–62.

9361. Dombrowski, Daniel A. Thoreau, sainthood and vegetarianism. ATQ (60) 25–36.

9362. Farcet, Gilles. Henry Thoreau, l'éveillé de la nature. Paris: Sang de la terre. pp. 250. (Le Sentiment de la nature.)

9363. Fink, Steven. The language of prophecy: Thoreau's *Wild Apples*. NEQ (59:2) 212–30.

9364. Krieger, William Carl. Henry David Thoreau and the limitations of nineteenth-century science. Unpub. doct. diss., Washington State Univ. [Abstr. in DA (47) 2206a.]

9365. Machann, Clinton. The foliate pattern: evidence of natural process in Thoreau. TJQ (13:1/2) 1981, 35–56.

9366. McIlroy, Gary. *Pilgrim at Tinker Creek* and the social legacy of *Walden*. SAQ (85:2) 111–22.

9367. Marshall, Ian. Thoreau's Walden Odyssey. ATQ (59) 53–62.

9368. Martin, John. 'This is the ship of pearl . . .'. *See* **8284.**

9369. Murray, Met McGavran. Thoreau's moon mythology: lunar clues to the hieroglyphics of *Walden*. AL (58:1) 15–32.

9370. Okuda, Joichi. *Walden mori no seikatu* ni tuite no ichi kosatu. (A reflection upon *Walden*.) Tokyo: Kirihara. pp. iv, 144.

9371. Parris, Peggy. Lank ghost, odd uncle and old hero: Thoreau in contemporary poetry. TJQ (13:3/4) 1981, 24–37.

9372. Pratt, Peter Philip. The paradoxical wilderness: Mailer and American nature writing. Unpub. doct. diss. Univ. of Michigan, 1985. [Abstr. in DA (46) 3353a.]

9373. Rosenblum, Joseph. A cock fight between Melville and Thoreau. *See* **8943.**

9374. Rougé, Bertrand. La cabane et le chemin: *Walden* comme autoportrait. EA (39:2) 139–49.

9375. SAUNDERS, JUDITH P. 'A different angle': Thoreau and the problem of perspective. MSE (10:3) 184–96.

9376. SAVAGE, GEORGE E. 'Fronting it': radical realism in Whitman and Thoreau. Unpub. doct. diss., Univ., of Wisconsin–Madison, 1985. [Abstr. in DA (47) 182A.]

9377. SAYRE, ROBERT F. Charles Bird King's *Joseph Porus* and Thoreau's *Maine Woods* guide. TJQ (13/3:4) 1981, 111–14.

9378. —— (ed.). A week on the Concord and Merrimack Rivers; Walden, or life in the woods; The Maine woods; Cape Cod. New York: Library of America; Cambridge: CUP, 1985. pp. 1114. (Literary classics of the United States.) Rev. by Denis Donoghue in TLS, 25 Apr., 435.

9379. SCHARNHORST, GARY. 'He is able to write a work that will not die': W. R. Alger and T. Stan King on Thoreau. TJQ (13:1/2) 1981, 5–17.

9380. SCHUELLER, MALINI. Carnival rhetoric and extra-vagance in Thoreau's *Walden*. AL (58:1) 33–45.

9381. SHERWOOD, MARY P. Brief history of the Maine Thoreau Fellowship, Inc. TJQ (13:3/4) 1981, 7–9.

9382. THOMAS, CHARLES JOSEPH. Eliciting formal and personal responses to Henry David Thoreau's *Civil Disobedience* and *Walden*. Unpub. doct. diss., Columbia Univ. Teachers College. [Abstr. in DA (47) 2064A.]

9383. WALKER, LINDA K. Wild berries in Thoreau's *Journal*: the promise of America. TJQ (13:3/4) 1981, 15–22.

9384. WHALEN, MARGEE. Ktaadn revisited. TJQ (13:1/2) 1981, 29–33.

9385. YARBROUGH, STEPHEN R. From the vice of intimacy to the vice of habit: the theories of friendship in Emerson and Thoreau. *See* **8300.**

Thomas Bangs Thorpe
9386. HIGGS, ROBERT J. The sublime and the beautiful: the meaning of sport in collected sketches of Thomas B. Thorpe. SoS (25:3) 235–56.

Henry Timrod
9387. MURPHY, CHRISTINA. The artistic design of societal commitment: Shakespeare and the poetry of Henry Timrod. *In* (pp. 29–47) **51.**

Mabel Loomis Todd
9388. LONGSWORTH, POLLY. Mabel Loomis Todd. Legacy (3:1) 63–8.

John Horne Tooke
9389. MULVIHILL, JAMES. A Tookean presence in Peacock's *Melincourt. See* **9052.**

Richard Trench
9390. POSTON, LAWRENCE. Victorian elegiac stanzas: more on the Tennyson–Trench relationship. *See* **9322.**

Anthony Trollope
9391. BAREHAM, T. First and last: some notes towards a re-appraisal of Trollope's *The Macdermots of Ballycloran* and *The Landleaguers*. DUJ (78:2) 311–17.

9392. BAREHAM, TONY (ed.).   The Barsetshire novels: a casebook. (Bibl. 1984, 8383.) Rev. by Alan Shelston in NQ (33:1) 124.

9393. BARKER, A. D.   Women and independence in the nineteenth-century novel: a study of Austen, Trollope and James. *See* **7573.**

9394. BLAKE, A. J.   Fiction as history: an examination of the ideological content of the 19th century novel of manners, with a case study of the portrayal of the ruling class in Anthony Trollope's novels. *See* **7205.**

9395. BUTTON, MARILYN DEMAREST.   American women in the works of Frances Milton Trollope and Anthony Trollope. Unpub. doct. diss., Univ. of Delaware, 1985. [Abstr. in DA (47) 534A.]

9396. EPPERLY, ELIZABETH R.   Trollope and the young Austin Dobson. *See* **594.**

9397. FOX, ARNOLD B.   Nightmare to daydream to art. Review (7) 1985, 207–13 (review-article).

9398. HALL, N. JOHN; BURGIS, NINA (eds).   The letters of Anthony Trollope. (Bibl. 1985, 8137.) Rev. by W. Baker in EngS (67:3) 277–9; by R. C. Terry in Review (8) 215–29; by Juliet McMaster in JEGP (85:2) 282–4.

9399. HALPERIN, JOHN (ed.).   The American senator. Oxford: OUP. pp. 582. (World's classics.)

9400. —— The Belton estate. Oxford: OUP. pp. 480. (World's classics.)

9401. HEBERLEIN, KATE BROWDER.   Barbara Pym and Anthony Trollope: communities of imaginative participation. PCP (19) 95–100.

9402. HYNES, JOHN.   Anthony Trollope's creative 'culture-shock'. Éire–Ireland (21:3) 124–31.

9403. —— A note on Trollope's *Landleaguers.* Études irlandaises (11) 65–70.

9404. IKELER, A. ABBOTT.   That peculiar book: critics, common readers, and *The Way We Live Now.* CLAJ (30:2) 219–40.

9405. JORDAN, REBECCA.   The art in digressing: Anthony Trollope on the novel. Unpub. doct. diss., Univ. of Kansas. [Abstr. in DA (47) 2168A.]

9406. KELLY, EDWARD H.   Trollope's *Barchester Towers.* Exp (44:2) 28–9.

9407. LANSBURY, CORAL.   The reasonable man: Trollope's legal fiction. (Bibl. 1985, 8145.) Rev. by R. H. Super in MLS (16:3) 336–41.

9408. LENIHAN, PATRICIA DIANE.   Regionalism in the fictional debuts of Trollope, Gaskell, and Eliot. *See* **8232.**

9409. LUND, MICHAEL.   Literary pieces and whole audiences: *Denis Duval, Edwin Drood,* and *The Landleaguers. See* **8065.**

9410. McMASTER, R. D.   Trollope and the law. Basingstoke: Macmillan. pp. 144.

9411. MORSE, DEBORAH DENENHOLZ.   'Am I not doing it all for him?': Anthony Trollope's Palliser novels and Victorian ideals of womanhood. Unpub. doct. diss., Northwestern Univ. [Abstr. in DA (47) 914A.]

9412. NARDIN, JANE.   Comic convention in Trollope's *Rachel Ray*. PLL (22:1) 39–50.

9413. ROBICHEAU, JOAN MARGARET.   George Henry Lewes, George Eliot and Anthony Trollope: experiments in realism. *See* **8244.**

9414. SKILTON, DAVID.   The Trollope reader. *In* (pp. 142–155) **39.**

9415. —— (ed.).   The Claverings. Oxford: OUP. pp. 560. (World's classics.)

9416. SUPER, R. H.   A review essay: modern scholarship on the Trollopes. MLS (16:3) 336–41.

9417. SUTHERLAND, JOHN (ed.).   Is he Popenjoy? Oxford: OUP. pp. xxxv, 335. (World's classics.)

9418. TAYLOR, MARIAN ELIZABETH.   The void in Anthony Trollope's fiction. Unpub. doct. diss., Univ. of Notre Dame. [Abstr. in DA (47) 917A.]

9419. TERRY, R. C.   Living at a gallop. Review (8) 215–29 (review-article).

9420. TINGAY, LANCE O.   The Trollope collector: a record of writings by and books about Anthony Trollope. London: Silverbridge, 1985. pp. vi, 115.

9421. WRIGHT, ANDREW.   Anthony Trollope: dream and art. (Bibl. 1985, 8159.) Rev. by Arnold B. Fox in Review (7) 1985, 207–13; by Alan Shelston in NQ (33:1) 123–4.

Frances Trollope

9422. BUTTON, MARILYN DEMAREST.   American women in the works of Frances Milton Trollope and Anthony Trollope. *See* **9395.**

9423. HEINEMAN, HELEN.   Mrs Trollope: the triumphant feminine in the nineteenth century. (Bibl. 1983, 8766.) Second ed. (1982) rev. by R. H. Super in MLS (16:3) 336–41.

9424. SUPER, R. H.   A review essay: modern scholarship on the Trollopes. *See* **9416.**

John Lucas Tupper ('Outis')

9425. KAPOOR, SUSHMA.   John Lucas Tupper, 1865–79: the rise of 'Outis'. JPRS (6:2) 37–44.

9426. LANDOW, GEORGE.   A check list of the writings of John Lucas Tupper, friend of the Pre-Raphaelites. JPRS (7:1) 63–8.

'Mark Twain' (Samuel L. Clemens)

9427. ANDERSON, DAVID D.   Mark Twain, Sherwood Anderson, Saul Bellow, and the territories of the spirit. Midamerica (13) 116–24.

9428. ANDERSON, DOUGLAS.   Reading the pictures in *Huckleberry Finn*. *See* **64.**

9429. BIRD, JOHN CHRISTIAN, JR.   'One right form for a story': Mark Twain and the narrative I. Unpub. doct. diss., Univ. of Rochester. [Abstr. in DA (47) 1320A.]

9430. BLAIR, WALTER; FISCHER, VICTOR (eds).   Adventures of Huckleberry Finn. Berkeley: California UP in assn with Univ. of Iowa, 1985. pp. 432. (Mark Twain library.) Rev. by Hugh Kenner in TLS, 9 May, 490–1.

9431. BUDD, LOUIS J.   Our Mark Twain: the making of his public personality. (Bibl. 1985, 8181.) Rev. by Robert F. Lucid in Review (7) 1985, 113–18.

9432. —— The repopularizing of Mark Twain. RALS (15:1) 1985, 9–16 (review-article).

9433. —— (ed.).   New essays on *Adventures of Huckleberry Finn.* Cambridge: CUP, 1985. pp. viii, 136. (American novel.)

9434. CHANG, YOUNG-HEE.   Journeys between the real and the ideal. *See* **8269.**

9435. CHO, SUNG-KYU.   Mark Twain eui bigwanjueui was doduckjoek isangjueui. (Mark Twain's pessimism and moral idealism.) IKY (55) 31–77; (56) 1–40.

9436. COARD, ROBERT J.   Huck Finn and two sixteenth-century lads. MidQ (23:4) 1982, 437–46.

9437. COLLINS, WILLIAM J.   Hank Morgan in the garden of forking paths: *A Connecticut Yankee in King Arthur's Court* as alternative history. MFS (32:1) 109–14.

9438. COMARNESCU, PETRU (ed.).; MARIAN, EUGEN B. (trans.).   Un yancheu la curtes regelui Arthur. (A Connecticut Yankee in King Arthur's court.) Bucharest: Univers. pp. 353.

9439. COWARD, NANCY POTTS.   Mothers and sons in the fiction of Mark Twain, William Dean Howells, and Henry James. *See* **8563.**

9440. COX, JAMES M. (introd.).   Life on the Mississippi. New York; Harmondsworth: Penguin, 1984. pp. 450. (Penguin American library.)

9441. EBLE, KENNETH E.   Howells and Twain: being and staying friends. *See* **8568.**

9442. —— Old Clemens and W. D. H.: the story of a remarkable friendship. *See* **8569.**

9443. GARBAGNATI, LUCILE.   Une traduction anesthésiante pour un texte subversif: Mark Twain: *The Adventures of Huckleberry Finn* (1884) traduit par W. L. Hughes, 1886. *In* (pp. 215–22) **1.**

9444. GILLETTE, JAY EDWIN.   Mark Twain's literary production: the writer at work, 1876–1885. Unpub. doct. diss., Univ. of California, Berkeley, 1985. [Abstr. in DA (46) 2692A.]

9445. GRUNZWEIG, WALTER.   Reminiscences of the Arkansas legislature, back fifty years ago: Mark Twain's use of Austrian politics in *Stirring Times in Austria. In* (pp. 181–93) **17.**

9446. HEATH, WILLIAM.   Tears and flapdoodle: sentimentality in *Huckleberry Finn.* SoCR (19:1) 60–79.

9447. JHANG, GAP-SANG.   Munhak eui sahaejeok poongja: *Huck Finn* eul jungsim euro. (Social satire in *Huck Finn.*) UJH (28) Dec., 131–43.

9448. KASSER, STEPHEN JAY.   Speech into print: a structural account of Mark Twain's use of folklore. *See* **2459.**

9449. KAUFMAN, W. K.   Mark Twain, Lenny Bruce and Kurt Vonnegut: the comedian as confidence man. Unpub. doct. diss., Univ. of Wales, Aberystwyth, 1985. [Abstr. in IT (36) 24.]

9450. KETTERER, DAVID (ed.).   The science fiction of Mark Twain. (Bibl. 1985, 8216.) Rev. by John Lauber in ESCan (12:3) 360–4; by Eric Solomon in SAF (14:1) 114–15.

9451. KISKIS, MICHAEL J.   Purpose and pattern in Mark Twain's autobiography. Unpub. doct. diss., State Univ. of New York at Albany. [Abstr. in DA (47) 1325A.]

9452. KOLB, HAROLD H., JR.   Mere humor and moral humor: the example of Mark Twain. ALR (19:1) 52–64.

9453. LONG, E. HUDSON; LEMASTER, J. R.   The new Mark Twain handbook. New York; London: Garland, 1985. pp. xxii, 254. (Garland reference library of the humanities, 615.) (Revised ed.: first ed., as *Mark Twain Handbook*, 1957.)

9454. LUCID, ROBERT F.   Aesthetic sensibility and the idea of the imagination in America. Review (7) 1985, 113–18 (review-article).

9455. MACHAN, TIM WILLIAM.   The symbolic narrative of *Huckleberry Finn*. AQ (42:2) 131–40.

9456. MIHĂILĂ, RODICA (trans. and ed.).   Sub cerul liber. (Roughing it.) Bucharest: Sport-Turism, 1985. pp. 375.

9457. PARKER, R. N.   The notion of the outsider in the writings of Cooper, Hawthorne, Twain and Faulkner. *See* **7968.**

9458. PRATT, PETER PHILIP.   The paradoxical wilderness: Mailer and American nature writing. *See* **9372.**

9459. RICHARDSON, THOMAS J.   Is Shakespeare dead? Mark Twain's irreverent question. *In* (pp. 63–82) **51.**

9460. ROBINSON, DOUGLAS.   Joan of Orc: a reading of Twain's French fantasy through Blake's *America: a Prophesy*. *See* **6279.**

9461. ROBINSON, FORREST G.   Patterns of consciousness in *The Innocents Abroad*. AL (58:1) 46–63.

9462. ROSS, MEREDITH JANE.   The sublime to the ridiculous: the restructuring of Arthurian materials in selected modern novels. *See* **3655.**

9463. SATTELMEYER, ROBERT; CROWLEY, J. DONALD (eds).   One hundred years of Huckleberry Finn: the boy, his book, and American culture. (Bibl. 1985, 8234.) Rev. by Everett Emerson in SAQ (85:4) 394–5.

9464. SEIDEL, KATHRYN LEE.   Emblems of anxiety: similes in *Huckleberry Finn*. *See* **1243.**

9465. SEWELL, DAVID R.   Varieties of language in the writings of Mark Twain. *See* **1030.**

9466. STAHL, JOHN DANIEL.   American myth in European disguise: fathers and sons in *The Prince and the Pauper*. AL (58:2) 203–16.

9467. STROHMIDEL, KARL-OTTO.   'Tranquil ecstasy': Mark Twains pastoral Neigung und ihre literarische Gestaltung. Amsterdam: Grüner. pp. xii, 302. (Bochumer anglistische Studien, 20.)

9468. STRONG, WILLIAM FREDERICK.   Mark Twain's speaking in the dark years. Unpub. doct. diss., Univ. of Arizona, 1985. [Abstr. in DA (46) 2131A.]

9469. SUNG, JONG-TAE.   Mark Twain soseol eui jakjung inmul eui bokhap jaah. (The double self image of characters in Mark Twain's novels.) Unpub. doct. diss., Yeungnam Univ. (Korea).

9470. WARTH, ROBERT D.   Mark Twain and the Gorky affair. SAQ (85:1) 32–9.

9471. WESTENDORP, TJEBBE A.   'He backed me into a corner and blockaded me with a chair': strategies of Mark Twain's literary campaigns. DQR (16:1) 22–36.

9472. WILSON, JAMES C.   *The Great Dark*: invisible spheres, formed in fright. MidQ (23:2) 1982, 229–43.

Sukey Vickery

9473. DAVIDSON, CATHY N.   Female authorship and authority: the case of Sukey Vickery. EAL (21:1) 4–28.

Mrs Humphry Ward (Mary Augusta Arnold)

9474. COLLISTER, PETE.   Alpine retreats and Arnoldian recoveries: Mrs Humphry Ward's *Lady Rose's Daughter*. DUJ (78:2), 1985, 289–99.

9475. SNAITH, C. V.   Mrs Humphry Ward: woman and writer. Unpub. doct. diss., Univ. of Hull. [Abstr. in IT (36) 471.]

Susan Warner

9476. DOBSON, JOANNE.   The hidden hand: subversion of cultural ideology in three mid-nineteenth-century American women's novels. *See* **9254.**

Sir William Watson

9477. WILSON, JEAN MOORCROFT (ed.).   I was an English poet: a critical biography of Sir William Watson (1858–1936). (Bibl. 1982, 8948.) Rev. by Clyde de L. Ryals in YES (16) 343.

Daniel Webster

9478. ERICKSON, PAUL D.   The poetry of events: Daniel Webster's rhetoric of the Constitution and Union. New York; London: New York UP. pp. xv, 147. (Cf. bibl. 1985. 8256.)

Walt Whitman

9479. BERTHOLD, DENNIS; PRICE, KENNETH M. (eds).   Dear Brother Walt: the letters of Thomas Jefferson Whitman. (Bibl. 1985, 8269.) Rev. by Larry Gara in CWH (32:2) 181–2.

9480. CAVITCH, DAVID.   My soul and I: the inner life of Walt Whitman. Boston, MA: Beacon Press, 1985. pp. xvi, 193. Rev. by Vivian R. Pollak in WWQR (4:1) 44–6; by C. Carroll Hollis in AL (58:3) 445–6; by David S. Reynolds in NYTB, 2 Feb., 14.

9481. CHANG, YOUNG-HEE.   Journeys between the real and the ideal. *See* **8269.**

9482. DEDMOND, FRANCIS B. (ed.).   'Here among soldiers in hospital': an unpublished letter from Walt Whitman to Lucia Jane Russell Briggs. NEQ (59:4) 544–8.

9483. ERKKILA, BETSY.   The federal mother: Whitman as revolutionary. Prospects (10) 1985, 423–41.

9484. FOLSOM, ED.   An unknown photograph of Whitman and Harry Stafford. WWQR (3:4) 51–2.

9485. FREEDMAN, FLORENCE BERNSTEIN.   William Douglas O'Connor: Walt Whitman's chosen knight. *See* **9009.**

9486. GIANTVALLEY, SCOTT.   *Walt Whitman, 1838–1939: A Reference Guide*: additional annotations. WWQR (4:1) 24–40.

9487. GILBERT, SANDRA M.   The American sexual poetics of Walt Whitman and Emily Dickinson. *In* (pp. 123–54) **47.**

9488. GOLDEN, ARTHUR.   The ending of the 1855 version of *Song of Myself.* WWQR (3:4) 27–30.

9489. —— Nine early Whitman letters, 1840–1841. AL (58:3) 342–60.

9490. GOODBLATT, CHANITA; GLICKSOHN, JOSEPH.   Cognitive psychology and Whitman's *Song of Myself.* Mosaic (19:3) 83–90.

9491. GRANT, JOHN ARLINGTON, JR.   The nature of spirituality in Walt Whitman's *Leaves of Grass.* Unpub. doct. diss., Saint Louis Univ., 1984. [Abstr. in DA (46) 1941A.]

9492. GRIER, EDWARD F. (ed.).   Walt Whitman: notebooks and unpublished prose manuscripts. (Bibl. 1985, 8281.) Rev. by Ed Folsom in PQ (65:2) 287–91; by David Bromwich in TLS, 21 Mar., 291–2.

9493. HERNDON, JERRY A.   Emerson's *Nature* and Whitman's *Song of Myself. See* **8279.**

9494. HINZ, E. J.; TEUNISSEN, J. J.   Milton, Whitman, Wolfe and Laurence: *The Stone Angel* as elegy. *See* **5728.**

9495. HOLLIS, C. CARROLL.   Is there a text in this grass? WWQR (3:3) 15–22.

9496. HUDGINS, ANDREW.   *Leaves of Grass* from the perspective of modern epic practice. MidQ (23:3) 1982, 380–90.

9497. JACKSON, BRENDAN.   A reluctant American: Ezra Pound's response to Whitman, Whistler and Henry James. *See* **8687.**

9498. KAPLAN, JUSTIN (ed.).   Complete poetry and collected prose. (Bibl. 1984, 8537.) Rev. by David Bromwich in TLS, 21 Mar., 291–2.

9499. KIEFER, DANIEL REYNARD.   Figurations of poetic voice in Whitman and Wordsworth. Unpub. doct. diss., Yale Univ., 1985. [Abstr. in DA (47) 169A.]

9500. KILLINGSWORTH, M. JIMMIE.   Whitman's sexual themes during a decade of revision: 1866–1876. WWQR (4:1) 7–15.

9501. KIM, YOUNG HO.   Philosophies, themes and symbols in the poetry of Walt Whitman and Han Yong-Un. Unpub. doct. diss., Univ. of Illinois at Urbana-Champaign, 1985. [Abstr. in DA (46) 1932A.]

9502. KRIEG, JOANN P. (ed.).   Walt Whitman: here and now. Westport, CT: Greenwood Press, 1985. pp. viii, 248. Rev. by C. Carroll Hollis in WWQR (3:4) 31–8.

9503. LEONARD, DOUGLAS.   The art of Walt Whitman's French in *Song of Myself.* WWQR (3:4) 24–7.

9504. LI, XILAO.   A selected bibliography of Walt Whitman in Chinese (1919–1984). WWQR (3:4) 43–7.

9505. —— Walt Whitman in China. WWQR (3:4) 1–8.

9506. LOVING, JEROME.   Whitman in the (latest) Soviet view. WWQR (3:4) 9–15.

9507. MARTIN, ROBERT K.   Walt Whitman and Thomas Mann. WWQR (4:1) 1–6.

9508. MARTIN, ROBERT KESSLER.   The 'half-hid warp': Whitman, Crane, and the tradition of 'adhesiveness' in American poetry. Unpub. doct. diss., Brown Univ., 1978. [Abstr. in DA (46) 2693A.]

9509. NATHANSON, TENNEY J.   You who peruse me: writing and the voice in Walt Whitman. Unpub. doct. diss., Columbia Univ., 1983. [Abstr. in DA (47) 180A.]

9510. PEATTIE, ROGER W.   Whitman, Charles Aldrich and W. M. Rossetti in 1885: background to the Whitman subscription. *See* **272.**

9511. PERRY, DENNIS R.   Whitman's influence on Stoker's *Dracula*. *See* **9279.**

9512. PLUMLY, STANLEY.   The abrupt edge. *See* **7697.**

9513. POSTMA, PAMELA.   Self-marriage, dream children, and the poetic imagination: a new reading of Whitman's *Twenty-eight Young Men*. ATQ (61) 37–46.

9514. QUINLAN, KIERAN.   Sea and sea-shore in *Song of Myself*: Whitman's liquid theme. *In* (pp. 185–92) **28.**

9515. REYNOLDS, DAVID S.   Whitman's America: a revolution of the backgrounds of *Leaves of Grass*. CREL (3) 1985, 98–105.

9516. SAVAGE, GEORGE E.   'Fronting it': radical realism in Whitman and Thoreau. *See* **9376.**

9517. TAPSCOTT, STEPHEN.   American beauty: William Carlos Williams and the modernist Whitman. Guildford: Columbia UP, 1984. (Cf. bibl. 1984, 8552.) Rev. by Christopher Clausen in AL (57) 1985, 140–3.

9518. THOMAS, M. WYNN.   Walt Whitman's Welsh connection: Ernest Rhys. AWR (82) 77–85.

9519. TUERK, RICHARD.   Michael Gold on Walt Whitman. WWQR (3:4) 16–23.

9520. WEINGARDEN, LAUREN S.   Naturalized technology: Louis H. Sullivan's Whitmanesque skyscrapers. CR (30:4) 480–95.

9521. WELLS, DANIEL A.   Whitman allusions in *Harper's Monthly*: an annotated list of citations. *See* **722.**

9522. WHITE, WILLIAM.   About Walt Whitman: Apollinaire's April fool's hoax. Long-Islander, 1 May, 14.

9523. —— About Walt Whitman: found: a Whitman Long-Islander. Long-Islander, 31 July, 13.

9524. —— About Walt Whitman: John Ciardi and Walt Whitman. Long-Islander, 17 Apr., 18.

9525. —— About Walt Whitman: letters from Woodbury. Long-Islander, 3 Apr., 20–1.

9526. —— About Walt Whitman: Louisa Van Velsor Whitman, the poet's mother. Long-Islander, 9 Jan., 3.

9527. —— About Walt Whitman: *The Midnight Visitor* not by Walt Whitman. Long-Islander, 30 Oct., 6.

9528. —— About Walt Whitman: on Walter Whitman, Sr. Long-Islander, 23 Jan., 3.

9529. —— About Walt Whitman: one hundred years ago. Long-Islander, 2 Jan., 8.

9530. —— About Walt Whitman: opinions of famous authors on Whitman. Long-Islander, 13 Mar., 12.

9531. —— About Walt Whitman: parodies of *Leaves of Grass*. Long-Islander, 27 Feb., 20.

9532. —— About Walt Whitman: 'Saint Walt'. Long-Islander, 20 Nov., 3, 15.

9533. —— About Walt Whitman: teaching school on Long Island, 1836. Long-Islander, 25 Sept., 11.

9534. —— About Walt Whitman: Whitman's California. Long-Islander, 30 Jan., 14.

9535. —— About Walt Whitman: who is Walt Whitman? what did he do? Long-Islander, 20 Mar., 14.

9536. —— 'Morbid adhesiveness – to be kept down': unpublished MS. WWQR (4:1) 49.

9537. —— Whitman: a current bibliography. WWQR (3:3) 39–43; (3:4) 48–50; (4:1) 41–3.

9538. —— Whitman: unrecorded notes on health. WWQR (3:3) 44.

9539. YUKMAN, CLAUDIA. Speaking to strangers: Dickinson's and Whitman's poetics of historical presence. *See* **8157.**

9540. ZWEIG, PAUL. Walt Whitman: the making of the poet. (Bibl. 1985, 8331.) Rev. by Hermione Lee in LRev, Dec. 1985, 4–5; by David Bromwich in TLS, 21 Mar., 291–2.

Anne Whitney

9541. DOBSON, JOANNE. The hidden hand: subversion of cultural ideology in three mid-nineteenth-century American women's novels. *See* **9254.**

Oscar Wilde

9542. ACKROYD, PETER (ed.). The picture of Dorian Gray. Harmondsworth: Penguin, 1984. pp. 269.

9543. D'ALESSANDRO, JEAN M. ELLIS. Hues of mutability: the waning vision in Oscar Wilde's narrative. Florence: Florence UP, 1983. pp. xxii, 244. Rev. by John Stokes in YES (16) 338–40.

9544. DELSEMME, PAUL. Oscar Wilde et la Beligique fin de siècle. *In* (pp. 277–91) **12.**

9545. ELLIS, MARY LOUISE. Improbable visitor: Oscar Wilde in Alabama, 1882. AlaR (39:4) 243–60.

9546. ELLMANN, RICHARD. Four Dubliners: Wilde, Yeats, Joyce, and Beckett. Washington, DC: Library of Congress; London: Hamilton. pp. x, 106.

9547. HART-DAVIS, RUPERT (ed.). More letters of Oscar Wilde. (Bibl. 1985, 8338.) Rev. by Humphrey Carpenter in TLS, 18 Apr., 414.

9548. KIJINSKI, JOHN L. Values, assumptions, and persuasion in the literary criticism of Arnold, Pater, and Wilde. *See* **7559.**

9549. KLOTZ, VOLKER. Das europäische Kunstmärchen. Fünfund-zwanzig Kapitel seiner Geschichte von der Renaissance bis zur Moderne. *See* **2846.**

9550. LICH, GLEN E. 'Anything but a misprint': comments on an Oscar Wilde typescript. *See* **318.**

9551. POWELL, KERRY. Who was Basil Hallward? ELN (24:1) 84–91.

9552. RAPOZA, FRANCES. Oscar Wilde and the Oxford tradition. Unpub. doct. diss., Univ. of California, Los Angeles, 1985. [Abstr. in DA (46) 1952A.]

9553. SCHÖNFELD, EICKE.   Der deformierte Dandy. Oscar Wilde im Zerrspiegel der Parodie. Frankfurt: Lang. pp. 344. (Neue Studien zur Anglistik und Amerikanistik, 33.)

9554. SHEWAN, R.   Oscar Wilde's *Salome*: a critical variorum edition from three extant manuscripts, proofsheets and two early printed texts transcribed in parallel. *See* **336.**

9555. TREMPER, ELLEN.   Commitment and escape: the fairy tales of Thackeray, Dickens, and Wilde. *See* **8094.**

9556. TYDEMAN, WILLIAM (ed.).   Wilde: comedies. *Lady Windermere's Fan, A Woman of No Importance, An Ideal Husband, The Importance of Being Earnest*: a casebook. (Bibl. 1984, 8600.) Rev. by John Stokes in YES (16) 338–40.

9557. WORTH, KATHARINE.   Oscar Wilde. (Bibl. 1984, 8604.) Rev. by John Stokes in YES (16) 338–40; by Norman White in NQ (33:1) 125–6; by Joel H. Kaplan in CJIS (12:1) 104–5.

9558. ZEENDER, MARIE-NOELLE.   Miroir de l'âme irlandaise: aspects du fantastique chez Le Fanu, chez Wilde et chez Stoker. *See* **8871.**

Nathaniel Parker Willis
9559. KLIEWER, WARREN.   American theatrical taste as class warfare. SDR (22:1) 1984, 6–15.

9560. Entry cancelled.

Cardinal Wiseman (Nicholas Patrick Stephen Wiseman)
9561. DURAND, MICHEL.   Les héros des cimetières souterrains ou le mythe victorien des catacombes. CVE (23) 17–34.

Constance Fenimore Woolson
9562. DEAN, SHARON.   Constance Woolson's Southern sketches. SoS (25:3) 274–83.

9563. LUPOLD, HARRY FORREST.   Constance Fenimore Woolson and the genre of regional fiction. OhioanaQ (29:4) 132–6.

9564. WEIMER, JOAN MEYERS.   Women artists as exiles in the fiction of Constance Fenimore Woolson. Legacy (3:2) 3–15.

Dorothy Wordsworth
9565. DE SELINCOURT, ERNEST (ed.).   The letters of William and Dorothy Wordsworth: vol. 6, The later years; part 3, 1835–1839. (Second ed., revised by ALAN G. HILL.) (Bibl. 1982, 9048.) Rev. by P. H. Butter in MLR (81:3) 724–5.

9566. GITTINGS, ROBERT; MANTON, JO.   Dorothy Wordsworth. (Bibl. 1985, 8349.) Rev. by Victor N. Paananen in CR (30:3) 429–31; by I. A. Rabinowitz in UES (24:2) 44–6.

9567. HILL, ALAN G. (ed.).   Letters of Dorothy Wordsworth: a selection. Oxford: Clarendon Press, 1985. (Cf. bibl. 1985, 8350, where date of publication incorrect.) Rev. by I. A. Rabinowitz in UES (24:2) 46–7.

William Wordsworth
9568. ALEXANDER, J. H.   Scott's *The Chase* and Wordsworth's *Hart-Leap Well*. *See* **9155.**

9569. AVERILL, JAMES (ed.). An evening walk. Ithaca, NY: Cornell UP, 1984. pp. xii, 306. Rev. by James K. Chandler in MP (84:2) 196–208.

9570. BAKER, JOHN MILTON, JR. Myth and poetic statement: the myth as function of discursive temporality in texts of Hölderlin, Keats and Wordsworth. *See* **8799.**

9571. BANERJEE, JIBON KRISHNA. Moral concerns in the dramatic works of Wordsworth, Coleridge and Southey. *See* **7886.**

9572. BEWELL, ALAN J. A 'word scarce said': hysteria and witchcraft in Wordsworth's 'experimental' poetry of 1797–1798. ELH (53:2) 357–90.

9573. BIDNEY, MARTIN. *The Common Day* and the Immortality Ode: Cheever's Wordsworthian craft. SSF (23:2) 139–51.

9574. —— Solomon and Pharaoh's daughter: Blake's response to Wordsworth's prospectus to *The Recluse*. *See* **6221.**

9575. BIRDSALL, ERIC. Nature and society in *Descriptive Sketches*. MP (84:1) 39–52.

9576. —— ZALL, PAUL M. (eds). Descriptive sketches. (Bibl. 1985, 8356.) Rev. by James K. Chandler in MP (84:2) 196–208.

9577. BLANK, G. K. Shelley and the problem of Wordsworth's influence. *See* **9207.**

9578. —— Shelley's Wordsworth: the desiccated celandine. *See* **9208.**

9579. BRINKLEY, ROBERT A. On the composition of *Mont Blanc*: staging a Wordsworthian scene. *See* **9210.**

9580. BUTLER, JAMES (ed.). *The Ruined Cottage* and *The Pedlar*. Ithaca, NY: Cornell UP; Hassocks: Harvester Press, 1979. pp. xvi, 480. Rev. by James K. Chandler in MP (84:2) 196–208.

9581. CHAI, LEON CHRISTOPHER. Melville and European Romanticism: studies on Melville's relations to major European Romantic writers. *See* **7898.**

9582. CHANDLER, JAMES K. Wordsworth rejuvenated. MP (84:2) 196–208 (review-article).

9583. CHRISTIE, W. H. Francis Jeffrey, Samuel Taylor Coleridge's *Biographia Literaria* and the contemporary criticism of William Wordsworth. *See* **7900.**

9584. COLVILLE, DEREK. The teaching of Wordsworth. Berne: Lang, 1984. pp. 125. Rev. by Mary Wedd in CLB (53) 155–6.

9585. COOMBS, JAMES H. Wordsworth and Milton: prophet–poets. *See* **5693.**

9586. DAVIES, HUGH SYKES. Wordsworth and the worth of words. Ed. by JOHN KERRIGAN and JONATHAN WORDSWORTH. Cambridge: CUP. pp. xii, 324.

9587. DE BOLLA, P. L. Wordsworth and the rhetoric of power. Unpub. doct. diss., Univ. of Cambridge, 1985.

9588. EASSON, ANGUS. Statesman, dwarf and weaver: Wordsworth and nineteenth-century narrative. *In* (pp. 16–29) **39.**

9589. EIFRIG, GAIL MCGRAW. Balancing Wordsworth and Wodehouse. Cresset (49:8) 7–12.

9590. EILENBERG, SUSAN RUTH. Strange power of speech: usurping voices in Wordsworth and Coleridge. *See* **7902.**

9591. ELDRIDGE, RICHARD. Self-understanding and community in Wordsworth's poetry. PhilL (10:2) 273–94.

9592. ELLIS, DAVID. Wordsworth, Freud and the spots of time: interpretation in *The Prelude*. (Bibl. 1985, 8370.) Rev. by David Gervais in CamQ (15:2) 148–56; by John Woolley in Eng (35) 73–8.

9593. FITZ GERALD, J. M. P. Wordsworth's natural philosophy: phlogiston and physiology in Wordsworth's poetry, 1798–1800. Unpub. doct. diss., Univ. of Cambridge, 1985. [Abstr. in IT (35) 546.]

9594. FLEISSNER, R. F. Retaking *The Road Not Taken*: a comic byway to it? NCL (16:2) 2–5.

9595. FRIEDMAN, GERALDINE SIMA. Writing in stone: monumentality and fragmentation in Wordsworth, Baudelaire and Rilke. Unpub. doct. diss., Yale Univ., 1985. [Abstr. in DA (47) 1920A.]

9596. GALPERIN, WILLIAM H. Authority and deconstruction in Book v of *The Prelude*. SELit (26:4) 613–31.

9597. GAST, MARLENE. Wordsworth and Milton: varieties of connection. *See* **5716.**

9598. GHOSH, TAPAN KUMAR. The culture of the feeling: a study of Wordsworth and Mill. *See* **8969.**

9599. GILL, STEPHEN (ed.). *The Salisbury Plain Poems* of William Wordsworth. (Bibl. 1977, 8287.) Rev. by James K. Chandler in MP (84:2) 196–208.

9600. —— William Wordsworth. (Bibl. 1984, 8630.) Rev. by Mary Wedd in CLB (54) 185–90; by Karen McLeod Hewitt in NQ (33:2) 248–9.

9601. GRAVER, BRUCE E. Wordsworth and the language of epic: the translation of the *Aeneid*. *See* **5417.**

9602. HAMILTON, PAUL. Wordsworth. Brighton: Harvester Press. pp. xii, 159. (Harvester new readings.)

9603. HILL, JAMES L. Experiments in the narrative of consciousness: Byron, Wordsworth, and *Childe Harold*, cantos 3 and 4. *See* **7775.**

9604. INBODEN, ROBIN LOUISE. 'The music in my heart I bore': the ballad revival, Scott, and Wordsworth. *See* **2520.**

9605. JARVIS, R. J. The early *Prelude*: texts and contexts. Unpub. doct. diss., Univ. of Southampton, 1982.

9606. JOHNSTON, KENNETH R. Wordsworth and *The Recluse*. New Haven, CT: Yale UP, 1984. (Bibl. 1984, 8643.) Rev. by John E. Jordan in Review (8) 51–5.

9607. JUMP, HARRIET. Tendencies in Wordsworth's *Prelude* revisions. CLB (54) 175–85.

9608. KELLERMANN, HENRYK. The meaning of 'utterance' in Wordsworth's *Immortality Ode*. Archiv (223:2) 356–62.

9609. KELLIHER, W. H. (introd.). The manuscript of William Wordsworth's *Poems, in Two Volumes* (1807). *See* **158.**

9610. KIEFER, DANIEL REYNARD. Figurations of poetic voice in Whitman and Wordsworth. *See* **9499.**

9611. KIM, JAE-IN.   Wordsworth eui sangsangryeuk yeongu. (On Wordsworth's imagination.) Unpub. doct. diss., Yonsei Univ. (Seoul), 1985.

9612. KING, EVERARD H.   Wordsworth and Beattie's *Minstrel*: the progress of poetic autobiography. *See* **6200.**

9613. KISHEL, JOSEPH F. (ed.).   *The Tuft of Primroses* with other late poems for *The Recluse*. Ithaca, NY; London: Cornell UP, pp. xiv, 394. (Cornell Wordsworth.)

9614. KNEALE, DOUGLAS.   Milton, Wordsworth, and the 'joint labourers' of *The Prelude*. *See* **5744.**

9615. KNEALE, J. DOUGLAS.   Wordsworth's images of language: voice and letter in *The Prelude*. PMLA (101:3) 351–61.

9616. LANGBAUM, ROBERT.   The epiphanic mode in Wordsworth and modern literature. NLH (14:2) 1983, 335–58.

9617. LEE, CHONG-HO.   Wordsworth eui si e natanan wa hanggu eui imagery. (Imagery of potentiality and permanence in Wordsworth's poetry.) EngSt (10) 39–49.

9618. LENNON, J.   Wordsworth and death. Unpub. doct. diss., Univ. of St Andrews, 1985. [Abstr. in IT (35) 49.]

9619. LEPPARD, D. G.   An investigation into the theory and structure of metaphor, with special reference to Wordsworth and Yeats. *See* **2235.**

9620. LEVINSON, MARJORIE.   Wordsworth's great period poems: four essays. Cambridge: CUP. pp. x, 170.

9621. LOGAN, S. W.   The moral implications of Wordsworth's style. Unpub. doct. diss., Univ. of Oxford. [Abstr. in IT (35) 546.]

9622. LOUKIDES, MICHAEL KOSTA.   The world's metrics: repetitive modelling in Wordsworth's poetry. Unpub. doct. diss., Stanford Univ., 1985. [Abstr. in DA (46) 3727A.]

9623. McCRACKEN, DAVID.   Wordsworth and the Lake District: a guide to the poems and their places. (Bibl. 1985, 8391.) Rev. by John E. Jordan in Review (8) 50–1.

9624. MARCUS, STEVEN.   Some representations of childhood in Wordsworth's poetry. *In* (pp. 1–16) **40.**

9625. MARTIN, PHILIP W.   Lucid intervals: Dryden, Carkesse, and Wordsworth. *See* **5324.**

9626. MAYS, J. C. C.   The authorship of 'The Barberry Tree'. *See* **7413.**

9627. MORÈRE, PIERRE.   Mémoire et création dans les Préfaces des *Lyrical Ballads*: l'héritage du dix-huitième siècle. *In* (pp. 23–39) **34.**

9628. NAGASAWA, JIRO.   Dove Cottage Manuscript 98, 99 to the Forth and Clyde Canal. (Dove Cottage Manuscript 98, 99 and the Forth and Clyde Canal.) SEL (63:2) 257–70.

9629. NEWLYN, L. A.   The myth of loss: echo, allusion and interconnection in the poetry of Wordsworth and Coleridge, 1797–1807. *See* **7931.**

9630. OSBORN, ROBERT (ed.).   The borderers. (Bibl. 1985, 8396.) Rev. by James K. Chandler in MP (84:2) 196–208.

9631. OWEN, W. J. B. (ed.).   The fourteen-book *Prelude*. Ithaca, NY;

London: Cornell UP, 1985. pp. xii, 1222. (Cornell Wordsworth.) Rev. by Paul Hamilton in THES (687) 16.

9632. PATI, MADHUSUDAN. Wordsworth: an Indian view. Jadavpur University Essays and Studies (Calcutta) (4) 1984, 64–73.

9633. PIEŃKOWSKI, PIOTR. The idea of the mental garden in William Wordsworth's poetry. *In* (pp. 127–45) **17.**

9634. PRICKETT, STEPHEN. Macaulay's vision of 1930: Wordsworth and the battle for the wilderness. *See* **8877.**

9635. RIEDER, JOHN. Description of a struggle: Shelley's radicalism on Wordsworth's terrain. *See* **9240.**

9636. ROE, N. H. Wordsworth, Coleridge and the French Revolution, 1789–1795. *See* **7934.**

9637. ROSS, MARLON B. Naturalizing gender: woman's place in Wordsworth's ideological landscape. ELH (53:2) 391–410.

9638. RZEPKA, CHARLES J. The self as mind: vision and identity in Wordsworth, Coleridge and Keats. *See* **7936.**

9639. SCARFONE, SUZANNE. The architectonics of fate: equilibrium and the process of creation in the work of William Wordsworth and Virginia Woolf. Unpub. doct. diss., Wayne State Univ., 1985. 2 vols. [Abstr. in DA (47) 190A.]

9640. SETZER, SHARON M. Wordsworth's *The Excursion* and the discourse of the other. Unpub. doct. diss., Duke Univ., 1985. [Abstr. in DA (47) 915A.]

9641. SITTERSON, JOSEPH C., JR. The genre and place of the Intimations Ode. PMLA (101:1) 24–37.

9642. SPIEGELMAN, WILLARD. Wordsworth's heroes. Berkeley; London: California UP, 1985. pp. xi, 258. Rev. by Roger Sharrock in THES (720) 15.

9643. TAKANO, MASAO. Kansei no utage: Keats, Wordsworth, Blake. (A feast of sensibility: Keats, Wordsworth, Blake.) *See* **6282.**

9644. TAYLOR, ANYA. Religious readings of the Immortality Ode. SELit (26:4) 633–54.

9645. TURNER, JOHN. Wordsworth: play and politics; a study of Wordsworth's poetry, 1781–1800. London: Macmillan. pp. xiii, 230. (Macmillan studies in Romanticism.)

9646. WARD, J. P. Wordsworth's language of men. (Bibl. 1985, 8416.) Rev. by David Gervais in CamQ (15:2) 148–56.

9647. WATSON, J. R. Wordsworth's vital soul: the sacred and profane in Wordsworth's poetry. (Bibl. 1984, 8681.) Rev. by Peter Larkin in YES (16) 289–90.

9648. WINBERG, CHRISTINE. Imagining Wordsworth: De Quincey and the art of biography. *See* **8003.**

9649. WORDSWORTH, JONATHAN. 'The Barberry Tree' revisited. *See* **7437.**

9650. —— William Wordsworth: the borders of vision. (Bibl. 1985, 8421.) Rev. by Marcel Isnard in EA (39:1) 99–101.

Charlotte M. Yonge

9651. MOBERLY, P. J.   Charlotte Mary Yonge's Anglicanism: an examination of John Keble's influence on her literary development and achievement. *See* **8830.**

TWENTIETH CENTURY
GENERAL
General Literary Studies

9652. ADAMOWSKI, T. H. (ed.). Letters in Canada 1985. UTQ (56:1) 1–282.

9653. AMIRTHANAYAGAM, GUY (ed.). Writers in east–west encounter: new cultural bearings. (Bibl. 1983, 129.) Rev. by A. H. Qureshi in CanRCL (13:2) 303–8.

9654. AMIS, MARTIN. The moronic inferno and other visits to America. London: Cape. pp. xi, 208.

9655. ANTOR, HEINZ. The Bloomsbury group: its philosophy, aesthetics, and literary achievement. Heidelberg: Winter. pp. 148.

9656. ARMSTRONG, NANCY. Introduction: literature as women's history. Genre (19:4) 347–69.

9657. AWOONOR, KOFI. Caliban answers Prospero: the dialogue between Western and African literature. Ob (7) Summer/Winter 1981, 75–98.

9658. BABEAUX, KATHY. Latest books of Ohio authors and on the Ohio scene. OhioanaQ (29:3) S 18–S 33.

9659. BAKER, HOUSTON A., JR. Blues, ideology, and Afro-American literature: a vernacular theory. Chicago: Chicago UP, 1985. pp. xi, 227. Rev. by Johnnella E. Butler in Novel (20:1) 90–3; by John Cooley in AL (58:2) 290–2; by Kimberly Benston in CR (30:1) 109–10; by Minrose C. Gwin in JEGP (85:3) 476–8.

9660. BALOGUN, F. ODUN. Who is the audience of modern African literature: a reply. Ob (7) Summer/Winter 1981, 29–36.

9661. BANDIERA, MARY A. Sacco and Vanzetti in the arts. ItalA (8:1) 47–71.

9662. BARKER-NUNN, JEANNE BEVERLY. A more adequate conception: American women writers' quest for a female ethic. Unpub. doct. diss., Univ. of Minnesota, 1985. [Abstr. in DA (46) 3069A.]

9663. BARNES, JOHN. 'Through clear Australian eyes': landscape and identity in Australian writing. *In* (pp. 86–104) **31.**

9664. BEASECKER, ROBERT; PADY, DONALD (eds). Annual bibliography of Midwestern literature: 1984. *See* **6979.**

9665. BELL, IAN. Patter-merchants and chancers. Planet (60) 43–52. (Glasgow writing.)

9666. BENNETT, BRUCE. Place, region and community. Townsville, Qld.: Foundation for Australian Literary Studies, 1985. pp. 64. (Monograph/Foundation for Australian Literary Studies, 11.)

9667. BENSTOCK, BERNARD. The assassin and the censor: political and literary tensions. CLIO (11:3) 1982, 219–38.

9668. BERCOVITCH, SACVAN (ed.). Reconstructing American literary history. *See* **47.**

9669. BERGONZI, BERNARD. *The Calendar of Modern Letters. See* **561.**

9670. —— The myth of Modernism and twentieth-century literature. Brighton: Harvester Press. pp. 216. Rev. by Frank Kermode in LRB (8:9) 3, 5–6; by Philip Hobsbaum in THES (708) 18.

9671. BERMAN, JEFFREY. The talking cure: literary representations of psychoanalysis. New York; London: New York UP, 1985. pp. x, 362.

9672. BERTHOLD, DENNIS. Cape Horn passages: literary conventions and nautical realities. *In* (pp. 40–50) **28.**

9673. BERTRAM, JAMES. Flight of the phoenix: critical notes on New Zealand writers. (Bibl. 1985, 8446.) Rev. by W. H. Oliver in NZList, 8 Nov., 66–7.

9674. BINYON, MIKE; EDE, RAY; WILLIAMS, DI (eds). Turning points. Manchester: Commonword, 1985. pp. 104.

9675. BLAEN, A. A survey and analysis of some aspects of West Country folklore as found in selected writings of Eden Phillpotts, Thomas Hardy, John Cowper Powys, Arthur Quiller-Couch and Henry Williamson. *See* **2396.**

9676. BLAMIRES, HARRY. Twentieth-century English literature. (Bibl. 1982, 9115.) London: Macmillan. pp. 296. (Macmillan history of literature.) (Second ed.: first ed. 1982.)

9677. BLODGETT, EDWARD. Translation as a key to Canadian literature. NC (1) 93–103.

9678. BLOOM, HAROLD. Agon: towards a theory of revisionism. New York; Oxford: OUP, 1982. (Cf. bibl. 1984, 8713.) Rev. by Marjorie Perloff in MLR (81:2) 431–5.

9679. BOWERING, GEORGE. Baseball and the Canadian imagination. CanL (108) 115–24.

9680. BRINK, ANDRÉ. Apocalyps nu: 'Het besef dat er iets eindigt' in recente Zuidafrikaanse bellettrie. (Apocalypse now: 'the idea that something is coming to an end' in recent South African literature.) De Gids (149:4) 287–96.

9681. BROEGE, VALERIE. War with the United States in Canadian literature and visual arts. JAC (9:1) 31–6.

9682. BURR, NELSON R. New Eden and new Babylon: religious thoughts of American authors: a bibliography: religious naturalism: the religious mysticism of nature. *See* **6992.**

9683. —— New Eden and new Babylon: religious thoughts of American authors: a bibliography: the 'death of God'. HMPEC (55:3) 213–47.

9684. CARTER, CAROLYN. Young people and books: a review of the research into young people's reading habits. *See* **2880.**

9685. CASTAN, CON. Ethnic Australian writing: is it really Australian literature? Outrider (Indooroopilly, Qld) (3:2) 64–79.

9686. CHAMETZKY, JULES. Ethnicity and beyond: an introduction. MassR (27:2) 242–51.

9687. CHILESHE, J. D. Literacy, literature and ideological formation: the Zambian case. Unpub. doct. diss., Univ. of Sussex, 1983.

9688. CHINWEIZU; JEMIE, ONWUCHEKWA; MADUBUIKE, IHECHUKWU. Toward the decolonization of African literature: vol. 1, African fiction and poetry and their critics. Enugu, Nigeria: Fourth Dimension, 1980;

London: KPI; Toronto: OUP, 1985. pp. xx, 320. Rev. by G. D. Killam in QQ (93:2) 431–2.

9689. CHOWDHURY, KABIR. The romantic tradition: focus on the literature of Bangladesh. Jadavpur University Essays and Studies (Calcutta) (4) 1984, 153–8.

9690. CLARK, WILLIAM BEDFORD; TURNER, W. CRAIG (eds). Critical essays on American humor. *See* **6999.**

9691. CLEMENTS, PATRICIA. Baudelaire and the English tradition. *See* **7000.**

9692. CNUDDE-KNOWLAND, A. Maurice Maeterlinck and English and Anglo-Irish literature: a study of parallels and influences. *See* **7001.**

9693. COALE, SAMUEL. The heart of darkness in the American romance. *See* **7002.**

9694. COHEN, RALPH. The aims and roles of *New Literary History*. *See* **575.**

9695. COLLIER, EUGENIA. The African presence in Afro-American literary criticism. Ob (6) Winter 1980, 30–55.

9696. COLLINS, ROBERT A.; PEARCE, HOWARD D. (eds). The scope of the fantastic: selected essays from the First International Conference on the Fantastic in Literature and Film. *See* **7003.**

9697. CONNOLLY, CYRIL. 100 key books of the modern movement from England, France and America 1880–1950. *See* **7005.**

9698. COOKE, MICHAEL G. Afro-American literature in the twentieth century: the achievement of intimacy. (Bibl. 1985, 8471.) Rev. by Alice Deck in JEGP (85:2) 293–5.

9699. CUNNINGHAM, VALENTINE (ed.). Spanish front: writers on the Civil War. Oxford: OUP. pp. xxxiii, 380.

9700. DABYDEEN, DAVID; WILSON-TAGOE, NANA. A reader's guide to West Indian and black British literature. Århus: Dangaroo Press. pp. 178.

9701. DARBY, ROBERT. The fall of fortress criticism. *See* **7010.**

9702. DAVIES, BARRIE. *Dulce* vs. *utile*: the Kevin O'Brien syndrome in New Brunswick literature. *See* **7011.**

9703. DAVIS, ROBERT MURRAY. Bloomsbury – and after? SCR (3:2) 69–77.

9704. DAVIS, THADIOUS M. Southern writers: notes toward a definition of terms. SoQ (19:2) 1981, 10–16.

9705. —— HARRIS, TRUDIER. Afro-American writers after 1958: dramatists and prose writers. Detroit, MI: Gale Research, 1985. pp. xvi, 390. (Dictionary of literary biography, 38). Rev. by Errol Hill in TJ (38:3) 383–4.

9706. DAYMOND, M. J.; JACOBS, J. U.; LENTA, MARGARET (eds). Momentum: on recent South African writing. (Bibl. 1985, 8480.) Rev. by Piniel Viriri Shava in Ariel (17:2) 94–7.

9707. DEACON, RICHARD. The Cambridge Apostles; a history of Cambridge University's elite intellectual secret society. *See* **7012.**

9708. DENNISON, SALLY. [Alternative] literary publishing: five modern histories. *See* **459.**

9709. D'IÂKONOVA, N.   Shekspir i angliĭskaiâ literatura XX veka. (Shakespeare and twentieth century English literature.) *See* **4428.**

9710. DIEPEVEEN, LEONARD.   Folktales in the Harlem Renaissance. *See* **2443.**

9711. DOCKER, JOHN.   Antipodean literature: a world upside down? *See* **7014.**

9712. DONOGHUE, DENIS.   We Irish: essays on Irish literature and society. New York: Knopf. pp. 275. Rev. by Robert Boyes in NYTB, 21 Sept., 13.

9713. DuPLESSIS, RACHEL BLAU.   Writing beyond the ending: narrative strategies of twentieth-century women writers. Bloomington: Indiana UP, 1985. pp. 253. Rev. by Ellen E. Berry in Novel (20:1) 78–81; by Katherine Fishburn in CR (30:3) 420–2.

9714. EADEN, P. R.; MORES, F. H. (eds).   Mapped but not known: the Australian landscape of the imagination. Essays and poems presented to Brian Elliott, 11 April 1985. *See* **31.**

9715. EGEJURU, PHAUEL.   Who is the audience of modern Africa literature? Ob (5) Spring/Summer 1979, 51–8.

9716. EPSTEIN, JOSEPH.   Windy City letters. NCrit (2:5) 1983/84, 37–46. (Literature of Chicago.)

9717. FABRE, GENEVIÈVE; FABRE, MICHEL.   La littérature noire américaine. TM (42:485) 185–98.

9718. FAULKNER, PETER (ed.).   A Modernist reader: Modernism in England 1910–1930. *See* **8664.**

9719. FEATHERSTONE, SIMON.   The nation as pastoral in British literature of the Second World War. JEurS (16:3) 155–68.

9720. FENDER, STEPHEN.   *The New York Review of Books. See* **597.**

9721. FETHERLING, DOUG.   The blue notebook: reports on Canadian culture. Oakville, Ont.: Mosiac Press, 1985. pp. 161. Rev. by Alexandre L. Amprimoz in CanP (19) 120–3.

9722. FINCH, PETER.   Dwarf grapes? *See* **598.**

9723. FINDLAY, ALLAN H. (ed.).   Root and branch: an anthology of southern African writing. Basingstoke: Macmillan, 1985. pp. xi, 252.

9724. FISHER, MARVIN.   Continuities: essays and ideas in American literature. *See* **7022.**

9725. FOKKEMA, DOUWE W.   Literary history, Modernism and post-Modernism. Amsterdam; Philadelphia, PA: Benjamins, 1984. pp. viii, 63. (Utrecht pubs in general and comparative literature, 19.) Rev. by Uri Margolin in CanRCL (13:3) 518–23.

9726. FOSTER, JOHN BURT, JR.   Heirs to Dionysus: a Nietzschean current in literary Modernism. (Bibl. 1985, 8497.) Rev. by Graham Good in CanRCL (12:3) 1985, 556–7.

9727. FOSTER, STEPHEN C.; KUENSLI, RUDOLPH E. (eds).   Dada spectrum: the dialectics of revolt. Madison, WI: Coda Press, 1979. pp. 291. Rev. by Stephen Scobie in CanRCL (12:3) 1985, 447–8

9728. FOULKE, ROBERT.   The literature of voyaging. *In* (pp. 1–13) **28.**

9729. FRIBERG, HEDDA.   Irish writing in the late 20th century: a report of a conversation with two Irish critics. MS (80) 210–20. (Declan Kiberd and Fintan O'Toole.)

9730. FRIEDMAN, ALAN J.; DONLEY, CAROL C. Einstein: as myth and muse. Cambridge: CUP, 1985. pp. xiv, 224.

9731. FUENTES, CARLOS; FORCHÉ, CAROLYN; GILDNER, GARY. Modern literature conference: the politics of experience. CR (30:2) 125–35.

9732. FUROMOTO, ATSUKO. America kokujin bungaku to folklore. (Black American literature and folklore.) *See* **2383.**

9733. GATES, HENRY LOUIS, JR (ed.). Black literature and literary theory. (Bibl. 1985, 8500.) Rev. by Reginald Martin in SCR (3:1) 107–9; by Ralph Willett in NQ (33:2) 280–1.

9734. GELFANT, BLANCHE H. Women writing in America: voices in collage. Hanover, NH; London: New England UP, 1984. pp. ix, 278. Rev. by Fred G. See in AL (58:1) 124–5; by Sandra M. Gilbert in Novel (20:1) 82–3.

9735. GÉRARD, ALBERT. Essais d'histoire littéraire africaine. *See* **7029.**

9736. GOLDSTEIN, LAURENCE. The image of Detroit in twentieth century literature. MichQR (25:2) 269–91.

9737. GOODWIN, KEN LESLIE. A history of Australian literature. *See* **5960.**

9738. GOONETILLEKE, D. C. R. A. Beyond alienation: the efflorescence of Sri Lankan literature in English. JCL (21:1) 26–38.

9739. GRAHAM, DON; LEE, JAMES W.; PILKINGTON, WILLIAM T. The Texas literary tradition: fiction, folklore, history. Austin: Texas UP, 1983. pp. 238. Rev. by Dorys Crow Grover in SocSJ (23:2) 228.

9740. GRAY, RICHARD. Writing the South: ideas of an American region. *See* **7034.**

9741. GRIGORESCU, DAN; TOMA, FLORIN (eds). Kalokagathon. By PETRU COMARNESCU. Bucharest: Editura Eminescu, 1985. pp. lii, 663. (Anderson, O'Neill, Shaw, Sinclair, Synge, Whitman, Wilder.)

9742. GROSS, HARVEY. Understanding Modernism. Review (8) 47–57 (review-article).

9743. GUGELBERGER, GEORG M. (ed.). Marxism and African literature. London: Currey, 1985. pp. xiii, 226.

9744. GUPTARA, PRAHBU. Black British literature: an annotated bibliography. Århus: Dangaroo Press. pp. 176.

9745. GUTKIND, LEE (ed.). Our roots grow deeper than we know: Pennsylvania writers/Pennsylvania life. Pittsburgh, PA: Pittsburgh UP, 1985. pp. xv, 290. Rev. by John L. Marsh in PMHB (110:2) 289–90.

9746. HAILSTONE, CHARLES; BELL, NANCY. History of Putney Literary and Debating Society. London: Putney Literary and Debating Soc., 1983. pp. 17.

9747. HALE, DAVID G. Interviews from the Brockport writers forum. BB (42) 1985, 34–41.

9748. HAMILTON, IAN (ed.). The *New Review* anthology. *See* **613.**

9749. HAMILTON, VIRGINIA.   On being a black writer in America. LU (10) 15–17.

9750. HARRISON, CRAIG.   No laughing matter. New Outlook, Jan./Feb., 40–3.

9751. HASHMI, ALAMGIR.   The place of American literature in our time. PJAS (4:2) 1–14.

9752. —— (ed.).   The worlds of Muslim imagination. Islamabad: Gulmohar Press. pp. 270. Rev. by Yasmine Gooneratne in CRNLE Reviews Journal (Bedford Park, S. Australia) (1986:2) 87–8; by Harry Aveling in Asiaweek (Hong Kong), 10 May, 64.

9753. HAYLES, N. KATHERINE.   The cosmic web: scientific field models and literary strategies in the twentieth century. (Bibl. 1985, 8519.) Rev. by Charles Elkins in SFS (13:2) 209–11; by Stuart Peterfreund in JEGP (85:1) 156–9.

9754. HEADON, DAVID.   Eccentrics, explorers and evangelists: a camel ride through the literature of the Northern Territory: part 1, Eccentrics and explorers. See **7036.**

9755. HEATH, STEPHEN.   Realism, modernism, and 'language-consciousness'. In (pp. 103–22) **46.**

9756. HECHT, ANTHONY.   Obbligati: essays in criticism. New York: Atheneum. pp. 330. Rev. by Anthony Thwaite in BkW, 31 Aug., 9; by Louis Menand in NYTB, 7 Sept., 19.

9757. HEINEMANN, MARLENE E.   Gender and destiny: women writers and the Holocaust. New York; London: Greenwood Press. pp. 149. (Contributions in women's studies, 72.)

9758. HERGENHAN, LAURIE; DUWELL, MARTIN.   Annual bibliography of studies in Australian literature: 1985. ALS (12:3) 367–91.

9759. HESELTINE, HARRY.   The uncertain self: essays in Australian literature and criticism. See **7039.**

9760. HILSKÝ, MARTIN.   Angus Wilson a nové tendence současné britské prózy. (Angus Wilson and the new trends in contemporary British prose.) In (pp. 25–6) **4.**

9761. HIMMELFARB, GERTRUDE.   From Clapham to Bloomsbury: a genealogy of morals. See **7040.**

9762. HOMBERGER, ERIC.   American writers and radical politics 1900–39: equivocal commitments. Basingstoke: Macmillan. pp. xiii, 268. (Macmillan studies in American literature.)

9763. HOOLEY, RUTH (ed.).   The female line: Northern Irish women writers. Belfast: Northern Ireland Women's Rights Movement, 1985. pp. 200.

9764. HUGHES, ROGER.   Caribbean writing: a checklist. London: Commonwealth Inst. Library Services. pp. 49. (Checklists on Commonwealth literature, 4.)

9765. IANNONE, CAROL.   The political-literary complex. Commentary (81:6) 64–7.

9766. IKIN, VAN; WALKER, BRENDA.   Annual bibliography of Commonwealth literature 1984: Australia (with Papua New Guinea). See **7047.**

9767. INDYK, IVOR. Some uses of myth in Australian literature. *See* **2458.**

9768. ISER, WOLFGANG. Changing functions of literature. YREAL (3) 1985, 1–21.

9769. JABBI, BU-BUAKEI. Influence and originality in African writing. Ob (6) Spring/Summer 1980, 7–23.

9770. JAMES, TREVOR. English literature from the Third World. *See* **7048.**

9771. JONES, DOROTHY. Mapping and mythmaking: women writers and the Australian legend. Ariel (17:4) 63–86.

9772. JONES, NANCY BAKER. On solid ground: the emergence of the self-created woman in contemporary American literature. Unpub. doct. diss., Univ. of Texas at Austin. [Abstr. in DA (47) 2158A.]

9773. JURGENSEN, MANFRED. Multicultural literature. Outrider (Indooroopilly, Qld) (3:2) 80–90.

9774. JURIST, JANET. The scandal of the Anglo-American Authors' Association. ABC (7:4) 13–19.

9775. KARAKOSTAS, A. Forty years of Greek writing in Australia: 1943/1983. Outrider (Indooroopilly, Qld) (1:2) 1984, 138–48.

9776. KATO, TUNEHIKO. America kokujin jyosei sakka no sekai. (The world of American black women writers.) Tokyo: Sogensha. pp. xviii, 326.

9777. KEEFER, JANICE KULYK. Recent Maritime fiction: women and words. StudCanL (11:2) 168–81.

9778. KERNAN, ALVIN B. The imaginary library: an essay on literature and society. (Bibl. 1985, 8850.) Rev. by Laura A. Curtis in MLS (16:2) 78–80.

9779. KIBERD, DECLAN. Men and feminism in modern literature. London: Macmillan, 1985. pp. 250. Rev. by Elaine Showalter in LRB (8:5) 8–9.

9780. KIMBLE, MARY ELLEN. Literary presentations of pioneer women in Kansas and neighboring states. *See* **7055.**

9781. KLAUS, H. GUSTAV. The other short story: working-class tales of the 1920s. Journal of the Short Story in English (7) 29–42.

9782. KLEIN, LEONARD S. (ed.). Encyclopaedia of world literature in the 20th century: vol. 1, A–D; vol. 2, E–K; vol. 3, L–Q; vol. 4, R–Z. New York: Ungar; London: Lorrimer, 1981–4. pp. xxxv, 608; xxvi, 630; xxvi, 619; xxx, 726. (Second ed.: first ed. 1975.)

9783. KLEIN, NORMA. On being a banned writer. LU (10) 18–20.

9784. KLÍMA, VLADIMÍR. Made in Trinidad: SvL (31:6) 249–51.

9785. KOLIN, PHILIP C. (ed.). Shakespeare and Southern writers: a study in influence. *See* **51.**

9786. KRAMER, HILTON. Bloomsbury idols. NCrit (2:5) 1983/84, 1–9.

9787. KROETSCH, ROBERT; NISCHIK, REINGARD M. (eds). Gaining ground: European critics on Canadian literature. *See* **22.**

9788. KÜHNELT, HARRO H. Österreich-England/Amerika. Abhandlungen zur Literatur-Geschichte. Ed. by SYLVIA M. PATSCH. *See* **7058.**

9789. Kunene, Daniel P.   Language, literature and the struggle for liberation in South Africa. Staffrider (6:3) 36–40, 46–7.

9790. Lamb, W. Kaye.   *Seventy-Five Years of Canadian Bibliography*: bibliographical studies in reprint. *See* **7059.**

9791. Lamming, George.   The pleasures of exile. London: Alison & Busby, 1984. pp. 232.

9792. Lang, Peter Christian.   Literarischer Unsinn im späten 19. und frühen 20. Jahrhundert: systematische Begründung und historische Rekonstruktion. *See* **7060.**

9793. Larson, Charles R.   The precarious state of the African writer. WLT (60:4) 409–13.

9794. Lee, A. Robert.   Black on white: the emergence of an Afro-American literary voice. DUJ (78:2) 335–44.

9795. Lee, Dorothy H.   Black voices in Detroit. MichQR (25:2) 313–28.

9796. Lee, Hermione (introd.).   The Hogarth letters. *See* **402.**

9797. Liberman, Serge.   Creative writing by Jews in Australia. *See* **7061.**

9798. Limerick, Patricia Nelson.   Desert passages: encounters with the American deserts. *See* **7062.**

9799. Lodge, David.   Write on: occasional essays '65–'85. London: Secker & Warburg. pp. xii, 211. Rev. by Chris Baldick in TLS, 12 Dec., 1393.

9800. McCormack, W. J.   The battle of the books: two decades of Irish cultural debate. Millingar: Lilliput. pp. 94.

9801. McDougall, Russell.   Opinion on location: regionalism in Australian and Canadian literature. *See* **1011.**

9802. McGregor, Gaile.   The Wacousta syndrome: explorations in the Canadian langscape. *See* **7068.**

9803. McKernan, Susan.   Crossing the border: regional writing in Australia. Meanjin (45:4) 547–60.

9804. Mackworth, Cecily.   Tendințe în poezia engleză contemporană. (Directions in contemporary English poetry.) RomLit, 27 Nov., 21.

9805. McLeod, Aorewa.   An innocent's reading of New Zealand women writers. New Zealand Women's Studies Journal (2:2) 2–13.

9806. McNaughton, Trudie (comp.).   Countless signs: the New Zealand landscape in literature. Auckland: Reed Methuen. pp. xi, 389.

9807. Marek, Jiří.   Současná literatura ve Skotsku. (Contemporary Scottish literature.) *In* (pp. 38–9) **4.**

9808. Martin, Stoddard.   Art, Messianism and crime: a study of antinomianism in modern literature and lives. *See* **7073.**

9809. Mathews, Robin.   Literature and politics: a Canadian absolute. JCF (35/36) 44–55.

9810. Mathieson, K. G.   The influence of science fiction in contemporary American writing. Unpub. doct. diss., Univ. of East Anglia, 1983.

9811. Melman, B.   Superfluous woman, flapper, nymph: images of young womanhood in popular fiction and popular journalism, 1918–1928. Unpub. doct. diss., Univ. of London, University Coll., 1984.

9812. METCALF, FRED. The Penguin dictionary of modern humorous quotations. Harmondsworth: Viking Press. pp. 319. Rev. by D. J. Enright in TLS, 26 Sept., 1079.

9813. MEYER, BRUCE; O'RIORDAN, BRIAN (eds). In their words: interviews with fourteen Canadian writers. (Bibl. 1985, 8582.) Rev. by Gerald Lynch in CanL (110) 150–1; by W. J. Keith in JCanStud (21:1) 155.

9814. MILLER, KARL. The *London Review of Books. See* **650.**

9815. MIROIU, MIHAI; MIHĂILĂ, RODICA; PANCU, LELIA (eds). An anthology of English literature: the modern age. Bucharest: Bucharest Univ., 1984. pp. 594.

9816. MONTAGUE, JOHN. The unpartitioned intellect: Dante, Savonarola, and an old sign. CJIS (12:1) 5–9. (Cultural tradition of Ireland.)

9817. MONTEITH, MOIRA (ed.). Women's writing: a challenge to theory. Brighton: Harvester Press. pp. 192.

9818. MOORE, JACK B. White on black – a review essay. SoHR (20:2) 159–69.

9819. MORGAN, PATRICK. The literature of Gippsland. *See* **7082.**

9820. —— The literature of Gippsland: the social and historical context of early writings, with bibliography. *See* **7083.**

9821. MORRIS, ADALAIDE. Dick, Jane, and American literature, fighting with canons. CE (47:5) 1985, 467–81.

9822. MOSHER, HOWARD FRANK. Writing far from the madding crowd. BkW, 10 Aug., 3, 9. (Writing in New England.)

9823. NELSON, EMMANUEL S. Black America and the Australian Aboriginal literary consciousness. *See* **1014.**

9824. NENADÁL, RADOSLAV. Poznámky k recepci americké literatury u nás. (Notes on the reception of American literature in this country (Czechoslovakia).) CJa (30) 107–12.

9825. NGUGI WA THIONG'O. Decolonising the mind: the politics of language in African literature. London: Currey. pp. 128.

9826. NICHOLS, BROOKS ASHTON. The poetics of epiphany: nineteenth-century origins of the modern literary 'moment'. *See* **7089.**

9827. NISCHIK, REINGARD M. European publications on Canadian literature. *In* (pp. 279–96) **22.**

9828. O'NEALE, SONDRA. Speaking for ourselves: black women writers of the '80's. SE (9:2) 1981, 16–19.

9829. PADOLSKY, ENOCH. Place of Italian-Canadian writing. JCanStud (21:4) 138–52 (review-article.)

9830. PATRICK, JAMES. The Magdalen metaphysicals: idealism and orthodoxy at Oxford, 1901–1945. Macon, GA: Mercer UP, 1985. pp. xliii, 190. Rev. by Nancy-Lou Patterson in Mythlore (12:3) 57–8.

9831. PERL, JEFFREY M. The tradition of return: the implicit history of modern literature. (Bibl. 1985, 8597.) Rev. by Harvey Gross in Review (8) 33–46; by William E. Cain in CLIO (14:3) 1985, 341–3.

9832. PERRY, JOHN OLIVER.   Current shiftings in aims and relationships among Indo-English poets. WLT (60:1) 49–51.

9833. PFEFFERKORN, ELI.   Fractured reality and conventional forms in Holocaust literature. MLS (16:1) 88–99.

9834. PIVATO, JOSEPH (ed.).   Contrasts: comparative essays on Italian-Canadian writing. *See* **13.**

9835. POWE, B. W.   A climate charged: essays on Canadian writing. Oakville, Ont.: Mosaic Press, 1984. pp. 196. Rev. by W. J. Keith in JCanStud (21:1) 155–7.

9836. POZNAR, WALTER.   What ever became of Mr Pickwick? CLit (13:2) 186–98. (Twentieth-century humour.)

9837. PRECOSKY, DON.   Seven myths about Canadian literature. *See* **7096.**

9838. PRIESSNITZ, HORST.   Zukunftsperspektiven der Anglistik. Ang (104:3/4) 423–44.

9839. PROCHÁZKA, MARTIN.   Průvodce americkou černošskou literatureu. (A guide through black American literature.) Literární měsíčník (15:4) 137.

9840. QUINONES, RICARDO J.   Mapping literary Modernism: time and development. (Bibl. 1985, 8606.) Rev. by Jeffrey M. Perl in CLIO (14:3) 1985, 344–6; by Zack Bowen in DHLR (18:1) 1985/86, 92–3; by Harvey Gross in Review (8) 33–46; by Margaret Dickie in JEGP (85:3) 468–70.

9841. RAFROIDI, PATRICK.   The year's work in Irish-English literature Autumn 1985–Autumn 1986. *See* **5984.**

9842. RICE, MICHAEL.   British views of the Boers. *See* **7100.**

9843. RICHARDS, THOMAS KARR.   Large promises: a literary history of English advertising, 1887–1914. *See* **7101.**

9844. RIPLEY, GORDON; MERCER, ANNE V. (eds).   Who's who in Canadian literature 1983–84. Toronto: Reference Press, 1983. pp. xix, 425. Rev. by David Jackel in ECanW (33) 195–7.

9845. ROBBINS, J. ALBERT (ed.).   American literary scholarship: an annual, 1980. *See* **7103.**

9846. ROSS, BRUCE CLUNIES.   Landscape and the Australian imagination. *In* (pp. 224–43) **31.**

9847. ROSS, ROBERT L.   An American looks at the Australian 'renaissance'. Australian Book Review (Kensington Park, S. Australia) (79) 23–4.

9848. SCANLON, TONY.   Eccentrics, explorers and evangelists: a camel ride through the literature of Northern Territory: part 2, Evangelists: the Aborigines in missionary literature. *See* **7112.**

9849. SCHUELLER, MALINI JOHAR.   The mono-dialogic narrative in America. *See* **7113.**

9850. SCHWARTZ, STEPHEN.   Escapees in paradise: literary life in San Francisco. NCrit (4:4) 1985, 1–5.

9851. SCHWENGER, PETER.   Phallic critiques: masculinity and twentieth-century literature. (Bibl. 1984, 9404.) Rev. by Elaine Showalter in LRB (8:5) 8–9.

9852. —— Writing the unthinkable. CI (13:1) 33–48.

9853. SCRUGGS, CHARLES. The sage in Harlem: H. L. Mencken and the black writers of the 1920s. (Bibl. 1984, 8870, where title incorrect.) Rev. by Fred Hobson in Review (7) 1985, 191–6.

9854. SEDGWICK, ELLERY, III. The American genteel tradition in the early twentieth century. AmS (25) Spring 1984, 49–67.

9855. SEGREST, M. Lines I dare to write: lesbian writing in the South. SE (9:2) 1981, 53–62.

9856. SHARRATT, BERNARD. Reading relations: structures of literary production: a dialectical text/book. (Bibl. 1983, 9231.) Rev. by John O. Thompson in Australian Journal of Cultural Studies (Bentley, W. Australia) (3:2) 1985, 105–16.

9857. SHATTUCK, ROGER. The innocent eye: on modern literature and the arts. London: Faber & Faber. (Bibl. 1985, 8623.) Rev. by Frank Kermode in LRB (8:9) 3, 5–6; by Stephen Baum in TLS, 23 May, 573; by Patrick Brady in PhilL (10:1) 98–9.

9858. SIMON, JOHN. Speaking around literature. NewL (69:11) 14–16.

9859. SIMPSON, PETER. What is it makes the stranger? Making it strange in some New Zealand texts. Untold (6) Spring, 38–43.

9860. SMITH, EVANS LANSING. The descent to the underworld: towards an archetypal poetics of Modernism. Unpub. doct. diss., Claremont Graduate School. [Abstr. in DA (47) 1736A.]

9861. SMITH, PAUL. Classical modernism. DalR (65:4) 1985/86, 577–84 (review-article).

9862. SPICE, NICHOLAS (ed.). London reviews: a selection from the *London Review of Books* 1983–1985. See **697**.

9863. Entry cancelled.

9864. STEINER, WENDY. The colors of rhetoric: problems in the relation between modern literature and painting. (Bibl. 1984, 8887.) Rev. by Stephen Scobie in CanRCL (12:3) 1985, 442–7.

9865. STERN, RICHARD. Penned in. CI (13:1) 1–32.

9866. STŘÍBRNÝ, ZDENĚK. Několik poznámek o dekonstruktivismu. (Notes on deconstructivism.) *In* (pp. 61–2) **4**.

9867. SUMI, YAEKO; OKAMURA, NAOMI (eds). Gendai igirisu no jyosei sakka. (Women writers of contemporary Britain.) Tokyo: Keiso Shobo. pp. viii, 342.

9868. SWANICK, ERIC L. New Brunswick literature and the pursuit of bibliography. See **58**.

9869. TATE, CLAUDIA (ed.). Black women writers at work. Harpenden: Oldcastle, 1985. pp. 256. (Cf. bibl. 1984, 8891.)

9870. TAYLOR, CLYDE. Scoping the seventies: black writing in a comatose decade. Ob (5) Winter 1979, 41–7.

9871. TEMPLE, RUTH Z.; TUCKER, MARTIN (eds). Twentieth century British literature: a reference guide and bibliography. New York: Ungar; London: Lorrimer. pp. x, 261.

9872. TIMMS, EDWARD; KELLEY, DAVID (eds). Unreal city: urban experience in modern European literature and art. Manchester: Manchester UP, 1985. pp. vi, 268. Rev. by John Melmoth in TLS, 1 Aug., 845.

9873. TOTAH, M. F.   Consciousness versus authority: a study of the critical debate between the Bloomsbury Group and the Men of 1914, 1910–30. Unpub. doct. diss., Univ. of Oxford, 1985. [Abstr. in IT (35) 550.]

9874. TOTH, EMILY (ed.).   Regionalism and the female imagination. *See* **7129.**

9875. TREGLOWN, JEREMY.   Literary history and the *Lit. Supp.* *See* **714.**

9876. TURNER, GRAEME.   National fictions: literature, film and the construction of Australian narrative. *See* **7130.**

9877. TUTTLETON, JAMES W.   American literary radicalism in the twenties. NCrit (3:7) 1985, 16–30.

9878. TWITCHELL, JAMES B.   Dreadful pleasures: an anatomy of modern horror. New York: OUP, 1985. pp. viii, 353. Rev. by Jonna G. Semeiks in Criticism (28:4) 467–70.

9879. UPDIKE, JOHN.   Writers on themselves: magic, working secrets. NYTB, 17 Aug., 1.

9880. VAN LEEUWEN, HENDRIK.   The liaison of visual and written Nonsense. *See* **84.**

9881. VASSANJI, M. G. (ed.).   A meeting of streams: South Asian Canadian literature. (Bibl. 1985, 8641.) Rev. by G. D. Killam in QQ (93:2) 428–31.

9882. WATKINS, MEL.   Sexism, racism, and black women writers. NYTB, 15 June, 1.

9883. WEBBY, ELIZABETH.   New Zealand literature in Australia: the tyranny of closeness. Meanjin (44:3) 1985, 420–1.

9884. WEBER, RONALD.   Seeing earth: literary responses to space exploration. Athens: Ohio UP, 1985. pp. 138. Rev. by St George Tucker Arnold in SFS (13:2) 211–16.

9885. WEISGERBER, JEAN (ed.).   Les avant-gardes littéraires au XXe siècle: vol. 1, Histoire; vol. 2, Théorie. Budapest: Akadémiai Kiadó, 1984. pp. 1216. (Histoire comparée des littératures de langues européennes, sous les auspices de l'Association Internationale de Littérature Comparée, 4–5.) Rev. by Marjorie Perloff in MLR (81:2) 426–7.

9886. WILDE, WILLIAM H.; HOOTON, JOY; ANDREWS, BARRY.   The Oxford companion to Australian literature. *See* **6010.**

9887. WILLIAMS, MARK.   The anxiety of writing: language and belonging in New Zealand and Fiji. Span (22) Apr., 93–104.

9888. WILLSON, LAWRENCE.   American letters ii. *See* **7140.**

9889. WILSON, CHRISTOPHER P.   The labor of words: literary professionalism in the Progressive Era. (Bibl. 1985, 8656.) Rev. by David Paul Nord in JAH (72:4) 980–1; by Helen McNeil in TLS, 21 Feb., 180; by James L. W. West, III, in Review (8) 149–56; by Joseph R. McElreath, Jr, in AL (58:3) 453–5; by Susan Coultrap-McQuin in NEQ (59:3) 464–7.

9890. Wingrove, David (ed.). The science fiction film source book. Harlow: Longman, 1985. pp. v, 312.

9891. Wisker, G. Self-constructs and moral commitment: a study of the treatment of these concepts in selected works by contemporary English and American authors. Unpub. doct. diss., Univ. of Nottingham, 1983.

9892. Wiśniewski, Jacek. Components of the scene: English literature and the coming of the Second World War. KN (33) 175–88.

9893. Woodress, James (ed.). American literary scholarship: an annual, 1979. See **7143.**

9894. Wyatt, David. The fall into Eden: landscape and imagination in California. See **7144.**

9895. Young, Alan. Dada and after: extremist Modernism and English literature. (Bibl. 1983, 9277.) Rev. by Stephen Scobie in CanRCL (12:3) 1985, 449–50.

Drama, the Theatre, Cinema, and Radio and Television Drama

9896. Ackerman, Marianne. A crisis of vision: anglophone theatre in Montreal. CanTR (46) 21–7.

9897. Ahrends, Günter. Das moderne amerikanische Drama. Anglistik & Englischunterricht (28) 185–95.

9898. Aldgate, Anthony; Richards, Jeffrey. Britain can take it: the British cinema in the Second World War. Oxford: Blackwell. pp. 312.

9899. Andrew, Dudley. Hermeneutics and cinema: the issue of history. SLI (19:1) 21–38.

9900. Asagba, Austin. Roots of African drama: critical approaches and elements of continuity. Kp (8:3) 84–100.

9901. Ashby, Clifford; May, Suzanne de Pauw. Trouping through Texas: Harley Sadler and his tent show. Bowling Green, OH: Bowling Green UP, 1982. pp. 180. Rev. by Rosemarie K. Bank in TS (28/29) 1981/82–1982/83, 112–14.

9902. Aylesworth, Thomas G. Broadway to Hollywood: musicals from stage to screen. Twickenham: Hamlyn, 1985. pp. 256.

9903. Barnes, Philip. A companion to post-war British theatre. London: Croom Helm. pp. 384.

9904. Barr, Charles (ed.). All our yesterdays: 90 years of British cinema. London: BFI. pp. ix, 446.

9905. Beger, Lois Lee Stewart. John Donahue and the Children's Theatre Company and School of Minneapolis, 1961–1978. Unpub. doct. diss., Florida State Univ., 1985. [Abstr. in DA (47) 21A.]

9906. Bennett, Benjamin K. Cinema, theater and opera: modern drama as ceremony. ModDr (28:1) 1985, 1–21.

9907. Bernardoni, James. George Cukor: a critical study and filmography. Jefferson, NC; London: MacFarland, 1985. pp. ix, 180.

9908. Berry, Ralph. Resurgence at Stratford. QQ (93:4) 750–9.

9909. Bessai, Diane. Sackville: 'Theatre in Atlantic Canada' at Mount Allison. CanTR (48) 128–36.

9910. BIGSBY, C. W. E.   A critical introduction to twentieth-century American drama: 3, Beyond Broadway. (Bibl. 1985, 8678.) Rev. by Brenda Murphy in AL (58:3) 463–5.

9911. BIRDWELL, CHRISTINE.   America's last old time tent theater. MichH (70:1) 24–9.

9912. BLAU, HERBERT.   Take up the bodies: theatre at the vanishing point. Champaign: Illinois UP, 1982. pp. 328. Rev. by Jim Stacy in TS (28/29) 1981/82–1982/83, 104–6.

9913. BLAUGHER, KURT EDWIN.   The community theatre in north-western Ohio, 1932–1984. Unpub. doct. diss., Northwestern Univ., 1985. [Abstr. in DA (46) 3196A.]

9914. BOGARDE, DIRK.   Backcloth. London: Viking Press. pp. 313.

9915. BORDWELL, DAVID.   Narration in the fiction film. London: Methuen, 1985. pp. xiv, 370.

9916. BORLASE, TIM.   Newfoundland: 2, Giving culture a shape. CanTR (48) 16–18.

9917. BRADBURY, MALCOLM; PALMER, DAVID (eds); BIGSBY, C. W. E. (assoc. ed.).   Contemporary English drama. New York: Holmes & Miller, 1981. (Bibl. 1985, 8688.) Rev. by John Russell Brown in TS (30) 1983/84, 64–6.

9918. BRAND, MONA, et al.   Australian drama 1920–1955: papers presented to a conference at the University of New England, Armidale, Sept. 1–4, 1984. Armidale, N.S.W.: Univ. of New England. pp. 156.

9919. BRASK, PER.   Canadian dramaturgy 2/ Dran Turgia. CanTR (49) 11–14.

9920. BROWN, JARED.   The fabulous Lunts: a biography of Alfred Lunt and Lynn Fontanne. New York: Atheneum. pp. 523. Rev. by Faiga Levine in BkW, 10 Aug., 11.

9921. BRYDEN, RONALD; NEIL, BOYD (eds).   Whittaker's theatre: a critic looks at stages in Canada and thereabouts: 1944–1975. Green-bank, Ont.: Whittaker Project, 1985. pp. xxii, 190. Rev. by Rota Herzberg Lister in CanD (12:1) 231–2.

9922. BUCKROYD, PETER.   British drama 1975–1985. RMRLL (40:1/2) 49–66.

9923. CARNEY, BENJAMIN FRANKLIN, III.   The Baltimore Theatre Project, 1971–1983: toward a people's theatre. Unpub. doct. diss., Univ. of Missouri–Columbia, 1985. [Abstr. in DA (46) 3196A.]

9924. CARPENTER, CHARLES A.   Modern drama scholarship and criticism 1966–1980: an international bibliography. Toronto; London: Toronto UP. pp. xxxv, 587.

9925. —— Modern drama studies: an annual bibliography. ModDr (28:2) 1985, 223–327; (29:2) 291–353.

9926. CARROLL, DENNIS.   Australian contemporary drama 1909–1982: a critical introduction. New York: Lang, 1985. pp. viii, 271. (American univ. studies: ser. 4, English language and literature, 25.)

9927. CARTER, KATHRYN ELIZABETH.   A phenomenology of feminist theatre and criticism. Unpub. doct. diss., Southern Illinois Univ. at Carbondale, 1985. [Abstr. in DA (46) 2857A.]

9928. CONNIFF, RICHARD.   The stage manager: Off-Broadway or on, the buck stops here. Smithsonian (17:11) 92–4, 96, 98–102.

9929. COOK, PAM (ed.).   The cinema book. London: BFI, 1985. pp. vi, 377. Rev. by Zachary Leader in TLS, 6 June, 610.

9930. COREN, MICHAEL.   Theatre Royal: 100 years of Stratford East. *See* **7151.**

9931. CROWTHER, BRUCE.   Hollywood faction: reality and myth in the movies. London: Columbus, 1984. pp. 219.

9932. DAVIS, RONALD O.   A rhetorical study of four critically acclaimed black dramatic plays produced on and off-Broadway between 1969 and 1981. Unpub. doct. diss., Florida State Univ., 1985. [Abstr. in DA (46) 2486A.]

9933. DENITTO, DENNIS.   Film: form and feeling. New York; London: Harper & Row, 1985. pp. xv, 544.

9934. DEVERELL, RITA SHELTON.   When the performer is black. CanTR (47) 56–62.

9935. DILWORTH, THOMAS.   David Jones and fascism. JML (13:1) 149–62.

9936. DOWSE, SARA.   The impact of film and television on the novel. Island Magazine (Sandy Bay, Tas.) (22) 1985, 12–17.

9937. DOXTATOR, ROBERT LUCAS.   James Stetson Metcalfe's signed criticism of the legitimate theatre in New York City: 1888–1927. *See* **588.**

9938. DREW, WILLIAM M.   D. W. Griffith's *Intolerance*: its genesis and its vision. Jefferson, NC; London: McFarland. pp. x, 197.

9939. DUKORE, BERNARD F.   Film and theatre: some revisionist propositions. ModDr (28:1) 1985, 171–9.

9940. DUNN, SHEILA.   The theatres of Bromley: a century of theatre in Bromley. *See* **7155.**

9941. DUTTON, RICHARD.   Modern British tragicomedy and the British tradition: Beckett, Pinter, Stoppard, Albee and Storey. Brighton: Harvester Press. pp. ix, 227.

9942. ELLIS, JACK C.   A history of film. (Bibl. 1981, 9328.) Englewood Cliffs, NJ; London: Prentice-Hall, 1985. pp. xiii, 447. (Second ed.: first ed. 1979.)

9943. ESSLIN, MARTIN.   Drama and the media in Britain. ModDr (28:1) 1985, 99–109.

9944. ETHERIDGE, DAVID; FITCH, SHEREE; RUGANDA, JOHN.   New Brunswick: 3, Enterprise Theatre Inc. CanTR (48) 33–6.

9945. FALK, QUENTIN.   Travels in Greeneland: the cinema of Graham Greene. London: Quartet, 1984. pp. x, 229.

9946. FEINSOD, ARTHUR BENNETT.   The origins of the minimalist *mise-en-scene* in the United States. Unpub. doct. diss., New York Univ. [Abstr. in DA (47) 1117A.]

9947. FETHERLING, DALE; FETHERLING, DOUG (eds).   Carl Sandburg at the movies: a poet in the Silent Era 1920–1927. Metuchen, NJ; London: Scarecrow Press, 1985. pp. vii, 199.

9948. FIELD DAY THEATRE COMPANY.   Ireland's field day. London: Hutchinson, 1985. pp. viii, 120.

9949. FILEWOD, ALAN DOUGLAS.   The development and performance of documentary theatre in English-speaking Canada. Unpub. doct. diss., Univ. of Toronto, 1985. [Abstr. in DA (47) 713A.]

9950. FINNEY, GAIL.   Theater of impotence: the one-act tragedy at the turn of the century. ModDr (28:3) 1985, 451–61.

9951. FLOWER, HARRY MITCHELL, III.   The structuralist enterprise and Aristotle's *Poetics*. Unpub. doct. diss., Ohio State Univ. 2 vols. [Abstr. in DA (47) 1531A.]

9952. FLYNN, JOYCE.   Melting plots: patterns of racial and ethnic amalgamation in American drama before Eugene O'Neill. *See* **7158.**

9953. FORSYTH, JAMES.   Back to the Barn. Haywards Heath: Grainloft. pp. xii, 100. (Rural Sussex theatre.)

9954. FOSTER, GRETCHEN.   John Dos Passos' use of film technique in *Manhattan Transfer* and *The 42nd Parallel*. LitFQ (14:3) 186–94.

9955. GALESTIN, PAUL.   The Marx brothers: verbal and visual nonsense in their films. DQR (16:3) 237–48.

9956. GALLAGHER, PATRICIA M. LOUISE.   Book by the Bard: a study of four musical comedies adapted from the plays of Shakespeare. *See* **4455.**

9957. GARDNER, BONNIE MILNE.   The emergence of the playwright–director: a new artist in American theatre, 1960–1983. Unpub. doct. diss., Kent State Univ., 1985. [Abstr. in DA (47) 22A.]

9958. GAREBIAN, KEITH.   Questions of taste: the 1986 Shaw Festival. JCanStud (21:4) 122–32.

9959. GERMANOU, M.   Playwriting and dialectical thought: Brecht's concept of dialectical materialist theatre, and the work of John Arden and Margaretta D'Arcy, Edward Bond and Steve Gooch. Unpub. doct. diss., Univ. of Essex, 1984.

9960. GIFFORD, DENIS.   The golden age of radio: an illustrated companion. London: Batsford, 1985. pp. 319.

9961. GILBERT, SKY.   Rhubarb 1/ inside the Rhubarb! festival. CanTR (49) 40–3.

9962. GOLDIE, TERRY.   Newfoundland: 1, The powers that be. CanTR (48) 6–15.

9963. GOORNEY, HOWARD; MACCOLL, EWAN (eds).   Agit-Prop to Theatre Workshop: political playscripts 1930–50. Manchester: Manchester UP. pp. lvii, 205.

9964. GRAHAM, COOPER C., *et al.*   D. W. Griffith and the Biograph Company. Metuchen, NJ; London: Scarecrow Press, 1985. pp. vii, 333. (Film makers, 10.)

9965. GRANT, BARRY K.   Looking upward: H. G. Wells, science fiction and the cinema. LitFQ (14:3) 154–63.

9966. GRANT, BARRY KEITH (ed.).   Planks of reason: essays on the horror film. Metuchen, NJ; London: Scarecrow Press, 1984. pp. xiv, 428.

9967. GRAVES, JAMES B.   The American musical comedy: a theoretical discussion. JPC (19:4) 17–26.

9968. GREEN, STANLEY.   The great clowns of Broadway. New York; Oxford: OUP, 1984. pp. ix, 247.

9969. GREENE, GRAHAM; REED, CAROL.   The third man: a film. London: Lorrimer, 1984. pp. 120. (Classic film scripts.) (Second ed.: first ed. 1968.)

9970. HALLIWELL, LESLIE; PURSER, PHILIP.   Halliwell's television companion. London: Grafton. pp. xv, 941. (Third ed.: first ed. 1979.)

9971. HARBEN, N.   Twentieth century English history plays. Unpub. doct. diss., Univ. of London, Royal Holloway Coll., 1984.

9972. HARDY, PHIL.   The encyclopedia of science fiction movies. London: Octopus. pp. 408. (Second ed.: first ed. 1984.)

9973. —— The encyclopedia of western movies. New York: Morrow, 1983; London: Octopus, 1985. pp. 395.

9974. HART, STEVEN.   The theme of 'race" in inner-city/prison theatre: The Family, Inc. TJ (38:4) 427–40.

9975. HAYNES, DAVID.   Fear no more the heat o' the sun: developing drama in Southern Africa. Cape Town: Univ. of Cape Town. pp. 10. (Inaugural lecture, n.s. 118).

9976. HENDERSON, ROBERT M.   D. W. Griffith: his life and work. New York; London: Garland, 1985. pp. ix, 326. (Second ed.: first ed. 1982.)

9977. HERNADI, PAUL.   Interpreting events: tragicomedies of history on the modern stage. Ithaca, NY; London: Cornell UP, 1985. pp. 236.

9978. HEYS, SANDRA.   Contemporary stage roles for women: a descriptive catalogue. Westport, CT; London: Greenwood Press, 1985. pp. xix, 195.

9979. HIGHAM, CHARLES.   Orson Welles: the rise and fall of an American genius. New York: St Martin's Press, 1985; London: New English Library. pp. 384. Rev. by Gerald Weales in Smithsonian (16:10) 155–7.

9980. HILL, ERROL.   The revolutionary tradition in black drama. TJ (38:4) 408–26.

9981. —— (ed.).   Plays for today. Harlow: Longman, 1985. pp. 233. (*Ti-Jean and his Brothers* by Derek Walcott, *An Echo in the Bone* by Dennis Scott, *Man Better Man* by Errol Hill.)

9982. HILLIER, JIM (ed.).   *Cahiers du cinéma*: vol. 1, The 1950s: neo-realism, Hollywood, new wave. London: Routledge & Kegan Paul; BFI, 1985. pp. xiii, 312.

9983. —— *Cahiers du cinéma*: vol. 2, 1960–1968: New wave, new cinema, re-evaluating Hollywood: an anthology from *Cahiers du cinéma* nos 103–207, January 1960–December 1968. London: Routledge & Kegan Paul; BFI. pp. xiv, 363.

9984. HIRSCH, FOSTER.   A method to their madness: the history of the Actors Studio. New York: Norton, 1984. pp. 367. Rev. by Benedict Nightingale in TLS, 27 June, 717.

9985. HOGAN, ROBERT; BURNHAM, RICHARD.   The art of the amateur 1916–1920. (Bibl. 1985, 8762.) Rev. by Patrick Rafroidi in Études irlandaises (9) 1984, 334.

9986. HOSTETTER, ROBERT DAVID.   The American nuclear theatre, 1946–1984. Unpub. doct. diss., Northwestern Univ., 1985. [Abstr. in DA (46) 2132A.]

9987. Houseman, John.   Unfinished business: a memoir. London: Chatto & Windus. pp. x, 498.

9988. Jameson, Fredric.   On magic realism in film. CI (12:2) 301–25.

9989. Jökulsson, Illugi.   Vonin I deiglunni: um Arthur Miller og leikrit hans. (Hope in *The Crucible*: Arthur Miller and his plays.) LM (61:16) 6–7.

9990. Jones, David Richard.   Great directors at work: Stanislavsky, Brecht, Kazan, Brook. Berkeley; London: California UP. pp. x, 289.

9991. Kael, Pauline.   Taking it all in. New York: Holt, Rinehart, Winston, 1984; London: Boyars. pp. xiii, 527.

9992. Kareda, Urjo.   Canadian dramaturgy 1/ they also serve who only stand and wait for rewrites. CanTR (49) 6–11.

9993. Kaufman, Rhoda Helfman.   The Yiddish theatre in New York, 1880–1920: a secular revival. *See* **7167.**

9994. Kempson, Rachel, Lady Redgrave.   A family and its fortunes. London: Duckworth, 1986. pp. 242.

9995. Kendzora, Kathryn Louise.   Going between novel and film: Harold Pinter's adaptation of *The Go-Between*. Unpub. doct. diss., Univ. of California, Irvine. [Abstr. in DA (47) 898A.]

9996. Kihn, Patricia Lenehan.   Kenneth Tynan and the renaissance of post-war British drama. Unpub. doct. diss., Wayne State Univ. [Abstr. in DA (47) 1118A.]

9997. Kissel, Howard.   The wise counselor? The critic's role in contemporary theatre. TS (31/32) 1984/85–1985/86, 41–8.

9998. Kitman, Marvin.   Blurring the type. *See* **1176.**

9999. Klein, Michael; Parker, Gillian (eds).   The English novel and the movies. *See* **2845.**

10000. Knowles, Richard Paul.   The Mulgrave Road Co-op: theatre and the community in Guysborough County, N.S. CanD (12:1) 18–32.

10001. —— New Brunswick: life after TNB. CanTR (48) 25.

10002. Kobayashi, Norio.   Broadway engeki. (Broadway drama.) Kyoto: Appollon Press. pp. 244.

10003. Kott, Jan.   'The Theater of Essence' and other essays. (Bibl. 1985, 8780.) Rev. by Ron Eagle in TJ (38:1) 122–3.

10004. Lamont, Rosette C.   Murderous enactments: the media's presence in the drama. ModDr (28:1) 1985, 148–61.

10005. Larlham, Peter.   Black theater, dance, and ritual in South Africa. Ann Arbor, MI: UMI Research Press; Epping: Bowker, 1985. pp. xii, 171. (Theater and dramatic studies, 29.)

10006. Leaming, Barbara.   Orson Welles: a biography. London: Weidenfeld & Nicolson; New York: Viking Press, 1985. pp. xii, 562. Rev. by Gerald Weales in Smithsonian (16:10) 155–7.

10007. Leitch, Thomas M.   Murderous victims in *The Secret Agent* and *Sabotage*. LitFQ (14:1) 64–8.

10008. Leiter, Samuel L.; Hill, Holly.   The encyclopedia of the

New York stage, 1920–1930. Westport, CT: Greenwood Press, 1985. 2 vols. pp. xxxiii, 1331. Rev. by Don B. Wilmeth in TJ (38:2) 235–7.

10009. LEONARD, PAUL. Rhubarb 2/ towards a new dramaturgy. CanTR (49) 44–50.

10010. LEVINE, JUNE PERRY. Passage to the Odeon: too lean. LitFQ (14:3) 139–50.

10011. LIEBERMAN, SUSAN; CABLE, FRANCES (comps). Memorable film characters: an index to roles and performers, 1915–1983. Westport, CT; London: Greenwood Press, 1984. pp. ix, 291. (Bibliographies and indexes in the performing arts, 1.)

10012. LYNES, RUSSELL. The lively audience: a social history of the visual and performing arts in America, 1890–1950. *See* **7169.**

10013. MCARTHUR, BENJAMIN. Actors and American culture, 1880–1920. *See* **7170.**

10014. MCDONNELL, BRIAN. The translation of New Zealand fiction into film. Unpub. doct. diss., Univ. of Auckland.

10015. MCDOUGAL, STUART Y. Made into movies: from literature to film. New York; London: Holt, Rinehart, Winston, 1985. pp. x, 405.

10016. MCKENNA, ED. Nova Scotia: 1, The Halifax problem: inside and out. CanTR (48) 43–54.

10017. MCLENNAN, KATHLEEN ANN. American domestic drama 1870 to 1910: individualism and the crisis of community. *See* **7171.**

10018. MCMAHON, BARRIE; QUIN, ROBYN. Real images: film and television. London: Macmillan. pp. 242.

10019. MAIR, ELIZABETH. Prince Edward Island: 1, Theatre; who's it for? CanTR (48) 19–22.

10020. MARTIN, TROY KENNEDY. Sharpening the edge of TV drama. Listener (116) 28 Aug., 9–12.

10021. MAST, GERALD; COHEN, MARSHALL (eds). Film theory and criticism: introductory readings. (Bibl. 1979, 9208.) New York; Oxford: OUP, 1985. pp. xxi, 852. (Third ed.: first ed. 1974.)

10022. MAY, JOHN R. Louisiana writers in film. SoQ (23:1) 1984, 18–31.

10023. MIKOTOWICZ, THOMAS J. Oliver Smith: an American scenographer. Unpub. doct. diss., New York Univ., 1985. [Abstr. in DA (46) 2132A.]

10024. MILLER, JAMES. The magic curtain: the story of theatre in Inverness. *See* **7174.**

10025. MONTESQUE, BARON (ed.). Theatrical landmarks: vol. 2. London: Arcade Recording Circuit, 1985. Items paginated separately. (Inc. 'Eustace Lionheart', *What Might Have Happened*; Amanda Smee, *Fleas*; Desmond Wilcox, *The Year Two Billion*.)

10026. —— Theatrical landmarks: vol. 3. London: Arcade Recording Circuit. Items paginated separately. (Imogen Whaler, *Claptrap* (vernacular version); Clive Bassart, *A Myth is Good for a Smile* (versified version); Fergus McPhee, *Merely Players, a Farrago*; Robert Pendark, *The Case of Red Diamonds*.)

10027. MUNDAY, JENNY. New Brunswick: 1, The comedy asylum. CanTR (48) 26–31.

10028. NAREMORE, JAMES. Expressive coherence and the 'acted image'. SLI (19:1) 39–54.

10029. NATALLE, ELIZABETH J. Feminist theatre: a study in persuasion. Metuchen, NJ; London: Scarecrow Press, 1985. pp. vii, 155.

10030. NILSEN, VLADIMIR. The cinema as a graphic art. New York: Garland, 1985. pp. 226. (Cinema classics.)

10031. NOEL, KEITH (ed.). Caribbean plays for playing. London: Heinemann Educational, 1985. pp. 163. (Caribbean writers, 36.)

10032. NORDON, PIERRE. Le fou sur la scène anglaise contemporaine. *In* (pp. 333–39) **1.**

10033. O'CONNOR, GARRY. Ralph Richardson: an actor's life. London: Hodder & Stoughton. pp. 288.

10034. OFFORD, JOHN. The theatres of Portsmouth. *See* **7177.**

10035. OLDENBURG, CHLOE WARNER. Leaps of faith: history of the Cleveland Play House 1915–85. Cleveland, OH: Oldenburg, 1985. pp. 185. Rev. by Richard R. Centing in OhioanaQ (29:3) 127–8.

10036. OLIVIER, LAURENCE. Henry V. *See* **4681.**

10037. —— On acting. London: Weidenfeld & Nicolson; New York: Simon & Schuster. pp. x, 270. Rev. by Jonathan Yardley in BkW, 2 Nov., 3, 13.

10038. PAGE, MALCOLM. British Columbia: White Rock summer theatre, 1976–85. CanTR (46) 100–5.

10039. —— Canadian plays in Britain: 1972–85. CanD (12:1) 64–73.

10040. PAUL, JOHN STEVEN. The horror at the heart of farce. Cresset (50:1) 23–6.

10041. PAVIS, PATRICE. The classical heritage of modern drama: the case of postmodern theatre. ModDr (29:1) 1–22.

10042. PEACOCK, D. KEITH. Facts versus history: two attempts to change the audience's political perspective. TS (31/32) 1984/85–1985/86, 15–31.

10043. PEAT, HAL W. Beyond the limit: familiar shadows from the world of Graham Greene. LitFQ (14:2) 133–6.

10044. PHILLIPS, GENE D. Alfred Hitchcock. Boston, MA: G. K. Hall, 1984; London: Columbus. pp. 212. (Columbus filmmakers.)

10045. PICK, JOHN. The West End: mismanagement and snobbery. *See* **7179.**

10046. PIENAAR, JOHAN. *The Story of an African Farm*: the opportunity for study across the media. *See* **9152.**

10047. PIPER, JUDITH ANN. Visual theatre – San Francisco Bay area, 1975–1984: creating exceptional realities. Unpub. doct. diss., Univ. of California, Davis, 1985. [Abstr. in DA (47) 349A.]

10048. PISTOTNIK, V. Marlowe in performance: professional productions on the British stage, 1960–1982. *See* **4128.**

10049. POTEET, SUSAN. A matter of voice: new play development in Quebec. CanTR (46) 28–35.

10050. Powell, Michael. A life in movies: an autobiography. London: Heinemann. pp. 705.

10051. Pratt, Judith Stevens. The vaudeville criticism of Epes Winthrop Sargent, 1896–1910. *See* **673.**

10052. Preddy, Jane. Costumes and clowns: bizarre projects of Norman Bel Geddes. JPC (20:2) 29–39.

10053. Preu, Dana McKinnon. *Gal Young Un*: a transfer of the seriocomic tradition in American literature to film. LitFQ (14:3) 171–80.

10054. Pyzik, Teresa. Postać w dramacie: obraz człowieka w dramaturgii amerykańskiej. (Character in the drama: man's image in American drama.) Katowice: Uniwersytet Śląski. pp. 187. (Prace naukowe Uniwersytetu Śląskiego w Katowicach, 773.)

10055. Rabey, David Ian. British and Irish political drama in the twentieth century: implicating the audience. Basingstoke: Macmillan. pp. x. 237.

10056. Radell, Karen M. Charley Fortnum's descent into dignity: the common denominator in Greene's *The Honorary Consul* and Paramount's *Beyond the Limit*. LitFQ (14:3) 181–5.

10057. Rees, Leslie. Australian drama 1970–1985: a historical and critical survey. (Bibl. 1978, 8943.) Sydney: Angus & Robertson. pp. vi, 400. (Revised ed.: first ed. 1978 as *Australian Drama in the 1970s*.)

10058. Regan, Tom. Nova Scotia: 2, The start of a beautiful relationship? CanTR (48) 55–8.

10059. Reinelt, Janelle. Beyond Brecht: Britain's new feminist drama. TJ (38:2) 154–63.

10060. Reston, James. Coming to terms: American plays and the Vietnam War. New York: Theatre Communications Group, 1985. pp. 330. Rev. by Alexis Greene in TJ (38:1) 126–7.

10061. Robinson, Lennox; Ó hAodha, Micheál. Pictures at the Abbey. Dublin: Dolmen Press in assn with the Irish National Theatre Soc., 1983. pp. 64. Rev. by Andrew Parkin in CJIS (12:1) 80–1.

10062. Rod, David K. Kenneth Burke and Susanne K. Langer on drama and its audiences. QJS (72:3) 306–17.

10063. —— Kenneth Burke and Susanne K. Langer: dramatic theorists. Unpub. doct. diss., Univ. of Kansas, 1985. [Abstr. in DA (46) 2859A.]

10064. Rollins, Ronald Gene. Divided Ireland: bifocal vision in modern Irish drama. Lanham, MD: UP of America, 1985. pp. xi, 104. Rev. by Andrew Parkin in CJIS (12:1) 79–80.

10065. Rosenmeyer, Thomas G. Aristotelian ethos and character in modern drama. *In* (pp. 119–25) **11.**

10066. Ryall, Tom. Alfred Hitchcock and the British cinema. London: Croom Helm. pp. ix, 193.

10067. Sanford, Timothy Bryce. The search for lost time in contemporary drama: from Proust to Pinter. Unpub. doct. diss., Stanford Univ., 1985. [Abstr. in DA (46) 2133A.]

10068. Sarlós, Robert Károly. Jig Cook and the Provincetown players: theatre in ferment. (Bibl. 1983, 9522.) Rev. by Alan Woods in TS (28/29) 1981/82–1982/83, 118–19.

10069. SCHAFER, R. MURRAY.   Theatre of confluence II. CanTR (47) 5–19. (Cf. bibl. 1980, 10622.)

10070. SCHECHNER, RICHARD.   The end of humanism: writings on performance. New York; Performing Arts Journal Pubs, 1982. pp. 128. Rev. by Richard Finlay in TS (28/29) 1981/82–1982/83, 102–4.

10071. SCHIFF, ELLEN.   From stereotype to metaphor: the Jew in contemporary drama. (Bibl. 1985, 8841.) Rev. by Henry Kreisel in CanRCL (12:3) 1985, 563–6.

10072. SEKINE, MASARU (ed.).   Irish writers and the theatre. *See* **7186.**

10073. SELLER, MAXINE SCHWARTZ (ed.).   Ethnic theatre in the United States. (Bibl. 1984, 9127.) Rev. by Jorge A. Huerta in TS (30) 1983/84, 82–4.

10074. SELLEY, APRIL.   'I have been, and ever shall be, your friend': *Star Trek*, *The Deerslayer* and the American romance. *See* **7971.**

10075. SELMAN, JAN.   Workshopping plays. CanTR (49) 15–23.

10076. SETON, JO.   Subjects of the gaze: controlling and containing women in *The Scarecrow*. Illusions (1) Summer, 18–21.

10077. SHIPOW, SANDRA.   Depression-era trends in popular culture as reflected in the Yiddish theatre career of Molly Picon. TS (30) 1983/84, 43–56.

10078. SILK, ILKAY; YOUNG, VICKI.   New Brunswick: 2, TNB's contact theatre. CanTR (48) 31–3.

10079. SIMARD, RODNEY.   Postmodern drama: contemporary playwrights in America and Britain. Lanham, MD: UP of America, 1984. pp. xv, 150. Rev. by Thomas J. Taylor in TJ (38:1) 125–6.

10080. SIMONE, SAM P.   Hitchcock as activist: politics and the war films. Ann Arbor, MI: UMI Research Press; Epping: Bowker, 1985. pp. xii, 203. (Studies in cinema, 36.)

10081. SINYARD, NEIL.   Filming literature: the art of screen adaptation. London: Croom Helm. pp. vii, 304.

10082. SLIDE, ANTHONY (ed.).   Selected theatre criticism: vol. 1, 1900–1919. Metuchen, NJ; London: Scarecrow Press, 1985. pp. ix, 383.

10083. —— Selected theatre criticism: vol. 2, 1920–1930. Metuchen, NJ; Scarecrow Press, 1985. pp. ix, 270.

10084. —— Selected theatre criticism: vol. 3, 1931–1950. Metuchen, NJ; London: Scarecrow Press. pp. viii, 289.

10085. SLUSSER, GEORGE E.; RABKIN, ERIC S. (eds).   Shadows of the magic lamp: fantasy and science fiction in film. Carbondale: Southern Illinois UP, 1985. pp. 259. Rev. by Andrew Gordon in SFS (13:1) 89–92.

10086. SMITH, SUSAN HARRIS.   Twentieth-century plays using classical mythic themes: a checklist. ModDr (29:1) 110–34.

10087. SMITH, SUSAN VALERIA HARRIS.   Masks in modern drama. *See* **7188.**

10088. STEADMAN, IAN PATRICK.   Drama and social consciousness:

themes to black theatre on the Witwatersrand until 1984. Unpub. doct. diss., Univ. of Witwatersrand, 1985. [Abstr. in DA (47) 23A.]

10089. STOREY, A. Representations of class in modern British drama. Unpub. doct. diss., Univ. of Nottingham, 1985. [Abstr. in IT (36) 23.]

10090. STOURAC, RICHARD; McCREERY, KATHLEEN. Theatre as a weapon: workers' theatre in the Soviet Union, Germany and Britain, 1917–1934. London: Routledge & Kegan Paul. pp. xvi, 336.

10091. TANITCH, ROBERT. Olivier: the complete career. London: Thames & Hudson, 1985. pp. 191.

10092. TAYLOR, JOHN RUSSELL. Orson Welles: a celebration. London: Pavilion. pp. 176.

10093. TEMPERLEY, NICHOLAS. Film forum: *The Beggar's Opera* (1953 and 1983). *See* **6489.**

10094. TINDALE, JOAN. Some observations on the situation of contemporary British women dramatists. *In* (pp. 305–11) **18.**

10095. TROMLY, F. B. Awakening the faith: Stratford's thirty-fourth season. JCanStud (21:4) 112–22.

10096. TURVEY, SARAH. Barthes' *S/Z* and the analysis of film narrative: *The Searchers*. London: Univ. of London Inst. of Education, 1982. pp. iii, 30. (Media analysis papers, 3.)

10097. TUSKA, JON. Dark cinema: American film noir in cultural perspective. Westport, CT; London: Greenwood Press, 1984. pp. xxiv, 305. (Contributions to the study of popular culture, 9.)

10098. USIN, LÉA V. Creon's city: a history of Ottawa's Town Theatre. CanD (12:1) 8–17.

10099. VAN ERVEN, EUGENE ADRIANUS PETRUS BERNARDUS. The contemporary people's theater: a study of the radical popular theater from 1968 to the present. Unpub. doct. diss., Vanderbilt Univ., 1985. [Abstr. in DA (46) 2288A.]

10100. VENTER, S. F.; WEIDEMAN, A. J. A measure of texture: cohesion in English drama dialogue and actual conversation. *See* **1146.**

10101. VINEBERG, STEVE EDWARD. Method in performance: fifty years of American method acting. Unpub. doct. diss., Stanford Univ., 1985. [Abstr. in DA (46) 2486A–7A.]

10102. VINSON, JAMES (ed.).; LYON, CHRISTOPHER; FALLER, GREG S. (asst eds). The international dictionary of films and filmmakers: vol. 3, Actors and actresses. Chicago; London: St James. pp. 750.

10103. WADE, BRYAN. Down and out in the Can Lit ghetto. CanTR (46) 106–9.

10104. WAGNER, ANTON. A national or international dramatic art: B. K. Sandwell and *Saturday Night* 1932–1951. CanD (12:2) 342–50.

10105. —— (ed.). Contemporary Canadian theatre: new world visions. (Bibl. 1985, 8873.) Rev. by Richard Paul Knowles in CanL (109) 137–9.

10106. WALLACE, ROBERT. Tales of two cities. CanTR (46) 6–13.

10107. WANDOR, MICHELENE. Carry on, understudies: theatre and sexual politics. (Bibl. 1981, 9492.) London: Routledge & Kegan Paul. pp. xxi, 210. (Second ed.: first ed. 1981.)

10108. WATSON, D.   British socialist theatre, 1930–1979: class, politics and dramatic form. Unpub. doct. diss., Univ. of Hull, 1985. [Abstr. in IT (36) 901.]

10109. WEALES, GERALD.   Canned goods as caviar: American film comedy of the 1930s. Chicago; London: Chicago UP, 1985. pp. x, 386.

10110. WEARING, J. P.   The London stage 1920–1929: a calendar of plays and players: vol. 1, 1920–1924; vol. 2, 1925–1929; vol. 3, Indexes. (Bibl. 1985, 8882.) Rev. by Margaret Watson in NQ (33:4) 564–5.

10111. WEBB, MICHAEL (ed.).   Hollywood: legend and reality. London: Pavilion; Smithsonian Institution Travelling Exhibition Service. pp. xii, 212.

10112. WELLS, STANLEY.   Shakespeare scholarship and the modern theatre. *See* **4618.**

10113. WESKAMP, BIRGIT.   Drama als Interaktion. Fallanalysen des modernen britischen Dramas im Horizont ihrer Vergleichbarkeit mit der Interaktion der Lebenswelt. Frankfurt: Lang. pp. 285. (Europäische Hochschulschriften, Reihe 14; Angelsächsische Sprache und Literatur, 161.)

10114. WHITEHEAD, C. S.   A literary history of the Third Programme, 1946 to 1970. Unpub. doct. diss., Univ. of Oxford, 1985. [Abstr. in IT (35) 533.]

10115. WHITTAKER, HERBERT W.   Whittaker's Montreal: a theatrical autobiography, 1910–1949. CanD (12:2) 233–331.

10116. WILLIAMS, MANCE.   Black theatre in the 1960's and 1970's: a historical-critical analysis of the movement. Westport, CT; London: Greenwood Press, 1985. pp. 188. Rev. by David W. Beams in TJ (38:2) 247–8.

10117. WILLIS, DONALD (ed.).   *Variety*'s complete science fiction reviews. *See* **729.**

10118. WILMUT, ROGER.   From Fringe to Flying Circus: celebrating a unique generation of comedy, 1960–1980. London: Methuen, 1982. pp. xxiv, 259. Rev. by Arvid F. Sponberg in TJ (38:2) 249.

10119. WILSON, GEORGE M.   Narration in light: studies in cinematic point of view. Baltimore, MD; London: Johns Hopkins UP. pp. x, 223.

10120. WINSTON, MATHEW.   The incoherent self in contemporary comedy. ModDr (29:3) 388–402.

10121. YACOWAR, MAURICE.   Tennessee Williams and film. New York: Ungar; London: Lorrimer, *c.* 1977. pp. 168. (Ungar film library.)

Fiction

10122. ABRASH, MERRITT.   Through logic to apocalypse: science-fiction scenarios of nuclear deterrence breakdown. SFS (13:2) 129–38.

10123. ADAIR, TOM.   The fictional face of Belfast. Linen Hall Review (3:4) 10–12.

10124. ALBACON.   Albacon 85: Glasgow's 10th science fiction convention, Central Hotel Glasgow July 19th–22nd 1985. London: Albacon 85, 1985. pp. 50.

10125. ALBERT, WALTER. Les pulps américains: une littérature souterraine. Europe (62:664/65) 1984, 13–19.

10126. ALDISS, BRIAN W.; WINGROVE, DAVID. Trillion year spree: the history of science fiction. *See* **6035.**

10127. ALLEN, WALTER. Tradition and dream: the English and American novel from the twenties to our time. (Bibl. 1964, 6996.) London: Hogarth Press. pp. xxii. 358. (Hogarth critics.) (Second ed.: first ed., 1964.)

10128. ALTER, ROBERT. Motives for fiction. (Bibl. 1985, 2330.) Rev. by Kathryn Sutherland in CritQ (28:4) 105–7.

10129. ALTSHULER, HARRY. Souvenirs d'un lecteur de pulps. Trans. by J.-J. SCHLERET. Europe (62:664/65) 1984, 66–8.

10130. AMBANASOM, SHADRACH ATEKE. The adolescent protagonist in the African novel: an analysis of five African novels. Unpub. doct. diss., Ohio Univ., 1985. [Abstr. in DA (47) 1320A.] (*Weep Not Child, Houseboy, A Son of the Soil, The Dark Child, Without a Home.*)

10131. ANCONA, FRANCESCO ARISTIDE. Writing the absence of the father: undoing Oedipal structures in the contemporary American novel. Lanham, MD; London: UP of America. pp. 161.

10132. ANDERSON, DON (ed.). Transgressions: Australian writing now. Ringwood, Vic.; Harmondsworth: Penguin. pp. ix, 245.

10133. ANTCZAK, JANICE. Science fiction: the mythos of a new romance. New York: Neal–Schuman, 1985. pp. 233. Rev. by Perry Nodelman in SFS (13:2) 216–18.

10134. ASH, BETH SHARON. Philosophy and the narrative imagination: an interdisciplinary study of the modern novel and continental philosophy. Unpub. doct. diss., Univ. of Virginia, 1985. [Abstr. in DA (47) 526A.]

10135. ASIMOV, ISAAC; GREENBERG, MARTIN HENRY; WAUGH, CHARLES G. (eds). Sherlock Holmes through time and space. *See* **8167.**

10136. BACHINGER, KATRINA. Shedding the skins of *Kanaima* in the Commonwealth short story. *In* (pp. 14–22) PETER O. STUMMER (ed.), The story must be told. Würzburg: Königshausen & Neumann. pp. 197.

10137. BAINBRIDGE, WILLIAM SIMS. Dimensions of science fiction. *See* **7200.**

10138. BARR, MARLEEN; SMITH, NICHOLAS D. (eds). Women and utopia: critical interpretations. (Bibl. 1984, 113.) Rev. by Susan Gubar in SFS (13:1) 79–83.

10139. BARTTER, MARTHA A. Nuclear holocaust as urban renewal. SFS (13:2) 148–58.

10140. BARTTER, MARTHA TAYLOR. Symbol to scenario: the atomic bomb in American science fiction, 1930–1960. Unpub. doct. diss., Univ. of Rochester. [Abstr. in DA (47) 900A.]

10141. BAUDOU, JACQUES. Troisème génération: le retour du privé. Europe (62:664/65) 1984, 123–31.

10142. —— Schleret, Jean-Jacques.   Quelques approches du roman noir. Europe (62:664/65) 1984, 3–12.

10143. Bawer, Bruce.   Diminishing fictions: four decades of the novel. NCrit (3:Summer) 1985, 11–21.

10144. —— The novel in the academy: a paean to perplexity. NCrit (2) May 1984, 20–30.

10145. Beard, Pauline Winsome.   A riddling thing: a study of time in five 20th century novels. Unpub. doct. diss., State Univ. of New York at Binghamton. [Abstr. in DA (47) 526A.] (*The Sound and the Fury, Nightwood, The Alexandria Quartet, Slaughterhouse-five, If on a Winter's Night a Traveler.*)

10146. Beauchamp, Gorman.   Technology in the dystopian novel. MFS (32:1) 53–63.

10147. Beker, Miroslav.   The attack on character in modern fiction. *In* (pp. 255–9) **19.**

10148. Bendixen, Alfred.   It was a mess! How Henry James and others actually wrote a novel. *See* **7204.**

10149. Bennett, Bruce.   Asian encounters in the contemporary Australian short story. WLWE (26:1) 49–61.

10150. Ben-Yehuda, Nachman.   The revival of the occult and of science fiction. JPC (20:2) 1–16.

10151. Berry, Reginald.   A deckchair of words: post-colonialism, post-modernism, and the novel of self-projection in Canada and New Zealand. Landfall (40:3) 310–23.

10152. Blum, Joanne Danielle.   Defying the constraints of gender: the male/female double of women's fiction. *See* **7206.**

10153. Boll, R. W.   Dostoevsky and the English novel. Unpub. doct. diss., Univ. of Bristol, 1983.

10154. Bouterfa, F.   Dream and reality: a study in literature and ideology in West African fiction. Unpub. doct. diss., Univ. of Warwick, 1985. [Abstr. in IT (36) 472.]

10155. Boyers, Robert.   Atrocity and amnesia: the political novel since 1945. New York; Oxford: OUP, 1985. pp. 259.

10156. Bradbury, Ray (introd.); Haining, Peter (comp.).   Tales of dungeons and dragons. *See* **7207.**

10157. Breen, Jon L.   Novel verdicts: a guide to courtroom fiction. *See* **7208.**

10158. Brians, Paul.   Resources for the study of nuclear war in fiction. SFS (13:2) 193–7.

10159. Brown, D. A. Maughan.   Land, freedom and literature: history and ideology in the fiction about 'Mau Mau'. Unpub. doct. diss., Univ. of Sussex, 1983.

10160. Buckley, Vincent.   The Irish presence in the Australian novel. *In* (pp. 34–45) C. Kiernan (ed.), Australia and Ireland 1788–1988: bicentenary essays. Dublin: Gill & Macmillan. pp. 309.

10161. Burgess, Moira.   The Glasgow novel: a survey and bibliography. *See* **7213.**

10162. —— WHYTE, HAMISH (eds). Streets of stone: an anthology of Glasgow short stories. Edinburgh: Salamander, 1985. pp. ix, 182.

10163. BURSTON, C. D. Technical change in American social fiction since the 1930s. Unpub. doct. diss., Univ. of Manchester, 1980.

10164. BURT, JOHN. Romance, character and the bounds of sense (II). *See* **7214.**

10165. BUSIA, A. P. A. Representing 'Africa': patterns of experience in British novels, 1948 to 1980. Unpub. doct. diss., Univ. of Oxford, 1983.

10166. BUTLER, CHRISTOPHER. Scepticism and experimental fiction. EC (36:1) 47–67.

10167. CAMPBELL, PAUL. Respectable little green men. *See* **7216.**

10168. CANDELARIA, CORDELIA. Literary fungoes: allusions to baseball in significant American fiction. MidQ (23:3) 1982, 411–15.

10169. CARAMELLO, CHARLES. Silverless mirrors: book, self and postmodern American fiction. (Bibl. 1985, 8932.) Rev. by Khachig Toloyan in Novel (19:3) 264–7; by Joan DelFattore in SAF (14:1) 112–14; by Theo D'Haen in PT (7:3) 580–1.

10170. CARLSON, JULIA LOWELL. American women of the thirties: images of women in American fiction of the 1930s. Unpub. doct. diss., Univ. of North Carolina at Chapel Hill, 1985. [Abstr. in DA (46) 3350A.]

10171. CAWS, MARY ANN. Reading frames in modern fiction. Guildford: Princeton UP, 1985. (Cf. bibl. 1985, 8937.) Rev. by Vincent Kling in ELN (24:2) 83–6; by Carol Schloss in Novel (19:3) 267–9; by Gerhard Joseph in Review (8) 189–95.

10172. CAWTHRA, G. M. Developments in fictional prose from the late Victorian to the early modern period. *See* **7218.**

10173. CERVANTES, LINDA LEVALLEY. Women's stories: gender and the culture of fiction in the United States. Unpub. doct. diss., Stanford Univ., 1985. [Abstr. in DA (46) 2463A.]

10174. CHAINEY, GRAHAM. From Boniface to Porterhouse: Cambridge in fiction. *See* **7219.**

10175. CHAMBERS, ROSS. Story and situation: narrative seduction and the power of fiction. *See* **2910.**

10176. CHESSMAN, D. R. 'In defense of the human': the survival of moral optimism in post-war American fiction. Unpub. doct. diss., Univ. of Hull, 1985. [Abstr. in IT (36) 914.]

10177. CHUNG, YOUN-SON. War and morality: the search for meaning in American novels of World War I, World War II, and the Vietnam War. Unpub. doct. diss., Emory Univ., 1985. [Abstr. in DA (46) 2729A.]

10178. CLARESON, THOMAS D. Science fiction in America, 1870s–1930s: an annotated bibliography of primary sources. *See* **7220.**

10179. —— Some kind of paradise: the emergence of American science fiction. Westport, CT: Greenwood Press, 1985. Rev. by James P. Barry in OhioanaQ (29:1) 164.

10180. CLARK, JOHN R.; MOTTO, ANNA LYNN. The progress of cannibalism in satire. MidQ (25) 1984, 174–86.

10181. COALE, SAMUEL CHASE. In Hawthorne's shadow: American romance from Melville to Mailer. *See* **7221.**

10182. COBLEY, EVELYN. Narrating the facts of war: new journalism in Herr's *Dispatches* and documentary realism in First World War novels. JNT (16:2) 97–116.

10183. CONDER, JOHN J. Naturalism in American fiction: the classic phase. (Bibl. 1985, 8948.) Rev. by Donald Pizer in JEGP (85:2) 291–2.

10184. CONLON, FAITH; DA SILVA, RACHEL; WILSON, BARBARA (eds). The things that divide us. Seattle, WA: Seal Press, 1985; London: Sheba. pp. 191.

10185. CONN, STEWART (introd.). Scottish short stories 1985. London: Collins, 1985. pp. 173.

10186. COOPER-CLARK, DIANA. Interviews with contemporary novelists. Basingstoke: Macmillan. pp. 297. (Margaret Drabble, Nadine Gordimer, Robertson Davies, Erica Jong, Elie Wiesel, Toni Morrison, Colin Wilson, Mary Gordon: Isaac Bashevis Singer, Carlos Fuentes, Vasily Aksyonov, Julio Cortázar.)

10187. CORDESSE, GÉRARD. La nouvelle science-fiction américaine. (Bibl. 1984, 9224.) Rev. by Graham Dunstan Martin in EA (38:3) 1985, 360.

10188. COWAN, PETER. The novel in the nineteen thirties: a Western Australian view. Westerly (31:4) 22–9.

10189. COWLEY, J. M. Composing reality: the postmodern fiction of Barthelme, Reed, Sukenick, Federman, Katz and Sorrentino. Unpub. doct. diss., Univ. of London, King's Coll. [Abstr. in IT (36) 24.]

10190. COX, MICHAEL; GILBERT, R. W. (sels). The Oxford book of English ghost stories. *See* **7223.**

10191. CROFT, A. Socialist fiction in Britain in the 1930s. Unpub. doct. diss., Univ. of Nottingham, 1985. [Abstr. in IT (36) 912.]

10192. DEAN, JOHN. The city in science fiction since mid-century. *In* (pp. 557–66) **1.**

10193. DEFLAUX, PIERRE. Aspects idéologiques du roman américain de la seconde guerre mondiale. (Bibl. 1985, 8958.) Rev. by Peter Wagner in EA (39:3) 367–8.

10194. DETWEILER, ROBERT. Mass communication technology and postmodern fiction. *In* (pp. 489–95) **19.**

10195. DICKSTEIN, MORRIS. Popular fiction and critical values: the novel as a challenge to literary history. *In* (pp. 29–66) **47.**

10196. DOBSON, FRANK EDWARD. The use of oral tradition and ritual in Afro-American fiction. Unpub. doct. diss., Bowling Green State Univ., 1985. [Abstr. in DA (47) 177A.]

10197. DOCTOROW, E. L. Ultimate discourse. Esquire (106:2) 41.

10198. DORLING, A. Experimental forms in contemporary fiction. Unpub. doct. diss., Univ. of Nottingham, 1985. [Abstr. in IT (36) 24.]

10199. DOVE, GEORGE N. The locked room mystique. Clues (7:2) 33–8.

10200. DOWLING, D. H. The atomic scientist: machine or moralist? SFS (13:2) 139–47.

10201. Dowse, Sara. The impact of film and television on the novel. *See* **9936.**

10202. Drewe, Robert. 'A cry in the Jungle Bar': Australians in Asia. Meridian (5:2) 133–9. (Australian novels set in Asia.)

10203. Dunsford, Cathie (ed.). New women's fiction. Auckland: New Women's Press. pp. 156.

10204. Dutruch, Suzanne. Les lendemains: variations sur l'enfer: à propos de quelques romans de science-fiction. *In* (pp. 293–301) **2.**

10205. —— Les techniques et les thèmes du roman policier anglais: auteurs féminins 1920–1950. Paris: Didier. pp. 785.

10206. Duyfhuizen, Bernard. Diary narratives in fact and fiction. Novel (19:2) 171–8 (review-article).

10207. Ellison, Jennifer (ed.). Rooms of their own. Melbourne: Penguin. pp. 248.

10208. Epstein, Ellen. The graves of academe. Caliban (23) 55–72.

10209. Faulkner, Howard. Homespun justice: the lynching in American fiction. SDR (22:4) 1984, 104–19.

10210. Ferrier, Carole (ed.). Gender, politics and fiction: twentieth century Australian women's novels. (Bibl. 1985, 8974.) Rev. by Susan Gingell in Ariel (17:4) 154–9.

10211. Fick, Thomas Hale. An American dialectic: power and innocence from Cooper to Kosinski. *See* **7235.**

10212. Fisher, Philip. Hard facts: setting and form in the American novel. *See* **7238.**

10213. Fishkin, Shelley Fisher. From fact to fiction: journalism and imaginative writing in America. (Bibl. 1985, 8977.) Rev. by Jeffrey Steinbrink in AL (58:2) 281–2; by Helen McNeil in TLS, 21 Feb., 180; by Ronald Weber in VQR (62) 142–50.

10214. Fogel, Stanley. A tale of two countries: contemporary fiction in Canada and the United States. Toronto: ECW Press, 1984. pp. 143. Rev. by Russell Brown in QQ (93:4) 899–901.

10215. Foreman, Paul. Sharecropper novels. SE (9:2) 1981, 107–10.

10216. Franklin, H. Bruce. Strange scenarios: science fiction, the theory of alienation, and the nuclear gods. SFS (13:2) 117–28.

10217. Fraser, Walter Wayne. The dominion of women: the relationship of the personal and the political in Canadian women's literature. Unpub. doct. diss., Univ. of Manitoba, 1985. [Abstr. in DA (46) 3356A.]

10218. Frazier, Charles Robinson. The geography of possibility: man in the landscape in recent Western fiction. Unpub. doct. diss., Univ. of South Carolina. [Abstr. in DA (47) 1322A.]

10219. Fujita, Gayle Kimi. The 'ceremonial self' in Japanese American literature. Unpub. doct. diss., Brown Univ. [Abstr. in DA (47) 1727A.] (*A Daughter of the Samurai, Nisei Daughter, No-No Boy, Obasan.*)

10220. Gadd, Bernard (comp.). I have seen the future: New Zealand science, future, and fantasy fiction stories. Auckland: Longman Paul. pp. xi, 163.

10221. GAKOV, V. Razmyshlíaîa o nemyslimom: atomnyĭ kontekst amerikanskoĭ fantastiki. (Reflecting on the unthinkable: the atomic context of American fantasy.) InL (1986:11) 206–13.

10222. GARFIELD, BRIAN (ed.). The crime of my life: favorite stories, by presidents of the Mystery Writers of America. New York: Walker, 1984; London: Severn House. pp. x, 269.

10223. GARROD, C. M. Individuation of middle class women in British fiction, 1848–1914. *See* **7241.**

10224. GARVEY, JOHANNA XANDRA KATHRYN. City voyages: consciousness and reflexivity in the modern novel. Unpub. doct. diss., Univ. of California, Berkeley, 1985. [Abstr. in DA (46) 3345A.]

10225. GEHERIN, DAVID. The American private eye: the image in fiction. New York: Ungar, 1985. pp. 228. Rev. by Martin Roth in Review (8) 265–72.

10226. GOOD, HOWARD. Acquainted with the night: the image of journalists in American fiction, 1890–1930. *See* **7247.**

10227. GÖTZ, DIETER. Idioms and real texts. *See* **1224.**

10228. GRANOFSKY, RONALD. The contemporary symbolic novel. Unpub. doct. diss., Queen's Univ. at Kingston. [Abstr. in DA (47) 526A.]

10229. GRANT, RENA JANE. From Clarissa to Lady Chatterley: character in the British novel. *See* **6051.**

10230. GREENE, SUE N. The use of the Jew in West Indian novels. WLWE (26:1) 150–69.

10231. GREVEN-BORDE, HÉLÈNE. Formes du roman utopique en Grande-Bretagne (1918–1970): dialogue du rationnel et de l'irrationnel. (Bibl. 1984. 9267.) Rev. by Graham Dunstan Martin in EA (39:1) 108.

10232. GROSS, LOUIS S. The transformed land: studies in American gothic narrative. *See* **7253.**

10233. GULLASON, THOMAS A. The 'lesser' renaissance: the American short story in the 1920s. *In* (pp. 71–101) **3.**

10234. GURNAH, A. R. Criteria in the criticism of West African fiction. Unpub. doct. diss., Univ. of Kent, 1982.

10235. HAGUE, ANGELA. Picaresque structure and the angry young novel. TCL (32:2) 209–20.

10236. HAINING, PETER (ed.). Vampire: chilling tales of the undead. *See* **7255.**

10237. HALÁSZ, A. M. The genealogical novel: a 20th century genre. *In* (pp. 41–5) **19.**

10238. HAMILTON, C. S. American dreaming: the American adventure formula in the western and hard-boiled detective novel, 1890–1940. *See* **7257.**

10239. HANO, ARNOLD. J'étais un veinard, ou les souvenirs d'un directeur de paperbacks. *See* **466.**

10240. HARRIS, NORMAN. The black universe in contemporary Afro-American fiction. CLAJ (30:1) 1–13.

10241. HARTMAN, PATRICIA L. The politics of language in feminist utopias. Unpub. doct. diss., Ohio Univ. [Abstr. in DA (47) 1724A.]

10242. HASENBERG, PETER. 'The Teuton's inbred mistake'. Das Deutschlandbild im britischen Agentenroman. Anglistik & Englischunterricht (29/30) 217–45.

10243. HATCH, RONALD. Narrative development in the Canadian historical novel. *See* **8848.**

10244. HAURI, CAREY. A study of fiction written by and about Australian immigrants. Cabbages and Kings (Adelaide) (14) 55–60.

10245. HAWTHORN, JEREMY (ed.). The British working-class novel in the twentieth century. *See* **6.**

10246. HERGENHAN, LAURIE. War in post 1960's fiction: Johnston, Stow, McDonald, Malouf and Les Murray. ALS (12:2) 1985, 248–60.

10247. —— (ed.). The Australian short story: an anthology from the 1890s to the 1980s. *See* **7263.**

10248. HICKEN, MARILYN (comp.). Cumulated fiction index, 1980–1984. Peterborough: Assn of Assistant Librarians, 1985. pp. 168.

10249. HIGBIE, ROBERT. Character and structure in the English novel. Gainesville: Florida UP, 1984. pp. 202. Rev. by Logan Speirs in EngS (67:4) 376–7.

10250. HIGDON, DAVID LEON. Shadows of the past in contemporary British fiction. Athens: Georgia UP, 1985. (Cf. bibl. 1985, 9017.) Rev. by Robert Murray Davis in SCR (3:4) 114–16; by Phillip Ward-Green in TLS, 8 Aug., 861.

10251. HITEN, EDITH A. La jeune fille dans le roman de 1920 à 1960, en France et aux États-Unis. Unpub. doct. diss., Univ. de Paris IV, 1973. [Abstr. in DA (46) 2685A.]

10252. HÖBLING, WALTER. Fiktionale Texte in der Landes- und Kulturkunde: Pragmatische Überlegungen am Beispiel amerikanischer Romane zum Vietnamkonflikt. *In* (pp. 231–53) **15.**

10253. HOCHMAN, BARUCH. The test of character: from the Victorian novel to the modern. *See* **7266.**

10254. HOFFMANN, GERHARD. The fantastic in fiction: its 'reality' status, its historical development and its transformation in postmodern narration. YREAL (1) 1982, 267–364.

10255. HÖLBLING, WALTER. Fiktionen vom Krieg im neueren amerikanischen Roman. Unpub. Habil. diss., Univ. of Graz (Austria).

10256. HOPPENSTAND, GARY CARL. On the trail of the paper tiger: a sociological perspective of myth, formula and the mystery genre in the entertainment print mass medium. Unpub. doct. diss., Bowling Green State Univ., 1985. [Abstr. in DA (47) 565A.]

10257. HOSKING, RICK. The usable past: Australian war fiction of the 1950s. ALS (12:2) 1985, 234–7.

10258. HOSTY, T. F. P. A universe of death: images of science and technology in twentieth century science fiction. Unpub. doct. diss., Univ. of Exeter, 1983.

10259. HOVANEC, EVELYN. Reader's guide to coal mining fiction and selected prose narratives. *See* **7268.**

10260. HOWARD, JUNE. Form and history in American literary naturalism. *See* **7269.**

10261. HURST, MARY JANE GAINES. The voice of the child in American literature: linguistic approaches to fictional child language. *See* **7271.**

10262. HUSEMANN, HARALD. 'When William came; if Adolf had come': English speculative novels on the German conquest of Britain. Anglistik & Englischunterricht (29/30) 57–83.

10263. HUTCHEON, LINDA. Narcissistic narrative, the metafictional paradox. (Bibl. 1985, 9029.) Rev. by Anthony Cheal Pugh in PT (7:3) 578–80; by Ronald Carter in NQ (33:2) 282–3.

10264. JAŘAB, JOSEF. Early Afro-American fiction. *See* **7273.**

10265. JESSEE, SHARON ADELE. A monotony of fine weather: imagined worlds in contemporary American fiction. Unpub. doct. diss., Univ. of Tulsa. [Abstr. in DA (47) 1728A.]

10266. JESSUP, EMILY DECKER LARDNER. Embattled landscapes: regionalism and gender in Midwestern literature, 1915–1941. Unpub. doct. diss., Univ. of Michigan, 1985. [Abstr. in DA (46) 3351A.]

10267. JINDRA, MIROSLAV. Hledání kořenů. (The search for roots.) *In* (pp. 31–2) **4.**

10268. JOHNSON, CHARLES. Philosophy and black fiction. Ob (6) Spring/Summer 1980, 55–61.

10269. JOHNSTONE, RICHARD. The will to believe: novelists of the nineteen-thirties. (Bibl. 1983, 9684.) Rev. by Martin Stannard in YES (16) 360–2.

10270. JONES, ANN ROSALIND. Mills & Boon meets femininism. *In* (pp. 195–218) **45.**

10271. JONES, JOSEPH; JONES, JOHANNA. Canadian fiction. *See* **6055.**

10272. JONES, LAWRENCE. New Zealand realism: retrospect and prospect. Landfall (40:4) 472–86.

10273. JOSEPH, GERHARD. Framing Caws. *See* **7277.**

10274. KAETZ, JAMES PATRICK. The Southern gentleman in twentieth century Southern fiction. Unpub. doct. diss., Univ. of North Carolina at Chapel Hill. [Abstr. in DA (47) 1729A.]

10275. KARL, FREDERICK R. American fictions 1940–1980; a comprehensive history and critical evaluation. (Bibl. 1985, 9036.) Rev. by Miriam Fuchs in MLS (16:3) 373–5.

10276. KEATING, H. R. F. Writing crime fiction. London: Black. pp. 96.

10277. KEEPING, CHARLES (ed.). Charles Keeping's book of classic ghost stories. *See* **7278.**

10278. KER, D. I. An examination of point of view in selected British, American and African novels. Unpub. doct. diss., Univ. of Stirling, 1984. [Abstr. in IT (35) 1087.]

10279. KIMBEL, ELLEN. The American short story: 1900–1920. *In* (pp. 33–69) **3.**

10280. KING, THOMAS HUNT. Inventing the Indian: white images, native oral literature, and contemporary native writers. Unpub. doct. diss., Univ. of Utah. [Abstr. in DA (47) 1729A.]

10281. KLEIN, H. M. Fiction of the First World War and the problems of criticism. *In* (pp. 109–14) **19.**

10282. KLEIN, HOLGER; FLOWER, JOHN; HOMBERGER, ERIC (eds). The Second World War in fiction. (Bibl. 1985, 9046.) Rev. by Ruth Pulik in UES (24:1) 45–7.

10283. KLEIN, KATHLEEN GREGORY.; KELLER, JOSEPH. Deductive detective fiction: the self-destructive genre. Genre (19:2) 155–72.

10284. KLÍMA, VLADIMÍR. Rozmach nigerijského romanopisectví. (The upsurge of Nigerian fiction.) SvL (31:3) 253–5.

10285. KLINKOWITZ, JEROME. The self-apparent word: fiction as language/language as fiction. (Bibl. 1985, 9047.) Rev. by Philip Stevick in JEGP (85:1) 159–61.

10286. KLOOSTER, DAVID J. The art of the present moment: studies in the American short story. *See* **7285.**

10287. KORENEVA, MARIJA M. The novel of the First and Second World War in western Europe and the USA. *In* (pp. 63–6) **19.**

10288. KORT, WESLEY A. Modern fiction and human time: a study in narrative and belief. Tampa: South Florida UP, 1985. pp. 227. Rev. by Joe McClatchey in ChrisL (36:1) 41–3.

10289. KOWALEWSKI, MICHAEL JOHN. Violence and verbal form in American fiction. *See* **7287.**

10290. KUEHL, JOHN. The ludic impulse in recent American fiction. JNT (16:3) 167–78.

10291. LARÈS, MAURICE. De Lawrence à Learoyd. Exploitation littéraire ou approche cinématographique? RLC (58:1) 1984, 51–88.

10292. LeBow, DIANE. Selfhood in free fall: novels by black and white American women. Unpub. doct. diss., Univ. of California, Santa Cruz, 1985. [Abstr. in DA (46) 3034A.]

10293. LECKER, ROBERT; DAVID, JACK (eds). Annotated bibliography of Canada's major authors: vol. 5. Downsview, Ont.: ECW Press, 1984. pp. 480. Rev. by W. J. Keith in JCanStud (21:1) 154–5.

10294. —— —— QUIGLEY, ELLEN (eds). Canadian writers and their works: fiction series: vol. 6. *See* **7.**

10295. —— —— —— Canadian writers and their works: fiction series: vol. 7. *See* **8.**

10296. LeCLAIR, TOM; McCAFFERY, LARRY (eds). Anything can happen: interviews with contemporary American novelists. (Bibl. 1984, 9313.) Rev. by David Seed in EA (38:3) 1985, 360–1.

10297. LEDGERWOOD, MIKLE DAVE. The images of the Indian in four New-World literatures. *See* **7291.**

10298. LEMON, LEE T. Portraits of the artist in the contemporary fiction. Lincoln: Nebraska UP, 1985. pp. xvii, 261. Rev. by James Gindin in JEGP (85:4) 580–3.

10299. LENAR, FAYE MERTINE. The emergence of the passionate woman in American fiction, 1850–1920. *See* **7293.**

10300. LERNER, FREDERICK ANDREW. Modern science fiction and the American literary community. Metuchen, NJ: Scarecrow Press, 1985. pp. 325.

10301. LOCKWOOD, STEPHEN P.   The new wave in science fiction: a primer. Unpub. doct. diss., Indiana Univ., 1985. [Abstr. in DA (46) 2689A.]

10302. LONG, ELIZABETH.   The American dream and the popular novel. (Bibl. 1985, 9069.) Rev. by Thomas L. Hartshorne in JAH (72:4) 1003–4; by Brooke K. Horvath in AL (58:1) 130–2.

10303. LYONGA, PAULINE NALOVA.   Uhamiri, or a feminist approach to African literature: an analysis of selected texts by women in oral and written literature. Unpub. doct. diss., Univ. of Michigan, 1985. [Abstr. in DA (46) 1940A.]

10304. MCADAMS, RUTH ANN.   The Shakers in American fiction. See **7300.**

10305. MCCORD, PHYLLIS FRUS.   The ideology of form: the nonfiction novel. Genre (19:1) 59–79.

10306. —— News and the novel: a theory and a history of the relation between journalism and fiction. Unpub. doct. diss., New York Univ., 1985. [Abstr. in DA (46) 3719A.]

10307. MCDONNELL, BRIAN.   The translation of New Zealand fiction into film. See **10014.**

10308. MCEWAN, J. N.   Perspective in historical fiction by British writers, 1953–1983. Unpub. doct. diss., Univ. of Stirling, 1984.

10309. MCLAVERTY, JAMES.   Authorial revision. See **7302.**

10310. MCLEOD, MARION; WEVERS, LYDIA (eds).   Women's work: contemporary short stories by New Zealand women. (Bibl. 1985, 9077.) Rev. by Elizabeth Caffin in NZList, 3 May, 51.

10311. MACLULICH, T. D.   The animal story and the 'Nature Faker' controversy. ECanW (33) 112–24.

10312. MACMILLAN, CARRIE.   Seaward vision and sense of place: the Maritime novel, 1880–1920. See **7303.**

10313. MADDEN-SIMPSON, JANET (ed.).   Woman's part: an anthology of short fiction by and about Irish women 1890–1960. See **7304.**

10314. MALZAHN, MANFRED.   Aspects of identity: the contemporary Scottish novel (1978–1981) as national self-expression. (Bibl. 1985, 9080.) Rev. by Glenda Norquay in Cencrastus (22) 58.

10315. MANDEL, ERNEST.   Delightful murder: a social history of the crime story. See **7306.**

10316. MANLOVE, COLIN N.   Science fiction: ten explorations. Kent, OH: Kent State UP; London: Macmillan. pp. x, 249.

10317. MARGOLIS, RICHARD J.   Melody and mystery. NewL (69:18) 9–10.

10318. MARRA, JAMES LEE.   The lifelike 'I': a theory of response to first-person narrator/protagonist fiction. Unpub. doct. diss., Texas Tech Univ., 1985. [Abstr. in DA (47) 523A.]

10319. MARSHALL, TOM.   Re-visioning: comedy and history in the Canadian novel. See **7308.**

10320. MASNEROVÁ, EVA.   K problému vymezení prózy amerického Jihu: její historičnost a další charakteristické rysy. (The delimitation of fiction in the American South: its history and characteristics.) *In* (pp. 40–1) **4.**

10321. MASSEY, DENNIS.   The modern American prison novel. Unpub. doct. diss., Univ. of Cincinnati, 1985. [Abstr. in DA (46) 3034A.]

10322. MATHIESON, K. G.   The influence of science fiction in contemporary American writing. *See* **9810.**

10323. MATTHEWS, BRIAN ERNEST.   Romantics and mavericks: the Australian short story. *See* **7309.**

10324. MAUGHAN-BROWN, DAVID.   Land, freedom and fiction: history and ideology in Kenya. London: Zed Books, 1985. pp. x, 284. Rev. by Brenda Cooper in Social Dynamics (Cape Town) (12:1) 85–90; by John A. Wiseman in THES (693) 15.

10325. MENDES DA COSTA, M.   Dreamers of the real: transitional characters in the contemporary American novel. Unpub. doct. diss., Univ. of Sussex, 1982.

10326. MENENDEZ, ALBERT J.   The subject is murder: a selective subject guide to mystery fiction. *See* **7311.**

10327. MERNIT, SUSAN.   The state of the short story. VQR (62:2) 302–11.

10328. MESPLÈDE, CLAUDE.   La première génération du roman noir. McCoy, Tracy, Latimer et quelques autres. Europe (62:664/65) 1984, 38–52.

10329. MILLER, DANNY LESTER.   Images of women in southern Appalachian mountain literature. *See* **7312.**

10330. MILLER, DAVID M.   'Mythic', 'realist', and sf: a zero-sum game. MFS (32:1) 3–9.

10331. MILLER, JANE.   Women writing about men. *See* **7314.**

10332. MILLER, PAUL W.   Paris of the 1920s through Midwestern novelists' eyes. Midamerica (13) 84–93. (Anderson, Farrell, Fitzgerald, Hemingway, Lewis.)

10333. MILNE, GORDON.   Ports of call: a study of the American nautical novel. *See* **7315.**

10334. MINNI, C. D.   The short story as an ethnic genre. *In* (pp. 61–76) **13.**

10335. MODDELMOG, DEBRA ANN.   The Œdipus myth in twentieth-century fiction. Unpub. doct. diss., Pennsylvania State Univ., 1985. [Abstr. in DA (46) 3341A.]

10336. MORRISSEY, MICHAEL (ed.).   The new fiction. (Bibl. 1985, 9096.) Rev. by Patrick Evans in NZList, 15 Feb., 38; by C. K. Stead in Islands (3:1) 73–8; by David Dowling in Landfall (40:1) 121–4.

10337. MOTTO, ANNA LYDIA; CLARK, JOHN R.   Intrusion, obstruction and the self-reflexive narrator in so-called post-modern literature. CML (7:1) 31–8.

10338. AL-MOUSA, N.   Self-cultivation as a literary theme: the German Bildungsroman and its French and English counterparts. Unpub. doct. diss., Univ. of Essex, 1984.

10339. MOYLAN, TOM. Demand the impossible: science fiction and the utopian imagination. New York; London: Methuen. pp. viii, 242.

10340. MUKHERJEE, MEENAKSHI. Realism and reality: the novel and society in India. *See* **7317.**

10341. MÜLLER, WOLFGANG G. The erudite detective: a tradition in English and American detective fiction. *See* **7319.**

10342. MURRAY, ISOBEL; TAIT, BOB. Ten modern Scottish novels. (Bibl. 1985, 9099.) Rev. by Glenda Norquay in Cencrastus (22) 58.

10343. MYERS, THOMAS ROBERT. Envisaging a war: Vietnam and the American historical novel. Unpub. doct. diss., Purdue Univ., 1985. [Abstr. in DA (47) 180A.]

10344. MZAMANE, MBULELO VIZIKHUNGO (ed.). *Hungry Flames*: and other black South African short stories. Harlow: Longman. pp. xxvi, 162. (Longman African classics.)

10345. NEWMAN, CHARLES. The post-modern aura: the act of fiction in an age of inflation. Evanston, IL: Northwestern UP, 1985. pp. iii, 203. Rev. by Timothy Erwin in WHR (40:4) 368–70; by Maurice Beebe in AL (58:1) 137–9; by Jerry Herron in Criticism (28:4) 476–80.

10346. NEWMAN, JOHN; UNSWORTH, MICHAEL (eds). Future war novels: an annotated bibliography of works in English published since 1946. Phoenix, AZ: Oryx Press, 1984. pp. 102. Rev. by I. F. Clarke in SFS (13:2) 207–9.

10347. NOVAK, DAGMAR VALERIE. The Canadian novel and the two World Wars. Unpub. doct. diss., Univ. of Toronto, 1985. [Abstr. in DA (46) 2697A.]

10348. NWEZEH, E. C. Satire in post-Independence West African fiction. *In* (pp. 193–9) **19.**

10349. O'HEARN, DENIS. Freedom from Mother Church: the Stephen Hero image in Australian literature. *In* (pp. 24–33) C. KIERNAN (ed.), Australia and Ireland 1788–1988: bicentenary essays. Dublin: Gill & Macmillan. pp. 309.

10350. OLSEN, LANCE MARTIN. Nameless things and thingless names: an essay on postmodern fantasy. Unpub. doct. diss., Univ. of Virginia, 1985. [Abstr. in DA (47) 524A.]

10351. OLSON, CHRISTOPHER PETER. Narrational and temporal form in the nineteenth- and twentieth-century novel. *See* **7322.**

10352. OSTENDORF, BERNDT (ed.). Amerikanische Gettoliteratur. Zur Literatur ethnischer, marginaler und unterdrückter Gruppen in Amerika. (Bibl. 1984, 8847.) Rev. by Sepp Tiefenthaler in AAA (11) 131–3.

10353. PACHE, WALTER. 'The fiction makes us real': aspects of postmodernism in Canada. *In* (pp. 64–78) **22.**

10354. PACI, F. G. Tasks of the Canadian novelist writing on immigrant themes. *In* (pp. 35–60) **13.**

10355. PARKER, HELEN N. Biological themes in modern science fiction. Ann Arbor, MI: UMI Research Press, 1984. (Cf. bibl. 1985, 9113.) Rev. by Michael D. Rose in SFS (13:3) 398–400.

10356. PARRINDER, PATRICK. ''Tis new to thee': the strange and the familiar in the language of science fiction. *In* (pp. 587–97) **1.**

10357. PAUL, RONALD. 'Fire in our hearts': a study of the portrayal of youth in a selection of post-war British working-class fiction. Gothenburg: Acta Universitatis Gothoburgensis, 1982. pp. 225. (Gothenburg studies in English, 51.) (Cf. bibl. 1983, 10431.) Rev. by Stig-Lennart Godin in Samlaren (106) 1985, 97–9.

10358. PEARCE, SHARYN. Changing places: working-class women in the fiction of the Depression. Westerly (31:4) 41–51.

10359. PENNEY, S. G. The role of the narrator in selected first-person novels. Unpub. doct. diss., Univ. of London (Royal Holloway Coll.), 1984.

10360. PETZOLD, DIETER. Fantasy fiction and related genres. MFS (32:1) 11–20.

10361. PEYTON, RICHARD (ed.). Deadly odds: crime and mystery stories of the turf. *See* **7327.**

10362. PONS, XAVIER. The psychoanalytic approach to literature. *See* **3039.**

10363. PORTCH, STEPHEN R. Literature's silent language: nonverbal communication. New York; Berne; Frankfurt: Lang, 1985. pp. viii, 172. Rev. by John E. Bassett in AL (58:2) 297–9.

10364. POWELL, PHILIP E. Tyger burning bright: the French Revolution and historical imagination. *See* **7331.**

10365. POYNTING, JEREMY. Seeing with other eyes: reflections on Christian proselytization in Indo-Caribbean fiction. Kp (8:2) 97–108.

10366. PŘIDAL, ANTONÍN. K proměnám detektivky u G. K. Chestertona a K. Čapka. (Variations on the detective story in G. K. Chesterton's and Karel Čapek's work.) *In* (pp. 51–4) **24.**

10367. PROCHÁZKA, MARTIN. V záři a soumraku jazzového věku. (The radiance and twilight of the Jazz Age.) Kmen (suppl. to Tvorba, Prague) (39) 8–9.

10368. QUINN, JOHN (ed.); HEANEY, SEAMUS (introd.). A portrait of the artist as a young girl. London: Methuen. pp. xiv, 144. (Irish writers.)

10369. RADWAY, JANICE. Reading the romance: women, patriarchy, and popular literature. (Bibl. 1985, 9127.) Rev. by Annette Kolodny in CR (30:1) 119–20; by Jane E. Caputi in LQ (56:1) 78–80.

10370. RANDALL, NEIL FRANKLIN. Humour in all seriousness: techniques and effects of humour in six Canadian novels. Unpub. doct. diss., York Univ. (Canada), 1985. [Abstr. in DA (47) 1185A.] (*St. Urbain's Horseman, What the Crow Said, The Rebel Angels, The Diviners, The Swing in the Garden, Shoeless Joe.*)

10371. RATH, SURA PRASAD. Play as a formal paradigm in modern fiction. Unpub. doct. diss., Texas A&M Univ., 1985. [Abstr. in DA (46) 3025A.]

10372. RAYNAUD, JEAN. Science-fiction: genre, ou vision? Introduction à une problématique. *In* (pp. 599–609) **1.**

10373. RECKWITZ, ERHARD. Der Roman als Metaroman: Salman

Rushdie, *Midnight's Children*; Kazuo Ishiguro, *A Pale View of the Hills*; John Fowles, *Mantissa*. PoetA (18:1/2) 140–64.

10374. REILLY, JOHN M. (ed.). Twentieth-century crime and mystery writers. (Bibl. 1980, 10916.) London: St James, 1985. pp. xx, 1094. (Twentieth-century writers.) (Second ed.: first ed. 1980.)

10375. REILLY, ROBERT (ed.). The transcendent adventure: studies of religion in science fiction/fantasy. (Bibl. 1985, 9130.) Rev. by Joe R. Christopher in ChrisL (35:4) 32–4.

10376. REITZ, ANN L. Sawbones to savior to cynic: the doctor's relation to society in English fiction of the eighteenth, nineteenth, and twentieth centuries. *See* **6066.**

10377. RIGNEY, BARBARA HILL. Lilith's daughters: women and religion in contemporary fiction. (Bibl. 1983, 9785.) Rev. by Rosalind Miles in YES (16) 365–6; by Patricia Clements in CanRCL (13:3) 523–7.

10378. RIPLEY, JONATHAN GRANT. The treatment of burial rituals in the modern American novel. Unpub. doct. diss., St. John's Univ., 1985. [Abstr. in DA (46) 2694A.]

10379. RISSER, LYNN KATHERINE. The Mexican setting in the contemporary American novel. Unpub. doct. diss., Univ. of Arkansas, 1985. [Abstr. in DA (46) 3035A.]

10380. ROBINSON, DOUGLAS. American apocalypses: the image of the end of the world in American literature. *See* **7335.**

10381. ROGERS, EARL M. Fiction with an Iowa City setting: an annotated checklist. BkIA (44) 10–26.

10382. ROHRBERGER, MARY. The question of regionalism: limitation and transcendence. *In* (pp. 147–82) **3.**

10383. ROSINSKY, NATALIE M. Feminist futures: contemporary women's speculative fiction. (Bibl. 1985, 9137.) Rev. by Linda Leith in SFS (13:1) 92–4.

10384. ROTH, MARTIN. Popular criticism. Review (8) 265–72 (review-article).

10385. ROWLAND, DIANE BAKER. Sisterhood and social conscience: the emergence and evolution of the feminist New Woman in selected American fiction, 1864–1933. *See* **7336.**

10386. RUBIN, DAVID. After the Raj: British novels of India since 1947. Hanover, NH; London: New England UP. pp. xi, 197.

10387. SANDELS, ROBERT. UFOs, science fiction and the postwar utopia. JPC (20:1) 141–51.

10388. SAUERBERG, LARS OLE. Secret-agent fiction: a survey of its critical literature with a bibliography. Clues (7:2) 1–31.

10389. SAUNDERS, JAMES ROBERT. Greater 'truth' in fiction: a study of four black writers. Unpub. doct. diss., Univ. of Michigan. [Abstr. in DA (47) 2161A.] (Langston Hughes, Zora Neale Hurston, James Weldon Johnson, Richard Wright.)

10390. SCHIPPER, MINEKE. Réalisme et roman africain. *In* (pp. 193–205) **19.**

10391. Schleret, Jean-Jacques. *Manhunt*, la revue de la seconde génération. *See* **690.**

10392. —— La seconde génération. L'âge d'or du roman noir américain. Europe (62:664/65) 1984, 69–88.

10393. Schlobin, Roger C. (ed.). The aesthetics of fantasy literature and art. (Bibl. 1984, 9400.) Rev. by Josef Schmidt in CanRCL (13:3) 479–80.

10394. Schlueter, Paul; Schlueter, June (eds). The English novel: twentieth century criticism: vol. 2, Twentieth century novelists. (Bibl. 1983, 249.) Rev. by Jay L. Halio in YES (16) 348–9.

10395. Schnitzer, Deborah Jane. The use and abuse of pictorial terminology in discussions of Modernist fiction. Unpub. doct. diss., Univ. of Manitoba. [Abstr. in DA (47) 1319A.] (Hemingway, Joyce, Lawrence, Matthiessen, Woolf.)

10396. Segal, Howard P. Technological utopianism in American culture. *See* **7338.**

10397. Shostak, Debra B. Survivors: perspectives on transformative violence in contemporary American narrative. Unpub. doct. diss., Univ. of Wisconsin–Madison, 1985. [Abstr. in DA (46) 3036A.]

10398. Shwartz, Susan (ed.). Moonsinger's friends: an anthology in honor of Andre Norton. New York: Bluejay, 1985; London: Severn House. pp. 342.

10399. Skei, Hans. Den konstruerte virkeligheten: noen betraktinger over postmodernistisk litteratur. (The invented reality: some reflections on postmodernist literature.) Samtiden (95:5) 63–7.

10400. Slusser, George E.; Rabkin, Eric S. (eds). Shadows of the magic lamp: fantasy and science fiction in film. *See* **10085.**

10401. Smith, Curtis C. (ed.). Twentieth-century science-fiction writers. (Bibl. 1983, 9811.) London: St James. pp. xviii, 933. (Second ed.: first ed. 1982.)

10402. Smither, Elizabeth. The NZ short story: from flux to ashes to innocence. Islands (3:1) 65–73.

10403. Söderlind, Sylvia. Den kanadensiska litteraturen i dag. (Canadian literature today.) Artes (12:3) 3–26.

10404. —— Madeincanadamadeincanada. Artes (12:3) 78–90.

10405. Spivey, Ted R. Revival: Southern writers in the city. Gainesville: Florida UP. pp. 227. Rev. by Ann R. Morris in ChrisL (36:1) 43–4.

10406. Stanzel, Franz K. A theory of narrative. Trans. by Charlotte Goedsche. Cambridge: CUP, 1984. pp. xvi, 309. Rev. by Dieter Meindl in AAA (11:2) 246–50.

10407. Stepto, Robert B. Distrust of the reader in Afro-American narratives. *In* (pp. 300–22) **47.**

10408. Steuernagel, Trudy. Contemporary homosexual fiction and the gay rights movement. JPC (20:3) 125–34.

10409. Stevenson, Randall. The British novel since the thirties: an introduction. London: Batsford. pp. 257.

21

10410. STEVICK, PHILIP (ed.).   The American short story, 1900–1945: a critical history. *See* **3.**

10411. STOWE, WILLIAM W.   Popular fiction as liberal art. CE (48:7) 646–63.

10412. —— Sleuth and method: a review essay. CanRCL (12:3) 1985, 433–41 (review-article).

10413. STRUTHERS, J. R. (TIM) (ed.).   The Montreal story tellers: memoirs, photographs, critical essays. Montreal: Véhicule Press, 1985. pp. 225. Rev. in QQ (93:4) 950–1.

10414. STRYCHACZ, THOMAS FRANK.   Challenging mass culture: American writers and literary authority, 1880–1940. *See* **7347.**

10415. SUCHOFF, DAVID BRUCE.   Reciprocal testimonies: conservatism and change in the novel. *See* **7348.**

10416. SUGUNASIRI, SUWANDA.   Reality and symbolism in the South Asian Canadian short story. WLWE (26:1) 98–107.

10417. SUVIN, DARKO.   'Formal' and 'sociological' analysis in the aesthetics of the science-fiction novel. *In* (pp. 453–8) **19.**

10418. SWINDER, PATRICK.   The English novel of history and society, 1940–1980: Richard Hughes, Henry Green, Anthony Powell, Angus Wilson, Kingsley Amis, V. S. Naipaul. (Bibl. 1985, 9169.) Rev. by Mark Casserley in TLS, 7 Mar., 258.

10419. SWINFEN, ANN.   In defence of fantasy: a survey of the genre in English and American literature since 1945. (Bibl. 1984, 9428.) Rev. by Eugene Warren in ChrisL (35:4) 53–4.

10420. SZUBERLA, GUY.   Reborn in Babel: immigrant characters and types in early Chicago fiction. Midamerica (13) 31–48.

10421. TALLIS, RAYMOND.   Is realism still relevant to modern reality? Listener (115) 20 Feb., 15–16.

10422. THIHER, ALLEN.   Words in reflection: modern language theory and postmodern fiction. (Bibl. 1985, 680.) Rev. by Theo D'Haen in PT (7:3) 581–3.

10423. THOMAS, AUDREY.   A fine romance, my dear, this is. CanL (108) 5–12. (Romantic fiction for women.)

10424. THORNTON, LAWRENCE.   Unbodied hope: narcissim and the modern novel. *See* **7353.**

10425. TREMPER, ELLEN.   Black English in children's literature. *See* **881.**

10426. TRUMP, M. E.   South African short fiction in English and Afrikaans since 1948. Unpub. doct. diss., Univ. of London, SOAS, 1985. [Abstr. in IT (35) 1493.]

10427. VAREILLE, JEAN-CLAUDE.   Culture savante et culture populaire: brèves remarques à propos des horizons idéologiques, des structures, et de la littérarité du roman policier. *See* **7357.**

10428. VIDAN, IVO.   Time sequence in spatial fiction. *In* (pp. 271–5) **19.**

10429. VILJOEN, HEIN.   Die Suid-Afrikaanse romansisteem *anno* 1981: 'n vergelykende studie. (The 'system' of the South African novel *anno*

1981: a comparative study.) Potchefstroom, Transvaal: Potchefstroomse Universiteit vir CHO. pp. xiv, 439.

10430. VINSON, JAMES; KIRKPATRICK, D. L. (eds). Contemporary novelists. London: St James. pp. xix, 1003. (Contemporary writers of the English language.) (Fourth ed.: first ed. 1982.)

10431. VIPOND, MARY. Best sellers in English Canada: 1919–1928. *See* **441.**

10432. VON BORN, HEIDI. Mellan rymd och prärie: en studie i kanadensisk prosa. (Between space and the prairie: a study of Canadian prose.) Artes (12:3) 52–9.

10433. VORLAT, EMMA. Minoriteit en mainstream: recente verhalende literatuur in de Verenigde Staten. (Minority and mainstream: recent narrative literature in the US.) Louvain; Amersfoort: ACCO, 1985. pp. 254.

10434. WALKER, SHIRLEY. The Boer War: Paterson, Abbot, Brennan, Miles Franklin and Morant. ALS (12:2) 1985, 207–22.

10435. WALLE, ALF H. Devolution and evolution: hillbillies and cowboys as American savages. *See* **2496.**

10436. WATSON, JAMES G. The American short story: 1930–1945. *In* (pp. 103–46) **3.**

10437. WAUGH, CHARLES G.; GREENBERG, MARTIN H. (eds). Alternative histories: eleven stories of the world as it might have been. Postscr. by GORDON B. CHAMBERLAIN; bibliography by BARTON C. MACKER and GORDON B. CHAMBERLAIN. New York; London: Garland. pp. 363. (Garland reference library of the humanities, 623.)

10438. WAUGH, PATRICIA. Metafiction: the theory and practice of self-conscious fiction. (Bibl. 1985, 9195.) Rev. by Ann Jefferson in PT (7:3)574–6.

10439. WEBER, ROBERT W. Pour un mythopoétique du roman de l'inconscient. *In* (pp. 353–6) **19.**

10440. WEE, MORRIS OWEN. Specks on the horizon: individuals and the land in Canadian prairie fiction. SDR (19:4) 1982, 18–31.

10441. WEISS, ALLAN BARRY. The university and the English-Canadian short story, 1950–1980. Unpub. doct. diss., Univ. of Toronto, 1985. [Abstr. in DA (46) 2697A.]

10442. WEISS, DANIEL. The critic agonistes: psychology, myth, and the art of fiction. Ed. by ERIC SOLOMON and STEPHEN ARKIN. *See* **7364.**

10443. WESTFAHL, GARY WESLEY. The mote in Gernsback's eye: a history of the idea of science fiction. Unpub. doct. diss., Claremont Graduate School. [Abstr. in DA (47) 184A.]

10444. WEVERS, LYDIA. Changing directions: the short story in New Zealand. Meanjin (44:3) 1985, 352–6.

10445. WHITEMAN, BRUCE. Canadian issues of Anglo-American fiction: the example of H. G. Wells. PBSA (80:1) 75–81.

10446. WILDE, ALAN. Shooting for smallness: limits and values in some recent American fiction. Boundary 2 (13:2/3) 1985, 343–69.

10447. WILLARD, NANCY. High talk in the starlit wood: on spirits and stories. *See* **7366.**

10448. WIMMER, ADOLF. Auf der Suche nach dem verlorenen Krieg. US-Literatur zum Vietnamkrieg. Forum (Vienna) (33) 1985/86, 16–22.

10449. WONG, TAK-WAI. The theme of initiation in Chinese and Anglo-American fiction. In (pp. 375–80) **19.**

10450. WOODCOCK, BRUCE. Post-1975 Caribbean fiction and the challenge to English literature. CritQ (28:4) 79–95.

10451. YORK, LORRAINE MARY. 'The other side of dailiness': photography in recent Canadian fiction. Unpub. doct. diss., McMaster Univ., 1985. [Abstr. in DA (46) 3723A.] (Timothy Finley, Margaret Lawrence, Alice Munro, Michael Ondaatje.)

10452. ZIEGLER, HEIDE; BIGSBY, CHRISTOPHER (eds). The radical imagination and the liberal tradition: interviews with English and American novelists. (Bibl. 1985, 9213.) Rev. by Michael Wilding in YES (16) 347–8.

10453. ZIPES, JACK (ed.). Don't bet on the prince: contemporary feminist fairy tales in North America and England. Aldershot: Gower. pp. xiv, 270.

Literature for Children

10454. ANON. 50 years on. See **354.**

10455. BARKER, KEITH. In the realms of the gold: the story of the Carnegie Medal. London: Macrae for Youth Libraries Group, Library Assn. pp. 61. Rev. in Growing Point (25:4) 4719.

10456. BUTLER, DOROTHY. Five to eight. London: Bodley Head. pp. 210. Rev. in Growing Point (25:3) 4692; by M. C. in Junior Bookshelf (50:6) 213.

10457. CHAMBERS, NANCY (ed.). The Signal selection of children's books, 1985. Stroud: Thimble Press. pp. 55. Rev. in Growing Point (25:3) 4692.

10458. CHASSAGNOL, MONIQUE. La fantaisie dans les récits pour la jeunesse en Grande-Bretagne de 1918 à 1968. Lille: Atelier de reproduction des thèses. pp. 808.

10459. COHEN, JOHN. *Reading Time* review: a content analysis. See **574.**

10460. CROUCH, MARCUS. Early days. Junior Bookshelf (50:3) 97–101. (Children's books of the 30s.)

10461. DIXON, DIANA. From instruction to amusement: attitudes of authority in children's periodicals before 1914. See **585.**

10462. FISHER, MARGERY. The bright face of danger. London; Hodder & Stoughton. pp. 440. Rev. by David Grylls in TLS, 29 Aug., 948; by G. B. in Junior Bookshelf (50:9) 179.

10463. GOLDMAN, IRENE CAROLYN. Captains of industry and their mates: a new look at the American business novel from Howells to Dreiser. See **7374.**

10464. JARMAN, DAVID; VAN OSS, CELIA. Childhood's pattern. See **7376.**

10465. LACAMPAGNE, ROBERT J. From Huck to Holden to Dinky Hocker: current humor in the American adolescent novel. See **7378.**

10466. MacLeod, Anne Scott. An end to innocence: the transformation of childhood in twentieth-century children's literature. *In* (pp. 100–17) **40.**

10467. Molson, Francis. Portrait of the young writer in children's fiction. LU (1:2) 1977, 77–90.

10468. Pflieger, Pat. A reference guide to modern fantasy for children. *See* **7379.**

10469. Phelps, Ruth M. A comparison of Newbery Award winners in the first and last decade of the award (1922–31 and 1976–85). Unpub. doct. diss., Miami Univ., 1985. [Abstr. in DA (47) 453A.]

10470. Rasmussen, Bonnie. Literary criticism: explication of the picture book. *See* **81.**

10471. Shavit, Zohar. Poetics of children's literature. Athens: Georgia UP. pp. 200. Rev. by David Grylls in TLS, 29 Aug., 948.

10472. Young, Beverly Burgoyne. The young female protagonist in juvenile fiction: three decades of evolution. Unpub. doct. diss., Washington State Univ., 1985. [Abstr. in DA (46) 3276A.] (1930s, 1950s, 1970s.)

Poetry

10473. Altieri, Charles. Self and sensibility in contemporary American poetry. New York: CUP, 1984. (Cf. bibl. 1985, 9228.) Rev. by Stephen Fredman in ELN (24:1) 98–9.

10474. Amprimoz, Alexandre L.; Viselli, Sante A. Death between two cultures: Italian-Canadian poetry. *In* (pp. 101–20) **13.**

10475. Baker, Peter Nicholas, Jr. Poetic practice. Unpub. doct. diss., Brown Univ., 1985. [Abstr. in DA (46) 1930A.]

10476. Balcon, Jill (sel. and introd.). The pity of war: poems of the First World War. London: Shepherd–Walwyn, 1985. pp. xi, 68.

10477. Barker, Sebastian (ed.). Portraits of poets. (Photographs by Christopher Barker.) Manchester: Carcanet Press. pp. 125. Rev. by Russell Davies in Listener, 4 Dec., 23.

10478. Barry, Sebastian (ed.). The inherited boundaries: younger poets of the Republic of Ireland. Portlaoise: Dolmen Press. pp. 192. Rev. by Gerald Dawe in Linen Hall Review (3:2, incorrectly numbered 3:3) 14; by Maurice Harmon in IUR (16) 235–7.

10479. Bartlett, Lee. What is 'language poetry'? CI (12:4) 741–52.

10480. Baughman, Ronald (ed.). American poets. Detroit, MI: Gale Research. pp. xvi, 387. (Contemporary authors, bibliographical ser., 2.) Rev. by Bernard F. Engel in CR (30:4) 543.

10481. Bensko, John Richard. Narrative in the modern short poem. Unpub. doct. diss., Florida State Univ., 1985. [Abstr. in DA (46) 2297A.]

10482. Beom, Dae-Soon. Auden generation eui si e natanan jungchijeok gwanshim e gwahan yeongu. (A study of the political themes in the poetry of the Auden generation.) Unpub. doct. diss., Jeonbuk National Univ. (Korea).

10483. —— 1930 yeondae youngsi yeongu. (A study of English poetry in the 1930s.) Seoul: Hansin. pp. 241.

10484. BOGACZ, TED. 'A tyranny of words': language, poetry, and antimodernism in England in the First World War. JMH (58:3) 643–68.

10485. BOOTH, MARTIN. British poetry 1964–84: driving through the barricades. (Bibl. 1985, 9236.) Rev. by Andrew Swarbrick in CritQ (28:3) 111–12; by Blake Morrison in LRev, Nov. 1985, 50–1.

10486. BRESLIN, JAMES E. B. From modern to contemporary: American poetry, 1945–1965. (Bibl. 1985, 9239.) Rev. by Alan Golding in MP (84:2) 235–8; by Marjorie Perloff in ELN (23:4) 61–5.

10487. BROWN, FRANK BURCH. Transfiguration: poetic metaphor and the languages of religious belief. (Bibl. 1985, 9241.) Rev. by Kathleen Watson in NQ (33:1) 132–3.

10488. BROWN, HAMISH; BERRY, MARTYN (eds). Speak to the hills: an anthology of twentieth century British and Irish mountain poetry. Introd. by NORMAN NICHOLSON. Aberdeen: Aberdeen UP, 1985. pp. xxvii, 530.

10489. BRUGIÈRE, BERNARD (ed.). La poésie brittannique: 1970–1984. Paris: Didier. pp. xxii, 129–229. (Études anglaises, cahiers et documents, 7.) (Repr. of extracts from Études Anglaises, vol. 38.).

10490. BUTLER, SUSAN (ed.); CONRAN, ANTHONY (introd.). Common ground: poets in a Welsh landscape. (Bibl. 1985, 9249.) Rev. by Philip Pacey in Poetry Wales (21:1) 116–21.

10491. CAM, H. K. The confesser's art: a study of five American poets. Unpub. doct. diss., Univ. of Reading, 1983.

10492. CAMPBELL, ANDREW MARCHANT. Geology in modern poetry. Unpub. doct. diss., Univ. of Kentucky, 1985. [Abstr. in DA (46) 2689A.]

10493. CARRUTH, HAYDEN. Poetry and academicism. SewR (94:2) 335–6.

10494. CHAPMAN, MICHAEL. Soweto poetry. Planet (59) 9–16.

10495. —— (ed.). The Paperbook of South African English poetry. See **7386.**

10496. CHATTERJEE, SATI. Art and inspiration: the continuing debate. See **7387.**

10497. CLEARFIELD, ANDREW M. These fragments I have shored: collage and montage in early Modernist poetry. Ann Arbor, MI: UMI Research Press; Epping: Bowker, 1984. pp. xii, 150. (Studies in modern literature.)

10498. COLOMBO, JOHN ROBERT; RICHARDSON, MICHAEL (eds). We stand on guard: poems and songs of Canadians in battle. Toronto: Doubleday, 1985. pp. xiii, 210. Rev. by Eric Thompson in CanL (111) 202–4.

10499. COOK, ALBERT. Figural choice in poetry and art. Hanover, NH; London: UP of New England for Brown UP, 1985. pp. ix, 256.

10500. COUCH, WILLIAM, JR. Black poetry – and others. Ob (5) Spring/Summer 1979, 17–25.

10501. COUZYN, JENI (ed.). The Bloodaxe book of contemporary women poets: eleven British writers. Newcastle-upon-Tyne: Bloodaxe, 1985. pp. 240. Rev. by Michael Allen in Honest Ulsterman (82) 73–6.

10502. DACEY, PHILIP; JAUSS, DAVID (eds). Strong measures: contemporary American poetry in traditional forms. Introd. by RICHARD WILBUR. New York; London: Harper & Row. pp. xix, 492.

10503. DAVIE, DONALD. Reflections on *PNR*. *See* **581**.

10504. DAVIES, DIANE. 'Knowing their place': a reflection on the state of contemporary Anglo-Irish poetry. Poetry Wales (21:2) 43–50.

10505. DAWE, GERALD. Reaching the wider audience. Linen Hall Review (3:2) [misnumbered 3:3] 12–14 (review-article).

10506. DODD, WAYNE. The art of poetry and the temper of the times. OhioR (37) 6–14.

10507. DUNNE, SEÁN. Poets of Munster: an anthology. London: Anvil, 1985. pp. 224.

10508. DYSON, A. E. (ed.). Poetry criticism and practice: developments since the symbolists: a casebook. *See* **7395**.

10509. ELDER, JOHN. Imagining the earth: poetry and vision of nature. Urbana: Illinois UP, 1985. pp. 232. Rev. by David Robinson in AL (58:3) 475–6.

10510. FEATHERSTONE, S. Attitudes to war in British poetry, 1939–1945. Unpub. doct. diss., Univ. of Manchester, 1984. [Abstr. in IT (35) 51.]

10511. FOGELMAN, BRUCE. 'Pan with us': the continuity of the eclogue in twentieth century poetry. CML (6:2) 109–25.

10512. FRASER, ROBERT. West African poetry: a critical history. Cambridge: CUP, pp. 351.

10513. FREDMAN, STEPHEN. Poet's prose: the crisis in American verse. (Bibl. 1985, 9270.) Rev. by William Sharpe in EA (38:4) 1985, 357.

10514. GARRATT, ROBERT F. Modern Irish poetry: tradition and continuity from Yeats to Heaney. Berkeley; London: California UP. pp. xii, 322.

10515. GOLDBERG, S. L. Literary judgment: making moral sense of poems. Critical Review (28) 18–46.

10516. GOULD, JEAN. Modern American women poets. New York: Dodd Mead, 1984. pp. xviii, 398. Rev. by Amy Jo Zook in OhioanaQ (29:2) 64–7; by Margaret Dickie in AL (58:1) 119–21.

10517. HAGGSTROM, JOHN CHARLES. Négritude and Afro-Portugese poetry. Unpub. doct. diss., Univ., of Minnesota, 1985. [Abstr. in DA (46) 1940A.] (Harlem renaissance poetry in English.)

10518. HAGSTROM, JACK W. C. Collective poem by 103 American poets. *See* **55**.

10519. HARVEY, GEOFFREY. The Romantic tradition in modern English poetry: rhetoric and experience. *See* **7403**.

10520. HEANEY, SEAMUS. Place and displacement: recent poetry of Northern Ireland: Pete Laver Memorial Lecture delivered at Grasmere 2nd August 1984. Grasmere: Trustees of Dove Cottage, 1984. pp. 22.

10521. HESELTINE, HARRY. Poetry, nature, counterstatement. Overland (105) 46–53.

10522. HIBBERD, DOMINIC. A publisher of First World War poetry: Galloway Kyle. NQ (33:2) 185–6.

10523. HIBBERD, DOMINIC; ONIONS, JOHN (eds). Poetry of the Great War: an anthology. Basingstoke: Macmillan. pp. viii, 250.

10524. HONTON, MARGARET (ed.). The poet's job: to go too far. Columbus, OH: Sophia, 1985. pp. 244. Rev. by Richard R. Centing in OhioanaQ (29:1) 34–5.

10525. HULSE, MICHAEL. Narratives secret and modern: a vogue in recent British poetry. Quadrant (30:7/8) 119–25.

10526. HUTCHINGS, GEOFFREY. On defining South African poetry: Geoffrey Hutchings considers the notion of 'South African' poetry. Upstream (4:4) 23–6.

10527. IVĂNESCU, MIRCEA (ed.); STOENESCU, STEFAN (introd.). Poezie americană modernă și contemporană. (Modern and contemporary American poetry.) Cluj-Napoca: Dacia. pp. 375. Rev. by Nicolae Emil in Ateneu (211) 16.

10528. JACKAMAN, ROB. Contemporary British poetry: a personal view. Untold (6) Spring, 28–37.

10529. JAŘAB, JOSEF. Modernismus a současná americká poezie. (Modernism and contemporary American poetry.) In (pp. 30–1) **4.**

10530. JEROME, JUDSON. Poet's market: 1986. See **470.**

10531. JOHNSTON, DILLON. Irish poetry after Joyce. Notre Dame, IN: Notre Dame UP; Mountrath: Dolmen Press, 1985. pp. xiii, 336. Rev. by Gerald Dawe in Linen Hall Review (3:2) [incorrectly numbered 3:3] 12–14; by Michael Hofman in TLS, 30 May, 585; by Patricia Craig in LRB (8:13) 17–18.

10532. JONES, RICHARD (ed.). Poetry and politics: an anthology of essays. New York: Morrow, 1985. pp. 320. (Cf. bibl. 1985. 2456, where pagination incorrect.) Rev. by Lorraine M. York in CanL (108) 157.

10533. KIM, SANGMOO. *New Lines* eui chulgan gwa geu baneung. (Responses to the publication of *New Lines*.) YYY (3) 1985, 83–116.

10534. KING, BRUCE. The emergence of post-independence modern Nigerian and Indian poetry. WLWE (26:2) 331–40.

10535. KING, CHARLES; SMITH, IAIN CRICHTON (eds). Twelve more modern Scottish poets. London: Hodder & Stoughton. pp. 176.

10536. KODAMA, SANEHIDE. American poetry and Japanese culture. See **7407.**

10537. LECKER, ROBERT; DAVID, JACK; QUIGLEY, ELLEN (eds). Canadian writers and their works: poetry series: vol. 5. See **9.**

10538. —— —— —— Canadian writers and their works: poetry series: vol. 9. See **10.**

10539. LENTRICCHIA, FRANK. On the ideologies of poetic modernism, 1980–1913: the example of William James. In (pp. 220–49) **47.**

10540. LINDSAY, MAURICE (ed.). Modern Scottish poetry: an anthology of the Scottish renaissance 1925–1985. (Bibl. 1976, 10199.) London: Hale. pp. 250. (Fourth ed.: first ed. 1946.)

10541. LONGLEY, EDNA.   Poetry in the wars. Newcastle upon Tyne: Bloodaxe. pp. 264.

10542. LUCAS, JOHN.   Modern English poetry: from Hardy to Hughes: a critical survey. *See* **7412.**

10543. MANLEY, FRANK; WATKINS, FLOYD C.   Some poems and some talk about poetry. Jackson: Mississippi UP, 1985. pp. xvi, 134. Rev. by Sally Dee Wade in SCR (3:2) 120–2.

10544. MARGOLIS, RICHARD J.   Melody and mystery. *See* **10317.**

10545. MATTHEWS, J. H.   Surrealism, insanity, and poetry. Syracuse, NY: Syracuse UP, 1982. pp. xii, 154. Rev. by Willard Bohn in CL (38:1) 108–10.

10546. MATTHEWS, RICHARD J. H.   Classical New Zealand poetry based on Greek and Latin models. Dunedin: Dept of Classics, Univ. of Otago, 1985. pp. 112.

10547. MEYER, KINERETH.   The mythology of modern death. Genre (19:1) 21–33.

10548. MILLER, R. BAXTER.   Window on the night: etymology of the cultural imagination. Ob (6) Winter 1980, 68–79. (Langston Hughes, Robert Hayden, Amiri Baraka, Sonia Sanchez, Colleen McElroy.)

10549. MOSINA, V. G.   Tema grazhdanskoĭ voĭny v Ispanii 1936–1939 godov v tvorchestve angliĭskikh poėtov-interbrigadovtŝev. (The theme of the Spanish Civil War 1936–1939 in the works of English poets in the International Brigade.) NDFN (1986: 4) 29–34.

10550. MUKHERJEE, ARUN P.   South Asian poetry in Canada: in search of a place. WLWE (26:1) 84–98.

10551. MULDOON, PAUL (ed.).   The Faber book of contemporary Irish poetry. London: Faber & Faber. pp. 415. Rev. by Eamon Grennan in Honest Ulsterman (82) 58–66; by James Simmons in Linen Hall Review (3:3) 7–8; by Patricia Craig in LRB (8:13) 17–18.

10552. MURATORI, FRED.   Traditional form and the living, breathing American poet. NER (9:2) 217–41.

10553. MURPHY, MARGUERITTE SCHAEFER.   Genre as subversion: the prose poem in England and America. Unpub. doct. diss., Harvard Univ., 1985. [Abstr. in DA (46) 1932A.]

10554. MURRAY, LES A. (ed.).   The new Oxford book of Australian verse. *See* **7416.**

10555. MUSKE, CAROL.   Recent poetry: the habit of time (or fleshing out the *zeitgeist*). WHR (40:4) 353–65.

10556. NIKITINA, S. E.   Frantsuzskiĭ simvolizm i angliĭskiĭ imazhizm. (French symbolism and English imagism.) VMU (1986:4) 60–2.

10557. NORTH, MICHAEL.   The final sculpture: public monuments and modern poets. Ithaca, NY: Cornell UP, 1985. pp. 262. Rev. by David H. Hesla in AL (58:3) 470–2; by Lachlan Mackinnon in TLS, 28 Mar., 341; by Andrew Swarbrick in CritQ (28:3) 112–14.

10558. OAKES, KAREN KILCUP.   Reading the feminine: gender gestures in poetic voice. *See* **7417.**

10559. O'CONNOR, MARK.   The poetry of the North: finding the words. *See* **1556.**

10560. OLEMBO, WAVENEY (comp.).   The music of poetry: poems from Africa, the Caribbean and elsewhere. London: Arnold. pp. 90.

10561. O'LOUGHLIN, MICHAEL.   After Kavanagh: Patrick Kavanagh and the discourse of contemporary Irish poetry. Dublin: Raven Arts Press, 1985.

10562. OSMOND, JOHN (ed.).   The future of the word. Swansea: Welsh Union of Writers, 1985. pp. 120. (Welsh Union of Writers register, 1985.)

10563. OSTRIKER, ALICIA.   American poetry, now shaped by women. NYTB, 9 Mar., 1.

10564. OSTRIKER, ALICIA SUSKIN.   Stealing the language: the emergence of women's poetry in America. Boston, MA: Beacon Press. pp. 315. Rev. by Liz Rosenberg in NYTB, 20 July, 21.

10565. PACK, ROBERT; LEA, SIDNEY; PARINI, JAY (eds).   The *Bread Loaf* anthology of contemporary American poetry. Hanover, NH; London: New England UP, 1985. pp. xvii, 347.

10566. PARANJAPE, MAKARAND R.   Mysticism in Indian English poetry. Unpub. doct. diss., Univ. of Illinois at Urbana-Champaign, 1985. [Abstr. in DA (46) 3355A.]

10567. PARRIS, PEGGY.   Lank ghost, odd uncle and old hero: Thoreau in contemporary poetry. *See* **9371.**

10568. PASKIN, SYLVIA; RAMSAY, JAY; SILVER, JEREMY (eds).   Angels of fire: an anthology of radical poetry in the '80s. London: Chatto & Windus. pp. xxviii, 170.

10569. PEARN, JULIE.   Poetry in the Caribbean. London: Hodder & Stoughton, 1985. pp. 64.

10570. PERLOFF, MARJORIE.   The dance of the intellect: studies in the poetry of the Pound tradition. Cambridge: CUP, 1985. pp. xii, 243. (Cambridge studies in American literature and culture.)

10571. —— The poetics of indeterminacy: Rimbaud to Cage. (Bibl. 1985, 9323.) Rev. by Shirley Neuman in CanRCL (12:3) 1985, 553–6.

10572. RAIZIS, M. BYRON.   From Caucasus to Pittsburgh: the Prometheus theme in British and American poetry. *See* **7420.**

10573. REILLY, CATHERINE W.   English poetry of the Second World War: a bibliography. London: Mansell. pp. xxviii, 394. Rev. by John Byrne in BC (35:4) 524–6.

10574. RICHMAN, ROBERT.   Poetry and the return of seriousness. NCrit (3:Summer) 1985, 39–48.

10575. RICKETTS, HARRY (ed.).   Talking about ourselves: twelve New Zealand poets in conversation with Harry Ricketts. Wellington: Mallinson Rendel. pp. 176. Rev. by Iain Sharp in NZList, 7 June, 49–50; by Kevin Ireland in Islands (3:1) 78–82.

10576. ROSENTHAL, M. L.; GALL, SALLY M.   The modern poetic sequence: the genius of modern poetry. (Bibl. 1984, 9776.) Rev. by Paul Mariani in AL (58:3) 465–8.

10577. ROSS, ANDREW.   The failure of Modernism: symptoms of American poetry. New York; Guildford: Columbia UP, pp. xviii, 248.

10578. RUMENS, CAROL (ed.).   Making for the open: the Chatto book of post-feminist poetry 1964–1984. London: Chatto & Windus, 1985. pp. xviii, 151.

10579. SAUNDERS, R. G.   The sociological significance of British and Soviet poetry, 1945–1985. Unpub. doct. diss., City Univ., 1985. [Abstr. in IT (35) 1082.]

10580. SCOBIE, STEPHEN.   Signs of the times: concrete poetry in retrospect. Cencrastus (22) 24–6.

10581. SELLICK, ROBERT (series ed.); SHARRAD, PAUL (ed.).   Poetry of the Pacific region: proceedings of CRNLE/SPACLALS Conference. Adelaide: Centre for Research in New Literatures in English, 1984. pp. vii, 143. (CRNLE essays and monographs, 2.)

10582. SHERRY, VINCENT B., JR (ed.).   Poets of Great Britain and Ireland 1945–1960. Detroit, MI: Gale Research, 1984. pp. xvi, 393. (Dictionary of literary biography, 27.)

10583. —— Poets of Great Britain and Ireland since 1960. Detroit, MI: Gale Research, 1985. pp. xx, 702. (Dictionary of literary biography, 40.)

10584. SHIKINA, SEIJI.   The adaptation of the haiku form in the poetry of the imagists. Unpub. doct. diss., Univ. of Southwestern Louisiana. [Abstr. in DA (47) 2162A.]

10585. SHIRES, LINDA M.   British poetry of the Second World War. (Bibl. 1985, 9337.) Rev. by Rowland Smith in DalR (65:4) 1985/86, 589–93.

10586. SMITH, ROWLAND.   War and after: poetry in the forties. DalR (65:4) 1985/86, 585–93 (review-article).

10587. SMITH, VIVIAN.   Experiment and renewal: a missing link in Australian poetry. Southerly (46:1) 3–18.

10588. STANYON, CARL.   British poetry: how it strikes a contemporary. Meridian (5:1) 23–35 (review-article).

10589. STANZEL, FRANZ K.   Texts recycled: 'found' poems found in Canada. In (pp. 91–106) **22.**

10590. STEAD, C. K.   Pound, Yeats, Eliot and the Modernist movement. London: Macmillan; New Brunswick, NJ: Rutgers UP. pp. viii, 393. Rev. by Alan Robinson in THES (708) 18; by Frank Kermode in LRB (8:9) 3, 5–6; by Sam S. Baskett in CR (30:4) 539–40; by Paul Smith in DalR (65:4) 1985/86, 579–84; by Ian Wedde in NZList, 18 Oct., 66–7; by K. K. Ruthven in Landfall (40:4) 509–13.

10591. STITT, PETER.   The world's hieroglyphic beauty: five American poets. Athens: Georgia UP, 1985. pp. xi, 291. (Louis Simpson, William Stafford, Robert Penn Warren, Richard Wilbur, James Wright.) Rev. by Alan Feldman in AL (58:4) 668–9.

10592. SWARBRICK, ANDREW.   Modern perplexity. CritQ (28:3) 109–14 (review-article).

10593. TAYLOR, ANDREW.   War poetry: myth as de-formation and re-formation. ALS (12:2) 1985, 182–93.

10594. TAYLOR, CAROLE ANNE.   A poetics of seeing: the implications of visual form in modern poetry. New York; London: Garland, 1985. pp. 400. (Garland pubs in comparative literature.)

10595. THWAITE, ANTHONY.   Poetry today: a critical guide to British poetry, 1960–84. (Bibl. 1985, 9351.) Rev. by Andrew Swarbrick in CritQ (28:3) 112.

10596. TIGGES, WIM.   The limerick: the sonnet of Nonsense? DQR (16:3) 220–36.

10597. TOLLEY, A. T.   The poetry of the forties in Britain. (Pub. in UK as *The Poetry of the Forties*.) Ottawa: Carleton UP; Manchester: Manchester UP, 1985. pp. 394. Rev. by Rowland Smith in DalR (65:4) 1985/86, 588–9; by William Scammel in TLS, 2 May, 476.

10598. VINSON, JAMES; KIRKPATRICK, D. L. (eds).   Contemporary poets. Introd. to the first ed. by C. Day Lewis. Introd. to the third ed. by MARJORIE PERLOFF. (Bibl. 1976, 10968.) London: St James, 1985. pp. xviii, 1071. (Fourth ed.: first ed. 1970.) Rev. by Jonathan Barker in TLS, 15 Aug., 900.)

10599. VON HALLBERG, ROBERT.   American poet–critics since 1945. *In* (pp. 280–99) **47.**

10600. —— American poetry and culture 1945–1980. (Bibl. 1985, 9355.) Rev. by Marjorie Perloff in ELN (23:4) 61–5; by Alan Golding in AL (58:3) 468–70; by Sherman Paul in JEGP (85:4) 602–5; by Vernon Shetley in YR (75:3) 429–32; by Lachlan Mackinnon in TLS, 9 May, 506.

10601. Entry cancelled.

10602. WASSERMAN, ROSANNE.   Helen of Troy: her myth in modern poetry. Unpub. doct. diss., City Univ. of New York. [Abstr. in DA (47) 1340A.]

10603. WATERSTON, ELIZABETH.   Regions and eras in Ontario poetry. *See* **7434.**

10604. WATSON, RODERICK.   Scottish poetry 1979–1980. SSL (17) 1982, 218–41.

10605. WATSON, STEPHEN.   Poetry and politicization. Contrast (16:1) 15–28.

10606. WEATHERHEAD, A. KINGSLEY.   The British dissonance: essays on ten contemporary poets. (Bibl. 1984, 9797.) Rev. by Roger Bowen in CL (38:1) 110–12.

10607. WEGNER, JURGEN.   *Poetry Australia*: 21 years: 100 issues. *See* **443.**

10608. WEISS, THEODORE.   The man from Porlock: engagements 1944–1981. (Bibl. 1983, 10184.) Rev. by Peter Makin in MLR (81:4) 992–3.

10609. WESLING, DONALD.   The new poetries: poetic form since Coleridge and Wordsworth. *See* **7436.**

10610. WHEATCROFT, JOHN.   About the disappearance of the poem. CEACrit (48:3) 2–8.

10611. WHEELER, LESLIE W. (ed.).   Ten Northeast poets: an anthology. (Bibl. 1985, 9361.) Rev. by Ronald J. B. Garden in AUR (51) 500–2.

10612. WILLIAMS, JEFFREY C.   The myth of the lost generation: the British war poets and the modern critics. CLIO (12:1) 1982, 45–56.

10613. WILLIAMSON, ALAN. Introspection and contemporary poetry. (Bibl. 1985, 9362.) Rev. by Alan Golding in MP (84:2) 235–8.

10614. WILLIAMSON, J. W. Appalachian poetry: the politics of coming home. SE (9:2) 1981, 69–74.

10615. WOODS, G. Male homo-erotic themes in poetry in English, 1914–1980. Unpub. doct. diss., Univ. of East Anglia, 1983.

10616. WYKEHAM, J. M. The poetry of British soldiers on the Western Front: the limitations of 'the sentimental attitude'. Unpub. doct. diss., Univ. of London, Birkbeck Coll., 1985. [Abstr. in IT (35) 1089.]

10617. YORK, R. A. The poem as utterance. *See* **7438.**

10618. ZWICKY, FAY. The lyre in the pawnshop: essays on literature and survival 1974–1984. Perth: Univ. of Western Australia Press. pp. 297.

Prose

10619. BARBOUR, JAMES; DOWLING, WILLIAM C. The death of the game in contemporary baseball literature. MidQ (27:3) 341–60.

10620. DONALDSON, WILLIAM; YOUNG, DOUGLAS (eds). Grampian hairst: an anthology of Northwest prose. Foreword by CUTHBERT GRAHAM; essay on Northeast Scots by DAVID MURISON. *See* **893.**

10621. HARDWICK, ELIZABETH (ed.). The best American essays: 1986. New York: Ticknor & Fields. pp. 320. Rev. by Bruce Allen in Smithsonian (17:9) 157–8.

10622. LORIMER, WILLIAM LAUGHTON (trans.). The New Testament in Scots. *See* **910.**

10623. MASNEROVÁ, EVA. Some aspects of Southern prose between the First and Second World Wars. *In* (pp. 92–8) GÜNTHER KLOTZ and HEINZ WÜSTENHAGEN (eds), Potsdamer Forschungen, A, 72. Potsdam: Pädagogische Hochschule Karl Liebknecht. pp. 228.

10624. MURPHY, MARGUERITTE SCHAEFER. Genre as subversion: the prose poem in England and America. *See* **10553.**

10625. THUBRON, COLIN. Travel writing today: its rise and its dilemma. EDH (44) 167–81.

10626. TOMPKINS, JANE. 'Indians': textualism, morality, and the problem of history. CI (13:1) 101–19.

Biography and Autobiography

10627. ALLISTER, MARK CHRISTOPHER. Encounters with un-imagined existence: documentary and autobiography in recent American prose. Unpub. doct. diss., Univ. of Washington, 1985. [Abstr. in DA (46) 3717A.]

10628. BRAXTON, JOANNE MARGARET. Autobiography by black American women: a tradition within a tradition. Unpub. doct. diss., Yale Univ., 1984. [Abstr. in DA (47) 1785A.]

10629. DODD, PHILIP (ed.). Modern selves: essays on modern British and American autobiography. London: Cass. pp. 192.

10630. DUYFHUIZEN, BERNARD.   Diary narratives in fact and fiction. *See* **10206.**

10631. FINNEY, BRIAN.   The inner I: British literary autobiography of the twentieth century. London: Faber & Faber, 1985. pp. 386. (Bibl. 1985, 9383.) Rev. by P. N. Furbank in LRB (8:10) 11–12; by Alf Louvre in Prose Studies (9:3) 110–12.

10632. FUJITA, GAYLE KIMI.   The 'ceremonial self' in Japanese American literature. *See* **10219.**

10633. HOBERMAN, RUTH SARAH.   Biography in England between the wars: modernist literary strategies. Unpub. doct. diss., Columbia Univ., 1984. [Abstr. in DA (47) 911A.]

10634. KIRK-GREENE, ANTHONY.   West African historiography and the underdevelopment of biography. JCL (21:1) 39–52.

10635. NADEL, IRA B.   Canadian biography and literary form. ECanW (33) 144–60.

10636. SHEEHY, DONALD G.   The poet as neurotic: the official biography of Robert Frost. AL (58:3) 392–410.

10637. STONE, ALBERT E.   Two recreate one: the act of collaboration in recent black autobiography. YREAL (1) 1982, 226–66.

10638. TAUSKY, THOMAS E.   'A passion to live in this splendid past': Canadian and Australian autobiographies of childhood. Ariel (17:3) 39–62.

Related Studies

10639. ASTRO, ALAN MICHAEL.   Writing in tongues: translation in Beckett and other modern writers. Unpub. doct. diss., Yale Univ., 1985. [Abstr. in DA (46) 3344A.]

10640. ATLAN, MADY.   Manhattan: le nouveau Yiddishland d'Isaac Bashevis Singer. *In* (pp. 143–56) **5.**

10641. BAIZER, MARY MARTHA.   The Bloomsbury Chekhov. Unpub. doct. diss., Washington Univ., 1985. [Abstr. in DA (46) 2286A.]

10642. BAUMANN, GERD (ed.).   The written word: literacy in transition: Wolfson College Lectures 1985. Oxford: Clarendon Press. pp. x, 197.

10643. BENSON, DOUGLAS K.   Inner and outer realities of Chicano life: the New Mexican perspectives of Leroy V. Quintana. PCL (12) 20–8.

10644. BLOOM, ALEXANDER.   Prodigal sons: the New York Intellectuals and their world. New York: OUP. pp. xii 461. Rev. by Frank Kermode in NYTB, 27 Apr., 12.

10645. BROOKEMAN, CHRISTOPHER.   American culture and society since the 1930s. New York: Schocken, 1984. pp. xv, 241. Rev. by George H. Roeder, Jr, in JAH (73:3) 803–4.

10646. BRÜGGEMEIER, F.-J.   Sounds of silents: history, narrative and life-recollections. Poetics (15:1/2) 5–24.

10647. BURCHILL, JULIE.   Damaged gods: cults and heroes reappraised. London: Century. pp. 144.

10648. CASTEX, PEGGY.   Is there a reader in the house? The dilemma of Cajun literature. *In* (pp. 47–76) **5.**

10649. CERPANA. Littératures et anthropologie, Afrique anglophone. Nouvelles du Sud N° 4. Ivry: Silex. pp. 143. (Colloque C.E.R.P.A.N.A. 1985).

10650. COLLINS, RICHARD, *et al.* (eds). Media, culture and society: a critical reader. London: Sage. pp. 346.

10651. COLLS, ROBERT; DODD, PHILIP (eds). Englishness: politics and culture 1880–1920. *See* **7462.**

10652. CONN, PETER. The divided mind: ideology and imagination in America, 1898–1917. (Bibl. 1984, 9829.) Rev. by Volker Bischoff in Archiv (223:2) 423–6.

10653. COOPER, EMMANUEL. The sexual perspective: homosexuality and art in the last 100 years in the West. *See* **7463.**

10654. COOPER-CLARK, DIANA. Interviews with contemporary novelists. *See* **10186.**

10655. CORE, PHILIP. The original eye: arbiters of twentieth-century taste. London: Quartet, 1984. pp. 190.

10656. COWLING, MAURICE. Religion and public doctrine in modern England: vol. 2, Assaults. *See* **7465.**

10657. DEARBORN, MARY V. Pocahontas revisited: gender and ethnicity in American culture from the Civil War to the present. *See* **7467.**

10658. DE GRAZIA, EMILIO. The great plain: Rolvaag's New World sea. *In* (pp. 244–55) **28.**

10659. DENVIR, BERNARD. The late Victorians: art, design and society, 1852–1910. *See* **7469.**

10660. DOSE, GERD. 'The soul of Germany'. Bemerkungen zum angloamerikanischen Deutschlandbild vor und zu Beginn des Ersten Weltkrieges. Anglistik & Englischunterricht (29/30) 21–55.

10661. FIELDING, XAN (ed.). Best of friends: the Brenan–Partridge letters. London: Chatto & Windus. pp. 252.

10662. FISHWICK, MARSHALL W. Seven pillars of popular culture. Westport, CT; London: Greenwood Press, 1985. pp. 236. (Contributions to the study of popular culture, 10.)

10663. FOSTER, JOHN WILSON. Richard Kearney – a reply. Honest Ulsterman (82) 43–6. (*Refers to* **10672.**)

10664. FRANK, ARMIN PAUL, *et al.* Toward a cultural history of literary translation: an exploration of issues and problems in researching the translational exchange between the USA and Germany. YREAL (4) 1986, 317–80.

10665. GILBERT, R. A. A. E. Waite: a bibliography. Wellingborough: Aquarian Press, 1983. pp. 192. Rev. by Hugh Ormsby-Lennon in YES (16) 354–6.

10666. HEWISON, ROBERT. Too much: art and society in the sixties, 1960–75. London: Methuen. pp. xviii, 350. Rev. by David Caute in Listener, 11 Sept., 24–5.

10667. HOMOLA, PRISCILLA HEPLER. Following a leg of mutton: the pastoral in Rölvaag's *Giants in the Earth.* Unpub. doct. diss., Univ. of North Dakota, 1985. [Abstr. in DA (46) 2692A.]

10668. HOOLEY, DANIEL MATTHEWS. 'The classics in paraphrase': Ezra Pound and modern translators of classical poetry. Unpub. doct. diss., Univ. of Minnesota, 1985. [Abstr. in DA (46) 1932A.]

10669. HSIAO, RUTH YU. The stages of development in American ethnic literature: Jewish and Chinese American literatures. Unpub. doct. diss., Tufts Univ. [Abstr. in DA (47) 1324A.]

10670. HUMPHREY, RICHARD. The historical novel as philosophy of history: three German contributions: Alexis, Fontane, Döblin. *See* **7482.**

10671. KADAR, MARLENE. Partisan culture in the thirties: *Partisan Review*, the Surrealists and Leon Trotsky. *See* **628.**

10672. KEARNEY, RICHARD. The transitional crisis in Irish culture. Honest Ulsterman (82) 30–42.

10673. KRUGER, ALET. The translation of non-standard language in literary works. English Usage (17:2) 23–32.

10674. LANGER, LAWRENCE L. Versions of survival: the Holocaust and the human spirit. (Bibl. 1985, 9170.) Rev. by Ilan Avisar in CanRCL (13:2) 313–19.

10675. LONG, ELIZABETH. Women, reading, and cultural authority: some implications of the audience perspective in cultural studies. AmQ (38:4) 591–612.

10676. MacCABE, COLIN; STEWART, OLIVIA (eds). The BBC and public service broadcasting. Manchester: Manchester UP. pp. viii, 116. (Images of culture.)

10677. MacKENZIE, JEANNE. The children of the Souls: a tragedy of the First World War. London: Chatto & Windus. pp. 276.

10678. MACKENZIE, JOHN M. (ed). Imperialism and popular culture. *See* **7489.**

10679. MacKENZIE, NORMAN; MacKENZIE, JEANNE (eds). The diary of Beatrice Webb: vol. 4, 1924–1943. Cambridge, MA: Harvard UP. pp. 519. Rev. by Anthony Howard in NYTB, 6 Apr., 42.

10680. McMURTRY, JO. English language, English literature: the creation of an academic discipline. *See* **826.**

10681. MADDEN, DAVID. 'The cruel radiance of what is'. SoQ (22:2) 1984, 5–43. (Photography.)

10682. MALTZ, MINNA HERMAN. Point of view in Isaac Bashevis Singer's *The Penitent*. ESA (29:2) 131–9.

10683. MILBAUER, ASHER Z. Transcending exile: Conrad, Nabokov, I. B. Singer. Miami: Florida International UP, 1985. pp. xv, 141. Rev. by Jon Kertzer in Ariel (17:3) 120–2.

10684. MILLER, JOHN E. Epistemology in flux: embattled truth in an information age. SDR (24:3) 7–20.

10685. MOORE, CHARLES; HAWTREE, CHRISTOPHER (eds). 1936 as recorded by *The Spectator*. *See* **652.**

10686. MÜNZ, RAINER; PELZ, MONIKA. Narration in social research. Poetics (15:1/2) 25–41.

10687. NEWTON, JUDITH; ROSENFELT, DEBORAH (eds). Feminist criticism and social change: sex, class and race in literature and culture. New York; London: Methuen, 1985. pp. 192.

10688. NICHOLS, DAVID (ed.). Ernie's war: the best of Ernie Pyle's World War II dispatches. New York: Random House. pp. 432. Rev. by James D. Atwater in NYTB, 5 Oct., 16.

10689. POSSIN, HANS-JOACHIM. Begegnungen mit Deutschland 1928–1934. Deutschlandbilder in englischen Reiseberichten. Anglistik & Englischunterricht (29/30) 85–112.

10690. PRUVOT, MONIQUE. Apocalypse et temps mythique chez les peintres américains de l'école de New York. In (pp. 335–55) **2.**

10691. RACEVSKIS, KARLIS. Michel Foucault and the subversion of intellect. Ithaca, NY: Cornell UP, 1983. pp. 172. Rev. by Randall McGowen in CL (38:2) 181–3.

10692. ROOM, ADRIAN. Dictionary of Britain. Oxford: OUP. pp. viii, 423. (Second ed.: first ed. 1986.)

10693. RUSSELL, CHARLES. Poets, prophets and revolutionaries: the literary avant-garde from Rimbaud through postmodernism. See **7498.**

10694. SÁNCHEZ, MARTA ESTER. Contemporary Chicana poetry: a critical approach to an emerging literature. Berkeley: California UP, 1985. pp. xi, 377. Rev. by Norman S. Grabo in AL (58:3) 473–5.

10695. SANTRAUD, JEANNE-MARIE (ed.). Les aspects littéraires du biculturalisme aux États-Unis. See **5.**

10696. —— SAPORTA, MARC. Introduction à une étude du biculturalisme. In (pp. 3–10) **5.**

10697. SAPORTA, MARC. L'émigré de nulle part. In (pp. 119–28) **5.**

10698. SCOBIE, STEPHEN. Between the arts: Dada and after. CanRCL (12:3) 1985, 442–50 (review-article).

10699. SHAW, DONALD. 'American-ness' in Spanish American literature. See **7499.**

10700. SHERIDAN, JUDITH RINDE. Isaac Bashevis Singer: sex as cosmic metaphor. MidQ (23:3) 1982, 365–79.

10701. SOLLORS, WERNER. A critique of pure pluralism. In (pp. 250–79) **47.**

10702. TAFOLLA, CARMEN. Chicano writing: beyond beginning. SE (9:2) 1981, 49–52.

10703. VELASQUEZ TREVINO, GLORIA LOUISE. Cultural ambivalence in early Chicana prose fiction. Unpub. doct. diss., Stanford Univ., 1985. [Abstr. in DA (46) 2310A.]

10704. WEST, THOMAS. Culture, cultures and bi-culturalism. In (pp. 159–69) **5.**

10705. WIEDEMANN, PETER M. Don't tell any stories: theories and discoveries concerning story-telling in the therapeutic setting. Poetics (15:1/2) 43–55.

10706. WILKINSON, RUPERT. American tough: the tough-guy tradition and American character. Westport, CT; London: Greenwood Press, 1984; New York; London: Harper & Row. pp. xiv, 221, (plates) 38. (Perennial library.)

10707. YARBRO-BEJARANO, YVONNE. The female subject in Chicano theatre: sexuality, 'race' and class. TJ (38:4) 389–407.

10708.   ZAMORA, BERNICE B. ORTIZ.   Mythopoeia of Chicano poetry: an introduction to cultural archetypes. Unpub. doct. diss., Stanford Univ. [Abstr. in DA (47) 533A.]

Literary Theory

This section is intended to contain studies **about** the literary theory, literary historiography, literary criticism, etc., produced *in* the twentieth century. For modern works **of** literary history and criticism dealing generally with this period, see under 'Twentieth Century: General Literary Studies'.

10709.   ABRAMS, M. H.; ACKERMAN, JAMES.   Theories of criticism. Washington, DC: Library of Congress, 1984. pp. 53. Rev. by Stuart Sim in CritQ (28:4) 119–20.

10710.   ANCHOR, ROBERT.   Bakhtin's truths of laughter. CLIO (14:3) 1985, 237–57.

10711.   ANDERSON, WARREN.   'Influentia' and 'influence': the currents of Maeander. *In* (pp. 35–42) **11.**

10712.   ANDREW, DUDLEY.   Hermeneutics and cinema: the issue of history. *See* **9899.**

10713.   ARAC, JONATHAN; GODZICH, WLAD; MARTIN, WALLACE (eds). The Yale critics: deconstruction in America. (Bibl. 1984, 9457.) Rev. by Rob Wolfs in ForumL (27:1) 73–6; by Stuart Sim in CritQ (28:4) 118–20.

10714.   ARGYROS, ALEX.   The residual difference: Wallace Stevens and American deconstruction. NOR (13:1) 20–31.

10715.   BAACKE, D.   Narration and narrative analysis in education and educational sciences. Poetics (15:1/2) 57–72.

10716.   BAHTI, TIMOTHY.   Ambiguity and indeterminacy: the juncture. *See* **8797.**

10717.   BAILEY, R. F.   Some preoccupations of Australian literary criticism, 1945–83. Unpub. doct. diss., Univ. of London, External, 1985. [Abstr. in IT (35) 1493.]

10718.   BAKER, HOUSTON A., JR.   Caliban's triple play. CI (13:1) 182–96.

10719.   BAL, MIEKE.   Narratology: introduction to the theory of narrative. Trans. by CHRISTINE VAN BOHEEMEN of *De theorie van Vertellen en Verhalen: Inleiding in de Narratologie.* Toronto; London: Toronto UP, 1985. pp. xi, 164.

10720.   —— Tell-tale theories. PT (7:3) 555–64 (review-article).

10721.   BARKER, FRANCIS, *et al.* (eds).   Literature, politics and theory: papers from the Essex Conference 1976–84. *See* **29.**

10722.   BARNOUW, JEFFREY.   Peirce and Derrida: 'natural signs' empiricism versus 'originary trace' deconstruction. PT (7:1) 73–94.

10723.   BARTHES, ROLAND.   The responsibility of forms: critical essays on music, art and representation. Trans. by RICHARD HOWARD. Oxford: Blackwell; New York: Hill & Wang, 1985. pp. viii, 312. Rev. by Harold Brodkey in NYTB, 20 Apr., 13.

10724. —— The rustle of language. Trans. by RICHARD HOWARD of *Le Bruissement de la langue*. Oxford: Blackwell; New York: Hill & Wang. pp. ix, 373. Rev. by Harold Brodkey in NYTB, 20 Apr., 13.

10725. BATSLEER, JANET, *et al*. Rewriting English: cultural politics of gender and class. London: Methuen. pp. vii, 188. Rev. by Valerie Shaw in THES (702) 19; by Chris Baldick in TLS, 26 May, 539; by Steven Scobie in MalaR (75) 128–30.

10726. BEALE, DONALD A. 'Striving with systems': Romanticism and the current critical scene. *See* **6978.**

10727. BEATTY, AUDREY. List of Kristian Smidt's publications. *In* (pp. 351–73) **18.**

10728. BEERS, TERRY LYNN. Interpretive schemata and literary response. Unpub. doct. diss., Univ. of Southern California. [Abstr. in DA (47) 2155A.]

10729. BERCOVITCH, SACVAN. America as canon and context: literary history in a time of dissensus. AL (58:1) 99–107.

10730. —— The problem of ideology in American literary history. *See* **6981.**

10731. BERNSTEIN, J. M. The philosophy of the novel: Lukács, Marxism and the dialectics of form. Minneapolis: Minnesota UP, 1984. (Cf. bibl. 1984, 9467.) Rev. by Eva L. Corredor in PhilL (10:2) 338–40.

10732. BIALOSTOSKY, DON. The English professor in the age of theory. Novel (19:2) 164–70 (review-article).

10733. BIALOSTOSKY, DON H. Dialogics as an art of discourse in literary criticism. PMLA (101:5) 788–97.

10734. BLOOM, CLIVE. The 'occult' experience and the New Criticism: daemonism, sexuality and the hidden in literature. Brighton: Harvester Press. pp. x, 133.

10735. BOGDAN, DEANNE. Moncton, mentors, and memories: an interview with Northrop Frye. StudCanL (11:2) 246–69.

10736. —— Virtual and actual forms of literary response. JAE (20:2) 51–7.

10737. BROWN, LAURA. Contemporary theory and the defense of eighteenth-century studies: Brian McCrea, G. S. Rousseau, and Melvyn New. *See* **5940.**

10738. BRUNS, GERALD L. Inventions: writing, textuality, and understanding in literary history. (Bibl. 1985, 9450.) Rev. by Kathleen Henderson Staudt in MLS (16:3) 321–4.

10739. —— Writing literary criticism. IowaR (12:4) 1981, 23–43.

10740. BUCI-GLUCKSMANN, CHRISTINE. Catastrophic utopia: the feminine as allegory of the modern. Representations (14) 220–9.

10741. BÜRGER, PETER. Theory of the avant-garde. Trans. by MICHAEL SHAW. Ed. by JOCHEN SCHULTE-SASSE. Minneapolis: Minnesota UP; Manchester: Manchester UP, 1984. pp. lvi, 135. (Theory and history of literature, 4.) Rev. by Marjorie Perloff in MLR (81:2) 429.

10742. BURGESS, ANTHONY. The academic critic and the living writer. TLS, 14 Nov., 1275.

10743. BUTLER, CHRISTOPHER. Interpretation, deconstruction, and ideology: an introduction to some current issues in literary theory. New York: OUP, 1984. (Bibl. 1985, 9454.) Rev. by Rory Ryan in UES (24:1) 67–8; by Raman Selden in MLR (81:4) 960–1; by Michael Toolan in PT (7:1) 167–9; by Michael McKie in EC (36:3) 275–8.

10744. BUTTIGIEG, JOSEPH A. The dissemination of deconstruction. ECent (27:2) 182–8 (review-article).

10745. BUZZARD, SHARON KAY. Reader response criticism and the reflexive narrative: the reader/viewer role in creating a narrative. Unpub. doct. diss., Univ. of Missouri–Columbia, 1985. [Abstr. in DA (46) 3348A.]

10746. CAIN, WILLIAM E. The crisis in criticism: theory, literature and reform in English studies. (Bibl. 1985, 9456.) Rev. by Don Bialostosky in Novel (19:2) 169–70; by Wallace Martin in CL (38:4) 360–2; by Edward Proffitt in JAE (20:2) 116–19.

10747. —— (gen. ed.). Roland Barthes: a bibliographical reader's guide. Ed. by SANFORD FREEDMAN and CAROLE ANNE TAYLOR. New York: Garland, 1983. pp. xxxvi, 409. (Garland bibliographies of modern critics and critical schools, 6.) (Garland reference library of the humanities, 322.) Rev. by Jonathan Culler in CanRCL (12:3) 1985, 492–3.

10748. CAWS, MARY ANN. Literal or liberal: translating perception. CI (13:1) 49–63.

10749. CHATMAN, SEYMOUR. Characters and narrators: filter, center, slant, and interest-focus. PT (7:2) 189–204.

10750. CLARK, KATERINA; HOLQUIST, MICHAEL. Mikhail Bakhtin. (Bibl. 1985, 9466.) Rev. by Lionel Gossman in CL (38:4) 337–49; by Michael Sprinker in PT (7:1) 117–28.

10751. COHEN, MURRAY. Eighteenth-century English literature and modern critical methodologies. *See* **6174.**

10752. COOK, DAVID. Northrop Frye: a vision of the New World. Montreal: New World Perspectives, 1985. pp. 122. Rev. by George Woodcock in CanL (110) 153–6.

10753. CREADON, MARY ANN. Wittgenstein's door to historical criticism. Unpub. doct. diss., Northwestern Univ. [Abstr. in DA (47) 891A.]

10754. CREAGH, JOHN WALTHALL, III. Literature as phenomenon: attribution theory and the act of performance. Unpub. doct. diss., Louisiana State Univ. and Agricultural and Mechanical College, 1985. [Abstr. in DA (47) 709A.]

10755. CULLER, JONATHAN. On deconstruction: theory and criticism after structuralism. (Bibl. 1985, 9471.) Rev. by Timothy J. Reiss in CanRCL (12:3) 1985, 422–32.

10756. CUSIN, MICHEL. D'un usage possible du schéma de Jakobson pour questionner les textes de fiction. *In* (pp. 115–20) **1.**

10757. DAMROSCH, LEOPOLD, JR. Samuel Johnson and reader-response criticism. *See* **6565.**

10758. DANE, JOSEPH A. The defense of the incompetent reader. CL (38:1) 53–72.

10759. Das Gupta, Kalyan. Principles of literary evaluation in English Marxist criticism: Christopher Caudwell, Raymond Williams and Terry Eagleton. Unpub. doct. diss., Univ. of British Columbia, 1985. [Abstr. in DA (47) 1332A.]

10760. Davenport, Edward. Scientific method as literary criticism. ERGS (42:4) 1985, 331–50.

10761. Davenport, Guy. Claiming kin: artist, critic and scholar as family. Shen (36:1) 1985/86, 35–86.

10762. Davies, Alistair. An annotated critical bibliography of Modernism. Totowa, NJ: Barnes & Noble, 1982. (Cf. bibl. 1984, 167.) Rev. by Marjorie Perloff in MLR (81:4) 993–4.

10763. Davies, Tony. Unfinished business: realism and working-class fiction. *In* (pp. 124–36) **6.**

10764. Davis, Robert Con (ed.). Contemporary literary criticism: modernism through poststructuralism. New York; London: Longman. pp. xiii, 571. (Longman English and humanities.)

10765. —— Schleifer, Ronald (eds). Rhetoric and form: deconstruction at Yale. Norman: Oklahoma UP; London: Eurospan, 1985. pp. xii, 255. Rev. by Jack Stillinger in JEGP (85:4) 550–7.

10766. Dean, Carolyn. Law and sacrifice: Bataille, Lacan, and the critique of the subject. Representations (13) 42–62.

10767. deBolla, Peter. Marxism, ideology, and false scholarship: a reply to G. S. Rousseau. *See* **5952.**

10768. de Man, Paul. The resistance to theory. Introd. by Wlad Godzich. Manchester: Manchester UP. pp. xviii, 137. (Theory and history of literature, 33.)

10769. Dollimore, Jonathan. The dominant and the deviant: a violent dialectic. CritQ (28:1/2) 179–92.

10770. Donoghue, Denis. The promiscuous cool of postmodernism. NYTB, 22 June, 3.

10771. Dowling, William C. Jameson, Althusser, Marx: an introduction to *The Political Unconscious*. (Bibl. 1985, 9483.). Rev. by Patrick Parrinder in MLR (81:1) 157–8.

10772. duBois, Page. Antigone and the feminist critic. Genre (19:4) 371–83.

10773. Durant, Alan. Pound, Modernism and literary criticism: a reply to Donald Davie. CritQ (28:1/2) 154–66. (*Refers to* bibl. 1983, 12996.)

10774. Eagleton, Mary (ed.). Feminist literary theory: a reader. Oxford: Blackwell. pp. 226.

10775. Eagleton, Terry. Walter Benjamin, or, Toward a revolutionary criticism. (Bibl. 1983, 9913.) Rev. by Stanley Corngold and Michael Jennings in MLS (16:3) 367–73.

10776. Erlich, Bruce. Amphibolies: on the critical self-contradictions of 'pluralism'. CI (12:3) 521–49.

10777. Everman, Welch D. Long talking: the infinite text. NOR (13:2) 22–30.

10778. EWINGTON, JULIE. Past the post: postmodernism and post-feminism. Antic (1) June, 5–21.

10779. FALCK, COLIN. Saussurian theory and the abolition of reality. Monist (69:1) 133–45.

10780. FINDLAY, L. M. Paul de Man, Thomas Carlyle, and *The Rhetoric of Temporality. See* **7812.**

10781. FISCHER, MICHAEL. Does deconstruction make any difference? Poststructuralism and the defenses of poetry in modern criticism. (Bibl. 1985, 9494.) Rev. by Alfred Lou in PhilL (10:2) 325–33; by Jack Stillinger in JEGP (85:4) 550–7; by Evelyn Cobley in MalaR (77) 144–5.

10782. FLOWER, HARRY MITCHELL, III. The structuralist enterprise and Aristotle's *Poetics. See* **9951.**

10783. FOWLER, ROGER. Linguistic criticism. Oxford: OUP. pp. 224. (OPUS.)

10784. FRAWLEY, WILLIAM. Intertextuality and the dictionary: toward a deconstructionist account of lexicography. *See* **1751.**

10785. FREADMAN, ANNE. Taking things literally (sins of my old age). SoRA (18:2) 1985, 161–88.

10786. FROMM, HAROLD. The hegemonic form of othering; or, the academic's burden. CI (13:1) 197–200.

10787. FROW, JOHN. Marxism and literary history. *See* **7519.**

10788. —— Spectacle binding: on character. PT (7:2) 227–50.

10789. GALAN, F. W. Historic structures: the Prague school project, 1928–1946. Austin: Texas UP, 1985. pp. xiii, 250. Rev. by Karen Newman in PT (7:2) 362–4.

10790. GARVER, NEWTON. Structuralism and the challenge of metaphor. Monist (69:1) 68–86.

10791. GATES, HENRY LOUIS, JR. Talkin' that talk. CI (13:1) 203–10.

10792. GELFAND, ELISSA D.; HULES, VIRGINIA T. French feminist criticism: women, language and literature: an annotated bibliography. New York; London: Garland, 1985. pp. lii, 318. (Garland bibliographies of modern critics and critical schools, 9.) (Garland reference library of the humanities, 351.)

10793. GELLRICH, JESSE. The argument of the book: medieval writing and modern theory. *See* **3342.**

10794. GHISELIN, BREWSTER. Signéderrida: brief for Jacques Derrida. WHR (40:1) 1–8.

10795. GILLESPIE, GERALD. Bible lessons: the Gospel according to Frye, Girard, Kermode, and Voegelin. CL (38:3) 289–97 (review-article).

10796. GLANNON, WALTER. What literary theory misses in Wittgenstein. PhilL (10:2) 263–72.

10797. GLINGA, WERNER. *The River Between* and its forerunners: a contribution to the theory of the Kenyan novel. WLWE (26:2) 211–28.

10798. GLOGOWSKI, JAMES EDWARD. The *Oedipus Tyrannos* of Freud and Lacan: clinical reflections of literary structure. Unpub. doct. diss., State Univ. of New York at Buffalo, 1985. [Abstr. in DA (46) 1947A.]

10799. GLOVERSMITH, FRANK (ed.). The theory of reading. (Bibl. 1985, 9509.) Rev. by David Shepherd in PT (7:1) 134–45.

10800. GLUCK, MARY. Toward a historical definition of Modernism: Georg Lukács and the avant-garde. JMH (58:4) 845–82.

10801. GODDEN, RICHARD. 'What did you do in the study daddy . . . ?' PT (7:1) 147–56 (review-article).

10802. GOLDBERG, JONATHAN. Voice terminal echo: postmodernism and English Renaissance texts. *See* **3845.**

10803. GOODHEART, EUGENE. The skeptic disposition in contemporary criticism. (Bibl. 1985, 9513.) Rev. by Raman Selden in MLR (81:4) 961–3; by Lauriat Lane, Jr, in DalR (65:2) 1985, 293–9.

10804. GRAFF, GERALD; GIBBONS, REGINALD (eds). Criticism in the University. Evanston, IL: Northwestern UP, 1985. pp. 234. (*Tri-Quarterly* ser. on criticism and culture, 1.) Rev. by Jack Stillinger in JEGP (85:4) 550–7; by Hunter Jefferson in NER (9:2) 242–9.

10805. GREENE, GAYLE; KAHN, COPPÉLIA (eds). Making a difference: feminist literary criticism. London: Methuen, 1985. pp. ix, 273. (New accents.) Rev. by Valerie Shaw in THES (702) 19; by Steven Scobie in MalaR (75) 128–30.

10806. GROENING, LAURA JEANNE. Art, vision, and process: the literary criticism of E. K. Brown. Unpub. doct. diss., Carleton Univ., 1985. [Abstr. in DA (47) 911A.]

10807. GUNEW, SNEJA; SHERIDAN, SUSAN (eds). Feminist forum. AUMLA (65) 73–91.

10808. HAIDU, PETER. Idealism *vs* dialectics in some contemporary theory. CanRCL (13:3) 424–49 (review-article).

10809. HALLIBURTON, THOMAS LAUGHLIN. Why do English professors say such crazy things about the *Canterbury Tales*? An investigation of the rhetoric, logic, method, and history of academic exegesis of Chaucer's *Tales* in America, 1900–1984. *See* **3756.**

10810. HANDWERK, GARY J. Irony and ethics in narrative: from Schlegel to Lacan. *See* **7520.**

10811. HARDMEIER, CHRISTOF. Old Testament exegesis and linguistic narrative research. Poetics (15:1/2) 89–109.

10812. HARRIS, JOHN. Introduction. ECanW (32) 1–6. (Literary criticism in British Columbia.)

10813. HARRIS, WENDELL V. Toward an ecological criticism: contextual versus unconditioned literary theory. CE (48:2) 116–31.

10814. HARTMAN, GEOFFREY H. Easy pieces. (Bibl. 1985, 2151.) Rev. by Eugene Paul Nasser in ModAge (30:2) 170–3.

10815. HAUPTMEIER, HELMUT; SCHMIDT, SIEGFRIED J. (eds). Einführung in die empirische Literaturwissenschaft. Wiesbaden: Vieweg, 1985. pp. viii, 215. Rev. by Johan Strutz in Spr (17) 305–8.

10816. HENRICKSEN, BRUCE (ed.). Murray Krieger and contemporary critical theory. New York; Guildford: Columbia UP. pp. xvi, 307. (Irvine studies in the humanities.)

10817. HESELTINE, HARRY. The uncertain self: essays in Australian literature and criticism. *See* **7039.**

10818. HOLUB, ROBERT C.   Reception theory, a critical introduction. (Bibl. 1985, 9529.) Rev. by David Shepherd in PT (7:1) 129–34.

10819. HORROCKS, ROGER.   'Reading' and 'gender': watching them change. Antic (1) June, 114–28.

10820. HOŠEK, CHAVIVA; PARKER, PATRICIA (eds).   Lyric poetry: beyond new criticism. See **2927.**

10821. HOWES, CRAIG.   Rhetorics of attack: Bakhtin and the aesthetics of satire. Genre (19:3) 215–43.

10822. HUMM, MAGGIE.   Feminist criticism. Brighton: Harvester Press. pp. xi, 218.

10823. HUTCHEON, LINDA.   Formalism and the Freudian aesthetic: the example of Charles Mauron. Cambridge: CUP, 1984. pp. 249. Rev. by Donald Morton in WHR (40:3) 287–92; by Robert R. Wilson in ESCan (12:4) 491–7.

10824. —— A theory of parody: the teachings of twentieth-century art forms. (Bibl. 1985, 9530.) Rev. by Koenraad Kuiper in PhilL (10:2) 343–4; by Richard Terry in EC (36:2) 160–5.

10825. IRELAND, K. R.   Towards a grammar of narrative sequence: the model of *The French Lieutenant's Woman*. PT (7:3) 397–420.

10826. JACOBUS, MARY.   Reading woman: essays in feminist criticism. London: Methuen. pp. 350.

10827. JAMESON, FREDRIC.   The political unconscious: narrative as a socially symbolic act. (Bibl. 1985, 9533.) Rev. by Stanley Corngold and Michael Jennings in MLS (16:3) 367–73.

10828. JAPP, PHYLLIS M.   Rhetoric and time: dimensions of temporality in theory and criticism. See **1170.**

10829. JOHNSTON, JOHN H.   The poet and the city: a study in urban perspectives. Athens: Georgia UP, 1984. pp. xx, 275. Rev. by Milton Birnbaum in ModAge (30:2) 177–80.

10830. JONES, JAMES T.   Wayward skeptic: the theories of R. P. Blackmur. Urbana: Illinois UP. pp. 216.

10831. KALAGA, WOJCIECH.   The literary sign: a triadic model. Katowice: Uniwersytet Śląski. pp. 112. (Prace naukowe Uniwersytetu Śląskiego w Katowicach, 750.)

10832. KAMUF, PEGGY.   Monumental de-facement: on Paul de Man's *The Rhetoric of Romanticism*. See **7052.**

10833. KEEFER, MICHAEL H.   Introduction. DalR (66:1/2) 5–13. (Introduction to special issue: *Literature and Politics/Literary Politics*.)

10834. KIM, CHONG-UN.   Sontag ea Kosinski: minimalism sogo. (Sontag and Kosinski: a study of minimalism.) JH (16) 3–20.

10835. KIM, SU-YONG.   Neo-Marxism eui munhak iron. (Neo-Marxist literary theory.) IKY (56) 71–98.

10836. KIPPERMAN, MARK.   The rhetorical case against a theory of literature and science. PhilL (10:1) 76–83.

10837. KNOBLOCH, FRANK A.   Criticism double bound: the uncanny, the Baconian ideal, and the semantics of indeterminacy. Unpub. doct. diss., Univ. of Wisconsin–Madison. [Abstr. in DA (47) 891A.]

10838. KONIGSBERG, IRA (ed.). American criticism in the post-structuralist age. Ann Arbor: Michigan UP, 1981. pp. xxvii, 186. (Michigan studies in the humanities, 4.) Rev. by Marike Finlay in CanRCL (13:1) 94–8.

10839. KRAMER, VICTOR A. (ed.). American critics at work: examinations of contemporary literary theories. Troy, NY: Whitston, 1984. pp. xii, 447. Rev. by James Whitlark in ChrisL (36:1) 48–9; by William E. Cain in PhilL (10:2) 337–8.

10840. KRIEGER, MURRAY. In the wake of morality: the thematic underside of recent theory. NLH (15:1) 1983, 119–36.

10841. KROKER, ARTHUR. Technology and the Canadian mind: Innis, McLuhan, Grant. Montreal: New World Perspectives, 1984. pp. 144. Rev. by Leslie Armour in CanL (110) 163–4.

10842. KUIPER, KOENRAAD; SMALL, VERNON. Constraints on fictions, with an analysis of M. K. Joseph's *A Soldier's Tale*. PT (7:3) 495–526.

10843. LANDON, ANTONY. Total Shakespeare: the vision of George Wilson Knight. *See* **4506.**

10844. LANG, BEREL. Hamlet's grandmother and other literary facts. *See* **4762.**

10845. LANGMAN, F. H. 'The critic without qualities': a personal response. Meridian (5:2) 140–4.

10846. LASSETÉR, ROLLIN A. Poetics and Christianity. SewR (94:2) 279–84 (review-article).

10847. LATHY, EDWARD DANIEL. Metaphor, symbol, and utterance: the reality of relation in Susanne Langer and Mikhail Bakhtin. Unpub. doct. diss., Ohio State Univ., 1985. [Abstr. in DA (46) 3637A.]

10848. LEFERINK, HEIN; VAN DER WOUDE, MARIUS. Comment faire, en 1979, l'histoire du roman? Quelques problèmes méthodologiques. *In* (pp. 91–5) **19.**

10849. LEVENSON, MICHAEL H. A genealogy of Modernism: a study of English literacy doctrine, 1908–1922. (Bibl. 1985, 8809.) Rev. by Tom Gibbons in AUMLA (65) 132–6; by Harvey Gross in Review (8) 33–46.

10850. LEVIN, RICHARD. Performance-critics *vs* close readers in the study of English Renaissance drama. *See* **3905.**

10851. LLOYD, GENEVIEVE. Texts, metaphors and the pretensions of philosophy. Monist (69:1) 87–102.

10852. LUCAS, JOHN. Absence into presence: changes in literary criticism. TLS, 14 Nov., 1280.

10853. LURY, C. E. Feminist literary theory and women's writing. Unpub. doct. diss., Univ. of Manchester, 1985. [Abstr. in IT (35) 1490.]

10854. MACCABE, COLIN. Broken English. CritQ (28:1/2) 3–14.

10855. MACHIN, R. C. Deconstruction at Yale: a reading of Geoffrey Hartman and Paul de Man. Unpub. doct. diss., Univ. of Wales, UWIST, 1984. [Abstr. in IT (35) 539.]

10856. MAGLIOLA, ROBERT. Derrida on the mend. West Lafayette, IN: Purdue UP, 1984. pp. xiv, 238. Rev. by Stuart Sim in CritQ (28:4) 114–16; by Clayton Koelb in CL (38:4) 366–7.

10857. MALMGREN, CARL D.   Reading authorial narration: the example of *The Mill on the Floss*. PT (7:3) 471–94.

10858. MARGOLIS, JOSEPH.   The threads of literary theory. PT (7:1) 95–110.

10859. MARSHALL, DONALD G.   The history of eighteenth-century criticism and modern hermeneutical philosophy: the example of Richard Hurd. *See* **6176.**

10860. MARTIN, WALLACE.   Recent theories of narrative. Ithaca, NY; London: Cornell UP. pp. 242.

10861. MAXWELL, ANNE.   Poststructuralist and feminist literary theories: the problematic relation. Antic (1) June, 59–72.

10862. MEHLMAN, JEFFREY.   Writing and deference: the politics of literary adulation. Representations (15) 1–14.

10863. MERQUIOR, J. G.   From Prague to Paris: a critique of structuralist and post-structuralist thought. London: Verso. pp. xi, 286.

10864. MEUTSCH, DIETRICH.   Mental models in literary discourse: towards the integration of linguistic and psychological levels of description. Poetics (15:3) 307–31.

10865. MEYER, MICHEL.   Meaning and reading: a philosophical essay on language and literature. (Bibl. 1985, 9579.) Rev. by Gerald Prince in PhilL (10:1) 101–2.

10866. MILEUR, JEAN-PIERRE.   Literary revisionism and the burden of modernity. Berkeley; London: California UP, 1985. pp. xiii, 271.

10867. MILLER, NANCY K. (ed.).   The poetics of gender. New York; Guildford: Columbia UP. pp. xv, 303. (Gender and culture.)

10868. MILNER, ANDREW.   The English ideology: literary criticism in England and Australia. Thesis Eleven (Glebe, N.S.W.) (12) 1985, 110–29.

10869. MITCHELL, W. J. T.   Against theory: literary studies and the new pragmatism. Chicago; London: Chicago UP, 1985. pp. 146. Rev. by Alexander Nehamas in LRB (8:9) 16–17.

10870. MOHANTY, SATYA PRAKASH.   Criticism as politics: the way(s) to history. Unpub. doct. diss., Univ. of Illinois at Urbana-Champaign, 1985. [Abstr. in DA (46) 3342A.]

10871. MOI, TORIL.   Feminist literary criticism: theory and practice. Unpub. doct. diss., Univ. of Bergen. Rev. by Birgitta Holm in Edda (86) 291–302; by Atle Kittang 303–14; reply by Toril Moi 315–33. (*See also* bibl. 1985, 9584.)

10872. —— Sexual/textual politics: feminist literary theory. (Bibl. 1985, 9584.) Rev. by Valerie Shaw in THES (702) 19; by Peter Barry in Eng (35) 89–96; by Helena Forsås-Scott in Edda (86) 87–90; by Steven Scobie in MalaR (75) 128–30.

10873. MONTEFIORE, ALAN.   Philosophy, literature and the restatement of a few banalities. Monist (69:1) 56–67.

10874. MORRIS, WESLEY.   Friday's footprint: structuralism and the articulated text. (Bibl. 1982, 9996.) Rev. by Marshall Grossman in CLIO (11:1) 1981, 91–3.

10875. MORTIER, ROLAND.   Cent ans de littérature comparée: l'acquis, les perspectives. *In* (pp. 11–17) **11.**

10876. MUKHERJEE, ARUN P.   The vocabulary of the 'universal': cultural imperialism and Western literary criticism. WLWE (26:2) 343–53.

10877. MURPHY, JOHN W.   Deconstruction and the subversion of 'affirmative culture'. NOR (13:2) 90–7.

10878. NATOLI, JOSEPH; RUSCH, FREDERIK L. (comps).   Psychocriticism: an annotated bibliography. Westport, CT; London: Greenwood Press, 1984. pp. xxiii, 267. (Bibliographies and indexes in world literature, 1.)

10879. NONKOVICH, FRANK A.   The New Criticism and Cold War America. SoQ (20:1) 1981, 1–24.

10880. NORRIS, CHRISTOPHER.   The contest of faculties: philosophy and theory after Deconstruction. London: Methuen, 1985. pp. viii, 247. Rev. by Alexander Nehamas in LRB (8:9) 16–17.

10881. —— The deconstructive turn: essays in the rhetoric of philosophy. (Bibl. 1985, 9587.) Rev. by Stuart Sim in CritQ (28:4) 118; by Beth S. Ash in MP (84:1) 109–12; by Raman Selden in MLR (81:4) 965–7.

10882. —— Suspended sentences: textual theory and the law. *See* **1021.**

10883. NOVITZ, DAVID.   The rage for deconstruction. Monist (69:1) 39–55.

10884. O'BANION, JOHN DAVID.   Kenneth Burke and the recovery of narration: the dialectic of list and story. Unpub. doct. diss., Northern Illinois Univ., 1985. [Abstr. in DA (46) 1917A.]

10885. O'HARA, DANIEL T.   The romance of interpretation: visionary criticism from Pater to de Man. *See* **7525.**

10886. OLSEN, LANCE.   Zombies and academics: the reader's role in fantasy. Poetics (15:3) 279–85.

10887. ORR, LEONARD.   Intertextuality and the cultural text in recent semiotics. *See* **2257.**

10888. PASANEN, OUTI; PRANTNER, WILFRIED.   Postmodernism: interview with William V. Spanos. AAA (11:2) 195–209.

10889. PECHEY, GRAHAM.   Bakhtin, Marxism and poststructuralism. *In* (pp. 104–25) **29.**

10890. PERLOFF, MARJORIE.   Recharging the canon: some reflections on feminist poetics and the avant-garde. APR (15:4) 12–20.

10891. PHEBY, KEITH CHARLES.   Deconstruction, praxis and the concept of self. Unpub. doct. diss., Marquette Univ. [Abstr. in DA (47) 1752A.]

10892. PIMENTEL-ANDUIZA, LUZ AURORA.   Metaphoric narration: the role of metaphor in narrative discourse. Unpub. doct. diss., Harvard Univ., 1985. [Abstr. in DA (46) 1933A.]

10893. PIVATO, JOSEPH.   Ethnic writing and comparative Canadian literature. *In* (pp. 17–34) **13.**

10894. RAJCHMAN, JOHN.   Lacan and the ethics of modernity. Representations (15) 42–56.

10895. RATH, SURA P.   Game, play, literature: an introduction. SCR (3:4) 1–4.

10896. RAVAL, SURESH.   Philosophy and the crisis of contemporary literary theory. Monist (69:1) 119–32.

10897. RAY, WILLIAM.   Literary meaning: from phenomenology to deconstruction. (Bibl. 1984, 9609.) Rev. by Raman Selden in MLR (81:4) 963–5; by Alan Kennedy in DalR (65:2) 1985, 314–17.

10898. REEVES, CHARLES ERIC.   'Conveniency to nature': literary art and arbitrariness. PMLA (101:5) 798–810.

10899. —— Literary conventions and the noumenal text: Stanley Fish's egalitarian poetics. Neophilologus (70:3) 334–40.

10900. —— Symbol and sign: the romantic articulation of convention. PT (7:2) 341–9 (review-article).

10901. REISING, RUSSELL J.   The unusable past: theory and the study of American literature. New York; London: Methuen. pp. xii, 290. (New accents.) (Cf. bibl. 1984, 9610.)

10902. REISS, TIMOTHY J.   On exposition. See **2272.**

10903. RHOADES, GEORGIA.   Literature and composition: using Michael Riffaterre's concept of ungrammaticality to relate text and context in the process of interpretation. Unpub. doct. diss., Univ. of Louisville, 1985. [Abstr. in DA (47) 892A.]

10904. RIESE, UTZ.   Umbrüche in den amerikanischen Literatur- ideologien zwischen Realismus und Postmodernismus. AAA (11:1) 3–18.

10905. ROONEY, ELLEN.   Who's left out? A rose by any other name is still red; or, the politics of pluralism. CI (12:3) 550–63.

10906. ROONEY, ELLEN FRANCES.   At 'the limits of pluralism': constructing the problematic of American literary theory. Unpub. doct. diss., Johns Hopkins Univ. [Abstr. in DA (47) 1718A.]

10907. ROPER, DEREK.   'Practical criticism': fifty years of an English teaching method. *In* (pp. 227–43) **17.**

10908. ROSE, GILLIAN.   Dialectic of nihilism: post-structuralism and law. Oxford: Blackwell, 1984. pp. 232. Rev. by Geoffrey Strickland in CamQ (15:1) 85–8.

10909. RUTHVEN, K. K.   The critic without qualities: forum. Merid- ian (4:2) 1985, 162–73.

10910. —— Feminist literary studies: an introduction. (Bibl. 1985, 9615.) Rev. by Peter Barry in Eng (35) 89–96.

10911. SACKS, HARVEY.   Some considerations of a story told in ordinary conversations. See **1392.**

10912. SCHMIDT, PAUL HENRY.   Newman and post-modernism: a study of Newman's prose non-fiction and its relation to poststructuralist literary theory. See **9004.**

10913. SCHOLES, ROBERT.   Textual power: literary theory and the teaching of English. (Bibl. 1985, 9619.) Rev. by Gerald Graff in Novel (19:2) 179–82; by Clarence Walhout in ChrisL (35:4) 51–3.

10914. SCHWARZ, DANIEL R.　The humanistic heritage: critical theories of the English novel from James to Hillis Miller. *See* **7526.**

10915. SELDEN, RAMAN.　Criticism and objectivity. (Bibl. 1985, 9621.) Rev. by R. J. Dingley in NQ (33:1) 133–4.

10916. —— A reader's guide to contemporary literary theory. Brighton: Harvester Press; Lexington: Kentucky UP, 1985. pp. vi, 153. Rev. by Terry Eagleton in MLR (81:4) 959–60.

10917. SHAWCROSS, JOHN R.　Literary revisionism and a case for genre. Genre (18:4) 1985, 413–34.

10918. SHEPHERD, DAVID.　The authority of meanings and the meanings of authority: some problems in the theory of reading. PT (7:1) 129–45 (review-article).

10919. SHERWOOD, JOHN C.　Derrida, formalism, and Christianity. ChrisL (35:4) 14–17.

10920. SHOWALTER, ELAINE (ed.).　The new feminist criticism: essays on women, literature, and theory. New York: Pantheon, 1985; London: Virago Press. pp. ix, 403. Rev. by Valerie Shaw in THES (710) 16.

10921. SHUSTERMAN, RICHARD.　Analytic aesthetics, literary theory, and deconstruction. Monist (69:1) 22–38.

10922. —— Poetics and current analytic aesthetics. PT (7:2) 323–9 (review-article).

10923. SHUSTERMAN, RONALD.　Blindness and anxiety: I. A. Richards and some current trends of criticism. EA (39:4) 411–23.

10924. SIEBERS, TOBIN.　Paul de Man and the rhetoric of selfhood. NOR (13:1) 5–9.

10925. SIM, STUART.　'Not quite philosophy': the situation of deconstruction. CritQ (28:4) 114–22 (review-article).

10926. SLINN, WARWICK.　The 'monsters' of deconstruction. Meridian (5:2) 109–16.

10927. SMIRNOV, IGOR P.　Jenseits des Poststrukturalismus oder lässt sich Literatur definieren? PoetA (17) 1985, 183–201.

10928. SMITH, ANNA.　Le féminin: a study of feminine textuality. Untold (5) Autumn, 10–20.

10929. SOSNOSKI, JAMES J.　Literary study as a field for inquiry. Boundary 2 (13:2/3) 1985, 91–104.

10930. SPANOS, WILLIAM V.; BOVÉ, PAUL A.; O'HARA, DANIEL (eds). The question of textuality: strategies of reading in contemporary American criticism. Bloomington: Indiana UP, 1982. pp. 372. Rev. by Linda Hutcheon in CanRCL (13:3) 461–5.

10931. SPIERS, LOGAN.　Terry Eagleton and 'the function of criticism'. CamQ (15) 57–63 (review-article).

10932. SPRINKER, MICHAEL.　Boundless context: problems in Bakhtin's linguistics. PT (7:1) 117–28 (review-article).

10933. —— What is living and what is dead in Chicago criticism. Boundary 2 (13:2/3) 1985, 189–212.

10934. STANLEY, KIMBERLY DIANE.　Language on holiday: twentieth-century literary critics define tragedy. *See* **2813.**

10935. STANZEL, FRANZ K.   A theory of narrative. Trans. by CHARLOTTE GOEDSCHE. *See* **10406.**

10936. STATEN, HENRY.   Wittgenstein and Derrida. Oxford: Blackwell. (Cf. bibl. 1985, 9638.) Rev. by Christopher Norris in CL (38:4) 350–9; by Stuart Sim in CritQ (28:4) 114–17.

10937. STEINER, DOROTHEA.   Feminist criticism, poetic theory and American poetry historiography. *In* (pp. 88–113) **21.**

10938. STEINER, PETER.   Russian formalism: a metapoetics. (Bibl. 1985, 9642.) Rev. by Milton Ehre in CL (38:1) 90–2.

10939. —— (ed.).   The Prague School: selected writings, 1929–1946. London: Texas UP, 1982. (Cf. bibl. 1983, 10030.) Rev. by René Wellek in MLR (81:3) 693–4.

10940. STEMPEL, WOLF-DIETER.   Everyday narrative as a prototype. Poetics (15:1/2) 203–16.

10941. STOUT, JEFFREY.   The relativity of interpretation. Monist (69:1) 103–18.

10942. STRUBE, PAUL.   Genre theory and textbook criticism: non fiction as literature. English in Australia (76) 28–32.

10943. STURROCK, JOHN.   Structuralism. London: Paladin. pp. xiii, 190. (Paladin movements and ideas.)

10944. SWINGEWOOD, ALAN.   Sociological poetics and aesthetic theory. Basingstoke: Macmillan. pp. 144.

10945. SYPHER, WYLIE.   A Modernist lexicon. *See* **7527.**

10946. SZEGEDY-MASZÁK, MIHÁLY.   Four aspects of the narrative text. *In* (pp. 129–33) **19.**

10947. TANNER, MICHAEL.   The test of time. Critical Review (28) 3–17.

10948. THURLEY, GEOFFREY.   Counter-modernism in current critical theory. (Bibl. 1985, 9650.) Rev. by John M. Ellis in CL (38:4) 374–5.

10949. TINDALE, CHRISTOPHER WILLIAM.   The speaking subject: speech acts, grammatology, and the phenomenology of speech. *See* **791.**

10950. TODOROV, TZVETAN.   'Race', writing, and culture. Trans. by LOULOU MACK. CI (13:1) 171–81.

10951. UDWIN, VICTOR MORRIS.   Experience interrupted: the dynamics of literary interpretation. Unpub. doct. diss., Univ. of California, Berkeley, 1985. [Abstr. in DA (47) 894A.]

10952. UNGAR, STEVEN.   Roland Barthes: the professor of desire. (Bibl. 1984, 9654.) Rev. by S. F. R. in CL (38:2) 191–3.

10953. VALDÉS, MARIO J.; MILLER, OWEN (eds).   Identity of the literary text. *See* **23.**

10954. VAN BOHEEMEN, CHRISTEL.   Tegendraads lezen of Is deconstructivisme destructief? (Reading against the grain, or is deconstructivism destructive?) De Gids (149:9/10) 827–37.

10955. VIEHOFF, REINHOLD.   How to construct a literary poem? Poetics (15:3) 287–306.

10956. VIGUERS, SUSAN T.   Commentaries: Monroe C. Beardsley, 1915–1985. JAE (20:1) 107–11.

10957. VON HALLBERG, ROBERT. American poet–critics since 1945.
In (pp. 280–99) **47.**

10958. WEIMANN, ROBERT. Structure and society in literary history:
studies in the history and theory of historical criticism. (Bibl. 1985,
2569.) Rev. by Sue Wienhorst in ChrisL (35:4) 54–5.

10959. WEISS, DANIEL. The critic agonistes: psychology, myth, and
the art of fiction. *See* **7364.**

10960. WELLEK, RENÉ. Four critics: Croce, Valéry, Lukács, and
Ingarden. (Bibl. 1984, 9665.) Rev. by George Bisztray in CanRCL
(13:2) 263–5.

10961. —— A history of modern criticism: 1750–1950: vol. 5, English
criticism, 1900–1950; vol. 6, American criticism, 1900–1950. New Haven,
CT; London: Yale UP. pp. xxiv, 343; viii, 345. Rev. by Robert M. Adams
in BkW, 23 Feb., 3, 11; by Claude Rawson in NYTB, 30 Mar., 8.

10962. WES, M. A. Contra George Steiner: een tegen rede. (Against
George Steiner: an opposing speech.) De Gids (149:2) 83–91.

10963. WEXLER, JOYCE. Who paid for Modernism? SewR (94:3)
440–9.

10964. WHEELER, SAMUEL C., III. The extension of deconstruction.
Monist (69:1) 3–21.

10965. WILSON, ROBERT R. Rules/conventions: three paradoxes in
the game/text analogy. SCR (3:4) 15–27.

10966. WOLIN, RICHARD. Walter Benjamin: an aesthetic of redemption. New York: Columbia UP, 1982. pp. 316. Rev. by Stanley Corngold
and Michael Jennings in MLS (16:3) 367–73.

10967. WREEN, MICHAEL J.; CALLEN, DONALD M. (eds). The
aesthetic point of view: selected essays by MONROE C. BEARDSLEY. (Bibl.
1985, 9669.) Rev. by Harold Osborne in JAE (20:1) 97–106.

10968. WRIGHT, ELIZABETH. Psychoanalytic criticism: theory in
practice. New York: Methuen, 1984. (Cf. bibl. 1985, 9670.) Rev. by
Barry Jordan in MLR (81:2) 417–19; by Annette Laver in PT (7:1)
170–2.

10969. YARBROUGH, STEPHEN R. Intrinsic criticism and deconstruction: their methods' legacy. SCR (3:1) 78–89.

10970. ZIPES, JACK. Don't bet on the prince: feminist fairy tales and
the feminist critique in America. *In* (pp. 69–99) **40.**

10971. Entry cancelled.

AUTHORS
Edward Abbey

10972. WESTRUM, DEXTER LYLE. The art of survival in the contemporary West: the fictions of Thomas McGuane, James Welch, and
Edward Abbey. Unpub. doct. diss., Univ. of Minnesota, 1985. [Abstr.
in DA (46) 3037A.]

Walter Abish

10973. BUTLER, CHRISTOPHER. Scepticism and experimental fiction.
See **10166.**

10974. PESTINO, JOSEPH FRANCIS. The reader/writer affair: instigating repertoire in the experimental fiction of Susan Sontag, Walter Abish, Réjean Ducharme, Paul West, and Christine Brooke-Rose. Unpub. doct. diss., Pennsylvania State Univ. [Abstr. in DA (47) 1314A.]

Peter Abrahams

10975. CHIWENGO, NGWARSUNGU. Peter Abrahams in perspective. Unpub. doct. diss., State Univ. of New York at Buffalo. [Abstr. in DA (47) 527A.]

10976. SCANLON, PAUL A. Dream and reality in Abrahams' *A Wreath for Udomo*. Ob (6) Spring/Summer 1980, 25–32.

Dannie Abse

10977. CURTIS, TONY. Dannie Abse. (Bibl. 1985, 9677.) Rev. by John Pikoulis in Poetry Wales (21:2) 111–16.

Chinua Achebe

10978. DOHERTY, JAIYEOLA. Die Satire im nigerianischen Roman. Die Rolle der Satire in den Romanwerken 4 nigerianischer Schriftsteller: T. M. Aluko, Chinua Achebe, Nkem Nwankwo und Wole Soyinka. Frankfurt: Lang. pp. 381. (Europäische Hochschulschriften: Reihe 14, Angelsächsische Sprache und Literatur, 151.)

10979. FRASER, ROBERT. A note on Okonkwo's suicide. Ob (6) Spring/Summer 1980, 30–3.

10980. HEYWOOD, CHRISTOPHER. Chinua Achebe, *Things Fall Apart*: a critical view. Ed. by YOLANDE CANTÙ. London: Collins; British Council, 1985. pp. 41. (Nexus.)

10981. LARSON, CHARLES R. The precarious state of the African writer. *See* **9793.**

10982. McDOUGALL, RUSSELL. Okonkwo's walk: the choreography of things falling apart. WLWE (26:1) 24–33.

10983. McDOUGALL, RUSSELL JOHN. A casement, triple-arch'd. Cultural kinetics: the fusion of music, the dance and the word in African and Caribbean culture. Unpub. doct. diss., Queen's Univ. at Kingston. [Abstr. in DA (47) 1721A.]

10984. OKAFOR, CLÉMENT A. Igbo narrative tradition and the novels of Chinua Achebe: transition from oral to written literature. *In* (pp. 483–7) **19.**

Kathy Acker

10985. COKER, JUDITH BRIGGS. Sexuality in discourse: feminine models in recent fiction by American women. Unpub. doct. diss., Univ. of Oklahoma. [Abstr. in DA (47) 1321A.]

Louis Adamic

10986. CHRISTIAN, HENRY ARTHUR. Louis Adamic: immigrant and American liberal. Unpub. doct. diss., Brown Univ., 1968. [Abstr. in DA (47) 176A.]

Harriet Stratemeyer Adams ('Carolyn Keene')

10987. BILLMAN, CAROL. The secret of the Stratemeyer syndicate: Nancy Drew, the Hardy Boys, and the million dollar fiction factory. *See* **355.**

Richard Adams
10988. KITCHELL, KENNETH F. The shrinking of the epic hero: from Homer to Richard Adams's *Watership Down*. CML (7:1) 13–30.

Robert Adamson
10989. SHARKEY, MICHAEL. Robert Adamson and the persistence of Mallarmé. Southerly (45:3) 1985, 308–20 (interview).

Seymour Adelman
10990. HARRINGTON, FRANK G. Recollections of Seymour. ABC (7:5) 21–6.

Renata Adler
10991. ETTER, KATHRYN. Genre of return: the short story volume. Unpub. doct. diss., Univ. of Iowa, 1985. [Abstr. in DA (47) 898A.]

James Agee
10992. ALLISTER, MARK. Seeing, knowing, and being: James Agee's *Let Us Now Praise Famous Men*. Prose Studies (9:3) 86–102.

10993. ALLISTER, MARK CHRISTOPHER. Encounters with unimagined existence: documentary and autobiography in recent American prose. *See* **10627.**

10994. KAZIN, ALFRED. A wounded life, a father 'perfect in death'. NYTB, 29 June, 3.

10995. MALAND, CHARLES. Agee, a film. SoQ (19:3/4) 1981, 225–8.

10996. SPEARS, ROSS. Regional film-making: the James Agee film project. SoQ (19:3/4) 1981, 223–5.

10997. WARD, J. A. American silences: the realism of James Agee, Walker Evans, and Edward Hopper. Baton Rouge: Louisiana State UP, 1985. pp. xvii, 210. Rev. by Milton A. Cohen in AL (58:1) 140–1.

10998. WYDEVEN, JOSEPH J. Photography and privacy: the protests of Wright Morris and James Agee. MidQ (23:1) 1981, 103–15.

Ama Ata Aidoo
10999. EKO, EBELE. Beyond the myth of confrontation: a comparative study of African and Afro-American female protagonists. Ariel (17:4) 139–52.

Conrad Aiken
11000. HAGENBÜCHLE, HELEN. Conrad Aiken's aesthetic theories: a tandem of methods. YREAL (2) 1984, 371–96.

11001. MOLIN, IRVING. Introduction: Aiken reflections. SoQ (21:1) 1982, 3–6.

11002. OLSON, STEVEN E. *Great Circle*: Conrad Aiken's autoplastic journey into childhood. SoQ (21:1) 1982, 38–63.

11003. PINSKER, SANFORD. The artist and the art novel: a reappraisal of Conrad Aiken's *Blue Voyage*. SoQ (21:1) 1982, 28–37.

11004. ROBILLARD, DOUGLAS. Conrad Aiken and the supernatural. SoQ (21:1) 1982, 119–31.

11005. ROUNTREE, MARY MARTIN. Conrad Aiken's fiction: 'an inordinate and copious lyric'. SoQ (21:1) 1982, 9–27.

11006. SPIVEY, TED R. Conrad Aiken and the life of reason. SoQ (21:1) 1982, 148–57.

11007. STORY, NANCY CIUCEVICH. Conrad Aiken: a functional basis for poetry and criticism. SoQ (21:1) 1982, 132–47.

11008. VOELKER, JOSEPH C. 'A collideorscape!': Sigmund Freud, Malcolm Lowry, and the aesthetics of Conrad Aiken's *A Heart for the Gods of Mexico*. SoQ (21:1) 1982, 64–81.

Edward Albee

11009. AHRENDS, GÜNTER. Stationen einer Odyssee. Edward Albees *The Zoo Story*. Anglistik & Englischunterricht (28) 81–96.

11010. BIGSBY, C. W. E. A critical introduction to twentieth-century American drama: 2, Tennessee Williams, Arthur Miller, Edward Albee. (Bibl. 1985, 9698.) Rev. by Brenda Murphy in AL (58:3) 463–5; by Rodney Simard in TJ (38:1) 123–4.

11011. FISCHER-SEIDEL, THERESE. Mythenparodie im modernen englischen und amerikanischen Drama. Tradition und Kommunikation bei Tennessee Williams, Edward Albee, Samuel Beckett und Harold Pinter. Heidelberg: Winter. pp. 216. (Anglistische Forschungen, 174.)

11012. FOUST, R. E. Desperate gambits, game theory, and modern American literature. *See* **11873.**

11013. MILLER, GABRIEL. Albee on death and dying: *Seascape* and *The Lady from Dubuque*. MLS (16:3) 149–60.

11014. MILLS, KATHLEEN. A transactional analysis of *Tiny Alice*: an alternative for the study of problematic scripts. Unpub. doct. diss., Florida State Univ., 1985. [Abstr. in DA (46) 3537A.]

11015. WASSERMAN, JULIAN (ed.). Edward Albee: an interview and essays. Houston, TX: Univ. of St Thomas, 1983. pp. 184. Rev. by Katherine Burckman in TS (30) 1983/84, 70–1.

Richard Aldington

11016. BARLOW, ADRIAN. Answers for my murdered self: the 'case for revaluing Richard Aldington's post First World War poetry'. Quadrant (30:11) 75–9.

11017. BURGESS, ANTHONY (introd.). The colonel's daughter. London: Hogarth Press. pp. 365. (Hogarth fiction.)

11018. CLEMENTS, PATRICIA. 'Transmuting' Nancy Cunard. DalR (66:1/2) 188–214.

11019. RIDGWAY, CHRISTOPHER (introd.). Death of a hero. London: Hogarth Press, 1984. pp. 375.

Nelson Algren

11020. PRINGLE, LAUREN HELEN. An annotated and indexed calendar and abstract of the Ohio State University collection of Simone de Beauvoir's letters to Nelson Algren. *See* **275.**

Walter Allen

11021. SILLITOE, ALAN (introd.). All in a lifetime. London: Hogarth Press. pp. 256.

'Woody Allen' (Allen Stewart Konigsberg)

11022. BENAYOUN, ROBERT. Woody Allen: beyond words. Trans. and introd. by ALEXANDER WALKER. London: Pavilion; Joseph. pp. 175.

11023. BRODE, DOUGLAS. Woody Allen: his films and careers. Secaucus, NJ: Citadel, 1985; London: Columbus. pp. 263.

11024. SCHAPIRO, BARBARA. Woody Allen's search for self. JPC (19:4) 47–62.

Phyllis Shand Allfrey

11025. CAMPBELL, ELAINE. *In the Cabinet*: a novelistic rendition of Federation politics. Ariel (17:4) 117–25.

Margery Allingham

11026. McDONOUGH, JILLMARIE ANN. 'The welfare of our country': social commentary in Margery Allingham's detective fiction. Unpub. doct. diss., Univ. of Michigan. [Abstr. in DA (47) 913A.]

T. M. Aluko

11027. DOHERTY, JAIYEOLA. Die Satire im nigerianischen Roman. Die Rolle der Satire in den Romanwerken 4 nigerianischer Schriftsteller: T. M. Aluko, Chinua Achebe, Nkem Nwankwo und Wole Soyinka. *See* **10978.**

Eric Ambler

11028. AMBLER, ERIC. Here lies: an autobiography. New York: Viking Press. (Cf. bibl. 1985, 9712.) Rev. by J. I. M. Stewart in BkW, 10 Aug., 4.

Kingsley Amis

11029. BARNIE, JOHN. The art of puffing: Kingsley Amis and his critics. Planet (60) 3–8.

11030. FAULKS, SEBASTIAN. The Old Devil takes the Booker. Independent, 23 Oct., 19.

Martin Amis

11031. IGNATIEFF, MICHAEL. Our valuation of human life has become thinner. Listener (115) 13 Mar., 18–19. (Interview.)

A. R. Ammons

11032. CLARK, MIRIAM MARTY. Not at all surprised by science: science and technology in Ammons, Nemerov, and Merrill. Unpub. doct. diss., Univ. of North Carolina at Chapel Hill. [Abstr. in DA (47) 1723A.]

11033. MILLS, ELIZABETH McGEACHY. Wording the unspeakable: Emily Dickinson and A. R. Ammons. *See* **8134.**

Mulk Raj Anand

11034. CHEW, SHIRLEY. Fictions of princely states and empire. Ariel (17:3) 103–17.

11035. MATHUR, O. P. Two modern versions of the Sita myth: Narayan and Anand. JCL (21:1) 16–25.

Rudolfo Anaya

11036. CLEMENTS, WILLIAM M. The way to individuation in Anaya's *Bless Me, Ultima*. MidQ (23:2) 1982, 131–43.

Jessica Anderson

11037. HAYNES, ROSLYNN D. Art as reflection in Jessica Anderson's *Tirra Lirra by the River*. ALS (12:3) 316–23 (review-article).

11038. SMITH, SHIRLEY. Image and theme in Jessica Anderson's *Tirra Lirra by the River*. Teaching of English (Rozelle, N.S.W.) (51) 17–21.

11039. SYKES, ALRENE. Jessica Anderson: arrivals and places. Southerly (46:1) 57–71.

Maxwell Anderson

11040. SHIVERS, ALFRED S. Maxwell Anderson: an annotated bibliography of primary and secondary works. Metuchen, NJ; London: Scarecrow Press, 1985. pp. xi, 287. (Scarecrow author bibliographies, 72.)

Patrick Anderson

11041. WHITNEY, PATRICIA.   From Oxford to Montreal: Patrick Anderson's political development. CanP (19) 26–48.

Sherwood Anderson

11042. ANDERSON, DAVID D.   Mark Twain, Sherwood Anderson, Saul Bellow, and the territories of the spirit. *See* **9427.**

11043. BREDAHL, A. CARL.   'The young thing within': divided narrative in Sherwood Anderson's *Winesburg, Ohio*. MidQ (27:4) 422–37.

11044. COLQUITT, CLARE.   The reader as voyeur: complicitous transformations in *Death in the Woods*. MFS (32:2) 175–90.

11045. MODLIN, CHARLES E.; CAMPBELL, HILBERT N.; TAKADA, KENICHI.   Sherwood Anderson: additions to the bibliography. SB (39) 266–8.

11046. SUTTON, WILLIAM A. (ed.).   Letters to Bab: Sherwood Anderson to Marietta D. Finley, 1916–1933. Urbana: Illinois UP, 1985. pp. xxii, 352. Rev by James H. Maguire in AL (58:1) 142–3; by David D. Anderson in NwOQ (58:1) 29–33.

Roger Angell

11047. GINDIN, JAMES.   Roger Angell and the annals of baseball. *See* **604.**

11048. PALMER, WILLIAM.   History, tradition, and hubris: the baseball universe of Roger Angell. *See* **664.**

Maya Angelou

11049. MAYER, SUSANNE.   Die Sehnsucht nach den anderen. Eine Studie zum Verhältnis von Subjekt und Gesellschaft in den Autobiographien von Lillian Hellman, Maya Angelou und Maxine Hong Kingston. Frankfurt: Lang. pp. 331. (Neue Studien zur Anglistik und Amerikanistik, 35.)

David Antin

11050. ALTIERI, CHARLES.   The postmodernism of David Antin's *Tuning*. CE (48:1) 9–26.

John Arden

11051. BAS, GEORGES.   Théâtre, histoire et politique d'une pièce radiophonique: *Pearl* (1978), de John Arden, et la question irlandaise. EA (39:4) 424–37.

11052. COHEN, MICHAEL.   The politics of the earlier Arden. ModDr (28:2) 1985, 198–210.

11053. GÖRING, MICHAEL.   Melodrama heute: die Adaptation melodramatischer Elemente und Strukturen im Werk von John Arden und Arden/D'Arcy. Amsterdam: Grüner. pp. 439. (Münchner Studien zur neueren englischen Literatur, 2.)

11054. MALICK, SHAH JAWEEDUL.   The dramaturgy of John Arden: dialectical vision and popular tradition. Unpub. doct. diss., McGill Univ., 1985. [Abstr. in DA (46) 3349A.]

Michael Arlen (Dikrān Kuyumjian)

11055. CLEMENTS, PATRICIA.   'Transmuting' Nancy Cunard. *See* **11018.**

Ayi Kwei Armah

11056. COOPER, B. L.   A theory of African literature and its application to texts by Wole Soyinka, Ayi Kwei Armah and Ngugi wa Thiong'o. Unpub. doct. diss., Univ. of Sussex, 1983.

11057. JACKSON, TOMMIE LEE.   Ayi Kwei Armah and French existentialism: a comparison. Unpub. doct. diss., Univ. of Nebraska–Lincoln, 1985. [Abstr. in DA (46) 3029A.]

11058. LIPENGA, KEN DISTON.   Alienation in the novels of Ayi Kwei Armah. Unpub. doct. diss., Univ. of New Brunswick, 1984. [Abstr. in DA (46) 2292A.]

11059. SABER, AHMED.   Political and social thought in the West African novel: Mongo Béti's *Perpétue*, Ousmane Sembène's *Xala* and Ayi Kwei Armah's *The Healers*. Unpub. doct. diss., Univ. of Georgia, 1985. [Abstr. in DA (46) 2686A.]

11060. SPENCER, NORMAN ALBRITTON.   Political consciousness and commitment in modern African literature: a study of the novels of Ayi Kwei Armah. Unpub. doct. diss., State Univ. of New York at Stony Brook, 1985. [Abstr. in DA (47) 527A.]

11061. WRIGHT, DEREK.   Flux and form: the geography of time in *The Beautyful Ones Are Not Yet Born*. Ariel (17:2) 63–77.

John Ashbery

11062. BENSKO, JOHN.   Reflexive narration in contemporary American poetry: some examples from Mark Strand, John Ashbery, Norman Dubie and Louis Simpson. JNT (16:2) 81–96.

11063. BROMWICH, DAVID.   John Ashbery: the self against its images. Raritan (5:4) 36–58.

11064. EDELMAN, LEE.   The pose of imposture: Ashbery's *Self-Portrait in a Convex Mirror*. TCL (32:1) 95–114.

11065. EICHBAUER, MARY E.   The visual arts as a myth of poetic origins in René Char and John Ashbery. Unpub. doct. diss., Univ. of California, Los Angeles, 1985. [Abstr. in DA (46) 3714A.]

11066. GARDNER, THOMAS.   Reading Ashbery. CEACrit (48:3) 50–7.

11067. JACKSON, RICHARD.   Many happy returns: the poetry of John Ashbery. Pl (12:3) 136–45.

11068. PICARD, CHRISTOPHER L.   The way of these lines: the poetry and poetic of John Ashbery. Unpub. doct. diss., Brown Univ., 1985. [Abstr. in DA (46) 1939A.]

11069. STAMELMAN, RICHARD.   Critical reflections: poetry and art criticism in Ashbery's *Self-portrait in a Convex Mirror*. NLH (15) 1984, 607–30.

Isaac Asimov

11070. GERDY, MARIA S.   The human–robot relationship theme in Isaac Asimov's robot trilogy. Unpub. doct. diss., Columbia Univ. Teachers College. [Abstr. in DA (47) 815A.]

Thea Astley

11071. CLANCY, LAURIE.   The fiction of Thea Astley. Meridian (5:1) 43–52.

11072. GOLDSWORTHY, KERRYN.   Voices in time: *A Kindness Cup* and *Miss Peabody's Inheritance*. ALS (12:4) 471–81.

11073. RICHEY, NORMA JEAN. An interview with Thea Astley. SCR (3:2) 90–102.

Margaret Atwood

11074. CARRINGTON, ILDIKÓ DE PAPP. Demons, doubles, and dinosaurs: *Life before Man, The Origin of Consciousness*, and *The Icicle*. ECanW (33) 68–88.

11075. DAVEY, FRANK. Alternate stories: the short fiction of Audrey Thomas and Margaret Atwood. CanL (109) 5–14.

11076. GODARD, BARBARA. Tales within tales: Margaret Atwood's folk narratives. *See* **2448.**

11077. GOETSCH, PAUL. Margaret Atwood's *Life Before Man* as a novel of manners. *In* (pp. 137–49) **22.**

11078. GRACE, SHERRILL E.; WEIR, LORRAINE (eds). Margaret Atwood: language, text and system. (Bibl. 1985, 9760.) Rev. by Barry Cameron in ESCan (12:3) 368–74.

11079. HOWELLS, CORAL ANN. Worlds alongside: contradictory discourses in the fiction of Alice Munro and Margaret Atwood. *In* (pp. 121–36) **22.**

11080. JENSEN, EMILY. Margaret Atwood's *Lady Oracle*: a modern parable. ECanW (33) 29–49.

11081. JOLLY, ROSLYN. Transformations of Caliban and Ariel: imagination and language in David Malouf, Margaret Atwood and Seamus Heaney. *See* **4987.**

11082. KLOVAN, PETER. 'They are out of reach now': the family motif in Margaret Atwood's *Surfacing*. ECanW (33) 1–28.

11083. MALLINSON, JEAN. Margaret Atwood. *In* (pp. 17–81) **10.**

11084. ROSENBERG, JEROME H. Margaret Atwood. Boston, MA: G. K. Hall, 1984. pp. 184. (Twayne's world authors, 740.) Rev. by Arnold E. Davidson in CanL (109) 105–7.

11085. ST ANDREWS, B. A. The Canadian connection: Frye/Atwood. WLT (60:1) 47–9.

11086. STOVEL, NORA FOSTER. Reflections on mirror images: doubles and identity in the novels of Margaret Atwood. ECanW (33) 50–67.

11087. VÁŇOVÁ, TAMARA. Ženské postavy v díle Margarety Atwoodové. (Margaret Atwood's female characters.) *In* (pp. 65–6) **4.**

11088. VARMA, DEVENDRA. Gothic shadows in the early novels of Margaret Atwood. AAS (6:1) 31–43.

11089. YORK, LORRAINE M. Lives of Joan and Del: separate paths to transformation in *Lives of Girls and Women* and *Lady Oracle*. UWR (19:2) 1–10.

W. H. Auden

11090. AQUIEN, PASCAL. Le théâtre de W. H. Auden: de l'artifice à l'impasse. EA (39:2) 163–73.

11091. —— W. H. Auden: nostalgie de l'Eden et apocalypse du moi. *In* (pp. 251–9) **2.**

11092. BELL, K. 'Throwing away the key': a study of the development of ideas and belief in the poetry of W. H. Auden, 1927–47. Unpub. doct. diss., Univ. of Reading, 1984. [Abstr. in IT (35) 547.]

11093. BOLD, ALAN (ed.).   W. H. Auden: the far interior. London: Vision Press; Totowa, NJ: Barnes & Noble. pp. 223. Rev. by Brian Finney in THES (689) 19; by Nicholas Jenkins in TLS, 13 June, 643.

11094. FARNAN, DOROTHY J.   Auden in love. (Bibl. 1985, 9772.) Rev. by Adam Mars-Jones in LRev, Apr. 1985, 18, 20–1.

11095. FORD, P. K.   The later W. H. Auden as a Christian poet. Unpub. doct. diss., Univ. of Aberdeen. [Abstr. in IT (36) 912.]

11096. HOUSTON, D. N.   Myths of place: the importance of landscape in the poetries of W. H. Auden and Seamus Heaney. Unpub. doct. diss., Univ. of Hull. [Abstr. in IT (36) 473.]

11097. ISMAEL, S. M. K.   A stylistic study of the vocabulary in W. H. Auden's poetry. Unpub. doct. diss., Univ. of Sheffield, 1985.

11098. JOHNSON, ALAN.   Toward the 'realm of malice': the sense of evil in Auden's poems of the late thirties. ELit (13:2) 247–61.

11099. McDIARMID, LUCY.   Saving civilization: Yeats, Eliot, and Auden between the wars. (Bibl. 1985, 9779.) Rev. by David Bradshaw in EC (36:4) 352–5; by Vincent Fitzpatrick in VQR (62) 360–5; by Nicholas Grene in NQ (33:3) 423–4.

11100. MYERSON, G. E.   The rhetorical achievement of W. H. Auden, with particular references to his poetry from the late twenties to the mid-thirties. Unpub. doct. diss., Univ. of Cambridge. [Abstr. in IT (35) 1087.]

11101. POGER, SIDNEY.   Berlin and the two versions of W. H. Auden's *Paid on Both Sides.* Ariel (17:2) 17–30.

11102. SHAPIRO, KARL.   *At Auden's Grave.* CEACrit (48:3) 10–20.

11103. SMITH, STAN.   W. H. Auden. Oxford: Blackwell, 1985. pp. 192. (Re-reading literature.) Rev. by Brian Finney in THES (689) 19; by Nicholas Jenkins in TLS, 13 June, 643.

11104. SNYDER, SUSAN.   Auden, Shakespeare, and the defence of poetry. *See* **4594.**

11105. WHITEHEAD, JOHN.   Auden and *All the Conspirators.* EC (36:4) 335–41.

Mary Austin

11106. LANGLOIS, KAREN S.   Mary Austin and Lincoln Steffens. HLQ (49:4) 357–84.

Kofi Awoonor

11107. MOODY, H. L. B.   Kofi Awoonor, *This Earth, My Brother*: a critical view. Ed. by YOLANDE CANTU. London: Collins; British Council, 1985. pp. 56. (Nexus.)

Alan Ayckbourn

11108. BARTSCH, UTA.   Alan Ayckbourns Dramenfiguren. Charakterisierung und Charakteristika. Hildesheim; Zürich; New York: Olms. pp. 296. (Anglistische und amerikanistische Texte und Studien, 1.)

11109. DUKORE, BERNARD F.   Craft, character, comedy: Ayckbourn's *Women in Mind.* TCL (32:1) 23–39.

Irving Babbitt

11110. NEVIN, THOMAS R.   Irving Babbitt: an intellectual study. (Bibl. 1985, 9788.) Rev. by Anthony Netboy in VQR (62) 355–9.

Enid Bagnold

11111. SEBBA, ANNE.   Enid Bagnold: the authorized biography. London: Weidenfeld & Nicolson. pp. xii, 317. Rev. by Nigel Williams in Listener, 13 Nov., 26; by Ann Chisholm in TLS, 26 Dec., 1442.

Alfred Goldsworthy Bailey

11112. LANE, M. TRAVIS.   An interview with Alfred Goldsworthy Bailey. StudCanL (11:2) 226–45.

11113. —— A sense of the medium: the poetry of A. G. Bailey. CanP (19) 1–10.

Beryl Bainbridge

11114. VALVERDE, GLORIA ANN DUARTE.   A textual study of Beryl Bainbridge's *Another Part of the Wood* and *A Weekend with Claude*. Unpub. doct. diss., Texas Tech Univ., 1985. 2 vols. [Abstr. in DA (47) 527A.]

Irene Baird

11115. HOPKINS, ANTHONY.   Thematic structure and vision in *Waste Heritage*. StudCanL (11:1) 77–85.

James Baldwin

11116. BALDWIN, JAMES.   The price of the ticket: collected non-fiction 1948–1985. London: Joseph, 1985. pp. xx, 690. Rev. by Tony Tanner in TLS, 24 Jan., 75–6; by Christopher Bigsby in THES (710) 16.

11117. BOBIA, ROSA.   L'ornière de James Baldwin en France. TM (42:485) 207–13.

11118. BOBIA, ROSA MAE WILLIAMSON.   James Baldwin and his francophone critics: an analysis and annotated bibliography (1952–1981). Unpub. doct. diss., Vanderbilt Univ., 1984. [Abstr. in DA (46) 2287A.]

11119. ESTES, DAVID C.   An interview with James Baldwin. NOR (13:3) 59–64.

11120. HARRIS, TRUDIER.   Black women in the fiction of James Baldwin. Knoxville: Tennessee UP, 1985. pp. viii, 229. Rev. by Charles Scruggs in AL (58:2) 293–5.

11121. LEEMING, DAVID ADAMS.   An interview with James Baldwin on Henry James. *See* **8697.**

Amiri Baraka (LeRoi Jones)

11122. LEVESQUE, GEORGE A.   LeRoi Jones' *Dutchman*: myth and allegory. Ob (5) Winter 1979, 33–40.

11123. WERNER, CRAIG.   Brer Rabbit meets the underground man: simplification of consciousness in Baraka's *Dutchman* and *Slave Ship*. Ob (5) Spring/Summer 1979, 35–40.

Owen Barfield

11124. HUNTER, JEANNE CLAYTON.   Owen Barfield: Christian apologist. Ren (36) 171–9.

Maurice Baring

11125. LETLEY, EMMA (introd.).   C. Oxford: OUP. pp. 784. (Twentieth-century classics.)

George Barker

11126. FRASER, R. H.   George Barker and the English poets: the minor bird on the bough. Unpub. doct. diss., Univ. of London (Royal Holloway Coll.), 1984.

J. M. Barrie

11127. GRIFFITH, JOHN.   Making wishes innocent: *Peter Pan*. LU (3:1) 1979, 28–37.

Iris Barry

11128. MEYERS, JEFFREY.   New light on Iris Barry. Paideuma (13:2) 1984, 285–9.

Philip Barry

11129. GILD, DAVID CARL.   An historical and critical study of the serious plays of Philip Barry. Unpub. doct. diss., Yale Univ., 1969. [Abstr. in DA (47) 2156A.]

John Barth

11130. CURWIN, JOYCE BETH.   'If only roads did end': the journey motif in the works of John Barth. Unpub. doct. diss., New York Univ., 1985. [Abstr. in DA (46) 2292A.]

11131. GARCÍA DÍEZ, ENRIQUE.   Pass me the 'boina': a conversation with John Barth. Atlantis (8) 103–8.

11132. GLADSKY, THOMAS S.   Good neighbours: history and fiction in John Barth's *The Sot-Weed Factor*. CLIO (14:3) 1985, 259–68.

11133. GUZLOWSKI, JOHN Z.   No more sea changes: four American novelists' responses to the sea. *In* (pp. 232–43) **28.**

11134. KENNEDY, COLLEEN STEPHANIE.   Footnotes and prefaces: ruses of authority in the postmodern fiction of Vladimir Nabokov and John Barth. Unpub. doct. diss., Univ. of California, Irvine. [Abstr. in DA (47) 1324A.]

11135. KIM, SUNG-GON.   Journey into the past: the historical and mystical imagination of Barth and Pynchon. Seoul: Seoul National UP, 1985.

11136. LAMPKIN, FRANCES LORETTA MURRELL.   Metaphor, motif, and the moment: form and human relationships in Laurence Sterne's *Tristram Shandy*, James Joyce's *Ulysses*, and John Barth's *Lost in the Funhouse. See* **6846.**

11137. LE REBELLER-MOUYEN, ANNIE.   Les mots et les choses ou les paradoxes du collectionneur dans *The Floating Opera* de John Barth. Fabula (Villeneuve d'Ascq) (6) 1985, 139–50.

11138. PFOFF, CHERYL KAY.   Love and art: the development of twin values in the fiction of John Barth. Unpub. doct. diss., Univ. of California, Los Angeles, 1985. [Abstr. in DA (46) 3720A.]

11139. PRUVOT, MONIQUE.   *The Floating Opera* de John Barth: le bateau-livre. EA (39:1) 62–77.

11140. RUCH, EDWARD DELAFIELD.   Techniques of self-reference in selected novels of Beckett, Nabokov, Vonnegut, and Barth. VNRN (5) 1980, 17–18.

11141. SHIPE, TIMOTHY.   Life/story: autobiographical modes in the fiction of Nabokov, Barth, and Frisch. VNRN (6) 1981, 41–3.

11142. SONG, CHANG-HO.   *The Floating Opera* e natanan ingan jonjae eui juje. (Human existence in *The Floating Opera*.) JELL (32:3) 521–44.

Donald Barthelme

11143. EVANS, WALTER.   Comanches and civilization in Donald Barthelme's *The Indian Uprising*. AQ (42:1) 45–52.

11144. HERRSCHER, WALTER.   Names in Donald Barthelme's short stories. *See* **1667**.

11145. STANLEY, DONALD HUTTON.   The self-conscious narrator in Donald Barthelme and Vladimir Nabokov. VNRN (5) 1980, 12–14.

11146. STENGEL, WAYNE B.   The shape of art in the short stories of Donald Barthelme. Baton Rouge: Louisiana State UP, 1985. pp. ix, 227. Rev. by Larry McCaffery in AL (58:3) 461–3; by William B. Warde, Jr, in SCR (3:2) 117–18.

Nancy Bauer

11147. KEEFER, JANICE KULYK.   Recent Maritime fiction: women and words. *See* **9777**.

Frank Baum

11148. EYLES, ALLEN.   The world of Oz. Harmondsworth: Viking Press, 1985. pp. 96.

11149. HEARN, MICHAEL PATRICK.   Discovering Oz (the great and terrible) at the Library of Congress. QJLC (39:2) 1982, 70–9.

James K. Baxter

11150. BAXTER, JAMES K. (postscr.).   Horse. Auckland; Oxford: OUP, 1985. pp. 125. (New Zealand classics.) Rev. by Trixie Te Arama Menzies in Landfall (40:4) 515–17; by Bill Manhire in NZList, 10 May, 45.

11151. SIMPSON, PETER.   'The trick of standing upright': Allen Curnow and James K. Baxter. WLWE (26:2) 369–78.

Barbara Baynton

11152. KRIMMER, SALLY; LAWSON, ALAN (eds).   Barbara Baynton. St Lucia: Queensland UP; Hemel Hempstead: Prentice-Hall, 1980. pp. xxxiii, 340. (Portable Australian authors.)

'BB' (D. J. Watkins-Pitchford)

11153. CROUCH, MARCUS.   'BB' at eighty. Junior Bookshelf (49) 165–8.

Julian Beck

11154. GELBER, JACK.   Julian Beck, businessman. TDR (30:2) 6–29.

Samuel Beckett

11155. ARMSTRONG, GORDON.   Symbols, signs, and language: the brothers Yeats and Samuel Beckett's art of the theater. CompDr (20:1) 38–53.

11156. ASTRO, ALAN MICHAEL.   Writing in tongues: translation in Beckett and other modern writers. *See* **10639**.

11157. BARGE, LAURA INEZ DEAVENPORT.   God, the quest, the hero: thematic structures in Beckett's fiction. Unpub. doct. diss., Univ. of Alabama, 1985. [Abstr. in DA (47) 1317A.]

11158–9. Entries cancelled.

11160. BEJA, MORRIS; GONTARSKI, S. E.; ASTIER, PIERRE. Samuel Beckett: humanistic perspectives. (Bibl. 1983, 10384.) Rev. by Germaine Brée in TS (30) 1983/84, 66–8.

11161. BEN-ZVI, LINDA. Samuel Beckett. London: Macmillan; Boston, MA: G. K. Hall. pp. 230. (Twayne's English authors, 423.) Rev. by Alan Jenkins in TLS, 14 Nov., 1281–2; by John Fletcher in THES (734) 20.

11162. —— Samuel Beckett's media plays. ModDr (28:1) 1985, 22–37.

11163. BRATER, ENOCH. Beckett at 80/Beckett in context. New York: OUP. pp. x, 238. Rev. by Alan Jenkins in TLS, 14 Nov., 1281–2.

11164. BREUER, ROLF; GUNDEL, HAROLD; HUBER, WERNER (eds). Beckett criticism in German: a bibliography. Munich: Fink. pp. 85. Rev. by J. C. C. Mays in IUR (16) 240–3.

11165. BUTLER, LANCE ST JOHN. Samuel Beckett and the meaning of being: a study in ontological parable. (Bibl. 1985, 9870.) Rev. by Felicity Horne in UES (24:1) 50–1.

11166. CALDER, JOHN (ed.). As no other dare fail: for Samuel Beckett on his 80th birthday by his friends and admirers. London: Calder; New York: Riverrun Press. pp. 135. Rev. by Alan Jenkins in TLS, 14 Nov., 1281–2.

11167. CALDERWOOD, JAMES L. Ways of waiting in *Waiting for Godot*. ModDr (29:3) 363–75.

11168. CHABERT, PIERRE (ed.). Samuel Beckett. Toulouse: Privat. pp. 336. (Special no. of *Revue d'Esthétique*.)

11169. DERRICK, PAUL SCOTT. The man behind the trilogy: revealing the voice of the void. RCEI (12) 97–111.

11170. DOBREZ, L. A. C. The existential and its exits: literary and philosophical perspectives on the work of Beckett, Ionesco, Genet, and Pinter. London: Athlone Press. pp. 392.

11171. ELLMANN, RICHARD. Four Dubliners: Wilde, Yeats, Joyce, and Beckett. *See* **9546.**

11172. —— Nayman of Noland. NYRB (33:7), 27–37.

11173. —— Samuel Beckett: Nayman of Noland. Washington DC: Library of Congress. pp. 31. Rev. by Alan Jenkins in TLS, 14 Nov., 1281–2.

11174. FISCHER-SEIDEL, THERESE. Mythenparodie im modernen englischen und amerikanischen Drama. Tradition und Kommunikation bei Tennessee Williams, Edward Albee, Samuel Beckett und Harold Pinter. *See* **11011.**

11175. GAUTAM, KRIPA K.; SHARMA, MANJULA. Dialogue in *Waiting for Godot* and Grice's concept of implicature. ModDr (29:4) 580–6.

11176. GIANNOTTI, THOMAS JOHN, JR. A language of silence: writing the self in Yeats and Synge, Joyce and Beckett. Unpub. doct. diss., Univ. of California, Riverside, 1985. [Abstr. in DA (46) 3725A.]

11177. GIBSON, ANDREW.   One kind of ambiguity in Joyce, Beckett and Robbe-Grillet. CanRCL (12:3) 1985, 409–21.

11178. GONTARSKI, S. E.   Company for *Company*: androgyny and theatricality in Samuel Beckett's prose. RCEI (12) 89–96.

11179. —— The intent of *undoing* in Samuel Beckett's dramatic texts. Bloomington: Indiana UP, 1985. pp. 221. Rev. by Edward Lense in OhioanaQ (29:2) 79.

11180. HAY, MALCOLM.   Happy birthday Beckett. Plays and Players (393) June, 5–6. (The radio plays.)

11181. HENNING, SYLVIE DEBEVEC.   Samuel Beckett's *Fin de partie*: variations on the hermeneutic theme. Boundary 2 (13:2/3) 1985, 371–91.

11182. HOMAN, SIDNEY.   Beckett's theaters: interpretations for performance. (Bibl. 1985, 9890.) Rev. by H. Porter Abbott in JEGP (85:4) 598–600.

11183. HRYNIEWICZ, EWA.   *Waiting for Godot*: Beckett's homo ludens. AQ (42:3) 261–70.

11184. HUTCHINGS, WILLIAM.   Abated drama: Samuel Beckett's *Breath*. Ariel (17:1) 85–94.

11185. JÖKULSSON, ILLUGI.   Nóbelshöfundurinn Samuel Beckett áttræður. Bráðum á að dimma. (The Nobel Prize author Samuel Beckett eighty years old. Darkness will soon come.) Morgunblaðið (73:102) B 28–9.

11186. JONES, K.   Schopenhauer and Beckett's *Proust*. Études irlandaises (11) 71–81.

11187. KENNER, HUGH.   Samuel Beckett: putting language in its place. NYTB, 13 Apr., 3.

11188. KNOWLSON, JAMES (ed.).   *Happy Days*: the production note-book of Samuel Beckett. London: Faber & Faber, 1985. pp. 206. (Facsims.)

11189. KRAMER, MIMI.   Stalemate in Cambridge. NCrit (3:6) 1985, 52–61. (American Repertory Theatre's performance of *Endgame*.)

11190. KREUTER, KATHERINE E.   Self and no-self: a psychoanalytical study of Beckettian man from *Murphy* to *How It Is*. PCL (12) 35–42.

11191. LIBERA, ANTONI.   Beckett's catastrophe! ModDr (28:3) 1985, 341–7.

11192. O'BRIEN, EOIN; KNOWLSON, JAMES.   The Beckett country: an exhibition for Samuel Beckett's 80th birthday. New York: Black Cat. pp. 97. Rev. by Patrick Parrinder in LRB (8:13) 16–17.

11193. O'DAIR, SHARON K.   'The contentless passion of an unfruitful wind': irony and laughter in *Endgame*. Criticism (28:2) 165–78.

11194. O'DONOVAN, PATRICK.   Beckett's monologues: the context and conditions of representation. MLR (81:2) 318–26.

11195. O'NEILL, KEVIN CHARLES.   The voyage from Dante to Beckett. Unpub. doct. diss., Univ. of California, Berkeley, 1985. [Abstr. in DA (46) 2709A.]

11196. PAINE, SYLVIA JEAN.   Sense and transcendence: the art of

Anaïs Nin, Vladimir Nabokov, and Samuel Beckett. VNRN (5) 1980, 15–16.

11197. RABATÉ, JEAN-MICHEL. Berkeley entre Joyce et Beckett. *See* **6211.**

11198. RABINOVITZ, RUBIN. The development of Samuel Beckett's fiction. (Bibl. 1985, 9906.) Rev. by John Pilling in NQ (33:2) 272–3.

11199. RUCH, EDWARD DELAFIELD. Techniques of self-reference in selected novels of Beckett, Nabokov, Vonnegut, and Barth. *See* **11140.**

11200. SHERINGHAM, MICHAEL. Beckett, *Molloy*. London: Grant & Cutler, 1985. pp. 88. (Critical guides to French texts, 48.) Rev. by Alan Jenkins in TLS, 14 Nov., 1281–2.

11201. STRICKLAND, GEOFFREY. The seriousness of Samuel Beckett. CamQ (15) 13–32.

11202. THOMAS, RONALD R. In the company of strangers: absent voices in Stevenson's *Dr Jekyll and Mr Hyde* and Beckett's *Company*. *See* **9274.**

11203. VAN LAAN, THOMAS F. *All That Falls* as a play for radio. ModDr (28:1) 1985, 38–47.

11204. WARGER, THOMAS A. Going mad systematically in Beckett's *Murphy*. MLS (16:2) 13–18.

11205. WATTS, EILEEN H. The language of doubt: post-Cartesian rationalism and the language of Beckett's novels. Unpub. doct. diss., Bryn Mawr College. [Abstr. in DA (47) 1724A–5A.]

John Beecher

11206. ADAMS, FRANK. John Beecher: a political poet. SE (9:2) 1981, 104–7.

11207. HELTEN, JAMES ALFRED. 'Do what the spirit say do': John Beecher and his poetry. Unpub. doct. diss., Univ. of North Dakota, 1985. [Abstr. in DA (47) 178A.]

Sir Max Beerbohm

11208. CAESAR, TERRY. Betrayal and theft: Beerbohm, parody, and modernism. Ariel (17:3) 23–37.

11209. HART-DAVIS, RUPERT (ed.). Letters to Max Beerbohm: with a few answers. London: Faber & Faber. pp. 114. (Letters from Siegfried Sassoon.)

Brendan Behan

11210. WITOSZEK, WALENTYNA. The funeral comedy of Brendan Behan. Études irlandaises (11) 83–91.

Frances Bellerby

11211. STEVENSON, ANNE (ed.). Selected poems. Biographical introd. by ROBERT GITTINGS. London: Enitharmon. pp. 178.

Hilaire Belloc

11212. PICKERING, SAM. Images and letters. SewR (94:2) 284–8 (review-article).

11213. REZNOWSKI, LORNE A. The 'Chesterbelloc' and Ezra Pound. Paideuma (13) 1984, 291–5.

Saul Bellow

11214. ALTER, ROBERT. Kafka's father, Agnon's mother, Bellow's cousins. Commentary (81:2) 46–52.

11215. ANDERSON, DAVID D.   Mark Twain, Sherwood Anderson, Saul Bellow, and the territories of the spirit. *See* **9427.**

11216. BAKKER, J.   Fiction as survival strategy: a comparative study of the major works of Ernest Hemingway and Saul Bellow. (Bibl. 1984, 10116.) Rev. by Hans Bertens in DQR (16:1) 77–80.

11217. BERGER, ALAN L.   Holocaust survivors and children in *Anya* and *Mr Sammler's Planet*. MLS (16:1) 81–7.

11218. DUTTON, ROBERT R.   Saul Bellow. Boston, MA: G. K. Hall, 1982. pp. xiv, 212. (Twayne's US authors, 181.) (Second ed.: first ed. 1971.) Rev. by Judie Newman in YES (16) 356–8.

11219. EHRLICH, REVA.   A study of Jewish literary identity in contemporary writers in America: a curriculum. Unpub. doct. diss., St. John's Univ., 1985. [Abstr. in DA (46) 3716A.]

11220. FOX, FRANCIS PATRICK.   Saul Bellow's city fiction. Unpub. doct. diss., Univ. of Pennsylvania. [Abstr. in DA (47) 1322A.]

11221. GLENDAY, M. K.   The modification of reality in the novels of Saul Bellow. Unpub. doct. diss., Univ. of Kent, 1985. [Abstr. in IT (36) 476.]

11222. GOLDMAN, L. H.   The Holocaust in the novels of Saul Bellow. MLS (16:1) 71–80.

11223. GUIEU, YVES.   Le machiavel et le mystique, ou les deux avatars du héros de Saul Bellow. EA (39:4) 444–50.

11224. IGNATIEFF, MICHAEL.   Our valuation of human life has become thinner. *See* **11031.**

11225. KIM, KYE-MIN.   Saul Bellow eui soseol e natanan reality instructor wa saviors e gwanhan bunsuk(II). (Observation and analysis of the advice and the lessons of 'reality instructors' and saviours in Saul Bellow's novels (II).) UJH (28) Dec., 1985, 103–30.

11226. LÉVY, CLAUDE.   Les romans de Saul Bellow: techniques narratives et stratégies œdipiennes. Paris: Klincksieck, 1983. pp. 262. (Cf. bibl. 1983, 10445, where pagination incorrect.) Rev. by Peter Wagner in EA (38:3) 1985, 359–60.

11227. MARCUS, STEVEN.   Reading the illegible: modern representations of urban experience. SoR (22:3) 443–65.

11228. PRICE, NANCY LAINE.   The serious self in a rhetorical world: affirmative ambiguity toward language in six novels of Saul Bellow. Unpub. doct. diss., Texas Christian Univ., 1985. [Abstr. in DA (46) 3353A.]

11229. WILSON, JONATHAN.   On Bellow's planet: readings from the dark side. Rutherford, NJ: Fairleigh Dickinson UP; London: Assoc. UPs, 1985. pp. 193. Rev. by Shaun O'Connell in AL (58:4) 663–4.

11230. YANG, KYOUNG-ZOO.   Saul Bellow eui soseol e natanan sowae yangsang. (Aspects of alienation in Saul Bellow's novels.) JUJH (22) 123–40.

11231. YETMAN, MICHAEL G.   Toward a language irresistible: Saul Bellow and the romance of poetry. PLL (22:4) 429–47.

Arnold Bennett

11232. BLAYAC, ALAIN. *The Lion's Share*, essai sur le réalisme d'Arnold Bennett. CVE (24) 47–61.

11233. DENJEAN, ALBERT. Analyse du discours réaliste dans les romans des cinq villes d'Arnold Bennett. CVE (24) 7–29.

11234. HEPBURN, JAMES (ed.). Letters of Arnold Bennett: vol. 4, Family letters. Oxford: OUP. pp. xxxviii, 638. Rev. by Sandra Kemp in THES (724) 20.

11235. LUCAS, JOHN. The marriage question and *Whom the Lord Hath Joined*. CVE (24) 31–45.

11236. McDONOUGH, MICHAEL JOHN. Arnold Bennett and Archibald Marshall: two letters from a forgotten literary friendship. ELT (29:4) 371–7.

11237. SIMPSON, ANNE B. Forster and the Edwardians: the literature of domestic failure. Unpub. doct. diss., City Univ. of New York, 1985. [Abstr. in DA (46) 3363A.]

Paul Lewis Bennett

11238. OSTER, BETSY. Paul Lewis Bennett. OhioanaQ (29:3) 121.

E. F. Benson

11239. BINYON, T. J. (introd.). As we are: a modern revue. London: Hogarth Press, 1985. pp. 307. (Hogarth fiction.)

11240. —— (introd.). As we were: a Victorian peep-show. London: Hogarth Press, 1985. pp. 355.

11241. HAWTREE, CHRISTOPHER (introd.). The freaks of Mayfair. London: Hogarth Press. pp. 256.

11242. KNIGHT, STEPHEN (introd.). The luck of the Vails. London: Hogarth Press. pp. 320. (Gaslight crime.)

11243. REAVELL, CYNTHIA (ed.). The tale of an empty house: and other ghost stories. Introd. by SUSAN HILL. London: Black Swan. pp. 231.

11244. SCALES, PRUNELLA (introd.). Dodo: an omnibus. London: Hogarth Press. pp. 532.

Thomas Berger

11245. SWEET-HURD, EVELYN CAROL. The roles of language in selected novels of Thomas Berger. Unpub. doct. diss., Baylor Univ., 1985. [Abstr. in DA (46) 3036A.]

11246. WALLACE, JON BERKLEY. The politics of style in fiction by Thomas Berger, Thomas McGuane and James Alan McPherson. Unpub. doct. diss., Univ. of Iowa, 1985. [Abstr. in DA (47) 902A.]

Alexander Berkman

11247. DEUTELBAUM, WENDY. Epistolary politics: the correspondence of Emma Goldman and Alexander Berkman. Prose Studies (9:1) 30–46.

Robert Berold

11248. GARDNER, SUSAN. Four South African poets: interviews with Robert Berold, Jeremy Cronin, Douglas Reid Skinner, Stephen Watson. Grahamstown: National English Literary Museum. pp. 71. (NELM interviews, 1.)

Wendell Berry

11249. CORNELL, DANIEL T. Practicing resurrection: Wendell Berry's georgic poetry, an ecological critique of American culture. Unpub. doct. diss., Washington State Univ., 1985. [Abstr. in DA (47) 951A.]

John Berryman

11250. BLOOM, JAMES D. The stock of available reality: R. P. Blackmur and John Berryman. Lewisburg, PA: Bucknell UP; London: Assoc. UPs, 1984. pp. vii, 216. (Cf. bibl. 1982, 10528.) Rev. by Bernard Duffy in SAQ (85:2) 204–5.

11251. GUSTAVSSON, BO. Dödsdriften som musa: om John Berrymans *Drömsångerna*. (Desire for death as the poet's Muse: on John Berryman's *Dream Songs*.) BLM (55) 250–2.

Alfred Bester

11252. WINGROVE, DAVID (introd.). Tiger! Tiger! Wendover: Goodchild, 1984. pp. 248. (SF alternatives.)

Ursula Bethell

11253. O'SULLIVAN, VINCENT (ed.). Collected poems. Oxford: OUP, 1985. (Cf. bibl. 1985, 9972.) Rev. by Fleur Adcock in NZList, 24 May, 54–6.

Sir John Betjeman

11254. HULSE, MICHAEL. The laureate business or the laureateship of Englishness. Quadrant (29:9) 1985, 45–9.

11255. KILMISTER, ANTHONY; LENOX, DONALD (eds). My favourite Betjeman: a selection of his poems by a selection of admirers. London: Lanthorn, 1985. pp. 51.

11256. RUDDICK, BILL. 'Some ruin-bibber, randy for antique': Philip Larkin's response to the poetry of John Betjeman. CritQ (28:4) 63–9.

11257. THWAITE, ANTHONY, et al. The teddy bear and the critics. Listener (113) 23 May 1985, 20–1.

Earle Birney

11258. AICHINGER, PETER. Earle Birney. *In* (pp. 27–71) 9.

Elizabeth Bishop

11259. CARLSON-BRADLEY, MARTHA ANN. Affinities in the poetry of Robert Lowell and Elizabeth Bishop. Unpub. doct. diss., Univ. of North Carolina at Chapel Hill, 1985. [Abstr. in DA (47) 176A.]

11260. CORN, ALFRED. Elizabeth Bishop's nativities. Shen (36:3) 21–46.

11261. LEITHAUSER, BRAD. The 'complete' Elizabeth Bishop. NCrit (1) Mar. 1983, 36–42.

11262. MILLIER, BRETT CANDLISH. Elizabeth Bishop: life and the memory of it. Unpub. doct. diss., Stanford Univ. [Abstr. in DA (47) 2160A.]

John Peale Bishop

11263. YOUNG, THOMAS DANIEL; HINDLE, JOHN J. (eds). The republic of letters in America: the correspondence of John Peale Bishop and Allen Tate. (Bibl. 1985, 9985.) Rev. by Daniel Aaron in YES (16) 350–2.

bill bissett

11264. HILMO, MAIDIE. Interview with bill bissett. ECanW (32) 134–46.

Douglas Blackburn

11265. RICE, MICHAEL. Douglas Blackburn's *A Burgher Quixote*. Kp (8:1) 70–86.

Paul Blackburn

11266. JAROLIM, EDITH (ed.). The collected poems of Paul Blackburn. New York: Persea, 1985. pp. xxxv, 687. (Cf. bibl. 1985, 9987.) Rev. by Paul Christensen in BkW, 5 Jan., 6.

R. P. Blackmur

11267. SAID, EDWARD W. The horizon of R. P. Blackmur. Raritan (6:2) 29–50.

Clark Blaise

11268. CAMERON, BARRY. Clark Blaise. *In* (pp. 21–89) **8.**

11269. LECKER, ROBERT. 'The other side of things': notes on Clark Blaise's *Notes Beyond a History*. CanL (111) 117–27.

Edward Blishen

11270. BLISHEN, EDWARD. The outside contributor. London: Hamilton. pp. 229.

Eliot Bliss

11271. BAILEY, PAUL (introd.). Saraband. London: Virago Press. pp. 316. (Virago modern classics.)

Robert Bloch

11272. COMPÈRE, DANIEL. Alice au pays des maléfices. Europe (62:664/65) 1984, 99–104.

11273. GUÉRIF, FRANÇOIS. Robert Bloch: du noir gothique au noir polar. Europe (62:664/65) 1984, 105–8.

Robert Bly

11274. DAVIS, WILLIAM V. 'In a low voice to someone he is sure is listening': Robert Bly's recent poems in prose. MidQ (25) 1984, 148–56.

11275. ROBERSON, WILLIAM H. Robert Bly: a primary and secondary bibliography. Metuchen, NJ; London: Scarecrow Press. pp. xxiii, 391. (Scarecrow author bibliographies, 75.)

Capel Boake

11276. DOWNER, CHRISTINE (introd.). Painted clay. London: Virago Press. pp. xiii, 343. (Virago modern classics, 231.)

Louise Bogan

11277. FRANK, ELIZABETH. Louise Bogan: a portrait. (Bibl. 1985, 9998.) Rev. by James E. B. Breslin in AL (58:1) 121–2.

11278. WILSON, ROBERT A. Louise Bogan: a bibliographical checklist. ABC (7:9) 31–6.

Edward Bond

11279. BULMAN, JAMES C. Bond, Shakespeare, and the absurd. *See* **4403.**

11280. CARDULLO, BERT. Bond's *Saved*. Exp (44:3) 62–4.

11281. CASTILLO, DEBRA A. Dehumanized or inhuman: doubles in Edward Bond. SCR (3:2) 78–89.

11282. CHOI, YOUNG.   Edward Bond's *Lear*: a modern Shakespeare offshoot. *See* **4826.**

11283. HIRST, DAVID L.   Edward Bond. London: Macmillan, 1985. pp. v, 165. (Macmillan modern dramatists.)

11284. ZAPF, HUBERT.   Gesellschaftsbegriff und dramatische Struktur in Edward Bonds *Lear*. Archiv (222:2) 1985, 306–20.

Herman Charles Bosman

11285. GRAY, STEPHEN (ed.).   Bosman's Johannesburg. Cape Town: Human & Rousseau. pp. 152.

11286. —— Herman Charles Bosman. Johannesburg: McGraw–Hill. pp. v, 204. (Southern African literature, 6.)

Vance Bourjaily

11287. FRANCIS, WILLIAM A.   A conversation about names with novelist Vance Bourjaily. *See* **1659.**

Elizabeth Bowen

11288. CRAIG, PATRICIA.   Elizabeth Bowen. Harmondsworth: Penguin. pp. 142. (Lives of modern women.)

11289. CRAMP, A.   Prose fiction in the 1930s: a study of Elizabeth Bowen, Rex Warner and Patrick Hamilton. Unpub. doct. diss., Univ. of Loughborough, 1985. [Abstr. in IT (35) 51.]

11290. HALPERIN, JOHN.   Elizabeth Bowen and Henry James. *See* **8681.**

11291. HAULE, JAMES M.   *She* and the moral dilemma of Elizabeth Bowen. *See* **8373.**

11292. LASSNER, PHYLLIS.   The past is a burning pattern: Elizabeth Bowen's *The Last September*. Éire–Ireland (21:1) 40–54.

11293. LEE, HERMIONE.   Elizabeth Bowen: an estimation. (Bibl. 1983, 10534.) Rev. by Jay L. Halio in MLR (81:1) 191–2.

11294. —— (ed.).   The mulberry tree: writings of Elizabeth Bowen. London: Virago Press. pp. 325. Rev. by Patricia Craig in TLS, 17 Oct., 1152.

11295. SULLIVAN, RITA MARIE.   The four corners of fiction: adolescent sensibility in the novels of Elizabeth Bowen and Rosamond Lehmann. Unpub. doct. diss., Brown Univ., 1985. [Abstr. in DA (46) 1953A.]

11296. WHEELER, ANN MARIE.   Shape and shapelessness: the symbolic function of setting in the fiction of Elizabeth Bowen. Unpub. doct. diss., Vanderbilt Univ., 1984. [Abstr. in DA (46) 2305A.]

Paul Bowles

11297. BUTSCHER, EDWARD.   Paul Bowles as poet: excursions of a minimal anti-self. TCL (32: 3/4) 350–72.

11298. DAGEL, GENA EMILY.   Paul Bowles: manufactured savage. Unpub. doct. diss., Univ. of Texas at Austin, 1984. [Abstr. in DA (47) 2205A.]

11299. DITSKY, JOHN.   *The Time of Friendship*: the short fiction of Paul Bowles. TCL (32:3/4) 373–87.

11300. GRABHER, GUDRUN M.   Existenzverlust durch den Tod des Anderen: ein Approach zu Paul Bowles' *The Sheltering Sky*. *In* (pp. 9–24)

RITA G. FISCHER (ed.). Beiträge zu den Sprach- und Literaturwissenschaften. Frankfurt: Fischer. pp. 78.

11301. HAMOVITCH, MITZI BERGER. Release from torment: the fragmented double in Bowles's *Let It Come Down*. TCL (32:3/4) 440–50.

11302. HIBBARD, ALLEN E. Expatriation and narration in two works by Paul Bowles. PhilP (32) 61–71.

11303. LESSER, WENDY. Murder as social impropriety: Paul Bowles's evil heroes. TCL (32:3/4) 402–7.

11304. MOSS, MARILYN. The child in the text: autobiography, fiction, and the aesthetics of deception in *Without Stopping*. TCL (32:3/4) 314–33.

11305. OLSON, STEVEN E. Alien terrain: Paul Bowles's filial landscapes. TCL (32:3/4) 334–49.

11306. POUNDS, WAYNE. Paul Bowles and Edgar Allan Poe: the disintegration of the personality. *See* **9083.**

11307. —— The subject of Paul Bowles. TCL (32:3/4) 301–13.

11308. WILLIAMS, MARCELLETTE G. 'Tea in the Sahara': the function of time in the work of Paul Bowles. TCL (32:3/4) 408–23. (*The Sheltering Sky*.)

Kay Boyle

11309. GRUMBACH, DORIS (postscr.). My next bride. London: Virago Press. pp. 330. (Virago modern classics, 226.)

11310. —— Year before last. London: Virago Press. pp. 329. (Virago modern classics, 225.)

David Bradley

11311. GLISERMAN, MARTIN. David Bradley's *The Chaneysville Incident*: the belly of the text. AI (43:2) 97–120.

11312. SADLER, LYNN VEACH. The black man's burden: the pursuit of non-conformity in David Bradley's *The Chaneysville Incident*. PhilP (32) 119–27.

Marion Zimmer Bradley

11313. ARBUR, ROSEMARIE. Marion Zimmer Bradley. Mercer Island, WA: Starmont House, 1985. pp. 138. Rev. by Edgar L. Chapman in SFS (13:3) 400–1.

11314. ROSS, MEREDITH JANE. The sublime to the ridiculous: the restructuring of Arthurian materials in selected modern novels. *See* **3655.**

Caryl Brahms

11315. SHERRIN, NED (ed.). Too dirty for the Windmill: a memoir of Caryl Brahms by Caryl Brahms and Ned Sherrin. London: Constable. pp. xvii, 286.

11316. —— (introd.). A bullet in the ballet. London: Hogarth Press. pp. 192.

11317. —— No bed for Bacon. London: Hogarth Press. pp. 288.

Ernest Bramah (Ernest Bramah Smith)

11318. LETHBRIDGE, H. J. (introd.). Kai Lung's golden hours. Hong Kong; Oxford: OUP, 1985. pp. xiii, 306. (Oxford paperbacks.)

11319. WHITE, WILLIAM. Ernest Bramah, Max Carrados, and *The News of the World. See* **724.**

Dionne Brand

11320. BRAITHWAITE, EDWARD KAMAU. Dionne Brand's *Winter Epigrams.* CanL (105) 1985, 18–30.

Charles Brasch

11321. GERAETS, JOHN. Kendrick Smithyman and Brasch's *Landfall. See* **603.**

Richard Brautigan

11322. GRIMAUD, ISABELLE. 'Stranger than paradise': *Dreaming of Babylon: a Private Eye Novel, 1942,* de Richard Brautigan. Caliban (23) 127–35.

11323. GROSSMAN, CLAUDIA. Richard Brautigan 'pounding at the gates of American literature'. Untersuchungen zu seiner Lyrik und Prosa. Heidelberg: Winter. pp. 262. (Reihe Siegen, Anglistische Abteilung, 66.)

11324. HORVATH, BROOKE KENTON. Dropping out: spiritual crisis and countercultural attitudes in four American novelists of the 1960s. Unpub. doct. diss., Purdue Univ. [Abstr. in DA (47) 2157A.]

11325. SWEATT, SUZANNE MITCHELL. Postmodernism in the fiction of Richard Brautigan. Unpub. doct. diss., Middle Tennessee State Univ., 1985. [Abstr. in DA (46) 2690A.]

Christopher Brennan

11326. STURM, TERRY. Christopher Brennan. St Lucia: Queensland UP, 1984. pp. xxxii, 477. (Portable Australian authors.) Rev. by J. J. O'Carroll in AUMLA (65) 119–22.

Howard Brenton

11327. CARDULLO, BERT. Three notes on drama. *See* **4925.**

11328. SOTO-MORETTINI, DONNA. Disrupting of the spectacle: Brenton's *Magnificence.* TJ (38:1) 82–95.

Breyten Breytenbach

11329. ROBERTS, SHEILA. Breyten Breytenbach's prison literature. CR (30:2) 304–13.

Robert Bridges

11330. HASAN, IQBAL. Robert Bridges: a critical study of his poetry, masques and plays. (Bibl. 1985, 10032.) Rev. by Jean-Georges Ritz in EA (38:4) 1985, 475–6.

Walter Brierley

11331. HOLDERNESS, GRAHAM. Miners and the novel: from bourgeois to proletarian fiction. *In* (pp. 18–32) **6.**

Raymond Briggs

11332. RAHN, SUZANNE. Beneath the surface with *Fungus the Bogeyman.* LU (7/8) 1983/84, 5–19.

Vera Brittain

11333. BISHOP, ALAN (ed.). Chronicle of friendship: diary of the thirties, 1932–1939. London: Gollancz. pp. 448.

11334. MELLOWN, MURIEL. Vera Brittain: feminist in a new age (1896–1970). *In* (pp. 314–34) **20.**

Bertram Brooker

11335. GRACE, SHERRILL E.   Another part in the Brooker quartette.
CanD (11) 1985, 251–3.

Christine Brooke-Rose

11336. PESTINO, JOSEPH FRANCIS.   The reader/writer affair: instigating repertoire in the experimental fiction of Susan Sontag, Walter
Abish, Réjean Ducharme, Paul West, and Christine Brooke-Rose.
See **10974.**

David Brooks

11337. PERKINS, ELIZABETH.   Metaphor and meaning in David
Brooks' *The Cold Front* and Andrew Lansdown's *Windfalls*. Linq (14:2)
35–47.

Gwendolyn Brooks

11338. GREASLEY, PHILIP A.   Gwendolyn Brooks's *Afrika*. Midamerica (13) 9–18.

Dee Brown

11339. HAGEN, LYMAN B.   Dee Alexander Brown. BB (43:3) 172–8.

E. K. Brown

11340. GROENING, LAURA JEANNE.   Art, vision, and process: the
literary criticism of E. K. Brown. *See* **10806.**

Fredric Brown

11341. COMPÈRE, DANIEL.   Alice au pays des maléfices. *See* **11272.**

George Mackay Brown

11342. ANNWN, DAVID.   Inhabited voices: myth and history in the
poetry of Geoffrey Hill, Seamus Heaney and George Mackay Brown.
(Bibl. 1985, 10049.) Rev. by Andrew Swarbrick in CritQ (28:3) 111.

11343. MURRAY, ROWENA E. G.   Style as voice: a reappraisal of
George Mackay Brown's prose. Unpub. doct. diss., Pennsylvania State
Univ. [Abstr. in DA (47) 1336A.]

Dennis Brutus

11344. OJAIDE, TANURE.   The troubador: the poet's persona in the
poetry of Dennis Brutus. Ariel (17:1) 55–69.

John Buchan

11345. McCLEERY, ALISTAIR.   John Buchan and the path of the keen.
ELT (29:3) 277–86.

Ernest Buckler

11346. BATTARBEE, KEITH.   Portraits of the artist as a young
Canadian. Pubs of the Dept of English, Univ. of Turku (7) 1985, 13–26.

Charles Bukowski

11347. COONEY, SEAMUS (ed.).   The Bukowski/Purdy letters, 1964–
74: a decade of dialogue. Sutton West, Ont.; Santa Barbara, CA: Paget,
1983. pp. 117. Rev. by Michael Peterman in ECanW (33) 181–4.

Anthony Burgess

11348. BURGESS, ANTHONY.   Homage to Qwert Yuiop. (Pub. in USA
as *But Do Blondes Prefer Gentlemen? Homage to Qwert Yuiop and Other
Writings.*) London: Hutchinson. pp. xiv, 589. Rev. by Robert Craft in
TLS, 6 June, 608; by Robertson Davies in BkW, 9 Mar., 1–2.

11349. COALE, SAMUEL. Anthony Burgess. (Bibl. 1983, 10592.) Rev. by Jay L. Halio in YES (16) 364–5.

11350. GHOSH-SCHELLHORN, MARTINA. Anthony Burgess: a study in character. Frankfurt: Lang. pp. 255. (European University studies: ser. 14, Anglo-Saxon language and literature, 155.)

11351. HELLER, ARNO. Anthony Burgess, *A Clockwork Orange* (1962). *In* (pp. 236–52) HARTMUT HEUERMANN (ed.), Der Science-Fiction Roman in der anglo-amerikanischen Literatur. Düsseldorf: Bagel. pp. 399.

11352. PORÉE, MARC. Le roman des derniers jours: Anthony Burgess, *The End of the World News*. *In* (pp. 273–92) **2.**

11353. SHISHKIN, A. Apostol massovoĭ belletristiki. (The apostle of popular fiction: notes on the work of Anthony Burgess.) VLit (1986:11) 113–32.

Kenneth Burke

11354. ELDER, DANA CRAIG. A Burkeian approach to D. H. Lawrence: perspectives on human motivation. Unpub. doct. diss., Washington State Univ., 1985. [Abstr. in DA (46) 3357A.]

11355. LEWIS, CLAYTON W. Identifications and divisions: Kenneth Burke and the Yale critics. SoR (22:1) 93–102.

11356. O'BANION, JOHN DAVID. Kenneth Burke and the recovery of narration: the dialectic of list and story. *See* **10884.**

11357. ROD, DAVID K. Kenneth Burke and Susanne K. Langer on drama and its audiences. *See* **10062.**

11358. —— Kenneth Burke and Susanne K. Langer: dramatic theorists. *See* **10063.**

11359. ROWAN, STEPHEN CHARLES. A dancing of attitudes: Burke's rhetoric on Shakespeare. *See* **4566.**

11360. WARNOCK, TILLY. Reading Kenneth Burke: ways in, ways out, ways roundabout. CE (48:1) 62–75.

W. R. Burnett

11361. DELOUX, JEAN-PIERRE. W. R. Burnett, D. H. Clarke: la loi des rues. Europe (62:664/65) 52–63.

William S. Burroughs

11362. BRYAN, JEFF. William Burroughs, and his faith in X. PhilP (32) 79–89.

11363. BURROUGHS, WILLIAM S. The adding machine: collected essays. London: Calder, 1985. pp. 201.

11364. SKERL, JENNIE. Ginsberg on Burroughs: an interview. MLS (16:3) 271–8.

11365. WILSON, TERRY. Here to go: planet R-101: Brian Gysin interviewed by Terry Wilson. Introd. and texts by WILLIAM S. BURROUGHS and BRIAN GYSIN. San Francisco, CA: Re/Search, 1982; London: Quartet, 1985. pp. xxii, 273.

Ron Butlin

11366. NICHOLSON, COLIN. 'Widdershins this life o mine': Ron Butlin's writing. Cencrastus (24) 34–40.

Alexander Buzo

11367. SIRMAI, GEOFFREY.   An interview with Alex Buzo. Southerly (46:1) 80–91.

Donn Byrne (Bernard Byrne, Brian Oswald Donn Byrne, Brian Donn-Byrne)

11368. BANNISTER, HENRY S.   Donn Byrne: a descriptive bibliography 1912–1935. New York; London: Garland, 1982. pp. xxvi, 311. Rev. by George Bixby in ABC (7:1) 47–50.

James Branch Cabell

11369. COLLINS, CARVEL.   Likeness within difference: Cabell and Faulkner. Kalki (8:4) 276–83.

11370. FLORA, JOSEPH M.   Cabell and Faulkner: connections literary and otherwise. Kalki (8:4) 271–5.

11371. JENKINS, WILLIAM D.   On keeping cool and keeping mum. Kalki (8:4) 305–6.

11372. SWOPE, ALLEN R.   The Cabell–Bailey correspondence: 1945–1949. Kalki (8:4) 293–300.

11373. TARRANT, DESMOND.   Cabell's journey to Antan. Kalki (8:4) 301–4.

11374. UMANSKY, HARLAN L.   Manuel as savior of Poictesme. Kalki (8:4) 284–90.

James M. Cain

11375. MADDEN, DAVID.   Cain's craft. Metuchen, NJ; London: Scarecrow Press, 1985. pp. xi, 162.

Erskine Caldwell

11376. THARPE, JAC.   Interview with Erskine Caldwell. SoQ (20:1) 1981, 64–74.

Morley Callaghan

11377. STAINES, DAVID (ed.).   The Callaghan symposium. (Bibl. 1984, 10308.) Rev. by Barbara Pell in JCF (35/36) 138–41.

Norman Cameron

11378. HOPE, WARREN THOMAS.   Norman Cameron's poems: a study of the contemporary plain style. Unpub. doct. diss., Temple Univ., 1985. [Abstr. in DA (46) 2300A.]

Roy Campbell

11379. ALEXANDER, PETER.   Roy Campbell: a critical biography. New York: OUP, 1982. (Cf. bibl. 1983, 10628.) Rev. by C. J. Rawson in YES (16) 360.

11380. CHAPMAN, MICHAEL.   Roy Campbell, poet: a defence in sociological times. Theoria (68) 79–93.

11381. RICHMAN, ROBERT.   The case of Roy Campbell. NCrit (2) Sept. 1983, 29–42.

Truman Capote

11382. BAWER, BRUCE.   Capote's children. NCrit (3:10) 1985, 39–44.

11383. BLADES, JOHN.   Capote still an enigma to his 'lost' friends. BW, 14 Dec., 3.

Peter Carey

11384. TURNER, GRAEME.   American dreaming: the fictions of Peter Carey. ALS (12:4) 431–41.

Bliss Carman

11385. McGillivray, Mary Beatrice.   Colour out of silence: a study of the poetry of Bliss Carman. Unpub. doct. diss., Queen's Univ. at Kingston, 1985. [Abstr. in DA (46) 2301A.]

Thomas Carnduff

11386. Gray, John.   Thomas Carnduff. Linen Hall Review (3:3) 18.

Emily Carr

11387. Kröller, Eva-Marie.   Literary versions of Emily Carr. CanL (109) 87–98.

Rachel Carson

11388. Gartner, Carol B.   Rachel Carson. New York: Ungar, 1983. pp. 161. Rev. by Joyce Wexler in MP (83:3) 330–3.

Catherine Carswell

11389. Carswell, John (introd.).   Open the door! London: Virago Press. pp. xviii, 400. (Virago modern classics, 201.) Rev. by Jean Ann Scott Miller in SLJ (supp. 25) 18–19.

Raymond Carver

11390. Bugeja, Michael J.   Tarnish and silver: an analysis of Carver's *Cathedral*. SDR (24:3) 73–87.

Joyce Cary

11391. Christian, Edwin Ernest.   Joyce Cary's major poems. Ariel (17:2) 33–46.
11392. Cook, Cornelia.   Joyce Cary: liberal principles. Totowa, NJ: Barnes & Noble, 1981. (Bibl. 1983, 10642.) Rev. by Jay L. Halio in MLR (81:1) 190–1.
11393. Fisher, Barbara.   The house as a symbol: Joyce Cary and 'the Turkish house'. Amsterdam: Rodopi. pp. 241. (Costerus, 55.)
11394. Makinen, M. A.   The faith and the plan: a study of the theme of social responsibility in the novels of Joyce Cary. Unpub. doct. diss., Univ. of London (Queen Mary Coll.), 1984.

Willa Cather

11395. Baker, Bruce.   From region to the world: two allusions in Cather's *A Lost Lady*. Midamerica (13) 61–8.
11396. Bender, Eileen T.   Pioneer or gadgeteer: Bergsonian metaphor in the work of Willa Cather. MidQ (28:1) 130–40.
11397. Busch, Beverley Gail.   The nature and extent of the influence of Sarah Orne Jewett on Willa Sibert Cather. *See* **8784.**
11398. Crane, John.   Willa Cather: a bibliography. (Bibl. 1983, 10652.) Rev. by Dean H. Keller in BB (43:1) 56–7.
11399. Dillman, Richard.   Tom Outland: Emerson's American scholar in *The Professor's House*. *See* **8273.**
11400. Epstein, Joseph.   Willa Cather: listing toward Lesbos. NCrit (2) Dec. 1983, 35–43.
11401. MacDonald, Phyllis Black.   The composed image: the house and the garden in the fiction of Willa Cather. Unpub. doct. diss., West Virginia Univ., 1985. [Abstr. in DA (47) 901A.]
11402. Mason, Julian.   An interesting Willa Cather letter. AL (58:1) 109–11.

11403. MIERENDORF, CONSTANCE C.	Southwest Indian art in Willa Cather's fiction. Unpub. doct. diss., Univ. of Nebraska–Lincoln, 1985. [Abstr. in DA (47) 179A.]

11404. NOVAK, FRANK G., JR.	Crisis and discovery in *The Professor's House*. CLQ (22:2) 119–32.

11405. O'BRIEN, SHARON.	Willa Cather: the emerging voice. New York: OUP. pp. 464. Rev. by Carolyn Heilbrun in NYTB, 14 Dec., 3.

11406. OEHLSCHLAEGER, FRITZ.	Willa Cather's *Consequences* and *Alexander's Bridge*: an approach through R. D. Laing and Ernest Becker. MFS (32:2) 191–202.

11407. PETRY, ALICE HALL.	Harvey's case: notes on Cather's *The Sculptor's Funeral*. SDR (24:3) 108–16.

11408. SHUBIK, VALERIE REID.	Willa Cather: an Emersonian angle of vision. *See* **8295.**

11409. STRYCHACZ, THOMAS F.	The ambiguities of escape in Willa Cather's *The Professor's House*. SAF (14:1) 49–61.

11410. VAN GASTEL, ADA L.	An unpublished poem by Willa Cather. RALS (14:1/2) 1984, 153–9.

11411. YUVAJITA, PHACHEE.	The changing images of women in Western American literature as illustrated in the works of Willa Cather, Hamlin Garland, and Mari Sandoz. Unpub. doct. diss., Univ. of Oregon, 1985. [Abstr. in DA (46) 3354A.]

'Christopher Caudwell' (Christopher St John Sprigg)

11412. DAS GUPTA, KALYAN.	Principles of literary evaluation in English Marxist criticism: Christopher Caudwell, Raymond Williams and Terry Eagleton. *See* **10759.**

11413. DUPARC, JEAN; MARGOLIES, DAVID (eds).	Scenes and actions: unpublished manuscripts. London: Routledge & Kegan Paul. pp. viii, 241.

11414. SULLIVAN, ROBERT JOHN.	Christopher Caudwell: one man in his time. Unpub. doct. diss., Brown Univ., 1985. [Abstr. in DA (46) 2702A.]

11415. YOUNG, ALAN (ed.).	Collected poems: 1924–1936. Manchester: Carcanet Press. pp. 180.

Raymond Chandler

11416. DEMOUZON, ALAIN.	Sur un air de paradoxe: à propos du polar noir, de Phil Marlowe et Ray Chandler. Europe (62:664/65) 1984, 30–8.

11417. LE PELLEC, YVES.	Marlowe narrateur, Chandler complice. Caliban (23) 95–110.

Sid Chaplin

11418. PICKERING, MICHAEL; ROBINS, KEVIN.	The making of a working-class writer: an interview with Sid Chaplin. *In* (pp. 138–50) **6.**

Fred Chappell

11419. LANG, JOHN.	Illuminating the stricken world: Fred Chappell's *Moments of Light*. SCR (3:4) 95–103.

James Hadley Chase

11420. SCHWEIGHAEUSER, JEAN-PAUL.	Le noir dévoyé: Cheyney et Chase. Europe (62:664/65) 1984, 63–6.

John Cheever

11421. BIDNEY, MARTIN. *The Common Day* and the Immortality Ode: Cheever's Wordsworthian craft. *See* **9573.**

11422. CHANEY, BEV, JR. John Cheever in Ossining. ABC (7:8) 21.

11423. —— BURTON, WILLIAM. John Cheever: a bibliographical checklist. ABC (ns 7:8) 22–31.

11424. CHEEVER, SUSAN. Home before dark. (Bibl. 1985, 10149.) Rev. by R. G. Collins in RALS (13:1) 1983, 33–40.

11425. HUNT, GEORGE W. John Cheever: the hobgoblin company of love. (Bibl. 1985, 10154.) Rev. by R. G. Collins in SAF (14:2) 237–9.

11426. VANCIL, DAVID EUGENE. The quest for the native self: the novels of John Cheever. Unpub. doct. diss., Univ. of Southwestern Louisiana, 1985. [Abstr. in DA (47) 532A.]

G. K. Chesterton

11427. BRAYBROOKE, NEVILLE. Master of topsy-turvydom. Cweal (113:13) 407–8.

11428. COATES, JOHN D. Chesterton and the Edwardian cultural crisis. (Bibl. 1985, 10157.) Rev. by Tony Brown in Prose Studies (9:1) 81–3.

11429. DALE, ALZINA STONE. The art of G. K. Chesterton. Chicago: Loyola UP, 1985. pp. 114.

11430. DENIS, YVES. Father Brown, prêtre détective. Caliban (23) 21–6.

11431. FFINCH, MICHAEL. G. K. Chesterton. London: Wiedenfeld & Nicholson. pp. 369. Rev. by J. I. M. Stewart in LRB (8:16) 15; by Hilary Spurling in TLS, 15 Aug., 885.

11432. ISLEY, WILLIAM L., JR. The adventure of life: romance in the writings of G. K. Chesterton. Unpub. doct. diss., Drew Univ. [Abstr. in DA (47) 1734A.]

11433. MILWARD, PETER; NAKANO, KII; YAMAGATA, KAZUMI (eds). G. K. Chesterton no sekai. (The world of G. K. Chesterton.) Tokyo: Kenkyusha Press. pp. x, 308. (Revised ed.)

11434. MOLYNEUX, M. A critical assessment of G. K. Chesterton as a literary critic. Unpub. doct. diss., CNAA, 1985. [Abstr. in IT (36) 474.]

11435. PŘIDAL, ANTONÍN. K proměnám detektivky u G. K. Chestertona a K. Čapka. (Variations on the detective story in G. K. Chesterton's and Karel Čapek's work.) *In* (pp. 51–4) **24.**

11436. REZNOWSKI, LORNE A. The 'Chesterbelloc' and Ezra Pound. *See* **11213.**

11437. VODIČKA, VAVŘINEC. Gilbert Keith Chesterton: čili filozofie zdravého rozumu. (Gilbert Keith Chesterton: the philosophy of common sense.) Purley: Rozmluvy. pp. 132.

11438. WALCZUK, ANNA. Gilbert Keith Chesterton's europeanism. *In* (pp. 207–15) **17.**

Peter Cheyney

11439. SCHWEIGHAEUSER, JEAN-PAUL. Le noir dévoyé: Cheyney et Chase. *See* **11420.**

Alice Childress

11440. ARTIZ, MIGUEL A. The politics of poverty in young adult literature. LU (2:2) 1978, 6–15.

Marquis Childs

11441. ERLER, H. RAPHAEL. Interpretation of the Mississippi River. Palimpsest (67:6) 175–93.

Steve Chimombo

11442. NAZOMBE, A. J. M. Malawian poetry in English from 1970 to the present day: a study of myth and socio-political change in the work of Steve Chimombo, Jack Mapanje, Frank Chipasula and Felix Mnthali. Unpub. doct. diss., Univ. of Sheffield, 1983.

Frank Chipasula

11443. NAZOMBE, A. J. M. Malawian poetry in English from 1970 to the present day: a study of myth and socio-political change in the work of Steve Chimombo, Jack Mapanje, Frank Chipasula and Felix Mnthali. *See* **11442.**

Agatha Christie

11444. SANDERS, DENNIS; LOVALLO, LEN. The Agatha Christie companion: the complete guide to Agatha Christie's life and work. New York: Delacorte Press, 1984; London: Allen, 1985. pp. xxiii, 519.

Caryl Churchill

11445. KRAMER, MIMI. Want in the midst of *Plenty*. NCrit (1) May 1983, 55–63.

11446. RUSSELL, ELIZABETH. Caryl Churchill: sexual politics and *Cloud Nine*. RCEI (12) 153–60.

11447. SWANSON, MICHAEL. Mother/daughter relationships in three plays by Caryl Churchill. TS (31/32) 1984/85–1985/86, 49–66.

John Ciardi

11448. WHITE, WILLIAM. About Walt Whitman: John Ciardi and Walt Whitman. *See* **9524.**

Amy Clampitt

11449. KORELITZ, JEAN HANFF. What Amy Clampitt was like: an interview. Honest Ulsterman (81) 41–51.

Tom Clancy

11450. SIGURÐSSON, JÓN ÁSGEIR. Tom Clancy: rætt við höfund bókanna *Leitin að Rauða október* og Rauði Stormur, en Island kemur við í þeim báðum. (Tom Clancy: an interview with the author of *The Hunt for Red October* and *Red Storm Rising*; Iceland is a theme in both.) Morgunblaðið (73:258) B 1–3.

Eleanor Clark

11451. PARINI, JAY. Splendid dragon. Horizon (29:4) 53–4.

John Pepper Clark

11452. ANPE, THOMAS VWETPAK. An investigation of John Pepper Clark's drama as an organic interaction of traditional African drama with Western theatre. Unpub. doct. diss., Univ. of Wisconsin–Madison, 1985. [Abstr. in DA (46) 1781A–2A.]

11453. BANHAM, MARTIN. Three plays: a critical view. Ed. by YOLANDE CANTU. London: Collins; British Council, 1985. pp. 55. (Nexus.)

Austin Clarke

11454. CRAIG, TERRANCE. Interview with Austin Clarke. WLWE (26:1) 115–27.

D. H. Clarke

11455. DELOUX, JEAN-PIERRE. W. R. Burnett, D. H. Clarke: la loi des rues. *See* **11361.**

Jack Clemo

11456. LOWMAN, P. J. Supernaturalistic causality and Christian theism in the modern English novel. Unpub. doct. diss., Univ. of Wales, Cardiff, 1985. [Abstr. in IT (36) 23.]

Charmian Clift

11457. KINNANE, GARRY (ed.). *Strong-man from Piraeus* and other stories. Melbourne: Nelson, 1983; Ringwood, Vic.; Harmondsworth: Penguin. pp. xiv, 192.

J. M. Coetzee

11458. MARTIN, RICHARD G. Narrative, history, and ideology: a study of *Waiting for the Barbarians* and *Burger's Daughter*. Ariel (17:3) 3–21.

11459. PENNER, DICK. Sight, blindness and double-thought in J. M. Coetzee's *Waiting for the Barbarians*. WLWE (26:1) 34–45.

11460. ZAMORA, LOIS PARKINSON. Allegories of power in the fiction of J. M. Coetzee. Journal of Literary Studies (2:1) 1–14.

Leonard Cohen

11461. SWARD, ROBERT; SMITH, PAT KEENEY. An interview with Leonard Cohen. MalaR (77) 55–63.

Matt Cohen

11462. MATHEWS, LAWRENCE. *The Colours of War*: Matt Cohen's ironic parable. CanL (110) 98–108.

11463. Entry cancelled.

John Stewart Collis

11464. INGRAMS, RICHARD. John Stewart Collis: a memoir. London: Chatto & Windus. pp. 157.

Pádraic Colum

11465. MACLAINE, KAY DIVINEY. Elements of the folk hero-tale in the fiction of Padraic Colum. Unpub. doct. diss., Univ. of British Columbia, 1985. [Abstr. in DA (47) 1335A.]

Jack Common

11466. PICKERING, MICHAEL; ROBINS, KEVIN. 'A revolutionary materialist with a leg free': the autobiographical novels of Jack Common. *In* (pp. 76–92) **6.**

Ivy Compton-Burnett

11467. LIDDELL, ROBERT. Elizabeth and Ivy. Introd. by FRANCIS KING. London: Owen. pp. 126. Rev. by Mervyn Jones in Listener, 16 Jan., 29.

11468. SPURLING, HILARY. Ivy: the life of I. Compton-Burnett. (Bibl. 1985, 10195.) Rev. by Robert Leiter in ASch (55) 1985/86, 140–2.

Stewart Conn

11469. ANON. From the editor. Upstream (2:3) 1984, 1–5. (Interview.)

Cyril Connolly ('Palinurus')

11470. LARKIN, PHILIP (introd.). The condemned playground: essays 1927–1944. London: Hogarth Press, 1985. pp. 287. (Hogarth critics.)

11471. OZICK, CYNTHIA. Cyril Connolly and the groans of success. NCrit (2) Mar. 1984, 21–7.

Joseph Conrad

11472. ABEDI, RAZI. *Hamlet* and 19th century sensibility. *See* **4737.**

11473. ARMSBY, LESLIE. Sujets et objets dans le roman post-symboliste: Gide, Alain-Fournier et Conrad revisités. CanRCL (13:1) 64–75.

11474. BAE, JONG-UN. Joseph Conrad eui dodeukjeok gaksung. (The moralistic awakening of Joseph Conrad.) Unpub. doct. diss., Kyungpook National Univ. (Korea).

11475. BARZA, STEVEN. Bonds of empathy: the widening audience in *Lord Jim*. MidQ (25) 1984, 220–32.

11476. BATCHELOR, JOHN (ed.). Victory: an island tale. Introd. by TONY TANNER. Oxford: OUP. pp. 464. (World's classics.)

11477. BENDER, TODD K.; PARINS, JAMES W. A concordance to Conrad's *Romance*. New York; London: Garland, 1985. pp. x, 406. (Garland reference library of the humanities, 576.)

11478. BREBACH, RAYMOND. Joseph Conrad, Ford Madox Ford, and the making of romance. Ann Arbor, MI: UMI Research Press; Epping: Bowker, 1985. pp. xii, 125. (Studies in modern literature, 46.)

11479. CHEVEREŞAN, CONSTANTIN. Functionality of discourse in the writings of Joseph Conrad. SLRC (7) 1985, 117–28.

11480. CHON, SOOYOUNG. Imperialism as metaphor in Joseph Conrad's fiction. Unpub. doct. diss., Univ. of Michigan. [Abstr. in DA (47) 2167A.]

11481. COHEN, MICHAEL. Sailing through *The Secret Sharer*: the end of Conrad's story. MSE (10:2) 1985, 102–9.

11482. CONROY, MARK. Modernism and authority: strategies of legitimation in Flaubert and Conrad. Baltimore, MD: Johns Hopkins UP, 1985. pp. ix, 193. Rev. by Gregory L. Ulmer in Novel (19:3) 275–7; by Paul B. Armstrong in Conradiana (18:1) 64–9; by Edward Wasiolek in MP (84:1) 104–6; by Todd K. Bender in Criticism (28:2) 226–9.

11483. CONSTANTINESCU, LIGIA. Joseph Conrad and James Joyce: epiphany and irony in short fiction. AnUILit (32) 79–83.

11484. CORONEOS, C. The modern novella: James, Conrad and Lawrence. *See* **8646.**

11485. COUSINEAU, THOMAS J. The ambiguity of Razumov's confession in *Under Western Eyes*. Conradiana (18:1) 27–40.

11486. DAZEY, MARY ANN. Shared secret or secret sharing in Joseph Conrad's *The Secret Sharer*. Conradiana (18:3) 201–3.

11487. DE MILLE, BARBARA. *An Inquiry into Some Points of Seamanship*:

narration as preservation in *Heart of Darkness*. Conradiana (18:2) 94–104.

11488. DOBRINSKY, JOSEPH. Notes sur les symbolismes de la mer dans *Lord Jim*. CVE (23) 133–46.

11489. FOGEL, AARON. Coercion to speak: Conrad's poetics of dialogue. Cambridge, MA; London: Harvard UP, 1985. pp. 284. Rev. by Todd K. Bender in Criticism (28:2) 226–9.

11490. FOULKE, ROBERT. The elegiac structure of Conrad's *The Mirror of the Sea*. In (pp. 154–60) **28.**

11491. —— Life in the dying world of sail, 1870–1910. In (pp. 72–115) **28.**

11492. GILLON, ADAM. Conrad's satirical stance in *Under Western Eyes*: two strange bedfellows – Prince Roman and Peter Ivanovitch. Conradiana (18:2) 119–28.

11493. GOLDMAN, MICHAEL. *Under Western Eyes* and the satanic script. HUSL (13:1) 1985, 63–97.

11494. GRIBBLE, JENNIFER. The fogginess of *Heart of Darkness*. Sydney Studies in English (11) 1985/86, 83–94.

11495. HAMPSON, ROBERT G. Conrad, Guthrie, and *The Arabian Nights*. *See* **7548.**

11496. HARGREAVES, ALEX. Exoticism in literature and history. Text & Context (1:1) 7–18.

11497. HIGDON, DAVID LEON. 'Word for word': the collected editions of Conrad's *Under Western Eyes*. *See* **312.**

11498. HOLDERNESS, GRAHAM. 'Life doesn't stand much looking into': the secret of *The Secret Agent*. DUJ (78:2) 319–26.

11499. HUNTER, ALLAN. Joseph Conrad and the ethics of Darwinism: the challenges of science. (Bibl. 1985, 10223.) Rev. by Cedric Watts in MLR (81:3) 730; by Jan Verleun and Jetty de Vries in ELT (29:3) 245–8.

11500. HUNTER, ALLAN G. Conrad to Clifford: some unpublished letters. Conradiana (18:2) 83–93.

11501. HYNES, SAMUEL. A budget of letters. SewR (94:4) 639–44 (review-article).

11502. INGRAM, ALLAN (ed.). Joseph Conrad: selected literary criticism and *The Shadow Line*. London: Methuen. pp. x, 273. (Methuen English texts.)

11503. JONES, MICHAEL P. Conrad's heroism: a paradise lost. Ann Arbor, MI: UMI Research Press, 1985. pp. 154.

11504. KARL, FREDERICK R.; DAVIES, LAURENCE (eds). The collected letters of Joseph Conrad: vol. 1, 1861–1897. (Bibl. 1985, 10225.) Rev. by C. J. Rawson in MLR (81:1) 187–8.

11505. —— —— The collected letters of Joseph Conrad: vol. 2, 1898–1902. Cambridge: CUP. pp. 483. Rev. by P. N. Furbank in LRB (8:17) 22–3; by Peter Kemp in Listener, 21 Aug., 23–4; by John Lucas in TLS, 29 Aug., 931; by Michael Thorpe in Enc (67:4) 51–4; by Tony Tanner in THES (725) 19.

11506. KING, DON WAYNE. Exile in the fiction of Joseph Conrad and

Fyodor Dostoyevsky. Unpub. doct. diss., Univ. of North Carolina at Greensboro, 1985. [Abstr. in DA (46) 3346A.]

11507. KNOWLES, OWEN; MISKIN, G. W. S. Unpublished Conrad letters: the *HQS Wellington* collection. *See* **248.**

11508. KOWALSKA, ANIELA; JANION, MARIA (postscr.). Conrad i Gombrowicz w walce o swoją wybitność. (Conrad and Gombrowicz in their struggle for eminence.) Warsaw: Państwowy Instytut Wydawniczy. pp. 222.

11509. KRISHNAMURTI, G. (introd.). A letter to William Nicholson. London: Eighteen Nineties Soc., 1985. pp. 7. (Makers of the nineties.)

11510. LAND, STEPHEN K. Paradox and polarity in the fiction of Joseph Conrad. (Pub. in UK as *Conrad and the Paradox of Plot*.) New York: St Martin's Press, 1984. (Cf. bibl. 1985, 10233.) Rev. by Cedric Watts in JEGP (85:4) 579–80.

11511. LAW, T. A. Politics in Conrad's major fiction. Unpub. doct. diss., Univ. of Loughborough, 1983.

11512. LEITCH, THOMAS M. Murderous victims in *The Secret Agent* and *Sabotage*. *See* **10007.**

11513. LEONDOPOULOS, JORDAN. Still the moving world: *Intolerance*, Modernism, and *Heart of Darkness*. Unpub. doct. diss., Columbia Univ., 1985. [Abstr. in DA (46) 2108A.]

11514. LESSAY, FRANCK. Joseph Conrad et les chemins de l'empire. *In* (pp. 122–39) **35.**

11515. LEVENSON, MICHAEL. On the edge of the heart of darkness. SSF (23:2) 153–7.

11516. LOMBARD, FRANÇOIS. Joseph Conrad et la mer dans *The End of the Tether*. CVE (23) 147–55.

11517. LOTHE, JAKOB. Conrad's narrative method. Unpub. doct. diss., Univ. of Bergen.

11518. LOWENS, PETER J. The Conrad–Pinker relationship: an unpublished letter. Conradiana (18:1) 45–7.

11519. LUYAT-MOORE, ANNE. The Swedish connection to *Victory* and *Chance*. Conradiana (18:3) 219–23.

11520. LYNN, DAVID HAYDEN. Cries out of the darkness: heroic narrators in early-modern fiction. Unpub. doct. diss., Univ. of Virginia, 1984. [Abstr. in DA (46) 1939A.]

11521. LYON, J. M. Thought and the novel: James, Conrad and Lawrence. *See* **8700.**

11522. McCARTHY, PATRICK A. *Heart of Darkness* and the early novels of H. G. Wells: evolution, anarchy, entropy. JML (13:1) 37–60.

11523. McCLURE, JOHN A. Kipling and Conrad: the colonial fiction. (Bibl. 1983, 10766.) Rev. by C. J. Rawson in YES (16) 341–2.

11524. McLAUCHLAN, JULIET. Conrad's heart of emptiness: *The Planter of Malata*. Conradiana (18:3) 180–92.

11525. MADDEN, FRED. Marlow and the double horror of *Heart of Darkness*. MidQ (27:4) 504–17.

11526. MANICOM, DAVID. True lies/false truths: narrative perspective and the control of ambiguity in *The Nigger of the 'Narcissus'*. Conradiana (18:2) 105–18.

11527. MARSHALL, T. A. Private and public spaces: narrative strategies in Dostoyevsky and Conrad. Unpub. doct. diss., Univ. of East Anglia, 1982.

11528. MEYERS, JEFFREY. The Ranee of Sarawak and Conrad's *Victory*. Conradiana (18:1) 41–4.

11529. MILBAUER, ASHER Z. Transcending exile: Conrad, Nabokov, I. B. Singer. *See* **10683.**

11530. MILNE, FRED L. Conrad's *The Secret Sharer*. Exp (44:3) 38–9.

11531. MITCHELL, GILES. Lord Jim's death fear, narcissism, and suicide. Conradiana (18:3) 163–79.

11532. MOFFAT, KATHLEEN WENDY. Reader and resolution: ambiguity in the later novels of Conrad, Forster, and Woolf. Unpub. doct. diss., Yale Univ., 1985. [Abstr. in DA (47) 1335A.]

11533. MOORE, GENE M. Chronotopes and voices in *Under Western Eyes*. Conradiana (18:1) 9–25.

11534. MURFIN, ROSS C. (ed.). Conrad revised: essays for the eighties. University: Alabama UP, 1985. pp. 190.

11535. MURPHY, MICHAEL. *The Secret Sharer*: Conrad's turn of the winch. Conradiana (18:3) 193–200.

11536. NAJDER, ZDZISLAW. Conrad's Polish background, or, from biography to a study of culture. Conradiana (18:1) 3–8.

11537. —— Joseph Conrad: a chronicle. (Bibl. 1985, 10239.) Rev. by Raymond Brebach in JEGP (85:1) 145–7; by Douglas Hewitt in NQ (33:2) 265–7.

11538. —— (ed.). Conrad under familial eyes. (Bibl. 1985, 10240.) Rev. by Keith Carabine in Conradiana (18:1) 48–59; by Douglas Hewitt in NQ (33:2) 265–7; by Jon Dertzer in Ariel (17:2) 88–91.

11539. O'CONNOR, GERARD P. Three types of irony in the novels of Joseph Conrad. Unpub. doct. diss., Univ. of Canterbury.

11540. PACCAUD, JOSIANE. The name-of-the-father in Conrad's *Under Western Eyes*. Conradiana (18:3) 204–18.

11541. —— Trahison, parole et vérité dans *Under Western Eyes* de Joseph Conrad: l'œuvre comme métaphore de l'avènement d'un sujet de la parole. EA (39:4) 400–10.

11542. PAGE, NORMAN. A Conrad companion. London: Macmillan. pp. xvi, 185. (Macmillan literary companions.)

11543. PATTERSON, J. D. The representation of love in the novels of Joseph Conrad, 1895–1915. Unpub. doct. diss., Univ. of Oxford, 1984.

11544. RAVAL, SURESH. The art of failure: Conrad's fiction. Boston, MA; London: Allen & Unwin. pp. ix, 187. Rev. by Cedric Watts in THES (703) 18.

11545. RAY, MARTIN. Conrad, Wells, and *The Secret Agent*: paying old debts and settling old scores. MLR (81:3) 560–73.

11546. RENNER, STANLEY. *Sartor Resartus* retailored? Conrad's *Lord Jim* and the peril of idealism. *See* **7821.**

11547. Rogé, Raymond. Verne – Conrad: voyage littéraire dans le continent noir. Littératures (14) 87–98.

11548. Rude, Donald W. Joseph Conrad's typescripts at Falls Library. *See* **330.**

11549. —— Some ghosts laid to rest: a note on Gordon J. Lindstrand's survey of Conrad's manuscripts and typescripts. Conradiana (17:2) 1985, 147–8.

11550. —— Three bibliographical notes on Conrad. Conradiana (18:2) 144–6.

11551. —— Three lost pieces of Conradiana. AEB (8:3) 1984, 171–2.

11552. Scheid, Teresa Marie. Experimentations in temporal and spatial techniques in the nineteenth and early twentieth centuries: an examination of the work of J. M. W. Turner, Joseph Conrad, Wyndham Lewis and C. R. W. Nevinson. Unpub. doct. diss., Ohio Univ., 1985. [Abstr. in DA (47) 334A.]

11553. Schwartz, Nina. The ideologies of Romanticism in *Heart of Darkness*. NOR (13:1) 84–95.

11554. Simons, Kenneth. The ludic imagination: a reading of Jospeh Conrad. Ann Arbor, MI: UMI Research Press; Epping: Bowker, 1985. pp. xiii, 156. (Studies in modern literature, 41.)

11555. Stape, J. H. The date and writing of Conrad's *Stephen Crane: A Note Without Dates. See* **7985a.**

11556. —— The date of Conrad's *Turgenev.* NQ (32) 1985, 376. (Conrad's foreword to Garnett's *Turgenev: a Study.*)

11557. Tanner, Tony. Joseph Conrad and the last gentlemen. CritQ (28:1/2) 109–42.

11558. Tarnawski, Wit. Conrad and religion: two letters. Conradiana (18:2) 137–40.

11559. Toews, Aganetha Wall. 'The great code' in six twentieth-century European novels. Unpub. doct. diss., Univ. of Oregon, 1984. [Abstr. in DA (45) 2519A.]

11560. Toker, Leona. A Nabokovian character in Conrad's *Nostromo.* RLC (59:1) 1985, 15–29.

11561. Verleun, Jan; de Vries, Jetty. Conrad criticism today: an evaluation of recent Conrad scholarship. ELT (29:3) 241–75 (review-article).

11562. —— —— Conrad's *The Secret Agent* and the critics: 1965–1980. Groningen; Bouma, 1984. pp. 320.

11563. Watts, Cedric (ed.). *Typhoon* and other tales. Oxford: OUP. pp. xxxii, 324. (World's classics.)

11564. Zabierowski, Stefan. Conrad i Żeromski. (Conrad and Żeromski.) PH (29:9/10) 1985, 1–23.

Shirley Conran

11565. Fahlgren, Margareta. 'Det maskinsydda broderiet': *Lace* och 80-talets kvinnliga populärroman. ('The manufactured embroidery': *Lace* and popular women's fiction in the 80's.) Kvinnovetenskaplig tidskrift (Gothenburg) (7:3) 48–54.

Alfred Duff Cooper, First Viscount Norwich
11566. CHARMLEY, JOHN.   Duff Cooper: the authorised biography.
London: Weidenfeld & Nicolson. pp. 265. Rev. by John Bayley in LRB
(8:8) 10.

Robert Coover
11567. COPE, JACKSON I.   Robert Coover's fictions. Baltimore, MD;
London: Johns Hopkins UP. pp xi, 151.
11568. LEE, L. L.   Robert Coover's moral vision: *Pricksongs &
Descants*. SSF (23:1) 63–9.
11569. TRUCHLAR, LEO.   Robert Coover, *Spanking the Maid*. Eine
Leseerfahrung. *In* (pp. 114–32) **21.**
11570. WILCZYŃSKI, MAREK.   The game of response in Robert
Coover's fiction. KN (33:4) 513–23.

Jim Corbett
11571. BOOTH, MARTIN.   Carpet Sahib: a life of Jim Corbett. London:
Constable. pp. 320. Rev. by Andrew Robinson in Listener, 20 Nov.,
27–8.

Edwin Corle
11572. SHIRLEY, CARL R.   Edwin Corle and the white man's Indian.
AQ (42:1) 68–76.

Robert Cormier
11573. DeLUCA, GERALDINE; NATOV, RONI.   An interview with
Robert Cormier. LU (2:2) 1978, 109–35.

Joe Corrie
11574. MACKENNEY, LINDA (ed.).   Plays, poems and theatre writings.
(Bibl. 1985, 10280.) Rev. by David Hutchinson in SLJ (supp. 24) 15–16.

Peter Corris
11575. KNIGHT, STEPHEN.   Real pulp at last: Peter Corris's thrillers.
Meanjin (45:4) 446–52.

Harold Courlander
11576. JOHNSON, ABBY ARTHUR.   The big old world of Harold
Courlander. MidQ (25) 1984, 450–70.

Sir Noel Coward
11577. HALLQUIST, JON WILLIAM.   'Just say the lines and don't trip
over the furniture!': the acting theories of Noel Coward. Unpub. doct.
diss., Univ. of Michigan, 1985. [Abstr. in DA (46) 1782A.]
11578. MORLEY, SHERIDAN (introd.).   Noel Coward: autobiography.
London: Methuen. pp. xiii, 512.
11579. PAYN, GRAHAM; MORLEY, SHERIDAN (eds).   The Noel Coward
diaries. (Bibl. 1982, 10887.) Rev. by Margaret Doody in Smithsonian
(16:12) 174, 176.
11580. TICKNER, MARTIN (introd.).   The complete stories of Noel
Coward. London: Methuen, 1985. pp. ix, 630.
11581. —— Hay fever. London: Methuen, 1983. pp. xvi, 107.

Edward Gordon Craig
11582. NEWMAN-BOUVET, L. M. M. L.   Edward Gordon Craig and
Harry Graf Kessler: correspondence, 1903–1937. Unpub. doct. diss.,
Univ. of Lancaster, 1985. [Abstr. in IT (35) 1076.]

Hart Crane

11583. BENNETT, MARIA FRANCES. The unfractioned idiom: Hart Crane and Modernism. Unpub. doct. diss., City Univ. of New York. [Abstr. in DA (47) 1313A.]

11584. BRUNNER, EDWARD J. Splendid failure: Hart Crane and the making of *The Bridge*. (Bibl. 1985, 10294.) Rev. by L. S. Dembo in Review (7) 1985, 197–205.

11585. DEMBO, L. S. Failed splendor: Edward Brunner's remaking of *The Bridge*. Review (7) 1985, 197–205 (review-article).

11586. GABRIEL, DANIEL. Hart Crane's *The Bridge* as a hybrid form. Unpub. doct. diss., City Univ. of New York. [Abstr. in DA (47) 1322A.]

11587. GARDEN, DIANE BETH. Arthur Rimbaud and Hart Crane: a comparison of their poetic techniques and underlying aesthetic goals. Unpub. doct. diss., New York Univ., 1985. [Abstr. in DA (46) 2287A.]

11588. GILES, PAUL. Hart Crane: the contexts of *The Bridge*. Cambridge: CUP. pp. 288. (Cambridge studies in American literature and culture.) Rev. by Roger Pooley in THES (723) 18.

11589. —— Hart Crane: the contexts of *The Bridge*. Unpub. doct. diss., Univ. of Oxford, 1985. [Abstr. in IT (35) 55.]

11590. MARTIN, ROBERT KESSLER. The 'half-hid warp': Whitman, Crane, and the tradition of 'adhesiveness' in American poetry. *See* **9508.**

11591. MORGAN, VERONICA. Reading Hart Crane by metonymy. Unpub. doct. diss., Univ. of Michigan. [Abstr. in DA (47) 2160A.]

11592. PETTINGELL, PHOEBE. Hart Crane revisited. NewL (69:7) 21–2.

11593. SCHENCK, CELESTE M. When the moderns write elegy: Crane, Kinsella, Nemerov. CML (6:2) 97–108.

11594. WEBER, BROM (ed.). Complete poems. (Bibl. 1985, 10304.) Rev. by Anne Stevenson in AWR (82) 113–17.

11595. Entry cancelled.

D'Arcy Cresswell

11596. SHAW, HELEN (ed.). Dear Lady Ginger: an exchange of letters between Lady Ottoline Morrell and D'Arcy Cresswell: together with Ottoline Morrell's essay on Katherine Mansfield. (Bibl. 1985, 10311.) Rev. by David Bradshaw in NQ (33:1) 128.

Harry Crews

11597. DEBORD, LARRY W.; LONG, GEORGE L. Harry Crews on the American dream. SoQ (20:3) 1982, 35–53.

11598. JEFFREY, DAVID K.; NOBLE, DONALD R. Harry Crews: an interview. SoQ (19:2) 1981, 65–79.

11599. RANDISI, JENNIFER L. The scene of the crime: the automobile in the fiction of Harry Crews. SoS (25:3) 213–19.

Richmal Crompton (Richmal Crompton Lamburn)

11600. CADOGAN, MARY. Richmal Crompton: the woman behind William. London: Allen & Unwin. pp. xvii, 169. Rev by Gillian Avery in

TLS, 5 Dec., 1378; by Nigel Williams in Listener, 13 Nov., 26; by Penelope Fitzgerald in LRB (8:21) 18.

11601. WILLIAMS, KAY.   Just Richmal: the life and work of Richmal Crompton Lamburn. Guildford: Genesis. pp. x, 230.

Jeremy Cronin

11602. GARDNER, SUSAN.   Four South African poets: interviews with Robert Berold, Jeremy Cronin, Douglas Reid Skinner, Stephen Watson. *See* **11248.**

Ian Cross

11603. O'SULLIVAN, VINCENT.   Ian Cross: the God old boy. NZList, 29 Mar., 24–6.

e. e. cummings

11604. OSTROM, ALAN.   *Fairy Tales*: the other cummings. LU (2:1) 1978, 65–72.

Nancy Cunard

11605. CLEMENTS, PATRICIA.   'Transmuting' Nancy Cunard. *See* **11018.**

Allen Curnow

11606. SIMPSON, PETER.   A checklist of Allen Curnow's critical prose. JNZL (4) 48–55.

11607. ——— 'The trick of standing upright': Allen Curnow and James K. Baxter. *See* **11151.**

Carroll John Daly

11608. SCHLERET, JEAN-JACQUES.   Carroll John Daly, le père fondateur. Europe (62:664/65) 20–8.

Eleanor Dark

11609. GARNER, HELEN.   Dazzling writing: the arts. Australian Society (Fitzroy, Vic.) (5:8) 33–4, 38.

11610. ——— (introd.).   Lantana lane. London: Virago Press. pp. xv, 254. (Virago modern classics, 212.)

11611. MODJESKA, DRUSILLA.   Dialogue with Dark: a modern novelist, a feminist critique. Age Monthly Review (Melbourne) Apr., 3–6.

Guy Davenport

11612. ARIAS-MISSON, ALAIN.   Erotic ear, amoral eye. ChiR (35:3) 66–71.

11613. OLSEN, LANCE.   A guydebook to the last modernist: Davenport on Davenport and *Da Vinci's Bicycle*. JNT (16:2) 148–61.

Donald Davidson

11614. LePORE, ERNEST (ed.).   Truth and interpretation: perspectives on the philosophy of Donald Davidson. Oxford: Blackwell. pp. xii, 520.

Donald Davie

11615. OAKLAND, LEONARD A.   *A Winter Talent*: Donald Davie: the poet as dissenter. Unpub. doct. diss., Washington State Univ., 1985. [Abstr. in DA (46) 3362A.]

Idris Davies

11616. JENKINS, ISLWYN.   Idris Davies of Rhymney: a personal memoir. Llandysul: Gomer. pp. xix, 273.

Robertson Davies

11617. HAWKINS, PETER S. Robertson Davies: shaking hands with the devil. ChCen (103:18) 515–18.

11618. KÖSTER, PATRICIA. 'Promptings stronger' than 'strict prohibitions': new forms of natural religion in the novels of Robertson Davies. CanL (111) 68–82.

11619. MILLS, JOHN. Robertson Davies. *In* (pp. 19–78) **7.**

11620. MONK, PATRICIA. Somatotyping, scatomancy, and Sophia: the relations of body and soul in the novels of Robertson Davies. ESCan (12:1) 79–100.

11621. STONE-BLACKBURN, SUSAN. Robertson Davies, playwright: a search for the self on the Canadian stage. (Bibl. 1985, 10340.) Rev. by Neil Carson in CanL (108) 189–90; by Anton Wagner in CanTR (47) 147–8.

W. H. Davies

11622. BARKER, JONATHAN (ed.). Selected poems. (Bibl. 1985, 10343.) Rev. by Lawrence Normand in Poetry Wales (21:1) 133–6.

11623. NORMAND, LAWRENCE. 'Authentic W. H. Davies'. Poetry Wales (21:2) 68–77.

Gerald Dawe

11624. DAWE, GERALD. The enabling elements: an assessment of the poetry of Thomas Kinsella. Linen Hall Review (3:1) 8–9.

Ralph de Boissière

11625. SANDER, REINHARD W. The American invaders: Ralph de Boissière's *Rum and Coca-Cola.* JCL (21:1) 93–108.

Len Deighton

11626. MILWARD-OLIVER, EDWARD. Len Deighton: an annotated bibliography 1954–1985. London: Sammler; Maidstone: Oliver, 1985. pp. 64.

11627. SAUERBERG, LARS OLE. Secret agents in fiction: Ian Fleming, John le Carré and Len Deighton. (Bibl. 1985, 10349.) Rev. by Eric Homberger in THES (708) 18.

Walter de la Mare

11628. BENTINCK, A. Walter de la Mare: a study of his poetry. Unpub. doct. diss., Univ. of Edinburgh, 1984.

11629. BRIGHTON, CATHERINE (sel.). The voice: a sequence of poems. London: Faber & Faber. pp. 31.

11630. GRIFFITHS, J. The poetry of Walter de la Mare. Unpub. doct. diss., Univ. of Liverpool, 1983. [Abstr. in IT (35) 52.]

11631. LEVAY, JOHN. De la Mare's *The Riddle.* Exp (43:3) 1984, 23–4.

11632. LOGES, MARY KAISER. The poetry of Walter de la Mare: a re-evaluation. Unpub. doct. diss., Univ. of Denver, 1985. [Abstr. in DA (46) 3349A.]

Samuel R. Delany

11633. ANON. Samuel Ray Delany. SvL (31:3) 119–20.

Floyd Dell

11634. ROBA, WILLIAM H. Floyd Dell in Iowa. BkIA (44) 27–41.

Lester Del Rey

11635. GOIZET, ANNETTE. *Helen O'Loy* de Lester Del Rey: Helen est-elle femme ou robot? *In* (pp. 579–86) **1.**

W. Redvers Dent

11636. WHITEMAN, BRUCE. Raymond Knister's hand in W. R. Dent's *Show Me Death!* CanL (111) 228–32.

Anita Desai

11637. AFZAL-KHAN, FAWZIA. Genre and ideology in the novels of four contemporary Indo-Anglian novelists: R. K. Narayan, Anita Desai, Kamala Markandaya and Salman Rushdie. Unpub. doct. diss., Tufts Univ. [Abstr. in DA (47) 1328A.]

11638. KIRPAL, VINEY. An image of India: a study of Anita Desai's *In Custody*. Ariel (17:4) 127–38.

James Martin Devaney

11639. TAYLOR, CHERYL; SMITH, ROSS. James Martin Devaney (1890–1976): a bibliography. Linq (12:1/3) 1984, 83–109.

Peter De Vries

11640. DOWN, NANCY. The search for authenticity in the satiric worlds of Nathanael West and Peter De Vries. Unpub. doct. diss., Drew Univ. [Abstr. in DA (47) 1727A.]

John Dewey

11641. GRANT, JAMES DICKINSON. Ralph Waldo Emerson and John Dewey: a study of intellectual continuities and influence. *See* **8275.**

Herbert I. E. Dhlomo

11642. COUZENS, TIM. The New African: a study of the life and work of H. I. E. Dhlomo. Johannesburg: Ravan Press, 1985. pp. xvii, 382. Rev. by Leon de Kock in UES (24:2) 55–7; by Isabel Hofmeyr in EngA (13:1) 93–8.

11643. VISSER, NICK; COUZENS, TIM (eds). Collected works. Johannesburg: Ravan Press, 1985. pp. xvii, 500. Rev. by Leon de Kock in UES (24:2) 55–7; by Isabel Hofmeyr in EngA (13:1) 93–8.

Philip K. Dick

11644. TRUCHLAR, LEO. Philip K. Dick, *Ubik*. *In* (pp. 315–30) HARTMUT HEUERMANN (ed.), Der Science-Fiction Roman in der anglo-amerikanischen Literatur. Düsseldorf: Bagel. pp. 399.

James Dickey

11645. BARTLETT, LEE; WITEMEYER, HUGH. Ezra Pound and James Dickey: a correspondence and a kinship. Paideuma (11:2) 1982, 290–312.

11646. WRIGHT, STUART. James Dickey Ltd. SewR (94:2) 292–5 (review-article).

Joan Didion

11647. CARTON, EVAN. Joan Didion's dreampolitics of the self. WHR (40:4) 307–28.

11648. SCHOW, H. WAYNE. *Out of Africa, The White Album*, and the possibility of tragic affirmation. EngS (67:1) 35–50.

11649. SNYDER, LELA FERN KROPF. Joan Didion: a 'state of rather eerie serenity'. Unpub. doct. diss., Univ. of Oregon, 1985. [Abstr. in DA (46) 1943A.]

Annie Dillard

11650. MCILROY, GARY. *Pilgrim at Tinker Creek* and the social legacy of *Walden. See* **9366.**

Mary di Michele

11651. BILLINGS, ROBERT. Contemporary influences on the poetry of Mary di Michele. *In* (pp. 121–52) **13.**

'Isak Dinesen' (Karen Blixen)

11652. JUHL, MARIANNE; JØRGENSEN, BO HAKON. Diana's revenge: two lines in Isak Dinesen's authorship. Trans. by ANNE BORN of *Dianas haevn: to spor i Karen Blixens forfatterskab.* Odense: Odense UP, 1985. pp. 257. Rev. by Susan Hardy Aiken in SS (58:1) 89–90.

11653. MAXWELL, RICHARD. In praise of a modest preface. Cresset (49:7) 19–22.

11654. MOI, TORIL. 'Hele verden en scene': en analyse av Karen Blixens *Storme.* ('All the world's a stage': an analysis of Karen Blixen's *Tempests.*) Edda (86:2) 149–61.

11655. SCHOW, H. WAYNE. *Out of Africa, The White Album,* and the possibility of tragic affirmation. *See* **11648.**

11656. UPDIKE, JOHN. *Seven Gothic Tales:* the divine swank of Isak Dinesen. NYTB, 23 Feb., 3.

Doris Miles Disney

11657. DEMARR, MARY JEAN. Doris Miles Disney and the historical mystery. Clues (7:1) 111–25.

Thomas Dixon

11658. ARMOUR, ROBERT A. History written in jagged lightning: realistic South *vs* romantic South in *The Birth of a Nation.* SoQ (19:3/4) 1981, 14–19.

11659. SILVERMAN, JOAN L. *The Birth of a Nation:* Prohibition propaganda. SoQ (19:3/4) 1981, 23–30.

Stephen Dobyns

11660. KARR, MARY. Stephen Dobyns: black dog, red dog. APR (15:2) 20–2.

E. L. Doctorow

11661. IANNONE, CAROL. E. L. Doctorow's 'Jewish' radicalism. Commentary (81:3) 53–6.

11662. PLIMPTON, GEORGE. The art of fiction XCIV. ParisR (101) 23–47.

11663. TANNER, STEPHEN L. Rage and order in Doctorow's *Welcome to Hard Times.* SDR (22:3) 1984, 79–83.

11664. TOKARCZYK, MICHELLE MARIANNE. The Rosenberg case and E. L. Doctorow's *The Book of Daniel:* a study of the use of history in fiction. Unpub. doct. diss., State Univ. of New York at Stony Brook, 1985. [Abstr. in DA (46) 2295A.]

Stephen R. Donaldson ('Reed Stephens')

11665. RICH, CALVIN; INGERSOLL, EARL. A conversation with Stephen R. Donaldson. Mythlore (12:4) 23–6.

John Donovan

11666. GOLDMAN, SUZY. John Donovan: sexuality, stereotypes, and self. LU (2:2) 1978, 27–36.

Hilda Doolittle ('H.D.')

11667. BAWER, BRUCE. H.D.: the mother of us all? NCrit (2) Mar. 1984, 63–70.

11668. CRAWFORD, FRED D. Approaches to biography: two studies of H.D. Review (7) 1985, 215–38 (review-article).

11669. DOBSON, SILVIA. 'Shock knit within terror': living through World War Two. IowaR (16:3) 232–45.

11670. DUNN, MARGARET M. H.D.'s *Trilogy*: a portrait of the artist in full bloom. CEACrit (48:3) 29–37.

11671. DUPLESSIS, RACHEL BLAU. H.D.: the career of that struggle. Brighton: Harvester Press. pp. xxi, 161. (Key women writers.)

11672. —— Language acquisition. IowaR (16:3) 252–83.

11673. FRENCH, WILLIAM. 'Saint Hilda', Mr Pound, and Rilke's Parisian panther at Pisa. Paideuma (11:1) 1982, 79–87.

11674. FRIEDMAN, SUSAN STANFORD. Emergences and convergences. IowaR (16:3) 42–56.

11675. GUEST, BARBARA. Herself defined: the poet H.D. and her world. (Bibl. 1985, 10407.) Rev. by S. G. Kossick in UES (24:1) 43; by Fred D. Crawford in Review (7) 1985, 216–24.

11676. —— The intimacy of biography. IowaR (16:3) 58–71.

11677. HOLLENBERG, DONNA KROLIK. Art and ardor in World War One: selected letters from H.D. to John Cournos. IowaR (16:3) 126–55.

11678. —— Nursing the muse: the childbirth metaphor in H. D.'s poetry. Unpub. doct. diss., Tufts Univ. [Abstr. in DA (47) 537A.]

11679. KING, MICHAEL. Go, little book: Ezra Pound, Hilda Doolittle and 'Hilda's book'. Paideuma (10:2) 1981, 347–60.

11680. LINK, FRANZ H. Zwei amerikanische Dichterinnen: Emily Dickinson und Hilda Doolittle. *See* **8128.**

11681. MORRIS, ADALAIDE. Reading H.D.'s *Helios and Athene*. IowaR (12:2/3) 1981, 155–63.

11682. —— Writing. IowaR (16:3) 1–6.

11683. ROBINSON, JANICE S. H.D.: the life and work of an American poet. (Bibl. 1985, 10414.) Rev. by Fred D. Crawford in Review (7) 1985, 224–38.

11684. SIEVERT, HEATHER ROSARIO. H.D.: a symbolist perspective. Unpub. doct. diss., New York Univ., 1985. [Abstr. in DA (46) 2288A.]

11685. SMITH, PAUL. H.D.'s flaws. IowaR (16:3) 77–86.

John Dos Passos

11686. CARR, VIRGINIA SPENCER. Dos Passos, painter and playwright: new possibilities in research. RALS (13:2) 1983, 207–14.

11687. FOSTER, GRETCHEN. John Dos Passos' use of film technique in *Manhattan Transfer* and *The 42nd Parallel*. *See* **9954.**

11688. LUDINGTON, TOWNSEND. Dos Passos: new possibilities in biographical research. RALS (13:2) 1983, 195–200.

11689. MAINE, BARRY. Representative men in Dos Passos's *The 42nd Parallel*. CLIO (12:1) 1982, 31–43.

11690. MAIR, CHRISTIAN. Geschichtsverständnis und Textstruktur im sozialkritischen amerikanischen Roman der dreißiger Jahre – John Dos Passos, James T. Farrell, Josephine Herbst. Unpub. doct. diss., Univ. of Innsbruck, 1985.

11691. PIZER, DONALD. The Hemingway–Dos Passos relationship. JML (13:1) 111–28.

11692. SPAUNHORST, FRANZ-PETER. Literarische Kulturkritik als Dekodierung von Macht und Werten am Beispiel ausgewählter Romane von Upton Sinclair, Frank Norris, John Dos Passos und Sinclair Lewis. Ein Beitrag zur Theorie und Methode der Amerikastudien als Kulturwert. Frankfurt: Lang. pp. 382. (Europäische Hochschulschriften: Reihe 14, Angelsächsische Sprache und Literatur, 167.)

11693. STEVENS, S. C. The concepts and implications of individualism and citizenship in the fiction of John Dos Passos, 1920–1960. Unpub. doct. diss., Univ. of Leeds, 1985. [Abstr. in IT (36) 915.]

11694. WAGNER, LINDA W. Dos Passos: some directions in the criticism. RALS (13:2) 1983, 201–6.

Patricia Doubell

11695. MURPHY, CLIVE (ed.). At the Dog in Dulwich: recollections of a poet. London: Secker & Warburg. pp. 243.

Keith Douglas

11696. GRAHAM, DESMOND (ed.). A prose miscellany. (Bibl. 1985, 10428.) Rev. by Rowland Smith in DalR (65:4) 1985/86, 586–7; by Anthony Head in Eng (35) 180–3.

Norman Douglas

11697. COPELAND, JOSHUA PAUL. Subjective geography: form and content in the travel books of Norman Douglas. Unpub. doct. diss., Univ. of South Carolina, 1985. [Abstr. in DA (46) 3724A.]

Margaret Drabble

11698. BROMBERG, PAMELA S. The development of narrative technique in Margaret Drabble's novels. JNT (16:3) 179–91.

11699. MAYER, CHARLES W. Drabble and James: *A Voyage to Cythera* and *In the Cage. See* **8709.**

11700. RAINES, HELON HOWELL. The moving sphere: Margaret Drabble's novels of connection and contradiction. Unpub. doct. diss., Univ. of Denver, 1985. [Abstr. in DA (46) 2701A.]

11701. RICHER, CAROL FRENCH. Continuation and innovation in the contemporary British novel: the reflexive fiction of Margaret Drabble, Iris Murdoch, and John Fowles. Unpub. doct. diss., Purdue Univ., 1985. [Abstr. in DA (47) 174A.]

Theodore Dreiser

11702. GRIFFIN, JOSEPH. The small canvas: an introduction to Dreiser's short stories. Rutherford, NJ: Fairleigh Dickinson UP, 1985. pp. 172. Rev. by Vincent Fitzpatrick in AL (58:4) 644–7.

11702a. HAKUTANI, YOSHINOBU (ed.). Selected magazine articles of Theodore Dreiser: life and art in the American 1890s. Rutherford, NJ: Fairleigh Dickinson UP; London; Toronto: Assoc. UPs, 1985. pp. 288. Rev. by Helen McNeil in TLS, 21 Feb., 180.

11703. Hussman, Lawrence E., Jr.   Dreiser and his fiction: a twentieth-century quest. (Bibl. 1985, 10447.) Rev. by Stephen C. Brennan in MLS (16:3) 327–9.

11704. Lingeman, Richard.   Theodore Dreiser: at the gates of the city 1871–1907. New York: Putnam. pp. 478. Rev. by Cynthia Ozick in NYTB, 9 Nov., 3.

11705. Machor, James L.   Carrie's other sister. SAF (14:2) 199–204.

11706. Mizruchi, Susan Laura.   The power of historical knowledge: narrating the past in Hawthorne, James, and Dreiser. *See* **8485.**

11707. Schwartz, Carol Ann.   Class consciousness in the novels of Theodore Dreiser. Unpub. doct. diss., Columbia Univ., 1985. [Abstr. in DA (46) 2695A.]

Davis Dresser ('Brett Halliday', 'Robert Terrall', 'Peter Shelley', 'Anderson Wayne')

11708. Plummer, Bonnie.   Writing under a house name: Brett Halliday. Clues (7:2) 39–47.

Norman Dubie

11709. Bensko, John.   Reflexive narration in contemporary American poetry: some examples from Mark Strand, John Ashbery, Norman Dubie and Louis Simpson. *See* **11062.**

W. E. B. DuBois

11710. Howard-Pitney, David.   The enduring black jeremiad: the American jeremiad and black protest rhetoric, from Frederick Douglass to W. E. B. DuBois, 1841–1919. *See* **8164.**

11711. Jařab, Josef.   W. E. Burghart Dubois and the new negro movement. *In* (pp. 61–74) Günther Klotz, and Heinz Wüstenhagen (eds), Potsdamer Forschungen, A (72). Potsdam: Pädagogische Hochschule Karl Liebknecht. pp. 228.

Marilyn Duckworth

11712. McLeod, Marion.   Plots aplenty. NZList, 22 Nov., 34–7.

Louis Dudek

11713. Goldie, Terry.   Louis Dudek. *In* (pp. 75–139) **9.**

Paul Laurence Dunbar

11714. Okeke-Exigbo, Emeka.   Paul Laurence Dunbar and the Afro-American folk tradition. *See* **2389.**

Ralph Cheever Dunning

11715. Pound, Ezra.   Mr Dunning's poetry. Paideuma (10:3) 1981, 605–9. (Review pub. in *Poetry: a Magazine of Verse* (26:1) 1926.)

Edward John Plunkett, Lord Dunsany

11716. Duperray, Max.   Lord Dunsany: sa place dans une éventuelle littérature fantastique irlandaise. Études irlandaises (9) 1984, 81–8.

Lawrence Durrell

11717. Ali, Zahra Ahmed Hussein.   Between Shahrazad and Marcel Proust: narrative techniques in *The Alexandria Quartet*. Unpub. doct. diss., Brown Univ., 1985. [Abstr. in DA (46) 1945A.]

11718. Zahlan, Anne Ricketson.   The destruction of the imperial self in Lawrence Durrell's *The Alexandria Quartet*. PCL (12) 3–12.

Charles Judson Dutton
11719. KRAMER, JOHN E., JR. Harley Manners: a paragon of professional perfection. Clues (7:2) 113–45.

Eva Emery Dye
11720. SWANSON, KIMBERLY. Eva Emery Dye and the romance of Oregon history. PacH (29:4) 1985, 59–68.

'Bob Dylan' (Robert Zimmerman)
11721. HAVER, FRITZ WERNER. Bob Dylans surrealistische Songpoesie. Frankfurt: Lang. pp. 300. (Europäische Hochschulschriften: Reihe 14, Angelsächsische Sprache und Literatur, 165.)

Richard Eberhart
11722. PARINI, JOE. Richard Eberhart: personal notes. Paintbrush (11/12:21/24) 1984/85, 40–2.

Lauris Edmond
11723. WILSON, JANET. Catching up. NZList, 19 Apr., 26.

Dorothy Edwards
11724. MEREDITH, LUNED. Dorothy Edwards. Planet (55) 50–6.

Loren Eiseley
11725. PITTS, MARY ELLEN. Popularization and science: informing metaphors in Loren Eiseley. Unpub. doct. diss., Univ. of Florida, 1985. [Abstr. in DA (47) 1326A.]

T. S. Eliot
11726. ABRAHAM, IONA JOSEPH. From cosmogony to eschatology: a time-centered mythic structure for *Four Quartets* with significance for the teaching of literature. Unpub. doct. diss., Illinois State Univ. [Abstr. in DA (47) 1732A.]
11727. AGHA SHAHID, ALI. T. S. Eliot as editor. Ann Arbor, MI: UMI Research Press. pp. 173.
11728. BARR, A. F. M. A. Text and sub-text in T. S. Eliot (a general study of his practice, with special reference to the origins and development through successive drafts of *The Confidential Clerk*). Unpub. doct. diss., Univ. of St Andrews, 1985. [Abstr. in IT (35) 50–1.]
11729. BAWER, BRUCE. The Eliot riddle. NCrit (3:5) 1985, 55–62.
11730. BEDIENT, CALVIN. He do the police in different voices: *The Waste Land* and its protagonist. Chicago; London: Chicago UP. pp. xi, 225.
11731. BEHR, CAROLINE. T. S. Eliot: a chronology of his life and works. New York: St Martin's Press, 1983. (Cf. bibl. 1984, 10702.) Rev. by Ruth Z. Temple in Review (7) 1985, 338–40.
11732. BERARD, WAYNE STEPHEN. The detail of the pattern: music and the structural analogy in T. S. Eliot's *Four Quartets*. Unpub. doct. diss., Univ. of Rhode Island, 1984. [Abstr. in DA (46) 2297A.]
11733. BEUM, ROBERT. Five for Eliot. SewR (94:1) 124–7 (review-article).
11734. BILLMAN, CAROL. History versus mystery: the test of time in *Murder in the Cathedral*. CLIO (10:1) 1980, 47–56.
11735. BIZLEY, W. H. The decadent metropolis as frontier: Eliot, Laforge and Baudelaire. Theoria (68) 25–35.

11736. BRØGGER, FREDERIK CHR.   Modernism and antimodernism: Eliot's *The Waste Land* as an 'American' poem. *In* (pp. 225–38) **18.**

11737. BURR, NELSON R.   New Eden and new Babylon: religious thoughts of American authors: a bibliography: the Catholic heritage outside Roman allegiance. *See* **2605.**

11738. BUSH, RONALD.   T. S. Eliot: a study in character and style. (Bibl. 1985, 10505.) Rev. by Jewel Spears Brooker in MP (83:3) 325–30; by Ruth Z. Temple in Review (7) 1985, 332–4.

11739. CANARY, ROBERT H.   T. S. Eliot: the poet and his critics. (Bibl. 1985, 10506.) Rev. by Ruth Z. Temple in Review (7) 1985, 342–5.

11740. CHILDS, D. J.   The religious dimensions of T. S. Eliot's early life, poetry and thought. Unpub. doct. diss., Univ. of Hull, 1984. [Abstr. in IT (35) 51.]

11741. CHOI, JONG-SOO.   T. S. Eliot's intolerable wrestle with sense and sound. CAE (19) 401–24.

11742. CHOUINARD, TIMOTHY MARK.   T. S. Eliot: a philosophy of communication for literature and speech. Unpub. doct. diss., Saint Louis Univ., 1985. [Abstr. in DA (46) 3701A.]

11743. COUTOUVIDIS, JOHN.   T. S. Eliot's preface to *The Dark Side of the Moon*: his model of society in the light of Polish experience. Text & Context (1:1) 31–45.

11744. COWAN, S. A.   An allusion to Thomas Hood's *Mermaid of Margate* in T. S. Eliot's *Waste Land. See* **8543.**

11745. CRAWFORD, R.   The savage and the city in the work of T. S. Eliot. Unpub. doct. diss., Univ. of Oxford, 1984.

11746. CRAWFORD, ROBERT.   Rudyard Kipling in *The Waste Land*. EC (36:1) 32–46.

11747. DAVIDSON, HARRIET.   T. S. Eliot and hermeneutics: absence and interpretation in *The Waste Land*. Baton Rouge: Louisiana State UP, 1985. (Cf. bibl. 1983, 10991.) Rev. by Margaret Moran in AL (58:1) 114–17.

11748. DESMOND, JOHN.   Walker Percy and T. S. Eliot: the Lancelot Andrewes connection. *See* **5260.**

11749. ELLMANN, M.   Impersonality in the poetry and criticism of T. S. Eliot and Ezra Pound. Unpub. doct. diss., Univ. of Oxford, 1982.

11750. FORD, P. K.   The later W. H. Auden as a Christian poet. *See* **11095.**

11751. GEARY, EDWARD A.   T. S. Eliot and the *fin de siècle*. RMRLL (40:1/2) 21–33.

11752. GILLUM, MICHAEL.   Ennui and alienation in Eliot's poetry. MidQ (25) 1984, 386–96.

11753. GÖRANSSON, SVERKER; MESTERTON, ERIK.   Den orörliga lågan: T. S. Eliot's *The Love Song of J. Alfred Prufrock* – en strukturanalys. (The immobile flame: T. S. Eliots *The Love Song of J. Alfred Prufrock* – a structural analysis.) Artes (12:6) 21–6.

11754. GOTTLIEB, SIDNEY.   Eliot's *The Death of Saint Narcissus* and Herbert's *Affliction (1). See* **5482.**

11755. GRANT, MICHAEL (ed.). T. S. Eliot: the critical heritage. (Bibl. 1982, 11096.) Rev. by Ruth Z. Temple in Review (7) 1985, 340–2.

11756. GRUSZEWSKA-WOJTAS, LUDMIŁA. Funkcjonowanie struktur przestrzennych w *Pieśni miłosnej J. Alfreda Prufrocka* T. S. Eliota. (The function of spatial structures in *The Love Song of J. Alfred Prufrock*.) KN (33) 227–39.

11757. GUNNER, EUGENIA M. T. S. Eliot's romantic dilemma: tradition's anti-traditional elements. New York; London: Garland, 1985. pp. iii, 158. (Garland pubs in comparative literature.)

11758. HARMON, WILLIAM. Eliot and his problems. SewR (94:3) 510–17 (review-article).

11759. HAY, ELOISE KNAPP. T. S. Eliot's negative way. (Bibl. 1984, 10730.) Rev. by Diane S. Bonds in JEGP (85:1) 153–4.

11760. HELMS, RANDEL. T. S. Eliot on Gilbert Murray. ELN (23:4) 50–6.

11761. IKEYA, TOSHITADA. Hikaku bungaku ronshu: T. S. Eliot wo chushin ni. (Studies in comparative literature: with special reference to T. S. Eliot.) Tokyo: Kogaku Press. pp. 234.

11762. JAIN, M. Scepticism and belief: some aspects of T. S. Eliot's development and its intellectual context, 1911–1922. Unpub. doct. diss., Univ. of Cambridge, 1985.

11763. JOYCE, C. Critics in context: aspects of the work of T. S. Eliot, John Middleton Murry and F. R. Leavis. Unpub. doct. diss., Univ. of Reading, 1983.

11764. KARI, DAVEN MICHAEL. T. S. Eliot's dramatic pilgrimage: a growth in craft as an expression of Christian perpective. Unpub. doct. diss., Purdue Univ. [Abstr. in DA (47) 2154A.]

11765. KARLEKAR, RANAJAY. T. E. Hulme and T. S. Eliot: crisis and tradition. Jadavpur University Essays and Studies (Calcutta) (4) 1984, 130–45.

11766. KENNEDY, ANDREW. A young person's Eliot: a personal recollection, based on 1948–51. In (pp. 275–83) **18.**

11767. KIM, DONG-YONG. T. S. Eliot eui *Four Quartets* eui gujo. (The structure of T. S. Eliot's *Four Quartets.*) Unpub. doct. diss., Geonguk Univ. (Korea).

11768. Entry cancelled.

11769. KIM, MYONG-OK. Eliot eui Donne bipyeong gwa Donne si eui hyeondaesung. See **5377.**

11770. LEE, EUN-HWAN. T. S. Eliot eui *Four Quartets* a natanan jungsim image yeongu. (A study of the image of the 'centre' in T. S. Eliot's *Four Quartets.*) Unpub. doct. diss., Chonnam National Univ. (Korea), 1985.

11771. LICKINDORF, E. T. The literary relations of T. S. Eliot and Ezra Pound, 1914–1922. Unpub. doct. diss., Univ. of Oxford. [Abstr. in IT (35) 548–9.]

11772. LOJKINE, MONIQUE. T. S. Eliot: entre l'aspiration à l'éternel présent de l'Eden retrouvé et apocalypse now. In (pp. 213–29) **2.**

11773. McNAMARA, ROBERT JAMES.   Alternate selves: Pound, Eliot, and the constructivist ethos. Unpub. doct. diss., Univ. of Washington, 1985. [Abstr. in DA (46) 3716A.]

11774. MANGANARO, MARC.   Dissociation in 'Dead Land': the primitive mind in the early poetry of T. S. Eliot. JML (13:1) 97–110.

11775. —— T. S. Eliot and the primitive mind. Unpub. doct. diss., Univ. of North Carolina at Chapel Hill, 1985. [Abstr. in DA (46) 3361A.]

11776. MENAND, LOUIS.   T. S. Eliot and F. H. Bradley. Raritan (5:3) 61–75.

11777. MITCHELL, GILES.   T. S. Eliot's *The Waste Land*: death, fear, apathy, and dehumanization. AI (43:1) 23–33.

11778. NEMBHARD, L. S.   Spiritual quest as aesthetic vision: aspects of T. S. Eliot's poetics as related to his literary works. Unpub. doct. diss., Univ. of Hull, 1984.

11779. NERY, ANTONIO WAGNER.   T. S. Eliot and the myth of Christ: an analysis of Prufrock, Tiresias and Becket. Unpub. doct. diss., George Washington Univ. [Abstr. in DA (47) 526A.]

11780. OAKES, RANDY W.   Myth and method: Eliot, Joyce, and Wolfe in *The Web and the Rock*. TWR (10:1) 23–6.

11781. PERKINS, DAVID.   Johnson and modern poetry. *See* **6617.**

11782. PHELAN, VIRGINIA B.   Euripides' *Alcestis* and T. S. Eliot's *The Cocktail Party*: two ways of life and death. Unpub. doct. diss., Rutgers Univ. [Abstr. in DA (47) 2152A.]

11783. PINION, F. B.   A T. S. Eliot companion: life and works. Basingstoke: Macmillan, pp. xii, 304. (Macmillan literary companions.)

11784. RAFFEL, BURTON.   Possum and Ole Ez in the public eye: contemporaries and peers on T. S. Eliot and Ezra Pound 1892–1972. Hamden, CT: Archon, 1985. pp. 143. Rev. by Margaret Moran in AL (58:1) 114–17.

11785. RHEE, JOON-HAK.   Ingan gotong eui geunwon c daehan tamsaek: T. S. Eliot eui *The Family Reunion*. (The search for the origin of human suffering: T. S. Eliot's *The Family Reunion*.) JELL (32:3) 479–503.

11786. RICHARDS, MARY MARGARET.   The idea of Rome in the work of T. S. Eliot. Unpub. doct. diss., Univ. of North Carolina at Chapel Hill. [Abstr. in DA (47) 1736A.]

11787. ROBERSON, SUSAN L.   T. S. Eliot's symbolical woman: from temptress to priestess. MidQ (27:4) 476–86.

11788. ROMER, S. C. M.   T. S. Eliot: post-Symbolist. Unpub. doct. diss., Univ. of Cambridge, 1985. [Abstr. in IT (35) 53.]

11789. SCHWARTZ, SANFORD.   The matrix of Modernism: Pound, Eliot and early twentieth-century thought. Princeton, NJ: Princeton UP, 1985. pp. x, 235. Rev. by Andrew Vincent in THES (693) 16; by Alison Rieke in AL (58:4) 648–50; by Paul Smith in DalR(65:4) 1985/86, 577–9.

11790. SCOTT, ROBERT IAN.   T. S. Eliot and the original *Waste Land*. *See* **7851.**

11791. SPURR, DAVID.   Conflicts in consciousness: T. S. Eliot's poetry and criticism. (Bibl. 1985, 10597.) Rev. by Ruth Z. Temple in Review (7) 1985, 334–7.

11792. STAUDT, KATHLEEN HENDERSON. The language of T. S. Eliot's *Four Quartets* and David Jones's *The Anathemata*. Ren (38:2) 118–30.

11793. STEINER, WENDY. Collage or miracle: historicism in a deconstructed world. *In* (pp. 323–51) **47.**

11794. SUH, SOO-CHUL. T. S. Eliot eui sigan eui euisig: geu eui si e natanan sigan gwa mu-sigan eui segae. (T. S. Eliot's consciousness of time: the world of time and non-time in T. S. Eliot's poetry.) Unpub. doct. diss., Yeungnam Univ. (Korea), 1985.

11795. SYPHER, WYLIE. Mrs Post, may I present Mr Eliot. ASch (54) 1985, 250–2.

11796. TEMPLE, RUTH Z. Waste land indeed: Eliot in our time. Review (7) 1985, 329–45 (review-article).

11797. TETREAULT, JAMES. Parallel lines: C. S. Lewis and T. S. Eliot. Ren (38:4) 256–69.

11798. TETZELI VON ROSADOR, KURT. Christian historical drama: the exemplariness of *Murder in the Cathedral*. ModDr (29:4) 516–31.

11799. TOBIN, DAVID NED. The presence of the past: T. S. Eliot's Victorian inheritance. Ann Arbor, MI: UMI Research Press, 1983. (Cf. bibl. 1984, 10771.) Rev. by Ruth Z. Temple in Review (7) 1985, 337–8.

11800. TOMLINSON, JOHN. Poetry and metamorphosis. Cambridge: CUP, 1983. pp. xi, 97. Rev. by Ruth Z. Temple in Review (7) 1985, 331–2.

11801. TROTTER, DAVID. Modernism and empire: reading *The Waste Land*. CritQ (28:1/2) 143–53.

11802. TRUBOWITZ, RACHEL. The past in the present: T. S. Eliot's idea of the seventeenth century. *See* **5089.**

11803. UNGER, LEONARD. Eliot's compound ghost: influence and confluence. London: Pennsylvania State UP, 1981. (Cf. bibl. 1984, 10772.) Rev. by A. V. C. Schmidt in MLR (81:1) 188–90.

11804. VIANU, LIDIA. T. S. Eliot: an author for all seasons. Bucharest: Bucharest Univ., 1984. pp. 325.

11805. WARNER, MARTIN. Philosophical poetry: the case of *Four Quartets*. PhilL (10:2) 222–45.

11806. WILLIAMS, GEOFFREY BERNARD. The reason in a storm: a study of the notion of ambiguity in the writings of T. S. Eliot. Unpub. doct. diss., Univ. of Toronto, 1985. [Abstr. in DA (47) 917A.]

11807. YANCEY, PHILIP. T. S. Eliot's Christian society: still relevant today? ChCen (103:35) 1031–3.

'Elizabeth' (Mary Annette, Countess von Arnim)

11808. USBORNE, KAREN. 'Elizabeth': the author of *Elizabeth and her German Garden*. London: Bodley Head. pp. viii, 340. Rev. by David Pryce-Jones in TLS, 14 Nov., 1265; by Penelope Fitzgerald in LRB (8:21) 18; by Valerie Shaw in Listener, 4 Dec., 22.

Stanley Elkin

11809. BAILEY, PETER J.   Reading Stanley Elkin. Urbana: Illinois UP, 1985. pp. 220. Rev. by Steven Moore in ANQ (24:9/10) 156.

11810. ROBINS, WILLIAM M.   Stanley Elkin: the art of the novel. Unpub. doct. diss., Univ. of South Carolina. [Abstr. in DA (47) 1326A.]

Ralph Ellison

11811. ELLISON, RALPH.   New York, 1936. Esquire (106:1) 98–9, 101–3.

11812. FRANK, JOSEPH.   Ralph Ellison and a literary 'ancestor': Dostoevsky. NCrit (2) Sept. 1983, 11–21.

11813. LYNCH, MICHAEL FRANCIS.   Richard Wright, Ralph Ellison, and Dostoevsky: the choice of individual freedom and dignity. Unpub. doct. diss., Kent State Univ., 1985. [Abstr. in DA (47) 179A.]

11814. MARMORSTEIN, GARY.   Ralph Ellison's not-so-new novel. Ob (6) Winter 1980, 7–21.

11815. SAMUELS, WILFRED D.   Ellison's *Invisible Man*. Exp (44:2) 47–9.

James Emanuel

11816. McCONOCHIE, JEAN (gen. ed.).   A poet's mind. New York: Regents, 1983. pp. x, 85. (Regents readers.) Rev. by Anthony Suter in Caliban (23) 137–40.

11817. SUTER, ANTHONY.   A poet's self. Caliban (23) 137–43 (review-article).

Buchi Emecheta

11818. SLOMSKI, GENEVIEVE T.   Dialogue in the discourse: a study of revolt in selected fiction by African women. Unpub. doct. diss., Indiana Univ. [Abstr. in DA (47) 1721A.]

11819. Entry cancelled.

William Empson

11820. HAFFENDEN, JOHN (ed.).   *The Royal Beasts* and other works. London: Chatto & Windus. pp. 201. Rev. by Ann Pasternak Slater in TLS, 14 Nov., 1271–2.

11821. PIRIE, DAVID B. (ed.).   Essays on Shakespeare. *See* **4554.**

Howard Engel

11822. WHITE, ROBERT.   Borderline cases: the private eye novels of Howard Engel. JAC (9:1) 37–43.

Marian Engel

11823. HOWELLS, CORAL ANN.   Marian Engel's *Bear*: pastoral, porn, and myth. Ariel (17:4) 105–14.

Hubert Evans

11824. WOODCOCK, GEORGE.   Hubert Evans. CanL (111) 240–1.

Frederick Exley

11825. EXLEY, FREDERICK.   The laureate of Alexandria Bay. Esquire (105:3) 214–18.

A. R. D. Fairburn

11826. TRUSSELL, DENYS.   Fairburn. (Bibl. 1985, 10651.) Rev. by Peter Simpson in Landfall (40:1) 107–13.

Nuruddin Farah

11827. ADAM, IAN. The murder of Soyaan Keynaan. WLWE (26:2) 203–11.

Eleanor Farjeon

11828. FARJEON, ANNABEL. Morning has broken: a biography of Eleanor Farjeon. London: MacRae. pp. 315. Rev. in Growing Point (25:2) 4663; by Naomi Lewis in Listener, 3 July, 31–2.

J. G. Farrell

11829. BINNS, RONALD. Chronicler of the thin red line. THES (709) 15.

11830. —— J. G. Farrell. London: Methuen. pp. 96. (Contemporary writers.)

11831. HARTVEIT, LARS. Ideological stock-taking in J. G. Farrell's historical fiction. In (pp. 251–62) **18.**

James T. Farrell

11832. BUTLER, ROBERT JAMES. The Christian roots of Farrell's O'Neill and Carr novels. Ren (34:2) 1982, 81–99.

11833. CARINO, PETER ALFONSO. Plot in *Studs Lonigan*: the failure of manhood, the triumph of artistry. Unpub. doct. diss., Univ. of Illinois at Urbana-Champaign, 1985. [Abstr. in DA (46) 1940A.]

11834. LESSER, MATTHEW BERNARD. James T. Farrell as literary realist and social historian. Unpub. doct. diss., Univ. of New Mexico, 1985. [Abstr. in DA (46) 1942A.]

11835. LOUGHMAN, CELESTE. 'Old now, and good to her': J. T. Farrell's last novels. Éire–Ireland (20:3) 1985, 43–55.

11836. MAIR, CHRISTIAN. Geschichtsverständnis und Textstruktur im sozialkritischen amerikanischen Roman der dreißiger Jahre – John Dos Passos, James T. Farrell, Josephine Herbst. *See* **11690.**

William Faulkner

11837. AARSETH, ASBJØRN. Myth and metanarration in the modern novel: remarks on Faulkner's *Absalom, Absalom!* and Simon's *La Route des Flandres*. In (pp. 341–5) **19.**

11838. ARESU, BERNARD. Gilbert Durand and the mythical structure of time in three novels by Faulkner, Simon and Kateb. In (pp. 437–41) **19.**

11839. BARBERA, JACK. Tomorrow and tomorrow and *Tomorrow*. SoQ (19:3/4) 1981, 183–97.

11840. BARNETT, LOUISE K. The speech community of *The Hamlet*. CR (30:3) 400–14.

11841. BASSETT, JOHN E. Gradual progress and *Intruder in the Dust*. CLit (13:3) 207–16.

11842. BIRON, BETH DYER. Faulkner in French: a study of the translations of his major works and their influence in French literature. Unpub. doct. diss., Univ. of Georgia. [Abstr. in DA (47) 2153A.]

11843. BLEIKASTEN, ANDRÉ. Faulkner descripteur. RANAM (19) 147–64.

11844. —— Parcours de Faulkner. Paris: Ophrys, 1982. (Cf. bibl. 1983, 11087.) Rev. by Michael Millgate in EA (39:4) 485–6.

11845. —— Temps, mythe et histoire chez Faulkner. *In* (pp. 173–93) **2.**

11846. BLOTNER, JOSEPH; POLK, NOEL (eds). Novels 1930–1935: *As I Lay Dying, Sanctuary, Light in August, Pylon.* New York: Library of America; Cambridge: CUP, 1985. pp. 1034. (Library of America, 25.)

11847. BOSWELL, GEORGE W. North Mississippi contributions to Faulkner's fiction. *See* **2397.**

11848. BRENNAN, DAN. A visit with Faulkner. SatR, May/June, 72.

11849. BRODSKY, LOUIS D. The 1961 Andrés Bello Award: William Faulkner's original Acceptance Speech. SB (39) 277–81.

11850. BRODSKY, LOUIS DANIEL. Faulkner's life masks. SoR (22:4) 738–65.

11851. —— Twenty-five years as a Faulkner collector. *See* **199.**

11852. —— HAMBLIN, ROBERT W. Faulkner: a comprehensive guide to the Brodsky collection: vol. 3, *The De Gaulle Story* by William Faulkner. *See* **200.**

11853. —— —— Faulkner: a comprehensive guide to the Brodsky collection: vol. 4, *Battle Cry*: a screenplay by William Faulkner. *See* **201.**

11854. BROOKS, CLEANTH. William Faulkner: first encounters. (Bibl. 1985, 10675.) Rev. by Ilse Dusoir Lind in SAF (14:1) 109–10; by Pär Hellström in Samlaren (106) 1985, 116–18.

11855. BROWN, CALVIN S. These thirteen Faulkner books. SewR (94:1) 167–80 (review-article).

11856. BUCKWALTER, MICHAEL. Benjy's sound and fury: a critical study of four interpretations. YREAL (4) 265–90.

11857. CAROTHERS, JAMES. B. William Faulkner's short stories. Ann Arbor, MI: UMI Research Press, 1985. pp. xvii, 165. Rev. by Walter Taylor in AL (58:2) 277–9.

11858. CERQUEIA, NELSON. Hermeneutics and literature: a study of William Faulkner's *As I Lay Dying* and Graciliano Ramos's *Vidas secas.* Unpub. doct. diss., Indiana Univ. [Abstr. in DA (47) 1719A.]

11859. CHAE, KYU-TAE. Dokjaronjeok gwanjeom eseo bon Faulkner soseol eui gaebangsung. (The openness of Faulkner's novels: from the reader's viewpoint.) Unpub. doct. diss., Sungkyunkwan Univ. (Seoul).

11860. CHAPPELL, CHARLES. The Memphis lawyer and his spine: another piece of the *Sanctuary* puzzle. ELit (13:2) 331–8.

11861. COHEN, PHILIP. Horace Benbow and Faulkner's other early failed idealists. SoCR (18:2) 78–92.

11862. —— Some recent titles in Faulkner studies. RALS (15:11) 1985, 31–47 (review-article).

11863. COLLINS, CARVEL. Likeness within difference: Cabell and Faulkner. *See* **11369.**

11864. CONLEY, TIMOTHY KEVIN. Resounding fury: Faulkner's Shakespeare, Shakespeare's Faulkner. *In* (pp. 83–124) **51.**

11865. CORNELL, BRENDA G. Faulkner's *Evangeline*: a preliminary stage. SoQ (22:4) 1984, 22–41.

11866. CROWELL, RICHARD C. 'Whose woods these are': art and values in William Faulkner's Snopes trilogy. Unpub. doct. diss., Southern Illinois Univ. at Carbondale, 1985. [Abstr. in DA (46) 3032A.]

11867. DAVIS, THADIOUS M. Faulkner's 'Negro': art and the Southern context. (Bibl. 1985, 10686.) Rev. by Craig Werner in MLS (16:3) 329–36.

11868. DE MONTAUZON, CHRISTINE. Faulkner's *Absalom, Absalom!* and interpretability: the inexplicable unseen. New York: Long, 1985. pp. xvi, 325. Rev. by Doreen Fowler in AL (58:4) 658–9.

11869. DITSKY, JOHN. William Faulkner's *The Wishing Tree*: maturity's first draft. LU (2:1) 1978, 56–64.

11870. DONALDSON, SUSAN V. Isaac McCaslin and the possibilities of vision. SoR (22:1) 37–50.

11871. EMERSON, O. B.; HERMANN, JOHN P. William Faulkner and the Faulkner family name. *See* **1701.**

11872. FLORA, JOSEPH M. Cabell and Faulkner: connections literary and otherwise. *See* **11370.**

11873. FOLKS, JEFFREY J. William Faulkner and the silent film. SoQ (19:3/4) 1981, 171–82.

11874. FOUST, R. E. Desperate gambits, game theory, and modern American literature. SoCR (17:1) 1984, 96–108.

11875. FOWLER, DOREEN. Time and punishment in Faulkner's *Requiem for a Nun*. Ren (38:4) 245–55.

11876. —— ABADIE, ANN J. (eds). Faulkner and humor: Faulkner and Yoknapatawpha, 1984. Jackson; London: Mississippi UP. pp. xv, 243.

11877. —— —— New directions in Faulkner studies. Jackson: Mississippi UP, 1984. pp. xviii, 390. Rev. by Thomas Bonner, Jr, in SCR (3:1) 98–100.

11878. FRIEDMAN, ALAN WARREN. William, Faulkner. New York: Ungar, 1985. pp. 240. Rev. by Helen McNeil in TLS, 27 June, 704.

11879. GRESSET, MICHEL. A Faulkner chronology. Jackson: Mississippi UP, 1985. pp. xv, 120. Rev. by George W. Van Devender in SCR (3:1) 100–1; by Helen McNeil in TLS, 27 June, 704.

11880. —— SAMWAY, PATRICK (eds). Faulkner and idealism: perspectives from Paris. (Bibl. 1984, 10856.) Rev. by Joan Templeton in EA (38:3) 1985, 358–9.

11881. —— POLK, NOEL (eds). Intertextuality in Faulkner. Jackson: Mississippi UP, 1985. pp. 217. Rev. by Phillip Castille in SCR (3:2) 112–14.

11882. HAMM, NAN WIENER. The secret burden: race and narrative form in the novels of William Faulkner. Unpub. doct. diss., Univ. of Virginia, 1985. [Abstr. in DA (47) 1728A.]

11883. HARRISON, JAMES. Faulkner's *The Old People*. Exp (44:2) 41.

11884. HAYASHI, FUMIYO. Faulkner's another country: a study of *Pylon*, *The Wild Palms*, and *A Fable*. Unpub. doct. diss., Indiana Univ., 1985. [Abstr. in DA (46) 3719A.]

11885. HILL, JANE BOWERS. Beyond myth: sexual identity in *Light in*

August and other novels by William Faulkner. Unpub. doct. diss., Univ. of Illinois at Urbana-Champaign, 1985. [Abstr. in DA (46) 3351A.]

11886. HINKLE, JAMES.   Reading Faulkner's *The Unvanquished*. CLit (13:3) 217–39.

11887. HÖNNIGHAUSEN, LOTHAR.   Faulkner's poetry. YREAL (2) 1984, 355–69.

11888. HURCOMBE, R. A.   The phenomenon of Faulkner: myth, authority and melodrama: some readings and re-readings of Faulkner. Unpub. doct. diss., Univ. of York, 1984.

11889. JENKINS, LEE.   Faulkner and black–white relations: a psycho-analytic approach. (Bibl. 1985, 10709.) Rev. by Craig Werner in MLS (16:3) 329–36.

11890. JOHNSON, M. SUZANNE PAUL.   William Faulkner's *Pylon*: annotations for the novel. Unpub. doct. diss., Univ. of South Carolina, 1985. [Abstr. in DA (46) 3034A.]

11891. KIM, JONG-TACK.   William Faulkner yeongu: daejo gusung gwa jujae. (A study of William Faulkner: the contradictory structure and the theme.) Unpub. doct. diss., Hankuk Univ. of Foreign Studies (Seoul).

11892. KIM, WOOK-DONG.   Mobang gwa changjo: Faulkner eui si. (Faulkner as a failed poet.) JELL (32:3) 505–20.

11893. KLEINBARD, DAVID.   *As I Lay Dying*: literary imagination, the child's mind, and mental illness. SoR (22:1) 51–68.

11894. KRAUSE, DAVID.   Opening Pandora's box: re-reading Compson's letter and Faulkner's *Absalom, Absalom!* CR (30:3) 358–82.

11895. KREISWIRTH, MARTIN.   William Faulkner: the making of a novelist. (Bibl. 1985, 10711.) Rev. by Shyamal Bagchee in ESCan (12:3) 365–8; by André Bleikasten in EA (38:3) 1985, 358.

11896. KUHLMANN, DEBORAH JANE.   William Faulkner and Virginia Woolf: the movement of the moment, a dialectic. Unpub. doct. diss., Texas Christian Univ., 1985. [Abstr. in DA (46) 3346A.]

11897. KURTZ, ELIZABETH CARNEY.   Faulkner's *A Rose for Emily*. Exp (44:2) 40.

11898. KWON, KYUNG-DEUK.   William Faulkner eui soseol e natanan ingan sowoe eui munjee. (The problem of human alienation in William Faulkner's novels.) Unpub. doct. diss., Jeonbuk National Univ. (Korea).

11899. LALONDE, CHRISTOPHER ARDEN.   Faulkner's frontier: rites of passage in five novels. Unpub. doct. diss., State Univ. of New York at Buffalo. [Abstr. in DA (47) 2159A.]

11900. LIMONS, JOHN.   The integration of Faulkner's *Go Down, Moses*. CI (12:2) 422–38.

11901. LUCENTE, GREGORY L.   Narrative of realism and myth: Verga, Lawrence, Faulkner, Pavese. (Bibl. 1982, 11240.) Rev. by Armin Arnold in CanRCL (12:3) 1985, 558–9.

11902. McHANEY, THOMAS (ed.).   William Faulkner manuscripts: 14, *The Wild Palms*: vol. 1, Holograph manuscript and miscellaneous rejected holograph pages. *See* **164.**

11903. MATHEWS, LINDA. Shaping the life of man: Darl Bundren as supplementary narrator in *As I Lay Dying*. JNT (16:3) 231–45.

11904. MORTIMER, GAIL. Evolutionary theory in Faulkner's Snopes trilogy. RMRLL (40:4) 187–202.

11905. MORTIMER, GAIL L. Faulkner's rhetoric of loss: a study in perception and meaning. (Bibl. 1985, 10727.) Rev. by Peter Verney in DalR (65:4) 1985/86, 606–8.

11906. MOSELEY, MERRITT. Faulkner's Benjy, Hemingway's Jake. CLit (13:3) 300–4.

11907. NAH, YOUNG-GYUN. Mal, hangdong geurigo euishik: *As I Lay Dying* reul jungsim euro. (Word, action, perception: three modes of living in *As I Lay Dying*.) JELL (32:4) 843–57.

11908. NISHIYAMA, TAMOTU. Yoknapatawpha monigatari: watashi no Faulkner. (Yoknapatawpha saga: my Faulkner.) Tokyo: Furukawa Press. pp. x, 396.

11909. OHASHI, KENZABURO; ONO, KIYOYUKI (comps); McHANEY, THOMAS L. (ed.). Faulkner studies in Japan. Athens: Georgia UP, 1985. pp. xvii, 214. Rev. by Don L. Cook in AL (58:4) 660–1.

11910. PALLISER, CHARLES. Predestination and freedom in *As I Lay Dying*. AL (58:4) 557–73.

11911. PARK, YUP. Faulkner wa Logos eui segae. (Faulkner and the world of Logos.) JELL (32:2) 237–53.

11912. PARKER, R. N. The notion of the outsider in the writings of Cooper, Hawthorne, Twain and Faulkner. *See* **7968.**

11913. PARKER, ROBERT DALE. The chronology and genealogy of *Absalom, Absalom!*: the authority of fiction and the fiction of authority. SAF (14:2) 191–8.

11914. —— Faulkner and the novelistic imagination. Urbana: Illinois UP, 1985. pp. 168. Rev. by Walter Taylor in AL (58:2) 277–9.

11915. PETRY, ALICE HALL. Faulkner's *A Rose for Emily*. Exp (44:3) 52–4.

11916. PRATT, PETER PHILIP. The paradoxical wilderness: Mailer and American nature writing. *See* **9372.**

11917. PUTZEL, MAX. Genius of place: William Faulkner's triumphant beginnings. London: Louisiana State UP, 1985. (Cf. bibl. 1985, 10739.) Rev. by Judith L. Sensibar in CR (30:1) 120–1; by Helen McNeil in TLS, 27 June, 704.

11918. RABBETTS, J. The ache of modernism: a comparative study of the novels of Thomas Hardy and William Faulkner. *See* **8428.**

11919. RADLOFF, BERNHARD. *Absalom, Absalom!* An ontological approach to Sutpen's 'design'. Mosaic (19:1) 45–56.

11920. —— Time and timepieces: a note on Quentin's section in *The Sound and the Fury*. ELN (23:3) 51–7.

11921. RAGAN, DAVID PAUL. William Faulkner's *Absalom, Absalom!*: a critical study. Unpub. doct. diss., Univ. of South Carolina, 1985. [Abstr. in DA (46) 3720A.]

11922. ROLLYSON, CARL E., JR. 'Counterpull': Estelle and William Faulkner. SAQ (85:3) 215–27.

11923. ROUSSELLE, MELINDA McLEOD. William Faulkner's *Sanctuary*: annotations to both versions of the novel. Unpub. doct. diss., Univ. of South Carolina, 1985. [Abstr. in DA (47) 182A.]

11924. SCHWARTZ, LAWRENCE H. Publishing William Faulkner. SoQ (22:2) 1984, 70–92.

11925. SKEI, HANS H. William Faulkner: the novelist as short story writer: a study of William Faulkner's short fiction. (Bibl. 1985, 10750.) Rev. by Walter Taylor in AL (58:2) 277–9; by Helen McNeil in TLS, 27 June, 704.

11926. SNEAD, JAMES A. Figures of division: William Faulkner's major novels. New York; London: Methuen. pp. 224.

11927. SUNDQUIST, ERIC J. Faulkner: the house divided. (Bibl. 1985, 10757.) Rev. by Craig Werner in MLS (16:3) 329–36.

11928. SWARTZLANDER, SUSAN. 'That meager and fragile thread': the artist as historian in *Absalom, Absalom!* SoS (25:1) 111–19.

11929. TANAKA, TAKAKO. Silence and words in William Faulkner's *Light in August*. Unpub. doct. diss., Lehigh Univ. [Abstr. in DA (46) 3721A.]

11930. TANGUM, MARION MAST. Voices in *Go Down, Moses*: Faulkner's dialogic rhetoric. Unpub. doct. diss., Univ. of Texas at Austin. [Abstr. in DA (47) 1731A.]

11931. TAYLOR, WALTER. Faulkner's search for a South. (Bibl. 1985, 10758.) Rev. by Craig Werner in MLS (16:3) 329–36.

11932. TOKIMITSU, SANAE. Faulkner and/or writing: on *Absalom, Absalom!*. Tokyo: Liberu Press. pp. x, 152.

11933. URGO, JOSEPH R. William Faulkner: a literature of the life experience. Unpub. doct. diss., Brown Univ. [Abstr. in DA (47) 1731A.]

11934. WATSON, JAMES G. Literary self-criticism: Faulkner in fiction on fiction. SoQ (20:1) 1981, 46–63.

Brian Fawcett

11935. HARRIS, JOHN. Brian Fawcett: the routes of imagination. ECanW (32) 41–69.

11936. McKINNON, BARRY. Interview with Brian Fawcett. *See* **644.**

David Fennario

11937. DESSON, JIM; FILSON, BRUCE K. Where is David Fennario now? CanTR (46) 36–41.

Edward Fenton

11938. GLASSER, WILLIAM. Creative children: characterized and criticized. LU (1:2) 1977, 40–6.

James Fenton

11939. GÓMEZ LARA, MANUEL. A conversation with James Fenton. RCEI (12) 161–9.

Lawrence Ferlinghetti

11940. MASNEROVÁ, EVA. Nové setkání s Ferlinghettim. (A new meeting with Lawrence Ferlinghetti.) Literární měsíčnik (15:2) 129–30.

'Gabriel Fielding' (Alan Gabriel Barnsley)

11941. TALIAFERRO, FRANCES. Who is Gabriel Fielding? NCrit (2) Nov. 1983, 18–22.

Robert Finch

11942. TREHEARNE, BRIAN.   Finch's early poetry and the dandy manner. CanP (18) 11–34.

Timothy Findley

11943. BENSON, EUGENE.   Interview with Timothy Findley. WLWE (26:1) 107–15.

11944. BRYDON, DIANA.   A devotion to fragility: Timothy Findley's *The Wars.* WLWE (26:1) 75–84.

11945. —— 'It could not be told': making meaning in Timothy Findley's *The Wars.* JCL (21:1) 62–79.

11946. INGHAM, DAVID KEITH.   Mediation and the indirect metafiction of Randolph Stow, M. K. Joseph, and Timothy Findley. Unpub. doct. diss., Univ. of British Columbia, 1985. [Abstr. in DA (47) 2154A.]

11947. MCKENZIE, M. L.   Memories of the Great War: Graves, Sassoon, and Findley. UTQ (55:4) 395–411.

11948. VAUTHIER, SIMONE.   The dubious battle of story-telling: narrative strategies in Timothy Findley's *The Wars. In* (pp. 11–39) **22.**

Ian Hamilton Finlay

11949. ABRIOUX, YVES.   Ian Hamilton Finlay: a visual primer. Edinburgh: Reaktion, 1985. pp. 248. Rev. in Edinburgh Review (72) 94–6.

11950. BANN, STEPHEN.   Apollo in Strathclyde. Cencrastus (22) 39–42.

11951. EYRES, PATRICK.   'Hedgehog' Stonypath & the Little Spartan War. Cencrastus (22) 35–7.

11952. MORGAN, EDWIN.   Early Finlay. Cencrastus (22) 21–3.

Ronald Firbank

11953. MORTIMER, JOHN (introd.).   The flower beneath the foot. Harmondsworth: Penguin. pp. 127. (Penguin modern classics.)

Roy Fisher

11954. BARRY, PETER.   Language and the city in Roy Fisher's poetry. EngS (67:3) 234–49.

11955. SHEPPARD, ROBERT.   Turning the prism: an interview with Roy Fisher. London: Toads Damp. pp. 26.

Rudolph Fisher

11956. DEUTSCH, LEONARD J.   Rudolph Fisher's unpublished manuscripts: description and commentary. Ob (6) Spring/Summer 1980, 82–97.

Vardis Fisher

11957. STRONG, LESTER.   Vardis Fisher revisited. SDR (24:3) 25–37.

F. Scott Fitzgerald

11958. BRUCCOLI, MATTHEW J. (ed.).   New essays on *The Great Gatsby.* Cambridge: CUP, 1985. pp. viii, 120. (American novel.)

11959. BRYER, JACKSON R.   The critical reputation of F. Scott Fitzgerald: a bibliographical study: suppl. vol. 1, through 1981. (Bibl. 1985, 10775.) Rev. by William White in BB (43:3) 182–3.

11960. CHAMBERS, J. B.   F. Scott Fitzgerald and the idea of the novel.

Unpub. doct. diss., Univ. of Newcastle upon Tyne, 1985. [Abstr. in IT (36) 23.]

11961. CHRISTENSEN, BRYCE J.   The mystery of ungodliness: Renan's *Life of Jesus* as a subtext for F. Scott Fitzgerald's *The Great Gatsby* and *Absolution*. ChrisL (36:1) 15–23.

11962. CHUNG, JIN-NONG.   F. Scott Fitzgerald eui jakgaron. (On F. Scott Fitzgerald.) Seoul: Hanshin, 1985. pp. 220.

11963. CUMMINGS, KATHERINE M.   Reconstructing 'life with father': the daughter's novel seduction. See **6755.**

11964. DAHL, CURTIS.   Fitzgerald's use of American architectural styles in *The Great Gatsby*. AmS (25) Spring 1984, 91–102.

11965. DONALDSON, SCOTT.   Fool for love: F. Scott Fitzgerald. (Bibl. 1985, 10778.) Rev. by James L. W. West, III, in SAF (14:1) 117–18.

11966. ELBAZ, ROBERT.   Of absence and excess in the discourse of Scott Fitzgerald. Zagadnienia Rodzajów Literackich (Lódź) (28:2) 1985, 63–77.

11967. GREIFF, LOUIS K.   Fitzgerald's *The Great Gatsby*. Exp (44:3) 49–52.

11968. JÓNSSON, HELGI.   90 ár liðin frá fæðingu F. Scott Fitzgerald: fiðrildið sem flaug án átaks. (90 years have passed since F. Scott Fitzgerald's birth: the butterfly that flew effortlessly.) Morgunblaðið (73:218) B 12–13.

11969. KALETA, KENNETH CHARLES.   F. Scott Fitzgerald as cinematic novelist: a study in the problems of critical vocabulary. Unpub. doct. diss., New York Univ., 1985. [Abstr. in DA (46) 3516A.]

11970. KIM, HAK-CHEON.   F. Scott Fitzgerald eui sosel yeongu. (A study of the novels of F. Scott Fitzgerald.) Unpub. doct. diss., Chonnam National Univ. (Korea), 1985.

11971. LE VOT, ANDRÉ.   F. Scott Fitzgerald: a bibliography. (Bibl. 1985, 10786.) Rev. by Alice Hall Petry in MLS (16:2) 93–6.

11972. LYNN, DAVID HAYDEN.   Cries out of the darkness: heroic narrators in early-modern fiction. See **11520.**

11973. MARWICK, M. J.   Right and wrong in *The Great Gatsby*. Crux (20:3) 24–32.

11974. MURPHY, PATRICK D.   Illumination and affection in the parallel plots of *The Rich Boy* and *The Beast in the Jungle*. See **8717.**

11975. OGUNSANWO, OLATUBOSUN.   George Meredith and F. Scott Fitzgerald: literary affinities, narrative indirectness and realism. *In* (pp. 245–8) **19.**

11976. PARKINSON, KATHLEEN.   F. Scott Fitzgerald, *Tender is the Night*. Harmondsworth: Penguin. pp. 104. (Penguin masterstudies.)

11977. PROCHÁZKA, MARTIN.   V záři a soumraku jazzového věku. See **10367.**

11978. RING, FRANCES KROLL.   Against the current: as I remember F. Scott Fitzgerald. Berkeley, CA: Creative Arts, 1985. pp. xi, 151. Rev. by Tom Quirk in AL (58:3) 455–6.

11979. SEONG, BYEONG-HWIE.   *The Great Gatsby* reul tonghaesuh bon

American dream eui silchae. (The reality of the American dream through *The Great Gatsby*.) YYY (4) 99–132.

11980. SHRUBB, E. P. The girls and the money: reflections on *The Great Gatsby*. Sydney Studies in English (11) 1985/86, 95–102.

11981. SNOW, SARA E. 'Worthy of belief': *ethos* in F. Scott Fitzgerald's *The Great Gatsby* and Ernest Hemingway's *The Sun Also Rises*. Unpub. doct. diss., Northwestern Univ., 1985. [Abstr. in DA (46) 2485A.]

11982. SZANTO, GEORGE. Fictions, societies and laws of equal and unequal development: notes for a sociology of literary comparison. *In* (pp. 283–90) **19.**

Helen Fletcher

11983. POWELL, DILYS (introd.). Bluestocking. London: Pandora. pp. xii, 163.

Horton Foote

11984. BARR, TERRY; WOOD, GERALD. 'A certain kind of writer': an interview with Horton Foote. LitFQ (14:4) 226–37.

11985. HACHEM, SAMIR. Foote-work. Horizon (29:3) 39–41.

Carolyn Forché

11986. DARGAN, JOAN. Poetic and political consciousness in Denise Levertov and Carolyn Forché. CEACrit (48:3) 58–67.

11987. GREER, MICHAEL. Politicizing the modern: Carolyn Forché in El Salvador and America. CR (30:2) 160–80.

'Ford Madox Ford' (Ford Madox Hueffer)

11988. BATE, JONATHAN. Arcadia and Armageddon: three English novelists and the First World War. EA (39:2) 150–62.

11989. BREBACH, RAYMOND. Joseph Conrad, Ford Madox Ford, and the making of romance. *See* **11478.**

11990. BRENNAN, JOSEPH G. The imperceptive narrator. *In* (pp. 233–9) **19.**

11991. CHENG, VINCENT J. A chronology of *The Good Soldier*. ELN (24:1) 91–7.

11992. CREESE, RICHARD. Abstracting and recording narration in *The Good Soldier* and *The End of the Affair*. JNT (16:1) 1–14.

11993. EDWARDS, C. J. Ford Madox Ford: the writer as documentarist and adventurer. Unpub. doct. diss., Univ. of York, 1984.

11994. FREDRICK, JOHN ANDREW. Triumph and travesty: reflexivity and the artistic conquest of nothingness and the void in Virginia Woolf's *To the Lighthouse* and Ford Madox Ford's *The Good Soldier*. Unpub. doct. diss., Univ. of California, Santa Barbara, 1985. [Abstr. in DA (46) 3345A.]

11995. JAMESON, BRUCE DALIN. Generating selves: narration as creation of identity in the works of Ford Madox Ford. Unpub. doct. diss., Bryn Mawr College, 1985. [Abstr. in DA (46) 1949A.]

11996. LINDBERG-SEYERSTED, BRITA. Cher F.: another item in the correspondence between Ezra Pound and Ford Madox Ford. Paideuma (15:1) 71–3.

11997. LYNN, DAVID HAYDEN. Cries out of the darkness: heroic narrators in early-modern fiction. *See* **11520.**

11998. RADELL, KAREN MARGUERITE. Affirmation in a moral wasteland: a comparison of Ford Madox Ford and Graham Greene. Unpub. doct. diss., Kent State Univ., 1985. [Abstr. in DA (47) 189A.]

11999. RAY, MARTIN. Ford Madox Ford at Folkstone: some new biographical information. NQ (33:2) 178–9.

12000. SAUNDERS, M. W. H. Ford Madox Ford and the reading of prose. Unpub. doct. diss., Univ. of Cambridge. [Abstr. in IT (35) 1088.]

12001. SIDORSKY, DAVID. Modernism and the emancipation of literature from morality: teleology and vocation in Joyce, Ford, and Proust. NLH (15:1) 1983, 137–53.

12002. SMITH, GROVER. Ford Madox Ford and the Christina Rossetti influence. *See* **9110.**

12003. STANG, SONDRA J. (ed.); GREENE, GRAHAM (introd.). The Ford Madox Ford reader. Manchester: Carcanet Press. pp. xxvii, 515.

E. M. Forster

12004. ALSTER, J. Hidden patterns in E. M. Forster's novels. Unpub. doct. diss., Univ. of Reading, 1983.

12005. AL-BASSAM, E. A. S. Socio-political obstacles to the individual's search for identity: a comparative aspect of the novels of E. M. Forster and Najib Mahfuz. Unpub. doct. diss., Univ. of Exeter, 1984.

12006. BEER, JOHN (ed.). *A Passage to India*: essays in interpretation. Basingstoke: Macmillan, 1985. pp. xiii, 172. Rev. by Lachlan Mackinnon in TLS, 7 Mar., 258.

12007. BELL, MILLICENT. What happened in the cave. PR (53:1) 103–10.

12008. BHARUCHA, RUSTOM. Forster's friends. Raritan (5:4) 105–22.

12009. BROWN, A. D. A consideration of some parallels in the personal and social ideals of E. M. Forster and Edward Carpenter. *See* **7834.**

12010. CRONIN, RICHARD. *The Hill of Devi* and *Heat and Dust*. EC (36:2) 142–59.

12011. DE CARO, F. A. 'A mystery is a muddle': gnomic expression in *A Passage to India*. *See* **2410.**

12012. EBBATSON, ROGER; NEALE, CATHERINE. E. M. Forster, *A Passage to India*. Harmondsworth: Penguin. pp.138. (Penguin master studies.)

12013. EPSTEIN, JOSEPH. One cheer for E. M. Forster. Quadrant (29:12) 1985, 8–12, 15–18.

12014. GANGULY, A. P. E. M. Forster's *A Passage to India*: a detailed study of his treatment of India's landscape, history, social anthropology, religion, philosophy, music and art. Unpub. doct. diss., Univ. of London (Birkbeck Coll.), 1984.

12015. GARDNER, PHILIP (ed.). Commonplace book. London: Scolar Press; Palo Alto, CA: Stanford UP. pp. xxiii, 372. Rev. by Stephen Spender in NYTB, 23 Feb., 11; by A. S. Byatt in TLS, 7 Mar., 258.

12016. HEGAZI, SAFAA.   The date and first publication of two essays by E. M. Forster. NQ (33:2) 191–2.

12017. HENKE, SUZETTE A.   *Howards End*: E. M. Forster without Marx or Sartre. MS (80) 116–20.

12018. HJELMAA, V. H.   E. M. Forster's fictional sources: a study of the Edwardian novels. Unpub. doct. diss., Univ. of Newcastle upon Tyne, 1983.

12019. KIRKPATRICK, B. J.   A bibliography of E. M. Forster. Oxford: Clarendon Press. pp. xvi, 320. (Soho bibliographies, 19.) (Second ed.: first ed. 1968.)

12020. LEVINE, JUNE PERRY.   Passage to the Odeon: too lean. *See* **10010.**

12021. McDOWELL, FREDERICK P. W.   E. M. Forster. (Bibl. 1970, 10110.) Boston, MA: G. K. Hall, 1982. pp. xviii, 174. (Twayne's English authors, 89.) (Revised ed.: first ed. 1969.) Rev. by Elizabeth Heine in YES (16) 354.

12022. MOFFAT, KATHLEEN WENDY.   Reader and resolution: ambiguity in the later novels of Conrad, Forster, and Woolf. *See* **11532.**

12023. MOUSLEH, T.   The humanist dilemma: a study of liberal thought in some selected novels by E. M. Forster, Angus Wilson and Iris Murdoch. Unpub. doct. diss., Univ. of Warwick, 1981.

12024. RAHMAN, TARIQ.   Edward Carpenter and E. M. Forster. *See* **7835.**

12025. SCOTT, P. J. M.   E. M. Forster: our permanent contemporary. (Bibl. 1985, 10858.) Rev. by Joyce Rothschild in SoHR (20:3) 278–80.

12026. SIMPSON, ANNE B.   Forster and the Edwardians: the literature of domestic failure. *See* **11237.**

12027. SPEAR, HILDA.   *A Passage to India* by E. M. Forster. Basingstoke: Macmillan. pp. xii, 84. (Macmillan master guides.)

12028. SUMMERS, CLAUDE J.   E. M. Forster. (Bibl. 1985, 10863.) Rev. by Kathleen Watson in NQ (33:1) 129–30.

12029. WINKGENS, MEINHARD.   Die Funktionalisierung des Deutschlandbildes und seiner Konnotation einer idealistischen Kultur in E. M. Forsters *Howards End*. Anglistik & Englischunterricht (29/30) 113–42.

12030. —— Die Funktionalisierung des Italienbildes in den Romanen *Where Angels Fear to Tread* von E. M. Forster und *The Lost Girl* von D. H. Lawrence. Arcadia (21:1) 41–61.

12031. YONEDA, KAZUHIKO.   E. M. Forster. Tokyo: Yamaguchi Press. pp. vi, 276. (Seminars on modern English and American literature, 8.) (In Japanese.)

John Fowles

12032. BAKER, JAMES R.   An interview with John Fowles. MichQR (25:4) 661–83.

12033. CHERRY, ROGER DENNIS.   *Ethos* in written discourse: a study of literary and persuasive texts. *See* **1352.**

12034. DELBAERE-GARANT, JEANNE.   Prospero to-day: magus, monster or patriarch? *In* (pp. 293–302) **12.**

12035. GAGGI, SILVIO.   Pirandello and Brechtian aspects of the fiction of John Fowles. CLS (23:4) 324–34.

12036. GALVÁN REULA, FERNANDO.   El realismo y el género en *The Collector.* (Realism and genre in *The Collector.*) Atlantis (8) 9–19.

12037. GOTTS, I.   The quest for selfhood: the novels and short stories of John Fowles. Unpub. doct. diss., Univ. of Aberdeen, 1984. [Abstr. in IT (35) 548.]

12038. IRELAND, K. R.   Towards a grammar of narrative sequence: the model of *The French Lieutenant's Woman. See* **10825.**

12039. McSWEENEY, KERRY.   Four contemporary novelists: Angus Wilson, Brian Moore, John Fowles, V. S. Naipaul. (Bibl. 1984, 11011.) Rev. by G. D. Killam in ESCan (12:1) 119–22; by Frederick M. Holmes in Ariel (17:3) 126–31.

12040. OMMUNDSEN, WENCHE.   Self-conscious fiction and literary theory: David Lodge, B. S. Johnson, and John Fowles. Unpub. doct. diss., Univ. of Melbourne. [Abstr. in DA (47) 2170A.]

12041. ONEGA, SUSANA.   Form and meaning in *The Magus.* Misc (7) 69–112.

12042. RECKWITZ, ERHARD.   Der Roman als Metaroman: Salman Rushdie, *Midnight's Children*; Kazuo Ishiguro, *A Pale View of the Hills*; John Fowles, *Mantissa. See* **10373.**

12043. RICHER, CAROL FRENCH.   Continuation and innovation in the contemporary British novel: the reflexive fiction of Margaret Drabble, Iris Murdoch, and John Fowles. *See* **11701.**

12044. SHAHAN, RICHARD MARK.   The moral art of John Fowles: freedom through paradox. Unpub. doct. diss., Univ. of Colorado at Boulder, 1985. [Abstr. in DA (46) 2303A.]

12045. TĂNASE, MANUELA.   Fowles şi focul creaţiei. (Fowles and the heat of creation.) RomLit, 6 Mar., 20.

12046. TARBOX, KATHERINE M.   A critical study of the novels of John Fowles. Unpub. doct. diss., Univ. of New Hampshire. [Abstr. in DA (47) 2172A.]

John Fox, Jr

12047. PENNELL, MELISSA McFARLAND.   Between Hell fer Sartain and Kingdom Come: John Fox, Jr's preservation of the masculine ethos. *See* **1704.**

Janet Frame

12048. EVANS, PATRICK.   Janet Frame and the art of life. Meanjin (44:3) 1985, 375–83.

12049. —— The muse as rough beast: the autobiography of Janet Frame. Untold (6) Spring, 1–10.

12050. FINDLEY, TIMOTHY.   Legends. Landfall (40:3) 327–32.

12051. MERCER, GINA.   Exploring 'the secret caves of language': Janet Frame's poetry. Meanjin (44:3) 1985, 384–90.

12052. SMITH, SHONA.   Fixed salt beings: isms and *Living in the Maniototo.* Untold (5) Autumn, 24–32.

Miles Franklin (Stella Maria Sarah Miles Franklin, 'Brent of Bin Bin', 'Mrs Ogniblat l'Artsau')

12053. CARRUTHERS, VIRGINIA KIRBY-SMITH. An outback Sybil: the renegade heroine of *My Brilliant Career*. PhilP (32) 41–8.

12054. DUNCAN, ROY (introd.). On Dearborn Street. St Lucia; London: Queensland UP, 1981. pp. xv, 219.

12055. ROE, JILL (introd.). Some everyday folk and Dawn. London: Virago Press. pp. xix, 347. (Virago modern classics, 211.)

G. S. Fraser

12056. FLETCHER, IAN; LUCAS, JOHN (eds). Poems of G. S. Fraser. (Bibl. 1982, 11399.) Rev. by Roderick Watson in SSL (19) 1984, 194–9.

Michael Frayn

12057. KAUFMAN, DAVID. The Frayn refrain. Horizon (29:1) 33–6.

Joseph Freeman

12058. McCONNELL, GARY ROBERT. Joseph Freeman: a personal odyssey from romance to revolution. Unpub. doct. diss., Univ. of North Carolina at Chapel Hill, 1985. [Abstr. in DA (46) 3352A.]

Brian Friel

12059. DANTANUS, ULF. Brian Friel: the growth of an Irish dramatist. Gothenburg: Acta Universitatis Gothoburgensis, 1985. pp. vi, 235. (Gothenburg studies in English, 59.) (Cf. bibl. 1984, 11035.) Rev. by Christopher Murray in IUR (16) 84–6.

12060. NIEL, RUTH. Digging into history: a reading of Brian Friel's *Volunteers* and Seamus Heaney's *Viking Dublin: Trial Pieces*. IUR (16) 35–47.

12061. ROBBINS, RONALD. Friel's modern 'fox and the grapes' fable. Éire–Ireland (21:4) 66–76.

Robert Frost

12062. ABEL, DARREL. Robert Frost's *Range-Finding*. CLQ (22:4) 225–37.

12063. BAGBY, GEORGE F., JR. Frost's synecdochism. AL (58:3) 379–92.

12064. BELL, BARBARA CURRIER. Frost on humanity in nature. AQ (42:3) 223–38.

12065. BIEGANOWSKI, RONALD. Sense of time in Robert Frost's poetics: a particular influence of Henri Bergson. RALS (13:2) 1983, 184–93.

12066. BLUMENTHAL, JOSEPH. Robert Frost and his printers. See **455.**

12067. BURNSHAW, STANLEY. Robert Frost himself. New York: Braziller. pp. 342. Rev. by R. W. Flint in NYTB, 30 Nov., 24; by Paul Mariani in BkW, 2 Nov., 3, 14.

12068. FLEISSNER, R. F. Retaking *The Road Not Taken*: a comic byway to it? See **9594.**

12069. FLEISSNER, ROBERT F. Frost's ancient music. Paideuma (13) 1984, 415–18.

12070. —— Markin' the Frost line: on Robert Frost and Edwin Markham. SoCR (16:2) 1984, 120–4.

12071. FRANCIS, LESLEY LEE.   A decade of 'stirring time': Robert Frost and Amy Lovell. NEQ (59:4) 508–22.

12072. GERBER, PHILIP L.   Remembering Robert Frost: an interview with William Jewell. NEQ (59:1) 1–27.

12073. —— Robert Frost. Boston, MA: G. K. Hall, 1982. pp. xviii, 203. (Twayne's US authors, 107.) Rev. by Richard Gray in YES (16) 352.

12074. HADAS, RACHEL.   Form, cycle, infinity: landscape imagery in the poetry of Robert Frost and George Seferis. Lewisburg, PA: Bucknell UP; London: Assoc. UPs, 1985. pp. 221. (Cf. bibl. 1982, 11416.)

12075. HALL, DOROTHY JUDD.   Robert Frost: contours of belief. (Bibl. 1984, 11044.) Rev. by Ian Jackson in NQ (33:1) 138–9.

12076. HOLLAND, NORMAN.   The brain of Robert Frost. NLH (15) 1984, 365–85.

12077. LEHMANN, JOHN.   Three literary friendships: Byron & Shelley, Rimbaud & Verlaine, Robert Frost & Edward Thomas. *See* **7780.**

12078. McPHILLIPS, ROBERT T.   Diverging and converging paths: horizontal and vertical movement in Robert Frost's *Mountain Interval*. AL (58:1) 82–98.

12079. O'BRIEN, TIMOTHY D.   Archetypal encounter in *Mending Wall*. ANQ (24:9/10) 147–51.

12080. OEHLSCHLAEGER, FRITZ.   West toward heaven: the adventure of metaphor in Robert Frost's *West-running Brook*. CLQ (22:4) 238–51.

12081. ORLOV, PAUL A.   The world's disorder and the word's design in two poems by Frost. JMMLA (19:2) 30–8.

12082. PEAN, JAMES LOUIS.   Snow in Frost. Unpub. doct. diss., St John's Univ., 1985. [Abstr. in DA (46) 2694A.]

12083. PRITCHARD, WILLIAM H.   Frost: a literary life reconsidered. Oxford: OUP, 1984. (Bibl. 1985, 10922.) Rev. by Ruth Pulik in UES (24:2) 49–51; by Robert Crawford in EC (36:2) 175–80; by Louis A. Renza in SAQ (85:3) 303–6.

12084. REYERO FERNÁNDEZ, DOLORES.   De la naturaleza al símbolo: la imagen del bosque en la poesía de Robert Frost. (From nature to symbol: the forest in Robert Frost's poetry.) Atlantis (8) 53–69.

12085. SHAW, W. DAVID.   The poetics of pragmatism: Robert Frost and William James. *See* **8773.**

12086. SHEEHY, DONALD G.   The poet as neurotic: the official biography of Robert Frost. *See* **10636.**

12087. STILLER, WALTER N.   The measure of meaning: the concept of order in the poetry of Robert Frost. Unpub. doct. diss., City Univ. of New York. [Abstr. in DA (47) 1327A.]

12088. STORCH, MARGARET.   Robert Frost's *The Subverted Flower*. AI (43:4) 295–305.

12089. SULLIVAN, D. BRADLEY.   'Education by poetry' in Robert Frost's masques. PLL (22:3) 312–21.

Christopher Fry

12090. VOS, ALVIN.   Christopher Fry's Christian dialectic in *A Phoenix Too Frequent*. Ren (36) 1984, 230–42.

Daniel Fuchs

12091. KRAFCHICK, MARCELLINE. World without heroes: the Brooklyn novels of Daniel Fuchs. Unpub. doct. diss., Univ. of California, Davis, 1985. [Abstr. in DA (46) 3352A.]

Athol Fugard

12092. ANDERSON, LAURI. The audience as judge in Athol Fugard's *The Island*. NCL (16:1) 5.

12093. CARDULLO, BERT. Patterns of opposition in *People Are Living There*. NCL (16:1) 3–4.

12094. COMBRINK, ANNETTE. 'A man's scenery is other men... ': Athol Fugard's latest plays. Literator (7:1) 58–68.

12095. GRAY, STEPHEN. Athol Fugard's 'insubstantial pageant': *The Road to Mecca*. Australasian Drama Studies (7) 1985, 43–52 (review-article).

12096. —— 'A chair called Agamemnon': Athol Fugard's use of Greek dramatic myths. Standpunte (39:4) 19–27.

12097. SEIDENSPINNER, MARGARETE. Exploring the labyrinth: Athol Fugard's approach to South African drama. Essen: Blaue Eule. pp. 364.

12098. VANDENBROUCKE, RUSSELL. Truths the hand can touch. Johannesburg: Donker. pp. 306. Rev. by Anne Levy Sarzin in Contrast (16:2) 87–90.

12099. WALDER, DENNIS. Athol Fugard. (Bibl. 1985, 10933.) Rev. by L. de Kock in Crux (20:1) 77–8; by D. W. Lloyd in UES (24:1) 61–2.

12100. WERTHEIM, ALBERT. Political acting and political action: Athol Fugard's *The Island*. WLWE (26:2) 245–52.

Charles Fuller

12101. HUGHES, LINDA K.; FAULKNER, HOWARD. The role of detection in *A Soldier's Play*. Clues (7:2) 83–97.

John Fuller

12102. HULSE, MICHAEL. The new zest in British poetry: the influence of John Fuller. Quadrant (30:11) 70–4.

Roy Fuller

12103. FULLER, ROY. Home and dry: memoirs III. London: London Magazine Ed., 1984. pp. 165.

12104. —— *Twelfth Night*: a personal view. *See* **5026.**

Joseph Furphy

12105. HARTLEY, ROBERT. Tom Collins, clot or ham?: a literary contract re-examined. SoRA (19:2) 154–72.

12106. INOYK, IVOR. Reading men like signboards: the egalitarian semiotic of *Such is Life*. ALS (12:3) 303–15 (review-article).

12107. MALOUF, DAVID (introd.). Such is life: being certain extracts from the diary of Tom Collins. London: Chatto & Windus. pp. 384.

12107a. OSLAND, DIANNE. Life, and the opinions of Tom Collins. *See* **6856.**

William Gaddis

12108. GUZLOWSKI, JOHN Z. No more sea changes: four American novelists' responses to the sea. *In* (pp. 232–43) **28.**

12109. MOORE, STEVEN. A reader's guide to William Gaddis's *The Recognitions*. (Bibl. 1984, 11075.) Rev. by David Seed in YES (16) 363–4.

Tess Gallagher

12110. RINGOLD, FRANCINE.   Tess Gallagher: making connections.
Nimrod (27:2) 1984, 34–40.

Mavis Gallant

12111. BESNER, NEIL.   A broken dialogue: history and memory in
Mavis Gallant's short fiction. ECanW (33) 89–99.
12112. FABRE, MICHEL.   'Orphans' progress', reader's progress:
voice and understatement in Mavis Gallant's stories. *In* (pp. 150–60) **22.**
12113. KEEFER, JANICE KULYK.   Mavis Gallant and the angel of
history. UTQ (55:3) 282–301.

John Galsworthy

12114. FRÉCHET, ALEC.   John Galsworthy: a reassessment. (Bibl.
1983, 11346.) Rev. by Patrick Parrinder in YES (16) 344.
12115. HARGREAVES, ALEX.   Exoticism in literature and history.
See **11496.**
12116. McDONALD, JAN.   The 'new drama' 1900–1914: Harley
Granville-Barker, John Galsworthy, St John Hankin, John Masefield.
London: Macmillan. pp. viii, 203. (Macmillan modern dramatists.)
12117. SHIOMI, TOMOYUKI.   John Galsworthy: a study of his mind and
art. Tokyo: Kobundo. pp. 128.
12118. SIMPSON, ANNE B.   Forster and the Edwardians: the literature
of domestic failure. *See* **11237.**

John Gardner

12119. HENDERSON, JEFF.   John Gardner's *Jason and Medeia*: the
resurrection of a genre. PLL (22:1) 76–95.
12120. —— (ed.).   Thor's hammer: essays on John Gardner. Conway: Central Arkansas UP, 1985. pp. 193. Rev. by Lee Templin
Hamilton in SCR (3:1) 109–11.
12121. MORACE, ROBERT A.   John Gardner: an annotated secondary
bibliography. (Bibl. 1985, 10946.) Rev. by George Bixby in ABC (7:1)
47–50.
12122. —— VANSPANCKEREN, KATHRYN (eds).   John Gardner: critical perspectives. Carbondale; Edwardsville: Southern Illinois UP, 1982.
pp. xxviii, 171. Rev. by Max F. Schulz in MLR (81:2) 470–1.
12123. NATOV, RONI; DELUCA, GERALDINE.   An interview with John
Gardner. LU (2:1) 1978, 114–36.
12124. PALMER, R. BARTON.   The problem with Gardner's *On Moral
Fiction*. Ren (34:3) 1982, 161–72.

Nene Gare

12125. FERRES, KAY.   Keneally and Gare: boundary riders and fringe
dwellers. Linq (14:2) 48–56.

Leon Garfield

12126. NATOV, RONI.   'Not the blackest of villains ... not the
brightest of saints': humanism in Leon Garfield's adventure novels. LU
(2:2) 1978, 44–71.

Robert Garioch

12127. FULTON, ROBIN (ed.).   A Garioch miscellany. Edinburgh:
MacDonald. pp. 210. (Lines review ed.)

Hamlin Garland
12128. DUNLOP, M. H.   Unfinished business: Hamlin Garland and Edward MacDowell. OldN (10) 1984, 175–85.
12129. YUVAJITA, PHACHEE.   The changing images of women in Western American literature as illustrated in the works of Willa Cather, Hamlin Garland, and Mari Sandoz. *See* **11411.**

Hugh Garner
12130. STUEWE, PAUL.   Hugh Garner. *In* (pp. 79–127) **7.**

David Garnett
12131. ROSS, MICHAEL L.   Ladies and foxes: D. H. Lawrence, David Garnett, and the female of the species. DHLR (18:2/3) 1985/86, 229–38.

Edward Garnett
12132. EGGERT, PAUL.   Edward Garnett's *Sons and Lovers*. CritQ (28:4) 51–61.
12133. STAPE, J. H.   The date of Conrad's *Turgenev*. *See* **11556.**

George Garrett
12134. RUFFIN, PAUL.   Interview with George Garrett. SoCR (16:2) 1984, 25–33.

Jean Garrigue
12135. UPTON, LEE.   Jean Garrigue: a poetics of plenitude. Unpub. doct. diss., State Univ. of New York at Binghamton. [Abstr. in DA (47) 1724A.]

Catherine Gaskin
12136. BRIDGWOOD, CHRISTINE.   Family romances: the contemporary popular family saga. *In* (pp. 167–93) **45.**

William Gass
12137. HALEY, VANESSA.   Egyptology and entomology in William Gass's *Order of Insects*. NCL (16:3) 3–5.
12138. SALTZMAN, ARTHUR M.   The fiction of William Gass: the consolation of language. Carbondale: Southern Illinois UP. pp. xviii, 194. Rev. by Brooke K. Horvath in AL (58:4) 666–7; by Brian W. Shaffer in JMMLA (19:2) 49–52.

Maurice Gee
12139. MANHIRE, BILL.   Maurice Gee. Auckland; Oxford: OUP. pp. 73. (New Zealand writers and their work.)

William Gerhardie
12140. DAVIES, M. F. S. R. J. D.   William Gerhardie: a critical biography. Unpub. doct. diss., Univ. of Cambridge. [Abstr. in IT (35) 1087.]

Hugo Gernsback
12141. RUDDICK, NICHOLAS.   Out of the Gernsbackian slime: Christopher Priest's abandonment of science fiction. MFS (32:1) 43–52.
12142. WESTFAHL, GARY WESLEY.   The mote in Gernsback's eye: a history of the idea of science fiction. *See* **10443.**

Zulfikar Ghose
12143. KANAGANAYAKAM, C.   Zulfikar Ghose: an interview. TCL (32:2) 169–86.
12144. KANAGANAYAKAM, CHELVANAYAKAM.   Paradigms of absence:

the writings of Zulfikar Ghose. Unpub. doct. diss., Univ. of British Columbia, 1985. [Abstr. in DA (47) 2168A.]

12145. VASSANJI, M. G.   A conversation with Zulfikar Ghose. TSAR (4:3) 14–21.

'Lewis Grassic Gibbon' (James Leslie Mitchell)

12146. BURTON, DEIRDRE.   A feminist reading of Lewis Grassic Gibbon's *A Scots Quair. In* (pp. 34–46) **6.**

12147. CAMPBELL, IAN.   Gibbon and MacDiarmid at play: the evolution of *Scottish Scene*. Bibliotheck (13:2) 46–55.

12148. —— Lewis Grassic Gibbon. Edinburgh: Scottish Academic Press, 1985. pp. ix, 131. (Scottish writers, 6.)

12149. McGRATH, M. J.   James Leslie Mitchell (Lewis Grassic Gibbon): a study in politics and ideas in relation to his life and work. Unpub. doct. diss., Univ. of Edinburgh, 1983.

12150. YOUNG, DOUGLAS F.   Lewis Grassic Gibbon's *Sunset Song*. Aberdeen: Assn for Scottish Literary Studies, pp. 56. (Scotnotes, 1.)

Gary Gildner

12151. COLEMAN, JAMES.   'Eat everything!': a consideration of the work of Gary Gildner. CR (30:2) 269–80.

Charlotte Perkins Gilman

12152. LANE, ANN J.   Charlotte Perkins Gilman: the personal is political (1860–1935). *In* (pp. 203–17) **20.**

12153. RAWLS, MELANIE.   *Herland* and *Out of the Silent Planet*: a comparison of a feminist utopia and a male charactered fantasy. Mythlore (13:2) 51–4.

12154. SCHARNHORST, GARY.   Charlotte Perkins Gilman: a bibliography. Metuchen, NJ; London: Scarecrow Press, 1985. pp. ix, 219. (Scarecrow author bibliographies, 71.)

Allen Ginsberg

12155. GROSSMAN, RON.   The beat goes on. BW, 30 Nov., 1, 4.

12156. SKERL, JENNIE.   Ginsberg on Burroughs: an interview. *See* **11364.**

12157. VENDLER, HELEN.   A lifelong poem including history. NY, 13 Jan., 77–84.

12158. WIMMER, ADI.   Zwischen 'Revelation' und 'Revolution': ein Blick auf das poetische œuvre Allen Ginsbergs. Englisch-Amerikanische Studien (Cologne) (7) 1985, 674–84.

Ellen Glasgow

12159. BINDING, PAUL (introd.).   Barren ground. London: Virago Press. pp. x, 409. (Virago modern classics, 219.)

12160. DUNBAR, IRENE NICHOLSON.   Illusion and imagination: Ellen Glasgow's fictional truth. Unpub. doct. diss., Univ. of Rochester. [Abstr. in DA (47) 900A.]

12161. OEHLSCHLAEGER, FRITZ H.   Ellen Glasgow and Stuart Pratt Sherman: the record of a literary friendship. RALS (14:1/2) 1984, 143–51.

12162. PANNILL, LINDA.   Ellen Glasgow's allegory of love and death: *The Greatest Good.* RALS (14:1/2) 1984, 161–6.

12163. THIÉBAUX, MARCELLE. Ellen Glasgow. (Bibl. 1985, 10970.) Rev. by Richard Gray in YES (16) 353.

Louise Glück

12164. GORDON, GERALD. 'Summoned prey' in Louise Glück's *Thanksgiving*. CEACrit (48:3) 68–72.

Elinor Glyn

12165. ETHERINGTON-SMITH, MEREDITH; PILCHER, JEREMY. The 'It' girls: Lucy, Lady Duff Gordon, the *couturière* 'Lucile' and Elinor Glyn, romantic novelist. London: Hamilton. pp. xiv, 274.

'Michael Gold' (Irwin Granich)

12166. TUERK, RICHARD. Michael Gold on Walt Whitman. *See* **9519.**

Albert Goldbarth

12167. LAVAZZI, THOMAS. Riddle of being: Goldbarth's *The Importance of Artists' Biographies*. MidQ (27:4) 438–55.

William Golding

12168. CAREY, JOHN (ed.). William Golding: the man his books: a tribute on his 75th birthday. London: Faber & Faber. pp. 191. Rev. by Peter Reading in TLS, 17 Oct., 1153.

12169. CLEVE, GUNNEL. Elements of mysticism in three of William Golding's novels. Turku, Finland: Turku UP. pp. iv, 388. (Annales universitatis Turkuensis, ser. B, 175.) (Doct. diss., Univ. of Turku.)

12170. COY GIRÓN, JUAN JOSÉ. El terror del hombre moderno: *Lord of the Flies*. (Modern man's terror: *Lord of the Flies*.) Atlantis (8) 109–14.

12171. GOATLY, A. P. Metaphor in the novels of William Golding. Unpub. doct. diss., Univ. of London, University Coll., 1984.

12172. JOHNSON, B. R. William Golding's *The Inheritors*: dualism and synthesis. SoRA (19:2) 173–83.

12173. JOHNSON, BETTE REECE. Consciousness visible: the novels of William Golding. Unpub. doct. diss., Univ. of California, Riverside, 1985. [Abstr. in DA (46) 3716A.]

12174. KRAHÉ, PETER. Schiffbruch und Selbstaufgabe. Ein Vergleich von *Nichts in Sicht, Bericht eines Schiffsbrüchigen* und *Pincher Martin*. GRM (36:4) 433–54.

12175. NELSON, MARIE. Two narrative modes, two modes of perception: the use of the instrumental in Golding's *Inheritors*. Neophilologus (70:2) 307–15.

12176. OLSEN, STEIN HAUGOM. A glimpse into the darkness? The epistemological and ontological theme in William Golding's *Darkness Visible*. In (pp. 284–95) **18.**

12177. PAGE, NORMAN (ed.). William Golding: novels 1954–67. London: Macmillan, 1985. pp. 190. (Casebook series.) Rev. by Gérard Klaus in EA (39:4) 469–71; by Peter Reading in TLS, 17 Oct., 1153.

12178. REDPATH, P. Seeing Venus: a structural study of William Golding's fiction. Unpub. doct. diss., Univ. of Exeter, 1984.

12179. REDPATH, PHILIP. Tricks of the light: William Golding's *Darkness Visible*. Ariel (17:1) 3–16.

12180. —— William Golding: a structural reading of his fiction. London: Vision Press. pp. 222. (Critical studies.)

12181. SIMON, IRÈNE.   The theatre motif in William Golding's *Rites of Passage*. *In* (pp. 261–7) **12**.

12182. SUMNER, ROSEMARY.   *The Spire* by William Golding. Basingstoke: Macmillan. pp. ix, 78. (Macmillan master guides.)

12183. THOMAS, SUE.   Some religious icons and biblical allusions in William Golding's *The Spire*. AUMLA (64) 1985, 190–7 (review-article).

12184. WILSON, RAYMOND.   *Lord of the Flies* by William Golding. Basingstoke: Macmillan. pp. viii, 88. (Macmillan master guides.)

Emma Goldman

12185. DEUTELBAUM, WENDY.   Epistolary politics: the correspondence of Emma Goldman and Alexander Berkman. *See* **11247**.

Nadine Gordimer

12186. CLINGMAN, S.   The consciousness of history in the novels of Nadine Gordimer. Unpub. doct. diss., Univ. of Oxford, 1983.

12187. CLINGMAN, STEPHEN.   The novels of Nadine Gordimer: history from the inside. London: Allen & Unwin. pp. xi, 276.

12188. GORDIMER, NADINE; GOLDBLATT, DAVID.   Lifetimes: under apartheid. London: Cape. pp. 115.

12189. LEAKE, ALISON (ed.).   July's people. London: Cape, 1981; Harlow: Longman. pp. xxv, 166. (Longman study texts.)

12190. MARTIN, RICHARD G.   Narrative, history, and ideology: a study of *Waiting for the Barbarians* and *Burger's Daughter*. *See* **11458**.

12191. NOWAK, HELENA.   Soviet literary critics on Nadine Gordimer. Contrast (16:2) 65–8.

12192. VILJOEN, HEIN.   Die Suid-Afrikaanse romansisteem *anno* 1981: 'n vergelykende studie. *See* **10429**.

Caroline Gordon

12193. BRINKMEYER, ROBERT H., JR.   Three catholic writers of the modern South. (Bibl. 1985, 11004.) Rev. by Melvin J. Friedman in SAF (14:2) 234–5.

12194. DESMOND, JOHN F.   *The Malefactors*: Caroline Gordon's redemptive vision. Ren (35:1) 1982, 17–38.

12195. HALL, THELMA RUTH.   Escape from the abyss: order in the fiction of Caroline Gordon. Unpub. doct. diss., Univ. of Alabama, 1985. [Abstr. in DA (46) 3348A.]

Edward Gorey

12196. FILSTRUP, JANE MERRILL.   An interview with Edward St John Gorey at the Gotham Book Mart. *See* **73**.

12197. TIGGES, WIM.   The limerick: the sonnet of Nonsense? *See* **8866**.

Sir Edmund Gosse

12197a. GRANQVIST, RAOUL.   Edmund Gosse: the reluctant critic of John Donne. *See* **5372**.

12197b. —— The reception of Edmund Gosse's *Life of John Donne* (1899). *See* **5373**.

12198. PICKERING, SAM.   Images and letters. *See* **11212**.

12199. STEPPUTAT, J.   Introversion and extroversion in certain late Victorian writers. *See* **8361**.

12200. THWAITE, ANN.   Edmund Gosse: a literary landscape. (Bibl. 1985, 11011.) Rev. by Cicely Palser Havely in NQ (33:2) 264–5.

Keith Gottschalk

12201. ANON. Keith Gottschalk in conversation with *Upstream*. Upstream (4:4) 1–8.

Patricia Grace

12202. GUERIN, LOUISE. A teller of tales. NZList, 15 Mar., 20–1.

Harry Graham

12203. KINGTON, MILES (introd.). When grandmama fell off the boat: the best of Harry Graham, inventor of *Ruthless Rhymes*. London: Methuen. pp. 160. (Methuen humour classics.)

R. B. Cunninghame Graham

12204. WALKER, JOHN. Cunninghame Graham and the critics – a reappraisal. SSL (19) 1984, 106–14.

12205. —— (ed.). The North American sketches of R. B. Cunninghame Graham. Edinburgh: Scottish Academic Press. pp. x. 145.

W. S. Graham

12206. LOPEZ, A. C. The life and work of W. S. Graham. Unpub. doct. diss., Univ. of Cambridge. [Abstr. in IT (36) 23.]

Harley Granville-Barker

12207. KENNEDY, DENNIS. Granville-Barker and the dream of theatre. (Bibl. 1985, 11014a.) Rev. by Cary M. Mazer in TJ (38:4) 505–7; by Edward Braun in THES (695) 17.

12208. McDONALD, JAN. The 'new drama' 1900–1914: Harley Granville-Barker, John Galsworthy, St John Hankin, John Masefield. *See* **12116.**

12209. SALENIUS, ELMER W. Harley Granville-Barker. Boston, MA: G. K. Hall, 1982. pp. xvi, 167. (Twayne's English authors, 309.) Rev. by John Stokes in YES (16) 340–1.

12210. WEISS, RUDOLF. The Barker inheritance. Berte Thomas and Harley Granville-Barker: *The Family of the Oldroyds*. *See* **9349.**

Shirley Ann Grau

12211. DURBIN, ROGER WAYNE. Setting and the novels of Shirley Ann Grau: an analysis of technique and function. Unpub. doct. diss., Kent State Univ., 1985. [Abstr. in DA (47) 177A.]

Robert Graves

12212. AHEARN, ALLEN; HEARNE, PATRICIA. Author price guides: Robert Graves. Bethesda, MD: Quill & Brush, 1984. pp. 16. Rev. by George Bixby in ABC (7:1) 47–50.

12213. BILTON, PETER. Graves on lovers, and Shakespeare at a lovers' funeral. *See* **4943.**

12214. BOETTCHER, RALPH CARL. The romantic past: primitivism and some novels by Thomas Hardy, D. H. Lawrence, and Robert Graves. *See* **8380.**

12215. CARTER, D. N. G. 'The second-fated': a study of the poetry of Robert Graves, 1914–1947. Unpub. doct. diss., Trinity Coll. Dublin, 1985/86. [Abstr. in IT (36) 912.]

12216. GRAVES, RICHARD PERCEVAL. Robert Graves: the assault heroic 1895–1926. London: Weidenfeld & Nicolson. pp. xxi, 387. Rev.

by Martin Seymour-Smith in LRB (8:17) 19–20; by Dominic Hibberd in TLS, 21 Nov., 1299.

12217. JONES, MARGARET.   Through a cool web darkly: an early apparition of the white goddess in the poetry of Robert Graves. NCL (16:5) 10–12.

12218. McKENZIE, M. L.   Memories of the Great War: Graves, Sassoon, and Findley. *See* **11947.**

12219. MÁNEK, BOHUSLAV.   Robert Graves (1895–1985). SvL (31:6) 252–4.

12220. MARIAN, EUGEN.   Robert Graves. Contemporanul, 14 Nov., 15. (In Romanian.)

12221. O'PREY, PAUL (ed.).   Robert Graves: selected poems. Harmondsworth: Penguin. pp. 262.

12222. ROEFFAERS, HUGO.   Engels kwintet: essays over Ted Hughes, Geoffrey Hill, Seamus Heaney, Craig Raine en Robert Graves. (English quintet: essays on Ted Hughes, Geoffrey Hill, Seamus Heaney, Craig Raine, and Robert Graves.) Leuven; Amersfoort: ACCO. pp. 144.

12223. ROOKSBY, R.   In her praise: the Muse poetry of Robert Graves. Unpub. doct. diss., Univ. of Wales, Cardiff, 1983.

Alasdair Gray

12224. ACKER, KATHY.   Alasdair Gray interviewed. Edinburgh Review (74) 83–90.

Robert Gray

12225. HASKELL, DENNIS.   Humanism and sensual awareness in the poetry of Robert Gray. Southerly (46:3) 261–70.

Simon Gray

12226. SHAFER, YVONNE.   Aristophanic and Chekhovian structure in the plays of Simon Gray. TS (31/32) 1984/85–1985/86, 32–40.

'Henry Green' (Henry Vincent Yorke)

12227. GORRA, MICHAEL EDWARD.   The English novel at mid-century: Evelyn Waugh, Henry Green, Anthony Powell, and Graham Greene. Unpub. doct. diss., Stanford Univ. [Abstr. in DA (47) 536A.]

12228. HOLMESLAND, ODDVAR.   A critical introduction to Henry Green's novels: the living vision. London: Macmillan, 1985. pp. iii, 450. (Macmillan studies in twentieth-century literature.)

12229. —— The image of contradiction: an approach to the novels of Henry Green. Unpub. doct. diss., Univ. of Edinburgh, 1983.

Ishmael Green

12230. KOEPPEL, FREDERIC.   Ishmael Green, author. Nimrod (26:1) 1982, 14–23.

Paul Green

12231. ANON.   An interview with Paul Green. SE (7:4) 1979, 137–40.

12232. ILACQUE, ALMA A.   Paul Green – in memoriam: a bibliography and profile. SoQ (20:3) 1982, 76–87.

Graham Greene

12233. BRENNAN, JOSEPH G.   The imperceptive narrator. *In* (pp. 233–9) **19.**

12234. CHARLTON, D. Graham Greene: a poetics of composition. Unpub. doct. diss., Univ. of Birmingham, 1983/84.

12235. CLARKE, PETER P. Graham Greene's *The Destructors*: an anarchist parable. ELN (23:3) 60–3.

12236. CREESE, RICHARD. Abstracting and recording narration in *The Good Soldier* and *The End of the Affair. See* **11992.**

12237. DAVIS, ROBERT MURRAY. The rhetoric of Mexican travel: Greene and Waugh. Ren (38:3) 160–9.

12238. —— The struggle with genre in *The End of the Affair.* Genre (18:4) 1985, 397–411.

12239. —— ARGIRO, THOMAS. Reading in the thirties: reviews by Waugh and Greene. EWN (20:3) 6–7.

12240. FALK, QUENTIN. Travels in Greeneland: the cinema of Graham Greene. *See* **9945.**

12241. GASTON, GEORGE M. A. The pursuit of salvation: a critical guide to the novels of Graham Greene. Troy, NY: Whitston, 1984. Rev. by Mary Leutkemeyer in ModAge (30:3/4) 328–31.

12242. GORRA, MICHAEL EDWARD. The English novel at mid-century: Evelyn Waugh, Henry Green, Anthony Powell, and Graham Greene. *See* **12227.**

12243. Entry cancelled.

12244. —— (introd. and commentary). Graham Greene country. Illus. by PAUL HOGARTH. London: Pavilion. pp. 173.

12245. —— REED, CAROL. The third man: a film. *See* **9969.**

12246. HENRY, PATRICK. Cervantes, Unamuno, and Graham Greene's *Monsignor Quixote*. CLS (23:1) 12–23.

12247. JEON, HO-CHUN. Graham Greene eui soseol e natanan thriller pattern gwa religious faith e gwanhan yeongu. (A study of the thriller pattern and religious faith in Graham Greene's novels.) Unpub. doct. diss., Chungnam National Univ. (Korea).

12248. KELLY, RICHARD. Graham Greene. New York: Ungar, 1984. pp. x, 196. Rev. by Margaret Hallissy in ChrisL (35:2) 44–5.

12249. LAKIN, BARBARA. Greene's *The Honorary Consul* and Lowry's *Under the Volcano*: a study in influence. SCR (3:1) 68–77.

12250. MUNZAR, JIŘÍ. Angažovanost v tvorbě Grahama Greena. (Studies in the work of Graham Greene.) (Bibl. 1983, 11483.) Rev. by Ingeborg Kejzlar in AAA (11) 134–5.

12251. PEAT, HAL W. Beyond the limit: familiar shadows from the world of Graham Greene. *See* **10043.**

12252. RADELL, KAREN M. Charley Fortnum's descent into dignity: the common denominator in Greene's *The Honorary Consul* and Paramount's *Beyond the Limit. See* **10056.**

12253. RADELL, KAREN MARGUERITE. Affirmation in a moral wasteland: a comparison of Ford Madox Ford and Graham Greene. *See* **11998.**

12254. SHARROCK, ROGER. Saints, sinners and comedians: the novels of Graham Greene. (Bibl. 1985, 11048.) Rev. by Peter Miles in NQ

(33:2) 271–2; by Dennis Burke in NCathW (229) 45–6; by Keith Wilson in QQ (93:1) 203–5; by C. H. Muller in UES (24:1) 49–50; by Sylvère Monod in EA (38:4) 1985, 481.

12255. SMITH, GRAHAME. The achievement of Graham Greene. Brighton: Harvester Press. pp. 228. Rev. by John Fletcher in THES (698) 25; by Mark Casserley in TLS, 1 Aug., 845.

12256. SPURLING, JOHN. Graham Greene. (Bibl. 1984, 11199.) Rev. by David Bradshaw in NQ (33:1) 130–1.

12257. WHITEHOUSE, J. C. The human person in the novels of Graham Greene. YREAL (2) 1984, 397–443.

Walter Greenwood

12258. WEBSTER, ROGER. *Love on the Dole* and the aesthetic of contradiction. *In* (pp. 48–61) **6.**

Augusta, Lady Gregory

12259. FITZGERALD, MARY (introd.). Selected plays. Washington, DC: Catholic UP of America; Gerrards Cross: Smythe, 1983. pp. 377. Rev. by Jean Hamard in Études irlandaises (9) 1984, 337–8.

12260. KOHFELDT, MARY LOU. Lady Gregory: the woman behind the Irish renaissance. (Bibl. 1985, 11055.) Rev. by Robert E. Ward in Éire-Ireland (21:1) 155–8.

12261. KOSOK, HEINZ. Lady Gregorys *The Gaol Gate* und das anglo-irische Kurzdrama. Anglistik & Englischunterricht (28) 7–32.

12262. STALLWORTHY, JON (introd.). Mr Gregory's letter-box 1813–1831. Ed. by Lady Gregory. (Bibl. 1982, 11575.) Rev. by Mark Mortimer in Études irlandaises (9) 1984, 338–40.

Kate Grenville

12263. MERCER, GINA. Kate Grenville. Newer voices: 2. Southerly (45:3) 1985, 295–300.

Zane Grey

12264. GREY, LOREN. Zane Grey: a photographic odyssey. Bellingham, WA: Taylor, 1985. Rev. by Katharine R. Kienzle in OhioanaQ (29:1) 165–6.

Trevor Griffith

12265. JOHNSTONE, RICHARD. Television drama and the people's war: David Hare's *Licking Hitler*, Ian McEwan's *The Imitation Game*, and Trevor Griffith's *Country*. ModDr (28:2) 1985, 189–97.

Francis Griswold

12266. SLEDGE, MAILANDE CHENEY. The representation of the Gullah dialect in Francis Griswold's *A Sea Island Lady*. *See* **980.**

Frederick Philip Grove

12267. BADER, RUDOLF. Frederick Philip Grove and naturalism reconsidered. *In* (pp. 222–33) **22.**

12268. KNOENAGEL, AXEL. Grove's first translation. CanL (111) 214–20.

12269. STICH, K. P. Narcissism and the uncanny in Grove's *Over Prairie Trails*. Mosaic (19:2) 31–41.

John Guare

12270. SAUVAGE, LEO. Tragic misalliances. NewL (69:8) 21–2.

A. B. Guthrie
12271. SIMMONS, MICHAEL K. Boone Caudill: the failure of an American primitive. SDR (22:3) 1984, 38–43.
Brian Gysin
12272. WILSON, TERRY. Here to go: planet R-101: Brian Gysin interviewed by Terry Wilson. Introd. and texts by WILLIAM S. BURROUGHS and BRIAN GYSIN. See **11365.**
Julian Hall
12273. SCRIMGEOUR, PAT DALE. Philip Larkin's *Dockery and Son* and Julian Hall's *The Senior Commoner*. NQ (33:2) 193.
Radclyffe Hall
12274. OMROD, RICHARD. Una Troubridge: the friend of Radclyffe Hall. London: Cape, 1984. pp. xviii, 340.
12275. RADFORD, JEAN. An inverted romance: *The Well of Loneliness* and sexual ideology. *In* (pp. 97–111) **45.**
Roger Hall
12276. BERESFORD, ROSEMARY. Gliding off to other things. NZList, 9 Aug., 38–9.
12277. LENNOX, BILL. Hall's humour. NZList, 9 Aug., 39.
Patrick Hamilton
12278. CRAMP, A. Prose fiction in the 1930s: a study of Elizabeth Bowen, Rex Warner and Patrick Hamilton. *See* **11289.**
Dashiell Hammett
12279. GREGORY, SINDA. Private investigations: the novels of Dashiell Hammett. Carbondale: Southern Illinois UP, 1985. pp. xiv, 205. (Cf. bibl. 1985, 11088, where pagination incorrect.) Rev by Martin Roth in Review (8) 265–72; by Bernard Benstock in JEGP (85:1) 154–6.
12280. HAGEMANN, E. R. From *The Cleansing of Poisonville* to *Red Harvest*. Clues (7:2) 115–32.
12281. ROTH, MARTIN. Popular criticism. *See* **10384.**
St John Hankin
12282. McDONALD, JAN. The 'new drama' 1900–1914: Harley Granville-Barker, John Galsworthy, St John Hankin, John Masefield. *See* **12116.**
Barbara Hanrahan
12283. KIRKBY, JOAN. Daisy Miller down under: the old world/new world paradigm in Barbara Hanrahan. Kp (8:3) 10–28.
Lorraine Hansberry
12284. WILKERSON, MARGARET B. *A Raisin in the Sun*: anniversary of an American classic. TJ (38:4) 441–52.
12285. WOOD, DEBORAH JEAN. The plays of Lorraine Hansberry: studies in dramatic form. Unpub. doct. diss., Univ. of Wisconsin–Madison, 1985. [Abstr. in DA (46) 2859A–60A.]
Joseph Hansen
12286. FONTANA, ERNEST. Joseph Hansen's anti-pastoral crime fiction. Clues (7:1) 89–97.
David Hare
12287. CARDULLO, BERT. Brecht and *Fanshen*. SN (58:2) 225–30.

12288. —— Playing on words: four notes on the drama of David Hare. USFLQ (24:3/4) 44–6.

12289. JOHNSTONE, RICHARD. Television drama and the people's war: David Hare's *Licking Hitler*, Ian McEwan's *The Imitation Game*, and Trevor Griffith's *Country*. See **12265.**

12290. KRAMER, MIMI. Want in the midst of *Plenty*. See **11445.**

Michael Harlow

12291. EDMOND, MURRAY. The poetry of Michael Harlow. Landfall (40:1) 31–42.

Karen Harper

12292. BARRY, ANNE. Romancing history: Karen Harper's heroines are real-life royal mistresses. OhioanaQ (29:2) 50–3.

Wilson Harris

12293. DRAKE, SANDRA E. Wilson Harris and the modern tradition: a new architecture of the world. New York; London: Greenwood Press. pp. xvi, 213. (Contributions in Afro-American and African studies, 93.)

12294. SHARRAD, PAUL. Open dialogue: metropolitan–provincial tensions and the quest for a post-colonial culture in the fiction of C. J. Koch, Raja Rao and Wilson Harris. Unpub. doct. diss., Flinders Univ. of South Australia. [Abstr. in DA (47) 2152A.]

12295. SLEMON, STEPHEN. Revisioning allegory: Wilson Harris's *Carnival*. Kp (8:2) 45–56.

12296. THOMAS, ELIZABETH. Wilson Harris: leading the reader to the (garden) gate. Span (22) Apr., 105–113.

12297. WEBB, BARBARA J. Myth and history in the novels of Alejo Carpentier and Wilson Harris: theories of cultural transformation. See **2498.**

12298. WILENTZ, GAY. Wilson Harris's divine comedy of existence: miniaturizations of the cosmos in *Palace of the Peacock*. Kp (8:2) 56–77.

Kevin Hart

12299. CATALANO, GARY. The weight of things: the poetry of Kevin Hart. Overland (104) 23–6.

L. P. Hartley

12300. KENDZORA, KATHRYN LOUISE. Going between novel and film: Harold Pinter's adaptation of *The Go-Between*. See **9995.**

John Hawkes

12301. ANASTASOPOULOU, MARIA TH. Dream and reality in John Hawkes's *The Lime Twig*. Parousia (4) 215–23.

12302. GAULT, PIERRE (ed.). John Hawkes. Delta: Centre d'Études et de Recherches sur les Écrivains du Sud aux États-Unis, 1985. pp. 192.

12303. GORAK, JAN. Something like a war memorial': John Hawkes's *Travesty*. ESA (29:1) 53–72.

12304. GUZLOWSKI, JOHN Z. No more sea changes: four American novelists' responses to the sea. *In* (pp. 232–43) **28.**

12305. HENDERSON, ERIC PAUL. Structured visions in the novels of John Hawkes. Unpub. doct. diss., Univ. of Western Ontario, 1985. [Abstr. in DA (46) 3034A.]

12306. HRYCIW-WING, CAROL A. (comp.). John Hawkes: a research guide. New York; London: Garland. pp. xxi, 396. (Garland reference library of the humanities, 668.)

12307. LAING, JEFFREY.   The dictatorial voice in John Hawkes's *The Cannibal* and *The Owl*. NCL (16:4) 2–3.

12308. O'DONNELL, PATRICK.   John Hawkes. (Bibl. 1984, 11271.) Rev. by Judie Newman in YES (16) 356–8.

Robert Hayden

12309. CALLAHAN, JOHN F.   'Meant to be free': the illuminative voice of Robert Hayden. Ob (8) Spring 1982, 156–74.

12310. GIBBONS, REGINALD.   A man that in his writing was most wise. Ob (8) Spring 1982, 182–7.

12311. GLAYSHER, FREDERICK (ed.).   Collected poems. London: Liveright, 1985. (Cf. bibl. 1955, 11120.)

12312. GOLDSTEIN, LAURENCE.   The only name he would be happy with is poet. Ob (8) Spring 1982, 42–6.

12313. JONES, GAYL.   Restoring the perspective: Robert Hayden's *The Dream*. Ob (8) Spring 1982, 188–91.

12314. NICHOLAS, XAVIER.   Robert Hayden: a bibliography. Ob (8) Spring 1982, 207–10.

12315. ZEBRUN, GARY.   In the darkness a wellspring of plangency: the poetry of Robert Hayden. Ob (8) Spring 1982, 22–6.

Sterling Hayden

12316. HUGHES, JAMES M.   Popular imagery of the sea: lore is a four-letter word. *In* (pp. 215–24) **28.**

Shirley Hazzard

12317. KAVANAGH, PAUL.   Shirley Hazzard, astronomer of souls. Southerly (45:2) 1985, 209–19. (Interview.)

Bessie Head

12318. EKO, EBELE.   Beyond the myth of confrontation: a comparative study of African and Afro-American female protagonists. *See* **10999.**

12319. GARDNER, SUSAN; SCOTT, PATRICIA E.   Bessie Head: a bibliography. Grahamstown, South Africa: National English Literary Museum. pp. iv, 52. (NELM bibliographies, 1.)

12320. HAGGIE, DAVID.   Bessie Head (1937–1986). Edinburgh Review (73) 123–5.

12321. JOHNSON, JOYCE.   Structures of meaning in the novels of Bessie Head. Kp (8:1) 56–70.

12322. OLA, VIRGINIA U.   Women's role in Bessie Head's ideal world. Ariel (17:4) 39–47.

12323. PEEK, ANDREW.   Bessie Head in Australia: interviewed by Andrew Peek in Launceston, 14 March 1984. New Literature Review (Canberra) (14) 1985, 5–13.

12324. SLOMSKI, GENEVIEVE T.   Dialogue in the discourse: a study of revolt in selected fiction by African women. *See* **11818.**

Seamus Heaney

12325. BYRNE, J. M.   The significance of landscape and history in the poetry of Seamus Heaney, Derek Mahon and John Montague. Unpub. doct. diss., Univ. of Newcastle upon Tyne, 1984.

12326. CORCORAN, NEIL.   Seamus Heaney. London: Faber & Faber. pp. 192. (Faber student guides.)

12327. CURTIS, TONY (ed.).   The art of Seamus Heaney. (Bibl. 1983, 11585.) Bridgend: Poetry Wales Press, 1985. pp. 178. (Second ed.: first ed. 1982.)

12328. DI NICOLA, ROBERT.   Time and history in Seamus Heaney's *In Memoriam Francis Ledwidge*. Éire–Ireland (21:4) 45–51.

12329. DURKAN, MICHAEL J.   Seamus Heaney: a checklist for a bibliography. IUR (16) 48–76.

12330. GLEN, HEATHER.   Geoffrey Hill's 'England of the mind'. Critical Review (27) 1985, 98–109.

12331. HOUSTON, D. N.   Myths of place: the importance of landscape in the poetries of W. H. Auden and Seamus Heaney. *See* **11096.**

12332. JOLLY, ROSLYN.   Transformations of Caliban and Ariel: imagination and language in David Malouf, Margaret Atwood and Seamus Heaney. *See* **4987.**

12333. KEARNEY, RICHARD.   Poetry, language and identity: a note on Seamus Heaney. Studies (75:300) 552–63.

12334. LLOYD, DAVID.   'Pap for the dispossessed': Seamus Heaney and the poetics of identity. Boundary 2 (13:2/3) 1985, 319–42.

12335. LLOYD, DAVID THOMAS.   Lyric impulse and epic dimension in Heaney's *North* and Hill's *Mercian Hymns*. Unpub. doct. diss., Brown Univ., 1985. [Abstr. in DA (46) 1950A.]

12336. NIEL, RUTH.   Digging into history: a reading of Brian Friel's *Volunteers* and Seamus Heaney's *Viking Dublin: Trial Pieces*. *See* **12060.**

12337. O'BRIEN, GEORGE.   *Incertus redux*. CamQ (15:1) 70–6.

12338. ROEFFAERS, HUGO.   Engels kwintet: essays over Ted Hughes, Geoffrey Hill, Seamus Heaney, Craig Raine en Robert Graves. *See* **12222.**

James Hearst

12339. SEARS, JEFF.   The worth of the harvest: James Hearst and his poetry: part 1. SSMLN (16:1) 8–16.

John Heath-Stubbs

12340. CHRISTOPHER, JOE R.   John Heath-Stubbs' *Artorius* and the influence of Charles Williams. Mythlore (13:2) 56–61.

Anthony Hecht

12341. O'BRIEN, TIMOTHY D.   Hecht's *The Dover Bitch*. Exp (44:2) 52–4.

Robert A. Heinlein

12342. DICKINSON, DANIEL.   What is one to make of Robert A. Heinlein? MFS (32:1) 127–31.

Joseph Heller

12343. ALDRIDGE, JOHN W.   The loony horror of it all: *Catch-22* turns 25. NYTB, 26 Oct., 3.

12344. BOYER, A. D.   James Jones and Joseph Heller: an essay in contrasts. Unpub. doct. diss., Univ. of St Andrews, 1984.

12345. CARTON, EVAN.   The politics of selfhood: Bob Slocum, T. S. Garp and auto-American-biography. Novel (20:1) 41–61.

12346. CRAIG, DAVID M. Closure resisted: style and form in Joseph Heller's novels. CR (30:2) 238–50.

12347. MERRILL, ROBERT. The structure and meaning of *Catch-22*. SAF (14:2) 139–52.

Lillian Hellman

12348. BROE, MARY LYNN. Bohemia bumps into Calvin: the deception of passivity in Lillian Hellman's drama. SoQ (19:2) 1981, 26–41.

12349. DENHAM, CYNTHIA BAILEY. Lillian Hellman's revisions in *The Collected Plays*. Unpub. doct. diss., Auburn Univ. [Abstr. in DA (47) 897A.]

12350. GROSSMAN, ANITA SUSAN. Art versus truth in autobiography: the case of Lillian Hellman. CLIO (14:3) 1985, 289–308.

12351. MAYER, SUSANNE. Die Sehnsucht nach den anderen. Eine Studie zum Verhältnis von Subjekt und Gesellschaft in den Autobiographien von Lillian Hellman, Maya Angelou und Maxine Hong Kingston. *See* **11049.**

12352. PARRISH, RICHARD DALE. Style in Lillian Hellman's *Pentimento*: the rhetoric of elusiveness. Unpub. doct. diss., East Texas State Univ., 1985. [Abstr. in DA (46) 2285A.]

12353. SABINSON, ERIC MITCHELL. Script and transcript: the writings of Clifford Odets, Lillian Hellman and Arthur Miller in relation to their testimony before the U.S. House Committee on Un-American Activities. Unpub. doct. diss., State Univ. of New York at Buffalo. [Abstr. in DA (47) 2161A.]

12354. TAAVILA-WALTERS, PIA SEIJA. Moral questions in the life and work of Lillian Hellman. Unpub. doct. diss., Michigan State Univ., 1985. [Abstr. in DA (47) 527A.]

12355. WRIGHT, WILLIAM. Lillian Hellman: the image, the woman. New York: Simon & Schuster. pp. 507. Rev. by Frank Rich in NYTB, 23 Nov., 1; by David Richards in BkW, 23 Nov., 1, 11.)

David Helwig

12356. YORK, LORRAINE M. 'The progress of illumination': the design and unity of David Helwig's *Catchpenny Poems*. CanP (18) 55–65.

Ernest Hemingway

12357. ADAIR, WILLIAM. Lying down in Hemingway's fiction. NCL (16:4) 7–8.

12358. ALDRIDGE, JOHN W. *The Sun Also Rises* – sixty years later. SewR (94:2) 337–45.

12359. ATHERTON, JOHN. The itinerary and the postcard: minimal strategies in *The Sun Also Rises*. ELH (53:1) 199–218.

12360. BASKETT, BELMA. Hemingway's Turkish experience: prelude to Spain. AAS (6:1) 45–54.

12361. BEASLEY, CONGER, JR. Hemingway and the *Kansas City Star*. *See* **560.**

12362. BENSON, JACKSON. Down for the count: posthumous and revisionist Hemingway. RALS (15:1) 1985, 17–29 (review-article).

12363. BLADES, JOHN. Divided Hemingways agree: his art, not his life, is the key. BkW, 24 Aug., 39.

12364. BRASCH, JAMES D.   Hemingway's doctor: José Luis Herrera Sotolongo remembers Ernest Hemingway. JML (13:2) 185–210.

12365. CAGLE, CHARLES HARMON.   'Cézanne nearly did': Stein, Cézanne, and Hemingway. MidQ (23:3) 1982, 268–78.

12366. CAPELLÁN, ÁNGEL.   Hemingway and the Hispanic world. Ann Arbor, MI: UMI Research Press; Epping: Bowker, 1985. pp. xvi, 327. (Studies in modern literature, 51.) Rev. by John M. Muste in AL (58:4) 656–8.

12367. CASILLO, ROBERT.   The festival gone wrong: vanity and victimization in *The Sun Also Rises.* ELit (13:1) 115–33.

12368. COLLINS, WILLIAM J.   Taking on the champion: Alice as liar in *The Light of the World.* SAF (14:2) 225–32.

12369. COOPER, STEPHEN, JR.   The politics of Ernest Hemingway. Unpub. doct. diss., Univ. of North Carolina at Chapel Hill, 1985. [Abstr. in DA (47) 176A.]

12370. DYER, JOYCE.   Hemingway's use of the pejorative term 'nigger' in *The Battler.* NCL (16:5) 5–10.

12371. FLEMING, ROBERT E.   Perversion and the writer in *The Sea Change.* SAF (14:2) 215–20.

12372. FUENTES, NORBERTO.   Hemingway in Cuba. (Bibl. 1985, 11179.) Rev. by Robert A. Martin in CR (30:4) 530–1.

12373. GRIFFIN, PETER.   Along with youth: Hemingway, the early years. Oxford: OUP, 1985. pp. x, 258. (Cf. bibl. 1985, 11182.) Rev. by James Campbell in TLS, 1 Aug., 837–8; by Richard Gray in THES (705) 20; by Frank Kermode in LRB (8:7) 4–5; by Joseph Waldmeir in CR (30:4) 529–30; by Jackson R. Bryer in Novel (19:3) 270–3; by Townsend Ludington in AL (58:4) 653–6.

12374. GRIMES, LARRY E.   The religious design of Hemingway's early fiction. Ann Arbor, MI: UMI Research Press; Epping: Bowker, 1985. pp. viii, 156. (Studies in modern literature, 50.) Rev. by Kenneth Kuiper in ChrisL (35:4) 40–1.

12375. HANNUM, HOWARD L.   Nick Adams and the search for light. SSF (23:1) 9–18.

12376. HEMINGWAY, ERNEST.   The garden of Eden. New York: Scribner's. pp. 247. Rev. by R. Z. Sheppard in Time, 26 May, 77; by John Updike in NY, 30 June, 85–8.

12377. HERNDON, JERRY A.   *The Snows of Kilimanjaro*: another look at theme and point of view. SAQ (85:4) 351–9.

12378. HOLMESLAND, ODDVAR.   Structuralism and interpretation: Ernest Hemingway's *Cat in the Rain.* EngS (67:3) 221–33.

12379. KERNER, DAVID.   The alleged errors of dialogue indentation in *Islands in the Stream. See* **110.**

12380. KIM, YU-SANG.   Sangzingsung gheukmyon esco gochalhan Ernest Hemingway jakpum yeongu. (A symbolistic approach to Ernest Hemingway.) Unpub. doct. diss., Geonguk Univ. (Korea), 1985.

12381. LUCID, ROBERT F.   Aesthetic sensibility and the idea of the imagination in America. *See* **9454.**

12382. LYNN, DAVID HAYDEN. Cries out of the darkness: heroic narrators in early-modern fiction. *See* **11520.**

12383. McNEELY, TREVOR. War zone revisited: Hemingway's aesthetics and *A Farewell to Arms.* SDR (22:4) 1984, 14–38.

12384. MEYERS, JEFFREY. Hemingway: a biography. London: Macmillan. pp. xv, 644. (Cf. bibl. 1985, 11210.) Rev. by James Campbell in TLS, 1 Aug., 8378; by Frank Kermode in LRB (8:7) 4–5; by Townsend Ludington in AL (58:4) 653–6; by Jackson R. Bryer in Novel (19:3) 270–3; by Sarah Bradford in Spect, 29 Apr., 30–2.

12385. —— Memoirs of Hemingway: growth of a legend. EDH (44) 125–46.

12386. MONTEIRO, GEORGE. 'This is my pal Bugs': Ernest Hemingway's *The Battler.* SSF (23:2) 179–83.

12387. MOORHEAD, MICHAEL. Hemingway's *The Short Happy Life of Francis Macomber* and Shaw's *The Deputy Sheriff.* Exp (44:2) 42–3.

12388. MOSELEY, MERRITT. Faulkner's Benjy, Hemingway's Jake. *See* **11906.**

12389. MOTTRAM, ERIC. Hemingway and his biographers. Enc (67:5) 44–50.

12390. PARSONS, THORNTON. Hemingway's audacious technique. Prague Studies in English (18) 1984, 85–95.

12391. PIZER, DONALD. The Hemingway–Dos Passos relationship. *See* **11691.**

12392. RAEBURN, JOHN. Fame became of him: Hemingway as public writer. (Bibl. 1985, 11233.) Rev. by Robert A. Martin in CR (30:1) 117–18; by Robert F. Lucid in Review (7) 1985, 113–18.

12393. REYNOLDS, MICHAEL. The young Hemingway. Oxford; New York: Blackwell. pp. 291. Rev. by Frank Kermode in LRB (8:7) 4–5; by John M. Muste in AL (58:4) 656–8; by Jackson R. Bryer in Novel (19:3) 270–3; by Richard Gray in THES (705) 20; by James Campbell in TLS, 1 Aug., 837–8.

12394. REYNOLDS, MICHAEL S. A supplement to Hemingway's reading: 1910–1940. SAF (14:1) 99–108.

12395. SAMUELSON, ARNOLD. With Hemingway: a year in Key West and Cuba. (Bibl. 1985, 11241.) Rev. by Allen Josephs in SAF (14:1) 119–20.

12396. SHIN, MOON-SOO. Chaeheom eui sihak: Ernest Hemingway ron. (Poetics of experience: Ernest Hemingway.) CAE (19) 223–36.

12397. SMITH, PAUL. Hemingway's apprentice fiction: 1919–1921. AL (58:4) 574–88.

12398. SNOW, SARA E. 'Worthy of belief': *ethos* in F. Scott Fitzgerald's *The Great Gatsby* and Ernest Hemingway's *The Sun Also Rises. See* **11981.**

12399. SVOBODA, FREDERIC JOSEPH. Hemingway and *The Sun Also Rises:* the crafting of a style. (Bibl. 1985, 11246.) Rev. by Paul Smith in RALS (13:1) 1983, 65–8; by Robert W. Lewis in SAF(14:1) 110–12.

12400. WAINWRIGHT, J. ANDREW. The far shore: gender complexities in Hemingway's *Indian Camp.* DalR (66:1/2) 181–7.

12401. WHITLOW, ROGER. Cassandra's daughters: the women in Hemingway. London: Greenwood Press, 1984. (Contributions in women's studies, 51.) (Cf. bibl. 1985, 11251.)

12402. WILHELM, ALBERT E. Dick Boulton's name in *The Doctor and the Doctor's Wife*. See **1698.**

12403. WINCHELL, MARK ROYDEN. Fishing the swamp: *Big Two-Hearted River* and the unity of *In Our Time*. SoCR (18:2) 18–29.

12404. WYATT, DAVID. Inventing Hemingway. SewR (94:2) 289–91 (review-article).

12405. YAMAMOTO, SHOH. Hemingway's Macomber story: its structure and meaning. PoetT (23) 98–115.

12406. ZAPF, HUBERT. Die Leserrolle in Ernest Hemingways *The Short Happy Life of Francis Macomber*. AAA (11:1) 19–39.

Beth Henley

12407. HARGROVE, NANCY D. The tragicomedy vision of Beth Henley's drama. SoQ (22:4) 1984, 54–70.

'O. Henry' (William Sydney Porter)

12408. PREU, DANA MCKINNON. *Gal Young Un*: a transfer of the seriocomic tradition in American literature to film. See **10053.**

Rayner Heppenstall

12409. GOODMAN, JONATHAN (ed.). The master eccentric: the journals of Rayner Heppenstall 1969–81. London: Allison & Busby, pp. ix, 278.

Frank Herbert

12410. FJELLMAN, STEPHEN M. Prescience and power: *God Emperor of Dune* and the intellectuals. SFS (13:1) 50–63.

Xavier Herbert

12411. JAMES, TREVOR. Australia: Xavier Herbert (1901–1984). London Magazine (25:5/6) 1985, 111–18.

12412. MONAHAN, SEAN. Xavier Herbert's *Capricornia*: in praise of the swagman spirit. Westerly (30:4) 1985, 15–24 (review-article).

Josephine Herbst

12413. MAIR, CHRISTIAN. Geschichtsverständnis und Textstruktur im sozialkritischen amerikanischen Roman der dreißiger Jahre – John Dos Passos, James T. Farrell, Josephine Herbst. See **11690.**

12414. NELSON, JOHN. An introduction to Josephine Herbst's forgotten exposé of Nazi Germany. MassR (27:2) 334–62.

12415. WIEDEMANN, BARBARA K. Josephine Herbst's short fiction. Unpub. doct. diss., Univ. of South Florida. [Abstr. in DA (47) 1327A.]

'James Herriot'

12416. GONZALEZ, ARTURO F., JR. James Herriot. SatR, May/June, 56–9, 88–9. (Interview.)

John Hersey

12417. DEE, JONATHAN. The art of fiction XCII. ParisR (100) 210–49.

John Hewitt

12418. MULLAN, FIONA. 'Paved unerring roads': the poetry of John Hewitt. Threshold (36) 30–43.

Stefan Heym

12419. DUBE, INGE DOROTHEA. Stefan Heym's portrait of America. Unpub. doct. diss., Northwestern Univ. [Abstr. in DA (47) 2173A.]

12420. HUTCHINSON, PETER. Problems of socialist historiography: the example of Stefan Heym's *The King David Report.* MLR (81:1) 131–8.

Jack Hibberd

12421. SIRMAI, GEOFF. An interview with Jack Hibberd. Southerly (45:3) 1985, 260–5.

Aidan Higgins

12422. IMHOF, RÜDIGER; KAMM, JÜRGEN. Coming to grips with Aidan Higgins: *Killachter Meadow* – an analysis. Études irlandaises (9) 1984, 145–60.

12423. RAUCHBAUER, OTTO. Aidan Higgins, *Killachter Meadow* und *Langrishe, Go Down* sowie Harold Pinters Fernsehfilm *Langrishe, Go Down*: Variationen eines Motivs. WBEP (80) 135–62.

Patricia Highsmith

12424. HILFER, ANTHONY CHANNELL. 'Not really such a monster': Highsmith's Ripley as thriller protagonist and protean man. MidQ (25) 1984, 361–74.

Geoffrey Hill

12425. BARFOOT, C. C. Reading the word in Geoffrey Hill. DQR (16:1) 37–60.

12426. GERVAIS, DAVID. Geoffrey Hill, his critics and his criticism. CamQ (15:3) 236–45 (review-article).

12427. GLEN, HEATHER. Geoffrey Hill's 'England of the mind'. *See* **12330.**

12428. HART, H. The poetry of Geoffrey Hill. Unpub. doct. diss., Univ. of Oxford, 1983.

12429. LLOYD, DAVID THOMAS. Lyric impulse and epic dimension in Heaney's *North* and Hill's *Mercian Hymns. See* **12335.**

12430. RICHMAN, ROBERT. 'The battle it was born to lose': the poetry of Geoffrey Hill. NCrit (2) Apr. 1984, 22–34.

12431. ROBINSON, PETER (ed.). Geoffrey Hill: essays on his work. (Bibl. 1985, 11283.) Rev. by Andrew Swarbrick in CritQ (28:3) 110–11; by Peter Levi in Cambridge Review (107:2290) 26–7; by David Gervais in CamQ (15:3) 236–42; by Alastair Fowler in TLS, 4 Apr., 363–4.

12432. ROEFFAERS, HUGO. Engels kwintet: essays over Ted Hughes, Geoffrey Hill, Seamus Heaney, Craig Raine en Robert Graves. *See* **12222.**

James Hilton

12433. SCOTT, PATRICK. James Hilton's *Goodbye, Mr Chips* and the strange death of liberal England. SAQ (85:4) 319–28.

Chester Himes

12434. SCHWEIGHAEUSER, JEAN-PAUL. Chester Himes: romancier noir noir. Europe (62:664/65) 1984, 97—9.

Gladys Hindmarch

12435. BUTLING, PAULINE.   Gladys Hindmarch: pointillist prose. ECanW (32) 70–91.

Barry Hines

12436. HOLDERNESS, GRAHAM.   Miners and the novel: from bourgeois to proletarian fiction. *In* (pp. 18–32) **6.**

Russell Hoban

12437. GRANOFSKY, RONALD.   Holocaust as symbol in *Riddley Walker* and *The White Hotel*. MLS (16:3) 172–82.

Jack Hodgins

12438. LERNOUT, G.   Creation-science and Jack Hodgins's *The Invention of the World*. RBPH (64:3) 532–8.

12439. McCAIG, JOANN.   Brother XII and *The Invention of the World*. ECanW (28) 1984, 128–40.

12440. Entry cancelled.

12441. ZACHARASIEWICZ, WALDEMAR.   The invention of a region: the art of fiction in Jack Hodgins' stories. *In* (pp. 186–91) **22.**

12442. —— Jack Hodgins as a short story writer and the tradition of regional fiction in Canada. *In* (pp. 195–206) **17.**

12443. Entry cancelled.

Hugh Hood

12444. GAREBIAN, KEITH.   Hugh Hood. *In* (pp. 93–151) **8.**

Arthur Hopcraft

12445. LARSON, JANET KARSTEN.   Is it bleaker than we think? ChCen (103:4) 85–7.

A. D. Hope

12446. KUCH, PETER; KAVANAGH, PAUL.   Daytime thoughts about the night shift: Alec Hope talks to Peter Kuch and Paul Kavanagh. Southerly (46:2) 221–31.

12447. LEONARD, JOHN.   Accessibility and myth: Gig Ryan and A. D. Hope. Meanjin (44:3) 1985, 413–19.

12448. MORSE, RUTH.   Editing A. D. Hope: notes and documents. *See* **322.**

12449. —— (sel. and introd.).   Selected poems. Manchester: Carcanet Press. pp. 139. (Poetry signatures.)

12450. Entry cancelled.

Paul Horgan

12451. HANSEN, TERRY L.   The experience of Paul Horgan's *The Peach Stone*. SDR (22:2) 1984, 71–85.

Donald Horne

12452. BUCKLEY, VINCENT.   Donald Horne's confession: 'Watching shadows and listening to echoes'. Quadrant (30:3) 76–9.

12453. THOMAS, MARK.   Australian thinkers: part 2, Donald Horne. Canberra Bulletin of Public Administration (12:3) 1985, 172–7.

Frances Horovitz

12454. GARFITT, ROGER (ed.).   Collected poems. Newcastle upon

Tyne: Bloodaxe in assn with Enitharmon, 1985. pp. 128. Rev. by Jeremy Hooker in AWR (83) 123–6; by Philip Pacey in Poetry Wales (21:4) 99–101.

Harold Horwood

12455. MILLER, JUDITH. A conversation with Harold Horwood. JCF (35/36) 56–72.

William Stanley Houghton

12456. MORTIMER, P. The life and literary career of W. Stanley Houghton, 1881–1913. Unpub. doct. diss., Univ. of Salford, 1984.

12457. MORTIMER, PAUL. W. Stanley Houghton: an introduction and bibliography. ModDr (28:3) 1985, 474–89.

A. E. Housman

12458. ADELMAN, SEYMOUR. He didn't like us, but we like him: a book collector's A. E. Housman. *See* **190**.

12459. BRINK, C. O. English classical scholarship: historical reflections on Bentley, Porson and Housman. Cambridge: Clarke; New York: OUP, 1985. pp. x, 243. Rev. by Peter Jones in Enc (67:2) 51–4.

12460. CLUCAS, HUMPHREY. A note on A. E. Housman. Agenda (24:2) 91–3.

12461. GREENE, GHUSSAN R. Housman since 1936 – popular responses and professional revaluations in America. HSJ (12) 30–46.

12462. HOAGWOOD, TERENCE ALLAN. Poetic design in *More Poems*: Laurence and A. E. Housman, I. HSJ (12) 77–86.

12463. MARUYA, HARUYASU. A study of A. E. Housman with special reference to his pessimism, I. HSJ (12) 150–9.

12464. NAIDITCH, P. G. A. E. Housman and the Civil Service examinations. ANQ (24:9/10) 147.

12465. —— A. E. Housman in Paris. HSJ (12) 55–70.

12466. —— Corrections. *See* **264**.

12467. —— Notes on the life of M. J. Jackson. HSJ (12) 93–114.

12468. —— Some echoes and allusions in A. E. Housman's prose writings. HSJ (12) 131–42.

12469. NIELSEN, ROSEMARY M.; SOLOMON, ROBERT H. Horace and Housman: twisting conventions. CanRCL (13:3) 325–49.

12469a. NICKSON, M. A. E. Sloane's codes: the solution to a mystery. *See* **265**.

12470. PAGE, NORMAN. A. E. Housman: a critical biography. London: Macmillan, 1985. pp. 236. (Repr., with amendments, of bibl. 1984, 11316.) Rev. by P. G. Naiditch in CJ (81:4) 262–5.

12471. POWELL, J. ENOCH. The influence and repressed passion of A. E. Housman. Spect (256:8234) 31–2.

12472. STEVENSON, JOHN W. The durability of Housman's poetry. SewR (94:4) 613–19.

12473. WHITE, WILLIAM. Two 'new' *Shropshire Lad* reprints. HSJ (12) 146–9.

12474. —— An unpublished A. E. H. letter to Horatio F. Brown. HSJ (12) 144–5.

12475. WILSON, J. LARRY. The relevance of Housman's *The Name and Nature of Poetry*. HSJ (12) 121–8.

Lawrence Housman

12476. HOAGWOOD, TERENCE ALLAN. Poetic design in *More Poems*: Laurence and A. E. Housman, 1. *See* **12462.**

Susan Howatch

12477. BRIDGWOOD, CHRISTINE. Family romances: the contemporary popular family saga. *In* (pp. 167–93) **45.**

Tina Howe

12478. HAUG, INGRID. Art *vs* decay in Tina Howe's *Painting Churches*. *In* (pp. 263–74) **18.**

W. H. Hudson

12479. CHEETHAM, SIR NICHOLAS (introd.). Far away and long ago: a childhood in Argentina. London: Century, 1985. pp. xix, 332. (Century travellers.) (Facsim. of ed. pub. London, 1918.)

12480. MILLER, D. L. S. The elusive paradise: a study of W. H. Hudson. Unpub. doct. diss., Univ. of London (Royal Holloway Coll.). [Abstr. in IT (36) 474.]

12481. TOMALIN, RUTH. W. H. Hudson: a biography. (Bibl. 1983, 11741.) Rev. by Cedric Watts in MLR (81:3) 730–1.

Langston Hughes

12482. RAMPERSAD, ARNOLD. The life of Langston Hughes: vol. 1, 1902–1941: I, too, sing America. New York; Oxford: OUP. pp. viii, 468. Rev. by Gwendolyn Brooks in NYTB, 12 Oct., 7.

12483. TRACY, STEVEN CARL. The influence of the blues tradition on Langston Hughes's blues poems. Unpub. doct. diss., Univ. of Cincinnati, 1985. [Abstr. in DA (47) 183A.]

Richard Hughes

12484. HUMPHREY, RICHARD. Der historische Roman und das Feindbild. Zu Richard Hughes' unvollendeter Faschismus-Trilogie *The Human Predicament*. Anglistik & Englischunterricht (29/30) 157–72.

12485. MILLIGAN, IAN. Richard Hughes and Michael Scott: a further source for *A High Wind in Jamaica*. *See* **9154.**

12486. MORGAN, PAUL BENNETT. Richard Hughes and *Living in W'ales*. AWR (84) 91–103.

12487. SAVAGE, D. S. Richard Hughes, solipsist. SewR (94:4) 602–13.

Ted Hughes

12488. BRANDES, RANDY PAUL. The myth of the Fall in the poetry of D. H. Lawrence and Ted Hughes. Unpub. doct. diss., Emory Univ., 1985. [Abstr. in DA (46) 2697A.]

12489. HOLBROOK, DAVID. The crow of Avon? Shakespeare, sex and Ted Hughes. *See* **4484.**

12490. PONSFORD, MICHAEL. Christianity and myth in Ted Hughes's *The Golden Boy*. NCL (16:4) 11–12.

12491. Robinson, C. The poetry of Ted Hughes. Unpub. doct. diss., Univ. of Lancaster, 1984.

12492. Roeffaers, Hugo. Engels kwintet: essays over Ted Hughes, Geoffrey Hill, Seamus Heaney, Craig Raine en Robert Graves. *See* **12222.**

12493. Runcie, Catherine. On figurative language: a reading of Shelley's, Hardy's and Hughes's skylark poems. *See* **8430.**

12494. Sweeting, M. C. R. Patterns of initiation in the poetry of Ted Hughes from 1970 to 1980. Unpub. doct. diss., Univ. of Durham, 1984.

12495. Sym, Myung-Ho. Ted Hughes eui dongmul si. (Ted Hughes's animal poems.) JELL (32:4) 625–45.

12496. Wandor, Michelene. When the Muse refuses to appear in public. Listener (116) 31 July, 22.

Keri Hulme

12497. Prentice, Chris. Re-writing their stories, renaming themselves: post-colonialism and feminism in the fictions of Keri Hulme and Audrey Thomas. Span (23) Sept., 68–80.

T. E. Hulme

12498. Csengeri, K. E. The chronology of T. E. Hulme's *Speculations*. PBSA (80:1) 105–9.

12499. —— T. E. Hulme: an annotated bibliography of writings about him. ELT (29:4) 388–428.

12500. Karlekar, Ranajay. T. E. Hulme and T. S. Eliot: crisis and tradition. *See* **11765.**

12501. Rae, P. M. Some theories of creative process of the late nineteenth and early twentieth centuries: a context for T. E. Hulme. Unpub. doct. diss., Univ. of Oxford, 1984.

Fannie Hurst

12502. Wilentz, Gay. White patron and black artist: the correspondence of Fannie Hurst and Zora Neale Hurston. LCUT (ns 35) 21–43.

Zora Neale Hurston

12503. Byers, Marianne Hollins. Zora Neale Hurston: a perspective of black men in the fiction and non-fiction. Unpub. doct. diss., Bowling Green State Univ., 1985. [Abstr. in DA (47) 528A.]

12504. Fryar, Lillie B. The aesthetics of language: Harper, Hurston and Morrison. *See* **8439.**

12505. Martin, Dellita L. (introd.). Dust tracks on a road: an autobiography. London: Virago Press. pp. xvii, 348.

12506. Pondrom, Cyrena N. The role of myth in Hurston's *Their Eyes Were Watching God*. AL (58:2) 181–202.

12507. Wilentz, Gay. White patron and black artist: the correspondence of Fannie Hurst and Zora Neale Hurston. *See* **12502.**

R. C. Hutchinson

12508. Green, Robert. R. C. Hutchinson: the man and his books. Introd. by Sir Rupert Hart-Davis. Metuchen, NJ; London: Scarecrow Press, 1985. pp. xvii, 137. (Scarecrow author bibliographies, 70.) Rev. in BB (43:4) 264.

Aldous Huxley

12509. BURNESS, E. S.   *Eyeless in Gaza* and *Soles Occidere et Redire Possunt*: an undertone of war. NQ (31) 1984, 515–16.

12510. CLEMENTS, PATRICIA.   'Transmuting' Nancy Cunard. *See* **11018.**

12511. CUPERS, JEAN-LOUIS.   Aldous Huxley et la musique: à la manière de Jean-Sebastien. Brussels: Facultés Universitaires Saint-Louis, 1985. pp. 410.

12512. GREINACHER, KURT.   Die frühen satirischen Romane Aldous Huxleys. Frankfurt: Lang. pp. 242. (Neue Studien zur Anglistik und Amerikanistik, 34.)

12513. LEAL, R. B.   Huxley and Drieu La Rochelle: studies in commitment and mysticism. RLC (59:4) 409–24.

12514. REBIKOVA, L. D.   O kharaktere ironii v ranneĭ satiricheskoĭ proze Oldosa Khaksli. (The nature of irony in the early satirical prose of Aldous Huxley.) VLU (1986:3) 102–4.

12515. SEXTON, JAMES.   *Brave New World* and the rationalization of industry. ESCan (12:4) 424–39.

Robin Hyde

12516. MATTHEWS, JACQUELINE; HARDY, LINDA; BUNKLE, PHILLIDA (introds).   Nor the years condemn. Auckland: New Women's Press. pp. xxvi, 352. Rev. by Heather Roberts in NZList, 14 June, 49.

12517. SANDBROOK, PATRICK.   A descriptive inventory of some manuscripts and drafts of the work of Robin Hyde. JNZL (4) 21–47.

David Ignatow

12518. MAZZARO, JEROME.   David Ignatow's post-Vietnam war poetry. CR (30:2) 219–27.

Witi Ihimaera

12519. YOUNG, DAVID.   An end to the silence. NZList, 7 June, 24–5.

William Inge

12520. CENTOLA, STEVEN R.   Compromise as bad faith: Arthur Miller's *A View from the Bridge* and William Inge's *Come Back, Little Sheba*. MidQ (28:1) 100–13.

Arthur Crew Inman

12521. AARON, DANIEL (ed.).   The Inman diary: a public and private confession. Cambridge, MA; London: Harvard UP, 1985. 2 vols. pp. 1661.

David Ireland

12522. GREEN, KEVIN.   David Ireland and the predicament of the Australian writer. Commonwealth (Dijon) (7:2) 1985, 39–47.

John Irving

12523. CARTON, EVAN.   The politics of selfhood: Bob Slocum, T. S. Garp and auto-American-biography. *See* **12345.**

12524. HANSEN, RON.   The art of fiction XCIII. ParisR (100) 74–103.

12525. NENADÁL, RADOSLAV.   Násilí jako konstruktivní fabulační prvek u Johna Irvinga. (Violence as a constructional element in John Irving.) *In* (pp. 42–3) **4.**

Christopher Isherwood

12526. ELICK, CATHERINE LILLY. Isherwood and his critics: a historical reading of *Goodbye to Berlin* and its adaptations. Unpub. doct. diss., Vanderbilt Univ. [Abstr. in DA (47) 1317A–18A.]

12527. FALCONER, T. P. Christopher Isherwood: the history of a dandy. Unpub. doct. diss., Univ. of Reading, 1981.

12528. WADE, S. P. Themes of self-identity in the fiction and autobiography of Christopher Isherwood. Unpub. doct. diss., Univ. of Wales, Aberystwyth, 1983.

12529. WHITEHEAD, JOHN. Auden and *All the Conspirators. See* **11105.**

Kazuo Ishiguro

12530. RECKWITZ, ERHARD. Der Roman als Metaroman: Salman Rushdie, *Midnight's Children*; Kazuo Ishiguro, *A Pale View of the Hills*; John Fowles, *Mantissa. See* **10373.**

Violet Jacob

12531. GARDEN, RONALD. Violet Jacob in India. SLJ (13:2) 48–64.

Josephine Jacobsen

12532. PRETTYMAN, EVELYN SAVAGE. Josephine Jacobsen: commitment to wonder. Unpub. doct. diss., Univ. of Maryland, 1985. [Abstr. in DA (47) 1730A.]

Dan Jacobson

12533. GRAY, STEPHEN. In conversation with Dan Jacobson. Contrast (16:2) 30–41.

12534. JACOBSON, DAN. Time and time again: autobiographies. (Bibl. 1985, 11386.) Rev. by Aleck Goldberg in Jewish Affairs (41:3) 35–6.

C. L. R. James

12535. SANDER, REINHARD W. C. L. R. James and the Haitian revolution. WLWE (26:2) 277–90.

M. R. James

12536. COX, MICHAEL (sel.). The ghost stories of M. R. James. Oxford: OUP. pp. 224.

P. D. James

12537. PLA, SANDRA. P. D. James: a new queen of crime? Caliban (23) 73–86.

Randall Jarrell

12538. BORUCH, MARIANNE. Rhetoric and mystery. Field (35) 57–61.

12539. BOTTOMS, DAVID. The messy humanity of Randall Jarrell: his poetry in the eighties. SoCR (17:1) 1984, 83–95.

12540. BURNS, RALPH. The plain truth in *The Truth*. Field (35) 39–42.

12541. CHAPPELL, FRED. The longing to belong. Field (35) 23–9.

12542. CROSS, RICHARD K. Jarrell and the Germans. ModAge (29:3) 1985, 250–5.

12543. FERGUSON, SUZANNE. Narrative and narrators in the poetry of Randall Jarrell. SoCR (17:1) 1984, 72–82.

12544. JARRELL, MARY (ed.); WRIGHT, STUART (asst ed.). Randall Jarrell's letters: an autobiographical and literary selection. (Bibl. 1985, 11391.) Rev. by Herbie Butterfield in THES (702) 20; by James

Applewhite in AL (58:1) 117–19; by Patricia Beer in Listener, 13 Feb., 25–6; by Michael Hofmann in TLS, 11 July, 759.

12545. JENSEN, LAURA. Potential for whole totem. Field (35) 10–13.

12546. LENSING, GEORGE S. The modernism of Randall Jarrell. SoCR (17:1) 1984, 52–60.

12547. MAZZARO, JEROME. Logical and local differences. SewR (94:1) 143–8 (review-article).

12548. MORON, RONALD. Randall Jarrell as critic of criticism. SoCR (17:1) 1984, 60–5.

12549. PREIS-SMITH, AGATA. Randall Jarrell – modern romantic. KN (33) 155–64.

12550. QUINN, BERNETTA. Randall Jarrell and angels: the search for immortality. SoCR (17:1) 1984, 65–71.

12551. ST JOHN, DAVID. *Seele im Raum.* Field (35) 33–6.

12552. WALKER, DAVID. The shape on the bed. Field (35) 64–7.

12553. WEIGL, BRUCE. An autobiography of nightmare. Field (35) 15–18.

12554. WILLARD, NANCY. Radiant facts. Field (35) 51–4.

12555. WRIGHT, C. D. Mission of the surviving gunner. Field (35) 19–20.

12556. YOUNG, DAVID. Day for night. Field (35) 46–9.

12557. ZANDERER, LEO. Randall Jarrell: about and for children. LU (2:1) 1978, 73–93.

Robinson Jeffers

12558. MORRIS, DAVID COPLAND. Literature and environment: the inhumanist perspective and the poetry of Robinson Jeffers. Unpub. doct. diss., Univ. of Washington, 1984. [Abstr. in DA (46) 2694A.]

12559. SCOTT, ROBERT IAN (ed.). *What Odd Expedients* and other poems by Robinson Jeffers. Hamden, CT: Archon; Shoe String Press, 1981. pp. viii, 125. Rev. by David Bromwich in YES(16) 362–3.

12560. YOZZO, JOHN MICHAEL. *In illo tempore, ab origine*: violence and reintegration in the poems of Robinson Jeffers. Unpub. doct. diss., Univ. of Tulsa, 1985. [Abstr. in DA (46) 3717A.]

12561. ZALLER, ROBERT. The cliffs of solitude: a reading of Robinson Jeffers. (Bibl. 1985, 11401.) Rev. by Pierre Lagayette in EA (38:3) 1985, 355.

Robin Jenkins

12562. GIFFORD, DOUGLAS. 'God's colossal irony': Robin Jenkins and *Guests of War*. Cencrastus (24) 13–17.

12563. NORQUAY, GLENDA. Against compromise: the fiction of Robin Jenkins. Cencrastus (24) 3–6.

12564. —— Moral absolutism in the novels of Robert Louis Stevenson, Robin Jenkins and Muriel Spark: challenges to realism. *See* **9272.**

12565. SELLIN, BERNARD. Robin Jenkins: the making of the novelist. Cencrastus (24) 7–9.

Ruth Prawer Jhabvala

12566. CHEW, SHIRLEY. Fictions of princely states and empire. *See* **11034.**

12567. Cronin, Richard. *The Hill of Devi* and *Heat and Dust*. See **12010.**

12568. Summerfield, Henry. Holy women and unholy men: Ruth Prawer Jhabvala confronts the non-rational. Ariel (17:3) 85–101.

W. E. Johns

12569. Mählqvist, Stefan. Biggles i Sverige: en litteratursociologisk studie av W. E. Johns Bigglesböcker. (Biggles in Sweden: a literary-sociological study of W. E. Johns's Biggles books.) (Bibl. 1984, 11493.) Rev. by Lena Kåreland in Samlaren (106) 1985, 118–19.

B. S. Johnson

12570. Hassam, Andrew. True novel or autobiography? The case of B. S. Johnson's *Trawl*. Prose Studies (9:1) 62–72.

12571. Ommundsen, Wenche. Self-conscious fiction and literary theory: David Lodge, B. S. Johnson, and John Fowles. See **12040.**

Colin Johnson

12572. Nelson, Emmanuel S. Connecting with the dreamtime: the novels of Colin Johnson. Southerly (46:3) 337–43.

Georgia Douglas Johnson

12573. Stetson, Erlene. Rediscovering the Harlem renaissance: Georgia Douglas Johnson, 'the new Negro poet'. Ob (5) Spring/Summer 1979, 26–34.

James Weldon Johnson

12574. Canady, Nicholas. *The Autobiography of an Ex-Coloured Man* and the tradition of the black autobiography. Ob (6) Spring/Summer 1980, 76–80.

Denis Johnston

12575. Flot, Michel. *The Moon in the Yellow River* de Denis Johnston: texte et représentation. Études irlandaises (11) 93–109.

George Johnston

12576. Dever, Maryanne. Artist and nationality in G. Johnston's trilogy. Commonwealth (Dijon) (7:2) 1985, 19–30.

12577. Kinnane, Garry (ed.). *Strong-man from Piraeus* and other stories. See **11457.**

Jennifer Johnston

12578. Connelly, Joseph. Legend and lyric as structure in the selected fiction of Jennifer Johnston. Éire–Ireland (21:3) 119–24.

Elizabeth Jolley

12579. Daniel, Helen. Elizabeth Jolley: variations on a theme. Westerly (31:2) 50–63.

12580. Goldsworthy, Kerryn. Voices in time: *A Kindness Cup* and *Miss Peabody's Inheritance*. See **11072.**

12581. Riemer, A. P. Displaced persons: some preoccupations in Elizabeth Jolley's fiction. Westerly (31:2) 64–79.

12582. Ward, Elizabeth. An Australian novelist at home. BkW, 2 Nov., 10–11. (Interview.)

D. G. Jones

12583. Blodgett, E. D. D. G. Jones. *In* (pp. 85–130) **10.**

David Jones

12584. AUSTIN, D. L.   A study of *In Parenthesis* by David Jones. Unpub. doct. diss., Univ. of Oxford, 1982.

12585. BLISSETT, WILLIAM.   'There's a Welsh poet named Jones.' UTQ (55:2) 1985/86, 212–15 (review-article).

12586. —— To make a shape in words. Ren (38:2) 67–81.

12587. BRESLIN, JOHN B.   David Jones: the shaping of a poet's mind. Ren (38:2) 83–102.

12588. CORCORAN, NEIL.   The song of deeds: a study of *The Anathemata* of David Jones. (Bibl. 1985, 11416.) Rev. by William Blissett in UTQ (55:2) 1985/86, 214–15.

12589. DALY, CARSON.   The amphibolic title of *The Anathemata*: a key to the structure of the poem. Ren (35:1) 1982, 49–63.

12590. —— Hills as the sacramental landscape in *The Anathemata*. Ren (38:2) 131–9.

12591. DEANE, PATRICK.   Raising a valid sign: a defence of the form of David Jones's *Anathemata*. Unpub. doct. diss., Univ. of Western Ontario. [Abstr. in DA (47) 1719A–20A.]

12592. DILWORTH, THOMAS.   David Jones and fascism. *See* **9935.**

12593. —— Form versus content in David Jones's *The Tribune's Visitation*. Ren (38:2) 103–16.

12594. —— (ed.).   Inner necessities: the letters of David Jones to Desmond Chute. Toronto: Anson–Cartwright, 1984. pp. 101. Rev. by William Blissett in UTQ (55:2) 1985/86, 214.

12595. FRIEDMAN, BARTON.   Tolkien and David Jones: the great war and the war of the ring. CLIO (11:2) 1982, 115–36.

12596. GALLAGHER, E. J.   The mythopoeic impulse in the poetry of David Jones. Unpub. doct. diss., Univ. of Manchester, 1980.

12597. MILES, J.   Coherent eclecticism: intellectual disposition, form and content in the work of David Jones. Unpub. doct. diss., Univ. of Oxford, 1983.

12598. PACEY, PHILIP.   David Jones and other wonder voyagers. (Bibl. 1985, 11422.) Rev. by William Blissett in UTQ (55:2) 1985/86, 214–15.

12599. STAUDT, KATHLEEN HENDERSON.   The language of T. S. Eliot's *Four Quartets* and David Jones's *The Anathemata*. *See* **11792.**

12600. WARD, ELIZABETH.   David Jones, mythmaker. (Bibl. 1985, 11425.) Rev. by William Blissett in UTQ (55:2) 1985/86, 213–14.

James Jones

12601. BOYER, A. D.   James Jones and Joseph Heller: an essay in contrasts. *See* **12344.**

12602. MACSHANE, FRANK.   Into eternity: the life of James Jones, American writer. (Bibl. 1985, 11428.) Rev. by Joseph M. Flora in AL (58:3) 458–9; by Seymour Krim in BkW, 5 Jan., 4, 6.

Lewis Jones

12603. HOLDERNESS, GRAHAM.   Miners and the novel: from bourgeois to proletarian fiction. *In* (pp. 18–32) **6.**

Madison Jones

12604. GRETLUND, JAN NORDBY. The last agrarian: Madison Jones's achievement. SoR (22:3) 478–88.

Erica Jong

12605. COKER, JUDITH BRIGGS. Sexuality in discourse: feminine models in recent fiction by American women. *See* **10985.**

M. K. Joseph

12606. INGHAM, DAVID KEITH. Mediation and the indirect meta-fiction of Randolph Stow, M. K. Joseph, and Timothy Findley. *See* **11946.**

12607. KUIPER, KOENRAAD; SMALL, VERNON. Constraints on fictions, with an analysis of M. K. Joseph's *A Soldier's Tale*. *See* **10842.**

Elsa Joubert

12608. LENTA, MARGARET. Independence as the creative choice in two South African fictions. *See* **9151a.**

James Joyce

12609. ABBOTT, SALLY. Artemis: the pre-Homeric source of Marion Tweedy Bloom. JJQ (23:4) 497–502.

12610. ASTRO, ALAN MICHAEL. Writing in tongues: translation in Beckett and other modern writers. *See* **10639.**

12611. ATTRIDGE, DEREK; FERRER, DANIEL (comps). Post-structuralist Joyce: essays from the French. (Bibl. 1985, 11437.) Rev. by Charles Peake in CamQ (15) 141–7; by John Kidd in TLS, 5 Sept., 980.

12612. AUBERT, JACQUES; SENN, FRITZ (eds). James Joyce. Paris: L'Herne, 1985. pp. 540. (Cahiers de l'Herne, 50.)

12613. BAKER, HAROLD D. Rite of passage: 'Ithaca', style, and the structure of *Ulysses*. JJQ (23:3) 277–97.

12614. BAR-DAVID, YORAM. Joyce et Kafka. *In* (pp. 173–94) **1.**

12615. BASSOFF, BRUCE. Joyce's *Ulysses* and Plato's *Symposium*. Exp (44:2) 34–6.

12616. BAZARGAN, SUSAN. The headings in 'Aeolus': a cinematographic view. JJQ (23:3) 345–50.

12617. BEEKMAN, E. M. The verbal empires of Simon Vestdijk and James Joyce. (Bibl. 1983, 11847.) Rev. by H. Bekkering in DQR (16:2) 155–7.

12618. BEGNAL, MICHAEL H. Stephen's terrible parable. JJQ (23:3) 355–7.

12619. BENSTOCK, BERNARD. James Joyce. New York: Ungar; London: Lorrimer, 1985. pp. xvii, 202. (Literature and life.) Rev. by James Hurt in JEGP (85:3) 470–2; by Mark Mortimer in TLS, 5 Sept., 980.

12620. —— (ed.). Critical essays on James Joyce. Boston, MA: G. K. Hall, 1985. pp. x, 238. (Critical essays on modern British literature.)

12621. BRAY, PAUL CYRUS. The influence of theories of history on the style of James Joyce's *Finnegans Wake*. Unpub. doct. diss., City Univ. of New York. [Abstr. in DA (47) 907A.]

12622. BRIVIC, SHELDON. Joyce the creator. (Bibl. 1985, 11450.) Rev.

by Ronald Mason in NQ (33:4) 566–7; by John Kidd in TLS, 5 Sept., 980.

12623. Brown, Richard.   James Joyce and sexuality. (Bibl. 1985, 11451.) Rev. by Mark Shechner in JJQ (23:4) 503–7; by John Kidd in TLS, 5 Sept., 980; by Ronald Mason in NQ (33:4) 566–7.

12624. Buning, Marius.   Ulysses's textual homecoming. See **301.**

12625. Burgess, Anthony.   *Blooms of Dublin*: a musical play based on James Joyce's *Ulysses*. London: Hutchinson. pp. 95.

12626. Clark, Hilary Anne.   The idea of a fictional encyclopaedia: *Finnegans Wake, Paradis, The Cantos*. Unpub. doct. diss., Univ. of British Columbia, 1985. [Abstr. in DA (47) 1313A.]

12627. Cohn, Alan M.   Current JJ checklist (35–38). JJQ (23:2) 201–8; (23:3) 337–43; (23:4) 479–85; (24:1) 73–8.

12628. Constantinescu, Ligia.   Joseph Conrad and James Joyce: epiphany and irony in short fiction. See **11483.**

12629. Dangerfield, George.   James Joyce, James Connolly and Irish nationalism. IUR (16) 5–21.

12630. Dauphiné, James.   *A Portrait of the Artist as a Young Man* et le problème de l'autobiographie. Europe (62:657/58) 1984, 83–96.

12631. Deane, Seamus.   'Masked with Matthew Arnold's face': Joyce and liberalism. CJIS (12:1) 11–12.

12632. de Cortanze, Gérard.   Quand Joyce ira à la maternelle finis les petits plats. Europe (62:657/58) 1984, 48–51.

12633. Devlin, Kimberly Jerell.   Self, language, and the other: an integrative approach to the works of James Joyce. Unpub. doct. diss., Univ. of Michigan, 1985. [Abstr. in DA (46) 1938A.]

12634. Dilworth, Thomas.   Sex and politics in *The Dead*. JJQ (23:2) 157–71.

12635. Donoghue, Denis.   We Irish: essays on Irish literature and society. See **9712.**

12636. Duffy, Edward.   *The Sisters* as introduction to *Dubliners*. PLL (22:4) 417–28.

12637. Dumay, Manuela.   'Es-tu bien irlandais, oui ou non?' Europe (62:657/58) 1984, 13–19.

12638. Eckley, Grace.   The entertaining *Nights* of Burton, Stead, and Joyce's Earwicker. See **591.**

12639. Ellerström, Jonas (ed.).   Tema: Joyce. (Theme: Joyce.) Lund: Ellerström. pp. 102.

12640. Ellmann, Richard.   Finally, the last word on *Ulysses*: the ideal text, and portable, too. NYTB, 15 June, 3.

12641. —— Four Dubliners: Wilde, Yeats, Joyce, and Beckett. See **9546.**

12642. —— The new *Ulysses*. GaR (40:2) 548–56 (review-article).

12643. —— Ulysses am Main. *In* (pp. 239–49) **18.**

12644. Ferrer, Daniel.   Miroirs aux sirènes. Europe (62:657/58) 1984, 99–106.

12645. Fludernik, Monika.   Narrative and its development in *Ulysses*. JNT (16:1) 15–40.

12646. —— *Ulysses* and Joyce's change of artistic aims: external and internal evidence. JJQ (23:2) 173–88.

12647. FREDKIN, GRACE. S in *Finnegans Wake*. JJQ (23:2) 189–99.

12648. FÜGER, WILHELM. Bloom's other eye. JJQ (23:2) 209–17.

12649. GABLER, HANS WALTER; STEPPE, WOLFHARD; MELCHIOR, CLAUS (eds). Ulysses: the corrected text. Harmondsworth: Penguin; London: Bodley Head. pp. xiii, 649. (Penguin modern classics.) Rev. by David Lodge in THES (711) 15.

12650. —— —— —— Ulysses: a critical and synoptic edition. (Bibl. 1985, 11479.) Rev. by Marius Buning in DQR (16:2) 145–51; by Antony Hammond in Library (8:4) 382–90.

12651. GEORGI, HELEN. Covert riddles in *Ulysses*: squaring the circle. JML (13:2) 329–39.

12652. GIANNOTTI, THOMAS JOHN, JR. A language of silence: writing the self in Yeats and Synge, Joyce and Beckett. *See* **11176.**

12653. GIBSON, ANDREW. One kind of ambiguity in Joyce, Beckett and Robbe-Grillet. *See* **11177.**

12654. GILLIAM, D. M. D.; McCONCHIE, R. W. Joyce's *A Portrait of the Artist as a Young Man*. Exp (44:3) 43–6.

12655. GONZALES, ALEXANDER G. Seumas O'Kelly and James Joyce. Éire–Ireland (21:2) 85–94.

12656. GORDON, JOHN. *Finnegans Wake*: a plot summary. Dublin: Gill & Macmillan. pp. 302.

12657. GRODEN, MICHAEL. Les gribouillages significatifs de Joyce. (Trans. by JUAN MAREY.) Europe (62:657/58) 1984, 96–9.

12658. HARKNESS, MARGUERITE. The aesthetics of Dedalus and Bloom. Lewisburg, PA: Bucknell UP; London: Assoc. UPs, 1984. pp. 212.

12659. HARPER, MARGARET MILLS. The aristocracy of art and the autobiographical fiction of James Joyce and Thomas Wolfe. Unpub. doct. diss., Univ. of North Carolina at Chapel Hill. [Abstr. in DA (47) 1723A.]

12660. HASSAINE, F. Moore, Joyce and the modernist Anglo-Irish short story. Unpub. doct. diss., Univ. of Leeds, 1985. [Abstr. in IT (36) 913.]

12661. HASSAN, IHAB. ( ): *Finnegans Wake* et l'imagination postmoderne. Europe (62:657/58) 1984, 127–33.

12662. HAYASHI, TETSUMARO (ed.). James Joyce: research opportunities and dissertation abstracts. Jefferson, NC; London: McFarland, 1985. pp. x, 342. (Research opportunities and dissertation abstracts, 4.)

12663. HAYMAN, DAVID. The Joycean inset. JJQ (23:2) 137–55.

12664. HEDBERG, JOHANNES. Pieces on Joyce. Nyköping, Sweden: James Joyce Soc. of Sweden and Finland. pp. 84.

12665. HEININGER, JOSEPH C. Stephen Dedalus in Paris: tracing the fall of Icarus in *Ulysses*. JJQ (23:4) 435–46.

12666. HELMLING, STEVEN. Joyce the irresponsible. SewR (94:3) 450–70.

12667. HERMAN-SEKULIC, MAJA B. The fall of hyperbaton: parodic and revisionary strategies in Bely, Joyce and Mann. Unpub. doct. diss., Princeton Univ. [Abstr. in DA (47) 171A.]

12668. HERR, CHERYL.   Joyce's anatomy of culture. Urbana: Illinois UP. pp. xiii, 314. Rev. by George Watson in THES (738) 18.

12669. HERRING, PHILLIP.   Comment Joyce finit ses chapitres et ses livres. Trans. by NELLY STÉPHANE. Europe (62:657/58) 1984, 65–73.

12670. HOGAN, PATRICK COLM.   Lapsarian Odysseus: Joyce, Milton, and the structure of *Ulysses. See* **5730.**

12671. JACQUET, CLAUDE (ed.).   Genèse de Babel: Joyce et la création. Paris: Éditions du C.N.R.S., 1985. pp. 267. Rev. by Jacques Aubert in Études irlandaises (11) 238–9.

12672. —— Genèse et métamorphose du texte joycien. (Bibl. 1985, 11497.) Rev. by Jacques Aubert in Études irlandaises (11) 239–41.

12673. KATO, MIKIRO.   *Ulysses* no nazo: dai 15 souwa 'Circe' wo chushin ni. (Enigmas in *Ulysses*, with special reference to the 15th episode 'Circe'.) SEL (63:2) 299–313.

12674. KENNER, HUGH.   Beaufoy's masterplaster. JJQ (24:1) 11–18.

12675. KERSHNER, R. B.   The artist as text: dialogism and incremental repetition in Joyce's *Portrait*. ELH (53:4) 881–94.

12676. KIREMIDJUAN, DAVID.   A study of modern parody: James Joyce's *Ulysses*, Thomas Mann's *Doctor Faustus*. New York; London: Garland, 1985. pp. 254. (Garland pubs in comparative literature.)

12677. KNOWLES, SEBASTIAN.   The substructure of 'Sirens'; Molly as *nexus omnia ligans*. JJQ (23:4) 447–63.

12678. LAMPKIN, FRANCES LORETTA MURRELL.   Metaphor, motif, and the moment: form and human relationships in Laurence Sterne's *Tristram Shandy*, James Joyce's *Ulysses*, and John Barth's *Lost in the Funhouse. See* **6846.**

12679. LARSEN, MAX DEEN.   Joyce's narrative theater: *Ivy Day in the Committee Room*. WBEP (80) 93–108.

12680. LAWSON, DAVID.   *Chamber Music* XXXVI as prototaxic experience. JJQ (24:1) 83–5.

12681. LEMAIRE, GÉRARD-GEORGES.   La bataille du *Finnegans Wake*. Europe (62:657/58) 1984, 120–6.

12682. LEONARD, GARRY MARTIN.   William Blake's 'vegetable existence' and James Joyce's 'moral paralysis': the relationship between Blake's Romantic philosophy and Joyce's thematic concerns in *Dubliners* and *A Portrait of the Artist as a Young Man. See* **6258.**

12683. LEVITOW, JONATHAN SETH.   *Ulysses* and the possibility of meaning. Unpub. doct. diss., Princeton Univ. [Abstr. in DA (47) 2169A.]

12684. LUPAN, RADU.   Some notes on James Joyce and his Romanian connections. JJQ (24:1) 86–9.

12685. McARTHUR, MURRAY.   'Signs on a white field': semiotics and forgery in the 'Proteus' chapter of *Ulysses*. ELH (53:3) 633–52.

12686. McARTHUR, MURRAY GILCHRIST.   Language and history in Blake's *Milton* and Joyce's *Ulysses. See* **6262.**

12687. McGrath, F. C.　Laughing in his sleeve: the sources of Stephen's aesthetics. JJQ (23:3) 259–75.

12688. Mansell, Darrel.　William Holman Hunt's *The Awakening Conscience* and James Joyce's *The Dead*. JJQ (23:4) 487–91.

12689. Martin, Timothy P.　Joyce and Wagner's pale vampire. JJQ (23:4) 491–6.

12690. Melchiori, Giorgio (ed.).　Joyce in Rome: the genesis of *Ulysses*. Rome: Bulzoni, 1984. pp. 153.

12691. Minière, Claude.　La musique des îles. Europe (62:657/58) 1984, 140–1.

12692. Mitchell, Breon.　Ezra Pound and G. B. Shaw: a long wordy war. JJQ (23:2) 127–36.

12693. Morrissey, L. J.　Joyce's revision of *The Sisters*: from epicleti to modern fiction. JJQ (24:1) 33–54.

12694. Mosher, Harold F.　Ambiguity in the reading process: narrative mode in *After the Race*. Journal of the Short Story in English (7) 43–61.

12695. Myers, P. D.　The sound of *Finnegans Wake*. Unpub. doct. diss., Univ. of York, 1985.

12696. Newman, Robert D.　The left-handed path of 'Circe'. JJQ (23:2) 223–7.

12697. Nilsen, Kenneth.　Down among the dead: elements of Irish language and mythology in James Joyce's *Dubliners*. CJIS (12:1) 23–34.

12698. Oakes, Randy W.　Myth and method: Eliot, Joyce, and Wolfe in *The Web and the Rock*. See **11780**.

12699. O'Halpin, Eunan.　British patronage and an Irish writer: the award of a government grant to James Joyce in 1916. JJQ (24:1) 79–83.

12700. O'Hearn, Denis.　Freedom from Mother Church: the Stephen Hero image in Australian literature. See **10349**.

12701. Olofsson, Tommy (ed.).　Joyce i Sverige. (Joyce in Sweden.) Stockholm: Atlantis. pp. 337.

12702. O'Neill, William.　The rout of the suitors, the making of an artist: the meaning of parallel and parody in *Ulysses*. MidQ (27:4) 401–21.

12703. O'Sullivan, J. Colm.　And each hue had a differing cry: Joyce's use of colours in *Finnegans Wake*. Unpub. doct. diss., Univ. of Western Ontario, 1985. [Abstr. in DA (46) 3042A.]

12704. Paris, Jean.　Du monologue et de ses précurseurs. Europe (62:657/58) 1984, 52–64.

12705. Parrinder, Patrick.　James Joyce. (Bibl. 1985, 11537.) Rev. by Ronald Mason in NQ (33:2) 268–9; by James Hurt in JEGP (85:3) 470–2; by Charles Peake in CamQ (15:2) 141–7.

12706. —— Joyce sur mer. CVE (23) 87–97.

12707. Patell, Cyrus R. K.　Joyce's use of history in *Finnegans Wake*. Cambridge, MA: Dept of English and American Literature and Language, Harvard Univ.; London: Harvard UP, 1984. pp. 81. (LeBaron Russell Briggs Prize honors essays in English, 1983.)

12708. PECORA, VINCENT P.   *The Dead* and the generosity of the word. PMLA (101:2) 233–45.

12709. RABATÉ, JEAN-MICHEL.   Berkeley entre Joyce et Beckett. *See* **6211.**

12710. ——James Joyce: portrait de l'auteur en autre lecteur. Petit-Roeulx, Belgium: Cistre, 1984. (Cf. bibl. 1984, 11621.) Rev. by Robert Adams Day in EA (39:3) 364–5.

12711. —— Qu'il faut – la chute: chutes, lapsus et parachutes dans *Finnegans Wake*. Europe (62:657/58) 1984, 133–9.

12712. RAYNAUD, CLAUDINE.   Woman, the letter writer; man, the writing master. JJQ (23:3) 299–324.

12713. REA, JOANNE E.   A few observations on Plutarch and Rabelais in *A Portrait*. JJQ (23:3) 357–9.

12714. ——Joyce and Rabelais: Mallow, marrow and Molly. *See* **1621.**

12715. REIZBAUM, MARILYN BELLE.   James Joyce's Judaic 'other': text and contexts. Unpub. doct. diss., Univ. of Wisconsin–Madison, 1985. [Abstr. in DA (47) 914A.]

12716. RIIKONEN, HANNU.   James Joycen *Odysseus*: kielen ja kerronnan sokkelo. (James Joyce's *Ulysses*: a maze of language and narrative.) Helsinki: Gaudeamus Press, 1985. pp. 163. Rev. by Liisa Dahl in Kanava (Helsinki) (2) 126–7.

12717. RIX, WALTER T.   James Joyce's *The Dead*: the Symbolist inspiration. Threshold (36) 49–67.

12718. ROBINSON, DAVID WAYNE.   Joyce's nonce symbols. Unpub. doct. diss., Univ. of Washington, 1985. [Abstr. in DA (46) 3728A.]

12719. ROSENBERG, SAMUEL.   Conan Doyle et James Joyce. (Trans. by GÉRARD-GEORGES LEMAIRE.) *See* **8185.**

12720. SANDULESCO, C. GEORGES.   The polyvalency of Joyce's characters. Études irlandaises (9) 1984, 125–44.

12721. SANDULESCU, C. GEORGE; HART, CLIVE (eds).   Assessing the 1984 *Ulysses*. Gerrards Cross: Smythe; Totowa, NJ: Barnes & Noble. pp. 300. (Proceedings of the Conference 'A *Finnegans Wake* Approach to *Ulysses*' organized by the Princess Grace Irish Library in Monaco in May 1985.)

12722. SCHLOSSMAN, BERYL.   Joyce's Catholic comedy of language. (Bibl. 1985, 11552.) Rev. by Ronald Mason in NQ (33:4) 566–7; by Dominic Manganiello in ChrisL (35:2) 54–6; by John Kidd in TLS, 5 Sept., 980.

12723. SCHNEIDER, ULRICH.   James Joyce, *Dubliners*. Munich: Fink, 1982. pp. 106.

12724. SEED, DAVID.   *Ulysses*: the evolution of a definitive text. *See* **335.**

12725. SEGALL, JEFFREY ALAN.   The polemics of the portraits: politics and ideology in the criticism of James Joyce. Unpub. doct. diss., State Univ. of New York at Buffalo, 1985. [Abstr. in DA (46) 3029A.]

12726. SENN, FRITZ.   *The Boarding House* seen as a tale of misdirection. JJQ (23:4) 405–13.

12727. ——Joyce's dislocations: essays on reading as translation. (Bibl. 1985, 11558.) Rev. by John Kidd in TLS, 5 Sept., 980.

12728. Spoo, Robert E. Nestor and the nightmare: the presence of the Great War in *Ulysses.* TCL (32:2) 137–54.

12729. Steinberg, Erwin R. The religion of Ellen Higgins Bloom. JJQ (23:3) 350–5.

12730. Stéphane, Nelly. L'homme-fiction. Europe (62:657/58) 1984, 5–12.

12731. Stutman, Suzanne. Portrait of the artist: Thomas Wolfe's encounters with James Joyce. JML (13:2) 325–29.

12732. Sultan, Stanley. 'what the hell is he? says Ned': why Joyce answers the question with a question. JJQ (23:2) 217–22.

12733. Suzuki, Ryohei, Joyce no sekai: modernism bungaku no kaidoku. (The world of Joyce: a reading of Modernist literature.) Tokyo: Sairyusha. pp. 264.

12734. Swartzlander, Susan. Multiple meaning and misunderstanding: the material of Festy King. JJQ (23:4) 465–76.

12735. Szilárd, Léna. Der Mythos im Roman und der Wechsel der literarisch-stilistischen Formationen: von Joyce und A. Belyj zum späten Th. Mann und zu M. Bulgakov. *In* (pp. 347–52) **19.**

12736. Thomas, Brook. The balance of history. JJQ (23:3) 359–61.

12737. Tichý, Aleš. Vypravěč a styl u Jamese Joyce a Virginie Woolfové. (Narrator and style in James Joyce and Virgina Woolf.) *In* (pp. 64–5) **4.**

12738. Torchiana, Donald T. Backgrounds for Joyce's *Dubliners.* Boston, MA; London: Allen & Unwin. pp. xiv, 283. Rev. by Clive Hart in THES (711) 15.

12739. Uhlenbruch, Bernd. 'Heaps of dead language' und 'Friedhof der Worte'. Russische Parallelen zu James Joyce. Arcadia (21:2) 145–65.

12740. van Boheemen, Christel. Epos en identiteit: Molly Bloom als voetstuk. (Epic and identity: Molly Bloom as pedestal.) De Gids (149:9/10) 843–51.

12741. —— Tegendraads lezen of Is deconstructivisme destructief? *See* **10954.**

12742. van Caspel, Paul. Bloomers on the Liffey: eisegetical readings of Joyce's *Ulysses.* Baltimore, MD; London: Johns Hopkins UP. pp. xv, 281.

12743. Walkiewicz, E. P. Pound/Joyce: Dublin '82. Paideuma (11:3) 1982, 511–17.

12744. Wall, Richard. An Anglo-Irish dialect glossary for Joyce's works. *See* **942.**

12745. Warner, John M. Myth and history in Joyce's 'Nausicaa' episode. JJQ (24:1) 19–31.

12746. Weintraub, Stanley. A respectful distance: James Joyce and his Dublin townsman Bernard Shaw. JML (13:1) 61–75.

12747. Wight, Doris T. Stephen's villanelle: from passive to active creation. CLQ (22:4) 215–24.

12748. —— Vladímir Propp and *Dubliners*. JJQ (23:4) 415–33.

12749. WILLIAMS, EDWIN W.   Agendath Netaim: promised land or waste land. MFS (32:2) 228–35.

Manfred Jurgensen

12750. PERKINS, ELIZABETH.   Translating the next sentence: language as theme in some poetry of Manfred Jurgensen. Linq (13:2) 1985, 1–14.

Wilson Katiyo

12751. AMBANASOM, SHADRACH ATEKE.   The adolescent protagonist in the African novel: an analysis of five African novels. Unpub. doct. diss., Ohio Univ., 1985. [Abstr. in DA (47) 1320A.]

Patrick Kavanagh (1904–1967)

12752. DOYLE, OWEN P.   From simplicity back to simplicity: Patrick Kavanagh's poetic vision. CAE (19) 517–34.

12753. DUFFY, PATRICK J.   Patrick Kavanagh's landscape. Éire–Ireland (21:3) 105–18.

12754. O'LOUGHLIN, MICHAEL.   After Kavanagh: Patrick Kavanagh and the discourse of contemporary Irish poetry. *See* **10561.**

Molly Keane ('M. J. Farrell')

12755. KIELY, BENEDICT.   The various lives of Molly Keane. HC (23) Dec., 1–8.

H. R. F. Keating

12756. KEATING, H. R. F.   Writing crime fiction. *See* **10276.**

Weldon Kees

12757. ELLEDGE, JIM (ed.).   Weldon Kees: a critical introduction. Metuchen, NJ; London: Scarecrow Press, 1985. pp. xix, 241.

Antigone Kefala

12758. GUNEW, SNEJA.   Ania Walwicz and Antigone Kefala: varieties of migrant dreaming. Arena (Melbourne) (76) 65–80.

Thomas Keneally

12759. CHERNEKOFF, JANICE.   Thomas Keneally: an annotated, secondary bibliography, 1979–1984. BB (43:4) 221–7.

12760. FERRES, KAY.   Keneally and Gare: boundary riders and fringe dwellers. *See* **12125.**

12761. PIERCE, PETER.   The sites of war in the fiction of Thomas Keneally. ALS (12:4) 442–52.

William Kennedy

12762. GIBB, ROBERT.   The life of the soul: William Kennedy, magical realist. Unpub. doct. diss., Lehigh Univ. [Abstr. in DA (47) 1323A.]

12763. REILLY, EDWARD C.   The pigeons and circular flight in Kennedy's *Ironweed*. NCL (16:2) 8.

Jack Kerouac

12764. HOFFIUS, STEPHEN.   The Dharma bum of Rocky Mount. SE (9:2) 1981, 83–5.

12765. MONTGOMERY, JOHN (comp.).   The Kerouac we knew:

unposed portraits; action shots compiled by John Montgomery, honoring the Kerouac conference at Naropa Institute. Kentfield, CA: Fels & Firn, 1982. pp. 46. Rev. by Michael Wilding in MLR (81:2) 468–9.

Susan Kerslake

12766. KEEFER, JANICE KULYK. Recent Maritime fiction: women and words. *See* **9777.**

Ken Kesey

12767. BAURECHT, WILLIAM C. Separation, initiation, and return: schizophrenic episodes in *One Flew Over the Cuckoo's Nest.* MidQ (23:3) 1982, 279–93.

12768. KESEY, KEN. Demon box. London: Methuen. pp. 364.

12769. MADDEN, FRED. Sanity and responsibility: Big Chief as narrator and executioner. MFS (32:2) 203–17.

12770. OLESKY, ELZBIETA. Kesey and Pynchon: a trip to the wasteland. RBPH (64:3) 520–31.

Frances Parkinson Keyes

12771. EHLERS, LEIGH A. 'An environment remembered': setting in the novels of Frances Parkinson Keyes. SoQ (20:3) 1982, 54–65.

Ismith Khan

12772. COBHAM, RHONDA. *The Jumbie Bird* by Ismith Khan: a new assessment. JCL (21:1) 240–9.

Benedict Kiely

12773. CASEY, DAN. Benedict Kiely: an Irish storyteller. HC (23) Feb., 1–10.

12774. KERSNOWSKI, FRANK. Ben Kiely and his ball of malt. Journal of the Short Story in English (7) 17–27.

Stephen King

12775. KANFER, STEFAN. King of horror: the master of pop dread writes on . . . and on . . . and on . . . and on. Time, 6 Oct., 74–83.

12776. UNDERWOOD, TIM; MILLER, CHUCK (eds). Kingdom of fear: the world of Stephen King. New York: New American Library; Sevenoaks: New English Library. pp. 283.

Maxine Hong Kingston

12777. MAYER, SUSANNE. Die Sehnsucht nach den anderen. Eine Studie zum Verhältnis von Subjekt und Gesellschaft in den Autobiographien von Lillian Hellman, Maya Angelou und Maxine Hong Kingston. *See* **11049.**

Galway Kinnell

12778. DYER, JOYCE. The music of Galway Kinnell's *Mortal Acts, Mortal Words.* NCL (16:3) 5–8.

12779. KLEINBARD, DAVID. Galway Kinnell's poetry of transformation. CR (30:1) 41–56.

Thomas Kinsella

12780. DAWE, GERALD. The enabling elements: an assessment of the poetry of Thomas Kinsella. *See* **11624.**

12781. SCHENCK, CELESTE M. When the moderns write elegy: Crane, Kinsella, Nemerov. *See* **11593.**

Rudyard Kipling

12782. ALLEN, CHARLES. A fresh look at the champion of the underdog. Independent, 31 Dec., 16.

12783. BAYLEY, JOHN.   The false structure. ELT (29:1) 19–27.

12784. CAESAR, TERRY.   Suppression, textuality, entanglement, and revenge in Kipling's *Dayspring Mishandled*. ELT (29:1) 54–63.

12785. COATES, JOHN.   Thor and Tyr: sacrifice, necessary suffering and the battle against disorder in *Rewards and Fairies*. ELT (29:1) 64–75.

12786. COUSTILLAS, PIERRE.   *The Light that Failed*, or artistic Bohemia as self-revelation. ELT (29:2) 127–39.

12787. CRAWFORD, ROBERT.   Rudyard Kipling in *The Waste Land*. *See* **11746.**

12788. FOOTE, TIMOTHY.   Fifty years on, 'O Best Beloved,' Kipling is making a comeback. Smithsonian (16:10) 34–40, 42–7.

12789. GILBERT, ELLIOT L.   Silence and survival in Rudyard Kipling's art and life. ELT (29:2) 115–26.

12789a. HANQUART, ÉVELYNE.   'For the pride of their race and the peace of the land': les héros anglo-indiens du jeune Kipling. CVE (23) 47–58.

12790. HUNTER, ALLAN.   Kipling to Clifford: a rediscovered correspondence. NQ (33:2) 179–84.

12791. KEMP, S.   'Limits and renewals': transformations of belief in Kipling's fiction. Unpub. doct. diss., Univ. of Oxford, 1985. [Abstr. in IT (35) 548.]

12792. KRARUP, SØREN.   Kipling. Tidehverv (Copenhagen) (60) 6–13.

12793. LEWIS, LISA A. F.   Kipling's Jane: some echoes of Austen. *See* **7592.**

12794. MOORE-GILBERT, B. J.   Kipling and 'Orientalism'. London: Croom Helm. pp. 240.

12795. —— Rudyard Kipling: his theory of social solidarity considered in relation to the nineteenth-century Anglo-Indian literary tradition. Unpub. doct. diss., Univ. of Oxford, 1982.

12796. PAGE, NORMAN.   A Kipling companion. (Bibl. 1985, 11627.) Rev. by Brian Gasser in NQ (33:1) 126–7.

12797. —— What happens in *Mary Postgate*? ELT (29:1) 41–7.

12798. PINNEY, THOMAS.   Kipling in the libraries. *See* **273.**

12799. —— (ed.).   Kipling's India: uncollected sketches, 1884–88. London: Macmillan. pp. xiii, 302. Rev. by Nigel Andrew in Listener (115) 2 Jan., 24–5.

12800. RAGLE, THOMAS B.   Foreword to Kipling's *Vermont Period*. ELT (29:2) 148–9.

12801. RICE, HOWARD C.   Brattleboro in the 1880's and 1890's: Cabots, Balestiers, and Kiplings. ELT (29:2) 150–60.

12802. RICKETTS, HARRY.   Kipling and the war: a reading of *Debits and Credits*. ELT (29:1) 29–39.

12802a. ROSENTHAL, LYNNE M.   Boy-society in Rudyard Kipling's *Stalky & Co*. LU (2:2) 16–26.

12803. RUTHERFORD, ANDREW.   News and the muse: press sources for some of Kipling's early verse. ELT (29:1) 7–16.

12804. —— (ed.).   Early verse by Rudyard Kipling, 1879–1889: unpublished, uncollected and rarely collected poems. Oxford: Clarendon Press. pp. 400. Rev. by Paul Johnson in Listener, 3 Apr., 26.

12805. SCHEICK, WILLIAM J. Hesitation in Kipling's *The Phantom 'Rickshaw*. ELT (29:1) 48–53.

12806. STEWART, D. H. Shooting elephants right. SoR (22:1) 86–92.

12807. STOVEL, NORA FOSTER. The 'inky *gamin*' and the 'egotistical tongue': viewing Kipling the person and the poet through an unpublished poem. ELT (29:2) 140–7.

C. H. B. Kitchin

12808. KEATING, H. R. F. (introd.). Death of his uncle. London: Hogarth Press. pp. 191.

12809. —— Death of my aunt. London: Hogarth Press. pp. 247.

A. M. Klein

12810. DAVIES, ROBIN EDWARDS. 'A game's stances': questions of language and unity in Klein's *The Provinces*. CanP (19) 49–56.

12811. GINGELL, SUSAN. Prosodic signification in the longer poems of Klein's *Hath Not a Jew*. CanP (19) 11–25.

12812. HEALY, J. J. Auschwitz, Hiroshima and the shaping of A. M. Klein. Span (22) Apr., 4–23.

William Kloefkorn

12813. CICOTELLO, DAVID M. 'Stay against chaos': an interview with William Kloefkorn. MidQ (24:3) 1983, 274–82.

Etheridge Knight

12814. PRICE, RON. The physicality of poetry: an interview with Etheridge Knight. New Letters (52:2/3) 167–76.

12815. WERNER, CRAIG. The poet, the poem, the people: Etheridge Knight's aesthetic. Ob (7) Summer/Winter 1981, 7–17.

Raymond Knister

12816. KUROPATWA, JOY RACHEL. A handbook to Raymond Knister's longer prose fiction. Unpub. doct. diss., Univ. of Western Ontario, 1985. [Abstr. in DA (46) 3038A.]

12817. WHITEMAN, BRUCE. Raymond Knister's hand in W. R. Dent's *Show Me Death! See* **11636.**

Ronald Knox

12818. DAYRAS, SOLANGE. Apocalypse 1945: du thomisme à l'atomisme. *In* (pp. 261–71) **2.**

C. J. Koch

12819. McKERNAN, SUSAN. C. J. Koch's two-faced vision. Meanjin (44:4) 1985, 432–9.

12820. MAES-JELINEK, HENA. History and the mythology of confrontation in *The Year of Living Dangerously*. Kp (8:1) 27–53.

12821. MITCHELL, ADRIAN (ed.) Christopher Koch on *The Doubleman*: a conversation with Adrian Mitchell. Southerly (45:2) 1985, 129–51.

12822. SHARRAD, PAUL. Open dialogue: metropolitan–provincial tensions and the quest for a post-colonial culture in the fiction of C. J. Koch, Raja Rao and Wilson Harris. *See* **12294.**

12823. THIEME, JOHN. Re-mapping the Australian psyche: the Asian novels of C. J. Koch. Commonwealth (Dijon) (8:1) 1985, 81–90.

Kenneth Koch
12824. BARRETT, EDWARD. Intent and practice in Kenneth Koch's *Wishes, Lies and Dreams* and *Rose, Where Did You Get That Red?* LU (4:2) 1980/81, 93–104.

Arthur Koestler
12825. LEVENE, MARK. Arthur Koestler. New York: Ungar; London: Wolff, 1985. pp. xv, 176.

12826. SCHAEFFER, DAVID LEWIS. The limits of ideology: Koestler's *Darkness at Noon*. ModAge (29:4) 1985, 319–29; (30:1) 10–21.

Joy Kogawa
12827. GOTTLIEB, ERIKA. The riddle of concentric worlds in *Obasan*. CanL (109) 34–53.

John Kolia
12828. BAER, LYNETTE. Cultural syncretism in John Kolia's Papua New Guinea novels. WLWE (26:2) 379–89.

Jerzy Kosinski
12829. ANON. Exegetics. ParisR (97) 1985, 93–9. (Interview.)

12830. KIM, CHONG-UN. Sontag ea Kosinski: minimalism sogo. (Sontag and Kosinski: a study of minimalism.) *See* **10834.**

12831. LAVERS, NORMAN. Jerzy Kosinski. (Bibl. 1985, 11644.) Rev. by Judie Newman in YES (16) 356–8.

12832. LUPACK, BARBARA TEPA. Hit or myth: Jerzy Kosinski's *Being There*. NOR (13:2) 58–68.

12833. MILLER, JAMES E., JR. Kosinski and the lessons of hate and revenge. *In* (pp. 107–16) **5.**

12834. RHEIN, PHILLIP H. The search for sin. *In* (pp. 369–73) **19.**

Robert Kroetsch
12835. LECKER, ROBERT. Robert Kroetsch. Boston, MA: G. K. Hall. pp. 165. (Twayne's world authors, 768.) Rev. by Leon Surette in CanP (19) 109–11.

12836. NEUMAN, SHIRLEY; WILSON, ROBERT. Labyrinths of voice: conversations with Robert Kroetsch. (Bibl. 1985, 11658.) Rev. by Brian Edwards in CanRCL (12:3) 1985, 566–9.

12837. SCHÄFER, JÜRGEN. A farewell to Europe: Rudy Wiebe's *The Temptations of Big Bear* and Robert Kroetsch's *Gone Indian*. *In* (pp. 79–90) **22.**

Oliver La Farge
12838. KLEINPOPPEN, PAUL STEVEN. The Indian fiction of Oliver La Farge. Unpub. doct. diss., Columbia Univ., 1985. [Abstr. in DA (47) 178A.]

Alex La Guma
12839. KELMAN, JAMES. Alex La Guma (1925–1985). Edinburgh Review (73) 117–21.

Georges Lamming
12840. DELBAERE-GARANT, JEANNE. Prospero to-day: magus, monster or patriarch? *In* (pp. 293–302) **12.**

Patrick Lane
12841. WOODCOCK, GEORGE. Patrick Lane. *In* (pp. 133–85) **10.**

Susanne K. Langer
12842. ROD, DAVID K.   Kenneth Burke and Susanne K. Langer on drama and its audiences. *See* **10062.**

12843. —— Kenneth Burke and Susanne K. Langer: dramatic theorists. *See* **10063.**

Andrew Lansdown
12844. PERKINS, ELIZABETH.   Metaphor and meaning in David Brooks' *The Cold Front* and Andrew Lansdown's *Windfalls*. *See* **11337.**

Ring Lardner (1885–1933)
12845. BLYTHE, HAL.   Lardner's *Haircut*. Exp (44:3) 48–9.

12846. GILEAD, SARAH.   Lardner's discourses of power. SSF (22) 331–7.

Philip Larkin
12847. BEETON, RIDLEY.   The early Philip Larkin: a manuscript exploration. UCTSE (16) 35–65.

12848. BROWNJOHN, ALAN.   Poet who reluctantly came to the point. Listener (115) 13 Feb., 15–16.

12849. CHAMBERS, HARRY (ed.).   An enormous yes: in memoriam to Philip Larkin, 1922–1985. Calstock: Peterloo Poets. pp. 67.

12850. ELLIOTT, ROGER.   The bard as moping owl. *See* **6524.**

12851. HARRISON, JAMES.   Larkin's *Ambulances*. Exp (44:2) 49–51.

12852. LARKIN, PHILIP (introd.).   The condemned playground: essays 1927–1944. *See* **11470.**

12853. LATRÉ, GUIDO.   De winterslaap van Larkin. (Larkin's hibernation.) DWB (131:1) 53–7.

12854. PATTERSON, G.   A flung-up faith: the language and art of Philip Larkin. Unpub. doct. diss., Trinity Coll. Dublin, 1985/86. [Abstr. in IT (36) 913.]

12855. RUDDICK, BILL.   'Some ruin-bibber, randy for antique': Philip Larkin's response to the poetry of John Betjeman. *See* **11256.**

12856. SCRIMGEOUR, PAT DALE.   Philip Larkin's *Dockery and Son* and Julian Hall's *The Senior Commoner*. *See* **12273.**

12857. THOMAS, MICHAEL WYNDHAM.   Triple time: the role of the past in the poetry of Philip Larkin and the short fiction of William Trevor. Unpub. doct. diss., Univ. of Saskatchewan, 1985. [Abstr. in DA (46) 3717A.]

12858. TIERCE, MIKE.   Philip Larkin: secondary sources, 1950–1984. BB (43:2) 67–75.

12859. WAIN, JOHN.   The importance of Philip Larkin. ASch (55) 349–64.

12860. WHALEN, TERRY.   Philip Larkin and English poetry. London: Macmillan. pp. viii, 192. (Studies in twentieth-century literature, 17.) Rev. by Kingsley Amis in Independent, 31 Dec., 16.

12861. WOOLLEY, JOHN.   Larkin: romance, fiction and myth. Eng (35) 237–67.

12862. YOUNG, DAVID.   Larkin: an appreciation. Field (34) 103–13.

Margaret Laurence

12863. BATTARBEE, KEITH. Portraits of the artist as a young Canadian. *See* **11346.**

12864. CAPONE, GIOVANNA. *A Bird in the House*: Margaret Laurence on order and the artist. *In* (pp. 161–70) **22.**

12865. DELBAERE-GARANT, JEANNE. Prospero to-day: magus, monster or patriarch? *In* (pp. 293–302) **12.**

12866. HINZ, E. J.; TEUNISSEN, J. J. Milton, Whitman, Wolfe and Laurence: *The Stone Angel* as elegy. *See* **5728.**

12867. LeGENDRE, BARBARA. The metaphoric world of Margaret Laurence. Unpub. doct. diss., Case Western Reserve Univ., 1985. [Abstr. in DA (46) 2696A.]

12868. WOODCOCK, G. (ed.). A place to stand on: essays by and about Margaret Laurence. Edmonton, Alta.; Newest Press, 1983. pp. 302. Rev. by Jean-Michel Lacroix in EA (38:4) 1985, 487–8.

Ray Lawler

12869. HOOTON, JOY. Lawler's demythologizing of *The Doll*: *Kid Stakes* and *Other Times*. ALS (12:3) 335–46 (review-article).

D. H. Lawrence

12870. ANSARI, A. A. *Women in Love*: search for integrated being. AJES (10) 1985, 156–77.

12871. ANSARI, IQBAL A. *Lady Chatterley's Lover*: pattern of contrast and conflict. AJES (10) 1985, 178–87.

12872. BALBERT, PETER. Snake's eye and the obsidian knife: art, ideology, and *The Woman Who Rode Away*. DHLR (18:2/3) 1985/86, 255–73.

12873. BARON, HELEN. *Sons and Lovers*: the surviving manuscripts from three drafts dated by paper analysis. *See* **139.**

12874. BEER, JOHN. D. H. Lawrence and English Romanticism. AJES (10) 1985, 109–21.

12875. BLACK, MICHAEL. D. H. Lawrence: the early fiction: a commentary. Basingstoke: Macmillan. pp. ix, 280. (Macmillan studies in twentieth-century literature.) Rev. by Brian Finney in THES (712) 18.

12876. BOETTCHER, RALPH CARL. The romantic past: primitivism and some novels by Thomas Hardy, D. H. Lawrence, and Robert Graves. *See* **8380.**

12877. BOULTON, JAMES T. (gen. ed.). The letters of D. H. Lawrence: vol 3, October 1916–June 1921. (Bibl. 1985, 11707.) Rev. by Émile Delavenay in EA (38:4) 1985, 476–7.

12878. BRANDES, RANDY PAUL. The myth of the Fall in the poetry of D. H. Lawrence and Ted Hughes. *See* **12488.**

12879. BURGESS, ANTHONY. Flame into being: the life and work of D. H. Lawrence. Toronto: Stoddart, 1985. (Cf. bibl. 1985, 11709.) Rev. by Paul Boytinck in QQ (93:1) 201–3; by Melissa King in UES (24:1) 43–4; by Howard Mills in Eng (35) 173–9.

12880. CALONNE, DAVID STEPHEN. Euphoria in Paris: Henry Miller meets D. H. Lawrence. LCUT (34) 89–98.

12881. CAMERON, ALAN (ed.).   D. H. Lawrence: a life in literature: catalogue of the centenary exhibition held in the University of Nottingham, 7 September–13 October 1985. Nottingham: Nottingham Univ. Library, 1985. pp. ix, 61.

12882. CLAREY, JOELLYN.   D. H. Lawrence's *Moby-Dick*: a textual note. *See* **302.**

12883. CLARKE, BRUCE.   The fall of Montezuma: poetry and history in William Carlos Williams and D. H. Lawrence. WCWR (12:1) 1–12.

12884. COOPER, ANDREW (ed.).   D. H. Lawrence: 1885–1930: a celebration. Sherwood, Notts: D. H. Lawrence Soc., 1985. pp. 125.

12885. CORONEOS, C.   The modern novella: James, Conrad and Lawrence. *See* **8646.**

12886. COWAN, JAMES C.   Lawrence and touch. DHLR (18:2/3) 1985/86, 121–37.

12887. CUSHMAN, KEITH.   D. H. Lawrence in Chapala: an unpublished letter to Thomas Seltzer and its context. DHLR (18:1) 1985/86, 25–31.

12888. CUSIC, CARLA METTLING.   Jealousy and envy in D. H. Lawrence's Brangwen novels. Unpub. doct. diss., Stanford Univ. [Abstr. in DA (47) 908A.]

12889. DAVEY, CHARLES.   D. H. Lawrence: a living poet. London: Brentham Press, 1985. pp. 55. Rev. by Raymond Stephens in AWR (82) 126–7.

12890. DOHERTY, GERALD.   A 'very funny' story: figural play in D. H. Lawrence's *The Captain's Doll*. DHLR (18:1) 1985/86, 5–17.

12891. DORBAD, LEO JAMES.   Sexually balanced relationships in the novels of D. H. Lawrence. Unpub. doct. diss., Lehigh Univ. [Abstr. in DA (47) 1332A.]

12892. DRAPER, R. P.   *Sons and Lovers* by D. H. Lawrence. Basingstoke: Macmillan. pp. viii, 88. (Macmillan master guides.)

12893. EASSON, ANGUS.   'My very knees are glad': D. H. Lawrence and apocalypse again. AJES (10) 1985, 205–18.

12894. EGGERT, PAUL.   D. H. Lawrence and his audience: the case of *Mr Noon*. SoRA (18:3) 1985, 298–307 (review-article).

12895. —— Edward Garnett's *Sons and Lovers*. *See* **12132.**

12896. ELDER, DANA CRAIG.   A Burkeian approach to D. H. Lawrence: perspectives on human motivation. *See* **11354.**

12897. ENGELBERG, EDWARD.   The displaced cathedral in Flaubert, James, Lawrence and Kafka. *See* **8661.**

12898. GALEA, ILEANA.   D. H. Lawrence: the value of myth. CREL (3) 1985, 72–7.

12899. GEE, KATHLEEN.   A checklist of D. H. Lawrence art work at HRHRC [Harry Ransom Humanities Research Center]. LCUT (34) 61–73.

12900. GOOD, JAN.   Toward a resolution of gender identity confusion: the relationship of Henry and March in *The Fox*. DHLR (18:2/3) 1985/86, 217–27.

12901. HAEGERT, JOHN.   Lawrence's world elsewhere: elegy and history in *The Rainbow*. CLIO (15:2) 115–35.

12902. HARDY, GEORGE; HARRIS, NATHANIEL.   A D. H. Lawrence album. Ashbourne: Moorland, 1985. pp. 155.

12903. HARRIS, JANICE HUBBARD.   The short fiction of D. H. Lawrence. (Bibl. 1985, 11727.) Rev. by Joseph Voelker in SSF (23) 131.

12904. HILLS, S. J.   D. H. Lawrence 1885–1930: catalogue of an exhibition at Cambridge University Library, September–November, 1985. Cambridge: Cambridge Univ. Library, 1985. pp. 43.

12905. HIRAI, MASAKO.   Chichioya fuzai no paradox: *Sons and Lovers* wo megutte. (The absent father: the paradox of *Sons and Lovers*.) SEL (63:1) 75–94.

12906. HOLDERNESS, GRAHAM.   Miners and the novel: from bourgeois to proletarian fiction. *In* (pp. 18–32) **6.**   .

12907. HYNES, SAMUEL.   A budget of letters. See **11501.**

12908. IIDA, TAKERO.   D. H. Lawrence no shi. (The poetry of D. H. Lawrence.) Fukuoka, Japan: Kyushu UP. pp. x, 238.

12909. JACKSON, ALAN D.   D. H. Lawrence, 'physical consciousness' and Robert Burns. See **6333.**

12910. JANOUŠEK, MIROSLAV.   David Storey: un-Lawrentian comparative notes on *Saville* and *Sons and Lovers*. Germanica Olomucensia (6) 69–77.

12911. JANSOHN, CHRISTA.   Zu Schopenhauers Einfluss auf D. H. Lawrence. Arcadia (21:3) 263–75.

12912. JOFFE, PHIL.   *Sons and Lovers*: the growth of Paul Morel. Crux (20:3) 49–62.

12913. KALNINS, MARA (ed.).   D. H. Lawrence: centenary essays. Bristol: Bristol Classical Press. pp. xi, 210. Rev. by Howard Mills in Eng (35) 173–9.

12914. KANG, CHUNG-SUK.   D. H. Lawrence eui geunwonjeok saengmyung eui tamgu. (D. H. Lawrence's search for the root of life.) Unpub. doct. diss., Chonnam National Univ., Korea.

12915. KONG, DUK-YONG.   D. H. Lawrence eui buhwalron: *The Man Who Died* reul jungsim euro. (D. H. Lawrence's view of resurrection: a study of physical resurrection in *The Man Who Died*.) JELL (32:4) 831–41.

12916. LAIRD, HOLLY.   The poems of *Piano*. DHLR (18:2/3) 1985/86, 183–99.

12917. LARVIN, NORA.   D. H. Lawrence: Nottingham connections. Nottingham: Astra. pp. viii, 187.

12918. LEA, F. A.   Lawrence and Murry: a twofold vision. London: Brentham Press, 1985. pp. 76. Rev. by Brigid Vousden in AWR (82) 127–9.

12919. LYON, J. M.   Thought and the novel: James, Conrad and Lawrence. See **8700.**

12920. MACLEOD, SHEILA.   Lawrence's men and women. (Bibl. 1985, 11740.) Rev. by Margaret H. van Zyl in UES (24:1) 44–5; by Howard Mills in Eng (35) 173–9.

12921. MARTIN, GRAHAM. 'History' and 'myth' in D. H. Lawrence's Chatterley novels. *In* (pp. 62–74) **6.**

12922. MARTIN, MURRAY S. *Kangaroo* revisited. DHLR (18:2/3) 1985/86, 201–15.

12923. MARTIN, W. R. Hannele's 'surrender': a misreading of *The Captain's Doll.* DHLR (18:1) 1985/86, 19–23.

12924. MEHL, DIETER. Editing a 'constantly revising author'. *See* **8711.**

12925. MEYERS, JEFFREY. D. H. Lawrence and the experience of Italy. (Bibl. 1985, 11745.) Rev. by Michael Caesar in CL (38:1) 106–8.

12926. —— (ed.). D. H. Lawrence and tradition. (Bibl. 1985, 11747.) Rev. by Howard Mills in Eng (35) 173–9.

12927. MILLS, HOWARD. 'My best single piece of writing': Lawrence's memoir of Magnus. Eng (35) 39–53.

12928. MONELL, SIV. The molecule strategy: a study of the description of character in *The Rainbow* by D. H. Lawrence. *In* (pp. 75–87) **43.**

12929. MOORTHY, POLANKI RAMA. *St Mawr*: the third eye. AJES (10) 1985, 188–204.

12930. MORGAN, JAMES FREDERICK. Serpent of the sun: D. H. Lawrence's myth of manhood. Unpub. doct. diss., Tufts Univ. [Abstr. in DA (47) 1336A.]

12931. MOYNAHAN, JULIAN. Lawrence and Sicily: the place of places. Mosaic (19:2) 69–84.

12932. NORRIS, MARGOT. Beasts of the modern imagination: Darwin, Nietzsche, Kafka, Ernst, and Lawrence. *See* **7997.**

12933. PARMENTER, ROSS. Lawrence in Oaxaca: a quest for the novelist in Mexico. (Bibl. 1985, 11757.) Rev. by Charles Rossman in DHLR (18:1) 1985/86, 84–6.

12934. PITTOCK, MALCOLM. *Sons and Lovers*: the price of betrayal. EC (36:3) 235–54.

12935. PRYZBYLOWICZ, DONNA. D. H. Lawrence's *The Plumed Serpent*: the dialectics of ideology and utopia. Boundary 2 (13:2/3) 1985, 289–318.

12936. RAIZADA, HARISH. Paul Morel: architect of his own destiny. AJES (10) 1985, 122–40.

12937. REES, A. J. D. H. Lawrence – the politics of industry: a study of Lawrence's later novels, with special reference to the East Midlands Coalfield. Unpub. doct. diss., Univ. of Sheffield, 1985.

12938. RICE, THOMAS JACKSON. D. H. Lawrence: a guide to research. (Bibl. 1984, 11846.) Rev. by Jim E. Tanner in DHLR (18:1) 1985/86, 82–3; by J. G. Watson in NQ (33:1) 129; by Bobby L. Smith in BB (43:3) 185.

12939. ROBERTS, WARREN. A bibliography of D. H. Lawrence. (Bibl. 1985, 11763.) Rev. by Alvin Sullivan in DHLR (18:1) 1985/86, 79–81.

12940. —— D. H. Lawrence at Texas: a memoir. *See* **277.**

12941. ROBERTSON, ANDREW (ed.). The white peacock. (Bibl. 1984, 11848.) Rev. by Dieter Mehl in Archiv (222:1) 1985, 131–2.

12942. ROBINS, ROSS PORTER. Lawrence's *Women in Love*: the two

Ursulas. Unpub. doct. diss., Univ. of California, Santa Barbara, 1985. [Abstr. in DA (47) 1337A.]

12943. ROSENTHAL, RAE; JACKSON, DENNIS; HOWARD, BRAD. Checklist of D. H. Lawrence criticism and scholarship, 1979–1983. DHLR (18:1) 1985/86, 37–74.

12944. ROSS, MICHAEL L. Ladies and foxes: D. H. Lawrence, David Garnett, and the female of the species. *See* **12131.**

12945. RUDERMAN, JUDITH. D. H. Lawrence and the devouring mother: the search for a patriarchal ideal of leadership. (Bibl. 1985, 11767, where subtitle incorrect.) Rev. by Julian N. Hartt in ChrisL (35:2) 45–6.

12946. SAGAR, KEITH. D. H. Lawrence: life into art. Athens: Georgia UP, 1985. pp. 363. (Cf. bibl. 1985, 11768.) Rev. by L. D. Clark in Genre (19:2) 199–202; by Howard Mills in Eng (35) 173–9.

12947. —— (ed.). Poems. (Bibl. 1972, 11339.) Harmondsworth: Penguin. pp. 269. (Penguin poetry library.) (Revised ed.: first ed. 1972.)

12948. SCHECKNER, PETER. Class consciousness in the works of D. H. Lawrence: a new reading. MidQ (25) 1984, 434–49.

12949. SKLENICKA, CAROL. Lawrence's vision of the child: reimagining character and consciousness. DHLR (18:2/3) 1985/86, 151–68.

12950. SQUIRES, MICHAEL. The creation of *Lady Chatterley's Lover*. (Bibl. 1985, 11776.) Rev. by Émile Délavenay in EA (38:4) 1985, 477–8; by Helen Baron in EC (36:2) 166–74.

12951. —— JACKSON, DENNIS (eds). D. H. Lawrence's *Lady*: a new look at *Lady Chatterley's Lover*. (Bibl. 1985, 11777.) Rev. by Patrick D. Morrow in SoHR (20:4) 385–7.

12952. STEELE, BRUCE. The rise of D. H. Lawrence's *Phoenix*. LCUT (34) 75–87.

12953. STEVEN, LAURENCE. From thimble to ladybird: D. H. Lawrence's widening vision? DHLR (18:2/3) 1985/86, 239–53.

12954. STEWART, JACK F. Expressionism in *The Prussian Officer*. DHLR (18:2/3) 1985/86, 275–89.

12955. THOMAS, DAVID J. D. H. Lawrence's *Snake*: the Edenic myth inverted. CLit (13:2) 199–206.

12956. TOLAN, HOMER COOK TRIMPI. The quest for identity in the shorter fiction of D. H. Lawrence. Unpub. doct. diss., Rice Univ. [Abstr. in DA (47) 1724A.]

12957. TORGOVNIK, MARIANNA. The visual arts, pictorialism and the novel: James, Lawrence, and Woolf. *See* **8753.**

12958. TRIPATHY, B. K. *The Rainbow*: unfamiliar quest. AJES (10) 1985, 141–55.

12959. TROTTER, DAVID. Modernism and empire: reading *The Waste Land*. *See* **11801.**

12960. TROY, MARK. '... A wild bit of Egyptology': Isis and *The Escaped Cock* of D. H. Lawrence. SN (58:2) 215–24.

12961. URANG, SARAH. Kindled in the flame: the apocalyptic scene in D. H. Lawrence. Ann Arbor, MI: UMI Research Press, 1983.

(Cf. bibl. 1984, 11861.) Rev. by Lawrence Gamache in DHLR (18:1) 1985/86, 86–8.

12962. VAN SPANCKEREN, KATHRYN.   Lawrence and the uses of story. DHLR (18:2/3) 1985/86, 291–300.

12963. VASEY, LINDETH (ed.).   Mr Noon. Introd. by MELVYN BRAGG. London: Grafton. pp. xiii, 382. (Cf. bibl. 1984, 11863.)

12964. —— Mr Noon. (Bibl. 1985, 11783.) Rev. by Paul Eggert in SoRA (18:3) 1985, 298–307; by Dieter Mehl in Archiv (222:1) 134–5; by Émile Délavenay in EA (38:4) 1985, 478.

12965. VASEY, LINDETH SHIVELY.   The Cambridge edition of *Mr Noon* by D. H. Lawrence. Unpub. doct. diss., Univ. of Texas at Austin, 1984. [Abstr. in DA (47) 2172A.]

12966. VERDUIN, KATHLEEN.   Lawrence and the Middle Ages. DHLR (18:2/3) 1985/86, 169–81.

12967. WHELAN, P. T.   Orders of reality in *The Rainbow* and *Women in Love*: D. H. Lawrence's use in his fiction of myth, psychology and the occult. Unpub. doct. diss., Univ. of Exeter, 1983.

12968. WIDMER, KINGSLEY.   Desire and denial, dialectics of passion in Lawrence (with some caveats on the co-option of Lawrence to conservative pieties). DHLR (18:2/3) 1985/86, 139–49.

12969. WIENER, GARY ALAN.   Eternal delight: heroic energy in the fiction of D. H. Lawrence. Unpub. doct. diss., Univ. of Rochester. [Abstr. in DA (47) 1340A.]

12970. WINKGENS, MEINHARD.   Die Funktionalisierung des Italien-bildes in den Romanen *Where Angels Fear to Tread* von E. M. Forster und *The Lost Girl* von D. H. Lawrence. *See* **12030.**

12971. WOODMAN, LEONORA.   'The big old pagan vision': the letters of D. H. Lawrence to Frederick Carter. LCUT (34) 39–51.

12972. WORTHEN, JOHN (ed.).   The lost girl. (Bibl. 1985, 11788.) Rev. by James C. Cowan in AEB (8:4) 1984, 269–71.

12973. —— The Prussian Officer and other stories. (Bibl. 1984, 11869.) Rev. by Dieter Mehl in Archiv (222:1) 1985, 132–4.

12974. ZIGAL,   THOMAS.   D. H. Lawrence   making   pictures. LCUT (34) 53–9.

T. E. Lawrence

12975. TABACHNIK, STEPHEN E. (ed.).   The T. E. Lawrence puzzle. Athens: Georgia UP, 1984. pp. x, 342. Rev. by A. D. B. in Prose Studies (9:1) 88.

12976. TREVELYAN, RALEIGH (introd.).   Revolt   in   the   desert. London: Century. pp. vi, 336.

Henry Lawson

12977. BARNES, JOHN.   Henry Lawson's short stories. Melbourne: Shillington House, 1985. pp. 48. (Essays in Australian literature.)

12977a. GHIȚULESCU, ANGHEL (trans.).   Povestri din Australia. (Australian tales.) Bucharest: Univers. pp. 303. (Pub. in UK as *The Best of Henry Lawson*.)

Irving Layton

12978. FRANCIS, WYNNE.   Irving Layton. *In* (pp. 143–234) **9.**

Stephen Leacock

12979. ANDERSON, ALLAN. Remembering Leacock: an oral history. Ottawa: Deneau, 1983. pp. xviii, 229. Rev. by Carl Spadoni in ECanW (33) 161–6.

12980. EL-HASSAN, KARLA. Reflections on the special unity of Stephen Leacock's *Sunshine Sketches of a Little Town. In* (pp. 171–85) **22.**

12981. MORITZ, ALBERT; MORITZ, THERESA. Leacock: a biography. Don Mills, Ont.: Stoddart, 1985. pp. 363. Rev. by Gerald Noonan in CanL (109) 132–4.

12982. VÁVROVÁ-REJŠKOVÁ, ZDEŇKA. Stephen Leacock and the art of humour. Prague: Charles UP. pp. 112. (Acta Universitatis Carolinae; Philologica; Monographia, 89.)

The Leavises

12983. THOMPSON, DENYS (ed.). The Leavises: recollections and impressions. (Bibl. 1985, 11804, where title incorrect.) Rev. by Thomas L. Jeffers in WHR (40:1) 83–9; by Peter Faulkner in NQ (33:3) 424–5.

F. R. Leavis

12984. JOYCE, C. Critics in context: aspects of the work of T. S. Eliot, John Middleton Murry and F. R. Leavis. See **11763.**

12985. KEYS, K. J. F. R. Leavis: the development of a critical vocabulary. Unpub. doct. diss., Univ. of Edinburgh, 1985. [Abstr. in IT (35) 1081.]

12986. SINGH, G. (ed.). *Valuation in Criticism* and other essays. Cambridge: CUP. pp. vii, 309.

John le Carré

12987. BARLEY, TONY. Taking sides: the fiction of John le Carré. Milton Keynes: Open UP. pp. 192. Rev. by John Sutherland in LRB (8:6) 5–6; by Blake Morrison in TLS, 11 Apr., 381–2; by Eric Homberger in THES (708) 18.

12988. HOMBERGER, ERIC. John le Carré. London: Methuen. pp. 96. (Contemporary writers.)

12989. LEWIS, PETER. John le Carré. New York: Ungar; London: Lorrimer, 1985. pp. 228. Rev. by John Sutherland in LRB (8:6) 5–6; by Blake Morrison in TLS, 11 Apr., 381–2.

12990. MONAGHAN, DAVID. The novels of John le Carré: the art of survival. Oxford; New York: Blackwell, 1985. pp. 207. Rev. by John Sutherland in LRB (8:6) 5–6; by Kurt W. Back in SAQ (85:4) 413–14; by Blake Morrison in TLS, 11 Apr., 381–2; by Eric Homberger in THES (708) 18.

12991. —— Smiley's Circus: a guide to the secret world of John le Carré. London: Orbis. pp. 207.

Francis Ledwidge

12992. DI NICOLA, ROBERT. Time and history in Seamus Heaney's *In Memoriam Francis Ledwidge. See* **12328.**

Dennis Lee

12993. MIDDLEBRO', T. G. Dennis Lee. *In* (pp. 189–228) **10.**

Ursula K. Le Guin

12994. HULL, KEITH N.   What is human? Ursula Le Guin and science fiction's great theme. MFS (32:1) 65–74.

12995. SELINGER, BERNARD GEORGE.   Ursula K. Le Guin and the paradox of identity in contemporary fiction. Unpub. doct. diss., York Univ. (Canada), 1984. [Abstr. in DA (46) 3721A.]

Rosamond Lehmann

12996. CHILDERS, MARY.   Narrating structures of opportunity. *See* **7663.**

12997. GUPPY, SHUSHA.   The art of fiction LXXXVIII: Rosamond Lehmann. ParisR (96) 1985, 162–85. (Interview.)

12998. SIEGEL, RUTH.   Rosamond Lehmann: a thirties writer. Unpub. doct. diss., Columbia Univ., 1985. [Abstr. in DA (46) 2303A.]

12999. SULLIVAN, RITA MARIE.   The four corners of fiction: adolescent sensibility in the novels of Elizabeth Bowen and Rosamond Lehmann. *See* **11295.**

John Lennon

13000. WIENER, JON.   Come together: John Lennon in his time. New York: Random House, 1984; London: Faber & Faber, 1985. pp. xix, 379.

Elmore Leonard

13001. BLADES, JOHN.   Elmore Leonard makes out like a bandit with critics. BW, 21 Dec., 3.

Tom Leonard

13002. LEONARD, TOM.   How I became a sound-poet. Cencrastus (22) 44–5.

Doris Lessing

13003. BERTELSEN, EVE.   Doris Lessing. JCL (21:1) 134–61 (interview).

13004. BRUECK, ERIC T.   Doris Lessing: a bibliography of her first editions. (Bibl. 1985, 11837.) Rev. by George Bixby in ABC (7:1) 47–50.

13005. DAYMOND, M. J.   Areas of the mind: *The Memoirs of a Survivor* and Doris Lessing's African stories. Ariel (17:3) 65–82.

13006. FRIEDMAN, ELLEN G.   Doris Lessing: fusion and transcendence of the female and the 'great tradition'. CR (30:4) 452–70.

13007. HUNTER, EVA.   Tracking through the tangles: the reader's task in Doris Lessing's *The Grass is Singing*. Kp (8:3) 121–35.

13008. KNAPP, MONA.   Canopuspeak: Doris Lessing's *Sentimental Agents* and Orwell's *1984*. Neophilologus (70:3) 453–61.

13009. —— Doris Lessing. New York: Ungar, 1984. pp. 210. Rev. by Linda Leith in SFS (13:2) 220–1.

13010. PÁLSSON, HJÖRTUR.   Nokkur orð um Doris Lessing. Vitund nútímakonunnar veruleiki samtíðar.(Doris Lessing: modern woman's conscience: a contemporary fact.) Morgunblaðið (73:56) C 5–7.

13011. SINGER, SANDRA.   Unleashing human potentialities: Doris Lessing's *The Memoirs of a Survivor* and contemporary cultural theory. Text & Context (1:1) 79–95.

13012. STYLE, COLIN.   Doris Lessing's 'Zambesia'. EngA (13:1) 73–91.

13013. TAYLOR, JENNY (ed.).   Notebooks/memoirs/archives: reading and rereading Doris Lessing. (Bibl. 1984, 12242.) Rev. by Maria Del Sapio in MLR (81:2) 469–70.

Denise Levertov

13014. CROWDER, ASHBY BLAND; CHURCHILL, JOHN. The problem of interpretation: a case in point. CLit (13:2) 123–40.

13015. DARGAN, JOAN. Poetic and political consciousness in Denise Levertov and Carolyn Forché. *See* **11986.**

13016. DRISCOLL, KERRY. A sense of unremitting emergency: politics in the early work of Denise Levertov. CR (30:2) 292–303.

13017. HALLISEY, JOAN. Denise Levertov '... Forever a stranger and pilgrim'. CR (30:2) 281–91.

13018. JAŘAB, JOSEF. Modernismus a současná americká poezie. (Modernism and contemporary American poetry.) *In* (pp. 30–1) **4.**

Peter Levi

13019. BAYLEY, JOHN. Sometimes voices ... Agenda (24:3) 51–4.

13020. MACVEAN, JEAN. Peter Levi as elegist. Agenda (24:3) 57–61.

Philip Levine

13021. ST JOHN, DAVID. Where the angels come toward us: the poetry of Philip Levine. AR (44:2) 176–91.

C. Day Lewis ('Nicholas Blake')

13022. DUTRUCH, SUZANNE. Un roman policier en forme d'élégie: *The Private Wound* de Nicholas Blake. Caliban (23) 41–53.

C. S. Lewis

13023. BEVERSLUIS, JOHN. C. S. Lewis and the search for rational religion. (Bibl. 1985, 11858.) Rev. by Robert L. Hurd in ChrisL (35:3) 30–1.

13024. BROWN, ROBERT F. Temptation and freedom in *Perelandra*. Ren (37) 1984, 52–68.

13025. CHRISTOPHER, JOE R. An Inklings' bibliography. Mythlore (12:4) 57–9; (13:1) 51–4.

13026. DIEKMA, DOUGLAS. Yet still there is hell: damnation and hell in C. S. Lewis. Cresset (49:3) 15–19.

13027. GRIFFIN, WILLIAM. Clive Staples Lewis: a dramatic life. San Francisco, CA: Harper & Row. pp. xxv, 507. Rev. by Roger Lewis in NYTB, 2 Nov., 22; by Corbin Scott Carnell in ChrisL (36:1) 31–2.

13028. HENTHORNE, SUSAN CASSANDRA. The image of woman in the fiction of C. S. Lewis. Unpub. doct. diss., State Univ. of New York at Buffalo, 1985. [Abstr. in DA (46) 1948A.]

13029. HOOPER, WALTER (ed.). Present concerns. London: Fount. pp. 108.

13030. JOHNSON, WILLIAM G.; HOUTMAN, MARCIA K. Platonic shadows in C. S. Lewis' Narnia Chronicles. MFS (32:1) 75–87.

13031. KARIMIPOUR, ZAHRA. A descriptive bibliography of C. S. Lewis's fiction: 1938–1981. Unpub. doct. diss., Oklahoma State Univ., 1985. [Abstr. in DA (46) 3726A.]

13032. KING, DON. The childlike in George MacDonald and C. S. Lewis. *See* **8882.**

13033. LEWIS, C. S. Odrzucony obraz: wprowadzenie do literatury średniowiecznej i renesansowej. (The discarded image: an introduction to medieval and Renaissance literature.) Trans. by WITOLD OSTROWSKI. Warsaw: PAX. pp. 168.

13034. LINDSKOOG, KATHRYN. The first chronicle of Narnia: the restoring of names. Mythlore (12:4) 43–6, 63.

13035. LOWMAN, P. J. Supernaturalistic causality and Christian theism in the modern English novel. See **11456.**

13036. LUTTON, JEANNETTE HUME. The feast of reason: *Out of the Silent Planet* as the book of Hnau. Mythlore (13:1) 37–41, 50.

13037. MCMILLAN, LEX O., III. C. S. Lewis as spiritual autobiographer: a study in the sacramental imagination. Unpub. doct. diss., Univ. of Notre Dame. [Abstr. in DA (47) 913A.]

13038. MUSACCHIO, GEORGE. C. S. Lewis's *A Grief Observed* as fiction. Mythlore (12:3) 24–7.

13039. PATTERSON, NANCY-LOU. 'Some kind of company': the sacred community in *That Hideous Strength*. Mythlore (13:1) 8–19.

13040. PETERS, JOHN. C. S. Lewis: the man and his achievement. Exeter: Paternoster Press, 1985. pp. 143.

13041. PURTILL, RICHARD L. C. S. Lewis's case for the Christian faith. San Francisco, CA; London: Harper & Row, 1985. pp. xi, 146.

13042. RAWLS, MELANIE. *Herland* and *Out of the Silent Planet*: a comparison of a feminist utopia and a male charactered fantasy. See **12153.**

13043. SCHAKEL, PETER. Dance as metaphor and myth in Lewis, Tolkien, and Williams. Mythlore (12:3) 4–8, 23.

13044. SCHÜTZE, MARLI. Neue Wege nach Narnia und Mittelerde. Handlungskonstituenten in der Fantasy-Literatur von C. S. Lewis und J. R. R. Tolkien. Frankfurt: Lang. pp. 303. (Europäische Hochschulschriften: Reihe 14, Angelsächsische Sprache und Literatur, 156.)

13045. SIBLEY, BRIAN. Shadowlands: the story of C. S. Lewis and Joy Davidman. London: Hodder & Stoughton, 1985. pp. 176.

13046. SUTHAMCHAI, PHANIDA. The fusion of Christian and fictional elements in C. S. Lewis's chronicles of Narnia. Unpub. doct. diss., Oklahoma State Univ., 1985. [Abstr. in DA (47) 916A.]

13047. TETREAULT, JAMES. Parallel lines: C. S. Lewis and T. S. Eliot. See **11797.**

Sinclair Lewis

13048. CONNAUGHTON, MICHAEL (ed.). Sinclair Lewis at 100: papers presented at a centennial conference. St Cloud, MN: St Cloud State UP, 1985. pp. 270. Rev. by Roger K. Blakely in MinnH (50:3) 129–30.

13049. FRANK, LINDA PINSKER. Bovarysm, its concept and application to literature: Stendhal, Flaubert, Hardy, Alas, and Lewis. See **8391.**

13050. PARRY, SALLY E. Sinclair Lewis: the darkening vision of his later novels. Unpub. doct. diss., Fordham Univ. [Abstr. in DA (47) 1326A.]

13051. SPAUNHORST, FRANZ-PETER. Literarische Kulturkritik als Dekodierung von Macht und Werten am Beispiel ausgewählter Romane von Upton Sinclair, Frank Norris, John Dos Passos und Sinclair Lewis.

Ein Beitrag zur Theorie und Methode der Amerikastudien als Kulturwert. *See* **11692**.

Wyndham Lewis

13052. DASENBROCK, REED WAY. The literary vorticism of Ezra Pound and Wyndham Lewis: towards the condition of painting. (Bibl. 1985, 11900.) Rev. by Timothy Materer in JEGP (85:2) 298–301; by Lachlan Mackinnon in TLS, 21 Mar., 292.

13053. LAFOURCADE, BERNARD. Wyndham Lewis ou l'apocalypse immobile. *In* (pp. 195–212) **2**.

13054. —— (ed.). Snooty baronet. (Bibl. 1984, 11952.) Rev. by Jean-Jacques Mayoux in EA (38:4) 1985, 479.

13055. MATERER, TIMOTHY (ed.). Pound/Lewis: the letters of Ezra Pound and Wyndham Lewis. (Bibl. 1985, 11905.) Rev. by T. C. Duncan Eaves in AL (58:1) 112–14.

13056. MEYERS, JEFFREY. New light on Iris Barry. *See* **11128**.

13057. SCHEID, TERESA MARIE. Experimentations in temporal and spatial techniques in the nineteenth and early twentieth centuries: an examination of the work of J. M. W. Turner, Joseph Conrad, Wyndham Lewis and C. R. W. Nevinson. *See* **11552**.

Paul Stephen Lim

13058. BRENSNAHAN, ROGER J. Can these, too, be Midwestern? Studies of two Filipino writers. Midamerica (13) 134–47.

Joan Lindsay

13059. CRICK, MALCOLM. Corsets, culture and contingency: reflections on Joan Lindsay's *Picnic at Hanging Rock*. Mankind (15:3) 1985, 231–42 (review-article).

Vachel Lindsay

13060. WARD, JOHN. Walking to Wagon Mound: composing Booth. WHR (40:3) 230–44.

Eric Linklater

13061. PARNELL, MICHAEL. Eric Linklater: a critical biography. (Bibl. 1985, 11919.) Rev. by Nancy Curme in SLJ (supp. 25) 24–7.

Dorothy Livesay

13062. RELKE, DIANA M. A. The task of poetic mediation: Dorothy Livesay's early poetry. Ariel (17:4) 17–36.

Douglas Livingstone

13063. LEVEY, DAVID. Livingstone's poems in *The Wild Wave*. Crux (20:3) 11–14.

13064. LIVINGSTONE, DOUGLAS. Writing poetry. Crux (20:3) 8–10.

13065. THOMPSON, ELIZABETH. An interview with Douglas Livingstone. Crux (20:4) 3–12.

13066. UNTERSLAK, JANET. A discussion of two poems. Crux (20:3) 15–19. (*Vanderdecken* and *Not Waving But Drowning*.)

Taban Lo Liyong

13067. SCHULZE, FRANK. Taban Lo Liyong's short stories: a western form of art? WLWE (26:2) 228–35.

Richard Llewellyn

13068. PRICE, DERRICK. *How Green was My Valley*: a romance of Wales. *In* (pp. 73–94) **45**.

Arnold Stark Lobel

13069. NATOV, RONI; DeLUCA, GERALDINE. An interview with Arnold Lobel. LU (1:1) 1977, 72–96.

Caroline Lockhart

13070. FURMAN, NECAH STEWART. Western author Caroline Lockhart. Montana (36:1) 50–9.

Ross Lockridge, Jr

13071. GOIST, PARK DIXON. Habits of the heart in *Raintree County*. Midamerica (13) 94–106.

David Lodge

13072. OMMUNDSEN, WENCHE. Self-conscious fiction and literary theory: David Lodge, B. S. Johnson, and John Fowles. *See* **12040.**

13073. WICHTEL, DIANA. Skating with poise. NZList, 3 May, 52.

Jack London

13074. HAMILTON, DAVID MIKE. The tools of my trade: the annotated books in Jack London's library. *See* **230.**

13075. JOHNSTON, CAROLYN. Jack London: an American radical? London: Greenwood Press, 1984. (Cf. bibl. 1985, 11928.) Rev. by Alexander Saxton in PacHR (55:1) 132–5.

13076. MITCHELL, LEE CLARK. 'Keeping his head': repetition and responsibility in London's *To Build a Fire*. JML (13:1) 76–96.

13077. ZAMEN, MARK E. Jack London, orator. PacH (30:2) 34–49.

Anita Loos

13078. SCHRADER, RICHARD J. 'But gentlemen marry brunettes': Anita Loos and H. L. Mencken. Menckeniana (98) 1–7.

H. P. Lovecraft

13079. GOORDEN, BERNARD. H. P. Lovecraft: bibliographie. Contribution à une bibliographie de Lovecraft en langue française. Index des principales œuvres en langue originale. Brussels: Ides et Autres. pp. 18.

Earl Lovelace

13080. BROEK, AART G. Het Caraïbisch gebied: 'Idiote idealen, falen, corruptie en stom geluk', Lovelace versus Naipaul. (The Caribbean area: 'idiocy, ideals, failures, corruption and mere fluke'. Lovelace versus Naipaul.) De Gids (149:4) 297–301.

Amy Lowell

13081. FRANCIS, LESLEY LEE. A decade of 'stirring time': Robert Frost and Amy Lovell. *See* **12071.**

Robert Lowell

13082. AXELROD, STEVEN GOULD; DEESE, HELEN (eds). Robert Lowell: essays on the poetry. Cambridge: CUP. pp. xii, 269. (Cambridge studies in American literature and culture.)

13083. CARLSON-BRADLEY, MARTHA ANN. Affinities in the poetry of Robert Lowell and Elizabeth Bishop. *See* **11259.**

13084. DORESKI, WILLIAM. Borrowed visions: Robert Lowell's imitations of Baudelaire and Rimbaud in *History*. CEACrit (48:3) 38–49.

13085. FRANCINI, ANTONELLA. In the Longfellow line: some contemporary American poets as translators of Eugenio Montale: a study in theory and practice. Unpub. doct. diss., Drew Univ., 1985. [Abstr. in DA (46) 3714A.]

13086. GILES, RONALD K.   Symbol and tone in *For the Union Dead*. CLit (13:3) 266–71.

13087. McCONAHAY, MARY DAVIDSON.   'Heidelberry braids' and Yankee 'politesse': Jean Stafford and Robert Lowell reconsidered. VQR (62:2) 213–36.

13088. MARWICK, M. J.   *For the Union Dead* by Robert Lowell. Crux (20:1) 13–17.

13089. MATTERSON, S.   A reading of the poetry of Robert Lowell in relation to developments in poetics since 1930. Unpub. doct. diss., CNAA, 1983.

13090. PETERSON, DONALD.   The legacy of Robert Lowell. NCrit (1) Jan. 1983, 9–29.

13091. PETRY, ALICE HALL.   That 'Tudor Ford' reconsidered: Robert Lowell's *Skunk Hour*. PLL (22:1) 70–5.

13092. RUDMAN, MARK.   Robert Lowell: an introduction to the poetry. (Bibl. 1985, 11945.) Rev. by William Sharpe in EA (38:3) 1985, 356–7.

13093. SHIN, JEONG-HYUN.   Stylistics of survival in the poetry of Robert Lowell. Unpub. doct. diss., Univ. of Tulsa. [Abstr. in DA (47) 532A.]

13094. WALLINGFORD, KATHARINE.   Robert Lowell and free association. Mosaic (19:4) 121–32.

Malcolm Lowry

13095. ACKERLEY, CHRIS; CLIPPER, LAWRENCE J.   A companion to *Under the Volcano*. (Bibl. 1985, 11948.) Rev. by P. Mathew St Pierre in ECanW (33) 190–4; by Sue Vice in NQ (33:2) 269–70.

13096. GROVE, DANA ANTHONY.   Malcolm Lowry's 'design-governing postures': a rhetorical analysis of *Under the Volcano*. Unpub. doct. diss., Ball State Univ., 1985. [Abstr. in DA (46) 1939A.]

13097. HADFIELD, D. J.   Real and imaginary golf-courses: systems of order in Malcolm Lowry's *Under the Volcano*. Unpub. doct. diss., Univ. of Warwick, 1982.

13098. HORTON, ANDREW S.   Deconstructing the Oedipus myth in Malcolm Lowry's *Under the Volcano*. *In* (pp. 391–5) **19.**

13099. LAKIN, BARBARA.   Greene's *The Honorary Consul* and Lowry's *Under the Volcano*: a study in influence. *See* **12249.**

13100. MACLEOD, C. E.   Hell is where the heart is: a study of symbol, myth and motif in the fiction of Malcolm Lowry. Unpub. doct. diss., Univ. of Strathclyde. [Abstr. in IT (36) 913.]

13101. MOON, KENNETH.   Lowry's *Under the Volcano* and Coleridge's *Kubla Khan*. *See* **7927.**

13102. VOELKER, JOSEPH C.   'A collideorscape!': Sigmund Freud, Malcolm Lowry, and the aesthetics of Conrad Aiken's *A Heart for the Gods of Mexico*. *See* **11008.**

Pat Lowther
13103. MALLINSON, JEAN. *Woman on/against Snow*: a poem and its sources. ECanW (32) 7–26.

Mabel Dodge Luhan
13104. RUDNICK, LOIS PALKEN. Mabel Dodge Luhan: new women, new worlds. Albuquerque: New Mexico UP, 1985. pp. 384. Rev. by Thomas H. Pauly in WHR (40:3) 279–81.

Alison Lurie
13105. PARINI, JAY. The novelist at sixty. Horizon (29:2) 21–2.
13106. WELLS, GULLY. Profile: Alison Lurie. LRev, Feb. 1985, 35–7.

Andrew Lytle
13107. FOATA, ANNE. Time and eternity in Andrew Lytle's *The Velvet Horn*. SoLJ (19:1) 3–15.

Rose Macaulay
13108. FROMM, GLORIA G. Re-inscribing *The Years*: Virginia Woolf, Rose Macaulay, and the critics. JML (13:2) 289–306.

James McAuley
13109. MACAINSH, NOEL. The late poems of James McAuley. Southerly (45:3) 1985, 330–42.

'Ed McBain' (Evan Hunter)
13110. BAUDOU, JACQUES. Isola blues. Europe (62:664/65) 1984, 114–23.

Mary McCarthy
13111. EAKIN, PAUL JOHN. Fictions in autobiography: studies in the art of self-invention. *See* **2973.**

James McClure
13112. SCHLEH, EUGENE. Spotlight on South Africa: the police novels of James McClure. Clues (7:2) 99–107.

Fionn Mac Colla ('Tom MacDonald')
13113. CAIRD, JAMES B. Fionn Mac Colla. Edinburgh Review (74) 50–7.

Carson McCullers
13114. COOK, RICHARD M. Carson McCullers. New York: Ungar, 1975; London: Lorrimer, 1982. pp. x, 150. (Literature and life.)
13115. GONZÁLEZ GROBA, CONSTANTE. A heaven in the age of anxiety: the café as setting and symbol in the fiction of Carson McCullers. Atlantis (8) 85–100.
13116. LAZENBLATT, W. W. G. The female mind in modern Southern fiction: the treatment and expression of female consciousness in the work of Flannery O'Connor, Carson McCullers and Eudora Welty. Unpub. doct. diss., Queen's Univ., Belfast.
13117. MEYER, PAUL RAYMOND. The interplay of reader and text in *The Member of the Wedding*: an experiment in reading. Unpub. doct. diss., Univ. of Texas at Austin, 1985. [Abstr. in DA (47) 523A.]
13118. PERRY, CONSTANCE M. Carson McCullers and the female *Wunderkind*. SoLJ (19:1) 36–45.
13119. PETRY, ALICE HALL. Baby Wilson redux: McCullers' *The Heart is a Lonely Hunter*. SoS (25:2) 196–203.

13120. TOURNIER, JACQUES.   Carson McCullers. Paris: Manufacture. pp. 182. (Qui êtes-vous?)

13121. WESTLING, LOUISE.   Sacred groves and ravaged gardens: the fiction of Eudora Welty, Carson McCullers, and Flannery O'Connor. (Bibl. 1985, 11966.) Rev. by Diane Roberts in EC (36:2) 180–6; by Robert H. Brinkmeyer, Jr, in AL (58:2) 301–2; by Nancy M. Tischler in ChrisL (35:4) 46–7; by Claire Kahane in JEGP (86:4) 595–8.

Colleen McCullough

13122. BRIDGWOOD, CHRISTINE.   Family romances: the contemporary popular family saga. *In* (pp. 167–93) **45.**

'Hugh MacDiarmid' (C. M. Grieve)

13123. BEVERIDGE, A. H.   Hugh MacDiarmid and religion: a new approach to the poet's work through a study of his recondite spirituality. Unpub. doct. diss., Univ. of Edinburgh. [Abstr. in IT (36) 911.]

13124. BOUTELLE, ANN EDWARDS.   Thistle and rose: a study of Hugh MacDiarmid's poetry. (Bibl. 1983, 12402.) Rev. by Andrew Noble in YES (16) 358–9.

13125. BUTHLAY, KENNETH.   Hugh MacDiarmid. (Bibl. 1985, 11972.) Rev. by J. H. Alexander in YES (16) 231–4.

13126. CAMPBELL, IAN.   Gibbon and MacDiarmid at play: the evolution of *Scottish Scene*. *See* **12147.**

13127. CRIBB, T. J.   The Cheka's horrors and *On a Raised Beach*. SSL (20) 1985, 88–100.

13128. GISH, NANCY K.   Hugh MacDiarmid: the man and his work. (Bibl. 1985, 11974.) Rev. by David Norbrook in LRB (8:18) 24–6.

13129. GRIEVE, MICHAEL; AITKEN, W. R. (eds).   The complete poems of Hugh MacDiarmid. (Bibl. 1985, 11975.) Rev. by Alan Riach in Cencrastus (23) 53–4.

13130. McCULLOCH, MARGERY.   The undeservedly broukit bairn: Hugh MacDiarmid's *To Circumjack Cencrastus*. SSL (17) 1982, 165–85.

13131. MILTON, C.   Hugh MacDiarmid and North-East Scots. *See* **916.**

13132. ROSS, R. J.   Hugh MacDiarmid and the politics of consciousness: a study of nationalism psychology and materialism in the work and thought of Hugh MacDiarmid. Unpub. doct. diss., Univ. of Stirling, 1984. [Abstr. in IT (35) 1088.]

13133. SILVER, R. S.   Student culture in the 1930s and acquaintance with C. M. Grieve. Edinburgh Review (74) 63–75.

13134. WANG, ZUOLIANG.   Reflections on Hugh MacDiarmid. SSL (19) 1984, 1–16.

13135. WATSON, RODERICK.   MacDiarmid. Milton Keynes: Open UP, 1985. pp. x, 115. (Open guides to literature.) Rev. in Edinburgh Review (72) 135–6.

13136. WHYTE, HAMISH.   MacDiarmid and the Beatniks. SLJ (13:2) 87–90.

Cynthia Macdonald

13137. JAŘAB, JOSEF.   Cynthia Macdonaldová: Pohřbívání nemluvňat. (Burying the babies.) SvL (31:5) 63–5.

John D. MacDonald
13138. BRITTIN, NORMAN A. From the 1940s to the 1980s: John D. MacDonald's increasing use of scatological language. *See* **1529.**
13139. KALER, ANNE K. Cats, colors, and calendars: the mythic basis of the love story of Travis McGee. Clues (7:2)147–57.

'Ross Macdonald' (Kenneth Millar)
13140. BUSCH, SUSAN RUNHOLT. Ross Macdonald as chronicler of Southern California. SDR (24:1) 111–20.
13141. LEE, L. L. The art of Ross Macdonald. SDR (24:1) 55–66.
13142. LYNDS, DENNIS. Expanding the *roman noir*: Ross Macdonald's legacy to mystery/detective authors. SDR (24:1) 121–4.
13143. SKENAZY, PAUL. Bringing it all back home: Ross Macdonald's California. SDR (24:1) 68–109.
13144. SNODGRASS, RICHARD. Down these streets, I mean, a man must go. SDR (24:1) 7–27.
13145. STEINER, T. R. The mind of the hardboiled: Ross Macdonald and the roles of criticism. SDR (24:1) 29–53.

Ian McEwan
13146. JOHNSTONE, RICHARD. Television drama and the people's war: David Hare's *Licking Hitler*, Ian McEwan's *The Imitation Game*, and Trevor Griffith's *Country*. *See* **12265.**

Gwendolyn MacEwen
13147. BARTLEY, JAN. Gwendolyn MacEwen. *In* (pp. 231–71) **10.**

Patricia MacGerr
13148. ABITEBOUL, MAURICE. *Hamlet* aujourd'hui: du drame élisabéthain au roman policier moderne. *See* **4738.**

Patrick MacGill
13149. O'GRADY, BRENDAN. 'Like grains of corn under a mill-stone'. CJIS (12:1) 67–77.
13150. SHERRY, RUTH. The Irish working class in fiction. *In* (pp. 110–23) **6.**

John McGrath
13151. JÄGER, ANDREAS. John McGrath und die '7:84 Company Scotland': Politik, Popularität und Regionalismus in Theater der siebziger Jahre in Schottland. Amsterdam: Grüner. pp. 262. (Münchner studien zur neueren englischen Literatur, 1.)

Thomas McGrath
13152. MATCHIE, THOMAS. The functions of the Hopi kachina in Tom McGrath's *Letter to an Imaginary Friend*. SDR (22:3) 1984, 7–21.

Thomas MacGreevy
13153. SCHREIBMAN, SUSAN. A brief view into the poems of Thomas MacGreevy. Studies (75:299) 328–33.

Thomas McGuane
13154. LEAR, LIZ. A conversation with Thomas McGuane. Shen (36:2) 12–26.
13155. WALLACE, JON BERKLEY. The politics of style in fiction by Thomas Berger, Thomas McGuane and James Alan McPherson. *See* **11246.**

13156. WESTRUM, DEXTER LYLE.   The art of survival in the contemporary West: the fictions of Thomas McGuane, James Welch, and Edward Abbey. *See* **10972.**

Arthur Machen
13157. MICHAELS, WALTER BENN.   Corporate fiction: Norris, Royce, and Arthur Machen. *In* (pp. 189–219) **47.**

William McIlvanney
13158. CRAIG, CAROL.   On men and women in McIlvanney's fiction. Edinburgh Review (73) 42–9.

Claude McKay
13159. SMITH, ROBERT P., JR.   Rereading *Banjo*: Claude McKay and the French connection. CLAJ (30:1) 46–58.

Sir Compton Mackenzie
13160. LINKLATER, ANDRO (introd.).   Extraordinary women: theme and variations. London: Hogarth Press. pp. 400.

13161. THOMAS, DAVID; THOMAS, JOYCE.   Compton Mackenzie: a bibliography. London: Mansell. pp. x, 309.

Barry McKinnon
13162. PRECOSKY, DON.   Interview with Barry McKinnon. ECanW (32) 160–73.

Michael McLaverty
13163. SHERRY, RUTH.   The Irish working class in fiction. *In* (pp. 110–23) **6.**

Hugh MacLennan
13164. BATTARBEE, KEITH.   Portraits of the artist as a young Canadian. *See* **11346.**

13165. GARDEN, RONALD.   Hugh MacLennan: The Scottish-Canadian connection. AUR (51) 314–22.

Alistair MacLeod
13166. NICHOLSON, COLIN.   Alistair MacLeod. JCL (21:1) 188–200 (interview.)

Louis MacNeice
13167. MARSACK, ROBYN.   The cave of making: the poetry of Louis MacNeice. New York: OUP, 1982. (Cf. bibl. 1983, 12450.) Rev. by J. C. Beckett in MLR (81:2) 467–8.

John McPhee
13168. BEARD, JOHN.   Inside the whale: a critical study of New Journalism and the nonfiction form. Unpub. doct. diss., Florida State Univ., 1985. [Abstr. in DA (46) 2691A.]

James Alan McPherson
13169. DOMNARSKI, WILLIAM.   The voices of misery and despair in the fiction of James Alan McPherson. AQ (42:1) 37–44.

13170. WALLACE, JON BERKLEY.   The politics of style in fiction by Thomas Berger, Thomas McGuane and James Alan McPherson. *See* **11246.**

Derek Mahon
13171. BYRNE, J. M.   The significance of landscape and history in the poetry of Seamus Heaney, Derek Mahon and John Montague. *See* **12325.**

Margaret Mahy

13172. BALL, DUNCAN. Margaret Mahy: there are no rules for writers. Australian Author (Milson's Point, NSW) (17:4) 1985, 7–8. (Interview.)

Norman Mailer

13173. ALLISTER, MARK CHRISTOPHER. Encounters with unimagined existence: documentary and autobiography in recent American prose. *See* **10627.**

13174. BEARD, JOHN. Inside the whale: a critical study of New Journalism and the nonfiction form. *See* **13168.**

13175. CHEVIGNY, BELL GALE. Twice-told tales and the meaning of history: testimonial novels by Miguel Barnet and Norman Mailer. CR (30:2) 181–95.

13176. LOUVRE, ALF. The reluctant historians: Sontag, Mailer and the American culture critics in the 1960s. Prose Studies (9:1) 47–61.

13177. MANSO, PETER. Mailer: his life and times. (Bibl. 1985, 12022.) Rev. by Philip Bufithis in SAF (14:2) 236.

13178. PRATT, PETER PHILIP. The paradoxical wilderness: Mailer and American nature writing. *See* **9372.**

13179. STERK, HELEN M. In praise of beautiful women. WJSC (50:3) 215–26.

Roger Mais

13180. OGUNYEMI, CHIKWENYE OKONJO. From a goat path in Africa: Roger Mais and Jean Toomer. Ob (5) Winter 1979, 7–21.

13181. RAMCHAND, KENNETH (ed.). Listen, the wind. Harlow: Longman. pp. xxxii, 160. (Longman Caribbean writers.)

Clarence Major

13182. JABLON, MADELYN HYLA. The contemporary black aesthetic. Unpub. doct. diss., State Univ. of New York at Buffalo. [Abstr. in DA (47) 2158A.]

Bernard Malamud

13183. CHOTT, LAURENCE ROYCE. The artist as prisoner in the fiction of Bernard Malamud. Unpub. doct. diss., Ball State Univ., 1985. [Abstr. in DA (46) 2691A.]

13184. COLEMAN, ARTHUR. *The Iron Mistress* and *The Natural*: analogue or influence? NCL (16:1) 11–12.

13185. KIM, IL-JOO. Bernard Malamud soseol eui gusung e gwanhan yeongu. (A study of the structure of Bernard Malamud's novels.) Unpub. doct. diss., Donga Univ. (Korea).

13186. McCABE, BRIAN. Bernard Malamud (1914–1986). Edinburgh Review (73) 121–3.

13187. MAY, CHARLES E. Something fishy in *The Magic Barrel*. SAF (14:1) 93–8.

13188. OCHSHORN, KATHLEEN GILLIKIN. The heart's essential landscape: Bernard Malamud's *mensch*-hero. Unpub. doct. diss., Univ. of South Florida. [Abstr. in DA (47) 1325A.]

13189. OZICK, CYNTHIA. Bernard Malamud. PR (53:3) 464–6.

13190. PROCHÁZKA, MARTIN.   Za Bernardem Malamudem. (Bernard Malamud; an obituary). Kmen (Prague) (20) 9.

13191. ROTH, PHILIP.   Pictures of Malamud. LRB (8:8) 5–6.

13192. —— Pictures of Malamud. NYTB, 20 Apr., 1.

13193. SALZBERG, JOEL.   Irremediable suffering: a reading of Malamud's *Take Pity*. SSF (23:1) 19–24.

Manohar Malgonkar

13194. CHEW, SHIRLEY.   Fictions of princely states and empire. *See* **11034.**

David Malouf

13195. BUCKRIDGE, PATRICK.   Colonial strategies in the writing of David Malouf. Kp (8:3) 48–84.

13196. DEVER, MARYANNE.   Secret companions: the continuity of David Malouf's fiction. WLWE (26:1) 62–75.

13197. JOLLY, ROSLYN.   Transformations of Caliban and Ariel: imagination and language in David Malouf, Margaret Atwood and Seamus Heaney. *See* **4987.**

13198. MALOUF, DAVID.   12 Edmondstone Street. London: Chatto & Windus, 1985. pp. 134.

13199. SIMPSON, PETER.   Word places. NZList, 24 May, 60.

David Mamet

13200. KOLIN, PHILIP C.   Revealing illusions in David Mamet's *The Shawl*. NCL (16:2) 9–10.

13201. ROUDANE, MATTHEW C.   Public issues, private tensions: David Mamet's *Glen Garry, Glen Ross*. SoCR (19:1) 35–47.

Frederick Manfred ('Feike Feikema VII')

13202. McALLISTER, MARK.   The first covenant in *Conquering Horse*: syncretic myth in the *Buckskin Man Tales*. SDR (20:3) 1982, 76–88.

Olivia Manning

13203. SALMON, MARY.   Nowhere to belong: the fiction of Olivia Manning. Linen Hall Review (3:3) 11–13.

Katherine Mansfield

13204. ANGUS, BARBARA.   A guide to Katherine Mansfield's Wellington. Wellington: Wellington Regional Committee of the NZ Historic Places Trust, 1985. pp. 19.

13205. BARKER, A. L. (introd.).   Katherine Mansfield: the memories of LM. London: Virago Press, 1985. pp. xxx, 240.

13206. CRANE, NORA.   A portrait of Katherine Mansfield. Ilfracombe: Stockwell, 1985. pp. 348.

13207. FULLBROOK, KATE.   Katherine Mansfield. Brighton: Harvester Press. pp. xvi, 146. (Key women writers.)

13208. HANSON, C.   The aesthetic of Katherine Mansfield. Unpub. doct. diss., Univ. of Reading, 1981.

13209. HYNES, SAMUEL.   A budget of letters. *See* **11501.**

13210. NEAMAN, JUDITH S.   Allusion, image, and associative pattern: the answers in Mansfield's *Bliss*. TCL (32:2) 242–54.

Jack Mapanje

13211. NAZOMBE, A. J. M.   Malawian poetry in English from 1970 to

the present day: a study of myth and socio-political change in the work of
Steve Chimombo, Jack Mapanje, Frank Chipasula and Felix Mnthali.
See **11442.**

Kamala Markandaya

13212. AFZAL-KHAN, FAWZIA.   Genre and ideology in the novels of
four contemporary Indo-Anglian novelists: R. K. Narayan, Anita
Desai, Kamala Markandaya and Salman Rushdie. *See* **11637.**

13213. KUMAR, PREM.   Conflict and resolution in the novels of
Kamala Markandaya. WLT (60:1) 22–7.

Edwin Markham

13214. FLEISSNER, ROBERT F.   Markin' the Frost line: on Robert Frost
and Edwin Markham. *See* **12070.**

Archibald Marshall (Arthur Hammond Marshall)

13215. MCDONOUGH, MICHAEL JOHN.   Arnold Bennett and
Archibald Marshall: two letters from a forgotten literary friendship.
See **11236.**

Paule Marshall

13216. EKO, EBELE.   Beyond the myth of confrontation: a comparative study of African and Afro-American female protagonists. *See* **10999.**

13217. WALLINGER-NOWAK, HANNA.   The wild zone in Paule
Marshall's fiction. *In* (pp. 69–87) **21.**

Philip Martin

13218. ROWE, NOEL.   Emotions of a destiny: the poetry of Philip
Martin. Southerly (46:1) 93–113.

John Masefield

13219. MCDONALD, JAN.   The 'new drama' 1900–1914: Harley
Granville-Barker, John Galsworthy, St John Hankin, John Masefield.
See **12116.**

Bruce Mason

13220. DOWLING, DAVID (ed.).   Every kind of weather: selected
writings on the arts, theatre, literature and current events in New
Zealand, 1953–1981. Auckland: Reed Methuen, pp. 306.

R. A. K. Mason

13221. MASON, R. A. K.   R. A. K. Mason at twenty-five. Christchurch, NZ: Nag's Head Press. pp. 48.

Edgar Lee Masters

13222. BIDNEY, MARTIN.   Beethoven, the Devil and the eternal
feminine: Masters' Goethean typology of redemption. PLL (22:2)
187–205.

13223. NOE, MARCIA.   The Johari window: a perspective on the *Spoon
River Anthology*. Midamerica (13) 49–60.

John Joseph Mathews

13224. RICHTER, SARA JANE.   The life and literature of John Joseph
Mathews: contributions of two cultures. Unpub. doct. diss., Oklahoma
State Univ., 1985. [Abstr. in DA (47) 902A.]

Roland Mathias

13225. HOOKER, JEREMY.   Roland Mathias: 'The strong remembered
words'. Poetry Wales (21:1) 1985, 94–103.

F. O. Matthiessen

13226. MAEKAWA, REIKO. F. O. Matthiessen: after *American Renaissance*. Unpub. doct. diss., Case Western Reserve Univ., 1985. [Abstr. in DA (46) 3764A.]

W. Somerset Maugham

13227. BLATCHFORD, ROY (ed.). Short stories. Harlow: Longman. pp. xxxiii, 222. (Longman study texts.)

13228. BUDAI, KATALIN. Maugham világa. (Maugham's world.) Budapest: Európa. pp. 264.

13229. CURTIS, ANTHONY. Somerset Maugham. Windsor: Profile, 1982. pp. 47. (Writers and their work, 279.)

H. L. Mencken

13230. AMRHINE, KENNETH W. The day Mencken was arrested. Menckeniana (98) 10–12.

13231. DUBERMAN, JASON D. H. L. Mencken and the wowsers. ABC (7:5) 3–14.

13232. FITZPATRICK, VINCENT. Bibliographic check list. Menckeniana (97) 14–16; (99) 14–16.

13233. GERSHENOWITZ, HARRY. Mencken and Nicholas Murray Butler. Menckeniana (100) 14–16.

13234. —— A triangle of forces: Mencken, Teachers College and Horace Mann. Menckeniana (96) 1985, 1–3.

13235. HAHN, H. GEORGE. Twilight reflections: the hold of Victorian Baltimore on Lizette Woodworth Reese and H. L. Mencken. SoQ (22:4) 1984, 5–21.

13236. HOBSON, FRED. H. L. Mencken and the Harlem Renaissance. Review (7) 1985, 191–6 (review-article).

13237. JENKINS, WILLIAM D. On keeping cool and keeping mum. *See* **11371.**

13238. KAZIN, ALFRED. H. L. Mencken and the great American boob. Menckeniana (99) 1–8.

13239. POITRAS, JEAN-MAURICE. Leonard Keene Hirshberg and Henry Louis Mencken. Menckeniana (97) 1–7.

13240. SCHRADER, RICHARD J. 'But gentlemen marry brunettes': Anita Loos and H. L. Mencken. *See* **13078.**

13241. SCRUGGS, CHARLES W. Finding out about this Mencken: the impact of *A Book of Prefaces* on Richard Wright. Menckeniana (95) 1985, 1–11.

13242. WINGATE, P. J. Mencken, Shaw and honorary degrees. Menckeniana (98) 8–9.

William Meredith

13243. HIRSCH, EDWARD. The art of poetry XXXIV: William Meredith. ParisR (95) 1985, 36–64 (interview).

Louise Meriwether

13244. ARTIZ, MIGUEL A. The politics of poverty in young adult literature. *See* **11440.**

James Merrill

13245. CLARK, MIRIAM MARTY. Not at all surprised by science: science and technology in Ammons, Nemerov, and Merrill. *See* **11032.**

13246. MACDONALD, D. L.   Merrill and Freud: psychopathology of eternal life. Mosaic (19:4) 159–72.

Thomas Merton

13247. COOPER, DAVID D.   Recent Merton criticism. Ren (34:2) 1982, 113–28.

13248. HART, PATRICK (ed.).   The literary essays of Thomas Merton. (Bibl. 1985, 12093.) Rev. by Dewey Weiss Kramer in ChrisL (35:4) 39–40.

13249. LABRIE, ROSS.   The burgeoning Merton industry. RALS (15:11) 1985, 49–59 (review-article).

W. S. Merwin

13250. CHRISTHILF, MARK.   Expressionist imagery in the poetry of W. S. Merwin. MidQ (27:3) 277–93.

John Metcalf

13251. ROLLINS, DOUGLAS.   John Metcalf. In (pp. 155–211) **8.**

Edna St Vincent Millay

13252. FRIED, DEBRA.   Andromeda unbound: gender and genre in Millay's sonnets. TCL (32:1) 1–22.

Arthur Miller

13253. ANDERSON, M. C.   *Death of a Salesman*: a consideration of Willy Loman's role in twentieth-century tragedy. Crux (20:2) 25–9.

13254. CENTOLA, STEVEN R.   Compromise as bad faith: Arthur Miller's *A View from the Bridge* and William Inge's *Come Back, Little Sheba*. See **12520.**

13255. FELDMAN, ROBERT LEE.   The problem of evil in five plays by Arthur Miller. Unpub. doct. diss., Univ. of Maryland, 1985. [Abstr. in DA (46) 2293A.]

13256. HIRSCHHORN, CLIVE.   Memories of a salesman: Arthur Miller talks to Clive Hirschhorn in New York about his latest play and the state of Broadway theatre today. Plays and Players (394), 7–10.

13257. LONG, DEBORAH MARIE.   The existential quest: family and form in selected American plays. Unpub. doct. diss., Univ. of Oregon. [Abstr. in DA (47) 1119A.]

13258. MAHMOUD, MOHAMED A. W.   A stylistic, sociolinguistic, and discourse analysis of linguistic naturalism in selected plays of Arthur Miller and Eugene O'Neill. See **1233.**

13259. PAUL, JOHN STEVEN.   Offenders. Cresset (49:8) 26–9.

13260. SABINSON, ERIC MITCHELL.   Script and transcript: the writings of Clifford Odets, Lillian Hellman and Arthur Miller in relation to their testimony before the U.S. House Committee on Un-American Activities. See **12353.**

13261. SCHROEDER, PATRICIA R.   Arthur Miller: illuminating process. YREAL (3) 1985, 265–93.

13262. SMITH, LEONARD.   *The Crucible* by Arthur Miller. Basingstoke: Macmillan. pp. viii, 88. (Macmillan master guides.)

13263. WELLAND, DENNIS.   Miller: the playwright. (Bibl. 1983, 12553.) London: Methuen, 1985. pp. 186. (Third ed.: first ed. 1983, as *Miller: a Study of his Plays.*)

13264. ZEINEDDINE, N.   I search: problems of identity: woman, artist and breadwinner in the plays of Henrik Ibsen, Tennessee Williams and Arthur Miller. Unpub. doct. diss., Univ. of Leicester, 1984.

Henry Miller

13265. ANON.   Nihon ni okeru Henry Miller shoshi. (A bibliography of Henry Miller criticism in Japan.) Tokyo: Hokuseido. pp. xiv, 88.   ·

13266. CALONNE, DAVID STEPHEN.   Euphoria in Paris: Henry Miller meets D. H. Lawrence. *See* **12880.**

13267. SINDELL, GERALD SETH (ed.).   Dear, dear Brenda: the love letters of Henry Miller to Brenda Venus. New York: Morrow/Corwin-Sindell. pp. 191. Rev. by Erica Jong in BkW, 30 Mar., 1–2.

13268. TEMPLE, FREDERIC-JACQUES.   Henry Miller. Paris: Manufacture. pp. 200. (Qui suis-je?)

Walter M. Miller, Jr

13269. MANGANIELLO, DOMINIC.   History as judgment and promise in *A Canticle for Leibowitz*. SFS (13:2) 159–69.

13270. OWER, JOHN.   Theology and evolution in the short fiction of Walter M. Miller, Jr. Cithara (25:2) 57–74.

A. A. Milne

13271. MASON, BRUCE.   Mr Pim. VNRN (6) 1981, 31–2.

13272. TREMPER, ELLEN.   Instigorating *Winnie the Pooh*. LU (1:1) 1977, 33–46.

Julian Mitchell

13273. KRAMER, MIMI.   Want in the midst of *Plenty*. *See* **11445.**

Margaret Mitchell

13274. CURRAN, TRISHA.   *Gone with the Wind*: an American tragedy. SoQ (19:3/4) 1981, 47–57.

13275. PYRON, DARDEN ASBURY.   Margaret Mitchell: first or nothing. SoQ (20:3) 1982, 19–34.

13276. TAYLOR, HELEN.   *Gone with the Wind*: the mammy of them all. *In* (pp. 113–36) **45.**

13277. WICKER, TOM.   Why, Miss Scarlett, how well you've aged. NYTB, 25 May, 1.

W. O. Mitchell

13278. MITCHELL, O. S.   Tall tales in the fiction of W. O. Mitchell. *See* **2473.**

Naomi Mitchison

13279. BENTON, JILL KATHRYN.   Historical representation in the novels of Naomi Mitchison (1931–1935). Unpub. doct. diss., Univ. of California, San Diego. [Abstr. in DA (47) 897A.]

13280. MURRAY, ISOBEL (ed.).   Beyond this limit; selected shorter fiction of Naomi Mitchison. Edinburgh: Scottish Academic Press. pp. xix, 217.

Nancy Mitford

13281. MOSLEY, CHARLOTTE (ed.).   A talent to annoy: essays, articles and reviews 1929–1968. London: Hamilton. pp. xi, 217.

Felix Mnthali

13282. NAZOMBE, A. J. M.   Malawian poetry in English from 1970 to

the present day: a study of myth and socio-political change in the work of
Steve Chimombo, Jack Mapanje, Frank Chipasula and Felix Mnthali.
See **11442**.

N. Scott Momaday

13283. GEORGI-FINDLAY, BRIGITTE. Tradition und Moderne in der
zeitgenössischen indianischen Literatur der USA. N. Scott Momadays
Roman *House Made of Dawn*. Cologne: Pahl–Rugenstein. pp. 352.

13284. LINCOLN, KENNETH. Tai-me to rainy mountain: the makings
of American Indian literature. AIQ (10:2) 101–17.

13285. PAPOVICH, J. FRANK. Landscape, tradition, and identity in
The Way to Rainy Mountain. PCL (12) 13–19.

13286. SCARBERRY-GARCIA, SUSAN. Sources of healing in *House Made
of Dawn*. Unpub. doct. diss., Univ. of Colorado at Boulder. [Abstr. in
DA (47) 2161A.]

13287. SCHUBNELL, M. M. N. Scott Momaday: the cultural and
literary background. Unpub. doct. diss., Univ. of Oxford, 1983.

13288. SCHUBNELL, MATTHIAS. N. Scott Momaday: the cultural and
literary background. Norman: Oklahoma UP. pp. viii, 336. Rev. by
Arnold Krupat in AL (58:4) 667–8.

John Montague

13289. BYRNE, J. M. The significance of landscape and history in the
poetry of Seamus Heaney, Derek Mahon and John Montague.
See **12325**.

13290. JOHN, BRIAN. The healing art of John Montague. CJIS (12:1)
35–52.

L. M. Montgomery

13291. RUBIO, MARY; WATERSTON, ELIZABETH (eds). The selected
journals of L. M. Montgomery: vol. 1, 1889–1910. Toronto: OUP, 1985.
pp. xxiv, 424. Rev. by Hilary Thompson in CanL (111) 205–6; by
Clifford G. Holland in QQ (93:3) 667–8.

William Vaughn Moody

13292. KOLDENHOVEN, JAMES JOHN. A structuralist approach to the
realistic drama of William Vaughn Moody. Unpub. doct. diss., Univ. of
Minnesota. [Abstr. in DA (47) 348A.]

Michael Moorcock

13293. MOORCOCK, MICHAEL. Letters from Hollywood. London:
Harrap. pp. 231. Rev. by Troy Kennedy Martin in Listener, 11 Sept.,
23–4.

George Moore

13294. BECKER, R. S. George Moore: an exile from the Nouvelle
Athènes. Éire–Ireland (21:2) 146–51.

13295. EAKIN, DAVID B.; GERBER, HELMUT E. (eds). In minor keys:
the uncollected short stories of George Moore. Syracuse, NY: Syracuse
UP; London: Fourth Estate, 1985. pp. 229. Rev. by Janet Egleson
Dunleavy in Éire-Ireland (21:1) 147–9.

13296. GILCHER, EDWIN. A note on Arizona State University's
George Moore collection. *See* **223**.

13297. GRUBGELD, ELIZABETH.   George Moore's *The Lake* and the geography of consciousness. EngS (67:4) 331–44.

13298. HASSAINE, F.   Moore, Joyce and the modernist Anglo-Irish short story. *See* **12660.**

13299. LANGENFELD, ROBERT.   *Memoirs of My Dead Life*: George Moore's comic autobiography. Éire–Ireland (21:1) 73–88.

13300. MITCHELL, JUDITH.   Fictional worlds in George Moore's *A Mummer's Wife*. EngS (67:4) 345–54.

13301. —— Formal considerations in *Esther Waters*: early intimations of George Moore's 'melodic line'. CVE (24) 123–33.

13302. —— George Moore's Kate Ede. ESCan (12:1) 69–78.

13303. NOEL, JEAN-CLAUDE.   Modes du récit et modulation narrative dans les premières nouvelles de George Moore. CVE (24) 109–21.

Marianne Moore
13304. LEGGET, B. J.   Wallace Stevens and Marianne Moore: two essays and a private review. WSJ (10:2) 76–83.

13305. MORAN, EILEEN G.   Selected letters of Marianne Moore to Hildegarde Watson, edited, with a critical introduction. Unpub. doct. diss., Bryn Mawr College, 1985. [Abstr. in DA (46) 2290A.]

13306. WILLIS, PATRICIA C. (ed.).   The complete prose of Marianne Moore. New York: Sifton/Viking Press. pp. 723. Rev. by Grace Schulman in NYTB, 30 Nov., 13; by Anthony Hecht in BkW, 23 Nov., 1, 14.

Frank Moorhouse
13307. SMITH, GRAEME KINROSS.   Liberating acts: Frank Moorhouse, his life, his narratives. Southerly (46:4) 391–423.

David Patrick Moran
13308. FENNEY, WILLIAM J.   D. P. Moran's *Tom O'Kelly* and Irish cultural identity. Éire–Ireland (21:3) 17–26.

Charles Morgan
13309. SCHAEFER, JACQUELINE T.   Two medieval myths in the work of Charles Morgan. *In* (pp. 415–20) **19.**

Ronald Hugh Morrieson
13310. SETON, JO.   Subjects of the gaze: controlling and containing women in *The Scarecrow*. *See* **10076.**

13311. SHADBOLT, MAURICE (introd.).   Predicament. Auckland: Penguin. pp. 248.

Wright Morris
13312. ARNOLD, MARILYN.   Wright Morris's *Plains Song*: woman's search for harmony. SDR (20:3) 1982, 50–62.

13313. WYDEVEN, JOSEPH J.   Photography and privacy: the protests of Wright Morris and James Agee. *See* **10998.**

Toni Morrison
13314. BAUM, ROSALIE MURPHY.   Alcoholism and family abuse in *Maggie* and *The Bluest Eye*. *See* **7977.**

13315. DE ARMAN, CHARLES.   Milkman as archetypal hero. Ob (6) Winter 1980, 56–9.

13316. EDELBERG, CYNTHIA DUBIN. Morrison's voices: formal education, the work ethic, and the Bible. AL (58:2) 217–37.

13317. FIKES, ROBERT. Echoes from small town Ohio: a Toni Morrison bibliography. Ob (5) Spring/Summer 1979, 142–8.

13318. FRYAR, LILLIE B. The aesthetics of language: Harper, Hurston and Morrison. *See* **8439**.

13319. JABLON, MADELYN HYLA. The contemporary black aesthetic. *See* **13182**.

13320. JORDAN, SHIRLEY MARIE. An analysis of the female experience in the novels of Toni Morrison. Unpub. doct. diss., Univ. of Michigan, 1985. [Abstr. in DA (47) 901A.]

13321. OTTEN, TERRY. The crime of innocence in Toni Morrison's *Tar Baby*. SAF (14:2) 153–64.

13322. PORTALES, MARCO. Toni Morrison's *The Bluest Eye*: Shirley Temple and Cholly. CR (30:4) 496–506.

13323. TANIFÉANI, WILLIAM. Entretien avec Toni Morrison, mai 1985. Trans. by RALPH NICOLAS. TM (42:485) 199–206.

Tad Mosel

13324. OVERMYER, JANET. Tad Mosel, Ohio playwright. OhioanaQ (29:4) 137–9.

Howard Moss

13325. LARKIN, JOAN. For children with smart ears. LU (2:1) 1978, 137–40.

Andrew Motion

13326. HULSE, MICHAEL. 'I could have outlived myself there': the poetry of Andrew Motion. CritQ (28:3) 71–81.

R. H. Mottram

13327. BATE, JONATHAN. Arcadia and Armageddon: three English novelists and the First World War. *See* **11988**.

Es'kia Mphahlele (formerly Ezekiel Mphahlele)

13328. HAARHOF, DORIAN. The Southern African setting of *Chirundu*. EngA (13:2) 39–45.

13329. HODGE, NORMAN. 'The way I looked at life then': Es'kia Mphahlele's *Man Must Live and Other Stories*. EngA (13:2) 47–64.

13330. MPHAHLELE, ES'KIA; HAARHOF, DORIAN (transcriber). Remarks on *Chirundu*. EngA (13:2) 21–37.

13331. RUTH, DAMIAN. Through the keyhole: masters and servants in the work of Es'kia Mphahlele. EngA (13:2) 65–88.

13332. SKINNER, KATHERINE; CORNWELL, GARETH. Es'kia Mphahlele: a checklist of primary sources. EngA (13:2) 89–103.

Edwin Muir

13333. BOUSON, J. BROOKS. Poetry and the unsayable: Edwin Muir's conception of the powers and limitations of poetic speech. SSL (17) 1982, 23–38.

13334. DODD, PHILIP; LAPSLEY, M. Is man no more than this? A consideration of Edwin Muir's *The Story and the Fable*. SSL (17) 1982, 13–22.

John Muir

13335. COHEN, MICHAEL P. The pathless way: John Muir and the American wilderness. (Bibl. 1985, 12195.) Rev. by Craig W. Allin in PacHR (55:1) 130–1.

13336. TURNER, FREDERICK. Rediscovering America: John Muir in his time and ours. (Bibl. 1985, 7756.) Rev. by Robert W. Bradford in AL (58:4) 647–8; by Alfred Runte in PacH (30:1) 63–4.

Bharati Mukherjee

13337. NAZARETH, PETER. Total vision. CanL (110) 184–91.

Alice Munro

13338. DAHLIE, HALLVARD. Alice Munro. *In* (pp. 215–56) **8.**

13339. DAZIRON, HELIANE CATHERINE. Angles of vision on Alice Munro's short fiction. Unpub. doct. diss., York Univ. (Canada), 1985. [Abstr. in DA (46) 2296A.]

13340. ETTER, KATHRYN. Genre of return: the short story volume. *See* **10991.**

13341. HOWELLS, CORAL ANN. Worlds alongside: contradictory discourses in the fiction of Alice Munro and Margaret Atwood. *In* (pp. 121–36) **22.**

13342. TAUSKY, THOMAS E. 'What happened to Marion?': art and reality in *Lives of Girls and Women*. StudCanL (11:1) 52–76.

13343. WOODCOCK, GEORGE. The plots of life: the realism of Alice Munro. QQ (93:2) 235–50.

13344. YORK, LORRAINE M. Lives of Joan and Del: separate paths to transformation in *Lives of Girls and Women* and *Lady Oracle*. *See* **11089.**

Iris Murdoch

13345. ATKINS, THELMA. The satire of substitution: a study of Iris Murdoch's later novels. Unpub. doct. diss., Tufts Univ., 1985. [Abstr. in DA (46) 3723A.]

13346. BOVE, CHERYL BROWNING. A character index and guide to the fiction of Iris Murdoch. New York; London: Garland. pp. xiii, 272. (Garland reference library of the humanities, 607.)

13347. CHARPENTIER, COLETTE. L'étrange dans *The Unicorn* d'Iris Murdoch. Études irlandaises (9) 1984, 89–94.

13348. CONRADI, P. J. Iris Murdoch and the purification of Eros: a study of the moral structure of her fiction. Unpub. doct. diss., Univ. of London, University Coll., 1984. [Abstr. in IT (35) 547–8.]

13349. EDWARDS, S. L. Playful Platonist: the development of ideas in the novels of Iris Murdoch. Unpub. doct. diss., Open Univ., 1984.

13350. JĘDRZEJKIEWICZ, MARIA. Escape from freedom: 'enchanters' in Iris Murdoch's fiction. *In* (pp. 217–25) **17.**

13351. MOUSLEH, T. The humanist dilemma: a study of liberal thought in some selected novels by E. M. Forster, Angus Wilson and Iris Murdoch. *See* **12023.**

13352. RALIAN, ANTOANETA (trans.). Discopolul. (The philosopher's pupil.) Bucharest: Univers. pp. 655. Rev. by Maria Ana Tupan in RomLit, 2 July, 20.

13353. RICHER, CAROL FRENCH. Continuation and innovation in the contemporary British novel: the reflexive fiction of Margaret Drabble, Iris Murdoch, and John Fowles. *See* **11701.**

13354. SCANLAN, MARGARET. The problem of the past in Iris Murdoch's *Nuns and Soldiers*. Ren (38:3) 170–82.

13355. SNAPE, RAY. *Henry and Cato* and the 'intelligence' of Iris Murdoch. DUJ (78:2) 327–33.

Gerald Murnane

13356. SALUSINSZKY, IMRE. On Gerald Murnane. Meanjin (45:4) 518–29.

Les A. Murray

13357. BOURKE, L. H. Digging under the horse: surface as disguise in the poetry of Les A. Murray. Southerly (46:1) 26–41.

13358. BOURKE, LAWRENCE. Les A. Murray. JCL (21:1) 167–87 (interview).

13359. OLES, CAROLE. Les Murray: an interview. APR (15:2) 28–36.

13360. TAYLOR, ANDREW. Past imperfect?: the sense of the past in Les A. Murray. SoRA (19:1) 89–103.

John Middleton Murry

13361. BLENCH, J. W. (introd.). The novels of Henry Williamson. London: Henry Williamson Soc. pp. 78.

13362. JOYCE, C. Critics in context: aspects of the work of T. S. Eliot, John Middleton Murry and F. R. Leavis. *See* **11763.**

13363. LEA, F. A. Lawrence and Murry: a twofold vision. *See* **12918.**

13364. MURRY, KATHERINE MIDDLETON. Beloved Quixote: the unknown life of John Middleton Murry. London: Souvenir Press. pp. 219. Rev. by Hilary Spurling in TLS, 4 Apr., 352, by P. N. Furbank in Listener, 20 Mar., 26–7.

Vladimir Nabokov

13365. ANON. Nabokov papers: U. S. Library of Congress. *See* **192.**

13366. BARABTARLO, GENE. The Bohemian sea and other shores. Nabokovian (16) 32–7.

13367. —— A note on *Pale Fire*. Nabokovian (17) 47–50.

13368. —— Pushkin embedded. VNRN (8) 1982, 28–31.

13369. —— 'That main secret tra-tà-ta tra-tà-ta tra-tà-' (*Fame*, 105). VNRN (9) 1982, 34–5.

13370. BARABTARLO, GENNADY. Phantom of fact: Vladimir Nabokov's *Pnin* annotated. Unpub. doct. diss., Univ. of Illinois at Urbana–Champaign, 1985. [Abstr. in DA (46) 1940A.]

13371. BARTON JOHNSON, D. A Henry James parody in *Ada. See* **8621.**

13372. —— The labyrinth of incest in Nabokov's *Ada*. CL (38:3) 224–55.

13373. —— 'Murochka, the story of a Woman's Life.' Nabokovian (17) 42–4.

13374. —— A POSSIBLE ANTI-SOURCE FOR *Ada*, or did Nabokov read German novels? VNRN (7) 1981, 21–4.

13375. —— Worlds in regression: some novels of Vladimir Nabokov. Ann Arbor, MI: Ardis, 1985. pp. x, 233.

13376. —— The *'yablochko' chastushka* in *Bend Sinister*. VNRN (9) 1982, 40–2.

13377. BOEGEMAN, MARGARET BYRD.   Invitation to a metamorphosis. VNRN (2) 1979, 11–13.

13378. BOWIE, ROBERT.   A note on Nabokov's *Gogol*. Nabokovian (16) 25–30.

13379. BOYD, BRIAN.   Emigré response to Nabokov: (1), 1921–1930. Nabokovian (17) 21–41.

13380. —— Lost and found columns: some new Nabokov works. Nabokovian (16) 44–59.

13381. —— Lost in the lost and found columns. Nabokovian (17) 56–8.

13382. —— A marsh marigold is a marsh marigold is a marsh marigold. VNRN (1) 1978, 13–16.

13383. —— The mysterious dozen: a problem in *Ada*. VNRN (1) 1978, 16–17.

13384. —— *et al.* Bibliography. VNRN (4) 1980, 39–46.

13385. —— KARLINSKY, SIMON.   Bibliography. VNRN (2) 1979, 28–34.

13386. —— NABOKOV, VERA.   Bibliography. VNRN (1) 1978, 18–32.

13387. BRAND, DANA.   Vladimir Nabokov's morality of art: *Lolita* as (God forbid) didactic fiction. Nabokovian (17) 52–5.

13388. BRUCKMANN, PATRICIA.   The day after the fourth. VNRN (3) 1979, 31–2.

13389. —— Un squelette des ombres. VNRN (6) 1981, 28–30.

13390. CANNON, DIANE.   *Pnin*: a study of narrative voice. Unpub. doct. diss., Univ. of Utah. [Abstr. in DA (47) 2166A.]

13391. CLARK, BEVERLY LYON.   Contradiction and confirmations in *Ada*: 'Ah, yes! I remember it well'. VNRN (4) 1980, 17–19.

13392. —— The mirror worlds of Carroll, Nabokov, and Pynchon: fantasy in the 1860s and 1960s. *See* **7838.**

13393. CLIFTON, GLADYS M.   John Shade's poem: Nabokov's subtle parody. VNRN (8) 1982, 17–19.

13394. COHEN, WALTER.   The ideology of Nabokov's fiction. VNRN (2) 1979, 14–15.

13395. CONNOLLY, JULIAN W.   A note on the name 'Pnin'. VNRN (6) 1981, 32–3.

13396. —— The otherworldly in Nabokov's poetry. Nabokovian (16) 21–22.

13397. —— The real life of Zhorzhik Uranski. VNRN (4) 1980, 35–7.

13398. COUTURIER, MAURICE.   L'énonciation du roman nabokovien. VNRN (8) 1982, 36–7.

13399. DAVEYDOV, SERGEJ.   The 'matreshka-technique' in Nabokov's *Lips to Lips*. VNRN (8) 1982, 13–16.

13400. DRANCH, SHERRY A.   *Nikolai Gogol* as a critical ur-text. VNRN (2) 1979, 16–17.

13401. EDELNANT, JAY ALAN.   Nabokov's black rainbow: an analysis of the rhetorical function of the color imagery in *Ada; or, Ardor: a Family Chronicle.* VNRN (5) 1980, 23–5.

13402. EDELSTEIN, MARILYN. The art of consciousness. VNRN (4) 1980, 14–16.

13403. —— Nabokov's impersonations: the dialogue between forward and afterward in *Lolita.* Nabokovian (17) 59–61.

13404. ENGELKING, LESZEK. Nabokov in *Literatura na Swiecie* (Poland). VNRN (9) 1982, 30–3.

13405. FIELD, ANDREW. VN: the life and art of Vladimir Nabokov. New York: Crown. pp. 417. Rev. by R. Z. Sheppard in Time, 20 Oct., 91–2; by Joel Conarroe in NYTB, 2 Nov., 7.

13406. FIELD, DAVID. Fluid worlds: Lem's *Solaris* and Nabokov's *Ada.* SFS (13:3) 329–44.

13407. FOWLER, DOUGLAS R. Elphinstoned again. VNRN (5) 1980, 26.

13408. GARFINKEL, NANCY. The intimacy of imagination: a study of the self in Nabokov's English novels. VNRN (7) 1981, 38–9.

13409. GARRETT-GOODYEAR, J. H. 'The rapture of endless approximation': the role of the narrator in *Pnin.* JNT (16:3) 192–203.

13410. GEORGE, EMERY. Remembering Nabokov: an interview with Victor Lange. MichQR (25:3) 479–92.

13411. GREEN, GEOFFREY. 'Nothing will ever change, nobody will ever die': the speech of memory in Nabokov's fiction. VNRN (6) 1981, 21–3.

13412. GROSSMITH, ROBERT. Nabokov's horological hearts. Nabokovian (16) 38–43.

13413. JULIAR, MICHAEL. Notes from a descriptive bibliography. VNRN (8) 1982, 20–7; (9) 1982, 14–25.

13414. —— Vladimir Nabokov: a descriptive bibliography. New York; London: Garland. pp. xiii, 780. (Garland reference library of the humanities, 656.) Rev. by Stephen Jan Parker in Nabokovian (17) 18–20.

13415. KECHT, MARIA-REGINA. Die Elemente des Grotesken im Prosawerk von Vladimir Nabokov. VNRN (8) 1982, 46–8.

13416. KENNEDY, COLLEEN STEPHANIE. Footnotes and prefaces: ruses of authority in the postmodern fiction of Vladimir Nabokov and John Barth. *See* **11134.**

13417. KOPPER, JOHN MATTHIAS, JR. Family resemblances. Unpub. doct. diss., Univ. of California, Berkeley, 1985. [Abstr. in DA (47) 893A.]

13418. LARMOUR, DAVID H. J. *Subsidunt montes et inga celsa ruunt.* Nabokovian (16) 30–2.

13419. LAVABRE, SIMONE. Vladimir Nabokov: richesse et problèmes du biculturalisme. *In* (pp. 99–106) **5.**

13420. LOWE, DAVID. Nabokov's Hermann: *homme sans mœurs et sans religion!* VNRN (7) 1981, 16–18.

13421. MADDOX, LUCY B. Nabokov's novels in English. (Bibl. 1985, 12255.) Rev. by Beverly Lyon Clark in SAF (14:1) 118–19.

13422. MASON, BRUCE.   Mr Pim. *See* **13271.**

13423. MEYER, PRISCILLA.   Nabokov's *Lolita* and Pushkin's *Onegin*: a colloquy of muses. VNRN (7) 1981, 33–4.

13424. —— Nabokov's non-fiction as reference library: Igor, Ossian, Kinbote. Nabokovian (16) 23–4.

13425. MILBAUER, ASHER Z.   Transcending exile: Conrad, Nabokov, I. B. Singer. *See* **10683.**

13426. MORGAN, PAUL BENNETT.   The use of female characters in the fiction of V. Nabokov. VNRN (9) 1982, 26–7.

13427. NICOL, CHARLES.   Flaubert's understudy. VNRN (5) 1980, 27–8.

13428. O'HARA, J. D.   The Tamara theme. VNRN (6) 1981, 15–17.

13429. OLSEN, LANCE.   A Janus-text: realism, fantasy, and Nabokov's *Lolita*. MFS (32:1) 115–26.

13430. PAGE, NORMAN (ed.).   Nabokov: the critical heritage. Boston, MA; Melbourne: Routledge & Kegan Paul, 1982. (Bibl. 1985, 12261.) Rev. by Michael Bell in MLR (81:2) 465–6.

13431. PAINE, SYLVIA JEAN.   Sense and transcendence: the art of Anaïs Nin, Vladimir Nabokov, and Samuel Beckett. *See* **11196.**

13432. PARKER, STEPHEN JAN.   Bibliography. VNRN (6) 1981, 44–7.

13433. —— 1979 bibliography. VNRN (5) 1980, 29–38.

13434. —— 1980 bibliography. VNRN (7) 1981, 40–9.

13435. —— 1981 Nabokov bibliography. VNRN (9) 1982, 43–52.

13436. —— 1985 Nabokov bibliography. Nabokovian (17) 62–78.

13437. —— Professor Nabokov. VNRN (8) 1982, 38–45.

13438. —— Some Nabokov holdings in the Library of Congress. *See* **268.**

13439. PETERSON, DALE E.   Nabokov and the poetics of composition. Nabokovian (16) 17–20.

13440. PETERSON, RONALD E.   Time in *The Gift*. VNRN (9) 1982, 36–40.

13441. PIFER, ELLEN.   Consciousness and real life in *King, Queen, Knave*. VNRN (2) 1979, 18–19.

13442. —— Nabokov's *Gift*: the art of exile. VNRN (6) 1981, 18–20.

13443. —— Wrestling with doubles in Nabokov's novels: *Despair*, *Lolita*, and *Pale Fire*. VNRN (6) 1981, 37–40.

13444. RAMPTON, DAVID.   Vladimir Nabokov: a critical study of the novels. (Bibl. 1985, 12263.) Rev. by Judith Armstrong in AUMLA (66) 320–3; by Charles Lock in NQ (33:2) 270–1.

13445. REA, JOHN A.   Elphinstone. VNRN (3) 1979, 29.

13446. RIVERS, J. E.; WALKER, WILLIAM.   Notes to Vivian Darkbloom's 'Notes to *Ada*'. VNRN (3) 1979, 34–41.

13447. ROLLINS, JACK D.   A note on the Arabic etymology of Nabokov. VNRN (6) 1981, 27–8.

13448. ROSENGRANT, JUDSON.   Nabokov's autobiography: some questions of translation and style. VNRN (6) 1981, 34–6.

13449. ROSS, DIANE M.   Lo. Lee. Ta. VNRN (3) 1979, 27–9.

13450. RUCH, EDWARD DELAFIELD. Techniques of self-reference in selected novels of Beckett, Nabokov, Vonnegut, and Barth. *See* **11140**.

13451. RYLEY, ROBERT M. Will Brown, Dolores, Colo. VNRN (3) 1979, 30.

13452. SCHUMAN, SAM. Another 'Nova Zembla'. VNRN (6) 1981, 30–1.

13453. —— Whatever happened to Humbert: the transformation of *Lolita* from novel to screenplay. VNRN (2) 1979, 20–2.

13454. SHIPE, TIMOTHY. Life/story: autobiographical modes in the fiction of Nabokov, Barth, and Frisch. *See* **11141**.

13455. —— Nabokov's metanovel. VNRN (6) 1981, 24–6.

13456. SIKORSKI, HELENE (ed.). Perepiska s sestroĭ. (Letters to a sister.) Ann Arbor, MI: Ardis, 1985. pp. 125.

13457. SISSON, JONATHAN BORDEN. Cosmic synchronization and other worlds in the work of Vladimir Nabokov. VNRN (7) 1981, 35–7.

13458. STANLEY, DONALD HUTTON. The self-conscious narrator in Donald Barthelme and Vladimir Nabokov. *See* **11145**.

13459. STUART, MARY. Bibliography. VNRN (3) 1979, 42–8.

13460. SWEENY, S. E. Io's metamorphosis: a classical subtext for *Lolita*. CML (6:2) 79–88.

13461. TAMMI, PEKKA. A nosological note on *The Eye*. Nabokovian (17) 45–7.

13462. —— Problems of Nabokov's poetics: a narratological analysis. *See* **1247**.

13463. —— Some remarks on Flaubert and *Ada*. VNRN (7) 1981, 19–21.

13464. TOKER, LEONA. Ambiguity in Vladimir Nabokov's *Invitation to a Beheading*. VNRN (8) 1982, 49–51.

13465. —— A Nabokovian character in Conrad's *Nostromo*. *See* **11560**.

13466. —— Self-conscious paralepsis in Vladimir Nabokov's *Pnin* and *Recruiting*. PT (7:3) 459–69.

13467. VANDER CLOSTER, SUSAN. A discussion of *The Gift*, the novel in which Vladimir Nabokov artistically confronts Nikolay Chernyshevski. VNRN (8) 1982, 32–5.

13468. WILLIAMS, RONALD JOHN ANDREW. Maps, chronologies, and identities in three novels of Vladimir Nabokov. Unpub. doct. diss., York Univ. (Canada), 1985. [Abstr. in DA (46) 2291A.]

13469. YUN, SANG-HI. Vladimir Nabokov yeongu: *Lolita* reul jungsim euro. (A study of Vladimir Nabokov's *Lolita*.) IKS (15) 79–97.

Sarojini Naidu

13470. ALEXANDER, MEENA. Sarojini Naidu: 'Romanticism and resistance'. Ariel (17:4) 49–61.

Shiva Naipaul

13471. STUART, DOUGLAS (introd.). An unfinished journey. London: Hamilton. pp. 136.

V. S. Naipaul

13472. BERMAN, JAYE. V. S. Naipaul's *Guerillas* as a postmodern naturalistic novel. PCL (12) 29–34.

13473. BROEK, AART G.   Het Caraïbisch gebied: 'Idiote idealen, falen, corruptie en stom geluk', Lovelace versus Naipaul. (The Caribbean area: 'idiocy, ideals, failures, corruption and mere fluke'. Lovelace versus Naipaul.) *See* **13080.**

13474. DHAHIR, SANNA.   Women in V. S. Naipaul's fiction: their roles and relationships. Unpub. doct. diss., Univ. of New Brunswick. [Abstr. in DA (47) 1317A.]

13475. HASSAN, DOLLY ZULAKHA.   West Indian response to V. S. Naipaul's West Indian works. Unpub. doct. diss., George Washington Univ. [Abstr. in DA (47) 536A.]

13476. NAUGRETTE, J.-P.   L'Afrique à la courbe du temps: l'Apocalypse selon V. S. Naipaul. *In* (pp. 303–17) **2.**

13477. POCOCK, A. J.   V. S. Naipaul: a critical study. Unpub. doct. diss., Univ. of Cambridge, 1985.

13478. REDDY, Y. G.   Alienation and the quest for identity and order in the novels of V. S. Naipaul. Unpub. doct. diss., Univ. of South Africa.

13479. THIEME, JOHN.   V. S. Naipaul, *The Mimic Men*: a critical view. Ed. by YOLANDE CANTÙ. London: Collins; British Council, 1985. pp. 42. (Nexus.)

13480. THORPE, MICHAEL.   V. S. Naipaul, *A House for Mr Biswas*: a critical view. Ed. by YOLANDE CANTÙ. London: Collins; British Council, 1985. pp. 43. (Nexus.)

R. K. Narayan

13481. AFZAL-KHAN, FAWZIA.   Genre and ideology in the novels of four contemporary Indo-Anglian novelists: R. K. Narayan, Anita Desai, Kamala Markandaya and Salman Rushdie. *See* **11637.**

13482. MATHUR, O. P.   Two modern versions of the Sita myth: Narayan and Anand. *See* **11035.**

13483. NIVEN, ALASTAIR.   R. K. Narayan, *The Guide:* a critical view. Ed. by YOLANDE CANTÙ. London: Collins; British Council, 1985. pp. 39. (Nexus.)

13484. PANDIT, MANORMA.   Detachment and liberation in the novels of R. K. Narayan. Unpub. doct. diss., Univ. of Oregon, 1985. [Abstr. in DA (46) 3355A.]

13485. PROCHÁZKA, MARTIN.   Smutná komedie z indického provinčního života. (A sombre comedy of Indian provincial life.) Literární měsíčník (15:7) 136–7. (*The Guide.*)

13486. ROBINSON, ANDREW.   Talking to the ambassador for Malgudi. Independent, 24 Oct., 14. (Interview.)

13487. VANDEN DRIESEN, CYNTHIA.   R. K. Narayan's neglected novel: *Waiting for the Mahatma.* WLWE (26:2) 362–9.

John G. Neihardt

13488. DEMALLIE, RAYMOND J. (ed.).   The sixth grandfather: Black Elk's teachings given to John G. Neihardt. (Bibl. 1985, 12290.) Rev. by James McLaird in NDH (53:4) 41–2.

13489. RICHARDS, JOHN THOMAS.   Rawhide laureate: John G. Neihardt: a selected, annotated bibliography. (Bibl. 1984, 12338.) Rev. by Sanford E. Marovitz in BB (43:1) 58–9.

John Shaw Neilson

13490. ANDERSON, HUGH. The spinning of a dream: the story of John Shaw Neilson. Ascot Vale, Vic.: Red Rooster Press. pp. 231.

13491. BALLYN, SUSAN P. Nature and the concept of death in John Shaw Neilson's verse. RCEI (12) 113–21.

13492. MACAINSH, NOEL. John Shaw Neilson and the floral metaphor. Linq (13:2) 1985, 56–74.

Howard Nemerov

13493. CLARK, MIRIAM MARTY. Not at all surprised by science: science and technology in Ammons, Nemerov, and Merrill. *See* **11032.**

13494. SCHENCK, CELESTE M. When the moderns write elegy: Crane, Kinsella, Nemerov. *See* **11593.**

Frances Newman

13495. DUGGAN, MARGARET MANNING. *The Gold-Fish Bowl*: Miss Newman's five-finger exercise. Unpub. doct. diss., Univ. of South Carolina, 1985. [Abstr. in DA (46) 1941A.]

Ngugi wa Thiong'o

13496. AMBANASOM, SHADRACH ATEKE. The adolescent protagonist in the African novel: an analysis of five African novels. *See* **12751.**

13497. BAILEY, DIANA. Ngugi wa Thiong'o, *The River Between*: a critical view. Ed. by YOLANDE CANTÙ. London: Collins; British Council, 1985. pp. 42. (Nexus.)

13498. COOPER, B. L. A theory of African literature and its application to texts by Wole Soyinka, Ayi Kwei Armah and Ngugi wa Thiong'o. *See* **11056.**

13499. CREHAN, STEWART. The politics of the signifier: Ngugi wa Thiong'o's *Petals of Blood*. WLWE (26:1) 1–24.

13500. EYOH, HANSEL NOLUMBE. Ngugi wa Thiong'o. JCL (21:1) 162–6 (interview).

13501. GLINGA, WERNER. *The River Between* and its forerunners: a contribution to the theory of the Kenyan novel. *See* **10797.**

bp Nichol

13502. BARBOUR, DOUGLAS. Some notes in progress about a work in process: bp Nichol's *The Martyrology*. OpL (6:5/6) 215–24.

13503. BARRETO-RIVERA, RAFAEL. Random walking *The Martyrology*'s Book v. OpL (6:5/6) 101–7.

13504. BOWERING, GEORGE. bp Nichol on the train. OpL (6:5/6) 7–20.

13505. CURRY, J. W. Notes toward a beepliography. OpL (6:5/6) 249–70.

13506. DAVEY, FRANK. Exegesis/eggs à Jesus: *The Martyrology* as a text in crisis. OpL (6:5/6) 169–81.

13507. DEWDNEY, CHRISTOPHER. B. P. specific writing. OpL (6:5/6) 185–7.

13508. DUTTON, PAUL. Confronting conventions: the musical/dramatic works of bpNichol. OpL (6:5/6) 131–40.

13509. HENDERSON, BRIAN. Soul rising out of the body of language: presence, process and faith in *The Martyrology*. OpL (6:5/6) 111–28.

13510. McCAFFERY, STEVE.   *The Martyrology* as paragram. OpL (6:5/6) 191–206.
13511. SCOBIE, STEPHEN.   Surviving the parah-raise. OpL (6:5/6) 48–68.
13512. SHIKATANI, GERRY.   Briefly, to martyr and suffer. OpL (6:5/6) 227–36.
13513. SMITH, STEVEN.   bp Nichol: sonic snapshots, fragmentary movements. OpL (6:5/6) 69–72.
13514. TOSTEVIN, LOLA LEMIRE.   Paternal body as outlaw. OpL (6:5/6) 77–80.

Peter Nicholas
13515. WORTHEN, W. B.   'Deciphering the British pantomime': *Poppy* and the rhetoric of political theater. Genre (19:2) 173–91.

Lorine Niedecker
13516. PENBERTHY, JENNY LYNN.   Lorine Niedecker and Louis Zukofsky: her poems and letters. Unpub. doct. diss., Univ. of British Columbia, 1985. [Abstr. in DA (47) 1326A.]

Anaïs Nin
13517. PAINE, SYLVIA JEAN.   Sense and transcendence: the art of Anaïs Nin, Vladimir Nabokov, and Samuel Beckett. See **11196.**
13518. SCHOLAR, NANCY.   Anaïs Nin. Boston, MA: G. K. Hall, 1984. pp. 143. (Twayne's US authors, 460.) Rev. by Bettina L. Knapp in MichQR (25:3) 624–6.

Frank Norris
13519. DOVER, LINDA A.   Frank Norris' *A Man's Woman*: the textual changes. RALS (13:2) 1983, 165–83.
13520. HOCHMAN, BARBARA.   Loss, habit, obsession: the governing dynamic of *McTeague*. SAF (14:2) 179–90.
13521. HUG, WILLIAM JOSEPH.   Frank Norris and formula fiction: the author and two early novels examined in the context of formula stories and the popular attitudes they express. Unpub. doct. diss., Auburn Univ., 1985. [Abstr. in DA (46) 3034A.]
13522. LEITZ, ROBERT C., III.   *A Christmas in the Transvaal*: an addition to the Norris canon. SAF (14:2) 221–4.
13523. MEZZINA, FRANCIS MARK.   Frank Norris' *Wave* writings. *See* **649.**
13524. MICHAELS, WALTER BENN.   Corporate fiction: Norris, Royce, and Arthur Machen. *In* (pp. 189–219) **47.**
13525. MITCHELL, LEE CLARK.   'Little pictures on the lacquered surface': the determining vocabularies of Norris's *Vandover and the Brute*. PLL (22:4) 386–405.
13526. PONCET, ANDRE.   Procédures de sémantisation dans la production du texte de *McTeague*. EA (39:1) 50–61.
13527. SPAUNHORST, FRANZ-PETER.   Literarische Kulturkritik als Dekodierung von Macht und Werten am Beispiel ausgewählter Romane von Upton Sinclair, Frank Norris, John Dos Passos und Sinclair Lewis. Ein Beitrag zur Theorie und Methode der Amerikastudien als Kulturwert. *See* **11692.**

Leslie Norris

13528. JENKINS, MIKE. The inner exile: the Merthyr poems of Leslie Norris. Poetry Wales (21:3) 76–82.

13529. MINHINNICK, ROBERT. Leslie Norris – insistent elegist. Poetry Wales (21:3) 83–6.

13530. SIMPSON, MERCER. Leslie Norris: reluctant exile, discovered alien. Poetry Wales (21:3) 87–94.

Alden Nowlan

13531. COGSWELL, FRED. Alden Nowlan as regional atavist. Stud-CanL (11:2) 206–25.

Nkem Nwankwo

13532. DOHERTY, JAIYEOLA. Die Satire im nigerianischen Roman. Die Rolle der Satire in den Romanwerken 4 nigerianischer Schriftsteller: T. M. Aluko, Chinua Achebe, Nkem Nwankwo und Wole Soyinka. *See* **10978.**

Joyce Carol Oates

13533. ÅKERMAN, NORDAL. En eftermiddag med Gore Vidal: och en timme med Miss Oates. (An afternoon with Gore Vidal: and an hour with Miss Oates.) Allt om böcker (1986:7/8) 2–7.

13534. COKER, JUDITH BRIGGS. Sexuality in discourse: feminine models in recent fiction by American women. *See* **10985.**

13535. HENKINS, KATHRYN MARIE. Joyce Carol Oates's America. Unpub. doct. diss., Claremont Graduate School. [Abstr. in DA (47) 2157A.]

13536. LERCANGÉE, FRANCINE. Joyce Carol Oates: an annotated bibliography. Introd. and annotations by BRUCE F. MICHELSON. New York; London: Garland. pp. xxii, 272. (Garland reference library of the humanities, 509.)

13537. SEVERIN, HERMANN. The image of the intellectual in the short stories of Joyce Carol Oates. Frankfurt: Lang. pp. 196. (European univ. studies, ser: 14, Anglo-Saxon language and literature, 159.)

'Flann O'Brien' (Brian O'Nolan, 'Myles na gCopaleen')

13538. CLUNE, ANNE. Flann O'Brien twenty years on. Linen Hall Review (3:2) [misnumbered 3:3] 4–7.

13539. HOPLEY, M. A. The works of Flann O'Brien. Unpub. doct. diss., Univ. of Essex, 1984.

13540. HURSON, TERESA ROSE. Fictional strategies in the novels of Flann O'Brien. Unpub. doct. diss., York Univ. (Canada), 1985. [Abstr. in DA (46) 2301A.]

13541. IMHOF, RÜDIGER (ed.). Alive–Alive O!: Flann O'Brien's *At Swim-Two-Birds*. Dublin: Wolfhound Press; Totowa, NJ: Barnes and Noble. pp. 213. Rev. by Mark Mortimer in TLS, 1 Aug., 845.

13542. O'TOOLE, MARY ALICE. The savage indignation of Brian O'Nolan: the mind and works of Flann O'Brien and Myles na gCopaleen. Unpub. doct. diss., Univ. of Tulsa. [Abstr. in DA (47) 1336A.]

13543. SIMPSON, P. A. The sociolinguistic analysis of literary dialogue, with specific reference to Flann 'O'Brien's *The Third Policeman*. *See* **1031.**

13544. THRONE, MARILYN. The provocative bicycle of Flann O'Brien's *The Third Policeman*. Éire–Ireland (21:4) 36–44.

Kate O'Brien
13545. DALSIMER, ADELE M. A not so simple saga: Kate O'Brien's *Without My Cloak*. Éire–Ireland (21:3) 55–71.

Tim O'Brien
13546. ZINS, DANIEL L. Imagining the real: the fiction of Tim O'Brien. HC (23) June, 1–12.

Sean O'Casey
13547. AYLING, RONALD (ed.). Seven plays by Sean O'Casey: a student's edition. Basingstoke: Macmillan, 1985. pp. xl, 545.

13548. BLAKE, ANN. The fame of Sean O'Casey: a reconsideration of the Dublin plays. Sydney Studies in English (12) 64–77.

13549. KOSOK, HEINZ. O'Casey the dramatist. (Bibl. 1985, 12333.) Rev. by Christopher Murray in IUR (16) 238–9.

13550. SCHRANK, BERNICE. Anatomizing an insurrection: Sean O'Casey's *The Plough and the Stars*. ModDr (29:2) 216–28.

13551. —— Language and silence in *The Plough and the Stars*. MS (80) 289–96.

13552. THOMSON, LESLIE. Opening the eyes of the audience: visual and verbal imagery in *Juno and the Paycock*. ModDr (29:4) 556–66.

13553. WEBB, J. Last stop Kylenamoe: a re-assessment of Sean O'Casey's drama. Unpub. doct. diss., Univ. of Reading, 1983.

Flannery O'Connor
13554. ALLEN, WILLIAM RODNEY. The cage of matter: the world as zoo in Flannery O'Connor's *Wise Blood*. AL (58:2) 256–70.

13555. ARBEIT, MARCEL. Morální aspekty románů Flannery O'Connorové a Walkera Percyho. (The novels of Flannery O'Connor and Walker Percy: moral aspects.) *In* (pp. 18) **4.**

13556. BURKE, WILLIAM. Displaced communities and literary form in Flannery O'Connor's *The Displaced Person*. MFS (32:2) 219–27.

13557. BURNS, M. The ridiculous and the sublime: the fiction of Flannery O'Connor. Unpub. doct. diss., Univ. of Manchester, 1984. [Abstr. in IT (35) 54–5.]

13558. CHEW, MARTHA. Flannery O'Connor's double-edged satire: the idiot daughter versus the lady PhD. SoQ (19:2) 1981, 17–25.

13559. CIUBA, GARY MARTIN. The fierce nun of *The Last Gentleman*: Percy's vision of Flannery O'Connor. FOB (15) 57–66.

13560. DRAKE, ROBERT. The lady *Frum* somewhere: Flannery O'Connor then and now. ModAge (29:3) 1985, 212–23.

13561. DUCKWORTH, VICTORIA. The redemptive impulse: *Wise Blood* and *The Color Purple*. FOB (15) 51–6.

13562. GENTRY, MARSHALL BRUCE. Flannery O'Connor's religion of the grotesque. Jackson: Mississippi UP. pp. 177. Rev. by Sura P. Rath in FOB (15) 82–7.

13563. GIDDEN, NANCY ANN. Classical agents of Christian grace in Flannery O'Connor's *Greenleaf*. SSF (23:2) 201–2.

13564. HEHER, MICHAEL.   Grotesque grace in the factious commonwealth. FOB (15) 69–81.

13565. KESSLER, EDWARD.   Flannery O'Connor and the language of apocalypse. Princeton, NJ: Princeton UP. pp. 163. Rev. by Ralph C. Wood in FOB (15) 88–91.

13566. KINNEY, ARTHUR F.   Flannery O'Connor and the fiction of grace. MassR (27:1) 71–96.

13567. LAZENBLATT, W. W. G.   The female mind in modern Southern fiction: the treatment and expression of female consciousness in the work of Flannery O'Connor, Carson McCullers and Eudora Welty. *See* **13116.**

13568. McMILLAN, NORMAN.   Mrs McIntire, Mrs Shortley, and the priest: empathic understanding in Flannery O'Connor's *The Displaced Person*. PhilP (31) 1985, 97–103.

13569. MAY, JOHN R.   The methodological limits of Flannery O'Connor's critics. FOB (15) 16–28.

13570. MEYER, WILLIAM E., JR.   Flannery O'Connor's 'two sets of eyes'. SoS (25:3) 284–94.

13571. MOORE, SUSAN.   The art of Flannery O'Connor: the habit of being. Quadrant (30:7/8) 111–13.

13572. OLIVER, BILL.   Flannery O'Connor's compassion. FOB (15) 1–15.

13573. OWER, JOHN.   The penny and the nickel in *Everything That Rises Must Converge*. SSF (23:1) 107–10.

13574. RIIS, TORBEN.   Flannery O'Connor: kristen realisme er ikke sentimental. (Flannery O'Connor: Christian realism is not sentimental.) Tidens Tegn (Copenhagen) 1984, 46–50.

13575. SCOUTEN, KENNETH.   *The Partridge Festival*: manuscript revisions. FOB (15) 35–41.

13576. SMITH, LESLIE WRIGHT.   The elusive confessant: a study of author and character in Dostoyevsky, Mauriac, and O'Connor. Unpub. doct. diss., Univ. of Texas at Austin. [Abstr. in DA (47) 1722A.]

13577. SPIVEY, TED R.   Flannery O'Connor's quest for a critic. FOB (15) 29–33.

13578. STEPHENS, C. RALPH (ed.).   The correspondence of Flannery O'Connor and the Brainard Cheneys. Jackson: Mississippi UP. pp. 214. Rev. by Sarah Gordon in FOB (15) 92–5.

13579. TALLANT, CAROLE ELLSWORTH.   Disjunctive ambiguity and the performance of Flannery O'Connor's *The Displaced Person*. SSJ (51:2) 106–24.

13580. THOMPSON, TERRY.   The killers in O'Connor's *A Good Man Is Hard to Find*. NCL (16:4) 4.

13581. WESTLING, LOUISE.   Demeter and Kore, Southern style. PCP (19) 1984, 101–7.

13582. —— Flannery O'Connor's revelations to 'A'. SoHR (20:1) 15–22.

13583. WHITT, MARGARET.   Flannery O'Connor's ladies. FOB (15) 42–50.

'Frank O'Connor' (Michael O'Donovan)

13584. SHERRY, RUTH.   The Irish working class in fiction. *In* (pp. 110–23) **6.**

13585. STOREY, MICHAEL L.   The guests of Frank O'Connor and Albert Camus. CLS (23:3) 250–62.

Clifford Odets

13586. HAN, YOUNGLIM.   Clifford Odets eui yeongeuk i ginin sahoesung: *Paradise Lost* reul jungsim euro. (Clifford Odets's social play: the example of *Paradise Lost*.) JELL (32:2) 255–68.

13587. SABINSON, ERIC MITCHELL.   Script and transcript: the writings of Clifford Odets, Lillian Hellman and Arthur Miller in relation to their testimony before the U.S. House Committee on Un-American Activities. *See* **12353.**

Julia O'Faolain

13588. WEEKES, ANN.   Diarmuid and Gráinne again: Julia O'Faolain's *No Country for Old Men*. Éire–Ireland (21:1) 89–102.

Sean O'Faolain

13589. MUTRAN, MUNIRA H.   Sean O'Faolain's 'pleasure' principle. Threshold (36) 1–5.

Howard O'Hagan

13590. DAVIDSON, ARNOLD E.   Silencing the word in Howard O'Hagan's *Tay John*. CanL (110) 30–44.

13591. FEE, MARGERY.   Howard O'Hagan's *Tay John*: making new world myth. CanL (110) 8–27.

Seumas O'Kelly

13592. GONZALES, ALEXANDER G.   Seumas O'Kelly and James Joyce. *See* **12655.**

Christopher Okigbo

13593. MAJA-PEARCE, ADEWALE (introd.).   Collected poems. London: Heinemann. pp. xxvii, 99.

Edith Olivier

13594. GILSON, DAVID.   Edith Olivier: some uncollected authors, LIV. BC (35:3) 305–25. (Includes bibliography.)

Tillie Olsen

13595. JACOBS, N. M.   Olsen's *O Yes*: Alva's vision as childbirth account. NCL (16:1) 7–8.

13596. NIEHUS, EDWARD L.; JACKSON, TERESA.   Polar stars, pyramids, and *Tell Me a Riddle*. ANQ (24:5/6) 77–83.

Charles Olson

13597. LOVECCHIO, JOHN PAUL.   Geranos: Charles Olson and the dance of the projective. Unpub. doct. diss., Univ. of Iowa, 1985. [Abstr. in DA (46) 1627A.]

13598. MCPHERON, WILLIAM.   Charles Olson: the critical reception, 1941–1983; a bibliographic guide. New York; London: Garland. pp. xxi, 427. (Garland reference library of the humanities, 619.)

13599. WHITE, KENNETH.   Poetics of the open universe. Cencrastus (22) 17–19.

Michael Ondaatje

13600. JACOBS, NAOMI. Michael Ondaatje and the new fiction biographies. StudCanL (11:1) 2–18.

13601. SOLECKI, SAM (ed.). Spider blues: essays on Michael Ondaatje. Montreal: Véhicule Press. pp. 369. Rev. by Alice Van Wart in CanP (19) 112–16.

Eugene O'Neill

13602. ADLER, THOMAS P. 'Daddy spoke to me!': gods lost and found in *Long Days's Journey into Night* and *Through a Glass Darkly*. CompDr (20:4) 341–8.

13603. ALVIS, JOHN. On the American line: O'Neill's *Mourning Becomes Electra* and the principles of the founding. SoR (22:1) 69–85.

13604. BARLOW, JUDITH E. Final acts: the creation of three late O'Neill plays. Athens: Georgia UP, 1985. pp. vii, 215. Rev. by James A. Robinson in AL (58:2) 306–7.

13605. BLACK, STEPHEN A. Letting the dead be dead: a reinterpretation of *A Moon for the Misbegotten*. ModDr (29:4) 544–55.

13606. BOWER, MARTHA. The cycle women and Carlotta Monterey O'Neill. EON (10:2) 29–33.

13607. BOWER, MARTHA E. GILMAN. The making of Eugene O'Neill's cycle plays: an analysis of O'Neill's writing process and gender role reversal. Unpub. doct. diss., Univ. of New Hampshire, 1985. [Abstr. in DA (47) 528A.]

13608. BRYER, JACKSON R. (ed.); ALVAREZ, RUTH M. (asst ed.). 'The theatre we worked for': the letters of Eugene O'Neill to Kenneth Macgowan. (Bibl. 1984, 12450.) Rev. by Yvonne Shafer in TS (30) 1983/84, 68–70.

13609. DRUCKER, TRUDY. The return of O'Neill's 'play of old sorrow'. EON (10:3) 21–3.

13610. ÉGRI, PÉTER. Chekhov and O'Neill: the uses of short story in Chekhov's and O'Neill's plays. Budapest: Akadémiai Kiadó. pp. 182.

13611. —— Novel in the drama. Eugene O'Neill: *More Stately Mansions*. ActLitH (26:3/4) 1984, 339–64.

13612. —— The social and spiritual history of the American dream: Eugene O'Neill, *A Tale of Possessors Self-dispossessed*. ActLitH (28:1/2) 65–89.

13613. FAMBROUGH, PRESTON. The tragic cosmology of O'Neill's *Desire Under the Elms*. EON (10:2) 25–8.

13614. FLOYD, VIRGINIA. The plays of Eugene O'Neill: a new assessment. New York: Ungar, 1985. pp. xxvii, 605. Rev. by Stephen A. Black in AL (58:4) 652–3.

13615. FRENZ, HORST. Eugene O'Neill and China. TamkR (10) 1980, 5–16.

13616. GARVEY, SHEILA HICKEY. Rethinking O'Neill. EON (10:3) 13–20.

13617. GRIGORESCU, DAN; FILIP, MIRCEA (eds). O'Neill şi renaşterea tragediei. (O'Neill and the rebirth of tragedy). By PETRU COMARNESCU. Cluj-Napoca: Dacia. pp. 340.

13618. KIM, HI-SOO. O'Neill eui whogi geuk: bigeukjeok gonoe wa guwon. (Tragic suffering and salvation in O'Neill's later plays.) Unpub. doct. diss., Chungang Univ. (Seoul).

13619. KREUTZER, EBERHARD. Eugen O'Neills *Bound East for Cardiff.* Genese, Struktur und Kontext eines paradigmatischen Einakters. Anglistik & Englischunterricht (28) 33–47.

13620. LEE, HAENG-SOO. *Beyond the Horizon* eui sinhwa won- hyeongjeok bunsuk. (The archetypal analysis of *Beyond the Horizon.*) JUJH (21) 1985, 127–43.

13621. LEE, TAE-DONG. Realism gwa *Bam euro eui geen yeoro*: jeontong gwa byeonhyeuk. (Realism in O'Neill's *Long Day's Journey into Night.*) JELL (31:4) 1985, 643–57.

13622. LLOYD, D. W. Mystical experience in *Long Day's Journey into Night.* UES (24:2) 17–21.

13623. LONG, DEBORAH MARIE. The existential quest: family and form in selected American plays. *See* **13257.**

13624. McDONOUGH, EDWIN JOSEPH. Quintero directs O'Neill: an examination of eleven plays of Eugene O'Neill staged by Jose Quintero in New York City, 1956–1981. Unpub. doct. diss., New York Univ. [Abstr. in DA (47) 1119A.]

13625. MAHMOUD, MOHAMED A. W. A stylistic, sociolinguistic, and discourse analysis of linguistic naturalism in selected plays of Arthur Miller and Eugene O'Neill. *See* **1233.**

13626. MAUFORT, MARC. Communication as translation of the self: Jamesian inner monologue in O'Neill's *Strange Interlude* (1927). *In* (pp. 319–28) **12.**

13627. —— Visions of the American experience: the O'Neill–Melville connection. *See* **8931.**

13628. MOLESKI, JOSEPH J.; STROUPE, JOHN H. Jean Anouilh and Eugene O'Neill: repetition as negativity. CompDr (20:4) 315–26.

13629. RANALD, MARGARET LOFTUS. The Eugene O'Neill com- panion. Westport, CT; London: Greenwood Press, 1984. pp. xi, 827.

13630. SAUVAGE, LEO. Tragic misalliances. *See* **12270.**

13631. SCHMITT, PATRICK E. *The Fountain, Marco Millions*, and *Lazarus Laughed*: O'Neill's 'exotics' as history plays. Unpub. doct. diss., Univ. of Wisconsin–Madison, 1985. [Abstr. in DA (46) 3537A.]

13632. WAINSCOTT, RONALD H. Harnessing O'Neill's Furies: Philip Moeller directs *Dynamo*. EON (10:3) 3–13.

13633. WATT, STEPHEN. O'Neill and Otto Rank: doubles, 'death instincts', and trauma of birth. CompDr (20:3) 211–30.

George Oppen

13634. BARNETT, ANTHONY. A note about George Oppen. Paideuma (10:1) 1981, 22.

13635. CORMAN, CID. The experience of poetry. Paideuma (10:1) 1981, 99–103.

13636. CUDDIHY, MICHAEL. George Oppen: a loved and native rock. Paideuma (10:1) 1981, 25–6.

13637. FREEMAN, JOHN (introd.). Not comforts // but vision: essays on the poetry of George Oppen. Budleigh Salterton: Interim, 1985. pp. 104.

13638. GERBER, DAN. Of fathers. Paideuma (10:1) 1981, 149–51.

13639. GRIFFIN, JONATHAN. George and Mary Oppen. Paideuma (10:1) 1981, 27.

13640. LINENTHAL, MARK. An appreciation. Paideuma (10:1) 1981, 37–8.

13641. SILLIMAN, RON. Third phase objectivism. Paideuma (10:1) 1981, 85–9.

13642. SORRENTINO, GILBERT. George Oppen: smallness of cause. Paideuma (10:1) 1981, 23–4.

13643. WEINBERGER, ELIOT. A little heap for George Oppen. Paideuma (10:1) 1981, 131–6.

E. Phillips Oppenheim

13644. SNOW, E. E. E. Phillips Oppenheim: storyteller: 1866 to 1946. Leicester: Evington, 1985. pp. 21.

Joe Orton

13645. LAHR, JOHN (ed.). The Orton diaries: including the correspondence of Edna Welthorpe and others. London: Methuen. pp. 304. Rev. by Sue Townsend in Listener, 13 Nov., 23; by Tony Gould in TLS, 14 Nov., 1266; by Craig Raine in LRB (8:21) 3, 5–6.

'George Orwell' (Eric Blair)

13646. ATKINSON, WILLIAM. Big Brother George: the end of *1984*. SoCR (17:1) 1984, 16–27.

13647. BÖKER, UWE. Zur Namengebung in Orwells *1984*. Ang (104:1/2) 122–31.

13648. BONIFAS, GILBERT. George Orwell: l'engagement. (Bibl. 1985, 12463.) Rev. by Hena Maes-Jelinek in EA (39:1) 108–10.

13649. CARTER, M. A. Existential authenticity in the novels of George Orwell. Unpub. doct. diss., CNAA, 1983.

13650. CARTER, STEVE. 'Freedom is slavery': history, the reader, and *1984*. SoCR (17:1) 1984, 3–15.

13651. CRICK, BERNARD (introd.). Nineteen eighty-four. Text ed. by PETER DAVISON. (Bibl. 1985, 12470.) Rev. by Jenny Mezciems in MLR (81:4) 994–6.

13652. DAVISON, PETER (ed.). Homage to Catalonia. London: Secker & Warburg. pp. 272. (Complete works of George Orwell, 6.)

13653. ECKSTEIN, ARTHUR. *1984* and George Orwell's other view of capitalism. ModAge (29:1) 1985, 11–19.

13654. GOOD, GRAHAM. The structure of Orwell's world view. ESCan (12:3) 315–35.

13655. KIM, TAE-SUNG. Gurapa choehwo eui ingan: *1984* e daehan han gochal. (A study of *1984*: the last human being in Europe.) IKY (55) 79–90.

13656. KNAPP, MONA. Canopuspeak: Doris Lessing's *Sentimental Agents* and Orwell's *1984*. See **13008.**

13657. LANGE, BERND-PETER. Orwell und die Utopie. GRM (36:2) 195–208.

13658. METTINGER, ARTHUR. Unendurable unpersons unmask unexampled untruths: remarks on the functions of negative prefixes in Orwell's *1984*. *See* **2139.**

13659. PATAI, DAPHNE. The Orwell mystique: a study in male ideology. (Bibl. 1985, 12498.) Rev. by Erika Gottlieb in CR (30:1) 113–14.

13660. REILLY, PATRICK. George Orwell: the age's adversary. Basingstoke: Macmillan. pp. xiii, 316.

13661. ROSSI, JOHN. Orwell and the Irish. Éire–Ireland (21:4) 142–5.

13662. SLATER, IAN. Orwell: the road to airstrip one. New York; London: Norton, 1985. pp. 302.

13663. STEWART, D. H. Shooting elephants right. *See* **12806.**

13664. TEDLOCK, DAVID. Orwell's anti-fascists: real readers, not uncles. CCC (37:2) 212–16.

13665. TERUYA, YOSHIO. George Orwell: bungaku to seiji. (George Orwell: literature and politics.) Tokyo: Kojinsha. pp. 282.

13666. WARNER, J. C. Liberalism and Marxism in the work of George Orwell. Unpub. doct. diss., Univ. of Oxford, 1983.

13667. WATSON, GEORGE. Orwell's Nazi renegade. SewR (94:3) 486–95.

John Osborne

13668. BERGE, MARIT. Jimmy Porter – Osborne's Hedda Gabler? *In* (pp. 201–12) **18.**

13669. LAWSON, MARK. Looking back in anger. Independent, 30 Oct., 12. (Interview.)

13670. READER, ROBERT DEAN. Illusion and reality: an approach to the 'history play' using *Luther* by John Osborne as the model. Unpub. doct. diss., Columbia Univ. Teachers College, 1985. [Abstr. in DA (46) 3537A.]

13671. WATSON, GEORGE. Osborne, Pinter, Stoppard: a playful look at London since 1956. VQR (62) 271–84.

Vincent O'Sullivan

13672. BLACK, SEBASTIAN. Ways of seeing: Vincent O'Sullivan's *Shuriken*. Landfall (40:1) 57–75.

Jenny Overton

13673. GOUGH, JOHN. Jenny Overton's quiet masterpieces. Junior Bookshelf (49) 109–14.

Wilfred Owen

13674. BELL, JOHN (ed.). Selected letters. Oxford: OUP, 1985. pp. xviii, 376.

13675. HIBBERD, DOMINIC. Owen the poet. Basingstoke: Macmillan. pp. xii, 244.

13676. MACHINEK, ANNA. Smile, smile, smile – the study of laughter in Wilfred Owen's poetry. KN (33:4) 525–37.

13677. NORGATE, PAUL. *Dulce et Decorum Est* and some amendments to the dating of Wilfred Owen's letters. NQ (33:2) 186–90.

13678. SILKIN, JON (ed.). Wilfred Owen: the poems. Harmondsworth: Penguin, 1985. pp. 192. (Penguin poetry library.)

13679. STALLWORTHY, JON (ed.). The poems of Wilfred Owen. London: Hogarth Press, 1985. pp. 200. (Hogarth poetry.)

13680. WORMLEIGHTON, S. J. A study of the Romantic impulse in the work of Wilfred Owen, with particular reference to the idea of the hero and the images of darkness. Unpub. doct. diss., Univ. of Exeter. [Abstr. in IT (36) 476.]

13681. WORMLEIGHTON, SIMON. Some echoes of Barbusse's *Under Fire* in Wilfred Owen's poems. NQ (33:2) 190–1.

Ferdinand Oyono

13682. OGUNSANWO, OLATUBOSUN. The narrative voice in two novels of Ferdinand Oyono. ESA (29:2) 97–120.

Cynthia Ozick

13683. EHRLICH, REVA. A study of Jewish literary identity in contemporary writers in America: a curriculum. *See* **11219.**

13684. KIELSKY, VERA EMUNA. Inevitable exiles: Cynthia Ozick's view of the precariousness of Jewish existence in a Gentile world. Unpub. doct. diss., Arizona State Univ., 1985. [Abstr. in DA (46) 3719A.]

Frank G. Paci

13685. SCIFF-ZAMARO, ROBERTA. *Black Madonna*: a search for the Great Mother. *In* (pp. 77–99) **13.**

P. K. Page

13686. BENTLEY, D. M. R. 'A subtle mourning': P. K. Page's *The Permanent Tourists*. CanP (19) 68–73.

13687. NEUMAN, SHIRLEY. Teaching P. K. Page's *The Permanent Tourists*. CanP (19) 65–8.

13688. RICOU, LAURIE (introd.) Literary theory in the classroom: three views of P. K. Page's *The Permanent Tourists*. CanP (19) 57–9.

13689. STOCKHOLDER, KAY. Devouring eyes in *The Permanent Tourists* and *Cry Ararat!* CanP (19) 59–64.

Grace Paley

13690. MARCHANT, PETER; INGERSOLL, EARL (eds). A conversation with Grace Paley. MassR (26:4) 1985, 606–14.

Dorothy Parker

13691. BONE, MARTHA DENHAM. Dorothy Parker and *New Yorker* satire. *See* **563.**

13692. MITSCH, RUTHMARIE H. Parker's *Iseult of Brittany*. Exp (44:2) 37–40.

Kenneth Patchen

13693. NELSON, RAYMOND. Kenneth Patchen and American mysticism. (Bibl. 1985, 12530.) Rev. by Victor A. Kramer in AL (58:1) 136–7.

Katherine Paterson

13694. KNIGHT, K. FAWN. A study of the revision process as it is revealed in the manuscripts of Katherine Paterson's *The Great Gilly Hopkins*. Unpub. doct. diss., Oakland Univ., 1985. [Abstr. in DA (47) 2062A–3A.]

Alan Paton

13695. ELLIS, MARK SPENCER (ed.). Cry, the beloved country: a story of comfort in desolation. Harlow: Longman. pp. xxvi, 268. (Longman study texts.)

Orlando Patterson

13696. McDonald, Avis G.   The crisis of the absurd in Orlando Patterson's *An Absence of Ruins*. Kp (8:2) 85–97.

Elliot Paul

13697. Meral, Jean.   Elliot Paul, auteur de romans policiers. Caliban (23) 87–93.

Okot p'Bitek

13698. Ofuani, Ogo A.   The image of the prostitute: a reconsideration of Okot p'Bitek's Malaya. Kp (8:3) 100–21.

13699. Weinstein, Mark.   The Song of Solomon and *Song of Lawino*. WLWE (26:2) 243–4.

Lee Pennington

13700. Wills, J. Robert.   Prevailing shadows: the plays of Lee Pennington. SoQ (20:1) 1981, 25–34.

Walker Percy

13701. Arbeit, Marcel.   Morální aspekty románů Flannery O'Connorové a Walkera Percyho. (The novels of Flannery O'Connor and Walker Percy: moral aspects.) *In* (pp. 18) **4.**

13702. Baker, Lewis.   The Percys of Mississippi: politics and literature in the new South. (Bibl. 1984, 12630.) Rev. by Veronica A. Makowsky in Review (7) 1985, 324–5.

13703. Belsches, Alan T.   Life over death: the use of memory in Walker Percy's *The Second Coming*. SoQ (23:4) 1985, 37–47.

13704. Broughton, Panthea Reid (ed.).   The art of Walker Percy: stratagems for being. (Bibl. 1985, 12537.) Rev. by Veronica A. Makowsky in Review (7) 1985, 313–16.

13705. Ciuba, Gary Martin.   The apocalyptic vision in the fiction of Walker Percy. Unpub. doct. diss., Fordham Univ. [Abstr. in DA (47) 1321A.]

13706. —— The fierce nun of *The Last Gentleman*: Percy's vision of Flannery O'Connor. See **13559.**

13707. Coles, Robert.   Walker Percy: an American search. (Bibl. 1985, 12539.) Rev. by Veronica A. Makowsky in Review (7) 1985, 310–13.

13708. Davis, J. Madison.   Walker Percy's *Lancelot*: the Shakespearean threads. *In* (pp. 159–72) **51.**

13709. Desmond, John.   Walker Percy and T. S. Eliot: the Lancelot Andrewes connection. See **5260.**

13710. Gunter, Elizabeth Ellington.   The critical response to philosophical ideas in Walker Percy's novels. Unpub. doct. diss., North Texas State Univ., 1985. [Abstr. in DA (47) 178A.]

13711. Horvath, Brooke Kenton.   Dropping out: spiritual crisis and countercultural attitudes in four American novelists of the 1960s. See **11324.**

13712. Howland, Mary Deems.   The gift of the other: Gabriel

Marcel's concept of intersubjectivity in Walker Percy's novels. Unpub. doct. diss., Univ. of Maryland. [Abstr. in DA (47) 2158A.]

13713. LAWSON, LEWIS A. Moviemaking in Percy's *Lancelot*. SCR (3:4) 78–94.

13714. —— KRAMER, VICTOR A. (eds). Conversations with Walker Percy. (Bibl. 1985, 12542.) Rev. by J. Donald Crowley in SAF (14:2) 241–3; by Veronica A. Makowsky in SCR (3:2) 116–17.

13715. LUSCHEI, MARTIN. The sovereign wayfarer: Walker Percy's diagnosis of the malaise. Baton Rouge: Louisiana State UP, 1972. pp. viii, 261. Rev. by Veronica A. Makowsky in Review (7) 1985, 306–10.

13716. MAKOWSKY, VERONICA A. The message in the novels: Walker Percy and the critics. Review (7) 1985, 305–27 (review-article).

13717. PARK, JEONG-MI. Religious experience in the novels of Walker Percy. Unpub. doct. diss., Saint Louis Univ., 1984. [Abstr. in DA (46) 1943A.]

13718. POTEAT, PATRICIA LEWIS. Walker Percy and the old modern age: reflections on language, argument, and the telling of stories. (Bibl. 1985, 12546.) Rev. by Mark Johnson in PhilL (10:1) 129–30; by Lachlan Mackinnon in TLS, 26 May, 536.

13719. RHEIN, PHILLIP H. The search for sin. *In* (pp. 369–73) **19**.

13720. SCHREIBER, PAUL CLIFTON. Observing communion: an investigation of alienation and sacramental re-entry in the novels of Walker Percy. Unpub. doct. diss., Univ. of California, Santa Cruz, 1985. [Abstr. in DA (46) 1943A.]

13721. THARPE, JAC (ed.). Walker Percy: art and ethics. Jackson: Mississippi UP, 1980. pp. viii, 160. (Cf. bibl. 1984, 12636.) Rev. by Veronica A. Makowsky in Review (7) 1985, 319–22.

S. J. Perelman

13722. GALE, STEVEN H. S. J. Perelman: an annotated bibliography. New York; London: Garland, 1985. pp. xxviii, 162. (Garland reference library of the humanities, 531.)

13723. HERRMANN, DOROTHY. S. J. Perelman: a life. New York: Putnam. pp. 337. Rev. by Stefan Kanfer in Time, 13 Oct., 100; by Janice Harayda in BW, 10 Aug., 43–4; by Jonathan Yardley in BkW, 27 July, 3.

Lenrie Peters

13724. KLÍMA, VLADIMÍR. Lenrie Peters: selected poetry. SvL (31:4) 240–1.

Ann Petry

13725. WASHINGTON, GLADYS J. A world made cunningly: a closer look at Ann Petry's short fiction. CLAJ (30:1) 14–29.

Meredith Ann Pierce

13726. PHILLIPS, ROBERT; RIEGER, BRANIMIR. The agony and the ecstasy: a Jungian analysis of two vampire novels, Meredith Ann Pierce's *The Darkangel* and Bram Stoker's *Dracula. See* **9280.**

Marge Piercy

13727. NOWIK, NAN. Mixing art and politics: the writings of Adrienne Rich, Marge Piercy, and Alice Walker. CR (30:2) 208–18.

Harold Pinter

13728. CARDULLO, BERT. Anonymity in *The Birthday Party*. NCL (16:4) 9–10.

13729. —— Comedy and meaning in the work of Harold Pinter. NCL (16:3) 9–12.

13730. DE REUCK, J. A. *Old Times* and Pinter's dramatic method. ESA (29:2) 121–30.

13731. DIAMOND, ELIN. Pinter's comic play. Lewisburg, PA: Bucknell UP, 1985. pp. 241. Rev. by Austin E. Quigley in TJ (38:4) 513–14.

13732. DOBREZ, L. A. C. The existential and its exits: literary and philosophical perspectives on the work of Beckett, Ionesco, Genet, and Pinter. See **11170.**

13733. FISCHER-SEIDEL, THERESE. Mythenparodie im modernen englischen und amerikanischen Drama. Tradition und Kommunikation bei Tennessee Williams, Edward Albee, Samuel Beckett und Harold Pinter. See **11011.**

13734. HORNÁT, JAROSLAV. Pinterův návrat domů. (Pinter's *The Homecoming*.) *In* (pp. 27–8) **4.**

13735. JOHNSON, R. THOMAS. Harold Pinter: poet of anxiety. Unpub. doct. diss., Univ. of Delaware, 1985. [Abstr. in DA (46) 1634A.]

13736. KENDZORA, KATHRYN LOUISE. Going between novel and film: Harold Pinter's adaptation of *The Go-Between*. See **9995.**

13737. LECCA, DOINA. Human communication – models for analysis. Bucharest: Bucharest Univ., 1985. pp. 228.

13738. NISCHIK, REINGARD M. Das groteske Kurzdrama und der Anreiz zur Enträtselung. Harold Pinters *The Dumb Waiter*. Anglistik & Englischunterricht (28) 125–48.

13739. POPESCU, MARIAN. Cuvintele tăcerii: Harold Pinter. (The words of silence: Harold Pinter.) Ramuri, 15 Mar., 12.

13740. RAUCHBAUER, OTTO. Aidan Higgins, *Killachter Meadow* und *Langrishe, Go Down* sowie Harold Pinters Fernsehfilm *Langrishe, Go Down*: Variationen eines Motivs. See **12423.**

13741. SAKELLARIDOU-HADZISPYROU, E. Masks of women: a study of female characters in Harold Pinter's dramatic work. Unpub. doct. diss., Univ. of London (Royal Holloway Coll.), 1984. [Abstr. in IT (35) 549.]

13742. SALEM, DANIEL. The impact of Pinter's work. Ariel (17:1) 71–83.

13743. SCOTT, MICHAEL (ed.). *The Birthday Party, The Caretaker, The Homecoming*: a casebook. Basingstoke: Macmillan. pp. 208.

13744. WATSON, GEORGE. Osborne, Pinter, Stoppard: a playful look at London since 1956. See **13671.**

13745. YUN, MIDUCK. Harold Pinter eui heuigok jakpum e natanan blindness. (Blindness in Harold Pinter's plays.) JELL (32:1) 81–104.

Robert M. Pirsig

13746. BURNHAM, CHRISTOPHER C. Heroes obscured. *Zen and the Art of Motorcycle Maintenance*. SDR (24:2) 151–60.

'Jean Plaidy' (Eleanor Burford, 'Phillippa Carr', 'Elbur Ford', 'Victoria Holt', 'Kathleen Kellow', 'Ellalice Tate')

13746a. BAYER-BERENBAUM, LINDA. The gothic imagination: expansion in gothic literature and art. See **7202.**

Sylvia Plath

13747. AXELROD, STEVEN GOULD. Plath's literary relations: an essay and an index to the *Journals* and *Letters Home*. RALS (14:1/2) 1984, 59–84.

13748. HUGHES, TED (sel.). Sylvia Plath's selected poems. London: Faber & Faber, 1985. pp. 85.

13749. LARKIN, JOAN. For children with smart ears. *See* **13325.**

13750. LINDBERG-SEYERSTED, BRITA. Gender and women's literature: thoughts on a relationship illustrated by the cases of Emily Dickinson and Sylvia Plath. *See* **8127.**

13751. MAHLENDORF, URSULA R. The wellsprings of literary creation: an analysis of male and female 'artist stories' from the German Romantics to American writers of the present. *See* **7858.**

13752. MATOVICH, RICHARD M. A concordance to the collected poems of Sylvia Plath. New York; London: Garland. pp. xi, 623. (Garland reference library of the humanities, 618.)

13753. OWEN, WENDY. 'A riddle in nine syllables': female creativity in the poetry of Sylvia Plath. Unpub. doct. diss., Yale Univ., 1985. [Abstr. in DA (47) 1319A.]

13754. PLUMLY, STANLEY. The abrupt edge. *See* **7697.**

13755. WALBURG, LORI. Plath's *Brasilia*. Exp (44:3) 60–2.

William Plomer

13756. GRAY, STEPHEN. William Plomer's stories: the South African origins of new literature modes. JCL (21:1) 53–61.

13757. SKINNER, DOUGLAS REID. Problems of definition: some thoughts after reading William Plomer's *Selected Poems*. Upstream (4:1) 26–8.

Hal Porter

13758. BURNS, D. R. *The Watcher on the Cast Iron Balcony*: Hal Porter's triumph of creative contradiction. ALS (12:3) 359–66 (review-article).

Katherine Anne Porter

13759. BEVEVINO, MARY MARGARET. The metamorphosis of economic disillusionment in Katherine Anne Porter's society. Unpub. doct. diss., Pennsylvania State Univ., 1985. [Abstr. in DA (46) 3030A.]

13760. HATCHETT, JUDIE JAMES. Identity, autonomy, and community: explorations of failure in the fiction of Katherine Anne Porter. Unpub. doct. diss., Univ. of Louisville. [Abstr. in DA (47) 2157A.]

13761. HOŁOTA, MACIEJ. Wzorce struktur krótkiej prozy narracyjnej Katarzyny Anny Porter. (Structural patterns of Katherine Anne Porter's short narrative prose.) Lublin, Poland: Uniwersytet Marii Curie-Skłodowskiej, 1985. pp. 176. (Uniwersytet Marii Curie-Skłodowskiej. Wydzial Humanistyczny.)

13762. MEYERS, ROBERT. Porter's *The Jilting of Granny Weatherall*. Exp (44:2) 37.

13763. SCOTT, SHIRLEY CLAY. The mind of Katherine Anne Porter. Nimrod (25:1) 1982, 7–19.

13764. UNRUE, DARLENE HARBOUR. Truth and vision in Katherine Anne Porter's fiction. Athens: Georgia UP, 1985. pp. xiv, 267. Rev. by Carol MacCurdy in AL (58:3) 457; by George Hendrick in JEGP (85:3) 475.

Beatrix Potter

13765. CAVALIERO, GLEN (ed.).   Beatrix Potter's journal. Harmondsworth: Warne. pp. 317, (plates) 8. Rev. by M. C. in Junior Bookshelf (50:4) 137.

13766. HOBBS, A. S.; WHALLEY, J. I. (eds).   Beatrix Potter: the V & A Collection. *See* **233.**

13767. LANE, MARGARET.   The tale of Beatrix Potter: a biography. Harmondsworth: Warne, 1985. pp. 174. (Second ed.: first ed. 1946.)

13768. TAYLOR, JUDY.   Beatrix Potter: artist, storyteller and countrywoman. London: Warne. pp. 224. Rev. by Glen Cavaliero in TLS, 5 Dec., 1378.

Dennis Potter

13769. LENNON, PETER.   A man with a lash. Listener (116) 20 Nov., 14–15.

13770. MARS-JONES, ADAM.   The art of illness. Independent, 14 Nov., 11 (interview).

Ezra Pound

13771. ALMAGRO, MANUEL.   De lo temático a lo estructural: guerra y usura en la obra de Ezra Pound. (From theme to structure: war and usury in Ezra Pound's work.) Atlantis (8) 71–83.

13772. ANDERSON, DAVID.   Breaking the silence: the interview of Vanni Ronsisvalle and Pier Paolo Pasolini with Ezra Pound in 1968. Paideuma (10:2) 1981, 331–45.

13773. BACIGALUPO, MASSIMO.   Who built the temple? or, thoughts on Pound, *res* and *verba*. Paideuma (13) 1984, 49–63.

13774. —— (ed.).   Ezra Pound: un poeta a Rapallo. Genoa: San Marco dei Giustiniani, 1985. pp. 98.

13775. BAKER, EDWARD HARBAGE.   'Timing the thunder': Ezra Pound's poetic historiography. Unpub. doct. diss., Univ. of Michigan. [Abstr. in DA (47) 1329A.]

13776. BARTLETT, LEE; WITEMEYER, HUGH.   Ezra Pound and James Dickey: a correspondence and a kinship. *See* **11645.**

13777. BAUMANN, WALTER.   Carleton, Paquin and Salzburg. Paideuma (11:3) 1982, 442–5.

13778. —— Ezra Pound and magic: old world tricks in a new world poem. Paideuma (10:2) 1981, 209–24.

13779. —— Ezra Pound's metamorphosis during his London years: from late-Romanticism to Modernism. Paideuma (13) 1984, 357–73.

13780. —— 'Gerhart ..., with the Standebuch of Sachs in Yr/ Luggage' (74/450). Paideuma (10:3) 1981, 589–94.

13781. BELL, IAN F. A.   Pound's vortex: shapes ancient and modern. Paideuma (10:2) 1981, 243–71.

13782. BERNSTEIN, CHARLES.   Pound and the poetry of today. YR (75:4) 635–40.

13783. BERNSTEIN, MICHAEL ANDRE.   Image, word, and sign: the visual arts as evidence in Ezra Pound's *Cantos*. CI (12:2) 347–64.

13784. BERRYMAN, JO BRANTLEY.   Circe's craft: Ezra Pound's *Hugh*

Selwyn Mauberley. Ann Arbor, MI: UMI Research Press, 1983. pp. xii, 245.

13785. BOOTH, MARCELLA. Ezrology: the class of '57. Paideuma (13) 1984, 375–88.

13786. BORNSTEIN, GEORGE. 'What porridge had John Keats?': Pound's *L'Art* and Browning's 'popularity'. *See* **7717.**

13787. —— (ed.). Ezra Pound among the poets. Chicago; London: Chicago UP, 1985. pp. xiii, 238.

13788. BOSHA, FRANCIS J. Pound's references to Borah and Stalin in *Canto 84*. Paideuma (11:2) 1982, 284–6.

13789. BUNTING, BASIL. The village fiesta. Paideuma (10:3) 1981, 619–21.

13790. CANTRELL, CAROL HELMSTETTER. Obscurity, clarity and simplicity in the *Cantos* of Ezra Pound. MidQ (23:3) 1982, 402–10.

13791. CARPENTER, HUMPHREY. The madness of Ezra Pound. EDH (44) 147–66.

13792. CASILLO, ROBERT. The meaning of Venetian history in Ruskin and Pound. *See* **9124.**

13793. —— Nature, history, and anti-nature in Ezra Pound's Fascism. PLL (22:3) 284–311.

13794. —— The stone alive: Adrian Stokes and John Ruskin. *See* **9125.**

13795. CAYLEY, JOHN. Ch'eng, or sincerity. Paideuma (13:2) 1984, 201–10.

13796. CLARK, HILARY ANNE. The idea of a fictional encyclopaedia: *Finnegans Wake, Paradis, The Cantos*. *See* **12626.**

13797. COOKSON, WILLIAM. A guide to the *Cantos* of Ezra Pound. London: Croom Helm; New York: Persea, 1985. pp. xxiii, 177. Rev. by Sally M. Gall in JEGP (85:4) 593–5.

13798. CRISP, P. G. Time past and present, and its transcendence, in the *Cantos* of Ezra Pound. Unpub. doct. diss., Univ. of Reading, 1981.

13799. DAVIDSON, PETER. Giulio Romano at the spring marriage. Paideuma (11:3) 1982, 503–10.

13800. DAVIE, DONALD. 'Res' and 'verba' in *Rock-Drill* and after. Paideuma (11:3) 1982, 382–94.

13801. DAVIS, KAY. Fugue and *Canto LXIII*. Paideuma (11:1) 1982, 15–38.

13802. —— Ring composition, subject rhyme and *Canto VI*. Paideuma (11:3) 1982, 429–39.

13803. —— Three techniques made new. Paideuma (15:1) 47–53.

13804. DENNIS, HELEN M. The Eleusian mysteries as an organizing principle in *The Pisan Cantos*. Paideuma (10:2) 1981, 273–91.

13805. D'EPIRO, PETER. *Canto 74*: new light on Lucifer. Paideuma (10:2) 1981, 297–301.

13806. —— Whose vanity must be pulled down? Paideuma (13:2) 1984, 247–52.

13807. DE RACHEWILTZ, MARY. Pound as son: letters home. YR (75:3) 321–30.

13808. DURANT, ALAN.   Pound, Modernism and literary criticism: a reply to Donald Davie. *See* **10773.**

13809. EDWARDS, COLIN.   Ninth International Pound Conference report. Paideuma (13) 1984, 435–43.

13810. ELLIOTT, ANGELA.   Pound's *Isis Kuanon*: an ascension motif in the Cantos. Paideuma (13) 1984, 327–56.

13811. ELLMANN, M.   Impersonality in the poetry and criticism of T. S. Eliot and Ezra Pound. *See* **11749.**

13812. ENGELKING, LESZEK.   Ezra Pound in Poland. Paideuma (11:1) 1982, 105–31.

13813. ESPEY, JOHN.   Some notes on *The Return*. Paideuma (15:1) 33–9.

13814. FAULKNER, PETER.   Pound and the pre-Raphaelites. Paideuma (13) 1984, 229–44.

13815. FELDMAN, DAVID.   Ezra Pound: a poet in a cage. Paideuma (10:2) 1981, 361–3.

13816. FLEISSNER, ROBERT F.   Frost's ancient music. *See* **12069.**

13817. FREIDMAN, ERIC.   Sources of *Canto XIII*. Paideuma (10:2) 1981, 435.

13818. FRENCH, WILLIAM.   On E. Fuller Torrey, the baiting of dead giants. Paideuma (13) 1984, 131–7.

13819. —— Peacocks in Poundland. Paideuma (13) 1984, 139–48.

13820. —— 'Saint Hilda', Mr Pound, and Rilke's Parisian panther at Pisa. *See* **11673.**

13821. —— MATERER, TIMOTHY.   Far-flung vortices and Ezra's 'Hindoo' yogi. Paideuma (11:1) 1982, 39–53.

13822. FROULA, CHRISTINE.   To write paradise: style and error in Pound's *Cantos*. (Bibl. 1985, 12639.) Rev. by Hugh Witemeyer in ELN (23:4) 66–7; by Lawrence Scott Rainey in MP (83:4) 441–5; by M. A. Curr in UES (24:2) 48–9.

13823. FUKUDA, RIKUTARO; YASUKAWA, IKU (eds).   Ezra Pound seitan hyakunen ronbunshu. (Essays on Ezra Pound on the centenary of his birth.) Tokyo: Yamaguchi Press. pp. vi, 302.

13824. FURIA, PHILIP.   Pound and Blake on Hell. *See* **6232.**

13825. GALLUP, DONALD.   The Ezra Pound archive at Yale. *See* **220.**

13826. GARDNER, TRACI.   Pound's *Hugh Selwyn Mauberley*. Exp (44:3) 46–8.

13827. GENEROSO, JAMES.   Ezra Pound: American odyssey. Paideuma (13) 1984, 309–10.

13828. GINSBERG, ALLEN.   Pound's influence. APR (15:4) 7–8.

13829. GLENN, EDGAR M.   Pound and Ovid. Paideuma (10:3) 1981, 625–34.

13830. GOLDENSOHN, BARRY.   Pound and antisemitism. YR (75:3) 399–421.

13831. GORDON, DAVID.   'The City of Dioce' and China. Paideuma (11:1) 1982, 99–101.

13832. —— 'Corpus juris' and *Canto XCIV*. Paideuma (11:2) 1982, 313–24.

13833. —— Notes on 'Katze' and 'Wand'. Paideuma (15:1) 75–6.
13834. GRIEVE, THOMAS FRASER. Displacing the self: the progress of Ezra Pound's pre-*Cantos* poetics. Unpub. doct. diss., Johns Hopkins Univ. [Abstr. in DA (47) 1318A.]
13835. HARMON, WILLIAM. Beat, beat, whirr, pound. SewR (94:4) 630–9 (review-article).
13836. HENDERSON, ARCHIE. Pound's contributions to *L'Art libre* (1920). *See* **619.**
13837. —— Pound's 'Strelets' interview (1915). Paideuma (11:3) 1982, 473–86.
13838. HESSE, EVA. Helen's 'νόστος', the 'cup of white gold'. Paideuma (10:3) 1981, 585–6.
13839. —— Klages in *Canto* LXXV/450: a positive identification. Paideuma (10:2) 1981, 295–6.
13840. —— Raymond Collignon, or (apropos *Paideuma*, 7:1–2, pp. 345–6), the duck that got away. Paideuma (10:3) 1981, 583–4.
13841. HOFFMAN, DANIEL (ed.). Ezra Pound and William Carlos Williams. Philadelphia: Pennsylvania UP, 1983. pp. xx, 247. Rev. by Jacqueline Ollier in EA (38:3) 1985, 356.
13842. HOOLEY, DANIEL MATTHEWS. 'The classics in paraphrase': Ezra Pound and modern translators of classical poetry. *See* **10668.**
13843. HOOVER, PAUL. Two Pound letters. Paideuma (15:1) 95–7.
13844. JACKSON, BRENDAN. A reluctant American: Ezra Pound's response to Whitman, Whistler and Henry James. *See* **8687.**
13845. —— Seventh International Ezra Pound Conference. Paideuma (11:1) 1982, 157–66.
13846. JOHNSON, SCOTT. The 'tools' of the ideogramic method. Paideuma (10:3) 1981, 524–32.
13847. JOSEPH, TERRI BRINT. The decentered center of Ezra Pound's *Hugh Selwyn Mauberley*. YREAL (1) 1982, 121–51.
13848. —— *Neat Perigord*: a perplexity of voice. Paideuma (11:1) 1982, 93–8.
13849. KAYMAN, MARTIN A. The Modernism of Ezra Pound: the science of poetry. London: Macmillan. pp. xiii, 208.
13850. KAZIN, ALFRED. The fascination and terror of Ezra Pound. NYRB (33:4) 16–24.
13851. KÉRY, LÁSZLÓ. Ezra Pound versei elé. (A preface to the poetry of Ezra Pound.) Nagyvilág (30:12) 1985, 1800–4.
13852. KIMPEL, BEN D.; EAVES, T. C. DUNCAN. How the Medici went bust. Paideuma (11:2) 1982, 282.
13853. —— —— 'Messire Uzzano in 1442'. Paideuma (11:3) 1982, 449–50.
13854. —— —— Pound's research for the Malatesta Cantos. Paideuma (11:3) 1982, 406–19.
13855. —— —— *Tremaine at 2 in the Morning* and other little mysteries. Paideuma (10:2) 1982, 307–10.
13856. KODAMA, SANEHIDE. Third annual meeting of the Ezra Pound Society of Japan. Paideuma (11:1) 1982, 167.

13857. KOPPEL, ANDREW J.   Napoleon and Talleyrand in the *Cantos*. Paideuma (11:1) 1982, 55–78.

13858. LASH, JOHN.   Making sense of *Donna mi priegha*. Paideuma (15:1) 83–93.

13859. LAUGHLIN, JAMES.   Walking around a water-butt. ParisR (100) 309–18.

13860. LEIGH, JOHN.   Arthur Symons and the evolution of Pound's concepts of absolute rhythm and precision. *See* **9296.**

13861. LI, VICTOR P. H.   The vanity of length: the long poem as problem in Pound's *Cantos* and Williams' *Paterson*. Genre (19:1) 3–20.

13862. LICKINDORF, E. T.   The literary relations of T. S. Eliot and Ezra Pound, 1914–1922. *See* **11771.**

13863. LINDBERG-SEYERSTED, BRITA.   Cher F.: another item in the correspondence between Ezra Pound and Ford Madox Ford. *See* **11996.**

13864. —— (ed.).   Letters from Ezra Pound to Joseph Brewer. Paideuma (10:2) 1981, 369–82.

13865. LINK, FRANZ.   A note on 'the apparition of these faces' in *The House of Mirth* and *In a Station of the Metro*. Paideuma (10:2) 1981, 327.

13866. LITTLE, MATTHEW.   Pound's use of the word 'totalitarian'. Paideuma (11:1) 1982, 147–56.

13867. LITZ, A. WALTON.   'Remember that I have remembered': traces of the past in *The Pisan Cantos*. YR (75:3) 357–67.

13868. LONGENBACH, JAMES.   Ezra Pound's *Canzoni*: toward a poem including history. Paideuma (13) 1984, 389–405.

13869. McDOWELL, COLIN.   'As towards a bridge over words': the way of the soul in the *Cantos*. Paideuma (13) 1984, 171–200.

13870. McFARLAND, RONALD.   A note on Monsieur Verog. Paideuma (11:3) 1982, 446–8.

13871. McNAMARA, ROBERT JAMES.   Alternate selves: Pound, Eliot, and the constructivist ethos. *See* **11773.**

13872. MAKIN, PETER.   Pound's *Cantos*. Boston, MA: Allen & Unwin, 1985. (Cf. bibl. 1985, 12675.) Rev. by Neil Corcoran in MLR (81:2) 464–5; by Graham Clarke in NQ (33:4) 570–1.

13873. MARTZ, LOUIS L.   Pound: the prophetic voice. YR (75:3) 373–84.

13874. MATERER, TIMOTHY.   Doppelganger: Ezra Pound in his letters. Paideuma (11:2) 1982, 241–56.

13875. MATTHEWS, C. J.   Ezra Pound and the ideogrammic method. Unpub. doct. diss., Univ. of Durham, 1983.

13876. MERCHANT, MOELWYN.   Meeting Ezra Pound. Planet (58) 61–7.

13877. MEYERS, PETER.   The metre of *Canto XLVII*. Paideuma (11:1) 1982, 91–2.

13878. MIKREAMMOS, PHILLIPPE.   *Cantos*, traduction: les mésaventures de l'original. Paideuma (13) 1984, 445–52.

13879. MITCHELL, BREON.   Ezra Pound and G. B. Shaw: a long wordy war. *See* **12692.**

13880. MIYAKE, AKIKO.   Contemplation East and West: a defense of

Fenollosa's synthetic language and its influence on Ezra Pound. Paideuma (10:3) 1981, 522–70.

13881. Moody, A. D. *The Pisan Cantos*: making cosmos in the wreckage of Europe. Paideuma (11:1) 1982, 135–46.

13882. Morse, Jonathan. What's his name. Paideuma (10:3) 1981, 595–7.

13883. Nänny, Max. Ezra Pound and the Menippean tradition. Paideuma (11:3) 1982, 395–405.

13884. —— More Menippus than Calliope: a reply. Paideuma (13:2) 1984, 263–8. (*Refers to* bibl. 1984, 12695.)

13885. Nicholls, P. A. The relation of Ezra Pound's social economic thought to the writing of the *Cantos*. Unpub. doct. diss., Univ. of Cambridge, 1983.

13886. Oderman, Kevin. *Cavalcanti*: that the body is not evil. Paideuma (11:2) 1982, 257–79.

13887. —— Of vision, tennis courts, and glands. Paideuma (13) 1984, 253–60.

13888. Odlin, Reno. Dinklage. Paideuma (11:2) 1982, 283.

13889. Pearlman, Daniel. *Canto 52*: the Vivante passage. Paideuma (10:2) 1981, 311–14.

13890. Perkins, David. Johnson and modern poetry. *See* **6617.**

13891. Perret, N. M. 'God's eye art 'ou': Eleusis as a paradigm for enlightenment in *Canto* CVI. Paideuma (13) 1984, 419–32.

13892. Pound, Ezra. Mr Dunning's poetry. *See* **11715.**

13893. Pound, Omar; Litz, A. Walton (eds). Ezra Pound and Dorothy Shakespear: their letters 1909–1914. (Bibl. 1985, 12683.) Rev. by Michael Hastings in LRev, Feb. 1985, 8–9.

13894. Pratt, William C. The greatest poet in captivity: Ezra Pound at St Elizabeths. SewR (94:4) 619–29.

13895. Rabaté, Jean-Michel. Comment lire le texte poundien. EA (39:3) 302–7.

13896. —— L'énonciation apocalyptique des *Cantos Pisans*. *In* (pp. 231–49) **2.**

13897. —— Language, sexuality and ideology in Ezra Pound's *Cantos*. Basingstoke: Macmillan. pp. x, 339. (Language, discourse, society.)

13898. Rader, James J. The value of testimony: Pound at Wabash. Paideuma (13) 1984, 67–130.

13899. Raffel, Burton. Possum and Ole Ez in the public eye: contemporaries and peers on T. S. Eliot and Ezra Pound 1892–1972. *See* **11784.**

13900. Reid, Richard G. 'Discontinuous gods': Ezra Pound and the epic of translation. Unpub. doct. diss., Princeton Univ. [Abstr. in DA (47) 894A.]

13901. Reynolds, Lloyd G. Economics in history: the poetic vision of Ezra Pound. YR (75:3) 385–98.

13902. Reznowski, Lorne A. The 'Chesterbelloc' and Ezra Pound. *See* **11213.**

13903. Ricks, Beatrice. Ezra Pound: a bibliography of secondary works. Metuchen, NJ; London: Scarecrow Press. pp. xxii, 281. (Scarecrow author bibliographies, 74.)

13904. SCHMIDT, G.   Hieroglyphen in den *Cantos* Ezra Pounds. GRM (36:1) 92–4.

13905. SCHNEEMAN, PETER.   Pound in Romania. Paideuma (10:2) 1981, 421–34.

13906. SCHULTZ, ROBERT.   A detailed chronology of Ezra Pound's London years, 1908–1920. Part One: 1908–1914. Paideuma (11:3) 1982, 456–72.

13907. SCHWARTZ, SANFORD.   The matrix of Modernism: Pound, Eliot and early twentieth-century thought. See **11789.**

13908. SHEA, JOHN; ROMANO, TIMOTHY.   The Pound–Williams conference. Paideuma (10:2) 1981, 411–18.

13909. SOLT, MARY ELLEN (ed.).   Dear Ez: letters from William Carlos Williams to Ezra Pound. Bloomington, IN: Private Press of Fredric Brewer for Friends of Lilly Library, 1985. pp. 51. Rev. by Patrick Moore in WCWR (12:2) 14–16.

13910. STOICHEFF, R. PETER.   The composition and publication history of Ezra Pound's *Drafts & Fragments*. TCL (32:1) 78–94.

13911. SUTTON, WALTER.   Coherence in Pound's *Cantos* and William James's pluralistic universe. See **8774.**

13912. TERRELL, CARROLL.   Cabranez, the mystery man. Paideuma (11:3) 1982, 451–3.

13913. TERRELL, CARROLL F.   A companion to the *Cantos* of Ezra Pound: vol 2 (Cantos 74–117). Berkeley: California UP, 1985. pp. x, 361. Rev. by Sally M. Gall in JEGP (85:4) 593–5.

13914. —— Poetic madness or political treason. Paideuma (13) 1984, 149–53.

13915. —— Salta sin barra! Paideuma (13:3) 1984, 409–14.

13916. THOMAS, RON.   E. P.: Hellenic punster. SCR (3:1) 56–67.

13917. —— The Latin masks of Ezra Pound. Ann Arbor: Michigan UP, 1983. (Cf. bibl. 1984, 12752.) Rev. by Graham Clarke in NQ (33:1) 137–8.

13918. TOMLINSON, JOHN.   Poetry and metamorphosis. See **11800.**

13919. WALKIEWICZ, E. P.   Back to ABC: a report on the sixth International Ezra Pound Conference. Paideuma (10:1) 1981, 173–80.

13920. —— Pound/Joyce: Dublin '82. See **12743.**

13921. WALLACE, EMILY MITCHELL.   Some friends of Ezra Pound: a photographic essay. YR (75:3) 330–56.

13922. WARNER, MICHAEL LEE.   Cantomorphosis: multilingualism in the *Cantos* of Ezra Pound. Unpub. doct. diss., Univ. of Tulsa. [Abstr. in DA (47) 2155A.]

13923. WILHELM, J. J.   The American roots of Ezra Pound. New York: Garland, 1985. pp. 230. Rev. by Margaret Moran in AL (58:1) 114–17.

13924. —— Ezra Pound's tribute to Newark. NJH (104:3/4) 43–7.

13925. WITEMEYER, HUGH.   *Of Kings' Treasuries*: Pound's allusion to Ruskin in *Hugh Selwyn Mauberley*. See **9148.**

13926. Zimmerman, Hans-Joachim. Ezra Pound, *A Song of the Degrees*: Chinese clarity versus alchemical confusion. Paideuma (10:2) 1981, 225–41.

Anthony Powell

13927. Gorra, Michael Edward. The English novel at mid-century: Evelyn Waugh, Henry Green, Anthony Powell, and Graham Greene. *See* **12227.**

J. F. Powers

13928. Gordon, Mary (introd.). *Prince of Darkness* and other stories. London: Hogarth Press, 1985. pp. 228. (Hogarth fiction.)

John Cowper Powys

13929. Fawkner, H. W. The ecstatic world of John Cowper Powys. Rutherford, NJ: Fairleigh Dickinson UP, London: Assoc. UPs. pp. 257.

13930. Hughes, D. I. A critical edition of John Cowper Powys's *Maiden Castle*. Unpub. doct. diss., Univ. of Wales, Bangor, 1984. [Abstr. in IT (35) 52.]

13931. Lock, Charles. Polyphonic Powys: Dostoevsky, Bakhtin, and *A Glastonbury Romance*. UTQ (55:3) 261–81.

13932. Wood, R. L. The 'Welsh mythology' of John Cowper Powys. Unpub. doct. diss., Univ. of Wales, Aberystwyth, 1983.

13933. Young, Vernon. The immense inane. ASch (55) 248–58 (review-article).

T. F. Powys

13934. Buning, Marius. T. F. Powys, a modern allegorist: the companion novels *Mr Weston's Good Wine* and *Unclay* in the light of modern allegorical theory. Amsterdam: Rodopi. pp. 261. (Costerus, 56.)

E. J. Pratt

13935. Pitt, David G. E. J. Pratt: the truant years 1882–1927. (Bibl. 1985, 12720.) Rev. by R. Gordon Moyles in ESCan (12:4) 487–91.

Christopher Priest

13936. Ruddick, Nicholas. Out of the Gernsbackian slime: Christopher Priest's abandonment of science fiction. *See* **12141.**

J. B. Priestley

13937. Firth, Gary. Bygone Bradford: the 'lost world' of J. B. Priestley. Lancaster: Dalesman. pp. 84.

V. S. Pritchett

13938. Forkner, Ben; Séjourné, Philippe. V. S. Pritchett. Journal of the Short Story in English (6) 1–102 (special issue on V. S. Pritchett).

13939. Pritchett, V. S. The other side of a frontier: a V. S. Pritchett reader. London: Clark, 1984. pp. 583.

J. H. Prynne

13940. Reeve, N. H.; Kerridge, Richard. A note to J. H. Prynne's *Royal Fern*. Eng (35) 139–57.

Al Purdy

13941. Cooney, Seamus (ed.). The Bukowski/Purdy letters, 1964–74: a decade of dialogue. *See* **11347.**

James Purdy

13942. Brantlinger, Patrick. Missing corpses: the deconstructive mysteries of James Purdy and Franz Kafka. Novel (20:1) 24–40.

Barbara Pym

13943. BERNDT, JUDY. Barbara Pym: a supplementary list of secondary sources. BB (43:2) 76–80.

13944. COOLEY, MASON. *The Sweet Dove Died*: the sexual politics of narcissism. TCL (32:1) 40–9.

13945. HEBERLEIN, KATE BROWDER. Barbara Pym and Anthony Trollope: communities of imaginative participation. *See* **9401.**

13946. KANE, PATRICIA. A curious eye: Barbara Pym's women. SDR (24:2) 50–9.

13947. KAUFMAN, ANTHONY. The short fiction of Barbara Pym. TCL (32:1) 50–77.

13948. LYLES, JEAN CAFFEY. Pym's cup: Anglicans and anthropologists. ChCen (103:18) 519–22.

13949. SADLER, LYNN VEACH. The pathos of everyday living in the novels of Barbara Pym. PhilP (31) 1985, 82–90.

Thomas Pynchon

13950. BALDWIN, HELENE. The one great centripetal movement: empathy in *Gravity's Rainbow*. PhilP (31) 1985, 116–24.

13951. BAYERL, ELIZABETH ANN. Tangled hierarchies: *Gödel, Escher, Bach: An Eternal Golden Braid* and *Gravity's Rainbow*. Unpub. doct. diss., Syracuse Univ., 1985. [Abstr. in DA (46) 3712A.]

13952. BAYLON, DANIEL. *The Crying of Lot 49*: vrai roman et faux policier? Caliban (23) 111–25.

13953. BYUN, JONG-MIN. Thomas Pynchon's techniques of time dislocation in *Gravity's Rainbow*. JUJH (22) 215–24.

13954. CLARK, BEVERLY LYON. The mirror worlds of Carroll, Nabokov, and Pynchon: fantasy in the 1860s and 1960s. *See* **7838.**

13955. DAWSON, G. P. The dilemma of contemporary existence in the fiction of Thomas Pynchon. Unpub. doct. diss., Univ. of Nottingham, 1984. [Abstr. in IT (35) 55.]

13956. DUGDALE, JOHN. 'A burglar, I think. A second-story man'. CamQ (15) 156–64.

13957. GUZLOWSKI, JOHN Z. No more sea changes: four American novelists' responses to the sea. *In* (pp. 232–43) **28.**

13958. HORVATH, BROOKE KENTON. Dropping out: spiritual crisis and countercultural attitudes in four American novelists of the 1960s. *See* **11324.**

13959. HUME, KATHRYN; KNIGHT, THOMAS J. Pynchon's orchestration of *Gravity's Rainbow*. JEGP (85:3) 366–85.

13960. KHARPERTIAN, THEODORE D. 'A hand to turn the time': Menippean satire and the postmodernist American fiction of Thomas Pynchon. Unpub. doct. diss., McGill Univ., 1985. [Abstr. in DA (46) 3352A.]

13961. KIM, SANG-KOO. Thomas Pynchon eui poongja: *V* wa *The Crying of Lot 49* reul jungsim euro. (Thomas Pynchon's satire: *V* and *The Crying of Lot 49*.) JELL (32:1) 105–25.

13962. KIM, SUNG-GON. Journey into the past: the historical and mystical imagination of Barth and Pynchon. *See* **11135.**

13963. LYTTLE, I. S.   Awareness and uncertainty: a reader-response approach to theme and method in Thomas Pynchon's fiction. Unpub. doct. diss., Queen's Univ., Belfast, 1985. [Abstr. in IT (35) 1089.]

13964. McCARRON, WILLIAM E.   Pynchon and Hogarth. NCL (16:5) 2.

13965. MARRIOTT, A. D.   'Approximately related changes': the meanings of narrative in Thomas Pynchon's *Gravity's Rainbow*. Unpub. doct. diss., Univ. of Manchester, 1985. [Abstr. in IT (35) 1493.]

13966. OLESKY, ELZBIETA.   Kesey and Pynchon: a trip to the wasteland. *See* **12770.**

13967. PETILLON, PIERRE-YVES.   American graffiti: S = klogW. Critique (41:462) 1985, 1090–105.

13968. PRICE, PENELOPE.   *Gravity's Rainbow*: Thomas Pynchon's use of the media. Unpub. doct. diss., Arizona State Univ., 1985. [Abstr. in DA (46) 2690A.]

13969. REITZ, BERNHARD.   'A very German question'. Der Mitläufer als Voyeur und als Opfer in Pynchons *V* und *Gravity's Rainbow*. Anglistik & Englischunterricht (29/30) 173–98.

13970. STEINER, WENDY.   Collage or miracle: historicism in a deconstructed world. *In* (pp. 323–51) **47.**

13971. TOIA, ELAINE M.   Thomas Pynchon's *V*: a curious landscape. Unpub. doct. diss., Lehigh Univ. [Abstr. in DA (47) 1731A.]

13972. ZADWORNA-FJELLESTAD, DANUTA.   *Alice's Adventures in Wonderland* and *Gravity's Rainbow*: a study in duplex fiction. *See* **7850.**

Thomas H. Raddall

13973. AUSTIN, DIANA.   'Helping to turn the tide': an interview with Thomas H. Raddall. StudCanL (11:1) 108–39.

Craig Raine

13974. MANHIRE, BILL.   In dialect. NZList, 31 May, 37.

13975. ROEFFAERS, HUGO.   Engels kwintet: essays over Ted Hughes, Geoffrey Hill, Seamus Heaney, Craig Raine en Robert Graves. *See* **12222.**

Ayn Rand

13976. GLADSTEIN, MIMI RIESEL.   The Ayn Rand companion. Westport, CT; London: Greenwood Press, 1984. pp. xii, 130.

John Crowe Ransom

13977. HARDER, KELSIE B.   Southern formalism at Shakespeare: Ransom on the Sonnets. *In* (pp. 125–36) **51.**

13978. MACK, JAMES.   John Crowe Ransom's moments: a reconstruction in the post-scientific mode. YREAL (4) 233–64.

13979. MAZZARO, JEROME.   Logical and local differences. *See* **12547.**

13980. VESTERMAN, WILLIAM.   The motives of meter in *Bells for John Whiteside's Daughter*. SoQ (22:4) 1984, 42–53.

13981. YOUNG, THOMAS DANIEL; HINDLE, JOHN (eds).   Selected essays of John Crowe Ransom. (Bibl. 1985, 12763.) Rev. by George Core in SAQ (85:2) 205–6; by Michael Cohen in NQ (33:2) 278–9.

Raja Rao

13982. SHARRAD, PAUL.   Open dialogue: metropolitan–provincial tensions and the quest for a post-colonial culture in the fiction of C. J. Koch, Raja Rao and Wilson Harris. *See* **12294.**

Terence Rattigan

13983. YOUNG, B. A.   The Rattigan version: Sir Terence Rattigan and the theatre of character. London: Hamilton. pp. ix, 228. Rev. by Michelene Wandor in Listener, 20 Nov., 30.

Marjorie Kennan Rawlings

13984. STEPHENSON, WILLIAM.   Fawn bites lion: how MGM tried to film *The Yearling* in Florida. SoQ (19:3/4) 1981, 229–39.

Frank Reade

13985. BLEILER, E. F. (ed.).   The Frank Reade library: vol. 3, Nos. 36–49. New York; London: Garland, 1985. pp. 350, in various pagings.

Peter Reading

13986. JENKINS, ALAN (sel. and introd.).   Essential Reading. London: Secker & Warburg. pp. 128.

Henry Reed

13987. CLEVERDON, DOUGLAS.   Henry Reed. Independent, 11 Dec., 23. (Obituary.)

Ishmael Reed

13988. HARRIS, NORMAN.   Politics as an innovative aspect of literary folklore: a study of Ishmael Reed. Ob (5) Spring/Summer 1979, 41–50.
13989. JABLON, MADELYN HYLA.   The contemporary black aesthetic. *See* **13182.**
13990. MARTIN, REGINALD.   Reed's *Mumbo Jumbo*. Exp (44:2) 55–6.
13991. MARTIN, RICHARD.   Ishmael Reed: rewriting America. KN (33:4) 487–511.
13992. MUSGRAVE, MARIAN.   Black myth versus white myth in the novels of Ishmael Reed. *In* (pp. 381–4) **19.**
13993. MUSGRAVE, MARIAN E.   Ishmael Reed's black Oedipus cycle. Ob (6) Winter 1980, 60–7.

Lizette Woodworth Reese

13994. HAHN, H. GEORGE.   Twilight reflections: the hold of Victorian Baltimore on Lizette Woodworth Reese and H. L. Mencken. *See* **13235.**

Kenneth Rexroth

13995. HAMILL, SAM.   Kenneth Rexroth's *Selected Poems*. APR (15:3) 9–13 (review-article).

Charles Reznikoff

13996. LEONARD, TOM.   What happens in Reznikoff's poetry. Edinburgh Review (73) 34–41.

Ernest Rhys

13997. THOMAS, M. WYNN.   Walt Whitman's Welsh connection: Ernest Rhys. *See* **9518.**

Jean Rhys

13998. BRANDMARK, WENDY.   The power of the victim: a study of *Quartet, After Leaving Mr Mackenzie* and *Voyage in the Dark* by Jean Rhys. Kp (8:2) 21–45.
13999. CODACCIONI, MARIE-JOSÉ.   L'autre vie de Bertha Rochester. *In* (pp. 107–14) **1.**

14000. MELLOWN, ELGIN W. Jean Rhys: a descriptive and annotated bibliography of works and criticism. (Bibl. 1985, 12793.) Rev. by George Bixby in ABC (7:1) 47–50.

14001. RAMCHAND, KENNETH (ed.). Tales of the wide Caribbean. London: Heinemann, 1985. pp. 180. (Caribbean writers, 33.)

14002. SMILOWITZ, ERIKA. Childlike women and paternal men: colonialism in Jean Rhys's fiction. Ariel (17:4) 93–103.

Elmer Rice

14003. BROWN, RUSSELL E. Names and numbers in *The Adding Machine. See* **1652.**

Adrienne Rich

14004. GALBRAITH, LORNA MAY. The emerging consciousness of women as seen in the poetry of Adrienne Rich. Unpub. doct. diss., United States International Univ., 1978. [Abstr. in DA (47) 1728A.]

14005. NOWIK, NAN. Mixing art and politics: the writings of Adrienne Rich, Marge Piercy, and Alice Walker. *See* **13727.**

David Adams Richards

14006. CONNOR, WILLIAM. The river in the blood: escape and entrapment in the fiction of David Adams Richards. WLWE (26:2) 269–77.

I. A. Richards

14007. BREDIN, HUGH. I. A. Richards and the philosophy of practical criticism. PhilL (10:1) 26–37.

14008. SHUSTERMAN, RONALD. Blindness and anxiety: I. A. Richards and some current trends of criticism. *See* **10923.**

'Henry Handel Richardson' (Ethel Florence Lindesay Robertson)

14009. GREEN, DOROTHY. Henry Handel Richardson and her fiction. Canberra: Australian National UP. pp. xiii, 582.

14010. KIERNAN, C. Henry Handel Richardson and Ireland. *In* (pp. 46–57) C. KIERNAN (ed.), Australia and Ireland 1788–1988: bicentenary essays. Dublin: Gill & Macmillan. pp. 309.

Mordecai Richler

14011. DAVIDSON, ARNOLD E. Mordecai Richler. New York: Ungar, 1983. pp. 203. Rev. by Kerry McSweeney in ECanW (33) 172–3.

14012. LUCKING, DAVID. 'Between things': public mythology and personal identity in the fiction of Mordecai Richler. DalR (65:2) 1985, 243–60.

14013. McSWEENEY, KERRY. Mordecai Richler. *In* (pp. 129–79) **7.**

Laura Riding (Laura (Riding) Jackson)

14014. MARCUS, JANE. Laura Riding roughshod. IowaR (12:2/3) 1981, 295–9.

Kenneth Roberts

14015. HUGHES, JAMES M. Inner and outer seas in Dickinson, Dana, Cooper and Roberts. *In* (pp. 202–11) **28.**

Kevin Roberts

14016. LANE, M. TRAVIS. 'Emotion first! Understanding later!' The poetry of Kevin Roberts. ECanW (32) 27–40.

Edwin Arlington Robinson

14017. SULLIVAN, WINIFRED H.   The double-edged irony of E. A. Robinson's *Miniver Cheevy*. CLQ (22:3) 185–91.

Marilynne Robinson

14018. BACHINGER, KATRINA.   The Tao of *Housekeeping*: reconnoitering the utopian ecological frontier in Marilynne Robinson's 'feminist' novel. *In* (pp. 14–33) **21.**

Theodore Roethke

14019. JANSSEN, RONALD R.   Roethke's *My Papa's Waltz*. Exp (44:2) 43–4.

14020. NADEL, ALAN.   Roethke, Wilbur, and the vision of the child: Romantic and Augustan in modern verse. LU (2:1) 1978, 94–113.

14021. NEWMAN, ROBERT D.   Emily Dickinson's influence on Roethke's *In Evening Air. See* **8142.**

14022. PLUMLY, STANLEY.   The abrupt edge. *See* **7697.**

14023. SMITH, NANCY ANN.   Roethke's *Where Knock Is Wide Open*. Exp (44:3) 59–60.

'Criena Rohan' (Deirdre Cash)

14024. FACTOR, JUNE.   Welcome back Criena Rohan. Meanjin (45:3) 423–28.

'Betty Roland' (Elizabeth Maclean)

14025. MODJESKA, DRUSILLA.   Interview: Betty Roland talks to Drusilla Modjeska. Australasian Drama Studies (St Lucia, Qld.) (8) Apr., 63–80.

Frederick William Rolfe (Baron Corvo)

14026. ANDREWS, CLARENCE A.   The Baron in Iowa. BkIA (45) 26–31.

Edward Everett Rose

14027. FIELDER, MARI KATHLEEN.   Green and gold reconsidered: the identity and assimilation of the American Irish as reflected in the dramas of Edward Everett Rose. TS (30) 1983/84 29–42.

Isaac Rosenberg

14028. MENASCÉ, ESTHER.   Guerra e pace nell'opera di Isaac Rosenberg (1890–1918). Padua: Liviana, 1984. pp. vii, 295.

14029. SOMMER, JASON F.   Lamp in his blood: some Jewish motifs in the poetry of Isaac Rosenberg. Unpub. doct. diss., Saint Louis Univ., 1985. [Abstr. in DA (46) 3729A.]

Sinclair Ross

14030. HINZ, EVELYN; TEUNISSEN, JOHN J.   Who's the father of Mrs Bentley's child? *As for Me and My House* and the conventions of dramatic monologue. CanL (111) 101–13.

14031. KAYE, FRANCES W.   Sinclair's Ross's use of George Sand and Frederic Chopin as models for the Bentleys. ECanW (33) 100–11.

14032. McMULLEN, LORRAINE.   Sinclair Ross. (Bibl. 1983, 13188.) Rev. by Douglas Daymond in JCF (35/36) 142–6.

W. W. E. Ross

14033. KIZUK, A. R.   Canadian poetry in the 'twenties: dialectics and prophecy in W. W. E. Ross's *Laconics* and *Sonnets*. CanP (18) 35–54.

Philip Roth

14034. GLASSMAN, STEVE. Roth's *Goodbye, Columbus*. Exp (44:2) 54–5.

14035. GREINER, NORBERT. Parodie der Verwandlung oder: Der Komparatist als Romanheld. Philip Roths *The Breast*. Arcadia (21:2) 190–202.

14036. ROTH, PHILIP. Reading myself and others. (Bibl. 1975, 13760.) New York; Harmondsworth: Penguin, 1985. pp. x, 325. (Second ed.: first ed. 1975.)

14037. SEARLES, GEORGE J. Salinger redux via Roth: an echo of *Franny and Zooey* in *My Life as a Man*. NCL (16:2) 7.

14038. TIPPENS, DARRYL. The shechina theme in Roth's *Conversion of the Jews*. ChrisL (35:3) 13–20.

Norbert Ruebsaat

14039. MEZEI, KATHY. Interview with Norbert Ruebsaat. ECanW (32) 147–59.

Damon Runyon

14040. D'ITRI, PATRICIA WARD. Damon Runyon. Boston, MA: G. K. Hall, 1982. pp. 168. (Twayne's US authors, 407.) Rev. by Judie Newman in YES (16) 356–8.

Salman Rushdie

14041. AFZAL-KHAN, FAWZIA. Genre and ideology in the novels of four contemporary Indo-Anglian novelists: R. K. Narayan, Anita Desai, Kamala Markandaya and Salman Rushdie. *See* **11637.**

14042. FLETCHER, M. D. Rushdie's *Shame* as apologue. JCL (21:1) 120–32.

14043. HARRIS, MICHAEL. 'Transformation without end': Salman Rushdie's India. Meridian (5:1) 15–22.

14044. RECKWITZ, ERHARD. Der Roman als Metaroman: Salman Rushdie, *Midnight's Children*; Kazuo Ishiguro, *A Pale View of the Hills*; John Fowles, *Mantissa*. *See* **10373.**

14045. SWANN, JOSEPH. 'East is east and west is west': Salman Rushdie's *Midnight's Children* as an Indian novel. WLWE (26:2) 353–62.

Bertrand Russell

14046. HOPKINS, KENNETH. Bertrand Russell and Gamel Woolsey. Norfolk: Warren House, 1985. pp. 17.

14047. KUNTZ, PAUL GRIMLEY. Bertrand Russell. Boston, MA: G. K. Hall. pp. 186. (Twayne's English authors, 421.)

14048. SPADONI, CARL. Who wrote Bertrand Russell's *Wisdom of the West*? PBSA (80:3) 349–67.

George William Russell ('AE')

14049. KUCH, PETER. Yeats and AE: the antagonism that unites dear friends. Gerrards Cross: Smythe; Totowa, NJ: Barnes & Noble. pp. xiii, 291.

Willy Russell

14050. DEBUSSCHER, GILBERT. *Educating Rita*, or an Open University *Pygmalion*. *In* (pp. 303–17) **12.**

Gig Ryan

14051. LEONARD, JOHN. Accessibility and myth: Gig Ryan and A. D. Hope. *See* **12447.**

George Ryga

14052. GLAAP, ALBERT-REINER.   'I got no past . . . no future . . . nothing. I nobody.' *Indian*, a short play by George Ryga. Anglistik & Englischunterricht (28) 97–124.

14053. HOFFMAN, JAMES F.   A biographical and critical investigation of the stage plays of George Ryga. Unpub. doct. diss., New York Univ., 1985. [Abstr. in DA (46) 2132A.]

14054. MARTINEZ, JILL.   An interview with George Ryga. JCF (35/36) 106–21.

V. Sackville-West

14055. GLENDINNING, VICTORIA (introd.).   Family history. London: Virago Press. pp. xiv. 428. (Virago modern classics, 234.)

14056. HENNEGAN, ALISON (introd.).   Pepita. London: Virago Press. pp. 282.

Kay Sage

14057. SUTHER, JUDITH D.   The poetry of Kay Sage and French surrealism. CLS (23:3) 234–49.

George Saintsbury

14058. BELL, ALAN.   St George – scholarly slayer of 'pussyfoots'. Listener (115) 1 May, 13–14.

J. D. Salinger

14059. FEENY, THOMAS.   The possible influence of J. D. Salinger's *The Catcher in the Rye* upon Lorenza Mazzetti's *Con rabbio*. Neohelicon (12:2) 1985, 35–46.

14060. LISH, GORDON.   A fool for Salinger. AR (44:4) 408–15.

14061. SEARLES, GEORGE J.   Salinger redux via Roth: an echo of *Franny and Zooey* in *My Life as a Man*. See **14037.**

14062. STRONG, PAUL.   Black wing, black heart – betrayal in J. D. Salinger's *The Laughing Man*. PhilP (31) 1985, 91–6.

14063. SUBLETTE, JACK R.   J. D. Salinger: an annotated bibliography, 1938–1981. (Bibl. 1985, 12876.) Rev. by George Bixby in ABC (7:1) 47–50.

14064. WEXELBLATT, ROBERT.   Chekhov, Salinger, and Epictetus. MidQ (28:1) 50–76.

Carl Sandburg

14065. FETHERLING, DALE; FETHERLING, DOUG (eds).   Carl Sandburg at the movies: a poet in the Silent Era 1920–1927. See **9947.**

14066. MOORE, J. R.   The early prose and poetry of Carl Sandburg, 1901–1919. Unpub. doct. diss., Univ. of London, King's Coll., 1984.

Mari Sandoz

14067. OEHLSCHLAEGER, FRITZ.   The art of Mari Sandoz's *The Smart Man*. SDR (19:4) 1982, 65–75.

14068. YUVAJITA, PHACHEE.   The changing images of women in Western American literature as illustrated in the works of Willa Cather, Hamlin Garland, and Mari Sandoz. See **11411.**

Bernard K. Sandwell

14069. WAGNER, ANTON.   A national or international dramatic art: B. K. Sandwell and *Saturday Night* 1932–1951. See **10104.**

George Santayana

14070. GUTENDORF, VINCENT FRITZ, JR. George Santayana: the philosopher as critic of American culture. Unpub. doct. diss., Columbia Univ., 1984. [Abstr. in DA (47) 178A.]

14071. SCOTT, NATHAN A., JR. The poetics of belief: studies in Coleridge, Arnold, Pater, Santayana, Stevens, and Heidegger. *See* **7563**.

Bienvenido N. Santos

14072. BRENSNAHAN, ROGER J. Can these, too, be Midwestern? Studies of two Filipino writers. *See* **13058**.

Frank Sargeson

14073. DAALDER, JOOST. Violence in the stories of Frank Sargeson. JNZL (4) 56–80.

14074. —— DURING, SIMON; SIMPSON, PETER. Three readings of Sargeson's *The Hole that Jack Dug*. Span (22) Apr., 73–92.

William Saroyan

14075. EVERDING, ROBERT G. Shaw and Saroyan. IndS (24:2/3) 35–40.

May Sarton

14076. FLUG, CHRISTINE MARGARET. The journey inward: an examination of the non-fictional prose of May Sarton. Unpub. doct. diss., Harvard Univ. [Abstr. in DA (47) 2156A.]

Siegfried Sassoon

14077. HART-DAVIS, RUPERT (ed.). Letters to Max Beerbohm: with a few answers. *See* **11209**.

14078. —— Siegfried Sassoon: diaries, 1923–1925. (Bibl. 1985, 12896.) Rev. by Michael Thorpe in EngS (67:5) 459–60; by Peter Vansittart in LRev, Apr. 1985, 29–30.

14079. McKENZIE, M. L. Memories of the Great War: Graves, Sassoon, and Findley. *See* **11947**.

James Saunders

14080. SAMMELLS, NEIL. Giggling at the arts: Tom Stoppard and James Saunders. CritQ (28:4) 71–8.

Dorothy Scarborough

14081. SLADE, CAROLE. Authorship and authority in Dorothy Scarborough's *The Wind*. SAF (14:1) 85–91.

Susan Fromberg Schaeffer

14082. BERGER, ALAN L. Holocaust survivors and children in *Anya* and *Mr Sammler's Planet*. *See* **11217**.

R. Murray Schafer

14083. SCHAFER, R. MURRAY. Theatre of confluence II. *See* **10069**.

14084. Entry cancelled.

Delmore Schwartz

14085. BRANS, JO. The passion for Plato in Delmore Schwartz. CR (30:4) 507–28.

14086. MAZZARO, JEROME. Logical and local differences. *See* **12547**.

14087. POLLET, ELIZABETH (ed.). Portrait of Delmore: journals and notes of Delmore Schwartz 1939–1959. New York: Farrar, Straus & Giroux. pp. 633. Rev. by Stanley Moss in NYTB, 19 Oct., 12.

14088. ZOLOTOW, MAURICE.   'I brake for Delmore Schwartz': portrait of the artist as a young liar. MichQR (25:1) 1–22.

Duncan Campbell Scott

14089. SIMPSON, JANICE C.   Healing the wound: cultural compromise in D. C. Scott's *A Scene at Lake Manitou*. CanP (18) 66–76.

14090. WARE, TRACY.   D. C. Scott's *The Height of Land* and the greater Romantic lyric. CanL (111) 10–25.

14091. WEIS, L. P.   D. C. Scott's view of history and the Indians. CanL (111) 27–40.

F. R. Scott

14092. HEENAN, MICHAEL.   An interview with F. R. Scott. CanP (19) 92–101.

Paul Scott

14093. REECE, SHELLEY C. (ed.).   My appointment with the Muse: essays, 1961–75. London: Heinemann. pp. 175.

14094. SCANLAN, MARGARET.   The disappearance of history: Paul Scott's Raj Quartet. CLIO (15:2) 154–69.

Sipho Sepamla

14095. MZAMANE, M. V.   Black consciousness poets in South Africa, 1967–1980, with special reference to Mongane Serote and Sipho Sepamla. Unpub. doct. diss., Univ. of Sheffield, 1984.

14096. VILJOEN, HEIN.   Die Suid-Afrikaanse romansisteem *anno* 1981: 'n vergelykende studie. *See* **10429.**

Mongane Wally Serote

14097. MZAMANE, M. V.   Black consciousness poets in South Africa, 1967–1980, with special reference to Mongane Serote and Sipho Sepamla. *See* **14095.**

Ernest Thompson Seton

14098. ROHRBOUGH, MALCOLM J.   A dedication to the memory of Ernest Thompson Seton 1860–1946. ArizW (28:1) 1–4.

Anne Sexton

14099. BOEBEL, DAGNY MARIE HEXOM.   Metaphor in the poetry of Anne Sexton. Unpub. doct. diss., Purdue Univ., 1985. [Abstr. in DA (47) 175A.]

Peter Shaffer

14100. BIDNEY, MARTIN.   Thinking about God and Mozart: the Salieris of Puškin and Peter Shaffer. SEEJ (30:2) 183–95.

Karl Shapiro

14101. CARRUTH, HAYDEN.   A salute in time. CEACrit (48:3) 21–3.

14102. PHILLIPS, ROBERT.   Karl Shapiro and his latest poems. CEACrit (48:3) 24–8.

George Bernard Shaw

14103. AMALRIC, JEAN-CLAUDE.   Les métamorphoses du héros shavien. CVE (23) 59–69.

14104. BERST, CHARLES A.   *The Irrational Knot*: the art of Shaw as a young Ibsenite. JEGP (85:2) 222–48.

14105. CASH, WILLIAM F.   What they really said about G.B.S.: Shaw and Pearson's 'Retreat from Moscow'. JML (13:2) 211–24.

14106. COLTON, PATRICK (ed.).   Androcles and the lion. Introd. by JOHN RUSSELL BROWN. Harlow: Longman. pp. xxxix, 166. (Longman study texts.)

14107. CORRIGAN, FELICITAS.   The nun, the infidel, and the superman: the remarkable friendships of Dame Laurentia McLachan with Sydney Cockerell, Bernard Shaw, and others. Chicago: Chicago UP, 1985. (Cf. bibl. 1985, 12936.) Rev. by Ruth A. Cameron in ChrisL (35:3) 34–6.

14108. COX, ROBERT.   John the Baptist: a Shavian role model. IndS (24:1) 15–18.

14109. CREEL, JAMES MELTON.   The phonetic play: *Pygmalion* from manuscript to first printing. *See* **303.**

14110. DEBUSSCHER, GILBERT.   *Educating Rita*, or an Open University *Pygmalion. In* (pp. 303–17) **12.**

14111. DIETRICH, RICHARD F.   Deconstruction as devil's advocacy: a Shavian alternative. ModDr (29:3) 431–51.

14112. DUNN, D.   Shaw's Russia: a study of the attitudes, ideas and beliefs of George Bernard Shaw as they affected and were modified by the development of Soviet Russia. Unpub. doct. diss., Univ. of London, London School of Economics, 1984.

14113. EVERDING, ROBERT G.   Shaw and Saroyan. *See* **14075.**

14114. GANZ, ARTHUR.   George Bernard Shaw. New York: Grove, 1983. pp. 240. (Cf. bibl. 1985, 12939.) Rev. by Gladys M. Crane in TJ (38:4) 512.

14115. GAREBIAN, KEITH.   Questions of taste: the 1986 Shaw Festival. *See* **9958.**

14116. GEIST, EDWARD V.   Ann Whitefield and Hedda Gabler: two versions of Everywoman. IndS (24:2/3) 27–33.

14117. HULBAN, HORIA.   Logical and semantic paradoxes in G. B. Shaw's drama. AnUILingv (32) 67–73.

14118. LAURENCE, DAN H. (ed.).   Bernard Shaw's collected letters: vol. 3, 1911–1925. (Bibl. 1985, 12947.) Rev. by P. N. Furbank in LRB (8:4) 22.

14119. —— Plays political. Harmondsworth: Penguin. pp. 461. (Penguin plays.) (*The Apple Cart, On the Rocks, Geneva.*)

14120. —— QUINN, MARTIN (eds).   Shaw on Dickens. *See* **8062.**

14121. —— RAMBEAU, JAMES (eds).   Agitations: letters to the press, 1875–1950. New York: Ungar; London: Lorrimer, 1985. pp. xvi, 375. Rev. by Bernard F. Dukore in TJ (38:3) 385–6; by Roger Scruton in TLS, 21 Feb., 180.

14122. MARSH, JAN.   Jane and May Morris: a biographical story 1839–1938. *See* **8992.**

14123. MATHESON, T. J.   The lure of power and the triumph of capital: an ironic reading of *Major Barbara*. ESCan (12:3) 285–300.

14124. MAY, KEITH M.   Ibsen and Shaw. New York: St Martin's

Press, 1985. (Cf. bibl. 1985, 12951.) Rev. by Gladys M. Crane in TJ (38:4) 512–13.

14125. MITCHELL, BREON.   Ezra Pound and G. B. Shaw: a long wordy war. *See* **12692.**

14126. NICKSON, RICHARD.   The lure of Stalinism: Bernard Shaw and company. MidQ (25) 1984, 416–33.

14127. ROLL-HANSEN, DIDERIK.   Shaw's *Saint Joan* on the stage: a comparison of some early and some recent London productions. *In* (pp. 296–304) **18.**

14128. SAVA, IOSIF.   George Bernard Shaw şi publicistica pe teme muzicale. (George Bernard Shaw and music criticism.) *In* (pp. 213–24) IOSIF SAVA, Bucuriile muzicii. (The joy of music.) Bucharest: Editura muzicală, 1985. pp. 399.

14129. SHAWCROSS, JOHN T.   Further remarks on Milton's influence: Shelley and Shaw. *See* **5791.**

14130. SHIPTON, R. F.   Profession and commitment in the novels of Shaw. Unpub. doct. diss., Univ. of Wales, Swansea, 1984. [Abstr. in IT (35) 549–50.]

14131. STAFFORD, TONY J.   From hens' eggs to cinders: avian imagery in Shaw's *Saint Joan*. RMRLL (40:4) 213–20.

14132. TURNER, TRAMBLE T.   Bernard Shaw's 'eternal' Irish concern. Éire–Ireland (21:2) 57–69.

14133. VOGELER, MARTHA S.   *Widowers' Houses* and the London County Council. IndS (24:1) 3–11.

14134. WEINTRAUB, STANLEY.   A respectful distance: James Joyce and his Dublin townsman Bernard Shaw. *See* **12746.**

14135. —— The unexpected Shaw: biographical approaches to G. B. S. and his work. (Bibl. 1984, 12998.) Rev. by John Stokes in YES (16) 340–1.

14136. —— (ed.).   Bernard Shaw: the diaries 1885–1897. University Park: Pennsylvania State UP. 2 vols. pp. 1241. Rev. by Julia Briggs in THES (731) 15; by Ronald Bryden in LRB (8:22) 11–12.

14137. WINGATE, P. J.   Mencken, Shaw and honorary degrees. *See* **13242.**

Irwin Shaw

14138. MOORHEAD, MICHAEL.   Hemingway's *The Short Happy Life of Francis Macomber* and Shaw's *The Deputy Sheriff*. *See* **12387.**

14139. SUH, INJAE.   Irwin Shaw eui Violence: *The Young Lions* eul jungsim euro. (The violence of Irwin Shaw: *The Young Lions*.) JHY (7:3) 1985, 547–59.

Wilfrid Sheed

14140. SHEED, WILFRID.   Frank and Maisie: a memoir with parents. London: Chatto & Windus, 1985. pp. 296.

Sam Shepard

14141. ANON.   Sam Shepard: Motelové kroniky. (Sam Shepard: Motel chronicles). SvL (31:4) 2–3.

14142. CALLENS, JOHAN.   Memories of the sea in Shepard's Illinois. *See* **8262.**

14143. CARROLL, DENNIS. The filmic cut and 'switchback' in the plays of Sam Shepard. ModDr (28:1) 1985, 125–38.

14144. CIMA, GAY GIBSON. Shifting perspectives: combining Shepard and Rauschenberg. TJ (38:1) 67–81.

14145. DeROSE, DAVID JOSEPH. Lobster in the livingroom: the theatricality of Sam Shepard. Unpub. doct. diss., Univ. of California, Berkeley, 1985. [Abstr. in DA (47) 712A.]

14146. KRAMER, MIMI. In search of the good Shepard. NCrit (2) Oct. 1983, 51–7.

14147. KREKEL, MICHAEL. 'Von *Cowboys* bis *True West*': Sam Shepards Dramen. Dokumente einer amerikanischen Phantasie. Frankfurt: Lang. pp. 360. (Europäische Hochschulschriften: Reihe 30, Theater-, Film- und Fernsehwissenschaften, 25.)

14148. PROCTOR, ELIZABETH CLIFTON. The art of Sam Shepard. Unpub. doct. diss., Univ. of North Carolina at Chapel Hill, 1985. [Abstr. in DA (47) 181A.]

14149. SZILASSY, ZOLTÁN. A drámairó Sam Shepard. (Sam Shepard, the dramatist.) Nagyvilág (31:1) 110–13.

14150. WHITING, CHARLES. Inverted chronology in Sam Shepard's *La Turista*. ModDr (29:3) 416–22.

14151. ZINMAN, TOBY SILVERMAN. Sam Shepard and super-realism. ModDr (29:3) 423–30.

Nevil Shute (Nevil Shute Norway)
14152. ERISMAN, FRED. Nevil Shute and the closed frontier. WAL (21:3) 207–17.

Leslie Silko
14153. BROWN, PATRICIA CLAIRE. The spiderweb: a time structure in Leslie Silko's *Ceremony*. Unpub. doct. diss., East Texas State Univ. [Abstr. in DA (47) 1726A.]

Alan Sillitoe
14154. CRAIG, DAVID. The roots of Sillitoe's fiction. *In* (pp. 94–109) **6.**

14155. ROTHSCHILD, JOYCE. The growth of a writer: an interview with Alan Sillitoe. SoHR (20:2) 127–40.

James Simmons
14156. SIMMONS, JAMES. A boyhood in the colony. Threshold (36) 68–78.

14157. —— The roots of value. Linen Hall Review (3:3) 5–7.

Neil Simon
14158. HENRY, WILLIAM A., III. Reliving a poignant past: Neil Simon's best comedy looks homeward. Time, 15 Dec., 72–8.

14159. JOHNSON, ROBERT K. Neil Simon. (Bibl. 1985, 12987.) Rev. by Richard Toscan in TS (28/29) 1981/82–1982/83, 117–18.

14160. SAUVAGE, LEO. Simonized success. NewL (69:19) 17–18.

14161. —— Tragic misalliances. *See* **12270.**

S. J. Simon
14162. SHERRIN, NED (introd.). A bullet in the ballet. *See* **11316.**

14163. —— No bed for Bacon. *See* **11317.**

Louis Simpson
14164. BENSKO, JOHN. Reflexive narration in contemporary American poetry: some examples from Mark Strand, John Ashbery, Norman Dubie and Louis Simpson. *See* **11062.**

'Jo Sinclair' (Ruth Seid)
14165. SANDBERG, ELISABETH. Jo Sinclair: toward a critical biography. Unpub. doct. diss., Univ. of Massachusetts, 1985. [Abstr. in DA (46) 3720A.]

Upton Sinclair
14166. SPAUNHORST, FRANZ-PETER. Literarische Kulturkritik als Dekodierung von Macht und Werten am Beispiel ausgewählter Romane von Upton Sinclair, Frank Norris, John Dos Passos und Sinclair Lewis. Ein Beitrag zur Theorie und Methode der Amerikastudien als Kulturwert. *See* **11692.**
14167. VADON, LEHEL. Upton Sinclair fogadtatása. (Upton Sinclair's reception.) Budapest: Akadémiai Kiadó. pp. 202.

L. E. Sissman
14168. LEITHAUSER, BRAD. The fixed moment: the poetry of L. E. Sissman. NCrit (2) Oct. 1983, 36–42.

Edith Sitwell
14169. BOEHM, BARBARA ELLEN. Edith Sitwell: the hunt for the soul. Unpub. doct. diss., Princeton Univ. [Abstr. in DA (47) 186A.]

Sacheverell Sitwell
14170. RAEBURN, MICHAEL (ed.). Sacheverell Sitwell's England. London: Orbis. pp. 236.

Robin Skelton
14171. SKELTON, ROBIN. The collected longer poems 1947–1977. Victoria, B.C.: Sono Nis, 1985. pp. viii, 182. Rev. by Warren Stevenson in CanL (111) 201–2.

Douglas Reid Skinner
14172. GARDNER, SUSAN. Four South African poets: interviews with Robert Berold, Jeremy Cronin, Douglas Reid Skinner, Stephen Watson. *See* **11248.**
14173. JAMES, ALAN. From the editor. Upstream (3:1) 1985, 1–3. (Interview.)

George Sklar
14174. SEGAL, ERROL. George Sklar: playwright for a socially committed theatre. Unpub. doct. diss., Univ. of Michigan. [Abstr. in DA (47) 1929A.]

Elizabeth Smart
14175. MCMULLEN, LORRAINE. Elizabeth Smart 1913–1985. CanL (111) 238–40.
14176. VANWART, ALICE. *By Grand Central Station I Sat Down and Wept*: the novel as a poem. StudCanL (11:1) 38–51.

Dodie Smith
14177. SMITH, DODIE. Look back with gratitude. London: Muller; Blond & White, 1985. pp. 272.

Iain Crichton Smith
14178. FULTON, ROBIN (sel.). Selected poems 1955–1980. Edinburgh: Macdonald, 1981. pp. 119. Rev. by Roderick Watson in SSL (19) 1984, 207–14.

Pauline Smith
14179. COETZEE, J. M. Farm novel and *Plaasroman* in South Africa. *See* **9151.**

Stevie Smith
14180. BARBERA, JACK; MCBRIEN, WILLIAM. Stevie: a biography of Stevie Smith. London: Heinemann; New York: OUP. pp. 378. Rev. by Peter Kemp in Listener, 16 Jan., 27–8; by Susannah Clapp in LRB (7:22) 1985, 22–3; by Christopher Reid in TLS, 29 Nov. 1985, 1369; by Jo Russell in Eng (35) 285–9.
14181. BOSTOCK, PETER A. An analysis of the major personae in the poetry of Stevie Smith. Unpub. doct. diss., Fordham Univ., 1985. [Abstr. in DA (46) 2297A.]
14182. LAWSON, ELIZABETH. 'Not drowning but waving': Stevie Smith and the problem of simplicity. Meridian (5:1) 36–42.
14183. PUMPHREY, MARTIN. Play, fantasy and strange laughter: Stevie Smith's uncomfortable poetry. CritQ (28:3) 85–96.
14184. RANKIN, ARTHUR C. The poetry of Stevie Smith: 'little girl lost'. (Bibl. 1985, 13006.) Rev. by Joe Russell in Eng (35) 285–9.
14185. UNTERSLAK, JANET. A discussion of two poems. *See* **13066.**

Vivian Smith
14186. CATALANO, GARY. In terms of music: Vivian Smith's *Selected Poems*. Meanjin (45:1) 103–6 (review-article).
14187. ROWE, NOEL. Patience and surprise: the poetry of Vivian Smith. Southerly (46:2) 178–94.

William Gardner Smith
14188. HODGES, LEROY S., JR. Portrait of an expatriate: William Gardner Smith, writer. Westport, CT: Greenwood Press, 1985. pp. xvi, 130. Rev. by Nellie McKay in AL (58:4) 662–3.

Kendrick Smithyman
14189. GERAETS, JOHN. Kendrick Smithyman and Brasch's *Landfall*. *See* **603.**

Gary Snyder
14190. EASY, P. A. J. Tradition and innovation in the poetry of Gary Snyder, 1952–1982. Unpub. doct. diss., Univ. of Hull, 1983.
14191. KRAUS, JAMES W. Gary Snyder's biopoetics: a study of the poet as ecologist. Unpub. doct. diss., Univ. of Hawaii. [Abstr. in DA (47) 2159A.]

'Somerville and Ross' (Edith Somerville and Violet Martin)
14192. LEWIS, GIFFORD. Somerville and Ross: the world of the Irish R.M. London: Viking Press, 1985. pp. 251. Rev. by Patricia Craig in LRB (8:7) 19.

Susan Sontag
14193. KIM, CHONG-UN. Sontag ea Kosinski: minimalism sogo. (Sontag and Kosinski: a study of minimalism.) *See* **10834.**

14194. LOUVRE, ALF.   The reluctant historians: Sontag, Mailer and the American culture critics in the 1960s. *See* **13176.**

14195. PESTINO, JOSEPH FRANCIS.   The reader/writer affair: instigating repertoire in the experimental fiction of Susan Sontag, Walter Abish, Réjean Ducharme, Paul West, and Christine Brooke-Rose. *See* **10974.**

Charles Hamilton Sorley

14196. WILSON, JEAN MOORCROFT.   Charles Hamilton Sorley: a biography. London: Woolf, 1985. pp. 222. Rev. by Neil Corcoran in TLS, 28 Feb., 214.

Raymond Souster

14197. WHITEMAN, BRUCE.   Raymond Souster. *In* (pp. 237–76) **9.**

Bode Sowande

14198. AMBANASOM, SHADRACH ATEKE.   The adolescent protagonist in the African novel: an analysis of five African novels. *See* **12751.**

Wole Soyinka

14199. AWONUGA, C. O.   Language use and literary meaning: a study of linguistic and stylistic realisation of theme in Wole Soyinka's *The Interpreters*. Unpub. doct. diss., Univ. of Edinburgh, 1983.

14200. BROCKBANK, PHILIP.   Blood and wine, tragic ritual from Aeschylus to Soyinka. *See* **4399.**

14201. CERPANA.   Wole Soyinka et le théâtre africain anglophone. Nouvelles de Sud, N° 2. Ivry: Silex. pp. 1789. (Colloque C.E.R.P.A.N.A. 1984).

14202. COOPER, B. L.   A theory of African literature and its application to texts by Wole Soyinka, Ayi Kwei Armah and Ngugi wa Thiong'o. *See* **11056.**

14203. DOHERTY, JAIYEOLA.   Die Satire im nigerianischen Roman. Die Rolle der Satire in den Romanwerken 4 nigerianischer Schriftsteller: T. M. Aluko, Chinua Achebe, Nkem Nwankwo und Wole Soyinka. *See* **10978.**

14204. GIBBS, JAMES.   Wole Soyinka. Basingstoke: Macmillan. pp. ix, 170. (Macmillan modern dramatists.)

14205. HEPBURN, JOAN ELAINE.   Toward the reintegration of society: healers of the social breach in seven Soyinka plays. Unpub. doct. diss., Brown Univ., 1985. [Abstr. in DA (46) 1939A.]

14206. JABBI, BU-BUAKEI.   Mythopoeic sensibility in *The Interpreters*: a horizontal overview. Ob (7) Summer/Winter 1981, 43–74.

14207. LARSEN, STEPHAN.   A writer and his gods: a study of the importance of Yoruba myths and religious ideas to the writing of Wole Soyinka. (Bibl. 1983, 13390.) Rev. by Jöran Mjöberg in Samlaren (107) 121–2. (In Swedish.)

14208. MCDOUGALL, RUSSELL JOHN.   A casement, triple-arch'd. Cultural kinetics: the fusion of music, the dance and the word in African and Caribbean culture. *See* **10983.**

14209. OMOLE, JAMES OLUKAYODE.   A sociolinguistic analysis of Wole Soyinka's *The Interpreters*. *See* **1022.**

14210. SOYINKA, WOLE. Shakespeare and the living dramatist. *See* **4596.**

14211. WALDER, DENNIS. Strange that Soyinka is so little heard of. We are supposed to be in favour of writers. Listener (116) 30 Oct., 25.

Muriel Spark

14212. BOLD, ALAN. Muriel Spark. London: Methuen. pp. 96. (Contemporary writers.)

14213. —— (ed.). Muriel Spark: an odd capacity for vision. London: Vision Press, 1984. pp. 208. (Critical studies series.)

14214. NORQUAY, GLENDA. Moral absolutism in the novels of Robert Louis Stevenson, Robin Jenkins and Muriel Spark: challenges to realism. *See* **9272.**

14215. RICHMOND, VELMA BOURGEOIS. Muriel Spark. London: Lorrimer, 1984. (Cf. bibl. 1985, 13026.) Rev. by Joseph A. Quinn in ChrisL (35:4) 44–5.

Bernard Spencer

14216. CAESAR, A. D. Exploring the fence: the poetry and manuscripts of Bernard Spencer. UES (24:1) 24–30.

Stephen Spender

14217. ABLEMAN, PAUL. Paul Ableman talks to Stephen Spender. LRev, Nov. 1985, 47–50.

14218. GOLDSMITH, JOHN (ed.). Journals 1939–1983. New York: Random House, 1985. (Cf. bibl. 1985, 13030.) Rev. by R. Z. Sheppard in Time, 20 Jan., 68; by Monroe K. Spears in BkW, 12 Jan., 1, 7.

14219. SPENDER, STEPHEN. Collected poems, 1928–1985. (Bibl. 1985, 13031.) Rev. by John Whitehead in EC (36:2) 186–91.

14220. VENDLER, HELEN. Youth lost and kept. NY, 10 Nov., 138–44.

Mickey Spillane

14221. SANDELS, ROBERT. 'The machinery of government *vs* people who cared': rightism in Mickey Spillane's Tiger Mann novels. Clues (7:1) 49–109.

Jean Stafford

14222. LEARY, WILLIAM G. A tale of two titles: Jean Stafford's *Caveat Emptor*. SAQ (85:2) 123–33.

14223. McCONAHAY, MARY DAVIDSON. 'Heidelberry braids' and Yankee 'politesse': Jean Stafford and Robert Lowell reconsidered. *See* **13087.**

George Stanley

14224. THESEN, SHARON. Chains of grace: the poetry of George Stanley. ECanW (32) 106–13.

Olaf Stapledon

14225. CROSSLEY, ROBERT. Olaf Stapledon and the idea of science fiction. MFS (32:1) 21–42.

14226. LEM, STANISLAW. On Stapledon's *Last and First Men*. Trans. by ISTVAN CSICSERY-RONAY, JR. SFS (13:3) 272–91.

14227. SATTY, HARVEY J.; SMITH, CURTIS C. Olaf Stapledon: a bibliography. Westport, CT; London: Greenwood Press, 1984. pp. xxxviii, 167. (Bibliographies and indexes in world literature, 2.)

Dame Freya Stark

14228. MOOREHEAD, CAROLINE.   Freya Stark. (Bibl. 1985, 13041, where scholar's surname misspelt.) Rev. by Malise Ruthven in LRB (8:11) 10–11.

C. K. Stead

14229. DURIX, JEAN-PIERRE.   Memoirs of a self-reflective godwit: C. K. Stead's *All Visitors Ashore*. JCL (21:1) 80–92.

Christina Stead

14230. BLAKE, ANN.   Christina Stead's *Ocean of Story*. Meridian (5:2) 117–22.

14231. BRYDON, DIANA.   Resisting 'the tyranny of what is written': Christina Stead's fiction. Ariel (17:4) 3–15.

14232. HOLMES, BRUCE.   Character and ideology in Christina Stead's *House of All Nations*. Southerly (45:3) 1985, 266–79.

14233. WOODWARD, WENDY.   Writing differences and the ideology of form: narrative structure in the novels of Christina Stead. Theoria (68) 49–57.

Lincoln Steffens

14234. LANGLOIS, KAREN S.   Mary Austin and Lincoln Steffens. *See* **11106.**

Gertrude Stein

14235. BURNS, EDWARD (ed.).   The letters of Gertrude Stein and Carl Van Vechten. New York; Guildford: Columbia UP. 2 vols. pp. 432; 901. Rev. by William H. Cass in TLS, 7 Nov., 1235–6.

14236. CAGLE, CHARLES HARMON.   'Cézanne nearly did': Stein, Cézanne, and Hemingway. *See* **12365.**

14237. CARAMELLO, CHARLES.   Reading Gertrude Stein reading Henry James, or Eros is Eros is Eros is Eros. *See* **8636.**

14238. DUBNICK, RANDA.   The structure of obscurity: Gertrude Stein, language, and cubism. (Bibl. 1984, 13101.) Rev. by Ellen Quigley in CanL (111) 196–7; by Allon White in JEGP (85:2) 295–8.

14239. GALANES, PHILIP (ed.).   Gertrude Stein: letters to a friend. ParisR (100) 359–78.

14240. HOFFELD, LAURA.   Gertrude Stein's unmentionables. LU (2:1) 1978, 48–55.

14241. LEMAIRE, GÉRARD-GEORGES.   La bataille du *Finnegans Wake*. *See* **12681.**

14242. MAUBREY-ROSE, VICTORIA.   The anti-representational response: Gertrude Stein's *Lucy Church Amiably*. (Bibl. 1985, 13068.) Rev. by Douglas Robinson in SN (58) 267–70.

14243. ROBINSON, DOUGLAS.   Against representation. SN (58:2) 267–70 (review-article).

14244. WIGHT, DORIS TERESA.   Illuminations of woman in Stein's *Tender Buttons*, Vallejo's *Trilce*, and Artaud's *L'Ombilic des limbes*. Unpub. doct. diss., Univ. of Wisconsin–Madison, 1985. [Abstr. in DA (46) 2687A.]

John Steinbeck

14245. GENTRY, ROBERT WAYNE.   John Steinbeck's use of

non-teleological thinking in his Mexican-American characters. Unpub.
doct. diss., Baylor Univ., 1985. [Abstr. in DA (46) 3033A.]

14246. MEYER, MICHAEL JON. Darkness visible: the moral dilemma
of Americans as portrayed in the early short fiction and later novels of
John Steinbeck. Unpub. doct. diss., Loyola Univ. of Chicago. [Abstr. in
DA (47) 179A.]

14247. OWENS, LOUIS. John Steinbeck's re-vision of America. (Bibl.
1985, 13093.) Rev. by Yoshinobu Hakutani in AL (58:2) 303–5.

14248. WHITE, RAY LEWIS. *The Grapes of Wrath* and the critics of
1939. RALS (13:2) 1983, 134–64.

James Stephens

14249. SHERRY, RUTH. The Irish working class in fiction. *In*
(pp. 110–23) **6.**

Gerald Stern

14250. GARBER, FREDERICK. Pockets of secrecy, places of occasion:
on Gerald Stern. APR (15:4) 38–47.

Wallace Stevens

14251. ADLARD, A. 'Words of the world': the testimony of the hero in
the poems of Wallace Stevens. Unpub. doct. diss., Univ. of Lancaster.

14252. ALFANO, MARY F. COURTNEY. A certain order of forms: the
music of *Harmonium*. Unpub. doct. diss., Fordham Univ. [Abstr. in DA
(47) 1320A.]

14253. ARENSBERG, MARY. 'Golden vacancies': Wallace Stevens'
problematics of place and presence. WSJ (10:1) 36–41.

14254. ARGYROS, ALEX. The residual difference: Wallace Stevens
and American deconstruction. *See* **10714.**

14255. BATES, MILTON J. Wallace Stevens: a mythology of self.
London: California UP, 1985. (Cf. bibl. 1985, 13103.) Rev. by Edward
Neill in EC (36:4) 355–9; by Katherine T. Wallingford in AL (58:2)
274–5; by Helen Vendler in NEQ (59:4) 549–63; by John N. Serio in
Criticism (28:3) 354–7.

14256. BERGER, CHARLES. Forms of farewell: the late poetry of
Wallace Stevens. (Bibl. 1985, 13104.) Rev. by David H. Hesla in AL
(58:3) 470–2; by Sam S. Baskett in CR (30:1) 123–4.

14257. BROGAN, JACQUELINE VAUGHT. Stevens and simile: a theory of
language. Princeton, NJ; Guildford: Princeton UP. pp. xii, 214.

14258. —— Wallace Stevens' *Vacancy in the Park* and the concept of
similitude. WSJ (10:1) 9–17.

14259. BUTT, DAVID. Wallace Stevens and 'willful nonsense'. SoRA
(18:3) 1985, 279–97.

14260. DESAI, R. W. Stevens' *Peter Quince at the Clavier* and *Pericles*.
See **4938.**

14261. DOUGHERTY, JAY. Stevens' mother and *Sunday Morning*. WSJ
(10:2) 100–6.

14262. DOYLE, CHARLES (ed.). Wallace Stevens: the critical heritage.
London: Boston, MA: Routledge & Kegan Paul, 1985. pp. 480. (Critical
heritage.) Rev. by J. P. Ward in THES (705) 23.

14263. FILREIS, ALAN JAY. World without peculiarity: the life of

Wallace Stevens. Unpub. doct. diss., Univ. of Virginia, 1985. [Abstr. in DA (47) 529A.]

14264. FISHER, BARBARA M.   Advancing toward chaos in new Stevens criticism. Review (7) 1985, 77–87 (review-article).

14265. GALEF, DAVID.   Resemblance and change in Wallace Stevens' *Three Academic Pieces*. AL (58:4) 589–608.

14266. GELPI, ALBERT (ed.).   Wallace Stevens: the poetics of Modernism. Cambridge: CUP, 1985. pp. x, 165. (Cambridge studies in American literature and culture.) Rev. by Edward Neill in EC (36:4) 359–60; by Helen Vendler in NEQ (59:4) 549–63.

14267. HALLIDAY, MARK.   Stevens and heterosexual love. ELit (13:1) 135–55.

14268. HARVEY, GORDON.   'Cherished like the thought of heaven': sentiment and sentimentality in Stevens. ESCan (12:3) 301–14.

14269. HASSAN, IHAB.   Imagination and belief: Wallace Stevens and William James in our clime. *See* **8770.**

14270. HELLER, JÜRGEN.   William Carlos Williams, Wallace Stevens und die moderne Malerei. Ästhetische Entwürfe, Verfahren und Komposition. Frankfurt: Lang. pp. 255. (Studien zur englischen Literatur, 7.)

14271. KEITH, PATRICIA JANE.   A violence from within: Wallace Stevens' *Notes towards a Supreme Fiction*. Unpub. doct. diss., Brandeis Univ. [Abstr. in DA (47) 1729A.]

14272. KOMAR, KATHLEEN L.   The issue of transcendence in Rilke's *Duineser Elegien* and Stevens' *Notes toward a Supreme Fiction*. Neophilologus (70:3) 429–41.

14273. KWON, HYONG-CHANG.   Wallace Stevens eui *The Auroras of Autumn*. (Wallace Stevens's *The Auroras of Autumn*.) YYY (4) 3–30.

14274. —— Wallace Stevens eui *Esthétique du Mal*. (Wallace Stevens's *Esthétique du Mal*.) YYY (3) 1985, 117–54.

14275. LaGUARDIA, DAVID M.   Advance on chaos: the sanctifying imagination of Wallace Stevens. (Bibl. 1985, 13121.) Rev. by Barbara M. Fisher in Review (7) 1985, 77–87; by Peter Nicholls in NQ (33:2) 279–80.

14276. LEGGET, B. J.   Wallace Stevens and Marianne Moore: two essays and a private review. *See* **13304.**

14277. McDERMOTT, JOHN V.   Stevens' X: the mighty egoist. NCL (16:4) 5–6.

14278. MACDONALD, D. L.   Wallace Stevens and Victor Serge. DalR (66:1/2) 174–80.

14279. MUEUR, KINERETH.   Stevens' *The Idea of Order at Key West*. Exp (44:3) 41–3.

14280. PATKE, RAJEEV S.   The long poems of Wallace Stevens: an interpretative study. New York: CUP, 1985. pp. xiii, 263. (Cf. bibl. 1985, 13126, where pagination incorrect.) Rev. by Helen Vendler in NEQ (59:4) 549–63; by David Galef in AL (58:3) 472–3.

14281. PERLIS, ALAN D.   Wallace Stevens' reader poems and the effacement of metaphor. WSJ (10:2) 67–75.

14282. RICHARDSON, JOAN. Wallace Stevens: the early years, 1879–1923. New York: Morrow. pp. 591. Rev. by Katha Pollitt in NYTB, 21 Dec., 13; by David Young in BkW, 21 Sept., 1, 7.

14283. ROBINSON, FRED MILLER. Strategies of smallness: Wallace Stevens and Emily Dickinson. *See* **8147.**

14284. ROYLE, N. W. O. The romantic imagination in relation to war and apocalypse in the later poetry of Wallace Stevens. Unpub. doct. diss., Univ. of Oxford, 1984.

14285. SCHAUM, MELITA. 'Preferring text to gloss': from decreation to deconstruction in Wallace Stevens criticism. WSJ (10:2) 84–99.

14286. SCHWARTZ, RICHARD ALAN. A textual history of Wallace Stevens' *Three Travellers Watch a Sunrise*. *See* **334.**

14287. SCOTT, NATHAN A., JR. The poetics of belief: studies in Coleridge, Arnold, Pater, Santayana, Stevens, and Heidegger. *See* **7563.**

14288. SMITH, LYLE H., JR. The argument of *Sunday Morning*. CLit (13:3) 254–65.

14289. STEINMAN, LISA. Getting the world right: Stevens, science and the American context. WSJ (10:1) 18–26.

14290. WALKER, DAVID. The transparent lyric: reading and meaning in the poetry of Stevens and Williams. (Bibl. 1985, 13134.) Rev. by Eleanor Berry in WCWR (12:2) 20–8.

14291. WHITING, ANTHONY. Words of the world: Wallace Stevens' poetry of irony. Unpub. doct. diss., Columbia Univ., 1984. [Abstr. in DA (47) 903A.]

14292. WICKERS, JANINE NOEL. Sight and song: perception, creation, and the myth of Orpheus in Mallarmé, Valéry, Rilke, and Stevens. Unpub. doct. diss., Brandeis Univ. [Abstr. in DA (47) 172A.]

14293. WILDE, DANA. Romantic and symbolist contexts in the poetry of Wallace Stevens. WSJ (10:1) 42–57.

14294. WOODMAN, LEONORA. Stanza my stone: Wallace Stevens and the hermetic tradition. (Bibl. 1985, 13135.) Rev. by Barbara M. Fisher in Review (7) 1985, 77–87.

Adrian Stokes

14295. CASILLO, ROBERT. The stone alive: Adrian Stokes and John Ruskin. *See* **9125.**

14296. READ, R. The evocative genre of art criticism: a study of descriptive prose in the works of Hazlitt, Ruskin, Pater and Adrian Stokes. *See* **8521.**

Ruth Stone

14297. GILBERT, SANDRA M., *et al.* On Ruth Stone. IowaR (12:2/3) 1981, 323–30.

Tom Stoppard

14298. BRASSELL, TIM. Tom Stoppard: an assessment. New York: St Martin's Press, 1985. (Cf. bibl. 1985, 13138.) Rev. by John Harty in TJ (38:1) 127–8.

14299. HARTY, JOHN, III. Tom Stoppard and the literature of exhaustion. Unpub. doct. diss., Univ. of Maryland, 1985. [Abstr. in DA (46) 2300A.]

14300. KELLY, KATHERINE.   Tom Stoppard's *Artist Descending a Staircase*: outdoing the 'Dada' Duchamp. CompDr (20:3) 191–200.
14301. KIM, MIJA.   Stoppard's world of mysteries in *Jumpers*. CAE (19) 41–51.
14302. KIM, WOO-TACK.   Shakespeare wa post-modernism: *Hamlet* wa *Rosenkrantz and Guildenstern Are Dead* eui daebi reul tonghan Shakespeare eui hyeondaesung yeongu. *See* **4759.**
14303. KRAMER, MIMI.   No time for comedy. NCrit (1) Mar. 1983, 56–63. (*The Real Thing.*)
14304. KREPS, BARBARA.   How do we know what we know in Tom Stoppard's *Jumpers*? TCL (32:2) 187–208.
14305. LEVENSON, JILL L.   *Hamlet* andante/*Hamlet* allegro: Tom Stoppard's two versions. *See* **4764.**
14306. PAGE, MALCOLM (comp.).   File on Stoppard. London: Methuen. pp. 96. (Writer-files.)
14307. SAMMELLS, N. C.   Criticism as creation in the works of Tom Stoppard. Unpub. doct. diss., Univ. of London, University Coll., 1984.
14308. SAMMELLS, NEIL.   Giggling at the arts: Tom Stoppard and James Saunders. *See* **14080.**
14309. STEPHENSON, BARBARA JEAN.   In defense of play: a reassessment of Tom Stoppard's theaters. Unpub. doct. diss., Univ. of Florida, 1985. [Abstr. in DA (47) 1339A.]
14310. WATSON, GEORGE.   Osborne, Pinter, Stoppard: a playful look at London since 1956. *See* **13671.**
14311. WOLF, WERNER.   Geschichtsfiktion im Kontext dekonstruktivistischer Tendenzen in neuerer Historik und literarischer Postmoderne: Tom Stoppards *Travesties*. PoetA (18:3/4) 305–57.

David Storey

14312. HILTON, R. H.   David Storey: a personal view of social experience: reality and its transformation in the novels and plays. Unpub. doct. diss., Univ. of Lancaster, 1983.
14313. JANOUŠEK, MIROSLAV.   David Storey: un-Lawrentian comparative notes on *Saville* and *Sons and Lovers*. *See* **12910.**
14314. OLSSON, BARBARA.   Alienation in Storey and Chekhov: a reassessment of *In Celebration* and *The Farm*. WBEP (80) 119–33.

Rex Stout

14315. ANDERSON, DAVID R.   Rex Stout. New York: Ungar; London: Lorrimer, 1984. pp. x, 134.
14316. BLADES, JOHN.   You'd just never guess Nero Wolfe had been dead. BW, 16 Mar., 38.

Adrien Stoutenburg
('Barbie Arden', 'Lace Kendall', 'Nelson Minier')

14317. SLAVITT, DAVID R. (ed.); DICKEY, JAMES (introd.).   Land of superior mirages: new and selected poems. Baltimore, MD; London: Johns Hopkins UP. pp. xi, 122. (Johns Hopkins: poetry and fiction.)

Randolph Stow

14318. HASSALL, ANTHONY J.   Strange country: a study of Randolph Stow. St Lucia; London: Queensland UP. pp. xix, 213.

14319. INGHAM, DAVID KEITH.   Mediation and the indirect meta-fiction of Randolph Stow, M. K. Joseph, and Timothy Findley. *See* **11946.**

14320. MOORE, GERALD.   Islands of ascent: the Australasian novels of Randolph Stow. International Fiction Review (Fredericton, New Brunswick) (13:2) 61–8.

14321. PRIESSNITZ, HORST.   Probleme einer kolonialen Existenz als Themen im Romanwerk von Randolph Stow. AAA (11:1) 40–62.

John St Loe Strachey

14322. MORRIS, A. J. L.   A study of John St Loe Strachey's editorship of *The Spectator*, 1901–14. *See* **654.**

Mark Strand

14323. BENSKO, JOHN.   Reflexive narration in contemporary American poetry: some examples from Mark Strand, John Ashbery, Norman Dubie and Louis Simpson. *See* **11062.**

Lucien Stryk

14324. GUILLORY, DANIEL L.   The Oriental connection: Zen and representations of the Midwest in the collected poems of Lucien Stryk. Midamerica (13) 107–15.

Francis Stuart

14325. MOLLOY, F. C.   Francis Stuart's Australian connection: the life and death of Henry Irwin Stuart. IUR (16) 22–32.

14326. WHEALE, J. W.   Redemption in the work of Francis Stuart. Unpub. doct. diss., Univ. of Warwick, 1983. [Abstr. in IT (35) 54.]

Jesse Stuart

14327. SPURLOCK, JOHN HOWARD.   A sociocultural and rhetorical analysis of Jesse Stuart's fiction. Unpub. doct. diss., Univ. of Louisville, 1985. [Abstr. in DA (47) 890A.]

Howard Sturgis

14328. ANNAN, NOEL (introd.).   Belchamber. Oxford: OUP. pp. xii, 334. (Twentieth-century classics.)

William Styron

14329. BLEIKASTEN, ANDRÉ (ed.).   William Styron. Delta: Centre d'Études et de Recherches sur les Écrivains du Sud aux États-Unis. pp. 186.

14330. CAPUTO, PHILIP.   Styron's choice. Esquire (106:6) 136–8, 140, 150, 152, 154, 156–7, 159.

14331. CRANE, JOHN KENNY.   The root of all evil: the thematic unity of William Styron's fiction. (Bibl. 1985, 13158.) Rev. by Waldemar Zacharasiewicz in AL (58:3) 459–61; by Robert K. Morris in Review (8) 231–40.

14332. MORRIS, ROBERT K.   Styron and evil. Review (8) 231–40 (review-article).

14333. NENADÁL, RADOSLAV.   K osobnosti Williama Styrona. (On the personality of William Styron.) Literární měsíčník (15:1) 113–15.

14334. RICHARDSON, THOMAS J.   Art and the angry times: apocalypse and redemption in William Styron's *The Confessions of Nat Turner*. MFR (19:2) 1985, 147–56.

14335. WEST, JAMES L. W., III (ed.).   Coversations with William Styron. French interviews trans. by W. PIERRE JACOEBEE; introd. by WILLIAM STYRON. Jackson: London: Mississippi UP, 1985. pp. xvi, 280. (Literary conversations.) Rev. by John Lang in SCR (3:2) 114–15.

14336. WHITE, ROBERT TERRENCE.   Point of view in the novels of William Styron. Unpub. doct. diss., Univ. of Arkansas, 1985. [Abstr. in DA (46) 3029A.]

Ruth Suckow

14337. DEMARR, MARY JEAN.   Ruth Suckow's Iowa 'nice girls'. Midamerica (13) 69–83.

Montague Summers

14338. SMITH, TIMOTHY D'ARCH.   Montague Summers: a bibliography. Wellingborough: Aquarian Press, 1983. pp. 170. Rev. by Hugh Ormsby-Lennon in YES (16) 354–6.

Glendon Swarthout

14339. ELLIS, KIRK.   *The Shootist*: going in style. LitFQ (14:1) 44–52.

J. M. Synge

14340. BECKSON, KARL.   Arthur Symons on John Millington Synge: a previously unpublished memoir. *See* **9294.**

14341. DOLL, EILEEN JESSICA.   Celtic and Christian signs in dialogue: John M. Synge and Ramon del Valle-Inclán. Unpub. doct. diss., Purdue Univ. [Abstr. in DA (47) 2151A.]

14342. FLEMING, DEBORAH DIANE.   The Irish peasant in the work of W. B. Yeats and J. M. Synge. Unpub. doct. diss., Ohio State Univ., 1985. [Abstr. in DA (46) 3724A.]

14343. GIANNOTTI, THOMAS JOHN, JR.   A language of silence: writing the self in Yeats and Synge, Joyce and Beckett. *See* **11176.**

14344. KING, MARY C.   The drama of J. M. Synge. London: Fourth Estate, 1985. pp. 229.

14345. SADDLEMYER, ANN (ed.).   Collected letters of John Millington Synge. (Bibl. 1985, 13178–9.) Rev. by Toni O'Brien Johnson in CJIS (12:1) 101–3; by Patrick Rafroidi in Études irlandaises (9) 1984, 337.

14345a. VICHY, THÉRÈSE.   La mer dans le théâtre de Synge. CVE (23) 177–88.

Rabindranath Tagore

14346. HENN, KATHERINE.   Rabindranath Tagore: a bibliography. Metuchen, NJ; London: American Theological Library Assn; Scarecrow Press, 1985. pp. xvii, 331. (ATLA bibliographies, 13.)

14347. PONNUSWAMY, KRISHNA.   Yeats and Tagore: a comparative study of their plays. Unpub. doct. diss., Madurai Kamaraj Univ. (India), 1984. [Abstr. in DA (46) 1933A.]

14348. THOMPSON, E. P.   Memories of Tagore. LRB (8:9) 18–19.

Allen Tate

14349. CORE, GEORGE.   Mr Tate and the limits of poetry. VQR (62:1) 105–14.

14350. GILMORE, SUE CHANEY.   The Aeneas analogy: a study of the Aeneas tradition in the works of Dryden, Hardy, and Tate. *See* **5416.**

14351. SIMPSON, LEWIS P.   Allen Tate. SewR (94:3) 471–85.

Elizabeth Taylor

14352. LIDDELL, ROBERT. Elizabeth and Ivy. Introd. by FRANCIS KING. *See* **11467.**

A. S. J. Tessimond

14353. NICHOLSON, HUBERT (ed.). The collected poems of A. S. J. Tessimond. Reading: Whiteknights, 1985. pp. xviii, 188.

'Josephine Tey' ('Gordon Daviot', Elizabeth Mackintosh)

14354. LIGHT, ALISON. Writing fictions: femininity and the 1950s. *In* (pp. 139–65) **45.**

Sharon Thesen

14355. WAH, FRED. Subjective as objective: the lyric poetry of Sharon Thesen. ECanW (32) 114–21.

Audrey Thomas

14356. DAVEY, FRANK. Alternate stories: the short fiction of Audrey Thomas and Margaret Atwood. *See* **11075.**

14357. PRENTICE, CHRIS. Re-writing their stories, renaming themselves: post-colonialism and feminism in the fictions of Keri Hulme and Audrey Thomas. *See* **12497.**

D. M. Thomas

14358. COWART, DAVID. Being and seeming: *The White Hotel*. Novel (19:3) 216–31.

14359. FOSTER, JOHN BURT, JR. Magic realism in *The White Hotel*: compensatory vision and the transformation of classic realism. SoHR (20:3) 205–19.

14360. GRANOFSKY, RONALD. Holocaust as symbol in *Riddley Walker* and *The White Hotel*. *See* **12437.**

14361. HUTCHEON, LINDA. Literary borrowing... and stealing: plagiarism, sources, influences, and intertexts. ESCan (12:2) 229–39.

Dylan Thomas

14362. ACKERMAN, JOHN. La recherche du temps gallois: Dylan Thomas's development as a prose writer. AWR (83) 86–95.

14363. DAVIES, JAMES A. 'Crying in my wordy wilderness': *The Collected Letters of Dylan Thomas*. AWR (83) 96–105 (review-article).

14364. DAVIES, WALFORD. Dylan Thomas. Milton Keynes: Open UP. pp. 128. (Open guides to literature.) Rev. by James A. Davies in AWR (84) 143–5.

14365. —— Dylan Thomas: the poet in his chains. Swansea: University College. pp. 28. (W. D. Thomas Memorial Lecture.)

14366. FERRIS, PAUL. Dylan Thomas. Harmondsworth: Penguin, 1985. pp. 446. (Second ed.: first ed. 1977.) Rev. by Claude Rawson in TLS, 2 May, 475–6.

14367. —— (ed.). The collected letters of Dylan Thomas. (Bibl. 1985, 13206.) Rev. by James A. Davies in AWR (83) 96–105; by Paul Gray in Time, 21 Apr., 73; by Ian Hamilton in BkW, 4 May, 1, 4; by Claude Rawson in TLS, 2 May, 475–6.

14368. McKAY, DON. Crafty Dylan and the 'Alterwise' sonnets: 'I build a flying tower and I pull it down'. UTQ (55:4) 375–94.

14369. —— What shall we do with a drunken poet? Dylan Thomas' poetic language. QQ (93:4) 794–807.

14370. THOMAS, CAITLIN; TREMLETT, GEORGE.   Caitlin: a warring absence. London: Secker & Warburg. pp. xvi, 211.

Edward Thomas

14371. GRAY, PIERS.   The childhood of Edward Thomas. CritQ (28:3) 51–67.

14372. KIRKHAM, MICHAEL.   The imagination of Edward Thomas. Cambridge: CUP. pp. xi, 225.

14373. LEHMANN, JOHN.   Three literary friendships: Byron & Shelley, Rimbaud & Verlaine, Robert Frost & Edward Thomas. *See* **7780.**

14374. MITCHELL, PETER.   Edward Thomas and the Georgians. UTQ (55:4) 359–74.

14375. SMITH, STAN.   Edward Thomas. London: Faber & Faber. pp. 221. (Faber student guides.)

14376. THOMAS, R. GEORGE.   Edward Thomas: a portrait. Toronto: OUP, 1985. (Cf. bibl. 1985, 13214.) Rev. by Jeremy Hooker in AWR (83) 148–52; by Jonathan Barker in Poetry Wales (21:1) 104–8; by Judith Stanley-Smith in Planet (56) 108–10; by Keith Wilson in QQ (93:4) 906–7.

14377. —— (introd.).   A handful of letters. Edinburgh: Tragara Press, 1985. pp. 37.

14378. WILSON, ELAINE (comp.).   A mirror of England. London: Shepheard-Walwyn, 1985. pp. 158.

Gwyn Thomas

14379. PARNELL, MICHAEL.   Years of apprenticeship: the early life of Gwyn Thomas. Planet (59) 64–70.

14380. ROBINSON, JEFFREY; MCCANN, BRIAN (eds).   High on hope. Cowbridge, South Glamorgan: Brown, 1985. pp. 120. Rev. by Mercer Simpson in AWR (82) 122.

14381. WILLIAMS, RAYMOND (introd.).   All things betray thee. London: Lawrence & Wishart. pp. 332. Rev. by Michael Parnell in AWR (84) 134–5.

R. S. Thomas

14382. HASAN, H. M.   Jewels of blood: an Arab perspective on R. S. Thomas. Unpub. doct. diss., Univ. of Wales, Aberystwyth, 1985. [Abstr. in IT (36) 472.]

14383. RADNER, EPHRAIM.   Passing through hard facts: the poetry of R. S. Thomas. ChCen (103:35) 1027–30.

14384. VOLK, SABINE.   Grenzpfähle der Wirklichkeit: approaches to the poetry of R. S. Thomas. (Bibl. 1985, 13217.) Rev. by Sandra Anstey in AWR (82) 123–4.

Hunter S. Thompson

14385. BEARD, JOHN.   Inside the whale: a critical study of New Journalism and the nonfiction form. *See* **13168.**

Mervyn Thompson

14386. BLACK, SEBASTIAN (introd.).   Mervyn Thompson: selected plays. (Bibl. 1985, 13220.) Rev. by Richard Corballis in Landfall (40:1) 100–7. (*See also* Landfall (40:4) 527–9 (reply by Thompson).)

James Thurber

14387. BLYTHE, HAL; SWEET, CHARLIE. Coitus interruptis: sexual symbolism in *The Secret Life of Walter Mitty*. SSF (23:1) 110–13.

14388. CARNES, PACK. The American face of Aesop: Thurber's fables and tradition. MS (80) 3–17.

14389. THOMPSON, TERRY. Look out for that Buick! Mitty *vs* machine. NCL (16:2) 11–12.

14390. TOOMBS, SARAH ELEANORA. James Thurber: a research guide. Unpub. doct. diss., Univ. of Notre Dame. [Abstr. in DA (47) 2163A.]

'James Tiptree, Jr' ('Raccoona Sheldon', Alice Sheldon)

14391. BARR, MARLEEN. 'The *females* do the fathering!': James Tiptree's male matriarchs and adult human gametes. SFS (13:1) 42–9.

J. R. R. Tolkien

14392. BOENIG, ROBERT. Tolkien and old Germanic ethics. Mythlore (13:2) 9–12, 40.

14393. CHRISTOPHER, JOE R. An Inklings' bibliography. See **13025.**

14394. DEYO, STEVEN M. Niggle's leaves: *The Red Book of Westmarch* and related minor poetry of J. R. R. Tolkien. Mythlore (12:3) 28–37.

14395. EINHAUS, BARBARA. *The Lord of the Rings*. Logik der kreativen Imagination. Munich: tuduv-Verlagsgesellschaft. pp. 239.

14396. FLIEGER, VERLYN. Missing person. Mythlore (12:4) 12–15.

14397. FRIEDMAN, BARTON. Tolkien and David Jones: the great war and the war of the ring. See **12595.**

14398. HARGROVE, GENE. Who is Tom Bombadil? Mythlore (13:1) 20–4.

14399. HOLMBERG, ANNIKA. J. R. R. Tolkien, *Kalevala* och det finska språket. (J. R. R. Tolkien, *Kalevala* and the Finnish language.) Horisont (33:5) 73–4.

14400. HYDE, PAUL NOLAN. Leaf and key. Mythlore (12:4) 27–9, 36.

14401. KROGH, BODIL. 'Heorot revisited': håbløshed og heltemod i: brugen af *Beowulf* som litteratur og i litteratur i det 20 årh. med hovedvægt på J. R. R. Tolkiens forfatterskab. ('Heorot revisited': despair and valour: the use of *Beowulf* as literature and in literature in the 20th century, with special reference to J. R. R. Tolkien's writing.) See **3263.**

14402. LOWMAN, P. J. Supernaturalistic causality and Christian theism in the modern English novel. See **11456.**

14403. MENDE, LISA ANNE. Gondolin, Minas Tirith and the eucatastrophe. Mythlore (13:2) 37–40.

14404. PURTILL, RICHARD L. J. R. R. Tolkien: myth, morality and religion. (Bibl. 1985, 13246.) Rev. by August J. Fry in ChrisL (35:4) 34–5.

14405. RATELIFF, JOHN D. 'And something yet remains to be said': Tolkien and Williams. Mythlore (12:3) 48–54.

14406. SCHAKEL, PETER. Dance as metaphor and myth in Lewis, Tolkien, and Williams. *See* **13043.**

14407. SCHÜTZE, MARLI. Neue Wege nach Narnia und Mittelerde. Handlungskonstituenten in der Fantasy-Literatur von C. S. Lewis und J. R. R. Tolkien. *See* **13044.**

14408. THOMPSON, GEORGE H. (comp.). Early reviews of books by J. R. R. Tolkien. Mythlore (12:3) 61–2; (12:4) 59–61; (13:1) 54–9.

14409. TOLKIEN, CHRISTOPHER (ed.). The shaping of Middle-Earth: the Wuenta, the Ambarkanta and the annals: together with the earliest Silmarillion and the first map. London: Allen & Unwin. pp. 380. (History of Middle-Earth, 4.)

Melvin B. Tolson

14410. RUSSELL, MARIANN. Ghetto laughter: a note on Tolson's style. Ob (5) Spring/Summer 1979, 7–16.

John Kennedy Toole

14411. MARTIN, VALERIE. Publish the perished. SatR, May/June, 46–8, 50, 87–8.

Jean Toomer

14412. BRINKMEYER, ROBERT H., JR. Wasted talent, wasted art: the literary career of Jean Toomer. SoQ (20:1) 1981, 75–84.

14413. BYRD, RUDOLPH PAUL. Jean Toomer: portrait of an artist, the years with Gurdjieff, 1923–1936. Unpub. doct. diss., Yale Univ., 1985. [Abstr. in DA (46) 3350A.]

14414. OGUNYEMI, CHIKWENYE OKONJO. From a goat path in Africa: Roger Mais and Jean Toomer. *See* **13180.**

14415. RUSCH, FREDERIK L. The blue man: Jean Toomer's solution to his problem of identity. Ob (6) Spring/Summer 1980, 38–54.

'Torquemada' (Edward Powys Mathers)

14416. REYNOLDS, WILLIAM. The detective fiction review of Torquemada: a selective index. Clues (7:1) 147–67.

Mary Tourtel

14417. STROUD, DAPHNE J. In praise of Mary. Junior Bookshelf (50:6) 211–12.

John Tranter

14418. TAYLOR, ANDREW. John Tranter: absence in flight. ALS (12:4) 458–70.

'Robert Tressell' (Robert Noonan)

14419. MILES, PETER. The painter's bible and the British workman: Robert Tressell's literary activism. *In* (pp. xii, 1–17) **6.**

William Trevor

14420. MORTIMER, MARK. The short stories of William Trevor. Études irlandaises (9) 1984, 161–73.

14421. THOMAS, MICHAEL WYNDHAM. Triple time: the role of the past in the poetry of Philip Larkin and the short fiction of William Trevor. *See* **12857.**

Lionel Trilling

14422. DICKSTEIN, MORRIS. Lionel Trilling and *The Liberal Imagination.* SewR (94:2) 323–34.

14423. KRUPNICK, MARK.   Lionel Trilling and the fate of cultural criticism. Evanston, IL: Northwestern UP. pp. 207. Rev. by Robert Boyes in NYTB, 13 Apr., 19; by John Bayley in LRB (8:13) 14–15; by A. S. Byatt in Enc (67:4) 46–51; by Julian Symons in TLS, 5 Sept., 959–60; by James W. Tuttleton in AL (58:4) 669–70; by Milton Birnbaum in ModAge (30:3/4) 289.

John Tripp
14424. JENKINS, NIGEL.   An interview with John Tripp. Planet (60) 32–42.

Victor Witter Turner
14425. WALL, CAREY.   Eudora Welty's *Delta Wedding* and Victor Turner's liminality. SoS (25:3) 220–34.

Anne Tyler
14426. BLADES, JOHN.   For NutraSweet fiction, Tyler takes the cake. BW, 20 July, 37.

14427. BROCK, DOROTHY FAYE SALA.   Anne Tyler's treatment of managing women. Unpub. doct. diss., North Texas State Univ., 1985. [Abstr. in DA (46) 3350A.]

14428. JONES, ANNE G.   Home at last, and homesick again: the ten novels of Anne Tyler. HC (23) Apr., 1–13.

John Updike
14429. BERRYMAN, CHARLES.   Updike and contemporary witchcraft. SAQ (85:1) 1–9.

14430. DOUGHERTY, DAVID C.   The price of modern empathy: John Updike's *The Centaur*. PhilP (31) 1985, 104–10.

14431. HORVATH, BROOKE KENTON.   Dropping out: spiritual crisis and countercultural attitudes in four American novelists of the 1960s. *See* **11324.**

14432. NEARY, JOHN M.   *The Centaur*: John Updike and the face of the other. Ren (38:4) 228–44.

14433. PETRY, ALICE HALL.   The dress code in Updike's *A & P*. NCL (16:1) 8–10.

14434. STEPHEN, KATHY.   Writing like an angel about God. Independent, 15 Oct., 13. (Interview.)

14435. WILHELM, ALBERT E.   Narrative continuity in Updike's *Too Far to Go*. Journal of the Short Story in English (7) 87–94.

14436. ZHORDANIĬÂ, S.   *Kentavr*: mif, metafora, real'nost'. (*The Centaur*: myth, metaphor, reality.) Literaturnîâ Gruziîâ (Tbilisi, USSR) (1986:7) 192–5.

Arthur W. Upfield
14437. BROWNE, RAY B.   The frontier heroism of Arthur W. Upfield. Clues (7:1) 127–45.

Alison Uttley
14438. JUDD, DENIS.   Alison Uttley: the life of a country child (1884–1976): the authorised biography. London: Joseph. pp. xiii, 295. Rev. in Growing Point (25:4) 4720; by Nicholas Tucker in TLS, 5 Dec., 1378; by Penelope Fitzgerald in LRB (8:21) 18.

Jack Vance

14439. ANON.   Jack Vance: Dodkinovo zaměstnání. (Dodkin's profession.) SvL (31:4) 98.

Aritha van Herk

14440. NISCHIK, REINGARD M.   Narrative techniques in Aritha van Herk's novels. *In* (pp. 107–20) **22.**

Carl Van Vechten

14441. BURNS, EDWARD (ed.).   The letters of Gertrude Stein and Carl Van Vechten. *See* **14235.**

Gore Vidal

14442. ÅKERMAN, NORDAL.   En eftermiddag med Gore Vidal: och en timme med Miss Oates. *See* **13533.**

14443. ARMSTRONG, GEORGE (ed.).   Vidal in Venice. London: Weidenfeld & Nicholson; Channel 4 TV; Antelope, 1985. pp. 160.

14444. KIERNAN, ROBERT F.   Gore Vidal. New York: Ungar, 1982. pp. xvi, 165. Rev. by David Seed in YES (16) 363–4.

Elfrida Vipont ('Charles Vipont')

14445. WOODFIELD, E. R.   Way will open. Junior Bookshelf (50:5) 173–8.

Kurt Vonnegut, Jr

14446. COHEN-SAFIR, C.   Le doute chez K. Vonnegut, Jr. *In* (pp. 567–77) **1.**

14447. KAUFMAN, W. K.   Mark Twain, Lenny Bruce and Kurt Vonnegut: the comedian as confidence man. *See* **9449.**

14448. MUSTAZZA, LEONARD.   Vonnegut's Tralfamadore and Milton's Eden. *See* **5771.**

14449. RUCH, EDWARD DELAFIELD.   Techniques of self-reference in selected novels of Beckett, Nabokov, Vonnegut, and Barth. *See* **11140.**

14450. SIGMAN, JOSEPH.   Science and parody in Kurt Vonnegut's *The Sirens of Titan.* Mosaic (19:1) 15–32.

14451. ZINS, DANIEL L.   Rescuing science from technocracy: *Cat's Cradle* and the play of apocalypse. SFS (13:2) 170–81.

Helen Waddell

14452. CORRIGAN, FELICITAS.   Helen Waddell: a biography. London: Gollancz. pp. 363. Rev. by Patricia Craig in TLS, 28 Mar., 334.

Miriam Waddington

14453. STEVENS, PETER.   Miriam Waddington. *In* (pp. 279–329) **9.**

Derek Walcott

14454. BUCHANAN, JANE BRITTON.   Poetic identity in the New World: Anne Bradstreet, Emily Dickinson, and Derek Walcott. *See* **5295.**

14455. FIDO, ELAINE SAVORY.   Value judgements on art and the question of macho attitudes: the case of Derek Walcott. JCL (21:1) 109–19.

14456. HIRSCH, EDWARD.   The art of poetry XXXVII. ParisR (101) 197–230.

14457. ISMOND, PATRICIA.   North and south: a look at Walcott's *Midsummer.* Kp (8:2) 77–85.

14458. TAYLOR, PATRICK. Myth and reality in Caribbean narrative: Derek Walcott's *Pantomime*. WLWE (26:1) 169–77.

Alice Walker

14459. BREWER, KRISTA. Writing to survive: an interview with Alice Walker. SE (9:2) 1981, 12–15.

14460. DUCKWORTH, VICTORIA. The redemptive impulse: *Wise Blood* and *The Color Purple*. See **13561.**

14461. EARLY, GERALD. *The Color Purple* as everybody's protest art. AR (44:3) 261–75.

14462. HARRIS, TRUDIER. From victimization to free enterprise: Alice Walker's *The Color Purple*. SAF (14:1) 1–17.

14463. NOWIK, NAN. Mixing art and politics: the writings of Adrienne Rich, Marge Piercy, and Alice Walker. See **13727.**

14464. ROBINSON, DANIEL. Problems in form: Alice Walker's *The Color Purple*. NCL (16:1) 2.

14465. TAVORMINA, M. TERESA. Dressing the spirit: clothworking and language in *The Color Purple*. JNT (16:3) 220–30.

Edgar Wallace

14466. ADRIAN, JACK (ed.). The death room: strange and startling stories. London: Kimber. pp. 222.

14467. —— The road to London. London: Kimber. pp. 176.

Jill Paton Walsh

14468. GOUGH, JOHN. Bitter truths: the human realities of courage, betrayal and defeat: two historical novels by Jill Paton Walsh. Junior Bookshelf (50:1) 7–11.

Ania Walwicz

14469. GUNEW, SNEJA. Ania Walwicz and Antigone Kefala: varieties of migrant dreaming. See **12758.**

Rex Warner

14470. CRAMP, A. Prose fiction in the 1930s: a study of Elizabeth Bowen, Rex Warner and Patrick Hamilton. See **11289.**

Sylvia Townsend Warner

14471. BJØRHOVDE, GERD. Transformation and subversion as narrative strategies in two fantasy novels of the 1920s: Sylvia Townsend Warner's *Lolly Willowes* and Virginia Woolf's *Orlando*. In (pp. 213–24) **18.**

Robert Penn Warren

14472. BEDIENT, CALVIN. In the heart's last kingdom: Robert Penn Warren's major poetry. (Bibl. 1985, 13333.) Rev. by Gavin Cologne-Brookes in TLS, 5 Sept., 960.

14473. CLARK, WILLIAM BEDFORD. Robert Penn Warren's love affair with America. SoR (22:4) 667–79.

14474. LEATHERBARROW, RONALD. The dynamics of self-fulfillment: a study of the early fiction of Robert Penn Warren. Unpub. doct. diss., Univ. of Maryland, 1985. 2 vols. [Abstr. in DA (47) 901A.]

14475. LEVY, ALFRED J. The web and the twitch: images in *All the King's Men*. BSUF (25:2) 1984, 53–6.

14476. Lydon, Christopher.   Robert Penn Warren. PR (53:4) 608–12. (Interview with Derek Walcott and Seamus Heaney.)

14477. Miller, Mark Daniel.   Robert Penn Warren's early poetry, 1922–1953: an appreciation. Unpub. doct. diss., Univ. of Texas at Austin, 1985. [Abstr. in DA (47) 530A.]

14478. Spanos, William V.; Bové, Paul A.; O'Hara, Daniel (eds). The question of textuality: strategies of reading in contemporary American criticism. *See* **10930**.

14479. Spears, Monroe K.   The critics who made us: Robert Penn Warren. SewR (94:1) 99–111.

14480. Watkins, Floyd C.   Following the tramp in Warren's *Blackberry Winter*. SSF (22) 1985, 343–5.

14481. Winchell, Mark Royden.   Renaissance men: Shakespeare's influence on Robert Penn Warren. *In* (pp. 137–58) **51**.

Sheila Watson

14482. Scobie, Stephen.   Sheila Watson. *In* (pp. 259–312) **8**.

Stephen Watson

14483. Gardner, Susan.   Four South African poets: interviews with Robert Berold, Jeremy Cronin, Douglas Reid Skinner, Stephen Watson. *See* **11248**.

Evelyn Waugh

14484. Davis, Robert Murray.   The rhetoric of Mexican travel: Greene and Waugh. *See* **12237**.

14485. —— Subdividing the wilderness: guides to Waugh criticism. PLL (22:2) 216–20 (review-article).

14486. —— Argiro, Thomas.   Reading in the thirties: reviews by Waugh and Greene. *See* **12239**.

14487. Dooley, D. J.   New light on Waugh in Yugoslavia. EWN (20:2) 1–4.

14488. Gnerro, Mark L.   Echoes of the *Anima Christi* in a pivotal paragraph of Evelyn's *Men At Arms*. EWN (20:3) 3–6.

14489. Gorra, Michael Edward.   The English novel at mid-century: Evelyn Waugh, Henry Green, Anthony Powell, and Graham Greene. *See* **12227**.

14490. Greene, Donald.   Reality into art: some detective notes on Waugh. EWN (20:1) 1–5.

14491. —— Waugh and the Mountbattens. EWN (20:2) 6–7.

14492. Kirk, P. N.   The voice of authority: Evelyn Waugh's fiction. Unpub. doct. diss., Univ. of Warwick, 1983. [Abstr. in IT (35) 52.]

14493. Littlewood, I.   Strategies of defence in the work of Evelyn Waugh. Unpub. doct. diss., Univ. of Sussex, 1983.

14494. Littlewood, Ian.   The writings of Evelyn Waugh. (Bibl. 1985, 13366.) Rev. by Martin Stannard in MLR (81:2) 466–7.

14495. McDonnell, J. A.   Women in the novels of Evelyn Waugh. Unpub. doct. diss., Univ. of Edinburgh, 1983.

14496. McDonnell, Jacqueline.   Waugh on women. New York: St Martin's Press; London: Duckworth, 1985. pp. 239. Rev. by Donald Greene in EWN (20:1) 5–7.

14497. SCHLUETER, KURT.   Anno Domini 1943. EWN (20:2) 4–6.
14498. STANNARD, MARTIN.   Evelyn Waugh: the critical heritage.
Melbourne: Routledge & Kegan Paul, 1984. (Cf. bibl. 1984, 13390.)
Rev. by Alain Blayac in EA (38:4) 1985, 479–80.
14499. —— Evelyn Waugh: the early years 1903–1939. London: Dent.
pp. xiv, 537. Rev. by John Bayley in LRB (8:21) 14; by P. N. Furbank in
TLS, 7 Nov., 1237.
14500. TOEWS, AGANETHA WALL.   'The great code' in six twentieth-
century European novels. See **11559.**
14501. TOSSER, YVON.   Le sens de l'absurde dans l'oeuvre d'Evelyn
Waugh. Paris: Didier. pp. 444. (Atelier de reproduction des thèses.)
14502. WOLK, GERHARD.   Evelyn Waugh: a supplementary checklist
of criticism. EWN (20:2) 7–9.

Mary Webb

14503. BRALE, MICHELE AINA.   Daughters and lovers: the life and
writing of Mary Webb. Middletown, CT: Wesleyan UP. pp. viii, 197.

Phyllis Webb

14504. HULCOOP, JOHN.   Webb's *Water and Light*. CanL (109) 151–9.
14505. WOODCOCK, GEORGE.   In the beginning was the question: the
poems of Phyllis Webb. QQ (93:3) 527–45.

James Welch

14506. SCHECKTER, JOHN.   James Welch: setting up on the reserva-
tion. SDR (24:2) 7–19.
14507. WESTRUM, DEXTER LYLE.   The art of survival in the contemporary West: the fictions of Thomas McGuane, James Welch, and
Edward Abbey. See **10972.**

Paul I. Wellman

14508. COLEMAN, ARTHUR.   *The Iron Mistress* and *The Natural*: analogue or influence? See **13184.**

H. G. Wells

14509. ALLETT, JOHN.   *Tono-Bungay*: the metaphor of disease in H. G.
Wells's novel. QQ (93:2) 365–74.
14510. BATCHELOR, JOHN.   H. G. Wells. (Bibl. 1985, 13389.) Rev. by
John Huntington in SFS (13:2) 200–6; by Brian Gasser in NQ (33:4)
563–4.
14511. BRODIE, PETER (ed.).   The history of Mr Polly. Harlow:
Longman. pp. xxii, 235. (Longman study texts.)
14512. GRANT, BARRY K.   Looking upward: H. G. Wells, science
fiction and the cinema. See **9965.**
14513. GREENSLADE, W. P.   The concept of degeneration, 1880–1910,
with particular reference to the work of Thomas Hardy, George Gissing
and H. G. Wells. See **8352.**
14514. HAMM, ALBERT.   L'analyse discursive à l'épreuve du texte:
cohérence, cohésion et connecteurs. RANAM (19) 63–80.
14515. HAMMOND, J. R. (ed.).   *The Man with a Nose* and other
uncollected short stories of H. G. Wells. London: Athlone Press, 1984.
pp. ix, 212. (Bibl. 1984, 13411.) Rev. by John Huntington in SFS (13:2)
200–6.

14516. HUNTINGTON, JOHN. The logic of fantasy: H. G. Wells and science fiction. (Bibl. 1985, 13395.) Rev. by Patrick Parrinder in MLR (81:3) 731–2.

14517. —— Rethinking Wells. SFS (13:2) 200–6 (review-article).

14518. McCARTHY, PATRICK A. *Heart of Darkness* and the early novels of H. G. Wells: evolution, anarchy, entropy. *See* **11522.**

14519. PHILMUS, ROBERT M. *Futurological Congress* as metageneric text. SFS (13:3) 313–28.

14520. RAY, MARTIN. Conrad, Wells, and *The Secret Agent*: paying old debts and settling old scores. *See* **11545.**

14521. RYDEL, CHRISTINE A. *Russia in the Shadows* and Wells in the dark. MichA (18:3) 393–410.

14522. SCHEICK, WILLIAM J. The splintering frame: the later fiction of H. G. Wells. Vancouver: Victoria UP, 1984. pp. 134. Rev. by John Huntington in SFS (13:2) 200–6.

14523. SIMPSON, ANNE B. Forster and the Edwardians: the literature of domestic failure. *See* **11237.**

14524. SMITH, DAVID C. H. G. Wells: desperately mortal. New Haven, CT; London: Yale UP. pp. xviii, 634. Rev. by W. Warren Wagar in BkW, 14 Sept., 4; by J. I. M. Stewart in LRB (8:18) 20–1; by Bernard Bergonzi in THES (726) 18; by Stanley Weintraub in NYTB, 19 Oct., 34; by Eric Korn in TLS, 17 Oct., 1153.

14525. —— H. G. Wells: socialist, feminist, polymath, educator and hero. NYTB, 21 Sept., 12.

14526. WHITEMAN, BRUCE. Canadian issues of Anglo-American fiction: the example of H. G. Wells. *See* **10445.**

James C. Welsh

14527. KLAUS, H. GUSTAV. James C. Welsh, major miner novelist. SLJ (13:2) 65–86.

Eudora Welty

14528. COULTHARD, A. R. *Keela, the Outcast Indian Maiden*: a dissenting view. SSF (23:1) 35–41.

14529. DEVLIN, ALBERT J. Jackson's Welty. SoQ (20:4) 1982, 54–91.

14530. ETTER, KATHRYN. Genre of return: the short story volume. *See* **10991.**

14531. EVANS, ELIZABETH. Eudora Welty: the metaphor of music. SoQ (20:4) 1982, 92–100.

14532. IDOL, JOHN L., JR. Edna Earle Ponder's good country people. SoQ (20:3) 1981, 66–75.

14533. KREYLING, MICHAEL. Modernism in Welty's *A Curtain of Green and Other Stories*. SoQ (20:4) 1982, 40–53.

14534. LAZENBLATT, W. W. G. The female mind in modern Southern fiction: the treatment and expression of female consciousness in the work of Flannery O'Connor, Carson McCullers and Eudora Welty. *See* **13116.**

14535. McDONALD, W. U., JR. An unworn path: bibliographical and textual scholarship on Eudora Welty. SoQ (20:4) 1982, 101–8.

14536. MANNING, CAROL S. With ears opening like morning glories:

Eudora Welty and the love of storytelling. Westport, CT: Greenwood Press, 1985. pp. xi, 221. Rev. by Kimball King in AL (58:4) 664–5.

14537. MARK, REBECCA. From the 'I' of the hero to the eye of the story: Eudora Welty's search for the voice of the woman artist in *The Golden Apples*. Unpub. doct. diss., Stanford Univ. [Abstr. in DA (47) 2159A.]

14538. MARRS, SUZANNE. The metaphor of race in Eudora Welty's fiction. SoR (22:4) 697–707.

14539. VANDE KIEFT, RUTH M. Eudora Welty: the question of meaning. SoQ (20:4) 1982, 24–39.

14540. VAN NAPPEN, MARTHA. A conversation with Eudora Welty. SoQ (20:4) 1982, 7–23.

14541. WALL, CAREY. Eudora Welty's *Delta Wedding* and Victor Turner's liminality. See **14425.**

14542. WALTER, JAMES. Love's habit of vision in Welty's *Phoenix Jackson*. Journal of the Short Story in English (7) 77–85.

14543. WATKINS, FLOYD C. Eudora Welty's Natchez Trace in the New World. SoR (22:4) 708–26.

14544. WESTLING, LOUISE. Demeter and Kore, Southern style. *See* **13581.**

Arnold Wesker

14545. HAIGH, ANTHONY RUSSELL. The essential unity of Arnold Wesker's vision with special reference to his non-dramatic texts. Unpub. doct. diss., Michigan State Univ. [Abstr. in DA (47) 1117A–18A.]

14546. ZIMMERMANN, HEINZ. Wesker and utopia in the sixties. ModDr (29:2) 185–206.

Nathanael West

14547. DOWN, NANCY. The search for authenticity in the satiric worlds of Nathanael West and Peter De Vries. *See* **11640.**

14548. NILSEN, HELGE NORMANN. A novel of despair: a note on Nathaneal West's *Miss Lonelyhearts*. Neophilologus (70:3) 475–8.

14549. SHROYER, THOMAS. Compassion and nightmare in Nathanael West. CAE (19) 543–51.

14550. WALDEN, DANIEL. Nathanael West: novelist of the bizarre, dystopist of the 1930s. JAC (9:3) 49–54.

Paul West

14551. PESTINO, JOSEPH FRANCIS. The reader/writer affair: instigating repertoire in the experimental fiction of Susan Sontag, Walter Abish, Réjean Ducharme, Paul West, and Christine Brooke-Rose. *See* **10974.**

'Rebecca West' (Mrs H. M. Andrews)

14552. GLENDINNING, VICTORIA (introd.). The birds fall down. London: Virago Press, pp. xiv, 428. (Virago modern classics, 235.)

14553. OREL, HAROLD. The literary achievement of Rebecca West. Basingstoke: Macmillan. pp. xii, 235.

Donald Westlake ('Richard Stark')

14554. THIRARD, PAUL-LOUIS. Alias Donald Westlake. Europe (62:664/65) 1984, 109–14.

Edith Wharton

14555. BAUER, DALE MARIE. The failure of community: women and resistance in Hawthorne's, James's, and Wharton's novels. *See* **8448.**

14556. BELL, MILLICENT LANG. Edith Wharton: studies in a writer's development. Unpub. doct. diss., Brown Univ., 1955. [Abstr. in DA (46) 3718A.]

14557. CASERIO, ROBERT L. Edith Wharton and the fiction of public commentary. WHR (40:3) 189–208.

14558. COLAVECCHIO, BARBARA MARIE. Edith Wharton and the re-shaping of legend. Unpub. doct. diss., Univ. of Rhode Island, 1985. [Abstr. in DA (47) 529A.]

14559. DE ABRUÑA, LAURA NIESEN. Wharton's *House of Mirth*. Exp (44:3) 39–40.

14560. FRENCH, MARILYN (postscr.). Hudson River bracketed. London: Virago Press. pp. 547. (Virago modern classics, 218.)

14561. —— The mother's recompense. London: Virago Press. pp. 353. (Virago modern classics, 217.)

14562. GOODER, JEAN. Unlocking Edith Wharton: an introduction to *The Reef.* CamQ (15) 33–52.

14563. GOODWYN, J. P. The novelist and 'the intelligent amateur': a topographical study of the writings of Edith Wharton. Unpub. doct. diss., Univ. of Warwick, 1983. [Abstr. in IT (35) 55.]

14564. HOVEY, R. B. *Ethan Frome*: a controversy about modernizing it. ALR (19:1) 4–20.

14565. KAPLAN, AMY. Edith Wharton's profession of authorship. ELH (53:2) 433–57.

14566. LEERABHANDH, SIVAPORN. A study of women characters in Edith Wharton's fiction, 1905–1920. Unpub. doct. diss., Michigan State Univ., 1985. [Abstr. in DA (46) 3719A.]

14567. LINK, FRANZ. A note on 'the apparition of these faces' in *The House of Mirth* and *In a Station of the Metro*. *See* **13865.**

14568. MOORE, P. The age of experience: the moral and aesthetic sensibility in the fiction of Edith Wharton. Unpub. doct. diss., Univ. of Leicester, 1974. [Abstr. in IT (35) 56.]

14569. ROTARU, IOANA (trans. and ed.). Sufletul omului. (Human nature.) Bucharest: Minerva, 1985. pp. 276.

14570. SINGLEY, CAROL J. The depth of the soul: faith, desire, and despair in Edith Wharton's fiction. Unpub. doct. diss., Brown Univ. [Abstr. in DA (47) 1730A.]

14571. SPRINGER, MARLENE; GILSON, JOAN. Edith Wharton: a reference guide updated. RALS (14:1/2) 1984, 85–111.

14572. VITA-FINZI, P. J. Edith Wharton: precepts and practice in the life of the writer and the art of fiction. Unpub. doct. diss., Univ. of London (Queen Mary Coll.). [Abstr. in IT (36) 25.]

E. B. White

14573. EPSTEIN, JOSEPH. E. B. White, dark & lite. Commentary (81:4) 48–56.

Patrick White
14574. BLISS, CAROLYN. Patrick White's fiction: the paradox of fortunate failure. Basingstoke: Macmillan. pp. xvi, 192. (Macmillan studies in twentieth-century literature.)

14575. BRADY-PAPADOPOULOU, VALENTINI. The Christ figure as archetype in Kazantzakis' *Christ Recrucified* and Patrick White's *Riders in the Chariot. In* (pp. 409–13) **19.**

14576. COLMER, JOHN. Patrick White. London: Methuen, 1984. pp. 94. (Contemporary writers.) Rev. by Peter Quartermaine in NQ (33:4) 568–9.

14577. DOMMERGUES, ANDRÉ. Patrick White et le thème aborigène. *In* (pp. 663–74) **1.**

14578. DUPARC, CHARLOTTE. Images of the artist in *The Vivisector* by P. White. Commonwealth (Dijon) (7:2) 1985, 11–18 (review-article).

14579. EKMAN, HANS-GÖRAN. Patrick White före hemkomsten: kring ett tema i några tidiga romaner. (Patrick White before returning home: on a theme in some early novels.) BLM (55) 237–41.

14580. FINDLEY, TIMOTHY. Legends. *See* **12050.**

14581. KRAMER, LEONIE. A visit to White's sacred sites. Quadrant (30:9) 66–7.

14582. LEWIS, M. B. Figures in a landscape: a study of the novels of Patrick White, 1955–1979. Unpub. doct. diss., Univ. of Newcastle upon Tyne, 1984.

14583. MACAINSH, NOEL. Patrick White's aesthetic. Linq (12:1/3) 1984, 55–70.

14584. —— Patrick White's myth of the artist: Dionysos as vivisector. Quadrant (29:11) 1985, 77–81.

14585. MCCULLOCH, ANNE M. A tragic vision: the novels of Patrick White. New York: Queensland UP, 1983. (Cf. bibl. 1983, 13824.) Rev. by John B. Beston in Ariel (17:2) 91–4.

14586. OLIVERIUSOVÁ, EVA. Patrick White: *Flaws in the Glass.* SvL (31:5) 232–4.

14587. TEYSSANDIER, HUBERT. L'Apocalypse et le nouvel Eden dans *Riders in the Chariot* de Patrick White. *In* (pp. 319–33) **2.**

14588. TRACEY, DAVID J. Patrick White's *Voss*: the teller and the tale. SoRA (18:3) 1985, 251–71 (review-article).

14589. WILLIAMS, MARK. 'Design of darkness': the religious and political heresies of Captain Ahab and Johann Voss. *See* **8956.**

14590. WOLFE, PETER. Laden choirs: the fiction of Patrick White. (Bibl. 1984, 13506.) Rev. by Peter Quartermaine in NQ (33:4) 568.

T. H. White
14591. GALLIX, FRANÇOIS. T. H. White: an annotated bibliography. New York; London: Garland. pp. xlix, 148.

14592. ROSS, MEREDITH JANE. The sublime to the ridiculous: the restructuring of Arthurian materials in selected modern novels. *See* **3655.**

Rudy Wiebe

14593. GRACE, SHERRILL E.   Structuring violence: *The Ethics of Linguistics* in *The Temptations of Big Bear*. CanL (104) 1985, 7–22.

14594. HOEPPNER, KENNETH.   Politics and religion in Rudy Wiebe's *The Scorched-Wood People*. ESCan (12:4) 440–50.

14595. KLOOS, WOLFGANG.   Narrative modes and forms of literary perception in Rudy Wiebe's *The Scorched-Wood People*. In (pp. 205–21) **22.**

14596. SCHÄFER, JÜRGEN.   A farewell to Europe: Rudy Wiebe's *The Temptations of Big Bear* and Robert Kroetsch's *Gone Indian*. In (pp. 79–90) **22.**

14597. SPRIET, PIERRE.   Structure and meaning in Rudy Wiebe's *My Lovely Enemy*. In (pp. 53–63) **22.**

14598. VAUTIER, MARIE.   Fiction, historiography, and myth: Jacques Godbout's *Les Têtes à Papineau* and Rudy Wiebe's *The Scorched-Wood People*. CanL (110) 61–78.

Richard Wilbur

14599. NADEL, ALAN.   Roethke, Wilbur, and the vision of the child: Romantic and Augustan in modern verse. *See* **14020.**

Laura Ingalls Wilder

14600. LEE, ANN THOMPSON.   'It is better further on': Laura Ingalls Wilder and the pioneer spirit. LU (3:1) 1979, 74–88.

Thornton Wilder

14601. DEGERING, KLAUS.   'Landstreicher im Sonnensystem'. Thornton Wilders *Pullman Car Hiawatha*. Anglistik & Englischunterricht (28) 49–79.

14602. FRESE, PENELOPE ANNE.   The American dream in form and concept in Thornton Wilder's *Our Town*, Norman Rockwell's 'Saying Grace', and the architecture of Hudson, Ohio. Unpub. doct. diss., Ohio Univ., 1985. [Abstr. in DA (47) 3A.]

14603. GALLUP, DONALD (ed.).   The journals of Thornton Wilder 1939–61, with two scenes of an uncompleted play, *The Emporium*. (Bibl. 1985, 13493, where title incomplete.) Rev. by Jackson R. Bryer in NEQ (59:2) 301–5; by Dennis Welland in THES (690) 17; by Frederic Raphael in TLS, 14 Mar., 281.

14604. LIFTON, PAUL SAMUEL.   Thornton Wilder and 'world theatre'. Unpub. doct. diss., Univ. of California, Berkeley, 1985. [Abstr. in DA (46) 2486A.]

14605. POWERS, LYALL H.   Thornton Wilder as literary cubist: an acknowledged debt to Henry James. *See* **8726.**

14606. YOUNG, VERNON.   The skin of his teeth. NCrit (2) Jan. 1984, 61–7.

Michael Wilding

14607. ROSS, BRUCE CLUNIES.   Paradise, politics and fiction: the writing of Michael Wilding. Meanjin (45:1) 19–27.

Alan Williams

14608. SKENE, REG.   Alan Williams: the actor as playwright. CanTR (49) 51–7.

Charles Williams

14609. BOSKY, BERNADETTE. Even an adept; Charles Williams and the Order of the Golden Dawn. Mythlore (13:2) 25–35.

14610. ——Grace and *goetia*: magic as forced compensation in *All Hallows Eve*. Mythlore (12:3) 19–23.

14611. CHRISTOPHER, JOE R. An Inklings' bibliography. *See* **13025.**

14612. ——John Heath-Stubbs' *Artorius* and the influence of Charles Williams. *See* **12340.**

14613. FORD, P. K. The later W. H. Auden as a Christian poet. *See* **11095.**

14614. GOODKNIGHT, GLEN (ed.). A centennial retrospective on Charles Williams. Mythlore (13:2) 13–21, 40.

14615. KOLLMANN, JUDITH. The figure of Beatrice in the works of Charles Williams. Mythlore (13:2) 3–8.

14616. KRANZ, GISBERT. Charles Williams und seine Arthur-Gedichte. Univ (41:5) 463–70.

14617. NYMAN, AMY. A feminist perspective in Williams' novels. Mythlore (12:4) 3–10.

14618. RATELIFF, JOHN D. 'And something yet remains to be said': Tolkien and Williams. *See* **14405.**

14619. REYNOLDS, GEORGE. Dante and Williams: pilgrims in purgatory. Mythlore (13:1) 3–7, 50.

14620. SCHAKEL, PETER. Dance as metaphor and myth in Lewis, Tolkien, and Williams. *See* **13043.**

14621. SHEHAN, JOHN. Liver as well as heart: the theology of Charles Williams. Ren (37) 1984, 32–42.

14622. WARREN, COLLEEN. Wentworth in the garden of Gomorrah: a study of the anima in *Descent into Hell*. Mythlore (13:2) 41–4, 54.

Heathcote Williams

14623. CARDULLO, BERT. Three notes on drama. *See* **4925.**

Tennessee Williams

14624. FISCHER-SEIDEL, THERESE. Mythenparodie im modernen englischen und amerikanischen Drama. Tradition und Kommunikation bei Tennessee Williams, Edward Albee, Samuel Beckett und Harold Pinter. *See* **11011.**

14625. FREIS, RICHARD. Southern Exposure. Opera News, 24 June, 26.

14626. HOLDITCH, W. KENNETH. Surviving with grace: Tennessee Williams tomorrow. SoR (22:4) 892–903 (review-article).

14627. KOUTSOUDAKI, MARIA. The Dionysiac element in Tennessee Williams's *The Rose Tattoo*. Parousia (4) 203–13.

14628. KRAMER, MIMI. Tennessee Williams and the fiddle in the wings. NCrit (2) Feb. 1984, 52–7.

14629. LONG, DEBORAH MARIE. The existential quest: family and form in selected American plays. *See* **13257.**

14630. MELMAN, LINDY. A captive maid: Blanche Dubois in *A Streetcar Named Desire*. DQR (16:2) 125–44.

14631. RADER, DOTSON.   Tennessee: cry of the heart. (Bibl. 1985, 13517.) Rev. by Thomas H. Pauly in TJ (38:1) 124–5.

14632. SCHLUETER, JUNE.   Imitating an icon: John Erman's remake of Tennessee Williams' *A Streetcar Named Desire*. ModDr (28:1) 1985, 139–47.

14633. SPOTO, DONALD.   The kindness of strangers: the life of Tennessee Williams. (Bibl. 1985, 13521.) Rev. by Thomas H. Pauly in TJ (38:1) 125.

14634. VIDAL, GORE (introd.).   Collected stories. New York: New Directions, 1985. pp. xxv, 574. Rev. by Seymour Krim in BkW, 12 Jan., 3, 11.

14635. VLASOPOLOS, ANCA.   Authorizing history: victimization in *A Streetcar Named Desire*. TJ (38:3) 322–38.

14636. WILHELMI, NANCY OLIVIA.   Under one roof: the language of the power struggles in five of Tennessee Williams' plays. Unpub. doct. diss., Univ. of Arkansas. [Abstr. in DA (47) 1725A.] (*The Glass Menagerie, A Streetcar Named Desire, Cat on a Hot Tin Roof, Summer and Smoke, Suddenly Last Summer.*)

14637. YACOWAR, MAURICE.   Tennessee Williams and film. *See* **10121.**

14638. ZEINEDDINE, N.   I search: problems of identity: woman, artist and breadwinner in the plays of Henrik Ibsen, Tennessee Williams and Arthur Miller. *See* **13264.**

William Carlos Williams

14639. ANTONE, EVAN H.; REEVES, BILLY D.   Postcards from El Paso: William Carlos Williams' visit in 1950. WCWR (12:2) 9–13.

14640. BAKER, A. D.   The act of seeing: poem, image and the work of William Carlos Williams. Unpub. doct. diss., Univ. of Durham, 1983.

14641. BALDWIN, NEIL.   To all gentleness: William Carlos Williams, the doctor poet. (Bibl. 1985, 13523.) Rev. by Gary Grieve in WCWR (12:2) 32–3.

14642. BARRY, NANCY K.   Epic history and the lyric impulse in the *Paterson* manuscripts. WCWR (12:2) 1–8.

14643. BARRY, NANCY KEATING.   William Carlos Williams and the pursuit of *Paterson*. Unpub. doct. diss., Univ. of Illinois at Urbana-Champaign. [Abstr. in DA (47) 1723A.]

14644. BREMEN, BRIAN A.   'The radiant gist': 'the poetry hidden in the prose' of Williams' *Paterson*. TCL (32:2) 221–41.

14645. CLARKE, BRUCE.   The fall of Montezuma: poetry and history in William Carlos Williams and D. H. Lawrence. *See* **12883.**

14646. CUSHMAN, STEPHEN.   William Carlos Williams and the meanings of measure. (Bibl. 1985, 13527.) Rev. by Gay Sibley in AL (58:2) 275–7; by Richard D. Cureton in WCWR (12:2) 34–52.

14647. DICKIE, MARGARET.   Williams reading *Paterson*. ELH (53:3) 653–71.

14648. GILBERT, SANDRA M.   Purloined letters: William Carlos Williams and 'Cress'. WCWR (11:2) 1985, 5–15.

14649. HELLER, JÜRGEN.   William Carlos Williams, Wallace Stevens und die moderne Malerei. Ästhetische Entwürfe, Verfahren und Komposition. *See* **14270.**

14650. HOFFMAN, DANIEL (ed.). Ezra Pound and William Carlos Williams. *See* **13841.**

14651. KALLET, MARILYN. Honest simplicity in William Carlos Williams' *Asphodel, That Greeny Flower*. Baton Rouge: Louisiana State UP, 1985. pp. xiv, 163. Rev. by Nancy K. Barry in WCWR (12:2) 29–31; by Lachlan Mackinnon in TLS, 1 Aug., 838.

14652. KUTZINSKI, VERA MAGRET. From American literature to New World writing: myth and history in William Carlos Williams, Jay Wright, and Nicolás Guillén. Unpub. doct. diss., Yale Univ., 1985. [Abstr. in DA (46) 3352A.]

14653. LEE, JUNG-KEE. Autochthony wa si: William Carlos Williams e gwanhayeo. (Autochthony and poetry: on William Carlos Williams.) JELL (32:4) 603–23.

14654. LI, VICTOR P. H. The vanity of length: the long poem as problem in Pound's *Cantos* and Williams' *Paterson*. *See* **13861.**

14655. MARIANI, PAUL. Williams: La Giaconda's [*sic*] smile. WCWR (11:2) 1985, 55–60.

14656. MONTEIRO, GEORGE. A textual error in *White Mule*. WCWR (12:1) 21.

14657. MOORE, PATRICK. William Carlos Williams and the Modernist attack on logical syntax. ELH (53:4) 895–916.

14658. NAY, JOAN MCNEILLY. William Carlos Williams and the singular woman. Unpub. doct. diss., Univ. of Southern California. [Abstr. in DA (47) 2160A.]

14659. NEUMANN, ANNE WALDRON. Diagramming the forces in a 'machine made of words': Williams' *Red Wheelbarrow* as picture poem. WCWR (12:1) 13–20.

14660. OLIPHANT, DAVID; ZIGAL, THOMAS (eds). William Carlos Williams and others. Austin, TX: Harry Ransom Humanities Research Center, Univ. of Texas at Austin, 1985. pp. 128. Rev. by Henry Sayre in WCWR (12:2) 17–19.

14661. PIPER, DAN. An unpublished Williams letter. WCWR (12:1) 39–40.

14662. RAPP, CARL. William Carlos Williams and romantic idealism. (Bibl. 1985, 13554.) Rev. by Nancy K. Barry in WHR (40:2) 185–8.

14663. READ, DENNIS M. Three unpublished poems by William Carlos Williams. AL (58:3) 422–6.

14664. SAYRE, HENRY M. The visual text of William Carlos Williams. (Bibl. 1985, 13559.) Rev. by Graham Clarke in NQ (33:1) 136–7.

14665. SHEA, JOHN; ROMANO, TIMOTHY. The Pound–Williams conference. *See* **13908.**

14666. SOLT, MARY ELLEN (ed.). Dear Ez: letters from William Carlos Williams to Ezra Pound. *See* **13909.**

14667. WRIGHT, BARBARA HERB. Fourteen unpublished letters by William Carlos Williams. WCWR (12:1) 22–38.

David Williamson

14668. KAVANAGH, PAUL; KUCH, PETER. What are the shades of grey: David Williamson talks to Paul Kavanagh and Peter Kuch. Southerly (46:2) 131–41.

14669. KIERNAN, BRIAN. Comic satiric realism: David Williamson's plays since *The Department*. Southerly (46:1) 3–18.

14670. WILLIAMS, BRUCE. David Williamson: the powerless audience. Meridian (5:2) 123–32.

Henry Williamson

14671. BLENCH, J. W. The influence of Richard Jefferies upon Henry Williamson, part 1. *See* **8776.**

14672. —— (introd.). The novels of Henry Williamson. By J. MIDDLETON MURRY. *See* **13361.**

14673. CARON, SUE. A glimpse of the ancient sunlight: memories of Henry Williamson. Introd. and notes by BROCARD SEWELL. Wirral: Aylesford, pp. 34.

14674. HUGHES, TED. Henry Williamson: a tribute by Ted Hughes: given at the service of thanksgiving at the Royal Parish Church of St Martin-in-the-Fields. London: Rainbow, 1979. pp. 12.

14675. WILLIAMSON, HENRY. *The Weekly Despatch*: articles contributed by Henry Williamson in the years 1920–21. *See* **728.**

Angus Wilson

14676. HILSKÝ, MARTIN. Angus Wilson a nové tendence současné britské prózy. (Angus Wilson and the new trends in contemporary British prose.) *In* (pp. 25–6) **4.**

14677. MOUSLEH, T. The humanist dilemma: a study of liberal thought in some selected novels by E. M. Forster, Angus Wilson and Iris Murdoch. *See* **12023.**

14678. PĂDURELEANU, MIRCEA (ed.). Atitudini anglo-saxone. (Anglo-Saxon attitudes.) Trans. by GEORGETA PĂDURELEANU. Bucharest: Univers, 1985. pp. 445.

14679. SZÁSZ, ANNA MÁRIA. Between tradition and experiment: a study in Angus Wilson's novels. ActLitH (27:3/4) 1985, 343–63.

14680. WILSON, ANGUS. Reflections in a writer's eye: travel pieces. London: Secker & Warburg. pp. 183.

Edmund Wilson

14681. CASTRONOVO, DAVID. Edmund Wilson. (Cf. bibl. 1985, 13576, where scholar's surname incorrect.) Rev. by Neil Berry in TLS, 14 Feb., 170.

14682. COSTA, RICHARD HAUER. Talcottville, N.Y., and the sentence(ing) of Edmund Wilson. NYH (67:2) 210–23.

14683. DEPIETRO, THOMAS. Edmund Wilson, American. SewR (94:1) 160–6 (review-article).

14684. DOUGLAS, GEORGE H. Edmund Wilson's America. (Bibl. 1985, 13577.) Rev. by Roger Gard in NQ (33:1) 139–40.

14685. EDEL, LEON (ed.). The fifties: from notebooks and diaries of the period by Edmund Wilson. New York: Farrar, Straus & Giroux; London: Macmillan. pp. xxxii, 663. Rev. by Ian Hamilton in BkW,

14 Sept., 5; by Otto Friedrich in Time, 8 Sept., 77; by Phillip Whitehead in Listener, 20 Nov., 29.

14686. FARGNOLI, JOSEPH R. Edmund Wilson and the sociology of literature. Unpub. doct. diss., Univ. of Rhode Island, 1985. [Abstr. in DA (46) 3351A.]

14687. KIRKPATRICK, KENNETH JOHN. Edmund's castle: a study of Edmund Wilson's major works, 1945–1962. Unpub. doct. diss., Harvard Univ. [Abstr. in DA (47) 901A.]

14688. RABAN, JONATHAN (introd.). Europe without Baedeker: sketches among the ruins of Italy, Greece and England together with *Notes from a European Diary, 1963–1964.* London: Hogarth Press. pp. xv, 467.

14689. UPDIKE, JOHN (postscr.). Memoirs of Hecate County. London: Hogarth Press. pp. 457.

Ethel Wilson

14690. MITCHELL, BEVERLEY. Ethel Wilson. *In* (pp. 181–238) **7.**

14691. STOUCK, MARY-ANN. Structure in Ethel Wilson's *The Innocent Traveller.* CanL (109) 17–31.

Lanford Wilson

14692. BARNETT, GENE A. Recreating the magic: an interview with Lanford Wilson. BSUF (25:2) 1984, 57–74.

14693. KANE, LESLIE. The agony of isolation in the drama of Anton Chekhov and Lanford Wilson. PhilP (31) 1985, 20–6.

14694. PAUWELS, GERARD W. A critical analysis of the plays of Lanford Wilson. Unpub. doct. diss., Indiana Univ. [Abstr. in DA (47) 1533A.]

Kathryn Windham

14695. OXENDINE, JILL. Kathryn Windham: 'Something I wanted to tell you'. *See* **2475.**

Yvor Winters

14696. BAGCHEE, SHYAMAL. The Western-ness of Yvor Winters's poetry. SDR (24:4) 148–65.

14697. DOMITO, TERRY. In defense of Winters: the poetry of Yvor Winters. Madison: Wisconsin UP. pp. xxix, 329. Rev. by Thomas Parkinson in AL (58:4) 650–1.

14698. HILLMAN, A. J. The poetry and poetic theory of Yvor Winters. Unpub. doct. diss., Univ. of Manchester, 1981.

Tim Winton

14699. MATTHEWS, BRIAN. Burning bright: impressions of Tim Winton. Meanjin (45:1) 83–93.

Adele Wiseman

14700. GREENSTEIN, MICHAEL. Adele Wiseman. *In* (pp. 239–72) **7.**

Owen Wister

14701. PAYNE, DARWIN. Owen Wister: chronicler of the West, gentlemen of the East. (Bibl. 1985, 13590.) Rev. by James H. Maguire in AL (58:3) 452–3; by Anthony Arthur in ALR (19:1) 84–5.

14702. THOMPSON, GERALD. Musical and literary influences on Owen Wister's *The Virginian.* SAQ (85:1) 40–85.

P. G. Wodehouse

14703. EIFRIG, GAIL McGRAW. Balancing Wordsworth and Wodehouse. *See* **9589.**

14704. MURPHY, N. T. P. In search of Blandings. London: Secker & Warburg, 1985. pp. 258. (Second ed.: first ed. 1981.) Rev. by David Cannadine in TLS, 8 Aug., 861.

Thomas Wolfe (1900–1938)

14705. ARMSTRONG, REBECCA BROWN. The imprisonment motif in the novels of Thomas Wolfe. Unpub. doct. diss., Univ. of Alabama, 1984. [Abstr. in DA (45) 3637A.]

14706. BLACKWELDER, JAMES RAY. Literary allusions in *Look Homeward, Angel*: Eugene and chapter XXIV. TWR (10:1) 27–39.

14707. BOYER, JAMES. Thomas Wolfe's characters – another look. TWR (10:2) 26–35.

14708. CLARK, JAMES W., JR. The war between the Gants. TWR (10:1) 58–63.

14709. DEDMOND, FRANCIS B. Problems of putting *Look Homeward, Angel* on the stage. TWR (10:1) 44–57.

14710. FIELD, LESLIE. *The Web and the Rock*: the city, Esther, and beyond. TWR (10:2) 11–18.

14711. HAACK, DIETMAR. Thomas Wolfes 'Dark Helen found and lost'. Der Wandel des Deutschlandbildes in den späten Romanen. Anglistik & Englischunterricht (29/30) 143–55.

14712. HAMILTON, ALTAMESE PURIFY. Eliza Gant: misunderstood victim. TWR (10:2) 39–46.

14713. HARPER, MARGARET MILLS. The aristocracy of art and the autobiographical fiction of James Joyce and Thomas Wolfe. *See* **12659.**

14714. HINZ, E. J.; TEUNISSEN, J. J. Milton, Whitman, Wolfe and Laurence: *The Stone Angel* as elegy. *See* **5728.**

14715. MILLS, MICHAEL S. From 'O Lost' to *Look Homeward, Angel*: a generic shift. TWR (10:1) 64–72.

14716. OAKES, RANDY W. Myth and method: Eliot, Joyce, and Wolfe in *The Web and the Rock*. *See* **11780.**

14717. PHILLIPSON, JOHN S. Thomas Wolfe's 'poems': where they came from. TWR (10:2) 36–8.

14718. POWELL, W. ALLEN. Thomas Wolfe: form through dichotomies. TWR (10:1)40–3.

14719. REED, RICHARD. Real estate in *Look Homeward, Angel*. SoLJ (19:1) 46–55.

14720. STUTMAN, SUZANNE. The discovery of a missing Thomas Wolfe letter. HLB (33:2) 1985, 101–13.

14721. —— Portrait of the artist: Thomas Wolfe's encounters with James Joyce. *See* **12731.**

Tom Wolfe (1931–)

14722. BEARD, JOHN. Inside the whale: a critical study of New Journalism and the nonfiction form. *See* **13168.**

14723. COHEN, ED. Tom Wolfe and the truth monitors: a historical fable. CLIO (16:1) 1–11.

14724. HARTSHORNE, THOMAS L.   Tom Wolfe on the 1960's. MidQ (23:2) 1982, 144–63.
14725. LOUNSBERRY, BARBARA.   Tom Wolfe's negative vision. SDR (20:2) 1982, 15–31.

John Woods

14726. TAYLOR, HENRY.   In the grip of days: the poetry of John Woods. HC (23) Oct., 1–12.

The Woolfs

14727. RHEIN, DONNA E.   The handprinted books of Leonard and Virginia Woolf at the Hogarth Press, 1917–1932. *See* **126.**

Leonard Woolf

14728. TRAUB, EILEEN.   The early years of the Hogarth Press. *See* **439.**

Virginia Woolf

14729. ANASTASOPOULOU, MARIA TH.   To lyriko mythistorema kai e Virginia Woolf. (The lyrical novel and Virginia Woolf.) Diavazo (153) 21–7.
14730. BATE, JONATHAN.   Arcadia and Armageddon: three English novelists and the First World War. *See* **11988.**
14731. BISHOP, E. L.   The shaping of *Jacob's Room*: Woolf's manuscript revisions. TCL (32:1) 115–35.
14732. BISHOP, EDWARD.   Writing, speech, and silence in *Mrs Dalloway*. ESCan (12:4) 397–423.
14733. BJØRHOVDE, GERD.   Transformation and subversion as narrative strategies in two fantasy novels of the 1920s: Sylvia Townsend Warner's *Lolly Willowes* and Virginia Woolf's *Orlando*. *In* (pp. 213–24) **18.**
14734. BLACK, NAOMI.   Virginia Woolf: the life of natural happiness (1882–1941). *In* (pp. 296–313) **20.**
14735. BOREN, LYNDA S.   The performing self: psychodrama in Austen, James and Woolf. *See* **7575.**
14736. CASHDAN, SONYA HANNAH.   'A hint of the fang': Virginia Woolf's personal portraits of women. Unpub. doct. diss., Texas A&M Univ., 1985. [Abstr. in DA (46) 3172A.]
14737. CHUNG, DUK-AE.   'Some lovely glorious nothing': self in Virginia Woolf's novels. Unpub. doct. diss., State Univ. of New York at Albany, 1985. [Abstr. in DA (47) 186A.]
14738. CLARKE, MICAEL M.   Virginia Woolf's Thackerayan heritage. *See* **9336.**
14739. DA SILVA, MACHADO.   The lineage of modernism and Virginia Woolf. Unpub. doct. diss., Univ. of Birmingham, 1983/84.
14740. FLINT, KATE.   Virginia Woolf and the General Strike. EC (36:4) 319–34.
14741. FREDRICK, JOHN ANDREW.   Triumph and travesty: reflexivity and the artistic conquest of nothingness and the void in Virginia Woolf's *To the Lighthouse* and Ford Madox Ford's *The Good Soldier*. *See* **11994.**
14742. FROMM, GLORIA G.   Re-inscribing *The Years*: Virginia Woolf, Rose Macaulay, and the critics. *See* **13108.**

14743. FULTON, MARILEE LINE.   Virginia Woolf's use of the past: the early criticism to *To the Lighthouse*. Unpub. doct. diss., Univ. of New Hampshire, 1985. [Abstr. in DA (47) 536A.]

14744. GINSBERG, ELAINE K.   Virginia Woolf and the Americans. *See* **865.**

14745. GORDON, LYNDALL.   Virginia Woolf: a writer's life. (Bibl. 1985, 13625.) Rev. by Morris Beja in Novel (20:1) 88–90.

14746. GROEN, HEIN.   The problematic nature of the feminist criticism of Virginia Woolf. DQR (16:2) 109–24.

14747. HARPER, HOWARD.   Between language and silence: the novels of Virginia Woolf. (Bibl. 1984, 13659.) Rev. by Stella McNichol in MLR (81:2) 462–3.

14748. HUSSEY, M. F.   The philosophy of Virginia Woolf. Unpub. doct. diss., Univ. of Nottingham, 1982.

14749. JUSTICIA, NELLIE TERESA.   Poetics of *Between the Acts* by Virginia Woolf. Unpub. doct. diss., New York Univ. [Abstr. in DA (47) 1334A.]

14750. KARAYIORGA, OLYMPIA.   O Erotas sto ergo tes Virginia Woolf. (Love in Virginia Woolf's work.) Diavazo (153) 50–1

14751. KAZAKOU, SOPHIA I.   E feministike apopse tes Virginia Woolf mesa apo dyo dokimia tes. (Virginia Woolf's feminist view in two of her essays.) Diavazo (153) 52–4.

14752. KNOX-SHAW, PETER.   *To the Lighthouse*: the novel as elegy. ESA (29:1) 31–52.

14753. KORE, L.-K.   'The nameless spirit': the sketches of Virginia Woolf. Unpub. doct. diss., Univ. of London, Bedford Coll. [Abstr. in IT (36) 473.]

14754. KOUTSOUDAKI, MARIA.   O 'Ellenas' Iakovos: e Ellada sto *Domatic tou Iakovou*. (The 'Greek' Jacob: Greece in *Jacob's Room*.) Diavazo (153) 42–9.

14755. —— Poia einai e k.Dalloway? (Who is Mrs Dalloway?) Diavazo (153) 28–30.

14756. KUHLMANN, DEBORAH JANE.   William Faulkner and Virginia Woolf: the movement of the moment, a dialectic. *See* **11896.**

14757. LAMBADARIDOU, EFFIE.   Dianoia kai phantasia ston *Orlando* tes Virginia Woolf. (Intellect and imagination in Virginia Woolf's *Orlando*.) Diavazo (153) 34–8

14758. LEONARDI, SUSAN J.   Bare places and ancient blemishes: Virginia Woolf's search for new language in *Night and Day*. Novel (19:2) 150–63.

14759. McCORD, PHYLLIS FRUS.   'Little corks that mark a sunken net': Virginia Woolf's *Sketch of the Past* as a fictional memoir. MLS (16:3) 247–54.

14760. McNEILLIE, ANDREW (ed.).   The essays of Virginia Woolf: vol. 1, 1904–12. London: Hogarth Press. pp. xxviii, 411. Rev. by P. N. Furbank in TLS, 12 Dec., 1393.

14761. MARCUS, JANE.   Virginia Woolf: a feminist slant. (Bibl. 1985, 13640.) Rev. by Janis M. Paul in Genre (19:1) 81–3.

14762. MARDER, HERBERT.   Split perspective: types of incongruity in *Mrs Dalloway*. PLL (22:1) 51–69.
14763. MILLER, CAROLINE RUTH.   Chance arrangements: the frames of Virginia Woolf's writings. Unpub. doct. diss., Univ. of Toronto, 1985. [Abstr. in DA (47) 914A.]
14764. MOFFAT, KATHLEEN WENDY.   Reader and resolution: ambiguity in the later novels of Conrad, Forster, and Woolf. *See* **11532.**
14765. PANAGHIS, APHRODITE M.   To thema tou kallitechne sto *Pros to Pharo* tes Woolf. (The theme of the artist in *To the Lighthouse* by Woolf.) Diavazo (153) 31–3.
14766. PARK, HEE-JIN.   *The Waves* yeongu: tusa eui chosang. (A study of *The Waves*: a portrait of a warrior.) JELL (32:3) 461–77.
14767. PINKNEY, M. M.   Feminine writing and the problem of the self: an examination of Virginia Woolf's novels in the light of recent critical and psychoanalytical theories. Unpub. doct. diss., Univ. of Warwick, 1985. [Abstr. in IT (36) 474.]
14768. QUICK, JONATHAN R.   Virginia Woolf, Roger Fry and post-impressionism. MassR (26:4) 1985, 547–70.
14769. ROSENMAN, ELLEN.   The 'invisible presence' in the creative process of Virginia Woolf. AI (43:2) 133–50.
14770. SAKELLIOU-SCHULTZ, LIANA.   *Ta Kymata* kai e 'ypoyeia' metaphora tous. (*The Waves* and their 'underground' metaphor.) Diavazo (153) 39–41.
14771. SCARFONE, SUZANNE.   The architectonics of fate: equilibrium and the process of creation in the work of William Wordsworth and Virginia Woolf. *See* **9639.**
14772. SQUIER, SUSAN MERRILL.   Virginia Woolf and London: the sexual politics of the city. Chapel Hill: North Carolina UP, 1985. pp. xii, 220. Rev. by Elgin W. Mellown in SAQ (85:4) 406–7.
14773. TICHÝ, ALEŠ.   Vypravěč a styl u Jamese Joyce a Virginie Woolfové. (Narrator and style in James Joyce and Virgina Woolf.) *In* (pp. 64–5) **4.**
14774. TORGOVNIK, MARIANNA.   The visual arts, pictorialism and the novel: James, Lawrence, and Woolf. *See* **8753.**
14775. TRAUB, EILEEN.   The early years of the Hogarth Press. *See* **439.**
14776. TSATSOU, MARIA.   Ena gramma yes Virginia Woolf yia ten Ellada. (A letter from Virginia Woolf about Greece.) Diavazo (153) 55–7.
14777. TURNER, B. E.   Reading, writing and meaning in the work of Virginia Woolf. Unpub. doct. diss., Univ. of Cambridge, 1984. [Abstr. in IT (35) 53.]
14778. WALKER, RONALD G.   Leaden circles dissolving in air: narrative rhythm and meaning in *Mrs Dalloway*. ELit (13:1) 57–87.
14779. WRIGHT, GLENN P.   The Raverat proofs of *Mrs Dalloway*. *See* **134.**
14780. YOON, HWA-GI.   Duality of imagery in Virginia Woolf's novels. Unpub. doct. diss., Sogang Univ. (Seoul).

14781. ZWERDLING, ALEX.   Virginia Woolf and the real world.
Berkeley; London: California UP. pp. x, 374.

Cornell Woolrich
14782. SOITOS, STEPHEN.   Some psychological themes in one of
Cornell Woolrich's novels. Clues (7:1) 75–87.

Gamel Woolsey
14783. HOPKINS, KENNETH.   Bertrand Russell and Gamel Woolsey.
See **14046.**

Charles Wright
14784. FRANCINI, ANTONELLA.   In the Longfellow line: some contemporary American poets as translators of Eugenio Montale: a study in
theory and practice. *See* **13085.**
14785. WRIGHT, STUART.   Charles Wright: a bibliographic chronicle,
1963–1985. BB (43:1) 3–12.

David McKee Wright
14786. SHARKEY, MICHAEL.   *Apollo in George Street*: a reappraisal of
David McKee Wright. Southerly (46:4) 444–55.

Eric Wright
14787. WRIGHT, ERIC.   Detective fiction: letter to a student studying
English 666. CanL (108) 40–4.

James Wright
14788. MORRILL, DONALD DEAN.   Exile's home: the poetry of James
Wright. Unpub. doct. diss., Univ. of Florida. [Abstr. in DA (47) 2160A.]
14789. STERIN, KEVIN.   A redefinition of the poetic self: James
Wright's *Amenities of Stone*. OhioR (33) 1984, 9–28.

Jay Wright
14790. KUTZINSKI, VERA MAGRET.   From American literature to New
World writing: myth and history in William Carlos Williams, Jay
Wright, and Nicolás Guillén. *See* **14652.**

Richard Wright
14791. COLTON, CYRUS.   Wright revisited. BW, 21 Dec., 1, 4, 14.
14792. ENGEL, LEONARD W.   Alienation and identity: Richard
Wright's outsider in *The Man Who Lived Underground*. PhilP (32) 72–8.
14793. FABRE, MICHEL.   The world of Richard Wright. Jackson:
Mississippi UP, 1985. pp. 268. Rev. by Jane Gibson Brown in SCR (3:4)
110–11.
14794. HAKUTANI, YOSHINOBU.   Richard Wright's experiment in
naturalism and satire: *Lawd Today*. SAF (14:2) 165–78.
14795. KODAMA, SANEHIDE.   Japanese influence on Richard Wright
in his last years: English haiku as a new genre. TamkR (15) 1984, 63–73.
14796. LYNCH, MICHAEL FRANCIS.   Richard Wright, Ralph Ellison,
and Dostoevsky: the choice of individual freedom and dignity.
See **11813.**
14797. MAGISTRALE, TONY.   From St Petersburg to Chicago:
Wright's *Crime and Punishment*. CLS (23:1) 59–70.
14798. SCRUGGS, CHARLES W.   Finding out about this Mencken: the
impact of *A Book of Prefaces* on Richard Wright. *See* **13241.**

14799. TREMAINE, LOUIS. The dissociated sensibility of Bigger Thomas in Wright's *Native Son*. SAF (14:1) 63–76.

Stephen Wright

14800. RINGNALDIA, DONALD. Chlorophyll overdose: Stephen Wright's *Meditations in Green*. WHR (40:2) 125–40.

Elinor Wylie

14801. HOAGWOOD, TERENCE ALLAN. Wylie's *The Crooked Stick*. Exp (44:3) 54–7.

John Wyndham
(John Wyndham Parkes Lucas Beynon Harris)

14802. STEPHENSON-PAYNE, PHIL; BENSON, GORDON JR. John Wyndham Parkes Lucas Benyon Harris: (10/7/03–10/3/69, Knowle, Warwickshire): a bibliography. Leeds: Stephenson-Payne, 1985. 18 leaves.

W. B. Yeats

14803. ARKINS, BRIAN. Yeat's version of Colonus' praise. CML (7:1) 39–42.

14804. ARMSTRONG, GORDON. Symbols, signs, and language: the brothers Yeats and Samuel Beckett's art of the theater. *See* **11155.**

14805. BARKER, VARA SUE TAMMINGA. W. B. Yeats: poetry as meditation. Unpub. doct. diss., Univ. of Texas at Austin, 1984. [Abstr. in DA (47) 2165A.]

14806. BATTAGLIA, ROSEMARIE A. Yeats, Nietzsche, and the aristocratic ideal. CLit (13:1) 88–94.

14807. BILLIGHEIMER, RACHEL V. The dance as vision in Blake and Yeats. *See* **6222.**

14808. —— 'Passion and conquest': Yeats' swans. CLit (13:1) 55–70.

14809. —— Self and soul in W. B. Yeats. Éire–Ireland (21:4) 52–65.

14810. BLOCK, ED, JR. Walter Pater, Arthur Symons, W. B. Yeats, and the fortunes of the literary portrait. *See* **9027.**

14811. BRAMSBÄCK, BIRGIT. William Butler Yeats och Sverige. (William Butler Yeats and Sweden.) Tvärsnitt (Stockholm) (8:1) 4–13.

14812. BURTON, R. E. The 'spiring treadmill' and the 'preposterous pig': the accommodation of science in the political, occult and poetic development of W. B. Yeats, 1885–1095. Unpub. doct. diss., Univ. of London, Royal Holloway Coll., 1985. [Abstr. in IT (35) 1086.]

14813. CHADWICK, JOSEPH. Family romance as national allegory in Yeats's *Cathleen ni Houlihan* and *The Dreaming of the Bones*. TCL (32:2) 155–68.

14814. CHOI, YOUNG-JA. W. B. Yeats eui si wa jubyeon inmul. (Poems of W. B. Yeats and their relationship to the poet's circle.) CAE (19) 387–99.

14815. CLARK, DAVID R. Yeats at songs and choruses. (Bibl. 1985, 13709.) Rev. by George Bornstein in MLS (16:2) 82–7.

14816. COPENHAVEN, CARLA. Mastering the images: Yeats's Byzantium poems. YREAL (2) 1984, 319–53.

14817. CULLINGFORD, ELIZABETH (ed.). Yeats: poems, 1919–1935: a

casebook. (Bibl. 1984, 13730.) Rev. by Andrew Swarbrick in CritQ
(28:3) 112; by James Simmons in NQ (33:2) 267.

14818. DETTMAR, KEVIN J. H. 'Evil gathers head': Yeats' poetics of
evil. CLit (13:1) 71–87.

14819. DONOGHUE, DENIS. We Irish: essays on Irish literature and
society. *See* **9712.**

14820. EARLE, RALPH HARDING. Yeats's passionate syntax. Unpub.
doct. diss., Univ. of North Carolina at Chapel Hill, 1985. [Abstr. in DA
(47) 535A.]

14821. ELLMANN, RICHARD. Four Dubliners: Wilde, Yeats, Joyce,
and Beckett. *See* **9546.**

14822. FINNERAN, RICHARD J. W. B. Yeats: a commentary on the *New
Commentary.* Review (7) 1985, 163–89 (review-article).

14823. —— (ed.). W. B. Yeats: the poems: a new edition. (Bibl.
1984, 13736.) Rev. by George Bornstein in MLS (16:2) 82–7.

14824. FLEMING, DEBORAH DIANE. The Irish peasant in the work of
W. B. Yeats and J. M. Synge. *See* **14342.**

14825. FOX, S. Nationalism in the lives and works of W. B. Yeats and
Alexander Blok: a comparative study. Unpub. doct. diss., Univ. of
Manchester, 1982. [Abstr. in IT (35) 41.]

14826. GIANNOTTI, THOMAS JOHN, JR. A language of silence: writing
the self in Yeats and Synge, Joyce and Beckett. *See* **11176.**

14827. GOGGIN, EDWARD WILLIAM. Blest: cohesion and ironic de-
flation in six short poem sequences of W. B. Yeats. Unpub. doct. diss.,
Fordham Univ., 1985. [Abstr. in DA (47) 910A.]

14828. GOOD, M. P. W. B. Yeats and the creation of a tragic universe.
Unpub. doct. diss., Trinity Coll. Dublin, 1983/84.

14829. GRAMM, CHRISTIE DIANE. The development of prophecy in
the poetry of W. B. Yeats. Unpub. doct. diss., Univ. of Oregon, 1985.
[Abstr. in DA (46) 1948A.]

14830. GRIFFIN, JON. Profane perfection: *The Statues.* CLit (13:1)
21–8.

14831. GRIFFIN, JON NELSON. Profane perfections: Yeats' *Last Poems.*
Unpub. doct. diss., Univ. of Rochester. [Abstr. in DA (47) 1318A.]

14832. HASSETT, JOSEPH M. Yeats and the poetics of hate. New York:
St Martin's Press; Dublin: Gill & Macmillan. pp. ix, 189.

14833. HIRST, DESIRÉE. The theosophical preoccupations of Blake
and Yeats. *See* **6249.**

14834. HOPENWASSER, NANDA. Crazy Jane: writer of her own
justification. CLit (13:1) 9–20.

14835. ILIOPOULOUS, S. 'Out of a medium's mouth': Yeats's art in
relation to mediumship, spiritualism and psychical research. Unpub.
doct. diss., Univ. of Warwick, 1985. [Abstr. in IT (36) 473.]

14836. JEFFARES, A. NORMAN. A new commentary on the poems of
W. B. Yeats. (Bibl. 1985, 13719.) Rev. by Richard J. Finneran in Review
(7) 1985, 163–89.

14837. —— (ed.). Poems of W. B. Yeats: a new selection. (Bibl.

1984, 13753.) Rev. by Andrew Swarbrick in CritQ (28:3) 112; by James Simmons in NQ (33:2) 267–8.

14838.   JORDAN, CARMEL.   The stone symbol in *Easter 1916* and the Cuchlain plays. CLit (13:1) 36–43.

14839.   KELLY, JOHN (ed.); DOMVILLE, ERIC (assoc. ed.).   The collected letters of W. B. Yeats: vol. I, 1865–1895. Oxford: Clarendon Press. pp. xxxii, 548. Rev. by Conor Cruise O'Brien in Listener, 20 Mar., 24–5; by Frank Stack in THES (698) 23; by Tom Paulin in LRB (8:6) 9–10.

14840.   KIM, WOOK-WON.   W. B. Yeats eui *Last Poems* e natanah bigeukgwan. (The tragic vision of W. B. Yeats's *Last Poems*.) YYY (3) 1985, 53–82.

14841.   KLUG, M. A.   Pursuit of confusion in *The Tower*. CLit (13:1) 29–35.

14842.   KNOWLAND, A. S.   W. B. Yeats: dramatist of vision. Gerrards Cross: Smythe; Totowa, NJ: Barnes & Noble, 1983. pp. 256. (Irish literary studies, 17.) Rev. by Jacqueline Genet in Études irlandaises (9) 1984, 341–2; by Andrew Parkin in CJIS (12:1) 81–3.

14843.   KOMESU, OKIFUMI.   The double perspective of Yeats's aesthetic. Totowa, NJ: Barnes & Noble, 1985. (Cf. bibl. 1985, 13725.) Rev. by Andrew Parkin in CJIS (12:1) 83–4.

14844.   KUCH, PETER.   Yeats and AE: the antagonism that unites dear friends. *See* **14049.**

14845.   LEAMON, WARREN.   Yeats: skeptic on stage. Éire–Ireland (21:1) 129–35.

14846.   LEE, CHANG-BAE.   Yeats si eui ihae. (Understanding Yeats's poetry.) Seoul: Munhak gwa Gisung. pp. 321.

14847.   LEE, SE-SOON.   W. B. Yeats eui isang segae: unity of being eui chugu. (W. B. Yeats's ideal world: the search for Unity of Being.) JELL (31:4) 1985, 611–33.

14848.   LEE, SEUNG-DAE.   Jakpum yeongu: *Byzantium*. (An analytical study of *Byzantium*.) YYY (3) 1985, 1–23.

14849.   LENSING, GEORGE S.   *Among School Children*: questions as conclusions. CLit (13:1) 1–8.

14850.   LEPPARD, D. G.   An investigation into the theory and structure of metaphor, with special reference to Wordsworth and Yeats. *See* **2235.**

14851.   McVEIGH, P. J.   Mirror and mask: a study of the major autobiographical prose of William Butler Yeats. Unpub. doct. diss., Trinity Coll. Dublin, 1983/84.

14852.   McWHIRTER, DAVID B.   The rhythm of the body in Yeats' *Nineteen Hundred and Nineteen*. CLit (13:1) 44–54.

14853.   MARTIN, HEATHER C.   W. B. Yeats: metaphysician as dramatist. Gerrards Cross: Smythe. pp. xiv, 153. (Cf. bibl. 1981, 13694.)

14854.   MARVEL, LAURA.   Blake and Yeats: visions of apocalypse. *See* **6265.**

14855.   MEIHUIZEN, NICHOLAS.   Yeats, Frye, and the meeting of saint and poet. Theoria (67) 53–60.

14856. MILLER, SUSAN FISHER. Hopes and fears for the tower: William Morris's spirit at Yeats's Ballylee. *See* **8993**.

14857. MORAN, G. P. W. B. Yeats's *Autobiographies* in the context of other Irish autobiographical writings. Unpub. doct. diss., Univ. of London, Bedford Coll., 1984.

14858. MORGAN, C. Stanza structures in the poetry of Hugo von Hofmannsthal and W. B. Yeats. Unpub. doct. diss., Univ. of East Anglia, 1984. [Abstr. in IT (36) 468.]

14859. MURPHY, RUSSELL. Josef Strzygowski and Yeats' 'a starlit or a moonlit dome'. CLit (13:1) 106–11.

14860. —— A new source for *Veronica's Napkin*. ELN (23:4) 42–50.

14861. NESMY, C. J. William Butler Yeats: l'âme celtique et le rôle de l'art. RG (1) 97–9.

14862. OPITZ, MICHAEL J. Poetry as appropriate epistemology: Gregory Bateson and W. B. Yeats. Unpub. doct. diss., Univ. of Minnesota, 1985. [Abstr. in DA (46) 3042A.]

14863. ORR, LEONARD. Yeats's theories of fiction. Éire–Ireland (21:2) 152–8.

14864. PEARCE, DONALD. Shadows deep: change and continuity in Yeats. CLQ (22:4) 198–204.

14865. PETTINGELL, PHOEBE. Young Yeats. NewL (69:13) 14–15.

14866. PITTOCK, MURRAY. Falcon and falconer: *The Second Coming* and Marvell's *Horatian Ode*. *See* **5635**.

14867. PONNUSWAMY, KRISHNA. Yeats and Tagore: a comparative study of their plays. *See* **14347**.

14868. PRUITT, VIRGINIA D. W. B. Yeats: rage, order, and the mask. Éire–Ireland (21:2) 141–6.

14869. PUTZEL, STEVEN. Reconstructing Yeats: *The Secret Rose* and *The Wind Among the Reeds*. Dublin: Gill & Macmillan. pp. 242.

14870. RAINE, KATHLEEN. Yeats the initiate: essays on certain themes in the work of W. B. Yeats. Portlaoise: Dolmen Press; London: Allen & Unwin. pp. xxiv, 449.

14871. RAMRATNAM, MALATI. W. B. Yeats and the craft of verse. Lanham, MD; London: UP of America, 1985. pp. x, 135.

14872. RAO, N. M. Yeats's *Among Schoolchildren*: text and context. AJES (11) 98–108.

14873. RAVINDRAN, SANKARAN. William Butler Yeats and India: Indian ideas of art, religion, and philosophy in Yeats' works, 1885–1939. Unpub. doct. diss., Univ. of Kansas. [Abstr. in DA (47) 2171A.]

14874. RHEE, YOUNG SUCK. The poetics of etherealization: female imagery in the work of W. B. Yeats. Unpub. doct. diss., Univ. of Nebraska–Lincoln, 1985. [Abstr. in DA (46) 3043A.]

14875. RUDRA, ARUP. *A Vision*: between romantic and modern. Jadavpur University Essays and Studies (Calcutta) (4) 1984, 116–20.

14876. SCHLEIFER, RONALD. The pathway of *The Rose*: Yeats, the lyric, and the syntax of symbolism. Genre (18:4) 1985, 375–96.

14877. SCHRICKER, GALE C. A new species of man: the poetic persona of W. B. Yeats. London: Assoc. UPs, 1982. (Cf. bibl. 1984, 13787.) Rev. by Elizabeth Mackenzie in NQ (3:4) 565–6.

14878. SCHWENKER, G. L.   A commentary on the *Autobiographies* of W. B. Yeats. Unpub. doct. diss., Univ. of Stirling, 1980.

14879. SIEGEL, SANDRA F. (ed.).   *Purgatory*: manuscript materials including the author's [Yeats's] final text. *See* **180.**

14880. WEATHERBY, JOAN.   Yeats, the Tarot, and the fool. CLit (13:1) 112–21.

14881. YAMAZAKI, HIROYUKI.   Yeats: kettei fukanousei no shijin. (Yeats: the poet of indecisiveness.) Tokyo: Yamaguchi Press. pp. xiv, 208.

14882. YOH, SUK-KEE.   Yeats wa ilbon eui Noh geuk: bigyeo yeongeukjeok gochal. (Yeats and the Japanese Noh.) JELL (32:4) 741–66.

14883. YUN, SAM-HA.   Yeats si eui jeongchijeok jujae. (Political themes of Yeats's poetry.) Unpub. doct. diss., Hankuk Univ. of Foreign Studies (Seoul).

Andrew Young

14884. LOWBURY, EDWARD; YOUNG, ALISON (eds).   The poetical works of Andrew Young. (Bibl. 1985, 13751.) Rev. by Dick Davis in Listener (115) 30 Jan., 24.

David Young

14885. FOGEL, STANLEY.   Terra incognita. ECanW (28) 1984, 150–5.

Roger Zelazny

14886. MORRISSEY, THOMAS J.   Zelazny: mythmaker of nuclear war. SFS (13:2) 182–92.

Dale Zieroth

14887. BUITENHUIS, PETER.   Attempted Edens: the poetry of Dale Zieroth. ECanW (32) 92–105.

Paul Zindel

14888. HOFFMAN, STANLEY.   Winning, losing, but above all taking risks: a look at the novels of Paul Zindel. LU (2:2) 1978, 78–88.

Louis Zukofsky

14889. HOOLEY, DANIEL MATTHEWS.   'The classics in paraphrase': Ezra Pound and modern translators of classical poetry. *See* **10668.**

14890. LEGGOTT, MICHELE JOY.   Reading Zukofsky's *80 Flowers*. Unpub. doct. diss., Univ. of British Columbia, 1985. [Abstr. in DA (47) 1325A.]

14891. ODLIN, RENO.   Materials toward an essay on Zukofsky's *A*. Paideuma (10:2) 1981, 315–25.

14892. PENBERTHY, JENNY LYNN.   Lorine Niedecker and Louis Zukofsky: her poems and letters. *See* **13516.**

INDEXES

INDEX OF AUTHORS AND SUBJECTS

This index consists mainly of authors' names, titles and subjects which appear as headings in the main body of the work, with some explanatory additions, cross-references, etc. For a breakdown, by genre, of the various periods within the 'English Literature' section, see the Table of Contents.

Lowell, Amy, 13081
— James Russell, 8875
— Robert, 13082–94
Lowry, Malcolm, 13095–102
Lowther, Pat, 13103
Luhan, Mabel Dodge, 13104
Lurie, Alison, 13105–6
Lydgate, John, 3646–8
Lyly, John, 4108–9
Lytle, Andrew, 13107
Lytton, Lord, 7743–5

Macaulay, Rose, 13108
— Thomas Babington, Lord,
　8876–8
McAuley, James, 13109
'McBain, Ed', 13110
McCarthy, Mary, 13111
McClure, James, 13112
Mac Colla, Fionn, 13113
McCullers, Carson, 13114–21
McCullough, Colleen, 13122
'MacDiarmid, Hugh',
　13123–36
Macdonald, Cynthia, 13137
MacDonald, George, 8879–88
— John D., 13138–9
'Macdonald, Ross', 13140–5
'MacDonald, Tom', 13113
McEwan, Ian, 13146
MacEwen, Gwendolyn, 13147
MacGerr, Patricia, 13148
MacGill, Patrick, 13149–50
McGrath, John, 13151
— Thomas, 13152
MacGreevy, Thomas, 13153
McGuane, Thomas, 13154–6
Machen, Arthur, 13157
McIlvanney, William, 13158
McKay, Claude, 13159
Mackenzie, Sir Compton,
　13160–1
McKinnon, Barry, 13162
Mackintosh, Elizabeth, 14354
Maclaren, Archibald, 8889
McLaverty, Michael, 13163
Maclean, Elizabeth, 14025
MacLennan, Hugh, 13164–5
MacLeod, Alistair, 13166
'MacLeod, Fiona', 8890
MacNeice, Louis, 13167
McPhee, John, 13168
Macpherson, James, 6665–9
McPherson, James Alan,
　13169–70
Madden, Samuel, 6670
Mahon, Derek, 13171
Mahy, Margaret, 13172
Maidstone, Richard, 3649

Mailer, Norman, 13173–9
Mainwaring, Arthur, 6671–3
Mais, Roger, 13180–1
Major, Clarence, 13182
Malamud, Bernard, 13183–93
Malgonkar, Manohar, 13194
Mallet, David, 6674
Malory, Sir Thomas, 3650–9
Malouf, David, 13195–9
Mamet, David, 13200–1
Mandeville, Bernard, 6675
— Sir John, 3660
Manfred, Frederick, 13202
Mangan, James Clarence,
　8891–2
Manley, Mary de la Rivière,
　6676–8
Manning, Olivia, 13203
Mannyng, Robert, 3661–2
Mansfield, Katherine,
　13204–10
Manuscripts, 136–89
Mapanje, Jack, 13211
Marchant, John, 6679
Markandaya, Kamala,
　13212–13
Markham, Edwin, 13214
Marlowe, Christopher, 4110–36
'Marprelate, Martin', 4137
Marryat, Captain Frederick,
　8893
Marsh, James, 8894
Marshall, Archibald, 13215
— Arthur Hammond, 13215
— Paule, 13216–17
Marston, John, 5616–19
Martin, Violet, 14192
— Philip, 13218
Martineau, Harriet, 8895–7
Marvell, Andrew, 5620–43
Masefield, John, 13219
Mason, Bruce, 13220
— R. A. K., 13221
Massinger, Philip, 5644–6
Masters, Edgar Lee, 13222–3
Mather, Cotton, 5647–9
Mathers, Edward Powys, 14416
Mathews, John Joseph, 13224
Mathias, Roland, 13225
Matthiessen, F. O., 13226
Maturin, C. R., 8898–9
Maugham, W. Somerset,
　13227–9
Mayhew, Henry, 8900
Medwall, Henry, 3663–4
Melville, Herman, 8901–58
Mencken, H. L., 13230–42
Merbury, Francis, 4138
Meredith, George, 8959–66
— William, 13243

Meriwether, Louise, 13244
Merrill, James, 13245–6
Merton, Thomas, 13247–9
Merwin, W. S., 13250
Metcalf, John, 13251
Middleton, Thomas, 5650–69
Mill, John Stuart, 8967–80
Millar, Kenneth, 13140–5
Millay, Edna St Vincent, 13252
Miller, Arthur, 13253–64
— Henry, 13265–8
— Walter M., Jr, 13269–70
Milne, A. A., 13271–2
Milnes, Richard Monckton,
　8981
Milton, John, 5670–828
'Minier, Nelson', 14317
'Mira', 6463
Mitchell, James Leslie,
　12146–50
— Julian, 13273
— Margaret, 13274–7
— W. O., 13278
Mitchison, Naomi, 13279–80
Mitford, Mary Russell, 8982
— Nancy, 13281
Mnthali, Felix, 13282
Moir, John, 6680
Momaday, N. Scott, 13283–8
Monboddo, James Burnett,
　Lord, 6681–2
Montagu, Lady Mary Wortley,
　6683–4
Montague, John, 13289–90
Montgomery, L. M., 13291
Moodie, Susanna, 8983–4
Moody, William Vaughn,
　13292
Moorcock, Michael, 13293
Moore, Edward, 6685
— George, 13294–303
— Marianne, 13304–6
Moorhouse, Frank, 13307
Moran, David Patrick, 13308
More, Hannah, 6686
— Henry, 5829
— Sir Thomas, 4139–68
Morgan, Charles, 13309
— Lady, 8985–5a
Morphology,
— current, 2128–45
— historical, 1909–21
Morrieson, Ronald Hugh,
　13310–11
Morris, William, 8986–97
— Wright, 13312–13
Morrison, Toni, 13314–23
Morton, Thomas, 5830
Mosel, Tad, 13324
Moss, Howard, 13325

INDEX OF SCHOLARS

including compilers, critics, editors and translators.
Reviewers are included only when the item has been counted as an essay-review.

Barton Johnson, D., 8621, 13372–6
Bartram, M., 7455
Bartsch, Uta, 11108
Bartter, Martha A., 10139
— Martha Taylor, 10140
Barza, Steven, 11475
Bas, Georges, 11051
Baskerville, E. J., 3984
Baskett, Belma, 12360
al-Bassam, E. A. S., 12005
Bassett, Helen Barnes, 2990
— John E., 11841
Bassnett, Suzan, 2590
Bassoff, Bruce, 12615
Bastian, F., 6386
Basu, S., 8006
Bataille, Gretchen M., 2968
— Robert R., 6650
Batchelor, John, 11476, 14510
Bate, A. J., 4380
— Jonathan, 65, 4381, 5673, 6554, 11988
— W. Jackson, 7903
Bately, Janet, 802
Bateman, J. A., 1082
Bates, Milton J., 14255
— Richard, 5404
Bates-Mims, Merelyn B., 972
Bateson, M., 1655
Batsleer, Janet, 10725
Battaglia, Rosemarie A., 14806
Battarbee, Keith, 2329, 11346
Battersby, James L., 6555
Battestin, Martin C., 558, 5210, 5931
Battin, Patricia, 194
Baudou, Jacques, 10141–2, 13110
Bauer, Dale Marie, 8448
— Gero, 887
Baugh, John, 1044
Baughman, Ronald, 10480
Baum, Rosalie Murphy, 7977
— Shari R., 1265
Bauman, Michael E., 5674
— Richard, 2432
Baumann, Gerd, 10642
— Uwe, 4139
— Walter, 13777–80
Baumgart, Wolfgang, 4383
Baumler, Ellen R., 3069
Baumlin, James S., 5362–3
Baurecht, William C., 12767
Bawcutt, N. W., 4877
— Priscilla, 3591
Bawer, Bruce, 10143–4, 11382, 11667, 11729
Bax, Ingrid Pufahl, 1346
Bayer-Berenbaum, Linda, 7202

Bayerl, Elizabeth Ann, 13951
Bayley, John, 2777, 12783, 13019
Baylon, Daniel, 13952
Baym, Nina, 2591, 7203
Bazargan, Susan, 12616
Bazire, Joyce, 3070
Bázlik, Miroslav, 1974
Beadle, Richard, 3292, 3453–4
Beal, Joan C., 888
Beale, Donald A., 6978
— Peter, 5099
Beaman, Darlene Suzette, 8103
Beard, John, 13168
— Pauline Winsome, 10145
Beardsley, Monroe C., 3018, 10967
Beare, Geraldine, 559
Beasecker, Robert, 6979
Beasley, Conger, Jr, 560
— Jerry C., 6041–2, 6801
Beattie, Geoffrey, 1273
Beatty, Audrey, 10727
— C. J. P., 7621
Beaty, Frederick L., 7760
Beauchamp, Gorman, 10146
Beaver, Harold, 2991
Bechler, R., 5932
Beck, Bruce, 90
Becker, Allienne R., 8449
— R. S., 13294
Beckerman, Bernard, 4110
Beckett, Ruth, 4384
Beckman, Mary E., 1405
Beckson, Karl, 9294
Beckwith, Marc, 4085, 5675
— Sarah, 3612
Bedient, Calvin, 11730, 14472
Beecher, Donald, 4233
Beekman, E. M., 12617
Beer, Gillian, 8200, 8959
— John, 7384, 7889–91, 12006, 12874
Beers, Terry Lynn, 10728
Beesley, K. R., 1975
Beeton, Ridley, 12847
Beetz, Kirk H., 9302
Beger, Lois Lee Stewart, 9905
Begnal, Michael H., 12618
Behm, Carl, III, 6054
Behr, Caroline, 11731
Behrendt, Stephen C., 6216–17
Behrens, Susan Janet, 1266
Behrmann, Alfred, 5285
Beiderwell, Bruce, 9159
— Bruce John, 9160
Beier, A. L., 3998
Beilin, Elaine V., 4056
Beiner, G., 4385, 4848, 4907
Beith, Gilbert, 7833

Beja, Morris, 11160
Beker, Miroslav, 10147
Belcher, Margaret, 9303
Bell, Alan, 195, 14058
— Barbara Currier, 12064
— Ian, 9665
— Ian A., 6387
— Ian F. A., 8623, 13781
— John, 13674
— K., 11092
— Lawrence H., 1316
— Millicent, 2822, 8624, 12007
— Millicent Lang, 14556
— Nancy, 9746
Bellamy, John, 2433
Bellman, James Fredrick, Jr, 3240
Bellringer, Alan W., 8625
Belsches, Alan T., 13703
Belsey, Catherine, 3869, 5933
Belton, Ellen R., 4980
Benayoun, Robert, 11022
Bendarz, James P., 4194
Bender, Eileen T., 11396
— Todd K., 11477
Bender-Davis, Jeannine M., 3218
Bendixen, Alfred, 7204
Benedict, Barbara MacVean, 6443
Ben-Ephraim, Gavriel, 8007
Benert, Annette Larson, 8626
Benes, Jane Montague, 803
— Peter, 803
Benet, Diana, 5474
Benfey, Christopher E. G., 8104
Bennett, Benjamin K., 9906
— Bruce, 8201, 9666, 10149
— Gillian, 2551
— J. A. W., 3293
— Maria Frances, 11583
Bennetts, Shirley, 3483
Ben-Porat, Ziva, 8800
Bensel-Meyers, Linda Diane, 3870
Bensick, Carol Marie, 8450
Bensko, John, 11062
— John Richard, 10481
Benson, C. J., 196
— Douglas K., 10643
— Eugene, 11943
— Evelyn, 1731–2
— Gordon, Jr, 14802
— Jackson, 12362
— Larry D., 3294
— Morton, 1730–2
Benstock, Bernard, 9667, 12619–20
Benston, Kimberly W., 4111
Bentinck, A., 11628

Bentley, D. M. R., 2592, 13686
— G. E., Jr, 6218–20
— Gerald Eades, 3871
— Gregory Wayne, 4878
— Jerry H., 3999
Benton, Jill Kathryn, 13279
Ben-Yehuda, Nachman, 10150
Ben-Zvi, Linda, 11161–2
Beom, Dae-Soon, 10482–3
Berard, Wayne Stephen, 11732
Berce, Sanda, 4386
Berch, Victor A., 197
Bercovitch, Sacvan, 47, 6981,
    6983, 10729
Beresford, Rosemary, 12276
Berge, Marit, 13668
Berger, Alan L., 11217
— Charles, 14256
— Fred R., 8968
Bergeron, David M., 3872–3,
    4387, 5514
Bergh, Gunnar, 1045
Bergner, H., 3804
Bergonzi, Bernard, 561, 9670
Berkeley, David S., 5034, 5676
— Linda Eileen, 8202
Berkhout, Carl T., 3071–3,
    3241
Berkowitz, Steven Bennett,
    3831
Berkson, Dorothy, 8627
Berlin, Ira, 7456
Berman, David, 6204–5
— Jaye, 13472
— Jeffrey, 9671
Bermant, Chaim, 2992
Bermejo García, Fuenciscla,
    8203
Bernardoni, James, 9907
Berndt, Judy, 13943
— Rolf, 804
Bernsen, Michael, 6312
Bernstein, Charles, 13782
— J. M., 10731
— Michael Andre, 13783
Berry, Martyn, 10488
— N., 562
— Ralph, 4389, 4633–4, 9908
— Ralph M., 2823
— Reginald, 10151
Berryman, Charles, 14429
— Jo Brantley, 13784
Berschin, W., 3185
Berst, Charles A., 14104
Bertelsen, Eve, 13003
— Lance, 5934
Berthoff, Warner, 2593
Berthold, Dennis, 6984, 7700,
    9249, 9479
Bertolino, Jane Victoria, 6752

Bertram, James, 9673
— Paul, 4390
Berwick, Robert C., 1300–1
Besner, Neil, 12111
Bessai, Diane, 9909
Besserman, Lawrence, 3734,
    3805
Bessinger, Jess B., Jr, 3242
Betz, Renee Rebeta, 1157
Beukema, Frits, 2114
Beum, Robert, 11733
Beveridge, A. H., 13123
Beversluis, John, 13023
Bevevino, Mary Margaret,
    13759
Bevington, David, 491, 4391,
    4787
Bewell, Alan J., 9572
Bharucha, Rustom, 12008
Bialostosky, Don, 10732
— Don H., 10733
Biber, Douglas, 1083–4
Biddulph, Joseph, 805–7, 889
Bidney, Martin, 5677, 6221,
    9573, 13222, 14100
Bieganowski, Ronald, 12065
Bielawski, Larry, 7761
Bieman, Elizabeth, 4235
Bienz, John, 5475
Bigsby, C. W. E., 9910, 9917,
    11010
— Christopher, 10452
Bijvoet, Maria Christina, 4908
Billigheimer, Rachel V.,
    6222–3, 14808–9
Billings, Robert, 11651
Billingsley, Dale B., 91
Billman, Carol, 355, 11734
Bilton, Peter, 18, 4943
Binding, Paul, 8308, 12159
Bindman, David, 6224
Binns, J. W., 4317
— Ronald, 11829–30
Binstock, L. R., 7457
Binyon, Mike, 9674
— T. J., 11239–40
Bird, Graham, 8767
— John Christian, Jr, 9429
— Toby Anne, 8008
Birdsall, Eric, 9575–6
— Virginia Ogden, 6388
Birdwell, Christine, 9911
Birkett, J., 4635
— Julian, 9195
Birna, Vlaicu, 4334
Birnbaum, G., 5214
Birney, Earle, 3675
Birns, H. William, 862
Biron, Beth Dyer, 11842
Birrell, Thomas Anthony, 2595

Birringer, Johannes, 4392
Bishop, Alan, 11333
— E. L., 14731
— Edward, 14732
— George Jonathan, 8628
— Ian, 3295
— Jonathan, 8259
Biswas, D. C., 4202
Bizley, W. H., 11735
Bjelland, Karen Theresa, 3296
Bjørhovde, Gerd, 14471
Björk, Lennart A., 8379
Bjork, Robert E., 3074
Black, James D., 2902
— Jeremy, 198, 6292, 6354,
    6790, 6824
— John W., 986
— M. H., 356
— Michael, 12875
— Naomi, 14734
— Sebastian, 13672, 14386
— Stephen A., 13605
Blackall, Jean Frantz, 8629
Blackburn, John Meredith,
    5461
— Mark, 1686
Blackham, H. J., 2596
Blackwelder, James Ray, 14706
Blades, John, 11383, 12363,
    13001, 14316, 14426
Blaen, A., 2396
Blaicher, G., 2779
— Günther, 7762
Blaim, Artur, 3941
Blain, Virginia, 7951
Blainey, Ann, 8591
Blair, I. D., 1347
— Peter Hunter, 3186
— Rhonda L., 6374
— Sandra J., 92
— Walter, 9430
Blake, A. J., 7205
— Ann, 13548, 14230
— Kathleen, 6986
— N. F., 3391, 3582, 3676,
    3735–6
— Norman, 3297
— Norman F., 808
Blakemore, Steven, 5678–9,
    7957
Blamires, Harry, 9676
Blanch, Robert J., 3806–7
Bland, Susan Kesner, 1348
Blank, G. K., 9207–8
Blanpied, John W., 4393
Blassingame, John W., 8163
Blatchford, Roy, 13227
Blau, Herbert, 5456, 9912
— Rivkah Teitz, 5476
Blaugher, Kurt Edwin, 9913

— Ray, 7207
Braden, Gordon, 3876, 5168, 5741
Bradford, Alan T., 3877
— R. W., 5169
Bradley, J. L., 9122
— Leslie John Alexander, 9123
— S. A. J., 3077
Bradshaw, Graham, 4894
— Steve, 8011
Brady, Ann P., 7718
— Anne M., 2603
— Brigid, 3304
— Ciaran, 4238
— Frank, 2969, 6296
— Jennifer, 5539
Brady-Papadopoulou, Valentini, 14575
Braeger, Peter C., 3243
Bragg, Lois Marian, 3078
— Melvyn, 8433, 12963
Braithwaite, Edward Kamau, 11320
Brake, Laurel, 564
Brale, Michele Aina, 14503
Bramsbäck, Birgit, 2379, 14811
Brand, Dana, 8452, 13387
— Mona, 9918
Brandes, Randy Paul, 12488
Brandmark, Wendy, 13998
Branford, Jean, 949
Brans, Jo, 14085
Brantley, Richard E., 5604
Brantlinger, Patrick, 13942
Brasch, James D., 12364
Brashear, Lucy, 5833
Brask, Per, 9919
Brassell, Tim, 14298
Braswell, Laurel, 3498
— Mary Flowers, 3499
Brater, Enoch, 11163
Brătescu, G., 4405
Brattin, Joel J., 300
Braunmuller, A. R., 5198
Braverman, Richard, 5605
— Richard Lewis, 5049
Braxton, Joanne M., 8612
— Joanne Margaret, 10628
Bray, J. R., 3305
— Paul Cyrus, 12621
Braybrooke, Neville, 11427
Brebach, Raymond, 11478
Bredahl, A. Carl, 11043
Bredin, Hugh, 14007
Breen, Jon L., 7208
Breitenberg, Mark, 4169
Breitwieser, Mitchell Robert, 5647
Breivik, Leif Egil, 1865, 1982
— Leiv Egil, 1088

Brekle, Herbert E., 809
Bremen, Brian A., 14644
Bremner, S., 7209
Brener, R. Y., 1302
Brennan, Anthony, 4397
— Anthony S., 4743
— Dan, 11848
— Joseph G., 11990
— Michael G., 2507
Brensnahan, Roger J., 13058
Brereton, John C., 493
Breslin, James E. B., 10486
— John B., 12587
Bressler, Charles Edward, 8316
Breuer, Hans-Peter, 7753
— Rolf, 11164
Brewer, Derek, 3306, 3679
— Elisabeth, 7127
— Krista, 14459
— William Dean, 7764
Brians, Paul, 10158
Bridges, Margaret Enid, 3079
Bridgman, Richard, 7806
Bridgwood, Christine, 12136
Briggs, Asa, 8900
Briggs, Julia, 3834
Brighton, Catherine, 11629
Brink, André, 9680
— C. O., 12459
Brinkley, Robert A., 9210
Brinkmeyer, Bob, 456
— Robert H., Jr, 12193, 14412
Briscoe, E. J., 1089
Brissenden, Alan, 4398
Bristol, Michael D., 3878
Britain, Ian, 7459
Brittin, Norman A., 1529
Brivic, Sheldon, 12622
Brock, D. Heyward, 5540
— Dorothy Faye Sala, 14427
Brockbank, J. P., 4707
— Philip, 4399, 4638
Brode, Douglas, 11023
Brodetsky, Tessa, 8331
Brodhead, Richard, 8902
Brodie, Peter, 14511
Brodovich, O. I., 2129
Brodsky, Louis D., 11849
— Louis Daniel, 199–201, 11850
Brodwin, Stanley, 8600
Brody, M., 1984
— Miriam, 6955
Broe, Mary Lynn, 12348
Broege, Valerie, 9681
Broek, Aart G., 13080
Brogan, Jacqueline Vaught, 14257–8
Brøgger, Frederik Chr., 11736
Brolley, John E., 4400

Bromberg, Pamela S., 11698
Bromham, A. A., 5650
— Tony, 5651
Bromley, Laura G., 5515
Bromwich, David, 565, 8518, 11063
Brönnimann, Werner, 4401
Bronson, Larry, 3786
Brook, Clifford, 8350
Brooke, John, 6937
Brookeman, Christopher, 10645
Brooks, Cleanth, 6693, 11854
— Edward, 174
— Ellen J., 1303
— G. P., 6947
— Harold, 4812, 4825, 4887
— John, 2552
— Linda Marie, 7894
— Peter, 7210
Brooks-Davies, Douglas, 6701
Broome, F. H., 8879
Brophy, Brigid, 8985
Brosse, Monique, 8893
Broughton, Panthea Reid, 13704
Brown, A. D., 7834
— Calvin S., 11855
— Carolyn E., 4879–80
— Cedric C., 5684–5
— Charles T., 2508
— Clarence A., 8632
— D. A. Maughan, 10159
— Elizabeth A. R., 3500
— Frances, 2553
— Frank Burch, 10487
— George Hardin, 3080
— Gillian, 1090
— Hamish, 10488
— Iain Gordon, 6681, 6746
— Jared, 9920
— John Russell, 4113, 4402, 4857, 14106
— Keith, 1123, 4795
— Langdon, 4677
— Laura, 5940, 6702
— Lucy, 566
— Marc, 2575
— Marianne, 4240
— Mary Ellen, 6325
— Mary Jane, 567
— Mary Ruth, 5686
— Michelle P., 143
— Nicholas, 9229
— Patricia Claire, 14153
— Paula, 1047
— Phyllis Rugg, 36
— Richard, 12623
— Richard E., 5600
— Robert F., 13024
— Russell E., 1652

— J. M., 12325
Byun, Jong-Min, 13953
Bywaters, David, 5405

C., C. W., 6201
Cable, Frances, 10011
— Thomas, 812
Cadden, Joan, 3506
Cadogan, Mary, 11600
Cady, Edwin H., 8562
Caesar, A. D., 14216
— Terry, 11208, 12784
Cagle, Charles Harmon, 12365
Cahalan, James M., 7215
Cahill, Audrey F., 8206
Cain, William E., 10746–7
Caird, James B., 13113
Cairns, John C., 8976
— Scott, 568
Calcraft, M. B. M., 7719
Calder, Angus, 569
— Daniel G., 3083
— Jenni, 9332
— John, 11166
Calderwood, James L., 4744,
  4858, 11167
Caldwell, Ellen Cashwell, 4241
— Ronald J., 6137
— Roy Chandler, Jr, 6839
Calhoun, Randall Lee, 6800
Callahan, John F., 12309
Callen, Donald M., 10967
Callens, Johan, 8262
Calonne, David Stephen, 12880
Cam, H. K., 10491
Camée, Jean-François, 5308,
  6802
Cameron, Alan, 12881
— Barry, 11268
— Sharon, 8263, 9355
Camfield, Gregg, 6199
Caminero, Rosario, 1986
Campbell, Andrew Marchant,
  10492
— Elaine, 11025
— Felicia F., 2606
— Hilbert N., 11045
— Ian, 7807–8, 12147–8
— James, 3189
— Paul, 7216
Campion, Dan, 570
Camsell, Margaret, 1654
Canady, Nicholas, 12574
Canary, Robert H., 11739
Canavan, Francis, 5689
Candelaria, Cordelia, 10168
Candido, Joseph, 4824
Cann, R., 1987
Canning, John, 8900

Cannon, Diane, 13390
— Garland, 6646
Cantacuzino, I. I., 4405
Cantalupo, Charles, 2909, 5519
Cantor, Paul A., 4708
Cantrell, Carol Helmstetter,
  13790
Cantù, Yolande, 10980, 11107,
  11453, 13479–80, 13483,
  13497
Capellán, Ángel, 12366
Capone, Giovanna, 12864
Cappello, Mary, 8456
Capraro, Rocco L., 359
Caputo, Philip, 14330
Carafiol, Peter, 8264
Caramello, Charles, 8636,
  10169
Carducci, Jane Shook, 4709
Cardullo, Bert, 4925, 8342,
  11280, 12093, 12287–8,
  13728–9
Carey, Anna Kirwan Steck,
  3880
— Glenn O., 9104
— John, 12168
— Norman E., 8457
Cargill, Mary Terrell, 6816
Carino, Peter Alfonso, 11833
Carlet, Yves, 8265, 9356
Carley, James P., 144, 204,
  4104
Carlin, Patricia L., 4406
Carl-Mitchell, Charlotte, 206–7
Carlson, Julia Lowell, 10170
— Lauri, 1092–3
— Marvin, 4640
— Patricia Ann, 28
Carlson-Bradley, Martha Ann,
  11259
Carnes, Pack, 14388
Carney, Benjamin Franklin, iii,
  9923
— Raymond, 7530
Carnochan, W. B., 6000, 6327
Caron, Sue, 14673
Carothers, James B., 11857
Carpenter, C. T., 3315
— Charles A., 9924–5
— Humphrey, 497, 2879, 7370,
  13791
— Kenneth E., 208
— Lynette, 7535
Carr, R. P., 360
— Stephen Leo, 6138
— Virginia Spencer, 11686
Carré, Jacques, 6139
Carretta, Vincent, 6952
Carrington, Dorothy, 6298
— Ildikó de Papp, 11074

Carrive, Lucien, 4001
Carroll, D. Allen, 4909
— David, 8207
— Dennis, 9926, 14143
— Susanne, 1988
— William C., 4407
— William E., 3576
Carrott, Patricia M. C., 2500
Carruth, Hayden, 10493, 14101
Carruthers, Mary J., 3316
— Virginia Kirby-Smith, 12053
Carson, Ada Lou, 6935
— Ciaran, 2509
Carstensen, Broder, 1530
Carswell, John, 11389
Cartelli, Thomas, 4408
Carter, Carolyn, 2880
— D. N. G., 12215
— David, 571
— E. Graydon, 457
— John, 88
— Kathryn Elizabeth, 9927
— M. A., 13649
— Margaret Louise, 6044
— Steve, 13650
Carton, Evan, 8109, 8637,
  11647, 12345
Cartwright, Graham, 209
Carver, Larry, 6651
Cary, Meredith, 2826
Case, Carol Ann, 9334
Caserio, Robert L., 14557
Casey, Dan, 12773
— Francis, 4825
Cash, Arthur H., 6840
— William F., 14105
Cashdan, Sonya Hannah,
  14736
Casillo, Robert, 9124–5, 12367,
  13793
Cason, Robert Ernst, 9211
Cassidy, Frederic G., 863, 1737,
  3244
Castan, Con, 9685
Castelaz, Donald Richard, 8267
Castex, Peggy, 10648
Castillo, Debra A., 11281
Castle, Terry, 6045, 6753
Castronovo, David, 14681
Catalano, Gary, 12299, 14186
Cate, George Allan, 7809
Catto, J. I., 3493
Cavaliero, Glen, 13765
Cavanaugh, D., 1866
Cave, Richard Allen, 48, 7148,
  9212
— Roderick, 94, 361
Cavell, Richard Anthony, 8208
Cavill, Paul, 3085
Cavitch, David, 9480

— J. S., 9010
— Joseph Kelly, 3947
— Micael M., 9336
— Peter P., 12235
Clayborough, Arthur, 7687
Clayton, M. G., 4981
— Mary, 3090–2, 3219
— Thomas, 4642
Clearfield, Andrew M., 10497
Cleary, Thomas R., 6445
Cleaver, Alan, 2399
Cleeve, Brian, 2603
Clements, A. G., 8643
— Patricia, 7000, 11018
— William M., 11036
Clemoes, Peter, 3093
Cleve, Gunnel, 12169
Cleverdon, Douglas, 13987
Clifton, Gladys M., 13393
Clinch, Rosemary, 2554
Clingham, G. J., 210, 6560–1
Clingman, S., 12186
— Stephen, 12187
Clipper, Lawrence J., 13095
Clogan, Paul M., 3787
Cloitre, Marylene, 1269
Clot, S., 2440
Clough, Andrea, 3651
Clover, Carol J., 3190–1
Clucas, Humphrey, 12460
Clunas, A. B., 9259
Clune, Anne, 13538
Cluver, A. D. de V., 745, 950
Clyne, Michael G., 989
Cnudde-Knowland, A., 7001
Coale, Samuel, 7002, 11349
— Samuel Chase, 7221
Coard, Robert J., 9436
Coates, Jennifer, 990, 1931
— John, 4827, 12785
— John D., 11428
— Paul, 7391
— Richard, 1625, 1699, 1709
Coats, Daryl R., 8014
Cobban, Alex, 8015
Coberly, Mary Schramm, 1305
Cobham, Rhonda, 12772
Cobley, Evelyn, 10182
Cocchiarelli, Joseph John, 3094
Cochrane, Hamilton Edwards, 6689
Cockshut, A. O. J., 7447
Codaccioni, Marie-José, 7665
Coe, Richard N., 2970
Coetzee, J. M., 9151
Coffler, Gail H., 8909
Cogan, Frances B., 7222
Cogley, Richard W., 5445
Cogswell, Fred, 13531
Cohan, Steven, 6291

Cohen, Charles Lloyd, 5217
— David S., 8601
— Ed, 14723
— Eileen Z., 4700
— Hazel, 8460
— John, 574
— Marshall, 10021
— Michael, 6931, 11052, 11481
— Michael P., 13335
— Morton N., 7839
— Murray, 6174
— Paula Marantz, 8644
— Philip, 11861–2
— Ralph, 575, 5418, 6141
— Walter, 3883, 4411, 13394
Cohen-Mushlin, Aliza, 146
Cohen-Safir, C., 14446
Cohn, Alan M., 8016, 12627
Coiro, Ann Baynes, 5510–11
Cokely, Dennis Richard, 991
Coker, Judith Briggs, 10985
Colaco, Jill, 4960
Colacurcio, Michael J., 8461–2
Colavecchio, Barbara Marie, 14558
Colby, Robert A., 362
Cole, Garold L., 2995
— Howard C., 4701
— Richard C., 6364
— Richard Cargill, 363
— Roger W., 857
— Susan Letzler, 2788
Colebourne, Bryan, 6870
Coleman, Arthur, 13184
— Cynthia, 1048
— D. P., 576
— James, 12151
— Michael C., 1049
Coles, Robert, 13707
Colish, Marcia L., 3508
Colley, Ann, 8864
— Ann C., 9306
Collie, Michael, 7628–9, 8348
Collier, Eugenia, 9695
— Peter, 2610
Collin, Dorothy W., 364
— Finn, 746
Collinge, Neville E., 813
Collings, Frank, 6562
Collins, Andrew, 2441
— Carvel, 11369
— John, 88–9
— K. K., 8016
— Kathleen Rettig, 4975
— Norman, 8017
— Philip, 9307
— Richard, 10650
— Robert A., 7003
— William J., 9437, 12368
Collister, Pete, 9474

Colls, Robert, 7462
Colman, Fran, 1656, 1912
— John, 5607
Colmer, John, 14576
Colombo, John Robert, 10498
Coloşenco, Mircea, 4412
Colquitt, Clare, 11044
Coltheart, Max, 1276
Colthorpe, Marion, 3884–5, 4002, 4064
Colton, Cyrus, 14791
— Patrick, 14106
Colville, Derek, 9584
Comanzo, Christian, 7004
Comarnescu, Petru, 9438, 9741, 13617
Combrink, Annette, 12094
Comensoli, Viviana, 5354
Compère, Daniel, 11272
Comrie, Bernard, 1994, 2333
Conder, John J., 10183
Conley, Timothy Kevin, 4413
Conlon, Faith, 10184
Conn, Peter, 10652
— Stewart, 10185
Connaughton, Michael, 13048
Connell, Charles, 365
Connelly, Joseph, 12578
Conner, Edwin Lee, 3741
Conniff, Richard, 9928
Connolly, Cyril, 7005
— Julian W., 13395–7
Connor, Steven, 8018
— William, 14006
Conrad, Peter, 2611, 6841
Conradi, P. J., 13348
Conran, Anthony, 10490
— Tony, 3948
Conroy, Mark, 11482
Conser, Walter H., Jr, 8894
Constantinescu, Aurelia, 7121
— Ligia, 11483
Contamine, Philippe, 3192
Coogan, Robert, 4003
Cook, Albert, 10499
— Ann Jennalie, 3886
— Carol, 4922, 5015
— Cornelia, 11392
— David, 10752
— Donald N., 6563
— Elizabeth, 3949
— Guy, 1095
— Hardy M., 4643
— J. D., 1270
— Jon, 3742
— Judith, 3887
— Pam, 9929
— Richard M., 13114
— William R., 3193
Cooke, Michael G., 9698

— Peter, 2510
— W. G., 3318
— William G., 3319
Cook-Gumperz, Jenny, 992
Cookson, Linda, 4319
— William, 13797
Cooley, Edna Hammer, 7150
— Mason, 13944
Coombs, James H., 5693
Coon, Anne Christine, 8645
Coones, Paul, 1700
Cooney, Seamus, 11347
Cooper, Andrew, 12884
— B. L., 11056
— Charles R., 1102
— David D., 13247
— Emmanuel, 7463
— Helen, 3743
— M. A., 1739
— Robin, 1096, 1995
— Stephen, Jr, 12369
Cooper-Clark, Diana, 10186
Cope, Jackson I., 11567
— Kevin L., 5319
Copeland, James E., 38
— Joshua Paul, 11697
Copenhaven, Carla, 14816
Copley, Stephen, 5947
Coppens, Chris, 95
Corballis, Richard, 4320
Corbett, M. J., 7765
Corbin, Peter, 5107
Corcoran, Neil, 12326, 12588
Cordasco, Francesco, 6647–8
Cordesse, Gérard, 10187
Cordner, Michael, 5407
Core, George, 14349
— Philip, 10655
Coren, Michael, 7151
Corman, Catherine Talmage, 3687
— Cid, 13635
Corn, Alfred, 11260
Cornell, Brenda G., 11865
— Daniel T., 11249
Cornford, S. W., 6968
Cornilescu, Alexandra, 1353, 1996
Cornish, Francis, 1932, 2168
Cornwell, Gareth, 13332
Corodi, Vasile, 4414
Coroneos, C., 8646
Corrigan, Felicitas, 14107, 14452
Corse, Douglas Taylor, 5408
Corson, David, 1740
Cosslett, Tess, 7006
Costa, Richard Hauer, 14682
Costabile, Rita Mary, 8210
Cotkin, George, 8271

Cotner, Thomas Ewing, III, 4828
Cotrău, Liviu, 9062–3
Cotsell, Michael, 577, 8019
Cotter, C. A., 1254
Cottle, Basil, 1933
Couch, William, Jr, 10500
Coulomb, Claude, 1306
Coulon, Virginia, 2782
Coulthard, A. R., 14528
— Malcolm, 1097
Counsel, June, 7866
Countryman, Edward, 6142
Couper, Richard W., 9025
Couper-Kuhlen, Elizabeth, 1463
Coursen, H. R., 4416, 4644
Cousineau, Thomas J., 11485
Cousins, A. D., 1217
Coustillas, Pierre, 8349–51, 12786
Coutouvidis, John, 11743
Coutts, Catherine, 3096
Couture, Barbara, 498
Couturier, Maurice, 13398
Couzens, Tim, 11642–3
Couzyn, Jeni, 10501
Covaci, Aurel, 7773
Covella, Francis Dolores, 4116
Covington, Michael A., 1844
Cowan, Bainard, 8910
— Ian B., 3837
— James C., 12886
— Peter, 10188
— S. A., 8543
Coward, Nancy Potts, 8563
Cowart, David, 14358
Cowen, Anne, 7464
— Roger, 7464
Cowler, Rosemary, 6705
Cowles, David L., 8463
Cowley, J. M., 10189
Cowling, Maurice, 7465
Cox, C. B., 4417
— Catherine I., 4745
— Catherine Irene, 4418
— Don Richard, 8168
— J. H., 578
— James M., 8648, 9440
— Michael, 7223, 12536
— Robert, 14108
— Stephen, 5948
Coy Girón, Juan José, 12170
Craddock, Patricia B., 6491
Craft, William, 4204
Crafton, John Michael, 4308
Cragg, William E., 7743
Craig, Carol, 13158
— D. H., 4093
— David, 14154

— David M., 12346
— Holly K., 994
— Joanne, 4243
— Patricia, 11288
— Terrance, 11454
Craigie, James, 5533
Craik, R. J., 5896
Cramer, James Douglas, 3459
Cramp, A., 11289
Crampton, Georgia Ronan, 36
Cran, William, 771
Crane, D. E. L., 5595
— David, 5624
— John, 11398
— John Kenny, 14331
— Mary Thomas, 2408
— Nora, 13206
Cranny-Francis, A., 8988
Craven, Kenneth, 6871
Crawford, Fred D., 11668
— Iain, 8021
— R., 11745
— Robert, 8859, 11746
— Thomas, 6328, 9161
Crawley, R. A., 1809
Creadon, Mary Ann, 10753
Creagh, John Walthall, III, 10754
Creel, James Melton, 303
Creese, Richard, 7578, 11992
Crehan, Stewart, 13499
Creighton, Margaret Scott, 2426
Crépin, André, 3504
Cresswell, M. J., 2169
— Thomas, 1741
Crewe, Jonathan, 4052
— Jonathan V., 4170, 4192
Cribb, T. J., 13127
Crick, Bernard, 13651
— Brian, 2775, 8384
— Malcolm, 13059
— Patricia, 8716
Crisp, P. G., 13798
Crist, Timothy J., 5051
Croft, A., 10191
Crombie, Winifred, 1098
Crompton, Louis, 7766
Cronan, Dennis, 1218
— Dennis James, 3097
Cronin, Richard, 6496, 12010
Cronkhite, Gary, 748
Crook, N., 9216
— Nora, 9217
Cross, Anthony, 2613
— Charles B., 2170
— J. E., 211
— James E., 3070, 3099
— Nigel, 7007
— Richard K., 12542

Diamond, Elin, 13731
Dickenson, Donna, 8112
Dickey, James, 14317
— Stephen, 4939
Dickie, Margaret, 14647
Dickinson, Daniel, 12342
— Donald C., 212, 584
Dicks, Mark Jeffry, 2622
Dickson, Donald R., 5900
Dickstein, Morris, 7227, 14422
Diedrich, Maria, 7228
Diehl, Huston, 3840
Diekma, Douglas, 13026
Diensberg, Bernhard, 1467
Diepeveen, Leonard, 2443
Dierks, Karin, 8029
Dietrich, Richard F., 14111
Dietrichson, Jan W., 8913
Dietz, Klaus, 1587
Dietze, Walter, 11
Dillard, J. L., 1658
Diller, Hans-Jurgen, 7229
Dillingham, William B., 8914
Dillman, Richard, 8273
— Richard H., 9360
Dillon, Myles, 2444
Dilworth, Thomas, 9935,
    12593-4, 12634
DiMatteo, Anthony Joseph,
    4004
Dime, Gregory T., 5172
Dimíc, Milan V., 2623, 6146
Dingley, R. J., 8831
Di Nicola, Robert, 12328
Dinshaw, F. E., 5480
Dinzelbacher, Peter, 2555
Di Paolo, Marianna, 864
Dipiero, W. S., 8650
Di Pietro, Robert J., 2624
Dircks, Phyllis T., 6482
Dirda, Michael, 213
Dîrlău, Andrei, 6228
Dirven, René, 1191, 1535, 1810,
    2338
Disbrow, Sarah, 3745
Ditchfield, G. M., 6568-9
D'Itri, Patricia Ward, 14040
Ditsky, John, 11299, 11869
Dix, R. C., 6190
— Robin, 6191
Dixon, Diana, 585-6
— Geoffrey M., 2445
— M. V., 2979
— Peter, 6435, 6504
Dixsaut, Jean, 6505, 6759
Djwa, Sandra, 8651
Dobozy, Maria, 3022
Dobrez, L. A. C., 11170
Dobriner, Jill, 7230
Dobrinsky, Joseph, 11488

Dobrzycka, Irena, 7231
Dobrzyńska, Tereza, 1366
Dobson, Bob, 892
— Frank Edward, 10196
— Joanne, 8113, 9254
— Silvia, 11669
Docherty, Thomas, 5365
Docker, John, 7014
Doctor, R., 2411
Doctorow, E. L., 10197
Dodd, Philip, 2964, 7462,
    10629, 13334
— Wayne, 10506
Dodsworth, Martin, 4746
Doherty, Gerald, 12890
— Jaiyeola, 10978
Dolezal, Fredric, 1744-5
Dolin, Arnold, 464
Doll, Dan, 6873
— Eileen Jessica, 14341
Dolle, Raymond Francis, 5953
Dollimore, Jonathan, 4429-30,
    10769
Dombrowski, Daniel A., 9361
Dominicy, Marc, 2005
Domito, Terry, 14697
Dommergues, André, 14577
Domnarski, William, 6570,
    13169
Domville, Eric, 14839
Donaldson, E. Talbot, 3616,
    3690
— Graham, 2412
— Ian, 2625, 4431, 5409,
    5545-6, 6571
— Morag L., 1272
— Peter S., 4648
— Scott, 8313, 11965
— Susan V., 11870
— William, 893, 7544, 8372
Donegan, Patricia J., 1409
Donker, Marjorie, 3841
Donley, Carol C., 9730
Donner, Morton, 1872
Donoghue, Daniel, 3101
— Denis, 4966, 9712, 10770
Donohue, Agnes McNeill, 8466
Donovan, Josephine, 8317,
    8785
Doody, Margaret Anne, 5173
Doolan, Paul M., 9221
Dooley, D. J., 14487
— Patrick K., 8567
Dorbad, Leo James, 12891
Doreski, William, 13084
Dorling, A., 10198
Dorsey, Laurens M., 8652
Dorson, Richard M., 2380
Dose, Gerd, 10660
Doubleday, James F., 9107

Dougherty, David C., 14430
— Jay, 14261
Doughtie, Edward, 3950
Doughty, Catherine, 1129
Douglas, George H., 14684
— Jane, 367
— S., 894
Dove, George N., 10199
— Mary, 3326
Dover, Linda A., 13519
Dowling, Constance, 8030
— D. H., 10200
— David, 13220
— Linda, 70, 7016
— Maria, 4005
— Paul, 5698
— William C., 10619, 10771
Down, Nancy, 11640
Downer, Christine, 11276
Downes, David, 460
— David Anthony, 8544
— John, 895
Downey, James C., 2512
Downie, J. A., 6395, 6572, 6874
Dowse, Sara, 9936
Dowty, David R., 1356
Doxtator, Robert Lucas, 588
Doyle, A. I., 148
— Charles, 14262
— Charles Clay, 2413
— Edward Gerard, 3196
— James, 368, 589, 5954
— Owen P., 12752
Drabble, Margaret, 2626
Drakakis, John, 4432
Drake, Robert, 13560
— Sandra E., 12293
Dralle, Lewis A., 6938
Dranch, Sherry A., 13400
Draper, R. P., 4649, 12892
Drasku, Jennifer, 506
Draudt, Manfred, 4895
Dreher, Diane Elizabeth, 4433
Drennan, William R., 4205-6
Dresher, Bezalel E., 1434
Dressler, Roland, 4650
— Wolfgang, 1410
Drew, William M., 9938
Drewe, Robert, 10202
Drexler, R. D., 4896
Driscoll, Kerry, 13016
Driskell, Glenda Joy, 2513
Dromode, Grigore, 4207
Dronke, Peter, 3515-16
Drozdz, Gregory, 7637
Drucker, Trudy, 13609
Drumbl, Johann, 3462
Drummond, C. Q., 4196
Drury, Susan M., 2556
Dryden, Edgar A., 9162

Funnell, Catherine, 445
Furbank, P. N., 2643, 6398–9, 6411–13
Furia, Philip, 6232
Furman, Necah Stewart, 13070
Furomoto, Atsuko, 2383
Furrow, Melissa M., 3339
Furst, Lilian R., 6050
Fyler, John M., 3696

Gabel, Gernot U., 2644
— John B., 2965
Gabin, Jane S., 8861
Gabler, Hans Walter, 5282, 12649–50
Gabriel, Daniel, 11586
Gabrieli, Vittorio, 4145
Gabriner, P. J., 1537
Gadd, Bernard, 10220
Gaffney, C., 4251
Gagen, Jean, 5715
Gaggi, Silvio, 12035
Gailey, Alan, 2572
Gaines, Barry, 307, 3881
Gair, Reavley, 308, 5863
— W. Reavley, 3892
Gaiser, Gottlieb, 4832
Gakov, V., 10221
Gál, Gedeon, 3579
Galan, F. W., 10789
Galanes, Philip, 14239
Galbo, Thomas S., 8175
Galbraith, Lorna May, 14004
Gale, Steven H., 13722
Galea, Ileana, 12898
Galef, David, 14265
Galestin, Paul, 9955
Gall, Sally M., 10576
Gallagher, Catherine, 7240
— E. J., 12596
— Patricia M. Louise, 4455
— Susan Vanzanten, 8919
Gallet, Liliane, 527
Gallimore, Edith Angela, 8829
Gallix, François, 14591
Gallup, Donald, 220, 14603
Galperin, William H., 9596
Galván Reula, Fernando, 12036
Gamez, Luis Rene, 6183
Ganguly, A. P., 12014
Ganim, John M., 3340
Ganz, Arthur, 14114
Ganzel, Dewey, 4326
Garavaglia, James M., 8470
Garbagnati, Lucile, 2345
Garber, Frederick, 14250
— Marjorie, 4456
Garces, J. P., 8392
Garcia, Carmen Maria, 1161

García Díez, Enrique, 11131
Garden, Diane Beth, 11587
— Ronald, 12531, 13165
Gardiner, Anne Barbeau, 5412–13
— Patrick, 8673
Gardiner-Stallaert, Nicole, 1513
Gardner, Bonnie Milne, 9957
— Philip, 12015
— Philip Alan Tennant, 4252
— S. F., 1940
— Stanley, 6233
— Susan, 11248, 12319
— Thomas, 11066
— Traci, 9312, 13826
Garebian, Keith, 9958, 12444
Garfield, Brian, 10222
Garfinkel, Nancy, 13408
Garfitt, Roger, 12454
Gargano, James W., 8674
Garlick, Kenneth, 74
— Raymond, 2922
Garman, Michael, 1317
Garner, Helen, 11609–10
— L., 4730
Garnham, Alan, 1275
Garratt, Robert F., 10514
Garrett, John, 2923
— M., 5644
Garrett-Goodyear, J. H., 13409
Garrison, Virginia, 7707–8
Garrod, C. M., 7241
Garside, P. D., 9164–5
— Peter, 221, 9166
— Peter Dignus, 9167
Gartner, Carol B., 11388
Garver, Newton, 10790
Garvey, B. T., 2645
— Johanna Xandra Kathryn, 10224
— Sheila Hickey, 13616
Gash, Anthony, 3464
Gaskell, Philip, 378
Gaskill, Howard, 6665
Gaspar, Julia, 5037
Gast, Marlene, 5716
Gaston, George M. A., 12241
Gatch, M. McC., 3202
— Milton McC., 152
Gates, Henry Louis, Jr, 2972, 7028, 9733, 10791
Gathercole, Virginia C., 2190
Gatrell, Simon, 8393–5
Gatta, John, Jr, 7907
Gaudet, Marcia, 2400
— Paul, 4898
Gault, Pierre, 12302
Gaunt, Simon, 3522
Gaur, Albertine, 1514

Gautam, Kripa K., 11175
Gavriliu, Eugenia, 2966
Gawron, Jean Mark, 2191–2
Gay, Peter, 7474
Gburek, Hubert, 1436
Geary, Edward A., 11751
— Keith, 4899
Gee, Christina, 7162
— Elizabeth, 3341
— Kathleen, 12899
— R., 7242
Geens, Dirk, 528–9
Geherin, David, 10225
Geiger, Stephen R., 463
Geis, Michael L., 1162
Geiser, Elizabeth A., 464
Geist, Edward V., 14116
Gelber, Jack, 11154
Gelder, K., 9261
Gelfand, Elissa D., 10792
Gelfant, Blanche H., 9734
Gellert, James, 309
Gelling, Margaret, 1663
Gellrich, Jesse, 3342
— Jesse M., 3343
Gelpi, Albert, 14266
Geluykens, Ronald, 1470, 2015
Gendron, Charisse, 8365
Generoso, James, 13827
Genster, Julia Ann, 5414
Gentili, Vanna, 4107
Gentry, Marshall Bruce, 13562
— Robert Wayne, 14245
Genzel, Hans-Jochen, 4457
George, Alexander, 753
— Diana Hume, 6234
— Emery, 13410
— K. E. M., 1538
— Sharon, 602
Georgi, Helen, 12651
Georgi-Findlay, Brigitte, 13283
Geraets, John, 603
Gérard, Albert, 7029
Gerbaud, Colette, 6378
Gerber, Dan, 13638
— Helmut E., 13295
— Philip L., 12072–3
Gerdy, Maria S., 11070
Geri, Carl, 6507
Gerlach, John, 7243
Germanou, M., 9959
Gerrard, Christine, 6365
Gerritsen, Johan, 3893
Gershenowitz, Harry, 13233–4
Gervais, David, 12426
Gheorghiu, Mihnea, 4335, 4458
Ghiselin, Brewster, 10794
Ghiṭulescu, Anghel, 12977a
Ghosh, Tapan Kumar, 8969

— Ken Leslie, 5960
Goodwyn, J. P., 14563
Goonetilleke, D. C. R. A., 9738
Goorden, Bernard, 13079
Goorney, Howard, 9963
Goossens, Louis, 1164, 1635, 1876
Gorak, Jan, 12303
Göransson, Sverker, 11753
Gordon, David, 13831–3
— E., 955
— Gerald, 12164
— Ian A., 8324
— John, 12656
— Lyndall, 14745
— Mary, 13928
Goreau, Angeline, 5288
Gorecki, John E., 4814
Gorgis, D. T., 1941
Göring, Michael, 11053
Görlach, Manfred, 974
Gorra, Michael Edward, 12227
Gorzkowska, Regina, 4850
Gose, Elliot B., Jr, 2449
Gossett, Thomas F., 9283
Gottfried, Barbara, 8044
— Michael, 841
Gottlieb, Erika, 12827
— Sidney, 5473, 5482, 5718
Gotts, I., 12037
Götz, Dieter, 1224
Gough, John, 13673, 14468
Gould, Carol Grant, 9339
— Jean, 10516
— Karen, 207
Goulden, R. J., 76, 225–6, 380–1, 6016, 6094
Gourlay, Alexander S., 6239
Gournay, Jean-François, 7749
Gouws, John, 4209
Goy-Blanquet, Dominique, 4460
Grabes, Herbert, 3348
Grabher, Gudrun M., 11300
Grace, Sherrill E., 11078, 11335, 14593
Graff, Gerald, 10804
Grafton, Anthony, 3526
Graham, Carla J., 8547
— Cooper C., 9964
— Cuthbert, 893
— Desmond, 11696
— Don, 9739
— Dorothy Beth Harbin, 8472
— Peter, 7771
— Peter W., 7772
— Robert J., 8325
Grainger, Margaret, 7874
Grambs, David, 1540
Gramm, Christie Diane, 14829

Grandy, Richard E., 754
Granofsky, Ronald, 10228, 12437
Granqvist, Raoul, 5372–3
Grant, Barry K., 9965
— Barry Keith, 9966
— James Dickinson, 8275
— John Arlington, Jr, 9491
— Michael, 11755
— Patrick, 4007
— Rena Jane, 6051
Grantley, D. R., 3466
— Darryll, 5038
Grasso, Anthony Robert, 9313
Grauer, Neil A., 609
Graulich, Melody, 8311
Graver, Bruce E., 5417
— Suzanne, 8219
Graves, James B., 9967
— Richard Perceval, 12216
Gravil, Richard, 7908
Gray, B. M., 8220
— Douglas, 1566, 3293, 3349–50, 4008
— J. C., 4461
— J. E., 9314
— James, 6579
— John, 11386
— Margaret K., 9013
— N. J., 3621
— Nick, 3622–3
— Piers, 14371
— Richard, 7034
— Stephen, 11285–6, 12095–6, 12533, 13756
Graziani, René, 4851
Greaney, Vincent, 227
Greasley, Philip A., 11338
Greaves, Richard L., 5315
Greciano, Gertrud, 1165
Greco, Norma A., 6240
Green, A. L., 5719
— Donald C., 3754
— Dorothy, 14009
— Geoffrey, 13411
— J., 2649
— Jonathon, 1166
— Kevin, 12522
— Marian, 2470
— Mary Elizabeth, 5340
— R., 3579
— Richard Firth, 3813
— Richard Lancelyn, 8177–9
— Richard Lancelyn, 8176
— Robert, 12508
— Stanley, 9968
Greenbaum, Arlynn, 465
— Sidney, 755, 842, 1102, 1541
Greenberg, Martin H., 10437
— Martin Henry, 8167

— William J., 756
Greenblatt, Stephen, 3846, 4009
Greene, Donald, 6299, 6580, 14490–1
— Gayle, 10805
— Ghussan R., 12461
— Graham, 9969, 12003
— Mildred Sarah E., 6765
— Sue N., 10230
— Thomas M., 2650–1, 3955, 4852
Greenfield, Bruce, 6527
— Bruce Robert, 6122
— Sayre Nelson, 4256
— Stanley B., 3110, 3255
— Thelma N., 4210
Greenhill, Pauline Jane, 2450
Greenhut, Deborah Schneider, 4302
Greenman, David, 4462
Greenslade, W. P., 8352
Greenstein, Michael, 14700
Greenwald, Michael L., 2790, 4657
Greenwood, D. S., 5176
— James, 7476
Greer, Germaine, 2652, 4463
— Michael, 11987
Gregory, E. R., 5721
— P., 228
— Sinda, 12279
Greiff, Louis K., 11967
Greinacher, Kurt, 12512
Greiner, Norbert, 11915
Grenier, Cecilia Marie, 6053
Grennen, Joseph E., 3351, 3755, 3789
Grenville, Hugo, 77
Gresham, Gwendolyn Holloway Parham, 6241
Gresset, Michel, 11879–80, 11881
Gretlund, Jan Nordby, 12604
Greven-Borde, Hélène, 10231
Grey, J. David, 7583
— Loren, 12264
Gribble, Jennifer, 7251, 8678, 11494
Grier, Edward F., 9492
Grieve, Michael, 13129
— Thomas Fraser, 13834
Griffin, Dustin, 5722
— Dustin H., 5723
— Jaspar, 2653
— John R., 9000
— Jon, 14830
— Jon Nelson, 14831
— Jonathan, 13639
— Joseph, 11702

Hattaway, Michael, 3898
Haug, Ingrid, 12478
Haugland, Kari E., 1847
Haule, James M., 8373
Hauptmeier, Helmut, 10815
Hauri, Carey, 10244
Hauser, Gerard A., 3031
Havelock, Eric A., 2455
Haver, Fritz Werner, 11721
Havighurst, Walter, 467
Hawkes, Terence, 4475
Hawkins, Harriett, 4476–7
— John A., 1815
— Peter S., 11617
Hawley, John C., 617
— John Charles, 618
Hawthorn, Jeremy, 6, 39
Hawtree, Christopher, 652, 11241
Hay, Éloise Knapp, 11759
— Malcolm, 11180
Hayashi, Fumiyo, 11884
— Tetsumaro, 12662
Hayes, Bruce, 1475
— M. J., 8159
— T. Wilson, 4012
Hayles, N. Katherine, 9753
Hayley, Barbara, 7803
Hayman, David, 12663
Hayne, David M., 2655
Haynes, David, 9975
— Jonathan, 5864
— Roslynn D., 11037
Hays, Michael, 4478
Haythornthwaite, J. A., 9014
Hayward, Arthur L., 1758
— B. J., 2540
Haywood, I., 6351
Headon, David, 7036–7
Healy, J. J., 12812
— Philip, 8369
— T. F., 5343
Heaney, Michael, 1596
— Seamus, 10368, 10520
Hearn, Michael Patrick, 8865, 11149
Hearne, Patricia, 12212
Heath, Stephen, 9263, 9755
— William, 9446
Heberlein, Kate Browder, 9401
Hecht, Anthony, 9756
Heckelman, Ronald Joe, 3118
Hecksher, William S., 3849
Hedayet, A. A. el-A, 2656
Hedberg, Johannes, 868, 12664
Hedges, William L., 8600
Hedin, Raymond, 7038
Heenan, Michael, 14092
Hees, Edwin, 5419, 5556
Heffernan, Carol Falvo, 3699

— James A. W., 7912
Hegazi, Safaa, 12016
Heher, Michael, 13564
Heidelberger-Leonard, Irène, 2353
Heilman, Robert B., 4479
Heimert, Alan, 6429
Hein, Rolland, 8880
Heineman, Helen, 9423
Heinemann, Marlene E., 9757
Heininger, Joseph C., 12665
Helbo, André, 2184
Helgerson, Richard, 3850–1, 4259
Hellenbrand, Harold, 8920
Heller, Arno, 2384, 11351
— Erich, 758
— Jürgen, 14270
Hellie, Thomas Lowell, 8309
Helm, Alex, 2542–3
Helmling, Steven, 12666
Helms, Randel, 11760
Helsinger, Elizabeth K., 9132
Helten, James Alfred, 11207
Hemphill, Lowry Elizabeth, 1000
Hempstead, James L., 6331
Hendel, Richard, 106
Henderson, Archie, 619, 13837
— Brian, 13509
— Diana E., 5516
— Eric Paul, 12305
— Jeff, 12119–20
— Katherine Usher, 4013
— Lalitha Pauliah, 1477
— Robert M., 9976
Henke, Suzette A., 12017
Henkins, Kathryn Marie, 13535
Henn, Katherine, 14346
Hennegan, Alison, 14056
Henning, Hans, 4480
— Sylvie Debevec, 11181
Henricksen, Bruce, 10816
Henry, Avril, 3361–3
— Desmond Paul, 759
— John, 5829
— Patrick, 12246
— William A., III, 14158
Henson, E., 6587
— Gail, 620
Henthorne, Susan Cassandra, 13028
Heny, Frank, 2030
Hepburn, James, 11234
— Joan Elaine, 14205
Hergenhan, Laurie, 7262–3, 9758, 10246
Heritage, John, 1344
Hermann, Elisabeth, 7264

— John P., 1701, 3700
Herman-Sekulic, Maja B., 12667
Hermerén, Lars, 2031
Hernadi, Paul, 9977
Herndon, Jerry A., 8279, 12377
Hernlund, Patricia, 388
Herold, John C., 8400
Herou, Josette, 6017–18
Herr, Cheryl, 12668
Herring, Phillip, 12669
Herrmann, Dorothy, 13723
Herrscher, Walter, 1667
Hersey, William Robert, 5289
Herskovits, Annette, 1816
Herstein, Sheila R., 7481
Hertz, Alan, 621
Herzinger, Kim, 8183
Herzman, Ronald B., 3193
Herzog, Kristin, 7265
Heseltine, Harry, 7039, 10521
Hesse, Eva, 13838–40
Hetherington, T. B., 8401
— Tom, 8402
Heuermann, Hartmut, 11644
Hewett, Edward, 8046
Hewison, Robert, 7165, 10666
Hewitt, David, 231, 468
Heyns, Michiel, 7586
Heys, Sandra, 9978
Heywood, Christopher, 10980
Hibbard, Allen E., 11302
— G. R., 4755
Hibberd, Dominic, 10522–3, 13675
Hicken, Marilyn, 10248
Hickey, Raymond, 899, 1437–8
Hickin, Norman, 61
Hieatt, Constance B., 155
Hietaranta, Pertti, 1942
Higbie, Robert, 10249
Higdon, David Leon, 312, 10250
Higgins, Anne Thorn, 3469
— Ian, 6884
— Regina Kirby, 8344
Higginson, Roy Patrick, 1320
Higgs, Robert J., 9386
High, Peter B., 2657
Higham, Charles, 9979
Highfill, Philip H., Jr, 5118
Higley, Sarah Lynn, 3259
Hilbert, Betsy, 8921
Hildahl, Frances Erdey, 3470
Hilfer, Anthony Channell, 12424
Hill, Alan G., 9002, 9565, 9567
— Betty, 3364
— Beverly, 1002
— Bridget, 6150, 6195

Ing, Janet, 392
— Janet Thompson, 393
Ingersoll, Earl, 11665, 13690
Ingham, David Keith, 11946
— Patricia, 8050, 8406
Inglesfield, Robert, 6798
Ingram, Allan, 6713, 11502
— Kevin, 624
Ingrams, Richard, 6590, 11464
Innis, Robert E., 1277, 2207
Inoyk, Ivor, 12106
Insley, J., 1668
— John, 1669
Ireland, K. R., 10825
Ireys, Virginia Foote, 6099
Irons, Glenwood Henry, 5065
Irvine, Martin, 1848
Irving, Edward B., Jr, 3124
Isani, Mukhtar Ali, 6948
Iser, Wolfgang, 9768
Isley, William L., Jr, 11432
Ismael, S. M. K., 11097
Ismond, Patricia, 14457
Ison, Mary M., 78
Ito, Hiroyuki, 625
— Isao, 9030
— Shoko, 9070
Ivănescu, Mircea, 10527
Iwasaki, Haruo, 1544, 1882

Jabbi, Bu-Buakei, 9769, 14206
Jablon, Madelyn Hyla, 13182
Jack, Ian, 6591, 7723
— R. D. S., 2664, 5897, 6332
Jackaman, Rob, 10528
Jackendoff, R. S., 2208
Jackson, Alan D., 6333
— Brendan, 8687, 13845
— David H., 9265
— Dennis, 12943, 12951
— Fleda Brown, 8573
— H. J., 7913-14
— MacD. P., 4789, 5655
— MacDonald P., 5618
— Richard, 11067
— Russell, 4666
— Teresa, 13596
— Tommie Lee, 11057
— W. T. H., 3369
— Wallace, 6525, 6714-15
Jacob, James R., 5228
Jacobs, Geraldine, 7724
— J. U., 9706
— N. M., 7652, 13595
— Naomi, 13600
Jacobsen, Bent, 1883, 1946
Jacobson, Howard, 5733
— Marcia, 8688
— Sven, 43, 2036

— Wendy S., 8051
Jacobsson, Bengt, 2038
Jacobus, Mary, 10826
Jacoebee, W. Pierre, 14335
Jacquet, Claude, 12671-2
Jaeggli, Osvaldo A., 2039-40
Jaffe, Audrey, 8052
— Audrey Anne, 8053
Jagendorf, Zvi, 4492
Jäger, Andreas, 13151
Jahn, Karen Frost, 8054
Jain, M., 11762
— N. J., 6592
James, Alan, 14173
— Edward, 7272
— Francis, 1370
— Mervyn, 4017
— Trevor, 7048, 12411
Jameson, Bruce Dalin, 11995
— Fredric, 5734, 9988, 10827
— Mary Ann, 2928
Janes, Regina, 6963
Janik, Del Ivan, 9138
Janion, Maria, 11508
Jannetta, M. J., 240
— Mervyn, 6716
Janoušek, Miroslav, 2665, 12910
Jansohn, Christa, 12911
Janssen, Frans A., 107
— J., 545
— Ronald R., 14019
Janssens, G. A. M., 5066
Janzen, Henry D., 502
Japp, Phyllis M., 1170
Jarab, Josef, 7273, 8120, 10529, 11711, 13137
Jardine, Lisa, 3526
Jarman, David, 7376
Jarolim, Edith, 11266
Jarratt, Susan Carole Funderburgh, 7995
Jarrell, Mary, 12544
Jarvis, Donald K., 2041
— R. J., 9605
Jaspaert, Lieven, 536
Jasper, David, 7915-16
Jauslin, Christian, 4636, 4667
Jauss, David, 10502
Jawad, A. S., 626
Jaworski, Philippe, 8924
Jay, Paul, 7049
Jędrzejkiewicz, Maria, 13350
Jefcoate, Graham, 6480
Jeffares, A. Norman, 2666, 14836-7
Jeffrey, David K., 11598
— David Lyle, 3702
— Rebecca A., 7483
Jehlen, Myra, 6983

Jemie, Onwuchekwa, 9688
Jemielity, Thomas, 6593
Jenkins, Alan, 13986
— Elizabeth, 6483
— Harold, 4331
— Islwyn, 11616
— Lee, 11889
— Mike, 13528
— Nigel, 14424
— William D., 11371
Jennings, Humphrey, 5230
— Mary-Lou, 5230
Jensen, Ejner J., 5559
— Emily, 11080
— Gillian Fellows, 1670
— Hans, 3288
— Laura, 12545
Jeon, Ho-Chun, 12247
Jerome, Judson, 470
Jeske, Jeffrey, 5648
Jessee, Sharon Adele, 10265
Jessup, Emily Decker Lardner, 10266
Jestin, Catherine T., 241
— Loftus Hugh Dudley, 6203
Jewell, John Robert, 8408
Jhally, Sut, 1180
Jhang, Gap-Sang, 9071, 9447
Jindra, Miroslav, 10267
Jobe, Don, 4121
Joffe, Phil, 12912
Johannesson, Nils-Lennart, 1884
Johannsen, Robert W., 7485
Johanson, Graeme, 394
Johansson, Stig, 537, 1171
John, Brian, 13290
— Eric, 3189
Johnsen, Lars, 1947
Johns-Lewis, Catherine, 1479
Johnson, Abby Arthur, 11576
— Alan, 11098
— Anthony, 5254, 5561
— B. R., 12172
— Barry C., 243
— Bette Reece, 12173
— Bruce, 8409
— Charles, 10268
— Claudia D., 7166
— Deborah Meem, 7274
— E. D. H., 6153
— Gerald D., 395
— Greg, 8121
— I. R., 3645
— Joyce, 12321
— Lynn Staley, 3814
— M. Suzanne Paul, 11890
— Mary-Parke, 62
— Patricia, 7275
— R. Thomas, 13735

— Robert, 7881
— Robert K., 14159
— Scott, 13846
— Vernon E., 7166
— William G., 13030
Johnson Mills, Yvonne Latetia, 1322
Johnston, Carolyn, 13075
— Dillon, 10531
— John H., 10829
— Kenneth R., 9606
— W. T., 108
Johnstone, Richard, 10269, 12265
Jökulsson, Illugi, 9989, 11185
Jolicœur, Claude, 7754
Jolley, Nicholas, 5611
Jolliffe, John W., 7050
Jolly, James Lester, Jr, 4493
— Roslyn, 4987
Joly, André, 1371
Jonassen, Frederick B., 3815
Jones, Ann Rosalind, 10270
— Anne G., 14428
— Barry, 2979
— Bernard, 109
— Buford, 8475
— Charles Foster, 2043
— Charlotte D., 627
— Chris, 6498
— David Richard, 9990
— Dolores Blythe, 9019
— Dorothy, 9771
— Edward John, 5735
— F., 3370
— Gayl, 12313
— Harold Whitmore, 5523
— Henry Festing, 7755
— James T., 10830
— Jean, 6143
— Johanna, 6055
— Joseph, 6055
— K., 11186
— Kathleen Anne, 7587
— Lawrence, 10272
— Leonidas, 9097
— Margaret, 12217
— Meredith Joy, 3371
— Michael, 3192
— Michael P., 11503
— Nancy Baker, 9772
— Peter, 6143
— Richard, 10532
— Robert, 5123
— Robin F., 155
— T., 8410
— Vivien, 8689
— W. L., 6717
Jones-Davies, M. T., 37
Jongman, Allard, 1480

Jónsson, Helgi, 11968
Jordan, Carmel, 14838
— June, 6949
— Rebecca, 9405
— Richard D., 5258
— Shirley Marie, 13320
Jordanova, L. J., 5965
Jorgens, Elise Bickford, 3958
— Jack, 4668
Jørgensen, Bo Hakon, 11652
— Erik, 2044
— Ravn, 2840
Joscelyne, Trevor A., 4464
Jose, Nicholas, 4756
Joseph, Gerhard, 7277
— Michael, 396
— Richard, 397
— Sister, 8476
— Terri Brint, 13847–8
Joshi, Irene M., 7117
Jost, David, 1764–5
Joukovsky, Nicholas A., 9049
Jouve, Michel, 6154
Jowett, John, 4988
Joy, Susan E., 4101
Joyce, C., 11763
— Elizabeth, 4669
Joyner, Charles, 2386
Juckett, Elizabeth Cox, 7816
Judd, Denis, 14438
Judge, Jeannie Sargent, 5485
— Roy, 2560
Judkins, David C., 5562
Juhasz, Suzanne, 8122
Juhl, Marianne, 11652
Juhnke, Marlies, 4989
Juliar, Michael, 13413–14
Jump, Harriet, 6192, 9607
Juneja, Renu, 5563
Jurgensen, Manfred, 9773
Jurish, Alice Eileen, 8690
Jurist, Janet, 9774
Justicia, Nellie Teresa, 14749
Justin, Henri, 8055

Kabell, Inge, 1442
Kachru, Braj B., 858, 966
Kachur, Barbara Anne, 4670
Kadar, Marlene, 628
Kael, Pauline, 9991
Kaetz, James Patrick, 10274
Kahan, Gerald, 6863
Kahn, Coppélia, 10805
— John, 1546
— John Ellison, 1172
— Victoria, 4018–19
Kakietek, Piotr, 2045
Kalackal, Thomas, 1481
Kalaga, Wojciech, 10831

Kaldewaij, Jelle, 1885
Kaler, Anne K., 13139
Kaleta, Kenneth Charles, 11969
Kalinke, Marianne E., 3205
Kallen, J. L., 2046
Kallet, Marilyn, 14651
Kallsen, T. J., 629
Kalnins, Mara, 12913
Kamata, Seizaburo, 1924
Kamio, Mituo, 6743
Kamm, Anthony, 2916
— Jürgen, 12422
Kamuf, Peggy, 7052
Kamusikiri, Sandra Darlene, 6255
Kanaganayakam, C., 12143
— Chelvanayakam, 12144
Kane, George, 3373, 3703
— Harold, 3374
— Leslie, 14693
— Patricia, 13946
Kanfer, Stefan, 12775
Kang, Chung-Suk, 12914
— Yop, 6256
Kannapell, Barbara Marie, 1006
Kaplan, Amy, 8574, 14565
— Cora, 2667
— Fred, 7817, 8056
— Joel H., 5656, 5890
— Justin, 9498
Kapoor, Sushma, 9425
Karakostas, A., 9775
Karayiorga, Olympia, 14750
Kardux, Johanna Cornelia, 8925
Kareda, Urjo, 9992
Kari, Daven Michael, 11764
— James, 1697
Karimipour, Zahra, 5034, 13031
Karita, Motoji, 2668
Karl, Frederick R., 10275, 11504–5
Karlekar, Ranajay, 11765
Karlinsky, Simon, 13385
Karr, Mary, 11660
Kaser, David, 244
Kasser, Stephen Jay, 2459
Kastovsky, Dieter, 26, 1372, 2218
Kates, Judith A., 5736
Kato, Kazuo, 1373, 2220
— Mikiro, 12673
— Tunehiko, 9776
Katz, Adelaide E., 6810
Katzen, May, 471
Katzner, Kenneth, 762
Kauffman, Linda S., 2841

— George P., 7449
Lane, Ann J., 12152
— M. Travis, 11112–13, 14016
— Maggie, 7591
— Margaret, 13767
Lang, Berel, 4762
— John, 11419
— Peter Christian, 7060
Langbauer, Laurie, 6059, 8060
Langbaum, Robert, 9616
Lange, Bernd-Peter, 13657
— D. J., 7992
Langefeld, Brigitte, 3134
Langendoen, D. Terence, 844
Langenfeld, Robert, 13299
Langer, Lawrence L., 10674
Langhans, Edward A., 5118
Langlois, Karen S., 11106
Langman, F. H., 10845
Lanham, Richard A., 3854
Lanier, Douglas M., 5564
— Gregory Warren, 4507
Lanoix, Louis, 5844, 6718
Lansbury, Coral, 9407
Lanser, Susan Sniader, 2852
Lapidge, Michael, 25, 160, 249, 3208–9
LaPorte, Valerie Dorothy, 5380
Lappert, Stephen, 1765
Lapsley, M., 13334
Larès, Maurice, 10291
Larkin, Joan, 13325
— Philip, 11470
Larlham, Peter, 10005
Larmour, David H. J., 13418
Larsen, Max Deen, 12679
— Stephan, 14207
Larson, Charles, 5630
— Charles R., 9793
— David M., 6471
— Janet Karsten, 12445
— Janet L., 8061
Larvin, Nora, 12917
Lascelles, Mary, 7290
Lash, John, 13858
Lasker, G. W., 1673
Lasnik, Howard, 1972, 2054
Lass, Roger, 1416, 1446, 1644
Lasseter, Rollin A., 10846
Lassner, Phyllis, 11292
Latham, Robert, 5845
Lathy, Edward Daniel, 10847
Latré, Guido, 12853
Lau, Beth, 8808
Laughlin, James, 13859
Laurence, Anne, 6406
— Dan H., 250, 8062, 8658, 14118–19, 14121
Lauridsen, Hanne, 1442
Lavabre, Simone, 13419

Lavazzi, Thomas, 12167
Lavers, Norman, 12831
Law, Alan G., 1771
— Alexander, 5533
— T. A., 11511
— Vivien, 822
Lawler, Traugott, 3762
Lawless, Donald S., 5645
Lawry, J. S., 5565
Lawson, Alan, 11152
— David, 12680
— Edwin D., 1674
— Elizabeth, 958, 14182
— Jacqueline Elaine, 6407
— Lewis A., 13713–14
— Mark, 13669
— Tom O., 6598, 6773
Lawson-Peebles, R., 2683
Lawton, David, 3707
— David A., 3387
— L. S., 161
Layton, Lynne, 2684
Lazenblatt, W. W. G., 13116
Lea, F. A., 12918
— Sidney, 10565
Leacroft, Helen, 2797
— Richard, 2797
Leake, Alison, 12189
Leal, R. B., 12513
Leaming, Barbara, 10006
Leamon, Warren, 14845
Lear, Liz, 13154
Learmouth, Trevor, 251
Leary, Lewis, 6748
— William G., 14222
Leatherbarrow, Ronald, 14474
Leavell, Linda, 4265
Leavis, L. R., 7669, 8230
LeBow, Diane, 10292
Lecca, Doina, 13737
Lecercle, Jean-Jacques, 767
Lecker, Robert, 7–10, 10293, 11269, 12835
LeClair, Tom, 10296
Lecouteux, Claude, 3543
Leddy, Michael, 1376
Ledgerwood, Mikle Dave, 7291
Le Doeuff, Michèle, 5266
Lee, A. Robert, 7292, 7409, 9794
— Alvin A., 2685
— Ann Thompson, 14600
— B. S., 3763
— Byung-Choon, 1821
— Chang-Bae, 14846
— Chong-Ho, 8809, 9617
— Dae-Suk, 4931
— David, 1324
— Doris Douglas, 2686
— Dorothy H., 9795

— Eric J., 1325
— Eun-Hwan, 11770
— Haeng-Soo, 13620
— Hermione, 402, 11293–4
— James W., 9739
— Jongsook, 5566–7
— Judith, 6257
— Jung-Kee, 14653
— Keun-Sup, 5486
— Ki-Suk, 1822
— Kyung-Shik, 111
— Kyung-Soon, 8231
— L. L., 11568, 13141
— Se-Soon, 14847
— Seung-Dae, 14848
— Soon-Sung, 1280
— Tae-Dong, 13621
— Won-Goog, 1377
Leech, Geoffrey, 755
Leeds, Winifred, 907
Leeming, David Adams, 8697
Leerabhandh, Sivaporn, 14566
Lees, Rosemary Ann, 3389
Lefanu, William, 6804, 7950
Lefebure, Molly, 7920
Leferink, Hein, 10848
LeGendre, Barbara, 12867
Leggatt, Alexander, 3904, 4508, 4949, 5568
Legget, B. J., 13304
Leggott, Michele Joy, 14890
Lehiste, Ilse, 1485
Lehmann, John, 7780
— Winfred P., 1823
Lehr, Genevieve, 2522
Lehrer, Adrienne, 2055
Lehrman, Walter D., 5569
Lehto, Leena, 1178
Leigh, John, 9296
Leighton, Angela, 7710
Leinbaugh, Theodore H., 162, 3222
Leinwand, Theodore B., 4915, 5128
Leisi, Ernst, 1009
Leiss, William, 1180
Leitch, Thomas M., 10007
Leiter, Samuel L., 4677, 10008
Leites, Edmund, 5234
Leithauser, Brad, 11261, 14168
Leitner, Gerhard, 1062, 1379
Leitz, Robert C., III, 13522
Lem, Stanislaw, 14226
Lemaire, Gérard-Georges, 8185, 12681
LeMaster, J. R., 9453
Lemay, J. A. Leo, 5972, 6472
Lemmedu, Beverly, 3652
Lemon, Charles, 7670
— Lee T., 10298

Lenar, Faye Mertine, 7293
Lendinara, Patrizia, 3210
Lenihan, Patricia Diane, 8232
Lennon, J., 9618
— Peter, 13769
Lennox, Bill, 12277
Lenox, Donald, 11255
Lensing, George S., 12546, 14849
Lenstrup, Rita, 1950
Lenta, Margaret, 9706, 9151a
Lentricchia, Frank, 7410
Leonard, Douglas, 9503
— Douglas Novich, 8125
— Garry Martin, 6258
— J. K., 5748
— James S., 4124
— John, 12447
— Paul, 10009
— Tom, 13996
Leonardi, Susan J., 14758
Leondopoulos, Jordan, 11513
Leone, Leonard, 3900
Le Pellec, Yves, 11417
LePore, Ernest, 11614
Lepow, Lauren, 2523
Leppard, D. G., 2235
Le Prevost, Christina, 6945
Lepschy, Giulio, 845
Lercangée, Francine, 13536
Le Rebeller-Mouyen, Annie, 11137
Lerer, Seth, 4096
Lerner, Frederick Andrew, 10300
— Laurence, 2687
Lernout, G., 12438
Le Saux, Françoise, 3642
Lessa, Richard, 7560
Lessay, Franck, 5524–5, 11514
Lesser, Matthew Bernard, 11834
— Wendy, 11303
Lester, B., 2236
— G. A., 1588, 3390, 3544, 3665
— Geoffrey, 3473
Lethbridge, H. J., 11318
— Robert, 4763
Letley, A. E. C., 908
— E., 909
— Emma, 9266, 11125
LeTourneau, Mark Stephen, 2237
Levao, Ronald, 4212
LeVay, John, 11631
Levene, Mark, 12825
Levenson, Jill L., 4764
— Michael, 11515
— Michael H., 10849
Levere, Trevor H., 7921

Leverenz, David, 1232
Levesque, George A., 11122
Levey, David, 3474, 13063
Levi, Peter, 2932
Levin, Beth, 2056
— Carole, 4027
— Harry, 8698
— Nancy S., 2057
— Richard, 3905
— Richard A., 4510
Levine, George, 7296
— George R., 9354
— Joseph M., 6493
— June Perry, 10010
— Laura, 3906
— Philippa, 7488
— Rhonda Joy, 7411
— Robert, 3791
— Robert T., 5659
— Stuart, 9074
— Susan, 9074
Levinson, Harry Norman, 6599
— Joan Persily, 1518
— Marjorie, 9620
Leviţchi, Leon, 2688, 4334
— Leon D., 4334–5
Levitow, Jonathan Seth, 12683
Le Vot, André, 11971
Levy, Alfred J., 14475
— Anita, 7694
Lévy, Claude, 11226
Levy, David, 7922
— David W., 636
— F. J., 5267
Lévy, Maurice, 6060
Lewalski, Barbara K., 5599
— Barbara Kiefer, 5749
Lewandowska, Barbara, 1281
Lewandowska-Tomaszczyk, Barbara, 768
Lewis, Ann Clifford, 8479
— Clayton W., 11355
— Gifford, 14192
— Lisa A. F., 7592
— M. B., 14582
— Mary Jane, 5072
— Peter, 2689, 12989
— R. E., 3391
— W. S., 6940
Leyerle, John, 3708
Li, Victor P. H., 13861
— Xilao, 9504–5
Libera, Antoni, 11191
Liberman, Anatoly, 2390
— Serge, 7061
Lich, Glen E., 318
Lickindorf, E. T., 11771
Liddell, Robert, 11467
Liddle, I. A., 6335
Lieb, Michael, 5750

Lieberman, Susan, 10011
Liesenfeld, Vincent J., 6024
Lifton, Paul Samuel, 14604
Light, Alison, 14354
Lightman, Naomi, 8064
Lightner, Theodore M., 2138
Liliendahl, Ann, 8126
Lilly, Mark, 4887
Lim, C. S., 4864
Limbert, Claudia, 5834
Limerick, Patricia Nelson, 7062
Limon, Jerzy, 3907, 5131, 5660
Limons, John, 11900
Lincoln, Andrew, 6259
— Kenneth, 13284
Lindahl, Carl, 2463
Lindberg-Seyersted, Brita, 8127, 11996, 13864
Linde, Charlotte, 1115
Linden, Stanton J., 5178
Lindheim, Nancy, 4213
Lindholdt, Paul Jeffrey, 5593
Lindley, David, 5320, 5570
Lindow, John, 3191
Lindquist, Hans, 2377
Lindsay, D., 539
— David W., 6649
— Maurice, 10540
— W. A., 5422
Lindsey, Geoffrey Alan, 1380
Lindskoog, Kathryn, 13034
Line, Maurice B., 540
Linenthal, Mark, 13640
Lines, Rodney, 7871
Ling, Åge, 2058
Lingeman, Richard, 11704
Link, Franz, 13865
— Franz H., 8128
Linklater, Andro, 13160
Linnarud, Moira, 1063
Lintott, S., 7672
Lipenga, Ken Diston, 11058
Lipka, Leonhard, 1773
Lipski, John M., 978
Lish, Gordon, 14060
Lister, Raymond, 6260
Little, G. L., 8810
— Matthew, 13866
Littlefield, Daniel F., Jr, 637, 2690
Littlewood, I., 14493
— Ian, 14494
Litvak, Joseph, 7593
Litz, A. Walton, 13867, 13893
Livingston, Chella Courington, 6601
Ljolje, A., 1488
Ljungquist, Kent, 9075
Llasera, Margaret, 5268, 5381–2

Lloyd, D. W., 13622
— David, 8891, 12334
— David Thomas, 12335
— Genevieve, 2981, 10851
— Tom, 7818
Lo Bello, Nino, 1182
Lochhead, Marion, 2464
Lochman, Daniel T., 5751
Lochrie, Karma, 1650, 3138–9
Lock, Charles, 8413, 13931
— F. P., 6887
Lockwood, Stephen P., 10301
— Thomas, 6185
Lodge, David, 9799
— K. R., 1489
Loesberg, Jonathan, 7297
Loewenstein, Joseph, 4266,
    5571–2
Lofaro, Michael A., 2465
Löffler, Arno, 5341, 6655
— Christa Maria, 3545
Logan, George M., 4150
— S. W., 9621
Logarbo, Mona Lynn, 3141
Loges, Mary Kaiser, 11632
Logue, Christopher, 2933
Lohrli, Anne, 9276
Lojkine, Monique, 11772
Lomask, Milton, 2982
Lomax, M. A., 3908
— Marion, 4267
Lombard, François, 11516
Lomperis, Linda Susan, 3764
London, April, 6744
Long, Deborah Marie, 13257
— E. Hudson, 9453
— Elizabeth, 10302, 10675
— George L., 11597
Longacre, Robert E., 1116
Longenbach, James, 13868
Longley, Edna, 10541
Longsworth, Polly, 9388
Lonoff, Sue, 7952, 8972
Lonsdale, Roger, 638, 6102
Looby, Christopher, 6473
Looney, J. Anna, 3422
Lopez, A. C., 12206
— Longino Luis, 3392
Lorant, André, 4765
Lord, George deF., 5631
— George deForest, 3961
Lorimer, William Laughton,
    910
Losey, Jay B., 9035
Lothe, Jakob, 8414, 11517
Lough, J., 5595
— John, 6186
Loughman, Celeste, 11835
Loughrey, Bryan, 4990, 6487
Louis, Margot Kathleen, 9292

Loukides, Michael Kosta, 9622
Lounsberry, Barbara, 14725
Louvre, Alf, 13176
Lovallo, Len, 11444
Love, Glen A., 8576
— Harold, 112, 320
LoVecchio, John Paul, 13597
Loving, Jerome, 8129, 9506
— Jerome M., 8130
Low, Anthony, 3959, 5713
— Donald A., 6336–8
Lowbury, Edward, 14884
Lowe, David, 13420
Lowens, Peter J., 11518
Lowenthal, F., 1326
Lowman, P. J., 11456
— R. J., 8415
Loy, J. Robert, 2691
Lozes, Jean, 8869
Lu, Gu-Sun, 4766
Lubbers, Klaus, 2853, 7298
Lubin, David M., 8699
Lubkoll, Christine, 2692
Lucas, John, 5973, 7063, 7412,
    7872, 10852, 11235, 12056
— Patricia Diane, 5383
— Peter J., 3817
Lucazeau, Michel, 4991
Lucente, Gregory L., 11901
Lucid, Robert F., 9454
Lucking, David, 14012
Lucow, Ben, 5870
Ludington, Townsend, 11688
Ludlow, Peter Jay, 2242
Luey, Beth, 472
Lukacher, Ned, 2693
Lukacs, Barbara Ann, 5573
— Paul Braddock, 7299
Lukens, Rebecca, 9267
Lull, Janis, 5487
Lumiansky, R. M., 3475–6
Lumsden, M., 2059
Lund, Michael, 8065
— Niels, 3142
Lunsford, Ronald F., 505
Lupack, Barbara Tepa, 12832
Lupan, Radu, 12684
Lupold, Harry Forrest, 7855,
    9563
Lury, C. E., 10853
Luschei, Martin, 13715
Luschnig, C. A. E., 1552
— L. J., 1552
Lussier, Mark, 6261
Lustig, Irma S., 6302–4
Luther, Susan Militzer, 7923
Lutton, Jeannette Hume,
    13036
Lutz, Angelika, 1447
Luxon, Thomas Hyatt, 5310

Luxton, Andrea Thomasing
    Joy, 5752
Luyat-Moore, Anne, 11519
Lyall, R., 5897
Lydon, Christopher, 14476
Lyles, Jean Caffey, 13948
Lynch, Andrew, 3709
— Michael Francis, 11813
— Tony, 8066
Lynds, Dennis, 13142
Lynes, Russell, 7169
Lynn, David Hayden, 11520
— Steven, 639
Lyon, Christopher, 10102
— J. M., 8700
— Kim, 7644
Lyonga, Pauline Nalova, 10303
Lyons, Bridget Gellert, 4511
— John, 769
— John D., 2694
Lyttle, I. S., 13963

Maber, R. G., 5839
Mabey, Richard, 6951
McAdams, Ruth Ann, 7300
Macainsh, Noel, 13109, 13492,
    14583–4
McAlindon, T., 3765, 3909
— Thomas, 3393
McAllister, Mark, 13202
Macarie, Manuela, 9178
McArthur, Benjamin, 7170
— Lewis L., 1675
— Murray, 12685
— Murray Gilchrist, 6262
— Tom, 1774
McAvoy, William C., 4336
McBrien, William, 14180
McCabe, Brian, 13186
MacCabe, Colin, 770, 1519,
    10676, 10854
McCabe, Richard A., 4092,
    4098
McCaffery, Larry, 10296
— Steve, 13510
McCaig, Joann, 12439
McCallum, Lauren, 8067
McCandless, David Foley, 5040
McCann, Brian, 14380
— Wesley, 252, 640
McCarron, William E., 13964
McCarthy, John J., 1490
— Muriel, 253
— Patrick A., 11522
— Terence, 3653
— William, 6697
MacCary, W. Thomas, 4512
McCleery, Alistair, 11345
McClellan, William T., 3766

Parrinder, Patrick, 10356, 12705–6
Parris, Peggy, 9371
Parrish, Richard Dale, 12352
Parrott, E. O., 2716
Parry, Ann, 666
— Caroline Balderston, 2546
— Graham, 5076
— Sally E., 13050
Parsons, Nicholas, 420
— R. D., 4720
— Thornton, 12390
Pasanen, Outi, 10888
Paskin, Sylvia, 10568
Pass, Olivia McNeely, 8492
Passmann, Dirk, 6898
— Dirk F., 6899
Patai, Daphne, 13659
Patell, Cyrus R. K., 12707
Paterson, Linda, 3557
— Linda M., 3552
Patey, Douglas Lane, 5981, 6616, 6726–7
Pati, Madhusudan, 9632
Patke, Rajeev S., 14280
Patrick, James, 9830
Patrides, C. A., 3856, 5302
Patsch, Sylvia M., 7058
Patten, Bob, 2477
— Jacqueline, 2477
Patterson, Annabel, 3857, 4279, 5578
— G., 12854
— J. D., 11543
— J. Daniel, 5880
— Nancy-Lou, 13039
— Sally, 7653
Pattison, Robert, 9319
Patton, Marilyn, 8935
Paul, David, 3916
— John Steven, 10040, 13259
— Ronald, 10357
Paulin, Tom, 2718, 2941, 8424
Paulson, Ronald, 5270
Pauwels, Gerard W., 14694
Pavel, Thomas G., 2860
Pavis, Patrice, 10041
Pavlopoulos, Françoise, 6530
Paxton, Nancy L., 5011
Payn, Graham, 11579
Payne, Alma J., 8580
— Darwin, 14701
— Deborah C., 5922
— John P., 4042
— Roberta Louise, 3409
Peacock, Alan J., 5579–80
— D. Keith, 10042
Peake, Charles, 6900
Pean, James Louis, 12082
Pearce, Brian Louis, 9023

— Donald, 14864
— Howard D., 7003
— Sharyn, 10358
Pearcy, Lee T., 3968
Pearlman, Daniel, 13889
Pearn, Julie, 10569
Pearsall, Derek, 325, 3421, 3716, 3770, 3776
Pearson, David, 269–71, 5239
— Eloise, 1127
— Norman Holmes, 8512
— R. A., 2567
Peat, Hal W., 10043
Peattie, Roger W., 272, 667, 9113
Pebworth, Ted-Larry, 5453
Pechey, Graham, 10889
Pechter, Edward, 4815
Pecora, Vincent P., 12708
Pedersen, Clarence, 8277
— Viggo Hjørnager, 2719
Pederson, Lee, 1421
Peek, Andrew, 12323
Peereboom, J. J., 6531
Peltason, Timothy, 9320
Pelz, Monika, 10686
Penberthy, Jenny Lynn, 13516
Penfield, Joyce, 875
Pennala, Judy L., 7603
Pennell, Melissa McFarland, 1704
Penner, Dick, 11459
Penney, S. G., 10359
Pennick, Nigel, 3214
Peper, Jürgen, 2259
Pepper, John, 923
Pequigney, Joseph, 4973
Percival, W. Keith, 832
Percy, Walker, 8936
Pereiah, Alan R., 3558
Perfect, Christopher, 124
Perkin, M. R., 421–2
Perkins, C. D., 1192
— David, 6617
— Elizabeth, 8442, 11337, 12750
Perkinson, Grace, 8144
Perl, Jeffrey M., 9831
Perlis, Alan D., 14281
Perloff, Marjorie, 10570–1, 10598, 10890
Perret, N. M., 13891
Perry, Constance M., 13118
— Dennis R., 5211, 9279
— John Oliver, 9832
— Menahem, 3038
— Ralph Barton, 475
— Ruth, 6197
Persson, Gunnar, 1555
Pestino, Joseph Francis, 10974

Péter, Ágnes, 8812
Peterman, Michael, 8984
Peters, Hans, 1594
— John, 13040
Peterson, Dale E., 13439
— Donald, 13090
— Leland D., 6901
— Lennart, 1927
— Linda H., 7451
— Richard S., 5582
— Ronald E., 13440
— Susan Lynn, 849
— William S., 423
Petillon, Pierre, 5185
— Pierre-Yves, 13967
Petri, Lucreţia, 1493–4
Petrie, Bradford M. N., 2260
Petro, Pamela, 476–7
Petry, Alice Hall, 8289, 11407, 11915, 13091, 13119, 14433
Pettinari, Catherine Johnson, 1128
Pettingell, Phoebe, 7604, 8145, 11592, 14865
Pettit, Norman, 6432
Pettitt, Thomas, 2504
Petyt, Keith Malcolm, 924
Petzold, Dieter, 10360
Peverett, Michael, 1633
Peyre, Yves, 3858
Peyton, Richard, 7327
Pfaelzer, Jean, 7328
Pfefferkorn, Eli, 9833
Pfister, Joel, 8493
Pflieger, Pat, 7379
Pfoff, Cheryl Kay, 11138
Pfordresher, John, 7746–7
Pharies, David A., 1388
Pheby, Keith Charles, 10891
Phelan, Herbert J., 5777
— Virginia B., 11782
Phelps, Ruth M., 10469
Philip, M. F. E., 6502
— Neil, 8078
Phillipps, K. C., 1026
Phillips, Adam, 9036
— Catherine, 8556
— Gene D., 10044
— Helen, 3717–18
— J. C., 3628
— Michael, 6269, 8884–5
— Michael Joseph, 1557
— Robert, 9280, 14102
Phillipson, John S., 14717
Philmus, Robert M., 2861, 14519
Philp, Mark, 6503
Phipps, Christine, 5306
Phythian, B. A., 850

Piacentino, Edward J., 6793, 8832
Pica, Teresa, 1129
Picard, Christopher L., 11068
— Hans Rudolf, 2986
Picht, Heribert, 506
Pick, John, 7179
Pickering, Kenneth, 3483
— Michael, 2077, 11418, 11466
— Sam, 11212
— Samuel, Jr, 6080, 8588
Pickford, Christopher, 424
Pickrel, Paul, 7679
Pienaar, Johan, 9152
Pieńkowski, Piotr, 9633
Pierce, Peter, 12761
Pifer, Ellen, 13441–3
Piggott, Glyne L., 1422
Pigman, G. W., III, 3969
Pigrame, Stella, 6495
Pike, Burton, 8079
Pilch, Herbert, 1130
Pilcher, Jeremy, 12165
Pilkington, William T., 9739
Pimentel-Anduiza, Luz Aurora, 10892
Pinciss, Gerald, 4127
Pineas, Rainer, 4057
Pineau, Lois Isabel, 1680
Pinion, F. B., 11783
Pinker, Steven, 1332
Pinkham, Jessie E., 2078
Pinkney, M. M., 14767
Pinney, Thomas, 273, 12799
Pinnington, A. J., 5390
Pinsker, Sanford, 11003
Pinter, Harold, 2942
Pinto, Julio César Machado, 1239
Piper, Dan, 14661
— Judith Ann, 10047
Pirie, David B., 4554
Pironon, Jean, 5583
Pistotnik, V., 4128
Pitcher, E. W., 668–72, 1624, 6811, 6820, 6964, 7976
— Edward W., 1583
— Edward W. R., 4155
— George, 6210
— John, 5271
Pitt, David G., 13935
Pittock, Malcolm, 4994, 12934
— Murray, 5635
— Murray G. H., 5636, 8794
Pitts, Mary Ellen, 11725
Pivato, Joseph, 13, 10893
Pizer, Donald, 7093, 11691
Pla, Sandra, 12537
Plaisant, Michèle, 2720
Plank, Frans, 1558

— Jeffrey, 6189
Platizky, Roger S., 9321
Platt, John, 852
— Michael, 4555, 4796
Platz, Norbert H., 7329
Plett, Heinrich F., 1240
Plimpton, George, 11662
Płocińska, Barbara, 26
Plowden, G. F. C., 6728
Plumly, Stanley, 7697
Plummer, Bonnie, 11708
Pochard, J.-C., 970
Pocock, A. J., 13477
Podhoretz, Norman, 7533
Poger, Sidney, 11101
Poirier, Richard, 8290
Poitras, Jean-Maurice, 13239
Polański, Kazimierz, 1956
Poldauf, Ivan, 1423
Polk, Noel, 11846, 11881
Pollak, Ellen, 6729
— Vivian R., 8146
Pollard, Arthur, 8876
— Graham, 88
Pollet, Elizabeth, 14087
Pollin, Burton R., 7987
Pollock, J. Y., 1813
Pomeroy, Elizabeth, 274
Pomphrey, Cathy, 851
Poncet, Andre, 13526
Ponder, Melinda, 8494
Pondrom, Cyrena N., 12506
Ponnuswamy, Krishna, 14347
Pons, Xavier, 3039
Ponsford, M. J., 5256
— Michael, 8425, 12490
Poole, Richard, 2721
Poovey, Mary, 6962, 7497
Pop, Lia-Maria, 7773
Pope, J. C., 1602
— John C., 1605
Popescu, Marian, 13739
Popkin, Susan Marsha, 6065
Popplewell, Lawrence, 8426
Porée, Marc, 11352
Portales, Marco, 13322
Portch, Stephen R., 10363
Porte, Joel, 8581
Porter, Daniel R., 7742
— Dennis, 2862
— E., 3410
— Joseph A., 1389
— Peter, 6270, 9109
— Roy, 6494
Posner, Roland, 2265
Posnock, Ross, 7730
Poss, Richard Lee, 5143
Possin, Hans-Joachim, 6124, 10689
Post, Michał, 2266

Postal, Paul M., 844, 1957
Poster, Jem, 6376
Postlethwaite, Diana, 7094
Postlewait, Thomas, 7549
Postma, Pamela, 9513
Poston, Lawrence, 7095, 9322
Poteat, Patricia Lewis, 13718
Poteet, Susan, 10049
Potkay, Adam, 6618
Potter, A. M., 4777
— Lois, 5778
— Richard C., 2267
— Robert, 3484
Pottle, Frederick A., 6303–4
Poulsen, Richard C., 876
Poulson, Christine, 7836
Pound, Ezra, 11715
— Omar, 13893
Pounds, Wayne, 9083, 11307
Poupko, Chana Kasachkoff, 6315
Poussa, Patricia, 925–6
Pousseur, Jean-Marie, 5272
Povsic, Francis, 2892
Powe, B. W., 9835
Powel, Ralph Austin, 2175
Powell, David, 6692, 7873–4
— Dilys, 11983
— J. Enoch, 12471
— Jocelyn, 5144
— Kerry, 9551
— Kirsten, 2478
— M. J., 2268
— Marianne, 3608
— Michael, 10050
— Philip E., 7331
— W. Allen, 14718
— Walter W., 507
— William Gregory, 8937
Powers, Lyall, 8725
— Lyall H., 8659, 8726
Poyet, Albert, 5426–7
Poynting, Jeremy, 8781, 10365
Poznar, Walter, 9836
Prantner, Wilfried, 10888
Pratt, Annis, 2863
— Judith Stevens, 673
— Mary Louise, 1390
— Peter Philip, 9372
— William C., 13894
Precosky, Don, 7096, 13162
Preddy, Jane, 10052
Preisler, Bent, 1391
Preis-Smith, Agata, 12549
Prentice, Chris, 12497
Prentis, B. L., 7645
Prescott, Andrew, 674
— Anne Lake, 4035
Pressman, Richard S., 6936

Sammons, Todd H., 5784
Sampson, H. Grant, 6106
Sams, Eric, 3926
— Horace, Jr, 5314
Samson, A. R., 3777
Samuels, M. L., 931
— Shirley, 6068
— Wilfred D., 11815
Samuelson, Arnold, 12395
Samway, Patrick, 11880
Sánchez, Marta Ester, 10694
Sandberg, Elisabeth, 14165
Sandbrook, Patrick, 12517
Sandels, Robert, 10387, 14221
Sander, Reinhard W., 11625, 12535
Sanderlin, George, 3796
Sanders, Arnold Allen, Jr, 3656
— Charles Richard, 480
— Dennis, 11444
— Norman, 4348–9
— Valerie, 7452, 8896
Sanderson, Michael, 7184
— Stewart, 903
Sandler, Lucy Freeman, 137
— Robert, 4574
Sandness, Glen D., 1771
Sandqvist, Sven, 3564
Sands, Kathleen Mullen, 2968
Sandulesco, C. Georges, 12720
Sandulescu, C. George, 12721
Sandved, Arthur O., 3721
Sanford, Timothy Bryce, 10067
Saniewski, Ursula, 4575
Sanjek, David Louis Russell, 8583
Santraud, Jeanne-Marie, 5, 1074
Saporta, Marc, 1074, 10697
Sappenfield, James A., 8604
Sarafinski, Dolores J., 5569
Şarbu, Aladár, 8944
Šarčević, Susan, 2809
Sargent, Mark L., 5994
Sarkar, Malabika, 5786
— Shyamal Kumar, 4923
Sarlós, Robert Károly, 10068
Sasaki, Michiru, 4918
Sato, Taisei, 2737
— Toshihiko, 7937, 8816–17
Sattelmeyer, Robert, 9463
Satty, Harvey J., 14227
Sauer, Hans, 3215
— Liselotte, 7110
Sauerberg, Lars Ole, 2868, 10388, 11627
Saul, Nigel, 3565
Saunders, James Robert, 10389
— Judith P., 9087, 9375
— M. W. H., 12000

— R. G., 10579
Saussy, George Stone, III, 1789
Sauvage, Leo, 12270, 14160
Sava, Iosif, 14128
Savage, D. S., 12487
— Elizabeth, 5569
— George E., 9376
Savory, Jerold, 429, 688
Sawada, Paul Akio, 4159
Sawyer, Paul L., 9141
Saxby, Maurice, 2894
Sayre, Henry M., 14664
— Robert F., 9377–8
Saywood, Barrie, 8083
Scaglione, Aldo, 812, 2365
Scales, Prunella, 11244
Scanlan, Margaret, 13354, 14094
Scanlon, Paul A., 10976
— Tony, 7112
Scarberry-Garcia, Susan, 13286
Scarborough, George, 2738
Scarfone, Suzanne, 9639
Scarisbrick, J. J., 3566
Scattergood, John, 4226–7
Schaar, Claes, 5787
Schabert, Ina, 4576
Schach, Paul, 175
Schaefer, Jacqueline T., 13309
Schaeffer, David Lewis, 12826
Schafer, Elizabeth, 5357
Schäfer, Jürgen, 12837
Schafer, R. Murray, 10069
Schakel, Peter, 13043
Schalkwyk, David, 4919
Schapiro, Barbara, 11024
— Barbara A., 7424
— Barbara Ann, 2684
Scharnhorst, Gary, 7546, 8737, 9379, 12154
Schatzberg, Walter, 3012
Schaum, Melita, 14285
Schechner, Richard, 10070
Scheckner, Peter, 12948
Scheckter, John, 14506
Scheick, William J., 12805, 14522
Scheid, Teresa Marie, 11552
Schein, Barry, 1499
Scheler, Manfred, 835
Schenck, Celeste M., 11593
Schendl, Herbert, 1606
Schenkel, Daniel, 1198
Scheps, Walter, 3422
Scherer, Barrymore Laurence, 5788
Scherr, Arthur, 1681
— Jennifer, 1682
Scheuermann, Mona, 6069
Schevill, James, 4997

Schibanoff, Susan, 4228
Schiebinger, Londa, 6164
Schieffelin, Bambi B., 1029
Schiff, Ellen, 10071
Schiffrin, Deborah, 1134
Schindler, Walter, 5789
Schipper, Mineke, 10390
— W., 1603
— William, 176
Schirmer, Ruth, 4160
— Walter F., 4160
Schleh, Eugene, 13112
Schleifer, Ronald, 10765, 14876
Schleiner, Louise, 3972–3
Schleret, J.-J., 10129
— Jean-Jacques, 690, 10142, 10392, 11608
Schlesinger, George, 3778
Schless, Howard H., 3722
Schlicke, Paul, 8084
Schlobin, Roger C., 10393
Schlossman, Beryl, 12722
Schlueter, June, 10394, 14632
— Kurt, 14497
— Paul, 10394
Schmid, Herta, 2285
Schmidgall, Gary, 4998
Schmidt, A. V. C., 3630
— G., 13904
— Johann N., 7185
— Paul Henry, 9004
— Siegfried J., 10815
Schmitt, Charles B., 4040
— Patrick E., 13631
Schmitz, Götz, 6780
Schneeman, Peter, 13905
Schneider, Edgar W., 878
— Ulrich, 12723
Schnitzer, Deborah Jane, 10395
Schnucker, Robert V., 509
Schoeck, R. J., 4161
Schoenbaum, S., 333, 3861, 3900
— Samuel, 4578
Schoenfeldt, Michael Carl, 5498
Schofield, Charles Malcolm, 5527
Scholar, Nancy, 13518
Scholes, Robert, 10913
Schönfeld, Eicke, 9553
Schonhorn, Manuel, 6417–18
Schor, Esther Helen, 7425
— Hilary Margo, 8339
Schork, R. J., 6662, 8431
Schött, Roland, 6512
Schouten, M. E. H., 1500
Schow, H. Wayne, 11648
Schrader, Richard J., 13078
Schram, Glenn N., 8978

Schrank, Bernice, 13550–1
Schreiber, Paul Clifton, 13720
Schreibman, Susan, 13153
Schricker, Gale C., 14877
Schrickx, Willem, 3927, 5666
Schriner, Delores Korb, 481
Schroeder, Patricia R., 13261
Schubnell, M. M., 13287
— Matthias, 13288
Schueller, Malini, 9380
— Malini Johar, 7113
Schuldiner, Michael, 5882
Schulte-Sasse, Jochen, 10741
Schultz, Robert, 13906
Schulz, Max F., 6107
Schulze, Frank, 13067
— Rainer, 1135, 1393
Schuman, Sam, 13452–3
Schur, Owen Marius, 8432
Schütze, Marli, 13044
Schwanbom, Per, 4579
Schwartz, Carol Ann, 11707
— Lawrence H., 11924
— Nina, 11553
— Richard Alan, 334
— Richard B., 6687
— Sanford, 11789
— Stephen, 9850
Schwarz, C. M., 1790
— Daniel R., 7526
Schweickart, Patrocinio P.,
3028
Schweighaeuser, J.-P., 487
— Jean-Paul, 11420, 12434
Schweizer, Harold, 7797
Schwenger, Peter, 2739, 9851–2
Schwenker, G. L., 14878
Sciff-Zamaro, Roberta, 13685
Scobie, Brian W. M., 5518
— Stephen, 10580, 10698,
13511, 14482
Scodel, Joshua Keith, 5188
Scolnicov, Hanna, 4138
Scorza, Thomas J., 8945–6
Scott, Bill, 2485
— Forrest S., 1683
— John Walter, 6918
— Mary Jane, 6934
— Michael, 13743
— Nathan A., Jr, 7563, 9038
— P. G., 9325
— P. H., 8326
— P. J. M., 12025
— Patricia E., 12319
— Patrick, 341, 6934, 8843,
12433
— Paul H., 2962
— Robert Ian, 7851
— Robert Ian, 12559
— Shirley Clay, 13763

Scouten, Kenneth, 13575
Scragg, D. G., 177, 3163
— Leah, 4109, 4580
Scrimgeour, Pat Dale, 12273
Scriven, Karen, 1336
Scrivener, Michael, 9199
— Michael Henry, 9243
Scruggs, Charles, 9853
— Charles W., 13241
Seaman, David M., 3779
Searles, George J., 14037
Sears, Jeff, 12339
Seaton, M. A., 1790
Seaver, Paul S., 5245
Sebba, Anne, 11111
— Mark, 971
Sebeok, Thomas A., 2188,
2286–7, 8171
Secor, Robert, 2486, 8738, 9142
Sedge, Douglas, 5107
Sedgwick, Ellery, III, 9854
— Eve Kosofsky, 2740
Sedycias, Joao A., 7983
Seeber, Hans Ulrich, 7427
Seecombe, M., 658
Seed, David, 335, 8739–40
Seeger, Peggy, 2402
Segal, Errol, 14174
— Howard P., 7338
Segall, Jeffrey Alan, 12725
Segrest, M., 9855
Seidel, Kathryn Lee, 1243, 2869
— Michael, 2870
Seidenspinner, Margarete,
12097
Seigel, Catharine F., 4891
Seiler, Th. B., 2288
Séjourné, Philippe, 13938
Sekine, Masaru, 7186
Selaiha, N. M. K., 7798
Selden, Raman, 5433, 10915–16
Selig, Robert L., 8359
Selinger, Bernard George,
12995
Selkirk, Elizabeth O., 1501
Sell, Roger D., 2741, 8085
Seller, Maxine Schwartz, 10073
Selley, April, 7971
Sellick, Robert, 10581
Sellin, Bernard, 12565
— Paul R., 5395, 5587
Selman, Jan, 10075
Semmel, Bernard, 8979
Senelick, Laurence, 4688
Sen Gupta, S. C., 4582
Seniff, Dennis P., 3488
Senn, Fritz, 12612, 12726–7
Seong, Byeong-Hwie, 11979
Seppänen, Aimo, 2093–4
— Ruth, 2094

Serpell, Michael, 5790
Servotte, Herman, 2952
Sessa, Jacqueline, 5299
Seton, Jo, 10076
Setterfield, Sue, 2412
Setzer, Sharon M., 9640
Severin, Hermann, 13537
Seward, Adrienne Lanier, 2391
Sewell, Brocard, 14673
Sewell, David R., 1030
— Elizabeth, 2895
Sexton, James, 12515
Seyersted, Per, 7636
Seymour, Barbara Jean, 6109
— M. C., 178, 3723
Shadbolt, Maurice, 13311
Shaddy, Virginia M., 5434
Shady, Raymond C., 44
Shafer, Yvonne, 12226
Shahan, Richard Mark, 12044
Shaheen, Mohammad, 430
al-Shaikh-Ali, A. S., 9299
Shailor, Barbara A., 179
Shakman, Michael L., 4999
Shamsuddin, 1962
Shand, G. B., 44
Shankman, Lillian F., 9099
— Steven, 6733
Shannon-Mangan, Ellen, 8892
Shapiro, Ann R., 7339
— Barbara J., 5246
— Fred R., 1560–1, 1636
— Gary, 6538
— Karl, 11102
Sharkey, Michael, 691, 10989,
14786
Sharma, A. B., 6627
— L. N., 8293
— Manjula, 11175
Sharp, Michael Stewart, 7799
— Phillip David, 7714
— Ronald A., 4904
Sharpe, Kevin, 3862
— Richard, 3209
— William, 7564
Sharrad, Paul, 10581, 12294
Sharratt, Bernard, 4229, 9856
Sharrock, Roger, 5315, 12254
Shatto, Susan, 9326–7
Shattock, Joanne, 692
Shattuck, Roger, 9857
Shaumyan, Sebastian, 2003,
2289
Shavit, Zohar, 10471
Shaw, Catherine M., 5335
— Donald, 7499
— Duncan, 3837
— Gary Howard, 4583
— Harry E., 7340
— Helen, 11596

Szilagyi, Stephen, 5640, 6736
Szilárd, Léna, 12735
Szilassy, Zoltán, 14149
Szittya, Penn R., 3431
Szondi, Peter, 3052
Szuberla, Guy, 10420
Szwedek, Aleksander, 26, 1504

Taavila-Walters, Pia Seija,
  12354
Tabachnik, Stephen E., 12975
Tabakowska, Elżbieta, 1396
Tabossi, P., 790
Tafolla, Carmen, 10702
Tahal, Karel, 2102–3
Tailby, John E., 3479
Tait, Bob, 10342
— Heather F. C., 710
— James A., 710
— Margaret, 9189
Takada, Kenichi, 11045
— Shigeki, 4816
Takahashi, Yasunari, 7126
Takano, Masao, 6282
Takemae, Fumio, 827
Takemoto, Yukihiro, 4132
Taliaferro, Frances, 11941
Tallant, Carole Ellsworth,
  13579
Tallis, Raymond, 3053, 10421
Talmadge, Jeffrey D., 711
Tambling, Jeremy, 8091
Tammi, Pekka, 1247, 13461,
  13463
Tanaka, Seitaro, 2954
— Takako, 11929
Tănase, Manuela, 12045
Tangum, Marion Mast, 11930
Taniféani, William, 13323
Tanitch, Robert, 10091
Tanne, Stephen Leonard, 7627
Tannenbaum, Leslie, 6283
Tanner, Michael, 10947
— Stephen L., 11663
— Tony, 7610, 8748, 11476,
  11557
Tanselle, G. Thomas, 339
Tapscott, Stephen, 9517
Tarbox, Katherine M., 12046
Tarcov, Nathan, 5613
Tarnawski, Wit, 11558
Tarnay, László, 1113
Tárnyiková, Jarmila, 2104–5
Tarr, Rodger L., 7825
Tarrant, Desmond, 11373
— Dorothy, 82
— John, 82
Tarvers, Josephine Koster,
  3432

Tasch, Peter A., 5360, 5438,
  6972
Tatar, Maria, 2491
Tate, Claudia, 9869
— Shirley, 971
Tatlow, Antony, 2757
Tatum, James, 5805
— Stephen, 2492
Tausky, Thomas E., 10638,
  13342
Tavormina, M. Teresa, 3433,
  14465
Taylor, Andrew, 10593, 13360,
  14418
— Anthony Brian, 3992,
  4074–5, 4082–4
— Anya, 9644
— Beverly, 3414, 7127
— Carole Anne, 10594, 10747
— Charlotte, 6635
— Cheryl, 11639
— Clyde, 9870
— Gary, 4350–2, 4358–9, 4601,
  4839
— George, 6462
— H., 7863
— Hanni Ulrike, 880
— Helen, 13276
— Henry, 14726
— J. A., 5087
— Jane H. M., 3572
— Jenny, 13013
— John Russell, 10092
— Judy, 13768
— M., 7567
— Marian Elizabeth, 9418
— Mark, 4602, 4798
— Michael, 4736
— Neil, 4990
— Patrick, 14458
— Paul Beekman, 3276
— Richard C., 5326
— Richard H., 8434
— Simon, 3198
— Walter, 11931
Teague, Anthony G., 5806
— Frances, 4693, 4935, 5248,
  5807
Tedlock, David, 13664
Telle, Emile V., 4163
Temperley, Nicholas, 6489
Temple, Frederic-Jacques,
  13268
— Mary Kay, 3277
— Ruth Z., 9871, 11796
Tenbrunsel, William James,
  8504
Tener, Robert H., 712, 6783
Tennenhouse, Leonard, 4603
Teodorescu, Virgil, 4335, 7773

Terasawa, Yoshio, 1568
Terfloth, John H., 7189
Terhune, Alfred McKinley,
  8310
— Annabelle Burdick, 8310
ter Meulen, Alice, 2308
Terrell, Carroll, 13912
— Carroll F., 13913–15
Terris, Olwen, 4604
Terry, R. C., 9419
Teruya, Yoshio, 13665
Teskey, Gordon, 4288, 5809
Tetreault, James, 11797
Tetzeli von Rosador, K., 4134,
  4723
— Kurt, 7351, 11798
Teunissen, J. J., 5728
— John J., 14030
Teyssandier, Hubert, 14587
Tharpe, Jac, 11376, 13721
Thayer, C. G., 4605
Thesen, Sharon, 14224
Thickstun, Margaret Olofson,
  5317
Thiébaux, Marcelle, 12163
Thiel, Gudrun, 2815
Thieme, John, 12823, 13479
Thiher, Allen, 10422
Thinès, Georges, 6284–5
Thirard, Paul-Louis, 14554
Thoka, Thabang, 953
Thomas, Audrey, 10423
— Brook, 12736
— Caitlin, 14370
— Charles, 8447
— Charles Joseph, 9382
— David, 13161
— David J., 12955
— Donald, 7736
— Elizabeth, 12296
— J. E., 8435
— Jeanie Gayle, 8249
— John A., 5259
— Joyce, 13161
— M. Wynn, 9518
— Mark, 12453
— Michael Wyndham, 12857
— Noel Kennedy, 5904
— R. George, 14376–7
— Ron, 13916–17
— Ronald R., 8092, 9274
— Sue, 12183
— W. K., 5439
Thompson, Ann, 4353
— Denys, 12983
— Dorothy Jay, 6921
— E. P., 14348
— Elizabeth, 13065
— George A. J., 2758
— George H., 14408

Westerweel, Bart, 4872, 5507
Westervelt, L. A., 8759
Westfahl, Gary Wesley, 10443
Westley, Margaret Grace, 4695
Westling, Louise, 13121, 13581–2
Westlund, Joseph, 4620
Westney, Paul, 2317
Westrum, Dexter Lyle, 10972
Wetherbee, Winthrop, 3801
Wettstein, Howard, 2318
Wetzel, Claus-Dieter, 132
Wevers, Lydia, 10310, 10444
Wexelblatt, Robert, 14064
Wexler, Joyce, 10963
Whalen, Margee, 9384
— Terry, 12860
Whalley, George, 2775
— J. I., 233
Whallon, William, 4801
Wharton, T. F., 6642
Whatley, Gordon, 3444
Wheale, J. W., 14326
Wheatcroft, John, 10610
Wheeler, Ann Marie, 11296
— Charles B., 2965
— David M., 6425
— Helen, 8252
— Leslie W., 10611
— Richard P., 4377, 4621
— Samuel C., III, 10964
— Saundra Segan, 7570
— Thomas, 4905
Whelan, P. T., 12967
— Robert Emmet, 8510
Whigham, Frank, 4050
Whitaker, Muriel, 3658
— Richard, 3165
— Rosemary, 8611
Whitburn, M., 2376
Whitcut, Janet, 1541
White, Allon, 2748
— Bruce A., 723
— E. N., 3936
— Eugene E., 5649
— H. R. B., 3445
— Hayden, 3061
— Hugh, 1617
— Kenneth, 13599
— Pamela, 7106
— R. S., 3937, 4622–4, 4855
— Ray Lewis, 14248
— Robert, 8760, 11822
— Robert Terrence, 14336
— W. W. P., 3938
— William, 724, 8153, 9522–38, 12473–4
Whitebrook, M. F., 2776
Whitehead, C. S., 10114
— E. L., 1293

— John, 11105
— Maurice, 6688
Whitehouse, J. C., 12257
Whiteley, P., 6114
Whiteman, Bruce, 445, 725, 10445, 11636, 14197
Whiteside, Thomas, 486
Whiting, Anthony, 14291
— Charles, 14150
Whitlock, Baird W., 5508
Whitlow, Roger, 12401
Whitmore, Daniel, 9190
Whitney, Charles, 5277
— Patricia, 726, 11041
— Rosemarie, 2122
Whitt, Margaret, 13583
Whittaker, Herbert W., 10115
Whittington, Harry, 487
Whitworth, Charles Walters, 3939
Whyte, Hamish, 10162, 13136
Wichtel, Diana, 13073
Wickens, G. Glen, 8437
Wicker, Tom, 13277
Wickers, Janine Noel, 14292
Wickert, Maria, 3601
Wickham, D. E., 727
— Glynne, 2817
Widdicombe, Karen Elizabeth, 3980
Widdowson, J. D. A., 903, 2452
— Peter, 2662
Widmer, Kingsley, 12968
Wiedemann, Barbara K., 12415
— Peter M., 10705
Wieland, Gernot, 3229
Wiener, Gary Alan, 12969
— Jon, 13000
Wierzbicka, Anna, 856, 1401, 2320–1, 2323
Wiesenfarth, Joseph, 8761
Wieser, Elisabeth, 2123
Wight, Doris T., 12747–8
— Doris Teresa, 14244
Wihl, Gary, 9147
Wikander, Matthew H., 2818, 5030
Wilbur, Richard, 10502
Wilcher, Robert, 4721, 5641–2
Wilcox, H. E., 5509
Wilczyński, Marek, 11570
Wilde, Alan, 10446
— Dana, 14293
— William H., 6010
Wilding, Michael, 5823, 7880
Wilentz, Gay, 12298, 12502
Wilhelm, Albert E., 1698, 14435
— J. J., 13923–4
— James, 3446

— James J., 3447
Wilhelmi, Nancy Olivia, 14636
Wilkenfeld, Deborah Ceil, 1429
Wilkerson, Margaret B., 12284
Wilkes, G. A., 962–3, 3062, 8253
— J. C., 7365
— Joanne, 8827
Wilkie, Brian, 7529
Wilkins, Wendy, 1997
Wilkinson, Rupert, 10706
Wilks, Brian, 7651
— J. S., 3940
Willard, Nancy, 7366, 12554
Willbern, David, 4873
Willcox, William B., 6478
Williams, Anne, 6115
— Arthur E., 7191
— Bridget, 488
— Bruce, 14670
— Carol Anne, 8834
— Carolyn, 5037, 8966
— Di, 9674
— Edwin, 1837, 2124
— Edwin W., 12749
— Franklin B., Jr, 63
— G. L., 8974
— Geoffrey Bernard, 11806
— George Walton, 4361, 4845, 5282
— H. M., 7631
— Jeffrey C., 10612
— John, 2956
— John Rodger, 2407
— Katherine, 9293
— Kay, 11601
— M. A., 8762
— Mance, 10116
— Marcellette G., 11308
— Mark, 8956, 9887
— Merryn, 7878, 9016–17
— Michael, 7614
— Michael John Stuart, 9093
— Moelwyn I., 291
— N. R., 1593
— Nancy, 4080
— Raymond, 446, 5965, 7878, 14381
— Robert W., 6739–40
— Ronald John Andrew, 13468
— Simon, 4696–7
— Susan Millar, 7624
— W. E., 9332
— William Proctor, 59
Williamson, Alan, 10613
— Henry, 728
— J. W., 10614
— Karina, 6814
Williman, Daniel, 3578
Willis, Donald, 729

— James Leo, 3659
— Jennifer Fugett, 8513
— N., 2502
Wydeven, Joseph J., 10998
Wykeham, J. M., 10616
Wyler, S., 6290
Wylie, I. M., 7946
Wymer, Rowland, 4136, 5162
Wynn, Marianne, 3178
Wynne-Davies, M., 3982
Wyrick, Deborah Baker, 6927

Yachnin, Paul, 5669
Yacowar, Maurice, 10121
Yadugiri, M. A., 1402
Yaeger, Patricia S., 7682
Yagi, Toshio, 8958
Yamada, Akihiro, 135
— Yutaka, 7947
Yamagata, Kazumi, 11433
Yamakawa, Kozo, 3016
Yamamoto, Shoh, 12405
Yamauchi, Masakazu, 8828
Yamazaki, Hiroyuki, 14881
Yancey, Philip, 11807
Yang, James Min-Ching, 8299
— Kyoung-Zoo, 11230
— Woo-Jin, 1841
Yarbro-Bejarano, Yvonne, 10707
Yarbrough, Stephen R., 6434, 8300, 10969
Yarrow, Ralph, 2819
Yarwood, Vaughan, 7145
Yasukawa, Iku, 13823
Yaxley, Susan, 2550
Yazawa, Melvin, 6172
Yeager, Robert F., 3242
Yearling, E. M., 5874
— Elizabeth M., 5032
Yeats-Edwards, Paul, 294
Yeazell, Ruth Bernard, 8764
Yelling, J. A., 7513
Yenal, Edith, 3587
Yerkes, David, 1907, 3182
Yetman, Michael G., 11231
Yi, Duck-Soo, 4731, 4936, 5008
Yoh, Suk-Kee, 14882
Yolton, John W., 5615
Yoneda, Kazuhiko, 12031

Yonekura, Hiroshi, 1908, 3666
Yoon, Chung-Eun, 4718
— Hwa-Gi, 14780
— Ji-Kwan, 7571
— Kee-Ho, 5826
York, Lorraine M., 8775, 11089, 12356
— Lorraine Mary, 10451
— R. A., 7438
Yoshida, Sachiko, 4232
— Takao, 8098
Young, A. R., 5840
— Alan, 9895, 11415
— Alison, 14884
— B. A., 13983
— Beverly Burgoyne, 10472
— Bob, 1212
— Chris Higgins, 735
— David, 12519, 12556, 12862
— Douglas, 893
— Douglas F., 12150
— Gary Ramsey, 6644
— Lynne, 1153
— Philip, 8514
— R. V., 5346, 5643
— Richard, 1129
— Robert M., 7514
— Thomas Daniel, 4629, 11263, 13981
— Vernon, 13933, 14606
— Vicki, 10078
Youra, Steven J., 8515
Yozzo, John Michael, 12560
Yu, Sung-Gon, 1251
Yukman, Claudia, 8157
Yule, George, 1090
Yun, Miduck, 13745
— Sam-Ha, 2959, 14883
— Sang-Hi, 13469
Yuvajita, Phachee, 11411

Zabierowski, Stefan, 11564
Zabrocki, Tadeusz, 2126
Zach, Wolfgang, 2779
Zacharasiewicz, Waldemar, 2780–1, 12441–2
Zadworna-Fjellestad, Danuta, 7850
Zahlan, Anne Ricketson, 11718
Zall, Paul M., 9576

Zaller, Robert, 12561
Zamen, Mark E., 13077
Zamfirescu, Bianca, 8362
Zamora, Bernice B. Ortiz, 10708
— Lois Parkinson, 11460
Zanderer, Leo, 12557
Zanger, Jules, 9094
Zapf, Hubert, 8516, 11284, 12406
Zaret, David, 4051
Zatlin, Linda Gertner, 7369
Zboray, Ronald J., 449
Zebrun, Gary, 12315
Zeeman, Nicolette, 3421
Zeender, Marie-Noelle, 8871
Zehr, Janet Susan, 7543
Zeineddine, N., 13264
Zell, Hans M., 2782
Zeong, Yun-Shig, 4875, 5828
Zetterholm, Tore, 2724
Zettersten, Arne, 3183
Zhordaniiâ, S., 14436
Ziegler, Heide, 10452
Zigal, Thomas, 12974, 14660
Zim, R., 3983
— Rivkah, 4091, 8256
Zimmerman, Hans-Joachim, 13926
Zimmermann, Heinz, 4924, 14546
Zinman, Toby Silverman, 14151
Zins, Daniel L., 13546, 14451
Zipes, Jack, 2503, 10453, 10970
Zitner, S. P., 348
Zohrab, P. D., 1295
Zolotow, Maurice, 14088
Zomchick, John P., 6787
Zong-Qi, Cai, 6519
Zuengler, Jane Ellen, 1296
Zundel, Veronica, 2783
Zwanenburg, Wiecher, 2127
Zwaneveld, Agnes M., 6862
Zweig, Paul, 9540
Zwerdling, Alex, 14781
Zwicker, Steven N., 5443
Zwicky, Arnold M., 1496, 1508
— Elizabeth D., 1508
— Fay, 10618